CONSUMER BEHAVIOR

Seventh Edition

JAMES F. ENGEL
Eastern College

ROGER D. BLACKWELL
The Ohio State University

PAUL W. MINIARD
University of South Carolina

The Dryden Press
Harcourt Brace College Publishers
Fort Worth   Philadelphia   San Diego
New York   Orlando   Austin   San Antonio
Toronto   Montreal   London   Sydney   Tokyo

Editor in Chief   Robert A. Pawlik
Acquisitions Editor   Lyn Hastert
Developmental Editor   R. Paul Stewart
Project Editor   Cheryl Hauser
Production Manager   Diane Southworth
Book Designers   Sue Hart and Paula Goldstein
Photo/Permissions Editors   Annette Coolidge, Sheila Shutter, and
                                 Cindy Robinson

Cover photo: Crowd #2, Diana Ong/Superstock.

Address for Editorial Correspondence
The Dryden Press, 301 Commerce Street, Suite 3700, Fort Worth, TX 76102

Address for Orders
The Dryden Press, 6277 Sea Harbor Drive, Orlando, FL 32887
1-800-782-4479, or 1-800-433-0001 (in Florida)

ISBN: 0-03-076751-2

Library of Congress Catalog Number: 92-73429

Printed in the United States of America
3 4 5 6 7 8 9 0 1 2   039   9 8 7 6 5 4 3 2 1

The Dryden Press
Harcourt Brace Jovanovich

DEDICATION

The 25th Anniversary Edition

To David T. (Dave) Kollat, our partner in developing this book and coauthor of the first three editions. Without your vision and incisive analytical mind, *Consumer Behavior* never would have been a reality. Furthermore, you validated our efforts through the innovative contributions made during your distinguished career at The Limited Stores, Inc. Your influence is still visible in these pages.

THE DRYDEN PRESS SERIES IN MARKETING

Assael
Marketing: Principles and Strategy
Second Edition

Bateson
Managing Services Marketing:
Text and Readings
Second Edition

Blackwell, Blackwell, and Talarzyk
Contemporary Cases in
Consumer Behavior
Fourth Edition

Boone and Kurtz
Contemporary Marketing
Seventh Edition

Churchill
Basic Marketing Research
Second Edition

Churchill
Marketing Research:
Methodological Foundations
Fifth Edition

Czinkota and Ronkainen
International Marketing
Third Edition

Dunn, Barban, Krugman, and
Reid
Advertising: Its Role in
Modern Marketing
Seventh Edition

Engel, Blackwell, and Miniard
Consumer Behavior
Seventh Edition

Futrell
Sales Management
Third Edition

Ghosh
Retail Management

Hutt and Speh
Business Marketing Management:
A Strategic View of Industrial
and Organizational Markets
Fourth Edition

Ingram and LaForge
Sales Management: Analysis
and Decision Making
Second Edition

Kurtz and Boone
Marketing
Third Edition

Murphy and Cunningham
Advertising and Marketing
Communications Management:
Cases and Applications

Oberhaus, Ratliffe, and Stauble
Professional Selling:
A Relationship Process

Park and Zaltman
Marketing Management

Patti and Frazer
Advertising: A Decision-Making
Approach

Rachman
Marketing Today
Second Edition

Rogers, Gamans, and Grassi
Retailing: New Perspectives
Second Edition

Rosenbloom
Marketing Channels:
A Management View
Fourth Edition

Schellinck and Maddox
Marketing and Research: A
Computer-Assisted Approach

Schnaars
MICROSIM
Marketing simulation available for
IBM PC and Apple

Sellars
Role Playing:
The Principles of Selling
Second Edition

Shimp
Promotion Management and
Marketing Communications
Third Edition

Talarzyk
Cases and Exercises in Marketing

Terpstra and Sarathy
International Marketing
Fifth Edition

Tootelian and Gaedeke
Cases and Classics in
Marketing Management

Weitz and Wensley
Readings in Strategic
Marketing Analysis, Planning,
and Implementation

Zikmund
Exploring Marketing Research
Fourth Edition

PREFACE

In 1965 three of us (Jim Engel, Dave Kollat, and Roger Blackwell) committed together to write what turned out to be the very first textbook in the newly emerging field of consumer research. Our concern at the time was figuring out just what to say. It did not dawn on us that we were helping to launch a field that would grow to such maturity. At that point, none of us could think much past the next couple of years; 1993 was somewhere in the distant future.

Serious efforts to integrate behavioral sciences into marketing were in their infancy. George Katona at University of Michigan and John Howard then at Pittsburgh had pioneered in these uncharted waters only a few years before. In fact, it was about 1960 when a few other hardy pioneers broke into the literature. Included among these were Jim Engel then at Michigan; Steuart Henderson Britt and Sid Levy at Northwestern; Don Cox, Ray Bauer, and Joe Newman at Harvard; and Franco Nicosia at California/Berkeley.

Jim Engel left Michigan in 1963 to join the marketing faculty at Ohio State where he was shortly joined by Dave Kollat from Indiana and Roger Blackwell from Northwestern. Each of us had background in various areas of behavioral sciences with little overlap among us. Maybe it was this eclectic combination of backgrounds (or perhaps the raw enthusiasm of youth) that gave us courage to offer one of the first seminars on consumer behavior in the United States in 1966.

The literature used in that seminar consisted of a smattering of marketing-relevant books and articles plus a heavy dose of writings from social psychology and sociology. We were forced to do most of the integration into marketing ourselves because of the paucity of appropriate materials.

This began a series of seminars that allowed for rich collaboration between faculty and graduate students, many of whom went on to become genuine leaders in the field. We especially remember the impact of Larry Light, formerly Ted Bates, International; Brian Sternthal and Alice Tybout, Northwestern University; Orville Walker, University of Minnesota; C. Samuel Craig, New York University; Philip Kuehl, formerly University of Maryland; Beverlee Anderson, University of Wisconsin, Parkside; B. Venkatesh, The Burke Institute; Reza Moinpour, University of Washington; Jim Hensel, University of South Florida; Homer Spence, formerly University of Washington; and Robert Keggereis, formerly Wright State

University; and John Schlachter, Arizona State University. Others will be acknowledged later.

Somehow we gained courage to pool our efforts into what became the first edition of this book. It appeared in 1968 and was published by Holt, Rinehart and Winston. Subsequent editions reflecting changes in this newly emerging field were published by The Dryden Press and appeared in 1973, 1978, 1982, 1986, and 1990. One member of the original coauthor team, David Kollat, dropped out in 1982 because of pressures he faced as a business executive, first at Management Horizons and later at The Limited. Paul W. Miniard joined in 1986 and has become a valued partner.

Now that 25 years have passed, a bookshelf that held our textbook and one or two specialized books on consumer behavior now has become completely filled with consumer behavior textbooks alone. We are excited to see how the field of consumer behavior has grown into a standard subject in business schools and related disciplines.

The conceptual and methodological sophistication of consumer behavior research has burgeoned, making book revision a demanding task indeed. Fields of specialization such as information processing, multiattribute models, consumer satisfaction/dissatisfaction (CS/D), and involvement theory now generate as much or more relevant research than the entire body of marketing-related literature we reviewed for the first edition.

Our basic purposes remain unchanged from the first edition.

1. To explore and evaluate a rapidly growing body of published and unpublished research.
2. To advance generalizations and propositions from the evidence.
3. To assess the practical significance of what has been learned.
4. To pinpoint areas where research has been lacking.

We shortly added a fifth, however, which is of great importance:

5. To make the field of consumer behavior exciting, interesting, and relevant to both students and faculty.

Nothing can be more dull than wading through mountains of abstractions and theories. More than ever before, we have infused this edition with examples that illustrate the use of consumer behavior research and theory in marketing strategy. We hope you will find our Consumer in Focus sections especially interesting as we attempt to provide a vivid picture of how consumer research is applied and used.

Because of our backgrounds and interests, the primary perspective of this textbook continues to be marketing. However, we branch out in many other directions as well, reflecting the diversity of application of consumer behavior research. Therefore, those with differing perspectives will find much of value in this edition.

From the outset we have made use of a model of consumer behavior as a basic method of exposition. Although there have been changes since 1968, we still are convinced that the model is helpful in structuring knowledge in the field and guiding applications in both research and strategy. We maintain our conviction that one model is sufficient to explain all types of decision-process behavior, ranging from high involvement to low involvement.

NEW TO THIS EDITION

How, then, is this edition different? As usual, we have a thoroughly updated book from beginning to end. We have rethought the model, flow of topics, exposition, and subjects to include and exclude. Here are the major things you will notice:

1. As mentioned above, more than ever before our entire outlook has been shaped by one dominant question: "How helpful is a given concept, theory, or technique in the world beyond the classroom?" As our knowledge and experience have grown over these decades, so has our grasp of applications. Therefore, you will find many examples from the business world, from not-for-profit organizations, and from many countries beyond North America integrated throughout the textbook.

2. We keep our long-standing decision-process perspective and have honored the suggestion of many adopters that we return to our time-honored practice of presenting the EKB (**E**ngel, **K**ollat, and **B**lackwell) model upfront as the organizing paradigm for the textbook.

3. We have made every effort to reflect the growing belief within the field that sole reliance on a decision-process perspective can be unduly limiting. What about the needs and gratifications in the consumption process itself? This is referred to as the *hedonic* perspective. We are convinced that this perspective provides some much needed richness and intend to strengthen and expand our use of it in future editions as more relevant research becomes available.

4. We continue our return to the structuring of topics that begins with environmental influences and progressively narrows to individual differences, psychological processes, and decision processes. Those who prefer a differing order, however, will have no difficulty beginning with other sections and topics.

5. As in previous editions, we focus heavily on the future in terms of economic, demographic, and sociocultural trends and have placed even greater emphasis in this edition on the uses of futurism in strategic planning.

6. In recognition of the increasing globalization of consumer markets, we have expanded our coverage of the international dimensions of consumer behavior and marketing. This edition particularly reflects the extensive recent experience, first of all, of Jim Engel in Russia as well as his involvement in more than 50 developing countries since 1972. Also, Roger Blackwell has traveled worldwide as a consultant and speaker and brings his rich perspective to bear throughout the textbook.

7. We reflect our growing concern about the ethics of consumer influence at many points throughout the textbook. Chapter 24 is totally revised and presents an all-new perspective on ethical thinking in this crucial and sensitive area of contemporary life. We genuinely hope that this chapter will not be omitted in the usual end-of-term rush. Nothing is more important today than a proper grounding in what is "right" from the consumer's perspective.

SUPPLEMENTS

The supplementary material for this edition has been greatly expanded to help meet the needs of instructors. The *Instructor's Manual/Test Bank/Transparency Masters* include teaching suggestions, detailed lecture outlines, answers to discussion questions, approximately 2,000 test questions, and more than 80 transparency masters of new figures and in-class exercises as well as key figures and tables from the text. The *Test Bank*, originally written by Edward Laurie of San Jose State University, has been revised by Paul Miniard and Michael Barone. The *Transparency Masters* were prepared by JoAnn Linrud of Mankato State University. Chapter outlines were prepared by Deepak Sirdeshmukh. A *Computerized Test Bank* for use with IBM PC microcomputers is also available.

In addition, a companion casebook, *Contemporary Cases in Consumer Behavior*, Fourth Edition, by Roger Blackwell, Tina Blackwell, and Wayne Talarzyk, can be used to highlight the practical relevance of the concepts covered in the text.

ACKNOWLEDGMENTS

In this 25th year it seems especially appropriate to acknowledge once again everyone who has contributed written evaluations and suggestions. As we have written the various editions, these contributions have been of great importance to us. All have been taken seriously. This book has been improved by your help, and we thank you once again for your role in our professional lives. In addition to our graduate students mentioned earlier, special thanks go to

John Antil, University of Delaware
April Atwood, University of Washington
Kenneth Baker, University of New Mexico
John Bennett, University of Northern Colorado
Gordon Bruner, Southern Illinois University, Carbondale
Steven Burgess, The University of Witwatersrand
Robert Burnkrant, Ohio State University
Peter Chadraba, University of West Oshkosh
Robert Coleman, Kansas State University
Sayeste Daser, Wake Forest University
Rohit Deshpande, University of Texas, Austin
Peter Dickson, Ohio State University
Peter DiPaulo, University of Missouri, St. Louis
Michael Dorsch, Valdosta State College
Hershey Friedman, Brooklyn College
David Gardner, University of Illinois, Urbana/Champaign
Peggy Gilbert, Southwest Missouri State University
James Ginter, Ohio State University
John Grabner, Ohio State University
Donald Granbois, Indiana University
Paul Green, University of Pennsylvania

Nessim Hanna, Northern Illinois University
Betty Harris, University of Southwestern Louisiana
Salah S. Hassan, George Washington University
Douglass Hawes, University of Wyoming
Gail Hudson, Arkansas State University
Wesley Johnston, Georgia State University
Benoy Joseph, Cleveland State University
Harold Kassarjian, University of California, Los Angeles
Inder Khera, Wright State University
Tina Kiesler, University of Southern California
Philip Kotler, Northwestern University
Jim Leigh, Texas A&M University
Larry Lepisto, Central Michigan University
Roger Leyton, University of New South Wales
JoAnn Linrud, Mankato State University
Ken Lord, SUNY, Buffalo
Deanna Mader, University of Louisville
James McNeal, Texas A&M University
Dan McQuiston, Butler University
Lee Meadow, Bentley College
Allan R. Miller, Towson State University
Don Norris, Miami University
Terry O'Brien, Northern Illinois University
J. Paul Peter, University of Wisconsin, Madison
Richard Pollay, University of British Columbia
Robert Pratt, Avon Products
John Schouten, University of Portland
Dan Sherrell, Louisiana State University
Deepak Sirdeshmukh, Ohio State University
Doug Stayman, Cornell University
W. Wayne Talarzyk, Ohio State University
Robert Tamilia, University of Quebec
B. Venkatesh, Burke Marketing Research
Angelina Villarreal, Miller Brewing Company
Tillie Voegtli, University of Missouri, St. Louis
Hugh Wales, University of Illinois (emeritus)
Malcolm White, California State University, Sacramento
Tommy E. Whittler, University of Kentucky, Lexington
Ron Willett, Indiana University
Robert Woodruff, University of Tennessee

We also wish to encourage readers of this textbook to share with us any ideas or materials they might have for improvement. Those contributing ideas or materials used in the next edition will of course be acknowledged.

We continue to express our appreciation to the staff of Management Horizons, a division of Price Waterhouse, for the help provided from the very beginning. We have benefitted from use of its excellent library facilities and research resources. A former colleague on the marketing faculty at Ohio State, William R. Davidson, deserves special thanks as do Cyrus Wilson and Dan Sweeney who were outstanding graduate students at Ohio State and participants in the early seminars.

We are somewhat bewildered by rapid consolidation within the publishing field and now find ourself as part of the Harcourt Brace Jovanovich family. This is a long way from our 1968 beginning at Holt, Rinehart and Winston. We will always be grateful to Siebert (Sieb) Adams, our first developmental editor, who believed in us, signed a contract for the first three book series (text, cases, and readings) and pulled out all stops to make us a success. Those were good days, indeed, and we always will be grateful to Sieb and his tough and resourceful senior editor, Ros Sackof, for laying a solid professional foundation for all that we have done.

We welcome the expanded resources that the HBJ/Dryden team offers and look forward to a fruitful relationship. We acknowledge the conscientious efforts of Lyn Hastert, acquisitions editor; Paul Stewart, developmental editor; Cheryl Hauser, project editor; Diane Southworth, production manager; Sue Hart, designer; Annette Coolidge, photo permissions editor; and Sheila Shutter, text permissions editor, in helping us make a successful transition in this seventh edition.

Finally, we acknowedge our wives, Sharon, Tina, and Debbie. You have been true partners. Thanks!

James F. Engel   *Philadelphia, Pennsylvania*
Roger D. Blackwell   *Columbus, Ohio*
Paul W. Miniard   *Columbia, South Carolina*

ABOUT THE AUTHORS

James F. Engel (Ph.D., University of Illinois, Urbana; B.S., Drake) has a distinguished name in the study of consumer behavior. He was honored by his peers in 1980 as the founder of a field when he was named one of the first two Fellows of the Association for Consumer Research. He received a similar citation when he received the prestigious Paul D. Converse Award of the American Marketing Association. These honors were given in recognition of his pioneering research that first appeared in 1960, his role as senior author of this textbook, and other forms of leadership.

He presently is Distinguished Professor of Marketing and Director of the Center for Organizational Excellence at Eastern College, St. Davids, Pennsylvania, where he moved in 1990. Professor Engel has shifted his emphasis from consumer goods marketing to the application of nonprofit marketing principles to religious organizations worldwide. He also has published widely in that field and serves as Senior Vice President of Management Development Associates, a consulting group specializing in these applications. In that capacity he has served as a consultant to more than 200 groups in over 50 countries.

Roger D. Blackwell (Ph.D., Northwestern; B.S., Missouri) is Professor of Marketing at The Ohio State University where he has served since 1965. He is a well-known author, and his works include several casebooks also published by The Dryden Press. He is in constant demand as a business consultant and speaker in the area of the impact of changing environments on marketing strategy, for companies such as IBM, AT&T, CheckPoint, and The Limited. He serves on the board of directors for several firms in retailing, consumer services, manufacturing, and management consulting.

Dr. Blackwell was recipient of the Marketing Educator of the Year Award given in 1984 by Sales and Marketing Executives International. He also has received a number of awards for outstanding teaching at Ohio State, including the Alumni Award for Distinguished Teaching in 1988.

Paul W. Miniard (Ph.D., M.A., B.S., University of Florida) is Associate Professor of Marketing at the University of South Carolina where he has been since 1990 when he moved from Ohio State University. Over his career, he has received a number of undergraduate and graduate teaching awards.

Dr. Miniard is well known through his published research in the area of consumer behavior, which has appeared in such leading journals as *Journal of Consumer Psychology*, *Journal of Consumer Research*, *Journal of Marketing Research*, and *Journal of Experimental Social Psychology*. He also serves as a consultant and expert witness in areas involving consumer behavior. In 1992, Dr. Miniard visited the University of International Business and Economics in Beijing, China, to help set up a course in consumer behavior.

BRIEF CONTENTS

CONTENTS

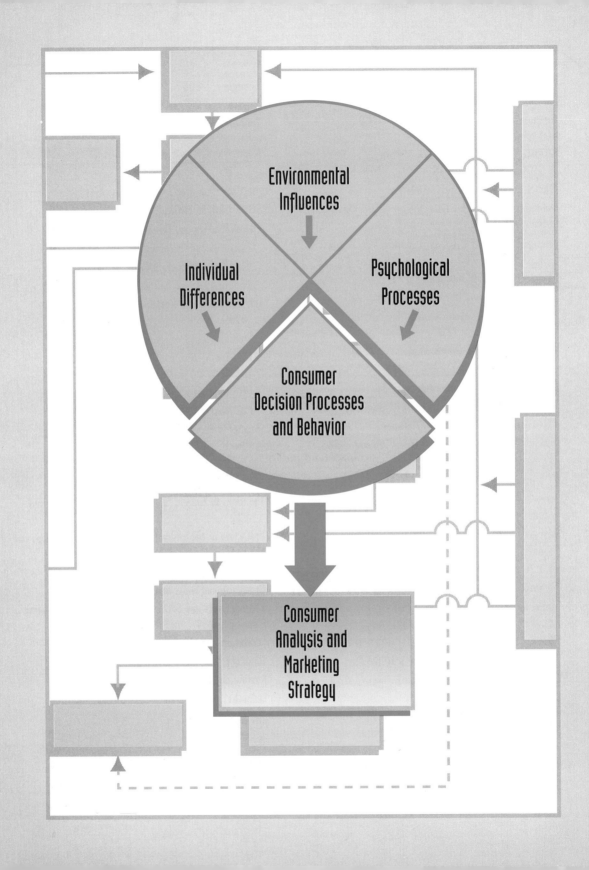

Environmental
Influences

Individual
Differences

Psychological
Processes

Consumer
Decision Processes
and Behavior

Consumer
Analysis and
Marketing
Strategy

PART 1

Introduction and Overview

What is consumer behavior all about? Why should it receive such widespread recognition as the key to modern marketing success? As an academic discipline? As a field of research? And how does this exciting field make a dynamic blend of economics, marketing, psychology, sociology, anthropology, and other related behavioral science disciplines? These and many other questions are considered in the first two chapters, which build a framework of essential principles, concepts, and variables.

Chapter 1 takes a broad perspective and introduces this field. Chapter 2 is of special importance, because it presents an overview of the model shown on the opposite page. You may not appreciate its richness at this point. Nevertheless, it gives you a quick picture of the primary variables and factors that must be understood by any serious student in the field. Take special time to understand this model as it is presented, because it provides the structure around which this textbook is organized.

Let your mind range far and wide as you read these chapters. Ask yourself how the content speaks to your life and career. There is no field which you could study which comes closer to daily life. Welcome to what we hope will be a real adventure for you.

1

The Consumer: Perspectives and Viewpoints

"You're the top, you're a lazy Sunday . . . you're a lunch on Monday, you're a blue-chip stock . . . ." Listen to the beguiling female voice croon a television commercial pitching Chivas Regal whiskey in Bangkok. The song continues: "You're the perfect deal, you're a Vietnamese meal . . . you're a Porsche, you're a firstborn son." In other words, you're a yuppie, Asian-style.

In Thailand, Taiwan, South Korea, and other fast-developing Asian countries, marketers are discovering a growing class of young professionals and entrepreneurs whose affluence defies the convenient broad-based statistics so often used to size up these markets. Their formidable earning power—and eagerness to buy—is stimulating sales of everything from sports cars and brand-name apparel to home furnishings, travel, and yes, Scotch whiskey.

Understanding what makes them tick is the hard part. "This young generation has grown up in an uninterrupted age of opportunity and prospects," says Kim Mun-Cho, a Korea University sociologist who at 40 is old enough to remember the hard years right after the Korean War. Kim's parents and the rest of that generation worked tirelessly, lived frugally, and saved religiously. In part, they had little choice because the government made sure through high tariffs and other restrictions that there were few ways for consumers to spend money.

Now, in a rush, everything that restrained their parents is disappearing. Money, the biggest constraint of all, is abundant. Such new freedom is leading the young Asians to question many traditional Asian values. Says Paul Lee, manager of the new Singapore Hard Rock Cafe: "People here are more able to express themselves, be

3

themselves, hang out." Many members of this rising Me Generation work five days a week, not the six or seven their parents toiled.

To make the most of their longer leisure hours, the yuppies spend money that their elders would have put in a bank. Asia's yuppies first dream of owning a car, then a house. Aaren Yu, 29, who owns a small Hong Kong ad agency, paid $40,000 for a new BMW 325i.

They crave big-name brands. A cruise through Sunrise Department Store in Taipei finds Ungaro, Boss, Ermenegildo Zegna, and Gianna Versace, to mention a few high-fashion names. You can also find Timberland deck shoes for $172; Ralph Lauren shorts for $90; Allen Edmonds shoes for $306; and a Giorgio Armani sport jacket for $1,280. All this on the same floor as a movie theater that sells popcorn and boiled chicken feet.

Source: Ford S. Worthy, "Asia's New Yuppies," *Fortune* (June 4, 1990), 223–235. © 1990 Time Inc. All rights reserved.

What's Consumer Behavior All About?

The story of Asia's new yuppies is interesting reading, isn't it? Just as the yuppie behavior pattern has come to be viewed with disdain in the United States, it is thriving on the Pacific Rim. Such stories are intriguing, because all of us are buyers and consumers. Much of what we do in this arena is central to our lifestyle and sense of well-being.

But this story is of even greater interest to manufacturers and distributors throughout the world who look covetously on this burgeoning market. Citibank found a lucrative opportunity in the Korean housing market.[1] Korean banks traditionally have required potential borrowers to pay into a savings account for several years before applying for a mortgage. The problem was that home prices often soar in this interim. Citibank waived this requirement and will approve a loan within 10 days if the buyer has a sufficient down payment. It has been flooded with inquiries, mostly from young professionals.

Therefore, it is not surprising that a large and expanding field of research has emerged focusing on consumer behavior. We define **consumer behavior** as those activities directly involved in obtaining, consuming, and disposing of products and services, including the decision processes that precede and follow these actions.

This subject can be approached from several perspectives, all of which are considered in this book: (1) consumer influence; (2) holistic; and (3) intercultural. As you will see, these categories overlap to some extent.

A Consumer Influence Perspective

Consumer behavior is of particular interest to those who, for various reasons, desire to influence or change that behavior, including those whose primary concern is marketing, consumer education and protection, and public policy.

Marketing   The economy of the Republic of Russia is a shambles after the failed coup attempt in 1991. Stores are empty; enormous lines form once there is a rumor that potatoes or some other item is suddenly available; potential buyers wait years for orders to be filled for durable goods such as refrigerators or automobiles. Shortages are so great that producers are fully aware everything they produce will be snapped up.

It is no exaggeration to state that the Russian economy parallels the American economy of 70 years earlier—there is a general and widespread excess of demand over supply. In such an environment most businesses can operate from a production orientation reflecting the philosophy that "a good product will sell itself."[2] Why ask consumers what they want when they will buy almost anything you produce?

Matters soon began to change in the United States as growing numbers of businesses discovered that they and their competitors possessed more productive capacity than the market could absorb. Consumer needs and wants began to assume an all-new importance as the search for ways to gain competitive advantage intensified.

While the onset of the Great Depression and World War II brought about a lengthy hiatus in the competitive scene, the scene shifted dramatically in the late 1940s as a new operating philosophy took center stage. Bottom-line competitive pressure forced widespread adoption of the marketing concept—the process of planning and executing the conception, pricing, promotion, and distribution of ideas, goods, and services to create exchanges that satisfy individual and organizational objectives.[3]

The key element in this definition is the *exchange* between the customer and the supplier. Each party gives something of value to the other with the goal of satisfying their respective needs, and, in the process, both parties gain. In the normal buying context money (or, increasingly, its plastic equivalent) is exchanged for a desired good or service.

Notice that the customer lies at the heart of the process. Everything that the supplier does in the way of product, price, promotion, and distribution (the marketing mix) is adapted to market demand. The consumer controls the exchange through the pocketbook. In 1954 Drucker sounded the clarion call: "There is one valid definition of business purpose: *to create a customer*" [italics ours].[4] Peters and Austin isolated the two factors that appear to distinguish the excellent business organization from the also-ran:

> In the private or public sector, in big business or small, we observe that there are only two ways to create and sustain superior performance over the long haul. First, take exceptional care of your customers . . . via superior service and superior quality. Second, constantly innovate. That's it.[5]

It is not surprising, then, that consumer behavior lies at the very center of business strategy, especially marketing. The underlying question guiding most of the writing in this field is, as Belk has noted, "What arrangement of the marketing mix will have what effects on the purchase behavior of what types of consumers?"[6] Therefore, the *buying process* is of more concern to marketers than the *consumption process*. And, consumer research must have distinct managerial relevance in this context before it will be considered. Yes, marketers will take the Asian yuppies very seriously and do everything possible to capitalize on the opportunities they present.

Returning now to the situation in the Republic of Russia, there is a true revolution underway as western firms act to capitalize on this potentially huge eastern European market. In the move from a command-directed to a market-controlled economy, the market now will set the competitive agenda, not the government. Those enterprises that fail to move away from a production orientation will face disaster in short order. A process that took many decades in the United States will occur in the incredibly short period of months or years. While the shakeout will be enormous, the ultimate consumer is the beneficiary of a changed way of life.

Consumer Education and Protection   Others also want to shape and influence consumer behavior but do so in an effort to help the consumer buy wisely. The consumer economist, in particular, will examine the behavior of Paul Lee, Aaren Yu, Kim Mun-Cho and their Asian yuppie counterparts in terms of whether they make the best choices in view of their motivations and goals. Here are some issues that might be raised:

1. Would the overall value received have been higher had there been better information at hand on other purchase alternatives?
2. Are they being misled through advertising to buy American?
3. Would these consumers have been better off to buy on the basis of price as opposed to brand name?

Through education the consumer can be taught how to detect the presence of deception and other abuses and be made aware of remedies that exist and opportunities for redress. Also, anyone can benefit from greater insight into money-saving strategies. Educational programs must be based on research into motivation and behavior if they are to be relevant in the real world of consumer life. Not surprisingly, consumer economists and home economists now rank among the most serious students of consumer behavior.[7]

The marketer and the consumer economist often take adversarial positions when analyzing the same behavior. Nevertheless, both desire to change that behavior when it is perceived from their perspective as being beneficial to do so. The only difference is in their respective agendas.

Public Policy   Education alone will not guarantee consumer welfare. The cornerstone of a free-enterprise economy is the right of any consumer to make an informed and unrestricted choice from an array of alternatives. When this right is curtailed because of business abuse, societal consensus affirms that government has the duty to influence consumer choice by restrictions in monopoly power and by curbing deception and other unfair trade practices.

Consumer protection legislation and regulation all too often are based on the opinions of a small group of advocates. The outcome can be ineffective or even counterproductive activity. There now is growing awareness that greater reliance must be placed on consumer research if consumer protection is to function as intended.[8]

A More Holistic Perspective

Those whose research motivation is consumer influence generally embrace the research paradigm of positivism in which rigorous empirical techniques are used to discover generalizable explanations and laws. Consumer decision processes and behavioral outcomes are studied to bring about prediction and change.[9] Indeed, most published consumer research until recently fell into this category.[10]

The domain of consumer research goes far beyond the managerial perspective, however, when primary focus is placed on consumption. Holbrook and Hirschman, among others, strongly advocate that the purchase decision is only a small component in the constellation of events involved in the consumption experience.[11] Holbrook has taken the lead in contending that it is time for consumer researchers to examine "all facets of the value potentially provided when some living organism acquires, uses, or disposes of any product that might achieve a goal, fulfill a need, or satisfy a want."[12] The decision process itself thus assumes a secondary importance as compared with consumption.

This broadened perspective has been recently reflected in the literature as published research into the subjectively based experiential aspects of the consumption experience such as sensation seeking, emotional arousal, and fantasizing.[13] This has come to be known as hedonic consumption—that undertaken purely for pleasure.[14] Research methodology moves beyond positivism to naturalism (ethnography, semiotics, literary criticism, and historicism) in order to achieve a broader understanding of the impact of consumption on individuals.[15]

If we were to analyze the behavior of the Asian yuppies from this point of view, our goal would be to understand what has taken place without any particular intent to change or influence the process:

1. Why are there such generational differences in outlooks?
2. What values are transmitted by the American products as opposed to domestic alternatives?
3. How can we understand the deeper meaning of the pleasures offered by the brand-name products?
4. Is it ethical for American and European firms to try to make these inroads into a culture with such different traditions?
5. What long-lasting effects will the consumer culture have on traditional Asian values?

While some of the outcomes may be significant to business managers as well, overall understanding is the goal.

This holistic perspective is a recent development. There is little doubt, however, that it will grow, because of the importance of understanding the nature of human behavior and values in this significant arena of life activity, over and above the pragmatic concerns of marketers, consumer educators, and regulators.

FIGURE 1.1 **Evidence of a Growing Consumer Culture Worldwide—Beijing, Nairobi, Berlin, Moscow**

An Intercultural Perspective

If one were to examine the literature, it would be easy to assume that consumer research is of primary importance only in North America, Europe, and Japan. Nothing could be further from the truth. On all continents, there is a striving toward economic development and greater self-sufficiency. Even in socialistic countries such as China, consumer goods are becoming increasingly important. As a consumer-oriented society emerges, an early manifestation is a middle class with disposable income. Unless political restrictions are imposed, a rising standard of living becomes a dominant concern.

A vogue word in China today is "*Huoli* 28," the Chinese pronunciation for "Power 28," which almost instantaneously has become the most popular detergent in that country.[16] Through television, radio, and newspaper advertising, sales increased by ten times when Huoli 28 was launched in the 1980s, resulting in a substantial profit. Until quite recently such a marketing success would have been unthinkable.

The middle-class counterparts of the Asian yuppies are seen on the streets of Kuala Lumpur, Nairobi, Quito, Beijing, New Delhi, Caracas, and elsewhere in the world. Therefore, marketers have been quick to capitalize on resulting opportunities, as the ads in Figure 1.1 demonstrate.

It is time to broaden horizons beyond the western world and view consumer research as a universal necessity. Basic human needs are universal, although there are undeniable and profound cultural differences in their expression.

The Perspective of this Book

Since the first edition we have tried to be eclectic in the best sense of the word and to reflect a broad orientation. Nevertheless, we approach the subject of consumer behavior from a marketing point of view. Our primary concern is phasing consumer research into marketing strategy. Increasingly, however, the other perspectives have changed our outlook. We welcome and affirm the enrichment that is taking place.

Right Thinking about the Consumer

Four significant principles underlie all that we say and do in these coming pages.

The Consumer Is Sovereign

Perhaps there was a time when a few "czars of fashion" could have a dominant influence in shaping consumer tastes. Although this may have been true in the past, the influence of fashion designers today is at an all-time low. Take time to read Consumer in Focus 1.1, which documents the marketing dilemma throughout the men's clothing industry.

The bottom-line issue is failure to recognize that *the consumer is sovereign*. He or she is not an unthinking pawn to be manipulated at will by the commercial persuader. Consumer behavior, as a rule, is purposeful and goal oriented. Products and services are accepted or rejected on the basis of the extent to which they are perceived as relevant to needs and lifestyle. The individual is fully capable of ignoring everything the marketer has to say.

It is astonishing to realize that a viewer watching 30 hours of television a week in the United States will be bombarded by more than 35,000 commercials a year.[17] Chapter 13 will demonstrate that consumers both possess and vigorously use inborn powers of selective screening. Television advertising, in particular, suffers as viewers use electronic remote controls to zap anything they do not want to see.[18] And, as the intriguing story in Consumer in Focus 1.2 makes clear, exactly the same thing happens in Russia in spite of burgeoning demand for anything western.

The effects of selective screening can be profound, and here is a case in point. There are limits on what advertising can do to change demand. Yet, anyone living in the United States would have to be fairly isolated if they failed to be exposed to the virulent advertising war among the three major long-distance telephone carriers. As one industry analyst put it, "Never before have consumers been bombarded by so many TV campaigns about telephone use, using tactics that range from warmth and humor to seriousness, direct comparison, and downright intimidation."[19] Yet in-

Consumer in Focus   1.1

Men's Suit Market Sags

The staple attire of traditional business—the two- or three-piece suit—is coming apart at the seams. Rising wool prices, a slumping economy, and a growing trend toward acceptance of casual attire in the workplace have broadsided the men's suit market.

Wool prices, which drive the price of men's tailored clothing, increased 30 percent in the late 1980s and consumers are balking at rising prices. And, because there have not been any dramatic fashion swings, what is in the closet is good enough for many consumers. According to Walter K. Levy, a New York retail consultant, men are in a wardrobe replacement mode, not a building mode.

Additionally, casual dress is working its way into the business world. Some companies, including a number of California securities firms, have declared Friday a "suit-optional" day. Executives of small businesses are as likely to be found wearing Dockers pants and knit shirts as they are to be found wearing suits.

Such habits spell trouble for those in the tailoring trade. Hartmarx Corp., which owns middle-income retail stores Wallachs in New York and Baskins in Chicago as well as Hart Schaffner & Marx, experienced a three-year slump even though it retains an 11 percent share of the U.S. men's suit market. Brooks Brothers experienced a 41 percent drop in operating profits in 1990. William V. Roberti, chief executive at Brooks Brothers, knows the business will remain tough: "The suit market as a total universe is getting smaller."

Sources: "The Suit Market Is Coming Apart at the Seams," *Business Week* (August 12, 1991), 42–43; "Bonfire of the Business Suits," *Time* (November 19, 1990), 83; and "Trying to Patch Up Menswear Sales," *The Wall Street Journal* (November 24, 1989).

flated ad spending has not altered market shares, apparently due to the way in which ad messages are offset in a cluttered context. AT&T still controls about 70 percent of this $55 billion industry, followed by MCI with a 16 percent share, and US Sprint with about 10 percent.[20]

Business history is full of wreckages that can be traced to a defective philosophy on the principle of consumer sovereignty. Purina Homestyle, "the quick dog dinner that's like homemade," was rejected almost as soon as it was introduced.[21] "So it's homemade. So what?" was the response. The Bristol-Myers Company introduced Small Miracle, which would allow the consumer to shampoo once or twice a

Consumer in Focus   1.2

An Adman's Wonderland Turns Sour

In theory it should be an adman's dream: 288 million product-starved consumers whose main experience of television commercials has been a lifetime of crude pitches for heavy machinery. In practice Russians may not turn out to be such pushovers. A study commissioned by J. Walter Thompson [JWT] shows that Muscovites are far less gullible—and more discriminating—than western marketers might have hoped.

Russia's biggest television channel, Gostelradio, broadcast five hours of typical British programming, and with it, a series of JWT's adverts [British lingo for *ad*]. Afterward, CRAM International, a research company, replayed the ads to small groups of young, well-educated, and affluent (hence more readily targeted) Muscovites to test their reactions.

Unlike naive westerners of 25 years ago, the Russians—weaned on propaganda and deeply distrustful of the media—were skeptical of the adverts' messages. Their interpretations were often quite sophisticated. A spot for Listerine mouthwash was seen as a morality play where evil (bad breath) was conquered by good (the product). And sensible: a harried, car-phone-toting yuppie was derided as unstable, hyperactive, and frivolous.

Source: "The Hidden Persuadees," *The Economist* (March 23, 1991), 79. Reproduced by special permission.

week. It achieved only 30 percent of market potential because most women are convinced of the necessity of more frequent shampooing.[22] And on the story goes.

It all comes down to this essential point: *Understanding and adapting to consumer motivation and behavior is not an option—it is an absolute necessity for competitive survival.* In the final analysis, the consumer is in control, and the marketer succeeds when the product or service is perceived as offering real benefits.

Consumer Motivation and Behavior Can Be Understood through Research

As we will discover in the coming pages, consumer behavior is a process, and purchase is only one stage. There are many underlying influences, ranging from internal motivations to social influences of various kinds. Yet, motivation and behavior can be understood, albeit imperfectly, through research. If this were not the case, this book would never have been written. Perfect prediction is never possible, but properly designed and used research efforts can significantly lower the risks of marketing failure.

FIGURE 1.2   Scotch Post-it Note Pads: A Product That Successfully Met and Activated Consumer Demand

Consumer Behavior Can Be Influenced

Consumer sovereignty presents a formidable challenge, but skillful marketing can affect both motivation and behavior *if the product or service offered is designed to meet consumer needs*. A sales success occurs because demand either exists already or is latent and awaiting activation by the right marketing offering.

A case in point is one of 3M's greatest successes, the Scotch Post-it Brand Note Pad (Figure 1.2). Quite by accident a researcher in the 3M laboratories discovered an adhesive that would bond two pieces of paper together while allowing quick and total separation with minimal effort. He believed there might be a market for removable, self-stick notes but was greeted with initial skepticism. However, perseverance, followed by marketing research, verified his hunch.

Once consumers had a chance to try the pad, large numbers of people quickly saw that this product met a need. Notes can be attached to something else without defacing or damaging it, and there proved to be a multitude of uses both at home and on the job.

It is worth noting that high promotional expenditures do not prevent the failure of most of the new products introduced on the market each year. Once again, consumer relevance is the central issue.

Consumer Influence Is Socially Legitimate

Consumer needs are real, and there is undeniable benefit from products or services that offer genuine utility. The consumer benefits while, at the same time, the economic system is energized. Leo Bogart, a well-known marketing strategist, stated it well over two decades ago:

> Apart from what a specific advertising [marketing] campaign does for a specific product, there is a broader combined effect of the thousands of advertising exhortations that confront every consumer in America each day, a constant reminder of material goods and services not yet possessed. That effect at the level of individual motivation is felt as a constant impetus toward more consumption, toward acquisition, toward upward mobility. At the collective level, it is felt in the economic drive to produce and to innovate which fuels our economic system.[23]

This proposition sounds both elegant and noble, but it assumes that all parties in the system act in accord with the highest ethical standards. Reality, of course, is something quite different. Fraud and manipulation abound, thus giving rise in 1960 to development of the Consumer Bill of Rights and its propagation and enforcement by the burgeoning consumerism movement in the United States.[24]

Take time to read the Consumer Bill of Rights, which appears in Figure 1.3. While we will discuss it at length in Chapter 25, it is important to grasp its scope and essence at this point. Rights are absolute, inviolable, and non-negotiable. Outright deception, low product quality, non-response to legitimate complaints, pollution, and other actions are nothing less than violation of legitimate rights and must be viewed as such.

There has been a shift in national consciousness leading to increased stridency in demands for moral and ethical behavior in business, professions, and politics. Consider these words:

> After the licentiousness of the Seventies and the materialism of the Eighties, the generation [the baby boomers born 1946–64] that coined the slogan "if it feels good, do it!" has concluded in middle age that if it feels good, it must be bad for you. With this realization has come a neo-prohibitionist impulse that militates against anything perceived as harmful, be it cigarettes, beer, cocaine, or cholesterol . . . "We're in a just-say-no mode."[25]

Manufacturers and retailers are increasingly faced with vigorous protest when actions go against social consensus. To take just one example, consumer backlash was unleashed after statistics showed a fourth straight drop in average longevity among African-Americans, attributable, at least in part, to higher instances of tobacco- and alcohol-related illnesses.[26] As a result, G. Heileman Brewing Co. was forced by public pressure to withdraw PowerMaster, its high-potency malt liquor

The Consumer Bill of Rights

1. *The Right to Safety*—protection against products or services that are hazardous to health and life.
2. *The Right to be Informed*—provision of facts necessary for an informed choice; protection against fraudulent, deceitful, or misleading claims.
3. *The Right to Choose*—assured access to a variety of products and services at competitive prices.
4. *The Right to be Heard (Redress)*—assurance that consumer interests receive full and sympathetic consideration in formulation and implementation of regulatory policy, and prompt and fair restitution.
5. *The Right to Enjoy a Clean and Healthful Environment.*
6. *The Right of the Poor and Other Minorities to Have Their Interests Protected.*

FIGURE 1.3   The Consumer Bill of Rights

aimed at inner-city consumers. Similarly, R. J. Reynolds dropped plans to market Uptown, a menthol cigarette aimed primarily at black consumers.

The key to social legitimacy is a guarantee that the consumer retains complete and unimpeded freedom throughout the buying and consumption process. This freedom is manifested when nothing induces the consumer to act in ways that would be regretted and even disavowed after more careful reflection.

Faith Popcorn, a popular marketing commentator, calls the 1990s the "decency decade," and demands that "corporate soul" be revealed in a four-part message:[27]

1. *Acknowledgment.* Our industry hasn't always done everything in its power to make the world a better place.
2. *Disclosure.* This is who we were. And this is the company we're trying, with your help, to become.
3. *Accountability.* Here is how we define our arena of responsibility and who can be held accountable.
4. *Presentation.* Here is what we pledge to you, the consumer: You'll find our corporate soul in all our products.

Improving Marketing Effectiveness

A central underlying premise of this book is that proper use of consumer research significantly sharpens the effectiveness of marketing efforts. We will try to show you in this section some of the managerial dynamics that are required for competitive survival.

FIGURE 1.4   Marketing Is Significant in the Not-for-Profit Organization

It is tempting to focus only on the research requirements of marketing strategy at the manufacturing level. Yet, retailers and not-for-profit organizations have marketing problems of their own.

Here are just some of the issues faced by retailers. What product mix should be handled? What image should be projected? What happens to sales when prices are raised? Is point-of-sale display sufficient, or is personal selling needed? It is not unusual to find continuing use of taste tests, surveys of store awareness and image, satisfaction evaluation, and panels of shoppers who evaluate potential new items.

Marketing concepts also have been adopted by not-for-profit organizations that provide public service in such forms as changed ideas (for example, religion, health, or social practices) and direct help (for example, famine relief or housing assistance). In many respects the challenges faced by these organizations are even greater than those of businesses because the former must contend with two markets: (1) the market for services and (2) the donor market.

For example, the Coalition for Literacy (Figure 1.4) must find ways to motivate and help the 27 million functionally illiterate Americans to overcome this handicap. In addition to that challenging goal, the Coalition must seek funds to raise public awareness that an illiteracy problem exists. The potential donor market must be segmented to find those who have the greatest interest in this appeal. Donor research now is finding widespread use.[28]

Right Thinking about Consumer Research

Eastman Kodak executive Raymond H. DeMoulin was in a Tokyo fish market one early morning when he observed a photographer trying to pry open a film container with his teeth while holding his camera. This observation quickly gave rise to a product change so that it now is possible to open containers of Kodak film with one hand.[29]

DeMoulin was doing consumer research that morning, even though he had no clipboard with him and engaged in no computerized analysis of data. He made enlightened use of observation which then was blended with experience and intuition (creative insight) to build practical, workable marketing strategy.

There are three foundations, then, for marketing decisions: (1) research, (2) experience, and (3) intuition; none is complete without the other. Frequently, however, consumer research is often ignored—with unfortunate consequences. To illustrate limitations on experience and intuition, consider the outcomes when marketing experts and complete marketing novices were asked to predict the interests and opinions of American consumers. The predictive accuracy of these hunches was very low, and experts did no better than novices.[30] Need we say more?

At times, it will be necessary to mount formal research investigations that can be complex and costly. We will give many examples of these throughout the book. However, do not mistakenly assume that formal research is always necessary. Some of the best research is done when executives engage in MBWA (Managing by Wandering Around).[31]

The goal of MBWA is to remove executives from their desks and keep them in touch with customers and employees. When this is done sensitively and perceptively, research becomes an attitude, and the benefits are real. Tom Peters calls for marketers to become obsessed with learning from and listening to their customers, and he recommends that they be in the field at least 25 percent of their time.[32]

MBWA is a major part of the remarkable success of Japanese companies in penetrating the U.S. market. For example, the Kao Corporation dominates the detergent and soap market in Japan by constantly monitoring the consumer environment and providing quick marketing responses when needed.[33] It is not unusual to find top-level management observing and talking with consumers at point of sale to find ways to serve them better. In this way Kao and other manufacturers countered Procter & Gamble, which introduced disposable diapers to Japan, and reduced P&G's market share from 90 percent in the mid-1970s to 8 percent by 1984.

When we move to the American scene, however, this observation by Calvin Hodock, past president of the American Marketing Association, is all too true:

> In American corporations today, marketing research is a discipline down there in the trenches with lots of other stuff. Senior executives have more important things to think about. Research is not revered in the corporate offices of America.[34]

Small wonder that Japan has made such stunning inroads into American markets. The implications are obvious—listening to and responding to the consumer is not an option!

An Entrepreneurial Commitment

Entrepreneurship is an "in word" today. This is because competitive survival demands a commitment to ongoing risk-taking and innovation. As Tom Peters puts it:

> No company's edge is commanding anymore. No transformation, no matter how dramatic, provides each five years' safety against the wildly gyrating forces at work. In today's fast-changing world, where we don't even know the names of next month's competitors, let alone their cost structure, no one has a safe lead. For the foreseeable future, organizations must learn to cherish change and to take advantage of constant tumult as much as they have resisted change in the past.[35]

American and European businesses seem to have become blinded by the quickness with which Japanese competitors have outdistanced them repeatedly. Why has this happened? In comparison with their British counterparts, Japanese firms gain advantage in four ways:[36]

1. Their focus is on changing markets and the opportunities presented rather than on production or finance.
2. Market changes are constantly monitored to detect emerging segments and opportunities.
3. Once these opportunities are in view, new models are brought onto the market almost instantly.
4. Decision making is decentralized so that rapid response is possible without endless management review.

The key lies in managerial commitment to adapt quickly to a rapidly changing environment. Without this commitment, there is no point in undertaking consumer research.

Entrepreneurship, however, can quickly be stifled by fear of failure. It is an ominous fact that about 90 percent of all product introductions ultimately either fail or fall short of potential. This happens, according to new-product consultant George Reider, because we have become myopic: "We're spending too much time looking at our computer screens instead of using the creativity and judgment of the people who are in direct customer contact each day."[37]

One significant source of innovation is ceaseless research scrutiny to uncover unmet needs and market "niches." Robert Bennett was a computer salesperson who spotted a real need in college dorm rooms and elsewhere—a small appliance that is a combination refrigerator/freezer and microwave. The MicroFridge was born and has gained significant inroads into the dormitory, no-frills hotels, and senior citizens' market.[38]

Many industries exist, however, in innovation-saturated, slow-growth markets. The entrepreneurial key here is to spot ways in which existing products can be improved or extended in small but significant ways. Kraft General Foods was the first company to market premeasured coffee packets for early-morning drinkers.

And Sara Lee, now a major conglomerate, introduced Just My Size pantyhose for larger women.[39]

Individualized Marketing

Rapp and Collins have challenged marketers to embrace a strategy of *individualized marketing*.[40] Here is what they mean:

> a very personal form of marketing that recognizes, acknowledges, appreciates, and serves the interests and needs of selected groups of consumers whose individual identities are or become known to the advertiser [marketer].[41]

In one sense there is little new here. For many decades it has been a commonplace policy to design an entirely different marketing strategy for smaller units or segments within a market that differ in meaningful ways from other groups. This strategy is known as **market segmentation**. The 18–24 age group becomes the target, for example, and different strategies are used for those who are older.

The Anheuser-Busch Company maintains industry dominance by "segmenting the market with a vengeance."[42] The company divides the United States into 210 markets, and there are regional strategy variations designed to position Anheuser-Busch products as "everyone's hometown beer." Sponsored events and advertising are specifically aimed at blacks, whites, blue-collar workers, computer buffs, and auto-racing fans, to mention only a few examples. The ad copy for one commercial event saluted waitresses and bartenders with, "This Bud's for everyone that serves them up cold."

You will find examples of segmentation research and strategies as we unfold the complex of influences on consumer behavior. Also, market segmentation is the subject of Chapter 21. Yet individualized marketing has come to take on an all-new meaning in the past decade—*data-base marketing*.[43] Through use of warranty cards and other means, names of individual customers or prospects are acquired and utilized. The individual, as a *micro segment*, then becomes the target.

Most enterprises aiming at micro segments have utilized a strategy of **direct marketing** whereby advertising and promotion are aimed at an identified individual. General Motors Corporation rolled out its new Cadillac Seville with a mailing that offered a videocassette to 170,000 young, affluent prospects.[44] You will learn more about this rapid-growth strategy in Chapter 19.

Direct marketing is only the beginning. The next step is **customized marketing**, which involves ongoing research dialogue between buyer and seller with full customization of product, price, promotion, and distribution. With the imminent widescale introduction of interactive video, no one can predict the future marketing possibilities.

Customer Satisfaction and Retention

In the past two decades, many American and West European marketers have been shaken by the realization that they were losing the product- and service-quality war to Japan. The outcome, of course, has been catastrophic loss of market share. Certainly, this did not happen overnight. What caused such myopia?

Consumer in Focus   1.3

How British Airways Butters Up the Passenger

It was our first transatlantic trip with our infant daughter, and my wife and I arrived at London's Heathrow Airport laden with luggage and baby gear. To our dismay, a computer failure had left check-in lines 40 deep. We were just about to settle in for an ordeal when a British Airways staffer pulled us aside. "You don't want to wait in those queues with a baby," he said. Grabbing our cart, he ushered us to a special desk and stood by until we checked in.

Experiences like ours have given British Airways one of the best service reputations in the business. A poll by the International Foundation for Airline Passengers Associations ranked it up with Singapore Airlines, Cathay Pacific, Swissair, and American Airlines. That's an impressive change for a carrier that in the early 80s was on many people's list of worst airlines. "The attitude was, 'This would be a great place to work if it wasn't for these bloody customers,'" says John J. Bray, chief executive of Forum Europe Ltd., a consulting firm BA hired in 1984.

The shift started in 1983, when Colin Marshall took over as chief executive. The British-born former CEO of Avis Inc. adopted a novel approach for BA: He asked customers what they wanted. Surveys showed that a friendly staff was twice as important as operational factors in food service and speed of check-in for generating goodwill. "We decided service excellence, not operations, was going to drive the business," says Liam Strong, BA's marketing director.

The next task was to convince BA's 35,000 employees that travelers should be treated as individuals, not components to be shunted down an assembly line. Marshall and his team tirelessly preached the gospel of focusing on the customer and launched an extensive training program.

Continued

Part of the answer relates to the earlier discussion of the Japanese managerial commitment to MBWA—Management by Wandering Around. However, there is more to it than that. Toyota has attained a 43 percent market share in Japan and the number-one import position in the United States by "total dedication to continuous improvement."[45] Everything is done to ensure that the customer is completely satisfied, and this, of course, is the key to retaining that customer over time.

Incontrovertible evidence shows that sustainable market share comes primarily through a commitment to ongoing leadership in quality and service.[46] This does not happen without ongoing consumer research, and the ramifications of this principle are far reaching. Take time to read Consumer in Focus 1.3, which documents how British Airways shed its old nickname, "Bloody Awful."

BA also dropped some of its old, military-style hierarchy in favor of more decentralized decision making. Marketing people helped decide which planes to buy and how to equip them. Money was poured into reservation systems, uniforms, and plane interiors. Employees, at first skeptical and still shaken by massive layoffs prior to Marshall's arrival, grew more responsive to the training. Privatization in 1987 made 74% of BA employees shareholders and provided further motivation.

Marshall has also focused on BA's most important group of customers: business travelers. Since upgrading business class in 1987—with wider seats, footrests, and expanded menus and wine list—revenues have doubled for long hauls and risen 13% in Europe. UBS Phillips & Drew Ltd. expects BA's pretax profits to grow 19%, to $544 million, on about $8.2 billion in sales for the fiscal year ending Mar. 31. Improved service accounts for part of the gain, but so does the Pan Am crash at Lockerbie, Scotland, which fed fears of flying U.S. carriers.

BA's record still isn't perfect: Capacity crowds on transatlantic flights since the Lockerbie disaster have overstretched staff. And complaints about on-board service continue to plague flights within Europe. But BA is trying harder. The airline employs 60 trained problem-solvers called "hunters" who roam BA's Heathrow terminals. Recently, a hunter spotted two women who had come off a delayed Lufthansa flight and had 20 minutes to catch a BA plane. After radioing ahead to preserve their seats, he snatched their hand luggage and ran with them to the gate.

Such service helps passengers forget BA's old nickname: Bloody Awful.

Source: Mark Maremont, "How British Airways Butters Up the Passenger," *Business Week* (March 12, 1990), 94. Reproduced by special permission.

The Point-of-Sale Battle

Markets in western countries are deluged with new products and services. The number of cereal brands that sell at least $1 million annually grew from 84 in 1979 to 150 in 1989. Over 10,000 new food and nonfood items are introduced for supermarkets each year at a cost of $15–20 million apiece.[47] Considering the fact that the average supermarket has space for only about 17,000 items, the outcome is a serious new-product glut.

How, then, does the manufacturer gain new-product distribution? One key is to pull the product through the system by building consumer interest through advertising. But media advertising faces a glut of its own through the increased clutter. The only recourse for many is to push the product through channels with special

Wired Consumers: Market-Researchers Go High-Tech

Joann Alter shops at the Weis Market near her home at least four times a week. But even if she's just dashing in for a quart of milk or a dozen eggs, she always remembers to give the cashier her Shopper's Hotline card. By showing the card, Mrs. Alter gets a chance at a variety of enticing prizes. "How could I ever forget to show my card, when with so little effort you can gain so much?" she asks.

That's the sort of thing the people at Information Resources Inc. like to hear. The card is a vital link in the program. It makes it possible to monitor purchases by consumers like Mrs. Alter and correlate them with information collected by gadgets on their television sets about what commercials they watch and with other data about what coupons they use.

Electronic testing techniques—such as those being used here, as well as in several other markets by Information Resources and two major competitors, A. C. Nielsen Co. and Burke Marketing Services Inc.—have made it possible to evaluate consumer tastes with much greater precision.

Continued

incentives. Indeed, it can cost $10,000 or more just to buy shelf space in some supermarkets.

Once distribution is attained, the battle now intensifies in the form of sales promotion—couponing, sampling, special displays, and so on. This is the nature of the competitive arena for the so-called **low involvement consumer behavior**, defined in the next chapter as a situation in which all brands are basically similar and the final choice is made on the basis of price or special incentive. This, in turn, can become competitively ruinous.

Is it any wonder that increasing numbers of marketers are searching for better distribution alternatives? This is a primary incentive for the burgeoning growth of direct marketing discussed earlier. Consumers also are tiring of the retail arena and are turning to in-home shopping. As Faith Popcorn has observed, the home is becoming a safe "cocoon."[48] This leads to some sharp changes in buyer behavior which will be discussed at many points in the following sections.

The Push for Cost Effectiveness

"I know that half of my advertising is effective. The only trouble is that I don't know which half." This statement has been attributed to several pre–World War II business pioneers. No matter who said it, bottom-line cost effectiveness has become an

The Williamsport, Pennsylvania, area, with a population of about 93,000 and an average annual discretionary income of $24,000, provides an unusual opportunity for electronic market testing. The extensive network of cable hookups is ideal for Information Resources' purpose. Clients buy local time to test new ads, or Information Resources can "overlay" a test ad or two in place of the client's national commercial, which the rest of the country is seeing.

Late each night, a computer calls the 3,000 Williamsport households participating in BehaviorScan to link up with the microprocessor inside each of their cable converters. Information Resources knows exactly what they watch each day and whether family members view an entire show or flip the channel several times.

Information Resources spent about $2 million in start-up costs to establish its electronic network here, equipping nine of the ten local supermarkets with bar-code scanning equipment that generates a computer file of each participating consumer's purchases.

Source: Michael Days, "Wired Consumers: Market Researchers Go High-Tech to Hone Ads, Weed Out Flops," *The Wall Street Journal* (January 23, 1986), 33. Reproduced by special permission.

even more crucial issue in the cost-conscious 1990s. As one commentator has pointed out:

> For many marketers, the 1980s stood for excess. They blitzed the U.S. consumer with sales pitches, collectively spending more than $6 a week on every man, woman and child in the U.S.—almost 50 percent more per capita than in any other nation. In retrospect, too much of it was wasted. Flawed products, inept ad campaigns, misguided gimmicks, poorly monitored promotions—these are the marketing legacies of the decade. Sales receipts often couldn't justify the soaring bills for advertising and promotion.[49]

Researchers have struggled to assess the impact of a specific marketing action on buying behavior. Fortunately, scanner technology has provided a breakthrough in behavioral measurement. With the onset of bar-coded prices, scanner data can be used to test buying response to instore promotional stimuli. With scanner technology, marketers can measure buying responses to promotional stimuli transmitted to selected cooperating homes which serve as a consumer panel.[50] Consumer in Focus 1.4 describes how this technology works.

While scanner research can be expensive, it quickly can pay for itself in cost savings. For example, Kraft General Foods discovered from a scanner test that 70 percent of its macaroni and cheese product would have sold *without* expensive promotion. Similarly, scanner data showed that a 40¢ coupon on toothpaste would yield a $147,000 profit increment, whereas a 50¢ coupon on the same item could mean a $348,000 loss.[51]

Scanner technology offers advantages that go beyond business practice. The evidence accumulated shows some stable and predictable patterns of consumer response. Rossiter and others contend with some justification that scanner data could lead to the rewriting of some basic tenets of consumer behavior theory.[52]

Save Our Society

The Save Our Society (S.O.S) issue is one of today's central marketing strategies.[53] Evidence shows that consumer pressures will increasingly force meaningful business response to the three critical E's—environment, education, and ethics.

As we pointed out earlier, the Consumer Bill of Rights is a clear declaration of consumer expectations. For many consumers, the environmental or "Green" movement lies at the heart of their concerns. A *Wall Street Journal*/NBC poll puts this issue in perspective:

> Eight in ten Americans regard themselves as "environmentalists" and half of those say they are "strong ones." Further, most aren't content to wait for future technological fixes to solve problems: They recognize the need for substantial, and in some cases profound, shifts in their own lifestyles.[54]

Business has responded by major efforts to reduce pollution, minimize the problems of waste disposal, and so on.[55] In fact, one study indicates the possibility that sales of so-called green consumer products will total $8.8 billion by 1995, a five-fold increase over 1990.[56]

While many evironmentally responsible firms are making profits, they have learned that consumers do not always back convictions with actions. When pressed to support their environmental courses by higher prices or taxes, a large percentage of citizens refuse.[57]

Also, many businesses have discovered that even responsible management decisions can boomerang. In 1989, Mobil Chemical Company introduced a biodegradable version of its popular Hefty trash bag line. Less than two years later, however, substances thought to be biodegradable become inert when buried too deeply for oxygen to enter. For that reason, the company has been widely criticized.[58] McDonald's and other environmentally concerned companies have faced similar dilemmas.

Internationalization

Overseas markets always have a special attraction, because the opportunities seem limitless. The easiest strategy is to engage in **global marketing**, where essentially the same strategy is used in all cultural contexts.[59] Certainly this approach, if it works, simplifies the whole process and brings about economies of scale.

Many companies have discovered, to their dismay, that it can be disastrous to ignore cultural differences that would have become apparent if they had conducted extensive consumer research. The principle that emerges, as stated in Chapter 14, is *think internationally, act locally.*

For example, Procter & Gamble Company entered the Japanese market in 1973 and lost money until 1987. As chairman and CEO Edwin L. Artzt put it, "P&G stormed into the Japanese market with American products, American managers, American advertising, and American sales methods and promotional strategies."[60] Finally a substantial investment in Japanese consumer research and marketing change has had such payout that Japan is now P&G's number-three market.[61] One of the simplest yet most profound lessons learned is that Japanese consumers, compared with their American counterparts, place far more importance on product performance than on price.

A far wiser strategy in nearly all cases is to engage in **contextualized marketing**, a strategy designed to take into account cultural differences in consumer motivation and behavior by adapting marketing efforts, where necessary, so that they are perceived as being culturally relevant.[62]

Recent research indicates that desirable product attributes vary from one Asian country to the next, thereby reflecting significant cultural differences.[63] Based on his research in China, Wang has shown that cultural variations range the least when products have high technological content (computers and household appliances are examples). Therefore, it would be appropriate for producers of such items to engage in a high degree of marketing standardization worldwide. Quite the opposite is the case, however, with food and clothing, which usually reflect cultural values.[64]

At one time many experts predicted that European Common Market (EEC) countries would represent a fertile field for uniform global marketing. Only 17 percent of companies competing in the EEC tailored their ads in 1973, but that figure leaped to 50 percent 10 years later and no doubt is even higher today.[65]

Evidence shows that some large multinational corporations can be successful with a uniform strategy in which a common image is presented worldwide.[66] Examples are Merrill Lynch & Company, Joseph E. Seagram & Sons, Digital Equipment Corporation, and Xerox Corporation. Nevertheless, most find customization necessary. Even Coca-Cola, with a seemingly universal appeal, has introduced 21 versions worldwide of its television spot featuring children singing the praises of Coke.[67]

Consumer Behavior as a Field of Academic Study

Our thrust so far has been on the uses and applications of consumer research, but it is also worth evaluating why it has become a significant academic discipline in its own right. The taproot of the field lies in economics. A more extensive historical review is given in Chapter 2, but it is worth emphasizing here that various theories about the consumer generally were not tested empirically until the middle twentieth century.[68] This distinctly practical emphasis awaited development of the field of marketing in the business curriculum and consumer studies in home economics.

Marketers, of course, always have acknowledged the significance of consumer sovereignty, but consumer research really came into its own after World War II.[69] A natural development at this time was a turning to behavioral sciences in the hopes of finding new insights into consumer behavior.

In the 1950s trained psychologists, often with a Freudian psychoanalytic perspective, found their way into the applied world and launched an era of inquiry known as **motivation research**. Although the outcome of this invasion (discussed in more detail in Chapter 2) was not especially notable, it did serve to stimulate awareness that behavioral sciences have something to contribute.

Consumer behavior emerged as a distinct field of study during the 1960s through the influence of such writers as Katona,[70] Ferber,[71] and Howard.[72] Suddenly, the behavioral sciences became the "in thing" in the schools of business. Marketers, in particular, borrowed rather indiscriminately from social psychology, sociology, anthropology, or any other field that might relate to consumer behavior in some way, no matter how remotely.

Although this borrowing process was counterproductive at times, it also was necessary for a field of study in its infancy. Soon this unfocused inquiry gave way to something far different, however, with publication of what Holbrook has referred to as the "landmark syntheses."[73] Serious attempts were made by Nicosia,[74] Howard and Sheth,[75] Engel, Kollat, and Blackwell,[76] and others to integrate what was known about consumer motivation and behavior in the form of systematic models.

Courses in consumer behavior quickly burgeoned throughout the western world. The numbers of active researchers increased geometrically from the initial handful. A major catalytic influence was formation of the Association for Consumer Research in 1969. Membership now exceeds 1,000, and the growing maturity of the field is reflected in its annual conference proceedings, entitled *Advances in Consumer Research*. You will sense the importance of these volumes by the frequency of citation in our endnotes.

The outcome is that consumer research is now an important field of study in its own right. The literature has grown sharply,[77] with the *Journal of Consumer Research* (first published in 1974) standing as a premier source. Most recently, the *Journal of Consumer Psychology* was launched in 1992.

What this means is that the field has grown from infancy to a healthy state of maturity in its 30-year life. With the onset of the holistic perspective discussed earlier, we can safely say that its impact will widen even further in the coming years.

Summary

Research into consumer motivation and behavior has assumed significance in contemporary societies worldwide. In the past 30 years a large and growing multidisciplinary field of study has emerged. The central concern of businesses, consumer economists, and others is to find more effective strategies to influence and shape that behavior. As a result, consumer research is of premier importance in this applied world.

Others have a more holistic perspective and are focusing efforts on studies of consumption in order to understand how humans think and behave in this important life activity.

When we factor in the more recent expansion of inquiry across cultural borders, the result is a rich and growing field of research.

The perspective of this book is primarily, though not exclusively, that of the field of marketing. As a result, our central concern is the practical relevance of principles and findings to business strategies. Everything done by marketers and others attempting to influence consumer behavior rests on four essential premises:

1. *The consumer is sovereign.* The consumer has full capability to screen out all attempts at influence, with the outcome that everything done by the business firm must be *adapted* to consumer motivation and behavior.
2. *Consumer motivation and behavior can be understood through research.* Perfect prediction is not possible, but strategic outcomes are notably improved through properly undertaken and utilized research.
3. *Consumer behavior can be influenced through persuasive activity that takes the consumer seriously as being sovereign and purposeful.*
4. *Consumer persuasion and influence has socially beneficial outcomes as long as legal, ethical, and moral safeguards are in place to curb attempts at manipulation.*

When these premises are disregarded, the consequences almost always are negative. We gave examples of the outcomes of both right and wrong thinking about the consumer. We further demonstrated that consumer research, properly conceived and interpreted, provides essential input for marketing strategies in both for-profit and not-for-profit organizations. Finally, research also serves as the basis for consumer education and protection, and furnishes important information for public policy decisions.

Review and Discussion Questions

1. Contrast the consumer influence and holistic perspectives in consumer research. How would the agendas of researchers from these two perspectives differ in an analysis of the decision processes and consumption behavior undertaken by new home purchasers?
2. Assume that new home buyers are studied in Chicago; New Orleans; Nairobi, Kenya; and Sao Paulo, Brazil. In each case, the target market segment is the upper middle class. What differences would you anticipate from one culture to the next?
3. Which of the following decisions should be considered legitimate topics of concern in the study of consumer behavior: (a) selecting a college, (b) purchasing a life insurance policy, (c) smoking a cigarette, (d) selecting a church to join, (e) selecting a dentist, (f) visiting an auto showroom to see new models, or (g) purchasing a college textbook.
4. Examine current advertisements for consumer products and select one for a new product. Will this product succeed in the long run in the consumer marketplace? What factors determine success?
5. A family has just come into the local office of a lending agency, asking for a bill consolidation loan. Payments for a new car, television, stereo, bedroom set, and central air conditioning have become excessive. The head of the family does not have a steady source of income, and real help is now needed. Is this an example of purposeful consumer behavior, or has this family been manipulated into making unwise purchases?
6. If it is true that motivations and behavior can be understood through research, is it also true that the marketer now has greater ability to influence the consumer adversely than would have been the case in an earlier era?

7. What contributions does the analysis of consumer behavior make to the field of finance? Of production? Of real estate? Of insurance? Of top management administration?

8. Would it be equally necessary to understand consumer behavior if the economic system were not one of free enterprise? In other words, is the subject matter of this book only of interest to those in capitalistic systems, or does it also have relevance for socialism and for communism where it still exists?

9. Consumer protection is an important issue. What areas of consumer behavior appear to be most in need of increased regulation and consumer education?

Endnotes

1. Fred S. Worthy, "Asia's New Yuppies," *Fortune* (December 4, 1990), 235.

2. Ronald A. Fullerton, "How Modern Is Modern Marketing? Marketing's Evolution and the Myth of the 'Production Era,'" *Journal of Marketing* 52 (January 1988), 108–125.

3. "AMA Board Approves New Marketing Definition," *Marketing News* (March 1, 1985), 1.

4. Peter F. Drucker, *The Practice of Management* (New York: Harper & Row, 1954), 37.

5. Tom Peters and Nancy Austin, *A Passion for Excellence* (New York: Random House, 1985), 4.

6. Russell W. Belk, "ACR Presidential Address: Happy Thought," in Melanie Wallendorf and Paul Anderson, eds., *Advances in Consumer Research* 14 (Provo, Utah: Association for Consumer Research, 1986), 2.

7. For a very interesting review, see Ruth E. Deacon and Wallace E. Huffman, eds., *Home Economics Research, 1887-1997, Proceedings* (Ames, Iowa: Iowa State University College of Home Economics, 1986), 7.

8. See E. Scott Maynes and ACCI Research Committee, eds., *The Frontier of Research in the Consumer Interest* (Columbia, Mo.: University of Missouri, American Council on Consumer Interests, 1988).

9. Julie L. Ozanne and Laurel Anderson Hudson, "Exploring Diversity in Consumer Research," in Elizabeth C. Hirschman, ed., *Interpretive Consumer Research* (Provo, Utah: Association for Consumer Research, 1989), 1–9; Craig J. Thompson, William Locander, and Howard R. Pollio, "Putting Consumer Experience Back into Consumer Research: The Philosophy and Method of Existential-Phenomenology," *Journal of Consumer Research* 16 (September 1989), 133–146.

10. Richard J. Lutz, "Editorial," *Journal of Consumer Research* 16 (September 1989), 32.

11. Morris B. Holbrook and Elizabeth C. Hirschman, "The Experiential Aspects of Consumption: Consumer Fantasies, Feelings, and Fun," *Journal of Consumer Research* 9 (September 1982), 132–140. Also see Elizabeth C. Hirschman and Morris B. Holbrook, "Hedonic Consumption: Emerging Concepts, Methods, and Propositions," *Journal of Marketing* 45 (Summer 1982), 92–101.

12. Morris B. Holbrook, "What Is Consumer Research?" *Journal of Consumer Research* 14 (June 1987), 130.

13. For an interesting and entertaining review, see Russell W. Belk, Melanie Wallendorf and John Sherry, Jr., "The Sacred and the Profane in Consumer Behavior: Theodicy on the Odyssey," *Journal of Consumer Research* 16 (June 1989), 1–38.

14. Morris B. Holbrook, "The Dramatic Side of Consumer Research: The Semiology of Consumption Symbolism in the Arts," in Melanie Wallendorf and Paul Anderson, eds., *Advances in Consumer Research* 14 (Provo, Utah: Association for Consumer Research, 1986), 2.

15. See Richard J. Lutz, "Presidential Address. Positivism, Naturalism and Pluralism in Consumer Research: Paradigms in Paradise," in Thomas K. Srull, ed., *Advances in Consumer Research* 16 (Provo, Utah: Association for Consumer Research, 1988), 1–8. Also Lawrence J. Marks, Susan Higgins, and Michael A. Kamins, "Investigating the Experiential Dimensions of Product Evaluation," *Advances in Consumer Research* 15 (Provo, Utah: Association for Consumer Research, 1987), 114–121; and Elizabeth C. Hirschman, "Humanistic Inquiry and Marketing Research: Philosophy, Method, and Criteria," *Journal of Marketing Research* 23 (August 1986), 237–249.
16. "Detergent Shows Power in Washing Market," *China Daily* (June 13, 1988), 6.
17. "Getting Inside Their Heads," *American Demographics* (August 1989), 20.
18. Joanne Lipman, "Ads on TV: Out of Sight, Out of Mind?" *The Wall Street Journal* (May 14, 1991), B1.
19. Kate Fitzgerald, "Hello? Is Anybody Listening?" *Advertising Age* (October 22, 1990), 34.
20. Fitzgerald, "Hello? Is Anybody Listening?"
21. Michael M. Miller, "What a Museum! Panda Punch, I Hate Peas, Nutrimate and More," *The Wall Street Journal* (December 15, 1986), 26.
22. Nancy Giges, "No Miracle in Small Miracle Story Behind Clairol Failure," *Advertising Age* (August 16, 1982), 76.
23. Leo Bogart, "Where Does Advertising Research Go from Here?" *Journal of Advertising Research* 9 (March 1969), 10.
24. For a fascinating history, see Robert J. Lampman, "JFK's Four Consumer Rights: A Retrospective View," in Maynes et al., *The Frontier of Research in the Consumer Interest*, 19–36.
25. Frank Rose, "If It Feels Good, It Must Be Bad," *Fortune* (October 21, 1991), 92.
26. Rose, "If It Feels Good, It Must Be Bad."
27. Faith Popcorn, *The Popcorn Report* (New York: Doubleday, 1991).
28. For a review of donor-related research done in one field of not-for-profit marketing, see James F. Engel and Jerry Jones, *Baby Boomers and the Future of World Missions* (Orange, Calif.: Management Development Associates, 1989) and James F. Engel, *Averting the Financial Crisis in Christian Organizations: Insights from a Decade of Donor Research* (Wheaton, Ill.: Management Development Associates, 1983).
29. "Why Kodak Is Starting to Click Again," *Business Week* (February 23, 1987), 134.
30. Stephen J. Hoch, "Who Do We Know? Predicting the Interests and Opinions of the American Consumer," *Journal of Consumer Research* 15 (December 1988), 315–324.
31. Peters and Austin, *A Passion for Excellence*, Chapter 2.
32. Tom Peters, *Thriving on Chaos* (New York: Alfred A. Knopf, 1987).
33. Johnny Johansson and Ikujiro Nonaka, "Market Research the Japanese Way," *Harvard Business Review* (May–June 1987), 16–23.
34. Calvin L. Hodcock, "The Decline and Fall of Marketing Research in Corporate America," *Marketing Research* 2 (June 1991), 15.
35. Tom Peters, "There Are No Excellent Companies," *Fortune* (April 27, 1987), 382.
36. Peter Doyle, John Saunders, and Veronica Wong, "A Comparative Investigation of Japanese Marketing Strategies and the British Market," in Robert F. Lusch et al., eds., *1985 AMA Educators' Proceedings* (Chicago: American Marketing Association, 1985), 256–262.
37. Howard Schlossberg, "Fear of Failure Stifles Product Development," *Marketing News* (May 14, 1990), 1.
38. Howard Schlossberg, "No 'Me Too' for These Two," *Marketing News* (May 14, 1990), 1.
39. Patricia Sellers, "Winning Over the New Consumer," *Fortune* (July 29, 1991), 113–124.

40. Stan Rapp and Tom Collins, *The Great Marketing Turnaround—The Age of the Individual and How to Profit from It* (Englewood Cliffs, N.J.: Prentice-Hall, 1990).

41. Rapp and Collins, *The Great Marketing Turnaround*, 37.

42. Patricia Sellers, "How Busch Wins in a Doggy Market," *Fortune* (June 22, 1987), 99–111.

43. Susan Krafft, "The Big Merge," *American Demographics* (June 1991), 44–48.

44. "What Happened to Advertising?" *Business Week* (September 23, 1991), 67–72.

45. Alex Taylor III, "Why Toyota Keeps Getting Better and Better and Better," *Fortune* (November 19, 1990), 66–79.

46. Two books shed particularly valuable light on the issue of quality. See Jan Carlzon, *Moments of Truth* (Cambridge, Mass.: Ballinger, 1987) and Peters, *Thriving on Chaos*. Also, see "King Customer," *Business Week* (March 12, 1990), 88–94.

47. Rapp and Collins, *The Great Marketing Turnaround*, 16.

48. Popcorn, *The Popcorn Report*.

49. Richard Gibson, "Marketers' Mantra: Reap More with Less," *The Wall Street Journal* (March 22, 1991), B1.

50. Martha Farnsworth Riche, "Look before Leaping," *American Demographics* (February 1990), 18–19.

51. Gibson, "Marketers' Mantra."

52. John R. Rossiter, "Consumer Research and Marketing Science," in Srull, *Advances*, 407–413. Also see Patrick G. Buckley, "An S-O-R Model of the Purchase of an Item in a Store," in Rebecca H. Holman and Michael R. Solomon, eds., *Advances in Consumer Research* 18 (Provo, Utah: Association for Consumer Research, 1991), 491–500.

53. Popcorn, *The Popcorn Report*.

54. Rose Gutfeld, "Shades of Green. Eight of 10 Americans Are Environmentalists, At Least So They Say," *The Wall Street Journal* (August 2, 1991), 1.

55. For a comprehensive review of the issues, see Patrick Carson and Julia Moulden, *Green Is Gold* (Toronto, Canada: Harper Collins, 1991).

56. Joseph M. Winski, "Big Prizes, But No Easy Answers," *Advertising Age* (October 28, 1991), GR 3.

57. Gutfeld, "Shades of Green."

58. Jennifer Lawrence, "The Green Revolution. Mobil Case Study," *Advertising Age* (January 29, 1991), 12–13.

59. Theodore Levitt, "The Globalization of Markets," *Harvard Business Review* (May-June 1976), 106–118.

60. Laurie Freeman, "Japan Rises to P&G's No. 3 Market," *Advertising Age* (December 10, 1990), 42.

61. Freeman, "Japan Rises."

62. James F. Engel, "Toward the Contextualization of Consumer Behavior," in Chin Tong Tan and Jagdish N. Sheth, eds., *Historical Perspectives in Consumer Research: National and International Perspectives* (Singapore: National University of Singapore, 1985), 1–4.

63. See David K. Tse, Russell W. Belk, and Nan Zhou, "Becoming a Consumer Society: A Longitudinal and Cross-Cultural Content Analysis of Print Ads from Hong Kong, the People's Republic of China, and Taiwan," *Journal of Consumer Research* 15 (March 1989), 457–472. Also, Wang Zhengyuan, "Toward Some Standardized Cross-Cultural Consumption Values: An Empirical Investigation" (unpublished MBA thesis, University of International Business & Economics, Beijing, People's Republic of China); and David K. Tse, John K. Wang, and Chin Tong Tan, "Toward Some Standardized Cross-Cultural Consumption Values," *Advances in Consumer Research* 15

(Provo, Utah: Association for Consumer Research, 1987), 387–395. Both of these sources refer to a common series of studies; hence the nearly identical titles.

64. Wang Zhengyuan, "Toward Some Standardized Cross-Cultural Consumption Values."

65. Julie Skur Hill and Joseph M. Winski, "Goodbye Global Ads," *Advertising Age* (November 16, 1987), 16ff.

66. See John S. Hill and William L. James, "Effects of Selective Environmental and Structural Factors on International Advertising Strategy: An Exploratory Study," in James H. Leigh and Claude R. Martin, Jr., eds., *Current Issues & Research in Advertising* 12 (Ann Arbor, Mich.: Division of Research, School of Business Administration, The University of Michigan, 1991), 136–153. Also, Gary Levin, "Ads Going Global," *Advertising Age* (July 22, 1991), 4ff.

67. Hill and Winski, "Goodbye Global Ads."

68. A good contemporary source is Paul J. Albanese, ed., *Psychological Foundations of Economic Behavior* (New York: Praeger, 1988).

69. For a helpful historical review, see Sidney J. Levy, "President's Column," *ACR Newsletter* (March 1991), 3–6.

70. George Katona, *The Powerful Consumer* (New York: McGraw-Hill, 1960).

71. Robert Ferber's writings ranged from advanced statistical techniques to applications of principles of psychology and economics to various phases of consumer behavior. He was coeditor with Hugh G. Wales of an important early book, *Motivation and Market Behavior* (Homewood, Ill.: Richard D. Irwin, 1958).

72. John A. Howard, *Marketing Management Analysis and Planning*, rev. ed. (Homewood, Ill.: Richard D. Irwin, 1963).

73. Holbrook, "What Is Consumer Research?" 130.

74. Francesco M. Nicosia, *Consumer Decision Processes* (Englewood Cliffs, N.J.: Prentice-Hall, 1966).

75. John A. Howard and Jagdish N. Sheth, *The Theory of Buyer Behavior* (New York: John Wiley & Sons, 1969).

76. James F. Engel, David T. Kollat, and Roger D. Blackwell, *Consumer Behavior*, 1st ed. (New York: Holt, Rinehart and Winston, 1968).

77. See especially John C. Mowen, *Consumer Behavior*, 2d ed. (New York: Macmillan, 1990); J. Paul Peter and Jerry C. Olson, *Consumer Behavior—Marketing Strategy Perspectives*, 2d ed. (Homewood, Ill.: Richard D. Irwin, 1990); Del I. Hawkins, Roger J. Best, and Kenneth A. Coney, *Consumer Behavior—Implications for Marketing Strategy*, 4th ed. (Homewood, Ill.: BPI/Irwin, 1989); Henry Assael, *Consumer Behavior and Marketing Action*, 3d ed. (Boston: Kent Publishing Co., 1987); William L. Wilkie, *Consumer Behavior* (New York: John Wiley & Sons, 1986); and Thomas S. Robertson, Joan Zielinski, and Scott Ward, *Consumer Behavior* (Glenview, Ill.: Scott Foresman, 1984). An especially noteworthy theoretical contribution is James R. Bettman, *An Information Processing Theory of Consumer Choice* (Reading, Mass.: Addison-Wesley, 1979).

Understanding the Consumer

Bob and Joanne Zeidler and their newborn first child, Robyn Nicole, live in Plymouth, Minnesota, a suburban community on the northwest outskirts of Minneapolis. Bob is a sales executive with a sheet metal fabricator, and Joanne works (part time since Robyn's birth in July 1991) with junior and senior high girls through a local youth guidance organization. They are in their early 30s and have been married since 1989. Both agree that their primary life goal is to live comfortably while having the time to enjoy life and active ministry in their church and engage in volunteer service.

During the past month or so, Joanne and Bob have made a number of buying decisions, either alone as individuals or together as a couple along with Robyn. Here are six examples:

1. Although they have a good 35mm camera, Joanne and Bob agreed that they would enjoy the benefits of home video, especially since the birth of Robyn. After a couple of weeks of deliberation they decided to make this investment. Bob did a fair amount of comparison shopping, and they finally settled on the Sony Camcorder.
2. Bob stopped on the way home to get milk and a few other items from a nearby convenience store. His eye was caught by a display for a brand of milk they ordinarily do not buy, but there was a $.25 price reduction. Therefore, he thought, "why not try it," and added a carton to his shopping cart.

3. They attended a movie in downtown Minneapolis the previous
   Two interesting candidates were identified from newspaper ads,
   recommendation was the deciding factor in the one which they
4. Joanne picked up a bottle of chenin blanc wine from the Hunter Va.,
   Australia. Australian wine was totally unfamiliar to her, but she wanted to try
   something different for a change.
5. Joanne ran out of Aveda Flax Seed/Aloe hair gel. The first store she entered
   was out of this brand. Rather than switch to something else, she bought Aveda
   elsewhere. She didn't consider trying another brand because Aveda has all-
   natural ingredients and holds her hair the way she wants it.
6. Bob's shopping list reminded him that he was out of shaving cream. There
   were a dozen or more brands on display at Walmart, and he didn't see any real
   difference between any of them. He stuck with his usual brand, however, because none was on sale for a lower price.

Joanne and Bob Zeidler made six purchase decisions, each of which revealed
different decision-process dynamics and actions. The primary purpose of this chapter is to give you an overview of the dynamics and complexities that have been
illustrated here.

We focus on two major issues: (1) the ways in which *environmental influences,
individual differences*, and *psychological processes* shape and influence what takes place;
and (2) the nature of consumer decision processes. Then we pull everything together in the form of a flow-chart integrative model which will be used throughout
the book to help you understand the variables affecting behavior and the ways in
which they interact.

The Underlying Influences on Consumer Behavior

Consumer behavior is influenced and shaped by many factors and determinants
which fall into these three categories: (1) environmental influences; (2) individual
differences and influences; and (3) psychological processes. A summary follows of
the many variables under these headings. While each is covered in depth in later
chapters, the discussion here will provide you with a broad overview.

Environmental Influences

Consumers live in a complex environment. Their decision-process behavior is influenced by (1) culture; (2) social class; (3) personal influence; (4) family; and
(5) situation.

Culture In some tribal settings in East Africa, one of the worst curses a rural,
traditional woman can face is to be slim. Members of those particular cultures stipu-
late that "fat is beautiful." What a contrast to the Western world!

Culture, as used in the study of consumer behavior, refers to the values, ideas, artifacts, and other meaningful symbols that help individuals communicate, interpret, and evaluate as members of society. Chapter 3 illustrates vividly that a marketer with a defective knowledge of culture is doomed.

Americans would not normally view Minnesota as a separate culture in its own right, but those beyond the boundaries of this country would have a different outlook. Imagine the challenge that would confront a vodka manufacturer located in remote northern Russia attempting to break into the U.S. (and Minneapolis) market. Executives would be bewildered in contending with a mature consumer culture for the first time and would have few clues in marketing their product.

From a different perspective, it is worth noting that all forms of marketing are a channel through which cultural meanings are transferred to consumer goods.[1] Hence, marketing is a value transmitter that simultaneously shapes culture and is shaped by it. This relationship raises many ethical questions, because, as we will discover in Chapter 24, there are disturbing challenges to the social ethical validity of marketing as it is presently practiced.

Social Class   **Social classes** are divisions within society composed of individuals sharing similar values, interests, and behaviors. They are differentiated by socio-economic status differences ranging from low to high. Social class status often leads to differing forms of consumer behavior (for example, the types of alcoholic beverages served, the make and style of car driven, and the styles of dress preferred).

Social class differences, while still alive, are blurring somewhat in the United States and probably were not much of a factor in Joanne and Bob's purchases. But this certainly is not the case in emerging countries of the world. Therefore, the concepts reviewed in Chapter 4 still are of significance for the student of consumer behavior.

Personal Influence   As consumers, our behavior often is affected by those with whom we closely associate. We may respond to perceived pressure to conform with the norms and expectations provided by others.

Also, we value those around us as did Joanne and Bob for their counsel on buying choices. This influence can take the form of observation of what others are doing, with the result that they become a comparative reference group. When we actively seek advice from another, however, that person can serve as an **influential** or **opinion leader**. All of these forms of personal influence are discussed in Chapter 5.

Family   Since the field of consumer research was founded in the post–World War II era, the family has been a focus of research. The family often is the primary decision-making unit with a complex and varying pattern of roles and functions.

At this point, Bob and Joanne have a high degree of interaction and cooperation in decision making, but each plays a differing role from one product to the next. Bob, for example, was more involved in evaluating video camera alternatives.

As of this writing Robyn was not old enough to influence family buying decisions through verbal or nonverbal communication. But this is about to change!

Very soon her wants will be quite obvious, and she will exert real influence on buying actions as she ages.

Chapter 6 unfolds the significance of the family in shaping buying and consumption decisions.

Situation

It is obvious that behavior changes as situations change. Sometimes these changes are erratic and unpredictable, such as a job layoff. At other times they can be predicted by research and capitalized upon in strategy.

As you will see in Chapter 7, marketers often capitalize upon **situational influences**, particularly in retail settings, to influence consumer behavior. No doubt the wine merchant deliberately created the atmosphere to intrigue potential buyers such as Joanne about non-familiar wines. Following the initiative of Belk and others in the 1970s,[2] situation now is treated as a research variable in its own right.

Individual Differences

Now we move from the external environment to five individual differences that affect behavior: (1) consumer resources; (2) motivation and involvement; (3) knowledge; (4) attitudes; and (5) personality, values, and lifestyle.

Consumer Resources

Each person brings three resources into every decision-making situation—(1) time, (2) money, and (3) information reception and processing capabilities. Generally there are distinct limits on the availability of each, thus requiring some careful allocation. These and other issues are discussed in Chapter 8.

To take an example, dual career/family women such as Joanne may have an income sufficient to enable purchases that would not have been possible in earlier years. Yet there are restrictions on the time available for shopping and the ability to allocate attention to the information gathered in the process. As a result, many women are resorting to purchasing high-fashion items from catalogs. The so-called upscale busy woman is the primary target for leading catalog marketer Spiegel Inc.[3]

Motivation and Involvement

Psychologists and marketers alike have conducted considerable research to determine what takes place when goal-directed behavior is energized and activated. This is what we mean by motivation, the subject of Chapter 9.

It is helpful at this point to delve a bit more deeply into this subject, following up the discussion in Chapter 1. In addition, it is helpful to provide background to help you understand how marketers have wrestled with this subject over the years.

Motives

Turning to the subject of motivation as traditionally conceived, a central variable has always been **motive**—an enduring predisposition that arouses and directs behavior toward certain goals. Researchers are still investigating how consumer motives can be classified and the extent to which they are conscious or unconscious.

In the 1920s, marketing scholar Melvin Copeland introduced the classification of rational versus emotional motives.[4] If we were to use this system, we would

Symbols, Icons, and Semiotics: Snuggle Fabric Softener

In just a few years, Lever Brothers Co. built a $300 million fabric softener brand through the charms of a huggable teddy bear named Snuggle. Most marketers only dream of creating such a powerful advertising symbol, and Lever didn't want to do anything to jeopardize this little gold mine. It felt it needed to know more about why Snuggle was so successful and how the bear should be used in ads. So Snuggle got psychoanalyzed.

Carol Moog, a psychologist turned advertising consultant, did an analysis of Snuggle that went way beyond cuddliness. "The bear is an ancient symbol of aggression, but when you create a teddy bear, you provide a softer, nurturant side to that aggression," she says. "As a symbol of tamed aggression, the teddy bear is the perfect image for a fabric softener that tames the rough texture of clothing."

Lever had other questions about Snuggle: Should the bear be a boy or girl? Should it interact with humans in the ads? How about blinking its eyes, wiggling its ears and sniffing the laundry? Blinking, wiggling and sniffing were all deemed suitable behavior, but Ms. Moog recommended that Snuggle remain genderless and that people not be included in ads. "To keep the magic, it has to be just Snuggle and the viewer communicating," she says. "The teddy bear acts as a bridge between the consumer's rational and more instinctual, emotional side."

Ms. Moog calls her analysis of signs and symbols in advertising "psychological semiotics." Some people refer to it simply as semiotics; others prefer "iconology" or image decoding. Whatever academic jargon they use to describe it, more marketers are turning to social scientists to help them understand the many messages their advertising is transmitting to consumers on both a conscious and subconscious level. Ads have always been rich with psychological imagery, but advertisers now are trying harder to control and

Continued

classify as rational motives such preferred utilitarian vacuum cleaner features as lightweightness, ease of handling, and convenience of storing.[5]

Yet we also recognize that products have *symbolic values* that transcend economic considerations. This is what Copeland meant by emotional motives, but that term is seldom used today. In a landmark contribution to consumer behavior in 1959, Sidney Levy stated:

> The things people buy are seen to have personal and social meanings in addition to their functions. Modern goods are recognized as psychological things, as symbolic of personal attributes and goals, as symbolic of social patterns and strivings.[6]

manipulate the symbols. Even the penguins in a new Diet Coke commercial aren't there just for humorous effect. SSC&B, an ad agency that practices semiotics, notes that the birds symbolize coolness, refreshment and friendliness.

"It's mind boggling to try to control all the non-verbal symbols in our creative work," says Elissa Moses, a research executive at the BBDO ad agency. "But if advertisers aren't aware of subtleties, they may inadvertently communicate the wrong message." Consider an ad for Grey Flannel cologne. The marketer was startled to learn from a psychologist that the ad showing only a man's back could be perceived as "rudely giving the consumer the cold shoulder."

Some ad agencies, though, are skeptical of semiotics. They question whether social scientists read too much into commercials, and they chafe at efforts to transform the creative process from an art to a science. "These psychologists tend to be overly intellectual and a little tutti-frutti," says George Lois, chairman of Lois Pitts Gershon Pon/GGK, an ad agency.

Even companies that do semiotic research sometimes take it with a grain of salt. That was the case with executives at American Cyanamid Co., when Ms. Moog, the psychologist, studied a commercial for Pierre Cardin men's fragrance. The ad was designed to show men who are aggressive and in control, but Ms. Moog saw a conflict in an image of the cologne gushing out of a phallic-shaped bottle. She said it symbolized male ejaculation and lack of control. "We recognized that she probably was right," says a marketing official who worked with Ms. Moog, "but we kept the shot of the exploding cologne in the commercial anyway. It's a beautiful product shot, plus it encourages men to use our fragrance liberally."

Source: Ronald Alsop, "Agencies Scrutinize Their Ads for Psychological Symbolism," *The Wall Street Journal* (June 11, 1987), 25. Reprinted by permission of *The Wall Street Journal*, © Dow Jones & Co., Inc. 1987. All rights reserved.

While Levy was giving a broad, eclectic viewpoint, those from a more psychoanalytic persuasion soon uncovered hidden symbolism. An example would be the sexual connotations of changing the design of a bar of hand soap from a square to a round shape. Small wonder that Vance Packard seized the opportunity in 1959 to write his best-seller, *The Hidden Persuaders*,[7] which generated considerable interest in the press and among the general public.

Some psychoanalysts and other specialists admittedly may have gone to the extreme, but symbolism cannot be ignored. Certainly it is an important part of everyday life. Do you agree with the conclusion in Consumer in Focus 2.1 that the

FIGURE 2.1 The Pillsbury Doughboy—A Potent Symbol?

teddy bear, Snuggle, offers symbolism that triggers emotions leading to purchase of the fabric softener by that name?

The concept of motive is helpful in understanding consumer preferences because criteria used in alternative evaluation are best conceived as product-specific manifestations of motives. A wide range of motives is presented in Chapter 9, including variety seeking and risk avoidance.

The Motivation-Research Era Borrowing from the Freudian-oriented clinical psychology of that time, a group of psychologists entered the marketing field in the 1950s and attempted to explain behavior on the basis of unconscious motivations. The most famous by far was the late Ernest Dichter, who became a dominant voice during that period.[8]

"Women bake cakes because of an unconscious desire to give birth." This was one of the findings that marketers found most intriguing. Pillsbury soon introduced the legendary advertising theme, "Nothing says lovin' like something from the oven." This was followed by the Pillsbury Doughboy (Figure 2.1) who took first place in 1987 as the favorite commercial character. What do you think he symbolizes?

A More Balanced Point of View Marketers did not linger long in the Freudian world of Dichter and others. Researchers built on this foundation and broadened their concepts extensively in the following years as we will discuss in Chapter 9.

Knowledge

Knowledge, the outcome of learning, can be defined simply as the information stored in memory. As discussed in Chapter 10, consumer knowledge encompasses a vast array of information, such as the availability and characteristics of products and services, where and when to buy, and how to use products.

Recently, the importance of understanding consumer knowledge or expertise has been stressed anew within the consumer research field. One major goal of advertising and selling is to provide relevant knowledge and information, which often are needed in decision making, especially under extended problem solving. Certainly the Zeidlers were motivated to acquire as much knowledge as possible before buying the Camcorder. Therefore, stimulation of awareness and interest is an important and often-necessary marketing objective.

Attitudes

Once Bob and Joanne finished their search for information and began to evaluate video camera possibilities, the outcome was the formation of an **attitude** toward each alternative. As is usually the case in such situations, they eventually purchased the brand they evaluated most favorably, the Camcorder.

Marketers must strive to understand their current and potential customers' attitudes in order to predict their behavior. In Chapter 11 we will explore this topic more fully.

Personality, Values, and Lifestyle

Joanne and Bob Zeidler fall into that generation of 77 million people born between 1946 and 1964 classified by demographers as **baby boomers**. Demographers isolate market segments using such descriptors such as age, income, and education.

The goal is to isolate both differences and trends in behavior and expenditures. When this is accompanied by **psychographic** research (values, opinions, preferences and lifestyle), much light can be shed on the nature and composition of markets.

No doubt Bob and Joanne have lifestyles that are similar in many ways to other boomers. These variables are discussed in Chapter 12 and are elaborated in many other later chapters.

Psychological Processes

Marketers will not have much influence on consumers such as Bob and Joanne unless they have a good basic understanding of how humans process information, learn, and undergo changes in attitudes and behavior. In fact, it is here that some of the greatest contributions have been made to the understanding of consumer behavior.

Information Processing

Communication is the bottom-line marketing activity. Therefore, consumer researchers have long been interested in discovering how people receive, process, and make sense of marketing communications.

How, for example, did Joanne first become aware of the benefits of Aveda Flax Seed/Aloe hair conditioner? Does her brand preference mean that competitors will encounter difficulty trying to change her preferences? How does his low level of product interest affect the way in which Bob responds to new brands of shaving cream? Will he be open or resistant?

Studies during and since World War II have underscored our foundational principle of *consumer sovereignty—people see and hear what they want to see and hear*. Information processing research, discussed in Chapter 13, addresses ways in which information is transformed, reduced, elaborated, stored, recovered, and used.

Learning Anyone attempting to influence the consumer is trying to bring about **learning**—the process by which experience leads to changes in knowledge, attitude, and behavior. How, for example, did Joanne come to prefer chenin blanc wines? How have her brand preferences for hair care products developed?

The marketing significance of learning theory became apparent when one of its leading proponents, John B. Watson, entered the advertising field in the 1930s.[9] Learning theory (Chapter 14) has an even greater practical relevance today given what we now know about products and services that are of low personal relevance to the consumer (see the discussion of involvement later in the chapter).

Attitude and Behavior Change Changes in attitude and behavior are a common marketing objective. Certainly this happened as Bob evaluated various brands of video recorders. This process reflects basic psychological influences that have been the subject of decades of intensive research. Chapter 15 reviews this literature from the perspective of designing effective promotional strategies.

The Nature of Decision Processes

If we are to understand Bob and Joanne's actions, we must be familiar with the various processes underlying buying and consumption decisions. Over the years, researchers and specialists have produced many studies and theories regarding human choice behavior.

John Dewey's conceptualizations of decision-process behavior as problem solving have been especially influential.[10] By **problem solving** we refer to thoughtful, consistent action undertaken to bring about need satisfaction. As you have seen, many factors can shape the final outcome, including internal motivations and such external influences as social pressures and marketing activities. Somehow individuals sort though all of these factors and make decisions that are logical and consistent for them. Consider these words by Ajzen and Fishbein:

> Generally speaking . . . human beings are usually quite rational and make systematic use of the information available to them . . . people consider the implications of their actions before they decide to engage or not engage in a given behavior.[11]

At times, consumer problem solving involves careful weighing and evaluation of utilitarian (or functional) product attributes. Often the term **rational decision making** is used when this is the case.

At other times, concern for so-called **hedonic benefits** will dominate, and the consumption object is viewed *symbolically* in terms of emotional responses, sensory pleasures, daydreams, or aesthetic considerations.[12] Buying and consumption frequently reflect a mixture of both the utilitarian and the hedonic.

The problem-solving perspective encompasses all types of need-satisfying behavior and a wide range of motivating and influencing factors. Broadly speaking, consumer decision making has the following stages:

1. Need recognition—a perception of difference between the desired state of affairs and the actual situation sufficient to arouse and activate the decision process.
2. Search for information—search for information stored in memory (internal search) or acquisition of decision-relevant information from the environment (external search).
3. Alternative evaluation—evaluation of options in terms of expected benefits and narrowing the choice to the preferred alternative.
4. Purchase—acquisition of the preferred alternative or an acceptable substitute.
5. Outcomes—evaluation whether or not the chosen alternative meets needs and expectations.

The Decision-Process Continuum

The extent to which each of these steps is followed in the precise form and sequence suggested here can vary, however, from one situation to the next. Sometimes consumers undertake a complex decision process requiring substantial amounts of time and energy. More common, however, are rather simplistic processes where relatively little time and effort are devoted to the decision.

One way to think about these variations is to imagine a continuum of decision making complexity ranging from high to low (see Figure 2.2). In situations where

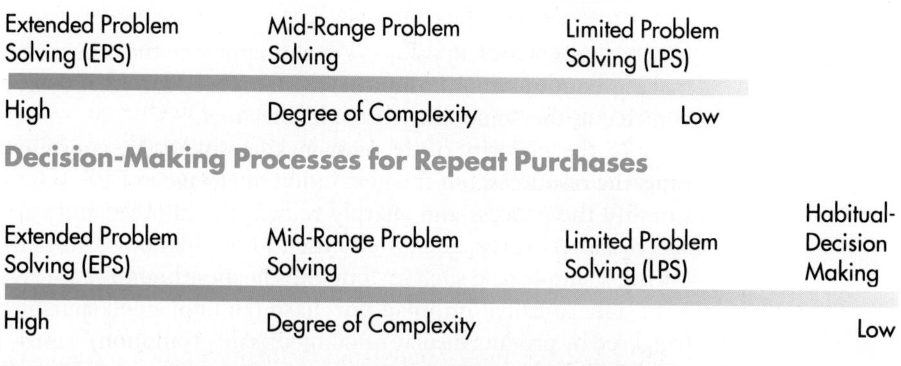

Decision-Making Processes for Initial Purchases

Extended Problem Solving (EPS)	Mid-Range Problem Solving	Limited Problem Solving (LPS)	
High	Degree of Complexity		Low

Decision-Making Processes for Repeat Purchases

Extended Problem Solving (EPS)	Mid-Range Problem Solving	Limited Problem Solving (LPS)	Habitual-Decision Making
High	Degree of Complexity		Low

FIGURE 2.2   The Consumer Decision-Process Continuum

consumers are making a decision for the first time, actions must be based on some form of problem solving. When this process is very complex, it is called **extended problem solving (EPS)**.

Limited problem solving (LPS), on the other hand, represents a lower degree of complexity. For convenience we refer to the process along the middle of the continuum as **mid-range problem solving**.

In Figure 2.2 we allow for the fact that the majority of consumer purchases are made on a repeated basis. When this is the case, the individual may engage in problem solving once again. Alternatively, he or she may greatly simplify the decisions by foregoing any deliberation of purchase alternatives and simply choosing the same brand purchased previously. What this represents is *habitual decision making*, the least complex of all decision processes.

When the initial decision was made by EPS, enduring buying patterns are often established on *brand loyalty*. On the other hand, limited problem solving leads to inertia-based habits—it's easier to do the same thing over again than switch. The reasons for these distinctions will become more clear as we proceed.

Initial Purchases

Extended Problem Solving (EPS)
When the decision process is especially detailed and rigorous, as it was when Joanne and Bob purchased the Camcorder, extended problem solving generally is a necessity. In addition, EPS also is commonly used by consumers purchasing automobiles, expensive clothing, stereo equipment, and other major products or services for which they feel it is essential to make the "right choice."

In this case, all stages in the process are followed, although not necessarily in any precise order. It is likely that many alternatives will be evaluated and a wide variety of information sources consulted. Furthermore, the decision on how and where to make the purchase also may require additional search and evaluation.

The process does not cease following purchase. If the item purchased is perceived as falling short of expectations, the outcome can be substantial and often vocal dissatisfaction. The desired outcome, of course, is satisfaction expressed in the form of positive recommendations to others and intention to repurchase should the occasion arise.

Limited Problem Solving (LPS)
We now approach the other extreme of the decision-making continuum (LPS) and arrive at what Harold Kassarjian has humorously depicted as the "muddling through consumer."[13]

In the majority of decision-making situations, consumers have neither the time, the resources, nor the motivation to engage in EPS. It is far more common to simplify the process and sharply reduce the number and variety of information sources, alternatives, and criteria used for evaluation. Choice often is made by following a simple rule such as "buy the cheapest brand."[14]

The so-called **impulse purchase** (an unplanned spur-of-the-moment action triggered by product display or point-of-sale promotion)[15] is the least complex form of LPS and represents the extreme on the continuum. When Bob saw the display and realized that a competitive brand of milk was cheaper, he bought it with little or no deliberation. His only thought was "Why not try it?" There was comparatively little information search, and the only real alternative evaluation took place *after* the milk was consumed, not before.

Mid-Range Problem Solving

As we have noted, EPS and LPS are extremes on a decision-process continuum, but many decisions range somewhere in between. An example is Joanne and Bob's choice of the movie. A minimum amount of information was required to know what was playing, which was easily found in the daily paper. Because several options looked promising, they needed to evaluate which comedy to choose. Their friend's recommendation helped. All of this was accomplished quickly and was far different from the deliberations required to purchase the Camcorder or the spur-of-the-moment decision to buy the milk.

The Special Case of Variety Seeking

Buying behavior also is initiated for a much simpler reason—**variety seeking**. This is why Joanne tried the unfamiliar brand of Australian wine. "Why not do something different for a change?" This response is most often seen when there are many similar alternatives.[16]

Repeat Purchases

Thus far, we have not addressed the issue of what happens when the buying process is repeated over time. Referring back to Figure 2.2, you will notice that there are two decision-making possibilities: (1) **repeated problem solving** (EPS, LPS, and mid-range) and (2) **habitual decision making**.

Repeated Problem Solving

Repeat purchases often require continued problem solving. Several factors can lead to this outcome. One of the most important is dissatisfaction with the previously bought alternative. A brand switch is likely. But continued problem solving also is required when retail stock has been depleted. Now the buyer must weigh the consequences of investing time and energy in shopping elsewhere.

Habitual Decision Making

Repeat purchases also can be based on habits or routines that are formed to simplify decision-process activity and enable the consumer to cope more effectively with the pressures of life. EPS, in particular, requires allocation of scarce time and energy and hence is usually avoided as much as possible. You will enjoy the dilemma of the "choice enslaved consumer" profiled in Consumer in Focus 2.2.

Purchasing habits differ sharply, however, depending upon the degree of involvement. Therefore it is necessary to contrast buying habits based on **brand loyalty** and those based on **inertia**.

Brand Loyalty   Joanne consistently buys Aveda Flax Seed/Aloe hair gel, even though it costs more than most other brands. This product class has relatively

Freedom of Choice Enslaves Dazed Consumer

The woman is standing in the drugstore suffering from acute "consumeritis." This attack has been brought on by the excess of choices on the shelf before her. Its chief symptom is mental paralysis, the total inability to make a decision.

She came here on a quest for a refill of shampoo. But when her usual brand was no longer available, she was tossed willy-nilly into the chaos of the modern day world of shampoos.

What did she want after all? Which of the three-dozen options lined up before her would make the dead follicles that grow out of her busy head come alive? A moisturizing formula? A body-building protein? A mysterious chemical soup of Elastin? Collagen? Keratin? Balsam?

She was compelled by the labels to ask herself some penetrating questions. Was she the sort of person who needed her pH balanced? Or would she prefer her pH a bit off of kilter? Should she put essential fatty acids in her scalp? Did she want shampoo with a pectin extract? Or isn't that what she uses to make jelly?

This proliferation of personal products had turned shopping into a decision-making marathon. The competing claims of manufacturers had produced an information glut.

Informed consumers are propelled into examining their bodies in ever more minute detail. Does my skin need intensive care or not? Do I have plaque on my teeth or not? Ridges on my nails? Split ends on my hair? Am I normal or dry?

One thing is clear to the woman lathering the body-building protein into her scalp: What the advertisers call brand loyalty is a low-level consumer protest movement. It's our way of cutting through the bouts of decision-making, avoiding the barrages of useless information. It's a defense against the need to waste energy differentiating things that barely differ.

Source: Ellen Goodman, "Freedom of Choice Enslaves Dazed Consumer," *The Columbus Dispatch* (October 9, 1987), 13A. Copyright 1987, The Boston Globe Newspaper Company/Washington Post Writer's Group. Reprinted with permission.

high involvement for two reasons. First, Joanne's appearance is important to her, and Aveda has consistently proved superior in maintaining her hair as she likes it.

Second, Joanne is interested in the Green movement and buys natural ingredients whenever possible. Once she discovered that the Aveda brand could be trusted, this became important information to her. So she has no incentive whatsoever to switch brands.

Inertia   Bob's shaving cream purchase, on the other hand, reflected a habit of quite a different nature. He has little or no personal involvement in this product category and feels that all brands are pretty much the same. Therefore, he will not often switch unless there are price specials.

This buying habit reflects little more than inertia. Bob has no particular incentive to switch but could very well do so if prices are lowered or he sees something bannered as being "new." Hence, this habit is nonstable, reflecting little or no brand loyalty. Given sufficient reason, he probably will switch in the future.

The Implications of Strong Loyalty   A high degree of brand loyalty is one of the greatest assets a marketer can possess. This is because strongly favorable attitudes resist change, thus making competitive inroads both difficult and expensive.

Any marketer covets high loyalty and does everything possible to maintain it. Anyone who tries to dislodge loyal purchasers of a brand of 35mm film such as Fuji could face a tough challenge indeed. This loyalty is often based on both the high involvement nature of photography to many and a belief that Fuji offers the truest color and picture quality. Such buyers have no incentive to change unless there is a real and demonstrable competitive breakthrough.

Such loyalty can quickly erode, however, when it is taken for granted. The key to maintenance of market share is pervasive and continuing commitment to customer satisfaction. Quality standards must be maintained at all costs, with any failure to perform as expected followed by immediate retribution. Furthermore, a premium must be placed on innovation to maintain competitive superiority.

Manufacturers of paper towels, on the other hand, do not enjoy much loyalty based on high involvement. Towels are a household necessity and the brands are pretty much alike, regardless of what advertisers say. So, why not switch?

Any manufacturer offering a competitive distinction, no matter how small, can gain temporary advantage. Hence, the most commonly used advertising word is *new*. Market share often is dictated more by winning the battle of advertising recognition than anything else. Heavy point-of-sale sampling, display, couponing, and other devices also are used to trigger a brand switch. Yet, instability of preference rather than loyalty is the most common outcome.

Factors Influencing the Extent of Problem Solving

Extended problem solving is most often undertaken when three major conditions are met: (1) the alternatives are differentiated in relevant ways; (2) there is sufficient time available for deliberation; and (3) there is a high degree of *involvement* (personal relevance) accompanying the purchase.

Differentiated Alternatives
Bob, particularly, engaged in EPS in the Camcorder purchase for the reason that alternatives differed in such important respects as size, versatility in varying light conditions, complexity of operation, price, and so on. Also, many information sources were available to them, including published ratings, ads, point-of-sale information, and recommendations from friends.

The more similar the alternatives are perceived to be, on the other hand, the greater the likelihood of LPS or some form of mid-range problem solving.

Time Availability   EPS is inhibited by time pressures. Joanne and Bob might have acted differently in selecting their Camcorder if they had been forced by circumstances to make a quick decision. Certainly they would not have engaged in lengthy search and alternative evaluation. Perhaps they would have shifted to an LPS strategy such as "choose one that's recommended by our video-producer friend."

Involvement   It is apparent that EPS is not always followed, even when alternatives are differentiated and there is no time pressure. Joanne and Bob did not engage in EPS when they chose the movie they were to see or when Joanne tried the unknown brand of white wine. There is little incentive to engage in this decision-making effort unless there is a high degree of **involvement**—the degree of perceived relevance and personal importance accompanying the product and brand choice within a specific situation.

When involvement is high, it is important to make the "right choice." Involvement motivates information search to find out what others think, for example, as well as vigorous comparison of alternatives.

Involvement is a highly personalized consideration and varies from one person to the next. Furthermore, it varies in extent of transiency or permanence. In some cases it is stable over time, but it also can be situation-specific and less enduring. Therefore, it can have complex and diverse manifestations (see Chapter 9).

An EPS Renaissance?   While most consumer purchases in the Western world fall into the LPS category, there may be a return to greater consumer evaluation and deliberation. Consumer in Focus 2.3 raises the possibility that Americans are emerging from many years of passivism and are becoming increasingly demanding.

A Model of Consumer Decision Processes and Behavior

We move now to an expanded perspective in the form of a model of the decision-making process. We will take the building blocks discussed up to this point and put them together into a coherent structure showing cause-and-effect relationships. This model should provide a more comprehensive frame of reference for the discussion in forthcoming chapters.

We are using the same basic model for both EPS and LPS. As you know, the differences between these two extremes on the decision-process continuum do not lie in the stages of the process per se. Rather, EPS and LPS vary in the extent and rigor to which each stage is observed and followed. The model presented here was first introduced in 1968, but it has undergone many modifications since that time.

Tougher Customers Test Marketers' Mettle

They are a couple to make marketers drool: both 35—born smack in the middle of the baby boom—two incomes, two children, a home of their own. But they are testing marketers' mettle instead. Patrick and Jill McNellis have dramatically changed their buying habits over the past ten years, after they began to run and to read books like *Eat to Win*. No more processed foods. Nothing high in sugar, salt, fat, or nitrites darkens their kitchen.

Before making major purchases, the McNellises check consumer magazines that rate product quality. Says Jill: "We don't buy as much as we used to, but now we buy with knowledge. I like the best quality, but I also love a good deal."

When Patrick, a bank supervision officer at the Denver branch of the Kansas City Federal Reserve, and Jill are displeased with the quality of a product or the manufacturer's stance on a social or ethical issue, they take action. They wrote protest letters and boycotted Clorox bleach for eight months because the company advertised on *Miami Vice* which the couple thought promoted violence.

Meet the paradigm of today's tougher U.S consumers—demanding, inquisitive, discriminating. No longer content with planned obsolescence, no longer willing to tolerate products that break down, they are insisting on high-quality goods that save time, energy, and calories; preserve the environment; and come from a manufacturer they think is socially responsible. Consider:

- Americans are willing to pay a premium for quality.
- Americans are concerned about nutrition and want to know what's in their food.
- Americans worry that their disposable society is despoiling their environment.
- Americans no longer trust manufacturers.

As consumer demands become more complex, companies don't wait for customers to phone in, they go out and ask what they want. Colgate-Palmolive frequently polls consumers who call in on its 800 line, asks people who have lodged complaints to evaluate improved products, and has commissioned a performance audit this year of 75,000 consumers for all its products.

Chairman Reuben Mark believes the millions of dollars a year Colgate spends debriefing the consumer is well worth it. "Our customers want a specific product that does a specific job, and they are less willing to settle for the happy medium. We must interact with them to fill their needs."

Source: Faye Rice, "How to Deal With Tougher Customers?" *Fortune* (December 3, 1990), 39ff. Reproduced by special permission.

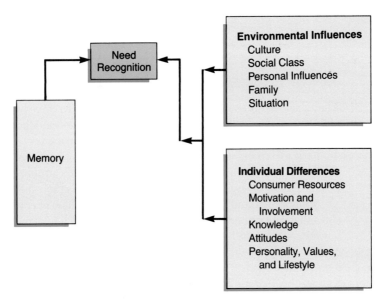

FIGURE 2.3   Need Recognition

A model is nothing more than a replica of the phenomena it is designed to represent. It specifies the building blocks (variables) and the ways in which they are interrelated (a solid arrow for a direct relationship and a broken arrow for an indirect or feedback relationship). Models of this type offer several advantages:

1. *Explanations are provided for behavior.* It is possible to grasp visually what happens as variables and circumstances change.
2. *A frame of reference is provided for research.* Gaps in knowledge and understanding become readily apparent, and research priorities can be established. It also is possible to relate individual research projects to one another.
3. *A foundation is provided for management information systems.* Proper use of a model discloses the kinds of information required to understand differing consumer decision processes and provides essential insights for marketing strategy.

Need Recognition   The initial stage in any decision-making process, of course, is **need recognition**, discussed in Chapter 16 and shown in Figure 2.3. There are three determinants of need recognition: (1) information stored in memory, (2) individual differences, and (3) environmental influences. Any of these working individually or in combination can trigger need recognition.

When involvement is low and EPS is not required, need recognition often is straightforward—"We're out of mouthwash. Pick up something on the way home." Out-of-stock conditions of this type are a primary purchase initiator. And, as we discussed earlier, a desire for variety also is common.

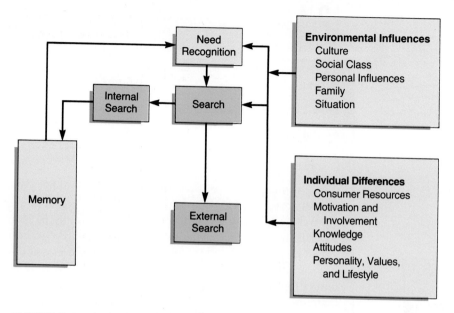

FIGURE 2.4   **Search for Information**

EPS, on the other hand, often is initiated by activation of motives centrally related to self-concept. Also, normative social influence can become relevant among consumers for whom the response of others is important. Therefore, need recognition is likely to be multifaceted and complex.

Search for Information   The next step following need recognition is **internal search** into memory to determine whether enough is known about available options to allow a choice to be made without further information search. **External search** usually will be required when this is not the case. Internal and external search, depicted in Figure 2.4, are discussed in Chapter 16.

When involvement is low, motivated information search prior to shopping, if undertaken at all, is often confined to such strategies as scanning the grocery ads for price specials. It would be a mistake to conclude, however, that advertising and other types of sales effort are without influence.

It is critically important to build brand awareness for the reason that *people are significantly less likely to consider or try an unfamiliar brand.*[17] When involvement is low, it is common for the shopper to truncate point-of-purchase search by confining themselves to brands they know. Because of this fact, an unknown brand is doomed in the supermarket competitive scene. For a vivid example of why "brand awareness is the name of the game," see Consumer in Focus 2.4. The strategy becomes one of increasing *share of mind*—relative familiarity of competitive brand names.

Figure 2.4 shows that propensity to engage in external search is affected by individual differences and environmental influences. For example, some potential buyers are cautious and unwilling to act without extensive and detailed information,

Consumer in Focus   2.4

Name of the Game: Brand Awareness

Is Avia International Ltd.:

a. a small Italian commuter airline?
b. an up-and-coming courier service?
c. a map exporter specializing in exotic spots?

None of the above. But if you're still stumped, you have plenty of company. Only 4 percent of U.S. consumers know that Avia makes sneakers and sports apparel—a dismally low percentage that Avia hopes to increase with a new advertising campaign poking fun at its low name recognition.

Given today's market clutter, name recognition is almost priceless. Selling a product that's not a household word "is like rowing a boat upstream," notes Frank Delano, chairman of Delano Goldman & Young, a corporate- and brand-image consultant in New York. "Movement is mostly backwards." Adds Jack Trout, president of Trout & Ries, Inc., an image-consulting firm, "To be anonymous is synonymous to being a No. 4 or a No. 5 in a category."

Approximately 90 percent of new products are pulled from the market within two to three years, according to Robert McMath, director of New Products Showcase and Learning Center, an Ithaca, N.Y., museum of 75,000 products that failed. "In most cases, failures were the result of a lack of product recognition," he says.

Source: Joseph Pereira, "Name of the Game: Brand Awareness," *The Wall Street Journal* (February 11, 1991), B8. Reproduced by special permission.

whereas other shoppers make purchases without even comparing alternatives. Search also can be inhibited by situational influence, an example being the urgent need for a new car when the current one breaks down and is not repairable.

Information Processing   What happens as the consumer is exposed to information during external search? In attempting to explain this impact, we turn once again to the subject of information processing. Now we will expand our discussion to include the stages in the process and their implications (Figure 2.5).

As a first step, information and persuasive communication must reach consumers where they happen to be. This is depicted in Figure 2.5 as **exposure**. Once exposure occurs one or more of the senses are activated and preliminary processing commences.

The next stage, **attention**, is defined as allocation of information-processing capacity to the incoming information. Attention is most likely to be attracted when the incoming message and its content are considered to be relevant. Consumers

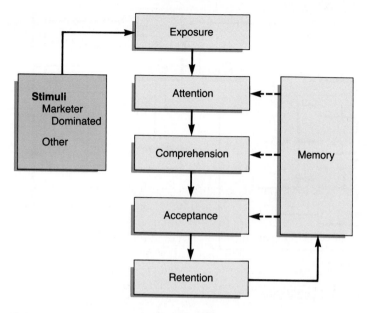

FIGURE 2.5   **Information Processing**

frequently ignore commercial persuasion at this stage and exercise their capabilities of *selective attention*.

If attention is attracted, the message is further analyzed against categories of meaning stored in memory. The marketer hopes, of course, that accurate **comprehension** will be the outcome.

As the incoming message is compared against existing beliefs, attitudes, and other factors stored in memory, any or all of these could be changed or modified in some way. If so, we can conclude that **acceptance** has taken place. If this new information is also stored in memory, then **retention** has taken place.

You can readily discern that information processing is a complex undertaking. The discussion in Chapter 13 will increase your understanding of its role in developing communication strategy.

Alternative Evaluation   Alternative evaluation (Figure 2.6) makes use of **evaluative criteria**—the standards and specifications used by consumers to compare different products and brands. In other words, these are the desired outcomes from purchase and consumption and are expressed in the form of preferred attributes.

Evaluative criteria are shaped and influenced by individual differences and environmental influences. As such, they become a product-specific manifestation of an individual's motives, values, lifestyles, and so on.

As you will discover in Chapter 17, a distinguishing characteristic of EPS is rigorous alternative evaluation. A common procedure is to process information one brand at a time, weighing each against the most important (salient) attributes. This is done following a **compensatory strategy** in which perceived weakness on one attribute can be compensated for or offset by strength on others.

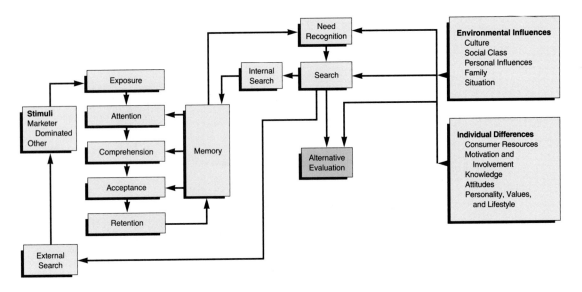

FIGURE 2.6 **Alternative Evaluation**

When consumers engage in LPS, on the other hand, alternative evaluation consists of little more than finding assurance that each competitive alternative "qualifies" in terms of the expected benefit. For example, "meets or exceeds car manufacturer's standards" is a central expected benefit when motor oil is purchased.

We now see **noncompensatory alternative evaluation** in which an option will be eliminated if it falls short. This is commonly done at the point of sale and is confirmed as the product is used or consumed.

Purchase and Its Outcomes Figure 2.7 completes the decision-process model by depicting purchase and its outcomes. Purchase most often takes place in some type of retail outlet, although our discussion in Chapter 18 demonstrates the remarkable growth of various forms of in-home shopping.

The LPS purchase usually is made with minimum deliberation and further decision making. Trial, of course, serves as a principal method of alternative evaluation, whereas this is not the case when EPS prevails.

Alternative evaluation does not cease once the purchase is made. If expectations are matched, the outcome is **satisfaction**. The feedback arrow in Figure 2.7 shows how satisfaction affects future alternative evaluation.

When the alternative is perceived as falling short in significant ways, **dissatisfaction** is the result. It is common when involvement is high to experience such doubts even before trial simply because of the presence of unchosen alternatives with desirable features. Often known as postdecision regret, this can be an incentive for further information search, as the dotted feedback arrow in Figure 2.7 indicates.

A product's failure to perform will not be accepted easily by the buyers, however, especially when the purchase has high perceived importance. Complaints and

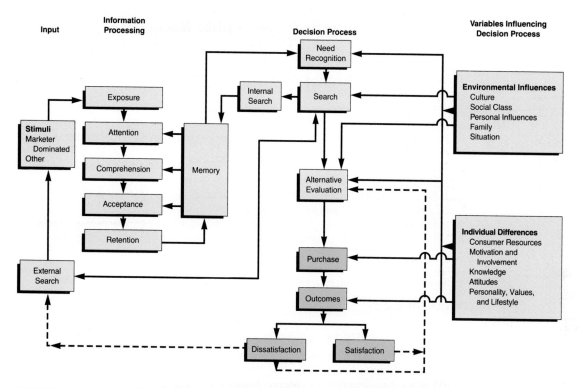

FIGURE 2.7 A Complete Model of Consumer Behavior Showing Purchase and Its Outcomes

efforts to achieve redress are common. The quality of postsale service can make a great difference.

Diagnosing Consumer Behavior

This chapter has covered a great deal. Figure 2.8 provides a set of questions that will help you diagnose what takes place in the consumer's world.

As you observe and try to explain the behavioral situations that are encountered every day in marketing, keep these points in mind:

1. Remember the continuum of initial purchase decision-process possibilities ranges from full-scale EPS on the one extreme to impulse buying (a "Why not try it?" response reflecting LPS) on the other. Similarly, habitual decision-making also is a continuum, with brand loyalty on one end and inertia on the other.

2. Consumers will differ from one to the next. One may be motivated by high involvement to engage in EPS, whereas this is not always the case with others.

FIGURE 2.8 Diagnosing the Consumer Decision-Making Process

Motivation and Need Recognition

1. What needs and motivations are satisfied by product purchase and usage? (i.e., What *benefits* are consumers seeking?)
2. Are these needs dormant or are they presently perceived as felt needs by prospective buyers?
3. How involved with the product are most prospective buyers in the target market segment?

Search for Information

1. What product- and brand-related information is stored in memory?
2. Is the consumer motivated to turn to external sources to find information about available alternatives and their characteristics?
3. What specific information sources are used most frequently when search is undertaken?
4. What product features or attributes are the focus of search when it is undertaken?

Alternative Evaluation

1. To what extent do consumers engage in alternative evaluation and comparison?
2. Which product and/or brand alternatives are included in the evaluation process?
3. Which product evaluative criteria (product attributes) are used to compare various alternatives?
   a. Which are most salient in the evaluation?
   b. How complex is the evaluation (i.e., using a single attribute as opposed to several in combination)?
4. What are the outcomes of evaluation regarding each of the candidate purchase alternatives?
   a. What is believed to be true about the characteristics and features of each?
   b. Are they perceived to be different in important ways, or are they seen as essentially the same?
5. What kind of decision rule is used to determine the best choice?

Purchase

1. Will the consumer expend time and energy to shop until the preferred alternative is found?
2. Is additional decision-process behavior needed to discover the preferred outlet for purchase?
3. What are the preferred models of purchase (i.e., retail store, in the home, or in other ways)?

Outcomes

1. What degree of satisfaction or dissatisfaction is expressed with respect to previously used alternatives in the product or service category?
2. What reasons are given for satisfaction or dissatisfaction?
3. Has perceived satisfaction or dissatisfaction been shared with other people to help them in their buying behavior?
4. Have consumers made attempts to achieve redress for dissatisfaction?
5. Is there an intention to repurchase any of the alternatives?
   a. If no, why not?
   b. If yes, does intention reflect brand loyalty or inertia?

Recognize multiple segments with differing motivations and decision-process behavior.

3. In some instances you will not have sufficient information to allow a proper diagnosis, in which case marketing research probably is needed.

Summary

The purpose of this chapter has been to introduce you to the nature of consumer decision making and the influences on this process. We began with discussion of the complex set of factors that influence and shape decision-process behavior.

The first of these is environmental influences, including (1) culture; (2) social class; (3) personal influence; (4) family; and (5) situation. The second is individual differences: (1) consumer resources; (2) motivation and involvement; (3) knowledge; (4) attitudes; and (5) personality, values, and lifestyle. The last component consists of the basic psychological processes of (1) information processing; (2) learning; and (3) attitude and behavior change.

Next we introduced you in a general way to the concept of consumer decision process and began with the principle that all decisions encompass the following stages: (1) need recognition; (2) search for information; (3) alternative evaluation; (4) purchase; and (5) outcomes or consequences of purchase.

We then focused on ways in which decision-process behavior can vary, and these are the important determining factors: (1) the extent to which alternatives are differentiated in significant ways; (2) the presence or absence of restricting time pressures; and (3) the degree of involvement—perceived relevance of the purchase in the context of important needs and motivations.

Extended problem solving (EPS) can be viewed as one end of a problem-solving continuum. It is characterized by intensive search for information and complex alternative evaluation. The opposite end of this continuum is anchored by limited problem solving (LPS). Here there is far less motivation to search widely for information and to engage in alternative evaluation.

A common form of LPS is the impulse purchase, in which the buyer acts on a "Why not try it?" response. We see this most often when alternatives are essentially similar, when there is unwillingness to devote time to the process, and when involvement is low. In short, there is little perceived risk of doing the wrong thing.

When the occasion arises for repeat purchases, however, many consumers quickly develop habitual decision processes. On occasion they are brand loyal and stay with their initial choice. This occurs mainly when there is high perceived involvement. When this is not the case, however, habits are built on inertia. If a consumer has no reason to switch, a repurchase will be made. But the consumer also is prone to switch if there is incentive to do so. Once again there is low involvement and little commitment to one alternative versus another.

We could begin our concentrated study of consumer behavior anywhere in this model, and we have tried different approaches in our previous editions. Experience over the years has shown, however, that it often is best to move from the general to the specific.

Therefore, our starting point (Part 2) is with environmental influences. Part 3 concentrates on individual differences, and we move from there to psychological processes in Part 4. Once we have this comprehensive grasp of the ways in which behavior is shaped and influenced, we return once again to the subject of consumer decision processes in Part 5. And the book concludes in Parts 6 and 7 with discussions of marketing strategies and organizational ethics.

Review and Discussion Questions

1. There are some who argue that consumers really do not pursue any kind of decision process but make their selections more or less randomly without any apparent reasoning. What is your position on this issue? Why?
2. In speaking of the problems that might result from psychological analysis of consumer behavior, one critic stated many years ago, "Much of it seems to represent regress rather than progress for man in his struggle to become a rational and self-guiding being." His point is that marketing persuaders now have new tools that enable them to manipulate the consumer and to circumvent his or her processes of reasoning. Comment.
3. Define the terms *extended problem solving* and *limited problem solving.* What are the essential differences? What type of decision process would you expect most people to follow in the initial purchase of a new product or brand in each of these categories: toothpaste, flour, men's cologne, carpeting, toilet tissue, bread, light bulbs, a 35mm camera, a sports car?
4. Referring once again to Question 3, is it possible that decision-process behavior could differ widely from one consumer to another in purchasing each of these items? Explain.
5. How might a manufacturer of automatic washers and dryers use a decision-process approach to better understand how consumers purchase these products?
6. Which of the following types of products do you think are most likely to be purchased on the basis of brand loyalty, on the basis of inertia: laundry detergent, motor oil, lipsticks, shoe polish, soft drinks, lawn care products (fertilizers, etc.), and spark plugs?
7. Assume you are responsible for marketing a new and previously unknown brand of 35mm slide film. You are up against Kodak and Fuji, both of which have built substantial brand loyalty. What strategies could you suggest to make market inroads?
8. Assume you have been called in as a marketing consultant to suggest an advertising strategy for a new brand of dry cat food. Which of the types of decision-process behavior discussed in this chapter do you feel is likely with most prospective buyers? Why do you say this? What difference will this make in marketing strategy?

Endnotes

1. Grant McCracken, "Advertising: Meaning or Information?" in Melanie Wallendorf and Paul Anderson, eds., *Advances in Consumer Research* 14 (Provo, Utah: Association for Consumer Research, 1987), 121–124.
2. For significant early writings on this subject, see Russell W. Belk, "An Exploratory Assessment of Situational Effects in Buyer Behavior," *Journal of Marketing Research* 11 (May 1974), 156–173; and Russell W. Belk, "Situational Variables and Consumer Behavior," *Journal of Consumer Research* 2 (December 1975), 157–164. Also Gordon R. Foxall, *Consumer Choice* (London: MacMillan, 1983), 86–97.
3. "Spiegel, Inc. (A)," in Roger D. Blackwell, W. Wayne Talarzyk, and James F. Engel, *Contemporary Cases in Consumer Behavior* (Hinsdale, Ill.: Dryden, 1985), 85–94.
4. Melvin Copeland, *Principles of Merchandising* (Chicago: A. W. Shaw, 1924), Chapters 6–7.
5. "New Vacuum Addresses Consumer Trends," *Marketing News* (November 21, 1986), 24.

6. Sidney J. Levy, "Symbols by Which We Buy," in Lynn H. Stockman, ed., *Advancing Marketing Efficiency* (Chicago: American Marketing Association, 1959), 410.
7. Vance Packard, *The Hidden Persuaders* (New York: McKay, 1957).
8. Ernest Dichter, *The Strategy of Desire* (New York: Doubleday, 1960).
9. For an interesting history of how this happened, see Peggy J. Kreshel, "John B. Watson at J. Walter Thompson: The Legitimization of 'Science' in Advertising," *Journal of Advertising* 19 (November 1990), 49–59.
10. John Dewey, *How We Think* (New York: Heath, 1910).
11. Icek Ajzen and Martjn Fishbein, *Understanding Attitudes and Predicting Social Behavior* (Englewood Cliffs, N.J.: Prentice-Hall, 1980).
12. Elizabeth C. Hirschman and Morris B. Holbrook, "Hedonic Consumption: Emerging Concepts, Methods, and Propositions," *Journal of Marketing* 46 (Summer 1982), 92–101.
13. Harold E. Kassarjian, "Consumer Research: Some Recollections and a Commentary," in Richard J. Lutz, *Advances in Consumer Research* 13 (Provo, Utah: Association for Consumer Research, 1986), 6–8.
14. Wayne D. Hoyer, "Variations and Choice Strategies Across Decision Contexts: An Examination of Continent Factors," in Lutz, *Advances*, 23–26.
15. Francis Piron, "Defining Impulse Purchasing," in Rebecca H. Holman and Michael R. Solomon, *Advances in Consumer Research* 18 (Provo, Utah: Association for Consumer Research, 1991), 512.
16. See Itamar Simonson, "The Effect of Purchase Quantity and Timing on Variety-Seeking Behavior," *Journal of Marketing Research* 27 (May 1990), 150–162. Also, Wayne D. Hoyer and Nancy M. Ridgway, "Variety Seeking as an Explanation for Exploratory Purchase Behavior: A Theoretical Model," in Thomas Kinnear, ed., *Advances in Consumer Research* 11 (Provo, Utah: Association for Consumer Research, 1984), 114–119.
17. Wayne D. Hoyer and Steven P. Brown, "Effects of Brand Awareness on Choice for a Common, Repeat-Purchase Product," *Journal of Consumer Research* 17 (September 1990), 141–148.

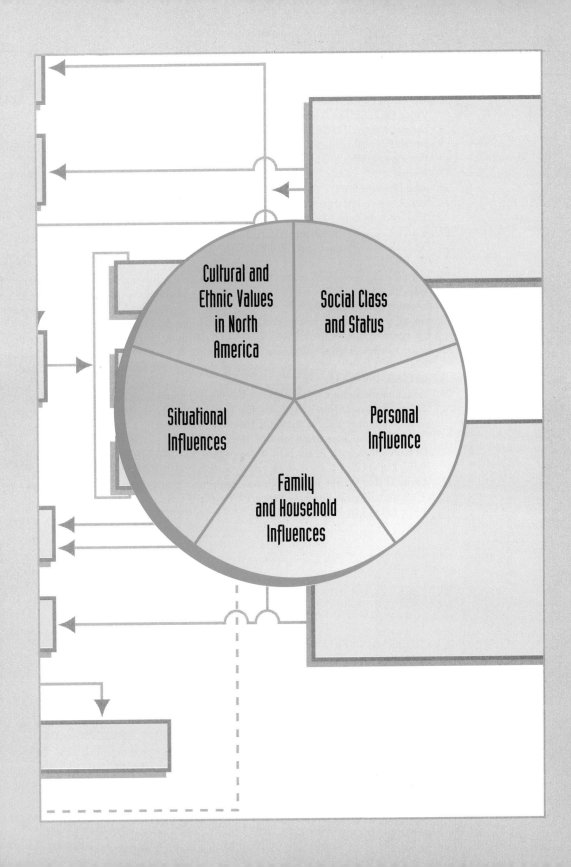

Environmental Influences

No person is an island. This statement certainly is true in the study of consumer behavior. Why are you what you are? Why do you do what you do? Is your behavior caused mostly by genetic predispositions, by the environment, or by some combination that is uniquely you? Scientists from many disciplines disagree on the answers to such basic questions.

Nevertheless, it is clear that consumers are shaped by their environment as they live and operate within it, while at the same time changing it through their behavior. The following chapters show you how this takes place by addressing the environmental influences highlighted in the model on the opposite page.

Most fundamental is an understanding of the nature and meaning of *culture*. This is the topic of Chapter 3, and you will see immediately how necessary cultural insight is in this era of globalized marketing. Also important is an understanding of *social class*, *personal influences*, *family*, and *consumption situations*, topics covered in Chapters 4–7.

These chapters are intended to cover the basic concepts and how they are related to buying and consumption behavior. Trends and specialized topics such as diffusion of new products and global marketing are discussed in Part 6.

3

The Cultural Context of Consumption

Procter & Gamble recently announced that its trademark man-in-the moon logo would be modernized—to keep in step with fashion. Although P&G officials insisted that the make-over had absolutely nothing to do with Satanism charges, the new design restyled the curls in the man's beard, which, when held upside down before a mirror (perhaps in a graveyard, on a dark and stormy night) had clearly formed Beelzebub's favorite Lotto number: 666.

P&G made the switch several months after Burger King capitulated to a boycott led by Christian Leaders for Responsible Television (ClearTV) and placed big newspaper ads to announce that, of course, the company did not, never had, and never would support "anti-family, anti-Christian" TV shows. A spokesperson said Burger King would never sponsor NBC's "Saturday Night Live" because "you certainly don't know, because it's live, what might be said."

NBC has gotten the message. Last month, the network warned Universal Television, the producer of "Quantum Leap," that Universal would be liable for lost revenues if any advertisers pulled their spots from a planned episode dealing with homosexuality and suicide. (The show's time-traveling body-snatcher hero was due to inhabit the body of a despondent gay teenager.) NBC's unprecedented move came after advertisers had yanked spots from the NBC movie "Roe v. Wade" and an episode of ABC's "thirtysomething" that featured two men in bed together.

Source: "Slants & Trends," *American Marketplace* (October 10, 1991), 199.

Cultural Values

Consumption decisions and consequently all aspects of marketing are affected by the culture of the marketing environment. In the opening scenario of this chapter, it is apparent that communications media and their advertisers are affected by cultural values and norms. It is arguable whether the values reported in the opening scenario reflect the majority of consumers or only a minority. Nevertheless, they clearly affect marketing decisions.

Marketing in Multicultural Markets

Cultural homogeneity varies greatly around the world. Some countries such as Japan are characterized by considerable homogeneity. An executive in Tokyo can look out his corporate window and know that nearly all consumers will have very similar views about honor, family, religion, education, and work habits. There is some variation, of course, but far less than the cultural diversity that is found in countries such as the United States and Canada. In Japan, consumers are even more likely to have similar incomes, cars, homes, and commuting patterns.

Marketing in North America is practiced in multicultural markets. When an executive in the United States or Canada looks out the corporate window, she or he may see a wide array of languages, religions, and ethnic backgrounds. Each of these variables may have significant influence on how consumers function. In this chapter, we examine both the concept of culture and how to analyze it as well as some of the ethnic variations that are found in North American markets.

North American Cultures

It is increasingly important to understand North American markets rather than simply those of the United States, Canada, or Mexico. In 1992, the European Community officially became a single market. Actually, only legal and trade barriers were reduced. The cultural and ethnic realities remained, but marketers can now consider these influences across national boundaries more than ever before.

The process that occurred in Europe in the early 1990s is likely to occur in North America in the rest of the decade. Marketing analysts will need therefore to focus on cultural and ethnic realities of the North American marketplace more than ever before. The political structures are not changed nor are all of the economic and trade barriers; but marketers increasingly need to consider the United States and Canada as one market, and eventually Mexico will probably be added to the process.

The North American culture reflects realities of three nations as well as many variations within each. In many ways, the United States and Canada are similar to each other to a much greater degree than are most nations in Europe. But the two countries are dissimilar to European or Asian markets, although Canadian values are more similar to European values than are U.S. values. There is enough similarity between the United States and Mexico to cause Wal-Mart and other retailers to enter Mexico with a strategy similar to the one that has created so much success in the United States.

Both the United States and Canada have significant ethnic populations which can be described as Asian-American or Asian-Canadian. Both countries have significant groups of African descent, although the influence is greater in the United States. While the United States has some French ethnic groups (principally in Louisiana), the influence is much greater in Canada. Mexico shares a majority culture with the fastest growing ethnic group in the United States—Hispanics.

This chapter discusses these influences on consumer behavior under the general rubric of culture and ethnicity in North America. We will save discussion of cultural influences on consumer behavior in other countries for a later chapter on Global Markets. But first, a look at some of the basic concepts that are important in understanding culture and values.

What Is Culture?

Culture refers to a set of values, ideas, artifacts, and other meaningful symbols that help individuals communicate, interpret, and evaluate as members of society. Culture does not include instincts, nor does it include idiosyncratic behavior occurring as a one-time solution to a unique problem.

Culture includes both abstract and material elements. **Abstract elements** include values, attitudes, ideas, personality types, and summary constructs, such as religion. **Material components** include such things as books, computers, tools, buildings, and specific products, such as a pair of Levi's 501 jeans. Material elements of culture are sometimes described as **cultural artifacts** or the material manifestation of culture, thereby restricting the use of **culture** to abstract concepts.

Culture provides people with a sense of identity and an understanding of acceptable behavior within society. Some of the more important attitudes and behaviors influenced by culture are the following:[1]

1. Sense of self and space
2. Communication and language
3. Dress and appearance
4. Food and feeding habits
5. Time and time consciousness
6. Relationships (family, organizations, government, and so on)
7. Values and norms
8. Beliefs and attitudes
9. Mental processes and learning
10. Work habits and practices

Values

Values are shared beliefs or group norms internalized by individuals, perhaps with some modification. **Norms** are beliefs held by consensus of a group concerning the behavior rules for individual members. Values play a major role in determining need recognition but may influence other stages of consumer decisions as well.

Cultural values are those shared broadly across a macroculture or microculture, while personal values are held by individuals but may not be shared by all or even many of the members of the group. Our concern in this chapter is on cultural values because they have impact on marketing strategies on such a widespread basis. In Chapter 12, we will examine how personal values influence individual decision making.

Macrocultures

Macroculture refers to the sets of values and symbols that apply to an entire society, or the largest proportion of its citizens. The term *society* usually refers to large and complex, yet organized, social systems, such as a nation or perhaps even Western civilization. In this chapter, we focus on the North American culture, especially as it exists in the United States.

Microcultures

Microculture refers to the sets of values and symbols of a restrictive group, such as a religious, ethnic, or other subdivision of the whole. (In older textbooks, microcultures were called *subcultures*, but some concern arose that identifying ethnic groups as subcultures might connote inferiority.) In this chapter, we look at some of the ethnic microcultures of North America such as Hispanic, African, Asian and French. In a later chapter, dealing with global marketing, we examine other cultures throughout the world.

Where Do People Get their Values?

Socialization

The processes by which people develop their values, motivations, and habitual activity is called **socialization**, the process of absorbing a culture. From the time a baby looks up and begins cooing and smiling, he or she starts forming values through socialization. The process continues throughout a lifetime, causing people to adopt values that influence consumption—such as thrift, pleasure, honesty, and ambition. These life forces also produce specific preferences—relating to choices of color, packaging, convenience, hours of shopping, and characteristic interactions with salespeople and many others. Attention can also be focused on **consumer socialization**, the acquisition of consumption-related cognitions, attitudes, and behavior. Earlier studies in consumer socialization focused on this process among young people, but increasingly the emphasis is on the lifelong development of such skills.[2] An examination of how people are socialized reveals some of the basic elements of the concept of culture.

Culture Is Learned

Unlike animals, whose behavior is more instinctive, humans are not born with norms of behavior. Instead, humans learn their norms through imitation or by observing the process of reward and punishment in a society of members who adhere to or deviate from the group's norms. Norms learned early in life may be highly resistant to promotional effort by marketers. When an advertiser is dealing with deeply ingrained, culturally defined behavior (about food, sex, basic forms of clothing, and so on), it is easier to change the marketing mix to conform with cultural values than to try to change the values through advertising. As an example, eating dogs, horses, sheep eyes, or even live fish is normal and healthy behavior in some cultures. Advertising would have great difficulty, however, in convincing typical North American consumers to buy these products.

Culture Is Inculcated

Culture is passed from one generation to the next, primarily by institutions such as family, religion, and schools. Early lifetime experiences and peers also transmit values; this process is shown in Figure 3.1. Predicting the values that will affect

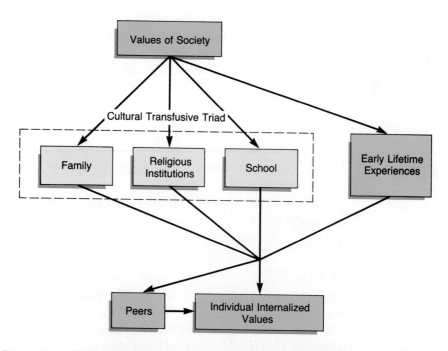

Figure 3.1   Environmental Influences on Consumer Decision and Marketing Strategy: Intergenerational Transmission of Values

consumer behavior in the future is based on understanding how these institutions are changing, a topic discussed later in this chapter.

Culture Rewards Socially Gratifying Responses

Culture develops and exists almost as if it were an entity in itself. Some anthropologists view culture as an entity serving humans in their attempts to meet the basic biological and social needs of the society. When norms no longer provide gratification in a society, the norms are extinguished.

Culture Is Adaptive

Culture is adaptive. Marketing strategies based upon values of society must also be adaptive. As change occurs in the traits that represent a society's ability to function, trends develop that provide marketing opportunities to those who spot the traits before competitors. Spotting these trends and maximizing marketing opportunities are among the topics discussed in a later chapter on Consumer Trends.

Understanding what types of consumer behavior will endure over time requires analysis of what "gratifying response," physical or social, is provided by a cultural norm. It may be possible to associate a product or brand with that cultural value or benefit. If that value is no longer gratifying in society, sales will suffer. For example, meat and potatoes used to be desired foods in the mass American culture. When most consumers worked on a farm or in strenuous manufacturing and labor jobs, high-energy and high-calorie foods were valued and gratifying. As those jobs were replaced increasingly by white-collar and other sedentary careers, the beef industry had to change its appeal to lean beef with less calories, fat, and cholesterol. McDonald's introduced a "McLean" burger to satisfy this change in North American values. Worthington Foods markets a wide variety of "meat analogues," such as "Grillers" and "Links," with no cholesterol and less fat—products that look and taste like meat but contain no animal fat.

How Culture Affects Consumer Behavior

Culture has a profound effect on why people buy. Culture affects the specific products people buy as well as the structure of consumption, individual decision making, and communication in a society.

Why People Buy Products

Consumers buy products to obtain *function, form, and meaning*. When supply exceeds demand, as is the case in most industrially advanced societies in the 1990s, marketers cannot be successful without attention to all three variables, as they are defined by the cultural context of consumption.

When consumers buy a product, they expect it to perform a *function*—to clean clothes in the case of laundry detergent or to provide nutrition in the case of food. A high level of consumer satisfaction and loyalty occurs only if expectations are met consistently. As a consequence, firms today must allocate significant resources to product-quality programs. They must also allocate resources to customer-contact programs to find out when functional expectations are not met or exceeded.

Appliances such as washing machines, as an example, may vary in function and form between cultures. In European cultures, washing machines are expected to last for decades. Highly efficient, top loading machines costing over $1,000 are marketed successfully by firms such as Miele, based in Germany. Yet when Miele introduced this same level of quality in North America, it found only limited success because, in the American culture, appliances should be priced at a few hundred dollars and are not expected to have much quality.[3] Americans move more frequently than Europeans, have lower quality of repair services available, and expect the more convenient but less efficient cleaning ability of top loading machines. Consequently, washing machines are almost a disposable product. When they break or if the consumer moves, they are often left behind or discarded. The cultural context of the consumer defines the meaning of quality in the function of the product.

But more than function determines success in marketing products. Successful products must also meet expectations about form. Nutritional requirements in food might be met in many ways, but some forms are much preferred by customers. Foods are expected to be "hot" or "cold" or "crisp" or "tender" or "microwavable." Shushimi or fish served raw may be a special treat in Japan but unacceptable to the majority markets of North America. Veal might be a special treat for Americans of recent European descent but an anathema to a California vegetarian. A front loading washing machine is a requirement for success in European markets but not desired in the United States. Such realities are determined by a consumer's culture.

Products also provide *symbols of meaning* in a society. Spinach may be associated with strength, possibly enticing children to eat an otherwise unappealing choice. Foods often represent symbols of family relationships, as in the case of a special recipe handed down through generations or associated with one's national or ethnic identity. Products sometimes are used in *ritual behavior*, as when certain foods are eaten during holidays or by candlelight for special occasions. Occasionally, products become so much of a symbol in a society that they are an *icon*, as in the case of foods eaten especially in religious observances. Sometimes the form of the product also acts as a symbol of the function, as the addition of "blue crystals" may do for a detergent that gets clothes "whiter."

The study of the symbolic qualities of products is defined in the marketing literature as **semiotics** or **product semantics**. Such an analysis focuses on cognitive meanings, symbolic functions, and cultural histories of products.[4] Cultural description is sometimes called **ethnographic research**, in which researchers place themselves in the culture or its artifacts in order to "soak up" meaning. These methods can be applied to any type of consumption behavior, even the accumulation of products by the homeless. Hill and Stamey, for example, found that the homeless may purchase some products but scavenge for most others. While some of these products are functional, such as food and shelter, other possessions are important for symbolic reasons. A precious few belongings such as photographs, books, or mementos may remind the homeless of happier days or significant others.[5]

The Structure of Consumption

Culture determines the structure of consumption by defining the choices available to consumers. Through the legal and governmental system, a nation's culture determines what suppliers can offer, the ways products can be marketed, and the degree to which consumers are allowed to act on their preferences. Shall countries put their resources into military, industrial, or consumer goods? Shall a nation produce good cars or good tanks? Good education or good health? Good computers or good music? And because insatiability of demand dictates there will never be enough goods for all, should these products be most available to the old or to the young? To which ethnic or religious groups? To the persons who are the best educated or to the members of the "right" families or to persons of the ruling party? Such choices are heavily affected by an individual's particular culture.

Individual Decision Making

Culture, along with other elements of the environment, affects all stages of consumer decision making. For example, the American culture may emphasize individual, competitive behavior, while the Japanese culture may emphasize cultural conformity in consumption and production rather than individual achievement.

Consumers place more weight on some product attributes than on others when they choose competing brands. The cause for such weights is often the culture to which the individual belongs. For example, some wealthy consumers may be found to place a great weight on low price, not because they lack money but because cultural values influence their choices. Conversely, a poor consumer may purchase an expensive pair of shoes because of personal or group values.

During the purchase process, the amount of price negotiation expected by both seller and buyer is culturally determined. In Greece and some middle-eastern countries, for instance, even the price of a physician's services is subject to negotiation.

Consumers' complaints or expressions of satisfaction may also be affected by cultural variables. Mexican-Americans, for example, are less likely than other consumers to complain about unsatisfactory service when they buy products. But they are more likely to protest delays in delivery, possibly because of a cultural value of obtaining things "today" or "right now."[6]

Communication and the Ideology of Consumption

Effective communication is influenced by how the culture provides an **ideology of consumption**, defined as the social meaning attached to and communicated by products. Research by Belk and his associates reveals that culture provides meaning not only to the advertising or communications about a product, but also to acts of consumption.[7] We can define consumer decision making broadly enough so we can understand not only why people purchase products but also why people enjoy attending museums and participating in athletic events, and the kinds of meaning that people attach to plots and character development when attending movies.[8]

The ideology of consumption can be further understood with an example from the research of Hirschman. She found that television programs communicate many forms of consumption, which vary between secular and sacred.[9] **Secular consumption** refers to the acquisition of human-made products, typically those resulting from technological process and those sought competitively by consumers. Consumption of secular products is typically associated with greed, avarice, and envy and is sought as an end in itself. In contrast, **sacred consumption** places primary importance on virtues such as love, honor, and integrity. Sacred consumers display little interest in acquiring technologically produced material goods. They are not fashion conscious and do not use products in a competitive manner. Sacred consumers in the media are usually involved in productive or natural careers rather than in management, and they often are portrayed as upholding values of family nurturance, friendship, loyalty, and honesty. Secular women characters dress in expensive couture apparel and fur coats, with jewelry, makeup, and well-coiffed hair. Secular men characters invariably wear conservative business suits, have closely trimmed hair, and often wear black tie and a dinner jacket, reflecting a symbolic commitment to capitalism and the management of technology.

In contrast, sacred consumption is portrayed with work clothes and cowboy gear or products constructed from inexpensive natural materials (flannel, denim, leather), obtainable from low-status sources. Food, residences, leisure activities, services, and many other aspects of consumption reflect the sacred-secular dichotomy in the ideology of consumption. In the television series "Dallas," Cliff Barnes and April Stevens symbolized the secular, Ray Krebs and Miss Ellie symbolized the sacred, and Bobby Ewing and Donna Krebs were mediating characters representing a synthesis of the two.

Meaning moves first from the culture of a nation or group to consumer goods and then from these goods to individual consumers. From the culture, products absorb meaning through advertising, fashion systems, retailing presentation, and many other ways not influenced by marketers. The individual consumer develops meaning through possession, exchange, grooming, and divestment rituals. McCracken explains:

> Culture constitutes the phenomenal world in two ways. First, culture is the "lens" through which the individual views phenomena; as such, it determines how the phenomena will be apprehended and assimilated. Second, culture is the "blueprint" of human activity, determining the co-ordinates of social action and productive activity, and specifying the behaviors and objects that issue from both.[10]

How Core Values Affect Marketing

Successful retailers know that a basic group of products is essential to the store's traffic, customer loyalty, and profits. These products are known as **core merchandise**. A group of values, called **core values**, also exists. These values are basic to understanding the behavior of people, and can be helpful to marketers in several ways.

Core values *define how products are used in a society*. Not only do core values determine what foods should be eaten but they also determine with what other foods they are appropriate, how they are prepared, and the time of day to eat them.

The core values of a nation *provide positive and negative valences for brands and for communications programs*. "As American as apple pie" communicated well in America for Chevrolet, but negative valences would surely result from associating cars with other foods such as bird nest soup or monkey gland stew (which have positive valences in China or Africa, respectively). Many marketers have used the Olympics to give positive valences to their company or product, appealing both to sports/health valences and to national pride. Core values frequently are *incorporated into advertising*, along with product benefits.

The core values of a nation also *define acceptable market relationships*. In Japan, the relationships between groups of firms—dating back to east and west dynasties—are so rigid and complex that outsiders have difficulty obtaining distribution unless they form a joint venture with one of the groups.

People in rich economies tend to assume that transactions probably will be completed as specified. If problems arise, they have agencies such as the Better Business Bureau, consumer protection agencies, and access to the legal system. In contrast, in poor countries, very little of this support structure may exist, and people may have little faith in trading with distant partners. Even when liberal laws exist, the social resources to protect economic transactions may not be available.

In peasant marketplaces, people develop long-term trading partnerships to provide reciprocating values to both buyers and sellers. These values include assured supply, reliable quality, employment of family members and neighbors, and price stability. In Haiti, trading partnerships are known as *pratik*. A buying *pratik* who knows that her selling counterpart is coming will wait at the proper place and time, refusing to buy from others the stock that she is sure her *pratik* is carrying. Similarly, a selling *pratik* will refuse to sell to others until she has met her *pratik* buyer. In Nigeria, similar partnerships are called *onibara* relationships; in Jamaica, they are "customers" rather than "higglers"; in the Philippines, such relationships are called *suki*. In Guatemala, growers bargain vigorously in the marketplace with middlemen with whom they do not have personal relationships. A *cliente* middleman, in contrast, will pay the prevailing price with no bargaining and will almost always buy the products unless he has absolutely no use for them. In return, the agricultural producer is expected to deliver the best produce to the *cliente* middlemen.[11]

Core values affect these and many other marketing functions. We discuss in Chapter 24 the core values of various nations around the world. There are, however, core values of the North American societies that affect consumption patterns and the marketing programs directed to the majority of U.S. consumers.

North American Core Values

Even in countries as diversely populated as the United States and Canada, core values can be observed that permeate most aspects of the two societies. However, both countries encompass diverse values within their populations, because they are so young, compared to Asian and European countries, and because they reflect many national origins. First, we'll examine U.S. values and then compare the two countries. Many values that are described as American also apply in Canada although there are important differences, as discussed in the second section. The term *American* includes Latin America as well, but in the following pages, we will restrict the discussion to only a part of America—the United States.

Some of the core values also apply to Mexican markets, although there is not yet sufficient data to allow in-depth discussion of consumer behavior in Mexico. The fact that emigration from Mexico to the United States is attractive to many people indicates acceptance of at least some U.S. values. Firms such as Wal-Mart and Amway have achieved success by translating marketing strategies based solidly on American values into the Mexican market. Consumer in Focus 3.1 provides more details of Amway's success in Mexico.

American Values: Their Influence on Consumers

The United States was an agrarian nation only two generations ago. Although it is now primarily urbanized and suburbanized, many core values are still traceable to the agrarian base. Daily living is now regulated more by the clock and the calendar than by the seasons or degree of daylight. Most people are employees of large, complex organizations rather than farmers or shopkeepers. Goods and services are purchased rather than produced, with money or plastic rather than property as the denominator of exchange. Yet many American values retain the agrarian base.

The origin of American values is described by Arensberg and Niehoff:

> Where does this American character come from? . . . The values derived from life on the frontier, the great open spaces, the virgin wealth, and the once seemingly limitless resources of a "new world" appear to have affected ideas of freedom. Individualism seems to have been fostered by a commitment to "progress" which in turn was derived from expansion over three hundred years. Much of the religious and ethical tradition is believed to have come from Calvinist (Puritan) doctrine, particularly an emphasis on individual responsibility and the positive work ethic. Anglo-Saxon civil rights, the rule of law, and representative institutions were inherited from the English background; ideas of egalitarian democracy and a secular spirit sprang from the French and American Revolutions. The period of slavery and its aftermath, and the European immigration of three centuries, have affected the American character strongly.[12]

What are the core values that provide appeals for advertising and marketing programs? Eight of the most basic are described in Table 3.1 (on pages 74–76). After you have studied the table, refer to Consumer in Focus 3.1, which discusses many of these values manifested in the successful Amway strategy.

Sometimes advertisers are accused of appealing mostly to fear, snobbery, and self-indulgence. Would advertisers be effective if they continually based their advertising on such appeals? As you examine Table 3.1, you will see that such an approach would have limited appeal. Marketers are more successful when they appeal to core values based on hard work, achievement and success, optimism, and equal opportunity for a better material standard of living.

Order and cleanliness are keys to the success of firms such as McDonald's and Stew Leonard's, in Connecticut, which is probably the largest family owned supermarket in the nation. Both firms appear to subscribe to the "rest room" theory of

Inspirational Marketing

"Amway is more than a company, it's a movement to help people help themselves," says Richard DeVos, founder of Amway, the world's second-largest door-to-door sales operation with $3.1 billion in retail sales. Amway manufactures and sells soap, cosmetics, vitamins, food products, and other household products as well as Coca-Cola machines, MCI service, clothing, and thousands of other items.

Although the average Amway distributor sells about $1,700 worth of goods a year, a few of the distributors at the top make really big money—$300,000 and more a year. The really big money is made not by selling goods so much as recruiting for Amway's sales force. In a world where many people find little satisfaction in the paychecks they receive, visions of financial independence are often compelling. But Amway goes a crucial step beyond mere money. It offers its recruits membership in a community of like-minded people—entrepreneurial, motivated, upwardly mobile—who believe in their country, in God, and in their family.

Amway rallies typically resemble a mix between a rock concert and a religious revival meeting. The evenings are often kicked off with inspiring

Continued

management: Firms that have dirty rest rooms are rarely successful. Sewell Cadillac in Texas has become America's largest Cadillac dealer by incorporating such values. One of the keys of this automobile company's success is a service area with floors scrubbed several times a day, literally clean enough to eat lunch off.[13]

Advertisers must understand values in order to avoid violating standards. Benetton, the Italian retailer, uses ads that reflect social issues. But most Americans never see some of Benetton's more provocative material. Figure 3.2 (on page 76) features some of these ads. In one, readers are presented with pastel-colored balloons. A closer look reveals that they are inflated condoms, part of a safe-sex blitz in which some stores give away condoms. In Europe, another ad displayed a white baby feeding at the breasts of a black woman. Although the advertisement was part of a long-running campaign stressing harmony among the races, the ad was considered too provocative for use in the United States and Britain. In the midst of the Gulf conflict, Benetton ran an ad in Europe with a lone Star of David in a cemetery full of white crosses. Many periodicals refused the ad on the basis that it was offensive to religion. Still another Benetton ad showed a black man and a white man chained together to promote the "united colors" theme. It was withdrawn in the United States after minority groups complained that the ad implied the black man was a criminal, and charged the company with racism.[14]

music—the theme from *Rocky* or *Chariots of Fire*—followed by much audience hand-holding, singing, swaying, and listening to testimonials. Some inspirational speeches last into the early morning hours. Hundreds of average working people are introduced and many of them recount how they became successful and became better people with Amway. DeVos says, "We have two forms of reward in this world. One is recognition and the other is dollars. We employ them both in the Amway business."

The company has been successful in a number of other countries, including Canada (where it experienced legal problems) and Mexico. DeVos is convinced that motivating foreigners is no different from motivating people in the United States. "In Mexico, people will ride a bus for hours to come to an Amway meeting because Amway will give them a shot at success. Most of these people have believed for generations that they would never be anybody, because the rich guy on the hill told them they'd never be anybody. But the Amway business has come to symbolize for great numbers of people their chance to get out of their rut."

Source: Based on Paul Klebnikov, "The Power of Positive Inspiration," *Forbes* 148 (December 9, 1991), 244–249.

U.S. and Canadian Variations in Values

Despite the numerous similarities between the two countries, Canadian and American values and institutions vary in important ways. For one, there is less of an ideology of Canadianism than there is one of Americanism. The emphasis on individualism and achievement can be traced to the American Revolution, an upheaval that Canada did not support. Canada presents a more neutral, affable face that distinguishes it from its more exuberant and aggressive neighbor. Canada's values may be an example of the kinder, gentler nation that President Bush hoped for.

What appear as significant differences when viewed through one lens may seem to be minor variations in the eyes of others. Canadians have much more awareness of American media and institutions than conversely. But the two countries have different situations and different histories. For example, law and order—enforced by the centrally controlled Northwest Mounted Police—tamed Canada's frontier much earlier than was the case in the United States. Seymour Lipset, one of the most prolific analysts of Canadian–U.S. relationships, believes this is the reason why Canadians generally have more respect for law and order today than do U.S. citizens.[15] We summarize other differences between the values of the two countries, based on Lipset's research, in Table 3.2.

TABLE 3.1   How Marketers Adapt to Core American Values

Material Well-Being

Americans believe in the marvels of modern comforts: swift and pleasant transportation, central heating, air conditioning, instant hot and cold water, and labor-saving devices of unending variety. It is almost a right to have such material things, and consumers reward Procter & Gamble, DuPont, McDonald's, and other firms who provide them. A familiar statement of core values says, "Cleanliness is next to godliness." As a consequence, marketers who expect to sell hotel space, food, or gasoline had better provide sanitary toilets and soft tissue.

Achievement and success are measured mostly by the quantity and quality of material goods. There is display value in articles that others can see: designer clothes, luxury personal cars, hot tubs, and personal computers for the children. Although rebellion against such values is expressed occasionally, well being is fundamental to the American value system—one that marketers and politicians can count on year after year. As the popular movie *Wall Street* opined, "In America, greed is good."

Twofold Moralizing

Americans believe in polarized morality. Twofold judgments are the rule: moral-immoral, legal-illegal, civilized-primitive, secular-sacred. This is not the yin-and-yang duality of the Chinese but a classification of actions as good or bad. Consequently, the evaluation that public officials do "bad" things causes enormous problems, whereas this behavior would be accepted as normal in other parts of the world. Most Americans may personally accept nonmonogamous sexual relationships, but accusations against a politician can end a presidential campaign. Public personalities are considered ethical or unethical—not a little of both.

Marketing strategy is affected in many ways. Advertising that is "a little deceptive" is considered bad even if the overall message is largely correct. Salespeople in many countries are expected to give gifts to managers of client firms, but in North America, most corporations have policies that severely restrict or totally exclude the acceptance of gifts. In many countries, it would be considered immoral for a manager not to give preference in hiring to members of the manager's family or ethnic group. In North America, managers are expected to give jobs to the best-qualified person and to impose severe sanctions against preference toward family or ethnic members, even though such preference may be common in the manager's social relationships. Gambling is "wrong" and often a criminal activity but "right" if organized as a state lottery to benefit a good cause.

Work Is More Important than Play

Work is serious, adult business. People are judged by their work. When strangers meet, often the first topic of conversation is the kind of work each does. People are supposed to "get ahead" and "make a contribution" to society through their work.

While work is associated in American values with high or necessary purpose and grim effort, play is associated with frivolity, pleasure, and children. In other cultures, festivals and holidays and children having fun are the most important events in the society. In America, even socializing is often work-related. Advertisements for most products appeal more to work situations than to having fun or "play." Saturday morning television ads, however, appeal to play values because they are for children.

Time Is Money

Americans' view of time is different from that of many other cultures. In some countries, people actually distinguish between *hora Americana* versus *hora Mexicana* or *among Amelikan* versus *among Lao*. In doing so, they mean that American time is exact—that people are punctual, activities are scheduled, time is apportioned for separate activities, and the measure is the mechanical clock. Americans are often irritated when other people miss appointments or delivery schedules for promised orders. In some cultures, people have difficulty understanding the values that produce a need to keep hours or appointments precisely.

TABLE 3.1   continued

Effort, Optimism, and Entrepreneurship

Americans believe that problems should be identified and effort should be expended to solve them. With proper effort, one can be optimistic about success. Europeans sometimes laugh at their American friends who believe that for every problem there is a solution. When Americans find a problem, they form a committee or start a fund to solve it.

This attitude is based on the concept that the universe is mechanistic, people are their own masters, and all is perfectible almost without limit. Thus, with enough effort, people can improve themselves and manipulate the part of the universe around themselves. This viewpoint produces a certain intolerance for people who have failed to do so by those who have succeeded. A failure in life is a person who "didn't have the guts" to "make a go of it" and "get ahead." American heroes are "can-do" people. Advertising often depicts the same attitudes of rugged toughness, from pick-up trucks to the Marlboro Man.

In the American culture, effort is rewarded, competition is enforced, and individual achievement is paramount. Activist, pragmatic values rather than contemplative or mystical ones are the basis of the American character. Entrepreneurship is one result of American values of effort and optimism. In such a competitive society, some people win and some people lose. And that is fine. Being the best is morally acceptable; more than acceptable, it is the goal. Football reflects American values, and Vince Lombardi said it well: "Winning is not everything; it is the only thing." In business, excellence and being number one is the goal.

Mastery over Nature

American core values produce a conquering attitude toward nature. In Buddhism and Hinduism, people and nature are one, and people work with nature rather than attempt to conquer it. In America, lack of water to grow crops is conquerable by irrigation. Chemicals are used to kill bugs and weeds with little regard for nature's balance. This conquering attitude toward nature appears to rest on at least three assumptions: that the universe is mechanistic; that people are the masters of the earth; and that people are qualitatively different from all other forms of life.

American advertising usually depicts people who are in command of the natural environment. It is the exception that proves the rule when an advertiser deviates from core values by saying, "It's not nice to fool Mother Nature." There are always people waiting to buy the latest product to reverse nature's battle to make men bald, old people wrinkled, and people overweight.

Egalitarianism

American core values support the belief that all people should have equal opportunities for achievement. This is more of a moral imperative than an actual condition, and many groups face discrimination by other groups and individuals. Yet the core values, codified legislatively and judicially, favor equality of all people, if those people accept the core values and behaviors of the social majority.

Americans often favor the "underdog," a trait that is difficult for people raised in some other cultures to understand. Open patterns of subordination, deference to royalty, or prestige based on variables other than personal achievement bother most Americans. People who receive advantages without "earning" them are objects to ridicule. Persons of inherited wealth are subjects of such ridicule in both advertising and television programming. Lee Iacocca became a folk hero in America partly because of his immigrant background and underdog "fighting the big boys" positioning.

Humanitarianism

An American trait of coming to the aid of the less fortunate is widespread. It expresses itself in the giving of donations to unknown individuals and groups; in the outpouring of aid to victims of famines, floods, and

Continued

TABLE 3.1 continued

epidemics; in contributions of time and money to the Heart Association and countless other causes (with the exception, initially, of AIDS, which conflicted with other mainstream values); and in the rebuilding of factories and homes of conquered enemies after world wars.

In some countries, humanitarianism is more personal and related to kinship obligations, but in America, giving is more organized and depersonalized. In India and other countries, the recipients of almsgiving are usually seen with outstretched palm; in the United States, homeless recipients are more likely to be unseen and reached through a committee or a direct mailing list. For marketers, humanitarianism is not only a social responsibility but an important communications and marketing program. McDonald's, with its sponsorship of Ronald McDonald houses, youth organizations, and other community and national humanitarian programs, is a prime example.

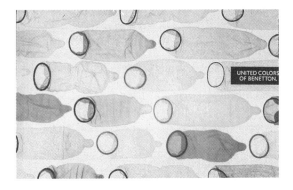

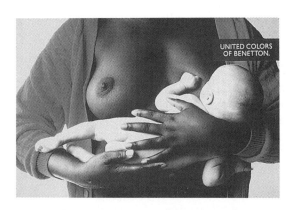

Figure 3.2 How Social Values Affect Advertising

Source: Courtesy of Benetton or "Benetton Ads: A Risqué Business," *Time* (March 25, 1991), 13.

TABLE 3.2   Variations in Values between Canada and the United States

Canada	United States
More observance of law and order	Less observance
Emphasis on the rights and obligations of community	More emphasis on individual rights and obligations
Courts are perceived as an arm of the state	Courts perceived as a check on the powers of the state
Lawful society	Greater propensity to redefine or ignore rules
Use the system to change things	Employ informal, aggressive and sometimes extra-legal means to correct what they think is wrong. "The greater lawlessness and corruption in the U.S. can also be attributed in part to a stronger emphasis on achievement."
Canadians find success in slightly bad taste	"Americans worship success."
Greater value of social relationships	Greater importance of work
	Higher commitment to work ethic
	Greater value of achievement (Goldfarb study)
Canadians more cautious	Americans take more risks
Corporate network denser in Canada. 1984—80% of companies on TSE controlled by 7 families. 32 families and 5 conglomerates control about 33% of all nonfinancial assets.	100 largest firms own about 33% of all nonfinancial assets, few controlled by individuals
5 banks hold 80% of all deposits	Literally thousands of small banks in the United States
Anti-combines legislation weakly enforced	Business affected by anti-elitist and anti–big business sentiments.
Favor partial or total government ownership.	Strong anti-trust laws
	Anti–big business, pro competition
Business leaders more likely to have privileged upbringing and less specialized education	Business leaders more likely to have a specialized education
Emphasis on social programs and government support	More laissez-faire
Canadian labor union density more than twice that of the American	
Fewer lobbying organizations in Canada even in proportion to smaller Canadian population. Since politicians toe party line, lobbying not as important.	7,000 lobbying organizations registered with Congress—since Congresspersons can vote as they choose on a bill, lobbying can be effective

Source: Summarized from Seymour Martin Lipset, *Continental Divide: The Values and Institutions of the United States and Canada* (New York: Routledge, 1990).

TABLE 3.3 Changing Values in Western Civilization

Traditional Values	New Values
Self-denial ethic	Self-fulfillment ethic
Higher standard of living	Better quality of life
Traditional sex roles	Blurring of sex roles
Accepted definition of success	Individualized definition of success
Traditional family life	Alternative families
Faith in industry, institutions	Self-reliance
Live to work	Work to live
Hero worship	Love of ideas
Expansionism	Pluralism
Patriotism	Less nationalistic
Unparalleled growth	Growing sense of limits
Industrial growth	Information/service growth
Receptivity to technology	Technology orientation

Note: Developed Western societies are gradually discarding traditional values, and are beginning to embrace emerging new values on an ever-widening scale.

Source: Joseph T. Plummer, "Changing Values," *The Futurist* 23 (January–February 1989), 10.

Changing Values

Society's values change continuously, even though the core values are relatively permanent. Marketers must pay special attention to values in transition because they affect the size of market segments. Changes in values may alter responses to advertising as well as responses to service offerings and preferred retailing formats. Some of the changes that are occurring in the 1990s have been identified in research at Young & Rubicam, shown in Table 3.3. They represent what Plummer calls a paradigm shift or a fundamental reordering of the way we see the world around us.[16]

Two types of forces explain both constancy and change in values. The first source of values is the triad of institutions: families, religious institutions, and schools. The second source is early lifetime experiences. Such experiences include wars, civil rights movements, economic realities, and many other factors. In addition, institutions such as government and the media transmit influences on values. Individuals internalize these values in a process affected by peers as well as by an individual's own decision and learning process. (See Figure 3.1.)

Changing Institutions

The triad of institutions known as family, religion, and education play a key role in understanding the values of a society. As long as these institutions are stable, the values transmitted are relatively stable. When these institutions change rapidly, the values of consumers change, creating the need for corresponding changes in marketing and communications programs.

Some of the dislocative changes in these institutions are described in the next few pages. Although discussed in the context of the United States, similar trends often are occurring in Canada, Europe, Japan, Australia, and other areas of the world.

Declining Family Influences

Family is the dominant transfusive agent of values in most cultures. Many changes are occurring in the family, which we will examine more closely later. We look at only a few basic influences on values now.

Less time for in-home or parent-child influence is available for children. This is partly due to increased enrollments in preschool or day-care facilities. Among three to four year olds, only 5.7 percent were enrolled in schools in 1965. Today that number is approaching 60 percent. In the past, children spent the first six formative years with their parents. Now children must increasingly learn their values outside the family. Substitute parents, such as babysitters, schools, and the media, now transmit values to children. Today's parents may have extensive travel responsibilities and longer, irregular working hours. With both parents away from home much of the time, especially among the higher social classes, the values of children—who will eventually become our future leaders—depend more heavily on sources outside the family.

Increasing divorce rates contribute to decreased family influence as children are socialized in one-parent households. The divorce rate has more than doubled in the past 20 years; current estimates are that about half of all marriages formed in recent decades will end in divorce. The majority of children are now raised part of their lives in single-parent households. Divorced men typically remarry younger women. Therefore, the husband's children from his first marriage are likely to be older than the wife's first children, causing problems for reconstituted families of different ages.[17]

The *isolated nuclear family* or geographical separation of the nuclear family from grandparents and other relatives (extended family) contributes to decline in family influences on value transmission. Due to the increase in young people attending college, a larger percentage of families seek employment in areas far removed from where the family grew up; they therefore lose the influence of their extended families. This removes an important stabilizing or traditionalizing influence on values. The result may be a lack of heritage or a yearning for roots.

Communications and travel companies may benefit from families' geographical separation, provided they have effective marketing programs. Delta Airlines has developed a senior citizen program with ads that proclaim, "Attend weddings and family reunions and be sure to allow enough time to visit the grandchildren."

How should businesses respond to the diminished influence of family? Some companies are reviewing their policies about job interference with family life; providing quality day-care centers for employees; encouraging families to travel out of town with executives; involving spouses in company seminars and newsletters; providing scholarships for employees' children; providing marital counseling; and in other ways recognizing the changing role of the family.

Changing Religious Influences

Judeo-Christian religious institutions historically played an important role in shaping the values of Western cultures. In recent years, these institutions have changed substantially.

Some religious groups necessarily grow at the expense of others. Catholics have risen from tiny levels in 1776 to a quarter of the U.S. population largely because of European immigration in the early 1900s and current immigration from Hispanic countries. Baptists have replaced Anglicans (Episcopalians) as the dominant Protestant group. More recently, rapidly growing groups, such as the Latter Day Saints (Mormons), have become a major influence on many of the values of their members. Non-Christian religions have gained influence in the United States, including many of the traditional Oriental religions and the New Age movement.

Groups declining in membership currently include moderate and liberal groups (Lutherans, Methodists, Presbyterians, Episcopalians, and others). The greatest gains in religious preference currently in the United States are among fundamentalists and among those with no religious preference.

Current trends in religious affiliation and attitudes are associated with the secularization of religious institutions—or loss of religious function. According to a thesis developed by Francis Schaeffer, religion has become compartmentalized and has lost some of its capacity to judge secular values and structure.[18] Although religion has weakened as an institutional influence in American society, it may still be very important for individuals. For example, women are more likely than men to define success in religious terms.[19]

Some evidence shows that a new sense of religious commitment and understanding is emerging in the United States, Canada, and some other countries. In a Gallup Poll, about one out of every three Americans indicated being a born-again Christian, and among families with children present, the following religious practices are reported:

42 percent of parents pray before meals with their children.
38 percent attend church services with their children.
28 percent attend church-related activities with their children.
17 percent read the Bible with their children.
44 percent talk about God and religion with their children.
31 percent pray or meditate with their children.
23 percent watch or listen to religious programs with their children.[20]

What are the effects of changing religious institutions upon marketing? The answer seems to be that in coming years, values of consumers will be more personal, diversified, and pluralistic. Retailers report more inventory shrinkage if religious institutions decline because employees may no longer think stealing is wrong. If the traditional Judeo-Christian value system declines, firms need to recruit more selectively and to develop programs, such as those of IBM, that inculcate values among employees.[21]

Religious values are major influences on marketing, but what about the ability of marketing to affect religion? Can religious institutions use marketing methods to enhance effectiveness? The answer is yes. Much of the material presented in this textbook has been developed by Engel into a book specifically designed for religious organizations.[22] Religious institutions are doing consumer research and applying the results to marketing plans.[23]

A successful application of consumer research by a religious organization is the Garden Grove Community Church in California. Started in a drive-in theater, the church now has thousands of members attending consecutive services each week in the multimillion-dollar Crystal Cathedral and a top-rated electronic ministry in the United States, Canada, and Australia. The church also supports hospitals, senior citizen centers, youth music schools, and relief programs throughout the world, as well as producing a television program that has survived the problems that other television evangelists faced in the late 1980s. The basic approach of the church is to research areas of life where people need help and then to develop a "shopping center for God—a part of the service industry to meet those needs."[24]

The Crystal Cathedral, shown in Figure 3.3, serves not only as a highly visible landmark to attract customers but also as a logo or symbol for the many ministries and programs.

Figure 3.3   The Crystal Cathedral: An Example of Successful Marketing by a Religious Organization
Source: Courtesy of Robert Schuller Ministries.

Changing Educational Institutions

The third major institution that transmits values to consumers is education. The influence of education appears to be increasing, due partly to the increased participation of Americans in formal education and partly to the vacuum left by families and religious institutions.

A dramatic rise in formal education has occurred at all levels. The result is a highly educated work force. Today, one in four workers in the United States is a college graduate, up from about one in eight in 1970. Fewer women workers are college graduates compared to men, but currently more women are enrolled in colleges and universities than are men. Weekend MBA programs, "Night Owl" and "Early Bird" programs, and other innovations in university continuing education departments encourage higher levels of education, even among those beyond the usual college age.

Another trend in education involves the emergence and proliferation of new teaching methods. Previously, teaching often emphasized description and memorization. This approach to learning implicitly, if not explicitly, says, "This is the way things are; just learn it," with no latitude for questioning. There has been a gradual but steady trend away from these methods toward analytical approaches emphasizing questioning of the old and the formulation of new approaches and solutions. There is no one correct answer; new horizons are encouraged. The case method in business schools is an example of this analytical, questioning approach. Another effect is described in *The Closing of the American Mind*, in which Bloom argues persuasively that American universities no longer provide much knowledge about values that arise from the great traditions of philosophy and literature.[25]

Consumers who have been socialized in the new teaching environment may reject rigid definitions of right or wrong. Individuals, particularly younger consumers, are no longer willing to lead unexamined lives. This leads to aggressive consumerism, a topic examined later in this text. Marketing organizations must develop sales programs and product-information formats that provide answers when customers ask about market offerings. Consumers may not complain to the firm but tell friends instead. Firms need complaint-management programs that seek out such complaints rather than just passively accept them. In a society where new consumers are increasingly scarce, it may be profitable to compensate complaints of existing customers, even when compensation exceeds the product's profit margin.[26] Nordstrom department stores and Stew Leonard's grocery stores are examples of firms that prosper with liberal refunds and complaint handling.

These three institutions—family, religion, and school—all contribute to transmitting traditional values as well as creating receptivity for changed lifestyles.

Intergenerational Motivating Factors

Consumers are products of their environment. People strive as adults to achieve what they feel they were deprived of in early stages of life. As a result, consumer analysts can further understand the socialization process by studying early lifetime influences of groups of people who experience similar influences while growing up.

Cohort analysis is a method for investigating the changes in patterns of behavior or attitudes of groups called **cohorts**. A cohort is any group of individuals linked as a group in some way—usually by age. Cohort analysis focuses on actual changes in the behavior or attitudes of a cohort, the changes that can be attributed to the process of aging, and changes that are associated with events of a particular period, such as the Great Depression or the Watergate scandal.[27] Many marketing organizations, for example, have focused on the baby boomers, a group of consumers of similar age and experiences.

Pre–World War II Consumers

Millions of mature consumers experienced the Great Depression of the 1930s. Even more experienced the upheavals of World War II. The severity of these cataclysmic events profoundly and indelibly affected the people who lived through them. These events affected their values of security, patriotism, and the acquisition and protection of material goods. Such values reflect the deprivations that individuals experienced during the depression and war.

Interpersonal Generation

The cohort of consumers who were children in the 1950s and 1960s—the Interpersonal Generation—express awareness and concern for other people. These aging baby boomers manifest themselves in social concern on issues of civil rights and equal opportunity. Fashion is also more important. They were not interested in fashion in the sense of keeping up with the Joneses, as had been true of their parents, but fashion that emerged because of so much social contact and interpersonal awareness.

The Self-Values Generation

The values of the most recent cohort of new consumers emphasize the self—self-expression, self-realization, self-help, and do-it-yourself. Critical influences on this cohort include the energy crisis, inflation, feminism, Watergate and the Iran cover-up, and federal deficits associated with an expanding tax and Social Security burden. Concern of the previous cohort was how to help others achieve the good life, but the most recent cohort is more concerned with the problem of maintaining the good lifestyle. You can see many of these values, likely to affect the 1990s, reflected in Table 3.3.

Self-interest and social concern are often blended on a personal basis. Consumers in today's cultural environment often express concern for the environment not so much because it is socially correct behavior but because they must take responsibility for their own survival. Among other things, self-interest also emphasizes nutrition and health. About 40 percent of Americans work out every day; a quarter take part in more than one sport; and wellness programs are increasingly supported by organizations as well as by individuals.[28] As a consequence, advertising frequently features such themes. Identification with healthy foods, personal appearance, and sports have surged in advertising usage for a broad array of products and services.

Figure 3.4   Advertising Sensitivity to Changing Values
Source: Courtesy of McDonald's and Amway.

Firms that built their success on traditional values must change. Notice how this is done by both McDonald's and Amway in Figure 3.4. McDonald's was built on what was often called junk food. Today they are one of the fast-food industry's leaders in providing nutritional information and developing innovative products related to health concerns. Amway, stressing individual effort and success motivation described earlier in the chapter, also demonstrates its sensitivity to environmental issues, including an awareness of Native American ethnicity.

Ethnic Influences on Consumer Behavior

The norms and values of specific groups within the larger society are called **ethnic patterns**. Individual consumers may be influenced slightly or extensively by an ethnic group. Ethnic groups may be formed around nationality, religion, physical attributes, geographic location, or other factors. Bikers or the Grey Panthers might even be an important ethnic group for some.

Figure 3.4   continued

Ethnicity is a process of group identification in which people use ethnic labels to define themselves and others. A "subjectivist" perspective reflects ascriptions people make about themselves. An "objectivist" definition is derived from socio-cultural categories. In consumer research, ethnicity is best defined as some combination of these, including the strength or weakness of affiliation which people have with the ethnic group.[29] To the degree that people in an ethnic group share common perceptions and cognitions that are different from those of other ethnic groups or the larger society, they constitute a distinct ethnic group or market segment.[30]

The values of an ethnic microculture may conflict with the values of the macroculture. Individuals exhibit a synthesis of the macroculture and perhaps more than one microculture. As an example, the lifestyles and consumption patterns of an African-American living in the western states may reflect both African-American and western microcultures and perhaps a religious group, as well as the values of the American macroculture. Keep in mind also that specific individuals may not reflect the values of the ethnic group with which they are commonly identified.

Native American Culture

In a sense, the truly "American" culture is that of Native Americans, although marketers view Native Americans as a minority ethnic group in today's majority culture. Almost two million people in the United States identified themselves as American Indian in the 1990 census and more than seven million claim some American Indian ancestry. The 1990 figure was 38 percent more than in 1980, a higher growth rate than for African-Americans (6 percent) but not as high as the growth rate for Hispanics (53 percent) or Asians (108 percent).[31]

After nearly a century of assimilation into white society, there is a resurgence of identification with Native American culture, both by Indians and *bahanas* (whites). Some American Indians dislike the idea of sharing their culture and spiritual practices with white people, but others welcome people of any race into their culture. The interest in Native American culture has increased consumer demand for products that reflect their ancient crafts and skills. The movie *Dances with Wolves* helped to stimulate demand in Native American literature and arts.

Other Nationality Groups

America is a montage of nationality groups. It has been called the greatest genetic pool of malcontents in the world, composed mostly of people or the descendants of people who were dissatisfied in their original nation and sought something better. England is the background nation for 26.34 percent of Americans, followed closely by Germany with 26.14 percent. The 50-million figure for English Americans is higher than the current population of England. The Irish are the third largest, with 17.77 percent, followed by African-Americans at 11.13 percent. Other nationality groups with significant numbers include French, Italian, Scottish, Polish, and Mexican, but recent census figures register 54 countries represented with 100,000 or more American residents.

Some immigrants identify with much of their culture of origin; others do not. A variable closely associated with national ethnic identity is the language spoken at home. Two groups of Americans who speak a language other than English are Chinese and Hispanics. Eighty-one percent of Chinese-Americans speak Chinese at home. About 43 percent of Hispanics speak Spanish at home, including Cuban-Americans at 92 percent, and Mexican-Americans at 77 percent of the households.[32]

A key issue is the degree to which immigrants embrace traditional American core values. Some nationality groups contribute to the cultural diversity of North America more than others, but frequently the variables that lead to success for majority Americans are the same as for immigrants who become nationality-market segments. When an immigrant family becomes American, the members often manifest and reinforce the work ethic that is at the core of American values.[33]

Religious Ethnic Groups

Religious groups have important influences on consumption. Mormons, for example, may refrain from purchasing tobacco, liquor, and other stimulants but may be prime prospects for fruit juices endorsed by Marie and Donnie Osmond. The *Christian Science Monitor* is not the best place for ads for Anacin or Tylenol. Seventh-Day Adventists limit their purchases of meat but may be prime targets for vegetable-based foods.

Born-again Christians are sometimes less materialistic and less interested in consumer goods than other Americans, have low use of credit, and weaker-than-average preferences for national brands. They have higher per capita consumption, however, of automobiles and motorcycles, groceries and fast food, apparel stores, sporting goods, insurance, and products from hardware or fabric and pattern stores.[34]

Jewish ethnicity is both religious and national and is an attractive market for many firms. Food products provide specific identification for kosher certification. Maxwell House Coffee and Tetley Tea have tried to appeal to Jewish consumers by featuring bagels in their ads. Star-Kist says, "Beautify a bialy with Star-Kist tuna salad surprise." Chef Boy-Ar-Dee promotes its macaroni shells with the line, "Treat your macaroni mayvin to real Italian taste."

Recent research has concentrated on differences in cognitive processing and other variables related to ethnicity. Hirschman found that Jewish norms create more childhood information exposure than among other groups, more adult information seeking, consumption innovativeness, consumption information transfer, and more active memory capacity. Jewish consumers are more disposed toward sensory gratification and arousal compared to other nationality groups, as evidenced by the types of leisure activities they prefer and their motives for engaging in these activities. Jewish (and also Hispanic) consumers appear more oriented toward sensual behavior (for example, making love) in leisure activity than do other nationality groups that have been examined, and they differ substantially from Christians in product-salience rankings. The research by Hirschman clearly indicates that ethnicity (Jewish or otherwise) is a variable of large potential influence. The more an individual consumer identifies with the ethnic group, the greater the influence is likely to be.[35]

Geographic Culture

Geographic areas in a nation sometimes develop their own culture. The Southwest area of the United States is known for casual lifestyles featuring comfortable clothing, outdoor entertaining, and active sports. The Southwest may also appear to be more innovative toward new products, such as cosmetic surgery, when compared to conservative, inhibited attitudes that characterize other areas of the nation. Climate, religious affiliations of the population, nationality influences, and other variables are interrelated to produce a core of cultural values in a geographic area.

Nine Nations of North America, as conceived by Joel Garreau,[36] cuts across national, state, and provincial borders of North America. This conceptualization incorporates the culture of each area, as well as its climate, institutions, business organizations, and resources such as minerals and water. In Garreau's system, North America is described as consisting of the following areas: The Foundry (industrial Northeast); Dixie; Ectopia (northern Pacific Rim); Mexamericana (Southwest wealthy area); Breadbasket; Quebec; The Empty Quarter (Northwest Canada); the Islands; and New England.

The application of geographic values to marketing is explained by Kahle:

> Contemporary marketing managers must also know that marketing activities often vary from one place to another. Because the underlying causes of success and failure in various places may not always be evident, understanding the values of various regions may provide an important clue to deciphering what sometimes seems like a regionally random pattern of successful experiences in marketing both new and established products. For example, an advertisement promoting the capacity for self-fulfillment (e.g., "Set yourself free with Stouffer's") of a product may be more successful in the West than in the South. Security, on the other hand, may be a more successful appeal in the South than in comparably urbanized areas of the West (e.g., "Protect your home from break-ins with Electronic Touch Alarm"). For personal computers, an advertising campaign emphasizing how computers can help one accomplish his/her goals or emphasizing the computer attributes that facilitate accomplishment will probably be more effective in the East than in the South, and particularly in the West South Central.[37]

Asian-American Culture

Asian-Americans are rapidly increasing as a desirable target for marketing organizations for two reasons. First, they are growing in number. Between 1980 and 1990 Asian-Americans in the United States increased from 3.8 million to almost 7 million. The U.S. Census Bureau estimates that number could reach 15 to 20 million by early next century. Second, Asian-Americans have higher incomes, more education, and are more likely to own a business than other minorities.[38] Asian-Americans are usually defined to include Chinese, Japanese, Koreans, Vietnamese, Cambodians, Laotians, Filipinos, Asian Indians, Pakistanis, Hawaiians, Samoans, Guamanians, Fiji Islanders, and other Asians and Pacific Islanders living in the United States. Some immigrants from Hong Kong, looking for safety and refuge before the 1997 change of control, bring substantial amounts of capital to the United States and Canada.

The Asian-American culture is characterized by hard work, strong family ties, appreciation for education, and other values that lead to success in entrepreneurship, technical skills, and the arts. The success also may bring conflict with more entrenched immigrants and other consumers. Japanese-Americans have a long history in America, including great suffering and discrimination associated with World War II. In recent years, immigration has been more extensive from other Asian countries than from Japan.

The socioeconomic characteristics of the Asian-American market attract marketers, but success in marketing programs hinges on understanding the distinctions of the microculture. Consumer in Focus 3.2 shows how a dentist—perhaps more sensitive to ethnic influence than others would be because of his own ethnic identity—achieved success in selling to Asian-American consumers. Careful reading of this box serves to indicate other details of most Asian microcultures.

Retailing and advertising are two areas of marketing directly affected by national ethnic groups. Many cities contain large groups of relatively homogeneous nationality groups, creating the opportunity for stores featuring ethnic foods and

Consumer in Focus   3.2

Can an Ethnic Dentist Find Happiness Selling German Cars to the Chinese?

San Francisco has long been the capital of Asian America. But Ron Greenspan, an orthodontist in a comfortable San Francisco neighborhood, had a small practice that had changed from 70 percent white in 1969 to 70 percent Asian a decade later.

Straightening teeth, however, was never Greenspan's great love—cars were. In 1981, he bought one of San Francisco's two Volkswagen dealerships for $250,000. At the time, this was a business going nowhere. The flocks of youthful, white San Franciscans, who once bought "Bugs" by the boatload, now were opting for more expensive German imports or cheaper cars from Japan.

It was natural that Greenspan would find former patients among his new customers. What was not so predictable is that this Jewish dentist from Cleveland could build a booming trade selling German cars to the Chinese. That required a good deal of ingenuity.

Greenspan started out by placing ads in such outlets as the *Asian Yellow Pages*. He mailed fliers into middle-class Asian neighborhoods such as the Richmond section of San Francisco, and the nearby suburb of Daly City, with its large concentration of Filipinos. Taking his cue from his salesman father, Nat, who had encouraged him as a youth to sell everything from shoe polish to toilet deodorizers door-to-door, Greenspan sent his salespeople out into the streets of the city to visit shops and hangouts frequented by the Asian bourgeoisie.

Bringing Asian customers into the showroom, however, was the easy part. Persuading them to buy was where the real challenge began. Most intimidating was the Chinese penchant for tough bargaining over price. To the Chinese, this is simply a normal part of the business culture. But to someone more accustomed to American business—even a car salesperson—the exchange can seem downright cutthroat. "When the guy comes in here and makes a ridiculous offer on a car, you don't get mad," Greenspan instructed his sales force. "You come back with something equally ridiculous and have a good laugh. Then start your real negotiation."

Another facet of Greenspan's "Asian Sensitivity Training" focused on dealing with the family. The Chinese prefer shopping in large family groups, with buying decisions usually made by the family elders. Greenspan explained to his salespeople that while the car might be for a teenage schoolgirl or a middle-aged engineer, the successful sales pitch may have to be directed to the grandfather or elderly uncle. To help things along, 75-year-old Nat Greenspan is often on hand to make the generational connection.

Continued

Consumer in Focus 3.2 continued

Largely as a result of sales to Asian-Americans, Greenspan has now boosted car sales from only 20 a month to more than 100, ranking among the top few VW dealers in America.

Source: Excerpted from Joel Kotkin, "Selling to the New America," *Inc.* (July 1987), 46–47. Reprinted with permission, *Inc.* magazine. Copyright © 1987 by Goldhirsh Group, *Inc.*, 38 Commercial Wharf, Boston, MA 02110.

other products. Staff may need to be bilingual. By making special appeals to Asians in their showrooms, Steinway now sells 15 percent of its product to Asian-Americans. National- and language-oriented media may promote greater loyalty among the readers and listeners, as well as provide excellent "cost-per-thousand" of concentrated market targets. Among Asian-Americans, 54 percent shop as a leisure activity compared with 50 percent of the general population. Asians also think quality is more important than price when they choose a store. They are far more likely to use technology such as automated teller machines, and many more own VCRs, CD players, microwave ovens, home computers, and telephone answering machines.[39]

Numbers are important to Asian-Americans, particularly the number 8 which symbolizes prosperity. Colors are also important, especially red. They believe that white envelopes should not be used around a holiday because white usually symbolizes death. Citibank effectively featured a dragon in one of its ads, instead of corks from champagne bottles, which are considered inappropriate. Celebrities, especially those of Asian background, can be very effective in appealing to Asian-American consumers. When Reebok featured Michael Chang in ads, shoe sales among Asian Americans greatly increased.[40] Kellogg's featured Olympic gold medalist Kristi Yamaguchi on their cereal boxes describing her as "California native" without reference to her Japanese ancestry.

Korean-Americans have substantially more education than other groups and may respond better to communications than less educationally oriented groups. Table 3.4 shows how clearly Koreans dominate the ownership of businesses. Koreans not only have a higher rate of business ownership than any other minority groups but also a higher rate of business success than nonminority consumers. A major study of Korean immigrants concludes that the values of hard work and merchant ability have been developed as a result of coming to America, rather than due to their Korean background.[41]

African-American or Black Culture

African-American or black culture refers to a common heritage rather than to a skin color. In the United States, the black heritage is conditioned by an American beginning in slavery, a shared history of discrimination and suffering, confined housing opportunities, and denial of participation in many aspects of the majority culture.

TABLE 3.4   Minority Business Owners

	1987	1982	Percent Change 1982–87
Blacks	14.6	11.3	29.2%
Hispanics	20.9	14.3	46.2
Mexican	18.8	13.7	37.2
Puerto Rican	10.9	6.3	73.0
Cuban	62.9	41.4	51.9
Other Hispanic	22.9	14.2	61.3
Asian*	57.0	43.2	31.9
Asian Indian	75.7	51.3	47.6
Chinese	63.4	49.1	29.1
Japanese	66.1	59.3	11.5
Korean	102.4	68.0	50.6
Vietnamese	49.6	14.6	239.7
Filipino	32.8	25.5	28.6
Hawaiian	21.5	16.6	29.5
American Indian	11.8	8.8	34.1
Aleut	54.0	58.5	−7.7
Eskimo	44.4	36.8	20.7
Native American	10.3	7.4	39.2
Nonminority	67.1	61.9	8.4

Note: Minority-owned firms per 1,000 population, for minority groups, and percent change 1982–87.
*Includes Pacific Islanders.

Source: Bureau of the Census, 1982 and 1987 Economic Censuses and population estimates quoted in William O'Hare, "Reaching for the Dream," American Demographics 14 (January 1992), 32–36.

Greater homogeneity in black markets than among white markets has been historically a valid assumption, although that may be challenged as well-educated black people achieve substantial separation in income and social status from other black people.[42]

The African-American market is worthy of serious marketing attention. It has a population base of over 26 million (and growing faster than the white population base) and buying power estimated as high as $225 billion. If U.S. black consumers were considered a separate country, that country would rank as eleventh largest in the free world. The African-American middle class is emerging as an important source of consumer buying power and influence. We look more closely at demographic changes occurring in the black population later in this book under the topic of Consumer Trends. In spite of the fact that African-Americans comprise 12.1 percent of the U.S. population and 11.3 percent of the readership of all magazines, on the average only 3.15 percent of the people shown in magazine advertising are black and only 7.5 percent of television ads include black actors. Blacks (and other minorities) are underrepresented, declining in representation, and frequently shown in stereotypical or menial roles.[43]

Structural influences shape African-American ethnic markets. They also inhibit some black consumer preferences or intentions. These structural influences include low income, educational deprivation, different family characteristics, and, of course, discrimination.

Income Deprivation   The African-American culture is sometimes associated with the low-income culture. This confusion is not difficult to understand because black consumers average less income than white consumers. About 30 percent of black families are below the poverty level, as defined by the U.S. Department of Commerce, compared to only about 10 percent of white families. More white families fall below the poverty level in absolute terms, but the percentage of black families is larger.[44]

Two factors related to low income among black families are significant in the study of consumer behavior. First, there is the direct effect derived from reducing spending power. Consumers often must buy from stores that welcome food stamps; many products are not financially within the reach of poor consumers; and, to a large degree, income must be spent on the basics of life.

The second factor is the methodological complexity of separating effects due to low income from those due to being African-American. Some studies attempt to correct for the income differences when reporting black-white differences, but many report "differences" between black and white consumers that are mostly differences in income levels. If marketers do not recognize this problem, it is easy to minimize the importance of middle- and higher-income black market targets. There are more similarities than differences in black and white spending. Most of the differences are linked to African-Americans' lower incomes and concentration in central cities.[45]

Educational Deprivation   Inadequate education places African-American consumers at a disadvantage not only in earning income but in acquiring consumer skills. Such skills must be learned on the street if not at school. Because of inadequate resources or by design, schools have often failed in helping black consumers master the educational skills needed for full participation in the market system.

Quality education can also provide a way out for black consumers. Some advertisers sponsor scholarship contests. Ads showing consumer durables and other expensive goods often use models portraying occupations that require education, knowing that many black customers recognize this is the best way to upward mobility and the middle-class lifestyle.

Family Characteristics   The African-American culture is influenced by unique family characteristics, primarily a highly mobile family structure. A high proportion of families are headed by females, perhaps twice as high as for white families. Therefore, black females influence purchases and create subtleties of relationships an advertiser must understand and consider in devising advertisements. Only 38 percent of black children live with two parents compared with 80 percent of white children.[46]

The typical black family is much younger than the typical white family. The median age is about five years younger, a factor accounting for differences in preferences for clothing, music, shelter, cars, and many other products and activities.[47]

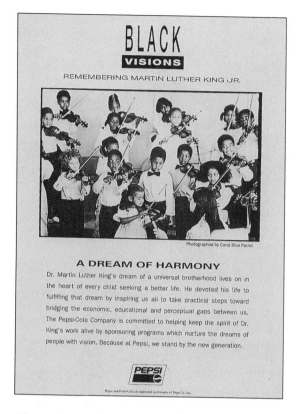

Figure 3.5   Advertisements from Ebony Magazine

Source: Courtesy of Pepsi and GM.

Discrimination   The effects of discrimination on the African-American culture are so massive and enduring that they cannot be ignored in the analysis of consumer behavior. Discrimination has been particularly restrictive on black consumption decisions in the area of housing.

As a result of years of discrimination, black consumers should have substantial skepticism toward white businesses. Many businesses contributed to segregated residential patterns and limited employment opportunities. They supported invisibility of blacks in the media until recent years. Today, firms that make a special effort to show sensitivity to the black culture, use black media wisely, and stand against discrimination may be able to turn a problem into an opportunity. Notice how Pepsi and General Motors attempt to build rapport with black consumers (see Figure 3.5). These ads appeared in *Ebony* magazine.

Many companies target black consumers through public relations and special promotions. Kraft publishes a free booklet featuring African-American cooking. For several years Budweiser has offered posters of "The Great Kings and Queens of Africa." Coca-Cola sponsors a "Share the Dream" scholarship program. American Airlines features ads with prominent black Americans such as Olympic runner

TABLE 3.5   Black Consumer Behavior

1. Socioeconomic deprivation leads black youths to behave differently than whites in an effort to upgrade their status. Black youths, in relation to their white counterparts, are more likely to
   a. have higher occupational aspirations
   b. have stronger desires for conspicuous consumption
   c. be more impatient regarding acquisition of socially conspicuous items
   d. be less likely to defer consumption gratifications
2. Black youths, compared to their white counterparts, are more likely to respond favorably to marketing stimuli. They tend to
   a. have more positive attitudes toward marketing stimuli
   b. be more susceptible to marketing practices
3. Black youths are more likely than white youths to use brand names when purchasing low involvement products.
4. The black youths' propensity to use brand name as a criterion in purchasing products declines with socioeconomic status.
5. White youths are more likely than their black counterparts to use price as a criterion when purchasing low involvement products.
6. Black girls in comparison with white girls are more likely to
   a. acquire greater independence than boys
   b. participate more in family purchasing decisions than boys
7. Black youths are more likely to have favorable orientations toward television than their white counterparts. Black youths are more likely than white youths to
   a. watch television
   b. evaluate television stimuli as being realistic
   c. use television for consumer information
   d. model after television characters

Florence Griffith Joyner and film maker Spike Lee. Most of these promotions are scheduled to appear around Black History Month in February.[48]

African-American Consumption Patterns

Do African-Americans differ in their consumption patterns from other market segments? The similarities are greater than the differences, especially among middle-income groups. Many differences in consumption are explained by income differences.

Many factors must be considered in developing marketing programs for the African-American. Numerous studies provide guidelines for developing effective programs.[49] Marketers must consider both cultural and structural elements. A fast-food chain, for example, completed a marketing research project among black consumers and found lower per capita purchases of hamburgers among black customers than among white consumers. The chain's stores located in predominantly black, inner-city areas, however, had the highest volume of any stores in the nation—apparently in conflict with the market research report. At first, executives were

TABLE 3.5   continued

8. White youths are more likely than black youths to use newspapers for information about consumption.
9. Black youths are less likely than white youths to interact with parents about consumption matters.
   a. Black youths discuss consumption less frequently than white youths.
   b. Black youths are less likely to model after their parents' consumer behavior than white youths.
10. White youths are socialized into the consumer role earlier than black youths.
11. Different socialization processes operate among black and white youths.
12. Black adult consumers are more likely than their white counterparts to emphasize consumption. Blacks are more likely than whites to
    a. hold materialistic values
    b. spend a larger proportion of their available income on items of social status and social significance
    c. be innovators of socially conspicuous products
    d. have higher occupational aspirations
13. Blacks are more likely than whites to trade goods and services among family members.
14. Black consumers are not likely to interact with the marketplace as effectively and efficiently as white consumers. Blacks are less likely than whites to
    a. seek information
    b. consider a larger number of alternatives
    c. evaluate alternatives on a large number of objective attributes
15. Black/white differences in consumer behavior are contingent on the adult person's socioeconomic status. When social class is taken into account
    a. Blacks are more likely to hold egalitarian sex role perceptions about household decisions.
    b. Black/white differences in consumer behaviors are greater among lower-class than higher-class adults.
16. With increasing age, older black consumers are more likely to experience declining activity in consumption than older white consumers.

Source: George P. Moschis, *Consumer Socialization* (Lexington, Mass.: Lexington Books, 1987), 247–258. Reprinted by permission of the publisher.

bewildered by the research findings. The answer lies, however, in the population-density ratios of the areas surrounding the store. While the average per capita consumption was lower, so many people living in the neighborhood bought hamburgers that the store's total volume was surprisingly high.

Consumer research has focused on similarities and differences between white and black people in the United States, starting with early reviews by Bauer and Cunningham and others.[50] For the most part, these studies failed to control for socioeconomic status or other structural variables.[51] Often they were conducted in a single city, quite a few years ago. Thus, for the consumer researcher a dilemma exists. Which of the studies are still valid? Which were valid to begin with? It would be incorrect to disregard all of them because some—such as the evidence that African-Americans are very loyal to specific brands—have been reported repeatedly.[52]

We solved the dilemma by reporting the findings about black and white differences in Table 3.5. Moschis consolidates many studies, focusing on the topic of black consumer socialization. Remember that some are based upon early research that may not be true today. There is no easy way to determine which findings are still valid or which need modification. Nevertheless, they provide propositions about black consumer behavior and ways to reach black markets. The propositions can be considered as hypotheses helpful in the design of marketing programs.

Hispanic Culture

Hispanics are the fastest-growing ethnic market in the United States, with buying power estimated as high as $100 billion. Between the 1980 and 1990 census, Hispanics increased from 14.6 million to 21.3 million. By 2015, experts believe Hispanics will outnumber African-Americans because of immigration and higher birth rates. The Hispanic market is 88 percent concentrated in cities, an attractive feature for media plans, distribution facilities, and other elements of marketing programs.

Who Is Hispanic?   Language and identity, rather than national origin, are the key elements in Hispanic culture. *Chicano* refers to persons of Mexican descent born in the United States. *Latino* is a more general term, which identifies those of Latin-American origin. The Census Bureau employs the term *Hispanic* to identify persons of Spanish origin with Spanish surnames. Hispanics may be of any color or racial group.

Hispanic consumers are often segmented into four groups. *Mexicans* are the largest segment, about 60 percent of all Hispanics. They are concentrated in the Southwest, and 53 percent were born in the United States. They tend to be young and have large families. *Puerto Ricans* are about 15 percent of all Hispanics. They are concentrated in the Northeast, especially in New York City. Most have arrived in the past 25 years, and many are now in middle age, with young children born in the United States. *Cubans* are about 7 percent of all Hispanics and are concentrated in the Southeast. Only 7 percent were born in the United States. Cubans are the oldest group, have fewer children, and are the aristocracy in terms of occupation, education, and income. *Other Hispanics* constitute 18 percent, heavily from Central America, and are dispersed geographically. They are 93 percent foreign-born and mostly young adults with few children.[53]

The diversity provides differences in values and motivations. Mexican-Americans are more likely to be assimilated into the U.S. culture, with less desire to return to Mexico. Cubans are more likely to consider themselves stranded in the host country. Although they may not want to return to Cuba, they are more likely than are other Hispanics to think of themselves as Hispanic first and American second.[54] Cuban income is much higher than that of any other Hispanic group, roughly at or above the average American income. Puerto Ricans have the lowest average of any Hispanic group.

Language is often described as a unifying factor, but even this is not always true. An advertiser describing brown sugar in Spanish would need to say *azucar negra* in New York, *azucar prieta* in Miami, *azucar cafe* in California, *azucar morena* in South Texas, and *azucar pardo* in other U.S. areas. In New York, an insecticide company advertised to Puerto Ricans that its product would kill all *bichos* (bugs), without realizing that for Puerto Ricans the colloquial *bichos* is a reference to male genitals.

Culturally unaware marketers might assume that because Hispanics are bilingual, it would be adequate to communicate with them in English. About 94 percent speak Spanish in the home, and studies show that Hispanics think in Spanish—

creating the need for marketers to communicate in Spanish-based forms to be most effective.[55]

Marketing to Hispanic Values

The Hispanic culture provides high value on quality. Many Hispanics emigrated from poorer countries. They seek status symbols that demonstrate that they have "arrived." For example, Bulova watches had an image in the Hispanic market of a "cheap American product." To counter this image, Bulova used Hispanic media to position its product as an expensive but affordable piece of jewelry. The revised advertisements emphasized Bulova's extensive line of 18-karat gold watches, because Hispanics view 14-karat as synonymous with gold-plated. Through these efforts Bulova achieved a 40 percent share in the Spanish-speaking market.

Coupons are thought to be not as effective with Hispanics as with non-Hispanic white and black consumers because of the stigma coupons have for people who came to this country poor. Hispanics are proud that they are now making a better living. They may not want to use coupons that are "for people who can't afford to pay the full price."[56]

Some products have made successful adaptations to the Hispanic market. Cudahy established a premium bacon called Rex based on the strategy that a lean, premium bacon could sell in a 12-ounce size for prices comparable to the biggest competitor's (Farmer John) 16-ounce package. The package shouts the message, *"Vale su peso en carne."* Beer companies such as Budweiser and Miller have battled to sponsor community celebrations such as *Cinco de Mayo* and the Independence Day Fair because of their importance in the Spanish culture.

The family is extremely important in Hispanic culture, and differs from non-Hispanic whites not only in values but also in size (larger) and age (younger).[57] Figure 3.6 shows how Ford Motor Company has adapted its advertising theme to this important value in the Hispanic culture.

Avoiding Marketing Blunders
Failure to understand the Hispanic culture can lead to marketing blunders. Humberto Valencia has identified three major types: translation blunders, culture misunderstandings, and Hispanic idiosyncrasies.[58]

Translation Blunders Translation blunders occur in Hispanic markets just as they often do in global markets. One cigarette advertisement wanted to say "less tar," but the translation actually said the brand claimed to have "less asphalt." A beer company found that the radio commercial they hoped would say "less filling, delicious" incorrectly came across in Spanish as "filling, less delicious" merely because of the way it was sung. Even market researchers blunder when they ask for the *"dama de la casa"* (madam of the house) rather than the *"señora de la casa"* (lady of the house).

Culture Misunderstandings Serious misunderstandings occur when marketers use stereotypes of their own self-reference criteria for designing strategies. A telephone company commercial portrayed a wife saying to her husband, "Run downstairs and phone Maria. Tell her we'll be a little late." Two serious culture

Figure 3.6   The Ford Advertisement Recognizes the Importance of the Family in Hispanic Culture
Source: Courtesy of Ford Motor Company, Agency: Hispania.

errors were committed. First, it is socially unacceptable for a Latin wife to give her husband orders. Second, Hispanics do not normally call to say they will not be on time; it is customary to arrive a little late.

A radio station ran a contest in which the prize was two tickets to Disneyland, but few Hispanics were interested. Giving away two tickets was not enough for the family-oriented Hispanic. When the number was increased, much more interest was generated.

Hispanic Idiosyncrasies   Marketing blunders sometimes occur from failure to understand the idiosyncrasies of each segment of the total Hispanic market. Just as the British, Canadians, South Africans, and frequently Americans have major differences even though English is the common language, so there are differences between Mexican-Americans, Puerto Rican–Americans, Cuban-Americans, and other Hispanics. A radio advertisement in Miami used the term *banditas*, which is a Puerto Rican term for Band-Aids. The ad failed because Miami's largely Cuban population did not recognize the term. Domino planned to add papaya flavor into its line of tropical-flavored drinks but dropped the idea because of the vulgar connotations papaya has for Cubans in Miami. A beer company filmed a Hispanic advertise-

Consumer in Focus   3.3

Kodak Develops Family Theme via Cultural Tie-ins

Kodak reaches Hispanic consumers via tie-ins with local cultural events, museums, and festivals. Kodak's "family fun" outings encourage picture-taking and provide fun activities and thematic photo backdrops. Family members can also borrow a Kodak camera for the day.

In 1989, the company tied in with a large Hispanic cultural festival in Miami. Since then, Kodak has refined its cultural tie-in approach to concentrate more on activities, workshops and, of course, picture-taking opportunities for Hispanic families with young children. Kodak also supports the California Museum of Latino History, said to be the largest repository of Hispanic-American documents and artifacts in the United States.

To provide a picture-taking opportunity that celebrated Hispanic performing arts, Kodak involved Telemundo (Spanish TV) soap opera stars and performances at Nuanu's Festival of the Americas, culminating in a fireworks display provided by Kodak. Festival-goers had the chance to have photos taken with stars of Hispanic TV and other celebrities.

Kodak ethnic marketing efforts are coordinated by UniWorld Group, Inc., a New York City–based communications company. For ethnic festivals, Kodak has developed a backdrop where families can pose for pictures. There is a kiosk where Kodak film is sold and cameras are demonstrated and loaned to consumers for the day. On a single day in Miami, Kodak sold more than 1,000 rolls of film.

Source: Summarized from Susan L. Fry, "Reaching Hispanic Publics with Special Events," *Public Relations Journal* 47 (February 1991), 12–13ff.

ment using the Paseo del Rio (Riverwalk) in San Antonio, Texas, as a background. The ad was well received among Hispanics living on the West Coast, who liked the Spanish atmosphere. In San Antonio itself, Hispanics did not like the ad because they considered the Paseo del Rio to be an attraction for non-Hispanic white tourists rather than for Hispanic residents.

The Hispanic market is being assimilated into older non-Hispanic markets, and many assumptions—such as higher brand-loyalty, lower coupon usage, more shopping enjoyment, and so forth—are increasingly questionable or need to be qualified.[59] Brand loyalty is increasingly questioned as typical of Hispanics, although price, product quality, and shopping ease appear to be important attributes to Hispanics.[60] Research findings about Hispanic or other ethnic groups are often confusing because they fail to consider the strength or weakness of identification with the ethnic group.[61] Consumer in Focus 3.3 shows, however, how Kodak has incorporated an understanding of the Hispanic market into its marketing and public relations strategy.

French-Canadian Culture

One of the largest and most distinct cultures in North America is the French-Canadian area of Canada, mostly in Quebec. This might be considered a nationality group or a geographic culture. The province of Quebec accounts for over 27 percent of the Canadian population and about 25 percent of income and retail sales.[62] For years, the French culture was somewhat ignored by English-oriented advertisers, thereby creating a social problem as well as limiting the potential effectiveness of communications to the French market. Some of the differential treatment may have been due to different social class groupings compared to Anglo markets.[63]

Marketing strategists should be concerned with whether advertising is transferable between the French-Canadian (FC) culture and the English-Canadian (EC) or Anglophone culture. Some marketers believe that separate advertising material must be developed to be effective in the FC microculture. Others believe materials can be developed that are effective with both groups. A minimum of verbal material is used, with emphasis on the visual.

Tamilia's research, which compared communications with FC and EC consumers on a cross-cultural basis, indicates the potential for increasing effectiveness in advertising communications. This is built upon some previous research by Tigert that indicated the French are more responsive to people-oriented than to message-oriented advertisements.[64] Tamilia's research led to the conclusion that French Canadians do react more to the source of the advertisement than do English Canadians, who are more message-oriented. Consumer in Focus 3.4 discusses other differences in marketing to French and English Canadians.

Because of the size and importance of the French-Canadian market, it has attracted the attention of many marketers. The process of understanding communications in a cross-cultural setting, however, is applicable to other situations where diverse ethnic groups are the target for marketing programs.

Summary

Marketing to consumers in North America must be done in an environment of multicultural diversity. This requires an understanding of the culture and values of these markets. This chapter has focused on the United States and Canada, although in the future the markets of Mexico will increasingly be important in viewing the entire North American market.

Culture is the complex of values, ideas, attitudes, and other meaningful symbols that allow humans to communicate, interpret, and evaluate as members of society. Culture and its values are transmitted from one generation to another. The core values of a society define how products are used, with regard to their function, form, and meaning. Culture also provides positive and negative valences for brands and for communications programs, and defines the ideology of consumption.

Core values in America include material well-being; twofold moralizing; the concepts that work is more important than play and that time is money; effort-optimism-entrepreneurship; mastery over nature; egalitarianism; and humanitarianism. Canadian and U.S. values are more similar to each other than to most other countries but differ in significant ways.

Consumer in Focus   3.4

Market Information Sources in French Canada

Market information can come from various sources including friends, family members, and the mass media. Where do French Canadians obtain their information? A recent study on the purchase of a car showed that, contrary to expectations, English Canadians used personal sources to a greater extent than French Canadians. Other interesting findings showed that

- French Canadians considered fewer cars than did English Canadians
- French Canadians devoted less time to search
- English Canadians made three times as many test drives as French Canadians
- Overall, English Canadians generally seem to conduct a more extensive information search than French Canadians, at least as it applies to the purchase of a new car

French Canadians traditionally have showed affinity for mass media preferences quite unlike their English counterparts. As a result, brand images, brand attitudes, product attributes, and positioning strategies in general may not achieve similar response patterns among the two groups. Language affects media choice, and obviously the marketing information contained therein impacts on the quantity and quality of the information received. For example, Quebec lags behind all other provinces and the United States in newspaper production per capita. The daily newspaper is not standard reading material for French Canadians as it is for the rest of Canadians. Television viewing is also heaviest among French Canadians, the heaviest in the world according to a source. Radio listening is also heaviest in Canada, with listening and television viewing habits showing marked contrast between Montreal and Quebec City, as an example, or between French Canadians working versus nonworking viewers and listeners, or between business executives living in Quebec City and Montreal. There is no doubt that media buying in Quebec is a complex decision process.

Source: Robert D. Tamilia, "The Duality of Canadian Culture: Toward an Understanding of the Quebec and French Canadian Markets," Working Paper No. 01-88 (Montreal: University of Quebec, Department of Administrative Sciences, 1988), 59–60.

The fundamental forces that form values include the cultural transfusive triad and early lifetime experiences. The former refers to the influence of the institutions of the family, religion, and schools. The latter refers to basic intergenerational influences, such as depressions, wars, and other major events. Contemporary consumers are oriented to self-fulfillment and satisfaction.

The norms and values of specific groups are called microcultures, in contrast to the macroculture of the nation. Ethnic groups may be formed around nationality, religion, physical attributes, or geographic location. Ethnicity is a process that may be defined objectively, based on sociocultural characteristics, or subjectively, based on identification that a person makes for self or others. Major microcultures in North America include Native Americans, Asian-Americans, African-Americans, Hispanics, and French Canadians.

Review and Discussion Questions

1. What is meant by the term *culture*? Why does this term create confusion about its meaning?
2. What is meant by the term *ideology of consumption*? Why should this concept be of concern to marketers?
3. Where do consumers get their values?
4. Examine the American core values described in this chapter. Consider how they might influence a marketer of consumer electronics products.
5. Select the topic of family, religious institutions, or schools, and prepare a report documenting the changes that are occurring in the institution you chose.
6. Describe ways in which advertising directed to consumers brought up during the Depression era might differ compared to that directed at consumers of the post–World War II era. What do you consider to be the most important changes that will occur in the future?
7. Asian-Americans are a small proportion of the total population of the United States. Why should they be given much importance in marketing strategies? What adaptations in a marketing plan should be made to reach Asian-Americans?
8. Assume that a soft drink marketer wanted to increase penetration into the Hispanic market. Prepare a set of recommendations for doing so.
9. Assume that a major retailer of shoes was considering a market program to make a special appeal to African-American consumers. Would you suggest such an approach? If so, what would be your recommendations?
10. Assume that a French manufacturer of women's apparel is seeking to expand markets by exporting to Canada. What marketing program should be recommended for maximum effectiveness?
11. What is the current status of markets in North America? Can the market be treated as one entity? If so, when? How?

Endnotes

1. Phillip R. Harris and Robert T. Moran, *Managing Cultural Differences* (Houston: Gulf Publishing Company, 1987), 190–195.
2. George P. Moschis, *Consumer Socialization* (Lexington, Mass.: Lexington Books, 1987), 9.
3. "Miele," in Roger D. Blackwell, Wayne W. Talarzyk and James F. Engel, *Contemporary Cases in Consumer Behavior* (Hinsdale, Ill.: Dryden Press, 1990), 473–480.
4. Ruby R. Dholakia and Sidney J. Levy, "Effect of Recent Economic Experiences on Consumer Dreams, Goals and Behavior in the U.S.," *Journal of Economic Psychology* 8 (1987).

5. Ronald Paul Hill and Mark Stamey, "The Homeless in America: An Examination of Possessions and Consumption Behaviors," *Journal of Consumer Research* 17 (December 1990), 303–321.

6. Bettina Cornwell, Alan David Bligh, and Emin Babakus, "Complaint Behavior of Mexican-American Consumers to a Third-Party Agency," *The Journal of Consumer Affairs* 25 (Summer 1991), 1–18.

7. Russell Belk, "Worldly Possessions: Issues and Criticisms," in Richard P. Bagozzi and Alice M. Tybout, eds., *Advances in Consumer Research* 10 (Ann Arbor, Association for Consumer Research, 1983), 514–519; and Russell Belk and Richard W. Pollay, "Images of Ourselves: The Good Life in Twentieth Century Advertising," *Journal of Consumer Research* 12 (June 1985), 887–897.

8. David Glen Mick, "Consumer Research and Semiotics: Exploring the Morphology of Signs, Symbols, and Significance," *Journal of Consumer Research* 13 (September 1986), 196–213. See also Morris B. Holbrook and Mark W. Grayson, "The Seminology of Cinematic Consumption: Symbolic Consumer Behavior in *Out of Africa*," *Journal of Consumer Research* 14 (December 1987), 374–381.

9. Elizabeth C. Hirschman, "The Ideology of Consumption: A Structural-Syntactical Analysis of 'Dallas' and 'Dynasty'," *Journal of Consumer Research* 15 (December 1988), 344–359.

10. Grant McCracken, "Culture and Consumption: A Theoretical Account of the Structure and Movement of the Cultural Meaning of Consumer Goods," *Journal of Consumer Research* 13 (June 1986), 71–81.

11. Stuart Plattner, "Equilibrating Market Relationships" (paper presented to Society for Economic Anthropology Conference, University of California-Davis, April 6–7, 1984).

12. Conrad M. Arensberg and Arthur H. Niehoff, "American Cultural Values," in James P. Spradley and Mihale A. Rykiewich, eds., *The Nacirema: Readings on American Culture* (Boston: Little, Brown and Company, 1980), 363–379. Table 3.1 builds on Arensberg and Niehoff.

13. Carl Sewell, *Customers for Life* (New York: Doubleday, 1990).

14. "Benetton Ads: A Risqué Business," *Time* (March 25, 1991), 13.

15. Seymour M. Lipset, *North American Cultures: Values and Institutions in Canada and the United States* (Orono, Maine: Borderlands, 1990), 6.

16. Joseph T. Plummer, "Changing Values," *The Futurist* 23 (January-February 1989), 8–13.

17. Karhyn A. Lond and Barbara F. Wilson, "Divorce," *American Demographics* 10 (October 1988), 23–26.

18. Francis A. Schaeffer, *How Should We Then Live?* (Old Tappan, N.J.: Fleming H. Revel Company, 1976).

19. "A Measure of Success," *American Demographics* 13 (April 1991), 9.

20. George Gallup and David Poling, *The Search for America's Faith* (Nashville: Abingdon, 1980), 51.

21. F. G. Buck Rogers, *The IBM Way* (New York: Harper & Row, 1986).

22. James Engel, *Contemporary Christian Communications* (Nashville: Thomas Nelson, 1979).

23. James F. Engel and H. Wilbert Norton, *What's Gone Wrong with the Harvest?* (Grand Rapids: Zondervan Publishing House, 1975); Donald McGavran, *Understanding Church Growth* (Grand Rapids: William B. Eerdmans, 1970).

24. Robert H. Schuller, *Your Church Has Real Possibilities!* (Glendale, Calif.: Regal Books, 1974). Also see "Possibility Thinking and Shrewd Marketing Pay Off for a Preacher," *The Wall Street Journal* (August 26, 1979), 1ff.

25. Allan Bloom, *The Closing of the American Mind* (New York: Simon and Schuster, 1987).
26. Claes Fornell and Birger Wernerfelt, "Defensive Marketing Strategy by Customers' Complaint Management: A Theoretical Analysis," *Journal of Marketing Research* 24 (November 1987), 337–346.
27. Norval D. Glenn, *Cohort Analysis* (Beverly Hills: Sage Publications, 1977).
28. Doris Walsh, "A Healthy Trend," *American Demographics* 6 (July 1984), 4–6.
29. Rohit Despande, Wayne D. Hoyer, and Naveen Donthu, "The Intensity of Ethnic Affiliation: A Study of the Sociology of Hispanic Consumption," *Journal of Consumer Research* 13 (September 1986), 214–219.
30. Elizabeth C. Hirschman, "An Examination of Ethnicity and Consumption Using Free Response Data," in AMA *Educators' Conference Proceedings* (Chicago: American Marketing Association, 1982), 84–88.
31. Dan Fost, "American Indians in the 1990s," *American Demographics* 13 (December 1991), 26–34.
32. Edith McArthur, "What Language Do You Speak?" *American Demographics* 6 (October 1984), 32–33.
33. Nathan Caplan, John K. Whitmore, and Marcella H. Choy, *The Boat People and Achievement in America: A Study of Family Life, Hard Work, and Cultural Values* (Ann Arbor: University of Michigan Press, 1989).
34. Brad Edmondson, "Bringing in the Sheaves," *American Demographics* 10 (August 1988), 28–32.
35. Findings in this paragraph are summarized from Elizabeth C. Hirschman, "American Jewish Ethnicity: Its Relationship to Some Selected Aspects of Consumer Behavior," *Journal of Marketing* 45 (Summer 1981), 102–109; and Elizabeth C. Hirschman, "Ethnic Variation in Leisure Activities and Motives," in AMA *Educators' Conference Proceedings* (Chicago: American Marketing Association, 1982), 93–98.
36. Joel Garreau, *The Nine Nations of North America* (Boston: Houghton Mifflin Company, 1981).
37. Lynn R. Kahle, "The Nine Nations of North America and the Value Basis of Geographic Segmentation," *Journal of Marketing* 50 (April 1986), 37–47.
38. Wendy Manning and William O'Hare, "Asian-American Businesses," *American Demographics* 10 (August 1988), 35–39.
39. Dan Fost, "California's Asian Market," *American Demographics* 12 (October 1990), 34–37.
40. Cyndee Miller, "Hot Asian-American Market Not Starting Much of a Fire Yet," *Marketing News* 25 (January 21, 1991), 12.
41. Ivan Light and Edna Bonacich, *Immigrant Entrepreneurs: Koreans in Los Angeles, 1965–1982* (Los Angeles: University of California Press, 1988).
42. Reynolds Farley and Suzanne M. Bianchi, "The Growing Gap Between Blacks," *American Demographics* 5 (July 1983), 15–18.
43. Mark Green, *Invisible People: The Depiction of Minorities in Magazine Ads and Catalogs* (New York: City of New York Department of Consumer Affairs, 1991).
44. U.S. Department of Commerce, *Current Population Reports*, Series P-20 (Washington, D.C.: U.S. Government Printing Office, 1988).
45. William O'Hare, "Blacks and Whites: One Market or Two?" *American Demographics* 9 (March 1987), 44–48.
46. Nancy Ten Kate, "Black Children More Likely to Live with One Parent," *American Demographics* 13 (February 1991), 11.
47. A collection of articles on this topic is found in Harriette Pipies McAdoo, ed., *Black Families* (Newbury Park, Calif.: Sage Publications, 1988).

48. Marilyn K. Foxworth, "Celebrating Black History," *Public Relations Journal* 47 (February 1991), 16–21.

49. Parke Gibson, *$70 Billion in the Black* (New York: Macmillan, 1978); B. G. Yovovich, "The Debate Rages On: Marketing to Blacks," *Advertising Age* (November 29, 1982), M-10; David Astor, "Black Spending Power: $140 Billion and Growing," *Marketing Communications* (July 1982), 13–18; P. A. Robinson, C. P. Rao, and S. C. Mehta, "Historical Perspectives of Black Consumer Research in the United States: A Critical Review," in C. T. Tan and J. Sheth, eds., *Historical Perspectives in Consumer Research* (Singapore: National University of Singapore, 1985), 46–50.

50. Raymond A. Bauer and Scott M. Cunningham, *Studies in the Negro Market* (Cambridge, Mass.: Marketing Science Institute, 1970). Also Donald Sexton, "Black Buyer Behavior," *Journal of Marketing* 36 (October 1972), 36–39.

51. Thomas E. Ness and Melvin T. Stith, "Middle-Class Values in Blacks and Whites," in Robert E. Pitts, Jr., and Arch G. Woodside, *Personal Values and Consumer Psychology* (Lexington, Mass.: Lexington Books, 1984), 255–270.

52. Alphonziz Wellington, "Traditional Brand Loyalty," *Advertising Age* (May 18, 1981), S-2.

53. Daniel Yankelovich, *Spanish USA* (New York: Yankelovich, Skelly & White, Inc., 1981). Also see reports on a repetition in 1984 of the same study in "Homogenized Hispanics," *American Demographics* 7 (February 1985), 16.

54. Yankelovich, *Spanish USA*.

55. Jim Sondheim, Rodd Rodriquez, Richard Dillon, and Richard Parades, "Hispanic Market: The Invisible Giant," *Advertising Age* (April 16, 1979), S-20. Also see Martha Frase-Blunt, "Who Watches Spanish Language TV?" *Hispanic* (November 1991), 26–27.

56. Examples are from Luiz Diaz-Altertini, "Brand-Loyal Hispanics Need Good Reason for Switching," *Advertising Age* (April 16, 1979), SX-23.

57. Lisa Penaloza Alaniz and Marcy C. Gilly, "The Hispanic Family—Consumer Research Issues," *Psychology and Marketing* (Winter 1986), 291–303.

58. Humberto Valencia, "Point of View: Avoid Hispanic Market Blunders," *Journal of Advertising Research* 23 (January 1984), 19–22.

59. Robert E. Wilkes and Humberto Valencia, "Shopping-Related Characteristics of Mexican-Americans and Blacks," *Psychology and Marketing* 3 (Winter 1986), 247–259.

60. Joel Saegert, Robert J. Hoover, and Marye Tharp Hilger, "Characteristics of Mexican American Consumers," *Journal of Consumer Research* 12 (June 1985), 104–109.

61. Deshpande, 1986.

62. Clarkson Gordon, *Tomorrow's Customers in Canada* (Toronto: Woods Gordon, 1984).

63. Pierre C. Lefrancois and Giles Chatel, "The French-Canadian Consumer: Fact and Fancy," in J. S. Wright and J. L. Goldstrucker, eds., *New Ideas for Successful Marketing* (Chicago: American Marketing Association, 1966), 705–717; Bernard Blishen, "Social Class and Opportunity in Canada," *Canadian Review of Sociology and Anthropology* 7 (May 1970), 110–127.

64. Robert Tamilia, "Cross-Cultural Advertising Research: A Review and Suggested Framework," in Ronald C. Curhan, ed., *1974 Combined Proceedings of the AMA* (Chicago: American Marketing Association, 1974), 131–134.

4

Social Class and Status

Consider the following biographies:

When Henry Ross Perot was a boy growing up in Texarkana, his mother tacked a Norman Rockwell print above his desk—"Boy Scout at Prayer." Perot became much more than the reverent boy above his desk; he became an Eagle Scout, a midshipman, a computer services entrepreneur worth $2.5 billion, a builder of modern Dallas, and nearly a candidate for U.S. president.

John Kluge is tied for second place, with H. Ross Perot, on the *Forbes* list of the 400 richest Americans. He is a self-made man. His entrepreneurial instincts seemed to have surfaced first at Columbia University where in addition to studying economics and working three shifts in the dining hall, he began to run small enterprises out of his dormitory room. Kluge decided to express his taste in consumption through his residence. He and his wife Patricia have spent five years creating Albemarle House, an immense English-style estate, out of more than 6,000 acres of rolling farmland in Virginia. In addition to their forty-five room Georgian country house, the Kluges have built a Gothic-style chapel, a glass conservatory, a stables and antique carriage house, a golf-course designed by Arnold Palmer, a tournament croquet lawn, several staff cottages and barns, a log cabin and a helicopter landing pad.

Descended from one of the immortal entrepreneurs, Jennifer Rockefeller led the Columbia University Marching Band in front of the Rockefeller Center. Jennifer is devoted to The Fund for Animals, especially its project to save America's wild horses. Her suit is Oscar de la Renta. Her stockings are Fogal. She wears Petrochi and Gorevic jewels with perfume by Oscar de la Renta. She is photographed in front of Rockefeller Center, one of her ancestor's notable secular monuments.

Source: Excerpts from Elizabeth C. Hirschman, "Secular Immortality and the American Ideology of Affluence," *Journal of Consumer Research* 17 (June 1990), 31–42.

Social Class and Consumer Behavior

Social class affects consumer behavior—how people spend their time, the products they buy, and where and how they shop. Magazines such as *Town & Country, Architectural Digest, Connoisseur,* and *Avenue* are read by certain consumers because the contents reflect the interests of the affluent social classes to which the readers belong, or to which they aspire. The magazines advertise upscale products for affluent consumers, and contain articles that reflect the themes and motivations of special significance to affluent social classes—articles about arts and craftsmanship, interior decoration, dominance of nature, the triumph of technology, fashions, and the ideology of affluence.[1]

Consumers associate brands of products and services with specific social classes. For instance, Heineken and Amstel Light are considered to be upper-middle-class drinks, while Old Style is perceived as a beer for "everyman," and is consumed mainly by middle- and lower-class drinkers. In the United States early in this century, beer was perceived as a lower-class beverage, but today it is popular with all classes—perhaps as a result of heavy marketing efforts.

Stores such as Bloomingdales and Marshall Field once had reputations as stores primarily for the upper or upper-middle classes, while K mart was mainly where the lower classes shopped. Target achieved much of its success as a discount department store positioned as more upscale than K mart. Among restaurants, Wendy's is considered more upscale than Burger King or Denny's.[2]

You may find this chapter unsettling because American traditions emphasize equality. In the United States and Canada, in one generation a family can rise from the lowest social/economic level to almost the highest; yet few could deny that there are enormous variations between the homeless of America and the individuals described in the opening scenario of this chapter.

In England, citizens can rarely change class rapidly and can never be royalty unless born into it. In India, the family can never change class but individuals may do so through reincarnation. In countries such as Russia and others such as China and Hungary, consumers formerly subscribed to the common man ideology of communism and socialism. Today, there are new stirrings and the emergence of a consumer culture that is demonstrated in homes, electronic equipment, cars, number of bodyguards, and clothes that no longer reflect the stereotyped view of a person as a cog in the societal mechanism.[3]

Even if it is uncomfortable for you to think about social status and inequality, it is necessary because consumer behavior is directly affected by such divisions in society. In this chapter, we will first analyze the basic concept of status and consider how to study it, then examine the effects of status on consumer behavior.

Social Stratification

Social classes and status systems exist in every country of the world. In Europe, the concept is so important to understanding consumer behavior that the European Society for Opinion and Marketing Research (ESOMAR) set up a working group to devise questions so that research about social class would be comparable from one country to another. Japan is a country with rigid expectations about social class, even though a large proportion of consumers are middle class. In Latin America, many countries have huge numbers of poorer classes struggling for existence, while the small but wealthy classes purchase a wide array of products that serve as visible symbols of class membership. Even in formerly Marxist societies, which were officially classless, the best of available consumer products went to privileged classes, based upon party affiliation, athletic ability, or educational attainment. Americans sometimes *believe* social class is unimportant but *act* as if class were quite important. Research indicates that Americans perceive effects of social class even more than in England, a country known for class importance.[4]

Even animals other than humans divide themselves into stratified societies. One famous study described a barnyard society in which each hen maintained a definite position in the pecking order of the group.[5] This is where the term *pecking order* apparently originated. Ries and Trout, in their influential book on positioning, extend this principle: "Consumers are like chickens. They are much more comfortable with a pecking order that everybody knows and accepts."[6]

Brand names and stores also have a pecking order by which they seek to lure customers, whose values and beliefs will lead them to say, "This brand (or store) is for me."

Beer advertisements illustrate how social-class positioning is achieved. In spite of recent inroads into the upper-middle classes, beer is still purchased mostly by middle and lower social classes, in contrast to wine. Miller once positioned its brand as "the champagne of bottled beer," but later Miller changed to the slogan, "When you've got the time, we've got the beer," to target the busy, active leisure activities of the upper-middle class. More recently, Miller switched to "the workingman's beer" to try to emulate Budweiser's success with less affluent drinkers. Budweiser ads feature people who don't have much fun in their jobs, but who relax with "The King of Beers" to forget their jobs. Budweiser's symbol of Clydesdale horses also ties in to the strong, physical demands on lower- and middle-class workers.

Few constructs are better documented in sociological literature than social inequality and the differential prestige or **deference** (granting of social honor) paid by some in society to members of higher classes. Most sociologists accept class inequality as a proven fact based on the empirical evidence.

Americans may hope that every person has equal opportunity to gain access to products and services. Yet, the empirical evidence indicates otherwise. Social class determines **life chances**, a term used by Max Weber to emphasize the fundamental aspects of an individual's future possibilities. Life chances range from the infant's chances for decent nutrition to the adult's opportunities to purchase the goods and services that marketers constantly urge her or him to buy.

Understanding the development of social class is important in understanding consumption, for lifestyles of the upper-middle class tend to filter down and become generally accepted by the rest of society. While most of us cannot afford Jennifer Rockefeller's clothes or jewels described in the opening scenario of this chapter, we can, for $10 an hour, have our picture taken skating on the ice at Rockefeller Center.

What Is Social Class?

Social class may be defined as relatively permanent and homogeneous divisions in a society into which individuals or families sharing similar values, lifestyles, interests, and behavior can be categorized. It refers to a grouping of people who are similar in their behavior based upon their economic position in the marketplace. Class membership exists and can be described as a statistical category whether or not individuals are aware of their common situation. **Status groups** reflect a community's expectations for style of life among each class as well as the positive or negative social estimation of honor given to each class. Max Weber, who along with Karl Marx might be regarded as the father of social class theory, clarified the distinction:

> With some over-simplification, one might thus say that "classes" are stratified according to their relations in the production and acquisition of goods, whereas "status groups" are stratified according to the principles of their consumption of goods as represented by special "styles of life."[7]

For marketers, status systems are of primary interest because they exert a major influence on what people buy and consume. However, what consumers are able to buy is determined by social class—namely the income or wealth of the consumer—and thus, our empirical emphasis in marketing research is on social class variables. For practical purposes, it is usually adequate in the study of consumer behavior to treat the terms *status* and *class* interchangeably, as we do in this chapter, although recognizing that status may be used in other contexts to describe differential respect given to an individual within a group.

Inequality Systems

All countries, except the smallest and most primitive, are stratified or have formal systems of inequality. Social class systems rank *families* rather than individuals. A family shares many characteristics among its members that affect relationships with outsiders, such as the same house, the same income, the same values, and thus much of the same buying behavior. *When a large group of families are approximately equal in rank to each other and clearly differentiated from other families, they form a social class.*

The *caste* system is more rigid. Only relatively controlled interaction is permitted between castes, and mobility between groups is limited. Caste is based upon hereditary status and, especially as it was practiced in India, upon religion.

The *estate system* was founded upon power and alliances—mainly the power of the lords and their warriors to offer protection from violence. Force was the basis of power, status, and a share of the land's produce. An extension of this system of inequality in contemporary societies is the power and deference given to people in the media, in professional athletics, and in organizations such as labor unions, political parties, and government agencies. Giant corporations, such as IBM, General Electric, and Mitsubishi, convey such status regardless of the other characteristics of the people who are employed by "status corporations."

Social Class Variables

Stratification occurs in order to develop and preserve collective social identity in a world characterized by pervasive economic inequality.[8] Social identity is achieved by establishing boundaries on interactions between people of unequal status.

Stratification involves many variables. An attempt to conceptualize these is shown in Figure 4.1, a model that can be examined vertically or horizontally. By looking down on the top of the model, you can identify the social institutions that

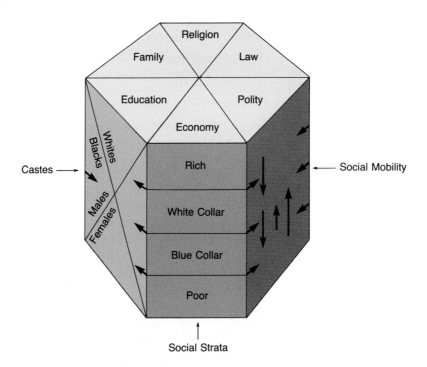

FIGURE 4.1   A Conceptual Model of Social Institutions and Social Strata in American Society

Source: Leonard Beeghley, *Social Stratification in America* (Santa Monica, Calif.: Goodyear Publishing Company, Inc., 1978), 102. Reprinted by permission.

generate goal-oriented activities of the society. The model's vertical dimension can be seen by looking at its side, where various levels of inequality, called strata or classes, are located. Individual consumers can be studied by examining their economic, political, legal, religious, familial, and educational characteristics. Social mobility can be studied by examining rates of intra- and intergenerational mobility in the population or market segments. The patterns of convergence among the variables create social classes. The patterns are tendencies or ideal types that, though not fully realized in any one situation, are discernible when one analyzes the underlying forces.

What Determines Social Class?

What causes your social status? The variables that determine social class have been identified in social stratification studies that began in the 1920s and 1930s. Early studies were descriptions of social classes in small towns of New England and the South. Today, social class research includes thousands of studies dealing with the measurement of social class in large cities; movement between social classes; interactions of social class with gender, race, ethnicity, and education; and the effects of social class on poverty and economic policy.

From extensive research on social class, nine variables have emerged as most important in determining social class. These nine variables were identified by Gilbert and Kahl in three categories.

Economic Variables	Interaction Variables	Political Variables
Occupation	Personal prestige	Power
Income	Association	Class consciousness
Wealth	Socialization	Mobility[9]

Some of these are more important than others in the study of consumer behavior and are described below.

Your social class is influenced mostly by the family in which you were raised. Your father's occupation probably had a significant effect upon your social class because a man's occupation historically has been the most important determinant, followed closely by the wife's occupation.[10] The primary role of the father may be less true in the future, especially among families in which wives have better paying or more prestigious careers than their husbands.

For consumer analysts, six variables of the above nine are especially useful in understanding a consumer's social class. These are based upon the original research of sociologist Joseph Kahl and include occupation, personal performance, interactions, possessions, value orientations, and class consciousness.[11]

It is very important to keep in mind that *social class is not determined by income*, even though there may be a correlation due to the relationship between income and other variables that determine social class. A senior garbage collector, for example, might earn more than an assistant professor of history. The professor typically would be ascribed higher social class, however. You can probably think of more examples of how income and social class differ.

Occupation

Occupation is the best single indicator of social class in most consumer research. You probably have had the experience of meeting someone, quickly followed by the question, "What do you do?" The answer provides a good clue to the social class of the individual. The work consumers perform greatly affects their lifestyles and is the single most important basis for according prestige, honor, and respect. Consumption varies considerably between occupations. Occupations such as service and blue collar workers spend a greater proportion of their income on food whereas managers and professionals spend a higher share of their income on eating out, clothing, and financial services.[12]

In most cultures of the world, physicians historically have been accorded respect and usually high financial reward. In more recent years some of the information occupations have gained status, such as television anchors, computer programmers, logistic managers, and so forth. Capitalist or entrepreneur is one of the occupations that offers the potential of "secular immortality" or more lasting effect upon the family's social class because of the possibility of building a store of capital that will continue the income for future generations.

Personal Performance

A person's status can also be influenced by her or his success relative to that of others in the same occupation—by an individual's personal performance. Statements such as "She is the finest trial lawyer in town," or "Frank is the only programmer that I trust to do it right," or "That professor is doing the most significant research in the field" are examples of evaluations of personal performance.

Even though income is not a good indicator of overall social class, it may serve as a gauge of personal performance within an occupation. The top 25 percent of income producers in any occupation are also likely to be the most highly respected as personally competent in their field.

Personal performance also involves activities other than job-related pursuits. Perhaps your father has a low-status occupation. Your family may still achieve more status if your father is perceived as one who helps others in need, is unusually kind and interested in fellow workers, or is a faithful worker in civic or religious organizations. The president of a corporation who serves as chairperson of the United Way or a trustee of a university may achieve higher social status than the president of a similar corporation not involved in such activities. A reputation as a good mother or a good father may contribute to one's status.

Interactions

People feel most comfortable when they are with people of similar values and behavior. Sociologists who emphasize analyses of social interactions are sometimes called the "who-invited-whom-to-dinner" school. In such an approach, group membership and interactions are considered a primary determinant of a person's social class.

The interaction variables of personal prestige, association, and socialization are the essence of social class. People have high **prestige** when other people have an attitude of respect or deference to them. **Association** is a variable concerned with everyday relationships, with people who like to do the same things they do, in the same ways, and with whom they feel comfortable. **Socialization** is the process by which an individual learns the skills, attitudes, and customs to participate in the life of the community. Social class behavior and values are clearly differentiated in children by the time they have reached adolescence, in variables that vary by social class such as self-esteem.[13] Interactions are the best validity check in social class research but are not used extensively in consumer research because they are difficult and expensive to measure.

Social interactions ordinarily are limited to one's immediate social class, even though opportunities exist for broader contact. Most marriages occur within the same or adjacent social classes. In public schools, open contact may be encouraged by the institution, but children usually reveal definite patterns of restricted association. Sometimes these groups have their own names—the "straights," the "grubbies," the "cheerleaders," and so forth. One of the most obvious examples of restricted social interaction is the *Social Register*, which contains rigid criteria for gaining and maintaining admission. Recently, it was changed from a series of local editions to a national edition listing socially prominent people throughout the United States.

Possessions

Possessions are symbols of class membership—not only the number of possessions, but the nature of the choices made. Thus, a middle-class family may choose wall-to-wall carpeting, whereas an upper-class family is more likely to choose Oriental rugs, even if the prices are equal. Thornston Veblen referred to such symbols as "conspicuous consumption." Consumption of products such as cars, homes, causes, clothing and so forth is affected because the ideology of affluence promotes seeking personal "secular immortality" through the cultural celebration of achievement, wealth, and the accumulation of possessions.[14]

Possessions and wealth are closely related. Wealth is usually a result of an accumulation of past income. In certain forms, such as ownership of a business or of stocks and bonds, wealth is the source of future income which may enable a family to maintain its (high) social class from generation to generation. Thus, possessions that indicate the family's wealth are important in reflecting social class.

The most important possession decision reflecting a family's social class is the choice of where to live. This includes both the type of home and the neighborhood. Notice the description of John and Patricia Kluge's house in the opening scenario of this chapter. Another important "possession" is the university one attends. Upper-class individuals select the "best" schools, which in turn reinforces class consciousness and cohesion.[15] Other possessions that serve as indicators of social status include club memberships (which also reflect interactions), preferred furniture styles, clothing, appliances, and types of vacations chosen.

The Brands to Buy to Reflect Increasing Social Status

THE WATCH: Rolex, for its Swiss accuracy, respectable name and gold-link band. THE RAINCOAT: Burberry. Check out the coatroom where the rich and powerful lunch and you'll find a sea of Burberry trench coats. THE SUIT: Armani. While the traditional status-conscious male may continue to have suits tailor-made, the new breed will plunk down as much as $1,500 for one of Giorgio Armani's couture suits. THE ATTACHE CASE: Mark Cross, because what's on the outside can be as important as what's on the inside. THE PEN: Montblanc. This top-dollar writing utensil starts at $12 for the ballpoint and reaches the $6,500 mark for a solid-gold fountain pen. THE CAR: Porsche, for those who are serious about power, performance and being out in front on the road. THE SUNGLASSES: Porsche, an extension of the car. THE SNEAKERS: Reeboks. Averaging about $55 a pair, these leather aerobic shoes are gracing the most graceful to work out in the trendiest health spas. THE RIGHT CREDIT: American Express platinum card. For $250 a year, the user gets a choice of billing dates, 24-hour customized travel service, and more. THE GOOD SOUND: Front row orchestra seats at a Wynton Marsalis or Sade concert. THE SWEET SMELL OF SUCCESS: For women, Giorgio, at $150 an ounce; for men, Lagerfeldt, at $30 for the four-ounce spray cologne. MAN'S BEST FRIEND: The Akita. They resemble German shepherds, but they're really Japanese guard dogs who will be your constant companion if you're willing to pay $750 to $2,000 for one.

Source: Monique Greenwood, "Status Symbols," *Black Enterprise* 16 (May 1986), 65.

People who lack the possessions or knowledge of them but who aspire to a higher social class may study diligently to learn more about the possessions of that class. Business students and others interested in making it "to the top," for example, may be prime prospects for books and courses that teach how to "dress for success" or the secrets "they didn't teach you in business school."

Products and brands often seek to be positioned as symbols of status—as the products used by upper-middle or upper classes. For people who are striving to become associated with those classes, the purchase of such brands may be partially based upon the desire for such affiliation or identification. Consumer in Focus 4.1 describes such status symbols, based upon a list prepared for consumers who may have been raised in social classes lower than their improved status.

Value Orientations

Values—shared beliefs about how people should behave—indicate the social class to which one belongs. When a group of people share a common set of abstract

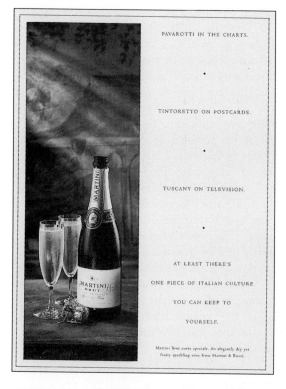

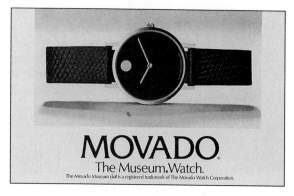

**FIGURE 4.2   Successful Advertisements Appeal to the Values of Particular Social Classes—
The Symbols in these Advertisements Appeal to Upper-Class Values**

Source: Courtesy of Movado; Martini & Rossi.

convictions that organize and relate a large number of specific attributes, it is possible to categorize an individual in the group by the degree to which he or she possesses these values. Some observers believe that in countries other than the United States, values are more important than possessions. Class is indicated more by merit derived from expressions in art, science, and religion and even in such mundane things as dressing and eating properly rather than defined in pecuniary terms. In contrast to Europe, people in the U.S. are believed to make a religion of money or using money as a "votive offering and pagan ornament."[16]

Consumer analysts need to answer the question, "What values characterize specific market segments?" These beliefs may refer to general values about political ideals, religious practices, work motivation, the capitalistic economic system, and so forth. Also included are more specific activities such as child rearing, family structure, sexual behavior, abortion, and impulsiveness in decision making.

Figure 4.2 shows ads that might appeal to upper social classes. Notice how Movado appeals to the interests of the upper classes in art and museums. Similarly, Martini & Rossi speaks of Pavarotti, Tintoretto, and Tuscany. Both ads use a minimum of words and a maximum of image.

Class Consciousness

One of the important political variables of social class is class consciousness. Class consciousness refers to the degree to which people in a social class are aware of themselves as a distinctive group with shared political and economic interests. As people become more group conscious, they are likely to organize political parties, trade unions, and other associations to advance their group interests.[17]

Americans often state they are not class conscious. To some extent, a person's social class is indicated by how conscious that person is of social class. Lower social class individuals may recognize the reality of social class but may not be as sensitive to specific differences. Thus, advertising for goods selling to upper class market targets are often rich with social class symbols but ads to middle and lower social class targets may not be well received if they use a direct class appeal.

Other political variables that are sometimes useful in understanding social class include power and mobility. **Power** is the potential of individuals or groups to carry out their will over others. **Mobility and succession** is a dual concept related to the stability or instability of stratification systems. Succession refers to the process of children inheriting the class position of their parents. Mobility refers to the process of moving up or down a class structure, relative to their parents. When mobility occurs in an upward direction, consumers may need to learn a new set of consumption behaviors—products and brands that are consistent with their new status, the kind of advice described in Consumer in Focus 4.1.

How to Measure Social Class

Consumer researchers have developed and borrowed a variety of methods to measure and describe social class. These methods have been developed to relate dependent variables, such as product usage, brand preference, attitudes, store image, and patronage, to the independent variable of social class. With such research it may be possible to define market segments on the basis of social class and to understand consumption and buying patterns of those segments.

Social class research methods are used for two purposes: *theoretical or validity research* and *practical marketing research*. A specific method might be used for either purpose, but the theoretical methods are often so costly and time consuming that market researchers do not use them on a day-to-day basis. They are designed to develop the theory and concepts of social class and to serve as a validity check on more practical methods.

Research methods may also be classified as *objective* when they involve quantitative variables of socioeconomic status (SES) measures such as occupation, education, and income. Methods may also be *subjective* when they involve reports by individuals of their perceptions of other people. Research methods may be described as *interpretive* in which researchers "read" society as a "text" by using novels, autobiographies, ads, and other materials much like literary criticism.[18]

Marketing researchers like objective methods because of the availability of data from census or representative surveys as well as the greater ease of using computerized, quantitative analytical techniques. Although objective methods may be preferred, the choice is sometimes at the expense of the richer insights and understanding provided by subjective or interpretive methods.

Theoretical and Validity Methods

Reputational methods involve asking people to rank the social position or prestige of other people. The reputational method was developed by Lloyd Warner, one of the pioneers in the study of social class in the United States.[19] This work was extended by Burleigh Gardner and his associates in the Deep South[20] and in the Midwest by Hollingshead.[21]

These studies also include **association or sociometric measures**, which count the number and nature of personal contacts of people in their informal relationships. These studies are also called **evaluative participation studies** because the researchers use not only the data they collect from respondents but the researchers' own observations gained from living in the community and participating in the informal networks and formal organizations of the community.

Warner and his colleagues developed the *Index of Status Characteristics* based upon the need for more objective and less laborious research techniques. After years of work with reputational, associational, and evaluative participation methods, which established the validity of social class, researchers concluded that, once the evaluated rankings were established, they could accurately predict such rankings on the basis of a family's *occupation, source of income, house type*, and *residential area*. By establishing the validity of these objective measures in social class research, marketing researchers can use updated and readily quantifiable methods.

The theoretical research provided a stream of empirical data and concepts that are central to our present efforts to relate social class to consumption. It was Warner, Gardner and their colleagues who described the six basic social classes found in the United States, which are detailed in Table 4.1.

Marketing Research Methods for Measuring Social Class

Marketing researchers measure social class as an independent variable in order to determine its association with dependent variables of interest in marketing. Objective methods assign status on the basis of respondents' possessing some value of a stratified variable. The most often used variables are occupation, income, education, size and type of residence, ownership of possessions, and organizational affiliations. Objective methods can be divided into those that are single indexes and those that are multiple indexes.

Subjective or self-reporting methods ask respondents to rate themselves on social class. These methods, although occasionally used, are of limited value to consumer analysts for two reasons: (1) respondents tend to overrate their own class position, and (2) respondents avoid the connotative terms of upper and lower classes and, thus, exaggerate the size of the middle class.

Single-Item Indexes   *Occupation* is the best single proxy indicator of social class. People who have similarly ranked (in prestige) occupations often share similar

TABLE 4.1 **Traditional Social Class Behavior in America**

Upper Upper. Upper uppers are the social elite of society. Inherited wealth from socially prominent families is the key to admission. Children attend private preparatory schools and graduate from the best colleges.

Consumers in the upper-upper class spend money as if it were unimportant, not tightly but not with display either, for that would imply that money is important. For some products a trickle-down influence may exist between social classes. The social position of these individuals is so secure that they can deviate from class norms if they choose to without losing status.

Lower Upper. Lower uppers include the very high-income professional people who have earned their position rather than inherited it. They are the *nouveaux riches*, active people with many material symbols of their status. They buy the largest homes in the best suburbs and the most expensive automobiles, swimming pools, and other symbols of conspicuous consumption, making them innovators and good markets for luxury marketing offerings.

Upper Middle. The key word for upper middles is career. Careers are based on successful professional or graduate degrees for a specific profession or the skill of business administration. Members of this class are demanding of their children in educational attainment.

The quality market for many products is the upper-middle class and gracious living in a conspicuous but careful manner characterizes the family's lifestyle. The home is of high importance and an important symbol of the family's success and competence.

Lower Middle. Lower-middle class families are typical Americans, exemplifying the core of respectability, conscientious work habits, and adherence to culturally defined norms and standards. They believe in attending church and obeying the law and are upset when their children are arrested for law violations. They are not innovators.

The *home* is very important to the lower-middle family and they want it to be neat, well-painted, and in a respected neighborhood. They may have little confidence in their own tastes and adopt standardized home furnishings—perhaps from Levitz or similar

access to the means of achieving a lifestyle. Leisure time, income independence, knowledge, and power are often common to occupational categories. They interact with one another and generally agree with each other concerning the types of activities, interests, and possessions that are important and how family resources should be allocated in order to implement the achievement of these goals.

Occupation is used in consumer research by asking respondents to write in their exact occupation, which can later be coded numerically according to its social class or status value. These values are established in one of two ways. One method is to use surveys of people asked to rank the prestige of people in various occupations or of the occupations themselves. A second method is to use objective measures, such as ranking of the average educational level and/or income of occupational groups.

There is a long history of studies of occupational prestige. They disclose stability of prestige ratings over time. High correlations between nations are also

TABLE 4.1   continued

furniture stores. This is in contrast to the upper-middle consumer who feels freer to experiment with new styles and new arrangements and with the upper-lower consumer who is not very concerned about the overall plan for furnishing the home: The lower-middle consumer reads and follows the advice of the medium-level shelter and service magazines in an attempt to make the house pretty.

The lower-middle class consumer works more at shopping than others and considers purchase decisions demanding and tedious. He or she may have a high degree of price sensitivity.

Upper Lower. Upper-lower social classes exhibit a routine life, characterized by a day-to-day existence of unchanging activities. They live in dull areas of the city, in small houses or apartments. The hard hats are included in this class, with many members working at uncreative jobs requiring manual activity or only moderate skills and education. Because of unions and security, many may earn incomes that give them considerable discretionary income.

The purchase decisions of the working class are often impulsive but at the same time may show high brand loyalty to national brands. Buying them is one way to prove knowledge as a buyer, a role in which he or she feels (probably correctly) that he or she has little skill. This consumer has little social contact outside the home and does not like to attend civic organizations or church activities. Social interaction is limited to close neighbors and relatives. If he or she takes a vacation, it will probably be to visit relatives in another city. Upper lowers are concerned that they not be confused with the lower lowers.

Lower Lower. The lower-lower social class contains people who may try to rise above their class but usually fail to do so. An individual in the lower-lower class often rejects middle class morality and gets pleasure wherever possible—and this includes buying impulsively. This lack of planning causes purchases that cost too much and may result in inferior goods. This person pays too much for products, buys on credit at a high interest rate and has difficulty obtaining quality or value. This group includes highly distressed families, some who have habitual legal problems and the homeless.

found. The key variables causing occupations to have prestige are the amount of education required as a prerequisite for entering the occupation and the reward (typically income) that society bestows on the occupation.

Government data relating to occupations are classified using the Standard Occupational Classification, or SOC.[22] The classification provides a coding system and nomenclature for identifying and classifying occupations in a system that can be used for marketing purposes as well as standard categories used by diverse governmental agencies. Information is included about the company and type of business in which the individual works; the kind of work and job duties as well as occupational title; and the classification of work as public, private, or self-employed.

One of the easiest scales for marketing researchers to use was developed by Nam and Powers and provides a precise, numerical status score for 589 occupations.[23] An example of some of the scores that are assigned to occupations using the Nam and Powers scale is shown in Table 4.2.

TABLE 4.2 Occupational Status Scores of Occupations

Occupation	Status Score
Accountants	89
Architects	97
Engineers	
Aeronautical	96
Industrial	93
Mechanical	93
Librarians	75
Physicians	
Chiropractors	95
Medical and Osteopathic	99
Registered Nurses	66
Clergymen	77
Social Scientists	
Economists	96
Sociologists	94
Social Workers	82
Teachers	
Chemistry	97
Business and Commerce	95
Elementary School, Public	80
Secondary School, Public	86
Sales Managers, Retail Trade	74
Sales Managers, Except Retail	94
Bank Tellers	49
Cashiers	29
Keypunch Operators	49
Typists	46
Mechanics	
Aircraft	72
Automotive	45
Office Machine	69
Bottling and Canning Operatives	22
Dry Wall Installers	51
Coal Mine Operatives	35
Bus Drivers	40
Taxicab Drivers	35
Farm Managers	52
Farm Laborers, Wage Workers	04
Bartenders	42
Busboys	12

Source: Excerpts from Table A1 of Charles B. Nam and Mary G. Powers, *The Socioeconomic Approach to Status Measurement* (Houston: Cap and Gown Press, 1983). See this source for a complete list of occupations.

Multiple-Item Indexes   Multiple-item indexes combine several indicators of social class into one index to provide a richer measure of social status. These indexes start with a single index, such as the Nam and Powers scores shown in Table 4.2, but are combined with additional scores for variables such as education and income of the consumer. The three scores (occupation, education, income) are then summed and divided by 3 to provide a multiple-item SES score. This provides an easy-to-use, numerical score of social class that can then be related to product purchase, brand preference, media processing, or other variables of interest to marketing researchers.

Coleman's CSI   Coleman's Computerized Status Index (CSI) is an index developed by Social Research, Inc., and which is extensively used in commercial consumer research. Figure 4.3 shows the format for administering the CSI. In this particular version, occupation is weighted double when computing the total scale. Other versions include an occupation scaling specifically for employed women, to be used whether they are the spouse or the household head. The status for conventional married couples with a male household head between 35 and 64 years of age is as follows: Upper American, 37 to 53; Middle Class, 24 to 36; Working Class, 13 to 23; and Lower American, 4 to 12. Additional refinements include adjustment for unusual income levels or abnormalities in occupation or neighborhood ratings.[24]

FIGURE 4.3   **Example of a Computerized Status Index (CSI)**

Interviewer circles code numbers (for the computer) which in his/her judgment best fit the respondent and family. Interviewer asks for detail on occupation, then makes rating. Interviewer often asks the respondent to describe neighborhood in own words. Interviewer asks respondent to specify income—a card is presented to the respondent showing the eight brackets—and records R's response. If interviewer feels this is overstatement or under, a "better-judgment" estimate should be given, along with explanation.

Education:	Respondent	Respondent's Spouse
Grammar school (8 yrs or less)	−1 *R's*	−1 *Spouse's*
Some high school (9 to 11 yrs)	−2 *age:*	−2 *age:*
Graduated high school (12 yrs)	−3	−3
Some post high school (business, nursing, technical, one yr college)	−4	−4
Two, three years of college—possibly Associate of Arts degree	−5	−5
Graduated four-year college (B.A./B.S.)	−7	−7
Master's or five-year professional degree	−8	−8
Ph.D. or six/seven-year professional degree	−9	−9
Ph.D. or six/seven-year professional degree	−9	−9

Continued

FIGURE 4.3 **continued**

Occupation Prestige Level of Household Head:

Interviewer's judgment of how head of household rates in occupational status. (Respondent's description—ask for previous occupation if retired, or if R. is widow, ask husband's: _____)

Chronically unemployed—"day" laborers, unskilled: on welfare	−0
Steadily employed but in marginal semiskilled jobs: custodians, minimum-pay factory help, service workers (gas attendants, etc.)	−1
Average-skill assembly-line workers, bus and truck drivers, police and firefighters, route deliverymen, carpenters, brickmasons	−2
Skilled craftsmen (electricians), small contractors, factory foreman, low-pay salesclerks, office workers, postal employees	−3
Owners of very small firms (2-4 employees), technicians, salespeople, office workers, civil servants with average level salaries	−4
Middle management, teachers, social workers, lesser professionals	−5
Lesser corporate officials, owners of middle-sized businesses (10-20 employees), moderate-success professionals (dentists, engineers, etc.)	−7
Top corporate executives, "big successes" in the professional world (leading doctors and lawyers), "rich" business owners.	−9

Area of Residence:

Interviewer's impressions of the immediate neighborhood in terms of its reputation in the eyes of the community.

Slum area: people on relief, common laborers	−1
Strictly working class: not slummy but some very poor housing	−2
Predominantly blue-collar with some office workers	−3
Predominantly white-collar with some well-paid blue-collar	−4
Better white-collar area; not many executives, but hardly any blue-collar either	−5
Excellent area: professionals and well-paid managers	−7
"Wealthy" or "society"-type neighborhood	−9

Total Family Income per Year:

Total Score _____

Under $5,000	−1	$20,000 to $24,999	−5
$5,000 to $9,999	−2	$25,000 to $34,999	−6
$10,000 to $14,999	−3	$35,000 to $49,999	−7
$15,000 to $19,999	−4	$50,000 and over	−8

Estimated Status _____

(Interviewer's estimate: _____ and explanation: _____)

Married _____ Divorced/Separated _____ Widowed _____ Single _____

(Code _____)

Source: Richard P. Coleman, "The Continuing Significance of Social Class to Marketing," *Journal of Consumer Research* 10 (December 1983), 265–280.

Zip Code Measures   Commercial marketing research firms and other organizations sometimes develop their own scales to measure social status or other variables such as lifestyles. These scales assign a status value to the zip postal code or other geographic designation of a respondent's residence. The values reflect geodemographic data based on the distribution of occupations, educational characteristics, income, condition of housing, and so forth, in zip code areas.

Zip methods are valuable because of their ability to measure status without the need to collect additional data from respondents beyond their addresses. This information can then be related to variables such as the class of customers that will be attracted to a shopping center or a specific store, or the type of people that may respond to types of merchandise offered by a direct-mail organization.

Which Scale Is Best?

Social class is a rich, multidimensional variable. Social status has many subtle nuances that can be valuable to creative strategies in marketing but that may be missed unless the right measure is used.

An ideal scale would satisfy the criteria offered by Dominquez and Page:

1. Validated Criterion Variable: The scale should be measured against the actual class or status rank of individuals, ascertained by independent means.
2. Appropriate Universe: Scales are validated against community or national samples. A community scale is not strictly applicable to different types of communities or to national samples.
3. Objective Predictors: Variables such as house type or dwelling area involve subjective, time-consuming, and potentially inaccurate evaluations by raters and should be avoided. Variables such as a subject's own perceived class membership are prone to serious biases and should also be avoided. Objective variables such as income, education, or occupation are preferred.
4. Detailed Fit: Because it is comparatively easy to separate the extremely high- and low-ranked cases, a scale will overstate its ability to order a class or status hierarchy. The acid test of a scale's goodness of fit is its ability correctly to order closely ranked cases.
5. Split Sample Validation: Ultimately the most critical test of a scale is its ability to rank cases correctly in a second sample.
6. Contemporaneousness: Major social and economic shifts, such as the baby boom, the movement to suburbia, increased educational levels, and the consequences of inflation and the energy crisis may render obsolete scales that were devised prior to the occurrence of those phenomena.[25]

Status Crystallization

One further complexity in measuring social class, as if any more were needed, is the problem of status inconsistency or consideration of people who rate high on one variable but low on another. Status inconsistencies are logical consequences of the normal growth processes in status hierarchies.

Lenski developed an index of status crystallization and concluded that some people have a low degree of status crystallization. An example might be Dave Thomas, founder of Wendy's, who is wealthy and powerful but possesses the language patterns and characteristics of a person with little formal education or family foundation. [26] Highly paid athletes and popular musicians often fit this category. At the other end of the spectrum of status inconsistency would include some professors who have little income but much education and cultural advantages. These people do not fit into many of the generalizations about social class. Lenski found, among other things, such people are more willing to support programs of social change.[27]

Are Social Classes Changing?

Are social classes as prevalent as they once were? Maybe social class is vanishing among working-class and middle-class people. This theory is sometimes called the **embourgeoisment** of society or the **massification theory**. Perhaps the prevalence of mass media and increasing income as well as the dissemination of economic and political power on a wider basis have eliminated many of the differences between working-class and middle-class people. This issue is usually addressed by examining economic indicators such as income and wealth. A major controversy exists concerning whether or not the middle class is shrinking in America,[28] but this topic will be discussed later, in Chapter 18.

An extensive review of factors such as power, income, wealth, status, and participation in the political process by Kriesberg concluded:

> Personal wealth has probably become more equally distributed in the past fifty years, but wealth in the form of corporate shares has not; concentration in ownership of the means of production has increased, as is reflected in the decline of self-employment.[29]

The Duncan studies at the University of Michigan indicate much more economic mobility than was generally thought to be true in the past.[30] These studies are based upon analysis of movement between quintiles of income and show that in a decade only about half of those who started out in the lowest income quintile ended up there. Conversely, of the individuals in families in the highest quintile, fewer than half stayed there. Thus, "riches to rags" is about as common in the United States as "rags to riches."

Perhaps most surprising in the Duncan studies—and important for consumer researchers—is the finding that consumers below the poverty line do not stay there. In the 10-year period of the study, with average poverty levels about 12 percent, about 25 percent of Americans were below the poverty line for at least 1 year, but only 2.6 percent stayed there. In their book *Years of Poverty, Years of Plenty,* Duncan and his fellow researchers reported that the 2 percent chronically below the poverty level tend to be heavily dependent on welfare; to live in rural areas; and to be black, elderly, disabled, or in households headed by women with limited job opportunities. For most consumers, economic mobility is as probable as is geographic mobility.

Marketers must realize that, except for the 2 to 3 percent that are chronically poor, poor consumers who have little purchasing power in one year may be individuals whom marketers may seek as valued customers in later years. Firms such as Wal-Mart have policies to treat all customers well, even poor ones. Many of the poor ones become more affluent and contribute to the reason Wal-Mart by 1991 had become the largest retailer in the United States. Social class has not been eliminated in the United States; it has just changed a little. After an exhaustive review of the literature in this field, two of the most influential commentators on social class, Gilbert and Kahl, concluded:

> Proportionately, the working class is declining while the upper-middle and middle classes, working poor, and the underclass are expanding. The blue-collar/white-collar distinction has lost force, and the fundamental cleavage in the class structure has moved upward. More generally, Americans in the top half of the class structure appear to be gaining privilege and power at the expense of those in the bottom half.[31]

How Likely Are You to Change Your Social Class?

You may change your occupation and income, but can you change them enough to attain a social class different from your parents? How often are changes such as those in Consumer in Focus 4.2 likely to occur? These are issues of intergenerational mobility.

The answer seems to be that, while it is possible to climb upward (or downward) in the social order as Consumer in Focus 4.2 indicates, the probabilities of this actually happening are not very high.[32] Both men and women are affected by the low probability of change in social class, although women may have a bit more mobility through marriage than do men through occupations, since a man is more likely to inherit his father's status.[33] Women are also more likely to be lowered in status by divorce than are men. Upper-class people are more likely to believe that poverty is a result of equity or wasting money, while lower-class people tend to believe that the rich resist social change that might end poverty.[34] Parental wealth is very important in determining the social class of the next generation, not only because of its direct effect but also because parental wealth has such a strong effect on the quality of education an individual receives.[35]

After reviewing the literature, Snarey and Vaillant concluded:

> Children's social class is a stubborn predictor of their social class as adults. Only 1.8% of the children of manual laborers, for instance, entered the professions. Research to date has impressively documented factors that derail lower- and working-class individuals from upward social mobility. Among these are restricted access to educational and employment opportunities; high school tracking; class-biased career counseling; residential segregation by social class; class-biased achievement and IQ tests; lower teacher expectations for lower-class youth; and, perhaps most serious of all, racial prejudice.[36]

Consumer in Focus   4.2

Overcome Your Upbringing

It is often overlooked that most Americans who are born in the ghetto aren't destined to die there. According to researchers at the University of Michigan, 56 percent of teenagers whose family income put them in the nation's lowest fifth of all families in the 1970s had climbed out of the basement a decade later. Indeed, 12 percent were among the country's top 40 percent of earners. Seattle attorney José Gaitan, 39, was one of them.

Gaitan grew up in the city's rough central neighborhood, the son of an illegal Salvadoran immigrant father, who was deported when José was five, and an American-born, heroin-addicted mother. Today Gaitan is co-owner of the law firm Gaitan & Cusak and an adjunct professor at the University of Washington's law school. He earns more than $100,000 a year and lives in a $225,000 house with his wife, Olive.

Growing up on welfare, Gaitan remembers that food was so scarce that he shared two turkey TV dinners with his mother and younger brother on Thanksgiving. He found the path to a better life at Seattle First Baptist Church, where a minister, a Boy Scout leader, and a Boeing engineer encouraged him to work hard in school.

His grades won him scholarships at Linfield College and later he worked his way through the University of Washington's School of Law. He worked as a county and federal prosecutor until he and a partner opened a private practice. Today his firm counts Nabisco and the Federal Deposit Insurance Corporation among its clients and employs 13 lawyers. Says Gaitan, "Social and economic mobility is a function of hard work, a can do attitude and being good to people."

Source: Excerpted from "Overcome Your Upbringing," *Money* (October 1991), 153.

How Large Are Social Classes?

There is no unqualified answer to the question of how large specific social classes are. Table 4.3 shows some recent estimates, using measures of class used in contemporary marketing research.

The Gilbert and Kahl definitions shown in Table 4.3 emphasize economic distinctions, especially the recent emphasis on capitalism and entrepreneurship, whereas the Coleman-Rainwater approach emphasizes how people interact with each other as equals, superiors, or inferiors, especially in their work relationships.

TABLE 4.3   Social Classes in America

Two Recent Views of the American Status Structure

The Gilbert-Kahl New Synthesis Class Structure: A situations model from political theory and sociological analysis[a]	**The Coleman-Rainwater Social Standing Class Hierarchy: A reputational behavioral view in the community study tradition[b]**
Upper Americans	*Upper Americans*
The Capitalist Class (1%)—Their investment decisions shape the national economy, income mostly from assets earned inherited, prestige university connections	Upper-Upper (0.3%)—The "capital S society" world of inherited wealth, aristocratic names
Upper Middle Class (14%)—Upper managers, professionals, medium businessmen; college educated; family income ideally runs nearly twice the national average	Lower-Upper (1.2%)—The newer social elite drawn from current professional corporate leadership
	Upper-Middle (12.5%)—The rest of college graduate managers and professionals; lifestyle centers on private clubs, causes, and the arts
Middle Americans	*Middle Americans*
Middle Class (33%)—Middle level white-collar, top level blue-collar: education past high school typical; income somewhat above the national average	Middle Class (32%)—Average pay white-collar workers and their blue-collar friends; live on "the better side of town," try to "do the proper things"
Working Class (32%)—Middle level blue-collar: lower level white-collar; income runs slightly below the national average; education is also slightly below	Working Class (38%)—Average pay blue-collar workers; lead "working class lifestyle" whatever the income, school background, and job
Marginal and Lower Americans	*Lower Americans*
The Working Poor (11–12%)—Below mainstream America in living standard, but above the poverty line; low-paid service workers, operatives; some high school education	"A lower group of people but not the lowest" (9%)—Working not on welfare; living standard is just above poverty; behavior judged "crude," "trashy"
The Underclass (8–9%)—Depend primarily on welfare system for sustenance; living standard below poverty line; not regularly employed; lack schooling	"Real Lower-Lower" (7%)—On welfare, visibly poverty-stricken, usually out of work (or have "the dirtiest jobs"); "bums," "common criminals"

[a]Abstracted by Coleman from Gilbert, Dennis, and Joseph A. Kahl, "The American Class Structure: A Synthesis," Chapter 11 in *The American Class Structure: A New Syntheses* (Homewood, Ill.: The Dorsey Press, 1982).
[b]This condensation of the Coleman-Rainwater view is drawn from Chapters 8, 9, and 10 of Coleman, Richard P. and Lee P. Rainwater, with Kent A. McClelland, *Social Standing in America: New Dimensions of Class* (New York: Basic Books, 1978).

Social Class Dynamics

Social class behavior is dynamic because it reflects the changing environment. Some people think a lot about upholding their social class; others actively rebel against it by becoming part of the "counterculture."

Parody display is a term used to describe the mockery of status symbols and behavior, such as when the well-to-do wear blue jeans, even ones with holes in the knees, to proclaim their distaste for class or their own security in the social status system. The "Yuppie" culture of the 1980s created young affluents who bought BMWs but exhibited parody display in the 1990s with a Honda.

Today, there is also more individualism or "doing your own thing" among the middle social classes, possibly as another example of the emulation of the same trend among the upper classes in earlier years. Coleman describes this situation:

> Through the 1960s and 1970s, the lifestyles and self-conceptions of people identified with the upper sixth of the nation appear to have changed more than those of people in the classes below. The lifestyle variations that have emerged exist vertically within Upper America, crossing the substrata and combining people from several status layers into one consumer group with common goals that are differentiated internally mainly by income. . . . The result is that Upper America is now a vibrant mix of many lifestyles, which may be labeled post-preppy, sybaritic, countercultural, conventional, intellectual, political, and so on. Such diversions are usually of more importance for targeting messages and goods than are the horizontal, status-flavored, class-named strata.[37]

Marketing to Social Class Segments

After reading the preceding pages, you should have a good grasp of what is meant by social stratification—how it is measured, how it is changing (both for individual consumers and in the society as a whole), and some reasonably specific descriptive ideas of how people in one social stratum differ in their behavior from people in higher or lower strata. Now it is time to bring this all together and ask, "How are buying decisions affected by social class? What does this mean for a marketing organization?"

Market Segmentation

Social class is useful for market segmentation, the process of understanding groups of customers in order to make an especially attractive offering to them. Social class was found to be a useful concept for the segmentation of markets in pioneering work by people such as Pierre Martineau (marketing researcher at the *Chicago Tribune*), Sidney Levy of Northwestern University, and Richard Coleman of Social Research Inc.[38]

The procedures for market segmentation include the following steps:

1. identification of social class usage of product,
2. comparison of social class variables for segmentation with other variables (income, life cycle, etc.),
3. description of social class characteristics identified in market target,
4. development of marketing program to maximize effectiveness of marketing mix based upon consistency with social class attributes.

Analysis of market segments by socioeconomic profile allows a marketer to develop a comprehensive marketing program to match the socioeconomic characteristics of the market target. This would include product attributes, media strategy, creative strategy, channels of distribution, and pricing. Notice in Table 4.4 the differences between social classes both in general statements about fashion and comfort as well as product specific statements such as how telephone design should coordinate with the room.

TABLE 4.4   Descriptions of Socioeconomic Market Segments

A General Psychographic Profile of Customer's Socioeconomic Status

Style/Color Statements	Lower Class Agreement (%) ($n=25$)	Lower-Middle Class Agreement (%) ($n=108$)	Upper-Middle Class Agreement (%) ($n=202$)	Upper Class Agreement (%) ($n=105$)
I am generally willing to try even the most radical fashion at least once.	32	25	42	37
When I must choose between the two, I usually dress for fashion not for comfort.	9	15	24	29
Our home is furnished for comfort, not style.	96	87	79	79
I have more modern appliances in my home than most people.	17	23	41	48
I prefer colored appliances.	57	73	87	92
I enjoy the better things in life and am willing to pay for them.	36	70	70	82

Note: All significant levels are based on x^2 with p .05, 3 d.f.

Continued

TABLE 4.4   continued

A Product-Specific Psychographic Profile of Customer's Socioeconomic Status

Style/Color Statements	Lower Class Agreement (%) (n=25)	Lower-Middle Class Agreement (%) (n=108)	Upper-Middle Class Agreement (%) (n=202)	Upper Class Agreement (%) (n=105)
Phones should come in patterns and designs as well as colors.	60	80	63	58
A telephone should improve the decorative style of a room.	47	82	73	77
Telephones should be modern in design.	58	85	83	89
A home should have a variety of telephone styles.	8	46	39	51
You can keep all those special phones. All I want is a phone that works.	83	67	68	56
The style of a telephone is unimportant to me.	86	54	58	51

Source: A. Marvin Roscoe, Jr., Arthur LeClaire, Jr., and Leon G. Schiffman, "Theory and Management Applications of Demographics in Buyer Behavior," in Arch G. Woodside, Jagdish N. Sheth, and Peter D. Bennett, eds., *Consumer and Industrial Buying Behavior* (Amsterdam: North-Holland, 1977), 74–75. Reprinted by permission.

Need Recognition and Evaluative Criteria

Consumer decision making is influenced by a person's social class, especially in the determination of needs and evaluative criteria. Look closely at Table 4.4 and you will see much more emphasis on form among upper classes than the functional needs of the lower social class. (Higher agreement with fashion than comfort, for example.) These influences can be observed in product decisions of consumers.

Clothing   The kind, quality, and style of clothing a person wears is closely linked to that person's social class, as Consumer in Focus 4.3 so vividly describes. Clothing furnishes a quick, visual cue to the class culture of the wearer. It serves well as a symbol of social differentiation because of its high visibility. When adolescent girls are asked to describe the characteristics of the popular girls, "dressed well" is the response most frequently given—that is, linked to social class characteristics.

Consumer in Focus **4.3**

Social Class Influences on Appearance Product: You Are What You Wear

There is an elite look in this country. It requires women to be thin, with a hairstyle dating back eighteen or twenty years or so. (The classiest women wear their hair for a lifetime in exactly the same style they affected in college.) They wear superbly fitting dresses and expensive but always understated shoes and handbags, with very little jewelry. They wear scarves—these instantly betoken class, because they are useless except as a caste mark. Men should be thin. No jewelry at all. No cigarette case. Moderate-length hair, never dyed or tinted, which is a middle-class or high-prole sign. . . . Never a hairpiece, a prole usage. Both women's and men's elite looks are achieved by a process of rejection—of the current, the showy, the superfluous. Thus the rejection of fat by the elite. It pays to be thin.

"Layering" is obligatory. It has generally been true that the more clothes someone has on, the higher his or her status; it is a fine way of displaying a large wardrobe. The upper-middle-class woman will appear almost invariably in a skirt of gray flannel, Stuart plaid, or khaki; a navy-blue cardigan, which may be cable stitched; a white blouse with Peter Pan collar; hose with flat shoes; hair preferably in a barrette. When it gets cold, she puts on a blue blazer, or for business, a gray flannel suit. But the color toward which everything aspires is really navy.

If navy is the upper-middle-class color, purple is the prole equivalent. The purple polyester pantsuit offends two principles that determine class in clothes: the color principle and the organic-materials principle. Navy blue aside, colors are classier the more pastel or faded, and materials are classier the more they consist of anything that was once alive. That means wool, leather, silk, cotton, and fur. Only. All synthetic fibers are prole, partly because they're cheaper than natural ones, partly because they're not archaic, and partly because they're entirely uniform and hence boring—you'll never find a bit of straw or sheep excrement woven into an acrylic sweater. (The organic principle also determines that in kitchens wood is classier than Formica, and on the kitchen table a cotton cloth "higher" than plastic or oilcloth.)

Source: Paul Fussell, *Class* (New York: Ballatine Books, 1983).

A 14-year-old student, attending a private high school in an upper-middle-class suburb, described the other students in the following manner:

There are three types of kids in our school. The rich kids wear Guess Jeans or clothes from the Limited. They have their parents' credit cards or their own, so they are used to getting what they want. They have to go to the bathroom after lunch to put on their makeup. They have seven Swatch watches, one for each day of the week. Their hair is curly or bobbed in a wave. At home they have waterbeds. The lower class kids don't dress as well. They don't hang around the cooler groups. They get made fun of a lot. They may have styles from the Limited but you know they bought them at T. J. Maxx. The lower class (at this school) have more money than the kids at public schools, but they don't dress well or act right. The middle class kids have money and dress nice but they are not really cool and they don't talk about themselves as much as the upper class kids.

Home Furnishings   The criteria used by consumers to furnish a home are closely related to social class. Higher social classes tend to feel most comfortable with worn Oriental rugs on parquet floors, middle classes love wall-to-wall carpeting and lower classes have vinyl floors. Originals—paintings, Tiffany lamps, or exhibits of ancient languages are favorites of upper classes. Lower classes buy reproductions of these things or display collections of various items. The contents of the home can be identified so closely by social class that a scale has been developed for calculating social class on the basis of such items as furniture, venetian blinds, periodicals displayed, family photographs present, and so forth.[39]

Leisure   Social class affects leisure in a variety of ways. The type of leisure preferred is based upon activities that occur primarily with people in the same or closely adjacent status levels. The influence to adopt new leisure activities will be from people with the same or slightly higher status than the adopters.[40]

The proportion of family income spent on leisure may not vary a great deal between social classes, but the type of recreation varies greatly. Polo is upper class, bridge is a middle- to upper-class game, whereas bingo is lower class. Squash is upper class, tennis and racquetball are middle to upper class, boxing is predominantly lower class. Opera is upper class, professional wrestling is lower class.

Prestige leisure time activities (jogging, swimming, tennis, and so on) involve fairly rapid movement, with extreme use of arms and legs, suggesting a compensatory form of leisure for the otherwise sedentary life of many prestige occupations. Most of these pursuits do not require much time to the degree that activities such as hunting, fishing, or boating would—typical leisure-time pursuits of lower social class. Time is a critical element in the prestige classes' use of leisure. Members of lower social classes tend to participate in team sports, whereas people of higher socioeconomic status tend to participate in individual or dual sports.[41] The heaviest users of both commercial leisure and public facilities (such as parks, museums, and swimming pools) are the middle classes, since upper classes frequently have their own facilities and the lower classes often cannot afford them or do not have the propensity to participate in them.

Chief executives of major corporations may have little time for leisure because of their long hours, typically 59 hours a week at work and increasing. Most senior managers enjoy leisure pursuits on a daily basis, however. Many take part in recreational sports; others paint, play musical instruments, photograph nature and family, or escape into the world of literature. Reading work-related books and listening to music are among the favorite pursuits of highest-ranking executives, with social class backgrounds reflected in their preferences. Executives with middle-class backgrounds prefer classical music more than do those with upper-class backgrounds.[42]

Information Processing

The amount and type of search undertaken and information processing by an individual varies by social class. Unfortunately, the lowest social classes often have limited information sources and may be at a disadvantage in filtering out misinformation and fraud in a complex, urbanized society. To compensate, working-class consumers often rely on relatives or close friends for information about consumption decisions. Middle-class consumers rely more on media-acquired information and actively engage in an external search of information from the media. As the level of social class increases, usually so does access to media information.

Media and messages can be tailored to specific social classes. The language and appearance, as well as how the product is used, communicate to each social class whether or not "this product is for me." At times, some TV networks have had stronger appeal in some social classes than in others, and many firms forgo direct commercial messages for the soft sell of "Funding provided by . . ." that can be placed upon the Public Broadcasting Service stations directed to upper-class audiences.

Magazines offer excellent potential for detailed positioning to social class segments. When the usage of a brand is correlated with purchases in these groups, zip code information can provide measures of the strength of various magazines in reaching each group.[43]

Social Language   The language patterns of individuals are closely correlated with their social class. In one set of experiments, the social classes of respondents were first measured before they were asked to make a 40-second recording of the fable, "The Tortoise and the Hare." These short recordings were played to groups of 15 to 30 regionally diverse college students who served as judges. The average ratings of social class by these judges correlated 0.80 with the speakers' social classes.[44]

When speakers were asked in role playing to alter their voices to sound upper class, the student judges' correlation with measured actual class was still 0.65. All of the subjects used proper grammar, but their choice of vocabulary, sentence length, sentence structure, and fluency varied by social class. In still another approach, speakers were asked to count from 1 to 20, and even in this situation, college students' rankings correlated 0.65 with social class of speakers.

The importance of language can be understood by analysis of the copy used in advertisements. Expensive cars such as Mercedes and Infiniti typically use longer words, fewer euphemisms, and more abstract language or visual materials. Lower- and middle-class car ads speak more of physical attributes, emphasize pictures rather than words, and are more likely to use slang or street language. These principles are often found in clothing and accessory ads. Notice in Figure 4.4 how two companies—Boss and Fendi—use almost no words at all except the company name.

FIGURE 4.4   The Social Language of Upper Class Advertising
Source: Courtesy of Boss and Fendi.

Purchasing Processes

Social status influences where and how people feel they should shop. Lower-status people prefer local, face-to-face places where they get friendly service and easy credit—often in the neighborhood. Upper-middle consumers feel more confident in their shopping ability. They will venture to new places to shop and will range throughout a store to find what they want.

The discount store traditionally appeals to the middle classes because they are careful and economy minded in their buying. In their early years, discount stores frequently did not carry prestige or designer brands, but as the middle classes' income grew and information influences broadened, firms such as J. C. Penney, K mart, and Target have added more designer brands. Major retail organizations such as The Limited need a portfolio of stores ranging from Lerner to Henri Bendel to appeal to the variety of social classes and lifestyles that exist in industrialized societies such as Canada and the United States.[45]

Consumers have an image of what social class a store attracts and have an understanding of what shopping should be like in a store that appeals to their own social class. People in upper classes want a pleasant store atmosphere featuring exciting displays and excellent service. Lower classes emphasize acquiring household items or clothing as the enjoyable part of shopping. Historically, upper classes shop more frequently than middle or lower classes but may be shopping more in the future with catalogues or videotex offerings such as CompuServe or other forms of direct marketing because of the time pressures felt by so many dual-income families. The greatest propensity for family members to shop together is among lower, white-collar, skilled, and semiskilled occupational classes. Shopping for many middle-class families, however, is a form of recreation. They are the ones willing to visit regional shopping malls. They are also most likely to experiment with store brands and respond most to variations in price offerings.

A Concluding Note

Social class is an important concept in developing positioning strategies—the creating of perceptions in consumers' minds about the attributes of a product or organization. To accomplish positioning effectively requires a good understanding of the class characteristics of the target market and the class attributes desired for the product. If you are marketing products or services to social class targets different from your own, be sure you do your homework to understand well the social class characteristics of your market target. Sometimes the process is uncomfortable but it is essential. The concepts and methods discussed in this chapter will be helpful to you in accomplishing the process.

Remember also that the number of consumers who aspire to higher social classes is much larger than those who are in them. Many of the middle classes can buy products with the symbols and allure of higher social classes—and often do for products as diverse as those of Russell Athletic or Godiva, shown in Figure 4.5. Market researchers at Grey Advertising estimate only a few million Americans have incomes that enable them to live affluent or rich lives. But far more—perhaps 10 times as many—partake of the good life some of the time, treating themselves to Godiva chocolates, Armani cologne, or Hermes scarves. Wanting it all is a hallmark of the middle class. Buying the best on at least a few occasions is a way to set themselves apart and bolster their self-image. Ads for premium-priced products need to be sensual, provocative, and elegant for these products.[46]

Summary

Social classes are relatively permanent and homogeneous groupings of people in society, permitting groups of people to be compared with one another. These groups are recognized as having inferior or superior positions by other people, often based upon economic position in the marketplace.

FIGURE 4.5 Appeals to the Upwardly Mobile
Source: Courtesy Russell Athletic.

Social class is determined by three types of variables: economic, interaction and political. For marketers, the most important determinants of social class are usually considered to be occupation, personal performance, interactions, possessions, value orientations, and class consciousness.

Measures of social class may be based on single variables or multiple variables. Multiple-variable measures provide the best theoretical information, but occupation is the best single proxy indicator of social class.

Social classes in the United States are traditionally divided into six groups: upper upper, lower upper, upper middle, lower middle, upper lower, and lower lower or marginal classes. Newer classification systems emphasize the enlarged capitalist or professional classes in the upper-middle or lower-lower classes. Social classes are always in transition, however, causing status and its symbols to be dynamic. Each group displays characteristic values and behaviors that are useful to consumer analysts in designing marketing programs. Social class analysis helps understand need recognition of consumers, search processes and information processing, evaluative criteria, and purchasing patterns of actual and aspiring social classes.

Review and Discussion Questions

1. What variables determine an individual's social class? In what order of importance should they be ranked?
2. In what way does income relate to social class? Why is it used so little as an indicator of social class? What should be its proper value as an indicator?
3. Prepare an outline of the major problems involved in the measurement of social classes. How would your outline differ for academic researchers as compared to business practitioners?
4. Some observers of contemporary America believe that social classes have declined in importance and presence, but others disagree. Outline your analysis of what has happened in recent years to social classes in the United States or in other countries.
5. A marketing researcher is speculating on the influence of upper classes on the consumption decisions of the lower classes for the following products: automobiles, food, clothing, and baby care products. What conclusions would you expect for each of these products? Describe a research project that could be used to answer this question.
6. The leisure products group of a large conglomerate is constantly seeking additional products for expanding markets and additional penetration for existing products. What conclusions that would be helpful in the design of marketing strategy might be reached concerning social class and leisure?
7. The operator of a large discount chain is contemplating a new store in an area of upper-lower class families. He asks for a consulting report defining the precautions he should take to ensure patronage among this group. What would you place in such a report? Assume that the area is mostly lower-lower class families. Would you recommend entry?
8. Prepare a research report comparing the search process of the major social classes of consumers in the United States or other countries.
9. Assume that you are preparing the advertisements for a home furnishings store. How would you vary the ads if the target segments are lower middle rather than upper middle?
10. In what social class would you place professional athletes? Actors and actresses?

Endnotes

1. Elizabeth C. Hirschman, "Secular Immortality and the American ideology of Affluence," *Journal of Consumer Research* 17 (June 1990), 31–42.
2. Kjell Gronhaug and Paul S. Trapp, "Perceived Social Class Appeals of Branded Goods," *The Journal of Consumer Marketing* 5 (Fall 1988), 25–30.
3. Natalya Prusakova, "Dress to Impress," *Business in the USSR* (December 1991), 90–93.
4. Robert V. Robinson, "Explaining Perceptions of Class and Racial Inequality in England and the United States of America," *The British Journal of Sociology* 34 (1983), 344–363.
5. T. Schjelderup-Ebbe, "Social Behavior of Birds," in C. Murchison, ed., *A Handbook of Social Psychology* (Worcester, Mass.: Clark University Press, 1935).
6. Al Ries and Jack Trout, *Positioning: The Battle for Your Mind* (New York: McGraw-Hill, 1981), 53.

7. Max Weber, in H. H. Gard and C. Wright Mills, *From Max Weber: Essays in Sociology* (New York: Oxford University Press, 1946), 193.

8. Max Haller, "Marriage, Women, and Social Stratification: A Theoretical Critique," *American Journal of Sociology* 86 (1981), 766–795.

9. Reprinted with permission of Wadsworth, Inc. From *The American Class Structure: A New Synthesis*, 3rd ed. by Dennis Gilbert and Joseph A. Kahl. © 1982, 1987 by Dennis Gilbert and Joseph A. Kahl. Although not cited in each instance, this excellent book has influenced the content of this chapter in numerous other points.

10. Stephen L. Nock, "Social Origins as Determinants of Family Social Status" (paper presented to the Mid-South Sociological Association, 1980).

11. Joseph A. Kahl, *The American Class Structure* (New York: Holt, Rinehart and Winston, 1957), 8–10. A more recent emphasis centers on the ownership of capitalistic assets and the role of occupations. See Gilbert and Kahl, 1982.

12. Robert Cage, "Spending Differences Across Occupational Fields," *Monthly Labor Review* 112 (December 1989), 33–43.

13. David H. Demo and Ritch C. Savin-Williams, "Early Adolescent Self-Esteem as a Function of Social Class," *American Journal of Sociology* 88 (1983), 763–773. Viktor Gecas and Monica A. Seff, "Social Class and Self-Esteem: Psychological Centrality, Compensation, and the Relative Effects of Work and Home," *Social Psychology Quarterly* 53 (1990), 165–173.

14. Hirschman, 1991.

15. Michael Useem and S. M. Miller, "The Upper Class in Higher Education," *Social Policy* 7 (January–February 1977), 28–31.

16. Lewis H. Lapham, *Money and Class in America* (Weidenfeld & Nicholson, 1988).

17. Reeve Vanneman and Lynn Weber Cannon, *The American Perception of Class* (Philadelphia: Temple University Press, 1987).

18. Barbara B. Stern, "Literary Criticism and Consumer Research: Overview and Illustrative Analysis," *Journal of Consumer Research* 16 (December 1989), 322–334. See also Russel W. Belk, Melanie R. Wallendorf, and John Sherry, Jr., "The Sacred and the Profane in Consumer Behavior: Theodicy on the Odyssey," *Journal of Consumer Research* 16 (June 1989), 1–38.

19. W. Lloyd Warner and Paul S. Lunt, *The Social Life of a Modern Community* (New Haven, Conn.: Yale University Press, 1941). See also the classic book by W. Lloyd Warner, *Yankee City* (New Haven, Conn.: Yale University Press, 1963).

20. Allison Davis, Burleigh B. Gardner, and Mary R. Gardner, *Deep South: A Social-Anthropological Study of Caste and Class* (Chicago: The University of Chicago Press, 1941).

21. August B. Hollingshead, *Elmtown's Youth* (New York: John Wiley & Sons, 1949).

22. U.S. Department of Commerce, *Standard Occupational Classification Manual* (Washington, D.C.: U.S. Government Printing Office, 1980).

23. Charles B. Nam and Mary G. Powers, *The Socioeconomic Approach to Status Measurement* (Houston: Cap and Gown Press, 1983).

24. Richard P. Coleman, "The Continuing Significance of Social Class to Marketing," *Journal of Consumer Research* 10 (December 1983), 265–280.

25. Louis V. Dominquez and Albert L. Page, "Stratification in Consumer Behavior Research: A Re-Examination," *Journal of the Academy of Marketing Science* 9 (Summer 1981), 257–258.

26. R. Dave Thomas, *Dave's Way: A New Approach to Old-Fashioned Success* (New York: G. P. Putnam's Sons, 1991).

27. Gerhard E. Lenski, "Status Crystallization: A Non-Vertical Dimension of Social Status," *American Sociological Review* 21 (August 1956), 458–464.

28. Dick Stevenson, "The Middle Class Comes Undone," *Ad Forum* 5 (June 1984), 32–39; Neal H. Rosenthal, "The Shrinking Middle Class: Myth or Reality?" *Monthly Labor Review* 108 (March 1985), 3–10; McKinley L. Blackburn and David F. Bloom, "What Is Happening to the Middle Class?" *American Demographics* 7 (January 1985), 19–25; Patrick J. McMahon and John H. Tschetter, "The Declining Middle Class: A Further Analysis," *Monthly Labor Review* 109 (September 1986), 22–26.

29. Louis Kriesberg, *Social Inequality* (Englewood Cliffs, N.J.: Prentice-Hall, 1979), 77–78.

30. Greg J. Duncan, ed., *Years of Poverty, Years of Plenty* (Ann Arbor: Institute for Social Research, 1984).

31. Gilbert and Kahl, *The American Class Structure*, 340.

32. Andrea Tyree and Robert W. Hodge, "Five Empirical Landmarks," *Social Forces* 56 (March 1978) 761–769. Some of the methodological issues in these studies are discussed in C. Matthew Snipp, "Occupational Mobility and Social Class: Insights from Men's Career Mobility," *American Sociological Review* 50 (August 1985), 475–492.

33. Ivan D. Chase, "A Comparison of Men's and Women's Intergenerational Mobility in the United States," *American Sociological Review* 40 (August 1975), 483–505.

34. Robert L. Leahy, "Development of the Conception of Economic Inequality: Explanations, Justifications, and Concepts of Social Mobility and Change," *Developmental Psychology* 19 (1983), 111–125.

35. Russell W. Rumberger, "The Influence of Family Background on Education, Earnings, and Wealth," *Social Forces* 61 (March 1983), 755–770.

36. John R. Snarey and George E. Vaillant, "How Lower- and Working-Class Youth Become Middle-Class Adults: The Association Between Ego Defense Mechanisms and Upward Social Mobility," *Child Development* 56 (1985), 904–908.

37. Richard P. Coleman, "The Continuing Significance of Social Class in Marketing," *Journal of Consumer Research* 10 (December 1983), 263–280, at 270.

38. Classic publications that in the 1990s are still valuable reading for consumer analysts include Pierre Martineau, "Social Classes and Spending Behavior," *Journal of Marketing* 23 (October 1958), 121–130; Sidney Levy, "Social Class and Consumer Behavior," in Joseph W. Newman, ed., *On Knowing the Consumer* (New York: John Wiley & Sons, 1966), 146–160; Richard P. Coleman and Bernice L. Neugarten, *Social Status in the City* (San Francisco: Jossey-Bass, 1971).

39. Paul Fussell, *Class* (New York: Ballantine Books, 1983), 230–233.

40. Patrick C. West, "Status Differences and Interpersonal Influence in the Adoption of Outdoor Recreation Activities," *Journal of Leisure Research* 16 (1984), 350–354.

41. Susan L. Greendorfer, "Social Class Influence on Female Sport Involvement," *Sex Roles* 4 (August 1978), 619–625.

42. Louis E. Boone, David L. Kurtz, and C. Patrick Fleenor, "Games CEOs Play," *American Demographics* 11 (January 1989), 43–45.

43. Hugh M. Canon and Gerald Linda, "Beyond Media Imperatives: Geodemographic Media Selection," *Journal of Advertising Research* 22 (June/July 1982), 31–36.

44. Dean S. Ellis, "Speech and Social Status in America," *Social Forces* 45 (March 1967), 431–437.

45. Roger Blackwell and Wayne Talarzyk, "Lifestyle Retailing: Competitive Strategies for the 1980's," *Journal of Retailing* 59 (December 1983), 7–27.

46. Jaclyn Fierman, "The High-Living Middle Class," *Fortune* 115 (April 13, 1987), 27.

5

Personal Influence

Weep for the Yuppie lifestyle. It is dead. Once it reigned supreme; now nobody wants it.

It was born in the 1970s of the Me Decade idea that one's things should reflect one's unique and fascinating self. It evolved in the '80s into an assumption that the self was the sum of stylish things—its clothes, car, house, vacations, amusing twig furniture.

Now it's gone out of style. What appeals now, as trendologist Faith Popcorn said in a recent interview, is "to be normal and have a regular life."

In other words, to wear blue jeans, eat tuna casserole, do yard work, go to PTA meetings, watch TV. Not that nobody did those things in the '80s, and not that nobody enjoyed them, but nobody thought they were cool. What was cool—or, if you prefer, hot—were la-di-da things like sun-dried tomatoes, halogen lamps, BMWs, Scaasi evening dresses that cost as much as a small house.

BMW probably suffered as much as anybody for its identification with the yuppie lifestyle. So look at the new BMW ads: Not only are there no yuppies in them, there are no people at all, only car parts. Now it's all "aerospace-style electric connectors" and "advanced motronics."

And how about the Subaru ad where Brian Keith piously insists that buying one "won't make you handsome, or prettier, or younger. And if it improves your standing with the neighbors, then you live among snobs with distorted values."

Consider the Revlon girl: She used to be an imperious beauty in a ballgown; now she's a motorcycle mama in a denim jacket, so much more accessible.

Today's Man has seen the light, too. He's "had it with designer water. He orders American coffee, not iced decaf cappuccino. He looks for substance, not superficiality." What a guy!

Of course, like Marie Antoinette, whose longing to experience downscale reality led her to dress up like a milkmaid and skip around the back yard at Versailles swinging a jeweled milk pail, some folks just don't get it. They're prisoners of style, looking for life in all the wrong places.

For fall, Lance Karesh, who designs the Basco menswear collection, showed clothes—based, he said, on "the immigrant look of yesterday"—that could've stepped right out of the famous Stieglitz photograph *The Steerage*. Designer Christian Francis Roth showed clothes that featured large, exquisitely set-in patches. He said they were inspired by the homeless.

Let them eat cake.

Source: Patricia McLaughlin, "Get a Life and Give Your Lifestyle a Rest," *Philadelphia Inquirer Magazine*, December 1, 1991, 43. Reproduced by special permission.

FIGURE 5.1 **The BMW—A Mechanical Wonder, Not a Yuppie Flagship**
Source: Courtesy of BMW.

Since the beginning of time, individual behavior has been affected and shaped by the expectations and direct input of others. Wise marketers in turn have discovered that personal influence often exceeds the power of company promotional efforts.

As you have just read, this never has been more true than during the height of the so-called *yuppie era.* Status was on constant public display through conspicuous consumption. Indeed a "programmed lifestyle" reigned supreme and was propagated through acute sensitivity to the offerings of savvy marketers, reinforced by vigilant comparison of personal preferences with the expectations of others. Nothing was more heinous for many than to lose social acceptance among their upwardly mobile peers.

As is so often the case, however, the pendulum has swung to an opposite extreme, and the yuppie influence is dead. As Judith Langer has noted, "There's a movement away from conspicuous consumption, a yuppie backlash."[1] The BMW now is promoted as a mechanical wonder, not as a symbol of yuppie social status (Figure 5.1). While "Shop Till You Drop" was the motto for many baby boom age consumers during the 1980s, it is rapidly being replaced by "Fashion Free and Proud of It."[2]

As you will learn in this chapter, personal influence takes two major forms. First, other people often are used as a *reference group*—a mirror, if you will, reflecting which choices are acceptable and which are not. Sometimes this input is viewed as binding, in which case it is referred to as *normative* influence. At other times it is only *comparative* and serves as yet another source of information to be weighed.

Personal influence also can come through word-of-mouth communication initiated or supplied by a person known as an opinion leader. Information from this source usually is viewed as being highly credible and often has the power to make or break a marketing campaign.

You will discover that the impact of personal influence varies directly with the degree of involvement. Involvement increases, of course, when the choices made are perceived as affecting one's social status and acceptance. It follows under these circumstances that personal input will be assigned high importance.

Reference Group Influence

A **reference group** is any "person or group of people that significantly influences an individual's behavior."[3] Reference groups provide standards (norms) and values that can become the determining perspective for how a person thinks and behaves.

Solomon Asch undertook a seminal study in 1951[4] that has been widely cited as demonstrating beyond doubt that most people are averse to behavior that contradicts group consensus.[5] In this experiment, subjects were required to choose which of three lines differing in length matched the length of a fourth line. Each person was seated with a group of confederates, all strangers, who were instructed to make an incorrect choice. When exposed to these incorrect choices, experimental subjects made a substantial number of errors consistent with group consensus. This was not the case, however, when other people were not present.

A similar study demonstrated the same personal influence pattern within a consumer behavior context. Venkatesan presented subjects with three identical suits and asked them to select the one they considered to be of highest quality.[6] Confederates always chose the suit labeled "B," and the experimental subjects were influenced to give the same response. Suit B was chosen least often, however, when other people were not present.

Types of Reference Groups

Social groups can take many forms. The classifications introduced here reflect standard terminology, but no category is mutually exclusive. It is possible, for example, for a person to be part of a formal, primary group.

Primary Versus Secondary

The Primary Group   The greatest influence and impact usually is exerted by **primary groups**, defined as a social aggregation that is sufficiently small to permit and facilitate unrestricted face-to-face interaction. They exist because "like attracts like." There is cohesiveness and motivated participation. As a result, members exhibit marked similarities in beliefs and behavior.[7] The family, of course, is the most obvious example of a strongly infuential primary group.

The Secondary Group   **Secondary groups** also have face-to-face interaction, but it is more sporadic, less comprehensive, and less influential in shaping thought and behavior.[8] Examples are professional associations, trade unions, and community organizations.

Aspirational versus Dissociative

The Aspirational Group   **Aspirational groups** exhibit a desire to adopt the norms, values, and behavior of others with whom the individual aspires to associate. On occasion there is anticipation of acceptance into membership and motivation to behave accordingly, although membership aspirations are not always present.

The influence of aspirational groups, while often indirect, can play a significant role in product choices. The ad in Figure 5.2 ran in Nairobi, Kenya, a typical non-Western urban center characterized by a predominance of families living at or only slightly above the poverty line. The lifestyle depicted here accurately reflects the dreams and aspirations of many, and it is not surprising that Cussons Imperial Leather has achieved significant market penetration.

The Dissociative Group   Influence also can be exerted by **dissociative groups** when the individual is motivated to *avoid* association. Certainly this has been the case among most baby boomers with respect to the yuppies whose lifestyles have been increasingly discredited.

Formal versus Informal

The Formal Group   **Formal groups** are characterized by a defined, known list of members, and the organization and structure are codified in writing. Examples are churches, fraternal bodies, and community service organizations. The influence exerted on behavior varies, depending upon the motivation of the individual to accept and comply with the group's standards. Also, there are wide latitudes in the degree to which specific conformity is expected and enforced.

The Informal Group   As would be expected, **informal groups** have far less structure and are likely to be based on friendship or collegial association. Norms can

a little
luxury
every
day

Cussons

FIGURE 5.2   **This Ad Is Designed to Capitalize on the Consumer Dreams and Aspirations in a Non-Western Urban Market**

be stringent, but they seldom appear in writing. The effect on behavior can be strong if individuals are motivated by social acceptance. There also is a high degree of intimate, face-to-face interaction, which further strengthens the power with which expectations and sanctions are expressed and enforced.

Three Forms of Reference Group Influence

Reference groups affect consumer choice in three principal ways: (1) normative compliance, (2) value-expressive influence, and (3) informational influence.

Normative Compliance   When reference groups affect behavior through pressures for conformity, this is referred to as **normative influence**. Conformity pressures become most potent when there is both positive motivation to maintain group identity and the motivation of threats of sanctioning power in the form of rewards and punishments. Further, some evidence suggests that susceptibility to interpersonal influence is a personality trait.[9]

Sociologist George Homans has shed useful light on the dynamics of normative compliance.[10] He has put forth an equation of human exchange that is built on the relationship between the rewards of compliance as compared with the costs. Symbols of esteem or approval can provide rewards and incentives, thereby reinforcing that behavior and encouraging its repetition. There also are costs, however, such as association with certain undesirable people, lost time, or restriction on freedom of choice.

The outcomes will be determined by an individual's perception of the *profit* inherent in the interaction (that is, rewards minus costs). Examples would be a college fraternity member who perceives that the rewards of acceptance outweigh the costs of not wearing a high school letter jacket, or the marketing manager who willingly endures the sometimes abusive responses of dissatisfied customers knowing full well that future advancement is based on high customer retention.

Normative influence can occur even when others do not control tangible outcomes because people are concerned with their perceptions of what others *think* of them. Mason Haire's classic 1950 study is a case in point.[11] Haire showed that perceptions of users of regular coffee were evaluated favorably, whereas purchasers of instant coffee (a new product at that time) were perceived as lazy and incompetent homemakers.

A number of other marketing studies over the years have demonstrated that conformity pressures do impact buying decisions,[12] and this is especially true when the product is conspicuous in its purchase and use and when group social acceptance is a strong motivator.[13] Fashion-conscious women, for example, receive clear signals from their peers which makes further information search unnecessary; many needed even further point-of-sale reinforcement that their choices were socially correct.[14]

Conspicuousness is not a fixed product characteristic but depends on how the product is used. Consequently, the impact of personal influence varies depending upon the usage situation. Miniard and Cohen found, for example, that normative influence on brand choice is important when beer is to be served to friends but not when it is consumed privately.[15]

Marketers have learned the potency of appealing to the "in thing," and this is not confined to North America, as the German ad in Figure 5.3 demonstrates ("calories are out, slim is in"). It is interesting to note, however, that normative compliance seems to be declining in its impact in much of the Western world.[16]

A major factor, we feel, is the worldwide growth of urbanization, which leads to greater social isolation and individualism. Grandparents, uncles, aunts, and other members of the extended family have far less face-to-face influence. Also, urban living arrangements, often in high-rises, minimize the social interaction that takes place much more readily when living in the country or the bush. Finally, television and other mass media open windows to the world and thereby broaden horizons and interests beyond normal social circles. A clear demonstration of this growing reality appears in Consumer in Focus 5.1.

Another factor leading to diminished normative compliance is a weakened respect for social norms rather than a complete denial of their existence or impact.

Coca-Cola light.
Kalorien sind 'out'. Geschmack ist 'in'.

Coca-Cola light

FIGURE 5.3   An Appeal to Conform to the "In-Thing": The Pressure for Social Acceptance Is Strong throughout the World

Source: Courtesy of the Coca-Cola Company.

Consumer in Focus   5.1

A Vanishing Sense of Community: Bolingbrook, Illinois

The business of life is to go forward.
—Samuel Johnson

For many years, the residents of Ottawa Drive in Bolingbrook, Ill., did just that.

In the townhouses of this suburban Chicago street, families shared in the heritage of the middle class: the guarantee of progress. Most would be promoted at work; most would buy more and better products for their homes.

Continued

Consumer in Focus 5.1 continued

One longtime resident remembers the neighborhood surrounding Ottawa Drive as a nest of young families who shared in wine-tasting parties, spaghetti dinners, and block dances. Neighbors, she says, were the best of friends.

Today, however, neighbors hardly know one another, and progress—when it comes—benefits individuals, not the community. "We used to have a lot of fun in this neighborhood," says Debie Weingarden, who has lived here for 14 years. "But now everybody's going his own way."

Ottawa Drive and its families reflect some of the changes that have splintered the middle class. Where upward mobility was once a given, middle-class households here and elsewhere now find themselves heading both up and *down* the economic ladder.

At the same time, the lifestyles of the people on the block have become as varied as their bank accounts. At one home, the wife is the breadwinner and works the night shift. Next door, three unmarried people share a house. Another address down, a young woman lives by herself. And, across the street, one family is building an addition for their 20-year-old son. As they come and go, most people here barely see or talk to each other.

The result, among other things, is a disappearing sense of community. Neighbors no longer share common aspirations or values. Although it still has the appearance of a traditional middle-class neighborhood, Ottawa Drive has become a site of differing expectations, values, and financial prospects.

Unlike the families who first lived here in the 1960s, most residents now find little agreement on what constitutes success, how they should live their lives, or how they should raise their children. "Everybody's rushing around trying to do their own thing, trying to get their own life settled."

Source: Alex Kotlowitz, "Changes Among Families Prompt a Vanishing Sense of Community," *The Wall Street Journal* (March 11, 1987), 33. Reprinted by special permission of *The Wall Street Journal*, Dow Jones & Company, Inc. 1987. All rights reserved worldwide.

This is referred to by sociologists as **anomie**.[17] People so affected are apt to conform grudgingly or, in certain instances, to engage in motivated evasion and failure to conform. The ad in Figure 5.4 is a good example of how Mazda Motor of America, Inc., has capitalized upon anomie and turned it into an effective appeal.

It is also interesting to observe ways in which some people seek to reverse the effects of anomie by deliberately seeking relationships in which others invoke rewards and sanctions designed for a person's own good. Alcoholics Anonymous and Weight Watchers are two examples in which membership is sought in recognition that changes in undesirable behavior can be nearly impossible to accomplish without stringent social pressure.

FIGURE 5.4   An Example of How One Company Is Fighting Normative Social Influence

Source: Mazda Motor of America. Reprinted by special permission.

Value-Expressive Influence   Reference groups also can perform a value-expressive function, whereby a need for psychological association with a group is evidenced by acceptance of its norms, values, or behavior and a conforming response is made, even though there may be no motivation to become a member. One desired outcome is enhanced image in the eyes of others. Another is identification with people who are admired and respected. Both of these benefits are captured in an advertising campaign by Martini & Rossi Corporation (Figure 5.5).

Another example appears in Figure 5.6, this time from an East African country. The picture says it all—"smoking is cool for everybody, young and old alike." What a contrast to the warning from the Ministry of Health about the dangers of smoking! As Consumer in Focus 5.2 makes completely clear, such an appeal would face immediate boycott pressures in the United States for what we consider to be

FIGURE 5.5 **In This Ad, Martini & Rossi Cutty Is Capitalizing on Value-Expressive Social influence**

Source: Courtesy Martini & Rossi Corporation.

FIGURE 5.6 **Value-Expressive Social Influence Also Is Used in East African Advertising**

good and proper reasons. Unfortunately, many businesses are adopting the principle that says *take it to the third world if you can't get away with it here*. What does this say about observance of the consumer's right to safety? We think it says plenty and deplore this practice.

Informational Influence Consumers often accept the opinions of others as providing credible and needed evidence about reality.[18] This is most apparent when it is difficult to assess product or brand characteristics by observation. Under these circumstances it is more likely that usage or recommendation by others will be perceived as thoughtful and valid.[19] We have more to say about this role of friends and relatives in the next section of this chapter.

If It Feels Good, It Must Be Bad

Representative Joe Kennedy is a man with a mission, a bellwether for the age. He and millions like him—baby-boomers whose focus has turned to health and children—have engineered a basic shift in the national consciousness.

After the licentiousness of the Seventies and the materialism of the Eighties, the generation that coined the slogan "If it feels good, do it!" has concluded in middle age that if it feels good, it must be bad for you. With this realization has come a neo-prohibitionist impulse that militates against anything perceived as harmful, be it cigarettes, beer, cocaine, or cholesterol.

Trend watchers see at least two forces at work: the emergence of health as a lifestyle and a new-found focus on kids. Americans of all stripes have broadened health to include such issues as emotional well-being, stress reduction, nurturing relationships, and a feeling of achievement, and they're seeking benefits that are increasingly long term—not just a runner's high or a slender figure, but also a stronger heart, cleaner arteries, a longer and happier life.

The other factor, a focus on children, is closely tied to health. "The baby-boomers have gone through enlightenment," says Leo Shapiro, a market researcher in Chicago. "Now they're looking at their children and they're really concerned." Cigarette smoking has come under increasingly strident attack: Responding to pressure from antismoking activists, convenience stores are more often carding minors in the 44 states where sales are illegal, and Iowa recently made it a crime for anyone under 18 to smoke.

Ultimately both concerns, health and children, stem from the boomer's realization that they are no longer young. "Two things are happening," says Shapiro. "They're developing a sense of their own mortality, and they're developing a sense that their immortality depends on their children." This makes the just-say-no mentality a very deep-rooted trend, since mortality is so fundamental, and a very broad-based one, since it transcends economic and ideological barriers.

But many inner-city residents have not absorbed the news about health and lifestyle. Enter Reverend Calvin Butts (the onetime black militant who now leads Harlem's Abyssinian Baptist Church), who has called for a nationwide ban on billboards advertising cigarettes and alcohol, and who recently led supporters in a whitewashing campaign against such billboards in Harlem. "Drugs kill! Alcohol and tobacco! All drugs!"

Source: Frank Rose, "If It Feels Good, It Must Be Bad," *Fortune* (October 21, 1991), 91–108 (selected pages). Reproduced by special permission.

FIGURE 5.7 **Appeals to Expertise Affect Consumer Opinion**
Source: Courtesy Columbia Crest Winery and Almond Board of California.

A commercial spokesperson's ability to exert informational influence will be affected by his or her perceived expertise. Woodside and Davenport varied the expertise of a music store salesperson who encouraged customers to purchase a tape-deck cleaning kit.[20] When the salesperson was seen as knowledgeable, two-thirds bought the product, but this dropped to only 20 percent when there was admission of unfamiliarity with the product.

This study illustrates the facilitating effect of perceived expertise on compliance, a fact that marketers have long recognized. Rigorous sales-training programs provide help in answering customers' questions and complaints. Ads often feature an expert spokesperson as a primary persuasive appeal or make reference to recommendations by groups of experts (Figure 5.7).

Determinants of Reference Group Impact

We have already stressed that social visibility is a factor in receptivity to the views of others. In other words, all things being equal, we expect greater social influence

FIGURE 5.8   Reference Group Influence as a Function of Product Type Consumption Situation

		Publicly consumed	
Brand	Product	Weak reference group influence (−)	Strong reference group influence (+)
Strong reference group influence (+)		*Public necessities* Influence: Weak product and strong brand Examples: Wristwatch, automobile, man's suit	*Public luxuries* Influence: Strong product and brand Examples: Golf clubs, snow skis, sailboat
Weak reference group influence (−)		*Private necessities* Influence: Weak product and brand Examples: Mattress, floor lamp, refrigerator	*Private luxuries* Influence: Strong product and weak brand Examples: TV game, trash compactor, icemaker

Necessity ———————————————————————— Luxury

Source: William O. Bearden and Michael J. Etzel, "Reference Group Influence on Product and Brand Purchase Decisions," *Journal of Consumer Research* 9 (September 1982), 185. Used with permission.

when the product is publicly displayed or consumed as opposed to its being privately displayed and used. Bearden and Etzel, however, have added one additional factor—whether the product is a luxury or necessity—the hypothesis being that luxuries are more susceptible to social influence than necessities.[21]

These two hypotheses were tested in a direct-mail survey of 800 households. Respondents were asked to consider 16 products that differed along the private-public and necessity-luxury dimensions. For each product they rated the extent of informational, value-expressive, and utilitarian reference group influence on both the choice of the product class and a brand. A summary of these results appears in Figure 5.8.

Figure 5.8 contains some interesting findings. Look at the upper left quadrant, for example. Here we encounter public consumption of a necessity in which there is weak reference group influence on choice of the *product* but strong influence on selection of the *brand*. A wristwatch is worn out of necessity, and it is of little consequence what others do. But brand choice is quite different, an example being the high social acceptability in some quarters signified by wearing a Rolex. As you read through these four quadrants, you gain helpful insights into the ways in which social influence becomes expressed.

Word-of-Mouth Influence

As we have already stated, consumers frequently turn to others, especially friends and family members, for opinions about products and services. The transmitter of this information is referred to as an **influential**. Over the years, the influential also has been labeled as an *opinion leader*, but we prefer to avoid this term because of the connotation that the transmitter has a dominant position over a so-called "follower." As you will see, word-of-mouth influence usually is not expressed in such a hierarchical pattern.

When are consumers most likely to accept and respond to word-of-mouth communication? Based on more than 30 years of research, it is safe to conclude that personal influence in the form of opinion leadership is most likely when one or more of these conditions and situations are present:

1. The consumer lacks sufficient information to make an adequately informed choice.
2. The product is complex and difficult to evaluate using objective criteria. Hence the experience of others serves as "vicarious trial."[22]
3. The person lacks ability to evaluate the product or service, no matter how information is disseminated and presented.
4. Other sources are perceived as having low credibility.
5. An influential person is more accessible than other sources and hence can be consulted with a saving of time and effort.
6. Strong social ties are in existence between transmitter and receiver.[23]
7. The individual has a high need for social approval.

Models of the Personal Influence Process

Personal influence has been theorized as working in three different ways: (1) trickle down, (2) a two-step flow, or (3) multistage interaction.

The Trickle-Down Theory
The oldest theory of personal influence alleges that lower classes often emulate the behavior of their higher-class counterparts.[24] In other words, influence is transmitted vertically through social classes, especially in the area of new fashions and styles. Presumably those in the higher classes express wealth through "conspicuous consumption," and their behavior is copied, when possible, by those in lower social strata.

The trickle-down theory is rarely seen demonstrated today in economically developed countries. The reason is that new fashions are disseminated overnight through mass media and quickly copied on a mass-merchandise basis. It still is observed, however, in underdeveloped economies when access to the mass media is restricted or absent altogether. Even here, however, it is rapidly disappearing.

It is far more common for this type of influence to occur among peers. This has come to be known as **homophilous influence**, a term that refers to information transmission between those who are similar in social class, age, education, and other demographic characteristics.[25] As we have demonstrated, reference group impact is often greatest when there is at least some degree of prior association and relationship.

A Two-Step Flow   In 1948, Lazarsfeld and his colleagues observed that new ideas and other influences flow from the mass media to influentials who, in turn, pass them on through word of mouth to others who are more passive in information seeking and far less exposed to the mass media and other sources.[26]

Although this model was a historic breakthrough for its time, there is ample reason now to question its accuracy. The primary reason is the audience is not as passive as the theory assumes. It is apparent, first of all, that the mass media have a widespread impact that is not confined to the influential. Furthermore, the initiative does not necessarily lie with the influential, as the theory assumed. Word-of-mouth communication is equally, if not more often, initiated by the receiver who is seeking the advice of a credible friend or relative.

A Multistage Interaction   Extensive research on the diffusion of innovations has largely invalidated the two-step flow model by demonstrating that both influential and seeker are affected by the mass media. In fact, mass media can motivate the seeker to approach someone else for advice rather than vice versa. Rarely does the influential mediate the flow of mass media content, as the two-step theory assumes.

At one time it was accepted that advertisers and other commercial persuaders would achieve greatest impact by concentrating only on the influential. It was assumed, of course, that they would pass on what they learned from the media. Current understanding shows that both the influential and the seeker are legitimate targets.

The Influential

How do we find the influentials? What type of people are they? What motivates them to share their experience? These questions have stimulated extensive research over the years in many countries of the world,[27] and it now is possible to advance some valid generalizations.

Research Methods   There are three basic ways to identify the influential:

1. *Sociometric*—people are asked to identify other people they seek out for advice or information in making a particular type of decision.
2. *Key informant*—knowledgeable people are used to identify the influentials within a social system.
3. *Self-designation*—people are asked to evaluate the extent to which they are sought out for advice.

The first two methods do not find widespread use in marketing research because of the focus on a specific, identifiable existing group. There are times, however, when a high-rise apartment complex or a neighborhood is the focus. When that is the case, the key-informant method is usually preferred because of greater ease of administration.

When many groups are targeted, the self-designation method is preferred. It is designed to be used on a wide scale, and it appears to have acceptable validity. The objective is to identify whether certain types or categories of people serve as influentials and not to designate the individuals themselves by name. If they can be identified and isolated from others as a distinct market segment, then it is possible to direct marketing efforts their way. An example of a multi-item scale designed for this purpose appears in Table 5.1.

TABLE 5.1 A Self-Designating Scale Used for Isolating an Influential Person

(1) In general, do you like to talk about _____ with your friends?
Yes _____— No _____—2

(2) Would you say *you give very little information, an average amount of information,* or *a great deal of information* about _____ to your friends?
You give very little information _____—1
You give an average amount of information _____—2
You give a great deal of information _____—3

(3) During the *past six months,* have *you told anyone* about some _____ ?
Yes _____—1 No _____—2

(4) Compared with your circle of friends, are you *less likely, about as likely,* or *more likely* to be asked for advice about _____ ?
Less likely to be asked _____—1
About as likely to be asked _____—1
More likely to be asked _____—3

(5) If you and your friends were to discuss _____, what part would *you* be most likely to play? Would you *mainly listen* to your friends' ideas or would *you try to convince them* of your ideas?
You mainly listen to your friends' ideas _____—1
You try to convince them of your ideas _____—2

(6) Which of these happens more often? Do *you tell your friends* about some _____, or do *they tell you* about some _____ ?
You tell them about _____—1
They tell you about _____—2

(7) Do you have the feeling that you are generally regarded by your friends and neighbors as a good source of advice about _____ ?
Yes _____—1 No _____—2

Source: Charles W. King and John O. Summers, "Generalized Opinion Leadership in Consumer Products: Some Preliminary Findings," paper no. 224 (Lafayette, Indiana: Institute for Research in the Behavioral, Economic and Management Sciences, Krannert Graduate School of Industrial Administration, January 1969), 16.

Characteristics   Extensive research on the characteristics of the influential is summarized in Table 5.2. It is safe to conclude that source and receiver are similar to one another in terms of demographic characteristics and lifestyle (that is, they are homophilous).[28] Evidence also shows that the person who provides the information also is a seeker in other situations.[29]

One issue of importance is whether the influence process is product-specific (**monomorphic**) or overlapping into other product areas (**polymorphic**). While much of the earlier literature supported the monomorphic hypothesis, there now is evidence that word-of-mouth influence is quasi-generalized, in that most serve as influentials for related products but not for all products in general.[30]

Motivations   Generally speaking, people will not share their experience with products or services unless the conversation produces some type of gratification. The motivations that drive such interactions fall into one or more of the following categories: (1) involvement, (2) self-enhancement, (3) concern for others, (4) message intrigue, and (5) dissonance reduction.

Involvement   First, the tendency to initiate conversations is directly proportional to the extent of interest or involvement in the topic under consideration.[31] A young executive is the first among his/her peers to have a new high-resolution television set complete with a built-in VCR. Telling others can serve as an outlet for pleasure or excitement caused by or resulting from its purchase and use.

TABLE 5.2   Characteristics of the Influential

Demographic
There is wide variation from one product category to another:
Young women dominate for fashions and movie-going.
Women with many children are consulted about self-medication.
Demographics usually show low correlation and are not a good predictor.

Social Activity
Gregariousness is the most frequently found predictor of opinion leadership.

General Attitudes
Opinion leaders are innovative and positive toward new products.

Personality and Lifestyle
Personality measures generally do not correlate with opinion leadership.
Opinion leaders tend to be more socially active, fashion conscious, and independent.

Product Related
Opinion leaders are more interested in the topic under discussion than others are. Fashion is an example.
They are active searchers and information gatherers, especially from the mass media.

Self-Enhancement   Many years ago Dichter suggested that word-of-mouth initiation can perform such functions as gaining attention, showing connoisseurship, suggesting status, giving the impression of possessing inside information, and asserting superiority.[32] For example, it is not uncommon for this to take the form of "insider information"—"I've just discovered the greatest Ethiopian restaurant."

Concern for Others   Conversation also is precipitated simply by a genuine desire to help a friend or relative make a better purchase decision. Old-fashioned altruism is not at all uncommon, especially when social ties are strong.

Message Intrigue   Some people find it entertaining to talk about certain ads or selling appeals. Who can deny the word-of-mouth that occurs when jokes are made of the Jolly Green Giant or the person who squeezes the Charmin?

Dissonance Reduction   Finally, research suggests that word of mouth is sometimes used to reduce cognitive dissonance (doubts) following a major purchase decision.[33] As we discuss in Chapter 18 and elsewhere, dissatisfied customers can be dangerous. It is not unusual for them to vent anger by disparaging the product or brand. Marketers worldwide are discovering that negative information of this type can have a decided impact on potential buyers.

The Impact of Word-of-Mouth Communication

Here is what we know about the effects of personal influence on consumer behavior.

Comparison with Other Media   First, research consistently demonstrates that personal influence generally has a more decisive role in influencing behavior than advertising and other marketer-dominated sources.[34] The issue of greater perceived credibility is most often the deciding factor. It is common to assume that another consumer has no ulterior or commercially motivated reasons for sharing information.

Source- versus Seeker-Initiated Conversation   Word of mouth can be initiated by either the source or the receiver, and the impact usually is strongest when the receiver plays this role.[35] The difference no doubt arises from the fact that a seeker is motivated to attend to and process the information, whereas that may not be the case when the source is the initiator.

Negative versus Positive Information   More than a third of all word-of-mouth information is negative in nature, and evidence indicates that it usually is given higher priority and assigned a greater weight in decision making.[36] No doubt this occurs because marketer-dominated communication will be uniformly positive, thus making the potential buyer all the more alert to anything that provides a different perspective. Also, the dissatisfied buyer is more motivated to share.[37]

Verbal versus Visual Information   Information can be passed interpersonally in either verbal or visual form. To the extent that information can be given visually, through observation or actual product demonstration, the greater will be the impact in terms of awareness and stimulation of interest. On the other hand, verbally communicated information has a stronger effect on thinking and evaluation.[38] Ideally, both visual and verbal will work in combination.

Marketing Strategy Implications of Personal Influence

Positive word of mouth can be one of the marketer's greatest assets, whereas the opposite can be true when the content is negative. Personal influence, of course, cannot be directly controlled by a business firm, but it can be stimulated and channeled in many ways.

Monitoring the Content of Word of Mouth
At the very least it is necessary to monitor whether or not word-of-mouth communication is occurring and the impact it is having. For example, Coca-Cola examined the communication patterns undertaken by those who had complained to the company.[39] Here are some of the major conclusions:

1. More than 12 percent told 20 or more people about the response they had received from the company.
2. Those who were completely satisfied with the response told a median of 4 to 5 others about their positive experience.
3. Nearly 10 percent who were completely satisfied increased their purchases of company products.
4. Those who felt they were not treated adequately communicated this fact to a median of 9 to 10 other people.
5. Nearly a third who felt their complaints were not dealt with adequately refused to buy any more company products, and another 45 percent reduced their purchases.

Although involvement is usually a predisposing factor for social influence, this example shows how extensive word of mouth can be, even for a low-involvement product such as a soft drink. This was further demonstrated during the now legendary "cola war," in which consumers overwhelmingly rejected "New Coke" and let their feelings be known (for more detail, see Chapter 18).

Focus-group research is often the best method for monitoring influence. From 8 to 12 people are brought together and guided by a moderator to discuss appropriate issues. When personal influence is taking place, its nature and impact quickly become evident because most people are willing to talk about products and their experiences. This is especially true when involvement is high.

Primary Reliance on Word of Mouth
On some occasions it is possible to rely on word-of-mouth communication as a substitute for advertising. This was done by Anheuser-Busch when a new ultrapremium beer was introduced into test market.[40] Admittedly, it is highly unusual to omit advertising and sales efforts entirely and few would risk this step. Wal-Mart Stores, on the other hand, has demonstrated that advertising can be sharply reduced when word of mouth is strong. This strategy is described in Consumer in Focus 5.3.

Consumer in Focus   5.3

No. 1 Retailer Relies on Word of Mouth, Not Ads

Wal-Mart Stores, the nation's new No. 1 retailer, plans to quadruple sales and be a $125 billion company by the year 2000.

The retailer's phenomenal growth won't necessarily be a windfall for the advertising and media industries, however. Wal-Mart has achieved its success while holding the lowest ratio of ad spending to retail sales among its peers.

The retailer's thrifty position isn't an indictment against advertising, industry analysts say. Instead, it's representative of Wal-Mart's superior management skills.

"I think [Wal-Mart's low ad budget] is a testimony to how well they run their stores," said William N. Smith, an analyst with Smith Barney, Harris Upham & Co. "Wal-Mart's got what the customer wants at the price they'll pay. They have not needed more advertising." Stacy Dutton, an equity research analyst with Morgan Stanley & Co., agreed: "Wal-Mart is a company built on word-of-mouth reputation."

"Most advertising in retail is for [price] specials," said William "Woody" Whyte, an analyst with Stephens Inc. "Since Wal-Mart has everyday low prices, it mitigates the needs to advertise specials." The consistent pricing, in turn, generates customer good will, he said. "If the retailer has an item at 40% off this week, the customer thinks, 'Why wasn't it 40% off last week? Are they raping, robbing, and pillaging all year?'

But low prices alone didn't make Wal-Mart a success. Its broad selection of merchandise, fully stocked shelves and superior customer service keep satisfied customers coming back, retail analysts say. Wal-Mart does use heavy media support for store grand openings, but advertising usually drops off to monthly circulars afterward.

But image advertising is important. When everyday low prices became the retail buzzword in the late 1980s, Wal-Mart introduced a TV and print image campaign asserting its longstanding pricing policies. "Always the low price on the brands you trust—always" is the theme of that campaign, still running from GSD & M, Austin, Texas.

Source: Christy Fisher, "Wal-Mart's Way," *Advertising Age* (February 18, 1991), 3 and 48.

Using the Influential as a Market Target   Although the two-step flow has largely been abandoned, it cannot be denied that influentials are sensitive to various sources of information, including advertising.[41] It is at least theoretically feasible to view them as a distinct market segment, *if they can be identified*. You will recall that identification can present quite a research challenge because of the similarity (homophily) between sender and receiver.

Even if they can be identified, however, their media exposure patterns often do not differ in any meaningful ways from those of receivers. Hence, it may be impossible to mount strategies that reach only this segment. The only exception is when certain types of social or organizational leaders are known to play the role of influentials. Examples are coaches, physicians, pharmacists, and pastors.

When identification is feasible, there are several possible strategies. One of the most common is to establish them as the target of space advertising, direct mail, and publicity releases aimed at them. As we discuss in Chapter 22, it is possible to buy mailing lists for coaches, teachers, and other specialized professions. Another option is to use the general media, knowing full well that there will be waste resulting from the large number of nonprospects. Sometimes there is no other option.

Stimulating Word of Mouth   At times there is benefit in either loaning or giving known influentials a product to display and use. The Ford Motor Company used this approach as part of its strategy to promote the 1984 Thunderbird.[42] Invitations were mailed to over 406,000 executives and professional people, giving them the opportunity to drive the car for a day, and about 15,000 took advantage. While only 10 percent became buyers, 84 percent indicated they would recommend the Thunderbird to a friend.

Creating Influentials   Next, it is sometimes possible to hire or directly involve those who seem to have the characteristics of an influential. Department stores and other clothing retailers, for example, have experimented with hiring the most popular young people who then receive substantial discounts on clothing they purchase. Hospitals have coped with excess capacity by forming alliances with physicians, who often hold the key to which hospital is chosen.

Yet another possible approach is to provide incentives for new customers to attract others to the point of sale. Sometimes this is done by offering attractive product premiums or even outright financial rebates.

At times it is possible to activate information seeking through word of mouth. This can be done through ads that capture imagination and intrigue, especially through phrases or characters that become part of the everyday vernacular. A famous early example is the "thousands of tiny time pills" theme used when Contac was first introduced as a cold remedy. This phrase in itself stimulated a great deal of conversation. More recently, Wendy's Clara Peller and the bucolic spokespersons for Bartle & Jaymes wine coolers have frequently been the subject of amused conversations.

Another tactic is to use ads asking consumers to seek information. "Ask the person who owns one" is an example of this approach.

Demonstrations, displays, and trial usage also are helpful methods. For example, color television manufacturers sell their sets to hotels and motels at low prices partly because it can help generate consumer interest and information seeking. And automobile manufacturers make deals with rental companies on cars like the Lincoln Continental featured at Budget Rent-a-Car.

Curbing Negative Word of Mouth   You have started your car and suddenly it surges, out of control, forward or backward. This is exactly what happened with the 1986 Audi 5000S, according to more than 500 complaints made to the National Highway Traffic Safety Administration. Audi management initially refused to acknowledge any culpability for this problem, even after a "60 Minutes" exposé on television activated public outrage.

It took a drastic drop in sales to induce acknowledgment of a problem, product recall, and remedial repair.[43] It later turned out that Audi management was vindicated in their claims of innocence, but it has taken years to recover from this unfortunate attitude of public insensitivity.

What can be done in an instance like this? Certainly stonewalling (denying the problem) is not the answer. The Toshiba Corporation found out that resignation and public disgrace of top management did little to mitigate U.S. public outrage over the release of important military secrets in product sales to Russia. The company decided to take the major face-losing step of running ads in several major papers that were headlined, "Toshiba Corporation Extends Its Deepest Regrets to the American People." This was a step in the right direction, but it may have been too little and too late.

The best strategy usually is an immediate acknowledgment of a problem by a credible company spokesperson. It is important to recognize that negative word of mouth rarely goes away by itself. If matters are not dealt with promptly, the financial results could be immediate and catastrophic. We return to this issue in Chapter 18.

Summary

Personal influence often plays an important role in consumer decision making, especially when there are high levels of involvement and perceived risk and the product or service has public visibility. This is expressed both through reference groups and through word-of-mouth communication.

Reference groups are any type of social aggregation that can influence attitudes and behavior, including primary (face-to-face) groups, secondary groups, and aspirational groups. The influence occurs in three ways: (1) utilitarian (pressures to conform to group norms in thinking and behavior), (2) value-expressive (reflecting a desire for psychological association and a willingness to accept values of others without pressure), and (3) informational (beliefs and behaviors of others are accepted as evidence about reality). When there is motivation to comply with group norms, it is important to make this a feature in marketing appeals.

Personal influence also is expressed through what has traditionally been referred to as "opinion leadership." What this means is that a credible person, referred to as an "influential," is accepted as a source of information about purchase and use. Usually the influential and the seeker are similar in characteristics, and both are influenced by mass media. The greater the credibility of the influential, the greater his or her impact upon other people.

Marketers can capitalize on personal influence by monitoring word of mouth and attempting to curb it when it is negative. Other strategies include creating new influentials, stimulating information seeking through this source, relying entirely on interpersonal influence to promote products, and combating negative word of mouth.

Review and Discussion Questions

1. For which of the following products would you expect personal influence to be a factor in buying decisions: soft drinks, motor oil, designer jeans, eyeliner, house paint, breakfast cereals, wine, carpeting, a dishwasher, and a 35mm camera? What are your reasons in each case?

2. Regarding each product listed in Question 1, do you think there could be a variation between personal influence on product choice and on brand name? Why do you say this?

3. Would any of the products in Question 1 be subject to personal influence coming from normative compliance? From value expression? From informational influence?

4. Assume that you are a consultant for a manufacturer of men's clothing. How would you go about identifying influentials on the college campus?

5. Recall the last time you volunteered information to someone about a brand or product that you purchased. What caused you to share in this way? How does your motivation compare with the motivations mentioned in the text?

6. In what ways do influentials differ from those who are information seekers?

7. Defend the conclusion mentioned in the text that influentials, as a rule, have a greater impact on consumer decision than advertising or personal selling.

8. Your company manufactures a full line of mobile homes in all price ranges. Several studies have indicated that word-of-mouth communication plays a role in the buying decision. Prepare a statement indicating the alternative strategies that can be utilized to harness and capitalize upon this source of consumer influence. Which strategy do you think would be most effective?

9. Assume that you are a public relations consultant for a state medical society concerned about public attitudes toward malpractice claims. The problem is to counteract a point of view, picked up through word-of-mouth monitoring, that filing a malpractice claim against a doctor is an easy way to pay medical bills or to get something for nothing. What can be done to attack this way of thinking?

Endnotes

1. Judith Langer as quoted in Gary M. Stern, "Future Forecasts," *USAir Magazine* (March 1991), 28.

2. Francesca Turchiano, "The (Un)Malling of America," *American Demographics* (April 1990), 39.

3. William O. Bearden and Michael J. Etzel, "Reference Group Influence on Product and Brand Purchase Decisions," *Journal of Consumer Research* 9 (September 1982), 184.

4. Solomon E. Asch, "Effects of Group Pressure on the Modification and Distortion of Judgments," in H. Guetzkow, ed., *Groups, Leadership, and Men* (Pittsburgh, Penn.: Carnegie Press, 1951).

5. Lee Ross, Gunter Bierbrauer, and Susan Hoffman, "The Role of Attribution Processes in Conformity and Dissent: Revisiting the Asch Situation," *American Psychologist* (February 1976), 148–157.

6. M. Venkatesan, "Experimental Study of Consumer Behavior Conformity and Independence," *Journal of Marketing Research* 3 (November 1966), 384–387.

7. Robert E. Witt and Grady D. Bruce, "Group Influence and Brand Choice," *Journal of Marketing Research* 9 (November 1972), 440–443.

8. James C. Ward and Peter H. Reingen, "Sociocognitive Analysis of Group Decision Making Among Consumers," *Journal of Consumer Research* 17 (December 1990), 245–262.

9. See William O. Bearden and Randall L. Rose, "Attention to Social Comparison Information: An Individual Difference Factor Affecting Consumer Conformity," *Journal of Consumer Research* 16 (March 1990), 461–472 and William O. Bearden, Richard G. Netemeyer, and Jesse E. Teel, "Measurement of Consumer Susceptibility to Interpersonal Influence," *Journal of Consumer Research* 15 (March 1989), 473–481.

10. George Homans, *Social Behavior: Its Elementary Forms* (New York: Harcourt, 1961).

11. Mason Haire, "Projective Techniques in Marketing Research," *Journal of Marketing* 14 (April 1950), 649–656.

12. Stephen A. LaTour and Ajay K. Manrai, "Interactive Impact of Informational and Normative Influence on Donations," *Journal of Marketing Research* 26 (August 1989), 327–335; Paul W. Miniard and Joel E. Cohen, "Modeling Personal and Normative Influences on Behavior," *Journal of Consumer Research* 10 (September 1983), 169–180. Also, Bearden and Etzel, "Reference Group Influence;" C. Whan Park and V. Parker Lessig, "Students and Housewives: Differences in Susceptibility to Reference Group Influence," *Journal of Consumer Research* 4 (September 1977), 102–109; George P. Moschis, "Social Comparison and Informal Group Influence," *Journal of Marketing Research* 13 (August 1976), 237–244; and M. Venkatesan, "Consumer Behavior: Conformity and Independence," *Journal of Marketing Research* 3 (November 1966), 384–387.

13. Bearden and Etzel, "Reference Group Influence."

14. David F. Midgley, Grahame R. Dowling, and Pamela D. Morrison, "Consumer Types, Social Influence, Information Search and Choice," in Thomas K. Srull, ed., *Advances in Consumer Research* 16 (Provo, Utah: Association for Consumer Research, 1989), 137–143.

15. Miniard and Cohen, "Modeling Personal and Normative Influence."

16. "31 Major Trends Shaping the Future of American Business," *The Public Pulse* 2 (1986), 1; Park and Lessig, "Students and Housewives"; and Robert E. Burnkrant and Alan Cousineau, "Informational and Normative Social Influence in Buyer Behavior," *Journal of Consumer Research* 2 (December 1975), 206–215.

17. Émile Durkheim, *Suicide*, trans. by George Simpson (New York: Free Press, 1951). For a cultural perspective, see Robert Merton, "Anomie, Anomia, and Social Interaction: Contexts of Deviate Behavior," in M. B. Clinard, ed., *Anomie and Deviate Behavior* (New York: Free Press, 1964).

18. Burnkrant and Cousineau, "Informational and Normative Social Influence."

19. Bobby Calder and Robert Burnkrant, "Interpersonal Influence on Consumer Behavior: An Attribution Theory Approach," *Journal of Consumer Research* 4 (June 1977), 29–38.

20. Arch G. Woodside and William Davenport, Jr., "The Effect of Salesman Similarity and Expertise on Consumer Purchasing Behavior," *Journal of Marketing Research* 11 (May 1974), 198–203. Also see Paul Busch and David T. Wilson, "An Experimental Analysis of a Salesman's Expert and Referent Bases on Social Power in the Buyer-Seller Dyad," *Journal of Marketing Research* 13 (February 1976), 3–11.

21. William O. Bearden and Michael J. Etzel, "Reference Group Influence on Product and Brand Purchase Decisions," *Journal of Consumer Research* 9 (September 1982), 181–186.

22. William L. Wilkie, *Consumer Behavior* (New York: Wiley, 1986), 160.

23. Jacqueline Johnson Brown and Peter H. Reingen, "Social Ties and Word-of-Mouth Referral Behavior," *Journal of Consumer Research* 14 (December 1987), 350–362.

24. Thorstein Veblen, *The Theory of the Leisure Class* (New York: Macmillan, 1899); and George Simmel, "Fashion," *International Quarterly* 10 (1904), 130–155.

25. Lazarsfeld and Robert K. Merton, "Friendship as Social Process: A Substantive and Methodological Analysis," in Monroe Berger, *et al.*, eds., *Freedom and Control in Modern Society* (New York: Octagon, 1964).

26. Paul F. Lazarsfeld, Bernard R. Berelson, and Hazel Gaudet, *The People's Choice* (New York: Columbia University Press, 1948), 151.

27. See, especially, Everett M. Rogers, *Diffusion of Innovations*, 3rd ed. (New York: Free Press, 1983). Also most of the pertinent references have been cited in the first five editions of this book.

28. See Brown and Reingen, "Social Ties and Word-of-Mouth."

29. Feick, Price, and Higie, "People Who Use People."

30. James H. Myers and Thomas S. Robertson, "Dimensions of Opinion Leadership," *Journal of Marketing Research* 9 (February 1972), 41–46; Charles W. King and John O. Summers, "Overlap of Opinion Leadership Across Consumer Product Categories," *Journal of Marketing Research* 7 (February 1970), 43–50; and Edwin J. Gross, "Support for Generalized Marketing Leadership Theory," *Journal of Advertising Research* (November 1969), 49–52.

31. Meera P. Venkatraman, "Opinion Leadership: Enduring Involvement and Characteristics of Opinion Leaders: A Moderating or Mediating Relationship," in Marvin E. Goldberg, Gerald Gorn, and Richard W. Pollay, *Advances in Consumer Research* 17 (Provo, Utah: Association for Consumer Research, 1990), 60–67.

32. Ernest Dichter, "How Word-of-Mouth Advertising Works," *Harvard Business Review* (November–December 1966), 147–166.

33. Hubert Gatignon and Thomas S. Robertson, "A Propositional Inventory for New Diffusion Research," *Journal of Consumer Research* 11 (March 1985), 849–867.

34. For a review of relevant research see Linda L. Price and Lawrence F. Feick, "The Role of Interpersonal Sources and External Search: An Informational Perspective," in Kinnear, ed., *Advances*, 250–255. Examples of current studies are Paul M. Herr, Frank R. Kardes, and John Kim, "Effects of Word-of-Mouth and Product-Attribute Information on Persuasion: An Accessibility-Diagnosticity Perspective," *Journal of Consumer Research* 17 (March 1991), 454–462; and Theresa A. Swartz and Nancy Stephens, "Information Search for Services: The Maturity Segment," in Kinnear, ed., *Advances*, 244–249.

35. Gatignon and Robertson, "A Propositional Inventory."

36. Marsha L. Richins, "Word of Mouth Communication as Negative Information," in Kinnear, ed., *Advances*, 697–702. Also Richard W. Mizerski, "An Attribution Explanation of the Disproportionate Influence of Unfavorable Information," *Journal of Consumer Research* 9 (December 1982), 301–310.

37. John H. Holmes and John D. Lett, Jr., "Product Sampling and Word of Mouth," *Journal of Advertising Research* 17 (October 1977), 35–40.

38. Gatignon and Robertson, "A Propositional Inventory."

39. *Measuring the Grapevine: Consumer Response and Word-of-Mouth*, the Coca-Cola Company, 1981.

40. Scott Hume, "Anheuser Beer Arrives Without Ads," *Advertising Age* (July 6, 1987), 2.

41. Jonathan Gutman and Michael K. Mills, "Fashion Lifestyle and Consumer Information Usage: Formulating Effective Marketing Communications," in Bruce J. Walker, *et al.*, eds., *An Assessment of Marketing Thought and Practice* (Chicago: American Marketing Association, 1982), 199–203.

42. Meg Cox, "Ford Pushing Thunderbird with VIP Plan," *The Wall Street Journal* (October 17, 1983), 37.

43. John E. Pluennecke and William J. Hampton, "Can Audi Fix a Dented Image?" *Business Week* (November 17, 1986), 81–82.

6

Family and Household Influences

Americans are waiting longer and longer to get married these days, the Census Bureau reports. The average first-time bride is older than at any time in the last century. Postponing nuptials is one way to cope with the increasing complexity of U.S. life. People are delaying marriage because their lives have become more entangled with school, career, and other things, said Martha Farnsworth Riche, a sociologist with the Population Reference Bureau in Washington, D.C.

Men typically are slightly older than 26 when they first marry and women are nearly 24, the bureau found. Twenty years ago, men on average were about 23 when they tied the knot for the first time; women were almost 21.

The Census Bureau survey also found the proportion of women in their early thirties who had never walked down the aisle nearly tripled to 16 percent in 1990 from 6 percent in 1970. There were 2.9 million unmarried couples living together, up 80 percent from 10 years earlier.

Besides deferring marriage, young adults also are putting off the day when they leave their parents' homes. One-third of people in their late twenties who had never married still lived with their parents in 1990.

The Census Bureau started compiling statistics on the average of first marriage in 1890, when men wed at 26 and women at 22. In those days, when most people farmed, a couple didn't get married until they could afford to buy a house. But as people moved from farms into cities, they shrugged off that custom and began marrying younger and younger. The marrying age declined until 1956, when grooms were six months over 22 and brides were barely 20. Since then the marriage age has risen steadily as the U.S. factory economy has given way to today's more complex enterprises.

Source: Excerpts from "People Are Waiting Longer To Get Married, Study Shows," Columbus *Dispatch* (June 7, 1991), 3A.

Families and the Study of Consumer Behavior

The study of families and their relationship to buying and consumption is very important in the analysis of consumer behavior. The importance of the family arises for two reasons.

First, *many products are purchased by multiple consumers acting as a family unit.* Homes are an example of products purchased by both spouses, perhaps with involvement from children, grandparents, or other members of the extended family. Cars are usually purchased by families, with both spouses and sometimes a teenager involved in various stages of the decision. A favorite form of leisure for many families is visiting a regional shopping mall. The visit often involves multiple family members buying a variety of household items, clothing, and perhaps groceries. The trip may also involve all members in deciding at which restaurant or outlet in the food court to spend the family's disposable income.

Second, even when purchases are made by an individual, *the buying decision of the individual may be heavily influenced by other members of the family.* Children may buy clothing that is financed and sanctioned by parents. The influence of a teenager may also be substantial on the clothing purchases of a parent. Spouses and siblings compete with each other in the decision of how the family's income will be allocated to their individual desires. The person responsible for buying and preparing the family's food may act as an individual in the supermarket but be influenced by the preferences and power of the other family members. Even when people are "on their own" as individual households, they may prefer the same furniture style (or perhaps the opposite) as the family in which they were raised. The consumer may like the same foods and leisure activities and may drive the same brand of car as other family members. The influence of family on consumer decisions is pervasive.

The study of family consumer decisions is less common than the study of individuals as consumers. The reason for neglect in studying family buying is the *difficulty of studying the family as an organization.* Surveys are easier to administer to individuals than to families. Administering a questionnaire to an entire family requires access to all members at approximately the same time (difficult in today's environment), using language that has the same meaning to all family members (difficult with discrepancies in age or education), and interpreting results when members of the same family report conflicting opinions about what the family buys or relative influence in the decision (a common finding in family research).

Environmental Influences

Part 2 explores the role played by environmental influences on consumer behavior. The manner by which such information affects marketing strategy and tactics is illustrated by the following set of full-color ads. A brief description of the specific environmental factor at work accompanies each ad.

Social Class & Status

Services such as hotels create their marketing mix with social or income strata as the primary means of targeting a segment. As the price of a hotel room goes down, so do the level of amenities. Shangri-La's ad uses concrete imagery to convey the high standards of their services.

Swatch turns time into something special. Swatch by day Swatch by night. Swiss quality made affordable. Water and shock resistant. Swatch tells more than time...it makes a statement.

swatch⊞

spring/summer collection '92

Personal Influence

Swatch watches are known for their exceptional variety in a market that was formally controlled either by utility or a formal and traditional sense of fashion. Swatch's variety caters to two apparently disparate influences--aspirational and dissociative. To comply with the rules of fashion is aspirational. To demand that one's fashion be unique is dissociative. Delivering diversity and following through with continual adaptation has revolutionized the watch industry.

He may give you
diamonds
this holiday season.

You can give him
a star.

ENGINEERED LIKE NO OTHER
CAR IN THE WORLD

© 1991 Mercedes-Benz of N.A., Inc., Montvale, N.J.

Family and Household Influences

Marketers are increasingly aware that women can and will buy items formerly relegated to male buyers. Mercedes is advertising directly to professional and affluent women with an appeal to a sense of prestige and of quality engineering.

Situational Influences

Companies sponsor events that enhance their corporate image. Not surprisingly, many companies sponsor the U.S. Olympic Team and feature that support in their ads during Olympic years. Beginning in 1994, the summer and winter Olympics will alternate every two years and advertised sponsorship will play a role, capitalizing on themes including patriotism, teamwork, and personal excellence.

What Is a Family?

A **family** is a group of *two or more persons related by blood, marriage, or adoption who reside together*. The **nuclear family** is the immediate group of father, mother, and child(ren) living together. The **extended family** includes the nuclear family, plus other relatives, such as grandparents, uncles and aunts, cousins, and in-laws. The family into which one is born is called the **family of orientation**, whereas the one established by marriage is the **family of procreation**.

What Is a Household?

Household is another term frequently used when describing consumer behavior. Household differs from family in that household describes *all persons, both related and unrelated, who occupy a housing unit*. There are significant differences between the terms household and family even though they are sometimes used interchangeably. It is important to distinguish between these terms when examining data.

Household is becoming a more important unit of analysis for marketers because of the rapid growth in nontraditional families and nonfamily households. Among nonfamily households, the great majority consist of people living alone. The remaining nonfamily households include those consisting of elderly people living with nonfamily members and the relatively new census category POSSLQ, "Persons of Opposite Sex Sharing Living Quarters." Families are the largest category of households but nonfamily households are growing faster. One way to avoid the problem of whether to study families or households is to simply use the term consumer unit (CU) or minimal household unit (MHU). It is easier and sometimes just as useful to avoid the distinctions between each group and refer to CU or MHU buying behavior.[1]

Variables Affecting Family/Household Purchases

Consumer purchasing is affected by various family or household variables. The most important structural variables are the age of head of household or family, marital status, presence of children, and employment status. For example, families have higher median incomes than do households because of the greater number of employed individuals in families.

A categorization of the major household/family variables related to economic and marketing analysis was developed by Haverty. The following variables are included:

A. Household Production Functions
1. Purchasing Function
2. Household Production
3. Consumption Function
4. Labor Market Function
5. Family Maintenance Function

    B. Household Stocks (Resources)
       1. Information
       2. Financial Resources
       3. Market Goods
       4. Characteristics
       5. Time
    C. Exogenous or Predetermined Variables
       1. Data
       2. Labor Market Opportunities
       3. Product Market Opportunities
       4. Household Structure
       5. Satisfaction[2]

In this chapter, our analysis is limited to the above items that are most directly relevant to the development of marketing strategy.

Families are like corporations; they are organizations formed to accomplish particular functions more effectively than individuals on their own. The most obvious function that two people can accomplish better than one is to have children. Although consumer analysts may have no opinion on whether or not families should have children, they have enormous interest in whether or not they do. The economic consequences of children create the demand structure for clothing, food, furniture, homes, medical care, education, and other products. Children in a family cause decreased demand for other products, such as travel, some restaurants, adult clothing, and many discretionary items.

Sociological Variables Affecting Families

The family is a "buying center" and reflects the activities and influences of the individuals who make up the family. Individuals often buy products for the family as well as their own use. Marketers can sometimes understand these decisions better by focusing on sociological dimensions of how families make consumer decisions. Three variables that help explain the functioning of families include cohesion, adaptability, and communication.

Cohesion is the emotional bonding that family members have toward one another. It is a measure of how close to each other family members feel on an emotional level. Cohesion reflects a sense of connectedness to or separateness from other family members.

Family adaptability is the ability of a marital or family system to change its power structure, role relationships, and relationship rules in response to situational and developmental stress. Family adaptability is a measure of how well a family can meet the challenges presented by changing needs.

Communication is a facilitating dimension, critical to movement on the other two dimensions. Positive communication skills (such as empathy, reflective listening, supportive comments) enable families to share with each other their changing needs and preferences as they relate to cohesion and adaptability. Negative communication skills (such as double messages, double binds, criticism) minimize the ability of a family to share feelings, thereby restricting movement on the dimen-

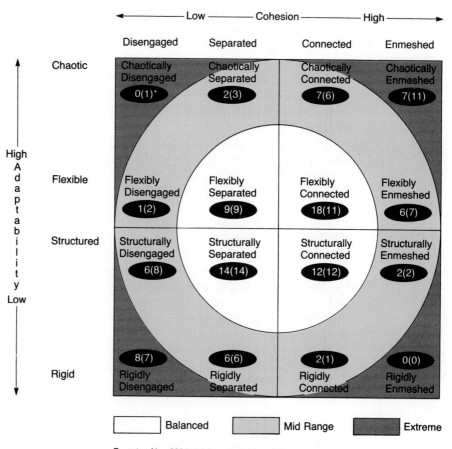

FIGURE 6.1   **This Classification of Families by Cohesion and Adaptability Is Useful to Marketers, Because These Factors Influence Consumption Decisions**

Source: David H. Olson et al., *Families: What Makes Them Work?* (Beverly Hills: Sage Publications, 1983), p. 90. Copyright 1983 by Sage Publications. Reprinted by permission.

sions of cohesion and adaptability. Understanding whether or not family members are satisfied with the products their families have purchased may require understanding communication within the family.

Families vary in their amount of cohesion and adaptability. In a major study of normal families in America, Olson and his associates found the 16 types of families shown in Figure 6.1, classified by whether couples are balanced, midrange, or extreme in cohesion and adaptability. The actual percentage of adults and adolescents falling into each of the 16 types is shown in the numbers in Figure 6.1 (the percentages for adolescents in the families studied are shown in parentheses). The four center cells represent the balanced types and the four corner cells, the extreme types. The mid-range types are represented by the other eight cells.[3]

Consumption decisions are influenced by the type of family in which an individual is a member. When cohesion levels are high (enmeshed systems), there is a high identification with the family. Such families do most things together and probably choose the same brands, colors, type of homes, and so forth. At the other extreme (disengaged systems), high levels of autonomy are encouraged and family members "do their own thing," with limited attachment or commitment to their family. In the central area of Figure 6.1 (separated and connected), individuals are able to experience and balance being independent from and connected to their family.

Some of the sociological research on how families function can be helpful in the development of marketing programs. For example, sociological research in recent years has increasingly focused on "resilient" families—those that are better able to negotiate their way through transitions and tragedies and to cope with or even thrive on life's hardships. Communication, social support, and hardiness (commitment to the family, ability to learn and grow together, and so on) are important variables in explaining how families cope. Of great interest to marketers, however, is that one of the most important variables in the development of resilient families is the importance given to family celebrations, family time and routines, and family traditions.[4]

Family celebrations are not only important to helping families survive crises, they are critically important to creating consumer demand for many products. Over 50 percent of retail sales and an even higher percentage of profits is normally generated by the Hannuka and Christmas holidays. Easter is a major factor in spring clothing sales and Valentine's Day, graduation, and other holidays usually are major events in annual marketing plans. Understanding gift giving and family holidays has become an important area of study by Belk, Hirschman, and others.[5] Advertising attempts to relate a family's holiday celebrations to consumption as do decorations by stores and shopping malls. Some of the most attractive attempts to relate to holidays are often ads by liquor brands as seen in Figure 6.2.

Who Determines What the Family Buys?

Families use products but individuals usually buy them. Determining what should be bought, how and when products are used, where they should be bought, and who should do the buying is a complicated process for most products involving a variety of roles and actors.

Role Behavior

Families and other groups exhibit what sociologist Talcott Parsons called instrumental and expressive role behavior. **Instrumental roles**, also known as functional or economic roles, involve financial aspects, performance characteristics, and other

FIGURE 6.2   Attempts to Stimulate Holiday Purchases

Source: Courtesy of Johnny Walker.

"functional" attributes such as conditions of purchase. **Expressive roles** involve support to other family members in the decision-making process and expression of aesthetic or emotional needs of the family, including upholding norms of the family. Choosing the color, product features, and retailer that fits most closely to the family's needs will be the outcome of role performance.

Marketing communications are usually directed to individuals but must take into consideration their roles in the families. Individuals are often influenced by other family members. For example, as Davis explains, "a husband may buy a station wagon, given the reality of having to transport four children, despite his strong preference for sports cars. . . . A housewife bases product and brand decisions to some extent on orders or requests from family members and on her judgment of what they like or dislike and what is 'good for them.'"[6]

Individual Roles in Family Purchases

Family consumption decisions involve at least five definable roles. These roles may be assumed by a husband, wife, children, or other members of a household. Both multiple roles and multiple actors are normal.

1. *Initiator/Gatekeeper*. Initiator of family thinking about buying products and the gathering of information to aid the decision.
2. *Influencer*. Individual whose opinions are sought concerning criteria the family should use in purchases and which products or brands most likely fit those evaluative criteria.
3. *Decider*. The person with the financial authority and/or power to choose how the family's money will be spent and the products or brands that will be chosen.
4. *Buyer*. The person who acts as purchasing agent: who visits the store, calls the supplier, writes the check, brings the products into the home, and so on.
5. *User*. The person or persons who use the product.

Marketers need to communicate with occupants of each role. Children, for example, are users of cereals, toys, clothing, and many other products but may not be the buyers. One or both of the parents may be the decider and the buyer, although the children may be important as influencers and as users. Parents may act as gatekeepers by preventing children from watching some TV programs or attempting to negate their influence by saying, "Toys don't really work like they appear on TV, you know." In Figure 6.3 you can see how a marketer is attempting to get agreement between parents and kids, recognizing the differing roles played by each.

Influencer roles may be taken by those with the most expertise. For example, a parent may be the decider about which car to purchase, but teenagers often play a major role as gatekeepers of information and as influencers because of greater knowledge about performance, product features, or social norms.

Spousal Roles in Buying Decisions

Which spouse is most important in family buying decisions? How does this vary by product category? How does this vary by stage of decision making? Generally, the following role-structure categories are used to analyze these questions:

1. Autonomic, when an equal number of decisions is made by each spouse, but each decision is individually made by one spouse or the other.
2. Husband dominant.
3. Wife dominant.
4. Syncratic, when most decisions are made by both husband and wife.

These categories are sometimes simplified to "husband more than wife," "wife more than husband," "both husband and wife," or simply "husband only," "wife only," or "children only." Which situation is likely to exist is influenced by the type of product, the stage in the decision process, and the nature of the situation surrounding the decision.

A landmark study investigating husband-wife influences was conducted by Harry Davis and Benny Rigaux.[7] Their findings are usually presented in the familiar triangular configuration shown in Figure 6.4 and have greatly influenced thinking about the relative influence of husbands and wives upon decision making and the extent of role specialization. This study was recently updated by Management Horizons, a division of Price Waterhouse, for use by businesses selling a wide variety of goods.[8]

FIGURE 6.3   Differing Roles in Family Purchases
Source: Courtesy of Kid Cuisine Mega Meals.

Overall Influence   Figure 6.4 displays measures of husbands' and wives' perceptions of their relative influence upon decision making across decision stages. Some product/service categories are wife dominant. They include women's clothing, children's clothing, pots and pans, and groceries. Two categories that are husband dominant include lawn mowers and hardware. Joint decisions tend to be made about vacations, television sets, refrigerators, and upholstered living room furniture. Autonomic decision making tends to be present in decisions about categories that include women's jewelry, men's leisure clothing, men's business clothing, sporting equipment, lamps, toys and games, indoor paint/wallpaper, and luggage.

Influence by Decision Stage   Figure 6.4 shows variation in the influence of spouses by stages in the decision-making process. This is indicated by the direction of the arrow, which shows movement from information search to final decision. This movement may be minimal in the case of many low-involvement goods but more pronounced for goods that are risky or have high involvement for the family. The decision process tends to move toward joint participation and away from autonomic behavior as a final decision nears. Movement is most pronounced

Relative Influence of Husbands and Wives

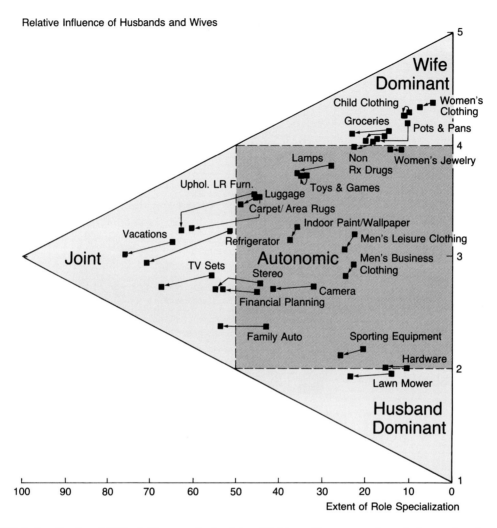

FIGURE 6.4 **Husband-Wife Influences in Decision Making: Movement from Information Search to Final Decision**

Source: © Management Horizons, a Division of Price Waterhouse. Reproduced with permission.

for refrigerators, a family auto, upholstered living room furniture, and carpets or rugs. Vacations are perhaps the most democratic of a family's purchase decisions.

Information-search stage is more autonomic than joint participation when compared to final decisions. Marketing plans thus require specialized use of media, such as magazines or other media having a strong appeal to either husbands or wives rather than both. Product or store design must reflect the evaluative criteria of both, however, as consensus on these must be achieved in the final decision. Separate campaigns may be timed to coincide with specialized interests, especially for products with a long planning cycle such as vacations and major purchases.

Consumer in Focus   6.1

Spousal Roles in the Supermarket

Men who have to ask a woman what's for dinner are on the way out. Women still do most of the food shopping. But men are getting more involved. Thirty-five percent of couples claim both the man and the woman are equally responsible for food shopping, according to a telephone survey of nearly 1,000 adults conducted by the Opinion Research Corporation for *Men's Health* magazine. Only 8 percent of couples say that the man does all or most of the food shopping, while 56 percent say the woman does all of the shopping.

Some experts say that men are helping take the burden off their overworked working wives and that men and women want egalitarian relationships. Peter Stein of William Paterson College in New Jersey says that a man might even experience a hunter-like feeling when he's shopping—like the primordial male coming home with the catch. Herb Goldberg, an L.A.-based psychologist, agrees: "I see food shopping as a latter-day version of food gathering. Instead of going into the woods, we go to the supermarket."

Source: Excerpted from "Tarzan of the Foodmart," *American Demographics* 12 (May 1990), 13.

Decline of Gender Differences

Changes in family structure over time are causing husband and wife decisions increasingly to be made jointly or syncratically. Qualls studied family decisions concerning vacations, automobiles, children's education, housing, insurance, and savings. All of these products had been studied extensively in prior decades and generally were reported to involve a minority of joint decisions. Qualls found overwhelmingly that joint decisions are now the norm for children's education and housing in 80 percent or more households. The majority shared decisions for the other products as well, although not as dramatically.[9] The Management Horizons Family Purchasing Study also found that increasing resources of women and shifts toward egalitarianism are producing more joint decision making in product/service categories of perceived high risk. In contrast, however, time pressures, brought about by larger numbers of dual-worker families, may produce more autonomic decisions in categories of perceived low risk. Notice in Consumer in Focus 6.1 the changing roles of men and women.

Consumer researchers must recognize that gender differences, despite movement away from sex-role dominance, still exist for some products and in some situations.[10] Also, advertising still includes sex-role dominance, perhaps by companies insensitive to such issues. Literature reviews of these areas are available in Jenkins;[11] Burns and Granbois;[12] and Gupta, Hagerty, and Myers.[13] But psychological gender differences in household decision making today is a low-yield area of research. Roberts explains: "It has never been very productive, and it will be even less productive in the future."[14]

There are many causes for the demise of gender differences in family buying decisions. Most have to do with the changing employment status and roles of women. The resource-contribution theory suggests that the greater the relative contribution of an individual, the greater the influence in decision making. A variation of this theory is called the "least interested partner" hypothesis, which states that the greater the value of one partner relative to the other as valued by society, the greater influence that partner will have. Gender-related consumer behavior still exists and is even pervasive in some types of purchasing decisions. Such roles are not determined by biological sex so much as the socialization experiences a person is likely to have and thus the consumer activities that will be learned by men and women.[15]

Family Life Cycles

Families change over time, passing through a series of stages. This process historically has been called the **family life cycle (FLC)**. The concept may need to be changed to Household Life Cycle (HLC) or Consumer Life Cycle (CLC) in the future to reflect changes in society, but for now we will continue using the most frequently researched term FLC popularized in marketing research by Wells and Gubar,[16] and later in a book by Reynolds and Wells showing how life cycle affects consumer behavior.[17]

Traditional FLC

The traditional FLC describes patterns found among families as they marry, have children, leave home, lose a spouse, and retire. These stages are described in Table 6.1, along with consumer behavior associated with each stage. Other versions, such as Murphy and Staples's, recognize contemporary developments of divorce, smaller sizes of families, and delayed age of marriage.[18]

Modified FLC Matrix

Marketing organizations may need to modify the traditional FLC to make it more specific to their analytical needs. Adding socioeconomic data, especially income, improves predictions about product choices such as clothing and helps in using the traditional FLC to explain consumer behavior.[19]

An example of a modified model reflecting contemporary lifestyles is the Consumer Market Matrix developed by Management Horizons, a division of Price Waterhouse. This matrix of consumer markets analyzes the interaction of income

TABLE 6.1   Traditional Life Cycles and Buying Behavior

Single Stage

Although earnings are relatively low, they are subject to few rigid demands, so consumers in this stage typically have substantial discretionary income. Part of this income is used to purchase a car and basic equipment and furnishings for their first residence away from home—usually an apartment. They tend to be more fashion and recreation oriented, spending a substantial proportion of their income on clothing, alcoholic beverages, food away from home, vacations, leisure time pursuits, and other products and services involved in the mating game.

Newly Married Couples

Newly married couples without children are usually better off financially than they have been in the past and will be in the near future because the wife is usually employed. Families at this stage also spend a substantial amount of their income on cars, clothing, vacations, and other leisure time activities. They also have the highest purchase rate and highest average purchase of durable goods, particularly furniture and appliances, and other expensive items, and appear to be more susceptible to advertising in this stage.

Full Nest I

With the arrival of the first child, some wives stop working outside the home, and consequently family income declines. Simultaneously, the young child creates new problems that change the way the family spends its income. The couple is likely to move into their first home; purchase furniture and furnishings for the child; buy a washer, dryer, and home maintenance items; and purchase such products as baby food, chest rubs, cough medicine, vitamins, toys, wagons, sleds, and skates. These requirements reduce family savings and the husband and wife are often dissatisfied with their financial position.

Full Nest II

At this stage the youngest child is six or over, the husband's income has improved, and the wife often returns to work outside the home. Consequently, the family's financial position usually improves. Consumption patterns continue to be heavily influenced by the children as the family tends to buy food and cleaning supplies in larger-sized packages, bicycles, pianos, and music lessons.

Full Nest III

As the family grows older, its financial position usually continues to improve because the husband's income rises, the wife returns to work or enjoys a higher salary, and the children earn money from occasional employment. The family typically replaces several pieces of furniture, purchases another automobile, buys several luxury appliances, and spends a considerable amount of money on dental services and education for the children.

Empty Nest I

At this stage the family is most satisfied with their financial position and the amount of money saved because income has continued to increase, and the children have left home and are no longer financially dependent on their parents. The couple often make home improvements, buy luxury items, and spend a greater proportion of their income on vacations, travel, and recreation.

Empty Nest II

By this time the household head has retired and so the couple usually suffers a noticeable reduction in income. Expenditures become more health-oriented, centering on such items as medical appliances; medical care products that aid health, sleep, and digestion; and perhaps a smaller home, apartment, or condominium in a more agreeable climate.

Continued

TABLE 6.1   continued

The Solitary Survivor

If still in the labor force, solitary survivors still enjoy a good income. They may sell their home and usually spend more money on vacations, recreation, and the types of health-oriented products and services mentioned above.

The Retired Solitary Survivor

The retired solitary survivor follows the same general consumption pattern except on a lower scale because of the reduction in income. In addition, these individuals have special needs for attention, affection, and security.

and lifestages on consumer behavior. It recognizes the increasing importance of aging of the population as well as the increased tendency for women either to delay having children to a later age or to choose not to have children.[20]

The major lifestages of households represent important market segments and are described as follows:

Younger Singles: Head of household single and under 45 with no children present.
Younger Couples: Married couple with head of household under 45 and no children present.
Younger Parents: Head of household under 45, with child(ren).
Mid-Life Families: Head of household between the ages of 45 and 64 with child(ren) either present in or financially supported by the household.
Mid-LifeHouseholds: Head of household between the ages of 45 and 64 with no child(ren) either present in or financially supported by the household.
Older Households: Head of household age 65 or older or retired.

The lifestage segments in the matrix are divided by income into

Down Market: The lower quartile of household income for a specific lifestage.
Middle Market: The two middle quartiles of household income for a specific lifestage.
Up Market: The upper quartile of household income for a specific lifestage.

This type of contemporary FLC matrix permits a quantitative analysis of the size of each market. Additional data are collected concerning preferences, expenditures, and shopping behavior of each segment. The objective is to attract core customers in the lifestage most profitable as the firm's target market. Close examination of the firm's marketing mix might reveal, for example, lack of a clearly defined offer, suggesting that the current marketing mix may be aimed at fringe rather than core customers.

The FLC helps explain how a specific family changes over time and modified forms are useful to identify core market targets. But the basic structure of families and households is changing in the United States, Canada, and other industrialized countries. In the next section, we examine trends in family and household structure. Many of these changes greatly affect marketing strategies and tactics.

FIGURE 6.5   Need Recognition Stage in the Changing Family
Source: Courtesy of State Farm.

Changing Family and Household Structure

What is the structure of contemporary families? How is that structure changing? How does structure affect consumption? Are the developing realities of family structure a problem or an opportunity for marketing organizations? These are some of the questions that consumer researchers try to answer. Many of the answers involve data from the decennial census and interim reports by the Bureau of Census. Figure 6.5, an ad for an insurance company, addresses the need recognition stage of the changing family. There are other topics relating to the family that could be mentioned such as the effects on families due to the aging of the population but we will cover these in later chapters on Consumer Resources and Consumer Trends.[21]

Married or Single?

Marriage: To be or not to be? That is the question. The answer is that marriage is in the cards for most consumers although they are delaying the age of first marriage, as the opening scenario of this chapter indicated. Approximately 90 percent of American adults marry at some time in their lives, but the proportion of consuming households composed of nonmarried individuals is increasing rapidly because of the delay in marriage and remarriage. Table 6.2 estimates changes in number of households by type in 1990 and 2000 and shows how rapidly the nonfamily households are increasing.

Smaller Households

Average household size is falling in most industrialized countries. In the United States it dropped from to 2.63 in 1990, down from 2.76 in 1980 and 3.14 in 1970. One-person households are now about 24 percent of the total, compared to 18 percent in 1970, and households with six or more persons dropped from 19.5 percent of all households to less than 6 percent today. Recent Census surveys disclose that only 26 percent of American households consist of a married couple with a child under 18, compared with 31 percent in 1980 and 40 percent in 1970.

Marketers are increasingly interested in single parent households. About 11 million of these are headed by a female with no husband present and about 3 million by a male householder with no wife present. Women without husbands maintain 13 percent of all white family households, 44 percent of all black family households and 23 percent of all Hispanic family households. The rate of increase in single black parenthood slowed during the last decade to 3.8 percent per year, while the rate for Hispanics more than doubled to 7 percent per year, the highest rate of increase for any racial group. About 24 percent of all American children, and about 55 percent of all black children, live in a single parent household.

Later Marriages

The median age at which people get married has increased substantially. Among males, the median age at first marriage was 22.8 in 1950 but increased to over 26 by 1990. For women, the median age increased from 20.3 to almost 24. In older mar-

TABLE 6.2   Households by Type: 1990–2000 Projections

	1990	2000	% Change 1990–2000
All households	95.2[a]	110.2	15.8
Family households	65.9	70.0	13.8
Married couples	51.7	52.3	1.1
Male householder	2.7	3.8	40.7
Female householder	11.5	13.9	20.9
Nonfamily households	29.3	40.2	37.2
Male householder	13.0	19.5	50.0
Female householder	16.3	20.7	27.0

[a]Numbers refer to millions.
Source: U.S. Bureau of the Census, Current Population Reports, Series P-25, No. 986, Series A Assumptions (reflecting recent changes in marriage and divorce trends).

riages, consumers may have to buy fewer of the basic furnishings and products needed for housekeeping but are able to buy better merchandise: higher-quality furniture, designer services, and so forth. Older marriages produce more extensive travel capabilities—perhaps a honeymoon in Grenada; a higher probability of owning two cars; and firmer preferences for styles, colors, and product designs since both the bride and the groom are likely to bring more housekeeping experience into the marriage.

Divorce and Consumer Behavior

The number of divorces increased for many years in the United States and in most other countries. A slight decrease in the rate has begun to occur attributed to various causes, such as later ages of marriage or the possibility that the pent-up demand of previous decades has simply been satisfied. Divorce contributes an added dimension to an analysis of consumer decision making. Consumers who have been previously married, sometimes called the "single again" market, carry with them preferences and shopping patterns learned in a family situation. They often carry financial problems that restrict their ability to buy the things that married couples or never-married singles might.[22]

In spite of recent declines in divorce rate, 51.6 percent of today's marriages end in divorce.[23] If a couple completes 10 years of marriage, the odds of divorce fall to 30 percent. Thus, while most people live most of their lives married, about half live part of their lives divorced.

Divorce creates markets. One family unit becomes two—with two households and two sets of household equipment. There are fewer divorced men because more men than women remarry and because men remarry sooner. Studies show that a man's income usually rises after a divorce while a woman's income usually falls, especially if she gets custody of children. For this reason, some divorced adults spend freely while others are forced into frugality. Both parties learn new patterns of consumer behavior.[24]

Remarriages and Redivorce

Most divorced people remarry. Markets in total, therefore, remain mostly married. Once-divorced couples are more likely, however, to be redivorced than are couples who have been married only once. Consumers who remarry, however, are more complex to analyze because they are often subject to the family influences from stepchildren. Also, there is potential conflict between siblings of the multiple families as well as continuing influences from former spouses on the children of their own households.

The problem of analyzing resource distribution and other consumption problems can make analysis of consumer behavior complex:

When a person enters into a remarriage, financial decision-making becomes more complex. After having spent some time in independent households, remarried partners must find some compatible way to handle their two economies. This may necessitate incorporating people from two separate households and two different generations who have different and/or opposing earning, spending, and saving habits. An additional factor complicates the family economy . . . financial responsibilities after remarriage may involve three or four adults across several households. In addition, the remarried family may be experiencing several different family stages simultaneously (for example, the newly married couple stage and the adolescent child stage). These two stages may conflict in their demands for resource distribution. That means problems may arise over whether to spend money for new household items versus a teenage child's request for a used car.[25]

Cohabiting Singles

Another category exists that is difficult to categorize as either family or single. Legally composed of singles, but functioning more as a family, cohabiting singles are the fastest-growing segment of the singles market. Although their numbers are small in proportion to the total number of households, the number of unmarried couples tripled from 523,000 in 1970 to 1.6 million in 1980, and increased by 80 percent to 2.9 million in 1990. Most are young and likely to have less income than married couples but nearly a third have at least one child. One study found that 8 percent are married to someone other than the person with whom they are cohabiting.[26]

A study financed by the National Institute of Health found that almost half of all Americans 25 to 35 have lived with an individual of the opposite sex outside of marriage, with a prediction that in the 1990s this practice will be a majority experience.[27]

Marketing to Singles

Some singles maintain their own households. Others live with their families or with other singles. Regardless of where they live they are a major target for marketing organizations and increasing in importance every year. Consumer in Focus 6.2 describes some of the ways companies seek to attract singles.

Singles Boom

There are more singles in the United States than ever before. Nearly 73 million adult Americans are not in married relationships, according to Census Bureau reports, an increase of 35 million from just 20 years ago. When those who are single due to death or divorce are included, the percentage of adult Americans who are not married has leaped from 28 percent in 1970 to 41 percent today. About one-fourth of men aged 30 to 34 have never been married and 1 in 6 aged 35 to 39 has never been married. The numbers of never-married women, while slightly smaller, have grown just as dramatically. These levels have tripled in 20 years. About 1 of every 4 occupied dwelling units has only 1 person in it. The notion that people must be married to be happy and productive is fading away in American society.

Marketing to Singles

Mary Kowalski dug into her savings account and packed her bags recently for two months in Italy and France. At 46, Mary has been divorced for years with no relationship on the horizon and travels with her two best women friends. A high-powered professional and torch carrier for new trends, Mary may be the perfect consumer for the 1990s. Free of the costs of braces, soccer shoes, Nintendos, and college tuition, singles like Mary Kowalski are an increasingly important market for products from furs and jewelry to real estate, foreign travel, cars, and even Drano.

Marketing successfully to singles means straddling traditional values and speaking about buying cars and whipping up dinner without talking down. Campbell Soup, for example, introduced "Soup for One," a single-serve portion. Singles liked the soup but they hated the name. They called it "The Lonely Soup" in focus groups. Campbell corrected the problem by expanding the line but dropped the reference to being for singles.

Honda invested heavily in ads in women's magazines and created a how-to guide for first-time women buyers. Today women account for more than half the sales of some Honda models. Two-thirds of the customers for jewelry are women. Not all of those are single but many are. Consequently, the World Gold Council runs ads that say, "When you really want to treat yourself, nothing makes you feel as good as gold."

Drano is running spots of an obviously single young man bouncing in the tub to the strains of "Splish, Splash" and then, after discovering the drain's clogged, pouring in a slug of Drano without skipping a beat. A generation ago, you would've had a guy saying, "Honey, I can't fix the drain," says Ann Clurman of Grey Advertising, the agency that created the spot.

According to research by ad agency Backer Spielvogel Bates, 32 percent of single Americans rely on brands from their youth. Only 23 percent of married parents responded similarly. Brands from childhood make them feel less lonely. "Without a mate," says psychologist Ross Goldstein, "single people look for products or services to satisfy their psychological needs—things like companionship, stimulation, security, connectedness."

Source: Excerpts from Jon Berry, "Forever Single," *Adweek's Marketing Week* 31 (October 15, 1990), 20–24.

Another reason for more singles is the increasing time between divorce and remarriage. Divorced women wait an average of 3.6 years before remarrying and divorced men wait an average of 3.2 years, figures that are both more than a year longer than in prior decades.[28]

Older Singles

Most singles (61 percent) are women, and of the 12 million women who live alone, the median age is 66. For the men the median age is 45. The demographics of single men and women are dramatically different because they are single for different reasons. Women live alone more because their husbands have died. Nearly half of all women over 75 are widows. Men live alone because they have not yet married or they are divorced.

The gap in life expectancy between men and women means that the largest fraction of singles in the foreseeable future will be elderly widows—with a median income of $8,000. Single men aren't exactly wealthy, either; their median annual income is only $14,000, but it is more likely to be from wages and salaries, whereas single women are more likely to receive monies from Social Security, other pensions, interest, and dividends. Consumer analysts will find most of this part of the "booming singles market" buying home-security devices, treatment for chronic health problems, congregate care facilities, and perhaps a sedate Caribbean cruise.

Younger Singles

Specialized media and products are often directed to the younger portions of the singles market. Magazines such as *Living Single* are examples. Resorts such as Club Med started out directed mostly to young singles but in recent years have broadened their appeal. There are miniaturized appliances for the condominium-size kitchen, and Corning Glass Works's small microwaveproof bowls for the cook who eats alone. Singles can list preferred birthday gifts in the Bloomingdale's Self-Registry, which works as any bridal registry does.

Home builders are also adapting since singles account for a fourth of first-time home buyers. Design changes include a lower number of bedrooms; decreasing dining room space; and an increase in kitchen area, which is becoming a living room to the single. Master bedrooms are more luxurious, bathrooms more spa like, and living space better equipped for high-tech entertainment.[29]

Gay Markets

Gay or lesbian consumers represent a segment of the market receiving increasing attention by marketing organizations. Most are classified as singles, although some jurisdictions may recognize the married status of some gay households and some gay individuals live in traditional family settings at least part of their lives. Reliable data concerning the size of the market are not available although it is estimated that as few as 6 percent or as high as 16 percent of adult Americans may be part of this market.[30]

The difficulty believed to exist for some marketers is how to target effectively the gay market without alienating their heterosexual customers. The risk may be worthwhile, however, because gay consumers are above average in income, relatively well-educated, and are likely to have higher proportions of disposable income. Gay and lesbian consumers are likely to travel extensively, spend considerable money on clothing, and express more interest in the arts. Often they are more aware of current social issues and politically active.

For the first time in history, the 1990 Census provides information on the number of same-sex couples and included a question in which gay couples had the opportunity to designate each other as an "unmarried partner" as opposed to "housemate/roommate." While this does not directly measure sexual orientation, the National Gay and Lesbian Task Force hopes to use the data to influence policy making in the areas of corporate health benefits, probate, adoption law, and AIDS treatment and prevention. Some private companies, such as Overlooked Opinions, Inc., conduct ongoing panels reporting data on homosexual consumers.[31]

Targeting gay and lesbian markets can be accomplished in a variety of ways. Understanding their needs is the preface to each. Commercial research firms such as Overlooked Opinions have created a panel of 12,000 gay men, lesbians, and bisexuals, representing every state and all major markets. Research from this panel indicates that the gay market is not only very affluent but is very image conscious. Targeting gays, for example, might show a refrigerator stocked with Beck's Dark and brie instead of an ad targeted to straights that would show a mass market beer and Cheese Whiz.

The primary marketing technique in reaching the gay market is simply to recognize that the market exists and to be willing to establish a relationship with this segment of the market. This can be done by participation in or sponsorship of activities considered important by gay consumers, such as sponsorship of AIDS research or community events relating to AIDS. Corporations can also create considerable awareness among the gay community by sponsorship of operas, ballets, classical concerts, and museums that attract high participation among the gay community, while at the same time also reaching the wider community.

Marketers may also advertise in gay-oriented media which exist at both the local and national levels. It is believed that such advertisers generate high loyalty among gay readers for advertising in those media without alienating homophobic consumers who do not read such media.[32] One of the largest of 175 gay newspapers is the *Advocate* which also rents its subscription list for direct mail promotions. Other advertisers use the straight media but design ads with a sensitivity that attracts gays. An ad for Paco Rabanne cologne, for example, has an ad that shows a man sprawled on a bed. The copy makes no specific mention of gender, which sends a message to gay men without offending straight customers.[33]

Changing Roles of Women

Marketing managers have always been interested in women because female consumers buy so many products. Interest in female consumers has intensified in recent years because of greater numbers of women, improved purchasing and employment status, and changed roles of women.

The female population is growing faster than the male population due to a higher survival rate for women. Life expectancy has increased more for women than for men. Controversy exists about why women live so much longer than men. Many observers thought that when women have equal representation in high-stress jobs, such as corporate executives, their life expectancy would be similar to men's. In fact, women handle stress better than men, possibly because estrogen may be better adapted than testosterone for the flight-or-fight situations of modern life. Whatever the reasons, females now exceed males by 6.5 million. This figure is expected to be 7.5 million by the year 2000.

More women attend colleges or universities than do men, in sharp contrast to the past. The principal reason females outnumber males on college campuses today is the greater number of women over 25 returning to campus. Some other differences between men and women are described in Table 6.3, some culturally determined and some genetically determined. Some of these may explain differences in the greater purchase of perfume based on greater sensitivity to smell, why health-care organizations have women as their primary market target, and other common differences in marketing to women and to men.

Feminine roles are of great concern today to consumer analysts and marketers. A **role** specifies what the typical occupant of a given position is expected to do in that position in a particular social context.[34] Consumer analysts are especially concerned with gender roles of women in the family and in their position as purchasing agents for the family.

TABLE 6.3   Differences between Women and Men

Remarkable Differences

Between 130 and 150 males are conceived for every 100 females. About 105 boys are born for every 100 girls. But by the time they reach the age of 20, there are only about 98 males per 100 females. And among those 65 and older, just 68 men survive for every 100 women.

Females have a better sense of smell than males from birth onward. They are also more sensitive to loud sounds. But males are more sensitive to bright light, and can detect more subtle differences in light.

It is physiologically more difficult for women than for men to maintain a desirable weight and still meet their nutritional needs.

Women on average spend 40 percent more days sick in bed than do men.

Sexual perversions—foot fetishes, for instance—are an almost exclusively male phenomenon.

Boys get more than 90 percent of all perfect scores of 800 on the math section of the Scholastic Aptitude Test. And the gap between SAT math scores for boys and girls is greatest—about 60 points higher for males—among students who are in the top 10 percent of their class.

Infant girls show a strong, early response to human faces—at a time when infant boys are just as likely to smile and coo at inanimate objects and blinking lights.

Boys are far more likely than girls to be left-handed, nearsighted, and dyslexic (more than 3 to 1). Males under 40 are also more likely than females to suffer from allergies and hiccups.

Source: "Men vs. Women," *U.S. News & World Report* 105 (August 8, 1988), 52. Copyright U.S. News & World Report.

Female Employment

Women today have much higher rates of employment outside the home than in past eras. Women have left hearth and home to bring home some of the bacon. Today over 56 percent of women are employed, in contrast to less than 25 percent in 1950. When movement in and out of the labor force is considered, the proportion of women working outside the home within a 2-year period may be as high as 80 percent.[35] In 1995, more than 80 percent of all mothers with children at home are expected to be working outside the home.[36]

How does female employment status affect buying? The most important impact is due to income. Analysis of the employment variable sometimes uses the following nomenclature: NWW = the wife is not employed outside the home; FWW = the wife works full time, 35 hours or more per week; and PWW = the wife works part time, less than 35 hours per week. FWW families average more than $10,000 additional income than NWW families. Today, the wife's work status is less of a determinant to how a family spends its income than is the total amount of net income the family has to spend.[37]

Other than differences due to income, some other variation occurs due to employment. Child care is a primary example with both PWW and FWW families spending 17 percent more than NWW families, although the gap narrows as the age of the family increases. Families in which the wife is employed also spend significantly more on food away from home and gasoline and motor oil than do NWW families, although not more on vehicles. FWW families spend more on shelter than do one-earner families.[38]

A major limitation in the purchasing power of women is that they face a "dual labor market," the term used to describe the situation in which women receive less for the same work than do men. This condition occurs across all industries and almost all jobs, including marketing. In a recent study, the incomes of males in marketing management exceeded females by $18,300, by $12,000 in marketing research, and by $25,200 in advertising management. Some of the gap can be attributable to factors other than gender such as years of business experience (5 years more for males), older age, higher corporate rank, more likely to work in manufacturing, and more education but gender discrimination is still the underlying problem.[39]

Some change is occurring. Women in some occupations are perceived by young consumers more positively than are men[40] and among dual-income families, more than 6 million women earn more than their husbands.[41] One of the factors most frequently cited as important in equalizing incomes of women and men is the availability of good, reasonably priced child care. For marketers, factors such as this are not only a social responsibility but increasingly an entrepreneurial opportunity. If you turn to the section of this book containing color prints of ads, you will see an ad for Mercedes. Notice that the ad is directed toward women, presumably highly paid professionals, who have enough money to buy a Mercedes motor car for the man in her life.

Career Orientation   Employed individuals are sometimes classified by orientation toward their careers. Rena Bartos finds two groups of working women:

those who think of themselves as having a career and those to whom work is "just a job." There are also housewives who prefer to stay at home and those who plan to work in the future. For marketers this may be important because homemakers and "just a job" women are more likely to read traditional women's magazines, whereas professional women are more likely to read general-interest and business-oriented magazines and newspapers.[42]

The primary reasons women and men work are similar—for the income. A growing proportion of women regard their work as a career rather than "just a job." Today, 45 percent of women think of their work as a career, up from 41 percent in 1985. About 57 percent of men regard their work as a career, a level that has remained constant in recent years.[43]

Women and Time

Married working women experience many time pressures. They often have two jobs: household responsibilities plus their jobs in the marketplace. Studies show they have significantly less leisure time than either their husbands or full-time homemakers.[44] This would suggest that working wives would buy more time-saving appliances, use more convenience foods, spend less time shopping, and so forth. Actually, Weinberg and Winer found that working and nonworking wives are similar in such behavior if income, life cycle, and other situational variables are held constant.[45] Bellante and Foster report that, although understanding employment effects is complex, working-wife families appear to spend more on food away from home, child care, and some services.[46]

Today's retail facilities must be open longer hours, not only because of so many women working but also because they frequently work different shifts than their spouses. One study found that among mothers who work full time, 45 percent work different shifts than their spouse. Among part-time working women, 57.4 percent work different shifts than their husbands.[47] Split shifts may cause retailers to be open longer hours but also aid the marketing programs of direct marketers with "800" numbers for catalogues as well as the newer technologies of shopping on television and other time-flexible forms of shopping.

Role Overload   **Role overload** exists when the total demands on time and energy associated with the prescribed activities of multiple roles are too great to perform the roles adequately or comfortably.[48] Much of the role overload felt by contemporary women occurs when they work more total hours than men. This creates the possibility of their solving the problem by purchases of products or services from marketing organizations.[49]

Data from three major studies of families, classified by gender and employment, are shown in Table 6.4. These studies examined paid work versus family work and disclosed that employed women work more hours each day than husbands who are employed and wives who are not employed. Sex-role ideology, especially found in feminism, and other forces are creating pressures toward more equality in work loads between men and women.

The 1990 Virginia Slims Opinion Poll found that the most tangible way for women to balance jobs and family is for men to take on more household work.

TABLE 6.4   Employed Husbands' and Wives' Time Use (Hours/Day) in Paid Work, Family Work, and All Work

Study	Time Use Category	Employed Husbands		Wives	
		Wife Employed	Wife Not Employed	Employed	Not Employed
Walker & Woods (1976)	Family Work	1.6	1.6	4.8	8.1
	Paid Work	6.3	7.8	5.3	.5
	All Work	7.9	9.4	10.1	8.6
Robinson (1977a)	Family Work	1.1	1.0	4.0	7.6
	Paid Work	5.8	6.5	5.3	0
	All Work	6.9	7.5	9.3	7.6
Meissner et al. (1975)	Family Work	.6	.6	2.3	4.6
	Paid Work	7.1	7.7	6.5	1.9
	All Work	7.7	8.3	9.0	6.5

Source: Joseph H. Pleck, *Working Wives/Working Husbands* (Beverly Hills: Sage Publications, 1985), 30.

Token help with the dishes or children no longer inspires women's gratitude. As women contribute more to the family income, they expect in return a more equal division of the household responsibilities.[50] There is evidence, especially among younger families, of a shift in attitudes toward work and housework that is causing a move toward more household equality between the sexes.[51]

Marketers must find ways of communicating with women who feel role overload. Figure 6.6 shows such an ad by Whirlpool. The ad recognizes the increasing number of employed women and their perceptions of lives that are busier than ever. Yet the ad avoids referring to employed women. To do so might alienate nonemployed women. Whirlpool makes products of high quality, targeted especially to families with the income to purchase quality—a situation most likely to occur among families with employed women. The ad is positioned to this target market, both in copy and illustration.

Feminine Roles

Consumer researchers are interested in measuring the multiple roles of women, which may provide clues to the development of effective marketing programs. The extent to which women hold feminist attitudes and values, for example, may be related to consumer behavior.

A typical method used to divide women into feminist or traditionalist categories is the Smith and Self scale.[52] The scale consists of 21 items, such as the achievements of women in history, whether or not women or men tend to have more common sense, and a biological drive for sex. Using the Smith and Self scale with more specific behaviors than other studies, Koch found that attitudes toward clothing and the way a woman dresses is significantly related to feminist orientation.[53]

FIGURE 6.6 **Ad Designed to Appeal to Employed Women without Alienating Nonemployed Women**

Source: Courtesy of Whirlpool Corporation.

Differences in feminine roles can be observed in a study by Venkatesh, in which women were categorized as traditionalists, moderates, and feminists.[54] Venkatesh was able to reduce a large amount of data into ten factors. Two factors, "sex stereotyping" and "fashion and personal appearance," are displayed in Table 6.5. Look at the factor on sex stereotyping and you will see that responses to every statement are statistically significant between groups. Look at the fashion and appearance factor, however, and you will see that no statistically significant differences exist between groups of women in the study except one concerning beauty parlors.

Marketers can use such information to make themselves sensitive to the topics that can be the same or must be different for different segments. An ad appearing in a magazine appealing to feminists might show boys playing with dolls, but the same illustration would have little appeal in magazines whose readers were mostly traditionalists. Concerning fashion, however, about 90 percent of all types of women say,

TABLE 6.5   **Feminine Roles**

Factor Analysis of Lifestyle Variables			
	Percent in Each Group Who Agree with the Statements		
Extracted Factor	Traditionalists	Moderates	Feminists
Sex Stereotyping			
American advertisements picture a woman's place to be in the home.	38[a]	64	89[b]
American advertisements seem to have recognized the changes in women's roles.	48	33	22[b]
American advertisements depict women as sexual objects.	44	56	81[b]
American advertisements depict women as independent without needing the protection of men.	14	8	4[b]
I would like to see more and more young girls play with mechanical toys.	18	42	75[b]
I would like to see boys playing with dolls just the way girls do.	10	30	66[b]
Boys and girls should play with the same kind of toys.	30	64	80[b]
Fashion and Personal Appearance			
An important part of my life and activities is dressing smartly.	39	38	38
I like to feel attractive.	86	92	90
I would like to go to the beauty parlor as often as I can.	17	12	5[c]
I enjoy looking through fashion magazines to see what is new in fashions.	60	63	57
I like to do a lot of partying.	26	39	38
I love to shop for clothes.	49	46	47

[a]Based on Chi-square tests results.
[b]Significant at 0.01 level.
[c]Significant at 0.05 level.
Source: Alladi Venkatesh, "Changing Roles of Women: Life-Style Analysis," *Journal of Consumer Research 7* (September 1980), 192–193.

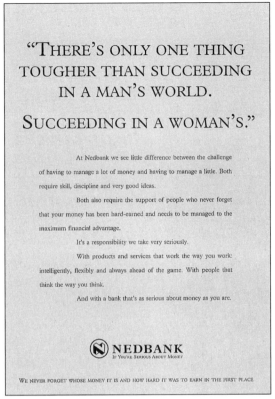

FIGURE 6.7   Self-Fulfillment Themes in Ads for Women

Source: Courtesy of Calgon, Nedbank, Toyota and Asics.

"I like to feel attractive." Ads with such an appeal are likely to cut across almost all types of women.

Women's Roles in Marketing   Advertising has often portrayed women in limited, stereotyped roles. Generally, women were shown as purchasers of low-unit-price items and as homemakers rather than career persons. Contemporary women are increasingly oriented toward self-realization, self-expression, and personal fulfillment. In Figure 6.7 you can see how a variety of firms have translated these needs into ads. Calgon emphasizes to busy women that "You deserve a little CalgonTime." Nedbank addresses those women who succeed in a "woman's world," emphasizing that they have to use skill, discipline, and good ideas in their household finances. Toyota indicates that women are playing hard as well as working hard and are discovering the "liberating versatility" of pickup trucks. Asics plays on the phrase that indicates that the country would be better if it were run by women.

Women's roles in the purchase of major durable products is very important in contemporary society. Women may represent about half the automobile buyers in

FIGURE 6.7   Continued

this country, according to the Motor Vehicle Manufacturers Association. Marketers are responding to these roles by targeting women in their ads, as Figure 6.7 shows. Among other programs to target this audience, training programs are being conducted to help dealers better service the female market. Training videotapes teach dealers how to attract and work with women customers, and individual dealers are sponsoring special events to bring women into their showrooms. Automakers are also offering mail-in credit applications in print ads in order to counteract discrimination women have felt in relation to financing.[55]

The "new traditionalist" is a term used by some advertisers to describe the career woman of the 1990s. *Good Housekeeping* used this concept to redesign the magazine. After examining Yankelovich Monitor studies, *Good Housekeeping* concluded that the American contemporary woman feels strongly about building a strong family and has a strong commitment to her husband, her home, and the values her mother had. These traditional values are synthesized with an emphasis on individuality and on tolerance for diverse ideas, lifestyles, and beliefs. While many marketers have accepted this concept of the "new traditionalist," other observers and women's scholars see the repetition of "traditional values" as reviving former stereotypes of the dependent housewife. Feminist Betty Friedan warns that this new "feminine mystique" defines women once again in terms of their husband, family, and home. Other feminists see such efforts of marketers as antifreedom, as anti-liberty, and as anti-self-actualizing.[56]

The reality facing marketers in the period between now and 2000 is that there is no mass market of women anymore, if there ever was. New options, economic realities and changes in the family structure have torn stereotypes to bits. A review of how marketers are responding to new roles reveals six core groups of women, even though there is great variation within each category. Consumer in Focus 6.3 describes these market segments and some of the ways marketers are reaching them.

Consumer in Focus   6.3

Reaching Six Female Market Segments

New Moms

Whether to work or to stay at home is a raging debate among new mothers. Some 49 percent of mothers said preschool kids need their mothers' full-time care; another 49 percent said it didn't make any difference so long as the care they got was loving. Marketers need to approach the "nurturers"—the stay-at-home mothers—as women who will try new products and pay a premium price if the products show value in what they do with their baby. The working mothers are more realistic and respond best to appeals that help control their time. Instead of the picture-perfect mom whipping up a pitcher of Kool-Aid for kids, a new spot shows a group of parents hanging around a comfortably disheveled kitchen talking about life and Kool-Aid.

50-Plus

Older women want to be shown in connection with their wisdom and abilities, not their limitations and disabilities, according to George Moschis at Georgia State University. Johnson & Johnson introduced Affinity shampoo with ads claiming, "the first shampoo created for hair over 40." The product failed because consumers did not want to be reminded that they had old hair. More successful approaches show attractive, silver-haired women riding with their husbands on motorcycles to a softball game. Models such as Cybil Shepherd, 40, appear in ads for L'Oreal and Linda Evans, 47, sells for Clairol.

Entrepreneurs

By the year 2000, women will own at least half of 30 million businesses in the United States, up from 5 percent a few decades earlier. These businesses pur-
Continued

chased over half of PBX equipment, copiers, telephones, fax machines, and personal computers. Female entrepreneurs have been overlooked in the past but marketers are targeting them for a wide variety of business and personal goods and services, often in a variety of new magazines targeted to working women.

Blue/Pink Collars

Working-class women are still the keepers of the family dinner and they want products that are satisfying, convenient, and, most important, fast. She is 31 years old on average, has a young family and annual household earnings of about $34,000, has a husband in the industrial labor force, and has to work outside the home to help pay the bills. Marketers often ignored this prime target by focusing on more affluent segments. These generally patriotic families began buying Toyotas because American cars weren't giving them what they wanted: a quality product at an affordable price. Shows like "Roseanne" and "The Simpsons" demonstrated the influence of this market segment and firms such as Sears, Roebuck & Co and K mart are working hard to regain this customer by stressing both quality and reasonable prices.

Teenagers

Today's teenagers are searching a little less for personal excellence and a little more for clean air. Marketers are forced to recognize their thirst for information. They're talking *to* them, rather than *at* them. They are savvier shoppers with a new sense of materialism believing that only "dumb" kids will spend $40 for a T-shirt at Benetton when they could buy it for $10 at The Gap. They are willing to pay more for "green" products at the Body Shop, a pricy British cosmetics company that promises none of its products have been tested on animals.

Homemakers

Once a homogeneous American segment, this group is diverse and demanding. Marketers are only beginning to recognize and contend with the unexpected diversity among this consumer group with some 43 million people who control billions in spending power. Advertising should replace the bonbon-eating, soap-opera-watching female stereotype with advertising that recognizes the intelligence and economic power of women at home. While still rare, a more intellectual approach was used by Dakin toys. Instead of purely emotional and visual approaches, its ads included an intellectual discussion about what stimulates a child's imagination. Cathi Mooney, a principal at the ad agency that created the ads, said, "I don't think we would have done an ad like this eight years ago, but there is now a growing respect for women who stay at home."

Source: Excerpts from "The Many Faces of Eve," *Adweek's Marketing Week* (June 25, 1990), 44–49.

Changing Masculine Roles

Roles of men in families are changing substantially. As women increasingly participate in the labor force and as values shift in society, men are taking on new roles in consuming and purchasing products. In a survey of 1,000 American males by the advertising agency Cunningham & Walsh, more and more men could be observed as househusbands. The privately published survey disclosed that 47 percent of men vacuum the house, 80 percent take out the garbage, 41 percent wash dishes, 37 percent make beds, 33 percent load the washing machine, 27 percent clean the bathroom, 23 percent dust, 23 percent dry dishes, 21 percent sort laundry, 16 percent clean the refrigerator, and 14 percent clean the oven. Over 50 percent of men take part in regular shopping trips, suggesting that men are important targets for marketing activity for many types of household products.

Men not only participate in household and consumption activities but apparently are increasing their rate of participation. Men now do one-fifth of the cooking, cleaning, and laundry, and married men now do more housework than unmarried men. Fathers are doing more than they once did, and mothers are doing less than previously (although still more than men).[57]

Not all researchers accept the finding that the "new father" is widespread nor even beneficial.[58] Much literature, however, is focusing on new roles of men.[59] One of the primary contributors to this literature, Joseph Pleck, concludes that while some of these images reflect hype, there is also much of substantive change:

> A new image, summed up in the term "the new father," is clearly on the rise in print and broadcast media. This new father differs from older images of involved fatherhood in several key respects: he is present at the birth; he is involved with his children as infants, not just when they are older; he participates in the actual day-to-day work of child care, and not just play; he is involved with his daughters as much as his sons.[60]

Men in the 1990s see themselves as being more sensitive. They are more like Kevin Costner than John Wayne, according to Roper poll studies for male-oriented magazines.[61] Men remain interested in romance but they also express a high interest in fitness, health, helping raise the children, helping out with household chores, and finding a better balance between work and leisure. These new roles appear to be creating a male market that is more interested in products and brands and therefore more brand loyal than in earlier decades. Some of the methods, as well as the controversies of how to market to men, are illustrated in Consumer in Focus 6.4.

Childhood Socialization and Influence

Much of consumer behavior is learned as a child. Remember that, in Chapter 3, we studied the cultural transfusive triad and observed that the family is one of the primary institutions that transmit values from one generation to the next through both the nuclear and extended family. Delayed marriage and the increasing number

Consumer in Focus   6.4

How to Market to Men

The macho man, like the blond bimbo, is nearing extinction on the advertising landscape. Even after being "sensitized" to sexual stereotypes, Madison Avenue hasn't decided who should replace him. A peculiar set of fellows is showing up in commercials: from hyper-nurturing single dads to goofy, tongue-tied bachelors to artistic "animals."

Hulk Hogan, the huge and well-sculpted professional wrestler, was captured painting a sunset at the beach in a spot for Right Guard antiperspirant designed to reach a "rough-and-tumble audience" of men.

The infantile husband was portrayed in a commercial for Robitussin: he can't manage the house and kids for even one day while his wife is sick. In contrast, the rare, enlightened Dad is used to appeal to female consumers' fantasies as much as to men themselves. A Motrin ad features a man who, upon arriving home from the office, immediately administers the pain reliever to his wife and gives their child a bath. The ad is actually targeted to 24–44 year old women, the primary purchaser of the product.

Marketers nevertheless cannot lose sight of the "man thing"—that guys respond to sports, sex, and grooming no matter how sensitive they strive to be. For Procter & Gamble's Old Spice, the "Mariner Man" cruises through port, whistling a familiar jingle and attracting stares from lovely lasses. As he escorts one away, he tosses an Old Spice bottle to an envious nerd.

Bugle Boy Industries targets 16- to 20-year-old males with ads featuring sexy women trying on men's Bugle Boy jeans. The message reads, "Attention all guys. First the bad news. Bugle Boy is demanding we show their new Color Denims in this commercial. Now the good news. Nobody said we had to put them on men." The same company targets 25+ plus males with a spot that pokes fun at male bonding and makes the domestic guy look cool. Three golf buddies pity a fourth for staying home with his wife. Yet steamy shots of the couple frolicking seductively at home show they're having a fine time without the boys. The spot is a poke at Bugle Boy's archrival, Dockers from Levi Strauss, whose ads turned male bonding into a fashion occasion.

"During research men will spout all kinds of stuff," says Simon Silvester. When a woman leads an automobile focus group, men talk about wanting safety features and leg room, he says. But when a man leads the discussion, they say, "I just want something I can accelerate at traffic lights." He concludes: "A lot of men are going in for this New Man image, but deep down they're all the same."

Source: Excerpted from Laura Bird, "Madison Avenue Stalks Today's Archetypal Male," Wall Street *Journal* (March 5, 1992), B1–3.

FIGURE 6.8   **Children's Role in Purchasing**

Source: Courtesy of Eastman Kodak; Motorola.

of single consumer units places more attention on the role of the family in causing consumer preferences because single consumers tend to be loyal to the brands they learned to buy as children.

Co-shopping, or shopping done together by parent and child, is a direct influence on a person's consumer decisions. Studies by Grossbart, Carlson, and Welsh indicate some of the influences that can be expected. Their studies indicate co-shoppers have more concern with children's development as consumers. They also place more value on children's input in family consumer decisions—even decisions on products not encountered on typical co-shopping trips such as automobiles, major appliances, life insurance, and vacations. Co-shoppers explain more to their children why they don't buy products than do low co-shoppers and discuss the role of advertising more, which to some extent may mediate the influence of advertising.[62]

Marketers can stimulate the role of children in family decisions in many ways. Figure 6.8 shows how two advertisers appeal to the influence of children on family decisions. Kodak includes children in ads and gives reference to a mother because

FIGURE 6.9   Involving Children in Shopping in a Japanese Department Store

children provide a major motivation for photography. Even for an adult product, such as a cellular phone, Motorola recognizes the role of children in using (or abusing) the product.

Retailers can also benefit from understanding the role of children in buying. Some retailers may consider children as an interference with parents' shopping time and seek to minimize this by providing play space. Ikea and other stores provide such play areas. A more proactive approach is found in Japanese department stores which encourage children and parents, principally mothers, to interact. This approach is shown in Figure 6.9 in which Japanese children are encouraged to become involved in creative arts and computers while mothers are in the stores.

Many changes in family structure directly affect how marketers communicate to families with children and to children themselves. For example, delayed marriage and higher education is increasing the number of families with only one child. The increasing number of "only child" consumers creates families with children who are accustomed to communicating with adults more than with siblings or peers. Their preferences may be much more "adult" than marketers traditionally expected. Effective communications must take into consideration the higher verbal and creative skills associated with only children. Understanding children and their information-processing skills may require analysis of their developmental process as well as the use of research methodologies such as observational techniques, play behavior and storytelling, and specialized questioning techniques.[63]

Families in which both parents are employed may have little time to spend with children. They may be willing to spend more money on consumer products for children (and certainly they have more money available than single-earner families) in order to compensate for the lack of time to spend with their children. Studies based on Canadian data indicate that young children cause less participation in the labor force, change how families spend their money and reduce the amount of time and money available for leisure.[64]

Research Methodology for Family Decision Studies

When you prepare an analysis of family influences on buying or the consumption decisions of families, most of the research techniques will be similar to other marketing research studies. There are a few unique aspects of family decisions that should be considered, however, in these final pages of the chapter.

Decision-Process Framework

Role-structure studies have often viewed purchasing as an act rather than a process and have based findings on questions such as, "Who usually makes the decision to purchase?" or "Who influences the decision?" Yet, the role and influence of family members varies by stage in the decision process. An example of process methodology is provided by Wilkes, who found the following types of questions useful for measuring family influence:

1. Who was responsible for initial need-recognition?
2. Who was responsible for acquiring information about the purchase alternatives?
3. Who made the final decision as to which alternative should be purchased?
4. Who made the actual purchase of the product?[65]

Better results using this methodology were obtained than with more global measures. Husbands and wives are more likely to hold similar perceptions about their relative influence for a given phase than when questioning fails to ask about decision stages.

Role-Structure Categories

The relevant role-structure categories in a research project depend on the specific product or service under consideration, but in many product categories only the husband or wife is involved. In other categories it is useful to measure the amount of influence in different roles. Spiro found that influence strategies or persuasion depend on several variables, especially stage in the life cycle and lifestyles.[66] Children are involved in many types of purchase situations, but the nature of their influence has often been ignored.

Interviewer Bias

The sex of the interviewer or observer may influence the roles husbands and wives say they play in a purchase situation. To overcome this bias, either self-administered questionnaires should be used or the sex of the observer should be randomly assigned to respondents.

Respondent Selection

In measuring family buying, it is necessary to decide which member(s) of the nuclear family should be asked about the influence of family members. Results often vary considerably depending on which family members are interviewed. Most often wives are the ones interviewed, but the percentage of couples whose responses agree is often so low as to make interviewing only one member unacceptable.

Granbois and Summers found husbands' responses concerning purchase intentions to be better than those of their wives as predictors of total planned cost and number of items planned from joint responses, although wives predicted better for certain products such as appliances, home furnishings, and entertainment equipment plans.[67] The researchers concluded that joint responses are more likely to uncover more plans of the family. Multiple roles in the influence and purchase process are illustrated in a study of vacation decisions by Filiatrault and Ritchie, in which they found substantial differences in influence of each parent and of the children on different stages of decisions. This study also shows that differences exist in the perceptions that people have about their influence on others in the family.[68]

Demise of the Family?

After reading about all of the changes in family and household structure, you may have concluded that the family is finished. Don't make that conclusion. It is true that dramatic changes are taking place in family life in many industrialized countries. Urie Bronfenbrenner, one of the most influential analysts of family patterns, concludes that the underlying dynamics and ultimate effects of family change are occurring in many countries and are strikingly similar around the globe.[69]

The demise of the family is not imminent, at least in the foreseeable future. A Roper poll of U.S. consumers indicates that being a good spouse and parent is the most common measure of success for many people, even more important than being true to oneself, to God, or to wealth. These results are indicated in Figure 6.10.

Summary

Families or households are consumer units (CU) of critical importance in the study of consumer behavior for two reasons. First, families or households are the unit of usage and purchase for many consumer products. Second, the family is a major influence on the attitudes and behavior of individuals. As consumers, we are the creation of our families to a large extent.

A family is a group of two or more persons related by blood, marriage, or adoption who reside together. A household differs from a family by describing all the persons, both related and unrelated, who occupy a housing unit. Thus households outnumber families and are smaller in size; the average income is higher for families than households.

Family (or household) members occupy various roles, which include initiator (gatekeeper), influencer, decider, buyer, and user. The influence of spouses, children, or other

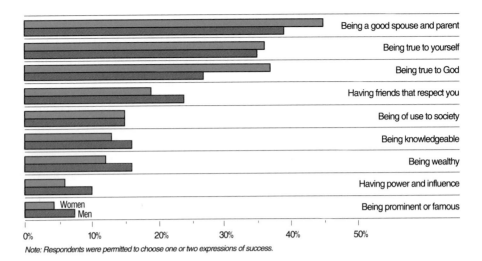

Note: Respondents were permitted to choose one or two expressions of success.

FIGURE 6.10 **Percent of Women and Men Who Believe Selected Achievements Express the Idea of Success**

Source: "A Measure of Success," *American Demographics* 13 (April 1991), 9.

family members varies depending on the resources of family members, the type of product, the stage in the life cycle, and the stage in the buying decision. These variables are more important in understanding family decisions than traditional roles ascribed to one gender or the other.

The family life cycle (FLC) describes how families change over time. Traditional approaches of analyzing FLC have been updated with a consumer market matrix of lifestages that emphasizes the relative income of a family in each stage. This matrix is built upon six stages: younger singles, younger couples, younger parents, mid-life families, mid-life households, and older households.

Families and households are changing in their structure and composition. Among more important recent changes are increases in the number of single households, smaller average family size, later marriages, divorce, remarriage and redivorce, cohabiting singles and the existence of the gay market. The increasing number of employed women has created role overload for employed women who work more hours (combining paid work and family work) each week than their husbands or nonemployed women.

Marketers are concerned with the roles performed by women, men, and children. Advertising to women increasingly reflects themes of increasing income and responsibility and drives for self-fulfillment and self-enhancement. Masculine roles increasingly reflect shared performance of household activities. Children learn much of their consumption and buying behavior from parents and exert considerable influence on family purchases.

Marketing research techniques useful in studying families and households give special consideration to the decision-process framework, questioning techniques, role-structure categories and relative influence, interviewer bias, and respondent selection. A methodological problem is created because husbands and wives often differ in their responses to questions about how their families buy consumer goods and services.

Review and Discussion Questions

1. What is meant by the term *family*? What is the importance of studying families to the understanding of consumer behavior?
2. Some studies of consumer behavior maintain that the family rather than the individual should be the unit of analysis in consumer behavior. What are the advantages and disadvantages of using the family as the unit of analysis?
3. Do husbands or wives have the most influence on buying decisions? Outline your answer.
4. How might an advertisement be designed that would appeal to the differences in instrumental and expressive roles within families?
5. Will there be more or fewer women employed outside the home in the future? What variables should be considered in answering this question? How does the answer affect demand for consumer products?
6. Analyze the statement, "Working women buy products and services essentially the same as nonworking women."
7. What is meant by the "singles" market? How would a food company appeal to the singles market?
8. Assume that an airline has asked for a research project to understand how families make vacation decisions. You are asked to prepare a research design for the project. What would you suggest?
9. Assume that you are the marketing manager for a clothing firm that wishes to attract the gay market. How would you assess the size of this market? Outline the marketing program you would recommend.
10. Children do not have much purchasing power. Yet, they are believed to be important in the understanding of consumer behavior. Why? What might firms do to be more profitable as a result of understanding the role of children in family buying?

Endnotes

1. For a discussion of these issues on a global perspective, see Nico Keilman, Anton Kuitsten, and Ad Vossen (eds.), *Modelling Household Formation and Dissolution* (New York: Oxford University Press, 1988).
2. John L. Haverty, "A Model of Household Behavior," in Russell W. Belk et al., 1987 *AMA Winter Educators' Conference* (Chicago: American Marketing Association, 1987), 284–289.
3. David H. Olson et al., *Families: What Makes Them Work?* (Beverly Hills: Sage Publications, 1983).
4. Hamilton I. McCubbin and Marilyn A. McCubbin, "Typologies of Resilient Families: Emerging Roles of Social Class and Ethnicity," *Family Relations* 37 (July 1988), 247–54.
5. Russel Belk, "A Child's Christmas in America: Santa Claus as Deity, Consumption as Religion," *Journal of American Culture* 10 (Spring 1987), 87–100; David Cheal, *The Gift Economy* (London: Routledge, 1988); Elizabeth Hirschman and Priscilla LaBarbera, "The Meaning of Christmas," in Elizabeth Hirschman, ed., *Interpretive Consumer Research* (Provo, Utah: Association for Consumer Research, 136–147).

6. Harry L. Davis, "Decision Making within the Household," *Journal of Consumer Research* 2 (March 1976), 241–260.

7. Harry L. Davis and Benny P. Rigaux, "Perception of Marital Roles in Decision Processes," *Journal of Consumer Research* 1 (June 1974), 5–14.

8. Mandy Putnam and William R. Davidson, *Family Purchasing Behavior: II Family Roles by Product Category* (Columbus, Ohio: Management Horizons Inc., a Division of Price Waterhouse, 1987).

9. William J. Qualls, "Changing Sex Roles: Its Impact upon Family Decision Making," in Andrew Mitchell, ed., *Advances in Consumer Research* 9 (Ann Arbor: Association for Consumer Research, 1982), 267–270.

10. For research on this topic from a wide variety of disciplines, see Beth B. Hess and Myra Marx Ferree, *Analyzing Gender* (Newbury Park, California: Sage Publications, 1987).

11. Roger Jenkins, "Contributions of Theory to the Study of Family Decision-Making," in Jerry Olson, ed., *Advances in Consumer Research* 7 (Ann Arbor: Association for Consumer Research, 1980), 207–211.

12. Alvin Burns and Donald Granbois, "Advancing the Study of Family Purchase Decision Making," in Olson, *Advances in Consumer Research* 7, 221–226.

13. Sunil Gupta, Michael R. Hagerty, and John G. Myers, "New Directions in Family Decision Making Research," in Alice M. Tybout, ed., *Advances in Consumer Research* 10 (Ann Arbor: Association for Consumer Research, 1983), 445–450.

14. Mary Lou Roberts, "Gender Differences and Household Decision-Making: Needed Conceptual and Methodological Developments," in Thomas C. Kinnear, ed., *Advances in Consumer Research* 11 (Provo, Utah: Association for Consumer Research, 1984), 276–278.

15. Eileen Fischer and Stephen J. Arnold, "More than a Labor of Love: Gender Roles and Christmas Gift Shopping," *Journal of Consumer Research* 17 (December 1990), 333–343.

16. William D. Wells and George Gubar, "The Life Cycle Concept," *Journal of Marketing Research* 2 (November 1966), 355–363.

17. Fred D. Reynolds and William D. Wells, *Consumer Behavior* (New York: McGraw-Hill, 1977).

18. Patrick E. Murphy and William Staples, "A Modernized Family Life Cycle," *Journal of Consumer Research* 6 (June 1979), 12–22.

19. Janet Wagner and Sherman Hanna, "The Effectiveness of Family Life Cycle Variables in Consumer Expenditure Research," *Journal of Consumer Research* 10 (December 1983), 281–291.

20. Mandy Putnam, Sharyn Brooks, and William R. Davidson, *The Expanded Management Horizons Consumer Market Matrix* (Columbus, Ohio: Management Horizons, a Division of Price Waterhouse, 1986).

21. Data in this chapter are mostly from the U.S. Bureau of the Census, Current Population Reports, Series P-20, No. 447 *Marital Status and Living Arrangements* (Washington, D.C.: Government Printing Office).

22. For a thorough analysis of the financial and other decision-making capabilities of these families, see Frank Furstenbert and Graham B. Spanier, *Recycling the Family* (Beverly Hills: Sage Publications, 1984).

23. "The Life of a Marriage," *American Demographics* 11 (February 1989), 12.

24. Kathryn A. London and Barbara Foley Wilson, "Divorce," *American Demographics* 10 (October 1988), 23–26.

25. Marilyn Ihinger-Tallman and Kay Pasley, *Remarriage* (Newbury, California: Sage Publications, 1987), 70.
26. Graham B. Spanier, "Living Together in the Eighties," *American Demographics* 4 (November 1982), 17–31.
27. Alan A. Otten, "People Patterns," *The Wall Street Journal* (June 14, 1988), 33.
28. Martha Farnsworth Riche, "The Postmarital Society," *American Demographics* 10 (November 1988), 23–26ff.
29. "Living Alone and Loving It," *U.S. News and World Report* (August 3, 1987).
30. W. Wayne Delozier and C. William Roe, "Marketing to the Homosexual (Gay) Market," in Robert L. King, ed., *Marketing: Toward the Twenty-First Century* (Richmond, Virg.: Southern Marketing Association, 1991), 107–109.
31. "Gay Community Looks for Strength in Numbers," *American Marketplace* (July 4, 1991), 134.
32. Richard V. Weekes, "Gay Dollars," *American Demographics* 10 (October 1989), 45ff.
33. Vyndee Miller, "Gays Are Affluent but Often Overlooked Market," *Marketing News* 24 (December 24, 1990), 2.
34. David Wilson, "Role Theory and Buying-Selling Negotiations: A Critical Review," in Richard Bagozzi, ed., *Marketing in the 1980s* (Chicago: American Marketing Association, 1980), 118–121.
35. Elizabeth Waldman, "Labor Force Statistics from a Family Perspective," *Monthly Labor Review* (December 1983), 16–20.
36. Bureau of National Affairs, *Work and Family: A Changing Dynamic* (Washington, D.C.: Bureau of National Affairs, 1986).
37. Rose M. Rubin, Bobye J. Riney, and David J. Molina, "Expenditure Pattern Differentials Between One-Earner and Dual-Earner Households: 1972–1973 and 1984," *Journal of Consumer Research* 17 (June 1990), 43–52.
38. Eva Jocobs, Stephanie Shipp, and Gregory Brown, "Families of Working Wives Spending More on Services and Nondurables," *Monthly Labor Review* 112 (February 1989), 15–23.
39. Pamela L. Kiecker, Shelby D. Hunt, and Lawrence B. Chonko, "Gender, Income Differences, and Marketing: Examining the 'Earnings Gap' in Three Areas of Marketing," *Journal of the Academy of Marketing Science* 19 (Spring 1991), 77–82.
40. Mary M. Brabeck and Karen Weisgerber, "College Students' Perceptions of Men and Women Choosing Teaching and Management: The Effects of Gender and Sex Role Egalitarianism," *Sex Roles* 21 (Nos. 11/12, 1989), 841–857.
41. Suzanne M. Bianchi, "Wives Who Earn More than Their Husbands," *American Demographics* 6 (July 1984), 18–23.
42. Rena Bartos, *The Moving Target: What Every Marketer Should Know About Women* (New York: Free Press, 1982).
43. Bickley Townsend and Kathleen O'Neil, "American Women Get Mad," *American Demographics* 12 (August 1990), 26–32.
44. Marianne Ferber and Bonnie Birnbaum, "One Job or Two Jobs: The Implications for Young Wives," *Journal of Consumer Research* 8 (December 1980), 263–271.
45. Charles B. Weinberg and Russell S. Winer, "Working Wives and Major Family Expenditures: Replication and Extension," *Journal of Consumer Research* 7 (September 1983), 259–263.
46. Don Bellante and Ann C. Foster, "Working Wives and Expenditure on Services," *Journal of Consumer Research* 11 (September 1984), 700–707.
47. Alan Otten, "People Patterns," *The Wall Street Journal* (June 14, 1988), 33.

48. Patricia Voydanoff, *Work and Family Life* (Newbury Park, California: Sage Publications, 1987), 83.

49. Alvin C. Burns and Ellen Foxman, "Role Load and Its Consequences on Individual Consumer Behavior," in Terence A. Shimp et al., *1986 AMA Educators' Proceedings* (Chicago: American Marketing Association, 1986), 18.

50. Townsend and O'Neil, "American Women Get Mad."

51. F. Thomas Juster, "A Note on Recent Changes in Time Use," in F. Thomas Juster and Frank P. Stafford, *Time, Goods, and Well-Being* (Ann Arbor: Institute for Social Research, 1985), 313–332.

52. M. D. Smith and G. D. Self, "Feminists and Traditionalists: An Attitudinal Comparison," *Sex Roles* 7 (1981), 182–188.

53. Kathryn E. Koch, "Dress-Related Attitudes of Employed Women Differing in Feminist Orientation and Work Status: Emphasis on Career Apparel" (unpublished Ph.D. dissertation, The Ohio State University, Columbus, 1985).

54. Alladi Venkatesh, "Changing Roles of Women: A Life-Style Analysis," *Journal of Consumer Research* 7 (September 1980), 189–197.

55. Frieda Curtindale, "Marketing Cars to Women," *American Demographics* 10 (November 1988), 29–31.

56. Connie Koenenn, "New Women's Ad Causes Stir," from the *Los Angeles Times*, in the *Columbus Dispatch* (January 15, 1989), 5F.

57. John P. Robinson, "Who's Doing the Housework," *American Demographics* 10 (December 1988), 24–28ff.

58. Charlie Lewis and Margaret O'Brien, eds., *Reassessing Fatherhood* (Newbury Park, California: Sage Publications, 1987).

59. Michael S. Kimmel, ed., *Changing Men: New Directions in Research on Men and Masculinity* (Newbury Park, California: Sage Publications, 1987).

60. Joseph H. Pleck, "American Fathering in Historical Perspective," in Kimmel, *Changing Men*, 93.

61. Laurie Freeman, "America's Man Has Gone Domestic," *Advertising Age* (April 15, 1991), S4.

62. Sanford Grossbart, Les Carlson and Ann Walsh, "Consumer Socialization and Frequency of Shopping with Children," *Journal of the Academy of Marketing Science* 19 (Summer 1991), 155–163.

63. James Garbarino, Frances M. Stott, et al., *What Children Can Tell Us* (San Francisco: Jossey-Bass Publishers, Inc., 1990).

64. Robin A. Douthitt and Joanne M. Fedyk, "Family Composition, Parental Time and Market Goods: Life Cycle Trade-Offs," *The Journal of Consumer Affairs* 24 (Summer 1990), 110–133.

65. Robert E. Wilkes, "Husband-Wife Influence in Purchase Decisions: A Confirmation and Extension," *Journal of Marketing Research* 12 (May 1975), 224–227.

66. Rosann L. Spiro, "Persuasion in Family Decision-Making," *Journal of Consumer Research* 9 (March 1983), 393–401.

67. Donald H. Granbois and John O. Summers, "Primary and Secondary Validity of Consumer Purchase Probabilities," *Journal of Consumer Research* 1 (March 1975), 31–38.

68. Pierre Filiatrault and J. R. Brent Ritchie, "Joint Purchasing Decisions: A Comparison of Influence Structure in Family and Couple Decision-Making Units," *Journal of Consumer Research* 6 (September 1980), 131–140.

69. Urie Bronfenbrenner, "What Do Families Do?" *Family Affairs* 4 (Winter/Spring 1991), 1–6.

7

Situational Influence

The next time you hear music in the air while shopping, there is a good chance that it was provided by Muzak. Muzak specializes in providing retailers the "right kind" of music for their customers. Retailers can choose among different types of music such as adult contemporary, light classical, Top 40, and New Age.

What is the "right kind" of music? The kind that sells. To demonstrate this payoff, Muzak conducted a test at a major department store. The company varied the presence and type of music played throughout the day. Shoppers, interviewed as they left the store, reported how long they were in the store, whether they stayed longer than expected, and the number of purchases they made.

The effect of the music depended on whether it matched the shopper's demographic characteristics. When they matched, consumers shopped an average of 18 percent longer. Longer shopping time could mean more buying. In this case, it did. The number of purchases rose by 17 percent.

Source: Cyndee Miller, "The Right Song in the Air Can Boost Retail Sales," *Marketing News* 25 (February 4, 1991), 2.

Our opening example provides a rather compelling demonstration of how situational influences within the purchase environment can shape consumer behavior. This chapter focuses on the role of situational influences as a determinant of consumer behavior and therefore marketing strategy. Indeed, situations exert some of the most pervasive influences on consumer behavior for one simple reason—behavior always occurs within some situational context. This is not to say that

TABLE 7.1 Characteristics of Consumer Situations

1. *Physical surroundings:* the tangible properties comprising the consumer situation. These features include geographical location, decor, sounds, aromas, lighting, weather, and visible configurations of merchandise or other material surrounding the stimulus object.
2. *Social surroundings:* the presence or absence of other people in the situation.
3. *Time:* the temporal properties of the situation such as the particular moment when behavior occurs (e.g., time of day, weekday, month, season). Time may also be measured relative to some past or future event for the situational participant (e.g., time since last purchase, time until payday).
4. *Task:* the particular goals or objectives consumers have in a situation. For instance, a person shopping for a wedding gift for a friend is in a different situation than when shopping for one's own personal use.
5. *Antecedent states:* the temporary moods (e.g., anxiety, pleasantness, excitement) or conditions (e.g., cash on hand, fatigue) which the consumer *brings* to the situation. Antecedent states are distinguished from those momentary states which occur in response to a situation as well as from more enduring individual traits (e.g., personality).

Source: Russell W. Belk, "Situational Variables and Consumer Behavior," *Journal of Consumer Research* 2 (December 1975), 157–164. Used with permission.

behavior is always shaped by situational influences. Die-hard Budweiser drinkers, for instance, might always buy a Bud regardless of whether they are out partying with friends or sitting home alone watching TV. In many, if not most, cases, however, situational factors will exert important influences.

Before proceeding any further, let us define what we mean by the term "situational influence." Because consumer situations also involve people and objects (for example, a product or advertisement), it is necessary to distinguish between influences due to consumers and objects from those that are unique to the situation itself. Accordingly, **situational influence** can be viewed as the influence arising from factors that are particular to a specific time and place that are independent of consumer and object characteristics.[1]

What are these situational factors or characteristics? Belk has suggested that consumer situations may be defined along the lines of five general characteristics, which are summarized in Table 7.1.[2] Although you probably can remember how each of these factors has, at one time or another, affected your own behavior as a consumer, additional examples of their influence can be found throughout the chapter.

Types of Consumer Situations

The music example described in the chapter opening centered around a very important type of consumer situation—namely, the purchase situation. Consumer situations can in fact be separated into three main types: communication, purchase, and usage situations.[3] Each of these is discussed in the sections following.

The Communication Situation

Communication situations can be defined as those settings in which the consumer is exposed to either personal or nonpersonal communications. Personal communications would encompass conversations consumers might have with others, such as salespeople or fellow consumers. Nonpersonal communications would involve a broad spectrum of stimuli, such as advertising and consumer-oriented programs and publications (for example, *Consumer Reports*).

To illustrate the potential impact of the communication situation, let us consider how it might determine the effectiveness of television advertising. We focus on this particular form of communication for two reasons. First, expenditures on TV advertising often receive a significant share of the promotion budget. Moreover, TV ads have often been employed in empirical investigations of the influences arising from the communication setting.

In the context of television advertising, a number of situational characteristics are likely to surface as potential determinants of an ad's effectiveness. The presence of others during message exposure may easily undermine the likelihood that the ad will receive much, if any, attention. Viewers often use commercial breaks as a time to interact with others in the immediate audience. Similarly, factors such as an ad's position within a commercial "string" (that is, a series of consecutive ads) or program might also be important. Reductions in audience size have been found to be greater for commercials in the middle of a string versus ads at the beginning or end.[4]

The sheer number of ads that are processed during television viewing can have an adverse impact on a given ad's effectiveness.[5] Given the recent trend toward shorter commercials (the industry standard has been shifting from 30 seconds to 15 seconds), which permits broadcasting more messages in a given time period, marketers have become increasingly concerned about the potential effects of advertising clutter.[6] *Clutter* refers to the problem of simply too many ads in the viewing environment. This increase in the number of ads can interfere with the consumer's ability to process an ad's selling points.

Situational influences may also arise from the particular program in which an ad appears. Sometimes a program may be so involving that consumers become preoccupied with the program (for example, avid football fans watching the Super Bowl), thus making them rather oblivious to anything that appears during the commercial breaks.[7] Programs can also alter how consumers feel, and these feelings may affect how they respond to advertising contained within the program. In one investigation, viewers' mood states while watching commercials were affected by the surrounding program. Happy programs induced happier moods during commercial exposure compared to sad programs. This more favorable mood state led subjects to have more positive thoughts while processing the ads, as well as better recall of the commercial information.[8] Note, however, that some ads may be more sensitive to their surrounding program than others.[9] Practitioners are very aware of the potential influences that a program may exert on the effectiveness of their advertising. Coca-Cola, for instance, avoids advertising during TV news programs because "there's going to be some bad news in there and Coke is an upbeat, fun product."[10] Similar concerns led to Chrysler's withdrawal of its advertising from ABC's miniseries "Amerika," the topic of Consumer in Focus 7.1.

Consumer in Focus   **7.1**

Programming Influences on Advertising Effectiveness: The Influence of the Communication Situation

One of the most popular, yet controversial miniseries to hit the airwaves during 1987 was ABC's "Amerika." This 14½ hour film, three years in the making at a cost of nearly $40 million, centers around the life of an American family living in a United States that has been peacefully taken over by the Soviet Union. The Chrysler Corporation had initially purchased roughly $7 million of air time for its commercials that pronounced "The Pride Is Back—Born in America." However, shortly before the program aired, Chrysler withdrew its ads, a decision supported by Lee A. Iacocca, the chairman of Chrysler, after viewing 6 hours of the film. The reason? According to a Chrysler spokesperson:

> We have concluded that the subject matter and its portrayal are so intense and emotional that our upbeat product commercials would be both inappropriate and of diminished effectiveness in that environment.

Source: Peter J. Boyer, "Chrysler Pulls Ads From 'Amerika,'" *The New York Times* (January 28, 1987), C26.

While the prior discussion has focused on television advertising, recognize that the communication situation is also an important consideration for other forms of advertising. In print advertising, the reputation and credibility of the magazine or newspaper carrying the ad may influence the ad's effectiveness. Such is the message carried by the ad for the *Wall Street Journal* appearing in Figure 7.1, which extolls the virtues of their publication as an advertising vehicle. For outdoor advertising, billboards must be designed to accommodate the fact that exposure will be quite brief in most instances. This communication situation is quite different from, say, being exposed to ads while seated in a theater. In the latter setting, consumers have far less stimuli competing for their attention, thereby diminishing the need for including attention-getting properties within the advertisement. The importance of gaining attention is considered further in Chapter 8.

The Purchase Situation

Purchase situations refer to those settings where consumers acquire products and services. Situational influences are very prevalent during purchasing. As a simple example, consider the tremendous change in consumers' price sensitivity across purchase situations. A grocer would find it extremely difficult to charge the prices that consumers pay for soda and snacks at a movie theater or ballpark.

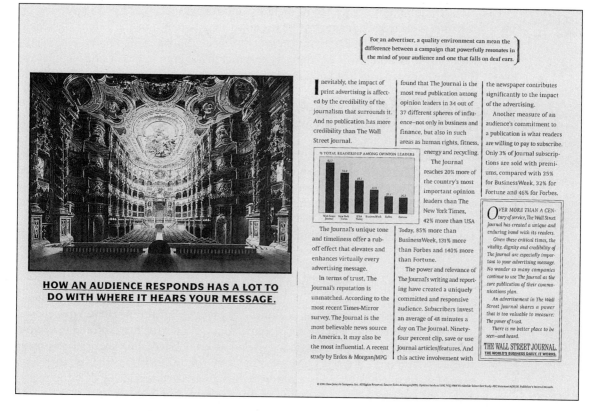

FIGURE 7.1   **This Ad Emphasizes the Importance of the Communication Situation in Print Advertising**

In examining how the purchase situation can affect consumer behavior, we first consider those influences arising from the information environment followed by a discussion of situational influences stemming from the retail environment in which purchase occurs.

The Information Environment   **Information environment** refers to the entire array of product-related data available to the consumer.[11] The nature of the information environment will be an important determinant of marketplace behavior when consumers engage in some form of nonhabitual decision making. Some of the major environmental characteristics include the availability of information, the amount of information load, and the modes in which information is presented and organized.

Information Availability   The availability of information is extremely important. The absence of information about the performance of competing brands on some attribute will preclude its use during decision making. Sometimes the availability of information will depend on the consumer's ability to retrieve the information from memory (the topic of memory and retrieval is considered more fully in Chapter 14). Research suggests that choice may depend on the extent to which product information is externally present during decision making versus being available only in memory (for example, a consumer at Sears trying to decide whether to buy the microwave in front of him or the one he examined yesterday at a competitive store). In one study, subjects were more likely to select the "best" brand when information about the brand was externally available than when they had to rely on their ability to recall this information, which had been presented previously but removed at the time of choice.[12]

Note that the issue of information availability is particularly relevant to those concerned with providing an information environment that allows consumers the opportunity to make well-reasoned and informed choices. In this regard, researchers have considered the potential value of providing consumers with information such as the energy consumption costs of appliances,[13] a product's life cycle cost (that is, purchase price plus operating costs),[14] unit price information,[15] and nutritional information.[16]

Information Load　The information load of a choice environment is determined by the number of choice alternatives and the number of attributes per alternative. Increases in the number of choice alternatives can alter the type of decision rule consumers employ during decision making,[17] a topic further explored in Chapter 17. Some have also argued that, beyond a certain level, information load may exceed consumers' ability to process accurately the information (that is, they become "overloaded") and, consequently, reduce their accuracy during decision making.[18] We return to this issue of information overload in Chapter 8.

Information Format　Information format, the manner in which it is organized, can also influence the behavior of consumers. Consumers' use of unit price information, for example, may depend on how it is organized or presented in the retail environment. Consumers have demonstrated greater use of unit price information when presented in the form of a list, which rank ordered the relative cost of competing brands on a single piece of paper, than when the unit price of each brand was posted on separate tags.[19] Research also indicates that format can influence the order in which information is acquired or processed, and the amount of time taken to reach a decision.[20]

Information Form　Even information form can play an important role. For some attributes (for example, gas mileage, nutritional properties), product information can be presented either numerically or semantically (for example, excellent, good, average, and so on). Numerical product ratings enable consumers to more easily estimate differences among products. Consequently, consumers are more inclined to compare brands on an attribute-by-attribute basis when brand information is presented in numerical rather than semantic form.[21]

The Retail Environment　The physical properties of the retail environment, often referred to as **store atmospherics**, are of particular interest to marketers for two

Consumer in Focus   7.2

The Grocery Store of the Future?

Anthony J. Adams says grocery shoppers in 2001 will step into a total environmental cubical near a product's display. The cubicles will be outfitted with music, holographic displays and appetizing smells, says Mr. Adams, vice president of market research at Campbell Soup Company. For a bar of soap, a shopper might stroll through the Irish countryside or swim in an alpine lake—all for the illusion of that clean-scrubbed feeling. "All the senses will be dazzled," Mr. Adams says.

Source: Excerpted from Kathleen Deveny, "The Soothsayers Have Their Say," *Wall Street Journal* (March 22, 1991), B6.

fundamental reasons. First, unlike many situational influences that are beyond the marketer's control, marketers have the ability to create the retail environment. Second, this influence is brought to bear on consumers at just the right place—inside the store. For a glimpse at what atmospherics might look like in the grocery store of the future, see Consumer in Focus 7.2.

From the marketer's perspective, a store's atmospherics can have a number of desirable effects on consumers.[22] First, it can help shape both the direction and duration of consumers' attention, thereby enhancing the odds of purchase for products that otherwise might go unnoticed. Second, the retail environment can express various aspects about the store to consumers, such as its intended audience and positioning (for example, the clothing store wishing to attract upscale customers with a fashion image). Finally, the store setting can also elicit particular emotional reactions from consumers (for example, pleasure and arousal). Research suggests that these feelings can influence the amount of time and money consumers spend while shopping.[23]

The retail environment is comprised of a variety of elements, including store layout, aisle space, placement and form of displays, colors, lighting, presence and volume of in-store music, smells (see Consumer in Focus 7.3), and temperature. Although much of the research documenting the influence of these factors is of a proprietary nature, published studies have gradually accumulated in this area.

Music   As revealed by the example at the beginning of the chapter, music in the retail environment can affect shopping behavior.[24] Indeed, some of the more interesting demonstrations of situational influence have used music. In an early study, the volume of music played by supermarkets was varied from loud to soft. Consumers exposed to the loud music took less time shopping but spent the same amount of money relative to those exposed to the soft music.[25] The effect of music

Consumer in Focus **7.3**

Smells That Sell

J'Amy Owens, whose Seattle-based firm is called Retail Planning Associates, helps design store interiors that will help retailers sell their products. "For years I've been specifying the lighting, music, and ambiance in stores," says Owens. "Why not add the dimension of aroma?"

There is growing evidence that supports the potential payoffs from using the right smells. Grocery stores that have pumped in the aroma of baked goods have found a threefold increase in sales for that department. Smells may also enhance the perceived value of a product. One study reports that consumers priced a pair of Nike shoes an average of $10 more when these judgments were made in a scented room than in an unscented room. Consumers also reported that they were more likely to buy the shoes when the room was scented.

Retailers are showing a greater appreciation for aroma as part of a store's atmospherics. Bigsby and Kruthers, a client of Owens, has used a leathery, oak-like aroma in three of its Knot Shop tie stores. President H. Gene Silverberg was so impressed that he plans on testing it in 19 other stores. According to Silverberg, "The employees find it very pleasant. A happier staff means a happier customer, and that means more sales."

Source: Pamela J. Black, "No One's Sniffing at Aroma Research Now," *Business Week* (December 23, 1991), 82–83; Cyndee Miller, "Research Reveals How Marketers Can Win by a Nose," *Marketing News* 25 (February 4, 1991), 1–2.

tempo (slow versus fast) has also been examined in a supermarket setting. Slow-tempo music increased both shopping time and expenditures compared to fast-tempo music.[26] Similar effects due to tempo have also been observed in a restaurant setting. Patrons spent nearly 25 percent more time and nearly 50 percent more on bar purchases when the tempo was slow rather than fast.[27]

Layout and In-Store Location　　Store layout and product location can be used to enhance the likelihood of consumers coming into contact with products. A supermarket, for instance, might design a layout that encourages a traffic flow that guides shoppers into particular areas. Similarly, the bakery department might be located close to the entrance and/or check out lines in the hope that the aromas of fresh-baked items will entice shoppers. Department stores will place product displays in high-traffic areas, such as at the end of an escalator. Vendors are extremely sensitive to a product's location because they recognize the incremental sales that can result from shelf position. And convenience stores strategically place impulse items near the check out in the hope that consumers will succumb to the buying urge.

Colors   The colors within the store are sources of potential influence on both consumers' perceptions and behavior. Warm colors, such as red and yellow, appear more effective in physically attracting people, relative to the cooler colors of green and blue. In one study where subjects were allowed to determine how close they sat to a colored wall, the distance was much shorter for warm than cool colors. Nonetheless, subjects rated retail interiors using cool colors as more positive, attractive, and relaxing than those employing warmer colors. The researchers concluded that warm colors were most suitable for a store's exterior color or display windows as a means of drawing customers into the store.[28] Additional support of color's behavioral impact comes from the finding that the shade of brown used in coloring walls altered the speed at which people moved through a museum.[29]

POP Materials   Point-of-purchase (POP) materials can serve as very powerful stimuli. Displays and signs can enhance the odds of capturing the consumer's attention, and thereby stimulate purchasing. Consistent with this, POP materials have been shown to increase sales.[30] It is likely that marketers will place greater emphasis on POP materials given that they are relatively inexpensive compared to other forms of promotion. In addition, informative and easy-to-use POP materials can partly help offset the recent declines in the quantity and quality of retail salespeople.[31] One example is the POP unit called Y.E.S. (which stands for "Your Extra Salesman"). This unit, which hangs on the shelf where the product is located, works like a window shade. Product information is printed on a self-retracting shade that rolls down from the canister unit.[32]

Salespeople   Although our discussion of the retail environment thus far has focused on nonpersonal stimuli, it is important to recognize the role of salespeople. The potential to influence consumers during shopping can be strongly affected by the retailer's front line staff. Indeed, a store's image and ability to build loyalty can heavily depend on the availability and characteristics (such as the attentiveness, expertise, friendliness, and appearance) of salespeople.

Crowding   Another aspect of the retail setting that may affect shopping behavior is the perceived level of crowding due to the density of shoppers within the store. High levels of crowding can lead to reductions in shopping time, postponement of unnecessary purchases, and less interaction with sales personnel.[33]

The Influence of Time   As noted in Table 7.1, time represents an important aspect of situational influence. This is particularly true for purchase situations. The demand for many products is highly time sensitive. The Christmas season is vitally important for many products, especially toys. Consumers' purchases of soft drinks, which peak during the summer, slow down considerably during the winter months (with the exception of the temporary spurts brought on by holidays such as Christmas and New Year). Moreover, products may be positioned differently depending on the

FIGURE 7.2 **Time-Dependent Product Positioning: An Example of Off Season Selling**

time of year. As reflected by the promotional piece appearing in Figure 7.2, Sanka attempted to overcome the sales lag typically experienced during warmer months by promoting a different way of consuming coffee.

The amount of time available for decision making can also be an important situational influence. A consumer whose refrigerator has broken down beyond repair will typically experience greater pressure to make a speedy decision than consumers shopping to replace an old but still working refrigerator.

Time pressure can affect consumer decision making in a couple of ways. First, it may "force" consumers to rely on existing knowledge and experience in making their decisions, rather than collecting additional information. Even if time pressures are not so great as to preclude some use of external information during decision making, they can still lead consumers to adopt simpler product evaluation strategies, such as relying on fewer attributes in comparing alternatives.[34] Time pressure has been found to reduce both the purchasing of products that consumers had initially planned to buy (that is, before time pressure manifested itself) and the frequency of unplanned purchases (that is, products that are acquired even though they were not on the shopping list).[35]

Time relative to prior events can also affect purchase behavior. A classic example is the effect of food deprivation (that is, time since last meal) on grocery shopping. The food expenditures of many consumers grow larger as the time since their last meal increases.[36] For this reason, home economists often recommend food shopping on a full stomach, so as to decrease the impulse buying hunger often motivates.

Finally, recent evidence suggests that advertising effectiveness can be affected by the particular time of day when consumers encounter an advertisement.[37] Shoppers at a suburban mall were shown a segment of a television news program containing six new 30-second TV commercials. Sessions were conducted in either the morning, afternoon, or early evening. When ad retention was measured immediately after the program, learning was best for the morning sessions and worst in the evening sessions. However, just the opposite pattern was observed when learning was not tested until nearly 2 hours had elapsed since viewing the commercials.

The Usage Situation

The remaining type of consumer situations considered here are **usage situations**, which refer to those settings where consumption occurs. In many instances, purchase and usage situations are virtually the same (for example, consumers who eat their meals at a fast-food restaurant). But product consumption often occurs in settings that are quite removed, both physically and temporally, from the setting in which the product is acquired.

Even when purchase and usage situations are distinct, the latter can still have a powerful influence as consumers take into account the "intended" usage situation during decision making.[38] Consider consumers purchasing rice, who might choose a brand based on whether they were planning to serve the rice as a stand-alone side dish, as an ingredient in recipes, or both.

The social surroundings that characterize a usage situation can have an important influence on consumer behavior.[39] In today's increasingly anti-smoking environment, the presence of nonsmokers will often serve as an impediment to smokers' "lighting up." Beer sales are particularly sensitive to whether consumption occurs in public versus private settings. Between 80 and 90 percent of import beer sales is "on premise" (for example, in bars and restaurants) where others can see the type of beer one consumes. In contrast, 70 percent of domestic brands' sales are generated by in-home consumption.[40]

The time at which usage occurs may also affect consumer behavior. For example, food consumption depends very heavily on the time of day. We rarely eat spaghetti for breakfast or cereal for dinner. Figure 7.3 shows how college students' preferences for various fruits depended on the time of day and context in which consumption occurred. Peaches were the most preferred fruit for breakfast or a daytime snack but were replaced by strawberries for a supper dessert.

FIGURE 7.3   **Students' Fruit Preferences by Eating Occasion Illustrates the Importance of Time in Consumption Decisions**

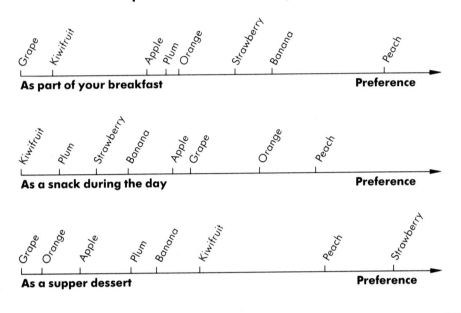

Source: Peter R. Dickson, "Person–Situation: Segmentation's Missing Link," *Journal of Marketing* 6 (Fall 1982), 56–64.

In order to understand why behavior is affected by usage situations, it is useful to examine how the importance consumers attach to product attributes and their beliefs about a product's performance may change across various settings. Consider, for example, Miller and Ginter's findings that patronage of a particular fast-food restaurant often depended on the usage situation.[41] While McDonald's had a market share of nearly 40 percent for leisurely evening meals with the family, its share of weekday lunches was less than 30 percent. This fluctuation in share was driven by two factors. First, consumers gave McDonald's its lowest convenience ratings when it was to be used for a weekday lunch. Second, convenience was viewed as more important in this situation.

Usage Situations and Marketing Strategy   Marketing strategy and tactics are affected by usage situations in several ways. First, it may often be vital that market segmentation schemes reflect the variety of usage situations. The apparel market, for instance, can be segmented in terms of the situation in which clothing is to be worn (for example, formal dinners, work, sports, casual). Targeting each of these segments will obviously necessitate changes in the product offering. Another, more detailed, example of segmentation based on the usage situation involving suntan lotion is presented in the next section of the chapter.

FIGURE 7.4
Changes in the Usage Situations for One Product Can Lead to New Opportunities for Another Product

The usage situation may often assume an important part in the positioning of a product. The advertising campaign that promotes the theme "The night belongs to Michelob" represents an attempt to position this beer as the one to use in nighttime social settings. Similarly, Wet Ones, a premoistened towelette, introduced itself to the marketplace with a series of ads which depicted the variety of situations (for example, at the beach, in the car, on a camping trip) in which the product would come in handy. Several examples appear in Figure 7.4. Given the growing

Consumer in Focus **7.4**

Pepsi's Courting of the Morning Market

What did you have to drink with breakfast this morning? Chances are it was not a soft drink. Coffee dominates the morning market with a 47 percent share of morning beverages sold. Soft drinks register a meager 4 percent share. During most other times of the day, however, soft drinks typically outsell most other beverages.

Soft drink manufacturers are fully aware of this untapped potential. Less obvious is the most effective strategy for enhancing consumption within this particular usage situation. Should the positioning of current offerings be expanded to incorporate morning consumption? Or would a new offering positioned specifically for morning use be more effective?

Pepsi has sought answers to these questions by test marketing a new brand extension called Pepsi A.M., which contains a higher-caffeine, low-carbonation flavor formula. The accompanying ad campaign centered around the theme: "The taste that beats coffee cold." In another test market, a similar ad campaign was launched that encouraged morning consumption of the regular Pepsi brand. A year later, Pepsi A.M. terminated the test market. Sluggish sales were attributed to the new formulation having a flat taste. According to a Pepsi spokeswoman, the test showed that "We don't need to introduce a reformulated [product] to encourage morning consumption." The company does intend to continue promoting morning consumption of their regular Pepsi brand.

Sources: Michael J. McCarthy, "Test Shows that Pepsi's Rival to Coffee So Far Isn't Most People's Cup of Tea," *Wall Street Journal* (March 30, 1990), B1–B2; "PepsiCo Discontinues Test of Higher-Caffeine A.M.," *Wall Street Journal* (October 15, 1990), B7.

restrictions on smoking in public, Wrigley's gum has positioned itself as something smokers can consume when they can't light up.

The discovery or development of new usage settings can be a vital source of new sales and often represents an important strategic option for revitalizing mature products.[42] Arm and Hammer baking soda is one product that has successfully broadened its appeal by promoting a variety of uses, ranging from dental care to a deodorizer for carpets and refrigerators. Orange juice producers attempted to enhance product consumption through an advertising campaign that claimed "It's not just for breakfast anymore." Even the refrigerator has benefitted from an expansion of potential usage situations by the development of very small models that easily fit into the office. Consumer in Focus 7.4 focuses on Pepsi's efforts to encourage consumption of their products in the morning.

Person–Situation Interactions

Thus far our discussion has implicitly assumed that all consumers respond in the same manner to a particular situation. Yet this may not be the case. While some consumers may be highly influenced by situational variations, others may often prove to be rather insensitive.

As an illustration of person–situation interactions, let us return to the previously discussed finding that consumers' grocery purchases escalated as the time since their last meal increased.[43] Whereas this effect was observed for average-weight consumers, it did not occur for overweight consumers. Thus, the situational influence of time since their last meal depended on the type of consumer.[44]

The notion that consumers are not homogeneous in their response to situational factors has important implications for market segmentation. Because different consumers may seek different product benefits, which can change across different usage situations, Dickson has argued that marketers may often need to employ **person–situation segmentation**.[45] An example of this form of segmentation in the context of suntan lotions appears in Figure 7.5. The columns represent different types of people who are consumers of suntan lotion. The rows identify various settings in which the product may be used. The benefits desired by a particular group or sought within a given usage situation are listed at the bottom of the column and at the end of the row. These are the benefits that the product should deliver in courting a specific person–situation segment. In addition, some person–situation segments seek unique benefits (for example, a scented winter lotion for female skiers), that are listed within that cell of the matrix. A suntan manufacturer interested in targeting dark-skinned adult women who use the product while snow skiing, for instance, should include ingredients that will provide special protection from the light rays and weather, an antifreeze formula, and a winter perfume scent that appeals to women.

Unexpected Situational Influences

Marketers sometimes ask target consumers their purchase intentions in order to forecast future demand for products. Although purchase intentions can, under the right conditions (see Chapter 11), be predictive of future behavior, one major threat to their predictive power is the disruption caused by unexpected situational influences.[46] For example, a consumer may fully anticipate buying a particular brand of potato chips during the next visit to the grocer. Yet this purchase intention may not be fulfilled if the product is out of stock or if another brand of similar quality is on sale. Conversely, a consumer may lack any interest in buying a product when surveyed at a particular point in time. Subsequently, however, purchase may occur because of some unanticipated event (for example, a noncoffee drinker who buys coffee for her visiting, coffee-drinking parents).

FIGURE 7.5 Person–Situation Segmentation Matrix for Suntan Lotion

Persons: / Situations	Young Children: Fair Skin	Young Children: Dark Skin	Teenagers: Fair Skin	Teenagers: Dark Skin	Adult Women: Fair Skin	Adult Women: Dark Skin	Adult Men: Fair Skin	Adult Men: Dark Skin	Situation Benefits/Features
Beach/boat sunbathing	Combined insect repellant				Summer perfume				a. Windburn protection b. Formula and container can stand heat c. Container floats and is distinctive (not easily lost)
Home-poolside sunbathing					Combined moisturizer				a. Large pump dispenser b. Won't stain wood, concrete, or furnishings
Sunlamp bathing					Combined moisturizer and massage oil				a. Designed specifically for type of lamp b. Artificial tanning ingredient
Snow skiing					Winter perfume				a. Special protection from special light rays and weather b. Antifreeze formula
Person Benefits/Features	Special protection a. Protection critical b. Non-poisonous		Special protection a. Fit in jean pocket b. Used by opinion leaders		Special protection Female perfume		Special protection Male perfume		

Source: Peter R. Dickson, "Person–Situation: Segmentation's Missing Link," *Journal of Marketing* 6 (Fall 1982), 56–64. Used with permission.

From a marketing perspective, the important point here is simply that one must recognize the potential for unexpected situational influences to undermine the accuracy of forecasts based on purchase intentions. While it is often hoped that such effects will tend to be counterbalancing (that is, the number of customers lost because of unexpected situational influences will be offset by the number gained for the same reasons), this may not be the case.

Summary

This chapter has focused on the influences that may arise from situational properties. The physical and social surroundings, time, task, and antecedent states are the major characteristics that comprise a given consumer situation.

In consumer behavior, it is useful to consider the potential impact of environmental factors in three main areas: communication, purchase, and usage situations. The effectiveness of marketing messages may often depend on the communication setting. The impact of a TV ad, for example, may in part be determined by the program in which it appears.

The purchase situation can have a strong influence on consumer behavior. Properties of the information environment, such as the availability, amount, format, and form of information, can affect decision making. Similarly, features of the retail environment, including music, layout, colors, POP materials, and crowding, will influence shopping and purchase behaviors.

The situation in which product consumption occurs can exert a major influence on consumer behavior. Consumers may often alter their purchasing patterns depending upon the usage situation. What is an acceptable brand of beer in one setting may be unacceptable in another. An understanding of the usage situation can be invaluable for segmenting markets and developing appropriate product positionings.

Review and Discussion Questions

1. What are the five basic characteristics of a consumer situation?
2. What are the three main types of consumer situations?
3. A recent test of advertising effectiveness has revealed that your television advertising was more effective when shown during program A than program B. How could you explain this finding?
4. A grocery chain has recently developed a set of private-label brands. These brands are comparable in product quality to their competition but offer the consumer a substantial price savings. How might this grocer structure the information environment so as to best convey this price differential to consumers?
5. What is meant by "store atmospherics"? Why is it important to marketers?
6. Many consumers will switch from one brand of rice to another depending on the usage situation. What explanations can you offer as to why this switching may occur?
7. Describe how the concept of the usage situation could be useful to a snack food manufacturer.

8. A manufacturer has discovered a new usage situation that offers considerable market potential. One strategy for tapping this potential is to broaden the positioning of the company's current products (for example, by showing consumption of their existing brands in the new situation). An alternative strategy is to develop a new brand positioned specifically for the new usage situation. Which strategy would you recommend? Why?

9. Returning to Figure 7.5, suppose a suntan lotion manufacturer was interested in targeting fair-skinned teenagers who use the product while sunlamp bathing. What benefits and features should the product deliver in courting this segment?

Endnotes

1. Russell W. Belk, "An Exploratory Assessment of Situational Effects in Buyer Behavior," *Journal of Marketing Research* 11 (May 1974), 156–163.
2. Russell W. Belk, "Situational Variables and Consumer Behavior," *Journal of Consumer Research* 2 (December 1975), 157–164.
3. Flemming Hansen, *Consumer Choice Behavior: A Cognitive Theory* (New York: Free Press, 1972), 53.
4. Burke Marketing Research Inc., "Viewer Attitudes Toward Commercial Clutter on Television and Media Buying Implications" (paper presented at the 18th Advertising Research Foundation Conference, New York, 1972).
5. Peter H. Webb, "Consumer Initial Processing in a Difficult Media Environment," *Journal of Consumer Research* 6 (December 1979), 225–236.
6. See, for example, "Emotional Impact Can Cut Clutter of 15-Second Spots," *Marketing News* 20 (December 5, 1986), 13; Michael L. Ray and Peter H. Webb, "Three Prescriptions for Clutter," *Journal of Advertising Research* 26 (February/March 1986), 69–77.
7. Gary F. Soldow and Victor Principe, "Response to Commercials as a Function of Program Context," *Journal of Advertising Research* 21 (April 1981), 59–65. Also see Kenneth R. Lord and Robert E. Burnkrant, "Television Program Elaboration Effects on Commercial Processing," in Michael J. Houston, ed., *Advances in Consumer Research* 15 (Provo, Utah: Association for Consumer Research, 1988), 213–218; C. Whan Park and Gordon W. McClung, "The Effect of TV Program Involvement on Involvement with Commercials," in Richard J. Lutz, ed., *Advances in Consumer Research* 13 (Provo, Utah: Association for Consumer Research, 1986), 544–548.
8. Marvin E. Goldberg and Gerald J. Gorn, "Happy and Sad TV Programs: How They Affect Reactions to Commercials," *Journal of Consumer Research* 14 (December 1987), 387–403. For an arousal explanation of programming effects, see Surendra N. Singh and Gilbert A. Churchill, Jr., "Arousal and Advertising Effectiveness," *Journal of Advertising* 16 (1987), 4–10.
9. Robert E. Burnkrant, H. Rao Unnava, and Kenneth R. Lord, "The Effects of Programming Induced Mood States on Memory for Commercial Information," (Working Paper Series, The Ohio State University, October 1987).
10. "GF, Coke Tell Why They Shun TV News," *Advertising Age* (January 28, 1980), 39.
11. James R. Bettman, "Issues in Designing Consumer Information Environments," *Journal of Consumer Research* 2 (December 1975), 169–177.

12. Gabriel Biehal and Dipankar Chakravarti, "Information Accessibility as a Moderator of Consumer Choice," *Journal of Consumer Research* 10 (June 1983), 1–14.

13. Dennis L. McNeill and William L. Wilkie, "Public Policy and Consumer Information: Impact of the New Energy Labels," *Journal of Consumer Research* 6 (June 1979), 1–11.

14. R. Bruce Hutton and William L. Wilkie, "Life Cycle Cost: A New Form of Consumer Information," *Journal of Consumer Research* 6 (March 1980), 349–360.

15. J. Edward Russo, "The Value of Unit Price Information," *Journal of Marketing Research* 14 (May 1977), 193–201; J. Edward Russo, Gene Krieser, and Sally Miyashita, "An Effective Display of Unit Price Information," *Journal of Marketing* 39 (April 1975), 11–19.

16. Bettman, "Issues in Designing Consumer Information Environments"; J. Edward Russo, Richard Staelin, Catherine A. Nolan, Gary J. Russell, and Barbara L. Metcalf, "Nutrition Information in the Supermarket," *Journal of Consumer Research* 13 (June 1986), 48–70. Also see Christine Moorman, "The Effects of Stimulus and Consumer Characteristics on the Utilization of Nutrition Information," *Journal of Consumer Research* 17 (December 1990), 362–374.

17. Denis A. Lussier and Richard W. Olshavsky, "Task Complexity and Contingent Processing in Brand Choice," *Journal of Consumer Research* 6 (September 1979), 154–165.

18. Jacob Jacoby, Donald Speller, and Carol Kohn, "Brand Choice as a Function of Information Load," *Journal of Marketing Research* 11 (February 1974), 63–69.

19. J. Edward Russo, "The Value of Unit Price Information," *Journal of Marketing Research* 14 (May 1977), 193–201; J. Edward Russo, Gene Krieser, and Sally Miyashita, "An Effective Display of Unit Price Information," *Journal of Marketing* 39 (April 1975), 11–19. See also Valarie A. Zeithaml, "Consumer Response to In-Store Price Information Environments," *Journal of Consumer Research* 8 (March 1982), 357–369.

20. James R. Bettman and Pradeep Kakkar, "Effects of Information Presentation Format on Consumer Information Acquisition Strategies," *Journal of Consumer Research* 3 (March 1977), 233–240; James R. Bettman and Michel A. Zins, "Information Format and Choice Task Effects in Decision Making," *Journal of Consumer Research* 6 (September 1979), 141–153. See also Scott Painton and James W. Gentry, "Another Look at the Impact of Information Presentation Format," *Journal of Consumer Research* 12 (September 1985), 240–244.

21. J. Edward Russo and Barbara Dosher, "Strategies for Multiattribute Binary Choice," *Journal of Experimental Psychology: Learning, Memory, and Cognition* 9 (1983), 676–696.

22. Philip Kotler, "Atmospherics as a Marketing Tool," *Journal of Retailing* 49 (Winter 1973–1974), 48–65.

23. Robert J. Donovan and John R. Rossiter, "Store Atmosphere: An Environmental Psychology Approach," *Journal of Retailing* 58 (Spring 1982), 34–57; Elaine Sherman and Ruth Belk Smith, "Mood States of Shoppers and Store Image: Promising Interactions and Possible Behavioral Effects," in Melanie Wallendorf and Paul Anderson, eds., *Advances in Consumer Research*, vol. 14 (Provo, Utah: Association for Consumer Research, 1987), 251–254.

24. For a review and analysis of music's usefulness to marketers, see Gordon C. Bruner II, "Music, Mood, and Marketing," *Journal of Marketing* 54 (October 1990), 94–104.

25. Patricia Cane Smith and Ross Curnow, "Arousal Hypotheses and the Effects of Music on Purchasing Behavior," *Journal of Applied Psychology* 50 (June 1966), 255–256.

26. Ronald E. Milliman, "Using Background Music to Affect the Behavior of Supermarket Shoppers," *Journal of Marketing* 46 (Summer 1982), 86–91.

27. Ronald E. Milliman, "The Influence of Background Music on the Behavior of Restaurant Patrons," *Journal of Consumer Research* 13 (September 1986), 286–289.

28. Joseph A. Bellizzi, Ayn E. Crowley, and Rondla W. Hasty, "The Effects of Color in Store Design," *Journal of Retailing* 59 (Spring 1983), 21–45.

29. Rajendra K. Scrivastava and Thomas S. Peel, *Human Movement as a Function of Color Stimulation* (Topeka: Environmental Research Foundation, 1968).

30. V. Kumar and Robert P. Leone, "Measuring the Effect of Retail Store Promotions on Brand and Store Substitution," *Journal of Marketing Research* 25 (May 1988), 178–185; Gary F. McKinnon, J. Patrick Kelly, and E. Doyle Robison, "Sales Effects of Point-of-Purchase In-Store Signing," *Journal of Retailing* 57 (Summer 1981), 49–63; Arch G. Woodside and Gerald L. Waddle, "Sales Effects of In-Store Advertising," *Journal of Advertising Research* 15 (June 1975), 29–33.

31. John A. Quelch and Kristina Cannon-Bonventre, "Better Marketing at the Point of Purchase," *Harvard Business Review* 61 (November–December 1983), 162–169.

32. Howard Schlossberg, "P-O-P Display Designer Wants to Keep Shoppers Shopping Longer," *Marketing News* 25 (November 11, 1991), 15.

33. Gilbert D. Harrell, Michael D. Hutt, and James C. Anderson, "Path Analysis of Buyer Behavior Under Conditions of Crowding," *Journal of Marketing Research* 17 (February 1980), 45–51. See also Michael K. Hui and John E. G. Bateson, "Perceived Control and the Effects of Crowding and Consumer Choice on the Service Experience," *Journal of Consumer Research* 18 (September 1991), 174–184.

34. Peter L. Wright and Barton Weitz, "Time Horizon Effects on Product Evaluation Strategies," *Journal of Marketing Research* 14 (November 1977), 429–443.

35. C. Whan Park, Easwar S. Iyer, and Daniel C. Smith, "The Effects of Situational Factors on In-Store Grocery Shopping Behavior: The Role of Store Environment and Time Available for Shopping," *Journal of Consumer Research* 15 (March 1989), 422–433.

36. R. E. Nisbett and D. E. Kanouse, "Obesity, Food Deprivation, and Supermarket Shopping Behavior," *Journal of Personality and Social Psychology* 12 (August 1969), 289–294.

37. Jacob Hornik, "Diurnal Variation in Consumer Response," *Journal of Consumer Research* 14 (March 1988), 588–591.

38. John L. Stanton and P. Greg Bonner, "An Investigation of the Differential Impact of Purchase Situation on Levels of Consumer Choice Behavior," in Jerry C. Olson, ed., *Advances in Consumer Research* 7 (Ann Arbor: Association for Consumer Research, 1980), 639–643.

39. For an interesting demonstration of how social situations may affect the relationships between consumer ethnicity and food choices, see Douglas M. Stayman and Rohit Deshpande, "Situational Ethnicity and Consumer Behavior," *Journal of Consumer Research* 16 (December 1989), 361–371.

40. Kevin T. Higgins, "Beer Importers Upbeat about Future, Despite Warning Signs," *Marketing News* (October 25, 1985), 1ff.

41. Kenneth E. Miller and James L. Ginter, "An Investigation of Situational Variation in Brand Choice Behavior and Attitude," *Journal of Marketing Research* 16 (February 1979), 111–123.

42. Jagdish Sheth and Glenn Morrison, "Winning Again in the Marketplace: Nine Strategies for Revitalizing Mature Products," *Journal of Consumer Marketing* 1 (1984), 17–28.

43. Nisbett and Kanouse, "Obesity, Food Deprivation, and Supermarket Shopping Behavior."

44. The manner in which situational influences vary across consumers and products has been examined in several studies. A review of this literature can be found in Belk, "Situational Variables and Consumer Behavior." See also Girish N. Punj and David W. Stewart, "An Interaction Framework of Consumer Decision Making," *Journal of Consumer Research* 10 (September 1983), 181–196.

45. Peter R. Dickson, "Person–Situation: Segmentation's Missing Link," *Journal of Marketing* 6 (Fall 1982), 56–64.

46. For an empirical demonstration of how unexpected situations affect the intention-behavior relationship, see Joseph A. Cote, James McCullough, and Michael Reilly, "Effects of Unexpected Situations on Behavior-Intention Differences: A Garbology Analysis," *Journal of Consumer Research* 12 (September 1985), 188–194.

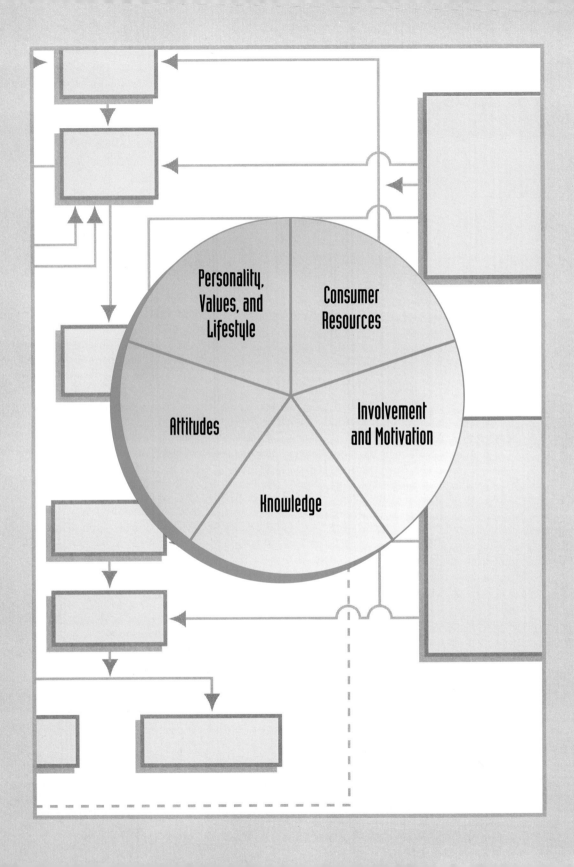

PART 3

Individual Differences

No two people are created the same. Certainly this is the case in consumer behavior. Which individual differences, however, are most crucial based on research and marketing experience? What difference do these variables make in our thinking and strategy? These are the issues covered in Part 3.

We begin in Chapter 8 with discussion of differences among individuals in terms of the *resources* they possess. A person with an income of $95,000 will have substantially different buying behavior from someone who barely scrapes by on $20,000. But they also differ in such resources as *time* and *information processing capability*.

Individuals also differ in other fundamental ways as you will notice in the highlighted section in the model on the opposite page. Chapter 9 examines the topics of *motivation and involvement*. Chapter 10 focuses on *knowledge and awareness*, and Chapter 11 introduces you to the important subject of *consumer attitudes* and their effects on behavior.

The final section of Part 3, Chapter 12, deals with a summary concept, *lifestyle*. Lifestyles are the patterns of living that are the outcomes of many other variables and influences, one of the most important of which is personality. You will find the discussion in Chapter 12 to be both interesting and practical in consumer research and marketing strategy.

8

Consumer Resources

O f the 40 percent of American women who color their hair, almost half do it themselves, generating a $500 million market. During a recession, however, women become more cautious with their discretionary income. Those who used to rely on professionals turn to home products, if not exclusively, at least as maintenance between less frequent salon visits.

As companies strive to keep their edge on the competition, favorite products are continually reevaluated and improved in the areas of shade selection, application ease, smell, and conditioning effect on the hair. At the same time, the industry is coming up with innovative new products that infiltrate traditional salon territory at a fraction of the cost. One recent introduction that goes directly after the salon dollar is L'Oreal's Color Weaving kit, which provides both highlights and low lights for the kind of dimensional color previously available only from a professional. At a retail cost of about $10, the kit offers a realistic alternative to the salon where prices for comparable services range from $40 to $350 for a top colorist.

Economic factors aside, the most obvious reason for at-home coloring's popularity is convenience. "We're aware that time is a woman's most precious commodity," says Karen Freeman, assistant vice president of marketing at L'Oreal. "So our at-home products are designed to give quick, easy, and consistent results in 40 minutes, compared with salon services, which can take up to three hours." For women who don't have time to eat lunch, much less schedule—and keep—an appointment with a salon, the at-home option simply makes a whole lot of sense.

Source: Excerpts from L. J. Kavanaugh, "The Business Side of Beauty," *Working Woman* (January 1992), 72.

In the previous chapters, we have focused primarily on *how* and *why* people buy. But this interesting story of the "business side of beauty" shows us that a consumer's perception of present or future resources profoundly affects *what* they buy. The key resources discussed in this chapter fall into the categories of (1) *economic*, (2) *temporaral* and (3) *cognitive* (ability to process and use information).

Economic Resources

"Money is what I need," echo the lyrics of a popular song. Credit cards also suffice. No other variable is as important in understanding what people buy as money. "Money is what I should study," could well be the theme song of every student of consumer behavior. Nearly every marketing research survey includes income as one of the key variables to explaining consumer behavior.

In an earlier era, barter—the trading of goods for goods—was common. Barter is still important in less developed societies and to a degree in the underground economies of all societies. There exists a substantial "informal economy" in which people barter or purchase goods and services in ways that may escape record keeping and taxation. The "heavy users" of the informal economy are affluent, well educated, and comparatively young.[1]

Economic resources—such as income or wealth—were the first variables to be analyzed in the study of consumer behavior, with studies traced back as far as 1672. The first with a reasonable statistical basis was published by Ernest Engel in 1857. The relationships between income and expenditures became popularized as Engel's Laws of Consumption. They contained propositions about the relationship between family income and the proportion spent on categories such as food, clothing, lodging, and "sundries" (education, health, recreation, and so forth).[2] Consumer in Focus 8.1 illustrates a current example of the relationship of family income and spending.

Substantial changes occur over time in the basic expenditures of families, depending on economic development of the country or income of individual families. Notice in Figure 8.1 the comparison in the United States between the early part of this century and today. The proportion of the budget spent on food and clothing has dropped dramatically, leaving money for upgraded housing and for the broad category of "other," similar to Engel's "sundries." It is this latter category that makes marketing dynamic and understanding consumers so challenging. Less developed countries of the world are likely to have a pattern of consumer expenditures more like the left side of Figure 8.1.

Measuring Economic Resources

Marketing involves exchange of economic resources. Measuring variables such as money income is complex because of the varied meanings of the term income. The objective is to develop measures that mean the same for everyone and that permit comparisons over time or across market segments. This objective is difficult to balance with the need to change definitions to fit changing conditions. Marketing

How Interest Rates Affect Consumer Behavior

Low interest rates are awfully nice. Just ask Michael and Rema Lichtenstein of Dracut, Mass. They're planning on refinancing their $165,000, 10.375 percent mortgage at something under 8.5 percent. That figures to put "$300 a month extra in our pockets," says Rema, a surgical nurse, "and that's better than in the bank's pocket." What will they do with the dough? Perhaps put some aside for their children's college education. Possibly step up their mortgage payments. Then again, says Michael, a 42-year-old furniture salesman, "Rema and I spend what we make, and the more we make the more we spend."

Source: "This May Be the Swift Kick the Economy Needs," *Business Week* (January 13, 1992), 30–31.

organizations usually develop their own definitions of income to use in questionnaires. Such questions need to be simple to understand by respondents but precise enough to provide reliable and valid data for analysis. Definitions of income in marketing studies may have different purposes than governmental research. Nevertheless, it is helpful to use similar definitions because marketing studies are often compared with census data or reference surveys by governmental agencies.

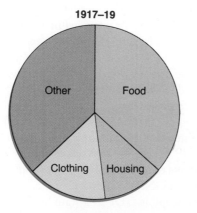

FIGURE 8.1   **Family Expenditures as Percent of Average Income, 1917–1919, and Today: The Larger the "Other" Category, the More Dynamic Marketing Becomes**

Note: Expenditure composition is not exactly comparable for the different time periods, but the data reflect differences in expenditures of the two time periods.
Sources: Bureau of Labor Statistics and Bureau of the Census.

Income   The Census Bureau defines income as money from wages and salaries as well as interest and welfare payments. The latter two, however, are often underreported. Official measures of income do not include other kinds of compensation such as employer or government benefits. Attempts to estimate the cash values of these benefits are difficult and raise consumer income substantially. Yet the failure to include them underreports changes in income in recent years. Similarly, if workers receive contractual rights to pensions in the future, no income is reported until such pensions are received, causing current income to be understated. The Census Bureau tries to equalize the rental value of a home to its owner by inputting a value to income for the home but ignores the mortgage tax subsidy that homeowners receive compared to renters. Changes in size of families, a rising number of nonfamily households, changing tax laws and other variables create problems that consumer researchers should always consider when analyzing data based on income measures.[3] Consumer researchers cannot always solve these definitional problems but, at a minimum, they need to be aware of such problems.

GDP and GNP   Economic conditions directly influence consumer behavior, as you saw in the opening scenario of this chapter. Consumer analysts, the media, and government policy makers want a single, easily understood measure of the economic condition of the nation. The official measures of production used for this purpose have recently changed in the United States.

Since 1941, the Commerce Department published the GNP, which was a measure of total goods and services produced or provided by the U.S. economy, valued at market prices. It was the broadest measure of the nation's economic health but also was used as a measure of the economic health of consumers when reported as per capita GNP. Since 1992, however, the Commerce Department releases statistics as the **Gross Domestic Product** or GDP which takes into consideration the location of production. The GDP measures goods and services produced in the United States including those produced or provided by foreign companies operating in the United States. GNP did not include these goods and services but did include goods and services produced by U.S. residents and corporations in other countries. Production of Ford of Europe as a wholly owned subsidiary, for example, was included in GNP but is excluded in GDP. Honda in the United States is part of GDP.

GDP is a more accurate gauge than GNP of what a nation's economy is actually doing. The disadvantage is that comparing per capita GDP statistics with the past may be difficult. Most industrialized nations have been using GDP for years, however, and the use of GDP by the United States makes global statistics more comparable. Marketing students today face a GDP world but face a computer full of statistics from the past based on GNP. A comparable measure is *Gross State Product* (GSP) reflecting the same concept as GDP at a state level.

Consumer Confidence

Consumers drive the economy. They account for more than two-thirds of all economic activity measured in GDP. In economies other than the United States or Canada, savings is much more important. In Japan and Germany, savings rates of about 15 percent are normal, but in the United States, savings were below 5 percent in the early 1990s. The combined inputs of American industry and federal and state or provincial governments are minimal compared to consumer spending.

What consumers do with their money is heavily influenced by what they believe will happen to their income in the future. Current income may be the primary determinant of products such as food at home but consumer confidence about future income is an essential element in understanding purchases of automobiles, major appliances, and other durable goods. Consumer confidence is a major factor influencing whether consumers will increase their debt levels or defer spending to pay off debt.

Measures of consumer confidence are reported periodically by various data services, such as the Conference Board. These data are very important to marketers making inventory decisions. During late summer, for example, retailers closely examine consumer confidence about future economic conditions in order to place inventory orders for the holiday selling season. The months of November and December account for over half of the sales or profits of many types of retailers. If inventories are too low, sales will be missed. If inventories are too high, price cuts may be needed so early in the season and so deep that few profits will be realized. Thus, consumer confidence is an important variable in the marketing decisions of retailers, their suppliers, and the entire economy. Consumer confidence may also be important in discerning trends about the future, a topic we will pursue further in a later chapter on Consumer Trends.

Whose Income?

Consumer behavior focuses on individuals, yet economic resources are often shared with others, in families or households. Consumer surveys usually ask entirely about individual behavior, except in the demographic section, where resource questions usually ask for family or household income. This is a matter of expediency in data collection, since the proportion is small of people whose income can be separated from family or household income. Recall some of the problems involved in this issue from Chapter 6. Although the trend is toward more emphasis on households, many surveys still ask resource questions with terminology such as "your family income last year before taxes." "Household" may be better terminology. When conducting marketing research, you will need to adjust family or household data by the number of members to determine per capita income. Carefully consider whether individual or consuming unit income is most relevant in understanding specific consumer decisions.

Where Is the Income?

Where would you go to find consumers who have the income to buy your product? This question could give you answers described on the basis of household size, occupation, racial or ethnic characteristics, or other variables.

A frequently used basis for targeting income segments is geographic area. Suburban areas or certain metropolitan counties contain consumers with high incomes. Table 8.1 shows the variation that exists between states. The Bureau of Economic Analysis reports that while average per capita personal income for Americans

TABLE 8.1   Per Capita Personal Income Projected to 2000

Region, Division, and State	Personal Income Per Capita		Average Annual Percent Change	
	1988	2000	1979–1988	1988–2000
United States	**$13,245**	**$15,345**	**1.53%**	**1.23%**
Northeast	**15,432**	**17,635**	**2.69**	**1.12**
New England	**16,205**	**18,154**	**3.41**	**0.95**
Maine	12,126	14,014	2.87	1.21
New Hampshire	15,449	17,363	3.69	0.98
Vermont	12,305	14,193	2.38	1.20
Massachusetts	16,736	18,694	3.69	0.93
Rhode Island	13,540	15,555	2.54	1.16
Connecticut	18,500	20,503	3.39	0.86
Middle Atlantic	**13,738**	**15,904**	**1.54**	**1.23**
New York	15,470	17,852	2.58	1.20
New Jersey	17,780	19,932	3.42	0.96
Pennsylvania	13,028	15,173	1.39	1.28
Midwest	**12,840**	**14,938**	**0.92**	**1.27**
East North Central	**13,042**	**15,098**	**0.93**	**1.23**
Ohio	12,486	14,531	0.96	1.27
Indiana	11,937	14,031	0.80	1.36
Illinois	14,126	16,131	1.01	1.11
Michigan	13,288	15,361	0.91	1.22
Wisconsin	12,490	14,575	0.82	1.29
West North Central	**12,362**	**14,562**	**0.89**	**1.37**
Minnesota	13,378	15,508	1.41	1.24
Iowa	11,777	13,849	0.14	1.36
Missouri	12,414	14,592	1.33	1.36
North Dakota	10,255	12,461	−0.49	1.64
South Dakota	10,244	12,330	−0.07	1.56
Nebraska	11,882	14,322	0.54	1.57
Kansas	12,645	14,986	0.70	1.43
South	**11,885**	**13,975**	**1.57**	**1.36**
South Atlantic	**12,927**	**15,009**	**2.27**	**1.25**
Delaware	14,217	15,747	2.14	0.86
Maryland	15,727	17,665	2.72	0.97
District of Columbia	17,149	19,823	1.88	1.21

Source: Bureau of Economic Analysis, *Survey of Current Business,* May 1990.

was $13,245 in a recent year, substantial variation exists. Income in the richest state, Connecticut, was more than twice that of the poorest state, Mississippi. Furthermore, even though the growth rate is expected to be much slower in the future than in the past, Connecticut is still projected to be the best market target in the year 2000, based on per capita personal income. You can examine the trends for other states in Table 8.1.

TABLE 8.1   continued

Region, Division, and State	1988	2000	Personal Income Per Capita Average Annual Percent Change 1979–1988	1988–2000
Virginia	$14,189	$16,345	2.72%	1.19%
West Virginia	9,393	10,921	0.19	1.26
North Carolina	11,481	13,481	2.33	1.35
South Carolina	10,372	12,304	1.83	1.43
Georgia	12,262	14,297	2.60	1.29
Florida	13,340	15,496	2.01	1.26
East South Central	**10,340**	**12,272**	**1.39**	**1.44**
Kentucky	10,304	12,178	0.97	1.40
Tennessee	11,138	13,192	1.84	1.42
Alabama	10,318	12,247	1.49	1.44
Mississippi	8,936	10,631	0.91	1.46
West South Central	**11,122**	**13,206**	**0.41**	**1.44**
Arkansas	9,812	11,594	1.11	1.40
Louisiana	9,876	11,680	0.08	1.41
Oklahoma	10,700	12,937	0.00	1.59
Texas	11,716	13,851	0.41	1.41
West	**13,811**	**15,844**	**1.02**	**1.15**
Mountain	**11,694**	**13,698**	**0.73**	**1.33**
Montana	10,364	12,474	−0.06	1.56
Idaho	10,119	12,181	0.14	1.56
Wyoming	10,956	12,898	−1.93	1.37
Colorado	13,220	15,311	1.00	1.23
New Mexico	10,037	11,949	0.57	1.46
Arizona	12,029	13,926	1.38	1.23
Utah	9,791	11,605	0.37	1.43
Nevada	14,076	15,855	0.55	1.00
Pacific	**14,566**	**16,607**	**1.10**	**1.10**
Washington	13,228	15,316	0.56	1.23
Oregon	11,953	13,908	0.21	1.27
California	15,070	17,113	1.26	1.06
Alaska	15,302	16,765	−0.56	0.76
Hawaii	13,449	15,219	1.13	1.04

Identifying Market Potential

The overall potential for many products may be identified with information about economic resources or other characteristics of consumers. Table 8.2 reveals how expenditures for major categories of consumer goods vary greatly by variables that

TABLE 8.2 Average Annual Income and Expenditures of U.S. Consumer Units

Line No.	Characteristic	Income before Taxes[1]	Total Expenditures	Food, Total	Food at Home Total[2]	Cereal and Bakery Products	Meats, Poultry, Fish, and Eggs	Dairy Products	Fruits and Vegetables	Food away from Home	Alcoholic Beverages	Housing Total	Shelter
1	All consumer units	28,540	25,892	3,748	2,136	312	551	274	373	1,612	269	8,079	4,493
	Age of reference person:												
2	Under 25 years old	14,827	16,373	2,455	1,121	166	249	152	176	1,334	312	4,746	3,004
3	25 to 34 years old	28,318	25,770	3,664	2,046	291	506	276	328	1,618	355	8,469	4,942
4	35 to 44 years old	36,428	33,078	4,636	2,599	387	661	333	434	2,037	281	10,467	6,147
5	45 to 54 years old	39,934	33,205	4,815	2,605	387	675	329	450	2,210	307	9,672	5,232
6	55 to 64 years old	29,979	25,765	3,952	2,355	334	648	295	433	1,597	239	7,757	3,929
7	65 to 74 years old	20,704	20,120	3,013	1,933	277	533	236	390	1,081	162	6,178	3,018
8	65 years old and over	13,707	13,339	1,939	1,373	215	357	175	290	566	89	4,682	2,276
	Husband and wife consumer units:												
9	Total husband and wife consumer units	37,299	32,314	4,727	2,761	407	710	353	475	1,967	263	9,731	5,174
10	Husband and wife only	33,825	27,955	3,815	2,148	302	558	266	413	1,667	259	8,453	4,433
	Husband and wife with children:												
11	Oldest child under 6	34,318	30,943	4,077	2,516	346	595	340	427	1,561	273	10,808	5,772
12	Oldest child 6 to 17	38,039	35,248	5,473	3,268	515	813	431	509	2,205	244	10,850	6,003
13	Oldest child 18 or over	45,596	37,764	5,966	3,313	484	929	408	546	2,653	299	9,819	4,901
14	One parent, at least one child under 18 years	16,276	18,616	3,005	1,931	291	511	256	314	1,074	167	7,113	4,249
15	Single person and other	18,509	17,951	2,452	1,265	179	328	163	235	1,187	292	5,903	3,576
	Income before taxes:												
16	Complete reporters of income	28,540	26,389	3,804	2,177	317	560	278	376	1,627	282	8,069	4,470
	Quintiles of income:												
17	Lowest 20 percent	4,942	10,893	1,950	1,322	194	347	164	247	628	144	3,957	2,209
18	Second 20 percent	12,872	16,880	2,815	1,831	269	499	234	323	984	185	5,510	2,982
19	Third 20 percent	22,570	23,290	3,545	2,074	303	521	272	352	1,471	264	7,051	3,850
20	Fourth 20 percent	34,974	32,084	4,633	2,570	371	636	337	442	2,063	343	9,370	5,171
21	Highest 20 percent	67,199	48,718	6,071	3,084	447	795	381	517	2,987	472	14,434	8,126
22	Incomplete reporting of income	(1)	23,360	3,545	1,977	293	517	260	360	1,568	219	8,236	4,628

[1]Income values derived from "complete income reporters" only. Represents the combined income of all consumer unit members 14 years or over during the 12 months preceding the interview. A complete reporter is a consumer unit providing values for at least one of the major sources of income.

[2]Includes other amounts not shown separately.

TABLE 8.2 Average Annual Income and Expenditures of U.S. Consumer Units (continued)

Line No.	Characteristic	Housing (continued) Fuel, Utilities, and Public Services	Household Operations and Furnishings[3]	Housekeeping Supplies	Apparel and Services	Transportation Vehicle Purchases	Gasoline and Motor Oil	All Other Transportation[4]	Health Care	Pensions and Social Security	Other Expenditures[5]	Personal Taxes
1	All consumer units	1,747	1,477	361	1,489	2,361	932	1,800	1,298	1,935	3,982	2,391
	Age of reference person:											
2	Under 25 years old	897	686	166	1,042	2,039	659	1,213	523	926	2,458	1,088
3	25 to 34 years old	1,545	1,635	347	1,504	2,794	923	1,763	777	2,052	3,469	2,390
4	35 to 44 years old	2,023	1,885	411	2,015	2,931	1,152	2,287	1,253	2,756	5,299	3,201
5	45 to 54 years old	2,173	1,818	450	2,112	3,016	1,248	2,376	1,258	2,991	5,410	3,935
6	55 to 64 years old	1,935	1,510	383	1,355	1,749	970	1,883	1,518	2,191	4,152	2,653
7	65 to 74 years old	1,739	1,039	382	977	1,849	729	1,397	2,005	682	3,129	1,021
8	65 years old and over	1,393	764	249	451	667	367	725	2,230	119	2,071	822
	Husband and wife consumer units:											
9	Total husband and wife consumer units	2,100	1,994	463	1,829	3,109	1,188	2,226	1,658	2,579	5,003	3,127
10	Husband and wife only	1,873	1,738	409	1,395	2,743	964	1,988	1,837	2,127	4,374	3,115
	Husband and wife with children:											
11	Oldest child under 6	1,841	2,719	477	1,764	3,224	1,054	1,971	1,206	2,502	4,065	2,585
12	Oldest child 6 to 17	2,197	2,159	491	2,182	3,054	1,279	2,236	1,479	2,878	5,572	3,046
13	Oldest child 18 or over	2,533	1,852	533	2,171	3,894	1,624	2,895	1,659	3,237	6,200	3,888
14	One parent, at least one child under 18 years	1,482	1,112	271	1,383	1,174	558	1,132	578	982	2,524	955
15	Single person and other	1,295	805	227	1,019	1,495	631	1,305	903	1,180	2,771	1,611
	Income before taxes:											
16	Complete reporters of income[1]	1,726	1,489	383	1,537	2,388	934	1,819	1,282	2,208	4,065	2,391
	Quintiles of income:											
17	Lowest 20 percent	1,121	455	173	574	588	459	613	831	159	1,620	88
18	Second 20 percent	1,432	793	302	901	1,422	659	1,061	1,320	626	2,383	563
19	Third 20 percent	1,675	1,171	354	1,356	2,282	926	1,674	1,286	1,580	3,326	1,396
20	Fourth 20 percent	1,928	1,807	464	1,826	3,334	1,204	2,306	1,425	3,007	4,636	2,849
21	Highest 20 percent	2,473	3,216	620	3,025	4,308	1,420	3,430	1,550	5,656	8,351	7,042
22	Incomplete reporting of income	1,875	1,455	277	1,310	2,194	920	1,716	1,397	289	3,535	(1)

[3] Includes household equipment.

[4] Includes other vehicle expenses and public transportation.

[5] Includes life insurance, entertainment, personal care, reading, education, tobacco and smoking supplies, cash contributions, and miscellaneous expenditures.

Source: U.S. Bureau of Labor Statistics, Consumer Expenditures in 1988 (BLS News Release, U.S.D.L.: 90–96).

might be used to define market segments. These data are for the most recent year available. Although numbers change from year to year, the relationships between spending and other variables are fairly stabile. In recent decades, the amount spent for housing and transportation has increased slightly, with small declines in the amounts spent for food and apparel. The share of expenditures devoted to life insurance, pensions, and other personal insurance has remained fairly constant.[4]

Who Has Buying Power?

It is much easier to hit a bull's-eye when you can see the target. That is why marketers place so much emphasis on knowing who has the buying power and how they are spending their money.

You may have questioned why so much attention in marketing is concentrated on *husband and wife consuming units* rather than single households or why marketers seem to emphasize consumers aged 45–54 so heavily. Examination of Table 8.2 quickly reveals the answer. *Consuming units with the reference person aged 45–54* average several thousand more dollars income to spend and save. Analysis of age segments shows that the 45–54 age spends almost the same on food at home as the 35–44 age group but considerably more for food away from home as well as somewhat more for alcoholic beverages, apparel, and some other categories. The younger group, however, spends more on housing. Consumers over 65 spend considerably more on health care.

Life cycle effects, discussed earlier in Chapter 6, are readily observable in Table 8.2. Husband and wife *consumer units with older children* have more income than other families. Single persons and single parent consuming units spend dramatically lower amounts on most items although relatively less on housing. Expenditures are higher than income among single parent consumers, indicating the distressed economic situation of this market segment.

Relationships between income and spending are revealed most readily by examining expenditures by quintiles of income. Notice in Table 8.2 the dramatic differences in income between the lowest quintile and the *highest quintile*. For some products such as food at home, the differences are relatively minor. The top 20 percent spend nearly 5 times as much as the lowest quintile, however, for food away from home. The top quintile spend over 5 times as much as the lowest 20 percent does for apparel and 7 times as much for vehicle purchases. You can easily understand why marketers place so much emphasis on the "up market."

Targeting the Up Market

Marketers increasingly target the up market, generally defined as the upper quintile or quartile of income (see Figure 8.2). These consuming units account for close to half of the sales of many product categories and far more than half for some luxury products.

The up market is likely to be dual-income households, time constrained (especially where children are present), and emphasizing quality in their product preferences. They are particularly important as target markets for products such as

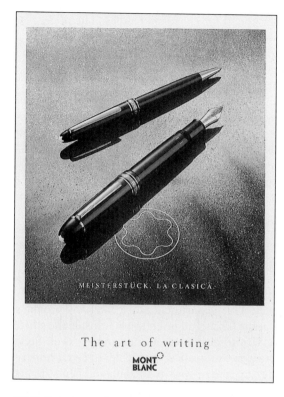

FIGURE 8.2   Ads Targeted to the Up Market
Source: Courtesy of Mont Blanc; Godiva.

men's wear, furniture, electronic and home entertainment, home furnishings, tableware, domestics, fine jewelry and tools, hardware, and building materials.[5]

Department stores are particularly strong competitors for apparel purchases by the up market. Firms such as Nordstrom have grown rapidly by providing excellent service to upscale consumers. Specialty stores are also beneficiaries of the purchasing power of the up market but so are some discount stores, especially factory outlet stores. Airport retailing provides a unique opportunity to reach the upscale, normally time-impoverished consumers in a unique situation where they have excess time to spend. Bloomie's Express, a Bloomingdale's branch at New York's Kennedy Airport, for example, grosses an average of $1,000 per square foot annually with items like $375 denim jackets and $100 infant overalls.[6]

Communicating to the up market is more print oriented than to other market segments. Readership of local weekday and Sunday newspapers is higher. So is readership of many magazines, creating effectiveness for ads such as that shown in Figure 8.2. Notice the ad for Mont Blanc, which assumes that its up market target will understand copy in German, Spanish, and English. The Godiva ad uses words such as "far-too-civilized" and "imaginative coatings" to communicate with an up market target willing to pay $25 per pound for chocolate truffles. The up market watches television less and listens to radio less than other segments, although up market consumers have a higher concentration subscribing to cable television and listening to public television and radio.

The highest end of the up market is sometimes described as "super affluents," defined as above income levels such as over $50,000, over $75,000, or even over $100,000. These market segments are increasingly the targets of specialized marketing programs. They are growing so rapidly that we will need to examine them again in the chapter on Consumer Trends.

A major implication of affluence in consumer resources is the rising importance of service marketing. The affluent can buy a wide variety of services that other consumers only wish they might buy—at beauty salons, dry cleaning shops, lawn care companies, and so forth. Many of the growth opportunities for marketing organizations are therefore in services. Additionally, excellence in service becomes especially important for many traditional marketers of a wide variety of products. The importance of such service was a major conclusion of the best seller by Albrecht and Zemke, *Service America*.[7]

Retailers such as Nordstrom have achieved enviable rates of growth and profitability by delighting the up market. This department store company provides classic products such as that shown in the Chanel ad in Figure 8.3. Inside the store, Nordstrom's employees provide service to customers at a legendary level. Stew Leonard's, a family owned grocery store in Connecticut, has achieved extraordinary success in serving the affluent suburban market with two commandments for its employees. One, the customer is always right. Two, when the customer is wrong, go back and read commandment number one.

Targeting the Down Market

The simultaneous success of luxury-good stores and off-price stores indicates that not everyone is affluent. There is a large down market. But even stores that appeal to the down market need to be attractive and stylish. Lerner Shops, for example, once targeted lower income women clothing shoppers with dowdy stores. When the Limited purchased Lerner, lower income women were still the target but the Limited added fashion and flair in the ambiance of the store. Sanford Goodkin explains, "Nobody wants to be reminded that they are not rich. Successful discounters have made their mark by convincing customers that they are smart and special, not poor riffraff."[8]

Value-oriented retailers have experienced rapid growth in recent years by providing good products at reasonable prices to the down market. The key to success for the best of these is to *treat consumers with respect and good service*, even though they may have less money than other market segments. In the Southeastern states, Food Lion became the nation's fastest growing grocery store chain with low prices, basic levels of product selection, and appeals to the economical shopper. The key, however, is that service is reliable and very respectful to consumers even though it is a basic, no frills approach. Wal-Mart has become the largest retailer in the United States (and has entered Mexico) with two basic themes. One theme, "Every Day Low Price," may naively be thought to be most important. The other theme, "Treat

FIGURE 8.3   Chanel Reaches the Up Market with Classic Products
Source: Courtesy of Chanel.

Every Customer as a Guest," is more difficult to understand functionally and difficult to imitate by competitors but is more important in understanding the success of Wal-Mart. Firms that treat the down market with respect and good service also attract some of the up market.

Opportunities for profit abound in economic adversity. One example is All For One, a division of Consolidated Stores shown in Figure 8.4. This chain buys "closeouts" from manufacturers or other retailers that have excess inventories or are in financial difficulty. It sells brand name merchandise for one price, currently a dollar. There have always been stores such as this, but the difference between All For One and many of its competitors is that the stores are light and bright, very clean, attractive, planned for logistical efficiency, provide good service, and are sometimes located in shopping centers willing to rent at low prices because of excess space. And because the inventory is ever-changing, consumers find different products to keep the enthusiasm alive.

There are other ways to profit from economic adversity. During a recession, marketers may be forced to focus on attributes of products or services that provide value for customers at the lowest price. Well-financed firms sometimes expand

FIGURE 8.4   All For One: Designed for Value Shoppers

Source: Courtesy of Consolidated Stores.

market share by maintaining advertising when competitors are forced to lower their promotional activities. Well-financed firms may be able to demand better terms from vendors or for retailing space, further benefitting from recessionary economic conditions. Campbell Soup Co. observed a consumer shift away from higher-priced foods such as ready-to-serve soups toward cheaper cook-at-home products. Campbell took cream of broccoli soup out of a higher-end Gold Label can, cut the price, and packed it in the familiar red-and-white can. They marketed it as a base for homemade meals. It sold more than 55 million cans and became the most successful new soup since 1935. Campbell also scored big by packing favorite soups in new, family-size, 26-ounce cans and cutting the unit price.[9]

Back to the basics marketing is the key to reaching down market consumers. About 40 percent of U.S. households earn less than $25,000. They are likely to be young or old and single or divorced. The poorest Americans spend heavily on education, prescription drugs, and tobacco. They are heavy users of products such as malt liquor, pancake syrup, whole milk, and laxatives. They are light users of dishwasher detergent, white wine, Diet Pepsi, skimmed milk, and Grey Poupon mustard.[10]

Other Economic Resources

Other economic resources besides income affect consumer behavior. The most important are wealth (net worth) and credit.

Wealth, measured by assets or net worth, is correlated with income. The government and private research organizations collect many statistics on income but relatively few about assets or net worth. Thus, it is more difficult to target consumers based on wealth. The primary variation is that older consumers tend to have a larger proportion of wealth than younger consumers. The primary asset of most Americans is their home—about 60 percent of total assets but only 9 percent of the assets of households with a net worth of more than $1 million. Millionaires are more likely to have their assets in stocks, bonds, and CDs. Although homes may appreciate, they are not readily available as a source of cash unless marketers can show consumers how to obtain a secondary mortgage. In today's environment, such loans may be tax advantaged.

Wealthy families spend their money on services, travel, interest, and investments more than do their less wealthy neighbors. Their expenditures on home furnishings, appliances, entertainment equipment, and similar products are not particularly high because wealthy families are usually in later stages of the life cycle and not concerned with furnishing new homes or making additional purchases of major equipment. Consumer in Focus 8.2 gives additional details about how to target affluent market segments.

Consumer in Focus   8.2

Consumer Behavior of Affluent Markets

As affluence increases, many households, particularly those with two earners, will place a premium on time. Improved customer service, immediate availability, trouble-free operation of products, and dependable maintenance and repair services will be valued. There will be a new willingness to pay the price for services that assure product performance and limit inconvenience.

In general, these income projections suggest that marketers should upgrade their focus and concentrate on higher-quality, higher-priced goods and services. Goods and services in demand will include the following:

■ Products that ease drudgery and household maintenance; automate homemaking chores; save time; and demonstrate quality, reliability, durability, and luxury.

■ Improved housing, including single-family homes and condominiums, that will appeal to more affluent, middle-aged, and preretirement husband-wife

Continued

Consumer in Focus 8.2 continued

households. Included here are quality furniture, fixtures, appliances, and household services.

■ Products and services designed to enhance the physical self, particularly those perceived as maintaining and restoring youthfulness: cosmetics, skin care products, health foods, vitamins, cosmetic surgery, spas, hair stylists, clothing consultants, exercise facilities, and diet and health programs.

■ Products and services that support the psychological self: counseling, education, skills analysis, stress management training, cultural activities, and self-improvement books and courses.

■ Products that support mobility and immediate gratification: instant photography, all-night restaurants, portable telephones and computers, emergency health centers, worldwide product services, rentals, 800 numbers, home entertainment centers, automated tellers, and instant credit.

■ Products and services that will secure and protect individuals and property: sensing devices, home protection systems, security guards, protected residential areas, insurance of various kinds, fire and burglar protection, financial security plans, air and water purifiers, and sanitation products.

■ Entertainment and leisure activities, including services as varied as participatory and spectator sports, travel, and gambling.

■ Products that permit us to differentiate ourselves and that appeal to the snob in all of us; products associated with taste, breeding, graceful lifestyles, culture, and the so-called "markets of the mind." Included are gourmet foods; wines; decorator and designer products and services; paintings; sculpture; and performing arts such as ballet, opera, symphony concerts, and drama.

Source: William Lazer, "How Rising Affluence Will Reshape Markets," *American Demographics* 6 (February 1984).

Targeting wealthy consumers is difficult. Usually marketers use income as a proxy for wealth. Government data are available from the Federal Reserve Board's Survey of Consumer Finances or the Census Bureau's Survey of Income and Program Participation. Donnelley Marketing Information Services of Stamford, Connecticut, keeps a master file of 82 million households which can be used to predict the overall affluence of a household. The annual Disposable Income and Net Worth Report from CACI of Fairfax, Virginia, shows how to find households with a high net worth by looking at the age of the householders, income distributions, and other factors.[11]

Credit extends the income resource, at least for a period of time (Table 8.3). Actually, because the cost of credit must be subtracted from the consumer's total resource availability, credit reduces the ability to buy goods and services in the long

TABLE 8.3 Consumer Willingness to Borrow

	Boats and Hobby Purchases	Auto Purchases	Expenses Due to Illness	Educational Expenses	Furniture Purchases	Vacation Expenses	Living Expenses When Income Is Cut	Consolidation of Bills	Fur Coat or Jewelry
All households	19%	82%	82%	79%	49%	13%	46%	48%	5%
Household income									
Under $10,000	10%	63%	77%	65%	39%	11%	54%	53%	3%
$10,000–19,999	14	86	81	81	49	13	46	52	4
$20,000–29,999	24	91	84	87	55	15	49	50	5
$30,000–39,999	32	93	84	88	58	15	41	48	6
$40,000–49,999	25	91	84	85	55	15	40	44	5
$50,000 and over	37	90	89	90	59	17	45	47	10
Age of householder									
< 25	27%	88%	91%	89%	56%	18%	68%	66%	8%
25–34	28	90	84	88	57	17	52	55	6
35–44	26	90	83	87	52	15	46	48	5
45–54	17	84	82	82	50	12	42	50	5
55–64	14	82	80	76	47	10	45	44	4
65+	5	61	74	58	33	9	37	35	2

ercent of householders who feel it is all right to use installment debt for different types of purchases, 1983)

David E. Bloom and Todd P. Steen, "Living On Credit," *American Demographics* 9 (October 1987), 22–29, at 25. Reprinted with permission.

run. Nevertheless, Americans are increasingly willing to use credit for temporary expansion of their economic resources. Younger householders are more likely to favor borrowing than older householders. About 90 percent of those younger than 45 feel it appropriate to borrow for an automobile purchase, compared to only 60 percent of those aged 65 and older. These data are shown in Table 8.3. Americans are most willing to borrow for cars, for medical bills, or for educational reasons. Younger households and those with higher incomes are more willing to borrow, no matter what the reason.[12]

Consumers' use of credit impacts the economic condition of a nation as well as specific expenditures. The 1980s in America was a boom time of consumer spending, stimulated by tax cuts and baby boomers setting up households but facilitated by credit. In 1980, total household debt was equal to about 70 percent of total household income but by 1990, household debt approached 90 percent of household income. The need to pay off this debt as well as declining values in commercial and residential real estate due to over building during the 1980s means that consumer spending is much slower in the 1990s than the previous decade.[13]

Other effects of economic resources on consumer buying could be analyzed. Some you have already thought about in the chapters on family, ethnicity, and social class and you will see more in other chapters of this book. We'll stop the discussion of economic resources now, however, and examine one of the other resources that facilitate and shape consumer decisions.

Temporal Resources

Time is important in understanding consumer behavior because of the increasing lack of time experienced by most Americans. Americans now value leisure time as highly as they value money. The most time-crunched Americans are women, parents, and minorities. Almost half of American workers say they would give up a day's pay to get an extra day off.[14] Are you one of these time-crunched consumers? Table 8.4 shows the questions that are used to measure the time crunch.

One of the most individual variables of human behavior is concerned with how a person spends her or his time budget. Most is spent on work, sleep, and other required activities. A portion, however, is spent on very personal activities called **leisure**, reflecting both personality and lifestyle preferences.

Consumer resources consist of two budget constraints: money budget and time budget. Income is a critical variable, as we saw earlier in this chapter. To understand consumer behavior fully, however, marketers must also examine how consumers spend their time budgets.[15] Although rising incomes might allow consumers to *buy* more of everything, they cannot conceivably *do* more of everything. Doing more things, as opposed to buying more things, requires an additional resource: ime. Whereas money budgets have no theoretical expansion limits, time has an imate restraint. It is a zero-sum game.

When discretionary incomes increase in a society, markets for time-related or services become more important. Scarcity creates value. For affluent con-

TABLE 8.4   Are You Time Crunched?

If you agree with more than three statements on the list below, consider yourself time crunched.

	Percent of Americans Who Agree with Selected Statements
1. I often feel under stress when I don't have enough time	43%
2. When I need more time, I tend to cut back on my sleep	40%
3. At the end of the day, I often feel that I haven't accomplished what I set out to do	33%
4. I worry that I don't spend enough time with my family or friends	33%
5. I feel that I'm constantly under stress—trying to accomplish more than I can handle	31%
6. I feel trapped in a daily routine	28%
7. When I'm working long hours, I often feel guilty that I'm not at home	27%
8. I consider myself a workaholic	26%
9. I just don't have time for fun anymore	22%
10. Sometimes I feel that my spouse doesn't know who I am anymore	21%

Source: John P. Robinson, "Your Money or Your Time," *American Demographics* 13 (November 1991).

sumers, the chief concern becomes buying more time rather than more products. The value of time increases as money budgets increase, thereby increasing the possibility that a marketer may enhance the value of products (and the corresponding price) more than the additional cost of doing so.

The consumer's time budget naively was regarded historically as having two components: work and leisure. This conceptualization is shown in the upper portion of Figure 8.5. A more contemporary conceptualization is shown in the lower portion. Here, consumer time budgets are divided into three blocks: "paid time," "obligated time," and "discretionary time." Lane and Lindquist use a similar classification system including income producing time, committed (obligated and nonobligated) time, and uncommitted (planned and unplanned) time.[16] It is only the latter block of discretionary or uncommitted time that can be truly regarded as leisure time. Voss concludes, "Leisure is a period of time referred to as discretionary time. It is that period when an individual feels no sense of economic, legal, moral, or social compulsion or obligation, nor of physiological necessity. The choice of how to utilize this time period belongs solely to the individual."[17]

An additional complication in defining leisure occurs when individuals are paid for activities they might otherwise choose as discretionary activities. Artists, professors, and professional athletes may be examples of individuals who are fortunate

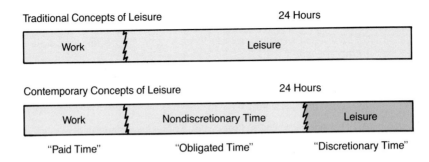

FIGURE 8.5 Conceptualizations of Consumer Time Budgets and Leisure: Only "Discretionary" Time Is Truly Leisure Time

to be paid for activities they would otherwise choose as leisure activities. Perhaps students might even view reading textbooks such as this one as leisure rather than obligated or paid activities! Then again, perhaps they might not.

Time Goods   A contemporary conceptualization of consumer time budgets leads to the recognition that goods and services have important time properties. Products and services classified by their time properties may be called time goods, and the time properties of goods have important marketing implications.

Time-Using Goods

Some products and services require the use of time with the product. Examples would be watching television, skiing, fishing, golfing, or playing tennis, all of which are usually classified as leisure-time activities. They fall in the category of time budgets called "discretionary time" or leisure.

Will consumers buy products that require the use of time? The answer requires consideration of the values associated with other categories of time usage in a typical 24-hour day. *Paid time* or work for example may be increasing for consumers with large money budgets because women enter the work force, workers get promotions (often the result of working longer hours), and the simple fact that people who work longer hours earn more income. For individuals, these trends may be contrary to popular opinion or government statistics that indicate shorter work weeks.

Belief in a reduced work week may be due to confusion caused by statistics based on payrolls. They usually include both full-time and part-time workers, which distorts the averages for all workers in times of increasing proportions of part-time workers. Payroll records do not distinguish second jobs, which understates the real work week for many consumers. The main increases in leisure time have been associated with earlier retirement as well as an increased number of holidays and length of vacations rather than reducing the hours worked in a normal week.[18]

Nondiscretionary or obligated time is a major block of nonmarket (nonwork) time that affects consumer purchases of time goods. Nondiscretionary time includes physical obligations (sleeping, commuting, personal care, and so forth), social obligations (which increase with urbanization and the rising proportion of professional and white-collar occupations), and moral obligations. Physical and social obligations increase with increasing income. Americans spend more time traveling today than they did ten years ago, especially those in high income households. Men who earn over $35,000 travel 12 hours a week compared to low income men who travel 8 hours. High income women travel 2 hours a week more than low income women.[19]

Harried American consumers cope with time-crunched lifestyles in many ways. The Hilton Time Values Study, described in Consumer in Focus 8.3, found that cutting back on sleep to "make" more time was true for 38 percent. Although Americans are facing a time-money dilemma, they have little ability to change their situations. For a marketer such as Hilton Hotels, this dilemma represents a market opportunity, as Consumer in Focus 8.3 describes. Other ways of coping may not result in the purchase of time goods. For example, "gross national housework" time is declining. People, especially women, are simply spending less time doing housework.[20]

Consumer in Focus   8.3

Hilton Hotels Targets Time-Crunched Consumers

The Hilton Hotels Corporation commissioned the 1991 Hilton Time Values Survey, a telephone survey of 1,010 adults age 18 and over. It focused on America's values and attitudes toward time and the reasons behind people's behavior.

The study disclosed that finding enough time for both work and personal lives has become so critical for most working Americans that nearly two-thirds say they would be willing to take less pay to get more time off. Working women, particularly those with children, feel the time crunch more than men. During the 1990s, respondents indicate spending time with family and friends will become more important than making money. More people (77 percent) selected "spending time with family and friends" than any other priority. More emphasis on "having free time" was the choice of 66 percent and "pursuing personal experiences such as traveling for pleasure and pursuing hobbies" was chosen by 59 percent. "Making money" came in fifth place (61) percent while "spending money on material possessions" came in last (29 percent). People in the eastern states placed more emphasis on making money than in the more relaxed western states.

Continued

Consumer in Focus 8.3 continued

Other findings that reveal America's current time-crunch attitudes include the following:

- Thirty-three percent said they are unlikely to be able to make time for their ideal weekend.
- Twenty-one percent said they don't have time for fun anymore.
- Thirty-three percent said they don't accomplish what they set out to do each day.
- Thirty-eight percent report cutting back on sleep to "make" more time.
- Twenty-nine percent constantly feel under stress.
- Thirty-one percent worry they don't spend enough time with family and friends.
- Twenty percent report calling in sick to work at least once during the past 12 months when they simply need time to relax.

As a response to the study, Hilton created the BounceBack Weekend to be an affordable, stress-relieving getaway. In essence, Hilton enables its guests to buy the free time they need in the form of a getaway weekend. Starting at $65 per night, BounceBack Weekends include free Continental breakfast for everyone in the party and kids stay free in their parents' room. The program emphasizes that consumers gain freedom from daily routine and the other time-crunch problems that rob them of their leisure hours. Families get a chance to step off the treadmill and gain new energy and perspective. Michael Ribero, Hilton's senior vice president for marketing, reports that the concept has proved so popular that Saturday has become Hilton's highest occupancy night.

Source: Materials courtesy of Hilton Hotels & Resorts.

Consumers may earn high incomes but live in time poverty. Such consumers require a lot of value from the limited hours available for leisure or discretionary activities. They may be willing to pay more money to enjoy their leisure time, thereby expanding market potential for such things as air travel, expensive sports equipment to maximize their enjoyment, top-notch exercise facilities, instruction to increase their exercise effectiveness, and so forth. They are likely to switch from less intense or active leisure activities such as fishing to more active sports such as racquetball or squash. This was shown in a study of leisure time satisfactions in which highly educated and high-income men (presumably busier) were more likely to derive satisfaction from tennis than from golf.[21]

The 41 million households that take one or more vacation trips per year spend an average of $3,000 a year on personal travel but the 19 million frequent traveling households (3 or more personal trips and at least one international trip per year) spend $4,000 a year.[22] Middle-aged consumers have the least amount of leisure but as they move toward retirement and become empty nesters, they begin to add to their budgets for leisure while at the same time they begin to decrease their budgets for necessary expenses.

Time-Saving Goods

Consumers can gain leisure time (discretionary time) if they can *decrease nondiscretionary time expenditures*. Fortunately for marketers, this may be done through the purchase of goods and services.

The purchase of services is one way to increase leisure or to have more discretionary time. Hiring either a neighborhood teenager or ChemLawn may free the consumer for either more work (which might increase income) or more nonmarket time to pursue leisure activities. Child care, housecleaning, restaurants, and a wide array of other services are direct substitutes for time obligations. They represent some of the greatest growth opportunities to be found in industrialized economies. Table 8.5 discloses that employment time-saving strategies have increased substantially in recent years. By 1991 over 60 percent of consumers save time by taking home meals, eating at fast-food restaurants, or simply postponing tasks such as housecleaning.

The purchase of durable and nondurable goods is another way to have more leisure or discretionary time. Dishwashers and microwave ovens are excellent examples of how time-saving attributes create enormous market opportunities. Nondurables are also affected, of course, since it is difficult to introduce new food products today that are not microwavable. Not only does this affect food industries, it also profoundly affects packaging products. Convenience stores and disposable products illustrate more market developments created by consumers' desire to buy time. A

TABLE 8.5   Saving Time

Consumers Are Increasing Time-Saving Activities

Percent of adults who "often or sometimes" choose time-saving activities, by type of activity, 1986–1991.

Type of activity	1986	1991
Housecleaning Put Off	64%	74%
Eat in Fast-Food Restaurants	59%	70%
Purchase Take-Out Food	48%	60%
Shop in Convenience Stores	44%	56%
Prepare Frozen Dinners/Foods	30%	42%
Shop by Mail, Computer, or Phone	22%	29%
Pay for Housekeeping	12%	14%

Source: "Time Savers," *American Demographics* 13, February 1992, 10.

comprehensive review of the literature and an econometric study of consumption related to time concluded:

> The rises in the prices of male and female time relative to other prices (annual increases of 6.1 percent and 6.5 percent in the prices of male and female time, respectively, versus annual 4.8 percent increases in the implicit price index for personal consumption expenditures) combined to alter American consumption patterns over the 30-year period from one in which nondurables played a large role to one in which durables and, increasingly, services play important roles. Unless some structural change occurs to disturb these results, increasing prices of time will continue to alter American consumption patterns.[23]

Polychronic Time Use

Polychronic time involves combining activities simultaneously, such as eating while watching television or working with a laptop computer while traveling on an airplane. By combining activities, individuals use their time resources to accomplish several goals at the same time. This concept has also been called "dual time usage" and contrasts with performing only one activity at a time (monochronic time use). Computers make some of these things possible. Figure 8.6, for example, shows how CompuServe allows travelers to use electronic mail even when they are traveling to another city.

Many products are marketed to facilitate polychronic time usage. Laptop computers, mentioned above, are one example. One of the most rapidly accepted innovations was the cellular phone, probably because it appealed to people with high incomes and therefore a high value on time by dual usage with an increasing amount of obligated time used in driving. Such products enrich the time budgets of consumers, producing a greater output of benefits than could be achieved in 24 hours of single or monochronic activities. Some of the stress that results from feeling one has too many things to do, or role overload, can be reduced with polychronic time usage. Drive-through cleaners, supermarkets offering planned assortments of food to simplify a consumer's need to plan and prepare meals, the addition of racks to facilitate reading while using exercise bikes, or the addition of beepers to allow medical or dental patients to shop in nearby stores while waiting for appointments are just a few of the marketing innovations stimulated by analysis of consumers' use of polychronic time.[24]

Communicating Time Prices

Some advertisers feature the "time price" of a product. Such ads may state that the product requires only two hours to install. Convenience due to a nearby location is also an attempt to reduce the time price. Some shopping malls announce the best ways to enter and exit the mall to attract shoppers unwilling to pay the time price of traffic congestion. New malls have a comprehensive regional plan to prevent such problems. Harried consumers—those who feel rushed and pressured for time—visit fewer stores and make few comparisons by considering fewer brands and attributes than those who are relaxed shoppers.[25]

Product attributes may communicate the ability to reduce the time price of the product. Examples include new "dry" deodorants, quick-dry paint, higher horse-

FIGURE 8.6   Traveling and Electronic Mail as Simultaneous Activities
Source: Courtesy of CompuServe Division of H&R Block.

power lawn mowers, and the Concorde airplane, which, although it has a high price in economic resources, is the cheapest plane in the air in temporal resources.

Some marketers offer a **time guarantee (TG)**, defined as a promise by the seller that assures customers they will not have to devote an unreasonable amount of time to getting product and service problems resolved. Any unusual problems would be handled at locations and times convenient to the customer. Koerner Ford in Rochester, New York, offers a TG which assures customers that if a problem with the vehicle is not fixed right the first time, the dealership will send a mechanic to the home or work location at times convenient to the customer to solve the problem. In a study of this offer, 63 percent of customers of the dealership rated the TG as very important, although most wanted it as an included service rather than something for which customers would pay extra.[26]

The Times, They Are a Changin'

Consumers are changing they way they spend their time. While some activitie stable, there are major changes, especially in the area of communications.

interpersonal conversations. For men between 25 and 44, Juster found that time on the telephone has almost doubled recently, and the gap between the sexes has narrowed. In other areas of time budgets, television viewing was increasing in prior years but now appears to be declining.[27]

In a major study comparing today's time budgets with those of the past, Hawes found that while women are spending less time in housework because of the entry to the labor force, men are spending more time doing things around the home.[28]

The importance of time must be recognized when developing marketing strategies as well as in communications programs. Fast-food restaurants capitalize on the rise of working women and one-person households with a resulting decline of traditional home-cooked meals and meals eaten away from home account for well over 40 percent of all food spending. Grocers, fed up with losing customers to fast-food outlets, are responding with convenience-driven efforts of their own. Giant and other supermarket chains are adding take-out dishes such as prepared salads, sandwiches, soup, and hot foods. Even five minutes in a microwave may be too slow compared to shelf-stable foods if consumers can accept the idea of getting a meal from an unrefrigerated package.

The analysis of temporary resources in marketing strategies is a contemporary recognition of the principle Benjamin Franklin in 1748 told a young tradesperson, "Remember that time is money." Franklin also commented, "Dost thou love Life? Then do not squander Time; for that's the stuff Life is made of."

Cognitive Resources

Walking through a supermarket in the mid-1990s, you may see a lot of consumers looking up and down the shelves, picking up products and comparing labels, spending minutes or even hours in the store, and, often, looking a bit confused. This is not a new form of ritual shopping behavior; it is an illustration that consumers have another resource from which they must spend in order to buy products and services. The other activity is information processing or spending cognitive resources.

Cognitive resource represents *the mental capacity available for undertaking various information-processing activities.* Just as marketers compete for consumers' money and time, so also do marketers compete for cognitive or information processing. Marketers need to get the attention of consumers and in today's market place, such a task may be difficult.

Capacity is a limited resource. We are able to process only a certain amount of information at a time. Capacity size is often described in terms of a **chunk**, which represents a grouping or combination of information that can be processed as a unit. Depending upon which source one chooses to draw upon, capacity varies from four or five chunks to as many as seven.[29] It has been rumored that the phone company selected seven-digit phone numbers because of the difficulties many consumers would have with more numbers. Consistent with this, learning declines as the number of words in a sentence increases beyond seven.[30]

The allocation of cognitive capacity is known as **attention**. Attention consists of two dimensions: **direction** and **intensity**.[31] Direction represents the **focus** of attention. Because consumers are unable to process all of the internal and external stimuli available at any given moment, they must be selective in how they allocate this limited resource. Some stimuli will gain attention, others will be ignored.

Intensity, on the other hand, refers to the *amount* of capacity focused in a particular direction. Consumers will often allocate only the capacity needed to identify a stimulus (for example, another car ad) before redirecting their attention elsewhere. On other occasions, consumers may pay enough attention to understand the basic gist of the ad. Sometimes consumers may give the ad their complete concentration and carefully scrutinize the message, such as a consumer in the market for a new car who is reading an automobile ad.

The fact that capacity is a limited resource carries a number of important implications concerning how consumers process information and make product choices. Some of these are discussed subsequently.

Gaining Attention

Gaining the consumer's attention represents one of the most formidable challenges a marketer may face. Consumers are bombarded continually by a substantial number of stimuli that compete for their limited capacity. Estimates of the number of ads consumers encounter in a typical day range in the hundreds, and are likely to increase as marketers continue to develop new avenues for reaching consumers (for example, the use of ads in rental videos) or video displays in shopping carts or at the checkout area of a store. A major determinant of an ad's success, then, is the likelihood of its gaining the consumer's attention.

Gaining attention at the point of purchase can be equally important. The use of eye-catching displays can be instrumental in helping a product stand out from the clutter of brands squeezed onto a retailer's shelf (see Consumer in Focus 8.4). Packaging can serve a similar function. Achieving a "louder voice on store shelves" was a major consideration in designing the cans for the various Coca-Cola brands.

Consequently, it is very important for marketers to understand what factors may influence the focus of attention. When you read Chapter 13 (Information Processing), you will find there are a number of stimuli at the marketer's disposal for gaining attention.

Shallow Attention

Another reality of the marketplace is that many products are simply not that important to consumers (see the concept of product involvement in Chapter 9) to warrant a "large" investment of their limited cognitive resources. In many respects, consumers are "cognitive misers" as they attempt to find acceptable rather than optimal solutions for many of their consumption needs. Thus, the cognitive demands required by an elaborate decision-making process are such that consumers will devote the needed capacity (as well as the time) for only a limited number of products.

Gaining Attention with Point-of-Purchase Displays: Olympia Brewing Company

Point-of-purchase (POP) displays are often used by marketers for attracting consumers' attention in a retail environment that is increasingly "cluttered" with new products. The Olympia Brewing Company conducted a study to determine the effects of POP displays on purchase behavior. The research involved both food and liquor stores located within two California cities. Some of the stores received a display while others did not (these latter stores provided a baseline for comparing the results for stores with displays). In addition, two types of POP displays were tested: motion displays (those with some movement being generated by the display) versus static displays (those without movement).

Sales in the stores were then monitored over a four-week period. The results (numbers represent the increase in sales over stores without displays) are presented as follows:

	Static Display	Motion Display
Food Store	18%	49%
Liquor Store	56%	107%

These findings clearly reveal the effectiveness of POP displays in generating sales. The presence of a display produced an average sales increase of more than 50 percent. The greater effectiveness observed for liquor stores relative to food stores suggests that the impact of POP displays is facilitated when consumers are already inclined toward purchasing the product (it seems safe to believe that those visiting the liquor store were so inclined). Further, the use of movement generated nearly three times the sales of the static display in food stores and nearly twice the sales in liquor stores.

Simplistic decision strategies (as discussed in Chapter 17) that lower the demands on capacity are more common.

This same barrier occurs for marketing communications. Even if one can succeed in gaining attention, consumers may not devote the amount of attention desired. Research indicates that failure to achieve an adequate degree of attention can reduce learning. For example, in a typical shadowing study, subjects wearing headphones receive a different message in each ear.[32] Subjects are then asked to "shadow" one of the messages: that is, repeat aloud the content. Despite hearing two different messages simultaneously, subjects can easily shadow one of them, although this task requires nearly all of their cognitive capacity.

The interesting question is what can be recalled about the message that is not shadowed. Some aspects of this message are absorbed, such as whether it contained human speech versus a nonspeech sound (for example, buzzing), or when the sex of the speaker changed during the message. However, recall of message content is nonexistent. Even changes from normal speech to a nonsense speech sound (for example, normal speech played backward) escape detection. These findings suggest that stimuli that fail to receive a sufficient amount of capacity are unlikely to leave a lasting impression on the consumer.

Persuasion as well as learning can depend on the amount of capacity allocated to a communication.[33] If consumers are unwilling or unable to devote the attention necessary for carefully evaluating an ad's claims, then persuasion can depend more heavily on reactions to the ad's executional features.[34] However, such features may have little influence when the claims receive the attention necessary for a thoughtful evaluation of their validity. We return to this issue in Chapter 15.

The Danger of Exceeding Cognitive Capacity

Because capacity is limited, it is possible that the demands of the information environment (see Chapter 7) may sometimes exceed this capacity. The Federal Trade Commission, for instance, once developed a proposal for increased disclosure of nutritional information within food advertisements. A fundamental flaw with the proposal was that it required the presentation of more information than could be processed within the time made available.[35]

What happens when the demands of the information environment exceed cognitive capacity? This question has led to a considerable amount of research and debate concerning the potential for **information overload**. Some have speculated that increased disclosure of product information may have undesirable effects. If the information "load" (that is, the amount of information) in a choice environment exceeds capacity, then consumers might become confused and make poorer choices. In an early study of overload by Jacoby and his colleagues, they concluded that

> It would appear that increasing package information load tends to produce: (1) dysfunctional consequences in terms of the consumer's ability to select that brand which was best for him, and (2) beneficial effects upon the consumer's degree of satisfaction, certainty, and confusion regarding his selection. In other words, our subjects felt better with more information but actually made poorer purchase decisions.[36]

This study and a similar investigation sparked a heated controversy.[37] Critics contended that the Jacoby studies overstated their findings and suggested that the data did not reflect overload as a result of increased product information, a conclusion with which we agree. This is not to say that overload cannot occur, only that the Jacoby studies did not demonstrate that more product information led to poorer decisions.

The information overload controversy has continued, although with somewhat different players.[38] Jacoby now maintains that information overload, while possible, is unlikely because consumers will stop processing information before they are overloaded.[39] However, a recent study suggests that consumers may be unable to stop short of overloading themselves when faced with a sufficiently rich information environment.[40]

The right amount of information will depend on factors such as involvement, situation, and personality or other variables as they vary between market segments. A consumer may allocate considerable amounts of information processing, for example, to a food product in a supermarket that attracts attention with a colorful display at a convenient location with a label that speaks of cholesterol, calories, fat, or other variables. A consumer with a heart problem that generates high involvement in the product category and an ample time budget may allocate a great deal of cognitive activity (and time) to consideration of alternatives. This consumer may eventually also allocate his or her money budget to the product that is successful in winning the consumer's cognitive budget.

Summary

Consumers possess three primary resources that they use in the exchange process of marketing. These resources are economic, temporal, and cognitive. Practically speaking, this means that marketers are competing for consumers' money, time, and information processing. A consumer's perception of available resources may affect the willingness to spend time or money for products. Thus, measures of consumer confidence may be useful in forecasting future sales by product category.

Buying is affected greatly by consumers' income. Affluence is a variable of major interest to marketers. The upper quintile or quartile or up market is often the focus of marketing programs. This group makes proportionately high purchases of products such as apparel, furniture, electronic and home entertainment, home furnishings, tableware, domestics, fine jewelry, tools, hardware, and building materials. Department stores are particularly strong competitors for affluent customers but so are some off-price retailers and specialty stores. These customers are reached relatively more effectively with print media, although they also have higher ownership of cable television. Americans have expressed a high propensity to use credit, which extends the income resource, at least for a period of time. The down market is also important, especially in difficult economic conditions. This market segment will lower prices and basic assortments but still expects to be treated with respect and good service.

The second major consumer resource is time. Products and services classified by their time properties may be called time goods. Time-using goods require the use of time with the product and include products such as attending a museum, watching television, and other activities often classified as leisure activities. Time-saving products allow consumers to increase their discretionary time, often through the purchase of services or goods that reduce the time required in other activities. Polychronic time usage involves more than one simultaneous activity and may be used to enhance consumers' time budgets. A contemporary conceptualization of time budgets includes paid time, obligated time, and discretionary time (or leisure).

The third major type of consumer resource is cognitive capacity. The allocation of cognitive capacity is known as attention. Because this capacity is limited, people must be selective in what they pay attention to and how much attention is allocated during information processing. Gaining the consumer's attention will often represent a major hurdle for marketers. Similarly, gaining "enough" attention can be equally challenging, particularly when the product is of limited importance. Finally, there is the possibility of consumers becoming "overloaded" when the information environment exceeds their cognitive capacity.

Review and Discussion Questions

1. Why is "perception" of economic resources a variable as important in explaining consumer behavior as actual resources? Analyze the opening vignette to predict how you think the household will spend its additional money.
2. Describe the relationships that can be expected between income and the purchase of major product categories.
3. When conducting marketing research, how should income be measured?
4. If a consumer goods manufacturer is seeking growth opportunities that may be expected from rising affluence, what advice would you provide?
5. What is meant by the term GDP? How does it differ from GNP?
6. How might the relationship between time budgets and economic budgets affect the marketing strategy of a major retailer?
7. A retailer has just completed a study of the effects due to the amount of shelf space given a product and where the product is located in the store. Whereas both the amount of space and location had significant effects on the sales for some items (for example, cookies), such effects were not observed for other items (for example, milk). How can you explain these differences?
8. Consider the manufacturer interested in determining which of two alternative ads would be most effective. Initially, target consumers were shown one of the ads along with several other ads and later tested for recall. The results revealed no difference in recall between the ads. However, in a later field test where target consumers encountered the ads in a "real world" setting, major differences were observed in the ads' effectiveness. How can you account for these inconsistencies between the two studies?
9. What is your opinion about the information overload controversy? Do you believe overload can occur? Do you believe it will occur?

Endnotes

1. Kevin F. McCrohan and James D. Smith, "Consumer Participation in the Informal Economy," *Journal of the Academy of Marketing Sciences* 13 (Winter 1987), 62–67.
2. Ernest Engel, "Die Productions and Consumptionsverhaltnisse des Königreichs Sacksen," *Zeitschrift des Statistischen Bureaus des Koniglich Sachsischen Ministeriums des Innern*, Nos. 8–9 (November 22, 1857), 8.
3. Martha Farnsworth Riche, "New Definitions of Income," *American Demographics* 12 (November 1990), 14–15.
4. David E. Bloom and Sanders D. Korenman, "Spending Habits of American Consumers," *American Demographics* 8 (March 1986), 22–25.
5. Mandy Putnam, "The Up Market" (Columbus, Ohio: Management Horizons, a Division of Price Waterhouse, 1988).
6. "Airport Retailing," *The Wall Street Journal* (December 29, 1988), A1.

7. Karl Albrecht and Ron Zemke, *Service America* (Homewood, Ill.: Dow Jones-Irwin, 1985).

8. "Real Estate, Retail Outlook," *American Marketplace* (July 4, 1991), 133.

9. "Seizing the Dark Day," *Business Week* (January 13, 1992), 26–28.

10. Jan Larson, "Reaching Downscale Markets," *American Demographics* 13 (November 1991), 38–41.

11. Joe Schwartz, "How to Find the Affluent," *American Demographics* 11 (June 1989), 22.

12. David E. Bloom and Todd P. Steen, "Living on Credit," *American Demographics* 9 (October 1987), 22–29.

13. James W. Hughes, "Understanding the Squeezed Consumer," *American Demographics* 13 (July 1991), 44–49.

14. John P. Robinson, "Your Money or Your Time," *American Demographics* 13 (November 1991), 22–26.

15. This conceptual framework is developed originally in Justin Voss and Roger Blackwell, "Markets for Leisure Time," in Mary Jane Slinger, ed., *Advances in Consumer Research* (Chicago: Association for Consumer Research, 1975), 837–845; and Justin Voss and Roger Blackwell, "The Role of Time Resources in Consumer Behavior," in O. C. Ferrell, Stephen Brown, and Charles Lamb, eds., *Conceptual and Theoretical Developments in Marketing* (Chicago: American Marketing Association, 1979), 296–311.

16. Paul M. Lane and Jay D. Lindquist, "Definitions for the Fourth Dimension: A Proposed Time Classification System," in Kenneth D. Bahn, ed., *Developments of Marketing Science* 11 (Blacksburg, Va.: Academy of Marketing Science, 1988), 38–46.

17. Justin Voss, "The Definition of Leisure," *Journal of Economic Issues* 1 (June 1967), 91–106.

18. Geoffrey H. Moore, "Measuring Leisure Time," *The Conference Board Record* (July 1971), 53–54.

19. John P. Robinson, "Americans on the Road," *American Demographics* 11 (September 1989), 10.

20. "How Americans Use Time," *The Futurist* (September–October 1991), 23–27.

21. Douglass K. Hawes, W. Wayne Talarzyk, and Roger D. Blackwell, "Consumer Satisfaction from Leisure Time Pursuits," in Mary J. Slinger, *Advances*, 822.

22. Blayne Cutler, "Where Does the Free Time Go?" *American Demographics* 12 (November 1990), 36–39.

23. W. Keith Bryant and Yan Wang, "American Consumption Patterns and the Price of Time: A Time-Series Analysis," *The Journal of Consumer Affairs* 24 (1990), 280–308.

24. Carol Felker Kaufman, Paul M. Lane, and Jay D. Lindquist, "Exploring More than 24 Hours a Day: A Preliminary Investigation of Polychronic Time Use," *Journal of Consumer Research* 18 (December 1991), 392–401.

25. Aida N. Rizkalla, "Consumer Temporal Orientation and Shopping Behavior: The Case of Harried vs. Relaxed Consumers," in Robert L. King, ed., *Retailing: Its Present and Future* 4 (Charleston, S.C.: Academy of Marketing Science, 1988), 230–235.

26. Eugene H. Fram and Andrew J. DuBrin, "The Time Guarantee in Action: Some Trends and Opportunities," *Journal of Consumer Marketing* 5 (Fall 1988), 53–60.

27. F. Thomas Juster, "A Note on Recent Changes in Time Use," in F. Thomas Juster and Frank P. Stafford, eds., *Time, Goods, and Well-Being* (Ann Arbor: University of Michigan, 1985), 316–317.

28. Douglass K. Hawes, "Time Budgets and Consumer Leisure-Time Behavior: An Eleven-Year-Later Replication and Extension," in Melanie Wallendorf and Paul Anderson, eds., *Advances in Consumer Research* 14 (Provo, Utah: Association for Consumer Research, 1987), 543–547.

29. Herbert A. Simon, "How Big Is a Chunk?" *Science* 183 (February 1974), 482–488; George A. Miller, "The Magical Number Seven, Plus or Minus Two: Some Limits on Our Capacity for Processing Information," *Psychological Review* 63 (March 1956), 81–97.

30. Alexander J. Wearing, "The Recall of Sentences of Varying Length," *Australian Journal of Psychology* 25 (August 1973), 156–161.

31. Scott B. MacKenzie, "The Role of Attention in Mediating the Effect of Advertising on Attribute Importance," *Journal of Consumer Research* 13 (September 1986), 174–195.

32. For example, see E. C. Cherry, "Some Experiments on the Recognition of Speech with One and Two Ears," *Journal of the Acoustical Society of America* 25 (1953), 975–979.

33. Anthony G. Greenwald and Clark Leavitt, "Audience Involvement in Advertising: Four Levels," *Journal of Consumer Research* 11 (June 1984), 581–592.

34. See, for example, Scott B. MacKenzie and Richard J. Lutz, "An Empirical Examination of the Structural Antecedents of Attitude-toward-the-Ad in an Advertising Pretesting Context," *Journal of Marketing* 53 (April 1989), 48–65; Richard E. Petty and John T. Cacioppo, *Communication and Persuasion: Central and Peripheral Routes to Attitude Change* (New York: Springer/Verlag, 1986).

35. James R. Bettman, "Issues in Designing Consumer Information Environments," *Journal of Consumer Research* 2 (December 1975), 169–177.

36. Jacob Jacoby, Donald Speller, and Carol Kohn Berning, "Brand Choice Behavior as a Function of Information Load," *Journal of Marketing Research* 11 (February 1974), 63–69.

37. Jacob Jacoby, Donald Speller, and Carol Kohn Berning, "Brand Choice Behavior as a Function of Information Load: Replication and Extension," *Journal of Consumer Research* 1 (June 1974), 33–42; J. Edward Russo, "More Information Is Better: A Reevaluation of Jacoby, Speller, and Kohn," *Journal of Consumer Research* 11 (November 1974), 467–468; William L. Wilkie, "Analysis of Effects of Information Load," *Journal of Marketing Research* 11 (November 1974), 462–466; Jacob Jacoby, Donald E. Speller, and Carol A. K. Berning, "Constructive Criticism and Programmatic Research: Reply to Russo," *Journal of Consumer Research* 1 (September 1975), 154–156; Jacob Jacoby, "Information Load and Decision Quality: Some Contested Issues," *Journal of Marketing Research* 15 (November 1977), 569–573.

38. Debra L. Scammon, "Information Load and Consumers," *Journal of Consumer Research* 4 (December 1977), 148–155; Naresh K. Malhotra, "Information Load and Consumer Decision Making," *Journal of Consumer Research* 8 (March 1982), 419–430; Naresh K. Malhotra, Arun K. Jain, and Stephen W. Lagakos, "The Information Overload Controversy: An Alternative Viewpoint," *Journal of Marketing* 46 (Spring 1982), 27–37; Naresh K. Malhotra, "Reflections on the Information Overload Paradigm in Consumer Decision Making," *Journal of Consumer Research* 10 (March 1984), 436–440.

39. Jacob Jacoby, "Perspectives on Information Overload," *Journal of Consumer Research* 10 (March 1984), 432–435.

40. Kevin Lane Keller and Richard Staelin, "Effects of Quality and Quantity of Information on Decision Effectiveness," *Journal of Consumer Research* 14 (September 1987), 200–213.

Involvement
and Motivation

Women who drink General Foods International Coffees take their ads light and sweet. Scenes that show best friends chatting do well. So do images of women relaxing with their husbands and kids. And women respond favorably when soft, relaxing music plays in the background.

How does General Foods know all this? Because the executives who market the brand conduct extensive tests that tell them how far they can push your hot buttons. They know, for instance, that high-tech images, blue light, or a close-up of an ice cube moving along a woman's neck will turn you off. They also know that you'll react warmly to an ad showing a man canceling a golf game to be with his wife, or one that shows a mother having a heart-to-heart with her daughter.

Scoff if you like, but the touchy-feely approach works. Between July 1989 and July 1990, sales of General Foods International Coffees (GFIC) were $115.9 million, an 11 percent rise over the same period a year earlier. This is startling when you consider that sales in the instant-coffee category as a whole, estimated to be worth $1.1 billion, are off by 9.4 percent. In fact, nearly all supermarket brands are down, the victims of rising health concerns about caffeine, the gourmet-bean trend, and morning cola consumption.

But GFIC isn't like other coffees. It's presweetened and positioned as a specialty product aimed at women, not a commodity. This gives it a designer image. GFIC is the closest coffee comes to the fashion or perfume business, says Tom

Pirko, president of Bevmark Inc., a Los Angeles consultancy. "It's selling the sizzle as much as the steak."

GFIC's marketers stress an emotional benefit—"more the feeling than the function," says Nancy Wong, director of marketing for General Foods' Maxwell House division, located in White Plains, New York. When it comes to GFIC, it's self-indulgence and traditional values represented by a series of emotional moments in commercials.

Over the years, GFIC's research techniques have become more complex as its audience has grown more sophisticated. It is no longer enough to ask, "What do you like about the taste?" "How do you feel before you've had a cup?" the psychologist might ask. "And after?" He or she then might direct women to draw pictures illustrating the transformation. "If you were having a dream in which GFIC played a part, what would it be?" " How old is GFIC?" "Is it male or female?"

Back in the early 1970s, actress Carol Lawrence was GFIC's spokeswoman and was chosen for her European looks. At that time, the General Foods marketers working on the brand wanted to emphasize its international personality. As Bill Burgess, a former member of the original GFIC team, recalls, "With Lawrence we were tapping into the heartbeat of the prime prospect at the time—homebodies who kaffeeklatsch, who are nurturers, who wanted to use this as an experience to treat themselves as they would company."

By the 1980s the ads positioned the brand as the coffee to drink when bonding with family, friends or co-workers. In one ad, a woman pauses in the kitchen while drinking a cup of GFIC to watch her husband and child snuggle in the living room. *It's a laugh, it's a cry . . . all the moments that you want to celebrate. . . . You don't need an invitation.*

Source: Bernice Kanner, "The Secret Life of the Female Consumer," *Working Woman* (December 1990), 69–71. Reproduced by special permission.

All marketers and others who want to shape and influence human behavior start with the question faced by General Foods' management—*what motivates the consumer?* Why do women buy this specialty coffee? What benefits are they seeking? What images and appeals are most effective?

A person can be said to be motivated when his or her system is energized (aroused), made active, and behavior is directed toward a desired goal. In short, the system is "turned on" and triggered to engage in need-satisfying activity. The marketing challenge is to discover the primary influences and to design strategies that both activate and satisfy felt needs.

This case illustrates that consumers often find it difficult to articulate their desires, feelings, wishes, dreams. The use of skillful research, however, can result in marketing strategies that effectively capture and build upon needs, values, and emotions. GFIC management has strongly highlighted the taste benefit of its new French Vanilla Cafe (Figure 9.1), but has also unleashed a rich set of emotions by its intriguing illustration of "mouths saying merci."

FIGURE 9.1 **French Vanilla Coffee Is Bought for More Than Taste**
Source: Courtesy Kraft General Foods, Inc.

In this chapter we explore some foundational concepts and theories of motivation. We begin with a discussion of the dynamics of the motivation process and the central importance of need activation and satisfaction.

Next, we demonstrate how the degree of involvement (perceived relevance) accompanying the purchase and consumption situation serves as an important motivating construct. When we are involved we respond in an entirely different manner than when this is not the case.

The remainder of the chapter focuses on some major needs that affect consumer behavior, various approaches to measurement and evaluation, and the primary implications for marketing strategy.

The Motivation of Human Behavior[1]

Motivated behavior is initiated by need activation (or need recognition). A need or motive (these terms often are used interchangeably) is activated when there is a sufficient discrepancy between the actual state and a desired or preferred state of being. As this discrepancy increases, the outcome is activation of a condition of arousal referred to as **drive**. The stronger the drive, the greater the perceived urgency of response.

Over time certain behavior patterns are recognized as more effective than others for need satisfaction, and these come to function as **incentives**. An incentive is an anticipated reward from a course of action that offers need-satisfying potential.

To take a simple example, a college student studying for a final examination says to her roommate, "I'm thirsty." First she perceives discomfort (felt need) that is recognized as thirst. This activated need leads to drive (arousal). A can of Diet Coke (her favorite beverage) from the machine down the hall is the incentive, and she behaves accordingly.

Dynamics of the Motivation Process

Felt need can be activated in different ways, one of which is entirely physiological, thirst or hunger being examples. The human being also possesses the capacity for thinking about a person or object not present at the immediate time or imagining the desirable consequences of a particular action. This thought process in itself can be arousing. All of us, for example, can feel hunger at times just by thinking about a favorite food. Finally, arousal can be triggered by outside information. You become hungry when your eye is stopped by a point-of-sale display announcing a special low price for Dove Bars.

Activated need or motive ultimately becomes expressed in buying behavior and consumption in the form of two types of expected benefits illustrated in Figure 9.2—(1) **utilitarian benefits** and (2) **hedonic/experiential benefits**.[2]

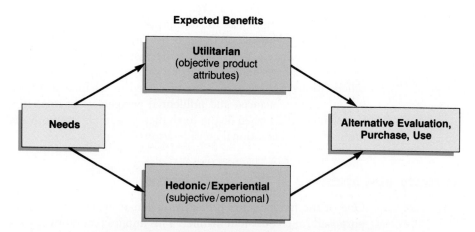

FIGURE 9.2   The Expression of Motivation in Product Purchase and Use: Utilitarian and Hedonistic Benefits

Utilitarian benefits are objective, functional product attributes. Hedonic benefits, on the other hand, encompass subjective responses, sensory pleasures, daydreams, and aesthetic considerations.[3] The criteria used when considering hedonic benefits are subjective and *symbolic*, centering on appreciation of the product or service for its own sake apart from more objective considerations. Both types of benefits become expressed as *evaluative criteria* used in the process of weighing and selecting the best alternative (see Chapter 17).

It is common for utilitarian and hedonic benefits to function simultaneously in a purchase decision. For example, a potential buyer compares European luxury cars on such objective dimensions as headroom, rear seat room, acceleration, and automatic locking systems. These attributes are stressed in specific terms in advertising and personal selling.

Hedonic benefits, on the other hand, can include experiential considerations such as a sense of status and prestige derived from owning a top-of-the-line car and the sheer sense of pleasure in driving. Alternative evaluation now becomes more spontaneous and holistic, focusing on overall symbolism, as opposed to specific features.[4]

The Influence of Affect

When a person is motivated there can be quite a range of accompanying feelings, emotions, and moods. Who can deny the power of the emotions expressed in the Pierre Cardin ad in Figure 9.3? These feeling states, referred at as **affect**,[5] influence consumer behavior in different ways: (1) positive effect (that is, a good mood) speeds up information processing and reduces the decision time in selecting appropriate products;[6] (2) activated mood leads to recall of products with positive associations;[7] and (3) emotions can, in and of themselves, activate a state of drive.[8]

What we have said thus far is largely common sense learned from the daily experience of each one of us. Yet, a reading of the literature in this field in the 1970s and early 1980s might lead you to think that emotions either do not exist or that they have little or no impact on buyer behavior.

Unfortunately, this reflects more than anything else a pendulum swing away from overemphasis on emotional and symbolic dimensions in vogue during the so-called "motivation-research" era discussed in Chapter 2. Once again we are returning to the balanced and influential perspective of marketing pioneer Melvin Copeland in 1924 when he put forth that consumers are motivated by both rational (utilitarian) and emotional considerations.[9]

The Unity and Stability of Motive Patterns

One of the fundamental premises of human behavior is that people behave in a purposeful and consistent manner. This implies that motives are integrated in some way. Over the course of this century, authorities have come to agree that the **self-concept** provides this unification.[10]

FIGURE 9.3   Emotions Are a Powerful Selling Appeal
Source: Courtesy Pierre Cardin.

The self-concept is an organized structure of perceptions of one's self, and it becomes a part of active memory. It is comprised of perceptions of abilities and characteristics and perceptions of one's self in relationship to the external environment. A central motive is to enhance this view of one's self. As a result, it has a direct influence on values, ideas, goals, and objectives.[11]

It is generally agreed that consumers engage in buying behavior that is consistent and congruent with their self-image.[12] When there is a positive affinity between self and product, it is probable that advertising appeals congruent with self-image will be more effective in terms of brand memory, brand attitude, and purchase intentions.[13]

Do you think that the Parker ad in Figure 9.4 is likely to be received favorably by many on the basis of self-image and product congruity? A good case can be made if you accept Russell Belk's contention that "we are what we have." In other words, he theorizes that there is an extended self-concept that encompasses possessions.[14]

FIGURE 9.4   Does the Appeal Establish Congruity between Product and Self-Image?

Source: Courtesy Parker Pen.

We agree with Belk that possessions in most cultures play the important role of helping us learn and define our sense of the past, who we are, and where we are going. Certainly the designers of the Parker ad reflect this same conviction and they made every effort to argue that a Parker Pen offers a unique way to express one's character, not merely to record thoughts.

The extent to which this ad succeeds, however, also may depend upon the extent to which a reader is a self-monitor.[15] High self-monitors tend to be responsive to appeals that reflect the image of the self they strive to be in social situations. Low self-monitors, on the other hand, will be more guided by inner dispositions such as beliefs, attitudes, and feelings.

There have been many published attempts to measure self-concept and relate it to aspects of buying behavior.[16] Most have confirmed that there usually is consistency between self-concept and behavior, but that the actual correlations are relatively low.[17] These low correlations are mostly a reflection of methodological difficulties and do not negate the hypothesis of congruence between self and possessions.

Belk and others produced quite different findings when they stepped away from the rigor of experimental design and carefully controlled research and made use of participant observation and other ethnographic methods more closely associated with anthropologists.[18] This often-quoted study, referred to as the "Consumer Behavior Odyssey," demonstrated the high personal significance attached to many possessions, and the authors used such terms as "sacred" and "ritual." They concluded that consumers sacramentalize products as they attempt to create transcendent meaning in their lives, and most of us will concur based on our own experience.

Can Needs Be Created?

Here is a question that has been debated in marketing classrooms probably since the first course was taught in 1904 at the University of Michigan: *Can marketers create needs?* More specifically, can the famous European confectioner, Lindt, somehow manipulate consumers to respond by creating a need through the ad in Figure 9.5? If so, some serious ethical questions are raised.

FIGURE 9.5   Does This Ad Create a Need?

FIGURE 9.6   Need Activation, Not Need Creation

Source: Courtesy of General Foods Corporation.

We contend that a purchase will never be made unless underlying needs (or motives) are activated and satisfied. Buying action, in turn, is not undertaken until an alternative is viewed positively in these terms. The need must already exist even though it may be dormant and largely unrecognized; *it is not created by the marketer*. It is true that marketing communication stimulates desire to buy a product or service to satisfy that need, but the need itself lies beyond the influence of the business firm.

As a broad generalization, we may conclude that a major role of marketing efforts is to position a product or service in the most favorable possible light in terms of potential to satisfy need. For example, many women no longer make homemade jam because of the effort required and the necessity of using large amounts of sugar to ensure the right jelling consistency.

Now Sure-Jell presents the option of Sure-Jell Light (Figure 9.6), which assures perfect homemade jam with one-third less sugar and no artificial sweeteners. This ad effectively tackles the obstacles and assures the buyer of success while reducing sugar as a significant way for meeting felt needs connected with nutrition and health.

Consumer in Focus **9.1**

An Old Lesson Relearned

Nineties customers will have to be coaxed to consume, and they will buy only what they really want. Kraft General Foods learned this lesson the hard way. Despite powerful brands like Oscar Mayer meats and Post cereals, the Philip Morris subsidiary had a disappointing record in the new product race. The reasons: it disregarded customer needs.

It ravaged its Maxwell House franchise a few years ago by using cheap beans when coffee drinkers were unambiguous about wanting a rich taste. It launched Philly Slices, even though people like to spread their [Philadelphia] cream cheese like butter, and Jello Microwave Pudding, when no one needed tapioca.

Two years ago Michael Miles, who becomes Philip Morris's CEO in September, overhauled product development to create what he calls his "TNCVV" strategy, and lately new-product winners have been popping out of the pantry. The awkward TNCVV, in case you wondered, stands for "taste, nutrition, convenience, value, and variety," which company researchers say are consumers' greatest concerns about food. Miles urges managers to out-do competitors in these areas and to create ads that highlight their brand's advantage.

The payoff? Kraft General Foods was first off the block with premeasured coffee (for bleary-eyed A.M. drinkers) and fat-free foods like cheese, salad dressing, mayonnaise, and baked goodies. Miles says KGF will sell $450 million of fat-free fodder this year, up from $310 million in 1990.

Source: Patricia Sellers, "Winning Over the New Consumer," *Fortune* (July 29, 1991), 114, 118.

Each generation of business executives apparently must relearn a historically validated principle: marketing efforts that ignore consumer need are destined to failure. This happens even at well-managed enterprises as Consumer in Focus 9.1 illustrates.

Involvement

You will recall from Chapter 2 that the concept of **involvement** is of major significance in understanding and explaining consumer behavior. This term was first popularized in marketing circles by Krugman in 1965 and has generated considerable interest since that time.[19]

Although it has been defined in many ways,[20] we like the following conceptualization put forward by Antil after careful consideration of multiple points of view: "Involvement is the level of perceived personal importance and/or interest evoked by a stimulus (or stimuli) within a specific situation."[21] To the extent that it is present, the consumer acts with deliberation to minimize risks and to maximize the benefits gained from purchase and use.

Involvement is best conceived as a function of *person*, *object*, and *situation*. The starting point always is with the person—underlying motivations in the form of needs and values, which, in turn, are a reflection of self-concept. Involvement is activated when the object (a product, service, or promotional message) is perceived as being instrumental in meeting important needs, goals, and values. But, as we will see, the perceived need-satisfying significance of the object will vary from one situation to the next. Therefore, all three factors (person, object, and situation) must be taken into account.

Involvement, then, is a reflection of strong motivation in the form of high perceived personal relevance of a product or service in a particular context. Depending upon the perceived linkage between the individual's motivating influences and the benefits offered by the object, it is a continuum ranging from low to high. Involvement becomes activated and felt when intrinsic personal characteristics (needs, values, self-concept) are confronted with appropriate marketing stimuli within a given situation.[22]

Some Antecedents of Involvement

Research on the factors that generate high or low involvement is extensive. Therefore, we will only highlight some main points here.

Personal Factors   Without activation of need and drive, there will be no involvement, and it is strongest when the product or service is perceived as enhancing self-image.[23] When that is the case, involvement is likely to be enduring and to function as a stable trait, as opposed to being situational or temporary.[24]

Richins and Bloch have shown, for example, that some consumers are auto enthusiasts, who attend races and rallies and subscribe to car magazines.[25] Others use their car continually but demonstrate low involvement through indifference to cars in general, including their own (unless perhaps it starts to self-destruct prematurely).

Product Factors   Products are not involving in and of themselves. Rather, it is how consumers respond to products that will determine their level of involvement. Nonetheless, product characteristics can shape consumer involvement.

First of all, involvement increases as choice alternatives are seen as being more differentiated.[26] Products or brands also become involving if there is some perceived risk in purchase and use. In 1960 the late Raymond Bauer advanced this important proposition: "Consumer behavior involves risk in the sense that any action of a consumer will produce consequences which he cannot anticipate with anything approximating certainty, and some of which are likely to be unpleasant."[27]

Many types of perceived risk have been identified, including *physical* (risk of bodily harm), *psychological* (especially a negative effect on self-image), *performance* (fear that the product will not perform as expected), and *financial* (risk that outcomes will lead to loss of earnings).[28]

As one would logically expect, the greater the perceived risk, the greater the likelihood of high involvement. When perceived risk becomes unacceptably high, there is motivation either to avoid purchase and use altogether or to minimize risk through the search and alternative evaluation stages in extended problem solving.

Finally, the hedonic value of the product also is a determining factor—that is, its emotional appeal and its perceived ability to provide pleasure quite apart from its objective benefits.[29] To the extent that these subjective considerations are important, involvement will increase.

Situational Factors   Whereas enduring involvement can be considered as a stable trait, situational (or instrumental) involvement changes over time. It is operational on a temporary basis and wanes once purchasing outcomes are resolved. This is often the case with fads such as trendy clothing items where involvement is high initially but quickly diminishes once the item is worn and fashions begin to change.

There also are times when an otherwise uninvolving product takes on a differing degree of relevance because of the manner in which it will be used.[30] For example, there can be a big difference between the perceived importance of a brand of hand soap purchased for home use as opposed to that given as a gift.

Finally, involvement can increase when social pressures are felt. Zaichkowsky demonstrated, for example, that consumers react quite differently when they purchase wine for ordinary personal consumption as opposed to wine that will be served at a dinner party.[31]

The Forms of Involvement and the Outcomes

Figure 9.7 shows the forms that involvement can take and the way it becomes expressed in consumer behavior. Notice, first of all, that consumers are motivated to search for relevant information and to process it more thoroughly when involvement is high[32] (see Chapter 13). Furthermore, they are more likely to be influenced by strength of argumentation as opposed to the way in which the appeal is expressed and visualized (see Chapter 15). This is represented in Figure 9.7 as message involvement.

Consumers also can become involved with the product (or brand). They are more likely to notice differences in the attributes offered by various products or brands, and a common outcome is greater loyalty when preference is grounded on high perceived involvement.

There is a greater likelihood of extended problem solving when involvement is high, whereas low involvement leads to the more simplified choice tactics of limited

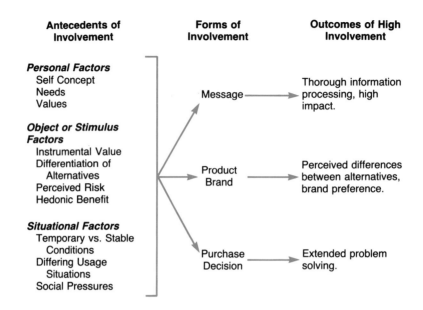

Antecedents of Involvement	Forms of Involvement	Outcomes of High Involvement
Personal Factors Self Concept Needs Values	Message	Thorough information processing, high impact.
Object or Stimulus Factors Instrumental Value Differentiation of Alternatives Perceived Risk Hedonic Benefit	Product Brand	Perceived differences between alternatives, brand preference.
Situational Factors Temporary vs. Stable Conditions Differing Usage Situations Social Pressures	Purchase Decision	Extended problem solving.

FIGURE 9.7   A Conceptualization of the Involvement Concept as Expressed in Consumer Behavior

Source: Adapted from Judith L. Zaichkowsky, "Conceptualizing Involvement," *Journal of Advertising* 15 (1986), 6.

problem solving.[33] This is expressed in the amount of effort expended in the search for information and alternative evaluation.

Finally, there is growing evidence that involvement is an important motivating influence across cultures. Zaichkowsy and Sood, for example, found that consumers in 15 countries were surprisingly similar in their degree of involvement and motivation toward a group of products and services.[34] The effects on information processing and decision making seem to be universal,[35] although there certainly will be cultural differences in interpretation and expression.

Measuring Involvement

Largely because of definitional disagreement, many ways have been proposed to measure involvement.[36] Ideally, any measurement should encompass the richness of the three categories of antecedents summarized in Figure 9.7. One of the first efforts to capture this paradigm was published by Laurent and Kapferer.[37] This scale was first designed for use in France, and it measured these dimensions (notice that they have used different wording and categorization):

TABLE 9.1   Involvement Profiles of 14 Consumer Products

	Importance of Negative Consequences	Subjective Probability of Mispurchase	Pleasure Value	Sign Value
Dresses	121	112	147	181
Bras	117	115	106	130
Washing machines	118	109	106	111
TV sets	112	100	122	95
Vacuum cleaners	110	112	70	78
Irons	103	95	72	76
Champagne	109	120	125	125
Oil	89	97	65	92
Yogurt	86	83	106	78
Chocolate	80	89	123	75
Shampoo	96	103	90	81
Toothpaste	95	95	94	105
Facial soap	82	90	114	118
Detergents	79	82	56	63

Source: Giles Laurent and Jean-Noël Kapferer, "Measuring Consumer Involvement Profiles," *Journal of Marketing Research* 22 (February 1985), 45. Used with special permission.

1. Importance of negative consequences—scale items evaluated both product importance and perceived risk of negative consequences.
2. Subjective probability of a mispurchase—the risk of making a bad choice.
3. Pleasure value—the hedonic value of purchase and use.
4. Sign value—the extent to which purchase and use makes a psycho/social statement about the person.

Table 9.1 shows you how 14 different products ranked on these four dimensions. As you would expect, dresses and bras rate at the top on all four dimensions, whereas detergents are quite low. The importance of using four dimensions is clearly demonstrated with vacuum cleaners and facial soap. The vacuum cleaner is not evaluated as having high pleasure or sign value; yet the perceived risk of purchase is high. Hence, there is relatively high involvement, whereas we see an exactly opposite situation with facial soap. Few had high concerns on product performance or risk, but pleasure and sign value were much higher.

Zaichkowsky also has designed a useful Involvement Inventory (Figure 9.8).[38] You might try this inventory yourself across a variety of products. Notice that her scale items mostly measure the product importance dimension. Follow the scoring directions at the bottom—the higher the score the greater the involvement. A maximum possible score is 140. Zaichkowsky found a mean score of 89.55 across 15 categories, with automobiles and calculators emerging as most involving and instant coffee, bubble bath, and breakfast cereals as least.

FIGURE 9.8 **The Personal Involvement Inventory**

(insert name of object to be judged)

important __ : __ : __ : __ : __ : __ : __ unimportant*
of no concern __ : __ : __ : __ : __ : __ : __ of concern to me
irrelevant __ : __ : __ : __ : __ : __ : __ relevant
means a lot to me __ : __ : __ : __ : __ : __ : __ means nothing to me*
useless __ : __ : __ : __ : __ : __ : __ useful
valuable __ : __ : __ : __ : __ : __ : __ worthless*
trivial __ : __ : __ : __ : __ : __ : __ fundamental
beneficial __ : __ : __ : __ : __ : __ : __ not beneficial*
matters to me __ : __ : __ : __ : __ : __ : __ doesn't matter*
uninterested __ : __ : __ : __ : __ : __ : __ interested
significant __ : __ : __ : __ : __ : __ : __ insignificant*
vital __ : __ : __ : __ : __ : __ : __ superfluous*
boring __ : __ : __ : __ : __ : __ : __ interesting
unexciting __ : __ : __ : __ : __ : __ : __ exciting
appealing __ : __ : __ : __ : __ : __ : __ unappealing*
mundane __ : __ : __ : __ : __ : __ : __ fascinating
essential __ : __ : __ : __ : __ : __ : __ nonessential*
undesirable __ : __ : __ : __ : __ : __ : __ desirable
wanted __ : __ : __ : __ : __ : __ : __ unwanted*
not needed __ : __ : __ : __ : __ : __ : __ needed

*Indicates item is reverse scored.

Items on the left are scored (1) low involvement to (7) high involvement on the right. Totaling the 20 items gives a score from a low of 20 to a high of 140.

Source: Judith L. Zaichkowsky, "Measuring the Involvement Construct," *Journal of Consumer Research* 12 (December 1985), 350. Used by special permission.

Understanding Consumer Needs

Need (or motive) is a variable of central importance to those whose goal is to influence consumer behavior. If needs can be measured and understood, it is possible to position marketing efforts more effectively in the context of consumer goals.

The Challenge of Measurement

Several methodological approaches to measurement are possible, including scaled AIO (activity, interest, and opinion) questions, indepth guided interviews, focus groups, and ethnography. Some earlier use was made of standardized research inventories developed for clinical counseling and psychotherapy. Experience has demonstrated, however, that tools designed for individualized diagnosis (an example being the Rorschach inkblot test) are not applicable in large-sample marketing research.

Scaled AIO Questions   A common approach makes use of a series of scaled agree–disagree questions covering varying areas of possible motivation and interest. Often these are referred to as AIO or psychographic questions (see Chapter 12). Basic needs are often uncovered by searching for a common pattern of interest across various questions.

Psychographic questions were used in a study of American college students, and here are three concerns that proved to be strongly correlated, in the sense that all three were mentioned by many people:[39]

How to overcome performance stress here on the campus.
How to get better grades.
How to be free from financial worries when I graduate.

The common denominator here is a fear of future financial insecurity, which is expressed by strong motivation to get better grades (mentioned as being of major importance by over half of the students). It was found that over 10 percent of students responded positively to direct marketing appeals for a book offering help in getting better grades—an unusually high direct-marketing response.

Indepth Guided Interviews   Chapter 2 introduced you to an interesting era in marketing history—the motivation-research era. It was characterized by fairly widespread use of methods borrowed from clinical psychology, one of the most common being the so-called **indepth** (or **guided**) **interview**.[40] Only a small sample is interviewed (50 or less) one at a time in a lengthy, unstructured session. Attempts are made to probe below the surface to uncover the wealth of possible motivating influences.

As you may recall from Chapter 2, some early advocates contended that the guided interview enables researchers to plumb all levels of consciousness and even the unconscious, thus moving beyond the scope of conventional marketing research methods. Advocates alleged that the marketer has much to gain by appealing to motivating influences that cannot be consciously expressed. We still hear this claim, and here is an example. A clinically trained researcher contended that people in one European country disdain consumption of fluid milk because of unfavorable childhood imagery. The proposed solution, supposedly based on indepth, guided interviews, was to associate milk with motherhood. This was accomplished by naturelike packaging and advertising imagery, complete with rolling hills, suggesting a most obvious part of the female anatomy as viewed at the time of birth. Plausible? Well, sales *did* increase. Perhaps a more logical explanation is that greatly increased advertising enhanced name recognition.

Few today would contend that indepth interviewing has such magic qualities. After all, how much can be learned in a one-hour interview? But the use of unstructured, probing questions has survived to this day and is a helpful tool in the research arsenal.

Focus Groups   At other times, people are asked to discuss their motivations and behavior in small groups referred to as **focus groups**. Consumer in Focus 9.2 gives you an interesting example.

Consumer in Focus 9.2

Chatting up Customers

Eleven young women file silently into a room in Englewood, New Jersey. Behind a one-way mirror, three people watch them for clues about what single life is like in the 1990s.

As the focus group progresses, the women develop a rapport. They are all between the ages of 21 and 25, and each earns between $15,000 and $30,000 a year. Laughing easily, they become animated as the conversation takes off. They are guided almost imperceptibly by moderator Judith Langer, president of Langer & Associates.

The women agree that men their age have a lot of growing up to do. "My boyfriend still lets his grandmother take care of him, and she's 85 years old," says an attractive 22 year old with highly moussed hair. "I tell him, 'Grow up, make your bed.'" Over the two-hour session, Langer elicits their opinions on everything from sex in the age of AIDS to careers, marriage, childbearing, shopping, and media habits. A wisdom emerges, but it is as unorganized as the group's conversation. This and nine other focus group sessions will give Langer's client, Condé Nast, a fix on the mind of the young American single woman.

Condé Nast backs up its focus group findings with quantitative data from field surveys. Similar studies done for *Self* and *G.Q.* [*Gentlemen's Quarterly*] have given the magazines an extra plum for advertisers. "This research allows *G.Q.* and *Self* to be the authority on their respective markets," says Eckart Guthe, corporate marketing director of Condé Nast. "The data become more real when you can see the faces and gestures of the people involved."

Source: Rebecca Piirto, "Why They Buy. Chatting Up Customers," *American Demographics* (September 1990), 6. Used by special permission. © American Demographics (September 1990).

Groups of about ten people are brought together for a session that usually does not exceed one hour in length. The interviewer, a skilled discussion leader, lets conversation flow naturally but guides it in such a way that pertinent issues are covered. The group setting provides a relaxed atmosphere, and the thoughts of one person stimulate those of others. Participants soon find themselves talking freely about their concerns. The outcome is often a richer yield of information that cannot be gathered through structured questionnaires.

Ethnography The methods presented thus far all focus primarily on verbal or written responses to questions of various types. There is growing interest in more *natu-*

Consumer in Focus **9.3**

Socks, Ties, and Videotape

It may be useful to hear what consumers say, but it's essential to keep track of what they do. Sometimes the only way to find out why people really make specific purchase decisions is to catch people in the act and ask them. Says Allison Cohen, a psychologist and director of account planning for the Ally & Gargano agency in New York City, "You can get a more honest answer if you catch them off guard."

This form of direct observation is called ethnography. It's a technique borrowed from anthropology, and it helps market researchers identify the motivations that lie beneath the surface of the rational mind.

Today, a video camera is the consumer ethnographer's best friend. Allison Cohen has used ethnography to study products as diverse as Tampax tampons and Swiss chocolates, and she won't go anywhere without a video camera in tow. Typically, she'll go into someone's home, poke through their pantry, record the brands she finds, and interview the occupants.

In a study for a Swiss chocolate manufacturer, Cohen went into the homes of "chocoholics" to see how chocolate fit into their lives. "We saw some aberrant behavior in otherwise sane people," she says. Chocoholics hid their stashes in lingerie drawers, in freezers, on top of china cabinets, and under sofas. They ate chocolate in the same way other people drink wine—using domestic brands like Snickers every day and hoarding Godiva chocolates to savor only on special occasions or after a particularly bad day.

Source: Rebecca Piirto, "Socks, Ties, and Videotape," *American Demographics* (September 1991), 6. Used by special permission. © American Demographics (September 1991).

ralistic methods that concentrate on observation and interpretation of behavior as it happens.[41] Among the most popular in recent years has been the tried-and-true staple of cultural anthropologists—**ethnography**.

As you will discover in Consumer in Focus 9.3, the guided interview is supplemented by participant observation of buying and consumption behavior.[42] Inquiry is directed less by specific hypotheses and more by a determined attempt to understand what's taking place from a wide-ranging, interdisciplinary perspective.

Semiotics   The field of **semiotics** (or semiology) centers on how meaning is generated in communication messages.[43] This is done through analysis of the ways in which message elements (signs, symbols, and icons) are combined to create meaning.

Here is an example of semiotics used to clarify the advertising meaning of a very familiar symbol, the teddy bear named *Snuggle*.[44] Lever Brothers Co. built a $300 million fabric softener brand through the charms of this little bear and wanted to further capitalize upon this potent symbol. Here are the words of Carol Moog, a psychologist who made use of semiotics:

> The bear is an ancient symbol of aggression, but when you create a teddy bear, you provide a softer, nurturant side to that aggression. As a symbol of tamed aggression, the teddy bear is the perfect image for a fabric softener that tames the rough texture of clothing. To keep the magic, it has to be just Snuggle and the viewer communicating. The teddy bear acts as a bridge between the consumer's rational and more instinctual, emotional side.[45]

What do you think of this interpretation? Admittedly it is subjective and open to challenge, but insights of this type lie far beyond the realm of surveys. We think this is entirely plausible and welcome the richness to be found when we move beyond the confines of our traditional research boundaries.

It is helpful before proceeding further to refer to the concept of **prepotency**, most often attributed to the late Abraham H. Maslow.[46] He hypothesized that needs are organized in such a way as to establish priorities and hierarchies of importance. According to his theory, there are five levels of needs ranging in priority from lowest order to highest order. These fall into three basic categories: (1) survival and safety; (2) human interaction, love, and affiliation; and (3) self-actualization (competency, self-expression, and understanding). Each higher-order need, according to Maslow, is largely dormant until lower-level needs are satisfied.

A distinguished pioneer in consumer research, George Katona, showed that prepotency does affect consumer behavior to the extent that previously ignored desires exert themselves most frequently after purchases have satisfied a predominant (and perhaps lower-order) need.[47] This can help explain why an older, successful business or professional person in his or her 50s can move away from status as a dominant motive into a more leisurely pursuit of art and music.

Few researchers today would accept that lower-order needs somehow cease functioning once there is a satisfactory level of fulfillment in the sense that Maslow implied. Furthermore, actions can be impelled by a combination of needs across the hierarchy. Therefore, prepotency is accepted more as a helpful general principle than a determining rule of behavior.

Classification of Needs

For more than 60 years, psychologists and marketers alike have tried their hand at classifying needs. Some of their lists are quite lengthy and exhibit creative ingenuity. It is still common today to find detailed enumeration of needs as classified by Murray in 1938,[48] Maslow,[49] McClelland,[50] McGuire,[51] and others.

Unfortunately, such lists, especially from an earlier period, often reflected opinion more than empirical analysis. More recently, the literature has concentrated

TABLE 9.2   A Summary Classification of Consumer Needs

1. *Physiological:* the fundamentals of survival, including hunger, thirst, and other bodily needs.
2. *Safety:* concern over physical survival and safety.
3. *Affiliation and Belongingness:* a need to be accepted by others, to be an important person to them.
4. *Achievement:* a basic desire for success in meeting personal goals.
5. *Power:* a desire to gain control over one's destiny as well as that of others.
6. *Self-expression:* the need to develop freedom in self-expression and to be perceived by others as significant.
7. *Cognition:* the desire to achieve self-actualization through knowing, understanding, systematizing, and constructing a system of values.
8. *Variety Seeking:* maintenance of a preferred level of physiological arousal and stimulation often expressed as variety seeking.
9. *Attribution of Causality:* estimation or attribution of the causality of events and actions.

on specific needs that can be isolated and explained empirically. Hence we find such needs as variety seeking.

Rather than succumb to the usual textbook tendency of walking through endless lists, we have found it more useful to classify needs into the broad underlying categories that are most helpful in understanding consumer behavior. These appear in Table 9.2, and each is then discussed in more detail. It should be noted that we have not attempted to make this classification exhaustive.

Appealing to Consumer Needs

Physiological Needs

We accept Maslow's contention that physiological needs usually will be satisfied before others, especially if survival is at stake. These needs often dominate and receive priority in information processing. Have you ever noticed how differently you react in a grocery store when you are hungry? In fact, retailers gain by attracting shoppers in and around mealtimes.

Safety Needs

Caution is sometimes thrown to the wind when survival is the issue. After some degree of need satisfaction, safety can become a priority issue. Who, for example, counts calories when they have not had enough food for some period of time? An abundance of high-caloric food, on the other hand, is now a proven cause of heart

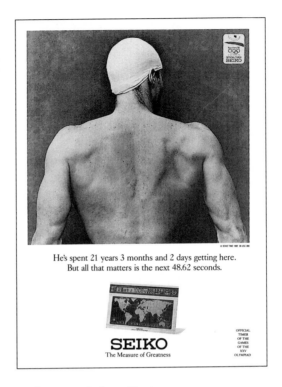

He's spent 21 years 3 months and 2 days getting here.
But all that matters is the next 48.62 seconds.

SEIKO
The Measure of Greatness

OFFICIAL
TIMER
OF THE
GAMES
OF THE
XXV
OLYMPIAD

FIGURE 9.9 Appealing to a Safety Motive
Source: Compliments of Seiko.

disease. For consumers of accurate timepieces safety may also be an issue. In Figure 9.9 the success of an Olympic dream depends on a Seiko's accuracy.

Affiliation and Belongingness

Little need be said about the importance of love and acceptance. Indeed, these needs seldom are fully satisfied. Once a society moves past a focus solely on physical survival, priorities quickly shift in this direction. A perusal of advertising themes in such popular Western magazines as *Vogue*, *Mademoiselle*, and *Elle* will quickly show that sexual attraction, belongingness, and love are dominant themes.

Achievement

The achievement motive has been researched extensively and found to be far reaching in its impact. Achievement, of course, is a basic and universal motivation, although it is expressed in varying ways from one culture to the next. It is evident that products and services providing ways to fulfill life goals stand an excellent chance of success. A good example appears in Figure 9.10.

FIGURE 9.10   Appeal to Achievement Motivation: Help in Reaching One's Goals Is a Universal Motivation

Power

Power as a motive stimulates some people to seek solutions to problems, to favor alternatives offering promise of real impact in gaining control. One can be motivated by achievement but be acquiescent on this dimension. Not many years ago, a manufacturer introduced a lawnmower with a muffler that really worked. There was only minimal noise as the mower did its job.

What do you think happened? It was later withdrawn from the market and the standard noisy motor reinstated. The reason was that many potential buyers ignored it on the belief that a quiet mower cannot possibly do the job. Noise was associated with power and potency in problem solution.

Continuing with a lawn care example, one of the greatest frustrations is a mower that will not start. Here the power-motivated person is defeated by an inanimate object. Therefore, Toro now guarantees a start each time. Not only is power gained in that manner, but ads show a dad achieving victory over his reluctant son, who now has no choice but to mow the lawn.

FIGURE 9.11   An Appeal to Those Who Dare to Be Different

Self-Expression

A common consumer motive is the need to express uniqueness—to make a statement to oneself and the world that "I am a person of significance." Westin Resorts has effectively captured this motive in its ad campaign which boldly proclaims, "Our resorts are for those who don't follow in anyone's footsteps" (Figure 9.11).

Need for Cognition

While all engage in thinking to some extent, there are real differences in the extent to which individuals exhibit a desire to know, understand, systematize, and prioritize. That is what we mean by need for cognition that recently has attracted the interest of researchers.[52] This has given rise to interesting practical applications. For example, those high in this need are more influenced by the quality of ad arguments than their counterparts, and their attitudes, once formed, are most persistent over time.[53]

FIGURE 9.12   Variety Can Be Fun

Variety Seeking

As you may recall from Chapter 2, consumers often will express satisfaction with their present brand of such items as potato chips or toothpaste but still will engage in brand switching. Why does this take place? There are several plausible explanations, all of which postulate that variety seeking is a fairly common consumer motive. Variety seeking is most common when there are many similar alternatives, low involvement, and high purchase frequency.[54]

A number of years ago Venkatesan argued that bordeom is often the root case of variety seeking.[55] In later years it became apparent that the theory of optimal stimulation provides a better explanation.[56] This theory assumes that everyone needs a certain degree of stimulation. When the expected or optimum stimulation level is not reached, then exploratory behavior is triggered.

In fact, many people appear to be **sensation seekers** who appear to be motivated by continued high-level stimulation and disdain anything that suggests boredom. Hence, we see the popularity of new and trendy restaurants offering exotic food and drink and highly stimulating lighting and music. Sensation seekers tend to be the first to adopt the new and the "trendy." Such individuals would be receptive to the "Hanes Her Way" ad in Figure 9.12.

There is good reason to hypothesize that both boredom and sensation seeking are plausible explanations for brand shifting undertaken without any dissatisfaction with existing choices and preferences. It is probable that using one brand repeatedly can create a satiation effect and decreases its utility.

When stimulation levels get too high, however, quite the opposite occurs. A television commercial shows a harried baseball umpire reaching the end of his tolerance. Then the music—"I need a vacation"—and we see him comfortably on his way 35,000 feet above sea level, saying "I'm out of there." This is a potent way to cope with overstimulation. Many such options are available for the popularly expressed malady of "burnout."

Attribution of Causality

A consumer has recently bought an expensive, top-of-the-line television set featuring new high-resolution picture technology. Within two weeks after purchase, it no longer is possible to receive sound with the picture. All of us will ask, "Why did this happen?" as we try to bring order into our world. Did I do something wrong? Is this set a lemon? Has something gone wrong with the antenna system? In other words, we try to attribute causes to events.

Various theories have been proposed attempting to explain this process, which falls under the broad category of **attribution theory**.[57] According to this theory, there is motivation to ascertain whether the causal influence in a situation is *internal* to the object or something *external*. In this situation, it is not unreasonable to assume that this particular set is a lemon (an internal attribution). The other two possible causes represent external attributions in that the fault is not inherent within the product itself.

You will find frequent reference to attribution theory throughout this book. It often gives clues needed to understand aspects of both motivation and behavior.

Some Additional Clues for Marketing Strategy

Our central objective has been to establish and reinforce the principle that marketers must accept needs as given. They are not likely to be created or modified by any type of marketing effort. Therefore, the goal always is to position a product or service within a target market as a valid and useful alternative for need satisfaction. This, of course, is the cardinal tenet of consumer sovereignty. There are several additional ways, however, to sharpen marketing impact.

Interpret Research with Caution

People have a tendency to give socially acceptable answers to questions probing their motivations. Where possible, make every attempt to determine whether or not actions match the words. As we have already stated, focus groups also can be useful in this context. Consumers often have a tendency to be more open when they sense that others are being candid. Analysis of response patterns thus allows a researcher to infer the true state of affairs. Unless this can be done, there always is the possibility of being misled by surface answers. Also participant observation may provide important clues on what really is taking place.

Be Alert to the Possibility of Motivational Conflict

It is common for several motives to function in a given situation. Kurt Lewin put forth the theory that some forces produce movement toward a goal object (he refers to this as **approach**), whereas others bring about **avoidance**.[58] Hence conflicts can occur, especially when involvement is high, and a skillful marketer often can anticipate and overcome them.

Here is an example. A female executive is attracted to a previously unknown brand of leisure clothing advertised in a catalog received through direct mail. While she is very interested in purchasing several items (*approach*), she is fearful about sizes and quality (*avoidance*). Her action will be dictated by a trade-off between these two forces, and one outcome may be no purchase. This conflict could easily be anticipated and diminished by a personalized service backed by a money-back guarantee.

Be Prepared to Provide Socially Acceptable Reasons for Choice

The most important buying motive may be one that, for varying reasons, the consumer does not want to acknowledge consciously. When that is the case, it can be wise to give a set of reasons that are more acceptable. The consumer thus is allowed to attribute a greater degree of objectivity or rationality to the choice.

Do you feel that the mechanical and technical details mentioned in the Mercedes-Benz 190 Class ad in Figure 9.13 are of central importance for all who buy a luxury car? Certainly there are some who base their actions, knowingly or unknowingly, more on the statement made to the world by Mercedes ownership about the driver and his or her lifestyle.

Exercise Caution when Marketing Cross-Culturally

In a general sense needs are universal, but priorities and means of expression and satisfaction can vary sharply. In many parts of Africa, for example, overly conspicuous consumption is frowned upon. While this may change as the middle class and affluence grow, less conspicuous means of satisfaction can be more appropriate. We discuss this issue in much more detail in Chapter 23.

Summary

This chapter examines, albeit briefly, the complex subject of involvement and motivation. Our purpose has been to identify the ways in which consumer behavior is activated, energized, and directed.

THE MERCEDES-BENZ 190 CLASS: THE SUBTLE DIFFERENCE BETWEEN MASTERING THE ROAD AND MERELY COPING WITH IT.

The road passes beneath you as always, but the sensations are markedly different. So is your state of mind. This is your first experience with a 190 Class sedan, but already you are driving with calm confidence. The car has earned your trust.

It feels resolutely stable, going precisely where you steer it, refusing to waver off course or wallow over potholes. Even the severest bumps seem only a minor disturbance as the suspension gently quells the violence underneath. Negotiating a run of switchback turns seems more routine business than high drama as the car shifts direction nimbly in response to your steering commands. Sports sedans might occasionally handle this adroitly, but they seldom feel this composed.

Suddenly the pavement deteriorates into washboard gravel, but the car tracks steadfastly ahead, curiously unfazed by the change in terrain. It occurs to you that you have yet to hear a squeak or rattle. The engine remains almost subliminally quiet, wind noise a faint whisper when you hear it at all. You normally feel an urge to stretch your legs after sitting for so long, but now you feel the urge to keep driving.

Even if you chose the automatic transmission, you still find it easy to shift manual-style when the mood strikes, locating each gear by feel without glancing downward. Your driving has become pleasurably instinctive, as driving at its best should be.

This ostensibly mystical exaltation of the driving experience springs from such technological advances as "the most sophisticated steel suspension ever put into volume production" (Britain's *Car* Magazine). And the simple fact that a 190 Class sedan is built like every Mercedes-Benz—not one ergonomic or safety principle sacrificed for the sake of cosmetic luxury or digital showmanship. Every detail of construction and assembly meeting universally envied standards.

The result is a sedan that does not "challenge" you in the macho sports-sedan tradition, but rather serves as a congenial and supremely capable ally—at once exciting and obedient, responsive and considerate. The road provides challenge enough.

Engineered like no other car in the world

© 1987 Mercedes-Benz of N.A., Inc., Montvale, N.J.

FIGURE 9.13   Are These the Real Reasons for Purchase or Reasons Consumers Want to Believe?

Need is a central variable in motivation. We defined need as a perceived difference between an ideal state and the present state, sufficient to activate behavior. When need is activated, it gives rise to drive (energized behavior), which is channeled toward certain goals that have been learned as incentives.

Involvement (perceived relevance or pertinence) is an important factor in understanding motivation. Involvement refers to the degree of perceived relevance in the act of purchase and consumption. When it is high, there is motivation to acquire and process information and a much greater likelihood of extended problem solving.

There are two types of involvement: (1) enduring (existing over time because of self-concept enhancement) and (2) situational (temporary involvement stimulated by perceived risk, conformity pressures, or other considerations).

Classification of needs is always a challenge, and we utilized eight summary categories without an attempt to be fully exhaustive (see Table 9.2).

1. Physiological—fundamental bodily needs.
2. Safety—concerns over survival.
3. Affiliation and belongingness—love and acceptance by others.
4. Achievement—desire for success in goal attainment.
5. Power—gaining control over one's destiny as well as that of others.
6. Self-expression—freedom in expressing one's uniqueness.
7. Cognition—desire to think, know, and understand.
8. Variety seeking—exploratory behavior undertaken to maintain a desired state of arousal.
9. Attribution of causality—estimation or attribution of the causality of events or actions.

The most important strategy is to accept these motivations as given and to find ways to present a product or service as a valid means of motive satisfaction. Many examples were given of how to identify needs through research and then capitalize upon them through skillful use of the marketing mix.

Review and Discussion Questions

1. Can needs be changed by marketing efforts? Why or why not?
2. Differentiate between utilitarian and hedonic benefits. How might these be expressed in purchase and use of a compact disc player? An electric can opener? Expensive perfume?
3. For which of these product categories would you expect high involvement for most buyers? A moped? Dry dog food? Lawn care products? A home computer? Dishwashing detergent? What reasons can you give?
4. What is meant by the concept of prepotency? Contrast the economies of Germany and Haiti. What differences would you expect in priorities within the need hierarchy?
5. Self-concept is said to be the source of motive integration and prioritizing. What is the self-concept? What is meant by the principle of congruence?
6. Would it be helpful for the marketing manager of a new line of detergents to have some insight into the self-concept of the average consumer, assuming this were possible through research?
7. Do you think there are intergenerational differences in the Western world in terms of sensation seeking? In other words, is this more a characteristic of the under-30 generation?
8. Using variety seeking as a need, to what extent do you think it influences the following types of buying behavior: soft drinks, lawn care products, eye makeup, motor oil, wine, choice of restaurant, and ballpoint pens?
9. Based on your own experience, would you agree that categories of needs are the same everywhere in the world? If so, how do you explain the widespread differences in buying behavior?
10. A survey was taken on college campuses throughout Scandinavia asking for beer brand preferences. When asked for the reasons, the most common answers were "flavor" and "price." If you were the brand manager for a brewery marketing in these countries, would you accept these findings as valid?

Endnotes

1. For a classic source on theories of motivation see David C. McClelland, *Personality* (New York: William Sloane, 1951).

2. See Brian T. Ratchford and Richard Vaughn, "On the Relationships between Motives and Purchase Decisions: Some Empirical Approaches," in Thomas K. Srull, ed., *Advances in Consumer Research* 16 (Provo, Utah: Association for Consumer Research, 1989), 293–299; T. C. Srinivasan, "An Integrative Approach to Consumer Choice," in Melanie Wallendorf and Paul Anderson, eds., *Advances in Consumer Research* 14 (Provo, Utah: Association for Consumer Research, 1987), 96–101; William J. Havlena and Morris B. Holbrook, "The Varieties of Consumption Experience: Comparing Two Typologies of Emotion and Consumer Behavior," *Journal of Consumer Research* 13 (December 1986), 394–404; Roberto Friedman and V. Parker Lessig, "A Framework of Psychological Meaning of Products," in Richard J. Lutz, ed., *Advances in Consumer Research* 13 (Provo, Utah: Association for Consumer Research, 1986), 338–342; and Morris B. Holbrook and Elizabeth C. Hirschman, "The Experiential Aspects of Consumption: Consumer Fantasies, Feelings, and Fun," *Journal of Consumer Research* 9 (September 1982), 132–140.

3. Elizabeth C. Hirschman and Morris B. Holbrook, "Hedonic Consumption: Emerging Methods and Propositions," *Journal of Marketing* 46 (Summer 1982), 92–101; and Holbrook and Hirschman, "The Experiential Aspects of Consumption."

4. Srinivasan, "An Integrative Approach to Consumer Choice."

5. Carl Obermiller and April Atwood, "Feelings and about Feeling-State Research: A Search for Harmony," in Marvin E. Goldberg, Gerald Gorn, and Richard W. Pollay, eds., *Advances in Consumer Research* 17 (Provo, Utah: Association for Consumer Research, 1990), 590–593; Mary T. Curren and Ronald C. Goodstein, "Affect and Consumer Behavior: Examining the Role of Emotions on Consumers' Actions and Perspectives," in Holman and Solomon, *Advances*, 624–626; and Meryl Paula Gardner and John Scott, "Product Type: A Neglected Moderator of the Effects of Mood," in Goldberg, Gorn, and Pollay, *Advances*, 585–589.

6. Rajeev Batra and Douglas M. Stayman, "The Role of Mood in Advertising Effectiveness," *Journal of Consumer Research* 17 (September 1990), 202–214; Haim Mano, "Emotional States and Decision Making," in Goldberg, Gorn, and Pollay, *Advances*, 577–589; and Meryl Paula Gardner, "Effects of Mood States on Consumer Information Processing," *Research in Consumer Behavior* 2 (May 1987), 113–135.

7. Gardner and Scott, "Product Type: A Neglected Moderator."

8. John C. Mowen, *Consumer Behavior*, 2nd ed. (New York: MacMillan, 1990), 150.

9. Melvin Copeland, *Principles of Merchandising* (Chicago: A. W. Shaw, 1924), Chapters 6–7.

10. See, for example, Lynn R. Kahle, "The Relationships among Consumer Attitudes, Self-Concept, and Behaviors: A Social Adaptation Approach," in Jerry Olson and Keith Sentis, eds., *Advertising and Consumer Psychology* 3 (New York: Praeger, 1986), 121–131; and Keith Sentis and Hazel Markis, "Brand Personality and the Self," in Olson and Sentis, *Advertising and Consumer Psychology*, 132–148.

11. Carl R. Rogers, *Client-Centered Therapy* (Boston: Houghton-Mifflin, 1951), 492.

12. Susan E. Schultz, Robert E. Kleine, III, and Jerome B. Kernan, "'These Are a Few of My Favorite Things: Toward an Explication of Attachment as a Consumer Behavior Construct," in Srull, *Advances*, 359–366. For a thorough review of earlier studies in the

marketing literature, see J. Paul Peter, "Some Observations on Self-Concept in Consumer Behavior Research," in Jerry C. Olson, ed., *Advances in Consumer Research* 7 (Ann Arbor, Mich.: Association for Consumer Research, 1980), 615–616.

13. Russell W. Belk, "Possessions and the Extended Self," *Journal of Consumer Research* 15 (September 1988), 139–168. Not everyone agrees with Belk, however. See, especially, Joel B. Cohen, "An Over-Extended Self?" *Journal of Consumer Research* 16 (June 1989), 125–128.

14. George N. Zinkhan and Jae W. Hong, "Self-Concept and Advertising Effectiveness: A Conceptual Model of Congruency, Conspicuousness, and Response Mode," in Holman and Solomon, *Advances*, 348–354.

15. Mark Snyder, "Selling Images versus Selling Products: Motivational Foundations of Consumer Attitudes and Behavior," in Srull, *Advances*, 306–311.

16. M. Joseph Sirgy, "Self-Concept in Consumer Behavior: A Critical Review," *Journal of Consumer Research* 9 (December 1982), 287–300; and Sak Onkvisit and John J. Shaw, "Image Congruence and Self Enhancement: A Critical Evaluation of the Self-Concept," in Robert F. Lusch, et al., eds., *1985 AMA Educators' Proceedings* (Chicago: American Marketing Association, 1985), 6.

17. Sentis and Markus, "Brand Personality and Self." Also see Nancy Giges, "Buying Linked to Self-Esteem," *Advertising Age* (April 13, 1987), 68.

18. Russell W. Belk, Melanie Wallendorf, and John H. Sherry, Jr., "The Sacred and the Profane in Consumer Behavior: Theodicy on the Odyssey," *Journal of Consumer Research* 16 (June 1989), 1–38.

19. Herbert Krugman, "The Impact of Television Advertising: Learning without Involvement," *Public Opinion Quarterly* 29 (Fall 1965), 349–356.

20. Two especially helpful sources are James A. Munch and Shelby D. Hunt, "Consumer Involvement: Definition Issues and Research Directions," in Thomas C. Kinnear, ed., *Advances in Consumer Research* 11 (Provo, Utah: Association for Consumer Research, 1984), 193–196; and Michael L. Rothschild, "Perspectives on Involvement: Current Problems and Future Directions," in Kinnear, *Advances*, 216–217.

21. John H. Antil, "Conceptualization and Operationalization of Involvement," in Kinnear, *Advances*, 204.

22. Richard L. Celsi and Jerry C. Olson, "The Role of Involvement in Attention and Comprehension Processes," *Journal of Consumer Research* 15 (September 1988), 210–224.

23. Meera P. Venkatraman, "Investigating Differences in the Roles of Enduring and Instrumentally Involved Consumers in the Diffusion Process," in Houston, *Advances*, 299–303.

24. Robin A. Higie and Lawrence F. Feick, "Enduring Involvement: Conceptual and Measurement Issues," in Srull, *Advances*, 690–696.

25. Marcia L. Richins and Peter H. Bloch, "After the New Wears Off: The Temporal Context of Product Involvement," *Journal of Consumer Research* 13 (September 1986), 280–285.

26. Giles Laurent and Jean-Noël Kapferer, "Measuring Consumer Involvement Profiles" *Journal of Marketing Research* 22 (February 1985), 41–53.

27. Raymond A. Bauer, "Consumer Behavior as Risk Taking," in *Dynamic Marketing for a Changing World* (Chicago: American Marketing Association, 1960), 389.

28. See George Brooker, "An Assessment of an Expanded Measure of Perceived Risk," in Kinnear, *Advances*, 439–441; and John W. Vann, "A Multi-Distributional, Conceptual Framework for the Study of Perceived Risk," in Kinnear, *Advances*, 442–446.

29. Laurent and Kapferer, "Measuring Consumer Involvement Profiles."

30. Russell W. Belk, "Effects of Gift-Giving Involvement on Gift Selection Strategies," in Andrew Mitchell, ed., *Advances in Consumer Research* 9 (Ann Arbor, Mich.: Association for Consumer Research, 1981), 408–411.
31. Judith L. Zaichkowsky, "Measuring the Involvement Construct," *Journal of Consumer Research* 12 (December 1985), 341–352.
32. J. Craig Andrews, "Motivation, Ability, and Opportunity to Process Information: Conceptual and Experimental Manipulation Issues," in Houston, *Advances*, 219–225; and Richard E. Petty, John T. Cacioppo, and David Schumann, "Central and Peripheral Routes to Advertising Effectiveness: The Moderating Role of Involvement," *Journal of Consumer Research* 10 (September 1983), 135–144.
33. Wayne D. Hoyer, "Variations in Choice Strategies Across Decision Contexts: An Examination of Contingent Factors," in Lutz, *Advances*, 32–36.
34. Judith L. Zaichkowsky and James H. Sood, "A Global Look at Consumers' Involvement and Use of Products," Discussion Paper 87-12-09, Faculty of Business Administration, Simon Fraser University, 1987.
35. Dana L. Alden, Wayne D. Hoyer, and Guntaless Wechasara, "Choice Strategies and Involvement: A Cross-Cultural Analysis," in Srull, *Advances*, 119–126.
36. See J. Craig Andrews, Srinivas Durvasula, and Syed H. Akhter, "A Framework for Conceptualizing and Measuring the Involvement Construct in Advertising Research," *Journal of Advertising* 19 (November 1990), 27–40; and Judith L. Zaichowsky, "Issues in Measuring Abstract Construct," in Goldberg, Gorn, and Pollay, *Advances*, 616–618.
37. Larent and Kapferer, "Measuring Consumer Involvement Profiles."
38. Zaichkowsky, "Measuring the Involvement Construct." For a validation of this scale, see Thomas D. Jensen, Les Carlson, and Carolyn Tripp, "The Dimensionality of Involvement: An Empirical Test," in Srull, *Advances*, 680–689.
39. Unpublished survey undertaken by Management Development Associates, Wheaton, Ill., 1987.
40. For an interesting history of the motivation research era, see Sidney J. Levy's comments in *ACR Newsletter* (March 1991), 3–6.
41. See Richard J. Lutz, "Positivism, Naturalism and Pluralism in Consumer Research: Paradigms in Paradise," in Srull, *Advances*, 1–8.
42. For further examples and explanation, see Neil M. Alperstein, "The Verbal Content of TV Advertising and Its Circulation in Everyday Life," *Journal of Advertising* 19 (November 1990), 15–22; and Laurel Anderson Hudson and Julie L. Ozanne, "Alternative Ways of Seeking Knowledge in Consumer Research," *Journal of Consumer Research* 14 (March 1988), 508–521.
43. This is a difficult and challenging field that involves many theories and conceptualizations. For a good introduction, see David G. Mick, "Consumer Research and Semiotics: Exploring the Morphology of Signs, 'Symbols, and Significance,'" *Journal of Consumer Research* 13 (September 1986), 196–213. Also the volume by Elizabeth C. Hirschman titled *Interpretive Consumer Research* will give some theoretical background (Provo, Utah: Association for Consumer Research, 1989) as will the proceedings of the First International Conference on Marketing and Semiotics: Jean Umiker-Sebeok, ed., *Marketing and Semiotics: New Directions in the Study of Signs for Sale* (Berlin: Mouton de Gruyter, 1987).
44. Ronald Alsop, "Agencies Scrutinize Their Ads for Psychological Symbolism," *The Wall Street Journal* (June 11, 1987), 25.
45. Alsop, "Agencies Scrutinize Their Ads."
46. Abraham H. Maslow, *Motivation and Personality*, 2nd ed. (New York: Harper & Row, 1970).

47. George Katona, *The Powerful Consumer* (New York: McGraw-Hill, 1962), 132.

48. A. H. Murray, *Explorations in Personality* (New York: Oxford University Press, 1938).

49. Maslow, *Motivation and Personality*.

50. David C. McClelland, *Personality* (New York: William Sloane, 1941).

51. William J. McGuire, "Psychological Motives and Communication Gratification," in J. G. Blumer and C. Katz, eds., *The Uses of Mass Communications: Current Perspectives on Gratification Research* (New York: Sage, 1974), 167–196.

52. For a review, see Sharon Shavitt, "Individual Differences in Consumer Attitudes and Behavior," in Srull, *Advances*, 51–55.

53. Curtis P. Haugtvedt and Richard E. Petty, "Need for Cognition and Attitude Persistency," in Srull, *Advances*, 33–36.

54. Wayne D. Hoyer and Nancy M. Ridgway, "Variety Seeking as an Explanation for Exploratory Purchase Behavior: A Theoretical Model," in Kinnear, *Advances*, 114–119.

55. M. Venkatesan, "Cognitive Consistency and Novelty Seeking," in Scott Ward and Thomas S. Robertson, eds., *Consumer Behavior: Theoretical Sources* (Englewood Cliffs, N.J.: Prentice-Hall, 1973), 354–384.

56. Erich A. Joachimsthaler and John L. Lastovicka, "Optimal Stimulation Level— Exploratory Behavior Models," *Journal of Consumer Research* 11 (December 1984), 830–835.

57. For a useful introduction to attribution theory, see Richard Mizerski, Linda Golden, and Jerome Kernan, "The Attribution Process in Consumer Behavior," *Journal of Consumer Research* 6 (September 1979), 123–140.

58. Kurt Lewin, *A Dynamic Theory of Personality* (New York: McGraw-Hill, 1935).

10

Knowledge

Let's test your knowledge. What effect does wine consumption have on a person's risk of chronic heart disease? Is this effect the same for both red and white wines?

According to a "60 Minutes" segment that aired in late 1991, moderate consumption of red (but not white) wine can cut the risk of heart disease in half. This reduction is due to a chemical within grape skins that lowers the amount of harmful cholesterol. Only red wines use grape skins in the fermentation process.

Apparently this new information did not go unnoticed by consumers. "We've seen a good 70 to 80 percent increase of people coming in wanting a red wine," says Joe Meyer of Seashore Package in Ocean Springs, Mississippi. "I asked them about it and right off the bat they would say they saw the story. They just started flowing in right after that."

Source: "'60 Minutes' Report Boosts Red Wine Sales," *The State* (December 14, 1991), 5A.

Our opening example provides a simple but useful illustration of the role consumer knowledge can play in determining consumer behavior. Indeed, what consumers buy, where they buy, and when they buy depends on the knowledge they possess about these basic decisions. Consequently, it is important for companies to acquire a thorough understanding of what consumers know (or don't know). Such an analysis may reveal significant gaps in consumer knowledge which, when filled in, will increase the likelihood of product purchase. Many dog owners, for instance,

FIGURE 10.1   **Expanding Consumers' Knowledge through Advertising**

may not appreciate the threat particular parasites can pose to their pet's health. For these consumers, educational efforts such as the ad appearing in Figure 10.1 may prove quite effective in stimulating product demand. Similarly, the newspaper insert ad that also appears in Figure 10.1 includes information designed to enhance knowledge about the advertised pharmacy among those consumers unaware of the pharmacy's pricing policies and services. We will see other examples of how marketers attempt to expand consumer knowledge throughout the chapter.

In addition to identifying gaps in what consumers know, marketers must also be on the lookout for errors in consumer knowledge. It is not at all uncommon to discover that a hefty number of consumers are misinformed and thus hold inaccurate knowledge. This inaccurate knowledge, typically referred to as **misperception**, may pose a significant barrier to the success of a business. A retailer that charges the same prices as a competitor, but is misperceived as being more expensive, is at a disadvantage.

When misperceptions exist that undermine the product's attractiveness to consumers, corrective actions will be necessary. An excellent example of one company's efforts to combat inaccurate knowledge is provided by Lever Brothers, the maker of

FIGURE 10.2   **Correcting Consumers' Knowledge about the Product Offering**

Dove soap. The company had identified a number of undesirable misperceptions about its product and responded by mailing target households a packet that contained, among other things, the brochure appearing in Figure 10.2. These misperceptions were listed inside the brochure, followed by an explanation as to why each was incorrect.

Understanding consumer knowledge is also important to public policy makers (see Consumer in Focus 10.1). Governmental agencies such as the Federal Trade Commission may commission a survey of consumer knowledge to help guide policies aimed at protecting the "uninformed" consumer. When consumers are judged to lack sufficient information to make an "informed choice," policy makers may enact legislation that requires the disclosure of appropriate information. Such was the motivation behind the government requiring the cigarette industry to replace the original warning required by law ("The Surgeon General has determined that cigarette smoking is dangerous to your health") with a series of warning labels describing specific dangers (for example, "Smoking causes lung cancer, heart disease, emphysema, and may complicate pregnancy") that are rotated periodically. At other times, consumers may hold inaccurate knowledge as a result of deceptive or misleading advertising. Corrective advertising may then be ordered by government agencies in order to remedy this erroneous knowledge.[1]

Consumer Knowledge and Public Policy

How well prepared are today's high school seniors who will shortly become full participants in the world of consumption? Answering this question is obviously important to public policy makers concerned with consumer education. And based on the findings of a recent study, it would appear they have good reason to be concerned.

Consumer Federation of America, the nation's largest consumer advocacy organization, and American Express sponsored a study in which seniors took a test of their consumer knowledge. The test covered six areas: consumer credit, checking/savings, auto insurance, housing rental, food purchasing, and car purchasing. Multiple questions were developed for each area, and each question was presented in a multiple-choice format with four answers. Consequently, chance alone would lead to a score of 25 percent.

The average score for the entire test was 42 percent. Seniors scored the highest (50 percent) on car buying, the lowest (36 percent) on checking/savings. In comparison, adults averaged 16 percentage points higher on a similar test. The report concluded that "high school seniors are not well prepared for the world of consumption." Apparently the same could be said for many adults as well.

Source: Student Consumer Knowledge: The Results of a Nationwide Test. Sponsored by Consumer Federation of America and American Express, 1991.

At a general level, **knowledge** can be defined as the information stored within memory. The subset of total information relevant to consumers functioning in the marketplace is called **consumer knowledge**. This chapter addresses three basic questions about consumer knowledge: What do consumers know? How is knowledge organized in memory? How can knowledge be measured? Questions concerning the processes and factors that govern how external information is transferred to memory (that is, becomes knowledge) and retrieved are deferred until later chapters on information processing (Chapter 13) and learning (Chapter 14). Similarly, the role played by knowledge during the cognitive processes that shape consumer decision making is described in subsequent chapters as well.[2]

The Content of Knowledge

A fundamental question that arises in a proper consumer analysis is "What do consumers know?" The answer to such a question rests upon understanding the contents of memory. Cognitive psychologists have suggested that there are two basic types of knowledge: declarative and procedural.[3] **Declarative knowledge** involves the subjective facts that are known, while **procedural knowledge** refers to the understanding of how these facts can be used. These facts are subjective in the sense that they need not correspond to objective reality. For instance, a consumer may believe price is an indicator of quality even when they are truly unrelated.

Declarative knowledge is divided into two categories: episodic and semantic.[4] **Episodic knowledge** involves information that is bounded by the passage of time. It is used for answering the question, "When did you last buy some clothes?" **Semantic knowledge**, on the other hand, contains generalized knowledge that gives meaning to one's world. It is the knowledge you would use, for example, in describing a videocassette recorder.

While these distinctions provide a general basis for categorizing knowledge content, a more useful typology is needed for the marketing practitioner. Although consumer researchers have largely ignored the development of such a typology,[5] our experience suggests that marketers will often find it useful to examine consumer knowledge within three general areas: product knowledge, purchase knowledge, and usage knowledge.

Product Knowledge

Product knowledge is itself a conglomerate of many different types of information. It would encompass:

1. Awareness of the product category and brands within the product category.
2. Product terminology (for example, "floppy disk" in computers).
3. Product attributes or features.
4. Beliefs about the product category in general and about specific brands.

In general, marketers are most interested in consumers' knowledge about their brand and competitive offerings. This information is provided by two types of analyses: awareness analysis and image analysis.

Awareness Analysis   A common approach to assessing brand awareness is the "top-of-the-mind" awareness measure. As the name suggests, consumers are asked to recall all of the brands that are applicable to the probe. The probe might be very general, such as a question asking you to name all of the toothpaste brands you can remember. Alternatively, the probe might limit the set of relevant brands by defining a particular benefit or usage situation (for example, the brands that would be best suited for someone going on a date).

Those brands familiar to the consumer comprise the **awareness set**. Obviously, it is difficult to sell an "unknown" product. For such unknown products, an important marketing objective must be to move the brand name into the awareness set. Enhancing awareness is a primary objective of the ad appearing in Figure 10.3.

Image Analysis   Each brand within the awareness set is likely to have a set of associations between itself and other bits and pieces of information that are stored in

Why you should invest your hard earned money with a company you've never heard of.

You shouldn't. That's why we're running this ad. To tell you who we are. To tell you we're one of the largest investment organizations in the world with a capital base of over 566 million dollars. And managing assets over 8 billion dollars. To tell you we have hundreds of investments to help you not only keep more of what you earn but earn more on what you keep.

So, while you may not have heard of us, it's obvious someone else has. 175,000 someones to be exact.

If you think those numbers were impressive, you should try these.

1-800-255-5550 ext. 600.

Integrated Resources

Because there's money to be made.

Circle No. 209 on Reader Service Card.

FIGURE 10.3 **Enhancing Brand Name Awareness Makes It Easier to Sell the Product**

memory. Crest may be strongly associated with decay and cavity prevention. Rolex and Mercedes-Benz are likely to be linked with prestige. McDonald's is the home of the golden arches and Ronald McDonald. Goodyear has the blimp. And for many consumers, the name Nike activates the slogan "Just do it."

Of course, each of these brands will possess additional associations beyond those mentioned. It is the entire array of associations that defines a brand's image. These associations may involve the brand's physical properties and attributes as well as the benefits and feelings that come from product consumption, symbols (for example, the Pillsbury Doughboy) and persons (for example, Andre Agassi and Nike) that are linked to the brand, advertising campaigns and slogans (for example, the Energizer ads with the drum-playing rabbit), and so on. The objective of an image analysis is to identify the particular associations that define a brand's image as well as the strength of these associations.

The BIP Approach to Understanding the Brand Image

According to Sal Randazzo, senior vice president/director of strategic planning at DMB&B advertising agency, there are two parts to understanding brand image: the easy part and the hard part. The easy part involves examining consumers' perceptions of the brand's physical qualities, attributes, benefits, and overall quality relative to the competition. The hard part is "trying to get a handle on the intangibles, the halo of psychological meaning and feelings." This is where the BIP (Brand Identity Profile) comes in handy.

Developing a BIP involves several steps. First, you need to identify all of the associations that come to the consumer's mind for a particular brand. For example, Budweiser's BIP might consist of the following associations: red and white can; beechwood aged; crisp, clean taste; Clydesdales; eagle; Spuds, the spotted dog; blue collar; macho.

Next, you need to find out how strongly each association is linked to the brand. Thus, consumers would report the degree to which the various Budweiser associations "connotes Budweiserness or somehow captures the essence of Budweiser." Says Randazzo, "What we ultimately end up with is a rank-ordered list of images, attributes, feelings, and things that are most strongly associated with our brand—a BIP."

The final step involves probing for a deeper understanding of what these associations represent in the consumer's psyche. Beyond knowing that Clydesdales are strongly associated with Budweiser, it is desirable to understand what Clydesdales symbolize to the consumer. For some, they may represent power, strength, and tradition: "They're working horses . . . that's the way they used to deliver beer." Others might view them as symbolizing the working-class male: "Strong, hard working, and proud." The end result of this type of probing is an enriched appreciation of the brand's meaning to the consumer.

Source: Sal Randazzo, "Build a BIP to Understand Brand's Image," *Marketing News* 25 (September 16, 1991), 18.

The basic steps and procedures that comprise an image analysis are presented in Consumer in Focus 10.2, which describes one company's approach to examining brand images. To illustrate some of the benefits afforded by an image analysis, suppose we were commissioned by bank A to assess the consumers' images of their bank and two competitors' banks. For simplicity, our example will focus on four specific attributes. In practice, many more attributes or dimensions may be used.

Figure 10.4 contains the results of the image analysis which represent consumers' average ratings of the three banks along scales representing each of the four attributes. Rather than aggregating the data across all respondents, it is useful to

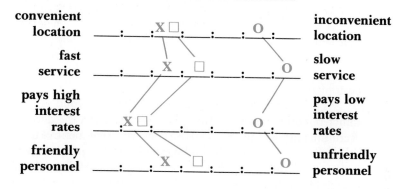

Results for Bank A Customers

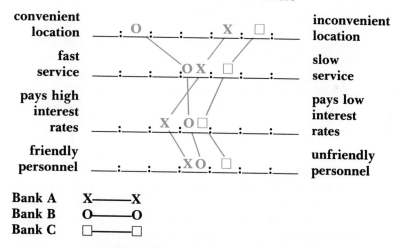

Results for Bank B Customers

Bank A	X———X
Bank B	O———O
Bank C	□———□

FIGURE 10.4   Image Analysis for Three Banks: How Consumers View the Competitors

separate the respondents into different groups. First, we would want to consider the findings based on bank A's customers. These are presented in the top half of the figure. In an absolute sense, the results indicate that bank A's customers generally hold favorable beliefs about the bank. Even so, there is room for improvement (assuming of course that consumers desire a bank to fall in the extreme left response category of each attribute scale), particularly in the areas of the speed of service and the personnel's friendliness toward customers. To the extent these attributes are important, improvements in them should enhance the bank's ability to retain customers.

A comparison of the three banks' ratings also carries implications for customer retention. For example, bank B receives very poor ratings. Consequently, this bank would pose little threat to bank A's customer base without substantial changes in its image. Bank C, on the other hand, represents a much more serious competitive threat, as it receives very similar ratings to bank A. Further, those areas where bank C is deficient might easily be improved. Bank A should, therefore, be much more sensitive to the threat posed by bank C and may wish to undertake activities that would help further differentiate the two banks within the minds of their current customers.

The benefits of this image analysis extend beyond their implications for customer-retention concerns. Indeed, it can also assist the development of customer-recruitment programs that focus on converting competitive users into our users. For this, we need to examine the findings based on competitive users. Ideally, this would be done for each competitor's customer base, as different competitive customers may hold very different beliefs. In our example, we consider the results based on bank B's customers, which are summarized in the bottom half of Figure 10.4.

These results indicate both opportunities and constraints for bank A in attempting to attract bank B's customers. Bank B holds a substantial location advantage. If this perceived advantage is false, in the sense that these customers hold a misperception of bank A's convenience (for example, they may be unaware of a nearby branch office), then correcting this misperception would be critical. On the other hand, if this disadvantage is real, bank A may be forced into building one or more branch offices in order to attract these customers. Alternatively, bank A may try to offset this location disadvantage by building their image on other attributes.

The approach used in our bank example is incomplete in that it does *not* provide needed information about the importance consumers place on the various attributes. There are, however, other approaches at the marketer's disposal that yield such information. Indeed, some of these techniques can even identify a brand's "ideal" positioning or image. These alternative approaches are presented in Chapter 11.

It is of course possible to assess consumers' brand knowledge at a more general level. Rather than measuring beliefs about each brand's quality, we could simply ask consumers whether they agree that all brands possess the same quality. However, when important differences exist between brands within the consumer's mind, measures of general knowledge are unable to identify the precise nature of these differences (for example, which brand is seen as having the best quality).

Price Knowledge   One aspect of product knowledge that deserves to be singled out is that involving product prices. An examination of what consumers know about an absolute price (for example, the price of a one-pound can of Maxwell House coffee) and a relative price (for example, whether this brand costs more than another or whether one store charges more than another for the same item) can provide important information for guiding marketing actions.

One example comes from a proprietary study undertaken by a consumer service firm. Consumers were asked to estimate the price of this service. As expected, users of the service gave very accurate estimates. This was not the case for nonusers. Their average price estimate was *twice* the actual price, and many nonusers exaggerated the price by a factor of three or four. This information resulted in a change in the company's advertising strategy, which previously had avoided price information.

Marketing executives' pricing decisions may also depend on their perceptions of how well informed consumers are about prices.[6] Marketers will be more motivated to hold prices down and respond to competitive price cuts when they believe consumers are knowledgeable about the prices charged in a market. Low levels of price knowledge, on the other hand, enable marketers to be less concerned about significant price differences relative to the competition. If consumers are largely ignorant of relative price differences, marketers may exploit this ignorance through higher prices.

Purchase Knowledge

Purchase knowledge encompasses the various pieces of information consumers possess that are germane to acquiring products. The basic dimensions of purchase knowledge involve information concerning the decisions of *where* the product should be purchased and *when* purchase should occur.

Where to Buy   A fundamental issue consumers must address during decision making is where they should purchase a product. Many products can be acquired through very different channels. Cosmetics, for example, may be purchased by visiting a retail store, ordering from a catalog, or contacting a field representative of a cosmetic firm that utilizes a sales force (for example, Avon, Mary Kay).

Because a given channel may consist of multiple competitors, the consumer must further decide which one to patronize. A consumer who has chosen to buy her cosmetics from a retailer can pick from a number of different department stores, mass merchandisers, and specialty stores.

Decisions of where to buy are determined largely by purchase knowledge. As in our prior discussion of product knowledge, awareness and image are important components of purchase knowledge. Low levels of patronage, for instance, may simply be due to a lack of store awareness among target consumers. Alternatively, it may reflect deficiencies in store image. The store may be seen as inferior to the competition in one or more key areas (for example, breadth of offering, price, convenience, availability of salespeople). Recognize that the image analysis described earlier can be easily adapted to examining consumers' knowledge about retailers.

Purchase knowledge also includes the information consumers have about the location of products within the retail environment. One aspect of this location knowledge involves the consumer's information about which stores carry which products. Another dimension concerns the knowledge about where the product is actually located within a store. In a study of the latter, shoppers were shown floor plans of a supermarket and asked to identify the location of various products.[7] Shoppers were more accurate for products placed on peripheral or exterior aisles than for those items located along central or interior aisles. Accuracy was also greater for smaller stores and shoppers reporting higher levels of store patronage.

Knowledge about the location of products in a store can affect purchase behavior.[8] When consumers are unfamiliar with a store, they have to rely more heavily on in-store information and displays for identifying product locations. This increased processing of in-store stimuli may activate needs or desires previously unrecognized, thereby leading to unplanned purchases.

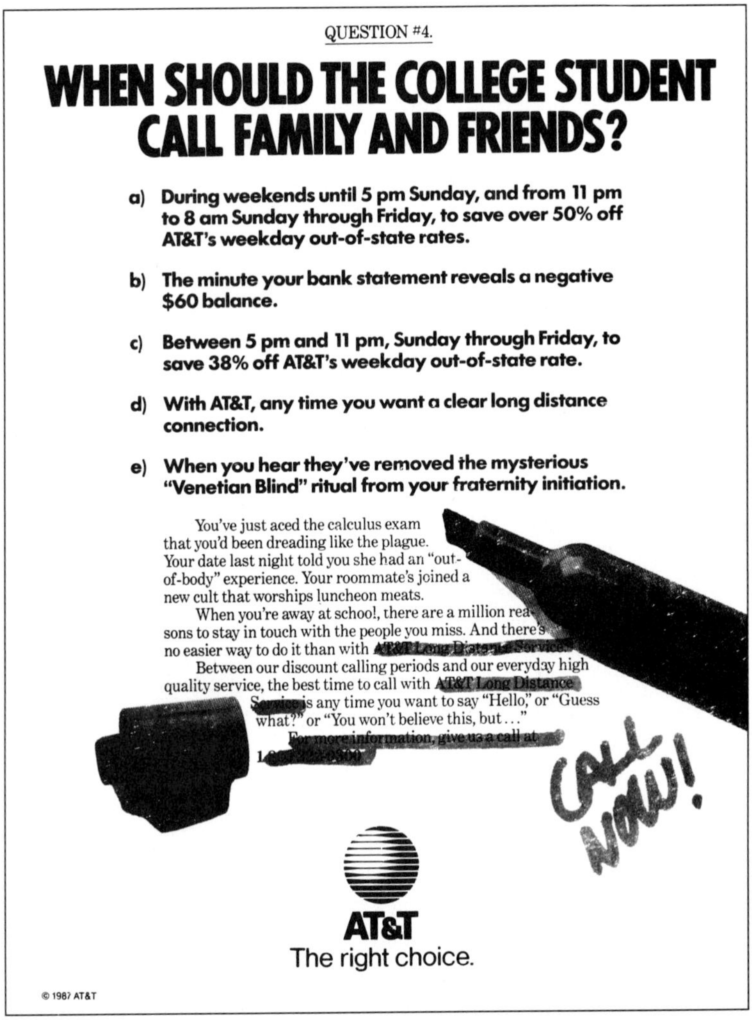

FIGURE 10.5   **Influencing Consumers' Knowledge about When to Buy a Product or Use a Service**

When to Buy   Consumers' beliefs about when to buy is another relevant component of purchase knowledge. Consumers who know that a product is traditionally placed on sale during certain times of the year may delay purchasing until such times. Knowledge about when to buy can be a very important determinant of purchase behavior for new innovations. Many consumers will not immediately acquire new products because they believe that prices may drop over time.

An ad aimed at influencing purchase knowledge appears in Figure 10.5. AT&T is attempting to modify the purchase behavior of college students by informing them about how price can vary depending on when they place their phone calls.

Usage Knowledge

Usage knowledge represents our third category of consumer knowledge. Such knowledge encompasses the information available in memory about how a product can be used and what is required to actually use the product. A consumer might know what a power saw can be used for but still lack the knowledge about how to operate the product.

The adequacy of consumers' usage knowledge is important for several reasons. First, consumers are certainly less likely to buy a product when they lack sufficient information about how to use it. Marketing efforts designed to educate the consumer about how to use the product are then needed. For example, some consumers avoid making conference calls simply because of a lack of knowledge about how to do so. One way of overcoming this barrier, shown in Figure 10.6, is to provide consumers with the necessary information on a plastic card that can be stored for future reference.

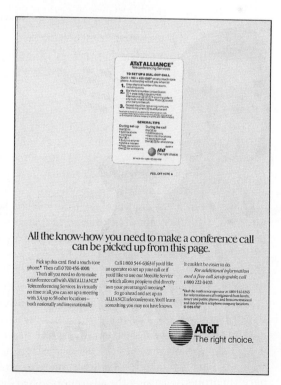

FIGURE 10.6   **Creating Knowledge about How to Use a Service**

FIGURE 10.7 **Expanding Consumers' Knowledge about Product Uses: New Uses for an Age-Old Product**

A similar barrier to purchase occurs when consumers possess incomplete information about the different ways or situations in which a product can be used. The discovery of aspirin's potential to reduce heart attack risks prompted Bayer to inform consumers of this new use. Similarly, the Morton Salt ad appearing in Figure 10.7 describes additional uses for the product beyond cooking and eating. Such efforts are quite common, as businesses often identify and promote new product uses to enhance demand, particularly in the case of mature products.

Note, however, that care must be taken in selecting new uses. A major concern is that a new use may in fact lower a product's attractiveness to consumers. For example, Avon employed a multiple-usage positioning for its bath oil, Skin So Soft. In addition to describing its use as an after-shower moisturizer, Avon also suggested that it could remove tar spots on automobiles. Some consumers may be less than enthusiastic about using a skin moisturizer that can also remove tar from a car.

Even if inadequate usage knowledge does not prevent product purchase, it can still have detrimental effects on consumer satisfaction. A misused product may not perform properly, causing the customers to feel dissatisfied. Even worse, misuse may lead to bodily injury, such as accidents involving hand-held power saws.[9]

Consumer in Focus 10.3

Coca-Cola Discovers Extra Benefits from Educating Consumers

Increasing consumer knowledge, even when the topic is quite removed from the company's products, can still be beneficial to a company. Ask Coca-Cola. The company published a pamphlet, *How to Talk to a Company and Get Action*, which explained what a consumer should do in approaching companies with a complaint or a request. The pamphlet did not refer directly to any of Coca-Cola's products. Even so, the company realized some important benefits.

One benefit stems from the reality that many unhappy customers never bother to make a complaint. Instead, they just take their business elsewhere. Studies suggest that around two-thirds of these dissatisfied customers switch brands without letting the company know why. By educating consumers on how to complain, CocaCola hopes that more of them will do so. This should at least provide the company with the opportunity to take corrective actions that will help retain customers.

In addition, many consumers gave Coca-Cola high marks for sponsoring the publication. Half of those who read the pamphlet reported feeling more confident about the company. And 15 percent claimed they would purchase more of the company's products.

Source: Judith Waldrop, "Educating the Customer," *American Demographics* 13 (September 1991), 44–47.

One final point before moving to the next topic. In considering how businesses attempt to increase consumer knowledge, our focus has been rather narrow in the sense that the examples have revolved around companies providing information about their products. Yet it is important to recognize that businesses may sometimes find it advantageous to educate consumers about topics that are unrelated to their products. To see how, read Consumer in Focus 10.3.

The Organization of Knowledge

In this section we consider how the various pieces of information within memory are structured or organized. Although there are many theories about memory organization, the literature largely favors the view of memory being organized in the form of an *associative network*.[10] According to this associative network concept, memory consists of a series of nodes (representing concepts) and links (which represent

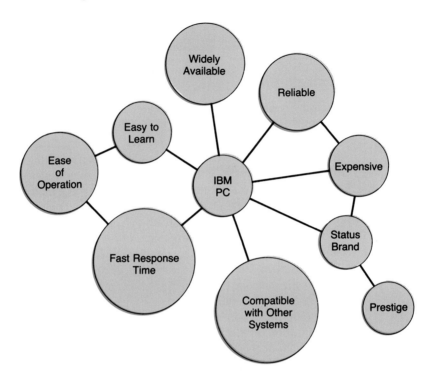

FIGURE 10.8 **An Associative Network of Knowledge for the IBM Personal Computer**

associations between nodes). Figure 10.8 displays a simplified associative network that might exist for an IBM personal computer. Recognize that the image analysis discussed earlier in the chapter (see in particular Consumer in Focus 10.2) attempts to identify the various nodes that are linked to the node representing the brand name.

The combination of various nodes within memory leads to more complex units of knowledge. A link between two nodes forms a *belief* or *proposition*, such as "IBM is an expensive brand." These beliefs will differ in the strength of the association between the two nodes. Thus, the consumer may strongly believe that IBM is an expensive brand but be far less convinced about the ease of learning how to operate an IBM.

These propositions or beliefs, in turn, can be combined to create a high-order knowledge structure called a **schema**.[11] Schemata are likely to exist for most brands familiar to the consumer. Schemata can also occur at various levels of abstraction. For example, consumers may possess a schema for a specific brand of automobile (for example, Mercedes-Benz) as well as the general concept of automobile.

One type of schema, known as a **script**, contains knowledge about the temporal action sequences that occur during an event.[12] Most of us have scripts for activities such as making a bank deposit, dining in a restaurant, or getting a prescription filled at a drug store. Schemata and scripts play an important role during information processing. In essence, activation of schemata or scripts during the processing of an incoming stimulus reduces the cognitive effort necessary for identifying what the stimulus is and how the person should respond to it.

One aspect of knowledge organization that has been examined in the research literature is whether product information is organized around brand names or product attributes. The associative network depicted in Figure 10.8 assumes a brand-based structure. Alternatively, the central node of such a network might involve a product attribute with surrounding nodes representing various brands within the product category. Research on this issue will typically expose subjects to a set of new information about the attributes of fictitious brands.[13] Later, subjects are asked to recall the information. The order in which this information is retrieved from memory is used to infer memory organization.[14]

The weight of current evidence supports a brand-based organizational structure.[15] Some have argued that this is to be expected, since most of consumers' product experiences are brand specific (for example, an ad discussing only one brand).[16] Consistent with this, research has shown a tendency to organize information within memory in a manner similar to how it is processed.[17] Thus, if information is presented one brand at a time (for example, all of the attributes for one brand are provided before turning to other brands), a brand-based memory structure is more likely to emerge. The fact that brand-based structures are also more likely to occur for subjects high rather than low in their knowledge provides further support for this experience explanation.[18]

The Measurement of Knowledge

Consumer researchers have employed a variety of approaches for measuring consumer knowledge. Some studies have relied on the amount of purchase or usage experience as an indicator of knowledge.[19] The assumption is that greater experience translates into great knowledge. Although product experience is obviously a rich source of information, consumers can possess some level of knowledge even though they have never used a particular product. Further, different types of experiences can create different types of knowledge. For these reasons, then, experience represents an imprecise indicator of knowledge.[20]

Perhaps the most obvious manner of measuring knowledge is to directly assess the contents of memory. Measures of *objective knowledge* are those that tap what the consumer actually has stored in memory.[21] This is by no means an easy task, given the vast array of relevant knowledge that consumers may possess. Indeed, our prior discussion of knowledge content provides some indication of the different pieces of information that may comprise consumer knowledge.

Figure 10.9 lists some of the questions that might be used in measuring consumers' objective knowledge. These questions represent various aspects of consumers' product, purchase, and usage knowledge. Which of them should be used

FIGURE 10.9   **Measuring Objective Knowledge**

Product Knowledge Measures

1. *Terminology*
   What is meant by the following terms?
   a. Basic
   b. Terminal
   c. CPU
2. *Attributes*
   What product features are important to you in deciding which brand of refrigerator to buy?
3. *Brand Awareness*
   List all of the brands of coffee you can remember.
4. *Product Beliefs*
   How fattening are potatoes?
   Which tastes better, Coke or Pepsi?
   How much does a McDonald's Big Mac cost?

Purchase Knowledge Measures

1. *Store Beliefs*
   Which stores carry JVC televisions?
   Which grocer offers lower prices, Big Bear or Kroger?
2. *Purchase Timing*
   Are some times better than others during the year for buying a new car?

Usage Knowledge Measures

1. *Usage Operation*
   Describe the steps involved in creating a data file on a personal computer.
2. *Usage Situations*
   What are the different ways a person can use baking soda?

will depend on the objective of the research. A study focusing on whether advertising has been successful in communicating a new product use would focus on usage knowledge. Research intended to aid pricing decisions, on the other hand, would focus on consumers' price knowledge.

A final option for assessing knowledge is to use measures of **subjective knowledge**.[22] These measures, as reflected by those appearing in Figure 10.10, tap consumers' perceptions of their own knowledgeability. In essence, consumers are asked to rate themselves in terms of their product knowledge or familiarity.

Unlike measures of objective knowledge, which focus on specific pieces of information that may be known to consumers, subjective knowledge measures center around the consumers' impressions of their total knowledge and familiarity. Thus, a consumer may feel very familiar with aspirins and still be unaware of the product's benefits in reducing the risks of heart attacks.

Research has revealed that subjective and objective knowledge measures, while related, are not substitutable.[23] That is, some people overestimate their

FIGURE 10.10 Measuring Subjective Knowledge

1. How knowledgeable are you about personal computers?
   very knowledgeable __:__:__:__:__:__ very unknowledgeable
2. Rate your knowledge of personal computers, as compared to the average consumer.
   one of the most knowledgeable __:__:__:__:__:__ one of the least knowledgeable
3. How familiar are you with personal computers?
   very familiar __:__:__:__:__:__ very unfamiliar
4. If you were going to buy a personal computer today, how comfortable would you feel
   making such a purchase based on what you know about personal computers?
   very comfortable __:__:__:__:__:__ very uncomfortable

knowledge, while others underestimate what they know. Apparently, subjective measures are affected by one's self-confidence such that people who are self-confident may over-report their level of knowledge.

In general, marketers will be most interested in what consumers actually know. As we have already seen, information about consumers' brand awareness and how they perceive the brand (that is, its image) can be very useful in formulating marketing activities. Implications for marketing action are also afforded by understanding the contents of consumers' purchase and usage knowledge.

This is not to say that measuring consumers' subjective knowledge is worthless. Subjective measures may be preferable when one is interested in anticipating the likelihood that consumers will search the environment for new information during decision making. This is because external search is less likely when consumers perceive themselves as possessing adequate amounts of information, regardless of how much they truly know (see Chapter 16). Conversely, even consumers who actually possess a high level of knowledge may search if they believe their knowledge is inadequate. Thus, subjective measures may outperform objective measures in forecasting consumers' propensity to acquire new information from their environment.[24]

Summary

Consumer knowledge consists of the information stored within memory. Marketers are particularly interested in understanding consumer knowledge. The information consumers hold about products will greatly affect their purchasing patterns. Awareness and image analyses are very useful for exploring the nature of product knowledge. Marketers should also consider purchase knowledge in terms of the beliefs consumers hold about where and when purchase should occur. Usage knowledge is another content area worthy of consideration. Expanding such knowledge can be a significant avenue for increasing sales.

Some attention has been given to understanding how consumer knowledge is organized within memory. Present findings suggest that memory is organized in the form of an associative network, with brand names serving as a central node for structures involving product knowledge.

Finally, consideration was given to alternative methods for measuring knowledge. Purchase or usage experience, while certainly related to knowledge, does not necessarily provide an accurate indication of just how much information consumers possess. Objective knowledge measures attempt to assess the actual contents of memory. Subjective knowledge measures, on the other hand, ask people to indicate how knowledgeable they perceive themselves to be.

Review and Discussion Questions

1. What is meant by the terms "product knowledge," "purchase knowledge," and "usage knowledge"? Give an example of how each might influence consumer behavior.
2. Consider the following set of results from an image analysis in which the customers of a competitive food product (brand A) rated their own brand, your brand (B), and another competitor (brand C).

good tasting __C_:_A_:_B_:__:__:__:__ poor tasting

high in nutrition __C_:__:__:_A_:_B_:__:__ low in nutrition

expensive __C_:__:__:_A_:__:_B_:__ inexpensive

easy to cook __:_B_:_A_:__:__:__:_C_ difficult to cook

What conclusions can you make based on this information?
3. Describe how advertising strategies may differ depending on consumer knowledge.
4. A grocer recently completed a study of consumers who patronize the store. One of the more intriguing findings was that the amount spent during a shopping trip depended on the number of times a consumer had shopped at the store. Consumers spent significantly more money when it was only their first or second trip. How can you explain this finding?
5. You have been asked to develop some brochures that describe a fairly sophisticated and technically oriented product. Results of market research indicate that the two primary target markets hold very different beliefs about how much product knowledge they possess. One segment perceives itself as very knowledgeable, while the other feels it is quite ignorant about the product. What implications does this difference in perceived knowledge carry for developing the brochures?
6. A recent market study suggests that consumers have very limited knowledge about the prices charged by your product and competitors. When asked to give a specific price, the majority were unable or unwilling to do so. Moreover, the average error of those giving a price was plus or minus 25 percent. What conclusions can you draw from these results about consumers' price sensitivity during decision making?
7. A recent survey of various target markets reveals important differences in both their level of product knowledge and use of friends' recommendations during decision making. Consumers having limited knowledge relied heavily on others' recommendations, while knowledgeable consumers did not. How can you explain this difference?

Endnotes

1. William L. Wilkie, Dennis L. McNeill, and Michael B. Mazis, "Marketing's 'Scarlet Letter': The Theory and Practice of Corrective Advertising," *Journal of Marketing* 48 (Spring 1984), 11–31.
2. A comprehensive and advanced discussion of how knowledge affects various cognitive processes can be found in Joseph A. Alba and J. Wesley Hutchinson, "Dimensions of Consumer Expertise," *Journal of Consumer Research* 13 (March 1987), 411–454.
3. John R. Anderson, "A Spreading Activation Theory of Memory," *Journal of Verbal Learning and Verbal Behavior* 22 (1983), 261–295.
4. Endel Tulving, "Episodic and Semantic Memory," in Endel Tulving, ed., *Organization of Memory* (New York: Academic Press, 1972).
5. For an exception, see Merrie Brucks, "A Typology of Consumer Knowledge Content," in Richard J. Lutz, ed., *Advances in Consumer Research* 13 (Provo, Utah: Association for Consumer Research, 1986), 58–63.
6. Joel E. Urbany and Peter R. Dickson, "Consumer Information, Competitive Rivalry, and Pricing in the Retail Grocery Industry" (working paper, University of South Carolina, 1988).
7. Robert Sommer and Susan Aitkens, "Mental Mapping of Two Supermarkets," *Journal of Consumer Research* 9 (September 1982), 211–215.
8. C. Whan Park, Easwar S. Iyer, and Daniel C. Smith, "The Effects of Situational Factors on In-Store Grocery Shopping Behavior: The Role of Store Environment and Time Available for Shopping," *Journal of Consumer Research* 15 (March 1989), 422–433.
9. For an example of research concerning product safety knowledge, see Richard Staelin, "The Effects of Consumer Education on Consumer Product Safety Behavior," *Journal of Consumer Research* 5 (June 1978), 30–40.
10. John R. Anderson, *The Architecture of Cognition* (Cambridge, Mass.: Harvard University Press, 1983).
11. For an evaluation of the schema concept, see Joseph W. Alba and Lynn Hasher, "Is Memory Schematic?" *Psychological Bulletin* 93 (March 1983), 203–231.
12. Research on consumer scripts can be found in George John and John C. Whitney, "An Empirical Investigation of the Serial Structure of Scripts," in *AMA Educators' Conference Proceedings* (Chicago: American Marketing Association, 1982), 75–79; Ruth Ann Smith and Michael J. Houston, "A Psychometric Assessment of Measures of Scripts in Consumer Memory," *Journal of Consumer Research* 12 (September 1985), 214–224; John C. Whitney and George John, "An Experimental Investigation of Intrusion Errors in Memory for Script Narratives," in Alice M. Tybout and Richard P. Bagozzi, eds., *Advances in Consumer Research* 10 (Ann Arbor, Mich.: Association for Consumer Research, 1983), 661–666.
13. An example of studying memory structure for existing knowledge can be found in J. Edward Russo and Eric J. Johnson, "What Do Consumers Know about Familiar Products?" in Jerry C. Olson, ed., *Advances in Consumer Research* 7 (Ann Arbor, Mich.: Association for Consumer Research, 1980), 417–423.
14. For an excellent discussion of the methodological limitations of this approach and alternative methods for testing memory structure, see John G. Lynch, Jr., and Thomas K. Srull, "Memory and Attentional Factors in Consumer Choice: Concepts and Research Methods," *Journal of Consumer Research* 9 (June 1982), 18–37.

15. Gabriel Biehal and Dipankar Chakravarti, "Information—Presentation Format and Learning Goals as Determinants of Consumers' Memory Retrieval and Choice Processes," *Journal of Consumer Research* 8 (March 1982), 431–441; Russo and Johnson, "What Do Consumers Know About Familiar Products?"

16. Eric J. Johnson and J. Edward Russo, "The Organization of Product Information in Memory Identified by Recall Times," in H. Keith Hunt, ed., *Advances in Consumer Research* 5 (Chicago: Association for Consumer Research, 1978), 79–86.

17. Biehal and Chakravarti, "Information—Presentation Format and Learning Goals as Determinants of Consumers' Memory Retrieval and Choice Processes"; Johnson and Russo, "The Organization of Product Information in Memory Identified by Recall Times"; Thomas K. Srull, "The Role of Prior Knowledge in the Acquisition, Retention, and Use of New Information," in Richard P. Bagozzi and Alice M. Tybout, eds., *Advances in Consumer Research* 10 (Ann Arbor, Mich.: Association for Consumer Research, 1983), 572–576.

18. Eric J. Johnson and J. Edward Russo, "Product Familiarity and Learning New Information," *Journal of Consumer Research* 11 (June 1984), 542–550.

19. Examples of experience-based measures can be found in James R. Bettman and C. Whan Park, "Effects of Prior Knowledge and Experience and Phase of the Choice Process on Consumer Decision Processes: A Protocol Analysis," *Journal of Consumer Research* 7 (December 1980), 234–248; Jacob Jacoby, Robert W. Chestnut, and William A. Fisher, "A Behavioral Process Approach to Information Acquisition in Nondurable Purchasing," *Journal of Marketing Research* 15 (November 1978), 523–544; Kent B. Monroe, "The Influence of Price Differences and Brand Familiarity on Brand Preferences," *Journal of Consumer Research* 3 (June 1976), 42–49; Joseph W. Newman and Richard Staelin, "Prepurchase Information Seeking for New Cars and Major Household Appliances," *Journal of Marketing Research* 9 (August 1972), 249–257.

20. See Merrie Brucks, "The Effects of Product Class Knowledge on Information Search Behavior," *Journal of Consumer Research* 12 (June 1985), 1–16; Catherine A. Cole, Gary Gaeth, and Surendra N. Singh, "Measuring Prior Knowledge," in Richard J. Lutz, ed., *Advances in Consumer Research* 13 (Provo, Utah: Association for Consumer Research, 1986), 64–66; Fred Selnes and Kjell Gronhaug, "Subjective and Objective Measures of Product Knowledge Contrasted," in Richard J. Lutz, ed., *Advances in Consumer Research* 13 (Provo, Utah: Association for Consumer Research, 1986), 67–70.

21. Examples of objective knowledge measures can be found in Brucks, "The Effects of Product Class Knowledge on Information Search Behavior"; Richard L. Celsi and Jerry C. Olson, "The Role of Involvement in Attention and Comprehension Processes," *Journal of Consumer Research* 15 (September 1988), 210–224; Akshay R. Rao and Kent B. Monroe, "The Moderating Effect of Prior Knowledge on Cue Utilization in Product Evaluations," *Journal of Consumer Research* 15 (September 1988), 253–264; Selnes and Gronhaug, "Subjective and Objective Measures of Product Knowledge Contrasted"; Mita Sujan, "Consumer Knowledge: Effects on Evaluation Strategies Mediating Consumer Judgments," *Journal of Consumer Research* 12 (June 1985), 31–46.

22. Examples of subjective knowledge measures can be found in Brucks, "The Effects of Product Class Knowledge on Information Search Behavior"; Johnson and Russo, "Product Familiarity and Learning New Information"; Arno J. Rethans, John L. Swasy, and Lawrence J. Marks, "Effects of Television Commercial Repetition, Receiver Knowledge, and Commercial Length: A Test of the Two-Factor Model," *Journal of Marketing Research* 23 (February 1986), 50-61; Selnes and Gronhaug, "Subjective and Objective Measures of Product Knowledge Contrasted."

23. Brucks, "The Effects of Product Class Knowledge on Information Search Behavior"; Cole, Gaeth, and Singh, "Measuring Prior Knowledge"; Selnes and Gronhaug, "Subjective and Objective Measures of Product Knowledge Contrasted."

24. Selnes and Gronhaug, "Subjective and Objective Measures of Product Knowledge Contrasted."

11

Attitudes

What are the 10 most powerful brand names in the world? Landor Associates, a firm specializing in the management of brand and corporate identity, attempted to answer this question by interviewing nearly 10,000 consumers in the United States, Japan, and Western Europe. Nearly 6,000 brands were tested. The top 10, in order, are:

1. Coca-Cola
2. Sony
3. Mercedes-Benz
4. Kodak
5. Disney

6. Nestlé
7. Toyota
8. McDonald's
9. IBM
10. Pepsi-Cola

What makes a brand name powerful? Two things, according to Landor Associates. One is how well known the brand is to consumers. The other is how highly consumers regard the brand.

Source: Bernard Ryan, Jr., *It Works! How Investment Spending in Advertising Pays Off* (New York: American Association for Advertising Agencies, 1991), 8–10.

In the prior chapter you learned why it is important for businesses to understand what consumers know and don't know. Equally important is the need to understand what consumers like and dislike. These likes and dislikes are called **attitudes**. More formally, attitude can be defined as simply an overall evaluation. As illustrated by the chapter opener, these attitudes play an important part in determining a product's standing among consumers.

Attitudes usually play a major role in shaping consumer behavior. In deciding which brand to buy, or which store to shop, consumers will typically select the brand or store that is evaluated most favorably. Consequently, in building an understanding of why consumers do or do not buy a particular product or shop a certain store, attitudes can be quite useful. This is especially true when attitudes are linked to the knowledge consumers possess about a product or store, as we shall see later in the chapter when we discuss attitude models.

Attitudes can also be useful to marketers in many other ways. They are often used for judging the effectiveness of marketing activities. Consider an advertising campaign designed to increase sales by enhancing consumers' attitudes. Relying solely on sales for evaluating the campaign's success can be potentially misleading, as sales are affected by many factors beyond advertising (for example, a competitor who slashes prices in response to the campaign). Consequently, it is possible for advertising to have a positive impact on attitudes without influencing sales. If, however, the ads failed to have the desired effect on attitudes, then it would probably be necessary to revise the campaign.

Attitudes can help evaluate marketing actions even before they are implemented within the marketplace. A packaging decision is one example. Establishing which version of several alternative packages evoked the most favorable attitudes from consumers could prove quite useful in making the final selection.

Attitudes can also be used to segment markets and choose target segments. One approach to segmentation involves dividing the market based on how favorable consumers are toward the product (see Consumer in Focus 11.1). All other things being equal, a firm would target the segment holding favorable attitudes, since these consumers should be more responsive to the product offering than those possessing less favorable attitudes. Even if some other base is used to segment a market (for example, geographic), one should still attempt to examine the relative favorability of various segments toward the product. The barriers to success become smaller as a segment's liking for a product grows larger.

Product attitudes are, of course, one of many different types of attitudes that marketers concern themselves with. Attitudes toward health and fitness, for instance, can carry potent implications for many industries, including cigarettes, exercise equipment, and diet foods. In the realm of persuasion, the attitudes formed toward an advertisement should also be considered as they can determine the ad's effectiveness (see Chapter 15).[1] A major study by the Advertising Research Foundation indicates that viewers' liking of a TV commercial is an important predictor of the ad's success in the marketplace.[2] Although this chapter's discussion and examples focus heavily on product attitudes, you should remember that these are only a part of the total picture.

Thus, an understanding of consumer attitudes can be beneficial in a number of ways. Fortunately, decades of attitude research have yielded a wealth of information upon which we can draw. Unfortunately, the amount of information necessary for even a basic appreciation of attitudes cannot fit within the constraints of a conventional textbook chapter. Consequently, we have devoted two chapters to this topic.

Identifying Potential Purchasers with Attitude Surveys

A company was interested in examining the attitudes of consumers who did not buy their product, even though they "qualified" for purchase (that is, they possessed the basic need that the product could satisfy and the income necessary for purchase). A national survey was therefore undertaken that included attitude measures that focused on a nonuser's likelihood of becoming a product user (for example, their agreement with statements such as "I would never buy this type of product"). Based on how they responded to the measures, nonusers were classified into one of the following segments:

"Best prospects"—segment members possess attitudes that indicate a very good chance of product purchase in the immediate future.
"Potentially convertibles"—members hold attitudes that indicate a good chance of product purchase at some point, but not in the near future.
"Neutrals"—members have attitudes that neither favor nor oppose product purchase.
"No ways"—members hold attitudes that indicate they are opposed to product purchase.

It was expected that consumers categorized as best prospects would be more likely to become product users, while those classified as no ways should be the least likely to do so. In order to validate this presumption, a follow-up survey was undertaken a year later in which respondents were asked to report whether they had purchased the product during the interim.

The results clearly supported the classification procedure. While a significant percentage of best prospects became users, very few of the no ways did. Findings such as these provide encouraging support for the potential to use attitudes as a means of identifying those consumers who are most inclined toward product purchase.

In this initial chapter, we explore some fundamental issues relevant to attitudes, such as their properties, their relationship with behavior, and their measurement. Chapter 15, on the other hand, builds upon this foundation and focuses on the variety of tactics available for influencing attitudes.

The Components of Attitude

Attitudes have traditionally been viewed as consisting of three components: cognitive, affective, and conative. A person's knowledge and beliefs about some attitude

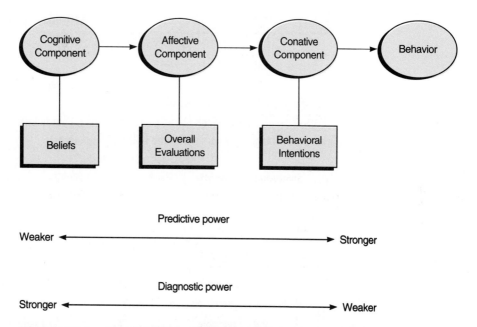

FIGURE 11.1   The Cognitive, Affective, and Conative Components of Attitude

object reside within the *cognitive* component. The *affective* component represents a person's like or dislike of the attitude object. The *conative* component refers to the person's action or behavioral tendencies toward the attitude object.

A more contemporary view of attitudes is reflected within Figure 11.1. Rather than conceptualizing attitudes as possessing three different components, attitudes are restricted to only the affective component, as reflected by the definition of attitude presented earlier. The remaining components, while closely related to attitudes, are viewed as distinct entities. Elements residing within the cognitive component are seen as a major determinant of the evaluations comprising the affective component which, in turn, is positioned as influencing the conative component. The conative component is viewed as the immediate determinant of actual behavior. Later in the chapter we will examine these relationships among the components more closely in our discussion of multiattribute attitude and behavioral intention models.

Note that each component is associated with its own unique set of measures, as illustrated in Figure 11.2. Measures that focus on a person's beliefs about the attitude object (for example, whether a product is perceived as possessing some attribute) represent the cognitive component. The affective component is represented by measures of the person's overall evaluation of the attitude object. Behavioral intention measures, representing the conative component, attempt to assess the perceived likelihood that some behavior involving the attitude object (for example, purchasing a product) will occur.[3]

FIGURE 11.2   **Alternative Measures of Beliefs, Attitudes, and Intentions**

Belief Measures

1. **How likely is it that Pepsi tastes sweet?**

   very likely __:__:__:__:__:__:__ very unlikely

2. **How would you rate the sweetness of Pepsi's taste?**

   very sweet __:__:__:__:__:__:__ very bitter

3. **Indicate how strongly you agree with the following statement:**

   "Pepsi has a sweet taste."

Strongly agree	Somewhat agree	Slightly agree	Neither agree nor disagree	Slightly disagree	Somewhat disagree	Strongly disagree

Attitude Measures

1. **How much do you like Pepsi?**

   like very much __:__:__:__:__:__:__ dislike very much

2. **How favorable is your overall opinion of Pepsi?**

   very favorable __:__:__:__:__:__:__ very unfavorable

3. **Pepsi is**

   good __:__:__:__:__:__:__ bad
   appealing __:__:__:__:__:__:__ unappealing
   pleasant __:__:__:__:__:__:__ unpleasant

4. **Indicate how strongly you agree with the following statement:**

   "I really like Pepsi."

Strongly agree	Somewhat agree	Slightly agree	Neither agree nor disagree	Slightly disagree	Somewhat disagree	Strongly disagree

Intention Measures

1. **Do you intend to buy Pepsi?**

   definitely intend to buy __:__:__:__:__:__:__ definitely intend not to buy

2. **How likely is it that you would buy Pepsi?**

   very likely __:__:__:__:__:__:__ very unlikely

3. **What is the probability that you will buy Pepsi?**

   0%   10%   20%   30%   40%   50%   60%   70%   80%   90%   100%

4. **Indicate how strongly you agree with the following statement:**

   "I intend to buy Pepsi."

Strongly agree	Somewhat agree	Slightly agree	Neither agree nor disagree	Slightly disagree	Somewhat disagree	Strongly disagree

As indicated in Figure 11.1, there are important predictive and diagnostic differences among the cognitive, affective, and conative components and measures. When prediction is of primary concern, then behavioral intention measures are most appropriate since they offer the greatest predictive power.[4] However, they are rather limited in their diagnostic power. This limitation stems from their inability to reveal *why* consumers intend or don't intend to perform a behavior. For example, a consumer may not intend to patronize a store for a number of reasons. The consumer may think that the store charges too much for its products. Or it may not have convenient shopping hours. And so on. Intention measures do not reveal these obstacles.

In contrast, belief measures offer such an understanding. They can reveal the reasons responsible for consumers' attitudes and intentions. As you will see, this is why the multiattribute attitude models covered later, which focus on beliefs, represent a powerful diagnostic tool. Thus, measures of the cognitive component offer greater diagnostic power than afforded by measures of the affective and conative components.

The Properties of Attitudes

Attitudes can vary along a number of dimensions or properties. One such dimension is **favorability**. A person may like Coke and Pepsi, dislike Shasta cola, and be fairly indifferent toward RC cola. Moreover, these attitudes may differ in their **intensity** (that is, the strength of the liking or disliking). Thus, while a consumer may hold a favorable attitude toward both Coke and Pepsi, she may be much more positive toward one brand than another.

Another important property of attitudes is the **confidence** with which they are held. Some attitudes may be held with strong convictions, while others may exist with a minimal degree of confidence. Although intensity and confidence are related, they are not the same. A consumer may, for example, be equally confident that she really likes Pepsi but is only slightly favorable toward Coke.

Understanding the degree of confidence associated with an attitude is important for two basic reasons. First, it can affect the strength of the relationship between attitudes and behavior.[5] Confidently held attitudes will usually be relied upon more heavily to guide behavior. When confidence is low, consumers may not feel comfortable with acting upon their existing attitudes. Instead, they may search for additional information before committing themselves. Second, confidence can affect an attitude's susceptibility to change. Attitudes become more resistant to change when they are held with greater confidence.[6]

Attitudes also differ in their **stability**. Whereas some are rather stable over an extended period of time, others will change, sometimes in dramatic fashion. Remember the surge of patriotism that occurred during and following the Gulf War? Manufacturers of the American flag had to greatly expand the hours of operation at their plants to keep up with the resulting increases in demand for their products.

This dynamic nature of attitudes is largely responsible for the changes in consumers' lifestyles (see Chapter 12). The clothing industry is highly sensitive to the reality that consumers' fashion attitudes are constantly changing. Manufacturers and retailers have often been left "holding the bag" after an abrupt shift in fashion preferences. Similarly, changes in consumers' health attitudes have been bad news for some industries (for example, cigarettes, liquor), but great news for others (for example, exercise and sporting equipment and clothing). Consequently, businesses can benefit from tracking consumer attitudes over time as one way of anticipating potential changes in product demand and shopping behavior.[7]

Finally, an attitude can vary in terms of whether it is based on the perceived utilitarian versus hedonic properties (see Chapter 9) of the attitude object.[8] For some products, attitude will depend very heavily on their utilitarian properties. Consumers' attitudes toward toothpaste, for instance, are likely to be driven primarily by their perceptions about the brand's functional benefits, such as reducing cavities. For other products, however, hedonic factors may dominate attitudes. Amusement parks, ballets, movies, music, and sporting events are valued for their ability to influence consumers' emotions. Understanding the relative influence of these utilitarian and hedonic properties on attitude provides useful guidance in developing effective advertising appeals (see Chapter 15).

Attitude Formation

The attitudes that consumers currently hold are, of course, a result of their prior experiences. Consumers who lived through the Depression era in the early 1930s, for example, typically have less favorable attitudes toward buying on credit. The origins of many attitudes can be traced back to childhood experiences, such as shopping trips with mom and dad. Thus, the family has a major influence on the development of attitudes during the consumer's early years. More generally, the environmental factors described in Part Two of the text will have a strong influence on attitude formation by shaping the type, amount, and quality of information and experience available to consumers.

The Role of Direct Experience

Attitudes are frequently formed as a result of direct contact with the attitude object. Consumers who enjoy a pleasant shopping trip to a retailer are likely to develop favorable attitudes toward the retailer. In contrast, a product that fails to perform as expected can easily lead to negative attitudes.

Recognize, however, that attitudes can be formed even in the absence of actual experience with an object. For example, many consumers have never driven a Mercedes-Benz or vacationed in Hawaii, but they still hold favorable attitudes toward this car and state as a vacation spot. Similarly, product attitudes may be formed even when consumers' experience with the product is limited to what they saw in an ad.

An important characteristic of attitudes based on direct experience is that they are usually held with more confidence.[9] Research has shown that consumers have much stronger convictions about their product attitudes when based on actual product usage than when based on advertising alone.[10]

In order to develop strategies and activities that will create, reinforce, or modify consumer attitudes, it is important to understand the processes that govern attitude formation. Space constraints prevent us from doing so here. Instead, these processes are explored in our discussion of information processing (Chapter 13) and learning (Chapter 14).

The Attitude–Behavior Relationship

In many situations, marketers are concerned with forecasting purchase behavior. Suppose your company had just developed a new product and was interested in determining whether there is sufficient demand in the marketplace to warrant introduction. One approach to making this determination involves introducing the product into one or more test markets. Depending on these results, you could then make a more informed judgment about the product's potential. Such a test can also cost millions of dollars, a very expensive price for discovering that your product has little appeal.

Alternatively, you could examine whether the product even merits the opportunity to go to test market by first considering consumers' attitudes toward the product. This approach is quite straightforward. Consumers from the target market would be asked to indicate their interest in buying the product. If few consumers express an interest, the product should be abandoned or modified and retested. On the other hand, if consumers are strongly attracted to the product, then it's time to consider a test market. Recognize that the costs of this attitude study will run thousands of dollars. Even so, such a price is far short of the millions you might spend on test markets, only to discover that your "star" was a "dog."

The use of attitudes to forecast demand is not limited to new products. Producers of existing products are also interested in predicting future sales. Indeed, knowledge about future consumption can be a critical determinant of many business decisions. For example, how interested would manufacturers operating at full capacity be in expanding their production facilities if they knew that sales were going to increase sharply? Conversely, discovering that demand was about to level off after several years of strong growth would reveal the need to begin exploring alternative avenues for achieving sales growth (for example, stealing competitors' customers).

The use of attitudes to predict behavior does, of course, presume that attitudes are related to behavior. The strength of the attitude–behavior relationship has long been a major area of inquiry within the social sciences. One of the first published studies on this topic was undertaken by LaPiere.[11] In the early 1930s, LaPiere traveled across the United States with a married Chinese couple. They were refused admittance by only one of the more than 200 restaurants and hotels patronized during their travels. After the trip, LaPiere mailed a questionnaire to these establishments asking if they would serve "members of the Chinese race." Nearly half of the businesses replied, and over 90 percent said they would *not* serve Chinese people.

This finding sparked a battle in the field of social psychology over attitude's predictive power. Hundreds of investigations have been undertaken on this issue, some supporting the attitude–behavior relationship, but many others confirming LaPiere's findings. In a review article published 35 years after LaPiere's study, the author concluded that "it is considerably more likely that attitudes will be unrelated or only slightly related to overt behaviors than that attitudes will be closely related to actions."[12]

Despite this pessimistic assessment, research has continued to explore the attitude–behavior relationship. It is now recognized that, under the proper circumstances, attitudes can predict behavior. Nonetheless, it has become evident that certain factors, as described subsequently, can affect the strength of this relationship.

Measurement Factors

The ability of attitudes to predict behavior very much depends on how attitudes are measured. To illustrate this point, suppose we wanted to predict whether consumers will buy a Mercedes-Benz automobile. What type of measure should work the best?

As suggested by our earlier coverage of attitude components, a measure of the intentions to buy a Mercedes-Benz should yield more accurate predictions than, say, an attitude measure that assesses how much consumers like this particular brand of automobile. The simple fact is that someone may like a Mercedes-Benz very much, but still not buy such a car due to a lack of need (for example, the person just bought a new car) or ability (for example, the person can't afford it). A measure of product liking would not register these purchase constraints. In contrast, consumers lacking the need or ability to buy a Mercedes-Benz would be unlikely to report that they intend to buy this car.

This simple example illustrates the importance of **measurement correspondence** in determining the strength of attitude–behavior relationships (also see Consumer in Focus 11.2). Measurement correspondence refers to how well a measure captures the action, target, time, and/or contextual elements that make up the to-be-predicted behavior. Greater correspondence leads to more accurate predictions. Each of these elements are discussed next.[13]

Action   This element refers to the *specific* behavior of interest (for example, buying, using, borrowing). It is imperative that attitude measures accurately represent the action element, since failure to do so can be very detrimental to their predictive accuracy. If one wants to predict automobile purchases, then the measure should focus on attitudes toward buying the car, not simply on whether they like the car. In general, measures of attitude toward an object (that is, measures omitting the action element) will be *inferior* to measures of attitude toward a behavior (that is, measures that specify the action element) in forecasting behavior.

Individual Differences

Individual differences, the topic of Part 3, are a major determinant of consumer behavior. The following full-color ads help demonstrate how individual differences shape marketing activities. Each one is accompanied by a short description of the relevant individual characteristic depicted by the ad.

Consumer Resources

A marketer of low involvement items like batteries is faced with countering the barrier of shallow attention. In this ad, Duracell uses Nolan Ryan, baseball's all-time strikeout leader, to project the quick message of durability and youthful energy.

Involvement & Motivation

This ad for Rollerblade balances utilitarian benefits with experiential benefits. The ad claims a health benefit if the product is used. To counter resistance to exercise as a form of work, juxtaposition of the visual and verbal messages shows that the health benefit is a by-product of having fun.

Attitudes

Buyer behavior can be deeply affected by social influences. Diet Pepsi's spokes-singer, Ray Charles, has been the focus of a campaign launched in the early 1990s. The campaign projects a feeling of fun, humor, and health while bridging gaps of age (his popularity as a performer spans four decades and includes fans of all ages), of lifestyle (his music ranges from country, to gospel, to jazz), of race (his audience is multi-ethnic), and of disability (he is blind). Both Ray Charles and the campaign embody the best conceptions of social homogeny.

Kinder? Gentler? No Way.

• *Shift-on-the-fly Insta-Trac,™ the most relied-upon 4x4 system in America.* • *Standard anti-lock brakes.* *
• *3-year/36,000-mile Bumper to Bumper Plus Warranty. No deductible.†*

Chevy S-10 Tahoe 4x4. The biggest V6 engine you can get. Take on any
mean street or unforgiving back road with Chevy S-10 Tahoe 4x4. Its big, 4.3 Liter Vortec V6 kicks out 160
horses at 4000 RPM. Nail it, and you know it's hammer time. Chevy S-10 Tahoe. Strong. Tall. Proud.
Chevrolet. The trucks you can depend on. The trucks that last.

The Heartbeat Of America Is Winning.™

Individual Differences

This ad for a Chevy S-10 Tahoe 4x4 might entice a consumer whose interpersonal orientation is aggressive. The rugged image and satirical wordplay are designed to appeal to people motivated by a need for power and a desire to take on any terrain or anyone.

Consumer in Focus **11.2**

Attitude Measures Receive Bad Press

It is not uncommon to find reports that, on the surface, seem to cast doubt on the relationship between consumers' attitudes and their behavior in the marketplace. NPD, a market research firm, has been tracking Americans' food attitudes and eating habits for more than a decade. These surveys report rather dramatic changes in attitudes with little corresponding effect on behavior. For example, while the number of consumers expressing concerns about french fries increased by nearly 40 percent between 1985–1989, the number eating fries at least once every two weeks dropped by only 7 percent. Similarly, the number of consumers who discourage fried chicken consumption more than doubled in a four-year period. Actual consumption declined by less than 10 percent.

What can account for these discrepancies between changes in attitudes and behaviors? According to Lois Kaufman, a vice president of Environmental Research Associates, "People lie consistently." She adds, "People's behaviors are going to lag behind what they say."

There is certainly some truth to Kaufman's observations. People may distort or hide their true feelings, particularly when the topic is heavily value laden such as alcohol and tobacco consumption, environmentalism, and nutrition. In many cases, however, the culprit is simply that the attitude measure did not correspond very well to the behavior of interest. The fact that consumers are becoming more concerned about the nutritional properties of french fries, for instance, need not imply that they will eat them less often. There are alternative ways these concerns may be expressed such as changing how french fries are prepared (for example, switching to a cholesterol-free oil) or eating fewer fries per consumption occasion. As discussed in the chapter, accurate prediction of specific behaviors (for example, eating french fries less often) requires the use of specific measures that correspond to the behavior (for example, asking the consumer whether he or she plans on eating fries less often).

Sources: Howard Schlossberg, "Americans Passionate about the Environment? Critics Say That's 'Nonsense'," *Marketing News* 25 (September 16, 1991), 8; Becky Townsend, "Consumers Don't Always Do What They Say," *American Demographics* 13 (April 1991), 12–13.

Target   Target elements can be very general (for example, buying *any* automobile) or very specific (for example, buying a Mercedes). The degree of target specificity depends upon the behavior of interest. For instance, the trade association for the automobile industry is primarily concerned with purchases of all automobiles. In contrast, General Motors would be more interested in purchases of its own models.

Returning to the LaPiere study, we can now understand the reported inconsistency between attitude and behavior. LaPiere's attitude measure involved a very general target (members of the Chinese race). In contrast, the actual behavior consisted of serving a married Chinese couple accompanied by a European male. This discrepancy, along with other problems (such as whether the person who answered the survey was the same one who served them), probably explains LaPiere's unsupportive findings.

Time   This element focuses upon the time frame in which the behavior is to occur. Suppose that on Monday you were asked about your attitude toward buying soft drinks. You report a very favorable attitude because you plan to purchase soft drinks on Wednesday, your normal day for grocery shopping. However, on Tuesday, you are asked to indicate which, if any, soft drinks you purchased since the day before. The apparent inconsistency between attitudes and behavior that would occur is simply due to the failure to specify this important timing factor. A more appropriate measure would have assessed your attitude toward buying soft drinks within the next 24 hours.

Context   The remaining element, context, refers to the setting in which the behavior is to occur. Soft drinks, for example, can be purchased in a variety of settings, such as a grocery store, vending machine at school, restaurant, and movie theater. If one is interested in predicting vending machine purchases, the attitude measure must incorporate this contextual element.

Time Interval

A very strong relationship between attitudes and behavior should occur whenever attitudes are measured just prior to actual behavior. Marketers, however, are interested in using today's attitudes to forecast behaviors that are somewhat distant in time. Retailers, for instance, place their orders for the Christmas buying season many months in advance.

The need to assess attitudes well in advance of actual behavior works against the strength of the attitude–behavior relationship. Attitudes are not static. They can easily change as a result of unexpected circumstances and situational influences.[14] A sudden budget crunch can lead to the postponement of a previously planned purchase, or an unanticipated increase in financial resources can result in purchases that were not seriously contemplated prior to this increase. The subsequent introduction of new products and brands can also influence previously formed attitudes.

This potential for change suggests that the strength of the attitude–behavior relationship will be affected by the time interval between the measurement of attitude and performance of the behavior. As this time interval increases, the opportunity for change becomes greater. Generally speaking, the shorter the time interval, the stronger the attitude–behavior relationship.[15]

Even a relatively short time interval does not necessarily ensure a strong relationship between attitude and behavior. Once again, unanticipated circumstances, such as out-of-stock conditions or an attractive in-store promotion by an alternative brand, can intervene. In such situations, it is unreasonable to expect that attitudes measured prior to this "new information" will provide a strong prediction of behavior.

Experience

As noted earlier, attitudes based on actual experience are likely to be more related to behavior than those based on "indirect" experience. Consequently, the attitudes of consumers who have purchased and consumed a product should prove more predictive of their future purchase behaviors than those lacking such experiences. Similarly, attitudes should be more indicative of a new product's potential when consumers are allowed actually to use the product as opposed to only being shown pictures or nonfunctional prototypes of the product. New product research may require the production of prototypes, even at high cost, and a simulated shopping context to achieve the greatest success in forecasting demand.

Accessibility

Before the attitudes stored in memory can influence behavior, they must first be retrieved from memory. However, simply because information is available in memory does not necessarily mean that it is always accessible. Indeed, only a fraction of this available information is actually accessible at any given moment. Accessibility represents the likelihood that information can be retrieved from memory. From this perspective, greater attitude accessibility should strengthen the attitude–behavior relationship.[16]

Social Influences

Behavior is sometimes more affected by pressures from the social environment than by personal attitudes. We have all probably experienced a situation where we did something not because of our personal desires but because of social influences (for example, smokers who try to avoid "lighting up" when accompanied by nonsmokers). Consequently, as we see later in our discussion of behavioral intention models, attitude measures are often accompanied by measures of social influence for predicting behavior.

Summary

Attitudes offer marketers a powerful predictive tool when used properly. By understanding the factors that influence the strength of the attitude–behavior relationship, we are better able to avoid pitfalls and situations that undermine attitude's predictive accuracy. While the marketer's needs may necessitate using attitude measures under less than optimal conditions (for example, forecasting behavior in the distant future), some potential problems can be easily minimized, such as avoiding the error of measuring the wrong attitude.

Multiattribute Attitude Models

While it is certainly important for businesses to know whether consumers hold favorable or unfavorable attitudes toward their products, it is also imperative for them to understand the basis or reasons for these attitudes. Knowing that consumers dislike your product does not tell you why this is so, or how you might go about overcoming this unfavorable evaluation.

Traditionally, consumer researchers have focused on the cognitive component of attitude in explaining the reasons behind favorable or unfavorable evaluations. From this perspective, attitude is seen as depending on knowledge about the attitude object. Consequently, emphasis is placed on ascertaining the important **beliefs** a person holds about the attitude object. Within multiattribute attitude models, these beliefs typically involve perceived associations between the attitude object and various features or attributes.

In addition to beliefs about an object's attributes, multiattribute attitude models also consider the **salience** of the attributes. Salience represents the relative influence an attribute can have on attitude. A product's attributes can vary substantially in how much weight they are given by consumers in forming their product attitudes. In evaluating soup, the color of the label on the can will be considered far less relevant than the taste of the soup inside.

Although several different multiattribute attitude models have been proposed in the literature, we will limit our focus to two versions.[17] After describing these different models, we will discuss some of the benefits they can offer marketers.

The Fishbein Model

Fishbein's formulation is perhaps the most well-known multiattribute model.[18] Symbolically, it can be expressed as

$$A_o = \sum_{i=1}^{n} b_i e_i \, ,$$

where

A_o = attitude toward the object,
b_i = the strength of the belief that the object has atttribute i,
e_i = the evaluation of attribute i,
n = the number of salient attributes.

The model therefore proposes that attitude toward a given object (such as a product) is based on the summed set of beliefs about the object's attributes weighted by the evaluation of these attributes. In order to illustrate the model's properties and operations, consider the situation where the model is used to understand consumers' preferences for three brands of running shoes. The first step would be to discover the target market's salient attributes. The most obvious and popular approach for identifying salient attributes is to ask consumers which ones they use in evaluating brands within the product category. The assumption is made that the person is aware of these salient attributes and will state them when asked. Those attributes receiving the most frequent mention or highest ranking are considered to be the most salient.

Sometimes, however, consumers may not divulge their true feelings.[19] People may distort their answers because of concerns over what others may think of them. For instance, consumers may underreport their use of price because they do not want to appear cheap.

One proposed remedy is to elicit a third-person response through some type of projective question.[20] An example would be, "What product features do most of the people around here consider to be important in buying a dishwasher?" Response biases presumably are minimized by making respondents feel that they are not revealing their personal opinions.

Returning to our running shoe example, assume that the following attributes are identified:

- whether the shoe is shock absorbent to permit running on hard surfaces,
- whether it is priced under $50,
- the durability of the shoe,
- how comfortable it is to wear,
- whether it is available in a desired color,
- the amount of arch support.

Next, the appropriate b_i and e_i measures would be developed. The e_i component, representing the evaluation of an attribute, is typically measured on a seven-point evaluative scale ranging from "very good" to "very bad." For instance,

Buying running shoes priced under $50 is

very good ___ : ___ : ___ : ___ : ___ : ___ : ___ very bad

　　　　　+3　+2　+1　0　−1　−2　−3

This would be done for each of the six salient attributes identified previously.

The b_i component represents how strongly consumers believe that a particular brand of running shoes possesses a given attribute. Beliefs are usually measured on a 7-point scale of perceived likelihood ranging from "very likely" to "very unlikely." For example:

How likely is it that brand A running shoes are priced under $50?

very likely ___ : ___ : ___ : ___ : ___ : ___ : ___ very unlikely

　　　　　+3　+2　+1　0　−1　−2　−3

For each brand, it would be necessary to assess consumers' beliefs for each attribute. Given 3 brands and 6 attributes, a total of 18 belief measurements would be necessary.[21]

Let us further assume that a survey containing these measures is administered to a sample of white-collar males earning more than $50,000. An average response could then be calculated for each b_i and e_i measure. A set of hypothetical results

TABLE 11.1 Hypothetical Results for Fishbein's Multiattribute Model

Attribute	Evaluation (e_i)	Beliefs (b_i) Brand A	Brand B	Brand C
Shock absorbent	+2	+2	+1	−1
Price under $50	−1	−3	−1	+3
Durability	+3	+3	+1	−1
Comfort	+3	+2	+3	+1
Desired color	+1	+1	+3	+3
Arch support	+2	+3	+1	−2
Total $\Sigma b_i e_i$ score		+29	+20	−6

appear in Table 11.1. It is important to keep in mind while interpreting these results that the b_i and e_i scales range from a maximum score of +3 to a minimum of −3.

In this example, durability and comfort are evaluated as the most desirable product attributes, followed by shock absorbent and arch support, with color a relatively minor although still salient consideration. Unlike the remaining attributes, low price (under $50) receives a negative score for this high-income sample. This does not mean that price is unimportant. Rather, it indicates that low price is viewed as an undesirable characteristic. This result is quite possible for a sample that perceives a price–quality relationship.

Findings involving brand beliefs suggest that brand A is viewed favorably by the sample because it receives a positive rating on all desired attributes. Indeed, brand A attains maximum ratings on both durability and arch support. The sample also believes that it is very unlikely (−3) that brand A costs less than $50. Given that low price is undesirable, this perception works in favor of brand A.

As a rule of thumb, marketers want consumers to perceive their brand as (1) possessing desirable attributes (that is, when e_i is positive, b_i should be positive) and (2) not possessing undesirable attributes (that is, when e_i is negative, b_i should be negative). Both strategies are commonly employed in advertising for creating favorable attitudes. The ad presented in Figure 11.3 attempts to convince consumers that the product contains desirable ingredients, while the ad in Figure 11.4 announces the absence of an ingredient that many consumers wish to avoid.

Although brand B outperforms brand A on comfort and color in Table 11.1, it is perceived as inferior to brand A on the remaining dimensions. Brand C is viewed as low priced, a perception that undermines attitude, given the negative evaluation of low price. The sample also believes that brand C is unlikely to absorb shock, be durable, or provide arch support. On the positive side, the brand is seen as somewhat comfortable and having a desired color.

To estimate the attitude toward each brand using the $\Sigma b_i e_i$ index, each belief score must first be multiplied by the corresponding evaluation score. For example, the brand A belief score of +2 for shock absorbency is multiplied by the evaluation

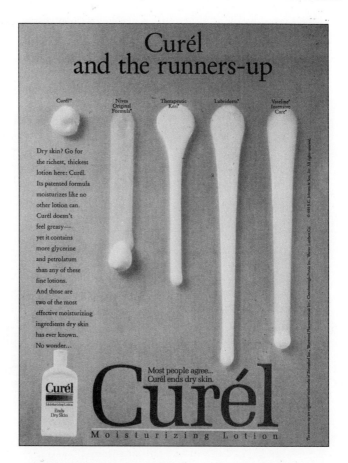

FIGURE 11.3   Communicating the Presence of Desirable Attributes Creates Positive Consumer Attitudes

of +2, which produces a value of +4 for this attribute. This same process is repeated for each of the five remaining attributes. This produces a total $\Sigma b_i e_i$ score of +29 for brand A. For brands B and C, the $\Sigma b_i e_i$ values are +20 and −6, respectively.

The score for brand A is very good, considering that the maximum score, given the current set of evaluations, is +36. The maximum score is derived by assuming the "ideal" belief score (that is, +3 or −3, depending upon whether the attribute is positively or negatively evaluated) and combining it with the existing evaluation scores.

We should note that market researchers who undertake a multiattribute analysis are typically much more interested in how a product is rated on various attributes than in the total $\Sigma b_i e_i$ score. Indeed, if one is only interested in consumers' overall product evaluations, then this information can be collected more easily by using the product attitude measures presented earlier in Figure 11.2.

FIGURE 11.4 **Communicating the Absence of Undesirable Attributes Also Improves Consumer Attitudes**

The Ideal-Point Model

A unique and important aspect of the ideal-point model is that it provides information concerning an "ideal brand" as well as information concerning how existing brands are viewed by consumers.[22] The model can be represented symbolically as

$$A_b = \sum_{i=1}^{n} W_i \mid I_i - X_i \mid ,$$

where

A_b = attitude toward the brand,
W_i = the importance of attribute i,
I_i = the "ideal" performance on attribute i,
X_i = the belief about the brand's actual performance on attribute i,
n = the number of salient attributes.

Under the ideal-point model, consumers are asked to indicate where they believe a brand is located on scales representing the various degrees or levels of salient attributes. Consumers would also indicate where the "ideal" brand would fall on these attribute scales (see Consumer in Focus 11.3). According to the model, the closer a brand's actual rating is to the ideal rating, the more favorable the attitude.

As an illustration, suppose we were to apply the model to soft drinks. Assume that the following attributes are identified as salient dimensions underlying soft drink evaluations:

- the sweetness of taste,
- the degree of carbonation,
- the number of calories,
- the amount of real fruit juices,
- the price.

Next, we would develop a scale representing various levels of an attribute for each salient dimension. Using sweetness as an example, the scale could look like

very sweet taste __:__:__:__:__:__:__ **very bitter taste**
            1   2   3   4   5   6   7

Consumer in Focus 11.3

Regional Differences in the Ideal Product

One of the reasons businesses vary their product offerings from one geographic region to another is because of regional differences in what consumers would prefer in their ideal product. Consumers living in the southwestern part of the country want a much spicier flavor than those living elsewhere. Food manufacturers accommodate this preference with slight changes in their product recipes. Coffee producers also vary their offerings in accordance with what is the ideal taste and strength within a region.

The ideal color for trucks and automobiles also differs by region. For trucks, dark blue is the most popular color among Northeasterners, followed by black and cabernet (medium red). In the southeast, scarlet (bright red) comes in first, followed by black and cabernet. Westerners prefer gray, bright blue, and dark blue. In the midwest, it is black, dark blue, and cabernet. Why such differences? One reason is climate. Given that the temperature of a car exposed to the sun can vary by 30 to 40 degrees depending on its color, darker colors sell better in colder climates.

Source: Frieda Curtindale, "A Red-Hot Mustang," *American Demographics* 11 (March 1989), 54, 56.

Consumers would then indicate their ideal or preferred taste by placing an "I" in the appropriate response category. This would be followed by ratings of where various brands fall along this taste continuum (that is, the X_i from the model equation). Consumers would also provide ratings of attribute importance on a scale such as:

not at all important __:__:__:__:__:__:__ **extremely important**
0   1   2   3   4   5   6

Unlike the bipolar coding scheme used for the Fishbein multiattribute model, unipolar coding is used for quantifying responses to the ideal-point model scales. Unipolar coding is necessary for importance measures, since a brand's performance on an unimportant attribute should not affect attitude. For this reason, we assign a zero to the "not at all important" response category. On the other hand, bipolar coding could be used for the ideal and actual brand ratings. Given that the difference between the ideal and actual brand ratings is converted to an *absolute* value, either coding scheme will produce the same results. We prefer unipolar coding since most people find it easier to work with mathematically.

You should also recognize that the Fishbein and ideal-point models use very different approaches in measuring beliefs. The ideal-point models belief measure focuses on perceptions of the brand's location along an attribute continuum. The Fishbein belief measure assesses the perceived likelihood that the brand is located at a single point on the continuum. For instance, the Fishbein counterpart to the ideal-point taste belief measure presented above might be "How likely is it that the soft drink has a very sweet taste?" While it is apparent what consumers mean when they indicate that it is very likely that the drink tastes very sweet, more ambiguous is what consumers mean when they report that it is very unlikely the product has a very sweet taste. This may indicate that they believe the taste is actually bitter. It may also indicate that they perceive the product to have neither a sweet nor a bitter taste. Either of these possibilities could lead to the same "unlikely" response on the Fishbein measure. Thus, the ideal-point measure can be more useful for understanding consumers' beliefs.

The models also differ in their measurement of attribute salience. Fishbein calls for an evaluation (that is, how good or bad) of the attribute, whereas the ideal-point model uses an importance measure. The two measures are not equivalent. Measures of importance can sometimes provide an incomplete picture of consumer motivation. This is because some attributes can be important for very different reasons. An attribute may be important because consumers want the product to have the attribute. In contrast, an attribute may be important because consumers do not want the product to possess the attribute. For example, "carbonation" in a soft drink may be very desirable for many consumers, but for those preferring an uncarbonated drink, it would be rather undesirable. Both segments are likely to rate carbonation as "important," although for very different reasons.

Note that this potential limitation with importance measures is avoided by measures that require evaluations of the attributes.[23] When an attribute is important and desirable, consumers will respond on the side of the evaluation scale anchored by "very good." If an attribute is important because it is undesirable, re-

TABLE 11.2   Hypothetical Results for the Ideal-Point Multiattribute Model

Attribute	Importance (W_i)	Ideal-Point (I_i)	Beliefs (X_i) Brand A	Brand B
Taste:				
sweet (1) — bitter (7)	6	2	2	3
Carbonation:				
high (1) — low (7)	3	3	2	6
Calories:				
high (1) — low (7)	4	5	4	5
Fruit juices:				
high (1) — low (7)	4	1	2	2
Price:				
high (1) — low (7)	5	5	4	3
Total $\Sigma W_i |I_i - X_i|$ **score**			16	29

sponses will move to the other side of the scale anchored by "very bad." When consumers really don't care whether or not the product possesses an attribute, their responses should fall on the midpoint of the scale. In general, measures of attribute evaluation are more informative because they capture both the importance and the desirability of an attribute.

Fortunately, this potential limitation is not a problem for the ideal-point model. This is because information about attribute desirability is provided by where the consumer locates the ideal performance of a product along the attribute continuum. For example, if carbonation is important because consumers prefer an uncarbonated drink, then they should place their ideal points along the low end of the carbonation continuum.

Continuing our soft drink example, suppose we found the results presented in Table 11.2. The first column specifies the attributes and the continuum (for example, sweet to bitter) along which the ideal (the third column) and actual brand (the fourth and fifth columns) ratings were taken. Attribute-importance ratings appear in the second column.

In this example, taste is the most important attribute, while carbonation is the least important. The ideal-point ratings indicate that the ideal soft drink would be sweet tasting, somewhat carbonated, fairly low in calories, very high in fruit juices (in actuality we would probably use a scale of juice content ranging from 0 percent to 100 percent), and toward the low side on price (again we might use a different scale, such as one containing specific price points). Brand A is perceived as being very close to the ideal brand. Brand B also performs well on some attributes (for example, calories) but suffers on others (such as carbonation).

Total brand attitude scores are estimated by first taking the difference between the ideal and actual brand ratings on an attribute. For taste, brand A has a difference of 0 (2 − 2), while the difference for brand B is −1 (2 − 3). This difference is converted to an absolute value as indicated by the symbol surrounding $I_i − X_i$ in the model equation and multiplied by the importance score. This operation would produce scores of 0 for brand A (0 × 6) and 6 for brand B (1 × 6) on the taste attribute. We would then repeat this process for the remaining attributes and sum the scores. For brand A, the total score is 16, while brand B's score is 29. Unlike Fishbein's multiattribute model where higher scores are preferred, lower scores are better under the ideal-point model. In fact, the best score a brand can receive is zero, which would indicate that the brand matches perfectly the ideal attribute configuration.

Benefits of a Multiattribute Analysis

A major attraction of multiattribute attitude models stems from their substantial diagnostic powers. That is, they provide richer insights into the reasons behind consumers' choices than afforded by measures of overall evaluations and behavioral intentions. One example of the type of diagnostic analyses provided by multiattribute models was presented in the image analysis section of Chapter 10. As we illustrated with the bank image example, examining consumers' beliefs can be very useful for identifying both undesirable misperceptions (for example, such as when consumers incorrectly perceive your brand as more expensive than another) and the relative competitive threat posed by competitors. It can also reveal the perceptual obstacles one must overcome in recruiting competitors' customers. You might want to return to this example in Chapter 10 and review it one more time so as to better appreciate how it fits within a multiattribute perspective.

Another way of thinking about the marketing implications of a multiattribute analysis is represented by the simultaneous importance-performance grid shown in Figure 11.5.[24] A brand is classified into one of eight cells. This classification depends on the attribute's importance (high versus low), the brand's performance on the attribute (good versus poor), and a competitive brand's performance on the attribute (good versus poor). Marketing implications are then drawn for each cell. For example, when a company's brand is truly superior to competitors on an important attribute, then this provides a competitive advantage that should be exploited, such as through a comparative advertising campaign. Poor performance by all brands on an important attribute signals a "neglected opportunity." By enhancing our brand's performance on this attribute, we could turn this into a competitive advantage. Poor performance by all brands on an unimportant attribute, however, represents little opportunity. Improving the brand's performance would have little, if any, impact on consumer choice as long as the attribute remained unimportant to consumers.

A multiattribute analysis can also provide the information necessary for some types of segmentation (see Chapter 21). For example, one might find it useful to segment consumers based on the importance they place on various attributes. Marketing activities will differ considerably when target consumers are primarily concerned with buying at a low price rather than buying the highest quality.

Another benefit of a multiattribute analysis is its implications for new product development.[25] Discovering that current offerings fall short of the ideal brand

FIGURE 11.5   **The Simultaneous Importance-Performance Grid**

Attribute Importance	Our Performance	Competitor's Performance	Simultaneous Result
High	Poor	Poor	Neglected Opportunity
	Poor	Good	Competitive Disadvantage
	Good	Poor	Competitive Advantage
	Good	Good	Head-to-Head Competition
Low	Poor	Poor	Null Opportunity
	Poor	Good	False Alarm
	Good	Poor	False Advantage
	Good	Good	False Competition

Source: Alvin C. Burns, "Generating Marketing Strategy Priorities Based on Relative Competitive Position," *Journal of Consumer Marketing* 3 (Fall 1986).

would reveal an opportunity for introducing a new offering that more closely resembles the ideal. A multiattribute model has also been used successfully by the Lever Brothers company to forecast the market shares of products such as Tone moisturizing soap and Coast deodorant soap prior to their market introduction.[26]

Attitude Change Implications

From a multiattribute model perspective, there are several ways to change consumer attitudes.[27] Returning to Table 11.2, suppose we wanted to increase consumers' attitudes toward brand B relative to brand A. Can you identify the different ways for doing this? They are: (1) changing brand beliefs, (2) changing attribute importance, and (3) changing ideal points.

Changing Brand Beliefs   As reflected by the ad appearing in Figure 11.6, companies often attempt to change consumers' beliefs about their products in the hope that this

FIGURE 11.6   IBM Designed this Ad to Change Consumers' Beliefs about Its Services

will enhance consumers' attitudes. In this ad, IBM is trying to persuade those who do not fully appreciate the full range of support services provided by the company.

Returning to Table 11.2, a change in the belief for brand B along any of the attributes *except* the brand's calories has the potential to improve attitudes. Since the brand belief for calories perfectly corresponds to the ideal point, any change here would only hurt attitudes. For the remaining attributes, any belief change in the direction of the ideal point would make the brand more attractive to consumers.

Recognize that the need to modify the product offering in order to change consumers' beliefs will depend on the accuracy of these beliefs. When consumers hold undesirable beliefs because they have misperceived the offering (for example, consumers who overestimate product price), then efforts should focus on bringing these beliefs into harmony with reality. If, however, consumers are accurate in their perceptions of a product's limitations, then it may be necessary to implement product changes.

Also recognize that brand B may be able to have an adverse influence on consumers' beliefs about brand A. Research indicates that comparative advertising, which touts the advantages of the advertised brand over a competitor, can undermine beliefs about the competitor's brand.[28] Consequently, if feasible, brand B could undertake a comparative ad campaign to reduce consumers' perceptions of brand A.

Changing Attribute Importance   Another way of altering attitudes is to change the importance consumers attach to various attributes in forming their overall evaluations. Depending on how the brand is perceived, one might wish either to increase or to decrease an attribute's importance. Research has demonstrated the potential to enhance the salience of an attribute already viewed as somewhat important.[29]

For brand B in Table 11.2, what changes in attribute importance would you recommend and in what direction (that is, an increase or decrease in importance)? In answering this question, you need to consider how each brand is perceived relative to the ideal performance. When the beliefs for both brands match the ideal point, then little is to be gained by altering the attribute's importance. No matter what importance is attached to fruit juices, the relative preference between brands A and B will not change given the current set of beliefs.

When, however, brand A is seen as closer to the ideal point for a particular attribute than brand B, decreasing the attribute's importance is to brand B's advantage. Such is the case for taste, carbonation, and price. Anything that can be done to make these attributes even less important to consumers will help reduce preferences for brand A relative to brand B.

Increasing attribute importance is desirable when the competitor's brand is farther from the ideal point than your offering. In Table 11.2, brand A is farther than brand B from the ideal point along the calories dimension. Consequently, enhancing the importance of calories would benefit brand B.

Another variant of changing the attribute importance approach to attitude change involves efforts to add a new attribute. That is, a company may try to create salience for an attribute that is currently unimportant. Flame broiling is unimportant to many consumers in selecting a fast-food burger restaurant, although Burger King's advertising has attempted to alter this feeling. Adding a new attribute to the set of salient attributes essentially amounts to increasing the importance of something that previously was nonsalient.

Changing Ideal Points   Another option for changing attitudes suggested by the ideal-point model involves altering consumers' preferences about what the ideal product would look like on each attribute. For example, in buying a television set, would your ideal brand be low priced, moderately priced, or expensive? Many consumers would place their ideal point somewhere other than on the expensive end. In an effort to persuade consumers that their ideal brand should indeed be expensive, Curtis-Mathis ran a campaign centered around the theme "The most expensive television set in America. And darn well worth it!"

There are several ideal-point changes in Table 11.2 that would help brand B. If consumers preferred either a more bitter taste, less carbonation, or a higher price, then attitudes toward brand B would increase. Such changes could also decrease attitudes toward brand A, depending on whether they broadened the gap between perceptions of brand A's performance and the ideal performance.

Changes for the remaining attributes, calories and fruit juices, would not be attractive to brand B. Given that brand B is seen as having the ideal amount of calories, altering the ideal point would be self-destructive. And while it is true that attitudes toward brand B would improve if consumers preferred a little less fruit juice in their beverage, this change would produce the same attitudinal impact for brand A. Because both brands are perceived as being the same on this attribute, any change in the preferred level of fruit juices cannot alter consumers' relative brand attitudes.

Estimating the Attitudinal Impact of Alternative Changes

As you have seen, there are many alternative changes that one might consider implementing in order to increase how much consumers like brand B relative to its competitor. Decisions about which changes to pursue should depend on a number of considerations. Some changes will be discarded because they will require product modifications that are prohibitively expensive to implement or that are virtually impossible to accomplish (for example, greatly improving product quality while maintaining a price lower than the competitor's).

Consumer resistance to change should also be considered, as some changes may be more likely than others. A belief based on inaccurate product information about the brand's price can be corrected fairly easily. In the absence of an actual product change, it may be nearly impossible to change beliefs derived from actual consumption about the taste of Spam. Nor should one underestimate how difficult it can be to change attribute importance and ideal points. An airline with a poor safety record may wish that consumers place less importance on safety in selecting a carrier, but it would be impossible for the company to actually accomplish this (not to mention the negative publicity that would accompany any effort to do so). Generally speaking, it is difficult to have a major impact on attribute importance and ideal points. Consequently, these typically should be taken as a given.

Another consideration in deciding which changes should be implemented is the potential attitudinal payoff that each change might deliver. A multiattribute model can help estimate this payoff. Let's go back to brand B in Table 11.2 one last time. Can you identify the one change which, if successful, would have the most favorable attitudinal impact from brand B's point of view?

Changing the ideal point for carbonation from 3 to 6 would be the single best change. The total multiattribute score for brand B would drop from 29 to 20 (remember lower total scores are better for the ideal-point model). This same change would increase the total score for brand A from 16 to 25. This is the only single change that would give brand B a more favorable total score than brand A.

The next best change would involve shifting the ideal point for taste from 2 to 3. The new total scores for brands A and B would be 22 and 23 respectively. This process would continue for each of the possible changes, thus yielding information about their relative attitudinal impact. All else being equal, those changes offering the greatest impact should be pursued.

Behavioral Intention Models

Earlier in the chapter we noted that the attitude–behavior relationship may be weaker when behavior is susceptible to social influences. Behavioral intention models represent one approach to examining the relative effects of attitudes and social influences. We again focus on Fishbein's formulation, which is the most widely known behavioral intention model.[30]

The Fishbein model postulates that intention, which is viewed as the immediate antecedent of behavior, is determined by an attitudinal or personal component, and a normative or social component.[31] This model can be expressed as

$$B \sim BI = W_1(A_B) + W_2(SN),$$

where

$$
\begin{aligned}
B &= \text{behavior,} \\
BI &= \text{behavioral intention,} \\
A_B &= \text{attitude toward performing behavior } B, \\
SN &= \text{subjective norm,} \\
W_1 \text{ and } W_2 &= \text{empirically determined weights representing the components'} \\
&\quad\ \text{relative influence.}
\end{aligned}
$$

Note that the model assumes that attitudes (A_B) and social influences (SN) do not directly affect behavior. Rather, their influence operates through intention, which directly determines behavior.

Earlier in the chapter we discussed the distinction between attitudes toward an object and attitudes toward a behavior and why the latter is a better predictor of how people may behave. For this reason, A_B is used to represent the attitude component of the intention model. Since the attitude measures presented in Figure 11.2 represent examples of how one might measure attitudes toward an object, an example of how attitudes toward a behavior (for example, such as buying Pepsi) could be measured is presented below:

Buying Pepsi is

good __:__:__:__:__:__:__ bad

appealing __:__:__:__:__:__:__ unappealing

pleasant __:__:__:__:__:__:__ unpleasant

The normative component, SN, represents a new concept. SN is intended to represent the influence of "important others." It is typically operationalized as the person's perception of what important others think the person should do with respect to a specific behavior. An example of how SN is measured follows:

**Most people who are important to me think
I should __:__:__:__:__:__:__ I should not
perform behavior B.**

The attraction of behavioral intention models stems from their diagnostic power in terms of estimating the relative importance of attitudes and social influences in determining behavior, thereby giving guidance to behavioral influence strategies. For example, when social pressures are a dominant force, then influencing behavior might require altering beliefs about referent expectations. Such efforts would hold little promise, however, if social others have minimal influence on behavior.

Research on the Fishbein intention model has been very extensive.[32] In many respects, the evidence has been quite supportive. Perhaps the strongest challenge to the model's validity has come from questions about how to isolate the influence of attitudes and social others.[33]

Summary

An analysis of consumer attitudes can yield both diagnostic and predictive benefits. Identifying receptive market segments, evaluating current and potential marketing activities, and forecasting future behaviors are some of the major ways in which attitudes can assist marketing decision making.

Attitudes are defined as an overall evaluation. Intensity, favorability, and confidence are important properties of attitude. Each of these properties will depend on the nature of a consumer's prior experiences with the attitude object. As the consumer accumulates new experiences, attitudes can change.

The extent to which attitudes provide accurate forecasts of behavior will depend on a number of factors. The attitude–behavior relationship should grow stronger when (1) attitude measurements specify correctly the action, target, time, and context components; (2) the time interval between attitude measurement and behavior becomes shorter; (3) attitudes are based on direct experience; (4) attitudes are accessible; and (5) behavior becomes less affected by social influences.

One approach to examining the basis for consumers' product attitudes in terms of product attributes is the multiattribute attitude model. Both the Fishbein and ideal-point models provide information about consumers' perceptions of existing products, but only the latter identifies consumers' preferred or ideal configuration of product attributes. Behavioral intention models, on the other hand, permit estimation of the relative impact of attitudes and social influences on behavioral intentions.

Review and Discussion Questions

1. A marketing research study undertaken for a major appliance manufacturer disclosed that 30 percent of those polled plan on purchasing a trash compactor in the next 3 months and 15 percent plan on purchasing a new iron. How much confidence should be placed in the predictive accuracy of these intention measurements? More generally, will predictive accuracy vary across products? Why or why not?

2. You are interested in predicting whether a person will purchase a new Chrysler from the Bob Caldwell dealership in the next month. Someone suggests the following phrasing for the intention measure: "How likely is it that you will buy a new automobile soon?" Why is this measure unlikely to predict the behavior of interest?

3. In January 1991, prior to market introduction, Mr. Dickson conducted a survey of consumers' attitudes toward his new product. The survey revealed that 80 percent of

those interviewed have favorable attitudes toward the product. The product was introduced in June 1992, and product sales have been very low. What explanations can you offer for this discrepancy between the attitude survey and product sales?

4. In order to determine which of two alternative celebrities should be used as the endorser for an upcoming ad campaign, a company assessed how much target consumers liked each celebrity. Based on these results, one of the celebrities was selected and the campaign was launched. Shortly thereafter, the campaign was withdrawn, as it proved ineffective. Interestingly, when the campaign was reintroduced using the celebrity who was liked less, it was found to be quite effective. How can you explain the greater effectiveness of the less-liked endorser?

5. Consider the following results for a TV set, based on Fishbein's multiattribute model:

Attribute	Evaluation	Brand Belief
Clear picture	+3	+2
Low price	+2	−1
Durable	+3	+1
Attractive cabinet	+1	+3

First, calculate the overall attitude score. Second, calculate the maximum overall score a brand could receive *given* the current set of attribute evaluations. Third, describe the product's strengths and weaknesses as perceived by consumers.

6. Using the multiattribute results presented in Question 5, identify all possible changes that would enhance brand attitude. Which change would lead to the greatest improvement in attitude?

7. Discuss the trade-offs between multiattribute models, measures of attitude toward a product, and intentions to purchase in terms of (a) their relative predictive power and (b) their usefulness in understanding consumer behavior.

8. Assume a company is trying to decide which consumer segments represent its best bet for future expansion. To help in this decision, the research department has collected information about segment members' product attitudes. The results show the following average attitude scores on a 10-point scale ranging from "bad product" (1) to "good product" (10):

Segment A   8.2
Segment B   7.5
Segment C   6.1

Which segment would you pick as being the most receptive to the company's offering? Why?

Endnotes

1. Scott B. MacKenzie, Richard J. Lutz, and George E. Belch, "The Role of Attitude toward the Ad as a Mediator of Advertising Effectiveness: A Test of Competing Explanations," *Journal of Marketing Research* 23 (May 1986), 130–143; Andrew A. Mitchell and Jerry C. Olson, "Are Product Attribute Beliefs the Only Mediators of Advertising Effects on Brand Attitudes?" *Journal of Marketing Research* 18 (August 1981), 318–332; Paul W. Miniard, Sunil Bhatla, and Randall L. Rose, "On the Formation

and Relationship of Ad and Brand Attitudes: An Experimental and Causal Analysis," *Journal of Marketing Research* 27 (August 1990), 290–303.

2. Cyndee Miller, "Study Says 'Likability' Surfaces as Measure of TV Ad Success," *Marketing News* 25 (January 7, 1991), 6, 14. Also see Cyndee Miller, "Researchers Balk at Testing Rough Ads for 'Likability'," *Marketing News* 25 (September 2, 1991), 2.

3. Research indicates that it is usually better to measure the perceived likelihood of performing a behavior than the intention to perform a behavior. See Paul R. Warshaw and Fred D. Davis, "Disentangling Behavioral Intention and Behavioral Expectation," *Journal of Experimental Social Psychology* 21 (1985), 213–228.

4. For research on the intention–behavior relationship, see Donald H. Granbois and John O. Summers, "Primary and Secondary Validity of Consumer Purchase Probabilities," *Journal of Consumer Research* 4 (March 1975), 31–38; Paul W. Miniard, Carl Obermiller, and Thomas J. Page, Jr., "A Further Assessment of Measurement Influences on the Intention–Behavior Relationship," *Journal of Marketing Research* (May 1983), 206–212; David J. Reibstein, "The Prediction of Individual Probabilities of Brand Choice," *Journal of Consumer Research* 5 (December 1978), 163–168; Paul R. Warshaw, "Predicting Purchase and Other Behaviors from General and Contextually Specific Intentions," *Journal of Marketing Research* 17 (February 1980), 26–33.

5. Russell H. Fazio and Mark P. Zanna, "On the Predictive Validity of Attitudes: The Roles of Direct Experience and Confidence," *Journal of Personality* 46 (June 1978), 228–243; Robert E. Smith and William R. Swinyard, "Attitude-Behavior Consistency: The Impact of Product Trial Versus Advertising," *Journal of Marketing Research* 20 (August 1983), 257–267.

6. Lawrence J. Marks and Michael A. Kamins, "The Use of Product Sampling and Advertising: Effects of Sequence of Exposure and Degree of Advertising Claim Exaggeration on Consumers' Belief Strength, Belief Confidence, and Attitudes," *Journal of Marketing Research* 25 (August 1988), 266–281.

7. For a discussion of different ways to track attitudes, see Mathew Greenwald and John P. Katosh, "How to Track Changes in Attitudes," *American Demographics* 9 (August 1987), 46–47.

8. Rajeev Batra and Olli T. Ahtola, "The Measurement and Role of Utilitarian and Hedonic Attitudes," working paper, University of Denver, 1987. Also see Elizabeth C. Hirschman and Morris B. Holbrook, "Hedonic Consumption: Emerging Concepts, Methods and Propositions," *Journal of Marketing* 46 (Summer 1982), 92–101.

9. Fazio and Zanna, "On the Predictive Validity of Attitudes: The Roles of Direct Experience and Confidence."

10. Marks and Kamins, "The Use of Product Sampling and Advertising: Effects of Sequence of Exposure and Degree of Advertising Claim Exaggeration on Consumers' Belief Strength, Belief Confidence, and Attitudes"; Smith and Swinyard, "Attitude–Behavior Consistency: The Impact of Product Trial versus Advertising."

11. Richard Tracy LaPiere, "Attitudes vs. Actions," *Social Forces* 13 (December 1934), 230–237.

12. Allan W. Wicker, "Attitudes vs. Actions: The Relationship of Verbal and Overt Behavioral Responses to Attitude Objects," *Journal of Social Issues* 25 (Autumn 1969), 41–78.

13. The literature is greatly indebted to the following article for its contribution concerning the importance of measurement correspondence: Icek Ajzen and Martin Fishbein, "Attitude–Behavior Relations: A Theoretical Analysis and Review of Empirical Research," *Psychological Bulletin* 84 (September 1977), 888–918. For an empirical demonstration, see James Jaccard, G. William King, and Richard Pomazal, "Attitudes

and Behavior: An Analysis of Specificity of Attitudinal Predictors," *Human Relations* 30 (September 1977), 817–824.

14. For research on how unexpected situations can influence the attitude–behavior relationship, see Joseph A. Cote, James McCullough, and Michael Reilly, "Effects of Unexpected Situations on Behavior–Intention Differences: A Garbology Analysis," *Journal of Consumer Research* 12 (September 1985), 188–194.

15. Icek Ajzen and Martin Fishbein, *Understanding Attitudes and Predicting Social Behavior* (Englewood Cliffs, N.J.: Prentice-Hall, 1980), Chapter 4; E. Bonfield, "Attitude, Social Influence, Personal Norms, and Intention Interactions as Related to Brand Purchase Behavior," *Journal of Marketing Research* 11 (November 1974), 379–389.

16. Russell H. Fazio, Martha C. Powell, and Carol J. Williams, "The Role of Attitude Accessibility in the Attitude-to-Behavior Process," *Journal of Consumer Research* 16 (December 1989), 280–288. Also see Ida E. Berger and Andrew A. Mitchell, "The Effect of Advertising on Attitude Accessibility, Attitude Confidence, and the Attitude–Behavior Relationship," *Journal of Consumer Research* 16 (December 1989), 269–279.

17. Discussion of additional multiattribute models can be found in Frank A. Bass and W. Wayne Talarzyk, "Attitude Model for the Study of Brand Preference," *Journal of Marketing Research* 9 (February 1972), 93–96; Jagdish N. Sheth and W. Wayne Talarzyk, "Perceived Instrumentality and Value Importance as Determinants of Attitudes," *Journal of Marketing Research* 9 (February 1973), 6–9; Milton J. Rosenberg, "Cognitive Structure and Attitudinal Affect," *Journal of Abnormal and Social Psychology* 53 (November 1956), 367–372; Olli T. Ahtola, "The Vector Model of Preferences: An Alternative to the Fishbein Model," *Journal of Marketing Research* 12 (February 1975), 52–59. For general reviews of multiattribute models, see Richard J. Lutz and James R. Bettman, "Multi-Attribute Models in Marketing: A Bicentennial Review," in Arch G. Woodside, Jagdish N. Sheth, and Peter D. Bennett, eds., *Consumer and Industrial Buying Behavior* (New York: North-Holland, 1977), 137–149; William L. Wilkie and Edgar A. Pessemier, "Issues in Marketing's Use of Multi-Attribute Models," *Journal of Marketing Research* 10 (November 1973), 428–441.

18. Martin Fishbein, "An Investigation of the Relationships between Beliefs about an Object and the Attitude toward that Object," *Human Relations* 16 (August 1963), 233–240; Martin Fishbein and Icek Ajzen, *Belief, Attitude, Intention, and Behavior: An Introduction to Theory and Research* (Reading, Mass.: Addison-Wesley, 1975); Ajzen and Fishbein, *Understanding Attitudes and Predicting Social Behavior.*

19. See, for example, Ernest Dichter, *The Strategy of Desire* (New York: Doubleday, 1960).

20. For an application of this technique, see Robert L. Thornton, "Selling the Hard Goods the Soft Way: American Versus Foreign Cars," *Journal of Consumer Marketing* 1 (1983), 35–44.

21. Evidence suggests that the order in which beliefs are measured (by attribute across brands versus by brand across attributes) can be important. See Eugene D. Joffee and Israel D. Nebenzahl, "Alternative Questionnaire Formats for Country Image Studies," *Journal of Marketing Research* 21 (November 1984), 463–471.

22. Examples of model application can be found in James L. Ginter, "An Experimental Investigation of Attitude Change and Choice of a New Brand," *Journal of Marketing Research* 11 (February 1974), 30–40; Donald R. Lehmann, "Television Show Preference: Application of a Choice Model," *Journal of Marketing Research* 8 (February 1972), 47–55.

23. Joel B. Cohen, Martin Fishbein, and Olli T. Ahtola, "The Nature and Uses of Expectancy-Value Models in Consumer Attitude Research," *Journal of Marketing Research* 9 (November 1972), 456–460.

24. Alvin C. Burns, "Generating Marketing Strategy Priorities Based on Relative Competitive Position," *Journal of Consumer Marketing* 3 (Fall 1986), 49–56.

25. For research on the model's usefulness in new product development, see Morris B. Holbrook and William J. Havlena, "Assessing the Real-to-Generalizability of Multi-attribute Attitude Models in Tests of New Product Designs," *Journal of Marketing Research* 25 (February 1988), 25–35.

26. "Lever Brothers Uses Micromodel to Project Market Share," *Marketing News* (November 27, 1981).

27. For an empirical demonstration, see Richard J. Lutz, "Changing Brand Attitudes through Modification of Cognitive Structure," *Journal of Consumer Research* 1 (March 1975), 49–59.

28. Cornelia Pechmann and S. Ratneshwar, "The Use of Comparative Advertising for Brand Positioning: Association versus Differentiation," *Journal of Consumer Research* 18 (September 1991), 145–160; Randall L. Rose, Paul W. Miniard, and Brian D. Till, "When Persuasion Goes Undetected: The Case of Comparative Advertising," working paper, University of South Carolina, 1992.

29. Scott B. MacKenzie, "The Role of Attention in Mediating the Effect of Advertising on Attribute Importance," *Journal of Consumer Research* 13 (September 1986), 174–195.

30. Alternative behavioral intention models can be found in Paul W. Miniard and Joel B. Cohen, "Modeling Personal and Normative Influences on Behavior," *Journal of Consumer Research* 10 (September 1983), 169–180; Paul R. Warshaw, "A New Model for Predicting Behavioral Intentions: An Alternative to Fishbein," *Journal of Marketing Research* 17 (May 1980), 153–172.

31. Ajzen and Fishbein, *Understanding Attitudes and Predicting Social Behavior*; Fishbein and Ajzen, *Belief, Attitude, Intention, and Behavior: An Introduction to Theory and Research*.

32. For a review of research from the consumer behavior literature, see Michael J. Ryan and E. H. Bonfield, "The Fishbein Extended Model and Consumer Behavior," *Journal of Consumer Research* 2 (September 1975), 118–136.

33. Paul W. Miniard and Joel B. Cohen, "Isolating Attitudinal and Normative Influences in Behavioral Intentions Models," *Journal of Marketing Research* 16 (February 1979), 102–110; Paul W. Miniard and Joel B. Cohen, "An Examination of the Fishbein-Ajzen Behavior Intention Model's Concepts and Measures," *Journal of Experimental Social Psychology* 17 (July 1981), 309–339; Miniard and Cohen, "Modeling Personal and Normative Influences on Behavior"; Michael J. Ryan, "Behavioral Intention Formation: A Structural Equation Analysis of Attitudinal and Social Influence Interdependency," *Journal of Consumer Research* 9 (December 1982), 263–278.

12

Personality, Values, and Lifestyle

From the Swiss village of Zermatt, a first glance at the Matterhorn is chilling. There are higher peaks nearby, but none stands so stark, so imposing as the defiant 14,692-foot granite pyramid. None says so brashly: "I dare you."

As many as 2,000 people a year climb the Matterhorn during a short summer season from mid-July to mid-September. A corps of 75 expert guides has made the adventure relatively safe for adults in good physical condition. You can hire one to make the two-day ascent for about $480 at the *Bergfuhrerburo* alpine guide office on Dorfstrasse, Zermatt's main street.

Guides say men and women from 30 to 45 are the best candidates because they have greater combined mental and physical strength than younger people. But there's no upper limit on age. One man climbed the Matterhorn at the age of 90. The climb itself takes two days, starting with a hike to the base camp. "Going down was very tough. I ran out of energy. Mental strength got me down," says Patricia Ruiz, a former IBM executive based in Paris who prepared by jogging up the steps to the top of the Eiffel Tower every day for six months.

The Matterhorn can be unforgiving. Each year, the mountain claims 10 to 20 lives of those who failed to respect the safety rules. "One mistake, and you are down," over the edge, says a guide who has scaled the mountain more than 200 times. Anyone who can run 10 kilometers has the basic endurance to make the ascent, but not without a week or two of special training at high altitude. Guides recommend a minimum of three days hiking in the surrounding mountains and one day training with a guide on snow and ice.

351

The worst candidates, guides say, are those who seek to prove something to others. The best are those who are driven by awe of the mountain and a reverence for nature. Ask any mountain guide to take you to the top, and he'll first look into your eyes to see which type you are. A guide explains, "I can usually tell standing in the office if someone can make it or not."

Source: Excerpted from Gail Schares, "A Peak Experience," *Business Week* (June 1, 1992), 118.

Relevance of Individuals for Marketing Programs

Do you wish you had the ability of the Matterhorn guide to look into the eyes of an individual and know if that person could make the climb or not? What is the guide looking for? Physical characteristics? Age? Gender? No, although they may have some effect. The guide is looking for something more determinant of behavior. That "something" might be called personality. Motivation and behavior are also related to values, as we saw in the opening scenario, when the guide described reverence for nature as a determinant of success. Whether or not the individual is successful is also a function of the person's lifestyle, as we also saw when the opening scenario referred to a person's jogging up stairs. These variables, which explain why a person actually wants, buys, and uses a product, are the topic of this chapter.

Consumer analysts might wish they could look into a consumer's eyes, as the Swiss guide does, and tell if the consumer will buy Fords or Chevrolets. In the absence of such ability, consumer analysts must use other methodologies in an attempt to predict the effects of internal or individual variables on behavior.

No one is like anyone else. A fingerprint check will quickly cure all doubts, should there be any. Even for such behaviors as choosing the clothing one wears, decorating a home, or pursuing leisure activities, few if any people have exactly the same preferences. Yet there must be some way to appeal to the needs of people at more than one at a time. The solution is to focus on the personality, values, and lifestyle of consumers.

Studying the influence of individual variables on consumer behavior is relevant to marketers in many ways. One of these is market segmentation. Although we address the topic in more detail in a later chapter, the goal is to design products which appeal to the *particulars* of consumers or groups of consumers.

Another reason for studying individual variables is the need for marketers to develop communications programs that possess *relevance*. "Relevance to consumers" became the hallmark of effective communications during the 1990s in many advertising agencies. One way to achieve relevance is to create an ad with a message that has an especially strong appeal to a consumer's personality, values, or lifestyle.

Marketing communications are "relevant" when consumers respond by saying "That product or that ad is for me." The product or message fits what I believe (values), the way I normally behave (personality), and my situation in life (lifestyle).

These variables are not necessarily more important than other variables you have studied—resources, motivation, attitudes, and so forth. However, lifestyle and the underlying personality or values they reflect are frequently more visible. Even personality is more visible than is motivation or knowledge. We speak in everyday terms of the nature of an individual as his or her "personality."

Marketing communications hope to evoke the response in an individual that the communicator truly understands him or her. One of the most admired advertisers in the 1990s is Nike. Its ads are usually oriented to lifestyle and personality themes rather than product attributes. Notice in Figure 12.1 the explicit recognition of how personalities develop over time, the values that have developed, and the realities of current behavior of many contemporary women.

As you saw in the previous chapter, some people place more weight or importance on an attribute (or have a different "ideal point") than other people. Attitude measures indicate that differences exist but generally do not explain why people exhibit such differences in attitudes. In this chapter, you have the opportunity to examine individual differences and how they relate to consumer behavior. These variables affect all aspects of consumer decisions but are particularly important in understanding need recognition.

Personality

Personality has many meanings. In consumer studies, personality is defined as *consistent responses to environmental stimuli.*[1] An individual's personality provides for orderly and coherently related experiences and behavior. Personality is the particular pattern of organization that makes one individual unique and different from all others. Personality provides a consistency of responses based on *enduring, inner psychological characteristics.*

Three major theories or approaches to the study of personality have been used in consumer research: psychoanalytic, socio-psychological, and trait-factor. Personality is sometimes related to the self-concept or the ideal self that individuals would like themselves to be, including Maslow's hierarchical theory in which people seek to achieve their fullest potential of self-actualization.[2]

Psychoanalytic Theory

Psychoanalytic theory posits that the human personality system consists of the id, ego, and superego.[3] The id is the source of psychic energy and seeks immediate gratification for biological and instinctual needs. The superego represents societal or personal norms and serves as an ethical constraint on behavior. The ego mediates the hedonistic demands of the id and the moralistic prohibitions of the superego. The dynamic interaction of these elements results in unconscious motivations that are manifested in observed human behavior.

The psychoanalytic theory served as the conceptual basis for the motivation-research movement that was described in Chapter 9 but which was also the forerun-

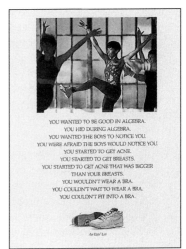

FIGURE 12.1   Nike Appeals to Personalities and Lifestyles Rather Than Product Attributes
Source: Courtesy of Nike.

ner of lifestyle studies. According to the philosophy of motivation researchers such as Dr. Ernest Dichter, consumer behavior is often the result of unconscious consumer motives, which can be determined through the indirect assessment methods described in Chapter 9 such as projective and related psychological techniques.

The motivation-research movement has produced some extraordinary findings.[4] Typical of the psychoanalytical explanations of consumer purchase motivations are these often-related examples: A man who buys a convertible sees it as a substitute mistress; a woman is very serious when baking a cake because, uncon-

FIGURE 12.1   Continued

sciously, she is going through the symbolic act of birth; and men want their cigars to be odoriferous to prove their masculinity.

These examples are interesting and perhaps even useful. They are subject to serious questions of validity, however. Certainly one must go further to gain a thorough, in-depth understanding of personality and consumer decision making. A consumer's personality is a result of more than subconscious drives. Yet a great deal of advertising is influenced by the psychoanalytic approach to personality, especially its heavy emphasis on sexual and other deep-seated biological instincts.

Socio-Psychological Theory

Socio-psychological theory recognizes the interdependence of the individual and society. The individual strives to meet the needs of society, while society helps the individual to attain his or her goals. The theory is therefore not exclusively sociological or psychological but rather the combination of the two. This theoretical orientation is associated with Adler, Horney, Fromm, and Sullivan.[5]

Socio-psychological personality theory differs from psychoanalytic theory in two important respects. First, social variables rather than biological instincts are considered to be the most important determinants in shaping personality. Second, behavioral motivation is directed to meet those needs.

A representative example of socio-psychological personality theory is the Horney paradigm. This model suggests that human behavior results from three predominant, interpersonal orientations: compliant, aggressive, and detached. Questions designed to measure these variables are referred to as a CAD scale. Compliant people are dependent on other people for love and affection and are said to move toward others. Aggressive people are motivated by the need for power and

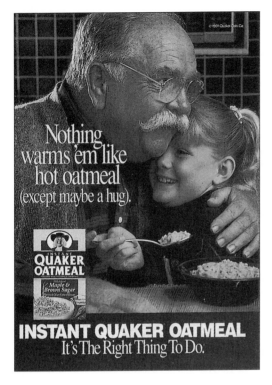

FIGURE 12.2   **Appeals to Compliant and Detached Personalities**
Source: Courtesy of Quaker Oats and Oliver Peoples.

move against others. Detached people are self-sufficient and independent and move away from others.[6]

You can see examples of appeals to these personalities in Figure 12.2. The ad for Quaker Oats appeals to the compliant, interpersonal needs of a hug and encourages consumers "to do the right thing." The ad for Oliver Peoples, in contrast, tries to appeal to detached people who "do not have to live like the crowd." If you want to see an ad with obvious appeal to aggressive people, turn to the color pages in this section and look at the ad for Chevrolet.

Personality structure or a person's self-concept may interact with external forces to lead to restructuring of lifestyles, relationships, and values. Especially at times when people are reconsidering and perhaps reconstructing their self-concept, they may become receptive to goods, services, or ideas that they formerly would have considered unnecessary. These interactions between external changes and internal motivations have been shown to be associated with the purchase of a product as extreme as cosmetic plastic surgery. Schouten found that such purchases are important to both the maintenance and the development of a stable, harmonious self-concept.[7]

Trait-Factor Theory

Trait-factor theory represents a quantitative approach to the study of personality. This theory postulates that an individual's personality is composed of definite predispositional attributes called traits. A **trait** is more specifically defined as any distinguishable, relatively enduring way in which one individual differs from another. Examples of such traits might be sociability, relaxed style, amount of internal control. Scale statements to measure such traits are shown in Table 12.1. Traits can alternatively be considered individual difference variables.[8]

Three assumptions delineate the trait-factor theory. It is assumed that traits are common to many individuals and vary in absolute amounts among individuals. It is further assumed that these traits are relatively stable and exert fairly universal effects on behavior regardless of the environmental situation. It follows directly from this assumption that a consistent functioning of personality variables is predictive of a wide variety of behavior. The final assumption asserts that traits can be inferred from the measurement of behavioral indicators.

A number of standard psychological inventories exist such as the California Psychological Inventory or the Edwards Personal Preference Scale (EPPS). Such tests are widely used for psychological testing and are sometimes applied to marketing applications. Borrowing standard scales that were designed for clinical purposes may produce poor results, however, when applied to marketing.[9] Modified tests, such as those shown in Table 12.1, are more likely to be useful for consumer research.[10]

TABLE 12.1   Test Items in the Modified Personality Instrument

Sociable

I am always glad to join a large gathering.
I consider myself a very sociable, outgoing person.
I find it easy to mingle among people at a social gathering.
When I am in a small group, I sit back and let others do most of the talking.
I have decidedly fewer friends than most people.
I am considered a very enthusiastic person.

Relaxed

I get tense as I think of all the things lying ahead of me.
Quite small setbacks occasionally irritate me too much.
I wish I knew how to relax.
I shrink from facing a crisis or a difficulty.

Internal Control

Sometimes I feel that I don't have enough control over the direction my life is taking.
Many times I feel that I have little influence over the things that happen to me.
What happens to me is my own doing.
Becoming a success is a matter of hard work; luck has nothing to do with it.
Getting a good job depends mainly on being in the right place at the right time.

Source: Kathryn E. A. Villani and Yoram Wind, "On the Usage of 'Modified' Personality Trait Measures in Consumer Research," *Journal of Consumer Research* 2 (December 1975), 223–228. Reprinted by permission.

Trait-factor theory has been the primary basis of marketing personality research. The typical study attempts to find a relationship between a set of personality variables and assorted consumer behaviors such as purchases, media choice, innovation, fear and social influence, product choice, opinion leadership, risk taking, and attitude change. Personality has been found to relate to specific attributes of product choice.[11] Research also indicates that people can make relatively good judgments about other people's traits and how these relate to such choices as automobile brands, occupations, and magazines.[12]

Predicting Buyer Behavior

Predicting consumer behavior has been the objective of most personality research, at least until very recently. The rich literature on personality in psychology and other behavioral sciences has enticed many researchers to theorize that personality characteristics should predict brand or store preference and other types of buyer activity. These studies generally fall into two classifications: (1) susceptibility to social influence, and (2) product and brand choice.

Much of the consumer researchers' interest in personality was stimulated by Evans, an early researcher who attempted to test the assumption that automobile buyers differ in personality structure.[13] A standard personality inventory, the Edwards Personal Preference Scale, was administered to owners of Chevrolets and Fords. There were only a few statistically significant differences between the two groups. Using a discriminant analysis, he was able to predict correctly a Ford or Chevrolet owner in only 63 percent of the cases, not much better than the 50 percent that would be expected by chance. Using 12 objective variables, such as age of car, income, and other demographics, he made a correct prediction in 70 percent of the cases. Evans concluded that personality is of relatively little value in predicting automobile brand ownership.

A number of other studies investigated the hypothesis that personality could be directly related to product choice and a few of these reported some relation between product use and personality traits. Most found only very small amounts of variance in product choice explained by personality. Looking back from today's vantage point, it is not surprising that these studies found little relationship between personality and product choice. After all, personality is but one variable in the process of consumer decision making. If any relationship were to be established, dependent variables such as intention would be better candidates than would behavior.

Even if personality traits were found to be valid predictors of intentions or behavior, would they be useful as a means of market segmentation? A positive answer would require that the following circumstances prevail:

1. People with common personality dimensions must be homogeneous in terms of demographic factors such as age, income, or location so that they can be reached economically through the mass media. This is necessary because data are available on media audiences mostly in terms of demographic characteristics. If they show no identifiable common characteristics of this type, there is no practical means of reaching them as a unique market segment.

2. Measures that isolate personality variables must be demonstrated to have adequate reliability and validity. The difficulties in this respect have been extensive.

3. Personality differences must reflect clear-cut variations in buyer activity and preferences, which, in turn, can be capitalized upon meaningfully through modifications in the marketing mix. In other words, people can show different personality profiles yet still prefer essentially the same product attributes.

4. Market groups isolated by personality measures must be of a sufficient size to be reached economically. Knowledge that each person varies on a personality scale is interesting but impractical for a marketing firm, which, of necessity, must generally work with relatively large segments.

The evidence to date falls short of these criteria, and personality has not been demonstrated convincingly as a useful means of market segmentation. There is no reason to assume, for example, that individuals with a given personality profile are homogeneous in other respects; nor does it seem reasonable to expect that they have enough in common to be reached easily through the mass media without attracting a large number of nonprospects.

Research on personality has failed to explain more than about 10 percent of variance in behavior, even in the most conclusive studies. Procter & Gamble conducted many studies in the 1970s using personality as a segmentation variable. They approached these studies with care, diligence, and the best resources available. After three years of effort, the attempt was abandoned because the brand and advertising managers could not generate results that allowed them to develop marketing strategies any more effectively than with other methodologies.

Research with the greatest ability to predict consumer behavior usually involves specific scales. Specific scales are developed for specific products or buying behavior. Naturally they will predict behavior better because they are so closely related to the behavior. Unfortunately, this causes such scales to lack generalizability—not to be useful for other products or other buying situations. More generalized scales or "pure" scales are derived from psychological tests with a history of validity and reliability evidence to support them. Although they have better support for use from a theoretical and methodological perspective, they generally do not predict consumer behavior as well as more specific scales.

The failure of personality measures to predict consumer behavior has stimulated development of more recent approaches. One approach is to study the personality of brands, rather than of people. The second approach is to relate personality measures to mediating variables or stages within the decision process, such as need recognition. The third approach is to develop broader, more behavioral concepts that are likely to be better targets for market segmentation—namely lifestyles, discussed later in the chapter.

Brand Personality

For marketing applications, a more effective use of the concept of personality may be to describe brands. The assumption is dropped that people have consistent patterns (drives or traits) that guide their decisions to all brands or consumption situations. Rather, brands have consistent responses evoked to them, not based upon assumptions about the personality of the consumers responding to the brands, although such responses will be stronger in some types of consumers or personalities than among others. Brand personality is a portion of the brand's overall image, understood perhaps by many consumers but more attractive (or repulsive) to some consumers than to others.

Brand personality refers to the communication goals concerning the attributes inherent in a product as well as the profile of perceptions received by consumers about specific brands.[14] Brands have three dimensions. One dimension is *physical attributes*, such as the color, price, ingredients, and so forth. Tang is an orange powder that costs 98 cents, for example. A second dimension is *functional attributes*, or the consequences of using a brand. Lemon-fresh Pledge polishes the consumer's furniture and repels dust. Both of these types of attributes are objectively verifiable.

The third dimension of brands is their *characterization*, their personality as perceived by consumers. Brands may be characterized as modern or old-fashioned, or lively or exotic, just as people are characterized. The Obsession brand of fragrance may be erotic to some consumers or pornographic to others, while the Poison brand of fragrance may evoke a perception of danger. These elements, mediated by the information processing of individuals interacting with the brand, are transformed into a consumer's head as making the brand "appropriate for me" or "not appropriate for me," or possibly, "me for it."[15] Consumer in Focus 12.1 illustrates how this approach affected the marketing of Dr Pepper in the cola wars of recent years.

Emotional Responses

Brand or product personalities may be further understood by focusing upon the emotional responses that are evoked among consumers. Such responses may be closely related to the drives or motives discussed in Chapter 9. Rather than speak of individual traits or drives that influence behavior, it may be useful to consider the categories of emotional responses that are evoked from the consumption of a product or a specific brand.

When consumers buy products, they often want more than functional or tangible attributes provided by the product. They also want a good experience, a good emotional response from usage of the product. This is described as "hedonic" benefits of consumption, as we saw in Chapter 9. Although subjective and intangible, emotional responses also evoke physiological reactions that can be measured with physiological research methods.[16]

A battery of psychological tests are used to understand emotional response to brands. Some of these are standard psychological approaches, such as focus groups and interviews. Some are more innovative. The Foote, Cone & Belding ad agency uses a technique in which consumers are given stacks of photographs of people's faces and asked to sort them into types of consumers who might be typical users of certain brands. Each face represents a different emotional reaction to a product.

The Dr Pepper Personality

Dr Pepper is a brand of soft drink in the difficult strategic position of facing Coke, Pepsi, 7-Up, and Royal Crown, all of which have larger market shares and larger media budgets. Research conducted at Young and Rubicam indicated that the Dr Pepper brand had high awareness but was often misperceived, with consumers believing it was made from prune juice, contained peppers or pepper sauce, or was in some way medicinal, and had a weak personality. As a result, a campaign was developed to develop a new personality for Dr Pepper as "America's Most Misunderstood Soft Drink." Dr Pepper's personality was developed as an underdog fighting to gain awareness though the use of fun, irreverent, and larger-than-life situations.

The campaign was successful not only in building a bright new characterization for Dr Pepper, but also a growth rate double that of the industry. Dr Pepper was no longer misunderstood. Therefore, the personality was no longer appropriate and had to be changed. The new campaign developed the personality of a contender, more positive and aggressive and sure of itself. Since the physical attributes gave Dr Pepper the most distinctive taste, the campaign was changed to "The Most Original Soft Drink Ever," and later to a brash, assertive personality of "Be a Pepper." Through the cola wars of Coke and Pepsi and considerable research at Y & R, the strategy evolved to a personality for Dr Pepper that would be integrated with the type of people who favored Dr Pepper. The brand personality was one appealing to fun, off-beat underdogs, transmitted through advertising expressed in radical, changing, fresh, creative approaches.

Source: Adapted from Joseph T. Plummer, "How Personality Makes a Difference," *Journal of Advertising Research* 24 (January 1985), 27–31.

At the McCann-Erickson ad agency, consumers are asked to draw pictures about products and to write stories about their sketches. For example, the agency was advising a client in the development of a new insecticide. To determine how people relate to roaches, the agency interviewed some low-income women about the insecticide brands they used. The women strongly believed a new brand of roach killer sold in little plastic trays was far more effective and less messy than traditional bug sprays. Yet they had never bought it, sticking stubbornly with their old sprays. Further research suggested that the women viewed roaches as symbolizing men whom the women said had abandoned them and left them feeling poor and powerless. The researchers concluded that killing the roaches with a bug spray and watching them squirm and die allowed the women to express their hostility toward men and have greater control over the roaches.[17]

In addition to these techniques, McCann-Erickson asks consumers to write newspaper obituaries for brands. The obituaries are interpreted depending on whether people describe the brand as young and virile and the victim of a tragic accident or as a worn-out product succumbing to old age.

Are there categories of emotional responses found among consumers just as there are traits in their personalities? Several systems for this purpose have been developed. At least two are being applied in consumer research.

The Mehrabian-Russell category of emotions represents three dimensions. The constructs of *pleasure*, *arousal*, and *dominance* define emotions in terms of continuous dimensions; this is called the **PAD paradigm**. A more extensive list was developed by Plutchik to include fear, anger, joy, sadness, disgust, acceptance, expectancy, and surprise.[18] Although the indices of these approaches are correlated, research by Havlena and Holbrook indicates that the Mehrabian-Russell PAD approach explains more about the emotional character of consumption experiences than does the approach of Plutchik.[19]

Personality and Decision Making

Personality can be used to explain intermediate stages in the decision process. Consumer researchers increasingly recognize that prediction of intermediate stages is better than attempting to explain behavioral outcomes with personality. The most promising of these attempts has been research focusing on the relationship between personality and information-processing variables.

The personality variable of **need for cognition** has been investigated and found to be related to how advertisements may influence the formation of attitudes toward a consumer product. Need for cognition (Ncog) is a measure of an individual's tendency to enjoy thinking. Marketing experiments by Haugtvedt, Petty, Cacioppo, and Steidley indicate that individuals high in Ncog are more influenced by the quality of arguments contained in an ad than are individuals low in Ncog. Individuals low in Ncog are more influenced by peripheral advertising stimuli such as endorser attractiveness than are individuals high in Ncog.[20]

Understanding personality variables such as need for cognition may be useful in several ways. Individuals with low need for cognition (Ncog) may require more repetitions before an ad is more effective. Individuals with high Ncog may need fewer repetitions but may need longer ads or ones with higher amounts of information. Individuals with high Ncog may rely more on newspapers and magazines for news, with television perhaps more useful for low Ncog individuals. While it is difficult to segment the market by the Ncog variable, understanding the type of individuals attracted may help design the communications program with greater effectiveness than not considering personality variables.

Risk taking is another variable that may improve our understanding of consumer decision making. As we saw in Chapter 9, there are risks in buying products that may be minimized by some types of marketing activities. But are there some types of individuals who are characteristically risk takers or avoiders? The answer seems to be yes.

Risk, as defined in personality research, is more than just uncertainty about outcomes. It is a personal expectation that a loss will occur. The greater a person's

FIGURE 12.3   Appeal to Risk Takers: Although a Small Group, Many Ads Are Designed for Type T Personalities

Source: Courtesy of Coty Wild Musk.

certainty for the loss, the more that person is a risk taker, a condition that may affect attitudes in the multiattribute models you read about in Chapter 11.[21]

Some consumers can be described on a personality profile as "Type T," for "Thrillseekers." Individuals high in Type T have a higher than average need for stimulation and become bored very easily. They are predisposed to pursue adventure. People who look for positive thrills are called T + individuals, whereas persons who seek thrills that are negative and destructive are T − personalities. Type T personalities are likely to list success and competence as their goals in life in contrast to risk avoiders, who list happiness as their first choice.[22] Risk takers are more likely to end up with health hazards such as those involving alcohol, drugs, and reckless driving, but are more likely to be self-motivated and well adjusted. It is easy to find advertisements directed to these people, who are believed to be about 25 percent of the American population. See Figure 12.3 for one example. Although such people are in the minority, some car ads emphasize the adventure and risk that appeal to Type T personalities, whereas most of the other car ads exhibit a less risky appeal.

Future consumer research seems headed toward more emphasis upon understanding the perceptions and responses of consumers in the consumption experience. Such research is focusing upon variables such as consumers' arousal-seeking tendencies and the manner in which they interact with sales personnel, especially as a determinant of planned and impulse purchasing and product/store situations.[23] This appears more effective than attempts to relate buying to the older, more general variables of personality based upon assumptions of pervasive traits or temperaments. Fortunately, as we see in the next few pages, more comprehensive concepts are available that were developed for the managerial interests of marketing organizations.

Personal Values

Why do some people make their consumption decisions differently than others? Personality is one answer but not an adequate answer. Some consumers seem to have patterns that are expressed in their decision making that indicate something more fundamental guiding these decisions. Personal values provide an improved answer.

It is important to recognize the difference between personal values and social values, which we discussed in Chapter 3. Social values are shared beliefs that characterize a group such as the "American core values" or the values of a microculture. An individual may or may not have similar values of the group, even though they are frequently related. As an example, in 1991 Clarence Thomas was nominated to the United States Supreme Court apparently because of his (presumably conservative) personal values. There was much discussion that some of his personal values might be in conflict with social values frequently ascribed to his African-American heritage. Social values define "normal" behavior in a society or group while personal values define "normal" behavior of an individual.

Not much is known about the exact process by which individuals develop their values. Certainly many are transferred to an individual through the institutions described in Chapter 3 as the Cultural Transfusive Triad as well as early lifetime experiences. Individuals may accept or may refuse the inculcation of these social values, however, even from their own family. The concept of values has evolved and is implicit or explicit in many of the psychological theories of Freud, Jung, Fromm, Adler, Horney, Erikson, Dichter, and others.[24]

The process of developing one's own values is illustrated in Figure 12.4 in the highly acclaimed advertising of Nike. Notice how this ad emphasizes that individuals are free to develop values different than those of their own families. As this ad indicates, a person's personal values are ultimately indicated not by their statements, but by their decisions.

Personal values answer the question, "Is this product for me?" They are particularly important in the need-recognition stage of consumer decision making. Values are also used by consumers in determining evaluative criteria, answering the

YOU DO NOT HAVE TO BE YOUR MOTHER UNLESS SHE IS WHO YOU WANT TO BE. YOU DO NOT HAVE TO BE YOUR MOTHER'S MOTHER, OR YOUR MOTHER'S MOTHER'S MOTHER, OR EVEN YOUR GRANDMOTHER'S MOTHER ON YOUR FATHER'S SIDE. YOU MAY INHERIT THEIR CHINS OR THEIR HIPS OR THEIR EYES, BUT YOU ARE NOT DESTINED TO BECOME THE WOMEN WHO CAME BEFORE YOU, YOU ARE NOT DESTINED TO LIVE THEIR LIVES. SO IF YOU INHERIT SOMETHING, INHERIT THEIR STRENGTH. IF YOU INHERIT SOMETHING, IN-HERIT THEIR RESILIENCE. BECAUSE THE ONLY PERSON YOU ARE DESTINED TO BECOME IS THE PERSON YOU DECIDE TO BE.

FIGURE 12.4   Personal Values Reflect an Individual's Own Decisions
Source: Courtesy of Nike.

question, "Is this brand for me?" Values also have an influence on the effectiveness of communications programs as consumers ask, "Is this situation (portrayed in the ad) one in which I would participate?" Values are the "ends" people seek in their lives. In a sense, marketing often provides the "means" to reach these ends.

Consumer research relating to values has been influenced by the work of Milton Rokeach. In his book, *The Nature of Human Values*, Rokeach defines a value as an *enduring belief that a specific mode of conduct or end-state of existence is personally or socially preferable to an opposite or converse mode of conduct or end-state of existence.*[25] Stated alternatively, values are relatively stable but not completely static beliefs about what a person should (but does not always) do. Values are concerned both with the goals (end-state or terminal elements) and the ways of behaving (instrumental components) to obtain goals.

Personal values are usually measured as instrumental or terminal. The easiest way to understand the difference is to examine Table 12.2. Rokeach surveyed American values and classified them by variables such as age, income, race, and gender,

TABLE 12.2   Rokeach's Personal Value Components Classified by Gender

Terminal Value Medians and Composite Rank Orders for American Men and Women

N=	Male 665	Female 744	p
A comfortable life	7.8 (4)	10.0 (13)	.001
An exciting life	14.6 (18)	15.8 (18)	.001
A sense of accomplishment	8.3 (7)	9.4 (10)	.01
A world at peace	3.8 (1)	3.0 (1)	.001
A world of beauty	13.6 (15)	13.5 (15)	—
Equality	8.9 (9)	8.3 (8)	—
Family security	3.8 (2)	3.8 (2)	—
Freedom	4.9 (3)	6.1 (3)	.01
Happiness	7.9 (5)	7.4 (5)	.05
Inner harmony	11.1 (13)	9.8 (12)	.001
Mature love	12.6 (14)	12.3 (14)	—
National security	9.2 (10)	9.8 (11)	—
Pleasure	14.1 (17)	15.0 (16)	.01
Salvation	9.9 (12)	7.3 (4)	.001
Self-respect	8.2 (6)	7.4 (6)	.01
Social recognition	13.8 (16)	15.0 (17)	.001
True friendship	9.6 (11)	9.1 (9)	—
Wisdom	8.5 (8)	7.7 (7)	.05

Continued

variables frequently used for market segmentation. Median ranks of importance for instrumental and terminal values by gender are shown in Table 12.2.

Values research in consumer behavior can be used for market segmentation studies. In a study of car buying, Vinson, Scott, and Lamont defined values in a marketing context as centrally held cognitive elements that stimulate motivation toward a behavioral response. For segmentation purposes, the attempt is to understand how consumption-related variables are related to global or core values.[26] Family influences may be important in such high-involvement purchases as cars but in the buying of routine or low-involvement purchases such as cereal or deodorants, other values may be more important. In a study of deodorants by Pitts and Woodside, for example, individuals who preferred Right Guard over Arrid were consumers with high importance on the Rokeach value scale measuring "mature love."[27] A number of studies have linked personal values to brand choice, product usage, or market segmentation. [28]

How can values be used to understand better the market for a product? Laddering is a recently developed technique useful in understanding product attributes.

TABLE 12.2   Continued

Instrumental Value Medians and Composite Rank Orders for American Men and Women

N=	Male 665	Female 744	p
Ambitious	5.6 (2)	7.4 (4)	.001
Broadminded	7.2 (4)	7.7 (5)	—
Capable	8.9 (8)	10.1 (12)	.001
Cheerful	10.4 (12)	9.4 (10)	.05
Clean	9.4 (9)	8.1 (8)	.01
Courageous	7.5 (5)	8.1 (6)	—
Forgiving	8.2 (6)	6.4 (2)	.001
Helpful	8.3 (7)	8.1 (7)	—
Honest	3.4 (1)	3.2 (1)	—
Imaginative	14.3 (18)	16.1 (18)	.001
Independent	10.2 (11)	10.7 (14)	—
Intellectual	12.8 (15)	13.2 (16)	—
Logical	13.5 (16)	14.7 (17)	.001
Loving	10.9 (14)	8.6 (9)	.001
Obedient	13.5 (17)	13.1 (15)	—
Polite	10.9 (13)	10.7 (13)	—
Responsible	6.6 (3)	6.8 (3)	—
Self-controlled	9.7 (10)	9.5 (11)	—

Figures shown in the first two columns are median rankings and, in parentheses, composite rank orders. Figures in the last column represent the level of significance between male and female rankings.
Source: Reprinted with permission of The Free Press, a Division of Macmillan, Inc. from Milton Rokeach, *The Nature of Human Values*, 57–58. Copyright 1973 by The Free Press.

Laddering refers to in-depth probing directed toward uncovering higher-level meanings at both the benefit (attribute) level and at the value level. Laddering seeks to uncover the *linkages between product attributes, personal outcomes (consequences), and values* that serve to structure components of the cognitive network in a consumer's mind.[29]

Figure 12.5 shows the attributes provided by wine coolers (carbonation, crisp, expensive, label, bottle, less alcohol, filling, smaller size) and how the consequences of those benefits (refreshing, thirst-quenching, more feminine, avoid negatives of alcohol, impress others, and so on) relate to the values (self-esteem, accomplishment, belonging, family life) of varying market segments. Any of these perceptual maps of the value structures could lead to developing alternative marketing strategies. Although the attributes might be the same, the image that should be developed for those with the self-esteem value would emphasize impressing others, perhaps with a sophisticated image, while the other image would be developed for the family life, emphasizing socializing without the negatives of alcohol. Additional analysis may indicate the size of segments, the degree of overlap between segments

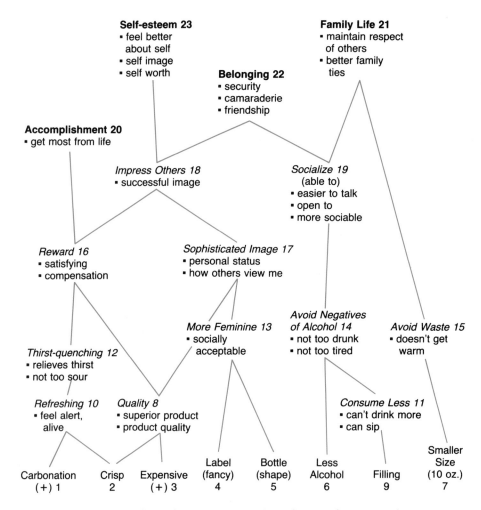

FIGURE 12.5 Hypothetical Hierarchical Value of Map of Wine Cooler Category

Source: Thomas J. Reynolds and Jonathan Gutman, "Laddering Theory, Method, Analysis, and Interpretation," Reprinted from the *Journal of Advertising Research* 28 (February/March 1988), 19. © 1988 by the Advertising Research Foundation.

or appeals that can be used to appeal to the widest number of consumers, as well as the level of abstraction that should be used in advertising and other elements of advertising strategy.[30]

Lifestyle Concepts and Measurement

Lifestyle is one of the most popular concepts in marketing as a way of understanding consumer behavior. Lifestyle is a concept more contemporary, more comprehen-

FIGURE 12.6   An Advertiser Adapts to Variations in Lifestyle
Source: Courtesy Nestlé Foods.

sive, and more useful than either personality or values. Lifestyle marketing attempts to relate a product, often through advertising, to the everyday experiences of the market target. Notice in the TV storyboards of Figure 12.6 how an ice cream product recognizes that everyday patterns of Friday and Saturday are different. Drumstick probably believes consumers will identify with its product because the company identifies with the lifestyles of its consumers.

     Lifestyle is a summary construct defined as *patterns in which people live and spend time and money*. Lifestyles reflect a person's activities, interests, and opinions (AIOs). People use constructs such as lifestyles to construe the events happening around them and to interpret, conceptualize, and predict events as well as to reconcile their values with events. George Kelly has noted that such a construct system is not only personal but also continually changes in response to a person's need to conceptualize cues from the changing environment to be consistent with his or her own values and personality.[31]

     Values are relatively enduring; lifestyles change more rapidly. Lifestyle researchers must, therefore, place attention on currency and flexibility in research methods and marketing strategies. Some of the most effective advertisers track trends in lifestyles of key market targets and reflect those lifestyles in their ads. Look at Figure 12.7 and you will see some popular ads, all designed by Pepsi's ad agency, BBDO, which reflect lifestyles from 1960 to 1991.

FIGURE 12.7 **Ads Change in Response to Changing Lifestyles**
Source: Courtesy PepsiCo, Inc.

If you are studying consumer behavior, you should recognize the differences between your own lifestyle and the lifestyles of other people. The responsibility of effective communicators is to understand the lifestyles of the audience, not just themselves. Perhaps you are thinking, do differences really exist? Look carefully at Table 12.3, which shows current lifestyles and values of the consumers in the United States. The table also shows lifestyle statements of advertising agency personnel.

Psychographics

Psychographics is an operational technique to measure lifestyles. Psychographics provide quantitative measures and can be used with the large samples needed for definition of market segments. In contrast, soft or qualitative research techniques such as focus-group interviews or in-depth interviews may provide richer insights or ideas for creative strategy even though they do not provide quantitative estimates.

TABLE 12.3   **Lifestyles of the Public and Advertising Agency Employees**

Lifestyle Activity, Interest, Opinion	Ad Agency Employees	Public
I went bowling last year.	46	30
I bought a lottery ticket last year.	75	61
I want to look different from others.	82	62
There's too much sex on prime time TV.	50	78
TV is my primary form of entertainment.	28	53
I went to a bar or tavern in the last year.	91	50
There should be a gun in every home.	9	32
My favorite music is classic rock.	64	35
My favorite music is easy listening.	27	51
Couples should live together before marriage.	50	33
My greatest achievements are still ahead of me.	89	65

Source: "Study: The Customer Ain't Me," *Advertising Age* (January 20, 1992).

Psychographics are more comprehensive than demographic, behavioral, and socioeconomic measures. Emanuel Demby, a researcher generally credited with inventing the term, explains:

> The use of psychological, sociological, and anthropological factors, such as benefits desired (from the behavior being studied), self-concept, and lifestyle (or serving style) to determine how the market is segmented by the propensity of groups within the market—and their reasons—to make a particular decision about a product, person, ideology, or otherwise hold an attitude or use a medium.[32]

Psychographics is a term often used interchangeably with **AIO measures,** or statements to describe the activities, interests, and opinions of consumers. Some researchers use the A to stand for attitudes, but activities are a better measure of lifestyles because they measure what people do. AIO components are defined by Reynolds and Darden as follows:

> An activity is a manifest action such as viewing a medium, shopping in a store, or telling a neighbor about a new service. Although these acts are usually observable, the reasons for the actions are seldom subject to direct measurement. An interest in some object, event, or topic is the degree of excitement that accompanies both special and continuing attention to it.
>
> An opinion is a spoken or written "answer" that a person gives in response to stimulus situations in which some "question" is raised. It is used to describe interpretations, expectations, and evaluations—such as beliefs about the intentions of other people, anticipations concerning future events, and appraisals of the rewarding or punishing consequences of alternative courses of action.[33]

Examples of each category are shown in Table 12.4. Demographics are also included in most psychographic or AIO studies.

TABLE 12.4   AIO Categories of Lifestyle Studies

Activities	Interests	Opinions	Demographics
Work	Family	Themselves	Age
Hobbies	Home	Social issues	Education
Social events	Job	Politics	Income
Vacation	Community	Business	Occupation
Entertainment	Recreation	Economics	Family size
Club membership	Fashion	Education	Dwelling
Community	Food	Products	Geography
Shopping	Media	Future	City size
Sports	Achievements	Culture	Stages in life cycle

Source: Joseph T. Plummer, "The Concept and Application of Life Style Segmentation," *Journal of Marketing* 38 (January 1974), 34. Reprinted from the *Journal of Marketing* published by the American Marketing Association.

AIO Statements

AIO statements may be general or specific. In either type, consumers are usually presented with Likert scales (named after the researcher who popularized the method of response) in which people are asked whether they strongly agree, agree, are neutral, disagree, or strongly disagree. Statements can be administered in person, by phone, or by mail. An efficient form of administration is with mail panels such as those operated by Market Facts of Chicago or NFO of Toledo.

General and Specific AIOs   AIO statements may refer to general activities and motivations or they may be specific. The specific approach focuses on statements that are product specific and that identify benefits associated with the product or brand.

One study concerned with health care services included both general and specific statements.[34] The study was concerned with predicting what types of consumers were likely to bring malpractice suits. Because attitude theory indicates that consumers try to behave in a way that will achieve consistency between their behavior and attitudes, it was necessary to determine specific attitudes toward physicians as well as toward malpractice. Thus, statements such as the following were included: "I have a great deal of confidence in my own doctor; about half of the physicians are not really competent to practice medicine; most physicians are overpaid; and in most malpractice suits, the physician is not really to blame."

In this study, respondents who indicated that they have a great deal of confidence in their doctors also reported a much lower likelihood of bringing a malpractice suit. Respondents agreeing with the statements that physicians are not really competent and that they are overpaid and disagreeing with the statements that physicians are not really to blame in malpractice suits were more likely to file a malpractice suit.

Analysis of this study also showed that respondents who agreed with general AIO statements such as "I generally do exercises" and "I am sick a lot more than my friends are" were found also to be more likely to bring malpractice suits. Such findings demonstrate how both general and specific AIOs can be used to profile consumers and relate their lifestyles to behavior.

Market Segmentation   Psychographic studies are used to develop an in-depth understanding of market segments. Sometimes marketers use psychographics to define segments, but a better practice is to avoid definition of the segments through AIOs in favor of using AIOs to better understand segments that have been defined with more traditional variables.

AIO statements can be analyzed by cross-tabulating each statement on the basis of variables believed important for market segmentation strategies, such as gender, age, and so forth. Factor analysis or other multivariate techniques may be used to group the statements into a more parsimonious format. Factor analysis is a mathematical technique for examining the intercorrelation between statements in an attempt to determine common or underlying factors that explain observed variation.[35]

Such techniques often reveal factors such as the "traditional" segment or the "modern" segment or perhaps the "frugal" segment or the "natural" segment or group within a segment defined by other variables. General Foods identified a health-conscious segment of consumers through psychographics to reposition its Sanka brand of decaffeinated coffee. Previously, decaffeinated coffee was associated with elderly people. Through psychographics, General Foods targeted active achievers of all ages, using advertising appealing to interests of adventurous lifestyles. The ads featured people in lifestyles such as running the rapids in a kayak with the copy line that Sanka "Lets you be your best."

Psychographic analysis allows marketers to understand consumer lifestyles of the core customers in order to communicate more effectively with people in that segment. The analysis may also lead to efforts to position new or existing products closely to consumers in a lifestyle segment, perhaps more effectively than if the segment were described only by demographics. The idea is to go beyond standard demographics to position the product in line with the activities, hopes, fears, dreams, and so forth of the product's best customers.

The "healthy" market segment is an example of a lifestyle that attracts many marketers currently. ConAgra brought out the Healthy Choice brand of food and became almost an instant success. McDonald's introduced a McLean sandwich in an attempt to appeal to the healthy lifestyle. Scramblers is a brand of frozen-egg product that provides the taste of real eggs without cholesterol. Kentucky Fried Chicken changed its name to KFC, dropping the word "fried," which many people consider an unhealthy way to cook. Even the image of Col. Harland Sanders' face was changed from brown ink to blue to fit changing lifestyles.[36] The objective in psychographic segmentation is to develop a marketing program that is consistent in all of its elements with many of the AIOs of the target market. Advertising in such programs often emphasizes the lifestyle elements rather than product attributes, as

FIGURE 12.8 **Appeal to Lifestyles Compatible with Beer Drinking**
Source: Courtesy of Anheiser-Busch, Inc.

in Figure 12.8. The ad targets drinkers of beer when they're not drinking beer by showing many of the lifestyle activities that are likely to create need recognition for a non-alcoholic beer.

VALS and the Nine American Lifestyles

A widely used approach to lifestyle marketing is the VALS and its most recent form, VALS II. The original program was developed by Mitchell at SRI and defined "nine American lifestyles." They are shown in Table 12.5 along with typical demographics and buying patterns. Another approach, called Monitor, is available from Yankelovich, Skelly, and White, although the SRI or VALS approach appears to be used more by marketers.[37] We will examine VALS more closely.

The VALS system defines a typology of three basic categories of consumer values and lifestyles, with nine more detailed types. SRI describes consumer market segments as need-driven, outer-directed, or inner-directed.

TABLE 12.5   VALS Lifestyle Segmentation

Percentage of Population (Age 18 and Over)	Consumer Type	Values and Lifestyles	Demographics	Buying Patterns
Need-Driven Consumers				
4%	Survivors	Struggle for survival Distrustful Socially misfitted Ruled by appetites	Poverty-level income Little education Many minority members Many live in city slums	Price dominant Focused on basics Buying for immediate needs
7	Sustainers	Concern with safety, security Insecure, compulsive Dependent, following Streetwise, determination to get ahead	Low income Low education Much unemployment Live in country as well as cities	Price important Want warranty Cautious buyers
Outer-Directed Consumers				
35%	Belongers	Conforming, conventional Unexperimental Traditional, formal Nostalgic	Low to middle income Low to average education Blue-collar jobs Tend toward noncity living	Family Home Fads Middle and lower mass markets
10	Emulators	Ambitious, show-off Status conscious Upwardly mobile Macho, competitive	Good to excellent income Youngish Highly urban Traditionally male, but changing	Conspicuous consumption "In" items Imitative Popular fashion
22	Achievers	Achievement, success, fame Materialism Leadership, efficiency Comfort	Excellent incomes Leaders in business, politics, etc. Good education Suburban and city living	Give evidence of success Top of the line Luxury and gift markets "New and improved" products

Continued

Source: Reprinted with permission of Macmillan Publishing Company from Arnold Mitchell, *Nine American Lifestyles: Who We Are and Where We Are Going* (New York: Macmillan, 1983). Copyright © 1983 by Arnold Mitchell.

TABLE 12.5   continued

Percentage of Population (Age 18 and Over)	Consumer Type	Values and Lifestyles	Demographics	Buying Patterns
Inner-Directed Consumers				
5%	I-Am-Me	Fiercely individualistic Dramatic, impulsive Experimental Volatile	Young Many single Student or starting job Affluent backgrounds	Display one's taste Experimental fads Source of far-out fads Clique buying
7	Experiential	Drive to direct experience Active, participative Person-centered Artistic	Bimodal incomes Mostly under 40 Many young families Good education	Process over product Vigorous, outdoor sports "Making" home pursuits Crafts and introspection
8	Societally Conscious	Societal responsibility Simple living Smallness of scale Inner growth	Bimodal low and high incomes Excellent education Diverse ages and places of residence Largely white	Conservation emphasis Simplicity Frugality Environmental concerns
2	Integrated	Psychological maturity Sense of fittingness Tolerant, self-actualizing World perspective	Good to excellent incomes Bimodal in age Excellent education Diverse jobs and residential patterns	Varied self-expression Esthetically oriented Ecologically aware One-of-a-kind items

Need-driven consumers exhibit spending driven by need rather than preference and are subdivided into survivors and sustainers, the former among the most disadvantaged people in the economy.

Outer-directed consumers, who are divided into three subgroups, are the backbone of the marketplace and generally buy with awareness of what other people will attribute to their consumption of that product.

Inner-directed consumers are divided into four subgroups. They comprise a much smaller percentage of the population (see Table 12.5). Their lives are directed more toward their individual needs than toward values oriented to externals. Although their numbers are small, they may be important as trend setters or groups through whom successful ideas and products trickle down. This segment is growing rapidly, whereas the number of need-driven consumers is declining and outer-directed is holding steady.

Advertising agencies and marketing organizations are using the VALS system in a variety of ways. At one time, Merrill Lynch Pierce Fenner & Smith used an advertising campaign, featuring a herd of galloping bulls with the slogan "Bullish on America." With the help of Young & Rubicam advertising agency, the theme was shifted to reach the achievers target audience, who are upwardly mobile and self-motivated. As a result, the thundering herds were replaced in the ads by a lone bull that wandered through the canyons of Wall Street or huddled in a cave where it found shelter while Merrill Lynch and its achiever customers were described as "A breed apart."

At Clairol, ads were developed for the inner-directed segment to make them feel in charge of their own lives with the theme "Make it happen" and for the outer-directed group the reassurance of "Sells the most, conditions the most." At General Foods, the belonger woman was the target for Jell-O ads that show women in the provider role who don't make just Jell-O for their families, they "Make some fun."

Global Lifestyles

The emergence of the European Single Market Initiative in 1992 and the rising importance of globalization require that marketing strategy increasingly be planned on a global basis. Rather than sell internationally, however, firms are selling to segments of the population—in whatever country they may be. Consumer research on topics as important as lifestyles, therefore, requires consideration of how lifestyle segments vary between countries. Table 12.6 displays such findings for several major markets of the world. As firms develop sophisticated, global strategies employing globalized media, increasingly they will need to use typologies such as this to develop products that appeal to segments of markets in many countries.[38] The VALS typology has been used very successfully to segment Canadian markets in a study reported by Ian Pearson.[39]

Limitations and Extensions

VALS gained rapid acceptance and widespread usage in marketing. Nevertheless, it has its limitations. Consumers are not "pure" in their type of lifestyle. Respondents are given a score that reflects the degree to which they share similar responses on lifestyles other than their primary lifestyle. Because VALS is a proprietary database, some consumer researchers also criticize the fact that researchers do not have full information on the factor loadings or rotations or the explained variance.

Although VALS is clearly useful to marketing organizations, other approaches might be better if they were more widely investigated. Kahle, Beatty, and Homer

TABLE 12.6 VALS Lifestyle Segments in Global Markets

Comparison of European/ U.S. Lifestyle Types	Survivor	Sustainer	Belonger	Emulator
United States	Old; intensely poor; fearful; depressed; despairing; far removed from the cultural mainstream; misfits.	Living on the edge of poverty; angry and resentful; streetwise; involved in the underground economy.	Aging; traditional and conventional; contented; intensely patriotic; sentimental; deeply stable.	Youthful and ambitious; macho; show-off; trying to break into the system, to make it big.
France	Negligible number, but attributes as in U.S., some older. Belongers and Sustainers share characteristics.	Old peasant women and retireds; poor; little education; fearful; live by habit; unable to cope with change.	Aging; need family and community; concerned about financial security, appearance, surroundings, health; able to cope with change, but avoid it.	Youthful, but older and quieter than in the U.S.; better educated; entertain at home rather than outside; consider ideologies to be dangerous; concerned about health.
Italy	Similar to U.S.; Survivors; live in northern urban slums.	Aging; uneducated; uprooted from agrarian society; dependent; concerned with health and appearance; escapist.	Aging; poorly educated; strongly authoritarian; self-sacrificing for family or church; fearful of change; fatalistic; save rather than spend; reject industrial society and its problems.	Youthful; mostly male; highly educated; reject family ties; highly materialistic; insensitive to nature; read more than average.
Sweden	Two categories: an older group similar to U.S.; a very young group of unemployed school dropouts who are alienated, apathetic.	Wealthier than others; fearful of children's economic future; concerned with own economic security and pensions; afraid of big government and big business.	As in the U.S., but more suspicious of government and big business.	Slightly older than others; concerned with prestige; want beautiful homes; prefer quieter lifestyles.

Achiever	I-Am-Me	Experiential	Societally Conscious	Integrated
Middle-aged and prosperous; able leaders; self-assured; materialistic; builders of the "American dream."	Transition state; exhibitionistic and narcissistic; young; impulsive; dramatic; experimental; active; inventive.	Youthful; seek direct experience; person-centered; artistic; intensely oriented toward inner growth.	Mission-oriented; leaders of single-issue groups; mature; successful; some live lives of voluntary simplicity.	Psychologically mature; large field of vision; tolerant and understanding; sense of fittingness.
Two groups: older, more mature are similar to U.S.; younger are more intuitive; both groups less materialistic than U.S. Achievers; both concerned about ecology, environment, etc.	Older (20–30); well-educated; contemplative; little concern for financial security, social success, or materialism; enjoy their work.	Young; predominantly male; highly educated; not fulfilled by work, but by leisure; enjoy the present; hedonistic.	Too few to be statistically significant, although most people have stronger Societally Conscious tendencies than in the U.S.	Same as in U.S.
Middle-aged; predominantly female; links to family and religion; indifferent to self-fulfillment from work; want success and prestige, but otherwise escapist.	Highly educated; middle- to upper-class; aged 25–35; reject both traditional and consumer/industrial societies; political extremists; live now; bored; take light drugs.	Too few to be statistically significant, although some I-Am-Me's exhibit Experiential characteristics.	Well-educated; generally fairly young; led by protagonists of 1968 protests; satisfied; want more education; socially committed.	Same as in U.S.
As interested in status as in money; save more than U.S. Achievers, buy valuables for their children to inherit; this group is the most middle-class of all.	Older than in the U.S.; entrepreneurial; self-expressive; concerned about self-improvement; reject drugs and alcohol; seek rich inner and emotional life, warm relationships.	Hedonists; risk-takers; crave experience and excitement; enjoy dangerous pursuits.	Want simpler, more basic ways of life; active in communities; questioning and critical; concerned about physical environment and impersonality of large organizations.	Same as in U.S.

Continued

TABLE 12.6 **Continued**

Comparison of European/ U.S. Lifestyle Types	Survivor	Sustainer	Belonger	Emulator
United Kingdom	Two groups similar to those in Sweden; older group is very similar to that in the U.S. The younger, unemployed, are more aggressive than those in Sweden—form cliques.	Working-class values; concerned about economic security; family centered; afraid of government and big business; mainly women; the youngest group is 35 years and older.	Two groups: one as in the U.S., with addition of wanting more satisfying work; the other traditional but more active, complaining; more concerned about education, creativity, emotions.	Older than others; mostly female; more interested in social status than job status; sacrifice comfort and practicality for fashion.
[Former] West Germany	Survivors in a psychological sense, not economic or demographic; fearful, envious, and alienated; concerned about social position, physical appearance; antibusiness; many are women.	Sustainers in a psychological sense only; negative feelings toward all aspects of life; resigned and apathetic; avoid risks; high level of hypochondria.	As in the U.S., although wealthier and better educated; more concerned about prestige and social standing.	Fairly young; well educated; mostly male; conscious about job status and social standing; concerned about physical safety.

Source: Arnold Mitchell, "Nine American Lifestyles: Values and Societal Change," *The Futurist* 18 (August 1984), 4–13.

compared VALS with the list of values (LOV) approach based on the Rokeach approach discussed earlier (see page 365). These researchers found that the LOV approach predicted consumer behavior better than VALS, possibly indicating better theoretical support for alternatives to VALS.[40] Used alone, VALS appears better than LOV but when demographic data are included with LOV, the latter approach is more effective.[41] When LOV is augmented with measures of more general values—such as materialism—the predictive power is further improved.[42]

Marketing organizations sometimes develop their own measurement systems in an attempt to be more specific to the organization's products and customers. ABC developed its own system to classify viewers into clusters relevant to television viewing, based more upon personality or fundamental psychological attributes than the attitudes and demographics they felt typified the VALS approach. ABC found, for

Achiever	I-Am-Me	Experiential	Societally Conscious	Integrated
Too few to be statistically significant; status geared to social position; wealthy become more inner-directed; older people are unwilling to change.	Too few to be statistically significant; exhibit self-expressive characteristics, but are more Societally Conscious.	Highly educated; want excitement and adventure; risk-takers; creative and self-expressive; want meaningful work; want to demonstrate abilities.	Family-oriented, young; well-educated; creative; want personal growth and meaningful, satisfying work; question authority and technology.	Same as in U.S.
As in the U.S., although more are politically active and more concerned about the environment.	Older than in the U.S.; find work meaningful and self-fulfilling; want to have an impact on society; have a high level of anxiety; emotional vacuum, looking for ideologies.	Too few to be statistically significant.	Too few to be statistically significant.	Same as in U.S.

example, a family-oriented group and a rigid-and-resistants group. While both groups had similar demographics, the family-oriented group watches a great deal of situation comedies, but the rigids group watches more action-adventure shows.[43] Other companies are extending the basic lifestyle profiles to reflect their special interests or marketing problems.

Multiple Measures of Individual Behavior

As you have seen in this chapter, a number of measures of individual behavior are used in the analysis of consumer behavior. Personality has an effect upon buying;

Max & Erma's Customers

Max & Erma's is a chain of dinner restaurants based in the Midwest with locations in Indianapolis, Dayton, Detroit, Canton, Columbus, Lexington, and Pittsburgh. The firm is targeted to those customers who seek a casual, contemporary, sophisticated, adult dining experience that is conducive to relaxation and fun. Major competitors include T.G.I.Friday's, Dalts, Houlihan's, Bennigans, Chi-Chi's, and others.

The firm grew rapidly in the late 1970s and the early 1980s, along with rapid growth in the restaurant industry. Losses were experienced in the 1980s, however, and the restaurant undertook extensive research to understand better its core customers and to develop a more effective marketing program.

Customers had previously been defined as the "18 to 45" age group with an emphasis on singles, but the firm felt the need for additional variables that would explain the individuals who were the core customers. A survey of 400 frequent customers (more than twice a month) was conducted to measure demographics, lifestyle variables (specifically VALS categories), and situation variables.

Using VALS categories, the Max & Erma core customer was described as 38 percent "inner directed" in contrast to only 20 percent of the population. They typically hold managerial or professional jobs, often with two professional incomes. They eat out a lot, will try anything, and are sophisticated and nonconformist. They care more about their personal tastes than status or what other people think. They like a wide choice of offbeat menu items that would make a "belonger" really uncomfortable.

The Max & Erma segment also contains more (38 percent) "achievers" than the population (31 percent). They are success oriented with a high educa-
continued

lifestyles have more. Certainly economic resources such as income and time, described in Chapter 8, are also very important. Which is best in the development of marketing strategy?

An eclectic approach to lifestyles is the most practical for developing marketing strategy. The goal is to understand consumers as thoroughly as possible. Consumer in Focus 12.2 illustrates how this was done by one company to achieve a turnaround in its market success. Rather than define its market segment as a specific income or age group or even a specific lifestyle, Max & Erma's Restaurants defined its segment as the "Max & Erma's customer" and conducted research using a variety of measures—demographics, lifestyles, and situation. With a comprehensive database for each of these variables, management was able to develop multiple marketing strategies to enhance the appeal of the restaurant to a number of segments of tion. They work hard, are motivated by good service, view value more in terms of quality than price, and have a high level of self-confidence. "Belongers" were more likely to choose the traditional offerings of Shoney's, Bob Evans, and other restaurants than Max & Erma's.

Individuals were also described by the situation in which they choose Max & Erma's. These occasions were convenience (24.8 percent), fun (20.4 percent), dates (19.6 percent), regulars (12.4 percent), fast (9.7 percent), families (7.9 percent), and business (4.2 percent). Max & Erma's was much stronger in the fun, dates, and regulars categories and much lower than other restaurants in the fast, families, and business situations.

A marketing plan was implemented targeted toward the key segments. The menu was tailored to inner-directed customers with "name your own burger," "top your own pasta," and "build your own sundae" items. Individualized local store programs of special promotions, coupons, and direct mail were used. The achievers were targeted for less formal occasions. An extensive TV advertising program was developed featuring a well-known achiever attorney and his respected but more inner-driven wife, who is also an attorney. They both are shown in TV ads eating frequently at Max & Erma's. Appeals emphasized time convenience, relaxed fun, and quality menu items. An extensive training program for store management and waiters was also implemented to ensure high levels of customer satisfaction.

The results: The firm achieved a turnaround in same-store sales at a time when industry sales were flat or declining. Profits were dramatically higher and generated the cash flow and debt capacity to open additional restaurants in several cities. The company attributed the success to its total marketing and operational program based upon a thorough understanding of the individual characteristics of its target of core customers.

core customers in ways that would not have been possible by focusing on only one of the individual influences on the behavior of its customers.

Summary

Purchase decisions vary between individuals because of unique characteristics possessed by each individual. One such variable is called personality. Personality is defined as consistent responses to environmental stimuli. Three major theories or approaches to the study of personality include psychoanalytic, socio-psychological, and trait-factor. Newer approaches to the use of personality include brand personality and more recent attempts to relate personality to elements of consumer decision making and information processing, such as the need for cognition.

Personal values also explain individual differences among consumers. Rokeach has identified such values as terminal and instrumental, or the ends to which behavior is directed and the means of attaining those ends. A promising approach of relating values to attributes of products is called laddering and appears to be useful in segmenting markets and the development of product and communications strategies to reach those markets.

Lifestyles are patterns in which people live and spend time and money. Lifestyles are the result of the total array of economic, cultural, and social life forces that contribute to a person's human qualities.

People develop constructs with which to interpret, predict, and control their environment. These constructs or patterns result in behavior patterns and attitude structures that minimize incompatibilities and inconsistencies in a person's life. Psychographics or AIOs measure the operational form of lifestyles. AIO stands for activities, interests, and opinions, and may be either general or product specific.

The practical solution to marketing mix problems often involves looking at multiple measures of individual characteristics. In addition to personality and lifestyle, such measures include economic resources such as money and time, as well as demographic measures such as age or nature of the household. All of these variables may interact with the usage situation for the product.

Review and Discussion Questions

1. Clearly distinguish between the following terms: lifestyles, psychographics, AIO measures, personality, benefits.
2. Explain the difference between a general lifestyle measure and a specific lifestyle measure. Give two examples of each for a research project involving a soft drink.
3. What is the basis for the VALS system? How might it be used by a marketing organization?
4. Describe the trait-factor theory of personality and assess its importance in past and future marketing research.
5. Should a restaurant segment its market by lifestyle, income, situation, or some other variable? Explain your answer.
6. Assume that you have recently been employed by a large department store and have been asked to prepare an analysis of the market for furniture in your city. The president of the store is interested in doing a psychographic study and has asked you to prepare a questionnaire. Be sure to indicate the specific content of the questionnaire, some sample questions, the method of data collection, and methods of analysis.
7. Assume that you are developing an advertising program for an airline. How would you use laddering to assist in the development of the program?
8. How might personal values be used to segment markets for financial services? Could similar approaches be used in less developed countries as well as industrialized markets?

Endnotes

1. H. H. Kassarjian, "Personality and Consumer Behavior: A Review," *Journal of Marketing Research* (November 1971), 409–418.

2. For descriptions of major personality theories, see Walter Mischel, *Introduction to Personality: A New Look* (New York: CBS College Publishing, 1986), and Larry Hjelle and Daniel Ziegler, *Personality Theories: Basic Assumptions, Research and Applications* (New York: McGraw-Hill, 1987).

3. For a marketing view of psychoanalytic theory, see W. D. Wells and A. D. Beard, "Personality and Consumer Behavior," in Scott Ward and T. S. Robertson, eds., *Consumer Behavior: Theoretical Sources* (Englewood Cliffs, N.J.: Prentice-Hall, 1973).

4. The classic example of this literature is Ernest Dichter, *Handbook of Consumer Motivations* (New York: McGraw-Hill, 1964). For a recent example of motivation research by Dr. Dichter, see the "Swan Cleaners" case in Roger D. Blackwell, James F. Engel, and W. Wayne Talarzyk, *Contemporary Cases in Consumer Behavior* (Chicago: Dryden, 1990), 135–142.

5. For a more complete explanation of this approach, see C. S. Hall and G. Lindzey, *Theories of Personality* (New York: John Wiley & Sons, 1970), 154–155.

6. J. B. Cohen, "An Interpersonal Orientation to the Study of Consumer Behavior," *Journal of Marketing Research* 4 (August 1967), 270–278; J. B. Cohen, "Toward an Interpersonal Theory of Consumer Behavior," *California Management Review* 10 (1968), 73–80. Also see Jon P. Noerager, "An Assessment of CAD: A Personality Instrument Developed Specifically for Marketing Research," *Journal of Marketing Research* (February 1979), 53–59.

7. John W. Schouten, "Selves in Transition: Symbolic Consumption in Personal Rites of Passage and Identity Reconstruction," *Journal of Consumer Research* 17 (March 1991), 412–423.

8. A good introduction to the theory and techniques of this approach is found in A. R. Buss and W. Poley, *Individual Differences: Traits and Factors* (New York: Halsted Press, 1976).

9. Raymond L. Horton, "The Edwards Personal Preference Schedule and Consumer Personality Research," *Journal of Marketing Research* 11 (August 1974), 335–337.

10. Kathryn E. A. Villani and Yoram Wind, "On the Usage of 'Modified' Personality Trait Measures in Consumer Research," *Journal of Consumer Research* 2 (December 1975), 223–226.

11. Mark I. Alpert, "Personality and the Determinants of Product Choice," *Journal of Marketing Research* 9 (February 1972), 89–92.

12. Paul E. Green, Yoram Wind, and Arun K. Jain, "A Note on Measurement of Social-Psychological Belief Systems," *Journal of Marketing Research* 9 (May 1972), 204–208.

13. F. B. Evans, "Psychological Objective Factors in the Prediction of Brand Choice: Ford Versus Chevrolet," *Journal of Business* 32 (1959), 340–369.

14. Joseph T. Plummer, "How Personality Makes a Difference," *Journal of Advertising Research* 24 (January 1985), 27–31.

15. Plummer, "How Personality Makes a Difference," 29.

16. James A. Muncy, "Psychological Responses of Consumer Emotions: Theory, Methods and Implications for Consumer Research," in Susan P. Douglas et al., *1987 AMA Educators' Conference Proceedings* (Chicago: American Marketing Association, 1987), 127–132.

17. Ronald Alsop, "Advertisers Put Consumers on the Couch," *The Wall Street Journal* (May 13, 1988), 17.

18. Robert Plutchik, *Emotion: A Psychoevolutionary Synthesis* (New York: Harper & Row, 1980).

19. William J. Havlena and Morris B. Holbrook, "The Varieties of Consumption Experience: Comparing Two Typologies of Emotion in Consumer Behavior," *Journal of Consumer Research* 13 (December 1986), 394–404.

20. Curt Haugtvedt, Richard E. Petty, John T. Cacioppo, and Theresa Steidley, "Personality and Ad Effectiveness: Exploring the Utility of Need for Cognition," in *Advances in Consumer Research* 16 (Provo, Utah: Association for Consumer Research, 1988).

21. Robert N. Stone and Frederick W. Winter, "Risk: Is It Still Uncertainty Times Consequences?" in Russell W. Belk et al., eds., *1987 AMA Winter Educators' Conference Proceedings* (Chicago: American Marketing Association, 1987), 261–265.

22. Frank Farley, "The Big T in Personality," *Psychology Today* 20 (May 1986), 44ff.

23. Patricia M. Anderson, "Personality, Perception and Emotional-State Factors in Approach-Avoidance Behavior in the Store Environment," in Terence A. Shimp et al., eds., *1986 AMA Educators' Conference Proceedings* (Chicago: American Marketing Association, 1986), 35–39.

24. An excellent review of how values are reflected in psychological theory is found in Steven M. Burgess, *Personal Values, Consumer Behaviour and Brand Image Perceptions* (Johannesburg: University of the Witwatersrand, 1990).

25. Milton Rokeach, *The Nature of Human Values* (New York: Free Press, 1973), 5. Also see M. Rokeach and S. J. Ball-Rokeach, "Stability and Change in American Value Priorities, 1968–1981," *American Psychologist* 44 (May 1989), 773–784.

26. Donald E. Vinson, Jerome E. Scott, and Lawrence M. Lamont, "The Role of Personal Values in Marketing and Consumer Behavior," *Journal of Marketing* 41 (April 1977), 44–50.

27. Robert E. Pitts and Arch G. Woodside, "Personal Values and Market Segmentation: Applying the Value Construct," in Pitts and Woodside, 1984, 55–67.

28. K. G. Grunert, S. C. Grunert and S. E. Beatty, "Cross-cultural Research on Consumer Values," *Marketing and Research Today* (February 1989), 30–39; J. M. Munson and E. F. McQuarrie, "Shortening the Rokeach Value Survey for Use in Consumer Research," *Advances in Consumer Research* 15 (Association for Consumer Research, 1988), 381–386; S. W. Perkings and T. J. Reynolds, "The Explanatory Power of Values in Preference Judgements Validation of the Means-End Perspective," in *Advances in Consumer Research* 15 (Association for Consumer Research, 1988), 122–126; G. Roehrich, P. Valette-Florence and B. Rappachi, "Combined Incidence of Personal Values, Involvement, and Innovativeness on Innovative Consumer Behavior," in *Is Marketing Keeping Up with the Consumer? Lessons from Changing Products, Attitudes and Behavior* (Vienna, Austria: ESOMAR, 1989), 261–279; D. K. Tse, J. K. Wong and C. T. Tan, "Towards Some Standard Cross-cultural Consumption Values," in *Advances in Consumer Research* 15 (Association for Consumer Research, 1988), 387–395; P. Valette-Florence and A. Jolibert, "Social Values, A.I.O. and Consumption Patterns: Exploratory Findings," *Journal of Business Research* 20 (March 1990), 109–122.

29. Thomas J. Reynolds and Jonathan Gutman, "Advertising Is Image Management," *Journal of Advertising Research* 24 (February/March 1984), 27–36.

30. Thomas J. Reynolds and Jonathan Gutman, "Laddering Theory, Method, Analysis, and Interpretation," *Journal of Advertising Research* 28 (February/March 1988), 11–31.

31. George A. Kelly, *The Psychology of Personal Constructs* 1 (New York: W. W. Norton, 1955). Also see Fred Reynolds and William Darden, "Construing Life Style and Psychographics," in William D. Wells, ed., *Life Style and Psychographics* (Chicago: American Marketing Association, 1974), 71–96.

32. Emanuel H. Demby, "Psychographics Revisited: The Birth of a Technique," *Marketing News* (January 2, 1989), 21.

33. Reynolds and Darden, "Construing Life Styles," 87.

34. This research is summarized from Roger Blackwell and Wayne Talarzyk, *Consumer Attitudes Toward Health Care and Malpractice* (Columbus, Ohio: Grid Publishing, 1977), Chapter 5.

35. Introductions to factor analysis are available in Joseph Hair et al., *Multivariate Data Analysis* (Tulsa: PPC Books, 1979); and George H. Dunteman, *Introduction to Multivariate Analysis* (Beverly Hills: Sage Publications, 1984).

36. "Kentucky Fried Chicken Redesigns for New Image," *Marketing News* (March 18, 1991), 6.

37. Rebecca Holman, "A Values and Lifestyles Perspective on Human Behavior," in Pitts and Woodside, 1984, 35–54; Sonia Yuspeh, "Syndicated Values/Lifestyles Segmentation Schemes: Use Them as Descriptive Tools, Not to Select Targets," *AMA Marketing News* 18 (May 25, 1984), 1ff; James Atlas, "Beyond Demographics," *Atlantic Monthly* (October 1984), 49–59.

38. Rebecca Holman, "A Values and Lifestyles Perspective on Human Behavior," in Pitts and Woodside, 1984, 35–54.

39. Ian Pearson, "Social Studies," *Canadian Business* 58 (1985), 67–73.

40. Lynn R. Kahle, Sharon E. Beatty, and Pamela Homer, "Alternative Measurement Approaches to Consumer Values: The List of Values (LOV) and Values and Life Style (VALS)," *Journal of Consumer Research* 13 (December 1986), 405–409. See also S. M. Burgess, "Personal Values and Consumer Behaviour: An Historical Perspective," Working Paper #89/7 (Johannesburg: Business Economics Research Group of the University of Witswatersrand, 1989) and Matthew Perri III, "Application of the List of Values Alternative Psychographic Assessment Scale," *Psychological Reports* 66 (July 1990), 403–406.

41. Thomas P. Novak and Bruce MacEvoy, "On Comparing Alternative Segmentation Schemes: The List of Values (LOV) and Values and Life Styles (VALS)," *Journal of Consumer Research* 17 (June 1990), 105–109.

42. Kim P. Corfman, Donald R. Lehmann, and Sarah Narayanan, "Values, Utility, and Ownership: Modeling the Relationships for Consumer Durables," *Journal of Retailing* 67 (Summer 1991), 184–204.

43. Bickley Townsend, "Psychographic Glitter and Gold," *American Demographics* (November 1985), 22–29.

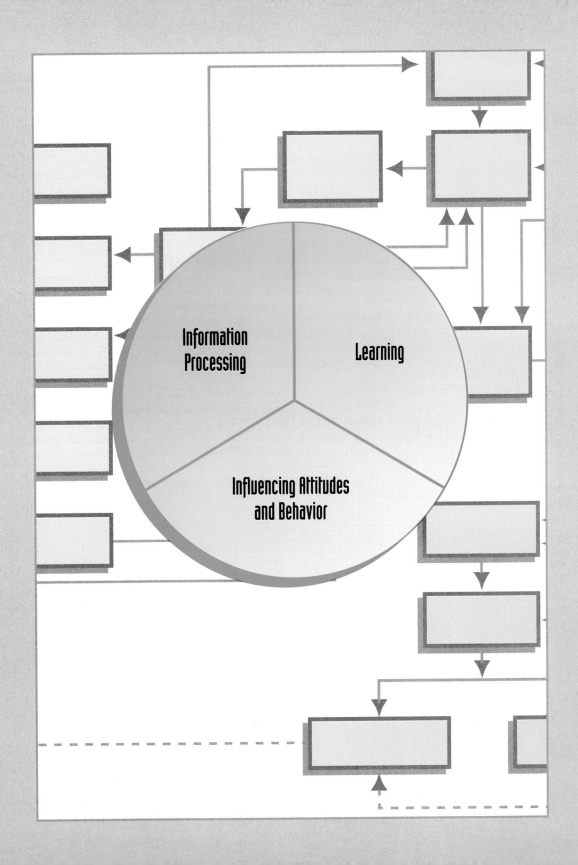

PART 4

Psychological Processes

Now our focus shifts to three central psychological processes that shape all aspects of consumer motivation and behavior: (1) *information processing* (Chapter 13); (2) *learning* (Chapter 14); and (3) *attitude and behavior change* (Chapter 15).

The information processing arena has attracted droves of behavioral science researchers in the past three decades, including those specializing in consumer behavior. This is understandable, because it focuses on the ways in which information is received, processed, and used in daily life. Nothing could be of greater practical significance. Chapter 13 covers a wide range of topics and issues in this field. You will find rewards from perseverance here, because the concepts developed are used extensively in chapters that follow.

Chapter 14 addresses the subject of learning. Certainly no single chapter can do justice to such a broad field of research, but you are introduced to various theories and concepts that have proven to have the greatest relevance for understanding the consumer.

Can consumer attitudes and choices be influenced? The answer obviously is yes, and much of the key lies in an understanding of persuasion. This is the subject of Chapter 15. An enormous range of literature is reviewed from the perspective of principles and strategies that offer the greatest practical payout.

13

Information Processing

Companies interested in enhancing the effectiveness of their advertising dollars have not been disappointed by their efforts to understand how consumers process and respond to their advertising messages. When Carillon Importers developed its print campaign for Bombay Gin, it turned to Perception Research Services, Inc. Using an invisible beam of light, the eye-tracking firm monitored consumers as they read the ad. The study discovered that a whopping 90 percent ignored the product's name. This problem was remedied by revising the ad using sharper graphics.

A different approach is offered by Inner Response, Inc. This advertising research company monitors electrical impulses in viewers' palms as they watch commercials. Tracking interest and attention levels can help separate the strong scenes from the weak ones. In one Eastman Kodak Co. film-processing ad, Inner Response determined that the viewers' interest level built slowly in the opening scenes, rose when a snapshot of an attractive young woman was shown, but spiked highest when a picture appeared of a smiling, pig-tailed girl. Kodak then knew which scenes had the highest impact, and could retain them when making changes in the spot or cutting it from 30 to 15 seconds.

Source: Excerpted from Annetta Miller and Dody Tsiantar, "Psyching Out Consumers," *Newsweek* (February 27, 1989), 46–47; Michael J. McCarthy, "Mind Probe," *Wall Street Journal* (March 22, 1991), B3.

Encountering stimuli relevant to their functioning as consumers is a daily experience for people. Ads, products, brand names, and prices are just some of the stimuli that continually impinge upon us. Estimates of the number of ads a typical consumer might encounter during a single day, for instance, range in the hundreds.

Because consumers' reactions to such stimuli, which will depend on how the stimuli are processed, can greatly shape their attitudes and behavior, an understanding of information processing can be very useful. **Information processing** refers to the process by which a stimulus is received, interpreted, stored in memory, and later retrieved. As you will see, an appreciation of information-processing principles and findings can yield some important lessons for the practice of marketing. Although advertising is perhaps the greatest beneficiary of what we know about how people process information, these lessons can be applied to many areas of communication, including personal selling, package design, branding, training of salespeople, and even consumer behavior classrooms.

Information processing can be broken down into five basic stages. These stages, shown in Figure 13.1, are based on the information-processing model developed by William McGuire.[1] These stages can be defined as follows:

1. *Exposure*: the achievement of proximity to a stimulus such that an opportunity exists for one or more of a person's five senses to be activated.
2. *Attention*: the allocation of processing capacity to the incoming stimulus.
3. *Comprehension*: the interpretation of the stimulus.
4. *Acceptance*: the degree to which the stimulus influences the person's knowledge and/or attitudes.
5. *Retention*: the transfer of the stimulus interpretation into long-term memory.

Figure 13.1 indicates that a stimulus must be present and available for processing in order for the first stage of information processing, exposure, to occur. Following exposure, the consumer may pay attention to or "process" the stimulus. During this processing, the consumer will attach meaning to the stimulus, which is the comprehension stage.

The next stage, acceptance, is of critical concern in the realm of persuasive communication. Although the consumer may accurately understand what a salesperson or advertisement is saying, the critical question addressed at this stage is whether the consumer actually believes this information.

The final stage, retention, involves the transfer of information into long-term memory. Note, however, that memory also influences prior stages as well. For example, the consumer who remembers an upcoming birthday of a family member is more likely to pay attention to gift ads. Similarly, the interpretation of stimuli depends upon stored knowledge and prior experiences.

An important implication of this information-processing model is that a stimulus must pass through each of the stages before it reaches memory. Consequently, the effectiveness of persuasive communications will hinge on their ability to survive all of the information-processing stages. This is not an easy task. In one study involving 1,800 TV commercials, only 16 percent of those exposed to an ad could

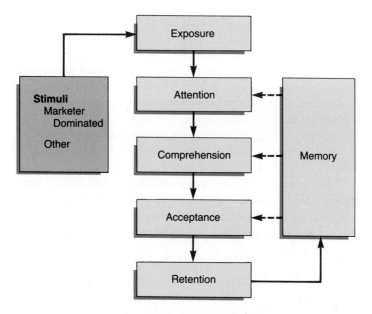

FIGURE 13.1   The Stages of Information Processing

remember the advertised brand.[2] Similarly, according to the Burke day-after recall test (described in Chapter 14), an average of only 24 percent of those people exposed to a television ad can give a sufficient response to reflect that retention of the ad has occurred 24 hours after exposure.[3] One benefit you should derive from this chapter is a better appreciation of the factors that influence the likelihood of a stimulus, such as an ad, passing through the separate stages of information processing.

Exposure

Information processing begins when patterns of energy in the form of stimulus inputs reach one or more of the five senses. **Exposure** occurs from physical proximity to a stimulus that allows the opportunity for one or more senses to be activated. This requires the communicator to select media, either interpersonal or mass, that reach the target market.[4]

Threshold Levels

Given exposure to a stimulus of sufficient strength, a person's sensory receptors are activated and the encoded information is transmitted along nerve fibers to the brain.

This activation is called a **sensation**, which is affected by the following three thresholds:[5]

1. *Lower or absolute threshold*: the minimum amount of stimulus energy or intensity necessary for sensation to occur.
2. *Terminal threshold*: the point at which additional increases in stimulus intensity have no effect on sensation.
3. *Difference threshold*: the smallest change in stimulus intensity that will be noticed by an individual.

Some consumer researchers maintain that stimuli must attain at least the lower or absolute threshold before they can have an impact on the person. Others argue that stimuli below the lower threshold can be influential. This controversial concept has become known as **subliminal persuasion**.

Subliminal Persuasion

Much of the interest in subliminal persuasion can be traced back to the late 1950s when Jim Vicary, the owner of a failing research business, claimed that he had discovered a way of influencing consumers without their conscious awareness. He reported Coca Cola sales increased by 18 percent and popcorn sales grew by 52 percent when the words DRINK COKE and EAT POPCORN were flashed on a movie theater screen at speeds that escaped conscious detection. However, when an independent replication of the study failed to show any effects, Vicary confessed to fabricating the results in the hope of reviving his business.[6]

For years the subject lay dormant until Wilson Bryan Key contended in a popularized book that erotic subliminal cues are implanted in advertisements (for example, the juxtaposition of ice cubes in a liquor ad) designed to appeal to subconscious sex drives.[7] Today, the use of subliminal stimuli is quite prevalent. Consumers spend millions of dollars each year on self-help tapes containing subliminal messages. Horror films have included subliminals in the form of death masks and other scary images to enhance their ability to frighten viewers. Retailers have incorporated subliminal messages within their in-store music designed to motivate employees and undermine shoplifting. Even some resorts have tried subliminals to help vacationers relax.[8]

Despite their prevalent use, the power of subliminal stimuli is still a strongly contested issue. There is some research to suggest that subliminal stimuli can be influential.[9] In a typical study, subjects are exposed to stimuli for very brief amounts of time (in the milliseconds). Exposure is so brief that subjects are unable to identify these stimuli in subsequent recognition tasks. Even so, subjects evaluate these previously seen but unrecognized stimuli more favorably than similar stimuli encountered for the first time. Such findings suggest the possibility of influencing attitudes without conscious cognitive activity.

Others, however, have challenged the effectiveness of subliminal stimuli. As stated by Moore:

> "A century of psychological research substantiates the general principle that more intense stimuli have a greater affect on people's behavior than weaker ones. . . . Subliminal stimuli are usually so weak that the recipient is not just unaware of the stimulus but is also oblivious to the fact that he/she is being stimulated. As a result, the potential effects of subliminal stimuli are easily nullified by other on-going stimulation in the same sensory channel whereby attention is being focused on another modality."[10]

Stated differently, why should one choose a weak method of persuasion when much more effective methods exist?

Weber's Law

It is often important to understand whether a change in some marketing stimulus (such as price) will be perceived by consumers. A retailer who promotes a special sale, for instance, will be disappointed unless consumers perceive the discounted price to be sufficiently lower than the normal price. Similarly, claims of product improvement will be ineffective when consumers fail to perceive a difference between the old and new versions.

In these situations, the **difference threshold**, representing the smallest change in stimulus intensity that will be noticed, is quite relevant. This threshold must be met in attempting to generate perceptions of change. According to Weber's law, as expressed in the following equation, the actual amount of change necessary to reach the difference threshold will depend on the initial starting point.

$$K = \frac{\Delta I}{I}$$

where

K = a constant that differs across the various senses,
ΔI = the smallest change in stimulus intensity necessary to produce a just noticeable difference (jnd),
I = the stimulus intensity at the point where the change occurs.

Weber's law suggests that, as the strength of the initial stimulus intensity increases, a greater amount of change is necessary to produce a just noticeable difference. Suppose that, in the area of price changes, K equals 10 percent. A discount of at least $5 would therefore be needed for a $50 item before consumers would perceive a real cost savings. This same $5 discount, however, would not be effective for a $150 item. In this instance, a discount of at least $15 would be necessary.

In some situations, a business may not wish to meet or exceed the difference threshold (see, for example, Consumer in Focus 13.1). Companies are sometimes

Difference Thresholds and Potato Chips

At Frito-Lay, the consumer is an obsession. Snack food research and development costs at the company have about doubled in the past decade—to between $20 million to $30 million a year. And to keep a close touch with the whims and fancies of the marketplace, the company undertakes nearly 500,000 consumer interviews a year.

This obsession is reflected throughout the company's operations, including how much difference consumers will tolerate in the thickness of a potato chip. Consumers have complained about chips that were cut 8/1000ths of an inch too thick or thin. In order to stay beneath this difference threshold, quality-control engineers measure the thickness of chips to 36/1000ths of an inch for flat chips and 91/1000ths for Ruffles, the company's brand of ridged potato chip.

Source: Excerpted from Robert Johnson, "In the Chips," *Wall Street Journal* (March 22, 1991), B1–B2.

interested in changing their products or prices *without* consumers noticing such changes. Price increases and reductions in product size (such as a shrinking candy bar) are changes that, if possible, should be undertaken without activating the just noticeable difference.

Attention

Not all of the stimuli that activate our sensory receptors during the exposure stage will receive additional processing. Because of limitations in our cognitive resources as discussed in Chapter 8, it is impossible for us to process all of the stimuli available at any given moment. Consequently, the cognitive system is constantly monitoring sensory inputs, selecting some of these for further processing. This screening occurs at a preconscious level and is referred to as **preattentive processing**.

Those stimuli that pass through this screening process enter into the second stage of the information processing model, **attention**. Attention can be defined as the allocation of processing capacity to a stimulus. Given the reality of selective attention, it is important to understand what factors influence the consumer's allocation of this limited resource, particularly for those seeking to attract the consumer's attention. Such factors can be grouped into two major categories: personal or individual determinants and stimulus determinants.

Personal Determinants of Attention

Personal determinants refer to those characteristics of the individual that influence attention. For the most part, these factors are not under the marketer's control. Rather, their existence should be recognized and viewed as constraints against which strategy should be evaluated.

Need/Motivation
Everyone is well aware from daily life that physiological needs have a strong influence on those stimuli that receive attention and those that do not. Hungry people, for example, are far more receptive to food stimuli than they would be on other occasions. Consumer economists have long contended that the worst time for food shopping is when one is hungry, because of the sharp increase in purchasing.

The nature of consumers' need states at the time of exposure to advertising should affect the emphasis placed on an ad's attention-getting properties. If it is possible for an ad to reach consumers when their needs are activated, then less emphasis on enhancing an ad's ability to gain attention is warranted since the consumer is already motivated to process the ad. Unfortunately, this can be difficult to achieve because the time span of consumer decision making is often quite small.[11] More often than not, it will be advantageous to develop advertising that contains stimuli (such as those described shortly) that enhance attention.

Attitudes
According to **cognitive consistency theories**, such as balance theory and congruity theory, people strive to maintain a consistent set of beliefs and attitudes (hence the name cognitive consistency).[12] Inconsistency in this cognitive system is believed to induce adverse psychological tension. Consequently, people are viewed as being receptive to information that maintains or enhances consistency, while avoiding information that challenges their beliefs and attitudes.

The principle of cognitive consistency suggests that attitudes may also influence the attention given to marketing communications. Consumers possessing unfavorable attitudes may allocate little attention, such as an avid antismoker exposed to the cigarette industry's campaign of "smokers' rights." On the other hand, smokers should be much more attentive to these messages. Thus, attitude can be a facilitator when consumers hold favorable feelings toward the product but may serve as a barrier when consumers are negative.

Adaptation Level
An important tendency people share is to become so habituated to a stimulus that it is no longer noticed—that is, they develop an **adaptation level** for the stimulus. Consider, for example, the couple who moves from a quiet, small town to an apartment in the middle of New York City. Initially, they will find the noise levels to be very disturbing and will suffer through many nights of restless

sleep. Eventually, however, they will grow accustomed or become adapted to the noise.

This same phenomenon occurs in marketing. Advertising is especially likely to fall victim to adaptation. Many products are familiar, and it is often difficult to say much that is really new. This can place some real demands on the design and format of the message. Similarly, repeated exposure to an ad may not be effective as consumers become habituated to this stimulus. A strategy of repetition must, therefore, be carefully conceived because of the danger of habituation.

Although adaptation level frequently represents a barrier between marketers and consumers, marketers can also employ it to their advantage. The use of unique product packaging, for instance, can help a product stand out on the shelf. Similarly, an advertising tactic for gaining attention is to include stimuli within an ad that deviate from the consumer's adaptation level. The use of the phrase "A bad ad" in the advertisement appearing in Figure 13.2 is contrary to what consumers expect to

FIGURE 13.2 Deviating from Consumers' Adaptation Level Can Help Capture Their Attention

see in an ad. As described subsequently, some of the stimulus factors that help capture attention do so because they capitalize on adaptation.

Span of Attention   The amount of time we can focus our attention on a single stimulus or thought is quite limited. You can easily demonstrate this to yourself by testing just how long you are able to concentrate on a particular thought before your mind begins to "wander." This limited span of attention may partly explain the increasing use of shorter commercials.

Stimulus Determinants of Attention

The second set of factors influencing attention, **stimulus determinants**, are characteristic of the stimulus itself. They represent "controllable" factors in the sense that they can be used for gaining and/or increasing attention.

Size   In general, the larger the stimulus, the more likely it will attract attention. Increasing a print ad's size will enhance the odds of gaining the consumer's attention.[13] A similar relationship holds for the size of the illustrations or pictures within an ad.[14]

The likelihood of a product being noticed in a store can depend upon the size or amount of shelf space allocated to the product. This can be particularly important for impulse items, whose sales may depend partly on how much space they receive.[15]

Color   The attention attracting and holding power of a stimulus may be sharply increased through the use of color.[16] In a field study involving newspaper advertising, one-color ads produced 41 percent more sales than did their black-and-white counterparts.[17] Color ads cost more, so their incremental effectiveness must be weighed against the additional expense.

Moreover, some colors may be more attention getting than others. Did you know that red colored cars get more speeding tickets than cars of any other color? Further testimony to the power of red comes from the fact that companies placing ads in the yellow pages are encouraged to use this color as a way of attracting attention.

Intensity   Greater stimulus intensity often produces more attention. Loud sounds and bright colors, for instance, can enhance attention. Radio and television commercials may begin with a loud noise to attract attention. Brightly colored print ads are quite common.

Contrast   People have a tendency to attend more closely to those stimuli that contrast with their background. The presentation of stimuli that are inconsistent or contrast with one another creates a perceptual conflict that enhances attention. An example of the use of contrast in print advertisement appears in Figure 13.3.

FIGURE 13.3   The Use of Contrast in Advertising Increases Consumer Attention

Techniques based on the contrast principle appear in a variety of forms in advertising. For example, a black-and-white ad preceded by color ads may be more noticed because of contrast. Similarly, a TV ad that is louder than the programming that preceded it may also attract greater attention. Note that both examples follow from adaptation level: that is, the person becomes adapted to color ads only or to a certain volume which, when violated, attracts their attention.

Position   Stimuli may also be more noticeable simply because of certain locational properties. Grocery vendors know this very well and compete for such prime grocery locations as the end of aisle and shelves located near eye level. Similarly, impulse items are strategically located near cash registers.

Position can also be important for print media. A recent study reports greater attention for ads located in the front rather than back part of the magazine, on right-hand pages rather than left-hand pages, and on the inside front, inside back, and outside back covers.[18] Presumably, these effects are due to the manner in which consumers typically flip through magazines.

Position within the printed page itself can also affect attention. A rule of thumb in advertising is that the upper left-hand corner of the page is the most likely corner to receive attention, whereas the lower right-hand corner is least likely.[19]

Position in broadcast advertising has received less attention in research, although it is a generally accepted rule that commercials perform better when included as part of the regular program rather than during the "clutter" of a program break.[20] Commercials at the beginning and end of a program suffer from the clutter of announcements and other distracting nonprogram material.

Directionality   The eye will tend to follow any signs within the stimulus that indicate directionality. Examples would be arrows or pointing devices. Examine the ad in Figure 13.4. Notice how it directs the eye to the brand name and pertinent copy.

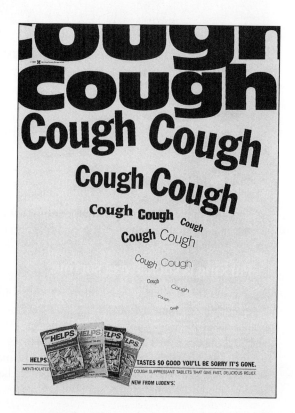

FIGURE 13.4   An Ad Design That Encourages Proper Eye Movement

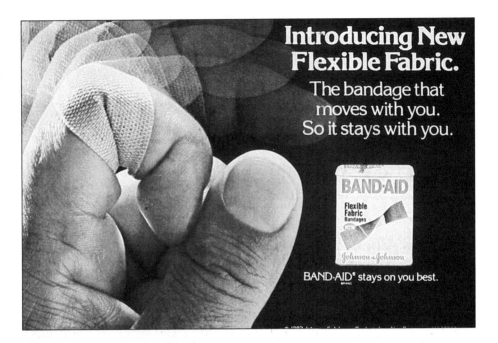

FIGURE 13.5 **Attracting Attention with Quasimotion**

Movement Stimuli in motion elicit greater attention than stationary stimuli. Even quasi or perceived motion, as illustrated by the ad in Figure 13.5, can enhance attention.

Isolation Isolation, which involves presenting a small number of stimuli in a relatively barren perceptual field, can also attract attention. The use of isolation in print advertising means that, rather than completely filling the ad with information and pictures, a substantial portion of the ad will remain "unused," such as the ad appearing in Figure 13.6.

Novelty Unusual or unexpected stimuli (for example, those that deviate from one's adaptation level) attract attention. Advertisers understand the value of novelty and frequently rely upon it for gaining attention, as illustrated by Figure 13.7. Recent applications include pop-up ads (such as the Dodge ad that showed three views of the Dakota pickup truck), 3-D ads (remember the Coke commercial during the halftime show of the 1989 Superbowl?), and print ads that play music thanks to microchip technology (such as a two-page whiskey ad containing a musical microchip activated by opening the ad).[21]

"Learned" Attention-Inducing Stimuli Some stimuli attract our attention because we have been taught or conditioned to react to them. A ringing phone or doorbell,

FIGURE 13.6 Gaining Attention with Isolation

FIGURE 13.7 Attracting Attention with Novelty

for example, typically elicits an immediate response from the person. Ringing phones or wailing sirens are sometimes included in the background of radio and TV ads to capture attention.

Attractive Spokesperson   A common attention-grabbing device is to employ an attractive model or celebrity as a spokesperson.[22] It is nearly impossible to watch TV for any length of time or flip through most magazines without encountering at least one ad with an attractive person. One company, in an effort to break through the clutter of products on supermarket shelves, has developed a line of common grocery products (for example, cereal, trash bags, light bulbs) named Star Pak, which features the faces of some very famous movie stars (Marilyn Monroe, Clark Gable) on the product packaging.[23]

One danger of using a spokesperson is that it can backfire when consumers perceive it as inappropriate for the product being advertised. Models attired in bathing suits, while seen as appropriate endorsers for suntan products, may evoke unfavorable reactions when used to promote furniture.

Scene Changes A new technique for capturing attention is the use of rapid-fire scene changes, which can cause an involuntary increase in brain activity.[24] In some Pontiac commercials, the viewer is exposed to a large number of scenes that last no longer than 1½ seconds, with some scenes as short as ¼ of a second. This same approach was used in the Goodyear commercials featured so prominently during the broadcast of the 1988 Summer Olympics. However, there is some concern that quick-cut commercials may be less memorable and persuasive than slower paced ads.[25]

Attracting Attention: A Precaution

As we have already pointed out, capturing the consumer's attention represents a major challenge to marketers. This will only become more difficult as consumers are bombarded with increasing numbers of products and promotions. Very often, marketers will have little choice but to rely on stimulus factors as bait for the consumer's attention.

We must be sensitive, however, to the fact that the use of stimulus factors is not without risk. A stimulus that dominates viewers' attention, while leaving the remaining message ignored, is self-defeating. The marketer must try to use stimuli that capture attention initially but that do not inhibit processing of the entire message. Whenever possible, stimuli should be employed that help reinforce the brand name or product positioning as well as gain attention. In this regard, the ad presented in Figure 13.3 provides an excellent illustration of using a stimulus that attracts attention while communicating the benefits of product use.

Comprehension

Comprehension, the third stage of information processing, is concerned with the interpretation of a stimulus. It is the point at which meaning is attached to the stimulus. This meaning will depend on how a stimulus is categorized and elaborated in terms of existing knowledge.

Stimulus Categorization

Stimulus categorization involves classifying a stimulus using concepts stored in memory.[26] Consumers' behavior can be affected by how they categorize marketing stimuli. Toro introduced a lightweight snowthrower named Snow Pup, which proved unsuccessful because the name led consumers to categorize the product either as a toy or as not powerful enough for the job. Changing the name (to first Snowmaster and then Toro) reversed this problem and made the product a success.[27]

Thus, influencing stimulus categorization can often be quite important. Consider, for example, the ad appearing in Figure 13.8. Note how it attempts to broaden the product's appeal by encouraging consumers to employ several categories during the categorization process.

FIGURE 13.8 **Encouraging Multiple Product Categorizations Can Broaden a Product's Appeal**

Stimulus Elaboration

In addition to classifying a stimulus, comprehension also involves the degree of elaboration that occurs during stimulus processing. **Elaboration** refers to the amount of integration between the new information and existing knowledge stored in memory or, as some have described it, the number of personal connections made between the stimulus and one's life experiences and goals.[28] Elaboration falls along a continuum ranging from low to high (or shallow to deep).[29]

Consumer researchers have typically focused on elaboration in the form of semantic or verbal elaboration. The amount and nature of elaboration during ad processing, for example, is often measured by asking subjects to write down the thoughts that occur while viewing the ad.[30] As discussed under the acceptance stage, these thoughts can determine the persuasive impact of a stimulus.

Recently, however, there has been a growing interest in the amount of **imagery** that occurs during information processing. Imagery is a process by which sensory information and experiences are represented in working memory.[31] An image may range from a single sensory dimension (for example, visualize a chocolate cake) to a combination of sensory dimensions (for example, imagine the smell and taste of the cake).

Stimulus Organization

Are there principles or rules governing the manner in which people organize incoming stimuli? This question is the domain of an area known as **Gestalt psychology**, which focuses on how people organize or combine stimuli into a meaningful whole. Three principles of stimulus organization are considered here.

Simplicity   People have a strong tendency to organize their perceptions into "simple" patterns. That is, people will opt for simple perceptions even when more complex perceptions can be derived from the stimulus. This principle is illustrated in Figure 13.9. Suppose you were asked to connect the dots in stimulus A. Most people would form a circle (B), even though the more complex pattern of two squares (C) can also be derived. This drive toward simplicity partly explains why consumers often perceive only a subset of the copy points contained in an ad.

Figure and Ground   People tend to organize their perceptions into two major patterns. The first is **figure**, which represents those elements within a perceptual field that receive the most attention. The remaining, less meaningful elements that comprise the background are referred to as **ground**. Many interesting experiments have been undertaken to determine what will be figure and what will be ground. Previous experience exerts a strong effect. The more familiar object tends to stand out. A familiar face, for example, can usually be recognized in a crowd. Similarly, the familiar brand symbol will stand out, thus underscoring the value of repetitive advertising.

The importance of the figure-ground principle in an advertising context is illustrated by consumers' reactions to the series of television commercials featuring James Garner and Mariette Hartley for the Polaroid One Step camera. The commercials built upon verbal sparring by a married couple, and there was no question that people liked them. However, many of those surveyed named Kodak as the

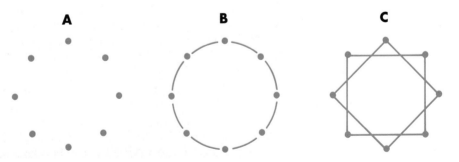

FIGURE 13.9   An Example of Simplicity

brand being advertised. For these consumers, Garner and Hartley became the figure while the product became ground, just the reverse of the advertiser's intent.

Closure   Another useful principle from Gestalt psychology is **closure**, which refers to our tendency to develop a complete picture or perception even when elements in the perceptual field are missing. Because of this drive to "fill in" the missing parts, the presentation of an incomplete stimulus provides marketers with a mechanism for increasing the effort and involvement that occur during information processing.[32]

Closure is a very popular technique in advertising. A classic example is the Salem musical jingle of "You can take Salem out of the country, but you can't take the country out of Salem." In the initial stages of the campaign, this jingle was strongly established in the consumer's mind. Subsequently, a new ad was developed that ended with that part of jingle up to the word "but." According to all reports, the campaign was quite successful.

Closure can be used in many other ways. Kellogg's, for instance, has developed ads as well as billboards in which either the bottom portion or last couple of letters of their name is missing. The ad appearing in Figure 13.10 employs the closure

FIGURE 13.10   **The Use of Closure in Advertising**

principle by obscuring a considerable portion of the brand name. Sometimes ads will present a partial picture of the product itself. Playing the soundtrack of well-known TV commercials may also evoke closure as the listener reproduces the visual portion.[33] Heavy viewers of MTV probably have a similar experience when the song from a familiar music video is played on the radio.

Personal Determinants of Comprehension

Comprehension, like attention, is influenced by many stimulus and personal factors. We first consider how personal factors can affect comprehension.

Motivation   Just as a person's motivational state during information processing can influence attention, so too can it exert an affect on comprehension. In a classic study, subjects who differed in the amount of elapsed time since their last meal were asked to describe what they saw in an "ambiguous" picture. As expected, subjects were more likely to categorize the stimulus as some type of food-related object the longer it had been since they had last eaten.[34]

Motivation can also influence the elaboration that occurs during comprehension.[35] When a stimulus is perceived as personally relevant (that is, the stimulus is seen as having some usefulness for need satisfaction), more elaborate processing should occur. An ad featuring a product that is irrelevant to a consumer's needs will typically be processed in a very shallow fashion. The relatively few thoughts that are generated during processing will focus more on the ad (for example, thoughts about the ad's executional properties) than the product. In contrast, when consumers are more motivated during ad processing, they will engage in more thinking, especially about the advertised product (for example, thoughts about the benefits of owning the product).

Knowledge   The knowledge stored in memory is obviously a major determinant of comprehension.[36] Categorization of a stimulus depends heavily on knowledge. The novice perceives a gold coin, the expert sees a rare and valuable St. Gaudens $20 gold coin in MS-65 condition (a grade for coins in near perfect shape).

Knowledge also enhances consumers' ability to understand a message. Unlike the expert, the novice may have difficulty with understanding the terminology (did you know what MS-65 meant?) and the significance of message claims. This beneficial effect on understanding is accompanied by a reduction in miscomprehension. Knowledge can help consumers recognize faulty logic and erroneous conclusions and avoid incorrect interpretations. Knowledgeable persons are also more likely to elaborate on message claims, whereas unknowledgeable consumers may focus on nonclaim cues (for example, background music, pictures) within the message.[37]

Expectation or Perceptual Set   Comprehension will often depend on prior conceptions or expectations of what we are likely to see. Suppose that you were asked to identify the stimulus shown in Figure 13.11. Many people would probably perceive the number 13, whereas others may interpret it as the letter B. However, what if

FIGURE 13.11 **The "Broken B" Stimulus: Prior Conceptions Affect Current Perceptions**

prior to encountering this stimulus you first viewed either four different capital letters or four pairs of digits? Research shows that those led to expect digits will report "13," whereas those who are primed to anticipate letters will report "B."[38]

This same phenomenon is often observed in marketing. In a classic study, consumers were asked to taste and rate various beers. These ratings were attained under both "blind" (no brand identification) and "labeled" (brands were identified) conditions. When the brands were unlabeled, the ratings were essentially the same for all brands. That is, consumers did not differentiate among the brands. However, significant rating differences emerged when the brands were labeled. Thus, the expectation created by the brand label was powerful enough to alter consumers' perceptions of the products.[39]

Expectations have recently been shown to influence how consumers process information provided by a salesperson. Subjects engaged in much more careful consideration of the information supplied by a salesperson who deviated from their expectations of the "typical" salesperson than in that supplied by one who matched their expectations.[40]

Stimulus Determinants of Comprehension

The actual physical properties of a stimulus play a major role in shaping how it is interpreted. The Apple computer company learned the hard way about the importance of size. Many consumers found it difficult to believe that the Apple IIc, a trimmer version of the Apple IIe, was more powerful, because of its smaller size. A new promotional program was developed to combat this perception (the basic theme being "It's a lot bigger than it looks"), and sales increased.

The color of a stimulus can serve as an important cue in consumers' perceptions. Appliance manufacturers, for instance, have discovered that they can reduce the consumer's perception of a product's weight such as a vacuum cleaner by using pastel rather than darker colors. Manufacturers of laundry soaps and cold capsules recognize the benefits of including colored granules as a visual reinforcement for product claims.

Similarly, comprehension can depend on a product's packaging and brand name. A grocery store discovered that the practice of prepackaging fresh fish with a plastic wrap undermined consumers' perceptions of the product's freshness. Many consumers interpreted the packaging to mean that the fish had been frozen. Consequently, a seafood bar was added where unwrapped fish were displayed on crushed

Is the Name to Blame?

In the immortal words of William Shakespeare, "A rose by any other name would smell as sweet." But would it? The experience of many businesses would suggest otherwise. Buncan MacRae, owner of the Yesterday's Tavern and Grill restaurant in Columbia, South Carolina, had a spicy dish called "Spanish chicken and rice" that would not sell. According to MacRae, after changing the name to "Lowcountry chicken and rice," the dish became so popular it "flew out of the window."

Bill Bricker and Ed Hensley have a similar story. In 1984, they began selling one of the richest organic manures available on the market. The source of this manure? Crickets, and lots of them. Two billion crickets played their part in the manufacturing process during the past year.

Originally, the product was named "CC-84." The CC stood for cricket crap, and the 84 represented the year they began selling it. Unfortunately, for those unfamiliar with the name's origins, the product was more likely to be perceived as a chemical than an organic fertilizer. Sales were dismal. In the words of Bricker's wife, "It was a bomb."

The name was changed to "Gotta Grow," but sales remain unchanged. One of Bricker's friends, an advertising salesman, then suggested a new name: "Kricket Krap." Once given this distinctive and memorable name, the product started selling. However, some were less than enthusiastic about the new name. The telephone company refused to list the full name in the phone book. Instead, it was listed as "Kricket #¢*?."

Source: "Fertilizer By Any Other Name Doesn't Sell as Well, By Jiminy," *The State* (September 28, 1991), 9A.

ice. Sales for the wrapped fish remained constant, while total sales, including those generated by the seafood bar, nearly doubled.

The importance of brand name is illustrated by Wendy's single hamburger. Although their single contains as much meat as a Whopper or Quarter Pounder and more than the Big Mac, its name fails to convey its size. Wendy's introduction of The Big Classic hamburger was intended to overcome this problem.[41] Additional illustrations of how a product's name can influence consumer perception is presented in Consumer in Focus 13.2.

Linguistics A rather substantial body of literature comprises the area known as **psycholinguistics**, the study of psychological factors involved in the perception of and response to linguistic phenomena. Listed next are findings that reflect the potential contribution psycholinguistics can make to understanding and enhancing message comprehension:[42]

1. Words used frequently in everyday language are more easily comprehended and remembered.[43]
2. Negative words such as "not" or "never" are less easily comprehended.[44]
3. The potential for misunderstanding is greater for passive sentences (for example, "The product was developed by Company X") than for active sentences (for example, "Company X developed the product").[45]

Psycholinguistics can also play a useful role in the development of brand names. Name Lab, a company that assists businesses in picking the right names for their products, has developed such names as Acura, Compaq, Sentra, and Zapmail through the use of "constructional linguistics," a method where basic word parts or morphemes (the smallest meaningful unit in a language) are combined to form the desired meaning.

Order Effects   Suppose that you and a friend were each given a list of the same personality traits describing a hypothetical individual, but the order of the traits on the lists were exactly opposite. Would different orderings cause a difference in how much you and your friend liked this person? According to Asch's research, the answer is yes.[46]

Two major types of order effects have been discussed in the research literature. One is **recency**, in which stimuli appearing at the end of a sequence are given more weight in the resulting interpretation. Alternatively, a **primacy** effect can occur. Primacy is consistent with the notion of "first impression" such that stimuli appearing at the beginning are given more weight. Unfortunately, it is presently impossible to predict which effect will emerge in a particular situation.

Context   The context, or surrounding situation in which the stimulus occurs, will in part determine what is comprehended.[47] In Chapter 7, we considered how context operates in communication situations, such as when the particular magazine or television program in which the ad appears affects how consumers respond to the ad.

The retail environment also represents a potential source of context effects. In the early 1980s, Levi jeans expanded distribution into mass merchandisers (for example, Sears, Penney's). Department stores viewed the move as damaging the brand's fashion image and threatening to their markups. Consequently, many stores turned to other jean manufacturers for a replacement, and Lee jeans benefitted considerably. Frito-Lay experienced undesirable context effects when displays for its new Cheetos "Paws," a corn snack in the shape of a cheetah's foot, were located near the pet food aisle. In the words of one confused consumer, "Are Paws for my cat, or for me?"[48]

Miscomprehension

Before turning to the acceptance stage, it is important to stress the potential for miscomprehension during information processing. Indeed, the meanings consumers attach to stimuli may differ considerably from those desired by marketers. For example, research suggests that a substantial number of people have some misunderstanding of what they view on TV, whether it is news, a regular program, or advertising.[49] Consequently, accurate comprehension of a message, even a relatively simple one, cannot be assumed.

Why does miscomprehension occur? In some cases, the consumer can be faulted, such as when inadequate attention is allocated to the stimulus during processing. At other times, however, miscomprehension may arise because of ambiguity in the stimulus itself. Consider the retailer that advertises "Lowest prices guaranteed." What does this mean to you? It could mean that the retailer is claiming lower prices than the competition. It may also mean that the retailer's prices are the lowest they have offered all year. There is even another possible meaning. When Montgomery Ward made this claim in newspaper ads, the company was referring to their policy of matching competitors' price. If customers found the same item at a lower price than they paid at Montgomery Ward within 30 days of purchase, then they would be refunded the difference.[50]

Miscomprehension can also occur because of misleading information. In a Tropicana orange juice ad, Olympic decathlon winner Bruce Jenner was shown squeezing oranges into the product carton. However, Tropicana juice is not squeezed directly into the carton. It is pasteurized and sometimes frozen first. Similarly, an ad for Jartran do-it-yourself moving trucks placed the trucks of its competitor, U-Haul, in the background. The result was that the U-Haul trucks looked small. Both the Tropicana and Jartran ads were ruled misleading by a court.

Acceptance

Suppose that an advertisement successfully captures attention and is accurately understood by viewers. Will persuasion occur? Not necessarily. The simple fact is that message comprehension is *not* the same as message acceptance. Consumers may understand perfectly all that is being communicated, but they may not agree with the message for any number of reasons. Indeed, many if not most consumers are very skeptical of advertising claims. One study reports that over 70 percent of consumers do not believe ads that use test results to support claims of product superiority.[51]

A key question, then, is what determines how much, if any, acceptance will occur during information processing. Research has shown that acceptance may heavily depend on the thoughts that occur during the comprehension stage.[52] Such thoughts are often referred to as **cognitive responses**.

Cognitive Responses

Consider a knowledgeable consumer who is highly motivated while processing an ad that contains a number of claims about a product that the consumer anticipates buying very soon. This consumer may engage in considerable thinking about the claims' validity. The nature of these cognitive responses will determine the acceptance of the claims. Of particular importance are those responses called support arguments and counterarguments. **Support arguments** are thoughts that are favorable to the claims. **Counterarguments** are thoughts that oppose the message claims. Acceptance is enhanced as support argumentation increases but is reduced by greater counterargumentation.

Of course, consumers may often be unmotivated or unable to carefully consider an ad's claims about the product. When this occurs, then acceptance may depend more heavily on the cognitive responses evoked by an ad's executional elements.[53]

Cognitive responses provide a valuable complement to standard attitude measures in evaluating communication effectiveness. Although standard attitude measures can reveal whether a communication leaves a favorable or unfavorable impression on the viewer, they often fail to reveal the reasons for this impression. If an ad flops, is it because of an ineffective spokesperson, the absence of compelling arguments, or poor visuals? Standard attitude measures may not answer such questions. Cognitive responses can give insights into these various concerns.

Nonetheless, cognitive responses are not without their limitations. There are some reasonable questions about the extent to which cognitive responses or, more generally, verbalizations of mental processes can fully reflect the content and activities that occur during processing.[54] A second concern is that focusing solely on cognitive thoughts is overly restrictive. This latter concern has led researchers to explore the role of affective responses.

Affective Responses

Although cognitive responses may often be the major determinant of an ad's persuasiveness, there are times when an ad's impact will depend much more heavily on how it makes us feel. **Affective responses** represent the feelings and emotions that are elicited by a stimulus.[55] It is these types of "hot" responses, rather than the "cold" cognitive responses, that are emphasized by much of today's advertising. The musical and visual elements within the "We build excitement" television advertisements for Pontiac are designed to elicit feelings of exhilaration and excitement.

As one example of the diversity of feelings that ads may elicit, consider those appearing in Table 13.1. In a recent study, subjects were exposed to a variety of television commercials and asked to indicate how strongly they experienced these feelings. The results indicated that this assortment of affective responses could be simplified into three primary dimensions: upbeat, negative, and warm. Some have recommended a larger set of primary emotions consisting of fear, surprise, sadness, disgust, anger, anticipation, joy, and acceptance.[56]

The role of affective responses has become a topic of considerable interest in the recent research literature. The findings thus far have been very supportive of the importance they play during the acceptance stage of information processing. For example, one study reports that both cognitive and affective responses were useful in predicting the attitudes formed after ad exposure.[57]

TABLE 13.1   Types of Feelings

Upbeat	Negative	Warm
Active	Angry	Affectionate
Adventurous	Annoyed	Calm
Alive	Bad	Concerned
Amused	Bored	Contemplative
Attentive	Critical	Emotional
Attractive	Defiant	Hopeful
Carefree	Depressed	Kind
Cheerful	Disgusted	Moved
Confident	Disinterested	Peaceful
Creative	Dubious	Pensive
Delighted	Dull	Sentimental
Elated	Fed-up	Touched
Energetic	Insulted	Warmhearted
Enthusiastic	Irritated	
Excited	Lonely	
Exhilarated	Offended	
Good	Regretful	
Happy	Sad	
Humorous	Skeptical	
Independent	Suspicious	
Industrious		
Inspired		
Interested		
Joyous		
Lighthearted		
Lively		
Playful		
Pleased		
Proud		
Satisfied		
Stimulated		
Strong		

Source: Julie A. Edell and Marian Chapman Burke, "The Power of Feelings in Understanding Advertising Effects," *Journal of Consumer Research* 14 (December 1987), p. 424, Table 1.

In developing effective communications, advertisers must consider the particular cognitive and affective responses that are likely to occur during information processing. Because acceptance depends on the favorability of these responses, the ad should only contain elements that evoke positive thoughts and feelings. Elements that elicit undesirable responses should be modified or eliminated from the ad. In Chapters 14 and 15 we will consider more carefully how advertisers try to influence affective and cognitive responses through their use of certain advertising elements.

Retention

The final stage of information processing is **retention**, which involves the transfer of information to long-term memory. Although much current knowledge about memory comes from the cognitive psychology literature, consumer researchers have become very interested in this area over the past decade. Indeed, articles relevant to memory issues are appearing at an increasing rate in the major consumer research journals and conferences.

Physiological Properties of the Human Brain

The human brain is divided into left and right hemispheres, which are connected by a large fiber tract known as the corpus callosum. Interestingly, the hemispheres differ in the types of cognitive operations performed during information processing. The left brain is viewed as the center for logical, abstract, and conceptual thinking, whereas the right brain focuses on creative, intuitive, and imaginal thinking. In addition, the right brain is involved with the processing of pictorial or visual information. Both hemispheres assist in processing verbal or semantic information, although differences do exist in the particular types of operations performed by each.[58]

Evidence for these distinctions comes from "split-brain" persons (those who have lost the corpus callosum). In such cases, the two hemispheres operate as independent units since the absence of the corpus callosum eliminates communication between the hemispheres. Consequently, it is possible to present stimuli so that only one hemisphere "receives" the information. If, for instance, a pair of scissors is processed by only the left hemisphere and the person is asked to identify the object, he or she can easily respond with the semantic concept of "scissors." However, when this same object is processed by the right hemisphere, the person is unable to give the answer.

People differ in the relative dominance of the two hemispheres. Some people are left-brain dominated, while others are right-brain dominated. In one test of hemispheric dominance, people are visually presented the word "red" in blue letters. They are then asked to verbalize the color of the letters. The left brain says red, whereas the right brain says blue. Whatever response finally emerges gives an indication of the hemispheres' relative dominance.

Advertisers have been particularly interested in examining how each hemisphere responds while consumers are processing advertising messages. Consumer in Focus 13.3 describes the benefits yielded by brain wave research for one company.[59] Some personnel consultants have also advocated the value of understanding hemispheric dominance in the recruitment and utilization of employees.[60]

Multiple-Store Theory of Memory

In addition to these physiological characteristics of memory, many believe that important psychological differences exist in the structure and functioning of memory.

Hemispheric Research and Advertising Effectiveness

In order to gain further insights into how their advertising messages are being processed by the brain, some advertisers use electroencephalograms (better known as EEGs), which trace electrical activity within the brain. Research on EEGs and advertising during the past decade or so has shown that emotional slice-of-life commercials tend to be processed mostly in the right hemisphere. More logical ads, such as product demonstrations, are handled predominantly by the left hemisphere.

That knowledge can help spot blunders that might turn an otherwise memorable commercial into a forgettable one. Neuro-Communication Research Laboratories Inc., a company that uses brainwave analysis to evaluate ads, cites a commercial in which a father and daughter were speaking. The father's affection produced a high level of processing activity in the right hemisphere. But just as the viewer was being drawn into that emotional scene, the commercial quickly cut to product information. And, deep inside the brain, that caused trouble.

The EEG showed the right hemisphere was still highly active, making it difficult for the brain to process words. Linguistic processing usually requires roughly equal activity in both the left and right hemispheres. In short, the timing may have muddled the message.

Source: Excerpted from Michael J. McCarthy, "Mind Probe," *Wall Street Journal* (March 22, 1991), B3.

One influential viewpoint, presented in Figure 13.12, is that memory consists of three different storage systems: (1) sensory memory, (2) short-term memory, and (3) long-term memory.[61]

Sensory Memory   In sensory memory, incoming information receives an initial analysis based largely on such physical properties as loudness, pitch, and so on. Visual processing at this stage is referred to as **iconic** and auditory processing as **echoic**. It takes place virtually instantaneously, with iconic processing requiring only one quarter of a second.[62]

Short-Term Memory   Once the stimulus passes through sensory processing, it enters short-term memory, which is viewed as the "workbench" for information-processing activities. In effect, it combines sensory input with the contents of long-term memory so that categorization and interpretation can take place.

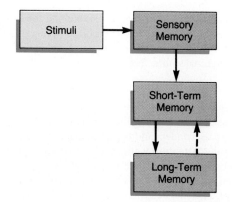

FIGURE 13.12 **The Multiple-Store Model of Memory: The Three Storage Systems**

Short-term memory is limited in several respects. First, it can hold only a limited amount of information at any given point in time. It has been estimated that this capacity is limited to as little as four and perhaps up to seven units of information.[63]

Short-term memory is also limited in how long information can exist without efforts to keep it activated. Suppose you were shown a phone number just long enough to process it and then were prevented from rehearsing the number. How much time would have to elapse before the number faded away? Information is typically lost in 30 seconds or less without rehearsal.[64]

Long-Term Memory   Long-term memory is viewed as an unlimited, permanent storehouse containing all of our knowledge. We have already examined two key properties of long-term memory, content and organization, in Chapter 10.

Given that marketers often attempt to implant information within the consumer's mind, it is very important for us to understand *how* retention takes place. That is, what factors influence the amount of retention that occurs during information processing? The answer to this question can be found in Chapter 14, under the topic of cognitive learning.

Summary

A model of the stages information passes through while being processed by consumers was presented in this chapter. This information-processing model consists of five stages: exposure, attention, comprehension, acceptance, and retention.

Exposure can be defined as the achievement of proximity to a stimulus such that an opportunity exists for activation of one or more of the five senses. Such activation results when a stimulus meets or exceeds the lower threshold: the minimum amount of stimulus intensity necessary for sensation to occur. Efforts to influence consumers with stimuli below the lower threshold are known as subliminal persuasion. Current evidence indicates that subliminal stimuli have, at best, minimal effects and suggests that fears of their persuasiveness are unfounded.

Attention represents the allocation of processing capacity to the incoming stimulus. Because of definite limitations in this capacity, consumers are very selective in what they pay attention to. Gaining the consumer's attention will often be a major hurdle.

An understanding of what factors influence attention can be very useful in jumping this hurdle. Attention is affected by two major types of determinants: personal and stimulus. Personal determinants are individual characteristics such as motivation, attitudes, adaptation, and span of attention. The net effect of personal influences is to make attention highly selective. Personal determinants are best viewed as constraints and barriers against which strategy should be evaluated.

Stimulus factors are characteristics of the stimulus itself. Size, color, intensity, contrast, position, directionality, movement, isolation, novelty, learned attention-inducing stimuli, attractive spokesperson, and scene changes can influence attention. These factors can be used by marketers in competing for the consumer's valuable attention.

Comprehension is concerned with the interpretation of the stimulus. Successful marketing will often depend on understanding the meaning consumers attach to stimuli such as price, packaging, brand names, as well as on advertising.

Gestalt psychology has uncovered several important principles about how people organize stimuli into a meaningful whole: simplicity, figure and ground, and closure. The most basic level of comprehension involves stimulus classification. Once classified, further elaboration may occur in the form of semantic or imaginal processing.

Comprehension is influenced by a number of factors. A consumer's level of knowledge and motivation or involvement and her or his expectations are critical determinants. Stimulus factors, such as the linguistic characteristics of a stimulus or the order in which stimuli are processed, can also affect comprehension.

The acceptance stage of information processing focuses on the extent to which persuasion occurs in the form of new or modified knowledge and attitudes. Acceptance will depend on the particular cognitive and affective responses experienced during processing. Acceptance is more likely as these responses become more favorable.

The final stage of information processing, retention, involves the transfer of information to long-term memory. Memory consists of three different storage systems: (1) sensory memory, (2) short-term memory, and (3) long-term memory.

Review and Discussion Questions

1. How can the concept of information processing be useful in understanding why ads are "successful" or "unsuccessful"?
2. Do you believe there are situations in which advertisers should consider the use of subliminal cues? Why or why not?
3. Many critics contend that too much advertising today is gimmicky and cute. The argument is that creative people are carried away by flashy attention-attracting devices and are forgetting that good advertising must sell. How would you respond to this criticism?
4. How does adaptation level create a barrier for advertising? How can it be used to increase advertising effectiveness?

5. A recent study reveals that a particular ad was much more effective in magazine A than in magazine B, even though the readership of the two magazines is virtually identical. How can you explain this finding?

6. A retailer of computer goods is puzzled by consumers' response to her recent fall sale. There was only one purchase of the $3,000 model (sale priced at $2,750). The $1,000 model (sale priced at $875), despite having only half the $250 savings offered by the more expensive model, sold out. How can you explain these results?

7. Two consumers are exposed to the same ad. One is in the market for this product, while the other is not. How might these two consumers differ in their processing of this ad?

Endnotes

1. William J. McGuire, "Some Internal Psychological Factors Influencing Consumer Choice," *Journal of Consumer Research* 2 (March 1976), 302–319.

2. Harry W. McMahan, "TV Loses the 'Name Game' but Wins Big in Personality," *Advertising Age* 51 (December 1, 1980), 54.

3. "To Burke or Not to Burke?" *TV Guide* 29 (February 7, 1981), 3.

4. For a detailed review of the principles of media selection, see James F. Engel, Martin R. Warshaw, and Thomas C. Kinnear, *Promotional Strategy*, 4th ed. (Homewood, Ill.: Richard D. Irwin, 1979), Chapter 13.

5. See W. N. Dember, *The Psychology of Perception* (New York: Holt, Rinehart and Winston, 1961), Chapter 2.

6. Walter Weir, "Another Look at Subliminal 'Facts'," *Advertising Age* (October 15, 1984), 46.

7. Wilson Bryan Key, *Subliminal Seduction: Ad Media's Manipulation of a Not-So-Innocent America* (Englewood Cliffs, N.J.: Prentice-Hall, 1972). Also see Wilson Bryan Key, *Media Sexploitation* (Englewood Cliffs, N.J.: Prentice-Hall, 1976). Key's claims have been strongly challenged. See Jack Haberstroh, "Can't Ignore Subliminal Ad Charges," *Advertising Age* (September 17, 1984), 3, 42, 44; Weir, "Another Look at Subliminal 'Facts.'" Research continues in this area and can be found in Ronnie Cuperfain and T. Keith Clark, "A New Perspective on Subliminal Advertising," *Journal of Advertising* 14 (July 1985), 36–41; Myron Gable, Henry T. Wilkens, Lynn Harris, and Richard Feinberg, "An Evaluation of Subliminally Embedded Sexual Stimuli in Graphics," *Journal of Advertising* 16 (1987), 26–31; Philip M. Merikle and Jim Cheesman, "Current Status of Research on Subliminal Perception," in Melanie Wallendorf and Paul Anderson, eds., *Advances in Consumer Research* 14 (Provo, Utah: Association for Consumer Research, 1987), 298–302.

8. Jo Anna Natale, "Are You Open to Suggestion?" *Psychology Today* (September 1988), 28, 30.

9. Robert B. Zajonc and Hazel Markus, "Affective and Cognitive Factors in Preferences," *Journal of Consumer Research* 9 (September 1982), 123–131. Also see Punam Anand and Morris B. Holbrook, "Reinterpretation of Mere Exposure or Exposure of Mere Reinterpretation," *Journal of Consumer Research* 17 (September 1990), 242–244; Punam Anand, Morris B. Holbrook, and Debra Stephens, "The Formation of Affective Judgments: The Cognitive-Affective Model Versus the Independence Hypothesis," *Journal of Consumer Research* 15 (December 1988), 386–391; Timothy B. Heath, "The Logic of Mere Exposure: A Reinterpretation of Anand, Holbrook, and Stephens (1988)," *Journal of Consumer Research* 17 (September 1990), 237–241; Chris

Janiszewski, "Preconscious Processing Effects: The Independence of Attitude Formation and Conscious Thought," *Journal of Consumer Research* 15 (September 1988), 199–209; Chris Janiszewski, "The Influence of Print Advertisement Organization on Affect Toward a Brand Name," *Journal of Consumer Research* 17 (June 1990), 53–65; Carl Obermiller, "Varieties of Mere Exposure: The Effects of Processing Style and Repetition on Affective Response," *Journal of Consumer Research* 12 (June 1985), 17–31; Yehoshua Tsal, "On the Relationship Between Cognitive and Affective Processes: A Critique of Zajonc and Markus," *Journal of Consumer Research* 12 (December 1985), 358–362.

10. Timothy E. Moore, "Subliminal Advertising: What You See Is What You Get," *Journal of Marketing* 46 (Spring 1982), 38–47.

11. National Advertising Bureau, *How America Shops and Buys* (June 1983), 23.

12. For a discussion of cognitive consistency theories, see William J. McGuire, "The Current Status of Cognitive Consistency Theories," in Joel B. Cohen, ed., *Behavioral Science Foundations of Consumer Behavior* (New York: Free Press, 1972), 253–274.

13. Adam Finn, "Print Ad Recognition Readership Scores: An Information Processing Perspective," *Journal of Marketing Research* 25 (May 1988), 168–177.

14. Ibid.

15. Keith K. Cox, "The Effect of Shelf Space upon Sales of Branded Products," *Journal of Marketing Research* 7 (February 1970), 55–58.

16. Finn, "Print Ad Recognition Readership Scores: An Information Processing Perspective."

17. Larry Percy, *Ways in Which the People, Words and Pictures in Advertising Influence Its Effectiveness* (Chicago: Financial Institutions Marketing Association, July 1984), 19.

18. Finn, "Print Ad Recognition Readership Scores: An Information Processing Perspective."

19. Sandra E. Moriarty, *Creative Advertising: Theory and Practice* (Englewood Cliffs, N.J.: Prentice-Hall, 1986). For research indicating that changes in the position of elements within an ad can also influence the ad's persuasiveness, see Janiszewski, "The Influence of Print Advertisement Organization on Affect toward a Brand Name."

20. For research on advertising clutter, see Peter H. Webb, "Consumer Initial Processing in a Difficult Media Environment," *Journal of Consumer Research* 6 (December 1979), 225–236. Also see Michael L. Ray and Peter H. Webb, "Three Prescriptions for Clutter," *Journal of Advertising Research* 26 (February/March 1986), 69–77.

21. Joe Agnew, "Musical Whiskey Ad to Chime in Time for Christmas," *Marketing News* 21 (October 9, 1987), 24–25; "Oh, What a 3-D Feeling from Toyota," *Marketing News* 21 (October 23, 1987), 9.

22. For research in this area, see M. Wayne Alexander and Ben Judd, Jr., "Do Nudes in Ads Enhance Brand Recall?" *Journal of Advertising Research* 18 (February 1978), 47–50; Michael J. Baker and Gilbert A. Churchill, Jr., "The Impact of Physically Attractive Models on Advertising Evaluations," *Journal of Marketing Research* 14 (November 1977), 538–555; M. Steadman, "How Sexy Illustrations Affect Brand Recall," *Journal of Advertising Research* 9 (March 1969), 15–18; Lynn R. Kahle and Pamela M. Homer, "Physical Attractiveness of the Celebrity Endorser: A Social Adaptation Perspective," *Journal of Consumer Research* 11 (March 1985), 954–961.

23. Joe Agnew, "Shoppers' Star Gazing Seen as Strategy to Slash Supermarket Shelf Clutter," *Marketing News* 21 (January 16, 1987), 1, 16.

24. David H. Freedman, "Why You Watch Some Commercials—Whether You Mean To or Not," *TV Guide* (February 20, 1988), 4–7.

25. Michael J. McCarthy, "Mind Probe," *Wall Street Journal* (March 22, 1991), B3.
26. Advanced discussions of categorization in the context of consumer information processing can be found in Joseph W. Alba and J. Wesley Hutchinson, "Dimensions of Consumer Expertise," *Journal of Consumer Research* 13 (March 1987), 411–454; Joel B. Cohen and Kunal Basu, "Alternative Models of Categorization: Toward a Contingent Processing Framework," *Journal of Consumer Research* 13 (March 1987), 455–472.
27. J. Neher, "Toro Cutting a Wide Swath in Outdoor Appliance Marketing," *Advertising Age* 50 (February 25, 1979), 21.
28. Herbert Krugman, "The Measurement of Advertising Involvement," *Public Opinion Quarterly* 30 (March 1966), 583–596.
29. Fergus I. M. Craik and Robert S. Lockhart, "Levels of Processing: A Framework for Memory Research," *Journal of Verbal Learning and Verbal Behavior* (December 1972), 671–684; Anthony G. Greenwald and Clark Leavitt, "Audience Involvement in Advertising: Four Levels," *Journal of Consumer Research* 11 (June 1984), 581–592.
30. For example, see Jerry C. Olson, Daniel R. Toy, and Philip A. Dover, "Do Cognitive Responses Mediate the Effectiveness of Advertising Content on Cognitive Structure?" *Journal of Consumer Research* 9 (December 1982), 245–262; Peter Wright, "The Cognitive Processes Mediating Acceptance of Advertising," *Journal of Marketing Research* 10 (February 1973), 53–62.
31. Deborah J. MacInnis and Linda L. Price, "The Role of Imagery in Information Processing: Review and Extensions," *Journal of Consumer Research* 13 (March 1987), 473–491.
32. James T. Heimbach and Jacob Jacoby, "The Zergarnik Effect in Advertising," in M. Venkatesan, ed., *Proceedings of the Third Annual Conference* (Urbana, Ill.: Association for Consumer Research, 1972), 746–758.
33. Julie A. Edell and Kevin Lane Keller, "The Information Processing of Coordinated Media Campaigns," *Journal of Marketing Research* 26 (May 1989), 149–163.
34. Robert Levine, Isidor Chein, and Gardner Murphy, "The Relation of the Intensity of a Need to the Amount of Perceptual Distortion," *Journal of Psychology* 13 (January 1942), 283–293.
35. Richard L. Celsi and Jerry C. Olson, "The Role of Involvement in Attention and Comprehension Processes," *Journal of Consumer Research* 15 (September 1988), 210–224.
36. Alba and Hutchinson, "Dimensions of Consumer Expertise."
37. Richard E. Petty and John T. Cacioppo, "The Elaboration Likelihood Model of Persuasion," in Leonard Berkowitz, ed., *Advances in Experimental Social Psychology*, vol. 19 (New York: Academic Press, 1986), 123–205.
38. Jerome S. Bruner and A. Leigh Minturn, "Perceptual Identification and Perceptual Organization," *Journal of General Psychology* 53 (July 1955), 21–28.
39. Ralph I. Allison and Kenneth P. Uhl, "Influence of Beer Brand Identification on Taste Perception," *Journal of Marketing Research* 1 (August 1964), 36–39.
40. Mita Sujan, James R. Bettman, and Harish Sujan, "Effects of Consumer Expectations on Information Processing in Selling Encounters," *Journal of Marketing Research* 23 (November 1986), 346–353.
41. "'Classic' Marketing Meets Whopper of a Challenge," *Marketing News* 21 (June 5, 1987), 22ff.
42. For a general discussion of the role of psycholinguistics in advertising copy, see Larry Percy, "Psycholinguistic Guidelines for Advertising," in Andrew Mitchell, ed., *Advances in Consumer Research* 9 (Ann Arbor: Association for Consumer Research, 1982), 107–111.

Also see Karen Ann Hunold, "Verbal Strategies for Product Presentation in Television Commercials," in Michael J. Houston, ed., *Advances in Consumer Research* 15 (Ann Arbor: Association for Consumer Research, 1988), 256–259.

43. Leo Postman, "Effects of Word Frequency on Acquisition and Retention Under Conditions of Free-Recall Learning," *Quarterly Journal of Experimental Psychology* 22 (May 1970), 185–195.

44. Philip B. Gough, "The Verification of Sentences: The Effect of Delay on Evidence and Sentence Length," *Journal of Verbal Learning and Verbal Behavior* 5 (October 1966), 492–496; Dan I. Slobin, "Grammatical Transformation and Sentence Comprehension in Childhood and Adulthood," *Journal of Verbal Learning and Verbal Behavior* 5 (June 1966), 219–227.

45. Percy, "Psycholinguistic Guidelines for Advertising."

46. Solomon E. Asch, *Social Psychology* (Englewood Cliffs, N.J.: Prentice-Hall, 1952), Chapter 8.

47. For research on how context can affect the way products are perceived, see Robert E. Kleine III and Jerome B. Kernan, "Contextual Influences on the Meanings Ascribed to Ordinary Consumption Objects," *Journal of Consumer Research* 18 (December 1991), 311–324.

48. Robert Johnson, "In the Chips," *Wall Street Journal* (March 22, 1991), B1–B2.

49. Jacob Jacoby and Wayne D. Hoyer, "Viewer Miscomprehension of Televised Communication: Selected Findings," *Journal of Marketing* 46 (Fall 1982), 12–26. Also see in this same journal issue Gary T. Ford and Richard Yalch, "Viewer Miscomprehension of Televised Communication: A Comment," 27–31; Richard W. Mizerski, "Viewer Miscomprehension Findings Are Measurement Bound," 32–34; Jacob Jacoby and Wayne D. Hoyer, "On Miscomprehending Televised Communication: A Rejoinder," 35–43. For an update, see "Warning: This Story Will Be Miscomprehended," *Marketing News* 21 (March 27, 1987), 1, 34. For research involving print communication, see Jacob Jacoby and Wayne D. Hoyer, "The Comprehension/Miscomprehension of Print Communication: Selected Findings," *Journal of Consumer Research* 15 (March 1989), 434–443.

50. Francine Schwadel, "Lowest-Price Claims in Ads Stir Dispute," *Wall Street Journal* (August 12, 1988), B1.

51. This figure comes from a study by Needham, Harper, and Steers as cited by Stephen J. Hoch and Young-Won Ha, "Consumer Learning: Advertising and the Ambiguity of Product Experience," *Journal of Consumer Research* 13 (September 1986), 221–233.

52. Rajeev Batra and Michael L. Ray, "Affective Responses Mediating Advertising Acceptance," *Journal of Consumer Research* 13 (September 1986), 234–249; George E. Belch, "The Effects of Television Commercial Repetition on Cognitive Response and Message Acceptance," *Journal of Consumer Research* 9 (June 1982), 56–63; Amitava Chattopadhyay and Joseph W. Alba, "The Situational Importance of Recall and Inference in Consumer Decision Making," *Journal of Consumer Research* 15 (June 1988), 1–12; Anthony G. Greenwald, "Cognitive Learning, Cognitive Response to Persuasion and Attitude Change," in Anthony G. Greenwald, Timothy C. Brock, and Thomas M. Ostrom, eds., *Psychological Foundations of Attitudes* (New York: Academic Press, 1968), 147–170; Manoj Hastak and Jerry C. Olson, "Assessing the Role of Brand-Related Cognitive Responses as Mediators of Communication Effects on Cognitive Structure," *Journal of Consumer Research* 15 (March 1989), 444–456; Jerry C. Olson, Daniel R. Toy, and Philip A. Dover, "Do Cognitive Responses Mediate the Effects of Advertising Content on Cognitive Structure?" *Journal of Consumer Research* 9 (December 1982), 245–262; Arno J. Rethans, John L. Swasy, and Lawrence J. Marks,

"Effects of Television Commercial Repetition, Receiver Knowledge, and Commercial Length: A Test of the Two-Factor Model," *Journal of Marketing Research* 23 (February 1986), 50–61; Daniel R. Toy, "Monitoring Communication Effects: A Cognitive Structure/Cognitive Response Approach," *Journal of Consumer Research* 9 (June 1982), 66–76; Peter Wright, "The Cognitive Processes Mediating Acceptance of Advertising," *Journal of Marketing Research* 10 (February 1973), 53–62.

53. Scott B. MacKenzie and Richard J. Lutz, "An Empirical Examination of the Structural Antecedents of Attitude-Toward-the-Ad in an Advertising Pretesting Context," *Journal of Marketing* 53 (April 1989), 48–65; Paul W. Miniard, Sunil Bhatla, Kenneth R. Lord, Peter R. Dickson, and H. Rao Unnava, "Picture-based Persuasion Processes and the Moderating Role of Involvement," *Journal of Consumer Research* 18 (June 1991), 92–107; Petty and Cacioppo, "The Elaboration Likelihood Model of Persuasion."

54. Richard E. Nisbett and Timothy D. Wilson, "Telling More Than We Can Know: Verbal Reports on Mental Processes," *Psychological Review* 84 (May 1977), 231–259; Peter Wright, "Message-Evoked Thoughts: Persuasion Research Using Thought Verbalizations," *Journal of Consumer Research* 7 (September 1980), 151–175; Raymond J. Smead, James B. Wilcox, and Robert E. Wilkes, "How Valid Are Product Descriptions and Protocols in Choice Experiments?" *Journal of Consumer Research* 8 (June 1981), 37–42.

55. David A. Aaker, Douglas M. Stayman, and Michael R. Hagerty, "Warmth in Advertising: Measurement, Impact, and Sequence Effects," *Journal of Consumer Research* 12 (March 1986), 365–381; Batra and Ray, "Affective Responses Mediating Acceptance of Advertising"; Marian Chapman Burke and Julie A. Edell, "The Impact of Feelings on Ad-Based Affect and Cognition," *Journal of Marketing Research* 26 (February 1989), 69–83; Julie A. Edell and Marian C. Burke, "The Power of Feelings in Understanding Advertising Effects," *Journal of Consumer Research* 14 (December 1987), 421–433; Meryl Paula Gardner, "Mood States and Consumer Behavior: A Critical Review," *Journal of Consumer Research* 12 (December 1985), 281–300; Morris B. Holbrook, "Emotion in the Consumption Experience: Toward a New Model of the Human Consumer," in Robert A. Peterson, Wayne D. Hoyer, and William R. Wilson, eds., *The Role of Affect in Consumer Behavior* (Lexington, Mass.: Heath, 1986), 17–52; Morris B. Holbrook and Rajeev Batra, "Assessing the Role of Emotions as Mediators of Consumer Responses to Advertising," *Journal of Consumer Research* 14 (December 1987), 404–420; Thomas J. Olney, Morris B. Holbrook, and Rajeev Batra, "Consumer Responses to Advertising: The Effects of Ad Content, Emotions, and Attitude toward the Ad on Viewing Time," *Journal of Consumer Research* 17 (March 1991), 440–453; Douglas M. Stayman and Rajeev Batra, "Encoding and Retrieval of Ad Affect in Memory," *Journal of Marketing Research* 28 (May 1991), 232–239; Patricia A. Stout and John D. Leckenby, "Measuring Emotion Response to Advertising," *Journal of Advertising* 15 (1986), 35–42; David M. Zeitlin and Richard A. Westwood, "Measuring Emotional Response," *Journal of Advertising Research* 26 (October/November 1986), 34–44.

56. Zeitlin and Westwood, "Measuring Emotional Response."

57. Batra and Ray, "Affective Responses Mediating Acceptance of Advertising."

58. Flemming Hansen, "Hemispheral Lateralization: Implications for Understanding Consumer Behavior," *Journal of Consumer Research* 8 (June 1981), 23–36; Chris Janiszewski, "The Influence of Nonattended Material on the Processing of Advertising Claims," *Journal of Marketing Research* 27 (August 1990), 263–278.

59. For research examining how hemispheric processing can influence advertising effectiveness, see the work of Chris Janiszewski cited in Footnotes 9 and 58. Also see

Michael L. Rothschild and Yong J. Hyun, "Predicting Memory for Components of TV Commercials from EEG," *Journal of Consumer Research* 16 (March 1990), 472–478.

60. Kevin McKean, "Of Two Minds: Selling the Right Brain," *Discover* 5 (April 1985), 30–40.

61. Lyle E. Bourne, Roger L. Dominowski, and Elizabeth F. Loftus, *Cognitive Processes* (Englewood Cliffs, N.J.: Prentice-Hall, 1979); Donald A. Norman, *Memory and Attention* (New York: John Wiley and Sons, 1969); Peter H. Lindsay and Donald A. Norman, *Human Information Processing* (New York: Academic Press, 1972); A. Newell and H. A. Simon, *Human Problem Solving* (Englewood Cliffs, N.J.: Prentice-Hall, 1972).

62. For more background, see Bourne, Dominowski, and Loftus, *Cognitive Processes*; Ulrich Neisser, *Cognitive Psychology* (New York: Appleton, 1966); Robert G. Crowsers, *Principles of Learning in Memory* (Hillsdale, N.J.: Lawrence Erlbaum, 1976); and Hershel W. Leibowitz and Lewis O. Harvey, Jr., "Perception," *Annual Review of Psychology* 24 (1973), 207–240.

63. Herbert A. Simon, "How Big Is a Chunk?" *Science* 183 (February 1974), 482–488; George A. Miller, "The Magical Number Seven, Plus or Minus Two: Some Limits on Our Capacity for Processing Information," *Psychological Review* 63 (March 1956), 81–97.

64. Richard M. Shiffrin and R. C. Atkinson, "Storage and Retrieval Processes in Long-Term Memory," *Psychological Review* 76 (March 1969), 179–193.

Psychological Processes

Efforts to influence consumer behavior should be grounded in an understanding of the psychological processes that shape learning, attitudes, and behavior. Part 4 examines these processes and how attitudes and behavior can be modified. The following full-color ads illustrate how psychological processes are considered in developing persuasive communications. Each one is accompanied by a brief description of the psychological process that shapes the ad.

Sometimes you have to get out and push a Range Rover.

There are, we admit, things in this world that can quite capably stop a Range Rover in its tracks.

Active tar pits. Brick walls. And yes, ten feet of water.

Beyond these, however, a Range Rover's spirited 3.9 liter V-8 engine, fully-articulated suspension system, and permanent four-wheel drive are designed to steer you through equally unpleasant, if far less far fetched, driving conditions.

From sleet and freezing rain, to the occasional blizzard and monsoon.

RANGE ROVER

In short, anything short of the impossible.

So why not call 1-800 FINE 4WD today for the dealer nearest you?

After all, for just under $39,000, you too could be driving off in a Range Rover.

And considering all that it has to offer, would you really want to be up the creek in anything less?

Information Processing

Answering the marketer's challenge to gain viewer attention, this Range Rover advertisement conjures a vision of adventure to be associated with the product.

Anti-Lock Brakes   *Traction Control*   *Front-Wheel Drive*

THE OLDSMOBILE EIGHTY EIGHT ROYALE LS HAS THREE ELEMENTS TO BEAT THE ELEMENTS.

We know that all your roads won't be sunny roads. That's why, when we re-engineered the Eighty Eight® Royale® LS, we gave it the intelligence to overcome the elements of rain, snow, sleet and ice. ‖ We call it Advanced Traction Engineering.™ Anti-lock brakes for more accurate stopping power; available traction control for slippery conditions; and the road-holding performance of front-wheel drive. In other words, the three elements to beat the elements. ‖ We also give you the Oldsmobile Edge.™ It's the most comprehensive owner satisfaction program in the industry. With it, you have the confidence of knowing you'll be taken care of...rain or shine. Visit your Oldsmobile® dealer for a test drive or call **1-800-242-OLDS**, Monday through Friday, 8 a.m.-7 p.m. EST.

EIGHTY EIGHT ROYALE LS

‖ Oldsmobile
THE POWER OF INTELLIGENT ENGINEERING

Cognitive Learning

Automobile marketers often rely on informational ads to increase customer awareness. Technical information is softened into nontechnical explanations of benefits. Such ads focus on cognitive learning processes.

Classical Conditioning

This advertisement illustrates the classical conditioning approach to learning. Sector associates strength, endurance, freedom of movement, and precision with their watches by the visual stimulus of a daring freeclimber.

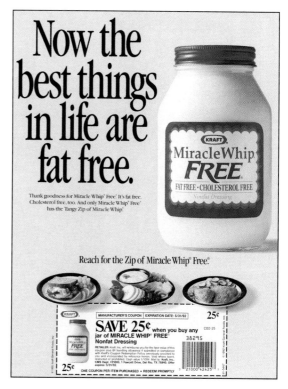

Operant Conditioning

Positive reinforcement in food product marketing is particularly competitive. A wary shopper can turn this 25 cent savings into a greater savings at stores offering double or triple coupon specials. Coupons attract both first-time and repeat buyers.

" In the Armed Forces, I earned a lot more than stripes... "

I also earned tuition assistance with the Montgomery GI Bill.

The GI Bill made higher education a reality for me. And it can for you too. By serving full-time in the Armed Forces, or part-time in the National Guard or Selected Reserves, you'll earn thousands of dollars in tuition assistance to help you get an education at an approved college, vocational or technical school.

But that's just part of the education, because in the Armed Forces you'll receive the kinds of skills, training and on-the-job experience that pay off, today and tomorrow. So if you're interested in the Montgomery GI Bill, call your local Armed Forces recruiter today.

U.S. ARMED FORCES

Influencing Attitudes and Behavior

The U.S. Armed Forces are neither a service nor a product, and yet they are marketed in a manner consistent with both. The strength of their beneficial claims are both tangible (money for college), and intangible (personal growth and experience). These strong claims encourage positive associations for the idea of joining.

14

Learning

"You've Got the Right One Baby, Uh-Huh!"
"I Love What You Do for Me."
"WOW! What a Difference."
"You Never Get a Second Chance to Make a First Impression."
"Sometimes You've Gotta Break the Rules."
"Just Do It."
"A Mind Is a Terrible Thing to Waste."

America has a bad case of ad nauseam. On any given day the average American is exposed to about 300 ad messages. That is 9,900 a month or 109,500 a year.

Little wonder that the clutter has helped create a case of national amnesia: Some 80 percent of Americans can't remember the typical commercial one day after they have seen it, according to Mapes & Ross, a company in Princeton, N.J., that measures advertising effectiveness.

That probably isn't such a bad thing. But it has inspired researchers to probe deeper than ever into the recesses of the brain on a quest for the Holy Grail of advertising: The secrets to making commercials memorable and effective.

Source: Excerpted from Michael J. McCarthy, "Mind Probe," *Wall Street Journal* (March 22, 1991), B3.

Why do consumers appear to have such a poor memory for advertising? Does failure to remember advertising mean that the advertising is ineffective? Are there ways to enhance the memorability of advertising?

425

Answers to these and other important questions must be founded in an understanding of how consumers learn. The significance of learning is captured by one simple but powerful observation: Consumer behavior is learned behavior. The tastes, values, beliefs, preferences, and habits that strongly influence consumers' shopping, purchase, and consumption behaviors are the result of prior learning. Consequently, an understanding of learning is an essential prerequisite for those responsible for diagnosing and influencing consumer behavior.

Learning is the process by which experience leads to changes in knowledge, attitudes, and/or behavior. This definition is quite broad in that it reflects the position of two major schools of thought about learning. One perspective on learning is known as the **cognitive approach**. Under this perspective, learning is reflected by changes in knowledge. Consequently, the focus is on understanding the mental processes that determine how people learn information (that is, how information is transferred to long-term memory).

In contrast, the **behaviorist approach** to learning is solely concerned with observable behaviors. Mental processes, which cannot be observed, and, thus, must be inferred are ignored under this approach. Rather, learning is shown by changes in behavior due to the development of associations between stimuli and responses.

Both approaches to learning are explored in this chapter. We begin with cognitive learning. This discussion is followed by an examination of two primary types of learning from the behaviorist perspective: classical and operant conditioning. Finally, we examine a hybrid type of learning, called vicarious learning, which combines elements of both the cognitive and behaviorist approaches.

Cognitive Learning

As indicated previously, mental processes are the focus under cognitive learning. These mental processes include a variety of activities ranging from the learning of information to problem solving. From this perspective, much of decision making can be viewed as cognitive learning in that such decisions essentially involve finding an acceptable solution to a consumption problem. Where should I spend my vacation? How should I go about selecting a doctor for the surgery I require? What is the best strategy for allocating my savings across the numerous investment options in today's financial markets? All of these represent problems that consumers must solve. Problem solving can also be important even after a purchase decision has been made. Trying to decipher the "easy-to-follow" instructions while assembling a product and understanding why a product breakdown occurs (Did I do something wrong or is this another instance of inferior craftsmanship?) are examples of postpurchase problem-solving activities in the consumer domain.

While acknowledging the importance of problem solving, this section focuses instead on the learning of information for a very important reason.[1] Quite simply, the objective of many marketing activities is to "implant" particular information within the consumer's mind. Sometimes this information takes the form of a brand name, store location, or upcoming sale. At other times marketers are interested in consumers retaining a particular image of their offering along one or more important dimensions (for example, the brand that claims to be the fastest and safest nonprescription relief available on the market).

Consequently, it is useful for us to understand how people learn information. Knowledge about those factors that influence cognitive learning can help marketers develop effective strategies for implanting the seeds of information within the garden of the mind. Two main determinants of learning are rehearsal and elaboration.

Rehearsal

Rehearsal involves the mental repetition of information or, more formally, the recycling of information through short-term memory. Some have described it as a form of inner speech.

Rehearsal serves two main functions. First, it allows for the maintenance of information in short-term memory. An example would be the rote repetition of a telephone number just acquired from a directory. Rehearsal is undertaken in order to keep the information activated long enough for the person to dial the number. The second function of rehearsal involves the transfer of information from short-term memory to long-term memory. Greater rehearsal will increase the strength of the long-term memory trace, thereby enhancing the likelihood that the trace can be later retrieved.

Elaboration

The degree of **elaboration** (that is, the amount of integration between the stimulus and existing knowledge) that occurs while a stimulus is processed will influence the amount of learning that takes place. At low levels of elaboration, a stimulus is processed in much the same form in which it is encountered. For instance, a person who wanted to remember a license plate numbered AJN-268 might encode this stimulus without any elaboration by simply repeating "A-J-N-2-6-8."

A more elaborate encoding of this license plate number could involve rearranging the letters into the name JAN, adding the numbers (which total 16), and then visualizing a 16-year-old girl named Jan. This in fact was the strategy a person reported using for remembering the license number of a car he witnessed leaving the scene of a bank robbery. After realizing he had seen the getaway car, he telephoned the police and gave them the license number. The suspects were apprehended, and he received a $500 reward.

Greater elaboration will generally lead to greater learning.[2] That is, the more a person elaborates upon a piece of information (or the more "deeply" it is processed), the greater the number of linkages that are formed between the new information and information already stored in memory. This in turn increases the number of avenues or paths by which the information can be retrieved from memory. In essence, the memory trace becomes more accessible given the greater number of pathways (linkages) that are available for retrieval. Many of the techniques suggested by memory experts and performers rely upon the benefits of elaboration.

FIGURE 14.1   **An Example of How an Ad Can Encourage Elaboration of the Company Name**

Although we will soon explore the different methods advertisers can use to enhance the memorability of their messages, at this point it is useful to acknowledge the advantages afforded by advertising that encourages elaboration. Quite simply, ads that encourage elaboration will be more memorable than those that don't. How can ads encourage elaboration? Consider Figure 14.1. Notice how the ad links the company name (Bull) to a word (formidable) likely to exist in the consumer's memory. Another example is the radio ad for an automotive parts supplier called Kar Part Outlet. This ad encouraged listeners to elaborate on the name by having the spokesperson say, "Kar, as in what you drive. Part, as in what you do to your hair. Outlet, as in what you stick a plug in."

The amount of elaboration that occurs during processing is strongly influenced by the person's motivation and ability.[3] Each of these is discussed below.

Motivation   A person's motivational state at the time of exposure to new information will have a considerable influence on what is remembered. Consider, for example, an automobile advertisement that is viewed by two consumers, one of whom is currently in the market for a new car. He or she would more actively process the ad, resulting in greater elaboration. Typically, the consumer more highly motivated during message processing will demonstrate greater learning than the less interested one.

This difference in learning depending on the level of motivation has been referred to as **directed** versus **incidental learning**.[4] Directed learning occurs when learning is the primary objective during information processing (for example, the student reading this text in preparation for the upcoming exam). Incidental learning, on the other hand, represents learning that occurs even when learning is not a processing objective (for example, the student flipping through a campus newspaper while waiting for class to begin). Research has consistently shown that increasing subjects' motivation to learn enhances their retention of material.

Ability   Knowledge is an important determinant of learning, as it enables the person to undertake more meaningful elaboration during information processing. In a classic study of how prior knowledge enhances learning, chess masters and novices were shown chess games in progress.[5] The masters generally held a substantial advantage over novices in remembering the board positions of the chess pieces. Interestingly, this superiority disappeared when subjects were exposed to games in which the pieces were randomly organized. Thus, the beneficial effect of knowledge materialized only when the information conformed to the person's organizational rules (that is, when the pieces' placement "made sense").

Even when knowledge is high, ability to process may still be low. This is because ability depends on both individual and environmental factors.[6] A knowledgeable consumer, for example, may be unable to engage in much elaboration of an ad appearing on TV if the room is filled with distractors (for example, a newborn crying for milk). Similarly, the aging process apparently reduces our learning abilities as suggested by a study reporting learning deficiencies among elderly consumers.[7]

Methods for Enhancing Retention

When consumers are both motivated and able to engage in elaboration during information processing, life for the marketer is much simpler. Efforts need be directed only toward ensuring that consumers are exposed to and accurately comprehend the information. However, consumers are often unwilling or unable to engage in much elaboration of marketing stimuli. When this occurs, efforts are needed for enhancing elaboration. Some of the ways in which this may be achieved are described subsequently.

Pictures   Researchers have only recently begun to examine the impact of stimuli that evoke mental imagery. While imagery can take many forms (for example, sight, smell, taste), visual imagery has been the focus of research thus far.[8] One obvious approach to activating visual imagery is the use of pictures. Two examples of providing visual representations of semantic concepts (in this case, brand names) are presented in Figure 14.2. The wisdom of this technique has been supported by research that indicates that the learning of brand names is greater when accompanied by pictorial representations.[9]

FIGURE 14.2 **Visual Representations Increase Retention of Brand Names**

Why do stimuli that elicit visual imagery have a facilitating effect on retention? One explanation rests upon the proposition that knowledge can be stored in both semantic and visual forms.[10] According to this perspective, information stored in both forms essentially doubles the pathways that can be traveled within memory for retrieving the information, relative to storage in only one form. While certainly plausible, some uncertainty exists over the validity of this explanation.[11] Nonetheless, the fact remains that stimuli that evoke imagery can provide marketers with a potent tool for enhancing learning.

An ad that capitalizes on visual imagery is presented in Figure 14.3. The woman's clothing, sofa pillows, as well as the material bordering the picture provide visual representations of the semantic concept "satin." Similarly, the television ad for Blue Polly car wax shows the product resting on the hood of a shiny blue automobile next to a blue parrot. Arctic Lights cigarette ads contain a cigarette package made out of ice. Ads for Firestone's Stones tires depict the brand name carved out of stone.

Whether pictures enhance memory for information in an advertisement will depend on their relationship to the ad copy. If the ad copy by itself evokes imagery, then pictures have less to offer than when the ad copy elicits little imagery. Research has shown greater recall when pictures are added to low imagery copy, but not when they are included in an ad containing high imagery copy.[12]

Concrete Words A less obvious approach to activating visual imagery is through the use of concrete words. **Concrete words**, such as tree or dog, are those that can be visualized easily. In contrast, **abstract words**, such as democracy or equality, do not lend themselves to a visual representation. Research has found that subjects exposed to a list of both concrete and abstract words will demonstrate greater retention of concrete words.[13]

FIGURE 14.3   An Ad That Encourages Visual Imagery Relevant to the Brand Name

The retention advantage of concrete words carries an important message for marketers. Far too often new products are introduced with rather abstract names. Consider, for instance, product names such as Actifed, Advil, Encaprin, and Nuprin, versus more concrete names such as Head and Throat, Easy Off, or Scrub Free. This lesson was learned by the Matex Corporation with its Rusty Jones rust-inhibitor product. Initially introduced as Thixo-Tex, the subsequent renaming of the product was one reason for sales climbing from $2 million in 1976 to about $100 million in 1980.[14]

Self-Referencing   Research in cognitive psychology indicates that learning is greater when subjects engage in self-referencing during processing. **Self-referencing** involves relating the information to one's own self and experiences. In a typical study, subjects are exposed to a series of words and asked whether each word describes them. These subjects exhibit greater recall than others who perform different tasks during information processing (for example, identify a synonym for the word).[15]

This facilitating effect of self-referencing is attributed to a more elaborate encoding of the stimulus information. The representation of the self in memory is believed to be a complex, highly organized structure that is activated by self-referencing. The use of this richer structure during encoding should enhance the number and strength of potential linkages that can be made between memory and the stimulus, which in turn increases the likelihood of retrieval.

Research supports the potential for encouraging self-referencing through advertising copy. This activation of self-referencing was achieved by using the word "you" and copy that prompted subjects to retrieve prior relevant product experiences. As expected, recall of the information from the ad was greater when the copy encouraged self-referencing.[16]

Mnemonic Devices

Quite often elaboration may be encouraged through simple mnemonic devices such as the use of rhymes. Brim coffee tells us to "fill it to the rim with Brim," while Shout stain remover asks us to "Shout it out." Similarly, B & B liqueur has encouraged elaboration of the brand name in advertisements that play on the name with phrases such as "B & Bewitch" and "B & Beloved" (see Figure 14.4).

Time-Compressed Speech

Technological advances have enabled advertisers to "compress" radio ads without distortion in speech or sound characteristics. For example, a 30-second ad can be reduced to 24 seconds. Initial research indicated that time-compressed ads can yield higher levels of recall than their longer counterparts, presumably because viewers are less likely to divert their attention elsewhere at this higher rate of information transmission.[17] More recent research, however, has been less supportive.[18] These studies have found time-compressed ads to be either equally or less effective than normally paced ads. Additional work is necessary to establish if and when time compression will be beneficial.

Repetition

When consumers are motivated and able to engage in meaningful elaboration during message processing, then only a single exposure to an advertisement may be necessary for the desired effect. Additional exposures will be desirable, however, if either motivation or ability is low. By continually repeating the message, marketers are increasing the odds that consumers will encounter it under more favorable circumstances.

A heavy reliance on repetition can be very desirable under a couple of conditions. When the communication conveys a large or complex set of information, consumers may be unable to comprehend fully the message during a single exposure, although this can depend on the type of medium in which the ad appears. Unlike radio and television ads, print ads can be processed at one's own rate and reprocessed if necessary. Thus, the additional opportunities for elaboration afforded by repetition may be more useful for ads appearing in broadcast than print media.

Repetition will also be more useful for some product categories than others. Many of the products consumers purchase at the grocery store, for instance, engender relatively low levels of involvement. Consequently, motivation to process intensively an ad will typically be quite limited. Marketers therefore employ repetition as a form of externally imposed rehearsal.

FIGURE 14.4   Enhancing Brand Name Memorability through Mnemonics

For these reasons, then, repetition is an important tool for enhancing learning. Indeed, a particular ad may rely heavily on repetition as reflected by the number of times the brand name or some other copy point is repeated throughout the ad. Ralston-Purina uses cats in TV commercials, for example, to repeat over and over the Meow Mix brand name. The same basic strategy was used in a television campaign for Rolaids antacid. The ads featured different persons being asked the question, "How do you spell relief?" Every time the person answered "R-O-L-A-I-D-S."

The facilitating effect of repetition has been well substantiated.[19] The standard research finding is that message learning will grow with additional exposures, although at a diminishing rate (that is, each successive exposure adds less than the preceding one). However, the effectiveness of repetition may depend on the level of competitive advertising. One study reports that repetition enhanced recall when competitive advertising was minimal or nonexistent. This effect disappeared, however, under higher levels of competitive advertising.[20]

It is also evident that too much repetition can have adverse effects. That is, after a certain number of repetitions, additional repetitions may reduce advertising

When Ads Wear Out Their Welcome

"April in Paris" may never be the same. Thanks to a commercial that has run over and over again for Maxwell House Rich French Roast coffee, the classic song and all-too-familiar sales pitch ("He spoke English like I spoke French") are chiseled into the minds of daytime television viewers. But for ad executives, a key question remains unanswered: Is this commercial still selling coffee?

Advertising has always relied on repetition to hammer a message home. But viewers simply don't watch commercials that are too familiar, and money spent to air them continually is wasted, says Karl Rosenberg, vice president of Research Systems Corp., an advertising testing firm. He argues agencies are playing it safe instead of smart, by relying on ads that were once effective but are now just plain stale.

Researchers point to a multitude of overused ads such as the one for Kaopectate, in which a wife meets her husband's plane and his first words to her are about diarrhea. In a much-aired spot for "I Can't Believe It's Not Butter," violins swell as a couple falls in love with margarine. And then there are entire categories that have grown tired, such as ads for local car dealerships with the predictable balloon-filled showrooms and tuxedo-clad men touting rebates.

Mr. Rosenberg says his research on tired ads offers a rule of thumb: after a given commercial accumulates 1,000 gross ratings points—the sum of all the ratings that a commercial gets based on the programs in which it appears—it loses half its effectiveness. At the 1,000 mark, an ad has reached some 42 percent of all U.S. households with TV sets at least 10 times.

Source: Excerpted from Laura Bird, "Researchers Criticize Overuse of Ads," *Wall Street Journal* (January 3, 1992), B3.

effectiveness. This phenomenon is called **advertising wearout**[21] and is the topic of Consumer in Focus 14.1.

Wearout can occur for two reasons. First, consumers may simply quit attending to an ad after a certain number of exposures. Alternatively, consumers may continue to pay attention, but they become more argumentative as a result of the tedium of seeing the same ad over and over.[22]

A simple solution to the wearout problem is the use of ads that differ in their executional strategies but that carry the same basic message.[23] The ad campaign for Energizer batteries featuring the drum-banging pink bunny consists of more than

20 commercials. Not to be outdone, competitor Duracell has developed more than 40 spots in which different battery-operated toys are shown to run longer when powered by a Duracell battery.[24] While additional expenses are incurred from the production of multiple ads, this cost may be a worthwhile investment for reducing the problems of advertising wearout.

Forgetting

Before reading past this sentence, stop and write down all of the brands of toothpaste you can remember. Once you have done this, consider the following set of toothpaste brands: Aim, Aquafresh, Check Up, Close Up, Colgate, Crest, Gleem, Pearl Drops, Pepsodent, Sensodyne, Topco, Topol, Ultrabrite, and Zact. It is probably safe to wager that you did not recall all of the brands just listed. It is also probably a safe bet that you did not write down some brands that you in fact "know" as reflected by your recognition of these names while reading the list.

Why, then, did you forget brands that are familiar to you? Two explanations have been offered for the lack of **retrieval**, defined as the process by which knowledge stored in long-term memory is activated.

The Role of Decay
It is well known that forgetting and time go hand in hand. The ability to retrieve learned information declines with the passage of time. According to **decay theory**, the strength of a memory trace will fade over time. Retrieval failure will occur when the trace lacks sufficient strength.

However, research has shown that forgetting may differ even when the influence of time is held constant. For example, forgetting will be much lower when the time is spent sleeping than if the person spends the same time awake.[25]

The Role of Interference
According to **interference theory**, forgetting is due to the learning of new information over time. One form of interference, where recently learned information inhibits the retrieval of previously learned information, is known as **retroactive inhibition**. Interference can also take the form of **proactive inhibition**, where prior learning hinders the learning and retrieval of new information. Both forms of inhibition were detected in an advertising study that reported that recall of the information presented in an ad was impaired when subjects were also exposed to ads for competitive products that either preceded (proactive inhibition) or followed (retroactive inhibition) the ad to be remembered.[26]

From this perspective, information can be available in memory (that is, the memory trace is of sufficient strength) and yet not be retrieved because of limitations in its accessibility. All of us have experienced situations where we have tried unsuccessfully to remember something, only to have it "pop" into our mind some time later. Similarly, hypnosis has been used to facilitate the retrieval of "lost" memories. This distinction between availability and accessibility has been supported by research showing that information that appeared to be forgotten could, in fact, be subsequently retrieved when subjects were provided with certain retrieval cues.[27]

The issue of information accessibility is particularly important to marketers. The influence of advertising, for instance, can depend on the consumer's ability to retrieve information from an ad seen some time ago while shopping at a store. More generally, research has suggested that consumers' product attitudes[28] and choices[29] may heavily depend on what information is retrieved from memory.

Two major determinants of information accessibility are (1) the amount of information stored in memory within the same "content domain" and (2) the particular retrieval cues available at the time.[30] The more brand names a consumer "knows," for instance, the more difficulty he or she will have in retrieving a particular name due to the greater number of competing responses.

Retrieval can be enhanced by the cues that are present at the time of such activity. Retrieval cues can be either self-generated or externally generated. In trying to retrieve a particular brand name, one might try to reconstruct the situation in which the product was last seen or used. A picture of the celebrity spokesperson who is strongly associated with the product may also trigger retrieval of the brand name.

Retrieval cues can help overcome one of the challenges to advertising effectiveness that arises from the time delay that typically occurs between ad exposure and product choice. An ad may elicit a very positive reaction from consumers sitting in their living rooms but have little influence on consumers who fail to remember the ad when making their choices at the point of purchase. In such cases, enhancing the retrieval of the ad information would be desirable.

One possible method for increasing consumers' memory for advertising is the use of retrieval cues at the point of purchase. An example of this comes from the popular Quaker Oats' "Mikey" commercial for its Life brand of cereal. For many years, the company placed a picture of one of the commercial's scenes in the lower right-hand corner of the product package. This cue would presumably serve as a prompt to help the consumer remember the ad.

The wisdom of this strategy has been supported in both laboratory and field settings. As expected, the presence of such cues enhances recall of an ad's claims. Moreover, given the favorable nature of the recalled information, the cues also led to more positive brand evaluations.[31] Similarly, the Campbell Soup Company reports that sales increased by 15 percent when point-of-purchase materials were directly related to television advertising.[32]

Although marketers typically are interested in enhancing consumers' abilities to retrieve information, there may be situations where they wish to achieve just the opposite—that is, to reduce the retrieval of information. Consider the situation where a consumer might normally consider four alternative brands during decision making. One approach a brand might adopt for gaining a competitive advantage would entail inhibiting the consumer's ability to recall one or more of the remaining brands. How could this inhibition be achieved?

Research has revealed that increasing the salience of a brand (that is, its prominence in short-term memory) will interfere with the retrieval of other brands within the same product category.[33] For instance, increasing a brand's salience by exposure to an ad for that brand was found to lower the number of recalled brands, including those brands that consumers would consider buying with one exception—it did not inhibit recall of whichever brand was most preferred by consumers. This inability to undermine consumers' retrieval of their preferred brand does reduce the potential value of marketing efforts to induce interference.

Measures of Cognitive Learning

The two major approaches to measuring cognitive learning are **recognition** and **recall**. Whereas recognition measures provide the person with some type of cue to prompt memory, this is not the case for recall measures. For example, asking a student on an exam to define the concept of elaboration would represent a recall measure. A recognition measure would involve asking the student to identify the correct definition from a set of possible answers.

Recognition tests generally reflect greater learning than recall measures, although there are exceptions.[34] Similarly, forgetting appears to occur more slowly when measured by recognition. This "superiority" of recognition measures is attributable to the additional retrieval cues inherent in such measures.

The Use of Learning Measures in Advertising
Recognition and recall are often used to evaluate advertising's effectiveness. There are a number of measurement versions that pose different degrees of retrieval difficulty.

Simple recognition measures involve presenting ads to people and asking them whether or not they remember seeing the ad previously.[35] This measure will yield the highest estimate of learning, since the presence of the original stimulus is a very strong retrieval cue. One problem with this approach is the potential for overestimating the amount of retention. People have been found to claim recognition of bogus ads that they could not possibly have seen before.[36]

Forced-choice recognition measures, on the other hand, offer a more realistic and informative appraisal of ad memory.[37] This approach focuses on the memorability of particular ad and brand elements, thus allowing a more detailed analysis of what is retrieved. In addition, respondents are forced to choose among a set of fixed answers in responding to questions about a specific element, much like a multiple-choice exam.

Alternatively, recall measures may be used as indicators of learning.[38] Recall measures differ in their use of retrieval cues. **Aided recall measures** (for example, "Do you remember the brand of soft drink advertised during last night's broadcast of the Academy Awards?") provide such cues. **Unaided recall measures** (for example, "Name all of the brands you have seen advertised during the past 24 hours") do not.

One of the most frequently used recall measures is the **demonstrated recall measure** developed by Burke, a major marketing research firm. The day after an ad has aired, households in the area are contacted by phone until 200 "qualified" persons (that is, those watching the program) are located. Each person is then asked to recall both the name of the advertised product and one copy point. The average Burke score is around 24 percent.[39]

Learning Measures: Are They Appropriate Indicators of Advertising Effectiveness? In the early stages of the product life cycle, establishing brand name awareness is a major objective of the promotion mix. Measures that tap brand name learning are very useful in determining whether this objective is being achieved. Similarly, cognitive learning measures are valuable indicators for evaluating advertising aimed at educating consumers about the brand's properties or uses.

In contrast, cognitive learning measures may have very little to say about an ad's impact on consumer attitudes. The fact that consumers can *remember* the claims made in an ad does not mean that they *believe* the claims. Obnoxious ads can be very memorable, but they may also have a negative effect on viewers' attitudes. Research has shown that recall alone may have very little relationship with attitude.[40] Thus, when an important objective of advertising is to influence product preferences, it is necessary to go beyond cognitive learning measures and assess brand attitudes.

Another concern with the validity of ad memory measures as indicators of ad effectiveness is the implicit assumption reflected in the chapter opener: an ad must be remembered before it can have an influence. If a person is unable to recall an ad, has the advertising been wasted? We don't think so. It seems quite possible for advertising to have an effect without establishing a strong link in the consumer's mind between the product and the ad itself. Certainly all of us retain certain bits and pieces of product knowledge as a result of prior advertising and yet cannot identify the source of such knowledge.

This is not to say that having such a linkage is undesirable. Indeed, as reported in Consumer in Focus 14.1, activating this linkage through retrieval cues can be very beneficial. We are saying that the "jury is still out" on the role of ad memory as a necessary prerequisite for ad impact.

Recognition or Recall: Which One? When learning measures are appropriate, one is faced with the choice of whether to rely on recognition or recall measures. It has been suggested that this choice should be based on whether brand recognition or brand recall is the important retrieval process during decision making.[41] Very often consumers make their choices within a retail environment filled with retrieval cues (for example, the product's packaging). However, when recognition is not a viable option, such as decision making that occurs at home (for example, the consumer deciding which restaurant to patronize), then brand name recall must be the focus.[42]

This decision can have a strong impact on the efficiency of advertising expenditures.[43] Dollars are likely to be wasted if only brand recognition is needed and brand recall is used as the advertising objective. This is because it will typically require fewer exposures (and hence dollars) to achieve a certain level of recognition than needed to reach the same level of recall.

Classical Conditioning

As noted in the beginning of the chapter, cognitive learning is but one of the ways in which learning occurs. The building of stimulus-response associations can also

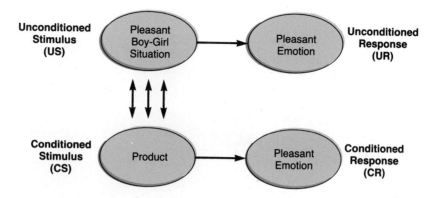

FIGURE 14.5 **The Classical Conditioning Approach to Influencing Product Attitudes**

lead to learning. The development of these associations is the focus of classical conditioning.

For many, the term *classical conditioning* elicits thoughts of Pavlov and his dogs. Pavlov, the father of classical conditioning, demonstrated this type of learning through the following procedures. First, an existing stimulus-response relationship is selected, such as food, referred to as the **unconditioned stimulus** (US), which elicits salivation, referred to as the **unconditioned response** (UR). A new stimulus, called the **conditioned stimulus** (CS), such as a bell, is then paired repeatedly with the food. Eventually, the conditioned stimulus will elicit a response, called the **conditioned response** (CR), that is quite similar to the response originally generated by the unconditioned stimulus.

Figure 14.5 presents the basic classical conditioning framework within a product context.[44] In this example, a boy-girl situation that elicits a pleasant emotion is paired with a product in the hope that these favorable feelings can be conditioned to the product. Thus, classical conditioning represents one mechanism by which attitude formation follows an affective-based rather than a cognitive-based process. This basic framework is illustrated by the ad appearing in Figure 14.6.

This simple principle of association between two objects or stimuli underlies much of today's advertising. A prime example is a scene from a Pepsi television commercial featuring a young boy playing with a pack of exuberant puppies. The pleasurable and warm emotions elicited by this scene will presumably generalize by association to the product. Similarly, retailers recognize the value of playing Christmas carols in order to evoke feelings that help overcome sales resistance.[45]

In product markets where competitive brands are virtually the same, it may be impossible to achieve brand differentiation through emphasizing product attributes. Differentiation may be possible, however, by conditioning brand attitudes through stimuli that evoke favorable responses. Accordingly, advertising in product categories comprised of fairly homogeneous offerings (for example, beer, cigarettes, liquor) often rely on a classical conditioning approach.

FIGURE 14.6   Using Classical Conditioning in Advertising to Create a Favorable Attitude toward the Product

Determinants of Classical Conditioning

Simply pairing a US with a product (that is, CS) does not guarantee that classical conditioning will occur. Indeed, as described subsequently, there are a number of factors that will influence the effectiveness of any efforts to induce conditioning.[46]

US Strength   The strength of the US will partly determine the amount of conditioning. By strength, we refer to the intensity of the feelings elicited by the US. A stronger US can enhance conditioning. When the US is weak, it may not be possible to induce conditioning.

There is, of course, considerable diversity among stimuli in their strength. In an interesting study of "thrills" (tingling sensations that occur in response to emotionally arousing stimuli), respondents were asked to indicate how often they experienced thrills for a variety of stimuli. Virtually everyone reported thrills for music, two-thirds had experienced thrills while viewing a beautiful painting, while parades elicited thrills from only one-fourth of the respondents.[47]

Number of Pairings   Just as repetition can play a major role in cognitive learning, it will also influence the degree of classical conditioning. Conditioning has been found for product preferences after a single CS-US pairing.[48] Even so, additional pairings are likely to be needed for maximum effectiveness. It has been suggested that as many as 30 pairings may be required for conditioning product preferences.[49]

CS-US Order   Conditioning can also depend on the order in which the CS and US are presented. There are three possible orders. **Forward conditioning** is when the CS precedes the US. **Backward conditioning** is when the US precedes the CS. Finally, presenting the CS and US at the same time is known as **simultaneous conditioning**.

Although conditioning may occur using any of these orders, forward conditioning appears to be the most effective.[50] This carries several implications for advertising practice. Suppose you were developing a TV ad that includes a well-liked musical tune. When should this tune (US) appear relative to the product (CS)? Superior results are expected when product presentation precedes rather than follows the tune or when the product is presented simultaneously with the tune.

It has also been suggested that some media are better suited for classical conditioning advertising because they allow more control of the order in which the US and CS are processed.[51] Broadcast channels (TV, radio) provide such control, while print media (magazines, billboards) do not. Simply because the product is positioned at the top of a page with the US appearing at the bottom does not guarantee that the viewer will process these stimuli in the desired order. The US may easily be viewed first. For this reason, then, print media may be less effective avenues for classical conditioning advertising.

Familiarity   Prior familiarity or experience with a stimulus can undermine conditioning.[52] A well-known song, for instance, may be less effective than a tune created specifically for the product (although this weakness in using a popular song may be more than offset by other considerations, such as greater liking for the music).

Similarly, classical conditioning may be more effective for new than existing products. Support for this proposition comes from research showing greater conditioning for unfamiliar brands.[53]

Elaboration   It has also been suggested that the degree of cognitive elaboration during message processing will moderate the impact of classical conditioning.[54] Classical conditioning is believed to occur only under low levels of issue-relevant thinking, such as when consumers are relatively uninvolved during message processing. Presumably, the presence of extensive issue-relevant thinking will override any possible effects of classical conditioning. However, this possibility has yet to be examined empirically.

Extinction

Extinction occurs when the conditioned stimulus no longer evokes the conditioned response. A classically conditioned response does not simply disappear over time. Rather, it will disappear when the relationship between the CS and US is broken.

How is the CS-US relation broken? One way is for the CS to be encountered *without* the US. Suppose a company uses classical conditioning in an ad by pairing music with the product. Encountering the product without the music will reduce the effectiveness of this ad. Accordingly, advertising that does not pair the product with the US will undermine advertising that does.

Many products, such as cars and clothing, are seen more frequently outside of commercials than other types of products, such as soaps and laundry detergents. These encounters encourage extinction since the CS (product) is seen without the US. Classical conditioning should therefore be better for less frequently encountered products.

Just as contact with the CS without the US will enhance extinction, so too will contact with the US without the CS. The Pepsi commercials featuring Hammer and his music suffer from this limitation. That is, many consumers will encounter Hammer and his music in situations where Pepsi is not present. This will encourage extinction. Consequently, "novel" unconditioned stimuli may often be preferable to familiar or popular ones, since the former are less likely to be encountered without the CS. Despite this limitation, the use of Hammer is very appropriate when we consider his strength as a US (that is, he can elicit very strong favorable reactions from many young consumers). Indeed, it is important to keep in mind that a stimulus, while deficient on one factor, can be very effective for inducing conditioning because of other factors that more than offset some limitation.

Generalization

Generalization occurs when, for an existing stimulus-response relationship, a new stimulus that is very similar to the existing one elicits the same response. In Pavlov's experiments, for instance, a noise that was very similar to the bell would evoke the salivation response.

Companies sometimes use generalization in the form of **family branding** by placing the same brand name on its different products. General Electric does so in the hope that consumers will generalize the favorable feelings developed toward one GE product to another.

There is currently a trend toward positioning new products as product-line extensions rather than developing separate brand identities.[55] Through consumer research, it was discovered that the Dole brand name, while traditionally associated with the fresh and canned fruit sections of a supermarket, could also work in the frozen section as well. This led to the launch of Dole Fruit & Juice Bars and other frozen desserts.[56] Other examples of this strategy include Crest Tartar Control, Duncan Hines cookies, Ivory Shampoo, Cherry 7Up, and Liquid Tide. Nabisco Brands also reaped the benefits of generalization when the company changed the name of its new offering from Apple Bars to Apple Newtons, a change that facilitated consumers connecting the product with the company's well established Fig Newtons brand. This trend is driven primarily by financial considerations. The cost of establishing a new brand name has been estimated between $50 million to $150 million, an expense far greater than incurred by extending an established name to a new product.[57]

Recognize, however, that a family branding strategy may not always be the best course of action. Separate brand identities are desirable for a company wishing to market products of varying quality. Gallo was concerned about the possibility that their new line of wine coolers would dilute the quality image of their wines' brand

Do Consumers Generalize Based on Color?

Do consumers generalize from one product to another based simply on the color of product packaging? The NutraSweet Company, manufacturer of the sugar substitute Equal, apparently thinks so. In 1989, the company filed suit against a major competitor for using a similar pastel shade of blue in the packaging for a new product named Sweet One. The company hoped to receive trademark protection for its packaging color, just as the Owens-Corning Corporation was granted a trademark for the pink color used to dye its fiberglass insulation.

The courts held a different opinion. According to the appeals court:

If each of the competitors presently in the tabletop sweetener market were permitted to appropriate a particular color for its product, new entrants would be deterred from entering the market. The essential purpose of trademark law is to prevent confusion, not to bar new entrants into the market.

Source: "Court Refuses Trademark for Package Color," *Marketing News* 25 (May 27, 1991), 25.

name. Consequently, the wine coolers were given a separate identity—Bartles & Jaymes.

In some cases, manufacturers try to encourage generalization through product packaging that is very similar to a leading competitor's packaging. This is the so-called **me-too product**. A soup manufacturer may produce a red and white can that is very similar to the Campbell's soup can. This use of generalization is intended to evoke the same favorable response that is typically associated with the Campbell's brand. Indeed, it is surprising just how often this form of generalization happens in the marketplace (see Consumer in Focus 14.2).

Consumers may also generalize between competitive products that possess very similar names (for example, Muffler King versus Speedy Muffler King, Country Inn versus Cross Country Inn). Legal battles often result in such situations. The Adolph Coors Brewing Company brought suit against the soft drink manufacturer of Corr's Natural Beverages on grounds that the names are indistinguishable to a substantial number of consumers.[58] Similarly, McDonald's filed suits against McTravel Travel Services and McSleep Hotels for infringing on the company name.[59]

Discrimination

Discrimination is the process whereby an organism learns to emit a response to one stimulus, but avoids making the same response to a similar stimulus. Using classical

FIGURE 14.7 **Canon Wants Consumers to Discriminate between Their Offering and Competing Brands**

conditioning, discrimination can be encouraged by pairing a positive US with one CS but not another CS. Conditioning should occur only for the CS paired with the US. Even greater discrimination could be encouraged by pairing the second CS (for example, a competitor's product) with a negative US.

Discrimination is obviously an important concept in marketing. As reflected by the ad shown in Figure 14.7, companies usually want consumers to distinguish between their products and those of competitors. When discrimination is desired, it is typically best achieved through endowing the product with unique benefits or features. While this may often be possible, sometimes it is not. As indicated by the beer label study described in Chapter 13 on information processing, consumers could not distinguish between various brands in blind taste tests.[60] When brands are fairly homogeneous, marketers must search for other means of differentiating their products.

A classic marketing example of discrimination on dimensions other than the product's benefits is the Goodrich advertising campaign of many years ago. Goodrich had discovered that many consumers did not distinguish between its name and

Rollerblade Wants Brand Name Discrimination

Rollerblade is not a verb or a noun, but a proper name for the company that has become America's trendiest vocabulary word. Since the Rollerblade name was coined in 1980 by two Minneapolis hockey players who developed a pair of in-line skates for off-season training, the name has become almost synonymous with the sport.

But by becoming too well known, the Minneapolis-based company that made in-line skating epitomize coolness could become too big for its skates and become a victim of the dreaded "genericide." To avoid becoming like a host of other words that were once company names but lost their trademark, Rollerblade Inc. is actively trying to avoid becoming the generic term for in-line skating.

If anyone uses Rollerblade in print as a general term or as a verb for in-line skating, the company sends a letter outlining correct usage, says spokesperson Mary Haugen. If an in-line skate manufacturer uses the term Rollerblade in any form with its product, it receives several warning letters and faces possible legal action.

It's "a great form of flattery when something becomes *the* word," but when a company loses its trademark, other companies can cash in on the name by using it to market their own products, says Michael Finn, communications manager for the U.S. Trademark Association. Finn also points out that if the courts were to declare Rollerblade a generic term for in-line skating "they will have lost a great marketing impetus."

Source: Excerpted from Carrie Goerne, "Rollerblade Reminds Everyone that Its Success is Not Generic," *Marketing News* 26 (March 2, 1992), 1–2.

that of a major competitor, Goodyear. Indeed, when exposed to Goodrich advertising, some consumers mistakenly perceived it as advertising for Goodyear. Consequently, it became critical for Goodrich to combat this confusion. This was accomplished by using the well-known Goodyear blimp in the campaign slogan "We're the one without the blimp."

Discrimination is also very important in the domain of brand name protection (see Consumer in Focus 14.3). Marketers that fail to encourage brand name discrimination run the risk of losing their trademarks. Courts can rule that a name has passed into the public domain (that is, the trademark is revoked) when it has become so common or generic that it has lost its specific meaning. Examples of lost trademarks include aspirin, cellophane, corn flakes, cube steak, dry ice, escalator, kerosene, linoleum, raisin bran, shredded wheat, shuttle, thermos, and yo-yo.[61]

PLEASE DON'T FOOL AROUND WITH OUR NAME.

Every now and then, the most confusing conversation in the world takes place. Here it is.
"Let's Federal Express it."
"Okay. Who should we use?"
"Let's just Federal Express it."
"Okay. Who should we use?"
Please. "Federal Express" is not a phrase that refers to anybody and everybody in the over-night package business.
Federal Express is a name. Our name. In fact, our trademark. Which is why when you ask for Federal Express, you should get no one but Federal Express. A single, specific air express com-pany that happens to deliver more packages to more places overnight than any other air express company. And, for the last ten years, has earned its reputation as the most reliable in the business.
So, let's make a deal.
We'll try not to lose your packages.
Please try not to misplace our name.

FEDERAL EXPRESS
WHY FOOL AROUND WITH ANYONE ELSE?
"Federal Express" is a registered trademark of the Federal Express Corporation.
©1984 Federal Express Corporation.

FIGURE 14.8   Federal Express Is Encouraging Brand Name Discrimination

Firms are sometimes hired to monitor a name's use in public and take appropriate actions when potential problems arise (for example, one firm reports writing a letter to Johnny Carson about the difference between cat box filler and Kitty Litter). The Federal Express ad appearing in Figure 14.8 encourages consumers to discriminate between their company and competitors by not using their name in a generic sense.

Operant Conditioning

While shopping at the grocery store, a consumer notices a new brand of cereal and decides to buy it. The next morning she gives it a try and is very satisfied with the taste. She likes it so much that she makes a mental note to pick up another box during her next shopping trip.

Positive Reinforcement

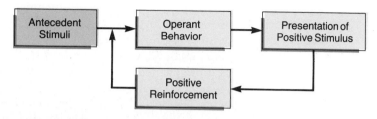

Negative Reinforcement

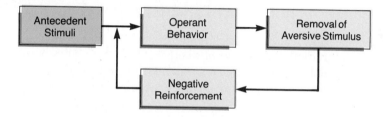

Punishment

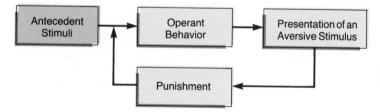

FIGURE 14.9   **Three Forms of Operant Conditioning**

Source: Adapted from Stanley M. Widrick, "Concept of Negative Reinforcement Has Place in Classroom," *Marketing News* 20 (July 18, 1986), 48–49.

This simple example illustrates how learning can occur as a result of **operant conditioning**. This form of conditioning, also called **instrumental learning**, is concerned with how the *consequences* of a behavior will affect the frequency or probability of the behavior being performed again. The satisfaction experienced by the consumer while eating the cereal increased the odds of repeat purchase. On the other hand, repeat purchasing would be unlikely if the cereal failed to satisfy the consumer.

Figure 14.9 reveals that consequences can affect behavior (called the operant behavior in the jargon of this literature) in one of three ways. To illustrate these distinctions, consider a typical operant conditioning experiment where a pigeon is placed in a cage containing a bar that, when pressed, produces some consequence. Under **positive reinforcement**, pressing the bar (the operant behavior) leads to receiving some positive stimulus (for example, food). Under **negative reinforcement**, bar pressing leads to the removal of some adverse stimulus (for example, stopping a low-level electrical shock). In both cases, the pigeon is more likely to repeat the behavior in the future. In contrast, **punishment** would reduce the odds of the behavior occurring again. In this case, pressing the bar would cause the appearance of an adverse stimulus (for example, a shock).

Although there may be occasions where marketers will employ punishers (for example, revoking a product warranty for failing to adhere to the maintenance schedule), reinforcement is the major focus of interest from a marketing perspective. In the following sections we examine the various reinforcers available for modifying consumer behavior and factors that influence their effectiveness.

Reinforcement from Product Consumption

The degree to which reinforcement occurs as a result of product consumption is a critical determinant of whether the product will be purchased again. Products that deliver reinforcement are more likely to be repurchased. Repeat purchasing is unlikely when product use does not reinforce the consumer or, even worse, punishes the consumer (for example, a lighter that explodes during use). The level of reinforcement provided by products can, and should, be monitored through the use of satisfaction measures, a topic considered in our later chapter on purchase and its outcomes.

Types of Product Reinforcement
Products differ in whether they provide positive or negative reinforcement.[62] For example, a consumer may eat candy because of the positive sensory experiences that result from this action. In contrast, eye drops might be used to remove the adverse feelings due to burning, irritated eyes. It is possible for a product to deliver both positive and negative reinforcement. An air freshener can replace odors (negative reinforcement) with a refreshing smell (positive reinforcement).

The type of reinforcement provided by a product can influence consumer behavior. Consumers are less likely to enjoy buying and using negative reinforcement products. Consequently, they will often spend less time and effort in buying these products.[63] This in turn limits a product's opportunity to break through the clutter of competitive brands and gain the consumer's consideration.

Marketers of negative reinforcement products should recognize the existence of three distinct consumer segments for their product. Obviously, consumers currently experiencing the problem solved by the product are the primary segment. Consumers who formerly suffered from the problem comprise a segment that may be receptive to appeals that encourage product use to ensure that the problem will not recur. Even consumers who have not faced the problem may be a viable segment. It might be possible to encourage product use as a means of reducing the odds that consumers would ever experience the problem, such as the consumer who takes aspirin daily because of its potential for reducing heart problems.

Product Reinforcement without Product Purchase
According to one old saying, "You can't get something for nothing." But what about getting something for almost

FIGURE 14.10 **Offering Consumers the Opportunity of Product Trial without Purchase**

nothing? The makers of Unisom offered consumers a free packet of their product if they mailed in the request form shown in Figure 14.10. In this same figure you will find an ad from the Apple Computer, Inc. which offered consumers the opportunity to take home and try a Macintosh.

Offering consumers the opportunity to try a product without having to buy it is a common occurrence in the marketplace, particularly when companies are introducing new products. When Duncan Hines was rolling out their new brand of cookies, target households received free samples in the mail. Similarly, when Coca-Cola developed the new versions of Coke, it arranged for packages containing single cans of the various brand extensions to be delivered to the consumer's doorstep. Food manufacturers also recognize the advantages of having someone pass out bite-sized servings of their products to shoppers strolling the aisles of supermarkets.

Why do companies incur the expense and trouble of doing this? Because it pays off. As suggested by the headline for the car ad shown in Figure 14.11, getting consumers to simply try a product, thereby enabling them to appreciate the reinforcement derived from consumption more fully, often enhances the odds of

FIGURE 14.11 **This Ad Provides Testimony to the Benefits of Offering Free Product Trial**

purchase. Further testimony of the benefits that can come from providing consumers a free product trial.

Further support for the effectiveness of providing free trial comes from research testing the impact of delivering free samples when rolling out a new product. Figure 14.12 summarizes the findings based on eight new product introduction tests conducted by National Panel Diary, a market research firm, in which one group of consumers received a free sample while another group did not.[64] The impact of free samples is reflected by a comparison of the two groups. The top graph in Figure 14.12 represents the results involving initial or trial purchasing. As can be seen, nearly 50 percent more households receiving a free sample engaged in initial purchasing relative to control households (that is, those not receiving a free sample). Moreover, as represented by the bottom graph in Figure 14.12, those who purchased after receiving the free sample were slightly more likely to buy it again. Overall, free samples yielded a penetration level of 5.7 percent after 6 months (trial rate of 16.0 percent times the repurchase rate of 35.7 percent) compared to a level of 3.6 percent when free samples were not used.

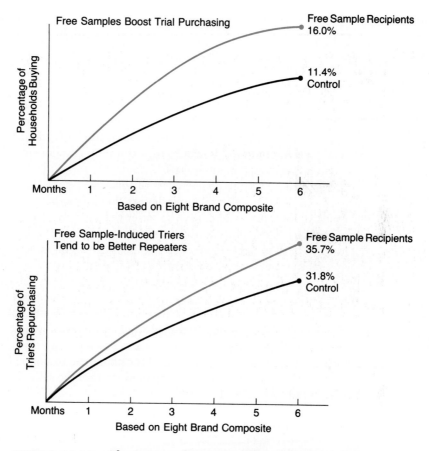

FIGURE 14.12   The Impact of Free Samples on Purchase Behavior

Nonproduct Reinforcement

While the degree of reinforcement a consumer experiences from using the product is critical, reinforcement can also be delivered in many other forms (see Consumer in Focus 14.4). Fast food restaurants often employ the tactic of including a small gift in children's meals for reinforcing the child who, in turn, influences Mom and Dad. MCL, a cafeteria-style restaurant, provides parents with a token that the child can use in a machine that dispenses small toys. Even adults can be the target of such reinforcers. The Sunflower Chinese restaurant in Columbus often bestows complimentary chocolate mints to their regular patrons.

Thanks for the Business

Perhaps one of the most underappreciated forms of reinforcement is to simply thank customers for their patronage. Many companies show this concern by sending new customers "thank you" notes. Similarly, the phrase "We thank you for your support" has become a common component of the Bartles & Jaymes wine cooler commercials.

Evidence of the effectiveness of thank you notes comes from a recent study of new life insurance purchasers. Following each monthly payment, some of the customers received a letter thanking them for their recent payment. Less than 9 percent of this customer group canceled their policy during the 6-month test period. In contrast, the cancellation rate of those customers not receiving this reinforcement was 23 percent.

Additional testimony to the power of thanking customers comes from a jewelry store that employed this tactic. After experiencing a considerable drop in sales, some of the store's prior customers were contacted by phone and thanked for their business, whereas other customers were not. Although sales did not increase among those customers not receiving this verbal reinforcement, the customers who did receive the phone call responded quite favorably. In fact, the store was able to completely reverse the sales decline during the test month.

Source: Adapted from Blaise J. Bergiel and Christine Trosclair, "Instrumental Learning: Its Application to Customer Satisfaction," *Journal of Consumer Marketing* 2 (Fall 1985), 23–28; J. Ronald Carey, Steven H. Clicque, Barbara A. Leighton, and Frank Milton, "A Test of Positive Reinforcement of Customers," *Journal of Marketing* 40 (October 1976), 98–100.

Reinforcing the Heavy User

To the extent that a company has decided to supplement the reinforcement from product consumption with additional reinforcers, special emphasis should be placed on heavy users when this segment exists. Heavy users are those consumers who account for a disproportionate amount of product consumption. All other things being equal, it is more desirable to attract and retain such consumers than moderate or light users.

The money-back program recently implemented by Harley Hotels, in which the consumer receives $25 for every seven nights of usage, is aimed at the heavy user (see Figure 14.13). Consumers who often take to the skies find the frequent flyer

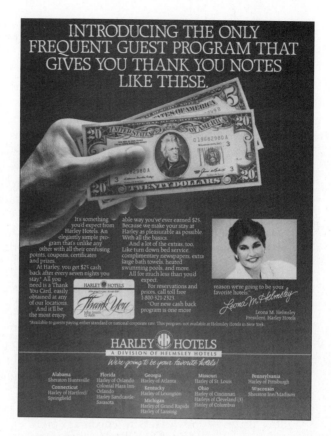

FIGURE 14.13 **One Way of Reinforcing the Heavy User Is a Money-Back Program**

programs offered by airlines very attractive. Similarly, the Zayre Corporation has introduced the "Frequent Z" points-for-purchase program. Customers earn points for their purchases, which can then be redeemed for catalog gift items. According to Stanley M. Adler, president, "We believe this program will attract new shoppers to our stores while building greater loyalty among current customers."[65]

Schedules of Reinforcement

Different schedules of reinforcement produce different patterns of behavior. Laboratory studies of animal behavior suggest that learning occurs most rapidly when the desired response is always reinforced (**total reinforcement**). However, when the response is reinforced only part of the time (**partial reinforcement**), learning is more lasting (that is, more resistant to extinction). A partial reinforcement schedule can be either systematic (for example, every third response is reinforced) or random (for example, the first and second responses are reinforced, the third is not, the fourth is, and so on).

The relative effectiveness of total versus partial reinforcement has been examined in the context of bus ridership.[66] Coupons offered as rewards were just as effective in enhancing ridership when given on a partial (every third person) schedule as when given on a continuous schedule (every person). Since it was much cheaper to offer the coupons only part of the time, considerable savings resulted from understanding the effectiveness of alternative reinforcement schedules.

This is not to say that partial reinforcement will always be the optimal strategy. Indeed, some have argued that partial reinforcement schedules may not work in many settings because the consumer may switch to another brand during the periods when the reinforcement is unavailable.[67] The best course of action is to examine empirically which schedule is best suited for a particular marketing situation.

Shaping

Shaping refers to the reinforcement of successive approximations of a desired behavior pattern or of behaviors that must be performed before the desired response can be emitted.[68] An animal that was expected to perform a complex trick would never succeed if the trainer waited for the animal to do the complete trick before rewarding it. Instead, the trainer rewards the animal for each step leading to the trick.

Shaping principles can be used to a marketer's advantage.[69] A retailer can offer door prizes or loss leaders to encourage store entry, a behavior that must occur before the desired response of buying the retailer's products can be achieved. Similar tactics can be employed by a car dealer offering free coffee and doughnuts for those visiting the showroom. The dealer might then give selected visitors a financial incentive for taking a test drive. Whatever the situation may be, shaping encourages marketers to think about what behaviors must precede the ultimate action of purchase and how these antecedent behaviors can be encouraged through appropriate reinforcements.

Discriminative Stimuli

As a result of prior association with reinforcers, **discriminative stimuli** can influence behavior even though they themselves do not provide reinforcement. Rather, they serve as cues about the likelihood that performing a particular behavior will lead to reinforcement. In marketing, discriminative stimuli can take the form of a brand or store name where the consumer has learned from prior experience that purchase behavior will be rewarded only when the distinctive cue is present. Examples of discriminative stimuli include such things as distinctive brandmarks (for example, the Levi tag), store signs (for example, 50 percent off sale), and store logos (for example, K mart's big red K).[70]

Vicarious Learning

A special type of learning that incorporates aspects of both cognitive and behavioral learning theories is vicarious learning. **Vicarious learning** (also called **modeling**) refers to a process that attempts to change behavior by having an individual observe the actions of others (that is, models) and the consequences of those behaviors.[71] This form of learning underlies much of today's advertising. Household products commonly promote themselves through ads that show the consumer receiving positive outcomes from product purchase and usage. Laundry detergent ads, for example, show a homemaker being drowned in praise from her family because their clothes are bright and clean. Similarly, dishwashing detergent ads offer users the promise of being noticed for young-looking and smooth hands.

Advertising will sometimes promote the product by focusing on negative consequences that may occur from using the competitive brand. In one of Wendy's advertisements, competitors are shown asking their customers to "step aside" and wait in long lines. Similarly, the ad in Figure 14.14 shows that the punishment (in the form of social disapproval) from not using the product disappears after consumption.

Summary

In this chapter, we examined four main types of learning. Cognitive learning is concerned with the mental processes that determine the retention of information. Classical conditioning focuses on learning through association. Operant conditioning considers how behavior is modified by reinforcers and punishers. Vicarious learning deals with learning through observation.

The retention of information will depend on the degree of rehearsal and elaboration that occurs during information processing. These in turn are affected by a number of individual (for example, motivation and ability) and stimulus (for example, pictures, concrete words, repetition, mnemonic devices, and time-compressed speech) characteristics. The fact that retention has occurred does not necessarily mean that the information can be retrieved. Retrieval failure may be due to either decay or interference in the form of proactive or retroactive inhibition.

Marketers often rely on classical conditioning, particularly in advertising, for influencing consumer preferences. The effectiveness of conditioning depends on a host of variables, including the strength of the US, the number of CS-US pairings, the order of the CS-US pairing, familiarity with the CS and US, and the amount of elaboration during stimulus processing. Extinction, on the other hand, will occur when the CS-US association is broken.

Operant conditioning emphasizes the importance of reinforcement as a tool for influencing consumer behavior. The degree of reinforcement consumers experience during consumption strongly determines future purchase behavior. Marketers can also provide additional reinforcers to consumers through tokens of appreciation (for example, gifts, thank you notes) for their patronage.

FIGURE 14.14 **Vicarious Learning in Advertising**

Review and Discussion Questions

1. Suppose you were developing a TV ad containing three main stimuli: (1) the product, (2) an attractive model, and (3) a well-liked musical jingle. Based upon classical conditioning principles, what order would you recommend for structuring these stimuli within the commercial?

2. Develop an advertisement containing your product and a competitor's product that would encourage discrimination.

3. A coffee producer is planning a new promotion to cover a 6-week period in which a small gift is attached to the outside of the package. Should this gift be offered every week or every other week?

4. When is classical conditioning most appropriate for promoting products? What factors are likely to limit the effectiveness of classical conditioning advertising?

5. Find advertising examples for the following concepts: (1) vicarious learning, (2) generalization, and (3) discrimination.

6. Are all reinforcers equally effective? If not, which are most effective?

7. The product manager for a new brand of skin softener is considering two possible names: Soft Skin versus Dickson's Skin Moisturizer. What name would you select? Why?

8. In this chapter we discuss many factors that can influence the memorability of ads. What do you perceive as the important principles that can be learned from this chapter for making ads more effective?

9. A company is trying to decide which of two alternative print ads should be adopted for an advertising campaign to be used during the market introduction phase for a new ice cream product called "Snowball." The only difference between the two ads is the type of picture that appears at the top of the ad. The picture for ad A shows the product sitting on top of snow and surrounded by a mound of snowballs. The picture for ad B shows a cute little girl consuming the product. To help decide which ad should be used, a study was undertaken in which target consumers were exposed to either ad A or ad B. (Assume that the method used to expose consumers to the ad was both valid and realistic.) The results indicated that ad A produced greater brand recall, but ad B generated more favorable product attitudes. Given these results, which ad would you recommend be used for introducing the product to the market, and why? Second, how can you explain that one ad is better for recall while the other is better for attitude given that the ads differed only in their picture?

Endnotes

1. For research on more complex forms of cognitive learning, see Robert J. Meyer, "The Learning of Multiattribute Judgment Policies," *Journal of Consumer Research* 14 (September 1987), 155–173; Peter Wright and Peter Rip, "Product Class Advertising Effects on First-Time Buyers' Decision Strategies," *Journal of Consumer Research* 7 (September 1980), 151–175.

2. Terry L. Childers and Michael J. Houston, "Conditions for a Picture-Superiority Effect on Consumer Memory," *Journal of Consumer Research* 11 (September 1984), 643–654; Fergus I. M. Craik and Endel Tulving, "Depth of Processing and the Retention of Words in Episodic Memory," *Journal of Experimental Psychology: General* 104 (September 1975), 268–294; Fergus I. M. Craik and Michael J. Watkins, "The Role of Rehearsal in Short-Term Memory," *Journal of Verbal Learning and Verbal Behavior* 12 (December 1973), 599–607; Meryl Paula Gardner, Andrew A. Mitchell, and J. Edward Russo, "Low Involvement Strategies for Processing Advertisements," *Journal of Advertising* 14 (1985), 4–12; Joel Saegert and Robert K. Young, "Comparison of Effects of Repetition and Levels of Processing in Memory for Advertisements," in Andrew A. Mitchell, ed., *Advances in Consumer Research* 9 (St. Louis: Association for Consumer Research, 1982), 431–434.

3. Richard E. Petty and John T. Cacioppo, "The Elaboration Likelihood Model of Persuasion," in Leonard Berkowitz, ed., *Advances in Experimental Social Psychology* 19 (New York: Academic Press, 1986), 123–205.

4. Gabriel Biehal and Dipankar Chakravarti, "Information-Presentation Format and Learning Goals as Determinants of Consumers' Memory Retrieval and Choice Processes," *Journal of Consumer Research* 8 (March 1982), 431–441; Eloise Coupey and Kent Nakamoto, "Learning Context and the Development of Product Category Perceptions," in Michael J. Houston, ed., *Advances in Consumer Research* 15 (Provo, Utah: Association for Consumer Research, 1988), 77–82; James H. Leigh and Anil Menon, "Audience Involvement Effects on the Information Processing of Umbrella Print Advertisements," *Journal of Advertising* 16 (1987), 3–12; Barry McLaughlin, "Intentional and Incidental Learning in Human Subjects: The Role of Instructions to Learn and Motivation," *Psychological Bulletin* 63 (May 1965), 359–376.

5. William G. Chase and Herbert A. Simon, "Perception in Chess," *Cognitive Psychology* 4 (January 1973), 55–81. For a more general discussion, see Joseph W. Alba and J. Wesley Hutchinson, "Dimensions of Consumer Expertise," *Journal of Consumer Research* 13 (March 1987), 411–454.

6. Rajeev Batra and Michael Ray, "Situational Effects of Advertising: The Moderating Influence of Motivation, Ability and Opportunity to Respond," *Journal of Consumer Research* 12 (March 1986), 432–445; Danny L. Moore, Douglas Hausknecht, and Kanchana Thamodaran, "Time Compression, Response Opportunity, and Persuasion," *Journal of Consumer Research* 13 (June 1986), 85–99; James M. Munch and John L. Swasy, "Rhetorical Question, Summarization Frequency, and Argument Strength Effects on Recall," *Journal of Consumer Research* 15 (June 1988), 69–76.

7. Catherine A. Cole and Michael J. Houston, "Encoding and Media Effects on Consumer Learning Deficiencies in the Elderly," *Journal of Marketing Research* 24 (February 1987), 55–63. Also see Gary J. Gaeth and Timothy B. Heath, "The Cognitive Processing of Misleading Advertising in Young and Old Adults," *Journal of Consumer Research* 14 (June 1987), 43–54.

8. For a recent review of this literature, see Deborah J. MacInnis and Linda L. Price, "The Role of Imagery in Information Processing: Review and Extensions," *Journal of Consumer Research* 13 (March 1987), 473–491.

9. Jose Biron and Stewart J. McKelvie, "Effects of Interactive and Noninteractive Imagery on Recall of Advertisements," *Perceptual and Motor Skills* 59 (May 1984), 799–805; Childers and Houston, "Conditions for a Picture-Superiority Effect on Consumer Memory"; Kathryn A. Lutz and Richard J. Lutz, "Effects of Interactive Imagery on Learning: Application to Advertising," *Journal of Applied Psychology* 62 (August 1977), 493–498.

10. Allan Paivio, "Mental Imagery in Associative Learning and Memory," *Psychological Review* 76 (May 1969), 241–263; Allan Paivio, *Mental Representations: A Dual Coding Approach* (New York: Oxford University Press, 1986).

11. See, for example, Childers and Houston, "Conditions for a Picture-Superiority Effect on Consumer Memory"; MacInnis and Price, "The Role of Imagery in Information Processing: Review and Extensions."

12. H. Rao Unnava and Robert E. Burnkrant, "An Imagery-Processing View of the Role of Pictures in Print Advertisements," *Journal of Marketing Research* 28 (May 1991), 226–231. For additional research in this general area, see Julie A. Edell and Richard Staelin, "The Information Processing of Pictures in Print Advertisements," *Journal of Consumer Research* 10 (June 1983), 45–61; Michael J. Houston, Terry L. Childers, and Susan E. Heckler, "Picture-Word Consistency and the Elaborative Processing of Advertisements," *Journal of Marketing Research* 24 (November 1987), 359–369; Lutz and Lutz, "Effects of Interactive Imagery on Learning: Application to Advertising;"

Biron and McKelvie, "Effects of Interactive and Noninteractive Imagery on Recall of Advertisements."

13. Roberta L. Klatzky, *Human Memory: Structures and Processes* (San Francisco: W. H. Freeman, 1975), 230.

14. Hooper White, "Name Change to Rusty Jones Helps Polish Product's Identity," *Advertising Age* (February 18, 1980), 47–48.

15. See, for example, T. B. Rogers, N. A. Kuiper, and W. S. Kirker, "Self-Reference and Encoding of Personal Information," *Journal of Personality and Social Psychology* 35 (September 1977), 677–688; Polly Brown, Janice M. Keenan, and George R. Potts, "The Self-Reference Effect with Imagery Encoding," *Journal of Personality and Social Psychology* 51 (November 1986), 897–906.

16. Robert E. Burnkrant and H. Rao Unnava, "Self-Referencing: A Strategy for Increasing Processing of Message Content," *Personality and Social Psychology Bulletin* 15 (December 1989), 628–638. Also see Kathleen Debevec, Harlan E. Spotts, and Jerome B. Kernan, "The Self-Reference Effect in Persuasion: Implications for Marketing Strategy," in Melanie Wallendorf and Paul Anderson, eds., *Advances in Consumer Research* 14 (Provo, Utah: Association for Consumer Research, 1987), 417–420.

17. Priscilla LaBarbera and James MacLachlan, "Time-Compressed Speech in Radio Advertising," *Journal of Marketing* 43 (January 1979), 30–36; James MacLachlan and Michael H. Siegel, "Reducing the Cost of TV Commercials by Use of Time Compressions," *Journal of Marketing Research* 17 (February 1980), 52–57.

18. Moore, Hausknecht, and Thamodaran, "Time Compression, Response Opportunity, and Persuasion"; Mary Jane Rawlins Schlinger, Linda F. Alwitt, Kathleen E. McCarthy, and Leila Green, "Effects of Time Compression on Attitudes and Information Processing," *Journal of Marketing* 47 (Winter 1983), 79–85.

19. For a general review, see Alan G. Sawyer, "The Effects of Repetition: Conclusions and Suggestions about Experimental Laboratory Research," in G. D. Hughes and Michael L. Ray, eds., *Buyer/Consumer Information Processing* (Chapel Hill: University of North Carolina Press, 1974), 190–219. Research on repetition effects can be found in Batra and Ray, "Situational Effects of Advertising Repetition: The Moderating Influence of Motivation, Ability, and Opportunity to Respond"; George E. Belch, "The Effects of Television Commercial Repetition on Cognitive Response and Message Acceptance," *Journal of Consumer Research* 9 (June 1982), 56–65; Arno J. Rethans, John L. Swasy, and Lawrence J. Marks, "Effects of Television Commercial Repetition, Receiver Knowledge, and Commercial Length: A Test of the Two-Factor Model," *Journal of Marketing Research* 23 (February 1986), 50–61; Surendra N. Singh, Michael L. Rothschild, and Gilbert A. Churchill, Jr., "Recognition Versus Recall as Measures of Television Commercial Forgetting," *Journal of Marketing Research* 25 (February 1988), 72–80; Esther Thorson and Rita Snyder, "Viewer Recall of Television Commercials: Prediction from the Propositional Structure of Commercial Scripts," *Journal of Marketing Research* 21 (May 1984), 127–136.

20. Raymond R. Burke and Thomas K. Srull, "Competitive Interference and Consumer Memory for Advertising," *Journal of Consumer Research* 15 (June 1988), 55–68.

21. For research on advertising wearout, see Bobby J. Calder and Brian Sternthal, "Television Commercial Wearout: An Information Processing View," *Journal of Marketing Research* 17 (May 1980), 173–186.

22. Richard E. Petty and John T. Cacioppo, "Effects of Message Repetition and Position on Cognitive Responses, Recall, and Persuasion," *Journal of Personality and Social Psychology* 37 (January 1979), 97–109; Rethans, Swasy, and Marks, "Effects of Television

Commercial Repetition, Receiver Knowledge, and Commercial Length: A Test of the Two-Factor Model."

23. Robert E. Burnkrant and Hanumantha R. Unnava, "Effects of Variation in Message Execution on the Learning of Repeated Brand Information," in Melanie Wallendorf and Paul F. Anderson, eds., *Advances in Consumer Research* 14 (Provo, Utah: Association for Consumer Research, 1987), 173–176; H. Rao Unnava and Robert E. Burnkrant, "Effects of Repeating Varied Ad Executions on Brand Name Memory," *Journal of Marketing Research* 28 (November 1991), 406–416.

24. Laura Bird, "Researchers Criticize Overuse of Ads," *Wall Street Journal* (January 3, 1992), B3.

25. John G. Jenkins and Karl M. Dallenbach, "Oblivescence during Sleep and Waking," *American Journal of Psychology* 35 (October 1924), 605–612.

26. Burke and Srull, "Competitive Interference and Consumer Memory for Advertising." Also see Kevin Lane Keller, "Memory and Evaluation Effects in Competitive Advertising Environments," *Journal of Consumer Research* 17 (March 1991), 463–476.

27. Endel Tulving and Zena Pearlstone, "Availability Versus Accessibility of Information in Memory for Words," *Journal of Verbal Learning and Verbal Behavior* 5 (August 1966), 381–391.

28. Amitava Chattopadhyay and Joseph W. Alba, "The Situational Importance of Recall and Inference in Consumer Decision Making," *Journal of Consumer Research* 15 (June 1988), 1–12; Jolita Kisielius and Brian Sternthal, "Detecting and Explaining Vividness Effects in Attitudinal Judgments," *Journal of Marketing Research* 21 (February 1984), 54–64; Jolita Kisielius and Brian Sternthal, "Examining the Vividness Controversy: An Availability-Valence Explanation," *Journal of Consumer Research* 12 (March 1986), 418–431; Barbara Loken and Ronald Hoverstad, "Relationships between Information Recall and Subsequent Attitudes: Some Exploratory Findings," *Journal of Consumer Research* 12 (September 1985), 155–168.

29. Gabriel Biehal and Dipankar Chakravarti, "Information Accessibility as a Moderator of Consumer Choice," *Journal of Consumer Research* 10 (June 1983), 1–14; Gabriel Biehal and Dipankar Chakravarti, "Consumers' Use of Memory and External Information in Choice: Macro and Micro Perspectives," *Journal of Consumer Research* 12 (March 1986), 382–405.

30. John G. Lynch, Jr., and Thomas K. Srull, "Memory and Attentional Factors in Consumer Choice: Concepts and Research Methods," *Journal of Consumer Research* 9 (June 1982), 18–37.

31. Kevin Lane Keller, "Memory Factors in Advertising: The Effect of Advertising Retrieval Cues on Brand Evaluations," *Journal of Consumer Research* 14 (December 1987), 316–333. Also see Kevin Lane Keller, "Cue Comparability and Framing in Advertising," *Journal of Marketing Research* 28 (February 1991), 42–57; Keller, "Memory and Evaluation Effects in Competitive Advertising Environments."

32. Joseph O. Eastlack, Jr., "How to Get More Bang for Your Television Bucks," *Journal of Consumer Marketing* 1 (1984), 25–34.

33. Joseph W. Alba and Amitava Chattopadhyay, "Effects of Context and Part-Category Cues on Recall of Competing Brands," *Journal of Marketing Research* 22 (August 1985), 340–349; Joseph W. Alba and Amitava Chattopadhyay, "Salience Effects in Brand Recall," *Journal of Marketing Research* 23 (November 1986), 363–369. Also see Paul W. Miniard, H. Rao Unnava, and Sunil Bhatla, "Investigating the Recall Inhibition Effect: A Test of Practical Considerations," *Marketing Letters* 2 (January 1991), 290–303.

34. Endel Tulving and Donald M. Thompson, "Encoding Specificity and Retrieval Processes in Episodic Memory," *Psychological Review* 80 (September 1973), 352–373.

35. For a review of the literature on recognition measures, see Surendra N. Singh and Catherine A. Cole, "Forced-Choice Recognition Tests: A Critical Review," *Journal of Advertising* 14 (1985), 52–58.

36. Eric Marder and Mort David, "Recognition of Ad Elements: Recall or Projection?" *Journal of Advertising Research* 1 (December 1961), 23–25. For an interesting discussion of recognition measures, see Adam Finn, "Print Ad Recognition Readership Scores: An Information Processing Perspective," *Journal of Marketing Research* 25 (May 1988), 168–177.

37. Surendra N. Singh and Gilbert A. Churchill, Jr., "Using the Theory of Signal Detection to Improve Ad Recognition Testing," *Journal of Marketing Research* 23 (November 1986), 327–336; Singh and Cole, "Forced-Choice Recognition Tests: A Critical Review"; Surendra N. Singh and Michael L. Rothschild, "Recognition as a Measure of Learning from Television Commercials," *Journal of Marketing Research* 20 (August 1983), 235–248; Singh, Rothschild, and Churchill, Jr., "Recognition Versus Recall as Measures of Television Commercial Forgetting."

38. There has been some criticism of recall measures' ability to provide an accurate assessment of the learning that occurs from emotional or feeling ads. See Hubert A. Zielske, "Does Day-After Recall Penalize 'Feeling' Ads?" *Journal of Advertising Research* 22 (February–March 1982), 19–22.

39. "To Burke or Not to Burke?" *TV Guide* 29 (February 7, 1981), 3ff.

40. Chattopadhyay and Alba, "The Situational Importance of Recall and Inference in Consumer Decision Making"; Loken and Hoverstad, "Relationships between Information Recall and Subsequent Attitudes: Some Exploratory Findings." Note, however, that the relationship between recall and attitude is stronger when attitudes are not formed during ad processing but are formed at a later time based on retrieval of the ad information. For a discussion of this issue, see Reid Hastie and Bernadette Park, "The Relationship Between Memory and Judgment Depends on Whether the Judgment Task Is Memory-Based or On-Line," *Psychological Review* 93 (June 1986), 258–268; Meryl Lichtenstein and Thomas K. Srull, "Processing Objectives as a Determinant of the Relationship between Recall and Judgment," *Journal of Experimental Social Psychology* 23 (March 1987), 93–118.

41. James R. Bettman, *An Information Processing Theory of Consumer Choice* (Reading, Massachusetts: Addison-Wesley, 1979).

42. For a discussion of advertising tactics to enhance brand recognition and recall, see John R. Rossiter and Larry Percy, "Advertising Communication Models," in Elizabeth C. Hirschman and Morris B. Holbrook, eds., *Advances in Consumer Research* 12 (Provo, Utah: Association for Consumer Research, 1985), 510–524.

43. Singh, Rothschild, and Churchill, Jr., "Recognition Versus Recall as Measures of Television Commercial Forgetting."

44. For an excellent translation of this literature into the marketing domain, see Frances K. McSweeney and Calvin Bierley, "Recent Developments in Classical Conditioning," *Journal of Consumer Research* 11 (September 1984), 619–631. For a recent review, see Terence A. Shimp, "Neo-Pavlovian Conditioning and its Implications for Consumer Theory and Research," in Thomas S. Robertson and Harold H. Kassarjian, eds., *Handbook of Consumer Behavior* (Englewood Cliffs, N.J.: Prentice-Hall, 1991), 162–187.

45. Walter R. Nord and J. Paul Peter, "A Behavior Modification Perspective on Marketing," *Journal of Marketing* 44 (Spring 1980), 36–47.

46. For a more detailed discussion of conditioning determinants, see Werner Kroeber-Riel, "Emotional Product Differentiation by Classical Conditioning," in Thomas C. Kinnear, ed., *Advances in Consumer Research* 11 (Provo, Utah: Association for Consumer Research, 1984), 538–543; McSweeney and Bierley, "Recent Developments in Classical Conditioning." For research on how conditioning may depend on conscious awareness of the CS-US relationship, see Chris T. Allen and Chris A. Janiszewski, "Assessing the Role of Contingency Awareness in Attitudinal Conditioning with Implications for Advertising Research," *Journal of Marketing Research* 26 (February 1989), 30–43.

47. Avram Goldstein, "Thrills in Response to Music and Other Stimuli," *Physiological Psychology* 8 (September 1980), 126–129.

48. Gerald J. Gorn, "The Effects of Music in Advertising on Choice Behavior: A Classical Conditioning Approach," *Journal of Marketing* 46 (Winter 1982), 94–101; Elnora W. Stuart, Terence A. Shimp, and Randall W. Engle, "Classical Conditioning of Consumer Attitudes: Four Experiments in an Advertising Context," *Journal of Consumer Research* 14 (December 1987), 334–349. Also see Chris T. Allen and Thomas J. Madden, "A Closer Look at Classical Conditioning," *Journal of Consumer Research* 12 (December 1985), 301–315; James J. Kellaris and Anthony D. Cox, "The Effects of Background Music in Advertising: A Reassessment," *Journal of Consumer Research* 16 (June 1989), 113–118; Terence A. Shimp, Eva M. Hyatt, and David J. Snyder, "A Critical Appraisal of Demand Artifacts in Consumer Research," *Journal of Consumer Research* 18 (December 1991), 273–283.

49. Kroeber-Riel, "Emotional Product Differentiation by Classical Conditioning."

50. McSweeney and Bierley, "Recent Developments in Classical Conditioning;" Stuart, Shimp, and Engle, "Classical Conditioning of Consumer Attitudes: Four Experiments in an Advertising Context."

51. McSweeney and Bierley, "Recent Developments in Classical Conditioning."

52. McSweeney and Bierley, "Recent Developments in Classical Conditioning."

53. Stuart, Shimp, and Engle, "Classical Conditioning of Consumer Attitudes: Four Experiments in an Advertising Context;" Terence A. Shimp, Elnora W. Stuart, and Randall W. Engle, "A Program of Classical Conditioning Experiments Testing Variations in the Conditioned Stimulus and Context," *Journal of Consumer Research* 18 (June 1991), 1–12.

54. Anthony G. Greenwald and Clark Leavitt, "Audience Involvement in Advertising: Four Levels," *Journal of Consumer Research* 11 (June 1984), 581–592; Richard E. Petty and John T. Cacioppo, "The Elaboration Likelihood Model of Persuasion," in Leonard Berkowitz, ed., *Advances in Experimental Social Psychology* 19 (New York: Academic Press, 1986), 123–205.

55. "Firm: Consumers Cool to New Products," *Marketing News* 20 (January 3, 1986), 1ff.

56. Elinor Selame and Greg Kolligian, "Brands Are a Company's Most Important Asset," *Marketing News* 25 (September 16, 1991), 14, 19. For research on factors that may influence the success of brand extensions, see David A. Aaker and Kevin Lane Keller, "Consumer Evaluations of Brand Extensions," *Journal of Marketing* 54 (January 1990), 27–41.

57. Selame and Kolligian, "Brands Are a Company's Most Important Asset," 19.

58. "Coors vs. Corr's," *Time* 123 (February 6, 1984), 51.

59. Diane Schneidman, "Use of 'Mc' in Front of Travel Firms' Names Leads to Lawsuits," *Marketing News* 21 (November 20, 1987), 17.

60. R. I. Allison and K. P. Uhl, "Influence of Beer Brand Identification on Taste Perception," *Journal of Marketing Research* 1 (August 1964), 36–39.

61. Julia Keller, "These Are Not Q-Tips," *The Columbus Dispatch* (April 10, 1987), G1.
62. Stanley M. Widrick, "Concept of Negative Reinforcement Has Place in Classroom," *Marketing News* 20 (July 18, 1986), 48–49; Stanley Widrick and Eugene H. Fram, "Identifying Negative Products: Do Customers Like to Purchase Your Products?" *Journal of Consumer Marketing* 1 (Fall 1983), 59–66.
63. Widrick, "Concept of Negative Reinforcement Has Place in Classroom."
64. *Insights*, NPD Research, Inc., 1979–1982.
65. "Zayre Launches 'Frequent Z' to Make Points with Shoppers," *Marketing News* 21 (November 20, 1987), 1.
66. Brian C. Deslauriers and Peter B. Everett, "The Effects of Intermittent and Continuous Token Reinforcement on Bus Ridership," *Journal of Applied Psychology* 62 (August 1977), 369–375.
67. Michael L. Rothschild and William C. Gaidis, "Behavioral Learning Theory: Its Relevance to Marketing and Promotions," *Journal of Marketing* 45 (Spring 1981), 70–78.
68. Nord and Peter, "A Behavior Modification Perspective on Marketing."
69. There has been some controversy over the application of shaping principles. See Nord and Peter, "A Behavior Modification Perspective on Marketing"; Rothschild and Gaidis, "Behavioral Learning Theory"; J. Paul Peter and Walter R. Nord, "A Clarification and Extension of Operant Conditioning Principles in Marketing," *Journal of Marketing* 46 (Summer 1982), 102–107.
70. Nord and Peter, "A Behavior Modification Perspective on Marketing."
71. Ibid.

15

Influencing Attitudes and Behavior

Knowing the customer helps companies figure out which products consumers want and what influences their decisions to buy. Are shoppers motivated by cents-off coupons, splashy displays, free samples, or product literature? Answers to these questions go a long way in formulating promotional strategy.

To help answer questions such as these, companies have been formed that specialize in supplying and interpreting scanner data for packaged goods firms like Kraft USA, Frito-Lay, and Procter & Gamble. Every time a grocery store clerk whisks a purchase over the scanner at the checkout counter, it electronically records what was bought, who makes it, the size, and the price. Information Resources Inc. (IRI) of Chicago buys the raw scanner data from about 2,700 grocery stores in 66 markets ranging from big cities to small towns. Scanner data is then combined with other research into what shoppers watch on television, the type of neighborhood they live in, and the kind of supermarket they shop in. The end result is a better picture of the effectiveness and profitability of promotional activities.

For example, when analysts at IRI reviewed one of Kraft's promotional campaigns, they concluded that 7 of every 10 boxes of its macaroni and cheese would have been sold *without* the promotion. Two of the three incremental-sales boxes moved because of in-store displays, while the other was purchased with coupons. Since promotion campaigns are costly, such findings can save plenty. Similarly, it was discovered that while a 40-cent coupon on a tube of toothpaste could yield $147,000 in profits, a 50-cent coupon on the same item could mean a $348,000 loss. According to Gian Fulgoni, IRI chairman, "The availability of scanner data has caused an explosion in learning how promotion affects purchasing."

Source: Excerpted from Susan Caminiti, "What the Scanner Knows about You," *Fortune* (December 3, 1990), 51–52; Richard Gibson, "Marketers' Mantra: Reap More with Less," *Wall Street Journal* (March 22, 1991), B1–B2.

Influencing consumers' attitudes and behavior is one of the most fundamental and yet challenging tasks confronting businesses. Companies invest billions of dollars each year in efforts designed to modify or reinforce how consumers think, feel, and act in the marketplace. Consequently, knowing how to influence consumers' attitudes and behavior is one of the most valuable skills a marketer can possess.

This chapter attempts to provide a foundation for such knowledge. You will discover that many of the concepts and ideas presented in previous chapters are very germane to this discussion. We begin our journey with a consideration of the persuasive power of marketing communications.

Persuasion through Communication

Marketing communications, whether in the form of advertising, a salesperson's "pitch," a point-of-purchase brochure, or product packaging, represent a significant means for persuading consumers. The processes that underlie the persuasive impact of such communications were described in Chapters 13 (Information Processing) and 14 (Learning). Little attention, however, was given to understanding how persuasion can depend on certain elements of the communication, such as the source, types of claims, and so on. The persuasive impact of various message elements is explored in this section. But first, we consider a conceptualization of the role played by various communication elements during persuasion, known as the Elaboration Likelihood Model.

The Elaboration Likelihood Model of Persuasion

According to the **Elaboration Likelihood Model** (ELM) developed by Petty and Cacioppo, the influence exerted by various communication elements will depend on the elaboration (that is, issue-relevant thinking) that occurs during processing.[1] When elaboration is high, the **central route** to persuasion is followed, where only those message elements (called **arguments**) relevant to forming a "reasoned"

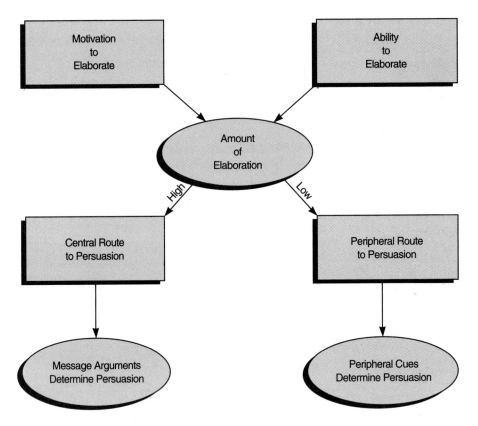

FIGURE 15.1   A Simplified Representation of the Elaboration Likelihood Model of Persuasion

opinion are influential. Conversely, the **peripheral route** to persuasion occurs under low levels of elaboration as elements (called **peripheral cues**) that are irrelevant to developing a reasoned opinion become influential. Both arguments and peripheral cues may have an effect under moderate levels of elaboration.

Elaboration, in turn, depends on the person's motivation and ability during message processing. A person motivated and able to elaborate will take the central route. The peripheral route is traveled when motivation or ability is lacking. Figure 15.1 provides a diagram of the basic model.

Research on the ELM has been largely supportive of its validity.[2] In one such study, subjects were exposed to a series of print ads.[3] The properties of one of these ads, featuring a fictitious razor product, were systematically manipulated. Some versions of the razor ad listed strong arguments (that is, claims about the product), while others contained weak arguments. Different endorsers were also used in the

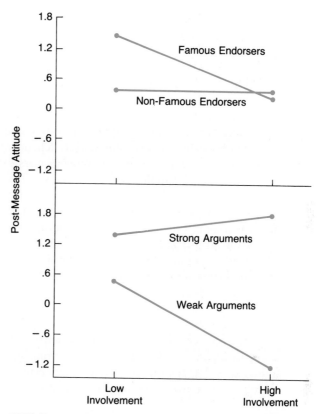

NOTE: Top panel shows interactive effect of involvement and endorser status on attitudes. Bottom panel shows interactive effect of involvement and argument quality on attitudes.

FIGURE 15.2   Brand Attitude Favorability as a Function of Involvement, Argument Strength, and Endorser Status

Source: Richard E. Petty, John T. Cacioppo, and David Schumann, "Central and Peripheral Routes to Advertising Effectiveness: The Moderating Role of Involvement," *Journal of Consumer Research* 10 (September 1983), 135–146. Used with permission.

ad versions. Some contained celebrity endorsers; other versions featured noncelebrity endorsers. Finally, subjects' involvement was also manipulated in order to vary the amount of elaboration that occurred while processing the razor ad. Only those subjects assigned to a "high-involvement" condition were told that they would eventually make a choice among razors.

The results involving postcommunication attitudes are presented in Figure 15.2. As prescribed by the ELM, the influence of the message elements varied across involvement. The attitudes of high-involvement subjects were affected only by the differences in the message arguments. In contrast, low-involvement subjects' attitudes were influenced by both the arguments (although to a lesser extent than the attitudes formed under high involvement) and endorser.

The ELM highlights the importance, in developing persuasive communications, of anticipating how much elaboration is likely to occur during message processing. If elaboration is likely to be high, then more emphasis on including compelling arguments that support the advocated position is appropriate. When this is not the case, other techniques less dependent on the degree of message processing may be desirable. Ads employing classical conditioning or an attractive spokesperson are examples.

The ELM provides a very useful perspective for understanding why research has often obtained seemingly inconsistent results concerning the influence of a persuasion variable. The fact that source (endorser) attractiveness, for instance, affects persuasion in one study but not another may simply reflect differences in the amount of elaboration that occurred within each study and, thus, the reliance on peripheral cues in forming attitudes.

Source Effects

Suppose you were in the market for a new car. While visiting a car dealership, a salesman explains why you should buy from his lot rather than from one of his competitors. His salespitch includes many claims about the virtues of his cars, including the statement that they are the most reliable automobiles on the market. Would you believe him?

Now suppose you received the same basic information from a close friend who possessed considerable expertise in this area. Would you be any more likely to believe the information is valid? Chances are you would. Although the message remains unchanged, the difference in the source of the message could determine whether or not you believe it. Unlike your friend, the salesman has a vested interest in what he says. Consumers realize this, thus making them more skeptical about the information being fed to them.

Such skepticism is not restricted simply to the pitches of salespersons. It can occur for any communication, especially those seen as originating from the business environment. For example, one study reports that over 70 percent of consumers do not believe ads that use test results to support claims of product superiority.[4] Consequently, it is not surprising why the Oldsmobile ad in Figure 15.3 states, "We couldn't print this if it weren't true." Advertisers are continually looking for ways to reduce consumer skepticism toward their messages.

To illustrate how the source of a message can determine its persuasive impact, consider the study in which subjects processed a comparative ad and then ranked the advertised brand. Prior to ad exposure, subjects received information that created either a positive or negative reputation for the advertiser. The study also varied the extremity of the claims made by the ad. Out of 100 brands, the advertised brand was claimed to be either the top rated brand in a taste test, the third best, the fifth best, or the twentieth best tasting brand.

FIGURE 15.3   Combatting Consumer Skepticism toward Advertising Claims

The research findings are displayed in Figure 15.4. Subjects ranked the brand more favorably when the source possessed a positive reputation. This was particularly true when the ad contained the most extreme claim of the brand tasting better than all of the remaining brands included in the test. Not only do these results demonstrate how important the message source can be, they also reveal the skepticism consumers hold toward advertising claims. All of the average rankings shown in Figure 15.4 are substantially lower than what would be expected if consumers completely accepted the advertising claims. Thus, even when the source had a positive reputation and the ad claimed the brand had the best taste, subjects still ranked the brand, on average, as the twenty-sixth best.

Source Characteristics   Given the impact a source can have on a communication's persuasiveness, researchers have long been interested in understanding which characteristics of a source will be influential during persuasion. A long-standing principle of persuasion is that a credible source will usually facilitate persuasion.[5] In Chapter 13 we described how the cognitive and affective responses that occur when

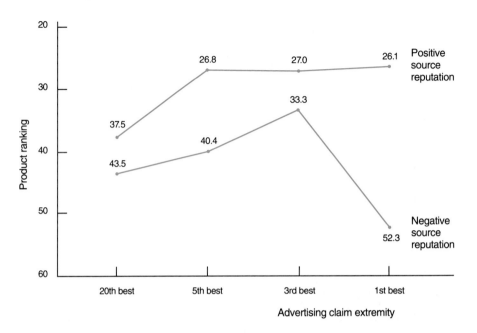

FIGURE 15.4 **Ranking of the Advertised Brand as a Function of Advertiser Reputation and Advertising Claim Extremity**

Source: Marvin E. Goldberg and Jon Hartwick, "The Effects of Advertiser Reputation and Extremity of Advertising Claim on Advertising Effectiveness," *Journal of Consumer Research* 17 (September 1990), 172–179.

consumers are processing a message can determine the amount of message acceptance. Credible sources inhibit counterargumentation (that is, unfavorable thoughts about the message claims), while sources lacking credibility may foster counterargumentation and undermine consumers generating support arguments.

Credibility is really a function of two separate source characteristics: expertise and trustworthiness. A car salesman may be seen as very knowledgeable, but his credibility will suffer when consumers doubt his trustworthiness. Conversely, close friends may be very trustworthy, but they may lack the expertise in a product category for them to function as a credible source.

A compelling demonstration of how expertise can influence a source's persuasive power is provided by research focusing on the purchase behavior of music store shoppers.[6] In this study, the salesperson asked customers if they were interested in purchasing a cleaning product for stereo equipment. The number agreeing to buy the item heavily depended on the expertise conveyed by the salesperson. Whereas two-thirds of the consumers bought the product when the salesperson acted knowledgeable about the product, only one-third of them did so when the salesperson admitted to being unfamiliar with the product.

Bo Jackson, professional baseball and football player.

THE JACKSON 5.

See Bo cross-train. See Bo cross-train in a shoe with Nike-Air® cushioning and plenty of support.   See Bo cross-train in the Air Trainer SC. See if you can do everything Bo can do in it.

For further information on Nike Cross-Training products call 1-800-344-NIKE, Monday through Friday, 7am-5pm Pacific Time.   Air Trainer SC

FIGURE 15.5   Celebrity Endorsements Can Enhance Persuasion

Although expertise and trustworthiness are important, they are not the only source characteristics that can determine communication effectiveness. Physically attractive sources can be more persuasive.[7] The same is true for sources that are likeable,[8] hold celebrity status,[9] or are similar to the target audience.[10]

Spokespersons   As we have noted, consumers can be quite skeptical of sources that have vested interests in the communication. One way businesses try to overcome such skepticism is to use spokespersons that are highly regarded by consumers. According to Marketing Evaluations/TV Q, a market research company that evaluates the recognition and appeal of celebrities, one of the most credible and appealing celebrities available is Bill Cosby.[11] Little wonder that we see him so often as the spokesperson for someone's product.

Of course, an effective spokesperson can do more than enhance the credibility of the sales message. In Chapter 13 we discussed how a spokesperson can serve as an attention-getting device. Moreover, the simple association of the product with the spokesperson can enhance the desirability of the product itself. When Bo Jackson endorses Nike athletic shoes (see Figure 15.5), many young consumers are likely to see product ownership as a way of linking themselves to this star athlete.

Consumer in Focus 15.1

Celebrity Endorsements That Went Awry

In an effort to stimulate beef consumption, the beef industry developed an advertising campaign in which celebrities told consumers that beef was "Real food for real people." One of these celebrities was Cybil Sheppard. Imagine how the industry felt when it was later publicized that Cybil was a vegetarian.

When Seagram's entered the wine cooler market, it relied on Bruce Willis to help develop the right feel and image for its new product. While the ads themselves were quite flashy and appealing, problems arose when rumors started circulating that the star had a drinking problem.

Remember when Madonna hooked up with Pepsi? The Madonna commercial, which reportedly cost somewhere in the range of $2–$5 million to produce, used the same song that appeared in her "Like A Prayer" music video. Some consumers became confused, thinking they saw some of the controversial images from the video in the Pepsi ad. Pepsi quickly pulled the ad off the airwaves. According to one industry insider, "If you have a Madonna or Michael Jackson endorsing your product, you have to worry about what weird thing they might do next."

Source: Iris Cohen Selinger, "Celebrity Overexposure," *Adweek* (March 4, 1991), 12–13.

One important consideration in selecting a celebrity endorser is whether there is a good fit between the product and the endorser.[12] When the late John Houseman (who played the hardnosed law professor on the TV series "Paper Chase") told us, on behalf of the Smith Barney investment firm, "We make money the old-fashioned way, we earn it," the ad raised the company's image and sales. The same could not be said for his appearance in a McDonald's spot.[13] Bill Cosby is very effective in promoting Jell-O food products and Kodak film, but he was far less persuasive when he appeared in a commercial for the E. F. Hutton investment company.[14] Thus, the use of a celebrity endorser does not guarantee success. Indeed, as described in Consumer in Focus 15.1, celebrity endorsements have sometimes had embarrassing consequences for the sponsoring product.

Message Effects

Additional characteristics of the message beyond the source can play a significant role in the persuasion process. Of particular interest here are the claims and executional elements that comprise the communication.

Strength of Claims   The strength of message claims will strongly determine how much yielding occurs under the central route to persuasion. Strong claims will inhibit negative thoughts while encouraging positive thoughts. Just the opposite holds for weak claims.

What makes a claim strong? *Relevancy* is critical. Claims that focus on dimensions that carry little or no weight in the decision process lack relevancy. One industry study reports that relevancy was the most important determinant of new product advertising's success in persuading consumers to try the product.[15]

Another important characteristic is a claim's *objectivity*. **Objective claims** focus on factual information that is not subject to individual interpretations. **Subjective claims**, on the other hand, are ones that may evoke different interpretations across individuals. Consider a product's price or weight. Claims such as "low-priced" or "lightweight" would be considered subjective, inasmuch as what is low or light for one person may not be for the next. These same attributes could be expressed objectively by giving the actual price and weight.

Objective claims are preferred by consumers over subjective claims because they are more precise and more easily confirmed. Research has shown that objective claims are perceived as more believable, reduce counterargumentation while increasing the number of support arguments, and create more favorable product beliefs and attitudes.[16]

The *verifiability* of claims can also be significant. **Search claims** are those that can be accurately evaluated prior to purchase. **Experience claims** are those that can be fully evaluated only after product consumption. **Credence claims** differ from the prior two types in that accurate evaluation is beyond the consumer's capabilities. Table 15.1 presents some examples of claims differing in their verifiability and objectivity.

TABLE 15.1   Claims That Differ in Their Objectivity and Verifiability

	Objective	Subjective
Search	• We offer five styles of cedar chests • Our brand has no cholesterol	• We offer an extraordinary collection of jewelry • There are a variety of attractive styles
Experience	• Our tent keeps you dry • Our test gives you results in 30 minutes	• We offer delicious meals • Easy to use with professional results
Credence	• We invested over $5 billion in our long-distance network • Our polish is used by 77 leading galleries and museums	• Our tire has been extensively tested • Our wine is naturally fermented

Source: Gary T. Ford, Darlene B. Smith, and John L. Swasy, "Consumer Skepticism of Advertising Claims: Testing Hypotheses from Economics of Information," *Journal of Consumer Research* 16 (March 1990), 433–441.

Consumers will presumably be less skeptical of a message when the claims lend themselves to confirmation. A recent study has shown that consumers perceive search claims to be much more truthful than either experience or credence claims.[17] Consumers' skepticism differed very little, however, between these latter two types of claims.

Substantiation of claims is also important. Consider the experience claim of great taste. This claim is more likely to be accepted if supported by credible taste-test findings than when such substantiation is lacking.

Number of Claims

The quantity, as well as the strength or quality, of the claims made in a message can influence persuasion. Petty and Cacioppo have reasoned that whereas claim quality is critical under the central route to persuasion, claim quantity might serve as a persuasion cue under the peripheral route.[18] Consistent with this, they report that variations in the number of message claims affected yielding when the message was processed under low-involvement conditions. Claim quantity was unimportant, however, when message processing occurred during high involvement.

Message Sidedness

What may come as a surprise is that including some weak claims along with strong claims can enhance a message's persuasiveness. **Two-sided messages** (those including pros and cons) increase perceptions of advertiser truthfulness and believability relative to **one-sided messages** (those presenting only pros).[19]

Comparative Messages

Claims can also vary in their use of brand comparisons. Comparative advertising, in which the advertised brand is implicitly or explicitly compared against one or more competitors, is often employed by new brands seeking to take business away from existing brands. It also is used by established brands, as evidenced by the advertising campaigns during the burger and cola wars. Although comparative ads have been shown to outperform noncomparative ads,[20] even in terms of producing greater sales,[21] this is not always the case. Sometimes comparative ads are no better or even worse than their noncomparative versions.[22]

Affective Messages

Whereas informationally oriented messages attempt to evoke favorable cognitive responses during processing, affective messages are designed to elicit favorable emotions and feelings. Such is the case for the ad presented in Figure 15.6. To the extent consumers experience favorable emotions when looking at the picture which become associated with the advertised product, then persuasion will be facilitated.

Figure 15.7 contains the findings from one study of the emotionality evoked by television commercials. It is not surprising that the positive emotions of joy, acceptance, and anticipation were observed most frequently. The results also revealed considerable diversity among the ads in their emotional intensity. Some ads evoked very little emotion from viewers, although all ads elicited at least some level of emotional response. This latter observation indicates that even so-called informational ads are likely to evoke some degree of emotional response.

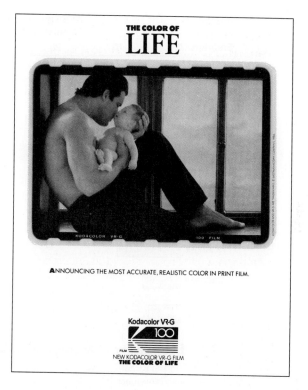

FIGURE 15.6   **Affective Messages Try to Persuade through Emotion**

Ray and Batra have suggested several potential advantages of affective or emotional advertising.[23] People may pay greater attention to emotional ads because of affect's role in guiding attention. Emotional ads may also increase the viewer's arousal, which, as discussed later, can enhance message processing. Affective executions can lead to more favorable attitudes than might otherwise be obtained.[24] The March of Dimes departed from their traditional institutional-style advertising in favor of "emotional response" ads for targeting less literate segments.[25] These new ads contained powerful visuals (for example, a liquor label on a baby bottle filled with alcohol) with little or no copy.

Executional Elements   Although persuasion may often depend on what you say in your message, how you say it can be equally, if not more, important in many situations. Message execution must therefore be carefully considered in the development of persuasive communications. Indeed, **executional elements** such as visuals, sounds, colors, and pace can play a critical role during persuasion, particularly for ads designed to elicit emotional responses.

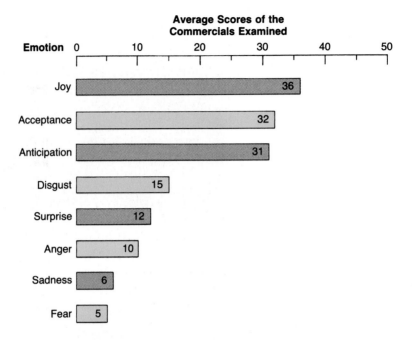

Average Scores of the Commercials Examined

Emotion	Score
Joy	36
Acceptance	32
Anticipation	31
Disgust	15
Surprise	12
Anger	10
Sadness	6
Fear	5

FIGURE 15.7   Emotionality of Average Television Commercial

Source: David M. Zeitlin and Richard A. Westwood, "Measuring Emotional Response," *Journal of Advertising Research* 26 (October/November 1986), 34–44, Table 3.

Existing research has largely focused on the persuasive impact of pictorial elements. Pictures can also influence consumers' perceptions of the product.[26] The fluffy cat resting comfortably on the recliner in Figure 15.8 is intended to enhance beliefs about the product's softness and comfort. Similarly, the Armstrong Tire Company includes pictures of "Tuffy the Rhino" in its advertising to reinforce perceptions of the product's strength, durability, and toughness.[27]

Research has also shown that the use of an attractive or unattractive picture in an ad can change product attitudes without affecting product beliefs.[28] When an ad contained an unattractive picture, subjects were puzzled by the picture's presence and expressed unfavorable thoughts about its appropriateness. However, when the ad contained a picture of an attractive tropical setting, they reported experiencing favorable imagery during ad processing.

The Influence of Attitudes toward the Ad

The ability of advertising to create favorable attitudes toward a product may often depend on consumers' attitudes toward the ad itself. Ads that are liked or evaluated favorably can lead to more positive product attitudes. Disliked ads may lower consumers' product evaluations. Research has demonstrated repeatedly that attitudes toward an ad serve as a significant predictor of product attitudes.[29]

FIGURE 15.8   What Does this Picture Convey about the Product?

This is not to say that consumers must always like an ad in order for it to be effective.[30] There can be ads that are disliked but still successful. Indeed, advertisers sometimes make ads deliberately annoying in the hope that the message can break through the clutter. A good example is the "Mr. Whipple" commercials for Procter & Gamble's Charmin toilet tissue that began in 1968 and ran for 14 years.[31] Consumers reported that they couldn't stand watching the ads. Even so, the campaign was very effective in communicating the brand's softness positioning and certainly helped it become the dominant brand in its category.

Repetition Effects

Research on the persuasive effects of message repetition has produced a mixed set of findings. Indeed, the literature has reported that repetition has a positive,[32] negative,[33] null,[34] or inverted-U[35] (that is, attitude increases up to some point, beyond which attitude declines) relationship with persuasion.

Perhaps the most promising explanation for how repetition affects persuasion is the two-stage attitude-modification process proposed by Cacioppo and Petty.[36] Early exposures are believed to provide the person with additional opportunities to evaluate the position advocated by the message. Once the person has fully evaluated the message's implications for her or his attitudes, the second stage takes over and tedium with the message becomes dominant. This tedium will lower message acceptance.

This view carries several implications about the persuasive role of repetition. First, additional repetitions are needed only if the person is unable or unwilling to fully evaluate the message's position after a single exposure.[37] For example, an informationally complex television ad may require several exposures, especially when the consumer is not highly motivated to carefully process the ad.

Moreover, when additional repetitions are required, the effect of repetition will depend on the strength of the message. More repetition should produce a greater amount of positive cognitive responses for messages using strong claims. Just the opposite should occur for weak claims, where repetition will increase the number of negative cognitive responses.

The point at which tedium begins will depend on the amount of processing that occurs during prior exposures. If the ad is fully evaluated after one exposure, tedium will set in immediately. If such thinking does not occur until after many exposures, the negative impact of tedium is delayed.

Evidence germane to this view has been largely supportive.[38] Cacioppo and Petty's initial study focused on the acceptance of a message containing strong arguments in favor of increasing university expenditures.[39] Subjects were exposed to the message a low (once), moderate (three), or high (five) number of times. Agreement with the message increased from one to three exposures but then decreased after five exposures. This pattern was consistent with the cognitive response data. Favorable thoughts followed the same pattern, while unfavorable thoughts moved in the opposite manner (that is, negative thoughts decreased from one to three exposures and increased after five exposures).

The role of message strength as a moderator of repetition effects has also been demonstrated. Whereas acceptance was greater after three exposures for a message presenting strong claims, acceptance was lower after three exposures for a message based on weak claims.[40] Finally, responses reflecting tedium have been found to increase in intensity and frequency with greater amounts of repetition.[41]

Consumer Considerations

Although marketers are able to enhance the persuasiveness of their communications by bringing together the appropriate blend of source and message elements, the ultimate impact of any communication will depend heavily on how consumers respond to it. These responses, in turn, are shaped by a multitude of consumer characteristics, such as the person's motivation or knowledge at the time of exposure. Consequently, the characteristics of the consumer at the time of exposure to a persuasive communication should be taken into account in designing the communication. In this section we examine some of the more important consumer characteristics.

Motivation   There is a tremendous diversity in consumers' motivational states when they are receiving marketing communications. Sometimes consumers will be highly motivated to carefully process and evaluate such communications. Quite often, however, this is not the case, as consumers either ignore or expend little cognitive effort during processing.

The importance of the consumer's motivational state during message processing was illustrated earlier in the chapter by the research of Petty, Cacioppo, and Schumann (see Figure 15.2).[42] Recall that when subjects were more strongly motivated to process the ad (that is, the high-involvement condition), persuasion depended solely on the strength of the message claims. However, when this motivation was lacking (that is, low involvement), the celebrity status of the endorser featured in the ad became influential.

The extent to which the product is purchased because of utilitarian versus hedonic considerations (see Chapter 9) is another important consideration in developing persuasive communications. If the product is purchased primarily for its utilitarian benefits (for example, its ability to solve current problems or eliminate potential problems), informational appeals (for example, how the product solves the problem and why it should be chosen over others) should be emphasized. Products that are bought primarily for their hedonic benefits (for example, those that provide sensory gratification or intellectual stimulation) should rely more heavily on affective appeals.[43]

It is, of course, possible that both types of appeals will be necessary for promoting the product. Automobiles are a good example. Print ads are typically filled with considerable amounts of details and facts about the car's characteristics that can be processed at the consumer's leisure. Television ads, on the other hand, may focus on the sensory pleasures that can be obtained by driving the car.

Arousal   Physiological arousal, representing a person's degree of alertness along a continuum ranging from extreme drowsiness to extreme wakefulness, can moderate the persuasion process. Arousal presumably has both facilitating and inhibiting effects on the amount of elaboration during message processing. Little processing can occur when the person is drowsy. A certain level of arousal is, therefore, desirable. However, increases in arousal lead to more processing of internal cues sent by the nervous system, thereby reducing the cognitive capacity available for message elaboration. These considerations suggest an inverted-U relationship between arousal and elaboration. Elaboration should be stronger at moderate levels of arousal than when arousal is very low or very high.

Research has supported the persuasive role of arousal.[44] When arousal was moderate, attitudes formed following message processing depended only on the strength of the message claims. In contrast, attitudes formed under high arousal were based more heavily on the celebrity status of the product endorser.

Such findings indicate the need to consider the arousal level of consumers when exposed to persuasive communications. Message elements other than the product claims may play a much greater role in determining persuasion when arousal is very high. High arousal may characterize a number of situations in which consumers receive persuasive communications, such as sporting events, action-packed movies, and workout shows where viewers actively participate.

Knowledge As discussed in Chapter 10, consumer knowledge is a major determinant of consumer behavior. The same holds true in the realm of persuasion. When consumers are knowledgeable about the topic of some persuasive communication, they are better able to evaluate the strengths and weaknesses of the message claims. Consistent with this, knowledgeable consumers have been shown to respond more favorably as advertising content becomes more technical.[45] Just the opposite was observed for unknowledgeable consumers.

This line of reasoning carries important implications for the content of a communication.[46] Because knowledgeable consumers already know the benefits of product ownership and usage, less emphasis on benefits relative to more technical features may be desirable. Camera ads aimed at experts, for instance, often emphasize technical product features. However, when target consumers lack such knowledge, communications that focus on easily understood product benefits are likely to be more successful.

Similarly, knowledgeable consumers are more likely to focus on information most relevant for evaluating a product's strengths and weaknesses. Those less informed may be more persuaded by information that is peripheral or less relevant. In one study, experts' evaluations of a camera were strongly affected by a description of the product's attributes but were unaffected by a label of the camera type (that is, 110 or 35mm SLR). The opposite was true for novices, as their product evaluations depended only on the product type label.[47]

Mood Another consumer characteristic that can influence persuasion is the consumer's mood state at the time of exposure to a communication. Moods refer to transient feelings (for example, sadness, anticipation) that exist at a particular time and place.[48] Research suggests that favorable moods can enhance persuasion, while unfavorable moods reduce persuasion.[49]

How can a communicator encourage favorable moods? One approach is to include within the communication certain executional elements that tend to evoke the desired mood state, as is commonly done in affective messages. A second approach is to place the communication in a context that encourages favorable moods. For example, as noted in Chapter 7, the program in which a commercial appears can affect the moods consumers bring to the communication situation.[50]

Personality Traits As noted in Chapter 12, a consumer's personality may also shape her or his responsiveness to persuasive communications. A person's **need for cognition** representing an individual's tendency to undertake and enjoy thinking, is one such personality trait.[51] Persons scoring high on need for cognition measures are more influenced by message claims, while those having a low need for cognition display greater sensitivity to peripheral message cues such as source attractiveness.[52]

Self-monitoring has also been linked to persuasion. High self-monitoring persons are very sensitive to situational and interpersonal considerations. They are quite willing and adept at modifying their behavior in order to be the "right person in the right place at the right time." At the other end are low self-monitoring individuals who do not try to modify their behavior to fit circumstantial situations. Rather, they rely more heavily on their own internal feelings and attitudes to guide behavior.[53]

The relative effectiveness of appeals based on a product's image versus claims about a product's quality can depend on self-monitoring.[54] High self-monitors have been found to respond more favorably to image advertising, whereas advertising of product quality was received more favorably by low self-monitors. Similar differences were also observed between high and low self-monitors in their willingness to try and how much they would pay for products associated with either an image or quality appeal. When Mercury abandoned its image-oriented advertising in favor of a new campaign emphasizing more substantive aspects of the cars themselves, the primary target market was low self-monitors.[55]

Existing Attitudes   The success of a persuasive communication will also depend on the attitudes presently held by the target audience. A fundamental distinction is whether persuasion takes place under **attitude formation** or **attitude change** conditions. When the person has yet to develop an attitude toward the topic of the message, then we are dealing with attitude formation. Attitude change characterizes settings in which the person holds a pre-existing attitude that differs from the position advocated by the message.

This distinction is important because of its implications for persuasion. In general, persuasive communications will be more successful at creating attitudes than in changing attitudes. Changing attitudes is more difficult simply because of the additional resistance that results from the commitment to the existing attitude. The stronger this commitment, the greater the resistance, as reflected by greater counterargumentation with the message.

Commitment will be stronger for attitudes anchored in a person's sense of self-worth or ego.[56] Similarly, attitudes based on actual product consumption will be held more firmly than those formed through indirect product experience (for example, advertising).[57]

One demonstration of how existing attitudes moderate persuasion comes from a study in which initial attitudes were formed toward a brand of peanut butter by either providing subjects with some product information or allowing them actually to taste the product.[58] Afterward, they were exposed to a communication favoring the product delivered by either a high- or low-credibility source. The impact of source credibility depended on the method of initial attitude formation. Source credibility affected postcommunication attitudes only when subjects did not first taste the product. These findings suggest that a message's peripheral cues may have little effect when the message is attempting to change firmly held attitudes.

The favorability of existing attitudes can also determine the relative effectiveness of different persuasive communications. Suppose you were trying to change the attitudes of consumers who currently hold a negative opinion of your product. Should you use a humorous ad to do so, or would a nonhumorous ad be more effective? The nonhumorous ad has been shown to be more persuasive in this situation. However, when prior attitudes were initially favorable, then the humorous ad was more effective.[59]

Product Considerations

Thus far our discussion has largely neglected how characteristics of the product can affect persuasion strategy. However, just as characteristics of the target consumer can affect the form and effectiveness of persuasion strategy, so too must various aspects of the product be taken into account.

Stage in the Product Life Cycle
Advertising strategy will vary over a product's life cycle. Gaining awareness and product trial are primary objectives for new products. Whereas building favorable brand attitudes is critical during the growth stages, maintaining or reinforcing these attitudes is paramount when the product reaches maturity.

Product Experience
The impact of persuasive communications will depend on consumers' subsequent experiences with the product. A poor tasting beverage is unlikely to be favorably evaluated, no matter how much advertising claims otherwise.

In some cases, however, consumers are limited in their ability to assess product performance accurately. Can the consumer truly evaluate the benefits that may arise from taking a vitamin a day? And how do we know whether the person who repaired our car or TV took advantage of us by unnecessarily replacing parts that were in working condition?

Research suggests that the "ambiguity" of product experiences can shape the impact of prior advertising. In one study, advertising's potential to affect perceptions of product quality was examined for two products—polo shirts and paper towels.[60] Following ad exposure, subjects were allowed to either visually inspect different brands of polo shirts or actually test the water absorption properties of various paper towel brands. The water test yielded clear evidence about the paper towels. Consequently, subjects based their product quality perceptions on this evidence alone and ignored the advertising. In contrast, the ambiguous information provided by visually inspecting the shirts enabled advertising to exert a favorable influence.

Product Positioning
A major determinant of persuasion strategy is the particular positioning desired for a product. That is, what product image does the marketer wish to create in the consumer's mind? The answer to this question will strongly dictate the type of message one uses to influence consumers. A product built around a status positioning will use very different messages than the product that competes based on price.

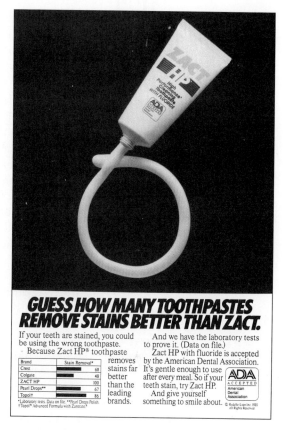

FIGURE 15.9   **The Influence of Relative Product Performance on Advertising Strategy**

Relative Performance   Attention must also be given to the product's performance relative to competitive products in the areas representing the desired positioning. When the product is demonstrably superior to competitors, this advantage can be a potent selling point. In the absence of such superiority, other tactics must be employed for communicating the product offering.

The two ads appearing in Figure 15.9 illustrate this point. The apparent superiority of Zact over Topol in removing stains permits Zact to employ a comparative ad making strong claims along this dimension. In contrast, the Topol ad attempts to convey the desired positioning without reference to competitors. Instead, an appropriate visual image (the model dressed completely in white, with shining teeth) is combined with the claim that Topol "works more effectively."

The attractiveness of affective and informational appeals is also linked to the relative performance of competing brands. Informational appeals may be of limited value when consumers perceive competing brands to be homogeneous in their

Influencing Product Choice through Peripheral Advertising Cues

Earlier in the chapter you learned about how consumers may sometimes follow a peripheral route to persuasion in which their postcommunication attitudes are based on stimuli that are actually irrelevant to evaluating the true merits of a product (for example, a pretty picture that is devoid of product-relevant information). While the attitudinal impact of peripheral cues has been well documented, little is known about whether such cues can actually influence consumers' product choices.

Recent research supports the potential for peripheral cues to alter choice under certain conditions. In this study, subjects were exposed initially to a series of print ads. One of the ads featured a fictitious brand of soft drink called Sunburst. For some subjects, the ad contained an attractive picture, which pretesting revealed to be devoid of product meaning. For others, the ad contained an unattractive, peripheral picture.

After viewing the ads, subjects were given the results of a taste test in which consumers had tasted and rated Sunburst and two other brands along three important attributes. The study used three different taste test results. Some subjects received a version that revealed the presence of a dominant brand other than Sunburst (that is, this brand received vastly superior ratings on all attributes). The second version reported virtually the same taste ratings for all brands. In the final version, one brand received the best ratings on one of the three attributes used in the taste test, another brand was rated the highest on the second attribute, and the remaining brand received the best ratings for the third attribute. Subjects were told that they would receive a six pack of the brand they preferred.

The results indicated that the peripheral pictures had a strong influence on brand choices so long as the taste test results did not reveal a dominant brand. When the taste ratings were essentially the same for all three brands, thus indicating a lack of differentiation, twice as many subjects chose Sunburst when it had previously been paired with the attractive picture in the ad. Similar results occurred even when the ratings revealed important brand differences without one brand being dominant. However, when the ratings indicated that Sunburst was dominated by another brand, subjects' choices were insensitive to the peripheral advertising cues.

Source: Paul W. Miniard, Deepak Sirdeshmukh, and Daniel E. Innis, "Peripheral Persuasion and Brand Choice," *Journal of Consumer Research* 19 (1992), forthcoming.

product characteristics. Affective appeals may represent a more promising means for achieving differentiation in such settings. This issue is further explored in Consumer in Focus 15.2.

Behavior Modification Techniques

Persuasive communications represent but one of the many weapons in the marketer's arsenal for influencing consumers' attitudes and behavior. In this section we explore a number of additional techniques that have been successfully employed for modifying human behavior.

Prompting

Prompting is nothing more than simply requesting some action from the person. Probably everyone who has ordered from a fast food restaurant has encountered a prompt. Requests such as "Would you like to try our new Philly Beef and Cheese?" or "Would you also like a side order of french fries?" are examples. Similarly, shoe salespeople will often ask the female customer preparing to purchase shoes if she is interested in a matching handbag. Prompts require the consumer to at least consider the product. Product purchase is thus more likely than it would be if the product were never considered.

Multiple Request Techniques

Research suggests that compliance with a "critical" request can be enhanced when the person is first asked to comply with an initial request. There are two major types of multiple-request procedures: foot-in-the-door and door-in-the-face.[61]

Foot-in-the-Door   Foot-in-the-door (FITD) represents a technique where compliance with a critical request is increased if an individual first agrees to an initial small request. This paradigm was introduced by Freedman and Fraser, who examined its effectiveness in getting homeowners to temporarily display a large, ugly sign reading "Drive Carefully" in their front yards.[62] They found a substantial increase in compliance with this request among those who were first asked to do a smaller task, such as to place a small sign advocating safe driving in their front windows.

The typical explanation offered for the FITD effect is derived from self-perception theory,[63] which maintains that individuals come to know their own attitudes, emotions, and other internal states partially from inferring them from observations of their own behavior. The individual is viewed functionally as being in the same position as an outside observer who relies on external cues to infer one's own inner state.

The self-perception explanation for FITD is as follows. Getting a person to comply with an initial request produces a behavior that indicated favorableness toward the behavioral domain. For instance, agreeing to display a small sign may suggest that a person approves of behaviors of this type. This favorableness results in greater compliance with a second request involving the same behavioral domain. In contrast, those asked to comply only with the second request have not undertaken the behavior generated by the first request. Consequently, they are less likely to do what is asked of them.

Marketing investigations of foot-in-the-door's usefulness for enhancing compliance have focused on behaviors such as answering surveys and donating to charity. Results have been largely supportive. Most studies have found FITD to be more effective than a straight request,[64] although a few have not.[65] The amount of delay between the first and second request, the extent of the requests, whether the person actually undertakes the initial request or only agrees to do so, the similarity in topics between the first and second request, as well as many other factors may influence the effectiveness of FITD.[66] Further research is needed to identify precisely those conditions that limit its usefulness.

Door-in-the-Face   Door-in-the-face (DITF) is the flip side of foot-in-the-door. Under this approach, the person is first asked to do something that is substantially more complex than the second, critical request. In fact, this initial request is designed to be so extreme that the person will refuse. Following this refusal, the second request is proposed. Research has shown DITF will often increase compliance relative to simply asking the second request alone.

Why does DITF work? One reason is perceptual contrast. The second, small request is made to look even smaller when preceded by the initial, large request.

A second reason is the principle of **reciprocity**, which essentially says that we should try to repay what others have done for us.[67] Thus, when someone makes a concession to us, we should reciprocate. The dramatic reduction between the first and second request is intended to create the perception that the requester is making a concession. In return, it is hoped that the person will reciprocate by now agreeing to the second request. Research indicates that such concession making is a necessary prerequisite for the DITF effect.[68]

The basic DITF strategy of large-then-smaller-request sequence underlies the retail store sales practice of "talking the top of the line."[69] The shopper is first shown the deluxe model. If the shopper buys this model, so much the better. If not, then the salesperson can counteroffer with a less expensive model. When Brunswick used this approach by first showing customers the most expensive pool table, followed by the rest of the product line, the average sale was over $1,000. However, starting customers with the least expensive table and working up produced an average sale of $550.[70]

The Principle of Reciprocity

As just noted, the principle of reciprocity provides an important point of leverage for those attempting to influence behavior.[71] Religious groups, including the Hare Krishnas, have used this technique to enhance compliance with their requests for donations by first offering the person some gift, such as a flower. It also applies to marketing. A company that sells through in-home demonstrations, for instance, contacts prospects and offers some gift or cash prize to be delivered by the salesperson. Sometimes the gift comes in the form of a free product sample. Food companies often hire someone to stand in supermarket aisles and offer shoppers a taste of the product. Many consumers find it difficult to accept the sample without feeling a sense of obligation to buy the product (see Consumer in Focus 15.3).

Amway's Use of Reciprocity

A different version of the free-sample tactic is used by the Amway Corporation, a company that manufactures and distributes household and personal-care products in a vast national network of door-to-door neighborhood sales. The company, which has grown from a basement-run operation to a one and a half billion-dollar yearly sales business, makes use of the free sample in a device called the BUG. The BUG consists of a collection of Amway products—bottles of furniture polish, detergent, or shampoo, spray containers of deodorizers, insect killers, or window cleaners—carried to the customer's home in a specially designed tray or just a polyethylene bag. The confidential Amway Career Manual then instructs the salesperson to leave the BUG with the customer "for 24, 48, or 72 hours, at no cost or obligation to her. Just tell her you would like her to try the products.... That's an offer no one can refuse." At the end of the trial period, the Amway representative returns and picks up orders for those of the products the customer wishes to purchase. Since few customers use up the entire contents of even one of the product containers in such a short time, the salesperson may then take the remaining product portions in the BUG to the next potential customer down the line or across the street and start the process again. Many Amway representatives have several BUGs circulating in their districts at one time.

The customer who has accepted and used the BUG products has been trapped into facing the influence of the reciprocity rule. Many such customers yield to a sense of obligation to order those of the salesperson's products that they have tried and thereby partially consumed. And, of course, by now the Amway Corporation knows that to be the case. Even in a company with as excellent a growth record as Amway, the BUG device has created a big stir.

Source: Robert B. Cialdini, *Influence: How and Why People Agree to Things* (New York: William Morrow, 1984), 39–40.

The Role of Commitment

The very act of making a commitment can have a strong influence on subsequent behavior. This effect is aptly demonstrated by research asking subjects to estimate the length of various lines.[72] One group was required to write down their estimates, sign their names, and turn the form in to the experimenter. A second group wrote their estimates on a "magic" writing pad that could be erased before others could see what they had written. A final group kept their judgments in their mind.

Subjects were then given new evidence that challenged their initial estimates. The group who had turned in their original estimates to the experimenter showed the least amount of opinion change. The simple act of publicly committing themselves made them less willing to change their minds. Interestingly, the second group who made a private commitment also displayed less change than those who only made a mental note of their original estimates. Thus, the very act of writing something down, even though it was not made publicly available, induced a sense of commitment that carried over.

Gaining a person's commitment to an opinion or action is a very good way of enhancing the odds that he or she will behave in a consistent manner. Gaining commitment is the key element of the unethical "lowballing" procedure.[73] A car dealer, for example, might use this procedure by offering customers a great deal in order to gain their commitment to buying the car. Once the customer has agreed to do so, the deal is then changed. This can be done in a variety of ways. The salesperson might claim that he or she "forgot" to include the price of some option. Another story line is that the boss has canceled the deal because "we would be losing money." Some customers may walk away. Unfortunately, others will not. The act of committing to the purchase will lead them to complete the transaction despite this change in terms.

Earlier we noted that the simple act of writing something down can enhance one's commitment. This observation helps explain the attractiveness of contests that require consumers to submit essays on "Why I like this product." Door-to-door sales companies have also discovered the magic of written commitment. They are able to reduce their cancellation rates (that is, customers who void the contract during the "cooling-off " period guaranteed by law) by simply having the customer, rather than the salesperson, complete the sales agreement form.[74]

Labeling

Labeling involves attaching some description to a person, such as "You are kind." Labels presumably lead people to view themselves in the manner implied by the label. This, in turn, should increase the likelihood that they will undertake behaviors that are consistent with the label. Research in this area has been very supportive across a number of behavioral domains, including voting, littering, and charitable actions.[75] However, the influence of labeling may be fairly short lived. In one study, labeling had an effect on voting behavior that occurred one week after the label was attached but not on voting behavior eight months later.[76]

Labeling appears to hold considerable promise, although further research is needed, particularly with respect to its effects on purchase behavior. Labeling could prove to be very useful in the realm of personal selling. The encyclopedia salesperson might describe prospective buyers with children as "concerned parents." Similarly, charitable organizations might wish to label potential donors as "generous and compassionate." Recent evidence also supports the usefulness of advertising as a mechanism for labeling consumers.[77]

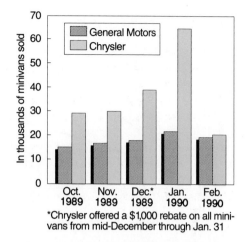

FIGURE 15.10   **Chrysler's Rebate Program Boosted Minivan Sales**

Source: Neal Templin, "GM Declares War on Chrysler Over Minivans," *Wall Street Journal* (March 23, 1990), B1, B6.

Incentives

Incentives encompass a broad range of promotional tools, such as price discounts, premiums, contests, sweepstakes, rebates, and coupons. Incentives typically represent an important component of the overall product-promotion strategy. Indeed, expenditures in this area have reached incredible levels.

To illustrate just how much influence incentives can have on consumer behavior, let's examine the effect of Chrysler's rebate program on sales of its minivans (see Figure 15.10). In the two months prior to the rebate, Chrysler was averaging nearly 30,000 sales per month. When the company began offering $1,000 rebates in mid-December, sales began to climb. In January, the last month rebates were offered, Chrysler sold nearly 64,000 minivans.

Packaged goods manufacturers often rely on coupons for influencing sales. In 1991, they distributed more than 300 billion coupons through the print media. Given the depressed economic conditions during this time, it is not surprising that consumers redeemed the most coupons since 1986, saving them $4 billion on their purchases.[78]

Evidence concerning the impact of coupons on purchasing behavior is presented in Figure 15.11. These results are based on four new product introduction tests undertaken by the National Panel Diary marketing research firm.[79] The influence of coupons is reflected by a comparison of those consumers who were sent coupons versus those who were not sent coupons.

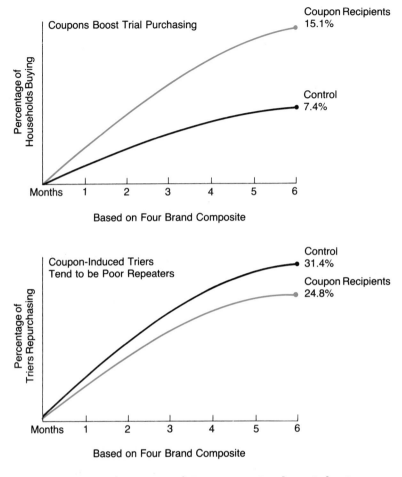

FIGURE 15.11   **The Impact of Coupons on Purchase Behavior**

The top graph in Figure 15.11 represents the findings involving initial or trial purchasing. As can be seen, coupons had a very strong effect on trial purchasing. Over twice as many households receiving a coupon engaged in product trial compared to those households not receiving the coupon.

What may come as a surprise are the findings involving repeat purchasing. The bottom graph in Figure 15.11 indicates that coupon-induced triers were *less* likely to repurchase the product than those who tried the product without the coupon inducement. Does this finding argue against the use of coupons? Not necessarily. In the present situation, coupons yielded a penetration level of 3.7 percent (trial rate of 15.1 percent times the repurchase rate of 24.8 percent), compared to a level of 2.3 percent when coupons were not used. The lower repurchase rates of coupon-induced triers is more than offset by the substantial boost in trial purchasing when coupons were used. Of course, this need not always be the case. Furthermore, even when coupons provide greater market penetration, this increase must be weighed against the costs of such gains.

Consistent with the repeat purchase results presented in Figure 15.11, a common finding in the literature is that repurchase rates are typically lower following a promotional purchase (that is, a purchase accompanied by an incentive) than a nonpromotional purchase.[80] Why does this occur? One explanation is that consumers who purchase a product accompanied by some incentive are less likely to attribute the purchase to favorable product attitudes than consumers who purchase without an incentive. As a result, consumers might hold less favorable product attitudes which, in turn, could lead to lower loyalty and repeat purchase rates.[81] However, a recent test of this possibility did not find incentives to have a detrimental effect on product attitudes.[82]

Alternatively, lower repurchase rates following promotional purchases may have little to do with reduced attitudes and loyalty. Rather, it may simply be a reflection of the type of customers that are attracted by incentives.[83] There is a segment of consumers whose purchase decisions are dictated by whatever brand is offering the best deal. They will buy a given brand only as long as it provides the best deal. Since deals come and go, so do they.

Single versus Multiple Incentives

"Single-shot" incentives may often be inadequate for modifying long-run behavior. Rather, a series of incentives may be necessary to produce more lasting effects on purchasing behavior.

The Coca-Cola promotional program used for introducing their new Coke formula was based on a multiple-application approach. Consumers were given both free samples (single cans of the product) and coupons (reproduced in Figure 15.12). Note that the coupon with the largest discount has the earliest expiration date, while the smallest discount coupon has the latest expiration date. This decline in the size of the price discount is very desirable. First, it enhances the proportion of reinforcement received from the product versus that stemming from the coupon. The gradual reduction also enhances the similarity of each purchase to the behavior ultimately desired (that is, buying at regular price).

Existing evidence supports the relative effectiveness of a multiple-incentive program versus the single-shot approach. For example, free samples with coupons have been shown to generate higher initial purchase rates than samples without the coupon.[84] Similarly, in-package coupons have been found to enhance repeat purchasing compared to media coupons and price discounts.[85] This observed superiority is consistent with the notion that incentives that help modify behavior over time will outperform those that do not. Further research is desperately needed to clarify the short- and long-run effects of alternative incentive programs.

Potential Problems with Incentives

As you have seen, incentives can be very effective in boosting sales. Even so, this increase in sales may come at the expense of a company's bottom line. Remember the examples in the chapter opener? Kraft discovered that the large majority of purchases made with coupons would have occurred even without the coupons being offered! Unless the profits made on the

FIGURE 15.12   A Multiple-Incentive Approach Can Be More Effective

incremental sales due to coupons covered the reduced profit on the remaining sales, Kraft lost money.

This same basic point can be made for Chrysler's rebate program discussed earlier. Returning to Figure 15.10, notice how the General Motors' minivan sales remained quite stable during this time, suggesting that the rebates had little impact on Chrysler's competitor. Where, then, did the increased Chrysler sales during December and January come from?

Perhaps these sales came from consumers who would have purchased a vehicle other than a minivan without the rebate. It is also possible that at least some of these sales represented "accelerated" purchases. Consumers who were planning on buying a Chrysler minivan later in the year may have moved up their purchase plans to take advantage of the rebate offer. The fact that sales after the rebates ended were substantially below the sales levels prior to the rebates being offered is a strong indication that many consumers purchased vans earlier than they would have. Each of these accelerated purchases represents a loss in profits that must be weighed against the profits generated by incremental sales in evaluating the incentive program's profitability.[86]

Consumers Wait for the Rebate

According to Jay Lewis, cruise industry consultant and president of Market Scope, "The auto industry taught the consumer to wait for a rebate. The cruise industry has taught the consumer to wait for the discount. You figure if you wait till the last possible moment, you get the best possible deal. That is how the consumer is thinking today."

And for good reason. Discounting in the cruise industry is averaging around 30 percent, with some cruise lines offering savings in the neighborhood of 50 percent.

But will consumers become conditioned to the lower rates? "I hope not," says Carol Morse, manager of Travel Is Fun. "Like the airlines, [cruise lines] can't keep undercutting their profit margin."

But once consumers have become conditioned to deals, weaning them is no easy matter. Automakers have been trying for several years to reduce their dependency on incentive programs, with little success. Ford, for example, tried to eliminate its direct-to-customer rebates in December 1990. Instead of offering discounts to consumers, Ford copied Japanese automakers, which typically offer discounts only to dealers.

The dealers are then free to pass on all the money, or use some of it to increase advertising, or keep some to boost their own profits. But the strategy didn't work. Ford was forced to resume customer incentives five months later because of sluggish sales. "In a way, incentive programs are like hard drugs," asserts Christopher Cedergren, an auto analyst at Auto Pacific Group Inc. "Once you get on, it's hard to get off."

Source: Excerpted in part from Krystal Miller, "Car Prices Start Turning Around as Firms Cut Rebates," *Wall Street Journal* (February 14, 1992), B1, B6; Philip Stelly Jr., "Winds of War Knock Wind Out of Sales for the Cruise Industry," *Adweek* (March 4, 1991), 2–3.

Another potential problem with incentives is that, if used too often, consumers may become conditioned to buy based simply on whatever product is offering the best deal (see Consumer in Focus 15.4). As Rothschild and Gaidis point out,

> Purchase may become contingent upon the presence of a promotional tool. Removal of the promotion may lead to the extinction of purchase behavior. If long-term behavior toward the product is desired, promotional tools should not overshadow the product. In a marketing situation, it is paramount that reinforcement for purchase be derived primarily from the product, lest purchase become contingent upon a never ending succession of consumer deals.[87]

Summary

This chapter has attempted to convey some sense of the richness and complexity of the vast literature concerning how one might influence attitudes and behavior. A substantial amount of attention has been given to understanding persuasion through communication. From an information-processing perspective, persuasion (that is, the degree of acceptance) depends on the cognitive (thoughts) and affective (feelings) responses that occur during message processing. These responses in turn are affected by a number of communication (for example, source, message, repetition) and consumer (for example, motivation, knowledge, prior attitudes) characteristics.

According to the Elaboration Likelihood Model, persuasion can be characterized as following one of two basic routes. Under the central route, consumers rationally evaluate the position advocated in a message. Consequently, the strength of message claims will determine the amount of acceptance. Persuasion in the absence of issue-relevant thinking is called the peripheral route. Other communication elements (that is, peripheral cues) now become important determinants of persuasion.

Characteristics of both the consumer and the product should be taken into account in developing communication strategy. Consumers' motivation, knowledge, arousal, moods, personality traits, and existing attitudes can strongly affect the impact of persuasive communications. Similarly, the product's life cycle stage, the desired positioning, and the product's performance relative to competition will play major roles in shaping such activities.

In addition to persuasive communications, consumers' attitudes and behavior can be influenced through any one of a number of behavior modification techniques. Single (prompts) and multiple (foot-in-the-door and door-in-the-face) requests can be effective devices for shaping behavior. Evoking the principle of reciprocity (for example, through a free gift) or commitment (for example, "why I like this product" contests) can also be very useful in modifying behavior. Incentives such as coupons and rebates are often employed by marketers to encourage purchase behavior.

Review and Discussion Questions

1. What is meant by central and peripheral routes to persuasion?
2. When is the source most likely to enhance the persuasive power of an advertisement?
3. Suppose you were faced with the choice between an ad that attempts to create favorable attitudes by making several strong claims about the product versus an ad devoid of such claims but filled with attractive visuals and favorable music. How might your preference for using a particular ad depend on: (a) consumer's involvement at the time of ad exposure, (b) consumer's product knowledge at the time of ad exposure, and (c) the product's performance relative to competition?
4. A pretest of two alternative commercials found that consumers liked commercial A better than commercial B but that commercial B produced more favorable product attitudes. Why might this difference occur? Which commercial would you select, and why?
5. In a laboratory study it is discovered that a foreign make of automobile is regarded more favorably when advertising messages feature positive selling points as well as the fact that problems have existed in the past with respect to brake fade, door leaks and rattles, faulty ignition, and spark plug fouling. Would you, as the director of advertising

research, recommend that this company use a two-sided campaign? What arguments might be advanced?

6. A cable TV company is trying to increase the number of new subscribers. One proposal under consideration is to provide interested consumers with free service for two weeks before asking them to subscribe. Would this enhance the likelihood of a person subscribing? What effect would you expect if receiving the free service was made contingent upon first completing an extensive survey of viewing habits?

7. A local charitable organization is planning its annual door-to-door fund-raising campaign. What suggestions would you make as to how the organization might enhance the effectiveness of its solicitors?

8. A recent study reveals that 20 percent of target households receiving a discount coupon tried the product compared to a 10 percent trial rate among those target households not receiving the coupon. Repeat-purchase rates, however, were far greater among noncoupon trier households (30 percent) relative to coupon-induced triers (15 percent). First, how can you explain this pattern of results? Second, do these results support the use of coupons as a means for increasing the customer base? Justify your position.

9. Consider the following proposals for using price-off coupons during the market introduction of a new food snack purchased weekly:

	Week			
Proposal	**1**	**2**	**3**	**4**
A	50% off	No coupon	No coupon	No coupon
B	50% off	50% off	50% off	50% off
C	50% off	35% off	20% off	5% off
D	5% off	20% off	35% off	50% off

Under proposal A, for instance, consumers would be supplied with a 50 percent discount coupon in the first week but no coupons in the second, third, and fourth weeks. Which proposal is likely to generate the greatest number of customers in week 5 when coupons are no longer available? Why?

Endnotes

1. For recent summaries of the ELM and associated literature, see Richard E. Petty and John T. Cacioppo, *Communication and Persuasion: Central and Peripheral Routes to Attitude Change* (New York: Springer/Verlag, 1986); Richard E. Petty and John T. Cacioppo, "The Elaboration Likelihood Model of Persuasion," in Leonard Berkowitz, ed., *Advances in Experimental Social Psychology* 19 (New York: Academic Press, 1986), 123–205. A similar conceptualization is offered by Shelly Chaiken, "Heuristic Versus Systematic Information Processing and the Use of Source Versus Message Cues in Persuasion," *Journal of Personality and Social Psychology* 39 (November 1980), 752–766. Also see Shelly Chaiken and C. Stangor, "Attitude and Attitude Change," *Annual Review of Psychology* 38 (1987), 575–630.

2. For research and critiques beyond those cited in the preceding footnote, see Charles S. Areni and Richard J. Lutz, "The Role of Argument Quality in the Elaboration Likelihood Model," in Michael J. Houston, ed., *Advances in Consumer Research* 15 (Ann

Arbor: Association for Consumer Research, 1988), 197–201; Mary J. Bitner and Carl Obermiller, "The Elaboration Likelihood Model: Limitations and Extensions in Marketing," in Elizabeth C. Hirschman and Morris R. Holbrook, eds., *Advances in Consumer Research* 12 (Ann Arbor: Association for Consumer Research, 1985), 420–425; Curt Haugtvedt, Richard E. Petty, John T. Cacioppo, and Theresa Steidley, "Personality and Ad Effectiveness: Exploring the Utility of Need for Cognition," in Michael J. Houston, ed., *Advances in Consumer Research* 15 (Ann Arbor: Association for Consumer Research, 1988), 209–212; Lynn R. Kahle and Pamela M. Homer, "Physical Attractiveness of the Celebrity Endorser: A Social Adaptation Perspective," *Journal of Consumer Research* 11 (March 1985), 954–961; Paul W. Miniard, Peter R. Dickson, and Kenneth R. Lord, "Some Central and Peripheral Thoughts on the Routes to Persuasion," in Michael J. Houston, ed., *Advances in Consumer Research* 15 (Ann Arbor: Association for Consumer Research, 1988), 204–208; Paul W. Miniard, Sunil Bhatla, Kenneth R. Lord, Peter R. Dickson, and H. Rao Unnava, "Picture-based Persuasion Processes and the Moderating Role of Involvement," *Journal of Consumer Research* 18 (June 1991), 92–107; Richard E. Petty and John T. Cacioppo, "The Effects of Involvement on Responses to Argument Quantity and Quality: Central and Peripheral Routes to Persuasion," *Journal of Personality and Social Psychology* 46 (January 1984), 69–81; Richard E. Petty, John T. Cacioppo, and David Schumann, "Central and Peripheral Routes to Advertising Effectiveness: The Moderating Role of Involvement," *Journal of Consumer Research* 10 (September 1983), 135–146; S. Ratneshwar and Shelly Chaiken, "Comprehension's Role in Persuasion: The Case of Its Moderating Effect on the Persuasive Impact of Source Cues," *Journal of Consumer Research* 18 (June 1991), 52–62; Richard F. Yalch and Rebecca Elmore-Yalch, "The Effect of Numbers on the Route to Persuasion," *Journal of Consumer Research* 11 (June 1984), 522–527.

3. Petty, Cacioppo, and Schumann, "Central and Peripheral Routes to Advertising Effectiveness: The Moderating Role of Involvement."

4. This figure comes from a study by Needham, Harper, and Steers as cited by Stephen J. Hoch and Young-Won Ha, "Consumer Learning: Advertising and the Ambiguity of Product Experience," *Journal of Consumer Research* 13 (September 1986), 221–233.

5. For a general review, see Brian Sternthal, Lynn Phillips, and Ruby Dholakia, "The Persuasive Effect of Source Credibility: A Situational Analysis," *Public Opinion Quarterly* 42 (Fall 1978), 285–314; Brian Sternthal and C. Samuel Craig, *Consumer Behavior: An Information Processing Perspective* (Englewood Cliffs, N.J.: Prentice-Hall, 1982), 295–304. Recent empirical investigations can be found in Danny L. Moore, Douglas Hausknecht, and Kanchana Thamodaran, "Time Compression, Response Opportunity, and Persuasion," *Journal of Consumer Research* 13 (June 1986), 85–99; Chenghuan Wu and David R. Shaffer, "Susceptibility to Persuasive Appeals as a Function of Source Credibility and Prior Experience with the Attitude Object," *Journal of Personality and Social Psychology* 52 (1987), 677–688. We should note that less credible sources have on occasion been found to induce more persuasion. See Robert R. Harmon and Kenneth A. Coney, "The Persuasive Effects of Source Credibility in Buy and Lease Situations," *Journal of Marketing Research* 19 (May 1982), 255–260; Brian Sternthal, Ruby Dholakia, and Clark Leavitt, "The Persuasive Effect of Source Credibility: Tests of Cognitive Response," *Journal of Consumer Research* 4 (March 1978), 252–260.

6. Arch G. Woodside and J. William Davenport, Jr., "The Effect of Salesman Similarity and Expertise on Consumer Purchasing Behavior," *Journal of Marketing Research* 11 (May 1974), 198–202.

7. Michael J. Baker and Gilbert A. Churchill, Jr., "The Impact of Physically Attractive Models on Advertising Evaluations," *Journal of Marketing Research* 14 (November 1977), 538–555; Shelly Chaiken, "Communicator Physical Attractiveness and Persuasion," *Journal of Personality and Social Psychology* 37 (August 1979), 752–766; Kahle and Homer, "Physical Attractiveness of the Celebrity Endorser: A Social Adaptation Perspective."

8. Kahle and Homer, "Physical Attractiveness of the Celebrity Endorser: A Social Adaptation Perspective."

9. Petty, Cacioppo, and Schumann, "Central and Peripheral Routes to Advertising Effectiveness: The Moderating Role of Involvement."

10. Woodside and Davenport, "The Effect of Salesman Similarity and Expertise on Consumer Purchasing Behavior."

11. Iris Cohen Selinger, "Celebrity Overexposure," *Adweek* (March 4, 1991), 12–13.

12. Grant McCracken, "Who Is the Celebrity Endorser? Cultural Foundations of the Endorsement Process," *Journal of Consumer Research* 16 (December 1989), 310–321.

13. Selinger, "Celebrity Overexposure."

14. Ibid.

15. David Olson, "The Characteristics of High-Trial New-Product Advertising," *Journal of Advertising Research* 25 (October/November 1985), 11–16.

16. See Julie A. Edell and Richard Staelin, "The Information Processing of Pictures in Print Advertisements," *Journal of Consumer Research* 10 (June 1983), 45–61; Gary T. Ford, Darlene B. Smith, and John L. Swasy, "Consumer Skepticism of Advertising Claims: Testing Hypotheses from Economics of Information," *Journal of Consumer Research* 16 (March 1990), 433–441; Morris B. Holbrook, "Beyond Attitude Structure: Toward the Informational Determinants of Attitude," *Journal of Marketing Research* 15 (November 1978), 545–556.

17. Ford, Smith, and Swasy, "Consumer Skepticism of Advertising Claims: Testing Hypotheses from Economics of Information."

18. Petty and Cacioppo, "The Effects of Involvement on Responses to Argument Quantity and Quality: Central and Peripheral Routes to Persuasion." Also see Joseph W. Alba and Howard Marmorstein, "The Effects of Frequency Knowledge on Consumer Decision Making," *Journal of Consumer Research* 14 (June 1987), 14–25.

19. For recent investigations on message sidedness, see Linda L. Golden and Mark I. Alpert, "Comparative Analysis of the Relative Effectiveness of One- and Two-Sided Communication for Contrasting Products," *Journal of Advertising* 16 (1987), 18–25; Michael A. Kamins and Lawrence J. Marks, "Advertising Puffery: The Impact of Using Two-Sided Claims on Product Attitude and Purchase Intention," *Journal of Advertising* 16 (1987), 6–15; Michael A. Kamins and Henry Assael, "Two-Sided Versus One-Sided Appeals: A Cognitive Perspective on Argumentation, Source Derogation, and the Effect of Disconfirming Trial on Belief Change," *Journal of Marketing Research* 24 (February 1987), 29–39.

20. Cornelia Droge and Rene Y. Darmon, "Associative Positioning Strategies through Comparative Advertising: Attribute Versus Overall Similarity Approaches," *Journal of Marketing Research* 24 (November 1987), 377–388; Gerald J. Gorn and Charles B. Weinberg, "The Impact of Comparative Advertising on Perception and Attitude: Some Positive Findings," *Journal of Consumer Research* 11 (September 1984), 719–727; Cornelia Pechmann and S. Ratneshwar, "The Use of Comparative Advertising for Brand Positioning: Association Versus Differentiation," *Journal of Consumer Research* 18 (September 1991), 145–160; Cornelia Pechmann and David W. Stewart, "The Effects of Comparative Advertising on Attention, Memory, and Purchase Intentions,"

Journal of Consumer Research 17 (September 1990), 180–191; Mita Sujan and Christine Dekleva, "Product Categorization and Inference Making: Some Implications for Comparative Advertising," *Journal of Consumer Research* 14 (December 1987), 372–378.

21. Z. S. Demirdijian, "Sales Effectiveness of Comparative Advertising: An Experimental Field Investigation," *Journal of Consumer Research* 10 (December 1983), 362–364.

22. A brief review of these findings is presented in Gorn and Weinberg, "The Impact of Comparative Advertising on Perception and Attitude: Some Positive Findings." Note, however, that research reporting equivalent persuasion between comparative and noncomparative advertising may be limited by measures that are insufficiently sensitive to the persuasive impact of comparative advertising. See Randall L. Rose, Paul W. Miniard, and Brian D. Till, "When Persuasion Goes Undetected: The Case of Comparative Advertising," working paper, University of South Carolina, 1992.

23. Michael L. Ray and Rajeev Batra, "Emotion and Persuasion in Advertising: What We Do and Don't Know About Affect," in Richard P. Bagozzi and Alice M. Tybout, eds., *Advances in Consumer Research* 10 (Ann Arbor: Association for Consumer Research, 1983), 543–548.

24. For additional citations of research on the role of affective responses in persuasion, see Footnote 52 in Chapter 13.

25. "Emotional Response Is Evoked for March of Dimes Campaign," *Marketing News* 20 (November 21, 1986), 6.

26. Andrew A. Mitchell and Jerry C. Olson, "Are Product Attribute Beliefs the Only Mediators of Advertising Effects on Brand Attitudes?" *Journal of Marketing Research* 18 (August 1981), 318–332.

27. "Armstrong Retreads 'Tuffy the Rhino,'" *Marketing News* 21 (November 20, 1987), 16.

28. Miniard, Bhatla, Lord, Dickson, and Unnava, "Picture-Based Persuasion Processes and the Moderating Role of Involvement;" Andrew A. Mitchell, "The Effect of Verbal and Visual Components of Advertisements on Brand Attitudes and Attitude toward the Advertisement," *Journal of Consumer Research* 13 (June 1986), 12–24.

29. Interest in this area was largely sparked by the following two articles: Mitchell and Olson, "Are Product Attribute Beliefs the Only Mediator of Advertising Effects on Brand Attitudes?"; Terence Shimp, "Attitude toward the Ad as a Mediator of Consumer Brand Choice," *Journal of Advertising* 10 (1981), 9–15. Recent research can be found in Marian C. Burke and Julie A. Edell, "Ad Reactions over Time: Capturing Changes in the Real World," *Journal of Consumer Research* 13 (June 1986), 114–118; Scot Burton and Donald R. Lichtenstein, "The Effect of Ad Claims and Ad Context on Attitude toward the Advertisement," *Journal of Advertising* 17 (1988), 3–11; Dena S. Cox and Anthony D. Cox, "What Does Familiarity Breed? Complexity as a Moderator of Repetition Effects in Advertisement Evaluation," *Journal of Consumer Research* 15 (June 1988), 111–116; Cornelia Droge, "Shaping the Route to Attitude Change: Central Versus Peripheral Processing through Comparative Versus Noncomparative Advertising," *Journal of Marketing Research* 26 (May 1989), 193–204; Edell and Burke, "The Power of Feelings in Understanding Advertising Effects"; Meryl P. Gardner, "Does Attitude toward the Ad Affect Brand Attitude Under a Brand Evaluation Set?" *Journal of Marketing Research* 22 (May 1985), 192–198; Larry G. Gresham and Terence A. Shimp, "Attitude toward the Advertisement and Brand Attitudes: A Classical Conditioning Perspective," *Journal of Advertising* 14 (1985), 10–17; Pamela M. Homer, "The Mediating Role of Attitude toward the Ad: Some Additional Evidence," *Journal of Marketing Research* 27 (February 1990), 78–86; Scott B. MacKenzie and Richard J. Lutz, "An Empirical Examination of Structural Antecedents of Attitude toward the Ad in an Advertising Pretesting Context," *Journal of Marketing* 53 (April 1989), 48–65;

Scott B. MacKenzie, Richard J. Lutz, and George E. Belch, "The Role of Attitude toward the Ad as a Mediator of Advertising Effectiveness: A Test of Competing Explanations," *Journal of Marketing Research* 23 (May 1986), 130–143; Thomas J. Madden, Chris T. Allen, and Jacquelyn L. Twible, "Attitude toward the Ad: An Assessment of Diverse Measurement Indices under Different Processing 'Sets,'" *Journal of Marketing Research* 25 (August 1988), 242–252; Paul W. Miniard, Sunil Bhatla, and Randall L. Rose, "On the Formation and Relationship of Ad and Brand Attitudes: An Experimental and Causal Analysis," *Journal of Marketing Research* 27 (August 1990), 290–303; Mitchell, "The Effect of Verbal and Visual Components of Advertisements on Brand Attitudes and Attitude toward the Advertisement"; Banwari Mittal, "The Relative Roles of Brand Beliefs and Attitude toward the Ad as Mediators of Brand Attitude: A Second Look," *Journal of Marketing Research* 27 (May 1990), 209–219; Whan C. Park and S. Mark Young, "Consumer Response to Television Commercials: The Impact of Involvement and Background Music on Brand Attitude Formation," *Journal of Marketing Research* 23 (February 1986), 11–24.

30. For an interesting discussion of consumers' irritation with advertising, see David A. Aaker and Donald E. Bruzzone, "Causes of Irritation in Advertising," *Journal of Marketing* 49 (Spring 1985), 47–57.

31. John R. Rossiter and Larry Percy, *Advertising and Promotion Management* (New York: McGraw-Hill, 1987), 235.

32. J. Lee McCullough and Thomas Ostrom, "Repetition of Highly Similar Messages and Attitude Change," *Journal of Applied Psychology* 59 (June 1974), 395–397; Carl Obermiller, "Varieties of Mere Exposure: The Effects of Processing Style and Repetition on Affective Response," *Journal of Consumer Research* 12 (June 1985), 17–30.

33. John T. Cacioppo and Richard E. Petty, "Central and Peripheral Routes to Persuasion: The Role of Message Repetition," in Linda F. Alwitt and Andrew A. Mitchell, eds., *Psychological Processes and Advertising Effects* (Hillsdale, N.J.: Lawrence Erlbaum, 1985), 91–111.

34. Belch, "The Effects of Television Commercial Repetition on Cognitive Response and Message Acceptance"; Rethans, Swasy, and Marks, "Effects of Television Commercial Repetition, Receiver Knowledge, and Commercial Length: A Test of the Two-Factor Model."

35. John T. Cacioppo and Richard E. Petty, "Effects of Message Repetition and Position on Cognitive Response, Recall, and Persuasion," *Journal of Personality and Social Psychology* 37 (January 1979), 97–109; Bobby J. Calder and Brian Sternthal, "Television Commercial Wearout: An Information Processing View," *Journal of Marketing Research* 17 (May 1980), 173–186; Gerald J. Gorn and Marvin E. Goldberg, "Children's Responses to Repetitive Television Commercials," *Journal of Consumer Research* 6 (March 1980), 421–424.

36. Cacioppo and Petty, "Central and Peripheral Routes to Persuasion: The Role of Message Repetition." For discussions of alternative explanations, see Calder and Sternthal, "Television Commercial Wearout: An Information Processing View"; Obermiller, "Varieties of Mere Exposure: The Effects of Processing Style and Repetition on Affective Response"; Rethans, Swasy, and Marks, "Effects of Television Commercial Repetition, Receiver Knowledge, and Commercial Length: A Test of the Two-Factor Model"; Alan G. Sawyer, "Repetition, Cognitive Response and Persuasion," in Richard E. Petty, Thomas Ostrom, and Timothy Brock, eds., *Cognitive Responses in Persuasion* (Hillsdale, N.J.: Lawrence Erlbaum, 1981), 237–261; Robert B. Zajonc and Hazel Markus, "Affective and Cognitive Factors in Preferences," *Journal of Consumer Research* 9 (September 1982), 123–131.

37. Also see Punam Anand and Brian Sternthal, "Ease of Message Processing as a Moderator of Repetition Effects in Advertising," *Journal of Marketing Research* 27 (August 1990), 345–353; Rajeev Batra and Michael L. Ray, "Situational Effects of Advertising Repetition: The Moderating Influence of Motivation, Ability, and Opportunity to Respond," *Journal of Consumer Research* 12 (March 1986), 432–445; Moore, Hausknecht, and Kanchana, "Time Compression, Response Opportunity, and Persuasion."

38. For a dissenting point of view, see Belch, "The Effects of Television Commercial Repetition on Cognitive Response and Message Acceptance"; Rethans, Swasy, and Marks, "Effects of Television Commercial Repetition, Receiver Knowledge, and Commercial Length: A Test of the Two-Factor Model."

39. Cacioppo and Petty, "Effects of Message Repetition and Position on Cognitive Response, Recall, and Persuasion."

40. Cacioppo and Petty, "Central and Peripheral Routes to Persuasion: The Role of Message Repetition."

41. Rethans, Swasy, and Marks, "Effects of Television Commercial Repetition, Receiver Knowledge, and Commercial Length: A Test of the Two-Factor Model."

42. Petty, Cacioppo, and Schumann, "Central and Peripheral Routes to Advertising Effectiveness: The Moderating Role of Involvement." Also see Durairaj Maheswaran and Joan Meyers-Levy, "The Influence of Message Framing and Issue Involvement," *Journal of Marketing Research* 27 (August 1990), 361–367; Gerald J. Gorn, "The Effects of Music in Advertising on Choice Behavior: A Classical Conditioning Approach," *Journal of Marketing* 46 (Winter 1982), 94–101; Alan G. Sawyer and Daniel J. Howard, "Effects of Omitting Conclusions in Advertisements to Involved and Uninvolved Audiences," *Journal of Marketing Research* 28 (November 1991), 467–474; David W. Schumann, Richard E. Petty, and D. Scott Clemons, "Predicting the Effectiveness of Advertising Variation: A Test of the Repetition-Variation Hypotheses," *Journal of Consumer Research* 17 (September 1990), 192–202.

43. For an expanded discussion of how persuasion tactics may depend on the type of motivation, see John R. Rossiter and Larry Percy, "Advertising Communication Models," in Elizabeth C. Hirschman and Morris B. Holbrook, eds., *Advances in Consumer Research* 12 (Provo, Utah: Association for Consumer Research, 1985), 510–524; Rossiter and Percy, *Advertising and Promotion Management.*

44. David M. Sanbonmatsu and Frank R. Kardes, "The Effects of Physiological Arousal on Information Processing and Persuasion," *Journal of Consumer Research* 15 (December 1988), 379–385. Also see Surendra N. Singh and Gilbert A. Churchill, Jr., "Arousal and Advertising Effectiveness," *Journal of Advertising* 16 (1987), 4–10.

45. Rolph E. Anderson and Marvin A. Jolson, "Technical Wording in Advertising: Implications for Market Segmentation," *Journal of Marketing* 44 (Winter 1980), 57–66.

46. Joseph W. Alba and J. Wesley Hutchinson, "Dimensions of Consumer Expertise," *Journal of Consumer Research* 13 (March 1987), 411–454.

47. Mita Sujan, "Consumer Knowledge: Effects on Evaluation Strategies Mediating Consumer Judgments," *Journal of Consumer Research* 12 (June 1985), 31–46. Also see Alba and Marmorstein, "The Effects of Frequency Knowledge on Consumer Decision Making."

48. Meryl Paula Gardner, "Mood States and Consumer Behavior: A Critical Review," *Journal of Consumer Research* 12 (December 1985), 281–300.

49. Thomas R. Srull, "Memory, Mood, and Consumer Judgment," in Melanie Wallendorf and Paul Anderson, eds., *Advances in Consumer Research* 14 (Provo, Utah: Association for Consumer Research, 1987), 404–407. Also see Rajeev Batra and Douglas M. Stayman, "The Role of Mood in Advertising Effectiveness," *Journal of Consumer Research* 17 (September 1990), 203–214.

50. Marvin E. Goldberg and Gerald J. Gorn, "Happy and Sad TV Programs: How They Affect Reactions to Commercials," *Journal of Consumer Research* 14 (December 1987), 387–403.

51. John T. Cacioppo and Richard E. Petty, "The Need for Cognition," *Journal of Personality and Social Psychology* 42 (1982), 116–131.

52. Haugvedt, Petty, Cacioppo, and Steidley, "Personality and Ad Effectiveness: Exploring the Utility of Need for Cognition." Also see Danny Axson, Susan Yates, and Shelly Chaiken, "Audience Response as a Heuristic Cue in Persuasion," *Journal of Personality and Social Psychology* 53 (1987), 30–40; Batra and Stayman, "The Role of Mood in Advertising Effectiveness;" J. Jeffrey Inman, Leigh McAlister, and Wayne D. Hoyer, "Promotion Signal: Proxy for a Price Cut?" *Journal of Consumer Research* 17 (June 1990), 74–81.

53. For a general review of self-monitoring, see Mark Snyder, "Self-Monitoring Processes," in Leonard Berkowitz, ed., *Advances in Experimental Social Psychology* 12 (New York: Academic Press, 1979), 85–128.

54. Mark Snyder and Kenneth G. DeBono, "Appeals to Image and Claims about Quality: Understanding the Psychology of Advertising," *Journal of Personality and Social Psychology* 49 (September 1985), 586–597.

55. Edward F. Cone, "Image and Reality," *Forbes* (December 14, 1987), 226, 228.

56. C. W. Sherif, M. Sherif, and R. E. Nebergall, *Attitude and Attitude Change* (New Haven: Yale University Press, 1961).

57. Robert E. Smith and William R. Swinyard, "Attitude-Behavior Consistency: The Impact of Product Trial Versus Advertising," *Journal of Marketing Research* 20 (August 1983), 257–267. Also see Lawrence J. Marks and Michael A. Kamins, "The Use of Product Sampling and Advertising: Effects of Sequence of Exposure and Degree of Advertising Claim Exaggeration on Consumers' Belief Strength, Belief Confidence, and Attitudes," *Journal of Marketing Research* 25 (August 1988), 266–281.

58. Wu and Shaffer, "Susceptibility to Persuasive Appeals as a Function of Source Credibility and Prior Experience with the Attitude Object."

59. Amitava Chattopadhyay and Kunal Basu, "Humor in Advertising: The Moderating Role of Prior Brand Evaluation," *Journal of Marketing Research* 27 (November 1990), 466–476.

60. Hoch and Ha, "Consumer Learning: Advertising and the Ambiguity of Product Experience."

61. A review of research on multiple request techniques can be found in Edward F. Fern, Kent B. Monroe, and Ramon A. Avila, "Effectiveness of Multiple Request Strategies: A Synthesis of Research Results," *Journal of Marketing Research* 22 (May 1986), 144–152.

62. Jonathan L. Freedman and Scott C. Fraser, "Compliance without Pressure: The Foot-in-the-Door Technique," *Journal of Personality and Social Psychology* 4 (August 1966), 195–202.

63. Daryl J. Bem, "Self-Perception Theory," in Leonard Berkowitz, ed., *Advances in Experimental Social Psychology* 6 (New York: Academic Press, 1972), 1–62. Also see William DeJong, "An Examination of Self-Perception Mediation of the Foot-in-the-Door Effect," *Journal of Personality and Social Psychology* 37 (December 1979), 2221–2239. For a dissenting point of view, see Peter H. Reingen, "On Inducing Compliance with Requests," *Journal of Consumer Research* 5 (September 1978), 96–102; Alice M. Tybout, Brian Sternthal, and Bobby J. Calder, "Information Availability as a Determinant of Multiple Request Effectiveness," *Journal of Marketing Research* 20 (August 1983), 280–290.

64. Chris T. Allen, Charles D. Schewe, and Gosta Wijk, "More on Self-Perception Theory's Foot Technique in the Pre-Call/Mail Survey Setting," *Journal of Marketing Research* 17 (November 1980), 498–502; Robert A. Hansen and Larry M. Robinson,

"Testing the Effectiveness of Alternative Foot-in-the-Door Manipulations," *Journal of Marketing Research* 17 (August 1980), 359–364; Peter H. Reingen, "On Inducing Compliance with Requests"; Peter H. Reingen and Jerome B. Kernan, "Compliance with an Interview Request: A Foot-in-the-Door, Self-Perception Interpretation," *Journal of Marketing Research* 14 (August 1977), 365–369; Carol A. Scott, "Modifying Socially Conscious Behavior: The Foot-in-the-Door Technique," *Journal of Consumer Research* 4 (December 1977), 156–164.

65. David H. Furse, David W. Stewart, and David L. Rados, "Effects of Foot-in-the-Door, Cash Incentives, and Followups on Survey Response," *Journal of Marketing Research* 18 (November 1981), 473–478; Peter H. Reingen and Jerome B. Kernan, "More Evidence on Interpersonal Yielding," *Journal of Marketing Research* 16 (November 1979), 588–593; Carol A. Scott, "The Effects of Trial and Incentives on Repeat Purchase Behavior," *Journal of Marketing Research* 13 (August 1976), 263–269.

66. Fern, Monroe, and Avila, "Effectiveness of Multiple Request Strategies: A Synthesis of Research Results."

67. Robert B. Cialdini, Joyce E. Vincent, Stephen K. Lewis, Jose Catalan, Diane Wheeler, and Betty Lee Darby, "Reciprocal Concessions Procedure for Inducing Compliance: The Door-in-the-Face Technique," *Journal of Personality and Social Psychology* 31 (February 1975), 206–215. For an alternative explanation, see Tybout, Sternthal, and Calder, "Information Availability as a Determinant of Multiple Request Effectiveness."

68. John C. Mowen and Robert B. Cialdini, "On Implementing the Door-in-the-Face Compliance Technique in a Business Context," *Journal of Marketing Research* 17 (May 1980), 253–258.

69. Robert B. Cialdini, *Influence: How and Why People Agree to Things* (New York: William Morrow, 1984), 57. This book is highly recommended reading for those interested in a well-written, interesting, and informative discussion of influence techniques.

70. John Vollbrecht, "To Get Volume Up, Sell Down," *Sales Management* (July 22, 1974), 29.

71. Also see Dennis T. Regan, "Effects of a Favor and Liking on Compliance," *Journal of Experimental Social Psychology* 7 (1971), 627–639.

72. Morton Deutsch and Harold B. Gerard, "A Study of Normative and Informational Social Influences upon Individual Judgment," *Journal of Abnormal and Social Psychology* 51 (November 1955), 629–636.

73. Cialdini, *Influence: How and Why People Agree to Things*, 102–103.

74. Ibid., 86.

75. For research on this topic, see Chris T. Allen, "Self-Perception Based Strategies for Stimulating Energy Conservation," *Journal of Consumer Research* 8 (March 1982), 381–390; Trudy Kehret-Ward and Richard Yalch, "To Take or Not to Take the Only One: Effects of Changing the Meaning of a Product Attribute on Choice Behavior," *Journal of Consumer Research* 10 (March 1984), 410–416; Robert Kraut, "Effects of Social Labeling on Giving to Charity," *Journal of Marketing Research* 14 (November 1977), 509–516; Ellen M. Moore, William O. Bearden, and Jesse E. Teel, "Use of Labeling and Assertions of Dependency in Appeals for Consumer Support," *Journal of Consumer Research* 12 (June 1985), 90–96; Alice M. Tybout and Richard F. Yalch, "The Effect of Experience: A Matter of Salience," *Journal of Consumer Research* 6 (March 1980), 406–413.

76. Tybout and Yalch, "The Effect of Experience: A Matter of Salience."

77. Allen, "Self-Perception Based Strategies for Stimulating Energy Conservation."

78. "Marketing Briefs," *Marketing News* 26 (March 2, 1991), 1.

79. *Insights*, NPD Research, Inc., 1979–1982.

80. Joe A. Dodson, Alice M. Tybout, and Brian Sternthal, "Impact of Deals and Deal Retraction on Brand Switching," *Journal of Marketing Research* 15 (February 1978), 72–

78; Anthony N. Doob, J. Merrill Carlsmith, Jonathan L. Freedman, Thomas K. Landauer, and Soleng Tom, "Effect of Initial Selling Price on Subsequent Sales," *Journal of Personality and Social Psychology* 11 (April 1969), 345–350.

81. Dodson, Tybout, and Sternthal, "Impact of Deals and Deal Retraction on Brand Switching."

82. Scott Davis, J. Jeffrey Inman, and Leigh McAlister, "Promotion Has a Negative Effect on Brand Evaluations—Or Does It? Additional Disconfirming Evidence," *Journal of Marketing Research* 29 (February 1992), 143–148.

83. Scott A. Neslin and Robert W. Shoemaker, "An Alternative Explanation for Lower Repeat Rates After Promotion Purchases," *Journal of Marketing Research* 26 (May 1989), 205–213.

84. This finding comes from a proprietary study undertaken by Ogilvy and Mather as reported by Rothschild and Gaidis, "Behavioral Learning Theory," 74.

85. Dodson, Tybout, and Sternthal, "Impact of Deals."

86. For research on those consumer segments most likely to become incremental purchasers due to coupons, see Kapil Bawa and Robert W. Shoemaker, "Analyzing Incremental Sales from a Direct Mail Coupon Promotion," *Journal of Marketing* 53 (July 1989), 66–78.

87. Michael L. Rothschild and William C. Gaidis, "Behavioral Learning Theory: Its Relevance to Marketing and Promotions," *Journal of Marketing* 45 (Spring 1981), 70–78.

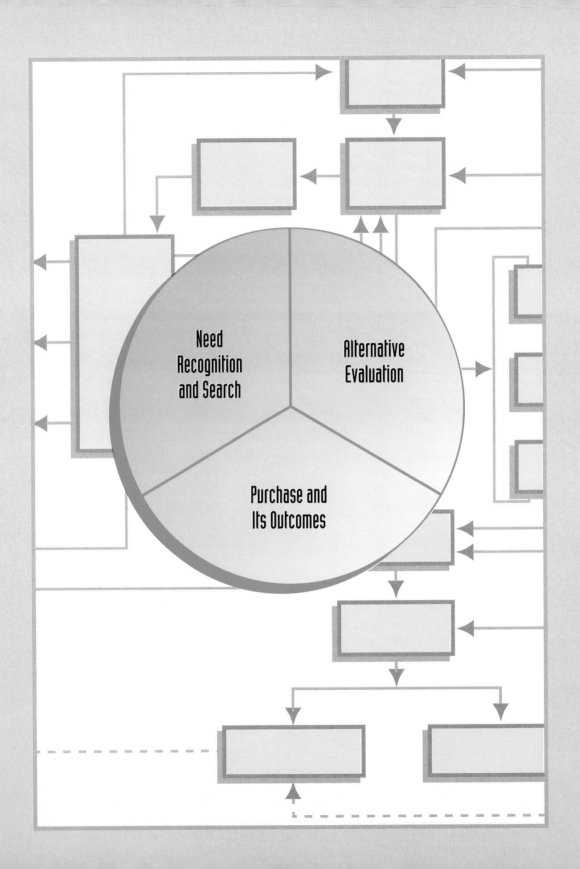

Need
Recognition
and Search

Alternative
Evaluation

Purchase and
Its Outcomes

PART 5

Consumer Decision Processes and Behavior

We have now completed our review of the various internal and external processes and influences that shape consumer behavior. It is necessary to return once again to the central component in our model on the opposite page—*the consumer decision process.*

The three chapters in this section build on and greatly expand the decision-process overview in Chapter 2. Our major objective here is to integrate the content of everything you have read up to this point. The goal is to help you have a comprehensive grasp of (1) the complexities of decision processes and (2) the many resulting implications for strategy.

Chapter 16 focuses on the first two stages in the decision process— *need recognition* and *search for information.* The nature and determinants of need recognition are discussed first. Then our focus shifts to the role and characteristics of both internal and external information search.

As you will see, the acquisition of information is just an initial step in *alternative evaluation*—the subject of Chapter 17. The heart of this process is comparison of alternatives against *evaluative criteria* (desired product attributes). The chapter describes how evaluative criteria are formed and the ways in which the evaluation process is undertaken in extended problem solving (EPS), limited problem solving (LPS), and habitual decision making.

Chapter 18 concludes the section by concentrating on the final two stages of the decision process—*purchase and its outcomes*. Purchase can be made in many different ways, ranging from use of interactive video to an instore visit. The variety of purchasing alternatives has grown rapidly in recent years, and there are many options for marketing strategy.

But the decision process continues after a product or service is bought and used into the outcome stage. Satisfaction and intention to repurchase are critically significant outcomes. Much of our discussion centers on satisfaction, because of the role it plays in determining business success.

16

Need Recognition and Search

D o you own a fax machine? Odds are you don't. Less than 1 percent of American households have fax machines. Contrast that with the 99 percent of American corporations that own one. Almost 60 percent of small- to mid-sized businesses—those with 5 to 99 employees—are equipped with fax.

Why don't you want a fax machine? "Don't need it" is a common reply. And this represents a major challenge to the fax industry. As the business market reaches saturation, future growth will heavily depend on stimulating consumer demand. And stimulating demand will require showing consumers how a fax machine could make their lives easier, more productive, and more entertaining.

Fax Interactive, a company offering fax services, has a couple of ideas about the types of services that consumers might want. One is a stock portfolio service that provides up-to-the-minute news and information on the market. Another service could focus on "triggering events." A subscriber would identify certain topics of interest, and when something happens related to those topics, he or she would automatically receive a fax with detailed information.

Another company, DataFax Communications Corp., plans to provide services where callers can request airline schedules, daily updates on their favorite soap operas, horoscopes, real estate information, recipes from food manufacturers, health information, movie schedules, weather updates . . . the list goes on. The company is also developing interactive fax games.

According to DataFax president Norberto Blumenscweig, "The key will be to begin offering all of these services simultaneously. The fax manufacturers want to be able to offer the consumer a package of several services as an enticement to buy the fax machine. If you only have one or two things available, it's not going to work."

Source: Excerpted in part from Kristine J. Tegethoff, "Fax Appeal," *Link* (March 1992), 22–25, 36–39.

The future of fax machines, as is the case for all goods and services, ultimately depends on whether consumers perceive them as fulfilling consumption needs. It is the activation and recognition of consumption needs that leads the consumer into a decision-making process that will determine product purchase and consumption. Accordingly, we label the first stage of the decision-making process as **need recognition**—defined as the perception of a difference between the desired state of affairs and the actual situation sufficient to arouse and activate the decision process. The first part of this chapter is devoted to this crucial stage of decision making.

Once need recognition has occurred, the consumer may then engage in a search for potential need satisfiers. These search activities constitute the second stage of decision making called **search** which is defined as the motivated activation of knowledge in memory or acquisition of information from the environment. Following discussion of need recognition, the remainder of this chapter is devoted to search.

Need Recognition

The simple diagram appearing in Figure 16.1 illustrates what happens during need recognition. Need recognition essentially depends on how much discrepancy exists between the actual state (that is, the consumer's current situation) and the desired state (that is, the situation the consumer wants to be in). When this discrepancy meets or exceeds a certain level or threshold, a need is recognized. For example, a consumer currently feeling hungry (actual state) and wanting to eliminate this feeling (desired state) will experience need recognition if the discrepancy between the two states is of sufficient magnitude. However, if the discrepancy is below the threshold level, then need recognition will not occur.

It is necessary to point out that the presence of need recognition does *not* automatically activate some action. This will depend on a couple of factors. First, the recognized need must be of sufficient importance. A hungry consumer may not feel that the rumblings in his stomach merit action at this point in time. Second, consumers must believe that a solution to the need is within their means. If need satisfaction is beyond a consumer's economic or temporal resources (see Chapter 8), for instance, then action is unlikely.

Need Activation

A need must first be "activated" before it can be "recognized." A host of factors will influence the likelihood that a particular need will be activated. Such factors operate by altering the person's actual and/or desired states.

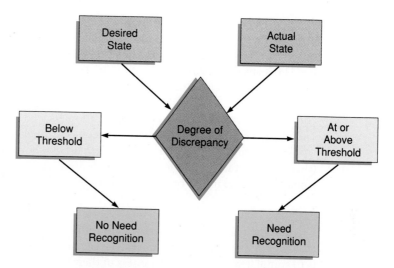

FIGURE 16.1   The Need Recognition Process Centers on the Degree of Discrepancy

Time   As anyone who has gone too long since their last meal well knows, the simple passage of time can be a potent activator of consumption needs. Similarly, the time since the smoker's last cigarette is a major influencer on his need to light up again. In both cases, time gradually deteriorates the consumer's actual state until it becomes sufficiently discrepant from the desired state to trigger need recognition.

Time can influence the desired state as well. As consumers grow older, they often experience changes in their tastes and values which, in turn, alter their desired state. Whereas many baby boomers get a haircut as soon as their hair starts touching their ears, in their younger days need recognition did not occur even though their hair was touching their shoulders!

Changed Circumstances   Needs will often be activated due to changes in one's life. Many students discover upon graduation and starting a new job that their current wardrobe needs to be expanded in order for them to function more comfortably within their work environment, particularly when there exists strong expectations within the firm as to what represents appropriate attire. Changes within the family can also trigger need recognition. The birth of a child, for instance, results in modified requirements for food, clothing, furniture, and housing.

Product Acquisition   The acquisition of a product may, in turn, activate the need for additional products. It is not uncommon to find that acquiring new furnishings will affect perceptions of the desirability of existing carpeting, wall coverings, and so on. Similarly, buying a new home will usually require the purchase of additional products, particularly for first-time buyers. It is for this reason that new home buyers are an important target market for many companies.

Product Consumption   Actual consumption itself can trigger need recognition. In many buying situations, a need is recognized simply because of an out-of-stock situation. The last slices of bread were toasted for breakfast, and more bread will be needed for tonight's dinner. Thus, need recognition occurs because of an *anticipated* need in the immediate future resulting from a change in the actual situation.

The extent to which the product lives up to consumers' expectations during consumption can also affect need recognition (as well as satisfaction—see Chapter 18).[1] When a product meets these expectations, then the actual and desired states will be in harmony. However, a product that falls short of consumers' expectations (that is, the actual state is less than the desired state) will trigger need recognition when repurchase in the product category is anticipated.

Marketing Influences   We noted in Chapter 9 that marketers are unable to "create" needs in the marketplace. Rather, their influence is constrained to activating needs that already exist within consumers. A basic objective of many advertisements, then, is to stimulate consumers' awareness of their needs. This stimulation may be either primary or selective in nature. An example of the former is the milk industry's recent advertising campaign to strengthen the primary demand for this product. Ads targeted at young consumers show a milk-drinking youngster maturing into an attractive young adult. Other ads tell older consumers they should drink milk "because you're not a kid anymore." Marketing activities that focus on primary demand are, in essence, attempting to elicit **generic need recognition**.

Selective need recognition, on the other hand, occurs when the need for a specific brand within a product category is stimulated. Consider the person holding a 13 percent loan and feeling quite satisfied with this rate. He then sees the ad appearing in Figure 16.2. Suddenly, he feels a bit uncomfortable. His perceptions of the desired state begin to change. He wonders why he should pay his current bank 13 percent when someone else is offering a lower rate. Thus, the ad has prompted both a redefinition of the desired state and selective need recognition for the advertised brand.

Sometimes need recognition can be prompted by marketing materials at the point of purchase. Consumers browsing a retailer's aisles may encounter a display that reminds them of a previously recognized but unfulfilled purchase need. Alternatively, the display may directly activate a need that leads to a previously unintended purchase.

Product innovations are another source of need recognition, which was certainly the case when Reebok came out with their pump athletic shoe (see Figure 16.3). This innovation changed the ideal state of many teenagers, leading them to view their current pair of shoes as inadequate.

Individual Differences   Bruner has recently proposed that consumers may often differ in whether need recognition results from changes in the actual state versus the desired state.[2] At one extreme are consumers (called **Actual State Types**) for whom need recognition is triggered typically by changes in the actual state. Consumers at the other extreme (called **Desired State Types**) usually experience need recognition produced by changes in the desired state. For example, Actual State Types tend

FIGURE 16.2   An Ad Designed to Stimulate Selective Need Recognition

to recognize a need for clothing only when their clothing does not perform satisfactorily. Desired State Types, on the other hand, will frequently experience need recognition as a result of their desires for something new.

Search

Once need recognition has occurred, the consumer may then engage in a search for potential need satisfiers. **Search**, the second stage of the decision-making process, can be defined as the motivated activation of knowledge stored in memory or acquisition of information from the environment. This definition suggests that search can be either internal or external in nature. **Internal search** involves the retrieval of

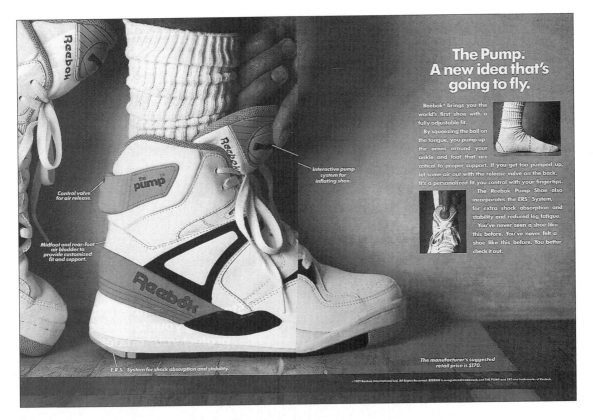

The Pump:
A new idea that's
going to fly.

Reebok* brings you the world's first shoe with a fully adjustable fit.

By squeezing the ball on the tongue, you pump up the areas around your ankle and foot that are critical to proper support. If you get too pumped up, let some air out with the release valve on the back. It's a personalized fit you control with your fingertips.

The Reebok Pump Shoe also incorporates the ERS™ System, for extra shock absorption and stability and reduced leg fatigue. You've never seen a shoe like this before. You've never felt a shoe like this before. You better check it out.

Interactive pump system for inflating shoe.

Control valve for air release.

Midfoot and rear-foot air bladder to provide customized fit and support.

E.R.S.™ System for shock absorption and stability.

The manufacturer's suggested retail price is $170.

© 1989 Reebok International Ltd. All Rights Reserved. REEBOK is a registered trademark and THE PUMP and ERS are trademarks of Reebok.

FIGURE 16.3   Stimulating Selective Need Recognition through Product Innovation

knowledge from memory, whereas **external search** consists of collecting information from the marketplace.

Internal Search

Search of an internal nature first occurs following need recognition (see Figure 16.4). Internal search is nothing more than a memory scan for decision-relevant knowledge stored in long-term memory (see Chapter 10).[3] If this scan reveals sufficient information to provide a satisfactory course of action, then external search is obviously unnecessary. Many times a past solution is remembered and implemented. For example, one study reports that many consumers needing an auto repair service relied on their existing knowledge in making their choice.[4] Only 40 percent turned to external search.

Whether consumers rely solely on internal search will heavily depend on the adequacy or quality of their existing knowledge. First-time buyers are obviously unlikely to possess the necessary information for decision making. Even experienced

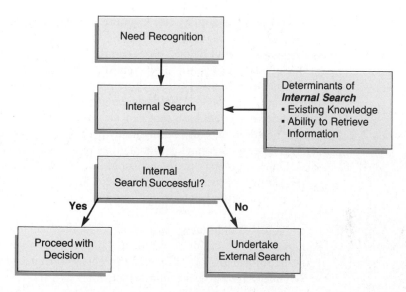

FIGURE 16.4   The Internal Search Process

buyers may need to undertake external search. Experienced buyers may find their knowledge to be inadequate for product categories characterized by large inter-purchase times (the amount of time between purchase occasions) during which there are significant product changes in terms of prices, features, and new brands and stores. Even if product changes have been minimal, internal search is hindered by large interpurchase times due to problems of forgetting. Nor may existing knowledge be sufficient when the present consumption problem is perceived to be different from those in the past.

The degree of satisfaction with prior purchases will also determine the consumer's reliance on internal search. If the consumer has been satisfied with the results of previous buying actions, then internal search may suffice.[5] Such is the case for habitual decision making, where the consumer simply remembers to buy the same brand as before.

External Search

When internal search proves inadequate, the consumer may decide to collect additional information from the environment. External search that is driven by an upcoming purchase decision is known as **prepurchase search**. This type of external search can be contrasted with another type called **ongoing search**, where information acquisition occurs on a relatively regular basis regardless of sporadic purchase needs.[6] For example, a consumer subscribing to automotive magazines would reflect an ongoing search activity. These same magazines might also be examined during prepurchase search, but only when the consumer is in the market for a new car. The fact that the same activity (for example, looking at a magazine) can occur during prepurchase and ongoing search, as well as the difficulty in establishing just when the decision process begins, poses significant problems for researchers attempting to distinguish between these two types of external search.

The primary motivation behind prepurchase search is the desire to make better consumption choices. Similarly, ongoing search may be motivated by desires to develop a knowledge base that can be used in future decision making. Ongoing search, however, may also occur simply because of the enjoyment derived from this activity. There is no denying that many consumers enjoy ongoing search for its own sake. Consumers may browse through a mall, without having specific purchase needs, simply because it is "fun" to them. A study reports that enjoyment was the driving force behind consumers' ongoing search for both clothing and personal computers.[7]

Note that ongoing search should affect the need for prepurchase search. Consumers active in ongoing search seem likely to possess greater amounts of decision-relevant information in memory, thereby lowering the amount of prepurchase search necessary for decision making.

Dimensions of Search

Table 16.1 indicates that consumer search can be characterized along three main dimensions: degree, direction, and sequence. **Degree** represents the total amount of

TABLE 16.1   Dimensions of Consumer Search

Degree of Search

- How many brands are examined?
- How many stores are visited?
- How many attributes are considered?
- How many information sources are consulted?
- How much time is spent on search?

Direction of Search

- Which brands are examined?
- Which stores are visited?
- Which attributes are considered?
- Which information sources are consulted?

Sequence of Search

- In what order are brands examined?
- In what order are stores visited?
- In what order is product attribute information processed?
- In what order are information sources consulted?

Consumer Search during Grocery Shopping

How much search do consumers undertake while grocery shopping? It would appear to be rather minimal based on the amount of time they stand in front of the shelving that displays the product. In one study, observers recorded the amount of time invested by consumers while making their purchase decisions within 4 different product categories: cereal, coffee, margarine, and toothpaste. On average, consumers took less than 12 seconds in making each decision. And nearly half spent 5 seconds or less.

After placing their selection in the cart, shoppers were approached by the observer and questioned about their choice. Less than 1 in 4 shoppers reported making a price comparison between their chosen brand and a competitive brand. Indeed, more than 40 percent did not bother to even check the price of the brand placed in their cart. Perhaps most surprising was the fact that less than half of the shoppers were aware they had chosen a brand that was being offered by the grocer at a reduced price.

Source: Peter R. Dickson and Alan G. Sawyer, "The Price Knowledge and Search of Supermarket Shoppers," *Journal of Marketing* 54 (July 1990), 42–53.

search. Search degree is reflected by the number of brands, stores, attributes, and information sources considered during search as well as the time taken in doing so. **Direction** represents the specific content of search. The emphasis here is on the particular brands and stores involved during search rather than simply the number. The third dimension, **sequence**, represents the order in which search activities occur.

Degree of Search   A common research finding is that many consumers engage in very little external search prior to purchase, even for major purchases involving furniture, appliances, and automobiles.[8] Indeed, these studies have found that significant numbers of consumers make major purchases after shopping at a single retailer and/or considering only one brand. Further testimony to just how limited consumer search may be is provided by Consumer in Focus 16.1.

The fact that consumers sometimes engage in minimal search has led some to suggest that purchase can occur without being preceded by a decision process.[9] The problem with this view is that it fails to consider the role of internal search. As noted earlier, internal search alone may sometimes suffice in making purchase decisions.

TABLE 16.2   Differences in the Degree of Search as a Function of the Decision-Making Process

Nature of Search	Decision-Making Process		
	Extended Problem Solving	Limited Problem Solving	Habitual
Number of brands	Greater	Fewer	One
Number of stores	Greater	Fewer	Unknown
Number of attributes	Greater	Fewer	One
Number of external information sources	Greater	Fewer	None
Amount of time	Larger	Smaller	Minimal

That consumers choose to rely on their existing knowledge would seem to provide inadequate grounds for suggesting that decision making has not occurred.

The degree of search is directly related to the type of decision-making process. Differences in search as a function of the decision process are summarized in Table 16.2. An extended problem-solving process will usually entail a considerable amount of search. The consumer may consider a number of brands, visit a number of stores, consult friends, and so on. At the other extreme is the habitual decision process. Here the consumer minimizes search time and effort by considering only one brand (the brand last purchased) and one attribute (brand name). Other sources of information are ignored. Uncertain, however, is the number of stores shopped, which may range from one (for example, if the consumer is also store loyal) to several. Search under a limited problem-solving process falls between these two extremes.

The amount of search related to a particular product can greatly vary from one consumer to the next. Consequently, it is possible to segment consumers based on their level of search. A study of new car purchasers, for instance, identified the following six segments:[10]

1. A low-search group, representing 26 percent of the respondents, with below-average activity on all search dimensions, especially out-of-store search activities.
2. A purchase-pal-assisted search group, representing 19 percent of the respondents.
3. A high-search group, with only 5 percent of the respondents, characterized by above-average activity on all search factors.
4. A high-self-search group, representing 12 percent of the respondents, who are above average on all out-of-store search activities in addition to the total number of visits to different car dealers.

5. A retail-shopper group comprising about 5 percent of respondents.
6. A moderate-search group, accounting for 32 percent of the respondents, characterized by moderate activity on all search factors, although slightly above average on out-of-store search activities and slightly below average on number of visits to car dealers.

Segmentation based on the degree of search can provide some insight into how search affects purchase behavior. Suppose that a car maker found that the segment characterized by very high levels of search was much more likely to buy one of the company's cars than segments that undertake less search. What implications does this finding suggest? Obviously, this segment would represent an attractive target relative to the remaining segments, given its demonstrated propensity to buy the company's products. Moreover, the company should also consider the possibility of enhancing consumers' search efforts, perhaps through advertising the potential advantages of search activity, since doing so will increase the likelihood that consumers will buy one of the company's offerings. Figure 16.5 presents two different advertisements that attempt to encourage consumer search.

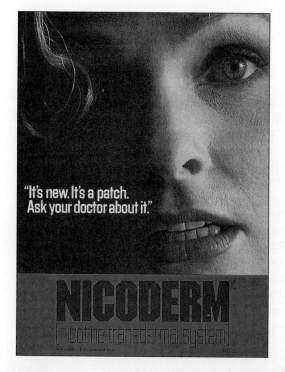

FIGURE 16.5   Ads Designed to Encourage Consumer Search

Even when markets are segmented on some other basis (see Chapter 21), it is still desirable to understand the search behavior of each segment. Segments that engage in considerable external search generally will be easier to reach. Marketers can feel more confident about the potential payoff of investments in advertising and in-store information. In contrast, such investments can be wasted on segments that rely on internal search. For these segments, free samples or substantial and well-publicized price discounts may be required to attract consumers.

Direction of Search   While it is important to understand how much consumers search before purchase, it is equally if not more vital to examine the direction of search. Knowing which brands consumers considered during decision making would be very useful in understanding the consumer's view of a firm's competitive set. Distribution decisions could benefit from information about which stores are visited.

Marketers are especially interested in the specific product attributes that consumers examine during search. Attributes receiving considerable attention might be emphasized more strongly in promotional materials unless, of course, they represent areas of product weaknesses. The emphasis placed on price during search can affect pricing strategies, as described in Consumer in Focus 16.2.

Consumer in Focus 16.2

The Influence of Comparison Shopping on Price Setting

Imagine that you are responsible for setting the prices charged by a supermarket. You have just discovered that a competitor has lowered prices on selected items. How might your response to the competitor's action depend on the level of comparison shopping undertaken by consumers? Would you be more likely to retaliate and cut prices when comparison shoppers constitute a majority of the market?

This basic issue was examined in a study of nearly 200 grocery executives responsible for making such pricing decisions. The executives reviewed a case situation where a competitor has cut prices for 8 products and they must now decide how to respond. They are also given information about the reactions

Continued

TABLE 16.3   Sources of Information

	Impersonal	Personal
Commercial	Advertising In-store information	Salespeople
Noncommercial	General purpose media	Social others

The particular information sources used during search will also influence marketing strategy. Table 16.3 indicates that information sources can be classified in terms of their source (personal versus impersonal) and type (commercial versus noncommercial). Each of these major sources is discussed subsequently.

Advertising   Once consumers recognize a need, they generally become more receptive to advertising, which they previously might have ignored completely. Ads are then often consulted for informational purposes. Although the informative role of advertising varies between products and consumers, the following are illustrative findings:

1. Consumers make considerable use of TV ads for information on style and design.[11]

(or inactions) of other competitors as well as a recent survey of comparison shoppers. Some are told that few consumers compare prices. The rest are informed that most consumers comparison shop.

The findings revealed that the influence of consumers' comparison shopping on the executives' pricing decisions varied across the eight products. The executives recommended lower prices for "high visibility" items (for example, soda, milk, bananas) as the amount of comparison shopping increased. In contrast, the level of comparison shopping was largely irrelevant in setting new prices for less visible items (for example, bologna, orange juice, mayonnaise). The pricing decisions for these products were more strongly influenced by the competitors' reactions to the initial price cut.

Source: Joel E. Urbany and Peter R. Dickson, "Consumer Information, Competitive Rivalry, and Pricing in the Retail Grocery Industry," working paper, University of South Carolina, 1988.

2. About 50 percent of those interviewed in one study actually purchased a product after seeing a magazine ad or a commercial for it. Information on price reduction was a major sales trigger.[12]
3. There is a distinct segment of the American public that relies heavily on advertising. They are likely to be male, young, single, and employed.[13]
4. Print and TV ads were found to be the primary information sources used in the purchase of small electrical appliances and outdoor products.[14]

The effects of advertising can be difficult to discern through questioning. People typically do not remember much about advertising unless it clearly stands out as decisive. A more definitive test is to do a field experiment, such as advertising in one market and not in another. This is expensive and methodologically demanding, but many companies will do it simply because there is no better way.

In-Store Information   Many buying decisions are actually made at the point of purchase. It has been reported that two-thirds of all food purchase decisions are made in the grocery store.[15] Consequently, in-store information can have a strong influence on consumer decision making. At least 40 percent of the buyers of housewares mentioned using in-store displays.[16] The informativeness of displays should increase sharply in the future as computerization becomes more common. Revlon and Estee Lauder introduced computerized displays several years ago, as it was found that consumers often want answers to questions that might be embarrassing to raise with a potentially ill-informed sales clerk. Hence, the display allows immediate feedback to these questions.

Package labels are often consulted (see Consumer in Focus 16.3) and, at times, the effects of this information source can be substantial. For example, nutritional labeling tends to improve consumer perception of such attributes as "wholesome" and "tender."[17] It has also been found that strictly promotional terms such as "sweet" and "succulent" leave people with an assurance of quality comparable to that of the more detailed nutritional data. This shows how easy it is for deception to take place.

On the other hand, there is evidence that sometimes labels are misperceived, used only in part, or disregarded altogether.[18] This is a particularly disturbing finding when the content consists of safety warnings or precautions. Moreover, consumers with lower socioeconomic status make less use of package information and vice versa—just the opposite of what policy makers usually intend.[19]

Salespeople   A number of situations exist in which personal selling still plays an important role, even in this era of mass merchandising. It becomes especially crucial when there is the necessity of some type of point-of-sale negotiation and information exchange between buyer and seller. The energy-use labeling program for major appliances, for instance, was found to be ineffective without the input

Consumer in Focus **16.3**

Food Labels and Consumer Search

If you think that consumers don't pay much attention to food labels, think again. On average, over one-third always read ingredient or nutritional information, although this varies across consumers. Women are more likely than men to read labels. Older consumers also make greater use of labels than younger ones.

Food labels are particularly important for products making a first impression. Nearly 80 percent of consumers report that they always or sometimes read labels prior to purchasing a food item for the first item. Many consumers also indicate that label information can influence what they buy. For instance, one-third report that their cereal purchases are influenced by what appears on the label.

Source: William Mueller, "Who Reads the Label?" *American Demographics* 13 (January 1991), 36–41. Reprinted with permission. © American Demographics (January 1991). For subscription information, please call (800) 828-1133.

from sales personnel to explain just what the ratings meant.[20] The druggist remains an important information source on various aspects of health care and medication usage.[21]

Consumers' reliance on the opinions of salespeople should be considered in developing promotional strategy. A basic decision confronting marketers is the relative emphasis they should place on **push** versus **pull strategies**. A pull strategy involves the manufacturer creating product demand by appealing to the ultimate consumer who, in turn, will encourage the channel to carry the product. Under a push strategy, manufacturers focus their selling efforts on the channel, which is then responsible for attracting consumers. This latter strategy makes more sense when the salesperson represents an important source of information.

General Purpose Media   The mass media frequently contain items of interest to those in the midst of the decision process. Some purchasers of houseware items, for example, reported that editorial articles in magazines and newspapers proved helpful.[22] Governmental agencies also generate a wealth of consumer relevant information.

Various product-rating agencies have risen to the forefront in recent years, the most widely known being Consumers' Union, which publishes *Consumer Reports*. A number of manufacturers have found, frequently to their dismay, that ratings by such agencies can have a potent effect, especially if the ratings are negative.[23]

Social Others   As seen in Chapters 5 and 6, social others such as friends and family can serve as significant sources of information. In a survey by J. D. Power and Associates, an automotive market research firm, two-thirds of new car buyers reported that their decision concerning which make of car to buy was most strongly influenced by their social contacts.[24]

Sequence of Search   The final search dimension, sequence, focuses on the order of search activities. Researchers have been particularly interested in the order in which product-attribute information is acquired.[25] When confronted with a set of brands described along several attributes, consumers may follow a **brand search sequence** (often referred to as **processing by brand**), where each brand is examined along the various attributes before search proceeds to the next brand. Alternatively, an **attribute search sequence** (or **processing by attribute**) may occur, in which brand information is collected on an attribute-by-attribute basis. For example, a consumer might first examine each brand's price, followed by an inspection of each brand's warranty. The sequence in which product-attribute information is acquired is an important property of the choice rules we consider in the following chapter.

The information source consumers consult at the beginning of external search may partly determine their purchase behavior. A study of consumers' appliance shopping behavior reports that those buying from Sears were most likely to begin their search process by consulting either newspaper ads or catalogs.[26] Purchases made at furniture stores, however, were most likely to start with discussing the situation with a friend or relative. Different sources can guide the consumer along different purchase paths.

Determinants of Search

A considerable amount of research has accumulated regarding the variety of factors that influence search. Some of these determinants are discussed next.

Situational Determinants   The manner in which situational forces can affect consumer decision making is considered in Chapter 7. As we note there, the information environment will play a significant role in shaping consumer behavior. External search is obviously constrained by the availability and quantity of information in the marketplace. Even the format in which information is presented can alter search behavior, as reflected by consumers' greater use of unit price information when presented on lists.[27]

Time pressures are another source of situational influence.[28] A refrigerator stuffed with food that breaks down beyond repair affords the consumer little time to pursue an extensive and deliberate search. Similarly, the person searching a new city for an upcoming move typically will have only a few days to locate living quarters.

Product Determinants   Features of the product can affect consumer search. The degree of product differentiation is very important. If consumers believe that all brands are essentially the same, then there is little need for extensive search. As brands become more distinct, then the potential payoff from search grows larger. However, such perceived differences must also be coupled with an uncertainty as to which brand is "best." For example, if consumers believe that a given brand offers the lowest prices, then they are unlikely to undertake price comparisons regardless of how much difference they perceive in the prices of competing brands.

Product price is another factor.[29] Higher prices will create greater concerns about the financial risks involved with the purchase, which in turn leads to greater search.

The stability of a product category may affect search. Experienced consumers can rely more heavily on their existing knowledge for categories (for example, milk, garden hoses, cigarettes) that change little relatively over time. In contrast, unstable categories characterized by product innovations or price changes (for example, personal computers, electronic games) may require consumers to "update" their knowledge through search.[30]

Consumer search may also vary between goods and services. Because consumers may perceive greater risk in buying services than goods, they may adopt somewhat different information search patterns to reduce perceived risk. In one study of this possibility, consumers relied more heavily on personal sources of information for decisions involving services.[31]

Retail Determinants   The retail environment will also influence consumer search. The distance between retail competitors can determine the number of stores consumers shop during decision making. Fewer stores will be visited as distance increases.

The similarity among retailers is another source of influence. Search is more likely when consumers perceive important differences across retailers.[32] This is particularly true when retailers differ in the prices charged for products.[33] Again, however, there must also be uncertainty about which store is best before perceptions of store differences will affect search.

Consumer Determinants   Characteristics of the consumer strongly determine search behavior. Some of the more important determinants are discussed subsequently.

Knowledge   Knowledge can have both inhibiting and facilitating effects on search behavior. It can allow the consumer to rely more heavily on internal search during decision making, thereby lowering the need for prepurchase search.

Consequently, knowledge or prior purchase experience is often found to have a negative relationship with external search.[34]

Alternatively, knowledge can enhance search, primarily by affording more effective utilization of newly acquired information. When consumers feel more confident about their ability to judge products, they will typically acquire more information.[35] Research has, therefore, found that knowledge may be related positively to external search.[36]

These positive and negative influences may combine to produce an inverted-U relationship between knowledge and external search.[37] Consumers possessing extremely limited knowledge (for example, first-time buyers) may feel incompetent to undertake an elaborate search and analysis. Instead, they may try to solve their consumption problem by relying on others. For example, in the "purchase-pal" car buying segment described earlier in the chapter, these inexperienced and unconfident consumers depended very heavily on the opinions of others (for example, dad) in making their decisions. Similarly, many first-time appliance buyers may decide to place their faith in the salesperson of a trusted retailer (for example, Sears).

Greater prepurchase search should occur for moderately informed consumers. They will possess sufficient knowledge to explore and understand the information environment. However, their knowledge is not so great that they feel comfortable relying heavily on memory. In contrast, a stronger reliance on memory may take place for those possessing high levels of relevant knowledge. Internal search may uncover most, if not all, of the information desired for decision making, thus leading to little prepurchase search for very knowledgeable consumers.[38]

Involvement   Search will also depend on the level of consumer involvement with the product and decision process. Product involvement, which reflects a more enduring interest in the product than that stimulated by purchase requirements, should exert a strong influence on ongoing search.[39] Prepurchase search, by contrast, will depend more heavily on consumers' involvement with the purchase decision stemming from their perceptions of the economic and psychological risks associated with product purchase. In both cases, higher involvement should lead to greater search.[40]

As one example of how involvement can influence consumer search, consider soup. It should come as no surprise that this product is rather uninvolving for many consumers. This lack of involvement is reflected by how little patience consumers have in locating what they want. According to Anthony Adams, vice president of marketing research at Campbell Soup Company, "After about 45 seconds, we find that consumers just give up." This simple fact prompted the company to streamline its soup selections to facilitate shoppers locating what they want as quickly as possible.[41]

One tactic that consumers frequently employ for low-involvement purchases is the use of product trial as a "substitute" for prepurchase search. Such is the case for many of the new products that find their way onto the grocer's shelves. Given the relatively low cost of these items, consumers will often decide that the most efficient utilization of their resources is to simply "buy it and try it." However, when consumers are highly involved with the purchase decision, a substantial amount of search may be undertaken in order to develop the conviction desired by consumers that they are making a good choice.

Beliefs and Attitudes   Search behavior, just like purchase behavior, is affected by consumers' beliefs and attitudes. For many consumers, shopping is a dreaded chore that is minimized whenever possible. Others hold very different attitudes, as exemplified by those consumers who proudly wear T-shirts proclaiming "Born to shop!" Generally speaking, consumers engage in more search as their attitudes toward shopping become more favorable.[42]

In the case of repeat purchases, consumer satisfaction with their prior choices may determine the perceived need for search while making their current choices. If the prior choice was satisfactory, consumers become less motivated to search. This simple fact goes a long way in explaining why grocery shoppers spent so little time in making the decisions described earlier in Consumer in Focus 16.1.

Of course, when prior choices turn out to be less than satisfying, or when consumers are making an initial purchase decision within the product category, at least some degree of search will be needed. In such cases, product attitudes can be important since search will tend to focus initially on brands with high prior attractiveness.[43]

The beliefs held by consumers are also important determinants.[44] Perceptions regarding the costs versus benefits of search play a major role in guiding search.[45] Consumers will usually invest more effort into search when the perceived benefits of this activity grow and the costs decline.

This cost-benefit view of search plays an important role in Wilkie and Dickson's model of appliance shopping behavior reproduced in Figure 16.6. Following need recognition (called "precipitating purchase circumstance" in their model), the consumer is seen as developing some preliminary specifications for the product purchase (for example, must be under $400). A store is then visited, perhaps because it is currently promoting sale prices. At this point a salesperson might influence the consumer to modify his initial specifications. If the "best" alternative (that is, the one coming closest to meeting the consumer's specifications) available at the store is exactly what the consumer wants, search will end and purchase takes place. If not, the consumer must then decide on the relative costs versus benefits of continued search.

Demographic Characteristics   Research indicates that search may be related to several demographic characteristics.[46] Age is often negatively related to search. Older consumers can call upon their greater experience. They may also be more brand loyal than their younger counterparts. Higher-income consumers search less than lower-income consumers. Higher-income consumers presumably value their time more highly, which increases search costs. Higher costs will reduce search.[47]

A positive relationship usually occurs between education and search. More educated consumers seem likely to have greater confidence in their ability to use search effectively. Such confidence will enhance search behavior.[48]

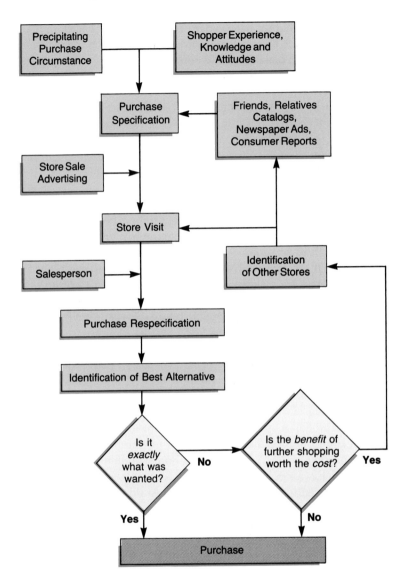

FIGURE 16.6 **A Dynamic-Adaptive Model of Appliance Shopping Behavior**

Measuring Information Search

There are basically two main approaches to measuring consumer search: **retrospective questioning** and **observation**. The most popular method, retrospective questioning, involves simply asking consumers to recall their search activities during decision making. This can be done through surveys and store exit interviews. Also, specifically designed warranty registration cards can be useful for this purpose.

Although this method finds widespread use, it suffers from the obvious limitation of reliance on recall. Unless the purchase is highly involving and recently made, it is probable that many details of the search process will be forgotten.

One way to overcome consumers' imperfect memory for their search behavior is through observation.[49] Evidence indicates that the incidences of actual information seeking are higher when they are observed than when indicated by a reliance on retrospective questioning.[50] Nonetheless, the observational method is not without its own set of limitations. Researchers can observe what consumers do within a specific store. But what about when consumers leave the store? Observational techniques are extremely limited in their potential to provide information about many aspects of consumer search, such as consulting with friends and reading relevant materials.

In addition to measuring what sources of information consumers consult during decision making, it is also useful to examine the extent to which consumers rely on a particular source. Consider two consumers, both of whom consult the same source (for example, a salesperson) during search. Suppose, however, that one consumer relies on the source's advice, while the other ignores this advice. Search measures that only capture whether consumers search a particular source without also gauging whether consumers use the source will provide an incomplete picture of the role information sources play during consumer decision making. For this reason, it is recommended that consumers should be asked to report both what sources they consult and how useful and influential they found each source to be.[51]

Summary

The decision process begins when a need is activated and recognized because of a discrepancy between the consumer's desired state and actual situation. Need recognition can be triggered by a number of factors. Changes in one's personal circumstances, such as the birth of a child, can activate new needs. Marketers can also influence the likelihood of need activation through advertising and product innovations.

Search for potential need satisfiers will occur following need recognition. If an internal search of memory provides a satisfactory solution to the consumption problem, then it will be unnecessary for consumers to seek information from their environment. Often, however, some degree of external search will be necessary. Just how much search will occur varies across consumers and depends on a host of situational, marketplace, and consumer characteristics.

Not all external search is driven by an immediate purchase need. Indeed, some consumers continually engage in ongoing search activities as a result of their involvement with the product category.

Consumer search can serve as an important determinant of marketing strategy. How much consumers search and the particular sources consulted during search can help shape a firm's pricing, promotion, and distribution strategies.

Review and Discussion Questions

1. Discuss how need recognition triggered your last soft drink purchase. Was this different from need recognition leading to the purchase of new shoes? What role, if any, do you feel marketing efforts played in both situations?
2. How did need recognition underlie your decision to attend college or graduate school?
3. Referring again to Question 2, describe how your institution could have influenced your need recognition through its marketing efforts.
4. Assume that you are a consultant to a national manufacturer of air conditioners. Your firm has 20 percent of the market. The remainder is divided among 7 competitors. Your firm wants to stimulate need recognition among those who own second homes for vacation and weekend purposes. What are your recommendations concerning, first of all, the desirability of such a strategy and, secondly, the techniques that should be used for this purpose?
5. What effect do you believe ongoing search has on consumers' use of internal search during decision making?
6. Explain how each of the following factors might affect consumer search: (a) brand loyalty, (b) store loyalty, (c) uncertainty about which brand best meets consumers' needs, and (d) the importance consumers place on paying a low price.
7. Consider two alternative target segments that differ only in their propensity for information search. One segment undertakes a substantial amount of external search during decision making. In contrast, consumers in the remaining segment are far less active in their search behaviors. Which segment, if either, would be a better target market? Assuming both were targeted, how could marketing activities differ in pursuing each segment?
8. The results of a consumer research project have just arrived on your desk. This study examined whether target consumers' brand preferences at the time of need recognition carried over to actual purchase. Consumers just beginning their decision process were asked about their preferences for the company's brand and two competitors. These results as well as each brand's share of purchase are presented below.

Brand	Consumers' Preference at Time of Need Recognition	Share of Purchases
Company's brand	50%	30%
Competitor A	30%	50%
Competitor B	20%	20%
Total	100%	100%

What conclusions would you reach from this information?

Endnotes

1. Sirgy has employed the concept of congruity between perceived and expected product performance to predict the strength of need recognition. See M. Joseph Sirgy, "A So-

cial Cognition Model of Consumer Problem Recognition," *Journal of the Academy of Marketing Science* 15 (Winter 1987), 53–61.

2. Gordon C. Bruner II, "The Effect of Problem Recognition Style on Information Seeking," *Journal of the Academy of Marketing Science* 15 (Winter 1987), 33–41; Gordon C. Bruner II, "Problem Recognition Styles and Search Patterns: An Empirical Investigation," *Journal of Retailing* 62 (1986), 281–297; Gordon C. Bruner II, "Recent Contributions to the Theory of Problem Recognition," in Robert F. Lusch, et al., eds., *1985 AMA Educators' Proceedings* (Washington, DC: American Marketing Association, 1985), 11–15.

3. Internal search has received relatively little attention in the consumer behavior literature. For exceptions, see James R. Bettman, *An Information Processing Theory of Consumer Choice* (Reading, Mass.: Addison-Wesley, 1979), 107–111; Gabriel J. Biehal, "Consumers' Prior Experiences and Perceptions in Auto Repair Choice," *Journal of Marketing* 47 (Summer 1983), 87–91. For research on how the adequacy of internal search will affect external search, see Girish Punj, "Presearch Decision Making in Consumer Durable Purchases," *Journal of Consumer Marketing* 4 (Winter 1987), 71–82.

4. Biehal, "Consumers' Prior Experiences and Perceptions in Auto Repair Choice."

5. Geoffrey C. Kiel and Roger A. Layton, "Dimensions of Consumer Information Seeking Behavior," *Journal of Marketing Research* 18 (May 1981), 233–239.

6. Peter H. Bloch, Daniel L. Sherrell, and Nancy M. Ridgway, "Consumer Search: An Extended Framework," *Journal of Consumer Research* 13 (June 1986), 119–126.

7. Bloch, Sherrell, and Ridgway, "Consumer Search: An Extended Framework."

8. John D. Claxton, Joseph N. Fry, and Bernard Portis, "A Taxonomy of Prepurchase Information Gathering Patterns," *Journal of Consumer Research* 1 (December 1974), 35–42; David H. Furse, Girish N. Punj, and David W. Stewart, "A Typology of Individual Search Strategies Among Purchasers of New Automobiles," *Journal of Consumer Research* 10 (March 1984), 417–431; Joseph W. Newman, "Consumer External Search: Amount and Determinants," in Arch G. Woodside, Jagdish N. Sheth, and Peter D. Bennett, eds., *Consumer and Industrial Buyer Behavior* (New York: North-Holland, 1977), 79–94.

9. Richard W. Olshavsky and Donald H. Granbois, "Consumer Decision Making—Fact or Fiction?" *Journal of Consumer Research* 6 (September 1979), 93–100.

10. Furse, Punj, and Stewart, "A Typology of Individual Search Strategies among Purchasers of New Automobiles." Also see David F. Midgley, "Patterns of Interpersonal Information Seeking for the Purchase of a Symbolic Product," *Journal of Marketing Research* 20 (February 1983), 74–83.

11. Michael A. Houston, "Consumer Evaluations and Product Information Sources," in James H. Leigh and Claude R. Martin, Jr., eds., *Current Issues and Research in Advertising* (Ann Arbor: University of Michigan Graduate School of Business, 1979), 135–144.

12. *A Study of Media Involvement* (New York: Magazine Publishers' Association, 1979).

13. "Whirlpool Corporation," in Roger D. Blackwell, James F. Engel, and W. Wayne Talarzyk, *Contemporary Cases in Consumer Behavior,* rev. ed. (Hinsdale, Ill.: Dryden Press, 1984), 365–388.

14. "Study Tracks Housewares Buying, Information Sources," *Marketing News* (October 14, 1983), 16.

15. Judann Dagnoli, "Heinz Marketing Gets $100M Boost," *Advertising Age* (September 16, 1991), 3, 45.

16. "Study Tracks Housewares Buying, Information Sources."

17. Edward H. Asam and Louis P. Bucklin, "Nutritional Labeling for Canned Goods: A Study of Consumer Response," *Journal of Marketing* 37 (April 1973), 32–37.

18. Gary T. Ford and Philip G. Kuehl, "Label Warning Messages in OTC Drug Advertising: An Experimental Examination of FTC Policy-Making," in James H. Leigh and Claude R. Martin, Jr., eds., *Current Issues and Research in Advertising* (Ann Arbor: University of Michigan Graduate School of Business, 1979), 115–128; Lorna Opatow, "How Consumers 'Use' Labels of OTC Drugs," *American Druggist* 177 (March 1978), 10ff; and Jo-Ann Zybtniewski, "Keeping Pace with the Nutrition Race," *Progressive Grocer* 59 (July 1980), 29.

19. James McCullough and Roger Best, "Consumer Preference for Food Label Information: A Basis for Segmentation," *Journal of Consumer Affairs* 14 (Summer 1980), 180–192.

20. John D. Claxton and C. Dennis Anderson, "Energy Information at the Point of Sale: A Field Experiment," in Jerry C. Olson, ed., *Advances in Consumer Research* 7 (Ann Arbor: Association for Consumer Research, 1980), 277–282.

21. "Public Goes on Strong 'Self-Medication Kick,'" *Marketing News* (June 27, 1980), 1.

22. "Study Tracks Housewares Buying, Information Sources."

23. Mark G. Weinberger and William R. Dillon, "The Effects of Unfavorable Product Rating Information," in Jerry C. Olson, ed., *Advances in Consumer Research* 7 (Ann Arbor: Association for Consumer Research, 1980), 528–532.

24. Cited in Bloch, Sherrell, and Ridgway, "Consumer Search: An Extended Framework," 121.

25. See James R. Bettman and Jacob Jacoby, "Patterns of Processing in Consumer Information Processing," in Beverlee B. Anderson, ed., *Advances in Consumer Research* 3 (Ann Arbor: Association for Consumer Research, 1976), 315–320; James R. Bettman and Pradeep Kakkar, "Effects of Information Presentation Format on Consumer Information Acquisition Strategies," *Journal of Consumer Research* 3 (March 1977), 233–240; James R. Bettman and C. Whan Park, "Effects of Prior Knowledge and Experience and Phase of the Choice Process on Consumer Decision Processes: A Protocol Analysis," *Journal of Consumer Research* 7 (December 1980), 243–248; Itamar Simonson, Joel Huber, and John Payne, "The Relationship between Prior Brand Knowledge and Information Acquisition Order," *Journal of Consumer Research* 14 (March 1988), 566–578.

26. William L. Wilkie and Peter R. Dickson, "Shopping for Appliances: Consumers' Strategies and Patterns of Information Search," Marketing Science Institute Working Paper No. 85–108, 1985.

27. J. Edward Russo, "The Value of Unit Price Information," *Journal of Marketing Research* 14 (May 1977), 193–201; J. Edward Russo, Gene Krieser, and Sally Miyashita, "An Effective Display of Unit Price Information," *Journal of Marketing* 39 (April 1975), 11–19.

28. Sharon E. Beatty and Scott M. Smith, "External Search Effort: An Investigation Across Several Product Categories," *Journal of Consumer Research* 14 (June 1987), 83–95; William L. Moore and Donald R. Lehmann, "Individual Differences in Search Behavior for a Nondurable," *Journal of Consumer Research* 7 (December 1980), 296–307.

29. Kiel and Layton, "Dimensions of Consumer Information Seeking Behavior."

30. Joel E. Urbany and Peter R. Dickson, "Information Search in the Retail Grocery Market," working paper, Ohio State University, 1987.

31. Keith B. Murray, "A Test of Services Marketing Theory: Consumer Information Acquisition Activities," *Journal of Marketing* 55 (January 1991), 10–25.

32. Calvin P. Duncan and Richard W. Olshavsky, "External Search: The Role of Consumer Beliefs," *Journal of Marketing Research* 19 (February 1982), 32–43.

33. Joel E. Urbany, "An Experimental Examination of the Economics of Information," *Journal of Consumer Research* 13 (September 1986), 257–271.

34. Beatty and Smith, "External Search Effort: An Investigation Across Several Product Categories"; Kiel and Layton, "Dimensions of Consumer Information Seeking Behavior"; Moore and Lehmann, "Individual Differences in Search Behavior for a Nondurable"; Joseph W. Newman and Richard Staelin, "Prepurchase Information Seeking for New Cars and Major Household Appliances," *Journal of Marketing Research* 9 (August 1972), 249–257; Girish N. Punj and Richard Staelin, "A Model of Consumer Information Search Behavior for New Automobiles," *Journal of Consumer Research* 9 (March 1983), 366–380.

35. Duncan and Olshavsky, "External Search: The Role of Consumer Beliefs."

36. Merrie Brucks, "The Effects of Product Class Knowledge on Information Search Behavior," *Journal of Consumer Research* 12 (June 1985), 1–16; Jacob Jacoby, Robert W. Chestnut, and William A. Fisher, "A Behavioral Process Approach to Information Acquisition in Nondurable Purchasing," *Journal of Marketing Research* 15 (November 1978), 532–544.

37. Bettman and Park, "Effects of Prior Knowledge and Experience and Phase of the Choice Process on Consumer Decision Processes: A Protocol Analysis." Also see Joel E. Urbany, Peter R. Dickson, and William L. Wilkie, "Buyer Uncertainty and Information Search," *Journal of Consumer Research* 16 (September 1989), 208–215.

38. Knowledge can also affect the sequence of search. See Simonson, Huber, and Payne, "The Relationship Between Prior Brand Knowledge and Information Acquisition."

39. Block, Sherrell, and Ridgway, "Consumer Search: An Extended Framework."

40. Beatty and Smith, "External Search Effort: An Investigation Across Several Product Categories"; Judith Lynne Zaichkowsky, "Measuring the Involvement Construct," *Journal of Consumer Research* 12 (December 1985), 341–352. For research on how involvement's influence may vary between functional versus expressive products, see Banwari Mittal, "Must Consumer Involvement Always Imply More Information Search?" in Thomas K. Srull, ed., *Advances in Consumer Research* 16 (Provo, Utah: Association for Consumer Research, 1989), 167–172.

41. Patricia Braus, "What Is Good Service?" *American Demographics* 12 (July 1990), 36–39.

42. Beatty and Smith, "External Search Effort: An Investigation Across Several Product Categories"; Punj and Staelin, "A Model of Consumer Information Search Behavior for New Automobiles."

43. Simonson, Huber, and Payne, "The Relationship between Prior Brand Knowledge and Information Acquisition Order."

44. Duncan and Olshavsky, "External Search: The Role of Consumer Beliefs"; Deborah Roedder John, Carol A. Scott, and James R. Bettman, "Sampling Data for Covariation Assessment: The Effect of Prior Beliefs on Search Patterns," *Journal of Consumer Research* 13 (June 1986), 38–47.

45. Urbany, "An Experimental Investigation of the Economics of Information." Also see Narasimhan Srinivasan and Brian T. Ratchford, "An Empirical Test of a Model of External Search for Automobiles," *Journal of Consumer Research* 18 (September 1991), 233–242.

46. For a brief review of the literature concerning demographics and search, see Beatty and Smith, "External Search Effort: An Investigation Across Several Product Categories."

47. John, Scott, and Bettman, "Sampling Data for Covariation Assessment: The Effect of Prior Beliefs on Search Patterns"; Urbany, "An Experimental Investigation of the Economics of Information."

48. Duncan and Olshavsky, "External Search: The Role of Consumer Beliefs."
49. Peter R. Dickson and Alan G. Sawyer, "The Price Knowledge and Search of Supermarket Shoppers," *Journal of Marketing* 54 (July 1990), 42–53; Wayne D. Hoyer, "An Examination of Consumer Decision Making for a Common Repeat Purchase Product," *Journal of Consumer Research* 11 (December 1984), 822–829; Joseph W. Newman and Bradley D. Lockman, "Measuring Prepurchase Information Seeking," *Journal of Consumer Research* 11 (December 1975), 216–222.
50. Newman and Lockman, "Measuring Prepurchase Information Seeking."
51. Jeff Blodgett and Donna Hill, "An Exploratory Study Comparing Amount-of-Search Measures to Consumers' Reliance on Each Source of Information," in Rebecca H. Holman and Michael R. Solomon, eds., *Advances in Consumer Research* 18 (Provo, Utah: Association for Consumer Research, 1991), 773–779.

17

Alternative Evaluation

The importance consumers attach to environmental considerations is changing. At the outset of the 1980s, environmental issues were not a major concern for most consumers. Today, they rank as the fourth most important issue among American consumers.

These attitudinal changes are affecting consumer behavior. Research indicates that one-third of consumers regularly check product labels for environmental information. And they want more. In a survey of females aged 21–54, 85 percent reported that product labels do not contain enough environmental information.

These changing attitudes have not gone unnoticed by businesses. What some have called "green marketing," businesses have begun catering to environmentally concerned consumers. Many of these green appeals have come in the form of new packaging. L'eggs, the world's largest maker of women's hosiery, has replaced its famous plastic egg container with an environmentally friendly cardboard package. McDonald's has discontinued using plastic foam cartons in favor of paper wraps.

Marketers are also changing what comes inside the package. Manufacturers of disposable diapers, for instance, have reformulated their products to ease the demands they place on landfill space.

Sources: Howard Schlossberg, "Latest Trend: Targeting Consumers According to Environmental Beliefs," *Marketing News* 26 (January 6, 1992), 5; Howard Schlossberg, "Americans Passionate about the Environment? Critic Says That's 'Nonsense'," *Marketing News* 25 (September 16, 1991), 8; Howard Schlossberg, "Survey: Consumers More Aware, Still Want More Info," *Marketing News* 25 (December 9, 1991), 6.

The chapter opener aptly illustrates that the importance consumers place on product features in evaluating choice alternatives affects a company's product offerings and marketing focus. This chapter examines the third stage of our consumer decision-making model, alternative evaluation. **Alternative evaluation** can be defined as the process by which a choice alternative is evaluated and selected to meet consumer needs. Although we have presented search and alternative evaluation as "separate" stages for pedagogical reasons, the reader should recognize that the two stages are intricately intertwined during decision making. The acquisition of product information from the environment, for instance, will normally lead to some evaluation (for example, "these prices are too high") that may then guide subsequent search (for example, "let's check the store across the street").

The complexity of alternative evaluation will vary dramatically depending on the particular process consumers follow in making their consumption decisions. When decision making is habitual in nature, alternative evaluation will simply involve the consumer forming an intention to repurchase the same product as before. Similarly, consumers lacking the knowledge needed for selecting an appropriate medicinal product may rely on the pharmacist's recommendations rather than try to decide for themselves. Under this scenario, alternative evaluation consists of the rather simple decision rule, "Buy what the expert recommends."

Sometimes alternative evaluation will be quite complex, as in the case of an experienced car buyer wishing to purchase a second family car. Figure 17.1 depicts the basic components of the alternative evaluation process. Decisions must be made initially about which choice alternatives to consider and the evaluative criteria (that is, dimensions or attributes) to use in judging the alternatives. The relative performance of the considered alternatives along the evaluative criteria must then be judged. A decision rule is then applied to these judgments in order to select a particular alternative. In the following sections we examine more fully these components of the alternative evaluation process.

Evaluative Criteria

Evaluative criteria are nothing more than the particular dimensions or attributes that are used in judging the choice alternatives. Evaluative criteria come in many forms. In purchasing a car, consumers may consider factors such as safety, reliability, price, brand name, country of origin (where it is made), warranty, and gas mileage. The consumer may also consider evaluative criteria more hedonic in nature, such as the feelings that come from owning (for example, prestige, status) and driving (for example, exhilaration, excitement) the car. Although it is beyond the scope of this text to provide a detailed review of the various evaluative criteria used by consumers, a couple deserve special comment.

Price

Certainly one of the more important evaluative criteria is price. Indeed, we have all experienced situations in which our product choice was heavily affected by pricing

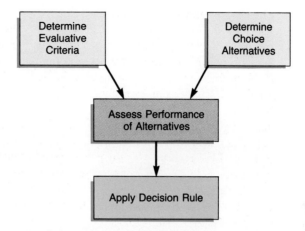

FIGURE 17.1   **Basic Components of the Alternative Evaluation Process**

considerations. Nonetheless, there is considerable variation in the importance of price across both consumers and products.[1] Consequently, consumers' price sensitivity is often used as a basis for market segmentation.

Note, however, that the role of price is often overrated. When supermarket shoppers were asked the price of an item they had just placed in their shopping basket, less than half of them could do so. Similarly, less than half were aware they had chosen a product offered at a reduced price.[2] Nor are consumers always looking for the lowest possible price or even the best price-to-quality ratio. Other factors such as convenience or brand name may assume greater importance.[3]

Brand Name

Brand name frequently emerges as a determinant criterion, as it did in a study of purchasing behavior involving dress shirts and suits.[4] It also proved to be significant in choosing over-the-counter drugs.[5] In these cases the brand name appears to serve as a surrogate indicator of product quality. Indeed, the potential for brand name to influence judgments of a product's quality has been well documented.[6]

The importance consumers place on brand name may vary with the ease with which quality can be judged objectively. For example, in the case of headache and cold remedies, the average consumer cannot judge purity and quality. Consequently, brand name becomes especially crucial as a surrogate indicator of quality. It is such a dominant factor with many consumers that they will pay much more for aspirin when it carries a well-known brand name, even though they are aware that government regulations require all aspirin products to contain the same basic therapeutic formulation.[7]

Brand name can also be influential when the name is seen as a status symbol and consumers are motivated by such considerations. For some consumers, having the Rolex name on a watch is just as important as any physical feature of the product itself.

FIGURE 17.2   Promoting the Product's Country of Origin

Country of Origin

In this age of intensifying international competition and the loss of many manufacturing jobs to cheaper foreign labor, it is not surprising that the country in which a
product is produced has become an important consideration among many American
consumers.[8] Consumer in Focus 17.1 describes the results of a study on the importance consumers would place on country of origin in buying a new car. Many
companies have tried to capitalize upon this concern by emphasizing the fact that
their product is "Made in the U.S.A." (see Figure 17.2). Others have taken this one
step further by advertising not only that the product is "American built" but also
that the manufacturer is "American owned."

The Salience of Evaluative Criteria

The concept of **salience** reflects the notion that evaluative criteria often differ in
their influence on consumers' product selections. Some criteria will have a greater
impact than others. A pleasant retail atmosphere may be a nice amenity, but the

Consideration of Imports versus American in New Car Buying

Are there differences in the likelihood that a car would be considered for purchase depending on its country of origin? The answer, based on a survey of 1,000 U.S. households by Market Facts, a Chicago-based market research firm, is a definite yes. Nearly 90 percent of the respondents indicated that they would either definitely or probably consider an American-built car if they were shopping today. This percentage drops to 32 percent for Japanese autos and 27 percent for European cars.

Further analysis revealed that consumers' receptiveness to imports varied by age. Younger consumers were more likely to consider imports than their older counterparts. Whereas less than 10 percent of those 55 or older would consider a European auto, nearly 40 percent of those under 35 would do so. Similarly, Japanese cars registered a 17 percent consideration rate among the 55 and older segment, compared to 43 percent among consumers under 35. These demographic differences suggest that U.S. manufacturers can anticipate even greater competition from imports as time passes due to the greater receptiveness of younger consumers.

Source: Larry Levin, "New Car Buying: Imports vs. American," *TeleNation Reports* (Fall 1987), 2.

prices charged by the retailer will usually carry more weight in consumers' decisions about where to shop.

Salience refers to the *potential* influence each dimension may exert during the comparison process. Whether this potential influence materializes depends on how consumers perceive the alternatives under consideration to perform along an evaluative criterion. Take airline travel as an example. An airline's ability to provide safe passage is of obvious importance to consumers. However, because most consumers perceive all airlines as providing relatively safe travel, safety is not a deciding factor in selecting a carrier. Similarly, consumers may rate price as a very important attribute, but if all brands cost the same amount, the impact of price essentially drops out. Salient attributes that actually influence the evaluation process (that is, attributes on which alternatives differ) are known as **determinant attributes**.[9]

An important aspect of understanding consumer decision making involves identifying the particular evaluative criteria consumers use when deciding among purchase alternatives. It is also necessary to assess the relative salience of these criteria. Note, however, that we have already discussed these issues during our coverage of the multiattribute attitude models in Chapter 11. You may wish to review this discussion to refamiliarize yourself with the different procedures for identifying salient attributes and measuring their salience.

Determinants of Evaluative Criteria

The particular evaluative criteria used by consumers during decision making will depend on a number of factors. Some of these are discussed below.

Situational Influences   Situational factors will often have an important influence on an evaluative criterion's salience.[10] Location convenience, for example, often assumes greater importance in the selection of a fast-food restaurant when the consumer is pressed for time than when time is not a factor. Similarly, many consumers will select a prestigious brand of liquor when it is to be served at a party but will opt for a less prestigious (and less expensive) brand for their own private use.

Similarity of Choice Alternatives   The similarity or comparability of alternatives from which consumers choose can vary substantially. A consumer deciding how to spend a tax refund may be considering such diverse alternatives as buying a new wardrobe, taking a vacation, or putting the money in the bank. Much greater similarity among choice alternatives will exist, on the other hand, for decisions about which brand to purchase within a product category.

Decisions involving noncomparable alternatives may require the consumer to employ more abstract evaluative criteria during alternative evaluation.[11] Consider, for instance, the consumer faced with choosing between a refrigerator, a television, and a stereo. These alternatives share few concrete attributes (price is an exception) along which comparisons can be made directly. Comparisons can be undertaken, however, using abstract dimensions such as necessity, entertainment, and status.

Consumers' reliance on price during decision making can be affected by the similarity of choice alternatives. If, for instance, consumers believe that all lawn care companies will provide essentially the same basic service and benefits, then they will depend much more heavily on price differences in making a choice. In general, price becomes more important in the absence of meaningful product differentiation.

Motivation   As noted in Chapter 9, a basic distinction in understanding motivation is whether consumers are driven by utilitarian versus hedonic considerations. The presence of such motivations will determine the type of evaluative criteria likely to be used during alternative evaluation. Utilitarian motivations during the purchase of athletic shoes could lead to examination of a shoe's price and construction, whereas hedonic motivations might lead to consideration of the feelings that come from product ownership and usage (for example, the person who buys Nike in order to project a desirable image).

Involvement   Consumers' involvement with the decision will influence the number of evaluative criteria used in alternative evaluation. A greater number of evaluative criteria are likely to enter into the decision as involvement increases.[12]

Involvement may also influence the relative salience of evaluative criteria. A recent study of the evaluative criteria used by Iowa farmers in selecting a retail outlet for supplies found that highly involved decision makers were more concerned with service attributes, whereas those less involved focused on low price and a retailer's size and reputation.[13]

Knowledge   Knowledge can have several effects on consumers' use of evaluative criteria. Knowledgeable consumers will have information stored in memory about the dimensions useful for comparing choice alternatives. This information is much less likely to exist in the memory of novices. Consequently, novices will be much more susceptible to external influences that attempt to shape the particular criteria used during decision making.[14] For example, advertisements that suggest the evaluative criteria that consumers should consider are likely to be more effective in this regard for first-time buyers.

Knowledge can also determine consumers' use of particular evaluative criteria. Consumers may rely much more heavily on brand name or others' recommendations, for instance, when they lack the knowledge necessary for directly evaluating product quality.

Determining Choice Alternatives

Not only must consumers decide on the criteria to use in alternative evaluation, they must also determine the alternatives from which choice is made. These alternatives define what is known as the **consideration set** (also known as the **evoked set**). As indicated by the results presented in Table 17.1, the consideration set will typically

TABLE 17.1   **Average Size of Consumers' Consideration Sets by Product Category**

Product Category	Average Consideration Set Size	Product Category	Average Consideration Set Size
Analgesic	3.5	Insecticides	2.7
Antacid	4.4	Laundry detergent	4.8
Air freshener	2.2	Laxative	2.8
Bar soap	3.7	Peanut butter	3.3
Bathroom cleaner	5.7	Razors	2.9
Beer	6.9	Shampoo	6.1
Bleach	3.9	Shortening	6.0
Chili	2.6	Sinus medicine	3.6
Coffee	4.0	Soap	4.8
Cookies	4.9	Soda	5.1
Deodorant	3.9	Yogurt	3.6
Frozen dinners	3.3		

Source: John R. Hauser and Birger Wernerfelt, "An Evaluation Cost Model of Consideration Sets," *Journal of Consumer Research* 16 (March 1990), 393–408.

FIGURE 17.3 **Gaining Consideration: A Necessary Prerequisite for Purchase**

contain only a subset of the total number of alternatives available to the consumer. Recognize that these results represent the *average* size of the consideration set. Thus, some consumers will have even larger consideration sets, while the consideration sets for other consumers will be smaller. Extremely brand loyal consumers, for instance, are likely to have only one brand in their consideration set.

Gaining entry into the consideration set is a top priority. Failure to do so means that a competitor's offering will be purchased. Marketers must, therefore, take steps to see that their products gain consideration during decision making. Examine the ad appearing in Figure 17.3. Notice how it plays upon consumers' fears about making a mistake during decision making as a means of gaining consideration.

Another tactic employed by companies for gaining consideration, as exemplified by Figure 17.4, is to offer incentives. Automobile manufacturers sometimes offer consumers gifts or money to simply test drive their cars. Coupons can play essentially the same role.

FIGURE 17.4   Offering Incentives Can Lead to Consideration

Constructing the Consideration Set

How does the consumer determine the alternatives that will receive consideration? The answer depends on both situational and individual factors. For example, suppose you were hungry and decided to go out for fast food. A search through memory is likely to yield a number of possibilities. In this situation, the consideration set would depend on your recall of alternatives from memory (that is, the **retrieval set**).[15]

Suppose we change the setting to a drugstore, where you have decided to resume taking vitamin pills after getting out of the habit for a couple of years. Perhaps the easiest way to construct a consideration set would be to simply scan the shelving containing the vitamins and see if anything looks familiar. Choice might then be made from the brands you recognize. Note that recognition of alternatives available at the point of purchase will determine the consideration set.

A common element in both hypotheticals is the assumption of prior knowledge of at least some alternatives. Yet, in the case of first-time buyers for some product categories, consumers may lack knowledge about what alternatives are available to choose from. When this occurs, the consideration set may be developed in any one of a number of ways. The consumer might talk to others, search through the yellow pages, consider all brands available at the store, and so on. Thus, external factors such as the retail environment have a greater opportunity to affect the consideration set of less knowledgeable consumers.[16]

The manner in which the consideration set is constructed can shape marketing strategy. Greater emphasis must be given to having consumers learn what the product packaging looks like when recognition at the point of purchase determines the consideration set. Conversely, brand name recall is the appropriate criterion when consumers rely on a recall retrieval process in selecting choice alternatives. There is also the possibility of undermining the competition by inhibiting the recall of competitive names (see Chapter 14).[17]

Influence of the Consideration Set

One area of recent research interest concerns how the evaluation and choice of a given alternative is affected by what other alternatives are included in the consideration set. Several studies have reported an **attraction effect** where a given alternative's attractiveness is enhanced when an inferior alternative is added to the set of choice alternatives.[18] Although the robustness of this effect is not well understood, it does suggest the possibility that a product might benefit from encouraging consumers to consider weaker offerings.

Assessing Choice Alternatives

Another component of the alternative evaluation process involves judging the performance of choice alternatives along salient evaluative criteria. There exists some rather interesting research, as reported in Consumer in Focus 17.2, which indicates that some consumers may be limited in their ability to "accurately" evaluate choice alternatives.[19] Such findings are, of course, a cause for concern among those involved with consumer protection (see Chapter 24).

In many cases, consumers already have stored in memory judgments or beliefs about the performance of the choice alternatives under consideration. The ability to retrieve this information may strongly affect which alternative is eventually chosen.[20] On the other hand, consumers lacking such stored knowledge will need to rely on external information in forming beliefs about an alternative's performance.

The Use of Cutoffs

In judging how well an alternative performs, consumers may often employ **cutoffs**.[21] A cutoff is simply a restriction or requirement for acceptable attribute values.

Can Consumers Determine the "Best Buy"?

Suppose you were asked to decide which of two bottles of garlic powder, identical except in price and size, represented the "best buy." Powder weight in the first bottle is 2.37 ounces or 67 grams at a cost of 77 cents. The powder in the smaller bottle weighs 1.25 ounces or 35 grams. This bottle normally costs 51 cents, but is currently on sale at 41 cents. Which bottle is the "best buy"?

The answer is the larger bottle. Its unit price is 32.5 cents per ounce compared to 32.8 cents for the smaller bottle. Recognition of the need to estimate the relative unit price and the ability to do so would determine the accuracy of one's choice.

This problem was actually used in a study of consumer skills where subjects were given the incentive of having a chance to win $50 for making the correct choice. Of 100 female supermarket shoppers, 39 did not rely on a comparison of relative unit price in making their choice. Rather, they employed different decision rules, such as inferring that an item on sale would be a better buy. Highly educated shoppers were much more likely to consider relative unit price than those less educated.

Source: Noel Capon and Deanna Kuhn, "Can Consumers Calculate Best Buys?" *Journal of Consumer Research* 8 (March 1982), 449–453.

One example is price. Consumers are likely to have a fairly defined range of prices they are willing to pay. A price that falls outside of this range or zone will be viewed as unacceptable.[22]

Cutoffs are used for many evaluative criteria other than price. A consumer may refuse to consider generic soft drink brands. Another may reject any soft drink exceeding a certain number of calories. Still another may insist that the drink contain some amount of real fruit juices.

The cutoffs employed by consumers during decision making will obviously have a strong influence on the final choice. Consequently, it is important for marketers to understand the presence and nature of cutoffs. A brand that fails to meet a cutoff may be rejected regardless of how well it performs on other dimensions.

The Use of Signals

Judgments about choice alternatives can depend on the presence of certain cues or signals. In the ad presented in Figure 17.5, for instance, Xerox is hoping that consumers will rely on the copier's warranty as an indicator of its quality. Since

FIGURE 17.5 **A Product's Warranty Can Serve as a Signal of Quality**

many prospective buyers may feel uncomfortable with their ability to evaluate a product's quality, they may use warranty as a signal of quality (see Consumer in Focus 17.3).

Of course, consumers might also use some other cue for judging product quality, such as price. Consider the lesson learned by one cosmetics manufacturer that introduced a new line of very low-priced cosmetics. Sales were virtually nonexistent, and the line was eventually withdrawn from the market. However, when essentially the same line was later reintroduced at a higher price, sales took off. Why? Because consumers used price as a signal of quality and were unwilling to run the risk of wearing low-quality cosmetics.

The use of price as a signal of quality has been substantiated repeatedly.[23] Even so, price may have little influence on perceived quality in some situations and for some consumers. For instance, price may have little signaling power when consumers are able to easily judge product quality or rely on other signals (for example, brand name, image of store carrying the product) to infer quality.

Is Whirlpool Missing the Signal?

Which brand of washing machines is best? To answer this question, *Consumer Reports* rated 16 brands along numerous dimensions: load capacity, water and energy efficiency, how well the machine could handle unbalanced loads, and so on. As reported in the February 1991 issue, products of the Whirlpool Corp. received the best ratings. In addition to selling washers that carry the Whirlpool name, the company also makes the washers that sell under the Sears' Kenmore and KitchenAid brand names. All three brands were at the top of the ratings.

    But what if consumers are unaware of the *Consumer Reports* ratings? How might they go about judging quality? As we noted in the chapter, a product's warranty can serve as a signal of quality. And this is where Whirlpool may be missing the signal. Consider the following warranty information based on a fact sheet developed by Amana which rested upon its washers being displayed by the retailer.

	Transmission Labor	Transmission Parts	Non-transmission Labor	Non-transmission Parts	Cabinet Rust
Amana	5 Years	10 Years	1 Year	2 Years	5 Years
Frigidaire	1 Year	5 Years	1 Year	1 Year	1 Year
GE/Hotpoint	1 Year	5 Years	1 Year	1 Year	1 Year
Kenmore	1 Year	5 Years	1 Year	1 Year	1 Year
Maytag	1 Year	10 Years	1 Year	2 Years	5 Years
Whirlpool	1 Year	5 Years	1 Year	1 Year	1 Year

Based on this information, consumers are likely to reach very different conclusions about which brand is best than implied by the *Consumer Reports* ratings. One can only wonder about how many sales Whirlpool may be losing because of the weak signal conveyed by its warranty.

Source: "Washing Machines," *Consumer Reports* (February 1991), 112–117.

Selecting a Decision Rule

The final element of the alternative evaluation process to be considered is the decision rule. **Decision rules** represent the strategies consumers use to make a selection from the choice alternatives.[24] Decision rules can range from very simplistic procedures that require little time and effort to very elaborate ones that involve considerably more time and processing effort on the part of the consumer.

When choice is habituated, the decision rule is very simple: buy the same brand as last time. Even when choice is not habituated, consumers may employ simplistic decision rules such as "buy the cheapest" or "buy the brand my spouse likes." This is because consumers continually make trade-offs between the quality of their choice (that is, buying the "best" brand) and the amount of time and effort necessary to reach a decision. In many cases the consumer will follow decision rules that yield a satisfactory (as opposed to optimal) choice while minimizing their time and effort. These simplistic decision rules are more likely to occur for repetitive product choices that are viewed as relatively low in importance or involvement.[25]

At other times, however, consumers are more highly motivated during decision making. Consequently, they will employ more elaborate or complex decision rules that require greater processing effort. A fundamental distinction between these more complex rules is whether they involve a compensatory versus a noncompensatory procedure.

Noncompensatory Decision Rules

Noncompensatory decision rules are characterized by the fact that a weakness in one attribute *cannot* be offset by a strength in another attribute. Consider snack foods. Manufacturers have the capability of meeting consumers' desires for healthier snacks by cutting the amount of oil and salt in the products. But eliminate too much of these ingredients, and the snacks taste lousy. While the reformulated product will score high marks on nutritional considerations, this strength cannot overcome the weakness in the product's taste. As observed by Dwight Riskey, a psychologist and vice president of market research at Frito-Lay, "Consumers won't sacrifice taste for health in snacks."[26]

The simplistic decision rules described earlier further illustrate the potential for consumer decision making to follow a noncompensatory strategy. For instance, a brand that is not the cheapest would not be chosen no matter how well it performs on other evaluative criteria when the decision rule is "buy the cheapest." That is, the brand's weakness in price is not compensated by its favorable performance in other attributes. Three additional types of noncompensatory rules are lexicographic, elimination by aspects, and conjunctive.[27]

Lexicographic   Under this decision strategy, brands are compared on the most important attribute. If one of the brands is perceived as superior based on that attribute, it is selected. If two or more brands are perceived as equally good, they are then compared on the second most important attribute. This process continues until the tie is broken.

To illustrate this rule, consider the information presented in Table 17.2. This table contains attribute-performance ratings (from excellent to poor) for four different food item brands and attribute-importance rankings (where "1" is the most important). Which brand would be chosen under the lexicographic rule?

TABLE 17.2   Hypothetical Ratings for Illustrating Decision Rules

Attribute	Importance Ranking	Brand Performance Ratings			
		Brand A	Brand B	Brand C	Brand D
Taste	1	Excellent	Excellent	Very Good	Excellent
Price	2	Very Good	Good	Excellent	Fair
Nutrition	3	Good	Good	Poor	Excellent
Convenience	4	Fair	Good	Good	Excellent

The answer is brand A. A comparison on the most important attribute, taste, produces a tie between brands A, B, and D. This tie is broken on the next most important attribute, price, because brand A has the highest rating of the three brands. Notice, however, what would happen if the attribute-importance rankings were slightly different. For instance, if price were most important, brand C would then be chosen.

The concepts of processing by brand (PBB) and processing by attribute (PBA), originally introduced in the discussion of search sequence in Chapter 16, are also relevant here. Recall that in PBB, information is acquired for one brand at a time. The person who learns all about one brand before learning about the next is processing by brand. PBA involves the acquisition of information about a particular attribute of the various brands. The person comparing brands on taste, then on price, and so forth, is processing by attribute.

Decision rules differ in whether they require PBB or PBA. The lexicographic procedure, for instance, involves PBA since brands are compared on one attribute at a time.

Elimination by Aspects   This rule closely resembles the lexicographic procedure. As before, brands are first evaluated on the most important attribute. Now, however, the consumer imposes cutoffs. The consumer may, for example, employ cutoffs such as "must be under $2" or "must be at least nutritious."

If only one brand meets the cutoff on the most important attribute, it is chosen. If several brands meet the cutoff, then the next most important attribute is selected and the process continues until the tie is broken. If none of the brands are acceptable, the consumer must revise the cutoffs, use a different decision rule, or postpone choice. Once again, processing by attribute is required.

Returning to Table 17.2, choice based on elimination by aspects would depend on the particular cutoff values imposed by the decision maker. Suppose the minimum acceptable values for taste and price were "excellent" and "very good," respectively. Brand A would again be chosen. But if the cutoff for taste was lowered to "very good" and the cutoff for price was raised to "excellent," then brand C would be selected.

Conjunctive   Cutoffs also play a prominent part in the conjunctive decision rule.[28] Cutoffs are established for each salient attribute. Each brand is compared, one at a time, against this set of cutoffs. Thus, processing by brand is required. If the brand meets the cutoffs for *all* the attributes, it is chosen. Failure to meet the cutoff for *any* attribute leads to rejection. As before, if none of the brands meet the cutoff requirements, then a change in either the cutoffs or the decision rule must occur. Otherwise, choice must be delayed.

To illustrate the conjunctive choice rule, assume that the consumer insists that the brand receive a rating of at least "good" on each attribute. In Table 17.2, brand A is rejected because of its inadequate rating (that is, does not meet the cutoff requirement of "good") on convenience, whereas brand C is inadequate on nutrition. Brand D is eliminated by the unacceptable price rating. Only brand B meets all the cutoff requirements and therefore would be evaluated as an acceptable choice.

Compensatory Decision Rules

Did you notice the plight of poor brand D in Table 17.2? Despite its excellent ratings in three of the four salient attributes (including the most important attribute), brand D never emerged as the top brand. Why? Because of its poor price performance; that is, none of the noncompensatory strategies permitted the brand's poor rating on price to be offset by its otherwise excellent performance.

This is not the case for compensatory decision rules. Under a compensatory strategy, a perceived weakness of one attribute may be offset or compensated for by a perceived strength of another attribute. Two types of compensatory rules are the **simple** and **weighted additive**.

Simple Additive   Under this rule, the consumer simply counts or adds the number of times each alternative is judged favorably in terms of the set of salient evaluative criteria. The alternative having the largest number of positive attributes is chosen. Research indicates that a simple additive rule is most likely when consumers' processing motivation or ability is limited.[29]

Weighted Additive   A far more complex form of the compensatory rule is the weighted additive. The consumer now engages in more refined judgments about the alternatives' performance than simply whether it is favorable or unfavorable. The relative salience of relevant evaluative criteria is also incorporated into the decision rule. In essence, a weighted additive rule is equivalent to the multiattribute attitude models described in Chapter 11. Consequently, discussion of their mechanics is not needed here (although the reader may wish to refresh her or his memory with a brief review of this material).

Phased Decision Strategies

Phased decision strategies involve the sequential use of at least two different decision rules as a means of coping with a large number of choice alternatives.[30] Phased strategies typically consist of a two-stage process. In the initial stage, one type of rule is used as a screening device to help narrow down the choice set to a more manageable number. A second decision rule is then applied to the remaining alternatives to make the final choice. For example, a consumer confronted with a very large number of brands might first eliminate those above a certain price from contention. The remaining brands would then be evaluated across a number of salient attributes.

Constructive Decision Rules

Many of the choice situations consumers encounter can be handled by simply retrieving the appropriate decision rule from memory. Stored rules are more likely to exist in memory as the consumer accumulates experience in making such choices. In other situations (for example, novel or unfamiliar choices), however, consumers may find it necessary to construct their decision rules at the time of choice.[31] That is, consumers build a **constructive decision rule** using elementary processing operations (that is, "fragments" of rules) available in memory that can accommodate the choice situation.

Affect Referral

A special type of decision rule is known as **affect referral**.[32] This rule assumes that the consumer has previously formed overall evaluations of each choice alternative. Rather than judging alternatives on various evaluative criteria, the consumer simply retrieves these global evaluations from memory. The alternative having the highest affect is then chosen. In essence, overall evaluation serves as the single evaluative criterion used in decision making.

Marketing Implications

At this point it is useful to stop and consider what all of this means for the practitioner. What value does knowledge about the particular decision rule consumers employ during alternative evaluation have for the development of marketing strategies?

Fundamentally speaking, marketers need to understand decision rules because these rules have an impact on consumer choice. An understanding of the decision rule (or rules) employed by current customers (that is, the rule that leads to the choice of one's product) may suggest actions that maintain or facilitate customers' use of this rule. It may also indicate actions that should be avoided because of their potential to change the customer's decision rule (and, hence, choice). For example, when the customer's decision rule is simply "buy the same brand as last time" (that is, choice is habituated), the marketer should avoid conditions that may trigger a change in the decision rule, such as a noticeable decline in product quality, significant price increases, or an out-of-stock situation.

The manner in which attribute information is organized and presented may also be important.[33] Presenting information about the brands' performance on one attribute at a time, while conducive to decision rules that require processing by attribute, should discourage the use of rules requiring consumers to process by

FIGURE 17.6   **Ads Offering Guidance Appeal to Consumers Lacking a Decision Strategy**

brand. Conversely, a brand-based presentation format should favor rules that involve processing by brand.

Even knowledge that consumers do not have a well-defined decision strategy (for example, a constructive method is employed) can be useful. Consumers who are uncertain about how they should make their decision may be receptive to those offering some guidance. For this reason, ads such as the one presented in Figure 17.6 may be very effective.

Understanding consumers' decision rules is also important in the development of attitude-change strategies.[34] This can be demonstrated by returning to Table 17.2. Suppose that brand C improved its taste perception from "very good" to "excellent." This change makes considerable sense if consumers use a lexicographic process in making their evaluation, since it would lead to brand C being chosen. Suppose, however, that consumers employ a conjunctive rule with cutoffs of "good." Improving the product's taste would be of little value since its nutritional rating of "poor" is unacceptable. Instead, it would be critical to enhance the brand's nutritional performance.

Recognize that changing consumers' decision rules provides marketers with another mechanism for influencing consumer choice. In some cases, this might involve changing the relative importance of salient evaluative criteria. For instance, assuming a lexicographic rule, brand C in Table 17.2 might consider altering the relative importance consumers attach to taste and price. A lexicographic rule with price being the most important attribute would lead to the selection of brand C, whereas this type of rule with taste being most important results in brand A being chosen.

Changing the cutoffs is another mechanism for altering the decision rule. As illustrated by the example considered in our prior discussion of elimination by aspects, changes in the minimum acceptable values for taste and price resulted in the selection of different brands from Table 17.2.

It may sometimes be desirable to encourage a change in the type of decision rule. In Table 17.2, for instance, brand D would want consumers to switch from lexicographic to some other procedure such as compensatory. Unfortunately, little is known about the likelihood of getting consumers to switch their decision strategies.

Summary

Alternative evaluation represents the decision-making stage in which consumers evaluate alternatives to make a choice. During this stage consumers must (1) determine the evaluative criteria to use for judging alternatives, (2) decide which alternatives to consider, (3) assess the performance of considered alternatives, and (4) select and apply a decision rule to make the final choice.

Consumers may employ a number of different evaluative criteria, including price, brand name, and country of origin, in making their decision. These criteria will usually vary in their relative importance or salience. Price may be a dominant dimension in some decisions and yet rather unimportant in others. The salience of evaluative criteria depends on a host of situational, product, and individual factors.

Consumers must determine the set of alternatives from which a choice will be made (that is, the consideration set). Sometimes the consideration set will depend on the consumer's ability to recall from memory viable alternatives. On other occasions an alternative will be considered if it is recognized at the point of purchase. When consumers lack prior knowledge about choice alternatives, they must then turn to the environment for assistance in forming their consideration set.

Consumers may also rely on their existing knowledge for judging how well alternatives perform along the salient evaluative criteria. Otherwise, external search will be required to form these judgments. The cutoffs or ranges of acceptable values that consumers impose for evaluative criteria will strongly determine whether a given alternative is viewed as acceptable. In addition, consumers may often use certain signals or cues in forming their judgments. Such is the case when price is used to infer product quality.

Finally, the strategies or procedures used for making the final choice are called decision rules. These rules may be stored in memory and retrieved when needed. Alternatively, they may be constructed to fit situational contingencies.

Decision rules vary considerably in their complexity. They may be very simple (for example, buy what I bought last time). They can also be quite complex, such as when the rule resembles a multiattribute attitude model. Another important distinction is between compensatory and noncompensatory decision rules. Noncompensatory rules, such as lexicographic, elimination by aspects, and conjunctive, do not permit product strengths to offset product weaknesses. In contrast, compensatory rules do allow product weaknesses to be compensated by product strengths.

Review and Discussion Questions

1. What are evaluative criteria? What criteria did you use when you purchased your last pair of shoes? How did these differ, if at all, from those used by others in your family?

2. In the chapter we indicate that offering incentives is one way for a product to gain consideration during consumer decision making. How else might a product try to enter the consideration set?

3. A restaurant is trying to decide on the appropriate method for assessing consumers' consideration set in deciding where to eat out. One person has argued for a recall method where consumers are asked to remember without any memory cues. Another person recommends a recognition method in which consumers are given a list of local restaurants and asked to circle the appropriate names. Which method would you recommend? Would your answer change if consumers normally consulted the yellow pages in making the decision?

4. Consider the company that currently offers a product warranty quite similar to the warranties offered by competitors, but is considering the merits of increasing the warranty coverage to make it superior to the competition. A market study was therefore undertaken to examine consumer response to an improved warranty. College students were shown the product accompanied by either the original warranty or the improved warranty. The results indicated that students did in fact perceive the improved warranty as much stronger, and that the product quality was rated higher when the product was paired with the improved warranty.

   Although the company viewed these results as very encouraging, concerns were raised about the appropriateness of using college students, most of whom have yet to make a purchase in the product category at this point in their life. Consequently, the study was replicated using older consumers who had made at least two purchase decisions in the product category. As before, the improved warranty was seen as providing much better coverage. However, judgments of product quality were not affected by the warranty. How can you explain this difference between the two studies' findings about the warranty's influence on perceived product quality? Also, what recommendations would you make to the company about whether or not it should offer the improved warranty?

5. Would you expect a price–quality relationship for each of the following product classes: hand soap, toilet paper, panty hose, men's shirts, china and glassware, and gasoline? Why?

6. Why is it important to understand the decision rules consumers use during alternative evaluation?

7. Identify which decision rule would lead to the selection of each of the brands in the table on the following page.

Attribute	Importance Ranking	Performance Ratings		
		Brand A	Brand B	Brand C
Price	1	Excellent	Very Good	Very Good
Quality	2	Poor	Very Good	Good
Convenience	3	Poor	Average	Good

Endnotes

1. Andre Gabor and C. W. J. Granger, "Price Sensitivity of the Consumer," *Journal of Advertising Research* 4 (December 1964), 40–44; Joel Huber, Morris B. Holbrook, and Barbara Kahn, "Effects of Competitive Context and of Additional Information on Price Sensitivity," *Journal of Marketing Research* 23 (August 1986), 250–260.
2. Peter R. Dickson and Alan G. Sawyer, "The Price Knowledge and Search of Supermarket Shoppers," *Journal of Marketing* 54 (July 1990), 42–53.
3. Huber, Holbrook, and Kahn, "Effects of Competitive Context and of Additional Information on Price Sensitivity"; Kent B. Monroe, "Buyer's Subjective Perceptions of Price," *Journal of Marketing Research* 10 (February 1973), 70–80.
4. David M. Gardner, "Is There a Generalized Price–Quality Relationship?" *Journal of Marketing Research* 8 (May 1971), 241–243.
5. J. F. Engel, D. A. Knapp, and D. E. Knapp, "Sources of Influence in the Acceptance of New Products for Self-Medication: Preliminary Findings," in R. M. Haas, ed., *Science, Technology and Marketing* (Chicago: American Marketing Association, 1966), 776–782.
6. William B. Dodd, Kent B. Monroe, and Dhruv Grewal, "Effects of Price, Brand, and Store Information on Buyers' Product Evaluations," *Journal of Marketing Research* 28 (August 1991), 307–319; Akshay R. Rao and Kent B. Monroe, "The Effect of Price, Brand Name, and Store Name on Buyers' Perceptions of Product Quality: An Integrative Review," *Journal of Marketing Research* 26 (August 1989), 351–357.
7. Engel, Knapp, and Knapp, "Sources of Influence."
8. For research on how this attribute can affect product evaluations, see Johny K. Johansson, Susan P. Douglas, and Ikujiro Nonaka, "Assessing the Impact of Country of Origin on Product Evaluations: A New Methodological Perspective," *Journal of Marketing Research* 22 (November 1985), 388–396; Sung-Tai Hong and Robert S. Wyer Jr., "Effects of Country-of-Origin and Product-Attribute Information on Product Evaluation: An Information Processing Perspective," *Journal of Consumer Research* 16 (September 1989), 175–187; Sung-Tai Hong and Robert S. Wyer Jr., "Determinants of Product Evaluation: Effects of the Time Interval between Knowledge of a Product's Country of Origin and Information about Its Specific Attributes," *Journal of Consumer Research* 17 (December 1990), 277–288.
9. Mark I. Alpert, "Identification of Determinant Attributes: A Comparison of Methods," *Journal of Marketing Research* 8 (May 1971), 184–191.
10. Peter R. Dickson, "Person-Situation: Segmentation's Missing Link," *Journal of Marketing* 6 (Fall 1982), 56–64; Kenneth E. Miller and James L. Ginter, "An Investi-

gation of Situational Variation in Brand Choice Behavior and Attitude," *Journal of Marketing Research* 16 (February 1979), 111–123.

11. James R. Bettman and Mita Sujan, "Effects of Framing on Evaluation of Comparable and Noncomparable Alternatives by Expert and Novice Consumers," *Journal of Consumer Research* 14 (September 1987), 141–154; Kim P. Corfman, "Comparability and Comparison Levels Used in Choices among Consumer Products," *Journal of Marketing Research* 28 (August 1991), 368–374; Michael D. Johnson, "Consumer Choice Strategies for Comparing Noncomparable Alternatives," *Journal of Consumer Research* 11 (December 1984), 741–753; Michael D. Johnson, "Comparability and Hierarchical Processing in Multialternative Choice," *Journal of Consumer Research* 15 (December 1988), 303–314; Michael D. Johnson, "The Differential Processing of Product Category and Noncomparable Choice Alternatives," *Journal of Consumer Research* 16 (December 1989), 300–309; C. Whan Park and Daniel C. Smith, "Product-Level Choice: A Top-Down or Bottom-Up Process?" *Journal of Consumer Research* 16 (December 1989), 289–299.

12. Michael L. Rothschild, "Advertising Strategies for High and Low Involvement Situations," in John C. Maloney and Bernard Silverman, eds., *Attitude Research Plays for High Stakes* (Chicago: American Marketing Association, 1979), 74–93; Michael L. Rothschild and Michael J. Houston, "The Consumer Involvement Matrix: Some Preliminary Findings," in Barnett A. Greenberg and Danny N. Bellenger, eds., *Contemporary Marketing Thoughts* (Chicago: American Marketing Association, 1977), 95–98.

13. Dennis H. Gensch and Rajshekhar G. Javalgi, "The Influence of Involvement on Disaggregate Attribute Choice Models," *Journal of Consumer Research* 14 (June 1987), 71–82.

14. Bettman and Sujan, "Effects of Framing on Evaluation of Comparable and Noncomparable Alternatives by Expert and Novice Consumers"; Peter Wright and Peter D. Rip, "Product Class Advertising Effects in First-Time Buyers' Decision Strategies," *Journal of Consumer Research* 7 (September 1980), 176–188.

15. Joseph W. Alba and Amitava Chattopadhay, "Effects of Context and Part-Category Cues on Recall of Competing Brands," *Journal of Marketing Research* 22 (August 1985), 340–349; Prakash Nedungadi, "Recall and Consumer Consideration Sets: Influencing Choice without Altering Brand Evaluations," *Journal of Consumer Research* 17 (December 1990), 263–276. For a different perspective on the formation of consideration sets, see John R. Hauser and Birger Wernerfelt, "An Evaluation Cost Model of Consideration Sets," *Journal of Consumer Research* 16 (March 1990), 393–408; John H. Roberts and James M. Lattin, "Development and Testing of a Model of Consideration Set Composition," *Journal of Marketing Research* 28 (November 1991), 429–440.

16. Joseph W. Alba and J. Wesley Hutchinson, "Dimensions of Consumer Expertise," *Journal of Consumer Research* 13 (March 1987), 411–454.

17. Alba and Chattopadhay, "Effects of Context and Part-Category Cues on Recall of Competing Brands"; Joseph W. Alba and Amitava Chattopadhay, "Salience Effects in Brand Recall," *Journal of Marketing Research* 23 (November 1986), 363–369. Also see Paul W. Miniard, H. Rao Unnava, and Sunil Bhatla, "Investigating the Recall Inhibition Effect: A Test of Practical Considerations," *Marketing Letters* 2 (January 1991), 27–34.

18. Joel Huber, John W. Payne, and Christopher Puto, "Adding Asymmetrically Dominated Alternatives: Violations of Regularity and the Similarity Hypothesis," *Journal of Consumer Research* 9 (June 1982), 90–98; Joel Huber and Christopher Puto, "Market Boundaries and Product Choice: Illustrating Attraction and Substitution Effects," *Journal of Consumer Research* 10 (June 1983), 31–44; Barbara Kahn, William L. Moore,

and Rashi Glazer, "Experiments in Constrained Choice," *Journal of Consumer Research* 14 (June 1987), 96–113; Srinivasan Ratneshwar, Allan D. Shocker, and David W. Stewart, "Toward Understanding the Attraction Effect: The Implications of Product Stimulus Meaningfulness and Familiarity," *Journal of Consumer Research* 13 (March 1987), 520–533; Itamar Simonson, "Choice Based on Reasons: The Case of Attraction and Compromise Effects," *Journal of Consumer Research* 16 (September 1989), 158–174.

19. For an additional empirical investigation in this domain, see Catherine A. Cole and Gary J. Gaeth, "Cognitive and Age-Related Differences in the Ability to Use Nutritional Information in a Complex Environment," *Journal of Marketing Research* 27 (May 1990), 175–184.

20. Gabriel Biehal and Dipankar Chakravarti, "Information Accessibility as a Moderator of Consumer Choice," *Journal of Consumer Research* 10 (June 1983), 1–14; Gabriel Biehal and Dipankar Chakravarti, "Consumers' Use of Memory and External Information in Choice: Macro and Micro Perspectives," *Journal of Consumer Research* 12 (March 1986), 382–405; John G. Lynch, Jr., Howard Marmorstein, and Michael F. Weigold, "Choices from Sets Including Remembered Brands: Use of Recalled Attributes and Prior Overall Evaluations," *Journal of Consumer Research* 15 (September 1988), 169–184.

21. For research on cutoff usage, see Barton Weitz and Peter Wright, "Retrospective Self-Insight on Factors Considered in Product Evaluations," *Journal of Consumer Research* 6 (December 1979), 280–294; Peter L. Wright and Barton Weitz, "Time Horizon Effects on Product Evaluation Strategies," *Journal of Marketing Research* 14 (November 1977), 429–443.

22. Susan M. Petroshius and Kent B. Monroe, "Effects of Product-Line Pricing Characteristics on Product Evaluations," *Journal of Consumer Research* 13 (March 1987), 511–519.

23. Dodds, Monroe, and Grewal, "Effects of Price, Brand, and Store Information on Buyers' Product Evaluations"; Gary M. Erickson and Johny K. Johansson, "The Role of Price in Multi-Attribute Product Evaluations," *Journal of Consumer Research* 12 (September 1985), 195–199; Michael Etgar and Naresh K. Malhotra, "Determinants of Price Dependency: Personal and Perceptual Factors," *Journal of Consumer Research* 8 (September 1981), 217–222; Zarrel V. Lambert, "Product Perception: An Important Variable in Price Strategy," *Journal of Marketing* 34 (October 1970), 68–76; Irwin P. Levin and Richard D. Johnson, "Estimating Price-Quality Tradeoffs Using Comparative Judgments," *Journal of Consumer Research* 11 (June 1984), 593–600; Kent B. Monroe, "The Influence of Price Differences and Brand Familiarity on Brand Preferences," *Journal of Consumer Research* 3 (June 1976), 42–49; Petroshius and Monroe, "Effects of Product-Line Pricing Characteristics on Product Evaluations"; Rao and Monroe, "The Effect of Price, Brand Name, and Store Name on Buyers' Perceptions of Product Quality: An Integrative Review."

24. For a detailed discussion of decision rules, see James R. Bettman, *An Information Processing Theory of Consumer Choice* (Reading, Massachusetts: Addison-Wesley, 1979), Chapter 7.

25. Wayne D. Hoyer, "An Examination of Consumer Decision Making for a Common Repeat Purchase Product," *Journal of Consumer Research* 11 (December 1984), 822–829. Also see Wayne D. Hoyer and Steven P. Brown, "Effects of Brand Awareness on Choice for a Common, Repeat-Purchase Product," *Journal of Consumer Research* 17 (September 1990), 141–148.

26. Robert Johnson, "In the Chips," *Wall Street Journal* (March 22, 1991), B1–B2.

27. For a discussion of other forms of noncompensatory rules, see Bettman, *An Information Processing Theory of Consumer Choice*, 181–182.

28. For a study of the conjunctive decision rule, see David Grether and Louis Wilde, "An Analysis of Conjunctive Choice: Theory and Experiments," *Journal of Consumer Research* 10 (March 1984), 373–385.

29. Joseph W. Alba and Howard Marmorstein, "The Effects of Frequency Knowledge on Consumer Decision Making," *Journal of Consumer Research* 14 (June 1987), 14–25.

30. Denis A. Lussier and Richard W. Olshavsky, "Task Complexity and Contingent Processing in Brand Choice," *Journal of Consumer Research* 6 (September 1979), 154–165.

31. Biehal and Chakravarti, "Consumers' Use of Memory and External Information in Choice: Micro and Macro Perspectives"; James R. Bettman and Michel A. Zins, "Constructive Processes in Consumer Choice," *Journal of Consumer Research* 4 (September 1977), 75–85.

32. Peter Wright, "Consumer Choice Strategies: Simplifying vs. Optimizing," *Journal of Marketing Research* 12 (February 1975), 60–67. Also see Bettman, *An Information Processing Theory of Consumer Choice*; Amitava Chattopadhyay and Joseph W. Alba, "The Situational Importance of Recall and Inference in Consumer Decision Making," *Journal of Consumer Research* 15 (June 1988), 1–12.

33. For research relevant to this issue, see James R. Bettman and Michel A. Zins, "Information Format and Choice Task Effects in Decision Making," *Journal of Consumer Research* 6 (September 1979), 141–153.

34. Peter L. Wright, "Use of Consumer Judgment Models in Promotion Planning," *Journal of Marketing* 37 (October 1973), 27–33.

18

Purchase and Its Outcomes

Would you rather eat a jar of hot peppers or earn a living by anticipating the desires of infants to 12-year-olds and their parents? If you chose the latter, prepare yourself for a fiery marketing battle. Sears, Roebuck and Co. has been selling children's merchandise since its first catalog more than 100 years ago. Today, what has changed is the retail environment in the United States and how consumers develop brand preference.

First, this country is overstored. In virtually every major market there's more square footage of retail space built than can be economically supported. Department stores compete with specialty retailers of every stripe plus discounters by the dozen.

Add to this proliferation of retail options the explosion of brands and private-label merchandise plus a multitude of media and you get a confused consumer. Or at least one who is bombarded by competing choices and claims—and with little time to analyze them, much less identify and bond with a brand. Hence, it's not surprising that 75 percent of consumers are not store loyal.

Within this marketing maelstrom is Sears' children's department. In a world where ever-younger kids are forming opinions about everything, including what they want to wear and where they want to shop, we decided the children's department needed a new marketing strategy and positioning.

The result of our research is Kids & More, a new power-format kids' store within Sears. What sets Kids & More apart from the competition? Here's what the direct mail advertising copy says:

> Walk in and one of the first things you'll notice is the unbelievable array of merchandise. We put everything you needed all in one place—so you don't have to drive

557

around like crazy from store to store anymore. Lots of big brand names (what *everybody's* wearing, so there's no grumbling).

And everything's top quality, made to stand up to wear and tear. Plus, you'll get great prices, every day: And what else? Super wide aisles. Fitting rooms that are more accessible and extra roomy. Friendly salespeople who can help out with fitting sizes and shoes.

Kid's & More at Sears. Finally, shopping without the struggle.

For this new retailing format, Ogilvy & Mather Direct created a series of power-format introductory mailers. Our marketing strategy is to tell the story of the new Kids & More to Sears customers selected on the basis of past purchase history plus non-Sears households with kids age 0 to 12. To generate store traffic, four limited-time, in-store offers were targeted to different age groups.

What can be said is that these direct-mail campaigns have been and continue to be extremely successful. An integral part of this educative process is the development and careful analysis of Sears' proprietary database. We are able to match purchase history by product category to a whole host of other attributes that will make future promotions even more targeted.

Source: Ray L. Velkers, "Sears' Strategy Matures," *Direct Marketing* (December 1990), 32ff. Reproduced by special permission.

The development of Kids & More was far more than someone's dream. It was based on growing evidence that shoppers are demanding some real changes in the way they make purchases. The numbers who are willing to "graze the malls" are dropping sharply.[1] In fact, a Harris Poll showed that 47 percent of those interviewed are spending less time shopping today than they did just 5 years ago.[2] Retailers are being forced by shoppers to rethink their business and to offer customers what they expect in the way of service, assortments, and sales assistance.[3]

The act of purchase is the last major stage in our model of consumer behavior (Figure 18.1). The consumer now must make three decisions: (1) when to buy, (2) where to buy, and (3) how to pay.

Some products are bought mostly on a seasonal basis. Air conditioners in northern climates, Christmas gifts, and Caribbean cruises are examples. Others, such as detergents and frozen foods, are often purchased only when stock is depleted. Marketers can change these patterns by offering special rebates and other price incentives.

Consumers have changed shopping and buying preferences in the last decade. In-home shopping, for example, has seen remarkable growth in most of the developing countries of the world. Many retailing establishments have been forced into direct marketing to complement their normal activities. Hence, the growing importance of "databased marketing" at both the manufacturer and retailer level.[4] Sears, Roebuck & Co. has the astonishing figure of 44,000,000 household accounts in its customer database.[5]

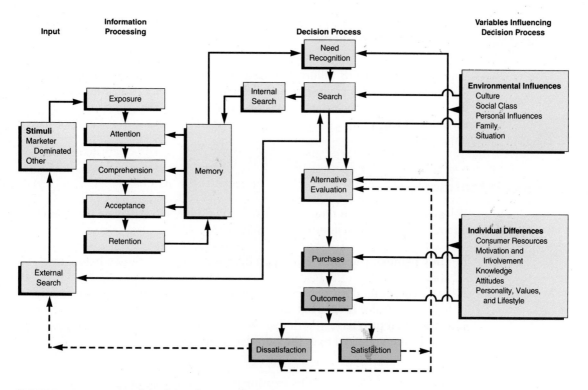

FIGURE 18.1   A Model of Purchase and Its Outcomes

Also there are other trends affecting retailing, such as an increasing shift of cosmetic purchases away from department stores to supermarkets. Thus, it has been necessary to develop packaging that is both eye catching and informative as retail display replaces the salesperson as a major persuasive influence.

Finally, the consumer must decide how to pay. Other chapters (especially Chapters 8 and 20) have demonstrated the relentless trend away from cash payment to use of credit cards and other forms of delayed payment.

The process does not stop once the purchase has been made, however. There often is substantial post-purchase evaluation, especially when high involvement has triggered extended problem solving. Sometimes buyers have doubts that the right choice was made. These doubts are designated in Figure 18.1 as *dissatisfaction*. This, of course, is the worst possible outcome as you have seen expressed many times in these pages.

The opposite response, of course, is one of *satisfaction*. Both depend upon the degree to which expectations have been fulfilled. The implications of buyer satisfaction (or dissatisfaction) for loyalty and word-of-mouth represent one of marketing's greatest challenges today.

The focus of this chapter is on two of these issues: (1) where to buy and (2) consumer satisfaction and dissatisfaction. The discussion continues in Chapter 19, which explores how consumer research is utilized in retailing strategy.

The Purchase Process

The model in Figure 18.1 illustrates that purchase is a function of two determinants: (1) intentions and (2) environmental influences and/or individual differences. Indeed, the act of purchase is a decision process in its own right.[6] Of the many variables which fall into the latter category, *situation* stands out as being of special importance.

Purchase Intentions

When asked to do so, it often is possible for consumers to articulate their purchase intentions, and these fall into three categories:

1. **Fully planned purchase**—both product and brand are chosen before the store visit.
2. **Partially planned purchase**—there is an intention to buy the product only but brand choice is deferred until shopping.
3. **Unplanned purchase**—both the items and brand are chosen in the store. This is often referred to as the **impulse purchase**.

The Fully Planned Purchase   On occasion this first category of intention is the outcome of high involvement and extended problem solving. In this situation, the consumer knows exactly what he or she wants and is willing to shop until it is found.

In most lower involvement purchases, however, the buyer prepares a shopping list beforehand and plans to buy both product and brand. The store visit, then, mostly consists of routine scanning of shelves. A recent nationwide survey of 4,200 shoppers by Willard Bishop Consulting Ltd revealed that 61 percent of supermarket purchases are made in this way.[7] This is in sharp contrast to a 1986 study by POPAI (Point-of-Purchase Advertising Institute) which found that only 34 percent of decisions were made outside the store.[8]

Whatever the true figure, it is likely that at least half of supermarket purchase decisions are fully planned. Whether or not this takes place, however, is affected by two factors: (1) knowledge of store layout and design and (2) time pressures that restrict browsing and in-store decision making.[9]

The Partially Planned Purchase   It also is correct to view category 2 (product only) as a planned purchase even though choice of brand is made at point of sale. Shopping now can become an important form of information search, especially when involvement is high.[10]

When involvement is low, on the other hand, the decision rule often is "buy one of the brands I already consider to be acceptable." The final decision now may hinge on promotional influences such as price reductions or special display and packaging.[11]

The Unplanned Purchase   Now we face a dilemma. Can we consider a purchase to be **unplanned** when a conscious intention was not articulated prior to the act of buying? Or is this strictly a matter of "impulse" or whim? This issue was first addressed empirically in 1967 by David T. Kollat, a member of the original author team of this book.[12] Because some estimate that up to 50 percent of purchases are made in this way,[13] it is important to understand the underlying dynamics.

It is important to note Kollat's important distinction, first of all, that a purchase can be planned in one sense even though a definite intention is not expressed verbally or in writing on a shopping list.[14] This is because shoppers often make intentional use of product display in mass merchandising outlets as a **surrogate shopping list**. In other words, display provides reminder of a need, and a purchase is triggered. Active processing of in-store information also can trigger new needs.[15]

There is growing evidence, however, that a true impulse action is something quite different, characterized by a unique set of influences. Consider Rook's clarification:

> Impulse buying occurs when a consumer experiences a sudden, often powerful and persistent urge to buy something immediately. The impulse to buy is hedonically complex and may stimulate emotional conflict. Also, impulse buying is prone to occur with diminished regard to its consequences.[16]

When defined in this way, some impulse purchasing is not based on consumer problem solving and is best viewed from an hedonic or experiential perspective.[17] According to Rook's research, impulse buying can have one or more of these characteristics:

1. *Spontaneity*. It is unexpected and motivates the consumer to *buy now*, often in response to direct point-of-sale visual stimulation.
2. *Power, compulsion, and intensity*. There can be motivation to put all else aside and act immediately.
3. *Excitement and stimulation*. These sudden urges to buy are often accompanied by emotions characterized as "exciting," "thrilling," or "wild."
4. *Disregard for consequences*. The urge to buy can be so irresistible that potentially negative consequences are ignored.[18]

Situational Influence

You are familiar with the role played by situational influence from the discussion in Chapter 7, which was devoted entirely to this subject. The primary ways in which situational influences can affect purchase actions are summarized in Table 18.1.

Many situational factors, such as weather and temporary unemployment, are beyond the influence of the marketer or retailer, but this is not always the case by any means. Marketers have direct control over display, product promotion and exposure, price reductions, store atmospherics, and out-of-stock conditions, to mention only a few. The most important point here is to be aware of the manner in which these situational considerations can affect choice and to avoid such unfortunate situations as out of stock and inadequate display.[19]

TABLE 18.1   A Summary of Situational Influences on Purchasing Behavior

1. The information environment.
    a. Information availability both internal (stored in memory) and external.
    b. Information load (or overload).
    c. Information format.
2. The retail environment.
    a. Store atmospherics.
    b. Layout and display.
    c. Point-of-purchase (POP) materials.
3. Time available for decision making.

Retail versus In-Home Shopping and Buying

At one point in time a large percentage of shopping and buying was done at home through use of the itinerant peddler. As convenient and inexpensive transportation methods became commonplace, however, the retail store gained ascendancy. The pendulum has swung once again in recent years to the point where both retailing and in-home buying are vigorous competitors. An interesting marketing challenge is presented.

Retail Shopping and Purchasing

Although exact figures are difficult to come by, our best estimate is that more than 90 percent of all consumer purchases are made through visits to a retail outlet or catalog showroom or through a vending machine.

Shopping has become a kind of national pastime, and as recently as 1987 about 70 percent of Americans visited a large shopping mall in a given week. Furthermore, about a third of these were men.[20] Why do people shop? One obvious primary motivation is information acquisition.[21] For those who want to discover and evaluate a full range of options, there really is no other alternative.

But the motivations for shopping are more diverse. Indeed, shopping has almost become a way of life in and of itself for some, although this is declining. Here are just some of the reasons frequent shoppers give: alleviating loneliness, dispelling boredom, shopping as a sport (that is, beating the system), spoils of the hunt (shopper as "the great provider"), escape, fantasy fulfillment, and relieving depression.[22]

Things have changed sharply since the middle 1980s. While the number of shopping malls increased 22 percent between 1986 and 1989, the number of shoppers going to malls each month rose only three percent.[23] The data in Table 18.2 further reveal a precipitous drop in average shopping mall usage each month. The major reasons seem to be diminishing leisure time, increased stress levels in life, and economic fears.

There also is a group which, to put it mildly, is not enamored with shopping. McNeal and McKee found a substantial segment, consisting of 20 percent of the population, who will avoid the marketplace whenever possible.[24] Anti-shopping seems to be a part of a generally negative world view. Moreover, such consumers are largely oblivious and nonresponsive to marketing efforts designed to lure them into the retailing net.

TABLE 18.2   Shoppers Are a Dwindling Species

Spare Hours

Compared to five years ago, do you personally feel you have less free time, more free time, or about the same free time you had back then?

More free time	21%	About the same	25%
Less free time	54%	Not sure	0%

At Leisure

Now which of these do you enjoy doing the most in your free time—watching TV, spending time with your family, going to movies, outdoor activities, shopping, or just relaxing at home?

Watching TV	7%	Shopping	6%
Spending time with your family	23%	Just relaxing at home	36%
Going to the movies	2%	Not sure	3%
Outdoor activities	23%		

Time at the Store

Compared to five years ago, are you spending more time than you were then, less time, or about the same time shopping?

Spending more time	18%	About the same time	34%
Spending less time	47%	Not sure	1%

A Pleasure or a Pain?

Now which one of these, if you had to choose, best describes how you feel about shopping?

Shopping gives me a real sense of pleasure and excitement	16%
While shopping sometimes is a chore, mostly I like doing it	20%
Even though from time to time it's a pleasure, mostly it's something I do because I have to	48%
I get no pleasure from shopping	15%
Not sure	1%

Where the Shoppers Are

Compared to five years ago, are you shopping more, less, or about the same amount . . .

	More	Less	About same	Not sure
In department stores	20%	36%	43%	1%
In specialty stores, which concentrate on a particular line of products, such as electronics, clothing, and toys	23%	38%	38%	1%
From catalogs and mail-order sources	25%	34%	37%	4%

Continued

TABLE 18.2 continued

Who's the Best?

Now, if you had to say, which of these three—department stores, specialty stores, or catalogs—do you think offers the best of each of the following?

	Department Stores	Specialty Stores	Catalogs	Not Sure
Overall service	52%	30%	15%	3%
Quality of merchandise	43%	38%	15%	4%
Variety of merchandise	64%	11%	23%	2%
Value for the money	56%	17%	25%	2%
Quality of sales people	47%	38%	10%	5%

Big-Store Mistakes

As you know, many well-known department stores have either gone out of business or are having financial trouble. Which one of these do you think is the main reason for this: They lost touch with their customers, their prices were too high, they opened too many stores, or they have poor management?

Lost touch with customers	14%	Poor management	33%
Prices too high	26%	Not sure	4%
Opened too many stores	23%		

Happy Holidays?

During this holiday season, do you think you will be buying as much as you did a year ago, will you be buying more, or will you be buying less than you did last year?

Buying as much	29%	Buying less	54%
Buying more	17%	Not sure	0%

Survey of 1,255 adults conducted Nov. 9-13 for *Business Week* by Louis Harris & Associates, Inc. Results should be accurate to within three percentage points.
Source: Business Week/Harris Poll, "Shoppers Are a Dwindling Species," *Business Week* (November 26, 1990), 144. Used by special permission.

In-Home Purchasing

A growing percentage of consumer shopping and buying activity now takes place in the home rather than in a retail store, through a vending machine, or in a catalog showroom. This type of buying annually represents about 16 percent of all general merchandise sales.[25]

Strategies used to reach the consumer in his or her home are referred to as **direct marketing**. *Direct Marketing* magazine estimates that nearly two-thirds of U.S. advertising dollars are undertaken to generate a direct response, including home and retail sales.[26]

Direct marketing also is growing rapidly in most developing countries of the world. Focusing only on mail-order statistics, 1990 sales in 17 countries in Europe and Asia totalled nearly $60.6 billion, as compared with almost $151 billion in the U.S. and Canada.[27]

There have been a number of studies profiling the in-home buyer.[28] While estimates vary, we feel it is safe to conclude that at least 60 percent of United States consumers have ordered from catalog, direct mail, or telephone courses in the past year.

Compared with the general population, they are somewhat younger, somewhat above average in terms of education and income, and are more likely to live in a smaller town or rural area. Items most frequently ordered are apparel, magazines, home accessories, home maintenance and kitchen equipment, and home office supplies. Also, most are active retail shoppers who shop at home for reasons other than deliberate avoidance of the store or shopping mall.

Here are some of the factors that have contributed to the rapid growth of this phenomenon:

1. Changing consumer lifestyles resulting from greater emphasis placed on leisure, the number of working wives, and demand for more services and conveniences in shopping.
2. The availability of credit, especially credit cards.
3. Problems encountered when shopping (examples are congested parking lots, inadequate parking, uninformed sales personnel, long lines, and in-store congestion during peak hours).
4. The trend toward a greater focusing of life within the circle of home family. This was referred to in Chapter 1 as *cocooning*.

The in-home shopper offers a unique opportunity to the marketer, because there is evidence that people may be more likely to buy when they are most contented. Studies by Retail Planning Associates show, for example, that those who have just finished a meal at home are 25 percent more likely to buy clothing than a person who is hungry.[29]

Direct-Marketing Methods   There are four primary ways in which consumers are reached to stimulate a direct response: (1) in-home personal selling, (2) direct-mail ads and catalogs, (3) other advertising media (especially telemarketing), and (4) interactive electronic media. All of these offer the unique benefit of precise segmentation.

In-Home Personal Selling   House-to-house personal selling now accounts for less than two percent of all general merchandise sales and still is declining. The greatest market penetration (31 percent of all sales) is in cosmetics, with housewares and electronics (24 percent) being a close second.[30]

Mary Kay Cosmetics, Incorporated has achieved a significant share of the cosmetics industry by concentrating exclusively on in-home presentations and sales.[31] All presentations are made to groups invited by a hostess. This situation adds social influence to the powerful benefit of firsthand observation of the personal effects of skin care. A definite segment of the market prefers this method over a similar presentation in a departament store.

Direct Mail Ads   Shopping in response to direct mail appeals has been shown to meet real consumer needs. The most often cited benefits are "availability of merchandise," "convenience," "low price," and "better quality." This may fall on deaf ears to many readers who often assume wrongly that direct mail is an unwanted invasion into the home. Polls consistently show that well over half welcome direct mail, open it, and read it, although this declines as education and income increase.

Catalogs Catalog buying has experienced dramatic growth in recent years, although it peaked during the recent recession. A 1991 survey of the readers of *Consumer Reports* showed that almost 90 percent of respondents had placed at least one catalog order in the previous year. Furthermore, 40 percent placed 8 or more, compared with only 25 percent 5 years earlier.[32]

The person most likely to buy from a catalog is a female with above average age, income, and education; married with children; a credit user; and an above average purchase frequency in the categories of housewares, appliances, men's clothing, and children's clothing.[33]

This type of purchasing has become so popular that some marketers now are offering their catalogs for sale at prices ranging from $1 to $5. Moreover, it has been discovered that between 5 and 15 percent of those who buy a catalog actually order merchandise, versus only 2 percent who receive them through the mail.[34]

Telemarketing Nearly 20 percent of direct-response orders now are triggered by a telephone call (referred to as **outbound telemarketing**). Homes can be targeted with great demographic precision using census data available within geographic zip codes. Also, real personalization can be achieved if the caller is skillful and sensitive.

Inbound telemarketing, on the other hand, refers to the use of an 800 number to place orders directly. A 1987 AT&T survey disclosed that the most frequently purchased items in the order of importance are clothing and accessories, records and tapes, housewares and cookware, and books and educational materials. The heaviest users are found among the younger and better educated families with higher incomes and children at home.[35]

Direct Response Ads Twenty-one percent of direct-response purchases in a recent year were stimulated by magazine ads (7 percent), newspaper ads (6 percent), yellow pages ads (5 percent), and TV commercials (3 percent).[36] These figures, however, do not reflect the recent upsurge in television home shopping. One authority estimates that sales through this medium will have experienced growth from $450 million in 1986 to $7.2 billion by 1991.[37]

Home Shopping Network Inc. was the pioneer in television, starting its operations in July 1985. Its average club member places 15 orders a year, with a typical purchase of $32.[38] Because of its success, home shopping options on cable TV are burgeoning, although there are some initial signs that sales could plateau once viewer novelty wears off.

Television home shopping efforts also are growing rapidly around the world.[39] Fujisankel Communications International Inc., for example, has put together a 1-hour TV shopping program with American-made merchandise. It is broadcast live to Tokyo via international satellite. European marketers are turning the tables, however. A program titled "Germany Today" can now be seen over video in 50 states, and it touts German-made products. Similarly, the French department store Galeries Lafayette has attempted to sell its products on Chicago area cable TV.

Interactive Electronic Media   Most Americans and increasing numbers in Europe can now order a wide range of merchandise through video if they choose to subscribe to an interactive system. Referred to as **videotex**, anything that can be typed on a computer terminal keyboard can be transmitted to the home screen and even copied if the TV set has facsimile capability. The purchases are transmitted in the same manner.

The availability of nearly instantaneous two-way communication offers consumer benefits, including convenience and opportunity to plan purchases through immediate access to needed information. The disadvantage has been the necessity of purchasing specialized equipment which, until recently, appears to have been too costly for most consumers. Also, there has been some understandable reluctance from those who are not familiar with computer hardware and software.

Of the 5 major videotex services started since 1969, CompuServe is the major survivor. All told, there are about 1.5 to 2 million videotex users and growth has been slow.[40] The problem seems to lie in low consumer awareness and interest, leading Major to suggest that technology preceded marketing.[41] In fact, only about 20 percent of all households have the necessary personal computer hardware. Nevertheless, there could be an upturn in consumer interest. As of this writing, the Prodigy system is engaged in direct marketing and has attracted over 200 advertisers.

Videotex was started in France, however, where it is known as Minitel.[42] Over 2 million terminals have been distributed free, and it is not surprising that consumers have responded enthusiastically. This experience does provide some encouragement for the future elsewhere if costs can be reduced.

An alternative approach is interactive cable TV. The J. C. Penney Company tested "Telaction," which allows consumers to communicate with their television monitor through a touchtone telephone. This allows pictures of items and their prices to appear on the screen. If this proves to be successful, the already dramatic growth of home shopping through cable programs may experience an even sharper increase.

Geodemography   **Geodemographic marketing** through direct mail offers especially intriguing possibilities.[43] As you may remember from earlier chapters, this procedure focuses on geographic clustering of present customers. Using computer-stored census data, it is projected that others in the same area will be similar in terms of income and other measures of buying potential. Mailing or telemarketing is then directed to these homes in the expectation that most are qualified prospects.

Direct Marketing's Growing Impact   It is important to note that an inexplicable bias against direct marketing in some circles in the past is now rapidly changing. Many leading advertising agencies finally have entered this field. In part this is a belated recognition that many efforts to reach the prospective consumer, especially through media advertising, are little more than what Leo Bogart refers to as **background noise**.[44]

Do Marketers Practice What They Preach?
Lessons to Be Learned from Two Weeks of Direct Mail

Seven-and-one-half inches! That's the altitude reached by the stack of direct mail I received when I was overseas from August 13 through August 30. The total was 110 direct mail pieces, including 40 catalogs and 70 packages/self-mailers. The onslaught was 7.9 pieces a day, up quite a bit from the national U.S. average of 4.3.

Fifty-five percent of the catalogs prospected for new customers, the remainder were triggered by pre-existing customer relationships. All of the prospecting catalogs were well-targeted demographically. Conventional targeting breaks down, of course, in the area of psychographics.

How is Brooks Brothers to know that wearing their clothes makes me look like a fireplug, and how is Gorsuch Ltd. to know I don't ski? Wouldn't it be a lot more cost-effective and a lot less wasteful if they sent me a card first asking if I'd like a catalog?

Favorite Catalog: "Victoria's Secret." They sent two, bless their souls. Hardly a week goes by without a Victoria's Secret catalog brightening the mailbox, even though neither I nor my wife have ever bought anything from them. I'm in love with the model on page 8, Winter '91 collection.

Oddest Single Picture: "The La Costa Spa," a model completely covered with "Energizing Face Mud" (blue), "Purifying Body Mud" (green) and "Contouring Body Mud" (pink). The model, clad only in multicolored gunk, looks like a Martian, an uncomfortable one at that.

Continued

The fact is that marketers are becoming fully aware that it is increasingly difficult to reach a target audience without the interference of a barrage of competitive efforts. As a result many are placing growing reliance on a combination of direct marketing methods.

What effects will this increasing barrage of mail and telephone communication have on the buyer, however? Direct marketing commentator James R. Rosenfield has some very real doubts and tongue-in-cheek comments in Consumer in Focus 18.1. Hopefully some of the errant direct marketers will take note of what he says.

There is much to be gained from integration of direct marketing with normal retail-based strategies. For example, the venerable Fuller Brush Company is now opening retail stores targeted for the middle-to-upper-middle-income woman aged 35 to 55 who no longer can be found through house-to-house selling. This beefed-up strategy is backed by local newspaper advertising.[45]

Single Biggest Catalog Design Flaw: much too much white type reversed out of light backgrounds. After reading through "The Peruvian Connection" I was squinting so much that I looked like an alpaca.

Worst Targeted Mailing: "Million Connections for Singles," sent to "Select Area Resident," promising that I, as a with-it single, can easily meet the with-it single of my dreams. I've been married a long, long time, and so has everybody else in my rather elderly neighborhood.

What does this flood tide of direct mail mean? Well, one thing it means is that we direct marketers are much better talking about database marketing than doing it. All 110 pieces are traditional direct mail programs. Not one of them is based on specific reactions to specific behavior, one of the defining qualities of database marketing.

It also indicates that American direct mailer users are mostly paying lip-service to environmental concerns. Fewer than 10 percent of the pieces received were on recycled paper.

And the fact that most of the solicitations were prospecting pieces, rather than customer-relationship communications, shows that we still consider sending out a thousand catalogs and getting 20 responses a viable way of doing business. Our PR is better than it used to be, but our practice is still in the Stone Age.

Source: James F. Rosenfield, "In the Mail," *Direct Marketing* (November 1991), 20–21. Reproduced by special permission.

Retailers, in turn, are finding that direct marketing is one key to restoring dwindling sales. Many historically have been reluctant to promote nonstore sales on the theory that this would detract from their regular business. Now some leaders, such as Saks and Neiman Marcus, are finding quite the opposite to be true. Failure to adapt strategies to consumer shopping preferences can be the worst kind of marketing myopia.

The Outcomes of Purchase

The marketing task does not cease once the sale has been made because the buyer will evaluate the alternative after purchase as well as before. When involvement is high, it is not uncommon to experience an immediate and often transitory period of doubt referred to as **buyer's regret**. This can have an impact on whether the buyer is satisfied or dissatisfied with the transaction (see Figure 18.1). The beliefs and attitudes formed at this stage have a direct influence on future purchase intentions, word-of-mouth communication, and complaint behavior.

Of far greater importance, however, is the degree to which the buyer is satisfied with the product, its performance, and service provided. The marketing literature today is flooded with research and commentary on this issue, far more than it was even a decade ago. There are several reasons for the priority placed on customer satisfaction/dissatisfaction (CS/D):

1. Customer retention has risen to the top of strategic priorities in today's competitive arena, because the difficulty and expense of attracting new customers are becoming formidable indeed.
2. *Customer satisfaction is the key to customer retention.*
3. Product and service quality lies at the heart of satisfaction and dissatisfaction.
4. Japanese industry has shifted priorities in the competitive arena to product and service quality at which they excel.
5. American industry has suffered dramatically and lost world market position because of widespread quality inferiority.

In our opinion, the enhanced customer satisfaction is the greatest challenge facing marketers today. Much of the concluding part of this section focuses on CS/D research and the strategic implications which emerge.

Buyer's Regret

Have you ever come to a decision under high-involvement conditions, say the selection of a college or university, only to experience doubts that you did the right thing? You think, perhaps, of several other schools that also were good options and find yourself troubled.

You are now experiencing postdecision doubt (or dissonance), a common initial outcome that can occur with or without a prior judgment of satisfaction or dissatisfaction. Here are the circumstances that can lead to buyer's regret:

1. a certain threshold of dissonance-motivated tension is surpassed,
2. the action is irrevocable,
3. there are other unchosen alternatives with qualitatively dissimilar but desirable attributes,
4. the choice is made entirely by free will or volition (that is, you have not been constrained by social or parental pressures).[46]

You now are motivated to do something to reduce this dissonance, and you have two basic options: (1) confirmation of your choice or (2) conclusion that you have made an unwise decision.[47]

One of the best ways to underscore that you have done the right thing is to search for supportive information, especially that provided by the manufacturer through ads or new buyer instructions. There is evidence that confirms that buyers experiencing regret indeed are more receptive to these types of materials.[48]

It makes marketing sense to recognize that buyer regret can occur and to take pains to reinforce the wisdom of choice by stressing product superiorities and other sources of uniqueness once again. A good place to do this is in owner manuals. Warranties also can be helpful for this purpose.

In other words, the buyer may need reassurance that he or she acted wisely. Doubts often can be counteracted if this can be put into their hands quickly. A personal letter or telephone call from the manufacturer or dealer also is an effective strategy.

The other option, concluding that a bad choice has been made, is painful and can have negative consequences for the marketer. At the very least, a repurchase is unlikely, and it is quite possible that the product will be returned. Even more critical is the possibility of negative word of mouth.

Bear in mind that these doubts usually are transitory and do not, as yet, signify dissatisfaction. They are an entirely normal consequence when there are attractive unchosen alternatives. There is no need for them to degenerate into dissatisfaction when it is so easy to provide reinforcement through a personal word or literature.

Consumer Satisfaction/Dissatisfaction (CS/D)

Everyone enters into purchase with certain expectations about what the product or service will do when it is used, and satisfaction is the hoped-for outcome. **Satisfaction** is defined here as a *post-consumption evaluation that a chosen alternative at least meets or exceeds expectations*. In short, it has done at least as well as you hoped it would. **Dissatisfaction**, of course, is the outcome of negatively confirmed expectations.

The pressures of consumerism and growing public disdain for shoddy product quality have brought this subject to the forefront in consumer research in the past decade. The response, not surprisingly, has been an increasingly militant response of customer outrage against seemingly calloused companies and the individuals who represent them at point of sale. Take time to read Cynthia Crossen's penetrating analysis in Consumer in Focus 18.2.

The Expectancy Disconfirmation Model Richard Oliver has spearheaded research on this subject with his **expectancy disconfirmation model**.[49] Briefly, this theory postulates that satisfaction or dissatisfaction is the outcome of a comparison of prepurchase expectations against actual outcomes.[50]

Consumers enter into purchase with *expectations* of how the product will actually perform once it is used, and these fall into three categories:

1. **Equitable performance**[51]—a normative judgment reflecting the performance one *ought* to receive given the costs and efforts devoted to purchase and use.
2. **Ideal performance**[52]—the optimum or hoped-for "ideal" performance level.
3. **Expected performance**[53]—what the performance probably will be.

Consumer in Focus 18.2

Simple Apology for Poor Service Is in Sorry State

I'm sorry to have to report that apologies have all but disappeared from America's commercial discourse.

In airports, hotels, restaurants, stores and offices across the country, consumers complain that even when service people make flagrant mistakes, they simply refuse to say they are sorry. In some cases, the expression of quick and sincere regrets could prevent a letter-writing campaign, an insurance claim or even a lawsuit.

"It's tragic that one of the fundamental human niceties has vanished," says Richard Whiteley, vice chairman of Forum Corp., a Boston service-quality consultant. "Organizations are larger and moving faster, and people just don't have the time for that kind of personal interaction."

The near extinction of the basic apology is the result of several recent cultural changes, including the litigation explosion and a diminishing sense of personal responsibility for the mistakes made by other parts of a large company. If the accounting department made the mistake, the customer-service people might think, "I didn't make the mistake, why should I apologize?"

Growing time and productivity pressures also contribute to the decline of service civility. "With new technology, clerks are getting very good at processing," says Mr. Whiteley. "They process customers the way data, meat or cheese are processed."

Consumers must also take a share of the blame. As consumers have learned to be more alert to their rights, more people have bought into the notion that the squeakier the wheel, the better the grease. Saying I'm sorry to customers who retort, "You should be," also dissuades service people from apologizing.

Some companies say they don't encourage apologies because they fear that such expressions will be interpreted as feeble substitutes for corrective action. "I'm sorry might be creeping out of the vocabulary because it normally indicates that you're not really doing anything about the problem," says Colson Turner, vice president of customer service for New York Telephone Co.

Most customers understand that accidents happen, even the best-laid plans sometimes go awry, and no one's perfect. They say they are prepared to accept misfortune at the hands of a service provider if someone simply acknowledges that a wrong has been done. "We can all be soothed by someone saying they're sorry," says Letita Baldrige, author of the "Complete Guide to the New Manners for the '90s." "An apology is like mommy kissing your hurt finger."

Source: Cynthia Crossen, "Simple Apology for Poor Service Is in Sorry State," *The Wall Street Journal* (November 29, 1990), B1 and B3.

Category 3, expected performance, is most often used in CS/D research, because this is the logical outcome of the alternative evaluation process discussed in Chapter 17.

Once the product or service has been purchased and used, outcomes are compared against expectancies and a judgment is made. Most researchers view this CS/D judgment as a subjective evaluation of the difference between expectancy and outcomes.

Others have shown that consumers make use of two basic criteria in arriving at this judgment. The first is an objective product-performance evaluation.[54] But consumers also experience differentiated emotions in the consumption experience as well as affective (pro/con) responses to the product as a whole and to its components.[55] Unless both the cognitive and affective elements are taken into account, the measurement process will be incomplete.

The CS/D judgment takes one of three different forms:

1. **Positive disconfirmation**—performance is better than expected.
2. **Simple confirmation**—performance equals expectations.
3. **Negative disconfirmation**—performance is worse than expected.

Positive disconfirmation, of course, leads to a response of satisfaction, and the opposite takes place when disconfirmation is negative. Simple confirmation implies a more neutral response that is neither extremely positive nor negative. The outcome directly affects repurchase intentions; the greater the positive disconfirmation, the better.

To take an example, a young executive jogger develops knee pain that is diagnosed as a result of improper foot movement (pronation) and stride. She is given the choice of six different shoes that will minimize the problem. She has tried each on and makes a selection believing that the problem will be solved. Her beliefs with respect to the chosen brand represent the prepurchase expectation, and it is positive. If actual running experience equals or exceeds that expectation, the outcome will be one of relative satisfaction. When this is not the case, there will be dissatisfaction.

It is interesting to note that high levels of satisfaction with a previously owned brand are often accompanied by some dissatisfaction following repurchase.[56] It appears that failure to exceed that high expectation can lead to mild dissatisfaction. At other times, however, those with poor prior experience are pleasantly surprised and indicate even higher levels of satisfaction than do their previously satisfied counterparts.[57]

An Attribution Theory Perspective   Although the expectancy-disconfirmation model (and its modifications) has achieved wide acceptance, there have been some suggested alternatives, especially attribution theory.[58] Attribution theory postulates that there are three bases used to classify and understand why a product does not perform as expected:

1. *Stability*. Are the causes temporary or permanent?
2. *Locus*. Are the causes consumer or marketer related?

3. *Controllability*. Are these causes under volitional control or are they constrained by outside factors that cannot be influenced?

In one study, Folkes discovered that the stability and locus of product failure influenced expectancies regarding future failure and preferences for an outright refund rather than replacement.[59] Customers apparently expected the product to fail if purchased again when the cause was perceived to be stable. For that reason, a refund was preferred. When the cause was perceived as unstable, however, they were less likely to react in this way.

In a more recent study, it was found that airline passengers were more prone to complain about flight delays when the problem was attributed to airline negligence as opposed to constraints such as bad weather.[60] Also, passengers were affected by their perception of whether the cause was stable and recurring. If the problem was attributed to a recurring problem, future flying intentions were negatively affected.

Consumer Response to Dissatisfaction

How extensive is dissatisfaction? What do consumers do when it occurs? Are complainers different from those who do not complain? These questions have been thoroughly researched in recent years.

Consumer Complaint Behavior   Evidence over the years has demonstrated the frequency of dissatisfaction to range from about 20 percent to around 50 percent of buyers depending on type of product, with an average of approximately one-third. A tally by Better Business Bureaus revealed that the frequency of consumer gripes in 1986 did not change much from preceding years, with the majority involving order or delivery foul-ups, home improvement firms, and auto repair shops.[61]

A number of studies have shown the major forms that dissatisfaction can take,[62] and a recent study by Singh suggests three different categories:[63]

1. Voice responses—for example, seeking redress from the seller.
2. Private responses—for example, negative word-of-mouth communication.
3. Third-party responses—for example, taking legal action.

"Once burned, twice shy" is a common reaction of Michigan consumers who no longer patronize businesses where they have had unpleasant experiences.[64]

These studies can be misleading, however, because they report only the complainers. There is solid evidence demonstrating that the majority never complain or seek redress. In fact, Day and his colleagues have shown that only one-third do so and are more likely instead to boycott or to complain to others.[65]

Dissatisfaction, in fact, often is a poor predictor of complaint behavior. Oliver has shown that the percentage of complaints among the dissatisfied directed toward the retailer range from 23 to 40 percent, and only 5 percent complain directly to the manufacturer.[66] In his research only 15 percent of variance in complaint behavior is explained by the satisfaction/dissatisfaction dimension.

Day and others have clarified the picture by demonstrating that attitude toward the act of complaining also must be taken into consideration.[67] Day has also shown that there are four additional factors that determine whether or not a complaint will be made:

1. Significance of the consumption event—product importance, price, social visibility, and time required in consumption.
2. Knowledge and experience—number of previous purchases, product knowledge, perception of ability as a consumer, and previous complaining experience.
3. Difficulty of seeking redress—time, disruption of routine, and costs.
4. Chances for success in complaining.[68]

Nevin and George also have found that consumers will complain to the degree that there is some likelihood of positive outcomes.[69] For example, they will readily do so when a warranty is offered.

Characteristics of Complainers

The type of person who complains and seeks redress tends to be younger, with higher-than-average income and education.[70] Also, they are positive about consumerist activities in general, prefer a lifestyle that demonstrates difference and individuality,[71] and experience little hesitancy in letting their problems be known.[72]

They do not keep these concerns to themselves. Over half share their experiences with friends and relatives, and evidence indicates that negative word of mouth can have a major influence on the buying behavior of others.[73]

Response to Complaints

What type of response can be expected when a complaint is registered? Overall, research studies indicate that 55 to 60 percent are resolved to the consumer's satisfaction.[74] In a recent study, for example, Cobb, Walgren, and Hollowed found a 58 percent response rate to complaint letters.[75] The vast majority were in the form of a personal letter. The greatest response came from pizza and snack manufacturers, whereas only one-fourth of clothing firms replied.

There is sufficient convincing evidence to support the principle that making a sincere effort to rectify problems will noticeably increase consumer assurance that the firm really cares. Not surprisingly, satisfaction and intent to repurchase are strengthened in the process.

Retaining the Customer

As we have stressed repeatedly, customer retention should receive even greater priority than new customer solicitation. First, it generally is less expensive to hold onto present customers than to attract new ones. Furthermore, customer loss can be disastrous in mature markets that are experiencing little real growth.

Therefore, customer loyalty based on genuine and ongoing satisfaction is one of the greatest assets a firm can acquire. Here are some of the ways in which marketers can strengthen their customer relationship.

Institute a Total Quality Control (TQC) Policy
The Strategic Planning Institute of Cambridge, Massachusetts, has analyzed the performance of nearly 2,600 businesses over a period of 15 years using such criteria as market share, return on investment, and asset turnover. Referred to as Profit Impact of Market Strategy (PIMS), this research led to one incontrovertible conclusion: *financial performance is tied directly to perceived quality of a company's goods and service*.[76]

Total quality control (TQC) is an operating philosophy that has its roots in the late 1970s when the Japanese took seriously the teachings of W. Edwards Deming on this crucial subject.[77] Deming called for a total commitment to excellence from top management exemplified by an effective system of quality circles (groups of employees regularly meeting to help solve problems), an employee suggestion system, wide use of statistical quality control principles, a goal of "zero defects," and constant training programs.

Toyota Motors is frequently cited as the premier example of a company that has built dominant market position by following the slogan of *kaizan*—constant improvement.[78] Taylor points out that:

> Extensive interviews with Toyota executives in the U.S. and Japan demonstrate the company's total dedication to continuous improvement. What is often mistaken for excessive modesty is, in fact, an expression of permanent dissatisfaction—even with exemplary performance. So the company is simultaneously restructuring its management, refining its already elegant manufacturing processes, planning its global strategy for the 21st century, tinkering with its corporate culture, and even becoming a fashion [automotive styling] leader.[79]

There has been an unfortunate period of Japan bashing in 1992, blaming the inroads of Japanese products into the American market on unfair trade practices. Most balanced commentators take quite an opposite viewpoint, however, and point with devastating accuracy to the extent to which Japan has beaten the U.S. at its own game. TQC is the reason why this has happened. Fortunately, executives in most industries (automobiles being the notable exception) have recognized this point and are responding creatively.[80]

A commitment to quality, however, is no small undertaking. It all begins with top management who must leave their offices, be close to the customer, and be accessible to operations in all phases. Employee turnover must be reduced, and incentives must be given for innovation and change.[81]

This can be both risky and costly, but competitive survival is at stake. All readers are painfully aware of widespread layoffs as one firm after another either goes out of business entirely or is totally restructuring in the hopes of regaining lost market position. But today's competitive world is forcing everyone to face these harsh realities.

Establish a Consumer Affairs Department with Clout
Someone within the enterprise has to be responsible for hearing the consumer's voice. This cannot be a public relations officer, however, primarily responsible to hear complaints and cool down

an irate customer. It must have clout, and this comes only if these stipulations are met:

1. a direct reporting line to top management,
2. power to give redress on the spot and to take other forms of action necessary to remedy damages which might have been done, and
3. access to all decision-making units within the company with top management-backed power to oversee changes to remedy deficiencies in quality and service.

The first step is to establish a guiding policy that *all complaints are taken seriously*. In the late 1980s, there was widespread public furor over the Audi 5000 model. There was a devastating exposé on the CBS "60 Minutes" program of an alleged problem with engine surge that was reported to have caused death and injuries.[82] The consistent response of Audi management was that the car was not at fault. They claimed instead that the blame lay with the driver who hit the accelerator instead of the brake.

Although there was opinion and evidence to the contrary, management stuck to this position for a long period of time. Finally, a recall was ordered and a minor transmission modification was made. Unfortunately, public confidence in Audi plummeted, and the future of the Audi 5000 model was doomed. Later evidence exonerated the company, incidentally.

What was the problem here? It was a total disregard of customer relations. The greatest sin was passing the buck to the consumer. What did the company have to gain by stonewalling on this issue? Absolutely nothing! An immediate and apologetic recognition that something was seriously wrong accompanied by a recall might have headed off the outrage. The point, of course, is that widespread dissatisfaction can prove fatal.

Notice the different tack taken by Chrysler Motors' Chairman Lee Iacocca when he publicly admitted that his management was grievously wrong in turning back the odometers on executive-driven cars, and apologized publicly. The issue was instantly and effectively defused.

Another good example of responsible action appears in Figure 18.2. After a series of lapses in flight safety procedures, Delta Airlines management admitted culpability and reassured its frequent-flier customers that everything possible was being done to restore public confidence. Once again the issue was addressed along with a pledge of company responsibility.

We wish we could be optimistic that business will accept the counsel given here. Unfortunately, data provided by Fornell and Westbrook argue to the contrary. After an extensive review of the way in which customer complaints are handled, they concluded that organizational willingness to listen and respond decreases as the numbers of complaints increase.[83] We see few signs of real change. We have more to say about this distressing problem in Chapter 24.

Analyze Lost Customers   The starting point lies in evaluation of overall sales growth. If sales are declining, then it is likely that problems exist in customer

DELTA AIR LINES, INC.
HARTSFIELD ATLANTA INTERNATIONAL AIRPORT
ATLANTA, GEORGIA 30320

W. WHITLEY HAWKINS
SENIOR VICE PRESIDENT
MARKETING

August 14, 1987

Dear Frequent Flyer:

You have selected Delta for a substantial amount of your travels
and we sincerely appreciate it. By your making this selection,
we have always thought of you as part of the Delta family - a
matter we take very seriously.

We also take very seriously our responsibility to provide you
with the finest and safest air transportation in the world. In
keeping with this responsibility, we feel an obligation to share
with you the attached memo written to all Delta personnel by
Ron Allen on July 31, 1987, regarding the incidents involving
Delta between June 18 and July 12 which have received so much
media attention. (At the time the memo was written, Ron was
our President and Chief Operating Officer. He has since become
our Chairman and Chief Executive Officer.)

Your overwhelming support during this very trying period has
been extremely gratifying to all of us here at Delta. The cards,
letters, phone calls and comments many of you have made to the
media have sustained us through these very difficult times. It
is during times like these that people's true colors are shown
and when real friends become highly visible.

We are proud to have you as friends and customers, and we renew
our pledge to you to provide you the finest airline service
possible. All of the slashing comments, jokes, political cartoons
and questionable reporting cannot erase the fact that Delta has
the finest service record of any airline in the world. We owe it
to you to keep it that way, and we will.

Thank you for being so special.

Sincerely,

Whit Hawkins

Attachment

FIGURE 18.2 Positive Corporate Response to a Quality Problem: Delta Pledges Company Responsibility

Source: Courtesy Delta Airlines, Inc.

satisfaction and retention. This assumes, of course, that the overall market is not experiencing a corresponding sales decay.

The best diagnostic criterion is the **cancellation rate**—the proportion of customers who have not repurchased. This becomes most meaningful, of course, when it is viewed in comparison with previous years and the experience of competitors.

TABLE 18.3   A Customer Portfolio Analysis for a Manufacturer of Major Household Appliances

	Customer Experience	
	Year-to-Date	Previous 5 Years
First time buyers	31%	33%
Switched from Brand A	7%	3%
Switched from Brand B	2%	5%
Switched from Brand C	3%	4%
Switched from all other brands	9%	12%
No previous buying history	10%	9%
Repeat buyers	34%	40%
Customers who switched brands	35%	27%
Switched to Brand A	6%	6%
Switched to Brand B	11%	7%
Switched to Brand C	12%	7%
All other brands	6%	7%

Cancellation rates indicate only *what* has happened, not *why*. Here is the crucial question: *Are customers being pushed away by company actions (or inaction), or are they being pulled away by competitors?* If they are being pushed away by inadequate handling of complaints, a defective product, and so on, the problem obviously is an internal one. If they are pulled away, on the other hand, this is clear indication that some form of marketing overhaul is needed.

In this context, it is helpful to undertake a "customer portfolio analysis" to provide an early warning of competitive problems. Table 18.3 provides an example of a portfolio analysis undertaken for a manufacturer of major household appliances. The focus here is on customer gain and loss relative to competitors for the current year as compared with the composite experience of previous years.

Notice, first of all, that the company is experiencing a decline overall in attracting customers from competitors, with the sole exception of brand A, where there has been a net gain this year. This is not a favorable indication. Even more ominous is the 6 percent decline in repeat buyers. Competitors B and C, in turn, are making some major inroads.

It is entirely possible that company actions are in some way causing customer alienation. Product quality could be slipping, prices may not be competitive, and so on. If this is the situation, then it is time for some remedial action in the marketing mix to remedy shortcomings. Further information obviously is required to detect where the problems lie.

There also is the possibility that competitors are making a more attractive offer to the consumer. If so, these losses could be permanent. It is necessary to make an immediate response based on further research into customer reactions and preferences.

A final possibility is that the problem lies in low consumer awareness of company distinctions. If this is the case, then the solution lies in revamped promotional strategy. Whatever the case, the early warning system has served its purpose.

These data also have their uses in an offensive rather than a defensive strategy. The inroads into the share of company A are encouraging. This is a good clue to a softening in its market position which can be further exploited once the reasons are clarified.

Anticipate Problems in Customer Retention   By the time a customer shows up as a cancellation, it normally is too late for retention measures to do much good. What is needed, then, is an "early warning system" that indicates problems with sufficient lead time for corrective actions to be taken. Ongoing surveys of consumer satisfaction lie at the heart of this warning system.

Many companies monitor quality and performance using an internally based technical perspective but miss a basic point: *quality is meaningful only if monitored through the eyes of the consumer*. A case in point is the financial services company that enforced a standard response time to consumer inquiries of 14–21 days only to find that 60 percent of customers expected seven-day responses.[84]

So here is the basic principle: *Learn what the customer expects in quality and performance and monitor customer response continually*. There are many ways that this can be done ranging from putting management on the road to focus groups and regular surveys. It is an excellent idea, in fact, to appoint and empower all sales people to be *relationship managers*.[85] Consumer in Focus 18.3 provides some helpful practical examples of other steps that can be taken.

Build Realistic Expectations   Remember that satisfaction is based on an assessment that prepurchase expectations were fulfilled. Consider what might happen if a consumer purchased a cellular car telephone on the basis of its offer of "clearest reception in the entire metropolitan area," only to find some real geographic limits on use. Even if all other brands have exactly the same problem, this company created an erroneous expectation through its promotion. Widespread dissatisfaction is altogether likely, and the blame lies with the advertising claim. The bottom line? Avoid exaggeration—the consumer might actually believe what you are saying and hold you accountable.

Provide Guarantees   "Quality comes first with us." This now is a common advertising message, but consumers often greet it with the bored response, "Oh yeah? Prove it!" Therefore, product guarantees are growing at "fever pitch."[86] Although there is evidence that warranties and guarantees have greater effects on product evaluations for new brands,[87] all companies can benefit from creative use of this strategy.

Consumer in Focus **18.3**

It's Basic but Necessary: Listen to the Customer

John McKitterick of General Electric said that "the principal task of the marketing function . . . is not so much to be skillful in making the customer do what suits the interest of the business, as to be skillful in conceiving and the making the business do what suits the interests of the customer."

Being customer focused can improve long-run profitability. A study has found that 54 percent of unhappy customers will buy again if they believe their complaint has been heard and resolved. Only about 19 percent will buy again if their complaint is heard, but not resolved. Fewer than 9 percent will be repeat buyers when a complaint is not heard.

Studies have shown that holding onto existing customers is about one-fifth the cost of acquiring new ones. Ford sees a 23 percent difference in repurchase decisions of customers satisfied with dealer service over those not satisfied.

Here are some examples of what management can do:

- Some Japanese firms have sales reps and design engineers spend half their time in the market place to see what customers want and need.
- Domino's Pizza Inc., Ann Arbor, Mich., pays 10,000 mystery customers to buy pizzas throughout the year in order to provide feedback.
- Embassy Suite Hotels interviews at least five customers daily and posts their remarks for the entire staff to see.
- Toll free numbers are installed at 50 percent of all companies with sales of at least $10 million. The phone calls are seen as the most effective forum for receiving complaint feedback. Companies believe they can respond faster and cheaper to the complaint or need through this mechanism.
- Focus groups are a popular way to obtain this feedback, but they can be expensive. They can be used to learn how a firm or its product are perceived, reaction to use of a product, reaction to new products, and other areas where a company would like to get additional information.
- Customer surveys have been popular for years. They can monitor opinions about the company and its goods and/or services. The problems with this method are that so many companies are using it that the public has become weary of surveys, and a significant amount of time and money must be invested to do a decent survey.

Source: Sharyn Hunt and Ernest F. Cooke, "It's Basic But Necessary: Listen to the Customer," *Marketing News* (March 5, 1990), 22. Reproduced by special permission.

This isn't just a baggage tag.
It's a contract.

We don't think a system of handling baggage
should leave anything to chance. Which is why
we take so many precautions. Like writing
baggage tags by computer and not by hand
(handwriting, unfortunately, is often subject
to interpretation).
     Our system works so well that we guarantee
you *and* your baggage a smooth trip. And we
back that guarantee with cash. If you or your baggage miss a connecting Lufthansa flight when
you fly Lufthansa First or Business Class across
the Atlantic, we will pay you $200.
     Call it a contract. We do. Everywhere we fly.
On 6 continents, in 82 countries, in 161 cities.

People expect the world of us.

Lufthansa
German Airlines

Lufthansa is a participant in the mileage programs of United,
Delta, and USAir. See your Travel Agent for details.

FIGURE 18.3   Customer Retention and Attraction through Use of a Guarantee
Source: Courtesy of Lufthansa German Airlines.

It is easy to conclude that Lufthansa German Airlines fully intends an on-time arrival complete with checked baggage (see Figure 18.3), given their stringent guarantee to first class and business class passengers. There could be no better way to retain present customers, to say nothing of making competitive inroads.

Provide Information on Product Use   Product designers should be aware of the ways in which the product fits into a consumer's lifestyle. How is it used? It should be designed and promoted in such a way that performance will be adequate under conditions actually experienced in the home. For example, buyers often use electric toasters for English muffins, rolls, and other types of baked goods as well as for bread. If the toaster will not properly handle these items, unconfirmed expectancies and dissatisfaction are likely.

Reinforce Customer Loyalty   You may recall from Chapter 14 how certain response patterns can be reinforced by reward. Bergiel and Trosclair have demonstrated the benefits of a very simple application of instrumental learning theory.[88] They found that the loyalty of insurance customers could be reinforced by occasional reminders that their company still is interested in them. All it takes is a periodic letter affirming the commitment of both the company and the broker.

Summary

This chapter examines the act of purchase and its outcomes. First, it is pointed out, making use of the model of consumer behavior, that purchase is a function of two factors: (1) purchase intentions and (2) environmental influences and/or individual differences. Often purchases are fully planned in the sense that there is intention to purchase both product and brand. At other times, intention encompasses only the product, with the choice of brand reserved for further deliberation at point of sale.

The so-called "unplanned" purchase is discussed at length. It was stressed that a purchase intention is not always consciously articulated, in which case product display provides a "surrogate shopping list." But many items also are bought purely on the basis of impulse, which can be spontaneous and hedonic in motivation.

A purchase can be made either at a retail outlet of some type or in the home. Retail outlets prosper in part because shopping has intrinsic value in and of itself. But there is also a dramatic growth of buying through direct mail, telephone, catalogs, and other non-retail sources. Strategies designed to reach the in-home buyer are referred to as direct marketing.

Decision-process behavior does not cease once a purchase is consummated, however. Further evaluation takes place in the form of comparing product or service performance against expectations. The outcome is one of satisfaction or dissatisfaction. Satisfaction serves to reinforce buyer loyalty, whereas dissatisfaction can lead to complaints, negative word of mouth, and attempts to seek redress through legal means.

This means that customer retention becomes a crucial part of marketing strategy. We stress how this can be done through such tactics as creating realistic expectations, ensuring that product and service quality meets expectations, monitoring satisfaction and customer-retention levels, offering guarantees, and meeting dissatisfaction head on by quick and appropriate response.

Review and Discussion Questions

1. You are the marketing manager for a manufacturer of specialty electronic items such as tiny lamps that illuminate only the page of a book, and a line of watches designed for runners. Would you seek to sell these items through retail stores or would you be inclined to try direct marketing (either alone or in combination with retail distribution)?

Why? Would your answer differ if the product line consisted mostly of costly "up-scale" women's fashion accessories (for example, gloves, scarves)?

2. Given the diverse reasons why many consumers genuinely enjoy shopping, how would you capitalize on this phenomenon if you are marketing a high-quality ice cream line?

3. Why would you say that many conventional marketers have been hesitant to enter into direct marketing? What case would you make for direct marketing to a book publisher? A distributor of French wines?

4. The brand manager for a laundry detergent has read about the phenomenon of buyer regret and asks the company marketing research department to undertake a survey to see if this happens when laundry products are purchased. Do you feel that research would disclose widespread buyer regret when purchasing and using this product? Would your answer be different if the product is a compact disc stereo system featuring an all-new speaker system design? Why?

5. Review the situation facing Audi Motors after the disclosure of widespread problems with engine surge in Audi 5000 models with automatic transmission. What might have been done differently to meet this problem? Make a case to management justifying your conclusions.

6. What influence do advertising and selling efforts have in forming buyer expectations? What advice can you give to an advertising manager if you are asked to suggest ways in which promotional strategy could help increase buyer satisfaction?

7. "Come to White Fence Farm where we offer the world's best chicken." This claim has been heard for many years on Chicago radio. Would you recommend its continuation from the perspective of consumer satisfaction? What are the possible dangers?

8. You are asked to recommend ways of getting small portable appliance designers and engineers to take quality seriously from the consumer's perspective. What would you suggest?

9. A manufacturer of do-it-yourself lawn care items is interested in understanding what happens to former customers. The issue is what brands they are now using, and why. What kind of research would you undertake to answer this question?

10. Consider a company that has experienced an increase in both cancellation rates and customer satisfaction over the past three years. What implications can be drawn from these findings?

Endnotes

1. Chip Walker, "Strip Malls; Plain But Powerful," *American Demographics* (October 1991), 48–51.

2. "Shoppers Are a Dwindling Species," *Business Week* (November 26, 1990), 144.

3. "Retailing: Who Will Survive?" *Business Week* (November 26, 1990), 134–144.

4. Laura Loro, "Data Bases Seen as 'Driving Force,'" *Advertising Age* (March 18, 1991), 39.

5. Arnold Fishman, "The Database Marketing 250," *Direct Marketing* (September 1990), 26.

6. Jeffrey J. Stoltman, James W. Gentry, and Kenneth A. Anglin, "Shopping Choices: The Case of Mall Choice," in Rebecca H. Holman and Michael R. Solomon, eds.,

Advances in Consumer Research 18 (Provo, Utah: Association for Consumer Research, 1991), 434–440.

7. "Cyndee Miller, "P-O-P Gains Followers as 'Era of Retailing' Dawns," *Advertising Age* (May 14, 1990), 2.

8. Miller, "P-O-P Gains Followers."

9. C. Whan Park, Easwar S. Iyer, and Daniel C. Smith, "The Effects of Situational Factors on In-Store Grocery Shopping Behavior: The Role of Store Environment and Time Available for Shopping," *Journal of Consumer Research* 15 (March 1989), 422–433.

10. Alain d'Asdtous, Idriss Bensouda, and Jean Guindon, "A Re-Examination of Consumer Decision Making for a Repeat Purchase Product: Variations in Product Importance and Purchase Frequency," in Thomas K. Srull, *Advances in Consumer Research* 16 (Provo, Utah: Association for Consumer Research, 1989), 433–438.

11. For a careful analysis of the impact of retail promotions, see Rodney G. Walters, "Assessing the Impact of Retail Price Promotions on Product Substitution, Complementary Purchase, and Interstore Sales Displacement," *Journal of Marketing* 55 (April 1991), 17–28.

12. David T. Kollat and Ronald P. Willett, "Customer Impulse Purchasing Behavior," *Journal of Marketing Research* 4 (February 1967), 21–31.

13. Joe Agnew, "P-O-P Displays Are Becoming a Matter of Consumer Convenience," *Marketing News* (October 9, 1987), 14.

14. Kollat and Willett, "Customer Impulse Purchasing Behavior."

15. Park, Iyer, and Smith, "The Effects of Situational Factors."

16. Dennis W. Rook, "The Buying Impulse," *Journal of Consumer Research* 14 (September 1987), 191.

17. Morris B. Holbrook and Elizabeth C. Hirschman, "The Experiential Aspects of Consumer Behavior: Consumer Fantasies, Feelings, and Fun," *Journal of Consumer Research* 9 (September 1982), 132–140.

18. Rook, "The Buying Impulse."

19. For more detail, see Gordon R. Foxall, *Consumer Choice* (London: Macmillan Press, 1983), 86–97.

20. Betsy Morris, "As a Favored Pastime, Shopping Ranks High with Most Americans," *The Wall Street Journal* (July 30, 1987), 1ff.

21. Jack A. Lesser and Sanjay Jain, "A Preliminary Investigation of the Relationship between Exploratory and Epistemic Shopping Behavior," in Robert F. Lusch et al., eds., *1985 AMA Educators' Proceedings* (Chicago: American Marketing Association, 1985), 75–81.

22. Morris, "As a Favored Pastime."

23. "Retailing: Who Will Survive?" *Business Week* (November 26, 1990), 135.

24. James U. McNeal and Daryl McKee, "The Case of Antishoppers," in Lusch et al., eds., *1985 AMA Educators' Proceedings*, 65–68.

25. See "Direct Marketing—An Aspect of Total Marketing," *Direct Marketing* (January 1992), 2. These are annual statistics published in each issue of this magazine.

26. "Direct Marketing—An Aspect of Total Marketing."

27. Arnold Fishman, "International Mail Order," *Direct Marketing* (October 1991), 36.

28. Martin P. Block and Tamara S. Brezen, "A Profile of the New In-Home Shopper," in Rebecca Holman, ed., *Proceedings of the 1991 Conference of the American Academy of Advertising* (New York: Rebecca H. Holman, D'Arcy Masius Benton & Bowles, Inc., 1991), 169–173; "Direct Marketing Sales Far Outpace Estimates," *Marketing*

News (November 23, 1984), 1 and 8; Paul I. Edwards, "Home Shopping Boom Forecast in Study," *Advertising Age* (December 15, 1986), 88; and Peter L. Gillet, "In-Home Shoppers: An Overview," *Journal of Marketing* 40 (October 1976), 81–88.

29. "Home Shopping. Is It a Revolution in Retailing—or Just a Fad?" *Business Week* (December 16, 1986), 68.

30. "1986 Mail Order Guide," 50.

31. "Mary Kay Cosmetics, Inc. (A)," in James F. Engel and W. Wayne Talarzyk, *Cases in Promotional Strategy*, rev. ed. (Homewood, Ill.: Irwin, 1983), 3–10.

32. "Bean, Lands' End Top Consumer Survey," *Direct Marketing* (November 1991), 8.

33. James R. Lumpkin and John R. Hawes, "Retailing without Stores: An Examination of Catalog Shoppers," *Journal of Business Research* 13 (1985), 139–151.

34. "Behavior and Attitudes of Telephone Shoppers," *Direct Marketing* (September 1987), 50ff.

35. "Behavior and Attitudes of Telephone Shoppers."

36. Eileen Norris, "Alternative Media Try to Get Their Feet in the Door," *Advertising Age* (October 17, 1985), 58.

37. Joe Agnew, "Home Shopping: TV's Hit of the Season," *Marketing News* (March 13, 1987), 1, 20.

38. Agnew, "Home Shopping: TV's Hit of the Season," *Marketing News* (March 13, 1987), 1, 20.

39. Agnew, "Home Shopping."

40. Michael J. Major, "Videotex Never Really Left, But It's Not All Here," *Advertising Age* (November 12, 1990), 2, 32.

41. Major, "Videotex Never Really Left," 2.

42. George Nahon and Edith Pointeau, "Minitel Videotex in France: What We Have Learned," *Direct Marketing* (January 1987), 64-69.

43. Dwight J. Shelton, "Birds of a Geodemographic Feather Flock Together," *Marketing News* (August 28, 1987), 13.

44. Leo Bogart, "Hitting the Right Consumer Target," *Advertising Age* (May 17, 1984), M-49–M-55.

45. Susan Garland, "Stores Brush up Fuller's Image," *Advertising Age* (September 14, 1987), 107.

46. Jack W. Brehm and Arthur R. Cohen, *Explorations in Cognitive Dissonance* (New York: Wiley, 1962), 300.

47. The literature here is dated. For an excellent review and clarification see Michael S. Latour, "Buyer's Regret," unpublished paper, College of Business and Public Administration, Old Dominion University, 1992.

48. For the first published study testing this theory in a practical marketing context, see James F. Engel, "The Psychological Consequences of a Major Purchase Decision," in William S. Decker, ed., *Marketing in Transition* (Chicago: American Marketing Association, 1963), 462–475.

49. The basic source is Richard L. Oliver, "A Cognitive Model of the Antecedents and Consequences of Satisfaction Decisions," *Journal of Marketing Research* 17 (November 1980), 460–469.

50. There have been many studies validating Oliver's theoretical model. One of the most recent is Ruth N. Bolton and James H. Drew, "A Multistage Model of Customers' Assessments of Service Quality and Value," *Journal of Consumer Research* 17 (March 1991), 375–384. For a thorough review of earlier evidence, see Richard L. Oliver and

Wayne S. DeSarbo, "Response Determinants in Satisfaction Judgments," *Journal of Consumer Research* 14 (March 1988), 495–507; and David K. Tse and Peter C. Wilton, "Models of Consumer Satisfaction Formation: An Extension," *Journal of Marketing Research* 25 (May 1988), 204–212.

51. Robert B. Woodruff, Ernest R. Cadotte, and Roger L. Jenkins, "Modeling Consumer Satisfaction Using Experience-Based Norms," *Journal of Marketing Research* 20 (August 1983), 296–304.

52. Morris B. Holbrook, "Situation-Specific Ideal Points and Usage of Multiple Dissimilar Brands," in Jagdish N. Sheth, ed., *Research in Marketing* 7 (Greenwich, Connecticut: JAI Press, 1984), 93–112.

53. M. Leichty and Gilbert A. Churchill, Jr., "Conceptual Insights into Consumer Satisfaction with Services," in Neil Beckwith et al., eds., *Educators' Conference Proceedings* (Chicago: American Marketing Association, 1979), 509–515.

54. Gilbert A. Churchill, Jr., and Carol Suprenant, "An Investigation into the Determinants of Customer Satisfaction," *Journal of Marketing Research* 19 (November 1983), 491–504. Also Peter C. Wilton and David K. Tse, "A Model of Consumer Response to Communication and Product Experiences," in Larry Percy and Arch G. Woodside, eds., *Advertising and Consumer Psychology* (Lexington, Massachusetts: Lexington Books, 1983), 315–332.

55. See Richard L. Oliver, "Cognitive, Affective, and Attribute Bases of Usage/Postpurchase Responses," in Holmon and Solomon, *Advances*, 54; Robert A. Westbrook, "Emotional Response, Involvement, and Satisfaction," in Holmon and Solomon, *Advances*, 54; and Laurette Dube and Bernd H. Schmitt, "The Processing of Emotional and Cognitive Aspects of Product Usage in Satisfaction Judgments," in Holman and Solomon, *Advances*, 52–56.

56. Robert A. Westbrook and Joseph W. Newman, "An Analysis of Shopper Dissatisfaction for Major Household Appliances," *Journal of Marketing Research* 15 (August 1978), 456–466.

57. Stephen A. LaTour and Nancy C. Peat, "The Role of Situationally Produced Expectations, Others' Experiences, and Prior Experience in Determining Consumer Satisfaction," in Jerry C. Olson, ed., *Advances in Consumer Research* 7 (Ann Arbor: Association for Consumer Research, 1980), 588–592.

58. Valerie S. Folkes, "Consumer Reactions to Product Failure: An Attributional Approach," *Journal of Consumer Research* 10 (March 1984), 398–409.

59. Folkes, "Consumer Reactions."

60. Valerie S. Folkes, Susan Kolestsky, and John L. Graham, "A Field Study of Causal Inferences and Consumer Reaction: The View from the Airport," *Journal of Consumer Research* 13 (March 1987), 534–539.

61. Research Recommendations, National Institute of Business Management, July 31, 1987.

62. Steven Brown and Richard F. Baltramini, "Consumer Complaining and Word of Mouth Activities: Field Evidence," in Thomas K. Srull, ed., *Advances in Consumer Research* 16 (Provo, Utah: Association for Consumer Research, 1989), 9–16; Bearden and Teel, "Selected Determinants of Consumer Satisfaction"; and Ralph L. Day, "Research Perspectives on Consumer Complaining Behavior," in Charles Lamb and Patrick Dunne, eds., *Theoretical Developments in Marketing* (Chicago: American Marketing Association, 1980), 211–215.

63. Jagdip Singh, "Consumer Complaint Intentions and Behavior: Definition and Taxonomical Issues," *Journal of Marketing* 52 (January 1988), 93–107.

64. "More than a Third of Michigan Consumers Have Been So 'Burned' that They Shy Away from Some Businesses," *Marketing News* (April 24, 1957), 20.

65. Ralph L. Day, Klaus Brabicke, Thomas Schaetzle, and Fritz Staubach, "The Hidden Agenda of Consumer Complaining," *Journal of Retailing* 57 (Fall 1981), 86–106.

66. Richard L. Oliver, "An Investigation of the Interrelationship between Consumer Dissatisfaction and Complaint Reports," in Melanie Wallendorf and Paul Anderson, eds., *Advances in Consumer Research* 14 (Provo, Utah: Association for Consumer Research, 1987), 218–222.

67. Ralph L. Day, "Modeling Choices among Alternative Responses to Dissatisfaction," in Thomas C. Kinnear, ed., *Advances in Consumer Research* 11 (Provo, Utah: Association for Consumer Research, 1984), 496–499; and Bearden and Mason, "An Investigation of Influences."

68. Day, "Modeling Choices."

69. George John and John R. Nevin, "The Role of Information Uncertainty, Disconfirmation and Disclosure Regulations as Determinants of Consumer Satisfaction and Complaint Behavior," in Terrance L. Shimp, ed., *1986 Educators' Proceedings* (Chicago: American Marketing Association, 1986), 68–73.

70. Michelle N. Morganowsky and Hilda Mayer Buckley, "Complaint Behavior: Analysis by Demographics, Lifestyle, Consumer Values," in Wallendorf and Anderson, *Advances*, 223–226.

71. Kathy J. Cobb, Gary C. Walgren, and Mary Hollowed, "Differences in Organizational Responses to Consumer Letters of Satisfaction and Dissatisfaction," in Wallendorf and Anderson, *Advances*, 227.

72. Marcia L. Richins, "An Investigation of Consumers' Attitudes towards Complaining," in Andrew Mitchell, ed., *Advances in Consumer Research* 9 (Ann Arbor: Association for Consumer Research, 1982), 502–506.

73. Brown and Baltramini, "Consumer Complaining and Word of Mouth Activities."

74. Cynthia J. Grimm, "Understanding and Reaching the Consumer: A Summary of Recent Research. Part II—Complaint Response Satisfaction and Market Impact," *Mobius* (Fall 1987), 18.

75. Cobb, Walgren, and Hollowed, "Differences in Organizational Responses."

76. John R. Hauser and Robert L. Klein, "Without Good Research, Quality Is a Shot in Dark," *Marketing News* (January 4, 1988), 1–2.

77. For a valuable summary of Deming's methods, see Mary Walton, *The Deming Management Method* (New York: Dodd, Mead, & Company, 1986).

78. Lex Taylor III, "Why Toyota Keeps Getting Better and Better and Better," *Fortune* (November 19, 1990), 66.

79. Taylor, "Why Toyota Keeps Getting Better," 67.

80. See, for example, Frank Rose, "Now Quality Means Service Too," *Fortune* (April 22, 1991), 98–110, and Gilbert Fuchsberg, "Gurus of Quality Are Gaining Clout," *The Wall Street Journal* (November 27, 1990), B1.

81. See Patricia Sellers, "What Customers Really Want," *Fortune* (June 4, 1990), 58–66.

82. For a review of the Audi story, see Fannie Weinstein, "One Foot in the Junkyard," *Advertising Age* (October 19, 1987), 92.

83. Claes Fornell and Robert A. Westbrook, "The Vicious Cycle of Consumer Complaints," *Journal of Marketing* 48 (Summer 1984), 68–78.

84. William Band, "Performance Metrics Keep Customer Satisfaction Programs on Track," *Marketing News* (May 28, 1990), 12.

85. Lawrence A. Crosby, Kenneth R. Evans, and Deborah Cowles, "Relationship Quality in Services Selling: An Interpersonal Influence Perspective," *Journal of Marketing* 54 (July 1990), 68–81.
86. Sara E. Stern, "Guarantees at Fever Pitch," *Advertising Age* (October 26, 1987), 3.
87. Daniel E. Innis and H. Rao Unnava, "The Usefulness of Product Warranties for Reputable and New Brands," in Holman and Solomon, *Advances*, 317–322.
88. Blaise Bergiel and Christine Trosclair, "Instrumental Learning: Its Application to Consumer Satisfaction," *Journal of Consumer Marketing* 2 (Fall 1985), 23–28.

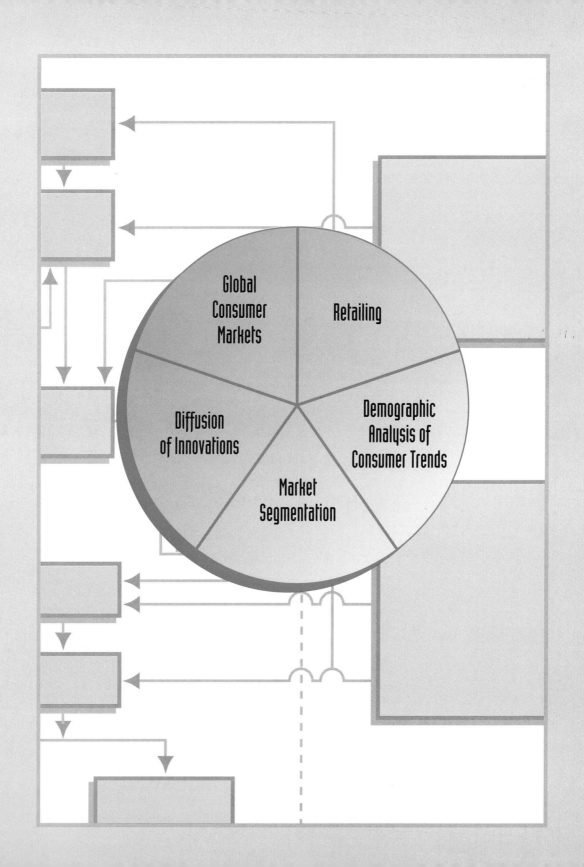

Global Consumer Markets

Retailing

Diffusion of Innovations

Demographic Analysis of Consumer Trends

Market Segmentation

Consumer Analysis and Marketing Strategy

W e now move from our model of consumer behavior and focus on the outcomes of proper research and strategic thinking. We have stressed outcomes at length, of course, in each chapter, and we have no intention of repetition here. Rather, we have chosen to highlight certain areas in which consumer research has special significance.

Chapter 18 opened the topic of consumer research as it is applied to distribution and retailing. There is much more to be said, however, about what has been learned regarding effective retailing and direct marketing strategies. This is the purpose of Chapter 19.

Chapter 20 then goes on to broaden our earlier discussion in Part 2 of demographic and psychographic analysis. It focuses on trends that are of greatest relevance. In a real sense, we enter the realms of *futurism*. But no one can avoid speculation on what will happen in the next decade.

Many other chapters have referred briefly to *market segmentation*. But we still must put this important phase of marketing analysis and strategic thinking into proper perspective. Chapter 21 summarizes and clarifies the earlier discussion and goes more deeply into this subject.

Up to now we have only referred occasionally to one area in which consumer research has had some of its greatest impact worldwide—*diffusion of innovations*. Thousands of published studies have led to a solid body of theory and practical applications. This important subject is reviewed in Chapter 22 from the perspective of new product strategy.

Finally, Chapter 23 refers to the issue of global and international marketing. You were given a thorough introduction to culture principles in Chapter 3, but this chapter builds on and expands on earlier discussion.

19

Retailing

In Mickey Drexler's idealized future, everybody would show up for work dressed as comfortably as he is now: soft leather shoes, rumpled khaki pants with pleats, and a wool sports coat. It is only natural Drexler would go casual. After all, he's president of The Gap, Inc., and these clothes are his business. At age 47, he has turned The Gap into the most popular and profitable specialty clothing chain in American retailing.

When other firms were stuck in recession and retailing retrenchment, sales at the Gap and its sibling stores, GapKids and Banana Republic, blasted up to $2.5 billion, an average earnings growth of 43 percent. The formula behind The Gap's rise is invoked by Drexler almost as a mantra: "Good style, good quality, good value."

That's good enough as far as it goes, but The Gap is a lot more than nice-looking T-shirts and denim jackets. It's a network of sites that have been shrewdly chosen by its founder. It's a carefully tended vision of a store that is a clean, well-lighted place where harried consumers can shop easily and quickly. It's a culture that fusses over the most mundane details, from cleaning store floors to rounding counter corners at GapKids stores for safety's sake. And it's a high tech distribution network that keeps 1,200 Gap stores constantly stocked with fresh merchandise. Buttressed by its acclaimed advertising, The Gap look is accepted equally by tots, teenagers, young adults, and graying baby boomers.

Source: Excerpted from Russell Mitchel, "The Gap," *Business Week* (March 9, 1992), 58–65.

Retailing: Ultimate Test of Consumer Research

In the last chapter, we examined the conceptual foundations of the purchase process—the final stage of decision making. This chapter "brings it home" with an applied analysis of the retailing environment. Here we examine questions such as: Where do consumers shop? Which stores do they choose? Which products and brands will be chosen as a result of in-store influences? How do the answers to these questions influence marketing strategy? How do consumers make decisions about retailers and retailing, and how is this related to the development of marketing strategy?

All of the material from preceding chapters is wasted unless consumer research can meet the ultimate test: Can retailers be persuaded to stock, price, service, and sell your product effectively? "Nothing happens of any value until someone sells something," the old adage states. And it's true. The best designed, produced, and advertised product is worthless unless retailers make it available to consumers in the format consumers are willing to buy.

Some retailers know how to do it all and do it right, as the opening scenario indicates. The Gap produces sales of over $2 billion with a return on equity averaging more than 25 percent over the past 10 years in its more than 1,000 stores, even during the tough recession years of the early 1990s. The Gap started out as a mostly jeans store with cluttered racks jammed with unrelated pants and shirts. Today, the Gap reflects the disciplined management that understands its customers and how to please them. The firm is absolutely fastidious about the style and quality of its merchandise and it doesn't play games with phony sales or messy stores. Would you be able to take control of a company and triple its sales and increase profits six-fold in just a few years? Mickey Drexler did.

The Gap is just one of many retailers who know how to win, even in the face of a tough environment and fierce competition. Others include The Limited, Wal-Mart, IKEA, Dillard's, Nordstrom, Home Depot, Circuit City, and the Disney Store. Have you ever noticed that when companies are successful, they attribute it to good management but when they are unsuccessful, they attribute it to problems beyond the control of management? In good times and in bad, in industries as diverse as discount stores, department stores, and specialty retailers, some win even when most lose. The purpose of this chapter is to help you sort out what it takes to win—that unique combination of understanding consumers and knowing how to delight them at the retail level.

The Power Struggle

A massive power struggle is occurring between manufacturers and retailers for access to consumers. Increasingly, retailers are winning.

The struggle for channel control is not new. Only the winner is new. The period in American history following the Revolutionary War was the era of the traders, the forerunners of today's wholesalers. The wealthy and powerful businesses were those that could seek manufacturers (mostly small, cottage industry) and match their goods with the small, decentralized retailers of the nation. In the era following the Civil War, the locus of power changed to large manufacturers, a condition that accelerated during the post–World War I era and continued until recently.

The emergence of massive mass merchants, often owned by a corporation with one or more billion-dollar chains, has put retailers in the driver's seat. Toys R Us recently announced that no manufacturer would be accepted as a supplier unless it conformed to the retailer's rules for packaging that, among other things, require information about what is inside the package on all four sides of the package. Why could the retailer dictate to the nation's largest toy manufacturers? Because Toys R Us accounts for 20 percent of the total market and is expected to double that market share during the 1990s.

When "power retailers" such as May, the Limited, or Wal-Mart speak, manufacturers and distributors listen. Mergers and acquisitions within retailing also cause the shift. May Department Stores once was a fairly small chain of regional stores but today is a $10 billion department chain with a return on equity of almost 22 percent in 1990. Its buyers are often described as the best in the business whether in the Lord & Taylor, May, or Payless Shoe divisions. The buyers know their customers well and buy in such volume that when they tell suppliers, "Change it" the suppliers do!

The concentration of volume among huge retail organizations is only part of the reason manufacturers are losing the power struggle to retailers. Among the best retail organizations, power is being concentrated internally as well. In the past, department organizations such as Federated, Macy's, and May were highly decentralized operations. Recent years have seen the development of centralized buying, national promotions, and sophisticated information and logistics systems that force manufacturers to conform to retailer requirements. Retailers such as The Gap and The Limited do more than just put their label on products. They control nearly every aspect of what manufacturers do from design through physical distribution, ending in advertising, merchandising, and in-store selling.

You might be thinking that manufacturers have such strong brands that retailers are dependent upon those brands. Certainly that used to be true. It is changing. No industry could be mentioned perhaps in which national brands dominate as much as soft drinks. Certainly a grocery store does not have much option but to stock Coca-Cola and Pepsi in large amounts. Or do they? Look at Consumer in Focus 19.1 and you will see that even with some of the best advertised brands in the world, retailers are beginning to grab some of the power for their own brands.

Retailing organizations such as May Department Stores aggressively recruit the brightest students from the nation's best business schools. Leading manufacturers have always done this. Retailers often were not competitive. But now when salespeople sit across from buyers and managers of the nation's best retailers, manufacturers are dealing with competent buyers backed with the power that arises from information systems and high-impact marketing programs to reach customers.

The Impact of Retailing on Your Career

The increasing power of retailers to impact consumers may interest you for two reasons. First, the most successful business persons are increasingly in the retailing

Retailer Brands Arise among Giants Coke and Pepsi

After decades of bruising battles with PepsiCo, Inc., Coca-Cola Co. is being distracted by a somewhat smaller rival: W POP.

A store-brand soft drink, W POP is now in New York stores belonging to Wegmans Food Markets Inc. Launched with TV spots, billboards, and store signs, W POP was walloping Coke and Pepsi, with a capital W. Today, the upstart W POP outsells both Coke and Pepsi in Wegmans stores. Coca-Cola formed a private-label task force in Atlanta to figure out how best to compete with a growing array of store-brand drinks.

Sales of store-brand sales are rising twice as fast as overall soda pop sales in supermarkets, according to Nielsen Marketing Research. The emergence of store brands is likely to affect pricing and product strategies at Coke and Pepsi more than ever before. And though store beverages normally thrive in recessions, they may now be building long-term staying power because of big improvements in taste and graphics, as well as increasingly powerful retailers and more value-conscious shoppers.

The cola giants insist publicly that private-label products are still a fairly small part of the $46 billion soft drink market. "This is an image business," adds Michael Weinstein, president of A & W Brands Inc., the rootbeer maker. "There's probably a limit to the number of people who want to walk around sipping a can of Wal-Mart cola."

But that hasn't stopped Wal-Mart Stores and other retailers—who think consumers are searching for greater value—from introducing their own colas. Sam's American Choice colas have red-and-white cans that resemble those of Coke and the message, "We believe these products . . . offer better value than the leading national brands." Even though store brands sell at an average discount of 35 percent compared to regular priced national brands, they are more profitable with margins of 30 percent compared to about 21 percent for Pepsi and Coke.

In Canada, Loblaw Co. grocery chain introduced its President's Choice cola in 1991 and boosted its cola market share in its 135 stores to more than 50 percent from around 10 percent. David Nichol, president of Loblaw's product-development division, says, "When there is no difference from a performance point of view, people aren't willing to pay the premium for Coke and Pepsi."

A Consumer Reports study recently found that store brands tasted just about as good as the Big Two. Private-label companies are betting that the cola leaders' traditional strengths—image and brand loyalty—are weakening amid price cutting and consumers' focus on value.

Source: Excerpted from Michael J. McCarthy, "Soft-Drink Giants Sit UP and Take Notice as Sales of Store Brands Show More Fizz," *Wall Street Journal* (March 6, 1992), B1ff.

sector rather than among manufacturing firms. The wealthiest person in the nation was once Sam Walton, founder of Wal-Mart, with personal assets of over $10 billion before his death. If discount retailing does not appeal to you, maybe you would enjoy specialty retailing as much as Les Wexner, Chairman of The Limited, who made the list of the top 5 billionaires, with assets of over $2 billion.

More importantly, retailing is involved in innovative, sophisticated marketing programs. A career with top retailing organizations offers, or requires, as much sophistication in understanding consumer behavior as does any manufacturing organization.

Another reason for studying consumer behavior at the retailing level is the importance of the retailer to promotional decisions of consumer goods manufacturers. Resources are being shifted from advertising to programs that are more retailing oriented. Leo Bogart, one of the nation's most respected advertising analysts, explains this shift:

> As companies expand into each other's traditional territories, the number of new brands and line extensions continues to grow, and competition intensifies for the limited amount of shelf and display space at the point of sale. Marketers' attention shifts from the struggle to influence the consumer to the primary battle to get products into the stores in the first place. Sheer presence and the visibility that can attract consumers count for a lot more than any amount of preconditioning through advertising. That is why a larger share of the marketing budget is going into promotion, much of it designed as a direct or indirect incentive to retailers to put the product where it can be bought. As the major retailers' market share expands, so does their power to dictate terms.[1]

The Retailing Revolution

A revolution began a few years ago and is exploding in the 1990s. The revolution is in retailing. Just as the Industrial Revolution dramatically affected the nature of manufacturing in the nineteenth century, so too the retailing revolution is affecting buying in the twentieth century. Retailers are pursuing innovations in effectiveness and productivity with aggressiveness and competitive fervor. Such competition requires more focus on how consumers buy.[2]

Two trends are especially dramatic. The first is the growth of the limited-line specialty store, which features narrow product lines but wide assortments. Hence, the service needs of customers can be met on a personalized basis. This is often tailored to specific lifestyle segments.

A second trend is the growth of mass merchandisers. They provide strong price appeal based on economies associated with self-service and operational efficiencies. They may also offer wide assortments to consumers. Caught in the middle are conventional outlets, which have increasing trouble competing and surviving.

The most successful firms in the retailing environment are increasingly building portfolios of retailing chains, each positioned to specific lifestyle segments. Companies such as Dayton-Hudson, Melville Co., Woolworth, and The Limited are examples of portfolio retailers.

The appeal of the specialty store is that everything it does is carefully tailored to meet a lifestyle segment with a unique product mix. Such stores achieve inventory

FIGURE 19.1 **Hypermarkets Provide Theater in Retailing**

turnover rates often twice those of conventional stores. Return on net worth follows suit. A good example is The Limited, which operates Limited stores in carefully selected locations throughout the nation, maintains an ongoing program of consumer research to determine product and store criteria used by its market segments, and creates an exciting in-store atmosphere for presentation of high-fashion merchandise in a portfolio of over 4,200 Limited and other specialty stores, including Structures, Abercrombie & Fitch, Cacique, and Bath & Body Works.

At the other end of the spectrum are the mass merchandisers. These include discount department stores such as Wal-Mart, one of the most successful retailers in the United States. Another successful example is Target, a division of Dayton-Hudson, which also operates major department stores. A number of newer forms are also emerging: Price Club and warehouse stores such as Cub, Biggs, Sam's Warehouse, and supermarkets for commodities other than foods (examples are Toys R Us, Standard Brands Paint, and Herman's World of Sporting Goods).

The most dramatic and innovative of mass-merchandising forms is the **hypermarket**. These are stores in the 60,000- to 200,000-square-foot range that carry both convenience and shopping goods, with a heavy emphasis on general merchan-

FIGURE 19.1   **continued**

dise as well as on food. They have incorporated breakthrough technology in materials handling in a warehouse operating profile that provides both a warehouse feel for consumers as well as strong price appeal.

The hypermarket has been most successful in countries other than the United States. Carrefour in France and Cara in Benelux are examples of hypermarkets which employ massive amounts of merchandise, total store graphics (graphics coordinated throughout the store), and classification dominance, all of which create excitement and price appeal. Hypermarkets also take advantage of operating economies involved in the technology of palletized product display and storage and the latest in scanning equipment at the cash registers. The largest single supermarket in the world is probably Pick 'n Pay, in a suburb of Johannesburg selling as much as R2–3 million (about $1 million in U.S. currency) in a single day![3]

In Figure 19.1 you can see some of elements of hypermarkets that cause them to be destination stores for consumers. Classification, dominance, and disciplined merchandise is a characteristic of the best. Pick 'n Pay has its own line of products that reflect graphics and packaging, sensitivity to environmental trends and value that are highly attractive to consumers. Unfortunately, photos cannot capture the full excitement created by the best of the hypermarkets. Their size and scope of activities illustrate the principle that great retailers provide theater for consumers.

These innovations underscore the rapidity of change in consumer purchasing and the consequent need for retailers to have a keen understanding of consumer research issues. How do consumers choose stores in which to shop? How important is location? How important is a store's image in determining store patronage? What factors determine image? What can be done to build store loyalty and to reduce shopper switching? We discuss these topics in the remaining pages of this chapter.

Where Will Consumers Shop?

Answering the questions about where consumers will shop involves several issues. How far will they travel to a retail location? Will they prefer regional shopping malls, neighborhood strip centers, or downtown shopping areas? After answering these questions, we can address the issue of which stores they will choose within acceptable categories. The strengths of individual stores will also influence consumer decisions about which shopping center may be chosen.

Number of Locations

Location strategies of retailers are one of the most important determinants of consumer behavior. More consumers buy fast food from McDonald's than any other organization, partially because McDonald's has two or three times more stores than its closest competitors. Attitude research may indicate consumers prefer Wendy's or taste tests may indicate consumers prefer Burger King's Whopper, but McDonald's, with over 12,000 stores, sells twice as much as the combined sales of both of its rivals. McDonald's opened 691 new stores in 1991 making it pretty difficult to find a place in the United States (and many other countries) where consumers are not close to a McDonald's.

Retailers with too few or too many stores often fail. So do retailers that locate on the wrong street, in the wrong shopping center, in the wrong city, or have the wrong parking spaces. An old adage says the three most important variables associated with retail success are: location, location, and location.

Retailer Strategies

Three levels of location decisions face marketing strategists: market selection, area analysis, and site evaluation. This process is shown in Figure 19.2. Understanding how consumers decide where to buy is a critical input in each of these levels. Retailers need a clear understanding of the **value platform** of the firm—the manner in which the firm differentiates itself from its competitors in the minds of the con-

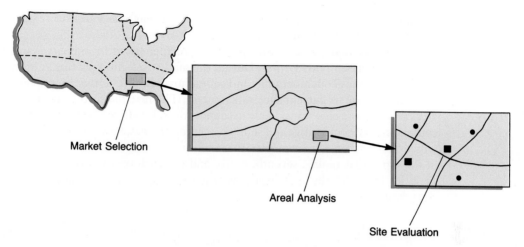

Market Selection

Areal Analysis

Site Evaluation

FIGURE 19.2   Three Levels of Spatial Analysis in Selecting Retail Locations

Source: Reprinted by permission of the publisher from *Location Strategies for Retail and Service Firms* by Avijit Ghosh and Sara L. McLafferty (Lexington, Mass.: Lexington Books, D. C. Heath and Company, 1987, 34, Copyright 1987; D. C. Heath and Company).

sumers it intends to serve, allowing it to achieve a sustainable differential advantage over competitors.[4] The marketing strategy of a firm is then developed to select the quantity and specific locations of retail facilities.

A strategic approach relates location issues to the overall marketing plan of the firm. Management Horizons, a division of Price Waterhouse, analyzed this process and formulated the following criteria for location decisions. Management Horizons concluded that location decisions for retailers and suppliers should be

1. Broad-based—incorporating the exploration of new markets, the penetration of existing markets, and other long-term growth issues.
2. Proactive—helping to meet long-term corporate goals.
3. On-going—occurring at all levels of the strategic planning process, from the development of corporate objectives to the monitoring of store location performance.
4. Consumer-oriented—based on a thorough knowledge of the target market population, including its desire for convenience in time and space.
5. Whole-market—maximizing market coverage within a market.
6. Functionally integrated—providing input for merchandising, customer communications, and especially market share management.[5]

In Figure 19.2, the process of spatial analysis appears sequential. First, markets are selected, then areas within those markets, and finally specific sites. In actual practice, the process is interactive. Site selection may affect market selection as much as the converse.

As an example, a successful computer retailer based in one city wanted to expand its success to other cities. During the market selection process, it identified 15 cities with the geodemographic and competitive conditions that corresponded to the conditions of its current successful market. The firm did further analysis of the areas within those cities most likely to support the sales of personal computers. After completing the competitive and shopping center analysis, however, some cities contained much more attractive sites than did others. The final selection was made in the cities that ranked seventh, tenth, and eleventh on the original ranking of 15 cities but were the best locations when specific sites and competitors were considered.

Cities and Trading Areas

The marketing literature has a stream of studies attempting to explain the impact of the location of a town, city, or trading area. Foundational work by William J. Reilly postulated that two cities attract retail trade from an intermediate town in the vicinity of the **breaking point** (where 50 percent of the trade is attracted to each city) in direct proportion to their population and in inverse proportion to the square of the distance from the two cities to the intermediate town.[6]

These early models were useful but simplistic. They ignored relative incomes of the populations, merchandise assortments in the two cities, and consumer preferences. More recent research by Huff, Applebaum, Nakanishi, and Cooper and others incorporated other variables.[7] **Product category** also influences how far people will travel. Consumers will travel farther for clothing than for household goods or products they feel need service locally.

What kind of person is the outshopper (one who shops outside a local trading area)? Today entire malls of stores containing factory outlet stores are located miles from major cities and attract consumers from distant points. Socioeconomic status appears to be a big factor as the "value oriented" malls actually attract people who are more affluent, better educated, and more experienced as shoppers. Socioeconomic status also helps explain the tendency of ghetto residents to shop in their neighborhood.[8]

Outshoppers also have these psychographic characteristics:

1. They are significantly more exposed to nonlocal media and exhibit greater knowledge of the outside world.
2. They are more innovative, fashion conscious, gregarious, and socially active.
3. They invest a great deal of time and effort in shopping and consult all relevant sources of information to a greater extent than their counterparts do.
4. They are more mobile and more cosmopolitan in their outlook.[9]

Marketers can attract shoppers away from their neighborhood or local town by using regional media and offering strong variety of both product lines and shopping options, especially with unique specialty stores.

Shopping Centers

The shopping center selected by consumers is influenced by travel time and the size of shopping facility. The foundational research on this topic was conducted by Huff. Huff's model estimates the probability that consumers in each relatively homogeneous statistical unit (neighborhood) will go to a particular shopping center for a particular type of purchase.[10]

The willingness to go to a shopping center declines as driving time to the center increases. Bruner and Mason found 15 minutes to be the maximum for approximately 75 percent of a center's patrons.[11] Other studies indicate wider variation depending on area of the country, normal traffic conditions, and other factors.

Cognitive Mapping

Cognitive maps or consumer perceptions of store locations and shopping areas are more important than actual location.[12] Cognitive maps refer both to cognized distances and cognized traveling times. Consumers generally overestimate both functional (actual) distance and functional time.

Variations between cognitive and actual distance are related to factors such as ease of parking in the area, quality of merchandise offered by area stores, and display and presentation of merchandise by stores and ease of driving to an area. Other factors affecting the cognitive maps of consumers include price of merchandise and helpfulness of salespeople.[13]

Individual Site Location

Where people shop is influenced by very specific details of the retail site. For example, two restaurants may have similar offerings but the selection of a site a block or so away from the main artery may cause as much as 10 to 20 percent variation in sales between the otherwise identical restaurants. Retailers sometimes fail because they succumb to a short-term strategy of leasing cheaper space, with the consequence of long-term reduced profitability.

Site Location Studies

What variables affect consumer decisions about location and should therefore be considered in selecting a retail site? Some of the more important components of a site evaluation include the following items:[14]

1. Site description (size, shape, etc.)
2. Lease requirements/land costs
3. Parking ratio
4. Pedestrian flow
5. Traffic flow (numbers and average speed)
6. Egress/Ingress
7. Public transportation access
8. Visibility, signage, ambience

9. Affinities (neighbors)
10. Access to trade area

Computer Analysis Site location studies are usually done with a computer. A ring around the site is drawn at a distance of 1.5 miles, 3 miles, or 5 miles. A refinement of this process is to compute the circles on the basis of 5, 10, or 20 minutes driving time to the store. An example of such an analysis is shown in Figure 19.3. The market within 1.5 miles of a proposed site at Santa Monica Boulevard and Wilshire in Beverly Hills is shown in this analysis, a computer printout by Urban Decision Systems. Note that Figure 19.3 shows the data (population, households, ethnic background, and so on) for both the primary area (1.5-mile ring) and the market

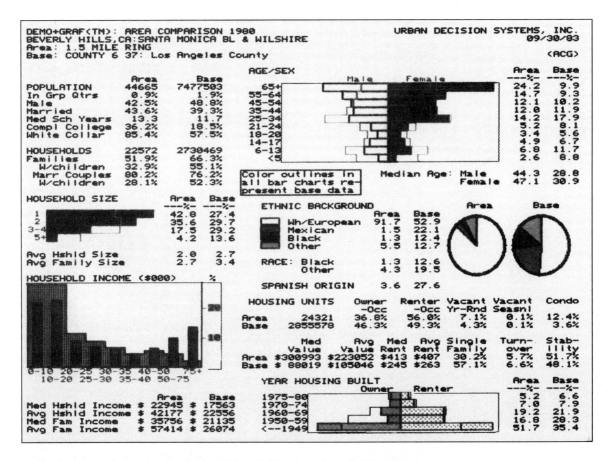

FIGURE 19.3 **Computer Analysis of Retail Site Based on Driving Time**

Source: Urban Decision Systems, Inc., Los Angeles, California.

base (Los Angeles County). Discriminant analysis or multiple regression models can be used to assess the probability of success in a specific site.

Density

An important variable in site location is density of population. Demand may seem to be high because of income, ethnic characteristics, family size, or other variables. Lack of density negates many of these effects.

An example of the density problem can be seen in the case of the restaurant chain Max & Erma's. The firm has a varied menu but its specialty is gourmet hamburgers. They are large, very tasty, and served in a fun atmosphere that appeals to young, upscale, well-educated consumers. The restaurant chain opened a restaurant in Johnson County, Kansas (a suburb of Kansas City) because the market analysis showed that market area to have one of the highest incomes in the Midwest, with households that are young and well educated. The market profile seemed ideal for the restaurant's consumer profile, but Max & Erma's failed to consider that the area was so upscale that there were few houses per square mile. Density was too low, and the location was eventually closed. The firm learned that even though the product is excellent, consumer attitudes are favorable, service is good, and the socioeconomic profile of the market is excellent, a retailer still fails when the market area lacks the density required for success.

Regional Density

On a regional basis, retailing organizations sometimes fail by choosing regions with low density. Sun Belt markets may be growing rapidly but lack density. The best retailing sites may still be east of the Mississippi because 60 percent of retail sales are transacted in the 29 percent of continental land area east of the Mississippi. The top states in population density are New Jersey, Rhode Island, Massachusetts, Connecticut, Maryland, New York, Delaware, Pennsylvania, Ohio, Illinois, Michigan, Indiana, and the District of Columbia. It was not until recently that a Sun Belt state, Florida, even came close to matching the population densities of the top states. After analyzing these data, Cooke concluded, "In spite of ongoing population shifts to the South and West, the best retail markets are still located in the North and East, and will be for years to come."[15]

Microspecialization

Retail location decisions are increasingly made through **microspecialization**—identification of specific market targets and development of specialized retailing formats that provide a high level of satisfaction to those market targets. With microspecialization, marketing organizations can access data on-line by networking their own computer with private firms specializing in data bases specific enough to be useful to retailers. A list of some of these firms is displayed in Figure 19.4 with the geographical areas for which data can be accessed, the coverage of variables, and other features. Marketing analysts can obtain instant access to some of these data bases through networking services such as CompuServe. Any market analyst with a personal computer, a modem, and an account can find the data with which to make retail location decisions instantly at any time of the day or night.

Legend:

□ Diaries are kept by cross section of the population.

▷ Includes sales reports from 20 different types of bullets including sales potential.

▶ Includes information on ten major U.S. markets.

○ U.S. household with incomes in the top 10%.

	VISION	UPPER DECK—THE AFFLUENT	TARGETSCAN	SUPERSITE	PRIZM	ONSITE	NPA/DEMOGRAPHIC	MRI-MEDIAMARKETS	MAX	MARKETPOTENTIAL	GRAPHIC PROFILE	CENSUS REPORTING PROGRAM	CENDATA	ARBITRON RADIO & TV	AMERICAN PROFILE	ACORN
SOURCES OF INFORMATION																
Census Data 1980	●		●	●	●	●		●		●	●	●	●		●	●
Census Data 1970			●		●	●		●					●		●	●
Demographic Reports				●				●						●	●	●
Projections/Estimates	●	●	●	●	●	●	●	●	●		●		●		●	●
Consumer Price Index				●	●				●	●						
Census of Retail Trade				●	●				●	●						
DATBASE COVERAGE																
Total population	●	○		●	●	●	●	▶	●	▷		●	□		●	●
Number of size of households	●	●		●	●	●	●	●	●			●	●	●	●	●
Median income	●			●	●	●			●			●	●	●	●	●
Race, Age, Sex	●	●		●	●	●	●	●	●			●	●	●	●	●
Level of Education	●	●		●	●	●			●	●		●	●	●	●	●
Housing Value	●	●		●	●	●			●	●		●	●	●	●	●
SPECIAL FEATURES																
Geo-demographics	●	●		●										●		●
Mapping software	●			●	●					●		●				
Mailing label production	●			●	●											
INFORMATION ACCESSED BY																
Zip Code	●		●	●	●	●			●	●			□		●	●
Counties	●		●	●	●	●	●	●	●	●					●	●
Census tracts			●	●	●						●	●	●	●		●
Entire U.S.	●	●	●	●							●	●	●		●	●
ADI									●		●	●		●	●	●
Geometric shapes				●	●	●										●
UPDATED																
Annually		●	●	●		●	●	●	●	●	●	●			●	●
Daily														●		

FIGURE 19.4   Profiles of On-Line Demographic Data Base for Retailers and Other Marketing Organizations

Source: "Tiny Targets: Pinpointing the Possibilities on Online Demographic Research," *Online Access* 2 (November/December 1987), 29 and 44.

The Competitive Battle between Shopping Areas

A war is raging to decide which shopping area consumers will choose. The major competitors include regional shopping malls, neighborhood strip centers, or CBD (downtown Central Business Districts) shopping centers. Currently, regional malls are under heavy attack. A "flanking action" by some retailers is to locate stores in freestanding locations, usually near regional shopping malls. Innovative hybrids also arise such as "power centers" combining the convenience of neighborhood centers and the selection and attractiveness (although smaller) of regional malls.

The Malling of America

Regional shopping malls have progressed dramatically since J. C. Nichols built the first one, Country Club Plaza, in Kansas City in 1922. That original shopping center is shown in Figure 19.5. Today it has changed so much that the Plaza is still one of the most exciting collections of upscale retailers in the nation. The ultimate progression of the original shopping center is shown in the remaining portion of Figure 19.5, West Edmonton Mall in Edmonton, Alberta, Canada.

The West Edmonton Mall is generally recognized as the largest in the world and was the first mega-mall, with 5.2 million square feet and 800 stores and services. One of the features is a 5-acre World Waterpark, the largest indoor waterpark in the world, shown in Figure 19.5. Other features include 19 movie theaters, a hotel, 110 food outlets, dozens of amusement rides, an ice rink, a miniature golf course, a chapel, a car dealership, and a zoo. Consumers arrive not only from nearby to shop; they arrive from all over North America to shop and play for a few days. West Edmonton Mall is a "destination shopping center." A somewhat similar mega-mall opened in 1992 in suburban Minneapolis, as "The Mall of America."

The Mall of America occupies a 78-acre site in suburban Minneapolis and is designed for 400 retail stores. Four major anchors include Bloomingdale's; Macy's; Nordstrom's; and Sears, Roebuck and Co. The 4.2 million-square-foot mall includes an 18-hole miniature golf course; a 14-unit theater; 13 restaurants; and Camp Snoopy, an amusement park operated by Knott's Berry Farm.[16]

There are over 28,500 shopping centers in America, compared to only 2,000 in 1957. This has produced a serious overbuilding problem. Between 1974 and 1984, the retail footage increased 80 percent while population increased only 12 percent. As a consequence, very few regional malls are being built today in sharp contrast with an average of 14 per year in the early 1980s and a high of 30 per year in the mid-1970s. Most of the new shopping centers are smaller and are sometimes called "mini-malls."

The competitive reality is that shopping centers are working as hard to attract consumers from other centers as are individual retailers competing with each other. The result is more emphasis on marketing. Southdale Center was opened in 1956 in suburban Minneapolis, described as the first enclosed mall. Today, not only has it

FIGURE 19.5   The Evolution of Shopping Malls from the Original Idea to the Newest Mega-Mall

Source: The Evolution of Regional Shopping Centers (Atlanta: Equitable Real Estate Investment Management Inc., 1987). Courtesy of J. C. Nichols Company.

been remodelled but it has a yearly marketing budget of about $424,000, with about 75 to 80 percent devoted to advertising and public relations.[17]

What can regional malls do to attract consumers? Many are adding the entertainment, merchandise, food, and ambience required to be competitive since regional malls became the "Main Street of America."

Mini-Malls and Strip Centers

The fastest growing shopping areas are small- and medium-sized centers of various formats, usually with less than 100,000 square feet. Some "strip" centers are still being built, containing mostly mom-and-pop stores. Some are neighborhood shopping centers with a variety of convenience merchandise stores accompanied also by substantial traffic flow problems, with concerns of the effects on neighboring residential areas. They emerged to serve homemakers who need basic items from the grocery store, dry cleaner and drugstore. Most are street oriented, pedestrian, and car friendly and account for 87 percent of all shopping malls and 51 percent of total shopping center retail sales in 1990.

FIGURE 19.5   continued
Courtesy of West Edmonton Mall.

Most were not designed to be architecturally "important" but a few of these are well planned and designed, sometimes in an enclosed or all-weather format, and are called **mini-malls** or **power malls**. Many older shopping centers have been "reformatted" by enclosing them and giving them a more contemporary appearance. Some have recaptured or maintained consumer patronage because of convenient location and density of population in the surrounding neighborhood.

Consumers for mini-malls and strip centers differ from others. Eighty-nine percent of adult Americans shop in these malls and 24 percent of Americans shop only at small shopping centers compared with just 5 percent who shop only at large regional centers. Small mall shoppers are more likely to be women, to have children, to be married, and to be homemakers. They usually have a specific purpose in mind. They are more likely to see shopping as a chore rather than a leisure activity as are the regional mall shoppers.[18]

Stores typically found in mini-malls or power strips include Blockbuster Video, Circuit City, and Pier One, or one of Mickey Drexler's Gaps or Banana Republics. Stores in strip malls have an edge over regional malls; stores in smaller malls have more opportunity to build relationships with individual consumers

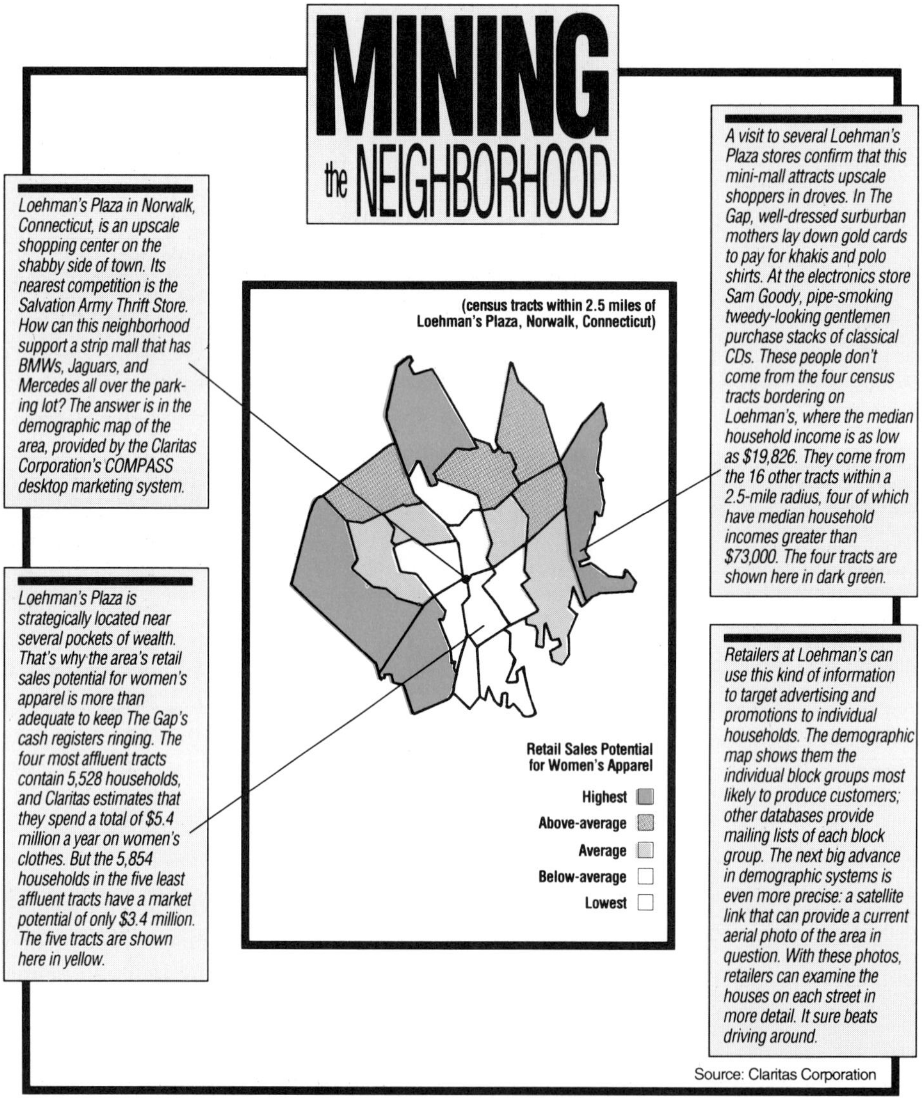
MINING the NEIGHBORHOOD
Loehman's Plaza in Norwalk, Connecticut, is an upscale shopping center on the shabby side of town. Its nearest competition is the Salvation Army Thrift Store. How can this neighborhood support a strip mall that has BMWs, Jaguars, and Mercedes all over the parking lot? The answer is in the demographic map of the area, provided by the Claritas Corporation's COMPASS desktop marketing system.
Loehman's Plaza is strategically located near several pockets of wealth. That's why the area's retail sales potential for women's apparel is more than adequate to keep The Gap's cash registers ringing. The four most affluent tracts contain 5,528 households, and Claritas estimates that they spend a total of $5.4 million a year on women's clothes. But the 5,854 households in the five least affluent tracts have a market potential of only $3.4 million. The five tracts are shown here in yellow.
(census tracts within 2.5 miles of Loehman's Plaza, Norwalk, Connecticut)
Retail Sales Potential for Women's Apparel
Highest
Above-average
Average
Below-average
Lowest
A visit to several Loehman's Plaza stores confirm that this mini-mall attracts upscale shoppers in droves. In The Gap, well-dressed surburban mothers lay down gold cards to pay for khakis and polo shirts. At the electronics store Sam Goody, pipe-smoking tweedy-looking gentlemen purchase stacks of classical CDs. These people don't come from the four census tracts bordering on Loehman's, where the median household income is as low as $19,826. They come from the 16 other tracts within a 2.5-mile radius, four of which have median household incomes greater than $73,000. The four tracts are shown here in dark green.
Retailers at Loehman's can use this kind of information to target advertising and promotions to individual households. The demographic map shows them the individual block groups most likely to produce customers; other databases provide mailing lists of each block group. The next big advance in demographic systems is even more precise: a satellite link that can provide a current aerial photo of the area in question. With these photos, retailers can examine the houses on each street in more detail. It sure beats driving around.
Source: Claritas Corporation

FIGURE 19.6 Mining the Neighborhood

Source: Chip Walker, "Strip Malls: Plain But Powerful," *American Demographics* 13 (October 1991), 48–52.

rather than relying on price or selection. Point-of-sale technology allows such stores to keep track of what's hot and what's not in their neighborhood. Combined with survey research, these stores can have a clear idea of exactly who their customer is and what he or she wants. Figure 19.6 shows how one of these, Loehman's Plaza in Norwalk, Connecticut, succeeds with careful analysis of its market.

Downtown Is Fun

The "big idea" of recent years has been the "festival marketplace." Of course, cities have always had markets and some specialized retail areas. The concept of recycling old buildings into a complex of shops and restaurants on a major scale was first done in the mid-1960s in Ghiradelli Square and the Cannery in San Francisco. However, it was James Rouse who fully conceptualized and implemented the festival marketplace concept with the development of Faneuil Hall Marketplace in Boston in 1976.

Other festival marketplaces and retail complexes already developed include Harborplace in Baltimore, the South Street Seaport in New York City, the Union Station project in St. Louis, the Waterside in Norfolk, Portside in Toledo, the 6th Street Marketplace in Richmond, and the Old Post Office in Washington, D.C. Almost every large city now has or is developing a marketplace.

While hugely successful as retail centers, the festival marketplaces have had a much more important role in creating new civic gathering places and in dramatically changing the image of American cities. A 1981 *Time* magazine cover story on James Rouse declared, "Cities Are Fun!"—a statement almost unthinkable in the atmosphere of the 1960s. The nurturing of this new spirit of fun and vitality at the core of cities has been a major factor in the resurgence of the American downtown in the past decade.

The success of the festival marketplace has spurred new interest in downtown retailing, which had been dormant or declining in most cities since the 1960s. Today, major retail complexes have been completed or are under construction in many cities, including development of new department stores. In many cases, the retail complexes connect existing stores. The Rouse Company has also been a pioneer in this movement, with the Gallery in Philadelphia, Grand Avenue Concourse in Milwaukee, The Shops in Washington, and the new Gallery at Harborplace in Baltimore.

Source: John Fondersmith, "Downtown 2040: Making Cities Fun," *Futurist* 22 (March–April 1988), 9–17.

CBD Centers

A major question about where consumers will shop is whether or not they will return downtown—to the **Central Business District** (CBD). There are many efforts to revitalize the downtown area as a place to shop as well as a place to work. Consumer in Focus 19.2 shows how "festival marketplaces" can be used to get people

JVJ'S GALLERIA AT ERIEVIEW.

Downtown Dazzles Again. If you haven't seen Cleveland lately, you haven't seen it. There's a bold and optimistic new spirit that's personified in Jacobs, Visconsi & Jacobs Co.'s Galleria at Erieview. Almost overnight, city shopping, dining, and entertainment have taken on a whole new light.
...And The Light Keeps Getting Brighter. The Galleria is redefining not only downtown Cleveland, but what retailers can expect from urban shopping centers. And the results have been excellent. Clevelanders are shopping downtown again — even at night and on weekends — producing record-breaking results for Galleria shops and restaurants.

The brave new energy that built the Galleria is the driving force behind Jacobs, Visconsi & Jacobs Co. In its own hometown, JVJ has achieved the reputation as *the* company that gets things done. And it's the standard that JVJ brings to every one of its developments across the country.

JACOBS, VISCONSI & JACOBS CO.
25425 Center Ridge Road
Cleveland, Ohio 44145 • 216/871-4800

FIGURE 19.7   **The Downtown Shopping Center Makes a Comeback**

Source: Courtesy of Jacobs, Visconsi, & Jacobs Co., Cleveland, Ohio.

shopping downtown again. Figure 19.7, an ad for a shopping center developer, shows what CBD shopping centers are doing to attract people back downtown.

The consumer has many places to shop—downtown, neighborhood malls, regional shopping centers, even in other towns. Retailers have many decisions to make in responding to these choices—regarding markets, areas, and specific sites. Now we move from these decisions to how consumers choose specific retailers.

How Consumers Choose Specific Retailers

Consumer decisions to buy a product, brand, or from a specific retailer are closely related. The sequence of decisions is often thought to be product category, brand, store, but this is not always true. Sometimes consumers simply go shopping with no specific product or brand in mind. This may reflect a desire to get out of the house, to window shop, or to spend leisure time with the family. Whether the product or the retailer is foremost in consumers' minds, how people decide to enter specific stores and what they do in those stores is of enormous consequence in analyzing consumer behavior.

Consumers shop for both personal and social motives. These motives are described in Table 19.1. Examination of these motives indicates many things retailers can do to attract consumers. Consider, for example, the motive of "Sensory Stimulation" described in Table 19.1. Successful grocery stores place a bakery near the front of the store, greeting people with the aroma of fresh-baked products. The Limited has been a leader in attracting consumers with an array of visual and auditory stimuli in The Limited and Limited Express stores. An addition to the sensory array is found in Victoria's Secret, where attractive scents whiff through the store, enhancing the appeal of entering and lingering in the store.

The Store-Choice Decision Process

Choosing a store is a process of interaction between retailers' marketing strategies and individual and situational characteristics of buyers. This process is described by Monroe and Guiltinan.[19] Store choice is similar to the general model of decision making used throughout this book.

Individual characteristics (such as lifestyles) cause general outlooks on and activities involved in shopping and search behavior. Retailers influence these activities with advertising and promotional strategies. Buyer characteristics also affect store image. Store image, in turn, affects store choice and the eventual product or brand purchase. If past experiences have been satisfactory, the choice will be fairly habitual, unless other factors have changed since the last visit.

Shopper Profiles

Store choice is affected by specific characteristics of buyers. Thus, some stores have customers with a particular profile while other stores attract differing shopper profiles. Demographics and psychographics are useful in describing shopper profiles. The Limited has many stores but the shopper profile of The Limited shopper is different from that of the Express shopper or the Lane Bryant or Lerner shopper. Similarly, the Structures shopper is different from the Abercrombie and Fitch shopper. While all stores are owned by the same company, managed by the same types of people, served mostly by the same distribution system, and have very similar financial objectives, each chain varies greatly by shopper profile.

Demographic Profiles   Retailers are most successful when they appeal to specific market segments. When stores understand the profile of their core customers with demographic variables such as age, income, and place of residence, the outlet can maximize its appeal through its product and service mix.[20] The Limited makes a strong appeal to women 25 to 40. The parent corporation targets younger women with Express and slightly older women with its Lane Bryant chain.

Geography is also important. In a study of grocery shopping for coffee, Winn and Childers found geographic regions and central city size as important correlates explaining shopping concentrations. Also important were social status variables

TABLE 19.1 Why Do People Shop?

Personal Motives

Role Playing
Many activities are learned behaviors, traditionally expected or accepted as part of a certain position or role in society—mother, housewife, husband, or student.

Diversion
Shopping can offer an opportunity for diversion from the routine of daily life and thus represents a form of recreation.

Self-Gratification
Different emotional states or moods may be relevant for explaining why (and when) someone goes shopping. Some people report that often they alleviate depression by simply spending money on themselves. In this case, the shopping trip is motivated not by the expected utility of consuming, but by the utility of the buying *process* itself.

Learning about New Trends
Products are intimately entwined in one's daily activities and often serve as symbols reflecting attitudes and life-styles. An individual learns about trends and movements and the symbols that support them when the individual visits a store.

Physical Activity
Shopping can provide people with a considerable amount of exercise at a leisurely pace, appealing to people living in an urban environment. Some shoppers apparently welcome the chance to walk in centers and malls.

Sensory Stimulation
Retail institutions provide many potential sensory benefits for shoppers. Customers browse through a store looking at the merchandise and at each other; they enjoy handling the merchandise, the sounds of background music, the scents of perfume counters or prepared food outlets.

Continued

Source: Excerpted from Edward M. Tauber, "Why Do People Shop?" *Journal of Marketing* 36 (October 1972), 46–59. Reprinted from the *Journal of Marketing* published by the American Marketing Association.

such as income, education, and occupation.[21] The on-line data sources described in Figure 19.4 can be used to profile customers whose addresses are known to the store. Other demographic variables such as race are correlated with type of store shopped, days of the week that shopping occurs, and degree of shopping activity.[22] Even religion has been found to have relevance in predicting purchase of certain types of furniture.[23]

Demographics and socioeconomic variables are also correlated with the amount of purchasing activity that consumers will undertake. A scale developed by Slama and Taschian measures purchasing involvement. It includes Likert-type statements such as, "It is part of my value system to shop around for the best buy," and "Being a smart shopper is worth the extra time it takes." Building on prior research investigating consumer involvement and search activity by Kassarjian and other researchers, Slama and Taschian found that the consumers most likely to be involved in purchasing activity (including search activities beyond the retailing environment) are women who have children, moderate incomes, and relatively high educations.[24]

TABLE 19.1   continued

Social Motives

Social Experiences Outside the Home
The marketplace has traditionally been a center of social activity and many parts of the United States and other countries still have market days, country fairs, and town squares that offer a time and place for social interaction. Shopping trips may result in direct encounters with friends (e.g., neighborhood women at a supermarket) and other social contact.

Communications with Others Having a Similar Interest
Stores that offer hobby-related goods or products and services such as boating, collecting stamps, car customizing, and home decorating provide an opportunity to talk with others about their interests and with sales personnel who provide special information concerning the activity.

Peer Group Attraction
The patronage of a store sometimes reflects a desire to be with one's peer group or a reference group to which one aspires to belong. For instance, record stores may provide a meeting place where members of a peer group may gather.

Status and Authority
Many shopping experiences provide the opportunity for an individual to command attention and respect or to be waited on without having to pay for this service. A person can attain a feeling of status and power in this limited master-servant relationship.

Pleasure of Bargaining
Many shoppers appear to enjoy the process of bargaining or haggling, believing that with bargaining, goods can be reduced to a more reasonable price. An individual prides himself in his ability to make wise purchases or to obtain bargains.

Psychographic Profiles   Psychographics allow retailers to profile the lifestyles of heavy users. Microspecialization, adapting the formats of retailing to specific market targets, is done by adapting the product and service mix of the store to the activities, interests, and opinions of customer groups. Observe the appeal in Consumer in Focus 19.3 to women who wear petite sizes.

Retail Image

Patronage is determined both by evaluative criteria of consumers and their perception of store attributes. The overall perception is referred to as **store image**. This concept has been defined in various ways,[25] but no one has improved much on Martineau's idea of store personality as "the way in which a store is defined in the shopper's mind, partly by its functional qualities and partly by an aura of psychological attributes."[26] Since image is the reality upon which consumers rely when making choices, image measurement is an essential tool for consumer analysts.

Petite Fashion Retailers

Fifty million American women are 5 feet 4 inches tall or under in sizes 2 to 12. Petite fashions cater to these shorter shoppers.

In 1983, The United States Shoe Corporation of Enfield, CT added the chain to its divisions: Casual Corner, Ups N'Downs, Caren Charles, August Max, Cabaret and Sophisticated Woman. To date, there are 160 Petite Sophisticate stores in most of the 50 states, with plans to open 10 to 15 this year. A long-term goal is to have 400 units by the early 1990s.

Says Skurow, "No one understands or knows how to dress the petite woman better than we do. Now we're going to use that expertise to offer great fashion to the 50 million American women who look to us as the authority on petites." According to the company, 50 million women translate into 54 percent of the American female population, aged 18 and over, in the 5 feet 4 inches or under category.

Skurow says the company looks at the demographics of the mall when deciding on locations for the 1,500-square-foot to 4,000-square-foot stores. "Ninety-five percent are in regional malls," he says.

The stores carry career separates, dresses, suits, coats, evening clothes, and active and leisure wear. Prices range from moderate to designer. "Most of the major designers have a petite line today," says Skurow. "There are more vendors and a broader selection now."

That broader selection is what some shoppers enjoy about the stores. Petite Sophisticate offers Club 5'4", PS Sport, Petite Sophisticate and Lauren Cole as private labels, in addition to the name brand and designer lines.

Selection, coupled with service, fashion and fit are hallmarks of the chain. "There are so many factors that lead to success, I can't pinpoint one," Skurow says. Fit includes scaling down the clothes to proportion, by adjusting waistlines, hemlines, sleeve lengths and pant rises. Also, the details are appropriately sized by narrowing lapels, reducing pocket size and shortening cuff depth.

Source: Jane A. Black, "Focus on Retailing," *Monitor* 18 (May 1988), 94 and 111.

Retail Image Measurement   Retail image is measured across a number of dimensions reflecting salient attributes. Not surprisingly, almost the entire gamut of attitude-research methods is used, including semantic differential,[27] customer prototypes,[28] the Q-sort,[29] the Guttman scale,[30] multidimensional scaling,[31] and psycholinguistics.[32]

Attitude-measurement techniques you learned in Chapter 11 are equally applicable for retail measurement. A multiattribute approach is appropriate for

TABLE 19.2   Belief and Importance Scores for Retail Stores

Attribute	Importance Scores	Store A	Store B	Store C	Store D	Store E	Store F	Store G	Store H
Price	6.13	3.71	3.91	4.48	5.14	3.93	4.11	3.92	4.06
Assortment	6.11	4.79	4.56	4.21	4.68	4.33	4.23	4.39	4.46
Personnel	5.15	4.70	4.56	4.31	4.40	4.39	4.34	4.34	4.43
Atmosphere	4.84	4.86	4.64	4.24	4.56	4.50	4.35	4.42	4.53
Service	5.63	4.89	4.67	4.23	4.47	4.62	4.47	4.49	4.50
Quality	6.37	5.15	5.02	3.97	4.35	4.80	4.65	4.71	4.69

Source: Don L. James, Richard M. Durand, and Robert A. Dreves, "The Use of a Multi-Attribute Attribute Model in a Store Image Study," *Journal of Retailing* 52 (Summer 1976), 23–32. Reprinted by permission.

retailing applications.[33] Many retailers develop their own proprietary image-measurement techniques.

An example of a multiattribute approach in retailing is presented in Table 19.2. This research focuses on men's clothing stores in a college town. Potential customers were asked to list attributes, characteristics, or terms that come to mind when one thinks of men's clothing stores. From that list, the attributes perceived as having the most salience were found to be assortment, personnel, atmosphere, service, quality, and price. Then stores were rated on a 1-to-7 scale along with each attribute, providing useful information for diagnostic purposes.[34] Store C, for example, rated poorly on quality, the most salient attribute. This could be a major cause of low patronage.

Determinant Attributes in Store Choice

The process of choosing a specific store is a function of consumer characteristics and store characteristics. That is, each market segment as defined by shopper profiles will have an image of various stores. The process is shown in Figure 19.8. Consumers sort out or compare perceived characteristics of stores with evaluative criteria of the core customers.

Store choice is a function of four variables shown in Figure 19.8: (1) evaluative criteria, (2) perceived characteristics of stores, (3) comparison process, and (4) acceptable and unacceptable stores. These processes are complex but understandable.

Determinants of store choice decision vary by market segment and by product class. Salient or determinant attributes usually fall into the following categories: (1) location, (2) nature and quality of assortment, (3) price, (4) advertising and promotion, (5) sales personnel, (6) services offered, (7) physical store attributes, (8) nature of store clientele, (9) store atmosphere, and (10) posttransaction service and satisfaction. Since location has been discussed in the context of market, area, and site selection, we go on to discuss the rest of the variables.

Nature and Quality of Assortment   Depth, breadth, and quality of assortment are often determinants of store choice. This is especially true for department stores and

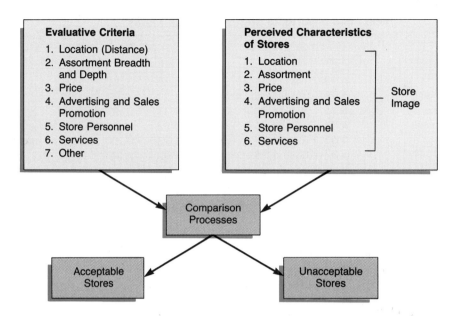

FIGURE 19.8 **Store Choice Process Is a Function of Salient Variables**

other stores in shopping centers.[35] Specialty stores have risen rapidly in competitive ability because of their ability to assemble and present dominant assortments, whether defined on the basis of classification, end-use, or lifestyle.[36]

The importance of assortments of merchandise is also important to the increase in retailers known as **"category killers."** They carry a broad assortment in one category of merchandise. An example is Toys R Us with hundreds of stores spread from Germany to Hong Kong. Its most profitable stores are not in the U.S., where it is very strong, but in Germany. In 1992, it had a highly publicized (along with President Bush) store opening in Japan and has added nearly 100 new units each year. Other category killers include Tower Records, Circuit City, Block Buster Video, Sportsmart, Lenscrafters, Home Depot, and Office Depot.

An alternative strategy for capitalizing on consumers' desires for quality or depth of assortment is found among **niche retailers**. These include Benetton, The Gap, Aca Joe, Esprit, Judy's, The Limited, Banana Republic, and many others. They have narrow but deep assortments.

Category killers and niche retailers compete effectively with department stores, which used to be the place for quality and quantity of assortments, because of the effect that narrow lines and disciplined merchandising have on turnover. In contrast, department stores typically have slower inventory turns along with higher operating expenses, lower sales per square foot, and larger inventory losses.

Price The importance of price as a determinant of store patronage varies by type of product. Supermarkets have placed great emphasis on price since the 1930s when King Kullen on Long Island, New York, pioneered the concept. Aldi's has built a

A Success Strategy Based on Low Prices and Lower Costs

Food Lion is generally recognized as the fastest growing chain in the supermarket business. Based in Salisbury, North Carolina, the chain's sales in 1991 were $6 billion in 700 stores and adding about 100 stores each year.

Its profits have grown at nearly 25 percent a year over the past 10 years and it maintains a profit percentage remarkably higher than other chains while keeping prices generally below other chains. The President, Tom Smith, explains, "We have a company that's run in a lean manner."

It achieves operating costs about a third less than the industry average by doing such things as controlling temperature for every store from its non-ostentatious headquarters building. Unlike other large supermarket chains, Food Lion does not divide responsibility for purchasing and distribution into large divisions in various locations. All a store manager has to worry about is labor and productivity.

Food Lion chooses locations for its stores, collecting information on population, real estate costs, and traffic before committing to a site. The stores are typically smaller than other supermarkets so they save on space and on land and construction. It avoids the flower shops and video counters found in other stores. The stores thrive on local convenience.

TV ads for Food Lion, which are produced at low cost in company headquarters, offer more of the company's cost-cutting secrets: recycling cardboard boxes to installing insulated cooler doors. Tom Smith explains, "Every supermarket says it has the lowest prices. This is why I'm on the ads—to show just how we do it. If a company officer explains it, it's more believable." Another officer explains, "We started out as a very poor company. We came very close to bankruptcy. We learned how to survive was to operate our stores very efficiently and lower our prices. We've kept these efficiencies up until today."

Source: Excerpted from "Food Lion Bares Its Teeth in Rapid Expansion Program," *Columbus Dispatch* (January 27, 1992), 2E and company annual reports.

worldwide supermarket chain based on merciless price competition backed by similar emphasis on cost reduction.

The fastest growing supermarket in the United States is the Belgium-founded chain Food Lion. Analysis of this company shows an amazing story of profitability based on low prices and even lower costs. Consumer in Focus 19.4 gives the details.

At one time price was not so important in consumer selection of department stores, which built their consumer franchise on product selection and service. Because of intense competition and often because of deterioration in service levels, price has become more important for some department stores. Some department stores—generally the least successful ones—develop "sales mania" in their attempt to buy back market share from competitors. Constant sales may have undermined the credibility of department stores and the confidence of customers in store prices. The importance of price depends on the nature of the buyer. Some customers preferring other factors, such as convenience, will, in effect, trade off that consideration against higher prices.[37] The consumer's perception of price, or subjective price, is usually more important than actual price.[38]

Price is an important variable upon which to build a marketing program but does not succeed without attention to other details such as quality products and services. Put them all together, however, and results can be dramatic. The Price Club is a prime example. On a base of 37 stores, it had 6 doing over $150 million per year and 2 doing over $200 million a year. For the 6 stores earning over $150 million, that is $1,550 per square foot turnover, an astounding achievement.

Wal-Mart is another prime example of a retailer using price as one of its many excellent attributes, as is Home Depot and Office Depot. Price appears to be important from these examples. But of the 37 warehouse chains operating in a recent year, only 3 made a profit. It is true that the 2 most profitable—Wal-Mart and Price Club—were enormously successful, but many retailers—almost all in this category—bet on low price as a competitive weapon and lost.

Price may be the most misunderstood variable in retailing. When Wal-Mart overtook Sears as the largest retailer in the United States, Sears cut its prices. What Sears may have failed to understand is that Wal-Mart not only has the policy of "Everyday low prices," it also has highly disciplined policies to enforce the policy "Treat every customer as a guest."

Every community provides examples of retailers and service providers that are the most successful in the trade area. Frequently, these successes are not due to having the lowest prices; they may even have some of the highest in prices. Alternately, retailers and services providers such as airlines that are near bankruptcy sometimes slash prices in an attempt to attract customers. Usually, they still go bankrupt. The common mistake is to assume that price is the determinant attribute of where consumers shop. This mistake may be understandable because historically economic analysis places primary attention on price. The reality of retailing is that low prices may attract consumers but it will not keep them unless other attributes such as convenience, location, product selection, and service are excellent. As Consumer in Focus 19.4 illustrates for Food Lion, when the other attributes are right, price can be a potent competitive weapon.

Advertising and Promotion   Advertising and promotion is an important, although controversial, variable associated with store choice. Its effectiveness varies by product category because some products and services are inherently more appealing than others. Men find restaurant ads and ads about tires and batteries most attention getting, for example, while women look most at ads for restaurants, women's shoes, and women's apparel.[39] Advertising has proved useful for some retailers, with results as dramatic as those for Farm Fresh, which tripled volume in 5 years without increasing the number of outlets.[40] Its advertising stressed low prices. Managers conscientiously monitored competitive ads to guarantee that Farm Fresh prices were always on a par or lower. The impact on consumers was backed up by testimonials appearing in the ads. Food Lion also uses price as an element in its advertising but does it in a more credible manner than the typical, "We will not be undersold" claims made, it seems, by nearly every other retailer, by explaining the specific reasons Food Lion has lower costs.

The effectiveness of price promotions is questionable, despite their widespread use.[41] Price promotion may only shift demand from one time period to another for a store. It may shift from one brand to another without increasing a store's total sales, or it may shift market share from one competitor to the next without increasing total demand. Nevertheless, price advertising is frequently done to maintain competitive parity. Apparently, a segment of the population—as large as a third or more—is affected by price advertising. But loyalty may last only until the next set of advertised prices attracts that segment elsewhere.

The effects of price advertising are filtered by recipients through the dimensions of their overall image. Keiser and Krum concluded that "other information cues besides advertised low price would seem to influence consumer choice of retailers. These information cues are received from personal shopping experience, from friends, and from many other sources besides newspaper advertisements."[42]

Advertising, along with other forms of sales promotion, can affect store choice, but its impact is difficult to assess. It depends on the type of purchase and the nature of the store itself. For example, a classic study documenting the sources of awareness of a new dairy products outlet found that advertising accounted for only 16.9 percent of this awareness, compared with 50.5 percent for visual notice and 32.6 percent for word of mouth.[43] Word of mouth, in turn, proved to be the most decisive influence on choice.

Questions about the relative effectiveness of price promotions, advertising, sales promotion, and so forth are increasingly answered more reliably by scanner data. Specifically, retailers who are equipped to do so can examine more closely brand and store substitution effects. Use of sophisticated scanner data analysis will shift power in the channel even more from manufacturers to retailers. Research on this topic seems to indicate that price promotions and to a lesser degree displays have brand substitution effects but also store substitution effects on a retailer and its competitors.[44]

Perhaps someday you will be manager of a large retailing chain. How important will advertising be to you? No clear answer is apparent. The Limited is highly successful. It uses almost no advertising. Yet Benetton is also successful and it has some of the most attention getting (and controversial) ads in the world. (See the Benneton ads in Figure 3.2.) The Gap is currently the most successful chain in the apparel category, as you saw in the opening scenario. Consumer in Focus 19.5 shows how The Gap successfully develops its advertising campaign.

Sales Personnel   "You win with people!" Coach Woody Hayes titled his book. It is as true in retailing as in football. Knowledgeable and helpful salespeople were rated

Consumer in Focus 19.5

Advertising Fills a Gap

Blonde, Beautiful, Boring. That's how Maggie Gross, The Gap Inc.'s senior vice president for advertising and marketing, reacted to the woman modeling a white Gap turtleneck. The idea for this 1988 Los Angeles-area campaign was to show some L.A. trendies in Gap garb. But album designer Lynn Robb looked like any other model.

Gross changed that. "Give me a shot of her with her own jacket on," she told photographer Matthew Rolston. Robb donned her well-worn motorcycle jacket, leaving it open to show the shirt. A fashion clone was transformed into something that communicated an individual sense of style.

That photo launched the Individuals of Style campaign—a series of black-and-white photos of personalities from jazz great Miles Davis to neo-country singer k. d. lang, all mixing Gap products with other clothes. The message was that Gap's fashions blended with everything from Armani sport coats to Grateful Dead headbands.

A Gap credo is not to overdo anything. So the Individuals of Style campaign went on hiatus replaced by simple ads of Gap items in striking colors. A new campaign aims at both big Gap and BabyGap customers showing an infant in blue jean jacket swaddling. Gross says Individuals of Style will be back "when the time is right"—but with a difference. In the 1990s, she figures, celebrities are out, and social activists could be in. The Dalai Lama in denim, perhaps?

Source: "How the Gap's Ads Got So-o-o Cool," *Business Week* (March 9, 1992), 64.

as an important consideration in choice of a shopping center by more than three-quarters of those interviewed in five major metropolitan areas.[45] The necessity of skillful personal selling was previously stressed under the discussion of search, so this finding is not surprising. But does performance match expectations?

Consumer confidence in retail salespeople is often low. But Home Depot has become the most successful do-it yourself, home improvement store. Part of its success is its policy of four weeks or more training for people walking the floors to help consumers—a rarity among most retailers. Before salespeople start they must learn about every item in their aisle and in two aisles adjacent. Salespeople, often recruited from the ranks of carpenters and electricians, are encouraged to spend all the time needed with customers, even if it takes hours.[46]

Perhaps no retailer is more successful at winning with personnel than Nordstrom's, the West Coast-based specialty department store. The secret of Nordstrom's success may be tied to a story, possibly apocryphal, about a retailer who asked a salesperson at Nordstrom's, "What can you be fired for?" The person replied: "Number one, for not taking care of the customer. Number two, for stealing." Many people believe that no retailer has a handle on customer service as well as Nordstrom's. Perception or fact? Most likely a halo effect has developed around the company's outstanding service. But the fact is, its service is excellent and is provided by highly trained and motivated sales personnel enmeshed in a culture that defines success as personal service to customers. It is consistent philosophy that gets communicated when hiring people and it is constantly reinforced.

You might be asking if these policies only apply to large, retailing chains. Frankly, these policies are probably the reason these organizations are large, because they all started out small and most of them relatively recently. Suppose you were given the responsibility for managing a single store, the smallest in the market and previously unsuccessful. Would you know how to turn it around to become the largest in the nation? Fred Ricart did, as Consumer in Focus 19.6 shows. The success story includes a major emphasis on training of personnel.

Services Offered

Convenient self-service facilities, ease of merchandise return, delivery, credit, and overall good service have all been found to be considerations affecting store image.[47] This varies, of course, depending upon the type of outlet and consumer expectations. For instance, the 90 Giant supermarkets in the Washington, D.C., area began a nutrition education program in cooperation with the National Heart, Lung, and Blood Institute with good results. The program is called "Foods for Health," and various tips are presented through shelf-talkers, posters, and other forms of display.[48] Similarly, a *Chain Store Age Executive* survey of managers revealed that the presence of in-store banking facilities such as automated teller machines raised traffic levels by 10 to 15 percent annually.[49] In-store restaurants increase sales in the range of 5 to 6 percent. Hardware and home supply stores that service their products increase sales. Grocery stores sell products such as stamps as a service because of the increase in traffic. Other stores add technology, personnel, and training in order to increase service and decrease the time consumers spend in waiting at the checkout or other places in the store.[50] These are just a few examples of the variety of services that warrant experimentation because of their high potential payout.

Physical Store Attributes

Facilities such as elevators, lighting, air conditioning, convenient and visible washrooms, layout, aisle placement and width, carpeting, and architecture have been found to be factors in and of themselves in store image and choice.[51] In a recent study, 61 percent of shoppers said convenient parking and 52.8 percent of shoppers said quick checkout would influence their decision about where to shop. Another physical store attribute of great importance was women's restrooms, rated by 50.7 percent of the women in the study as a factor influencing where they shop.[52]

Store Clientele

The type of person who shops in a store affects choice because of the pervasive tendency to attempt to match one's self-image with that of the store. The clientele of a restaurant makes it attractive or not so attractive to customers who

#1 Auto Dealer in the Nation

Auto Age magazine and *Automotive News* have both reported that Ricart Ford is the #1 Ford dealer in the world and the #1 Ford dealer in retail sales for multiple years. With annual sales of over $232 million and 22,000 cars in 1992, it might be expected that the #1 dealership would be in a major market such as New York or Los Angeles. Ricart Ford is in Canal Winchester, Ohio.

Ricart Ford was not always that successful. The average dealer in the U.S. sells about 500 cars in a year and in 1983, Ricart was below average. But during the 1980s, Ricart began to experiment with new forms of selling, training, and advertising. The firm conducted over 500 consumer experiments, carefully observing the results of each.

Experiments involving careful observation and analysis to evaluate causation were nothing new to the president of the dealership, Fred Ricart. Ricart studied at Case Western Reserve University earning a bachelor's degree in biochemistry. During graduate study, he became a lab scientist, spending years researching the light-sensitive chemical necessary to transmit light patterns from the retina to the brain for translation into a visual image. Working hours in a darkened laboratory with only a dim safelight bulb for illumination, he turned to music to pass the time, singing to himself and playing the guitar. When the family business ran into a crisis, Fred Ricart left the lab to help his father but brought his scientist's approach to understanding consumer behavior—and his guitar—to the Ford dealership.

He spent years, along with his younger brother Rhett, who is the accountant and information systems expert of the team, finding what works and what doesn't. They developed a training system for sales personnel that involves weeks of learning how "to sell yourself, instead of cars." They experimented with advertising media, learning what response could be expected if an ad was on the Bill Cosby show instead of Wheel of Fortune and the difference in response between 10 commercial ROS's (run-of-schedule) on one channel versus more expensive commercials carefully placed on channels selected to match market targets.

Continued

want to see or be seen by others. Some customers may avoid a restaurant because of the type of people who are generally there, such as an instance when adults avoid restaurants that are believed to attract children.

Store Atmosphere   An important determinant of store choice is store atmosphere. Its importance is recognized in the term **store atmospherics**, the conscious designing of space to create certain effects in buyers.[53] Intense competition between stores

They developed a system of selling whereby all visitors to the dealership are met with a parking plan as carefully orchestrated as parking at Disney World. Visitors are introduced to the well-trained salespersons and the information system starts. At the beginning of each day, the computer displays the "close ratio" for each of the nearly 100 salespersons. The results: while the national average of 17 percent is considered good in many dealerships, Ricart Ford achieves a close ratio over 50 percent. You can afford to spend more on advertising to get a potential customer into the store when you are well prepared for them when they arrive.

With information systems that permit management to identify what every person in the firm is accomplishing, it is no wonder that independent rating services report the customer satisfaction with Ricart's service area one of the highest of all dealerships in the nation. For both sales and service as well as other areas of the business, the Ricarts have detailed reports on the precise accomplishments of each person the preceding day. They don't threaten or intimidate employees with such information. Fred Ricart explains, "The advantage is derived simply from the fact that I know what our people are doing—and they know that I know."

Consumers are drawn from as far as Cleveland and Cincinnati. They see a friendly dealer having fun on TV, playing the guitar he picked up as a student and laboratory scientist, singing "We're dealing." The consumers may not see one of the most advanced training programs in the business, the careful design for the store and surrounding area, the cost-effective media plan, the computerized TV studio that allows changes in advertising (such as rebates or special service contracts) two to three weeks earlier than competitors, or the state-of-the-art information system by which the firm is managed.

Advertising is the tip of the iceberg. It's the rest of the story that explains why Ricart Ford is the #1 dealer in America.

Source: Excerpted from the Columbus *Daily Reporter* (December 16, 1987), 1; "Entrepreneur of the Year Awards," *Inc.* (January 1991), 51 and company interviews.

for young, upscale consumers has caused stores to discard their dowdy old formats for colorful, well-designed, image-enhanced selling environments. Even the masses of consumers want some class in their stores. You can see this principle in effect in Gap stores, described in the opening scenario.

Even supermarkets need revitalization of their atmospherics. Byerly's in Minneapolis has one of the most attractive stores in the United States. In Canada, Loblaws is an outstanding example of a store with coordinated graphics. The

FIGURE 19.9 **Atmospherics of Cheryl & Co.: The Conscious Design of Space to Attract Consumers**

Source: Courtesy of Cheryl & Co.

exterior signing invites people to come inside. When inside, customers are faced with super graphics as signing, clean and contemporary displays, and lighting and colors that encourage people to stay and shop. Products as ordinary as cookies can be exciting with the right atmospherics. Figure 19.9 shows a retail outlet for Cheryl & Co., a company that started with Cheryl Krueger making cookies in her kitchen for friends. The firm evolved into a successful entry in regional shopping malls, exciting not only because of the excellent taste of its cookies and other products but because of the bright red colors with designer-developed accents of black and white and carefully coordinated displays. While competitors sell cookies in "plain vanilla" stores, Cheryl & Co. has used atmospherics to make the store much more than just a "cookie store."

Posttransaction Service and Satisfaction Customers want service and satisfaction after the sale. This is especially true for those who purchase such high-involvement products as furniture, appliances, and automobiles. More and more retailers and service firms are providing comment cards and other forms of feedback to ensure that consumers are satisfied. Marriott Hotels go to great efforts to serve consumers well and to find out about unmet expectations through questionnaires in every room as well as additional questionnaires sent to some guests after their stay.

Posttransaction service and satisfaction programs are more important in an era of slower growth in the total market. Successful retailers have found that the best source of new business frequently is current customers. As the population of industrialized countries slows or declines, it becomes more justifiable economically to implement programs that will satisfy present customers than to spend money to obtain new customers. Growing profits require more attention to meeting customer expectations for service.[54]

McDonald's adheres to the philosophy that satisfied customers are the key to success. So McDonald's listens to customers and responds to changing tastes and priorities. The goal is to satisfy them so completely on every visit that they want to return for more delicious meals. The focus on customer care drives every aspect of the business, from product development to employee training to the design of restaurants. Since drive-thrus account for 53 percent of sales, the company is experimenting with a variety of technological improvements that permit face-to-face ordering. They are currently in more than 100 restaurants across the U.S. and about 30 restaurants outside the U.S. Customer surveys reveal that 90 percent of the individuals who experience the face-to-face system prefer this friendlier, more personal drive-thru configuration. Since clearer communications result, there is also a marked improvement in order accuracy. President and CEO Ed Rensi says, "Customers are very special to us; serving them is the reason we are in business. We know our customers have many choices and we want to be their first choice every time. Making them want to come back is the key to continued success and growth in the coming years."[55]

These are the reasons why consumers choose one store in preference to another. These reasons should also help explain some of the trends that are underway in retailing and suggest some of the actions that you will need to take if you are responsible for the marketing strategy of a retailer or supplier to retailers. Further insights into success requirements are described in the next section.

Marketing Strategies in Response to Consumer Decisions

How do you respond when you read of the successes created by people such as Sam Walton at Wal-Mart, Mickey Drexler at The Gap, Les Wexner at The Limited, or Cheryl Krueger at Cheryl & Co.? Would you like to create something similar? Such success is not a matter of luck.

Success in retailing is a matter of rigorously following certain principles. In the examples described in this chapter, people developed and executed retail strategies to interact with the decision processes of consumers to provide a satisfying and innovative interaction for both parties. You probably can do the same if you wish to do so by applying the same principles that can be observed in their firms. A number of characteristics of successful retailing firms were identified by Management Horizons as the following.

1. *Market-Driven*—These companies have identified pockets of high-growth opportunity in consumer, merchandise, and geographic markets and have well-defined marketing strategies geared to some form of dominance.
2. *Professional Entrepreneurial Management*—Managements have maintained a hands-on entrepreneurial approach to their businesses. The presence of an

individual who is a professional manager, as well as the driving force behind the company's success, who has a vision for the company and whose personal satisfaction is tied to the company's performance, is seen in many of the retailers who are "stayers."

3. *Programmed Resource Relationships*—Higher performance retailers tend to be the "captains" of their distribution channels, controlling the conditions under which they do business with suppliers. These companies have become powerful factors in the distribution channel because of an ability to deliver market share and/or through ownership of the source of supply.

4. *Productivity/Technology Leaders*—Technology represents a major commitment and a continuing investment for high-achievement retailers. Technological leadership contributes to efficiency in communications in marketing and operating activities, and often results in higher productivity.

5. *High-Value Offer*—The companies are high-value retailers, where value is defined as more for less. Such companies are compelling competitors because they greatly exaggerate the value equation in some way.[56]

Lifestyle Retailing Portfolios

The wheel of retailing goes round and round but not necessarily in the same place. The old general store of original American retailing was a composite of items closely related to the lifestyles of the locality; a general store in a small town carried quite different items from those of the downtown or neighborhood stores of the cities. Store operators were essentially purchasing agents for the citizens of a specific locality, reflecting closely those customers' lifestyles, brand preferences, sizes, and preferred shopping hours. Without awareness of the concept of lifestyles and without psychographic research, the operators of those stores a hundred or more years ago were practitioners of both the "marketing concept" and what is now called lifestyle retailing.[57]

Lifestyle Retailing   **Lifestyle retailing** may be defined as the policy of tailoring a retail offering closely to the lifestyles of specific target market groups of consumers. This contrasts with what might be called **supplier-style retailing**, in which the key to success in recent decades has been a focus on homogeneity in retailing operations.

A & P stores in a New Jersey city and a Midwestern suburb varied little in size, personnel, product line, or promotional methods. Similarly, K mart achieved its market dominance because of the tremendous distributional, promotional, and operational efficiencies brought about by market homogeneity.

While A & P may have been the best (or, more correctly, the worst) example of homogeneity with its emphasis upon supplier-style retailing, Sears, Woolworth, Western Auto, and many other major retailers were different from A & P only in degree. Managers could be moved from store to store (and frequently were), and with the exception of physical size, they would find little difference in products carried, advertising used, or any other significant area of operations. Even department stores, traditionally the finest "purchasing agents" of consumers, followed the same strategy, in most instances, by building suburban stores that were little more than miniature carbon copies of the downtown stores. Minimal, if any, recognition was given to the fundamentally different lifestyles of suburban customers compared with those of traditional or downtown customers.

Lifestyle retailers, conversely, base their strategy and operations on unique living patterns of their target customers rather than on demographics or merchandise strength. The most successful of lifestyle retailers often emphasize lifestyle strength over demographic and merchandise strengths to find a differential advantage.

Portfolios of Retailing Chains   In the 1990s, success requirements are increasingly for movement beyond a chain that is lifestyle based and more toward a *portfolio* of such chains. Figure 19.10 shows how Woolworth has converted its previous 10,000-foot Woolworth stores—which tried to appeal to everyone and as a consequence appealed very little to anyone—to a portfolio of stores such as Brookstone, Eddie Bauer, and Ki Clayton, each programmed for specific lifestyles. Woolworth now owns more than 8,600 stores in the U.S., Canada, Germany, Australia, England, Belgium, and the Netherlands in over 40 different formats ranging from Footlocker to Northern Reflections, with even a few of the original Woolworth stores left.

The Limited provides a premier example of a portfolio of lifestyle retailing groups. When men found the fashions in Limited Express more attractive than those available in men's stores, The Limited started new stores for men and also for

FIGURE 19.10   The Woolworth Evolution from a "Dime Store" to a Portfolio
Source: Courtesy Woolworth, Inc.

kids. For the expanding leisure markets, the company added Abercrombie & Fitch to its portfolio and expanded its offering of clothing. When the firm found that a lot of men were buying fashions for themselves at Express, it spun off a new division called Structures.

Integrated Marketing Communications

The search for productivity in retailing is leading in new directions. One direction is the integration of marketing communications of retailing organizations in a closely coordinated program relating to consumer behavior. Such programs can be described as **Integrated Marketing Communications** or IMC.[58] **Marketing communications** of retailers, defined as shared meanings between retailing organizations and persons, with exchange as their objective, are of increasing importance to retailing as well as other marketing organizations. The increased importance is due to the nature of the competitive environment as well as the enormous resources required to compete in contemporary retailing environments. One solution to the problem is an IMC.

Integrated marketing communications of retailers or other organizations differ from traditionally programmed communications in several ways:

1. IMC programs are comprehensive. Advertising, personal selling, retail atmospherics and in-store programs, behavioral modification programs, public relations, investor relations programs, employee communications, and other forms are all considered in the planning of an IMC.
2. IMC programs are unified. The messages delivered by all media, including such diverse influences as employee recruiting and the atmospherics of retailers, are the same or supportive of a unified theme.
3. IMC programs are targeted. The public relations program, advertising programs, in-store and point-of-purchase programs, all have the same or related target markets.
4. IMC programs have coordinated execution of all the communications components of the organization.
5. IMC programs emphasize productivity in reaching the designated targets when selecting communication channels and allocating resources to marketing media. One of the best examples of an IMC is The Limited.

Market Targeting   The Limited started in 1963 with a single store targeted to young, fashion-conscious, moderately affluent women. Unlike other retailers, who often define their targets in terms of merchandise carried, The Limited focused on the consumer. It organized all aspects of store operations and communications toward that consumer. When retailers define their target in terms of products rather than consumers, they must constantly win the loyalty of new consumers as the previous ones mature and move to other product lines over the family life cycle. The Limited moved with the target market, and today's Limited is far different than 20 years ago.

Unified Message   The Limited has achieved a unified message directed to a specific market target. The visual, auditory, and interpersonal environment is managed to provide a unified appeal. A market research firm selects exactly the right music to be played in each store for the defined consumer segment. A shopper might walk from a Limited next door to an Express, but the shopper's ears will tell her she has walked a decade away.

The most dramatic part of the in-store environment may be The Limited's high information content. Shoppers can walk into many competitive stores and fail to get help, personal or otherwise, in mixing and matching various items of apparel. That does not happen with The Limited. The information is on the walls. They are covered by carefully coordinated groups, assembled by expert designers. They are changed often; they are creative and persuasive as sale communications. The result is that shoppers may leave The Limited or its sister stores with several items rather than only one (as they might in competitive stores). Most importantly, the consumers probably are more satisfied because they have purchased items that truly do look better on them than if they had purchased mismatched items over time in a variety of stores.

Coordinated Personal Sales   The communications of The Limited are so integrated that they include specific criteria about the employees who are recruited to sell apparel and how they are trained. The employees are like the customers. They wear clothes The Limited sells and present the right image as they do their work, causing them to be effective opinion leaders to many of the customers.

At The Limited, sales associates are recruited to sell, trained to sell, given the time and opportunity to sell, and evaluated and compensated well when they do sell. This is not, however, "high pressure." Instead, sales communications are designed in the context of a philosophy that understands the best way to sell is to create customers so pleased they will be highly loyal. Even this philosophy is communicated simply and effectively at The Limited with the phrase, "No sale is ever final."

Information-Based Strategies   Changing demographics, especially more education, have created a consumer responsiveness to information-based marketing strategies. Understanding this can lead to higher margins as part of the IMC.

As the ratio of information increases relative to the physical mass of the product, the potential increases for higher margin selling of goods by retailers. The process is also appropriate for other marketing organizations as well. Higher margins are possible because information increases the value of products and services to consumers. Higher margins are possible assuming, of course, that the marginal cost of producing the information is less than the marginal value created for consumers.[59]

Information-based strategies take many forms. Some include more information on packaging; special inserts or hangtags accompanying products; more attention to information contained in advertising; special training programs for salespeople and other workers who have contact with customers; enhanced point-of-purchase materials, including videotapes and computerized displays; and seminars or training programs for customers and potential customers.

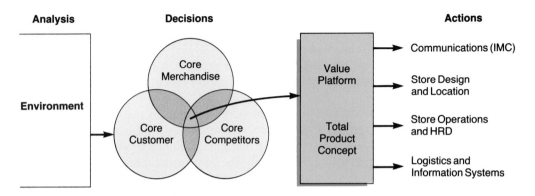

FIGURE 19.11   Developing a Core Retailing Strategy: Finding the Differential Advantage for a Particular Product

The Core Strategy

The key to long-term sustainable competitive advantage is to find a differential advantage that serves as a value platform for communicating the total product concept to customers. Retailing organizations with a long-term approach to markets take a process such as that portrayed in Figure 19.11.

The first step is analysis of the environment—all of the types of information discussed in previous chapters of this book as well as the demographic trends you will read about in the next chapter.

The second step is to make decisions. These decisions are fundamental. Who will be our core customer? What will be our core merchandise? Who is likely to be among core competitors? Focusing on the really important or core aspects of the situation is more likely to produce a differential advantage than trying to be all things to all people. From the intersection of these core concepts should evolve the total product concept and the value platform that serves to make it specific and observable to the consumer.

The final step is taking actions to implement this plan—communications (an IMC approach), store design and location, store operations and Human Relations Development (HRD), and the logistics management and information systems that are essential to highly profitable retailers in today's environment.

Once a firm "has it right," does that mean it can relax and reap the profits? Hardly. It is the best stores that keep changing things—that strive for continual improvement. "If it ain't broken, don't fix it," says an old adage. It is a false adage. It is the unsuccessful retailers that stay the same. The ones at the top are continually modifying their operations, experimenting with new products, new training programs, and new operating procedures. We end this chapter with an example of just such a process in Consumer in Focus 19.7.

Wal-Mart in the Future

When Sam Walton opened the first Wal-Mart discount store in Rogers, Arkansas, in 1962, the retail industry didn't notice. Shortly before his death in 1992, he wished his new store, also in Arkansas, would likewise escape attention. But with 1991 sales of $33 billion, Wal-Mart is likely to be noticed.

From the design and innovations built into the new prototype, Wal-Mart thinks its customers of the future will be as concerned about service as about low prices. With wide aisles and classy displays, it looks more like an upscale department store than a spartan discounter. One of the biggest distinctions between discount and department stores—self-service vs. full service—is blurred at this store; new technology provides information about products and helps customers locate them. The new store even has some designer names typically found only at upscale department stores, such as Estee Lauder and Calvin Klein.

Unlike department stores, however, the Wal-Mart store has the same bargain basement prices found in all its outlets. Trying out unproven devices such as shopping carts with video screens may seem odd for a retailer dedicated to low costs. But it's in keeping with a corporate tradition of disdain for the conventional—which extends back to when Walton, against the advice of virtually everyone, began opening discount stores in towns thought too small to support them. The corporate culture at Wal-Mart still encourages ideas that might seem downright "wacky."

Wal-Mart, long a leader in computerizing the distribution side of retailing, is putting technology in the hands of customers at this store. Consumerscan, found throughout the store, gives customers their own barcode scanners to check prices. The Wal-Mart Arts Report has a TV screen to let customers preview movies and music videos. Shoppers also can use the device to order titles that aren't in stock. Wal-Mart is becoming a leader in providing improved consumer information through technology, different from most self-service stores that provide little information.

The most popular gadget in the store is VideOcart, an information technology becoming available in supermarkets but until now not used elsewhere. As customers progress through the store, information about the department at hand flashes on the video screen attached to their cars.

At about 125,000 square feet, the store is the largest Wal-Mart store (50 percent bigger than most) and much of that space is devoted to wider aisles, less cramped displays and sitting areas for customers. Not all of the features of this store will turn up in the future in others but the new store gets good reviews from customers.

Source: Kevin Helliker, "Wal-Mart's Store of the Future Blends Discount Prices, Department-Store Feel," *Wall Street Journal* (May 17, 1991), B1.

Summary

Purchasing processes is a term that refers to the interaction between consumers and retail outlets. Decisions about stores are fundamentally the same as decisions about products or brands. Need recognition leading to shopping behavior may be initiated by product problem recognition or by nonproduct-related motives such as the desire to get out of the house or engage in family-related leisure activity.

The fundamental questions facing retailers are where people will shop and which stores they will choose. Store choice is a complex process consisting of four variables: (1) evaluative criteria, (2) perceived characteristics of stores, (3) comparison process, and (4) acceptable and unacceptable stores. In general, the variables involved in this process are location, nature and quality of assortment, price, advertising and promotion, sales personnel, services offered, physical attributes, store clientele, store atmosphere, and posttransaction service.

Store image is the perception of consumers about the objective characteristics of stores. Common methods of measuring store image include the semantic differential, multiattribute measures, multidimensional scaling, and other methods.

Shopper profiles are important for analyzing the comparison process by which consumers pick acceptable and unacceptable stores. Demographic variables, especially age, income, and place of residence, are often used to define patronage of a store, and many of these data are available from on-line computer data bases.

Review and Discussion Questions

1. Why is it important to understand purchasing processes as part of the decision-process approach to understanding consumer behavior?
2. Think of the last time you bought a product. How did you decide which store to patronize? How does your behavior compare with the conceptualization of the process as presented in this chapter?
3. Define the term *store image* and explain why it is important as a concept for retail management.
4. What is the image of the two largest stores in your area? How do your perceptions of these stores compare with those of your friends? Your parents? Why do these differences exist?
5. Assume you are a consultant for a major department store. Describe how you would go about evaluating the type of competition faced by the department store in the next few years.
6. Assume that you are asked to measure the image of the dominant grocery chain in your area. How would you recommend this be done? Why?
7. Of what importance is location in analyzing the patronage of retail stores?
8. Several marketing responses to consumer decisions about retailing were described in this chapter. Briefly outline the salient characteristics of each and list some examples other than those mentioned in the chapter.
9. Describe the importance of price in the patronage decision for supermarkets.
10. Evaluate the strategies of Food Lion. Why do you believe it has experienced such rapid growth? Will this continue in the future?

Endnotes

1. Leo Bogart, James Webb Young Fund Address, University of Illinois, April 7, 1988.
2. Much of the following material is based upon Roger D. Blackwell and W. Wayne Talarzyk, "Life-Style Retailing: Competitive Strategies for the 1980's," *Journal of Retailing* 59 (Winter 1983), 7–27.
3. Additional details of this innovative retail chain can be found in Roger D. Blackwell, Wayne Talarzyk and James F. Engel, *Contemporary Cases in Consumer Behavior*, 3rd ed. (Hinsdale, Ill.: Dryden Press, 1990), 389–402.
4. Avijit Ghosh and Sara L. McLafferty, *Location Strategies for Retail and Service Firms* (Lexington, Mass.: Lexington Books, 1987), 16.
5. Peter A. Doherty, *Location Strategies to Support the Marketing Management Function* (Columbus: Management Horizons, 1984), 4.
6. William J. Reilly, *Methods for the Study of Retail Relationships* (Austin, Tex.: Bureau of Business Research, University of Texas Press, 1929), 16.
7. For a review of this literature, see Avijit Ghosh and G. Rushton, "Progress in Location Allocation Models," in A. Ghosh and G. Rushton, eds., *Spatial Analysis and Location Allocation Models* (New York: Van Nostrand Reinhold, 1987).
8. Karen F. Stein, "Explaining Ghetto Consumer Behavior: Hypotheses from Urban Sociology," *The Journal of Consumer Affairs* 14 (Summer 1980), 232–242.
9. William R. Darden, John L. Lennon, and Donna K. Darden, "Communicating with Interurban Shoppers," *Journal of Retailing* 42 (Spring 1978), 51–64.
10. David L. Huff, "A Probabilistic Analysis of Consumer Spatial Behavior," in William S. Decker, ed., *Emerging Concepts in Marketing* (Chicago: American Marketing Association, 1962), 443–461. For an excellent discussion of other techniques for estimating shopping center patronage, see Bernard J. LaLonde, *Differentials in Super Market Drawing Power* (East Lansing, Mich.: Bureau of Business and Economic Research, Michigan State University, 1962). For dissenting findings about these types of models, see Joseph B. Mason and Charles T. Moore, "An Empirical Reappraisal of Behavioristic Assumptions in Trading Area Studies," *Journal of Retailing* (Winter 1970–1971), 31–37.
11. James A. Bruner and John L. Mason, "The Influence of Driving Time upon Shopping Center Preference," *Journal of Marketing* 32 (April 1968), 57–61.
12. David B. Mackay and Richard W. Olshavsky, "Cognitive Maps of Retail Locations: An Investigation of Some Basic Issues," *Journal of Consumer Research* 2 (December 1975); and Edward M. Mazze, "Determining Shopper Movements by Cognitive Maps," *Journal of Retailing* 50 (Fall 1974), 43–48.
13. R. Mittelstaedt et al., "Psychophysical and Evaluative Dimensions of Cognized Distance in an Urban Shopping Environment," in R. C. Curhan, ed., *Combined Proceedings* (Chicago: American Marketing Association, 1974), 190–193.
14. For additional details on store location decisions, see William R. Davidson, Daniel J. Sweeney, and Ronald W. Stampfl, *Retailing Management*, 5th ed. (New York: John Wiley & Sons, 1984), 179–197.
15. Ernest F. Cooke, "Why Most of the Retail Action Is East of the Mississippi," *American Demographics* 6 (November 1984), 20–23.
16. Kate Fitzgerald, "Mega Malls," *Advertising Age* (January 27, 1992), S-1.
17. George R. Puskar, "Regional Malls: A Preferred Institutional Investment," *The Real Estate Finance Journal* (Summer 1987), 77–83.

18. Chip Walker, "Strip Malls: Plain But Powerful," *American Demographics* 13 (October 1991), 48–51.

19. Kent B. Monroe and Joseph P. Guiltinan, "A Path-Analytic Exploration of Retail Patronage Influences," *Journal of Consumer Research* (June 1975), 19–28.

20. A. Coskun Samli, "Use of Segmentation Index to Measure Store Loyalty," *Journal of Retailing* 51 (Spring 1975), 51–60.

21. Paul R. Winn and Terry L. Childers, "Demographics and Store Patronage Concentrations: Some Promising Results," in Kenneth L. Bernhart, ed., *Marketing: 1776–1976 and Beyond* (Chicago: American Marketing Association, 1976), 82–86.

22. Donald E. Sexton, Jr., "Differences in Food Shopping Habits by Area of Residence, Race, and Income," *Journal of Retailing* 50 (Spring 1974), 37–49.

23. Howard A. Thompson and Jesse E. Raine, "Religious Denomination Preference as a Basis for Store Location," *Journal of Retailing* 52 (Summer 1976), 71–78.

24. Mark E. Slama and Armen Taschian, "Selected Socioeconomic and Demographic Characteristics Associated with Purchasing Involvement," *Journal of Marketing* 49 (Winter 1985), 72–82.

25. See Jay D. Lindquist, "The Meaning of Image," *Journal of Retailing* 50 (Winter 1974–1975), 29–38; Robert A. Hansen and Terry Deutscher, "An Empirical Investigation of Attribute Importance in Retail Store Selection," *Journal of Retailing* 53 (Winter 1977–1978), 59–72; and Leon Arons, "Does Television Viewing Influence Store Image and Shopping Frequency?" *Journal of Retailing* 37 (Fall 1961), 1–13; Ernest Dichter, "What's In an Image," *Journal of Consumer Marketing* 2 (Winter 1985), 75–81.

26. Pierre Martineau, "The Personality of the Retail Store," *Harvard Business Review* 36 (January–February 1958), 47.

27. G. H. G. McDougall and J. N. Fry, "Combining Two Methods of Image Measurement," *Journal of Retailing* 50 (Winter 1974–1975), 53–61.

28. W. B. Weale, "Measuring the Customer's Image of a Department Store," *Journal of Retailing* 37 (Spring 1961), 40–48.

29. See, for example, William Stephenson, "Public Images of Public Utilities," *Journal of Advertising Research* 3 (December 1963), 34–39.

30. Elizabeth A. Richards, "A Commercial Application of Guttman Attitude Scaling Techniques," *Journal of Marketing* 22 (October 1957), 166–173.

31. Peter Doyle and Ian Fenwick, "How Store Image Affects Shopping Habits in Grocery Chains," *Journal of Retailing* 50 (Winter 1974–1975), 39–52.

32. Richard N. Cardozo, "How Images Vary by Product Class," *Journal of Retailing* 50 (Winter 1974–1975), 85–98.

33. See, for example, Don L. James, Richard M. Durand, and Robert A. Dreves, "The Use of a Multi-Attribute Attribute Model in a Store Image Study," *Journal of Retailing* 52 (Summer 1976), 23–32; and Hansen and Deutscher, "An Empirical Investigation."

34. For a useful discussion, see Eleanor G. May, "Practical Applications of Recent Retail Image Research," *Journal of Retailing* 50 (Winter 1974–1975), 15–20.

35. Hansen and Deutscher, "An Empirical Investigation"; Lindquist, "The Meaning of Image"; Gentry and Burns, "How Important"; and John D. Claxton and J. R. Brent Ritchie, "Consumer Prepurchase Shopping Problems: A Focus on the Retailing Component," *Journal of Retailing* 55 (Fall 1979), 24–43.

36. Walter K. Levy, "Department Stores: The Next Generation," *Retailing Issues Letter* 1 (1987), 1.

37. Robert H. Williams, John J. Painter, and Herbert R. Nicholas, "A Policy-Oriented Typology of Grocery Shoppers," *Journal of Retailing* 54 (Spring 1978), 27–42.

38. Kent B. Monroe, "Buyers' Subjective Perceptions of Price," *Journal of Marketing Research* 10 (February 1973), 73–80.
39. Leo Bogart and B. Stuart Tolley, "The Search for Information in Newspaper Advertising," *Journal of Advertising Research* 28 (April–May 1988), 9–19.
40. Ronald Tanner, "Building a Store Image with Careful Ad Planning," *Progressive Grocer* (March 1979), 35.
41. Joseph N. Fry and Gordon H. McDougall, "Consumer Appraisal of Retail Price Advertisements," *Journal of Marketing* 38 (July 1974); V. Kumar and Robert P. Leone, "Measuring the Effect of Retail Store Promotions on Brand and Store Substitution," *Journal of Marketing Research* 25 (May 1988), 178–185.
42. Stephen K. Keiser and James R. Krum, "Consumer Perceptions of Retail Advertising with Overstated Price Savings," *Journal of Retailing* 452 (Fall 1976), 27–36.
43. Robert F. Kelly, "The Role of Information in the Patronage Decision: A Diffusion Phenomenon," in M. S. Moyer and R. E. Vosburgh, eds., *Marketing for Tomorrow . . . Today* (Chicago: American Marketing Association, 1967), 119–129.
44. V. Kumar and Robert P. Leone, "Measuring the Effect of Retail Store Promotions on Brand and Store Substitution," *Journal of Marketing* 25 (May 1988), 178–185.
45. "Service: Retail's No. 1 Problem," *Chain Store Age* (January 1987), 19.
46. Christopher Power and Laura Power, "Their Wish Is Your Command," *Business Week/ Quality 1991* (January 15, 1992), 126–127.
47. Lindquist, "The Meaning of Image."
48. Jo-Ann Zbtniewski, "Just-the-Facts-Ma'am on Health and Nutrition Posted in Giant Stores," *Progressive Grocer* (February 1979), 29.
49. "Retailers Asking: Is There Money in In-Store Banking?" *Chain Store Age Executive* 54 (October 1978), 35–39.
50. John V. Hummell and Ronald Savitt, "Customer Service in Retailing: A Temporal Approach," in Robert L. King, ed., *Retailing: Its Present and Future* (Charleston, S.C.: Academy of Marketing Science, 1988), 50–55.
51. "Retailers Asking: Is There Money in In-Store Banking?" 35–39.
52. "Service: Retail's No. 1 Problem," *Chain Store Age* (January 1987), 19.
53. Philip Kotler, "Atmospherics as a Marketing Tool," *Journal of Retailing* 49 (Winter 1973–1974), 48–63.
54. For expansion of this concept, see Roger D. Blackwell, "The Consumer Affairs Role in an Era of Slow Growth Markets," *Mobius: Journal of Consumer Affairs Professionals in Business* 7 (Fall 1988), 1–7.
55. McDonald's Fourth Quarter Report 1991, cover.
56. Robert E. O'Neill, "50 High Performance Retail Chains," *Monitor* 18 (May 1988), 55–66.
57. For additional details on this concept, see Roger D. Blackwell and W. Wayne Talarzyk, "Life-Style Retailing: Competitive Strategies for the 1980s," *Journal of Retailing* 59 (Winter 1983), 7–26.
58. This section is based upon Roger D. Blackwell, "Integrated Marketing Communications," in Gary L. Frazier and Jagdish N. Sheth, eds., *Contemporary Views on Marketing Practice* (Lexington, Mass.: Lexington Books, 1987), 237–250.
59. Paul Hawken, *The New Economy* (New York: Ballantine Books, 1983).

Demographic Analysis of Consumer Trends

The seats are covered in cowhide, pictures of the Judds and Hank Williams, Jr., grace the walls. The patrons, some 500 strong, are mostly outfitted in cowboy hats and Wrangler jeans. On the dance floor, an army of cowboy boots is stomping out a Texas two-step as Garth Brooks' song "Unanswered Prayers" blares from the disc jockey's booth.

A cowboy bar in Dallas? A honky-tonk in Nashville? Nope. It's Denim & Diamonds in trendy Santa Monica, one of the hottest new spots in the Los Angeles area. Less than a year ago Denim & Diamonds was a disco playing top 40 hits. Rock's out, country's in. "Country is better to dance to, and besides, it's more sentimental. It's much easier to listen to." And not just in Santa Monica. Over the last two years country music has taken over the airwaves and the record charts, as well as the bestseller lists.

Harold Zullow, a professor at Columbia University who specializes in consumer attitudes, credits the recession. "Country music focuses on the pathos in life, and so it makes sense that in times where people are focused on problems, country music will have a greater appeal."

Right in the eye of this popular storm is an unprepossessing-looking 30-year-old Oklahoman named Garth Brooks. He used to watch the rock group Queen and figured there was no reason he couldn't do those kinds of theatrics in country. "Garth is like Led Zeppelin meets Roy Rogers," says James Bowen of Liberty Records. One week in January Brooks records sold nearly 340,000 units, putting $500,000 in his wallet.

Brooks represents the new breed of country music entertainer. He was a marketing and advertising major in college, and the training shows—and it's not just in his stage antics. Brooks' ticket prices last year were $15, about half what the Rolling Stones charged on their last tour. "The less people pay at the gate, the more they'll spend inside," says Brooks. "That's just simple logic. I believe in the Wal-Mart school of business. The less people pay for a product that they are happy with, the happier they are with it." He pays attention to quality as well, selling T-shirts at $8.50 that are all 100 percent cotton, about the heaviest weight you can buy. Brooks says, "That shirt is an advertisement on someone's back. So we want to give people something that's going to last."

Good quality at a reasonable price. What more can you ask from the entertainment industry—or any other business?

Source: Excerpted from Lisa Gubernick and Peter Newcomb, "The Wal-Mart School of Music," *Forbes* (March 2, 1992), 72–76.

Firms that fail to plan generally plan to fail. Planning, however, requires some facts—a basis of assumptions about the future. Some of the most important facts relate to the structure of the market—its population, income, and lifestyles. For current marketing programs, facts can be collected about the current environment. In earlier chapters, for example, we examined such topics as consumer resources, ethnic make up of the population, and lifestyles. All are critical dimensions of the demographic analysis of markets. How will these facts change in the future? What are the trends in such market conditions? This is the topic of this chapter. In the opening scenario, we saw how country music has replaced rock music to some degree. At Denim & Diamonds, for example, the clientele is of mixed ages. There is a preponderance of young consumers but customers range from 21 to 60. As the young become older and richer, however, they may switch to something more mellow than rock. According to a study by Simmons Research, for example, more people with household incomes of $40,000 or above listen to country music radio than any other format, different from audiences of the past.

Planning for Change

Unless management acts, the more successful a firm has been in the past, the more likely it is to fail in the future. Why? Because of the basic psychological principle that people tend to repeat behavior for which they have been rewarded. It is natural therefore for organizations to continue strategies that have made them successful in the past. The problem arises because the reality of successful strategies is that they must fit the environment. Consequently, marketing programs that have been successful will continue to be so only to the degree that the environment remains the same in the future as it has been in the past.

Consumer analysts are charged with the responsibility of monitoring and interpreting the environment and how it may change in the future. It is a role of increasing importance in most organizations. It is also a role of profound importance in understanding how the entire economy or society functions. These two roles are sometimes described as **micromarketing** and **macromarketing**.

Macroanalysis of Trends and Demographics

Will more food or less be required to feed the population of a country in the future? Will politicians of the future need to appeal to the affluent or to the poor in order to be elected? Will people support the use of nuclear power and its risk of nuclear disaster to meet their energy needs in the future? Or will they continue to support coal-fired energy and its atmospheric pollution that may threaten flooding of coastal areas and droughts of inland areas due to the "greenhouse effect"? Will people spend their time in museums, at sporting events, or at home "cocooning" around their gardens and TV sets?

The answers to all of these questions will be provided by consumers. Finding those answers is the subject of macroanalysis of consumer behavior. Macromarketing applications of consumer behavior focus upon determining the aggregate performance of marketing in society, evaluating marketing from society's perspective, and understanding the consequences in a society of marketing actions and transactions. Marketing scholars generally agree that macromarketing issues also include comparison of the marketing systems of different nations, examining how marketing adapts to different cultures, and the impact of the marketing activities of influential firms such as General Motors on the quality of life in a society.[1]

Consumer Analysis and Marketing Strategy

The economic well-being of a country is directly related to the quantity and types of goods consumers decide to purchase. Consumers may decide to drive cars two or three years longer, which greatly affects employment and GDP in the country. A changed preference for Japanese or Korean cars has profound effects both domestically and globally, not only for managers and government officials but for labor organizations as well.

Many policy issues are related to macromarketing and trends in consumer decisions. If a tax cut is proposed by "supply-side" economists, what changes will result as consumers spend such reductions? What policies would cause consumers to save more and spend less on current consumption? When the average age of the population increases, will health prices increase for young working people who pay the bills or will prices decrease for young consumers because underutilized health care facilities are used more efficiently? If the white population of the United States has low birth rates in combination with high birth and immigration rates among minorities, what will be the effect on Social Security when most of the older (white) retirees are supported by young (black and Hispanic) members of the work force? When large numbers of people migrate to the Sun Belt, are consumers better served by the new but overcrowded facilities in the Sun Belt or by the older but less crowded (and possibly fully depreciated) facilities in the mature cities? What happens when the work force of a nation is primarily producing services (such as the entertainment described in the opening scenario) rather than manufactured goods?

You will not find the answers to these questions in this chapter, unfortunately. The reason is that we don't know the answers. Consumer analysts have focused mostly on micromarketing research even though the field of consumer behavior had its birth in such questions in the pioneering work of George Katona.[2] Today, there is a reawakening of interest in what Katona called behavioral economics and what is now called psychological economics. But frankly, not much is yet known. Perhaps you, as a reader of this book, will generate research that will be included as answers to these questions in future editions.

Microapplications of Trend Analysis

Micromarketing analysis of consumer trends and demographics focuses on marketing programs of specific organizations. **Trend analysis** focuses on discovering marketing opportunities that arise as a result of changes in the environment. Such opportunities include developing new or modified products, changing distribution channels, and improving communications with consumers.

ESV and the Criticality of Growing Profits

The chief financial goal of strong, well-managed corporations is **ESV—enhanced shareholder value**. The importance of long-term, consistent appreciation of shareholder value is observable in company annual reports and other communications with employees and the financial community.[3] If you have taken a financial management course, you will recognize that ESV is nothing new. What is new is the increased recognition that marketing personnel, especially consumer analysts, play a key role in discovering opportunities to grow profits and thus enhance shareholder value.

ESV reflects long-term strategies of a company—such things as investment in new products, joint ventures, and major capital investment.[4] Marketing objectives are much broader than market share, profits, sales increases, or other concepts that have traditionally been yardsticks by which marketing programs are evaluated. *The role of consumer research is to discover ways to increase profits in the future* rather than merely maintain profits. ESV occurs when financial markets believe a firm is well positioned for increasing its earnings in the future, often reflected in a high Price–Earnings (PE) ratio. ESV does not refer only to stock prices however, but to long-term value defined broadly. In the United States, financial performance has often been measured short term, possibly stimulated by government regulations requiring quarterly reporting of results. During the height of "Japan bashing" in the 1992 elections, an executive of a Japanese firm explained, "You Americans manage companies to achieve quarterly results to report. In Japan, we manage our companies from the perspective of what the corporation will be 1,000 years from now."

3 M's of Profit Growth

Three major ways of increasing profits exist in which the study of consumer trends plays a major role. The three ways of growing profits can be thought of as the 3 M's:

1. More markets
2. More market share
3. More margin

In this chapter we mainly examine the first M—markets. Much of the rest of this text focuses on the issue of the second M—gaining market share. The third M—margin—involves strategies to reduce costs or to increase the price that can be obtained for a product. Cost reduction is mostly outside the scope of our present study. Logistics or physical distribution management, which is often an important part of reducing costs, is closely related to consumer behavior, however, because of the need to define customer satisfaction standards. Increasing prices is closely related to consumer analysis, because consumer perceptions of value are directly related to pricing strategies.

Although the third M is mostly outside the scope of this text, it is essential that consumer analysts have an appreciation for the role of physical distribution and logistics. Both consumer behavior and logistics ultimately have the same objective: customer satisfaction. If a product is delivered in poor condition, is too high priced because of distribution and warehousing costs, or is out of stock—all major concerns of logistics management—the result is just as disastrous or more so than if consumer behavior analysts have designed the product or communicated its attributes poorly. Notice Figure 20.1. Consumer analysts might study how a stereo sounds and looks or how easy it is for consumers to connect the components. The Consolidated Freightways ad makes the point that customer satisfaction is just as much a function of distribution and logistics management.

ConAgra is an example of a company that has achieved remarkable growth in mature industries often thought to have limited possibilities for growing earnings. ConAgra has grown by searching for market opportunities and exploiting them to

FIGURE 20.1   Customer Satisfaction Depends on Logistics
Source: Courtesy of Consolidated Freightways, Inc.

their fullest. As you read Consumer in Focus 20.1, notice how ConAgra uses all three of the "M's" to enhance shareholder value.

More Markets   People and their ability to buy are the most basic determinants of markets. Thus, consumer analysts have a special responsibility of determining trends in population and buying power *to discover market segments that are growing.* Finding growth segments might include analysis of geographical growth areas, enlarging age groups, new sources of income, global opportunities to replace declining domestic markets, and other trends. Consumer trend analysis might also include methods of reaching growth segments more effectively or sooner than competitors.

Consumer trend analysis has an important application in industrial marketing because industrial demand is ultimately derived from consumer demand. Industrial firms (selling to other organizations) need to give attention to forecasting consumer markets likely to grow fastest. The purpose is to market industrial products and services needed by growth firms producing and marketing consumer goods.

Building Trend Line Earning Power: ConAgra's Strategy

ConAgra is a diversified family of companies with nearly $20 billion of sales in 1991. The company defines its business as helping to feed people better in a world expected to have 8.5 billion people to feed by the year 2025. The company also has a strong commitment to protect and nurture the environment in order to give our children and grandchildren a better future and environmentally sustainable forms of economic progress. In addition to operations in the U.S., ConAgra has extensive operations in the Asia-Pacific Rim, Latin America, Europe, Canada, Eastern Europe, and the former Soviet Union.

ConAgra concentrates on building trend line earning power to reward stockholders over the long haul. ConAgra's most important objective is to average better than a 20-percent return on beginning common equity. ConAgra's 10-year average return to investors has been 25.3 percent. By contrast, the median return on equity for the Fortune 500 food companies is less than 16 percent. For all the Fortune 500 companies the figure is less than 12 percent.

Spurred by new products including new Healthy Choice offerings, the prepared foods division increased profits 90 percent in 1991 over 1990 on a sales increase of 36 percent. The company emphasizes convenient, value-oriented foods that include Hunt's tomato products, Wesson cooking and salad oils, Manwich sloppy joe sandwich, Orville Redenbacher's popcorn, Peter Pan peanut butter, Snack Pack puddings, Swiss Miss puddings and cocoa mixes, La Choy Oriental products, and Rosarita and Gehardt Mexican products. The Hunt-Wesson group of brands boasts one of the most advanced and cost-efficient, shelf-stable grocery sales and distribution systems in the nation.

ConAgra Frozen Foods is a leading producer and marketer of frozen prepared foods, many of which appeal to changing lifestyles and demographic trends. Principal brands are Banquet, Healthy Choice, Kid Cuisine, Morton, Patio, Chun King, La Choy, Armour Classics, Country Skillet and Ultra Slim Fast frozen entrees. In 1991 and 1992, ConAgra introduced 122 new products including new frozen Healthy Choice dinners and entrees and a line of breakfast products including sandwiches, muffins and cholesterol-free egg products as well as Healthy Choice frozen dairy dessert. Healthy Choice soups, stews, pastas, and chilies in cans and micro-cups were in test market and in 1992 many of these products were introduced to Canada as well as rolled out throughout the U.S.

One of the reasons the company has grown in a fairly flat industry that is fraught with fierce competition is because managers understand their brand equity. They understand price/value relationships—they fill consumer needs, they know what consumers are looking for, and they deliver consistent quality that meets consumers' expectations.

A wide variety of products are marketed under brands such as Armour, Swift-Eckrich, Butterball poultry (primarily turkeys), Beatrice Cheese, Conagra Shrimp and Country Skillet catfish. Many of these products have focused on lower salt products. Armour is now the leader in the lower salt category with a line that includes lower salt ham, bacon, hot dogs, sausage, luncheon meats and cheeses.

Patio and Chun King are two good examples of applying research that helped know these brands had good equity in the ethnic arena. They found ways to build on it, introducing Patio microwave burritos and Chun King microwave egg rolls.

The microwave oven, for example, has changed the lifestyles of many consumers—more than 60 percent of U.S. households now have microwave ovens. Many frozen foods today are "dual oven," meaning you can prepare them in either a conventional oven or a microwave oven. So when ConAgra set out to restage the Dinner Classics line, research showed that consumers wanted microwaveability. It produced the new Dinner Classics so that it would be superior when prepared in a microwave. The new Dinner Classics can also be prepared in a conventional oven, but it's best when microwaved. ConAgra did not compromise microwave performance to focus on "dual ovenability."

Marketing is something that's been central to ConAgra's business philosophy for years. "When we use the term, we are talking about marketing in its broadest sense; it's much more than the eye-catching packages and the memorable advertising campaigns that get so much attention. We focus on the entire marketing process of determining what our customers or consumers need, then providing the right product or service at an appropriate price/value relationship—and in a timely, consistent, and dependable manner."

There are four keys that lead to long-term success and plans for the future at ConAgra. The company is built on these four enduring fundamentals:

1. Establish leading positions across the food chain.
2. Structure for entrepreneurial, results-oriented leadership.
3. Commit to premium long-term financial objectives.
4. Reward our stockholders.

The results? If you bought 10,000 shares of ConAgra in 1975 at $3, at the end of 1991 you would have owned 135,000 shares due to stock splits and your $30,000 investment would have grown to more than $6 million. Plus dividends along the way.

Source: 1991 ConAgra Annual Report and other company reports.

Focusing on consumer trends helps firms avoid artificial separation of industrial and consumer markets. Firms that concentrate on products or services for one or the other may find growth opportunities by focusing on the overall trend and moving aggressively between industrial and consumer marketing. ServiceMaster is a rapidly growing service firm with sales of over $2 billion. Ten years ago the company received 93 percent of its revenues from business services and only 7 percent from consumer services. After a decade of responding to changing markets, the company receives 24 percent of its operating income from consumer services and products. The process occurred because the company focused on health care, education, child care, and home care. Initially its expertise was mostly in management services to the firms in these growing industries but, over the years, the company has extended these areas of expertise to consumer markets through divisions such as Terminix termite and pest control services, Tru-Green and Chem Lawn lawn services, maid services through Merry Maids franchises, and residential and appliance repair or replacement through American Home Shield. This process is known at ServiceMaster as the "2 × 5" approach to markets—doubling the customer base every 5 years.

The Changing Structure of Consumer Markets   The search for growing profit opportunities leads to careful analysis of trends in the structure of markets. Markets are defined as having four major components:

1. People and their needs
2. Ability to buy
3. Willingness to buy
4. Authority to buy

Variables are examined in the following pages that help understand the first three of these components. First, we focus on people—forecasting how many are likely to exist as potential consumers and some understanding of their needs related to age and other demographic factors. Second, we focus on changes in buying power that have occurred and are likely to occur in the future. Third, we briefly describe social and technological trends that affect willingness to buy some products more than others or favor particular marketers. Additionally, we examine some other trends that affect the development of marketing, especially trends in the geography of demand and the rise of an information society. The chapter concludes with discussion of how consumer analysts keep aware of these trends with a process called environmental scanning.

People: Foundation of Market Analysis

People are the foundation of market analysis. How many will there be? What will be the age distribution? Where will they live? These issues involve the study of demographics, defined as the size, structure, and distribution of a population. When combined with data on purchasing power or wealth, this type of analysis is called **economic demographics**, the study of the economic characteristics of a nation's population.

The most important application of economic demographics is market segmentation strategies, the process of dividing a total market into groups of people who have relatively similar characteristics and behavior. The next chapter describes how to reach those market segments. In this chapter, look for market segments that are growing either in size or in purchasing power. If a firm can market effectively to growing segments, the firm's profits will grow even when the total market is slowing in growth or declining.

There are no more mass markets, it is often observed, only variations in the size of segments. That is the reason we spend the entire next chapter on the topic of segmentation. You can't sell everything to anybody and you can't sell anything to everybody. As an executive of Sears' information services recently observed, "There's this great big market out there called the United States. If you go after them, it's the death knell."[5] In this chapter, we analyze how to avoid going after the "great big market" and, instead, how to harvest growing profits from little markets.

Population is the foundation for market analysis because of its critical importance in determining demand. It is also reliably predictable. Population demographics move like celestial mechanics, a great advantage when compared to most variables studied by consumer analysts. There are unknowns, of course. Discontinuities include natural calamities, wars, and medical problems such as plagues in ancient times or AIDS in modern times. Ordinarily, though, populations of countries are reasonably predictable.

Births are the most important of the three variables (births, deaths, and net immigration) that determine the population of a country. Births are also the most volatile. Before looking at overall population projections, we need to examine the critical question of how many babies will be born in the future.

How Many Babies?

Slight changes in the birthrate have enormous impact on consumer demand. After years of decline, there has been an increase in the number of births in the early years of the 1990s decade. Is this a real increase in fertility or merely the result of women making up for delayed childbearing? These differences in opinion account for 27 different possible population totals by the Census Bureau ranging from 260 million to 278 million in the year 2000.[6]

Whether families spend money on food and education of children or on luxury goods and travel is greatly influenced by average family size. Consumption decisions for both individual families and the larger society are impacted by birthrates.

Causes of Babies

Birthrates are determined by four variables. First is *age distribution* of the population. Second is *family structure*. What proportion are married? What proportion of the women are employed outside of the home? What is the average age when people get married? The third cause of births is *social attitudes* toward family and children. Finally, birthrates are affected by *technology*, such as availability and cost of contraception.

Basic Concepts

Several terms are used by consumer analysts and others when describing and projecting future populations.[7] The **birthrate** (also called **crude birthrate**) is the number of live births per 1,000 population in a given year. The **fertility rate** (also called **general fertility rate**) is the number of live births per 1,000 women of childbearing age (defined as 15 to 44). Fertility rates are sometimes stated as age-specific rates (such as age 30 to 39 women) to facilitate comparison over time or to see differences in fertility at different ages. **Completed fertility rate** is the total number of children ever born to women of a specific age group. In 1910, the completed fertility rate for women aged 50 to 54 was 4.1, but by 1980 that number had dropped to 3.0 and probably will be less in the 1990 Census.

The **total fertility rate** (TFR) is the average number of children that would be born alive to a woman during her lifetime if she were to pass through all her childbearing years conforming to the age-specific fertility rates of a given year. Although it is a synthetic number and might seem complex, TFR is the most useful indicator of fertility because it answers the simple question: How many children are women having currently? In many developing countries, the number is over 6.0. Currently in the United States it is about 1.8 children. TFR is even lower in Europe and some other developed countries. A **replacement rate** is a fertility rate of 2.1 children, the number required for a couple to replace the current population, with allowance for some infant mortality.

The number of babies born in any year is a product of the fertility rate (generally declining in most countries) times the number of women of childbearing age (generally increasing). The result is increasing population in the United States and most countries. The birthrate is as high as 52 per 1,000 in Kenya but as low as 10 per 1,000 in Denmark, where population is now decreasing annually. In the United States, the birthrate dropped from historical levels of 25 to 30 per 1,000 to about 15 or 16 in the latter part of the 1980s.

Birthrates should not be confused with **natural increase**, which is the surplus of births over deaths in a given time period. An even more important concept is **growth rate** of a population due to natural increase and net migration, expressed as a percentage of the base population. The growth rate takes into account all components of population growth. Although the world's growth rate is about 1.7 percent (or stated alternatively, an increase of 17 per 1,000 population per year), the United States is at .9 and with some projections of a decline to about .6 by the year 2000. If the rate of .9 were to continue, the U.S. population would double in about 78 years. Length of time required to double in size based on current growth rates is called the **doubling rate**.

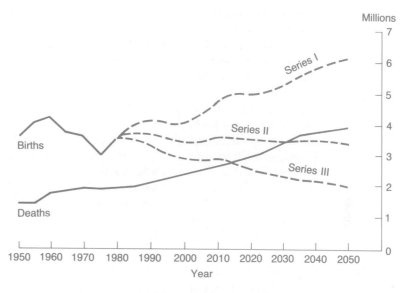

FIGURE 20.2   Births and Deaths in the United States
Source: Lowest, medium, and highest fertility series. U.S. Bureau of the Census.

Future Fertility

Forecasting births in future decades is difficult. Although fecundity, the physiological capability of couples to reproduce, is fairly predictable, fertility, which is actual reproductive performance, is more difficult. Fertility is affected by fecundity but also by age at marriage or cohabitation, the availability and use of family planning, economic development, the status of women, and the age-sex structure.

The solution to the problem of forecasting babies born—and thus total population—adopted by the Census Bureau is to provide several projections based upon different fertility assumptions. Series I assumes 2.7 children per woman, Series II assumes 2.1 children per woman, and Series III assumes 1.7. Calculating the number of births that will occur under each assumption produces radically different estimates (Figure 20.2), anywhere between 3 and 4 million births per year by the year 2050.

Fertility rates declined from a high of 3.7 in 1960 to 1.8 in 1978. After 1978, a slight increase in fertility occurred, and the large number of women of childbearing age caused total births to increase in a "mini-baby boom." However, fertility rates decreased in the latter part of the 1980s, increased slightly in the early 1990s and the picture for the future is uncertain. Greater labor force participation of females, later age of marriage, and increasing educational levels all are associated with lower fertility rate assumptions for the future. Wives aged 18 to 34 expect to have an average of 2.1 children in their lifetime, although the actual rate is consistently lower than expectations.

Attitudes toward marriage and children are also changing. A study by *Better Homes & Gardens* of its readers—who presumably are among the more family oriented consumers in the economy—investigated these attitudes. When asked the question, "Do you think a husband and wife must have children—either their own or adopted—in order to have a fulfilling and happy life?" 85 percent of the women and 74 percent of the men said "no."[8] If fertility rates continue at a low level and current trends in mortality rates also continue, there will come a time in the United States and other industrialized countries when deaths will outnumber births, as they already have in Germany and Scandinavian countries. Family size has been dramatically affected by attitudes and behavior toward contraception, a trend that is reasonably permanent considering that the leading method of contraception in the United States is now sterilization.[9]

Order Effects

Order effects produce significant consumption differences between families even when the total number of babies is the same. **First-order** (first-born) babies generate more economic impact than **higher order** (second, third, fourth, and so on) babies. First-order babies may generate $1,500 of retail sales, for example, compared to less than half of that for higher order babies. In 1960, only one child in four was first-born, but by 1990 this figure was nearly 50 percent.

The marketing programs of some companies are especially impacted by order effects. Eastman Kodak benefits from first-order babies because their happy parents buy cameras and take massive quantities of pictures. Higher order children may be lucky to get one picture at graduation. Families with one child can afford to eat at better restaurants and buy wanted products such as personal computers, extension phones in the child's room, new and better clothes instead of hand-me-downs, and services such as private education, ballet school, gymnastics or other sports lessons, and so forth.

You might ask if people really have enough money to buy all of these nice things for their children. The answer is most often yes in the special case of only children. One reason only children have such a disproportionately high achievement rate is the simple fact of resource constraints. A family with *only one child has more economic and temporal resources—money and time to spend on a child's development, education and health than the same family would if there were more than one child.*

Having one's first child at an older age—the trend for the foreseeable future—usually results in fewer children per family. Not only does this produce more money to spend on each child for a vast array of goods and services, but it also has macroeconomic effects associated with a slower growing population base in the society, including the possibility of Zero Population Growth (ZPG) in some countries. The social effects of ZPG, or near-ZPG, include fewer people available to serve in the military and to pay for Social Security (at the same time that the number of people receiving Social Security rises dramatically), less crime, higher productivity in offices and factories, lower unemployment rates, and other economic and social consequences.

Another factor affecting births is abortion. The Alan Guttmacher Institute in New York reports that abortions increased dramatically in the 1970s in the United States and other countries. The U.S. rate of abortion—28.2 per 1,000 women—ranks about mid-range internationally. Canada's rate, 11.3 per 1,000, is very low. Among the highest are Cuba, with a rate of 52.1, and Bulgaria, with a rate of 68.3, according to The Guttmacher Institute.

Childlessness has also become more prevalent. By the end of the 1980s, about 25 percent of college-educated working women were childless. In addition to college education and employment outside the home, other variables associated with childlessness tend to be marriage later in life, not actively religious, and urban residence. Some of the "baby busters" are those who have made a deliberate decision not to have children; others simply delay the decision for economic or other reasons until the opportunity to have children is greatly diminished. The practical consequence is more spending power available for travel, luxury products that pamper one's self, adult education and self-development services, and perhaps more need for savings and retirement planning.

Ethnic Variations

A key variable in understanding the number of consumers in the future is ethnic variation in fertility. The fertility rate among Hispanic women aged 18 to 44 was 95.8 compared to about 83 births per 1,000 black women and 69 per 1,000 among white women. The key difference is among younger women, however. Among black and white women over 30, currently there are not statistically significant differences in fertility.

White women typically have babies at older ages than other ethnic groups. Therefore, white families have fewer babies in total. By 1990, about 55 percent of births to black women were to women who were not married, a level about 4 times as high as that of white women (12 percent) and about twice as high as that reported by Hispanic women (26 percent). Approximately 11 percent of all births currently are to Hispanic women, although they constitute only 8 percent of all women 18 to 44 years old. Such ethnic variations markedly affect attractiveness of market segments as well as affecting total population in a country.

Most Likely Scenarios

The variables described above will determine the population of the future. No one knows exactly what will occur. Since we don't know how many people will be born, one approach for consumer researchers is to examine the consequences of alternative

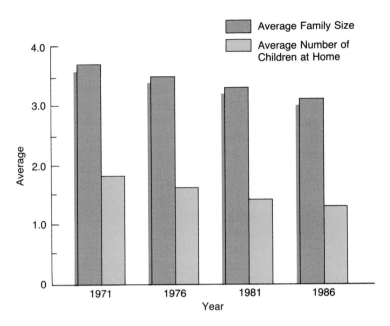

FIGURE 20.3 **Fewer Kids, Smaller Families in Canada**
Source: Statistics Canada, *The Daily,* July 9, 1987.

scenarios. Based upon an understanding of the variations in fertility, it is possible to develop the most likely scenarios in making projections. This is the approach reflected in Figure 20.3 and the following pages in discussing future population trends and their marketing implications in North America. Legal immigration was 530,000 per year in the 1980s and increases to 700,000 in 1992–1994 and 675,000 thereafter. Undocumented migrants boost the numbers but immigration is still a small part of the total U.S. population.

Trends in the Population of North America

The population base in North America is expanding but at a decreasing rate. In both Canada and the United States, the population is growing at less than 1 percent a year. Projections of the populations for both countries are presented in Table 20.1 (on pages 654–655) and Table 20.2 (on page 656), which serve as the basis for much of the following discussion. Differing years of census and other problems make it difficult to present the projections in the same format for both Canada and the U.S., but an examination of these tables reveals great similarities in changing age distribution and growth rates of the two countries.

U.S.-Canadian Markets

Important changes in tariff restrictions began to take effect in 1990, allowing freer access by Canadian and U.S. marketers to the consumers of the other country. Canadian marketers were often more aware of the U.S. market in the past than were U.S. marketers of Canadian markets, but in the future consumer analysts must understand both countries since all trade barriers are supposed to cease by 1998.

Freer exchange of marketing programs between Canada and the United States will provide opportunities for growth. In some instances, increased competition will also occur. Canadian beers (as well as Mexican beers) have made significant penetration in the U.S. market, for example. Automobile production and marketing is highly integrated by North American manufacturers. Windsor plants supply all of Chrysler's minivan products for North America, as an example. Canada and the United States have more than $150 billion of merchandise trade, more than any other pair of nations, and the future promises even more with movement toward a unified or single North American market in the 1990s, somewhat along the lines of the European Community.

Table 20.1 is a comprehensive and detailed description of the U.S. population in the year 2000. It also shows the effects of different scenarios about birthrates. Perhaps you will find it fascinating to look at all the numbers in that table, but don't be discouraged if it does not fascinate you. We explain the major trends contained in the table in the following pages. Since the Canadian population is smaller and the graphics less formidable, we examine Canadian trends first.

Canadian Population

The population of Canada is currently almost 27 million persons, based upon the most recent Census. Figure 20.3 shows that Canadians are having fewer children and smaller families, causing the growth rate to drop to .84 percent annually, the lowest in history and down from a high of about 3 percent annually in the 1950s. The number of immigrants is also declining, from 135,000 in 1981–1982 to 85,000 in more recent years. Women in Canada now average 1.6 births in their lifetimes. If present trends continue, Canada's population will peak at about 28 million sometime after the year 2000 and then begin to decrease in the next century.

The age structure of Canada is changing dramatically but in ways that are similar to what is happening in the United States, we will not discuss them separately. In Mexico, however, the population is much younger, much less affluent, and growing much more rapidly. As you read the following pages about the changing U.S. age structure, keep in mind that the basic trends occurring in the U.S. are similar in Canada. This is also true with reference to the trends toward more education and the emerging importance of women in the labor force. Women make up the majority (about 52 percent) of all Canadian university students, as is true in the United States. The majority of Canadian families are also dual-earner families. About 54 percent of women aged 25 and over were in the labor force.

TABLE 20.1 Projections of the Total Population by Age, Sex, Race, and Spanish Origin: 1990 to 2000 (in thousands as of July 1; includes Armed Forces overseas)

Age, Sex, Race, and Spanish Origin	Lowest Series			Middle Series			Highest Series		
	1990	1995	2000	1990	1995	2000	1990	1995	2000
Total population*	**245,753**	**251,876**	**256,098**	**249,657**	**259,559**	**267,955**	**254,122**	**268,151**	**281,542**
Under 5 years old	17,515	16,193	14,942	19,198	18,615	17,626	20,615	20,815	20,530
5–17 years old	44,486	46,125	44,951	45,139	48,518	49,763	46,055	50,990	54,434
18–24 years old	25,547	23,347	24,157	25,794	23,702	24,601	26,137	24,233	25,326
25–34 years old	43,147	39,887	35,596	43,529	40,520	36,415	44,329	41,672	37,850
35–44 years old	37,570	41,500	42,972	37,847	41,997	43,743	38,229	42,870	45,128
45–54 years old	25,226	31,044	36,533	25,402	31,397	37,119	25,578	31,763	37,813
55–64 years old	20,910	20,655	23,326	21,051	20,923	23,767	21,189	21,190	24,212
65 years old and over	31,353	33,127	33,621	31,697	33,887	34,921	31,989	34,618	36,246
16 years old and over	190,198	196,242	203,526	191,819	199,188	208,185	194,035	203,249	214,597
Male, total	**119,620**	**122,608**	**124,671**	**121,518**	**126,368**	**130,491**	**123,698**	**130,577**	**137,163**
Under 5 years old	8,964	8,288	7,647	9,827	9,529	9,022	10,550	10,653	10,508
5–17 years old	22,745	23,586	22,989	23,082	24,815	25,458	23,549	26,074	27,842
18–24 years old	13,016	11,904	12,314	13,127	12,072	12,530	13,283	12,325	12,881
25–34 years old	21,722	20,155	18,009	21,892	20,443	18,384	22,261	20,959	19,044
35–44 years old	18,598	20,649	21,508	18,732	20,879	21,866	18,927	21,322	22,537
45–54 years old	12,268	15,152	17,903	12,350	15,327	18,196	12,441	15,518	18,563
55–64 years old	9,804	9,733	11,046	9,871	9,865	11,272	9,936	10,000	11,511
65 years old and over	12,503	13,143	13,255	12,637	13,440	13,762	12,751	13,725	14,277
16 years old and over	91,205	94,152	97,779	91,929	95,480	99,906	92,964	97,378	102,913
Female, total	**126,133**	**129,268**	**131,427**	**128,139**	**133,191**	**137,464**	**130,424**	**137,574**	**144,379**
Under 5 years old	8,551	7,906	7,295	9,371	9,086	8,604	10,065	10,161	10,022
5–17 years old	21,741	22,539	21,962	22,056	23,703	24,305	22,506	24,915	26,592
18–24 years old	12,532	11,443	11,843	12,667	11,630	12,071	12,854	11,908	12,445
25–34 years old	21,426	19,731	17,586	21,637	20,077	18,031	22,068	20,713	18,806
35–44 years old	18,971	20,851	21,465	19,116	21,119	21,877	19,302	21,548	22,591
45–54 years old	12,958	15,891	18,630	13,051	16,071	18,923	13,137	16,245	19,251
55–64 years old	11,105	10,922	12,279	11,180	11,059	12,495	11,253	11,190	12,702
65 years old and over	18,850	19,984	20,366	19,061	20,447	21,158	19,238	20,893	21,969
16 years old and over	98,993	102,090	105,747	99,890	103,708	108,279	101,071	105,871	111,684

continued

*Includes other races not shown separately.

TABLE 20.1 continued

Age, Sex, Race, and Spanish Origin	Lowest Series			Middle Series			Highest Series		
	1990	1995	2000	1990	1995	2000	1990	1995	2000
White, total	**207,799**	**211,481**	**213,498**	**210,790**	**217,412**	**222,654**	**213,753**	**223,236**	**231,980**
Under 5 years old	14,046	12,884	11,760	15,390	14,797	13,843	16,451	16,417	15,958
5–17 years old	36,028	37,062	35,876	36,523	38,941	39,667	37,149	40,716	43,061
18–24 years old	20,989	19,008	19,485	21,170	19,267	19,806	21,369	19,578	20,238
25–34 years old	36,027	32,867	29,009	36,289	33,312	29,590	36,768	33,998	30,442
35–44 years old	32,097	35,037	35,822	32,292	35,379	36,355	32,509	35,895	37,180
45–54 years old	21,868	26,822	31,239	21,994	27,077	31,662	22,090	27,286	32,071
55–64 years old	18,432	18,014	20,273	18,536	18,213	20,605	18,605	18,362	20,868
65 years old and over	28,313	29,787	30,032	28,596	30,424	31,126	28,810	30,984	32,162
16 years old and over	162,971	166,987	171,734	164,160	169,181	175,245	165,486	171,695	179,346
Male	101,518	103,352	104,369	102,979	106,266	108,879	104,460	109,175	113,536
Female	106,281	108,129	109,129	107,811	111,146	113,775	109,292	114,061	118,445
Black, total	**30,836**	**32,506**	**33,957**	**31,412**	**33,651**	**35,753**	**31,974**	**34,780**	**37,602**
Under 5 years old	2,948	2,771	2,620	3,215	3,165	3,079	3,440	3,525	3,570
5–17 years old	6,942	7,498	7,553	7,042	7,871	8,321	7,159	8,222	9,031
18–24 years old	3,766	3,495	3,715	3,798	3,542	3,773	3,849	3,620	3,865
25–34 years old	5,809	5,683	5,208	5,860	5,768	5,316	5,932	5,884	5,479
35–44 years old	4,254	5,096	5,701	4,295	5,169	5,811	4,339	5,261	5,954
45–54 years old	2,600	3,210	4,036	2,626	3,262	4,124	2,646	3,307	4,211
55–64 years old	1,978	2,035	2,292	1,998	2,073	2,355	2,013	2,103	2,407
65 years old and over	2,538	2,717	2,833	2,579	2,802	2,975	2,597	2,857	3,085
16 years old and over	21,922	23,230	24,996	22,138	23,618	25,613	22,372	24,055	26,317
Male	14,645	15,451	16,156	14,926	16,013	17,040	15,204	16,573	17,958
Female	16,191	17,055	17,802	16,485	17,638	18,714	16,769	18,207	19,644
Spanish origin, total†	**19,148**	**21,149**	**23,065**	**19,887**	**22,550**	**25,223**	**22,053**	**26,475**	**31,208**
Under 5 years old	2,047	2,039	2,033	2,282	2,412	2,496	2,690	3,129	3,510
5–17 years old	4,682	5,158	5,436	4,825	5,554	6,206	5,337	6,605	7,973
18–24 years old	2,289	2,376	2,602	2,386	2,511	2,766	2,811	3,069	3,499
25–34 years old	3,517	3,514	3,529	3,629	3,717	3,804	4,242	4,782	5,129
35–44 years old	2,721	3,309	3,602	2,768	3,430	3,803	2,900	3,771	4,590
45–54 years old	1,629	2,091	2,687	1,688	2,165	2,811	1,720	2,262	2,993
55–64 years old	1,160	1,297	1,547	1,183	1,341	1,619	1,209	1,394	1,709
65 years old and over	1,101	1,367	1,627	1,126	1,419	1,719	1,144	1,463	1,804
16 years old and over	13,070	15,663	16,434	13,453	15,322	17,419	14,763	17,597	20,807
Male	9,580	10,586	11,548	9,947	11,285	12,627	11,137	13,425	15,869
Female	9,568	10,562	11,516	9,490	11,265	12,596	10,916	13,050	15,339

†Persons of Spanish origin may be of any race.
Source: U.S. Bureau of the Census, *Current Population Reports*, series P-25, No. 952.

TABLE 20.2 **Canadian Population Projections, 1981–2001**

Year	Population as of June 1, 2000	Annual Rate of Population Growth	Distribution by Age			
			9–19	20–44	45–64	65+
1981	24,041.4	1.1%	32.0%	39.6%	19.0%	9.4%
1986	25,382.9	1.1	29.3	41.9	18.7	10.1
1991	26,591.4	0.9	28.4	41.5	19.1	11.0
1996	27,569.7	0.7	27.8	39.8	20.9	11.5
2001	28,369.7	0.6	26.7	37.9	23.6	11.8

Source: Series C Projections, Statistics Canada. (Series C assumes total fertility will change to 1.80 by 1985 and remain constant through 2001, net migration gain of 60,000 per year and expectation of life at birth will increase gradually to 70.2 years for males and 78.4 for females by 1986 and then remain constant through 2001.)

Average income in Canada has been on a roller coaster in recent years. Between 1980 and 1984, average real income (expressed in 1984 Canadian dollars) declined from $37,950 to $35,770. It began to rebound in the latter part of the 1980s to around $38,000 but still lagged behind the rapid growth that had been seen in real income during the 1970s. Average income is highest in Alberta and Ontario and lowest in Newfoundland and Prince Edward Island. By age group, the young have not done so well, and the only families to gain purchasing power have been those headed by someone aged 65 or older.[10]

Caution and some lack of confidence exists among Canadian consumers because of inflation, decreased purchasing power, the increased risk of unemployment, and slower economic growth. The latter part of the 1980s saw a reversal of some of these trends, leading to more willingness to buy and optimism about markets of the future but during the 1990s, concern exists about Canadian retailing due to the G.S.T. (General Sales Tax), prompting many Canadian consumers to go south of the border for shopping.

As general trends, the Canadian market is characterized as one of slower growth population, an aging population, declining youth markets, maturing of the baby boom generation, more working women, and a changed family structure that features later marriage, more single young adults, more common-law unions, and more well-educated, dual-income households.

Changing Ages of Markets

The changing age distribution in North America affects consumer behavior in many ways essential to understanding how to develop effective marketing programs. Understanding these changes permits forecasting the consumption of some products as well as related behaviors, attitudes and opinions.[11]

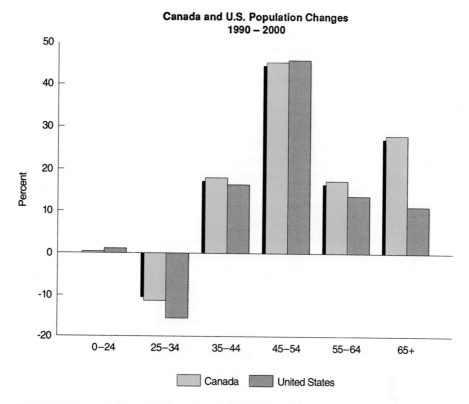

FIGURE 20.4   Projected Changes in Population by Age in Canada and the United States

Examine Table 20.1 carefully and you will notice that projections of age segments vary most among younger ages (not yet born at the time of the projection) but there should not be much variation from the projections for older ages. To help you get an overall picture of the next few pages, refer to Figure 20.4, which graphically shows the changes in population expected from 1990 to 2000.

Consuming Children

The number of young children may decline during the 1990s but their importance as consumers won't decline. Using the low series of population projections (in Table 20.1), the number of children under 5 will decline from 17.5 million to 14.9 million between 1990 and 2000. The high proportion of first-order babies will generate high demand for quality products and services. In addition to higher quality products, parents may expect more information about the product. Parents will pay for designer labels, shop more at specialty stores, and have higher expectations during usage of products.

Children don't sign checks but they do have a big influence on spending. A couple whose oldest child is under 6 years old spends 10 percent more money in total than the average couple without children. A couple whole oldest child is aged 6 to 17 spends 24 percent more and a couple whose oldest child is aged 18 or older spends 36 percent more.[12] On average, children influence 17 percent of family spending in many product categories with some categories such as fruit snacks influenced 80 percent of the time by children.[13]

Marketing programs emphasize style and attractiveness when clothing and other products are consumed by only one child. Attributes of durability and timelessness of style are not so important as when products are "handed down." J.C. Penney added designer clothes and discarded "hard lines" such as tires and auto supplies to create a fashion image that would appeal to children and parents who can afford and are willing to buy fashionable clothing.

Second-use stores and informal trading networks develop to achieve multiple use of beautiful and expensive products by multiple children—but in different families. Conversely, some products—such as diapers or other consumables—are more likely to be disposable, even in the face of environmental concerns about such products. Hotel chains such as Hyatt have targeted children to reach parents with a program called Camp Hyatt. Hyatt formed a Camp Hyatt Kids Council, ages 7 to 12, which told the firm, among other things, to have fun things to do besides just jumping on beds. Trends are important to study because kids love new things, whether it be songs, dances, food, toys, or computer games.[14] Research methods useful in understanding children are described in Consumer in Focus 20.2.

Fall and Rise of Teenagers

The tumultuous fall in number of teenagers that occurred during the 1980s should reverse in the 1990s with a rise of several million in the number of teenagers. During the decline, severe labor shortages occurred, as well as declining markets for fast food and other products appealing to teenagers. McDonald's changed its advertising that formerly featured teenagers to include mature individuals working in the restaurants. Salads and food appealing to young adults were added by McDonald's to compensate for a declining number of teenagers.

Marketers to teenagers can thrive by appealing to *spending power disproportionate to the number of teenagers*. In 1987, annual spending of teenagers was estimated at $234 billion and rising at the rate of $7 billion a year. Nearly $142 billion was created by the 75 percent of teenagers who claim that they urge their parents to buy products and services for the home.[15] Grocery marketers are now directing ads to teenagers, who are increasingly given the task of buying the family groceries in dual-income families. The Levi's! jeans ad in Figure 20.5 also shows the influence children and young teens may have on parents.

Consumer in Focus 20.2

Understanding the Child Consumer

The child consumer isn't just a pint-sized version of an adult. The methods used by researchers are designed to get to know how they, and only they, act and react; to understand their ever-changing tastes and desires. Focus groups can be useful in studying kids if moderators tune in properly and refine how to talk with kids on their own terms.

Unlike adults, youngsters provide information through more than conversation and focus group moderators who vary from conference table conversation can reap increased, better information. Techniques include role-playing and simulated shopping.

The key is knowing how they think. Does crunchy mean the same thing to a child as an adult? If kids are under 7, it's "crunchy" if they can hear it. You can't ask young children what food they have eaten in the last month, because they often don't know what a month is.

Peer pressure is one of the toughest obstacles for moderators; it can easily color kids' answers. One way to diminish peer pressure is to give the kids some anonymity by talking to kids when no kid sees another kid in that room they know or through individual interviews. If boys and girls are in the same room, differences in their reactions to products get muddled so it is usually best to separate the sexes.

Because kids look up to older kids, it is important to keep group members within a two-year age span. Nine and 10 year olds are most forthcoming with their own opinions. Younger children are more tied to their families. Older kids tend to be cynical.

Source: Excerpted from Betsy Spethmann, "Focus Groups Key to Reaching Kids," *Advertising Age* (February 10, 1992).

Young Adults from the Baby Bust

Young adults are declining in numbers at a rapid rate. In Figure 20.2, you can see that the age group of 25 to 34 will decline about 10 percent in Canada and 15 percent in the United States as a result of the birth dearth during the 1970s. From a consumption perspective, age 25 to 34 is the time when families form up, bear young and often buy their first home and their first new car.

Declines in young adults produces a vacuum in sales of new homes, new cars, and many other products. Some observers wonder why the beginning of the 1990s experienced slow sales in homes, cars and related products. Yet, consumer analysts

FIGURE 20.5   Influence of Children on Parental Purchasing

Source: Courtesy of Levi Strauss & Co.

who understand demographics find no surprise in such declining sales. This is also the age when young families spend all they can earn and most of what they can borrow to achieve the kind of standards of living they expect from watching their parents. They save little and use a lot of credit cards to support their "habit" of homes, microwaves, VCRs and similar consumer goods. They buy in value-oriented discount retailers. The demand will be diminished during the 1990s for such purchases. For stores selling to these consumers, there will be a new chapter written in the 1990s. Often the chapter will be 11!

Baby Boomers and Muppies

The most important year of the decade may be 1996 because that is when baby boomers start to hit age 50. *Baby boomers* is a term given to the cohort of people born in huge numbers following World War II. The soaring fertility lasted through 74 million births by 1964, which will continue to impact markets and all other aspects of society for decades. In the 1980s, marketers focused on Yuppies—young urban professionals—because of their discretionary income and their influence on market trends. Today, Yuppies have become Muppies—middle-aged, urban professionals creating different but even more profitable markets for marketers who understand the trend.

Baby boomers delayed getting married and having children, but eventually they entered the trap and brought with them a permanent propensity to consume. They know what they want—quality products that are aesthetically pleasing; personally satisfying; natural; and, if possible, noncaloric. The products and services must also be available in convenient and value-oriented distribution channels, such as off-price but quality retailers and catalogs. Baby boomers buy more and save less than other generations, spending on products that past generations would have considered luxuries, such as consumer electronics, second cars, household services, and a wide range of other products. When they were young, the instrument of choice for purchases by baby boomers was the credit card. Increasingly, it will be cash. Banks and other financial institutions will make their money not so much from credit cards as from asset accumulation products, bought with an increasing awareness of the need to prepare for future retirement.[16]

The lifestyle decisions of baby boom consumers are influenced greatly by trends in marriage, divorce, and consumption during the 1980s. They don't need a new car, but if they buy one, it will be higher quality than what they accepted as young adults. It may also be one that restores some of the "youth" they don't want to concede to the next generation. Infiniti ads show a Muppie being challenged by a young consumer on the highway, but the Muppie accelerates and goes ahead of the younger consumer. The Muppie often is a "quality" consumer, accepting compromises in earlier years because of budget constraints and the need to purchase products immediately. Now, this consumer is more likely to have money and less need for immediate purchase. You can see these themes illustrated in Figure 20.6 for Infiniti and Braun. When consumers buy homes or products for the home, they also face less immediacy and more ability to finance quality. They don't want to buy the split

FIGURE 20.6 Appealing to the Quality Demands of Aging Baby Boomers

Source: Courtesy of Infiniti and Braun.

level preferred in younger years. They want a nicer, but perhaps smaller home. The real estate boom of the 1990s is focused on second homes for leisure usage rather than the multi-family facilities needed by baby boomers in the 1970s or single family homes of the 1980s.[17]

The 45 to 55 age group is projected to grow by 11 to 12 million during the 1990s, and the 55 to 64 category will also grow substantially. Without an understanding of trends, this may catch marketers unprepared, since the 1980s experienced substantial declines in the 50 to 64 age group. Toward the end of the 1990s, many of these families will become empty nesters.

Empty-nesters, families whose children have not only left home but have also left the university, provide opportunities to grow profits for firms that understand this segment because of the per capita discretionary income of this age group. They have small families at home, are often at the height of their careers and earning power, and have low or no mortgages to pay and generally reduced family responsibilities.

FIGURE 20.7   An Appeal to Waiting for the Best

Source: Courtesy of Jaguar.

The key to understanding the empty-nesters is freedom. They already have an adequate inventory of housing products, cars, clothing, and such products. They not only have the *freedom to spend* on what they want; they have the *freedom to withhold* until they receive precisely what they want. In Figure 20.7, Jaguar appeals to a heritage that people want but could not afford until later in life.

Empty-nesters indulge in luxury travel, restaurants, and the theater—which often means they need more fashionable clothing, jewelry, and department stores. They watch their waistlines and diets, and are good prospects for spas, health clubs, cosmetics and beauty parlors, and healthier foods. As they approach retirement, they purchase condominiums and begin to take more frequent but less expensive vacations. They are a prime prospect for financial products oriented toward asset accumulation and retirement income.

Many of the families of the baby boomers will be **transgenerational couples**, of mixed ages. Either the husband or the wife may be substantially younger in age than the other. Such spouses choose each other because of similarity in values,

FIGURE 20.8 Appeal to Transgenerational Families

Source: Courtesy of Dewar's.

lifestyles, and interests rather than chronological age. Notice the ad for Dewar's in Figure 20.8 in which the ages are listed as 50 and 33. Some individuals might be considered transgenerational because of their appeal to many ages. Turn to the second color section and you will see an ad for Duracell featuring Nolan Ryan who just keeps going on and on and on.

The Young Again Market

A major trend during the 1990s is the mushrooming "young again" market, referring to consumers who have accumulated more chronological age than most others. Various terms are used to describe this segment such as maturity market, seniors, elderly and so forth but we have chosen the young again (YA) phrase in an attempt to capture the importance of a market that is chronologically older but has attitudes and economic resources to be highly attractive to marketers oriented toward the future. Millions of additional consumers in the 65-plus category will be added during the 1990s, increasing by 10.5 percent in the United States and 27.7 percent in Canada.

Older families have more to spend, but they need to spend less. Having money does not mean spending it, however. Moschis concluded older people are thrifty and careful with the money they spend.[18] Nevertheless, with home mortgages paid off or nearly so, no more college educations to finance, and an ample inventory of basic appliances and furnishings, mature families are especially good prospects for luxury goods, travel-related goods and services, health care, and a wide range of financial services.

Market segmentation is important in the maturity market.[19] Often this is done by age, with marked differences in spending patterns between those who are "older" (55 to 64), "elderly" (65 to 74), "aged" (75 to 84), and the "very old" (85 and older).[20] Discretionary income is also important as are other variables such as health, activity level, discretionary time and response to others. But the most useful segmentation may be psychographic. Segmentation may be on the basis of engagement with society or internal versus external locus of control, similar to the inner- versus outer-directedness differentiation in the VALS typology.[21]

Consumption patterns vary substantially between the retired and those still working.[22] Despite the trend toward early retirement, large numbers are capable of working beyond 65, may need to do so financially, and may in the future seek to work at some kind of job longer than they now do. In the 1990s, retirement may be just another work phase as people at 65 decide what job to do next, not what hobby to pursue.[23]

Women greatly outnumber men in the mature market because of greater life expectancy. Over 60 percent of women over 65 are not married. Many are widows who typically experience inability to earn an income, inadequate and often dangerous housing, and social and economic rejection.[24]

The YA market tends to be careful in shopping because of their experience and because of economic concerns. Inflation may cause the prices of what they buy to increase but not necessarily their income. They have the experience and ability to wait to find good value in their buying process. They may respond more to coupons and be willing to shift their buying to off-peak times if given an adequate incentive to do so.

Older consumers use the mass media more than younger consumers do and have less interpersonal contact. They may need special services such as delivery or telephone shopping, and they are more loyal to the firm that provides good service and value. In a comprehensive literature review of information processing among older consumers, Ross found many problems with the media because of declining sensory abilities. Older consumers are likely to be newspaper readers and AM radio listeners. They are more likely to shop at department or other traditional stores than in discount stores.[25] Older consumers are pretty much like younger segments in their brand loyalty and shopping behavior, however.[26]

Older markets are often affluent. On a per capita basis, consumers aged 65–69 have the highest level of discretionary income in the nation. People who are now retiring have lived their lives in decades of economic expansion that has often given them a comfortable retirement. There are over 15 million people who are "comfortably retired," with incomes twice the poverty level but with lower spending needs. The **pension elite** consist of another 3 million older persons, mostly in the 65 to 74 age category, with enough income from multiple sources to support buying of products and services for an active, independent, and healthy lifestyle.[27] Some states, such as California, New York, and Florida, are home to over a million or more of these upscale retired consumers. Some cities, such as Fort Lauderdale, Palm Beach, San Diego, and Mobile Bay, have particularly large concentrations of such consumers, making these markets increasingly attractive as targets for segmented marketing offerings.

Marketing to the Young Again Market

Young again or maturity markets are different from youthful markets in ways associated with their age, but not limited to their age. The maturity market currently reflects a cohort that was influenced by the Great Depression and World War II. The resulting emphasis was on saving and conservative consumption. The maturity market of the future, however, has experienced mostly prosperity since World War II and a willingness to spend as long as the credit cards were not over their limit.

Differences in consumption between older consumers and younger consumers go beyond attitudes. Some differences are physical. Eyes don't see as well, creating the need for larger print and bright colors rather than pastels or earth tones. Shiny paper in packaging or print ads should be avoided. TV commercials with visual changes every few seconds are annoying. Legs do not move as fast or as high, creating physical vulnerability that creates a booming home security market. Hands have less flexibility, causing doorknobs to be replaced with levers. Phones need larger buttons, as well as volume controls.

Young again markets are "experience" markets rather than "things" markets. Mature consumers already have enough things, as well as the maturity of attitude that does not associate things with happiness. The YA market therefore places more emphasis on experiences such as travel, activities with persons in similar situations, and staying in touch. Segmenting or predicting purchase within the YA market may not be so much based upon product/service attributes as upon the amount of life satisfaction experienced by mature consumers and the relationship of life satisfaction with familiar concepts and product/service satisfaction.[28]

Three qualities are especially important in products purchased by mature markets: comfort, security, and convenience. Young people may stuff their feet into high-heeled shoes that are trendy. Older people want to be comfortable in their clothing, as well as in the furniture in their homes and in their feelings about the institutions handling their assets. They are less willing to take risks, whether they be physical, social, or financial. Thus, need for security is higher than with other markets and rewarding to the marketers who understand this need. Convenience is also a price for which the mature market will reward marketers. They want a computer that is easy to understand. They want to go to stores where they are sure they will find what they expect. They don't want to struggle with the frustration of automated teller machines too complex to operate. Some banks recognize these trends and provide personal assistance at teller machines with heavy concentrations of mature customers. Some stores and shopping malls provide convenient, dependable bus or van service between their facilities and concentrations of mature customers. Examples of product positioning for the maturity market are also shown in Consumer in Focus 20.3.

Consumer in Focus 20.3

Redesigning Products for the Maturity Market

Ken Dychtwald, gerontologist specializing in marketing, explains how currently successful firms might change their offering to meet the trend toward the aging of consumers.

Holiday Inns

"For any company that wants to serve the senior market, the first step is to claim it, to let seniors know they are a market the company wants to serve. Holiday Inns could be first. The relationship can be built by promoting Holiday Inns through networks such as the American Association of Retired Persons, senior centers, and social clubs. I'd also establish a 24-hour medical emergency hot line. For some people, that service alone would be a deciding factor.

"Most of all, though, I'd work on positioning. Bring back the original Holiday Inns marketing campaigns, the ones that said, No matter where you are in America, you can pull into a Holiday Inn and it will be the same. You can trust us. There are no surprises here. The sell is sameness, comfort, security; this is a serious and profound psychological theme on the minds of many older people when they travel."

Porsche

"Forty-eight percent of the luxury cars in America are already purchased by people over 55, so certainly the money is there to buy a car as expensive as a Porsche. But to sell them, Porsche has to understand that the mature market is interested in *experiences*, not *things*. They've already done enough accumulating; they'll purchase things if they become a means to an experience.

"What I'd do is build a special line—maybe a new product, maybe just an ergonomically modified version of an existing one. Chairs might swivel 90 degrees and tilt for getting in and out. The dash and instruments could be set higher, bigger. Simple stuff. Then: Market it. Turn the experience into something a 50-or-60-year-old can see himself doing. Convince older people that Porsches may be for them."

Source: Curtis Hartman, "Redesigning America," *Inc.* 10 (June 1988), 58–74.

Among the "young old" there is a sensitivity to revealing one's age. Consequently, an ad that blasts out in pictures or words that the product is for 60 year olds won't work. Nor will advertising that is obviously directed to 30 year olds. The most effective way to get around that problem is to create affinities between the product and some interest of the mature generation. Dychtwald, a gerontologist specializing in marketing, explains:

> Quaker Oats is now very cleverly launching a campaign to get Quaker Oats viewed as a nutritious product for old people. They don't say, "Quaker Oats is good for you if you're old," What they say is, "Eating Quaker Oats lowers your cholesterol level." That's an affinity. That's an issue that anyone over the age of 50 is going to land right on. For 19-year-olds, it's invisible. They don't worry about their cholesterol levels.[29]

The Consequences of a Slow Growing, Older Consumer Base

North America and most other industrialized areas are becoming old; really old. While the United States has over 12 percent of its population above the age of 65 and Canada has 10.4 percent, that is young compared to Sweden, which has nearly 17 percent over age 65.[30] All European countries are older than the United States and Canada. The challenge for consumer analysts is to understand what this means, not only for products purchased by older consumers but for labor and retirement policies, political elections, family structures, health care, and many other areas of life.

The impact on the rest of consumers will also be substantial. As younger people are surrounded by older consumers and realize that life is going to last much longer than it used to, they may spend more money on health and appearance products and spend more time on healthier activities. As Mickey Mantle is reported to have said, "If I'd known I was going to live so long, I'd have taken better care of myself."

The impact of slow growth in population is on the value of retaining customers rather than attaining new customers. When there are few new consumers to attract, marketing budgets shift from advertising to developing human resources to provide good service to current customers. Retailers such as Nordstrom have shown that good service can be a winning strategy.

More resources will be needed for consumer affairs departments or other programs for soliciting and handling complaints.[31] **Defensive marketing** will be needed to encourage complaints. Higher economic value results from settling complaints quickly. The savings in offensive marketing may be high enough to justify additional costs associated with compensating dissatisfied customers. Economic models have been developed to calculate these trade-offs.[32]

One way to increase profits is to create a relationship to consumers through **network marketing**. Network marketing depends upon a relationship to the customer that becomes central in the marketing of several noncompetitive organizations. A good example of network marketing is found currently in the travel industry, especially the frequent traveler programs. All major airlines use them not only to create loyalty but also to track the behavior of the best customers—who are also the best customers of hotels, rental car companies, marketers of upscale consumer goods and credit cards. Many people who are the prime target for airline programs are the same for a hotel, even though they are not direct competitors. In fact, it is just the opposite in the sense that the more a customer buys from the airline, the more likely the customer is to buy from a hotel and use a credit card. Thus, a firm's success in the marketplace is determined not only by how effective its own marketing program is but the quality of the network to which the firm belongs.[33]

Money: Second Requirement for Markets

Willie Sutton, the infamous bank robber, said, "I go where the money is . . . and I go there often." So do marketers.

The search for growing market segments with ability to buy is essential for consumer analysts. Who has high income to spend on consumer products and services? Which segments are growing the fastest? What products and services do these segments value most? Where, when, and how do they buy?

These are critical questions for consumer analysts. Such questions are not meant to negate the macro issues or the social importance of studying people in poverty. For marketers, the simple reality lies in the truism that it is easier to sell to people with money than to people without money.

Proliferation of Affluence

What will consumer analysts primarily be studying in the future? At least half of their time will be spent in understanding what the affluent want to buy. The reason for this provocative statement is that the wealthiest 20 percent of U.S. families now command 50 percent of after-tax family income. Thus, assuming this trend continues, at least half of the activity of consumer analysts will have to be spent studying the affluent. Perhaps more than half because the spending behavior of the poor is much more predictable and the financial rewards for serving the affluent, despite the difficulty of doing so, are so much greater.

Price increases are easier for marketers to achieve among the affluent than the poor. The Moet Index measures the cost of a market basket of a dozen luxury products—such things as a Rolls-Royce, Dom Perignon champagne, and Beluga caviar. When the CPI increased 4.4 percent per year, for example, the Moet Index of luxuries increased 9.0 percent.[34]

The trend toward affluence both in the United States and in some other industrialized countries is very important in understanding market opportunities. Table 20.3 displays this dramatic shift in income. A study released by the Congressional Budget Office shows most of the increase in median family income concentrated in the top quintile. Inequality grew sharply. Most of the gains arose from the entry of wives as second earners rather than from changes in incomes of established workers. Such changes are important for marketers of many goods and services, of course, but they are also important to analysts in the growing field of political marketing. The trend toward affluence has created an erosion in the voting power of the poor and the working class, with attendant effects on labor unions and the Democratic Party.

TABLE 20.3   Average After-Tax Family Income (in 1988 dollars)

Income Category	Annual Household Incomes (after-tax, in 1990 dollars)		% Change
	1980	1990	
Richest 1%	$213,675	$399,697	87.1%
Richest 5%	100,331	151,132	50.6
Richest fifth	58,886	78,032	32.5
Next richest fifth	32,075	34,824	8.6
Middle fifth	24,031	24,691	2.7
Next poorest fifth	16,088	16,123	0.2
Poorest fifth	7,357	6,973	− 5.2

Source: U.S. Center on Budget & Policy Priorities.

Targeted Affluents   Affluent families increasingly are the targets for marketing programs. The number of over-$50,000 families is growing very rapidly. In 1980, only about 10 percent of families earned over $50,000, but the number, in constant dollars, is projected to be about 20 percent by 1995, nearly 15 million families to which to market goods and services.[35]

Selling to super affluents involves upscale products and retailers, but also high levels of service. The most affluent of the affluents survive recessions with little impact on their standard of living. Even though many products are impacted, Consumer in Focus 20.4 shows how to market to the most affluent. Even the dream of becoming a "millionaire" is more attainable for many Americans. Most of them made it themselves rather than inheriting it. Typically, they are entrepreneurs who own their own businesses. Many are physicians, dentists, or consultants. The average age is 57 years and most are likely to live in California, New York, Texas, or Illinois.

Millionaires are often considered to be the market for yachts, Rolls Royces, and so forth, but, in fact, these products are more likely to be purchased by corporations. Millionaires do not spend their fortunes on luxury goods; they are more likely to have a Sears credit card than American Express, Neiman-Marcus, Saks Fifth Avenue, or Lord and Taylor cards. They buy few home furnishings and appliances (because they already have them), but they do spend large amounts on services, travel, and college tuitions.[36]

Poverty

Marketing analysts cannot forecast a future very well if they do not consider "nonmarkets" as well as target markets. There should be concern among marketers about all people—not just those that have enough money to be attractive targets for marketing programs.

If the number of impoverished people in a society is increasing, it is difficult to market "as usual" to those who still have money for two reasons. First, the attitudes of people with money will be affected negatively, probably leading to decreased

Marketing to Lifestyles of the Rich

The rich don't let a sputtering economy crimp their travel plans. Travel agents say their super-rich clients—the kind who charter flights and sleep in $2,000-a-night suites—are vacationing just as much or more in a recessionary year as before.

Several hoteliers and cruise lines say their most expensive suites and cabins are selling out faster than before the recession. Royal Viking Line says the penthouse suite on its Sun ship is still "one of the first to go" even at $116,000 for a 97-day cruise.

In Chicago, the Ritz-Carlton's "State Suites," which cost $2,500 a night, are booked months in advance. "That kind of traveler just isn't affected by a recession as much," a spokeswoman says.

The sluggish economy didn't stop one couple from recently booking a $500,000, three-week honeymoon in Europe. Along with Concorde flights; royal suites in London, Paris and Rome; and Rolls-Royces waiting at every stop, the couple played tennis with the top teaching pros at Wimbledon and hired a personal shopper for antique and clothing shopping sprees. They also hired a helicopter so they could commute between Antibes, France, and Monte Carlo. The travel agent explains, "They wanted to stay in both places but they didn't want to get stuck in traffic."

The rich are a demanding clientele. It isn't unusual for clients to call the travel agent during a trip with a long list of demands from sending over a fax machine to shipping special baby formula. Some clients think nothing of calling from a cellular phone when they're rushing for a commercial flight (first class, of course) and asking them to hold the flight.

Source: Excerpted from Jonathan Dahl, "Travel Styles of the Rich Are Immune to Recession," *Wall Street Journal* (March 4, 1992), B1.

willingness to take on debt for durable goods and increased frugality in their decisions about nearly all goods and services. Second, if the number of impoverished people is increasing, increased demand for services will arise probably affecting tax rates, crime, and other variables that lead to decreased consumption among those with money.

Furthermore, even the impoverished buy many basic products and services. Poor consumers may be profitable to serve with products and distribution facilities adapted to their problems and resources. Some retailers operate profitably by accepting food stamps, offering realistic credit policies, employing high-security procedures and in other ways adapting to the realities of serving the poor. The grocery chain Aldi is one of the most successful in the world by offering limited

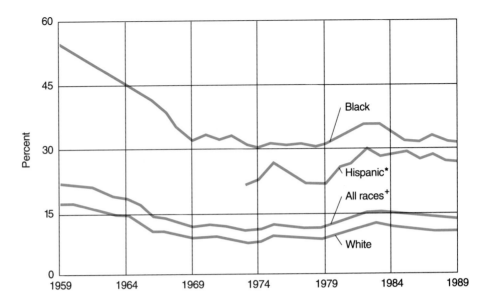

* Hispanic persons may be of any race.
+ Includes other races not shown separately.

FIGURE 20.9 **Persons Below the Poverty Level: 1959–1989**

Source: U.S. Bureau of the Census, *Current Population Reports*, series P-60, No. 168 and earlier reports.

selection, strictly cash, no acceptance of coupons, no free bags, requiring refundable deposits (coins that unlock shopping carts) on carts taken to parking lots and other methods usually unacceptable in stores selling more to the affluent. Whether in Germany, the United States, Belgium or other countries, the locations and operating procedures take into consideration the needs of the poor.

What is the trend concerning poverty? Figure 20.9 displays what has happened in the United States over time and among ethnic groups. Poverty decreased substantially in the 1960s and 1970s, rose in the early part of the 1980s and has been decreasing in recent years to less than 13 percent by 1990. What happens in the future will be determined by variables such as educational policies of the nation, value systems of consumers, global competitive effectiveness of business firms and the degree to which economic policies promote wealth distribution or wealth creation.

Consumer Behavior in a Depression

What if there were to be a major depression, similar to the worldwide depression that occurred in the years following 1929? Edward Cornish, a noted futurist, describes some of the effects on consumers of such an event. Some marketing researchers project the possibility of such a depression,[37] but another value of considering such possibilities is to understand how marketing strategies may deal with less severe but more probable recession periods.

Cornish believes business failures will soar. Declining sales will lead to distress selling and, eventually, to bankruptcies and liquidations. Workers who hang on to their jobs may also suffer, because their work weeks may be trimmed or their wages reduced. Cash will be king because people distrust financial institutions, causing stores to feature special "cash and carry" offers. People will decide it is smart to be thrifty, which will influence much of their saving and spending behavior. Born-again savers will save pieces of string, make baby blankets out of scraps of cloth, straighten and reuse nails, and so on. People will mend their clothing, grow their own vegetables, and repair products instead of buying new ones. Buying things secondhand will become more popular. Sales of "big ticket" goods such as cars and services will drop faster than those of less expensive items. Cornish believes the depression will reduce the standard of living of both the rich and the poor, but the rich will be better able to maintain their usual lifestyles.[38]

Time and Change in Spending

Time and change will surely prove how firm a foundation is found in spending patterns. Knowing how consumers spend their money is basic to making major macroeconomic policy decisions, as well as to understanding the microeconomic implications of marketing opportunities for individual firms.

A major study by the Office of Technology Assessment (OTA) of the U.S. government projects personal consumption expenditures in the year 2005, based upon important demographic, economic, lifestyle, and technological variables such as those discussed in this chapter.[39] This study discloses the close relationship between consumption and all economic variables, such as employment.

Early in the history of this country, Americans grew their own food. As manufacturing developed to reflect spending and production in the country, a specialized agricultural industry developed in which most of the nation derived their employment from either farming or manufacturing. Today, employment is much less derived from growing food and much more concentrated in its processing and serving. The OTA study shows, for example, that the number of scientists, lawyers, and computer professionals involved in supplying Americans with food is roughly equal to the number of farmers. In other areas, services that were once purchased, such as movies, are now provided at home through videocassette recorders. At the same time, services that once were provided at home are now purchased (care of children and the elderly, for example).

Scenario Development   Projections of the future often involve scenario development. The future cannot be known by consumer analysts, but they can project the consequences of various alternative paths of development. For example, if GDP growth is 3 percent, the proportion of the nation's expenditures on food will be different than if GDP growth is 1.5 percent. If prices of inputs such as energy rise at the rate they have for the past 50 years, different spending will occur than if prices of energy rise at the rate they did during the 1970s. Estimates of the number of people in different age groups (a very reliable number to estimate) can be converted to estimates of household types, given assumptions about future marriage and divorce

TABLE 20.4   The Effects of Demographic Change, Income Growth, and Price Change on U.S. Personal Consumption in 2005 (changes in percent of all spending)

Amenity or Item Purchased	Percent Change from 1983 Due to Various Factors				
	All	Demographic	Income	Price	Interactive
Food	−5.26	0.07	−3.37	−1.87	−0.10
Food and beverages at home	−4.41	0.04	−4.05	−0.45	0.06
Food and beverages away from home	−0.15	0.03	1.31	−1.30	−0.19
Tobacco	−0.70	0.00	−0.63	−0.11	0.04
Housing	−0.48	0.40	−1.91	1.72	0.11
Owner occupied	0.28	0.19	0.00	0.47	0.00
Renters	−1.91	0.32	−1.81	0.19	0.03
Maintenance services	0.01	0.01	0.10	−0.07	−0.01
Maintenance commodities	−0.49	0.02	−0.30	−0.24	0.03
Tenants insurance	−0.02	0.04	0.02	−0.09	0.01
House furnishings	0.95	0.03	0.06	0.84	0.02
House appliances	0.71	0.01	0.17	0.47	0.06
Water and sewer	−0.01	0.01	−0.15	0.16	−0.03
Transportation	−0.51	0.06	0.38	−0.96	0.02
New vehicles	−0.33	0.03	−0.00	−0.33	−0.02
Used vehicles	−0.24	0.01	0.05	−0.29	0.01
Vehicle maintenance	−0.13	0.04	−0.06	−0.14	0.04
Other private transportation	−0.02	0.00	−0.01	−0.01	0.00
					Continued

How To Read This Table:
Assuming 3 percent annual economic growth through 2005, 2005 household distribution, and prices and incomes adjusted to this growth, the percentage of American spending on food eaten at home (as a share of the items listed here—roughly three-quarters of all personal spending) would decline by 4.41 percentage points. Changing incomes would account for a drop of 4.05 points and changing prices would account for a 0.45 point drop, while demographic changes would exert a slight positive trend of 0.04 percentage points; the effect of interaction between these factors would be a rise of 0.06.

NOTES: This table estimates how U.S. consumer spending on selected items and amenities could change, and attempts to isolate what factors may contribute to that change. The "All" column assumes 3 percent annual economic growth through 2005, 2005 household structure as developed earlier in this chapter, and a set of possible price changes for these items in 2005 as outlined in the appendix. Incomes are then raised by 35.5 percent, the level at which Americans will have enough purchasing power to satisfy the estimate of personal spending in 2005.

rates. With the aid of computerized models, estimates of future purchases can be developed, given the development of alternative growth rates and assumptions—or scenarios. The results of such an analysis are shown in Table 20.4 for the major types of personal consumption expenditures in the year 2005. This table displays the most likely scenario, although the source document contains alternative scenarios given other assumptions about demographic, income, and price changes. Marketing analysts can use such data to spot trends such as the rising importance of owner-occupied housing compared to the declining importance of renter housing, or the

TABLE 20.4   continued

Amenity or Item Purchased	Percent Change from 1983 Due to Various Factors				
	All	Demographic	Income	Price	Interactive
Transportation continued					
Air fare	0.37	0.00	0.37	−0.01	0.00
Other public transportation	−0.17	0.00	0.02	−0.18	0.00
Clothing and Personal Care	1.84	0.10	1.63	0.01	0.10
Personal care commodities	0.06	0.00	0.06	0.00	0.00
Personal care services	0.11	0.01	−0.02	0.11	0.01
Men's and boys' clothing	0.39	0.02	0.38	−0.02	0.01
Women's and girls' clothing	0.94	0.06	0.87	−0.05	0.05
Other (including jewelry)	0.24	0.01	0.25	−0.01	0.01
Footwear	0.03	0.01	0.02	−0.01	0.01
Apparel services	0.06	0.00	0.06	0.00	0.00
Personal Business and Communication	0.95	0.07	1.26	−0.16	−0.23
Telephone	0.17	0.02	−0.35	0.61	−0.08
Personal business	0.78	0.09	1.61	−0.77	−0.15
Recreation and Leisure	3.47	0.10	2.02	1.26	0.09
Entertainment services	1.26	0.06	1.43	−0.21	−0.02
Entertainment commodities	0.89	0.02	0.20	0.64	0.03
TV and sound	0.83	0.00	0.11	0.68	0.03
Lodging	0.49	0.02	0.28	0.14	0.06

How To Read This Table continued:
For individual components of change:
• For demographic changes in 2005: see table 2-4; price and income held at 1983 levels.
• For income changes in 2005: incomes raised by 35.5 percent; demographics and prices held at 1983 levels.
• For price changes in 2005: see the appendix; demographics and income held at 1983 levels.
The effects of these three components that cannot be traced individually but are rather the result of a combination of factors are captured in the "Interactive" column.
Source: U.S. Congress, Office of Technology Assessment, "Consumer Expenditure Demand Projection Program," April 1986, based on data provided by the U.S. Department of Labor, Bureau of Labor Statistics; the U.S. Department of Commerce, Bureaus of Census and of Economic Analysis; and the U.S. Department of Health and Human Services, Social Security Administration.

rising importance of clothing and personal care, or the enormous growth in the importance of recreation and leisure industries.

Changing Geography of Demand

People and money. They are certainly the foundation of consumer demand. Where those people live and earn their money is also critical to understanding demand, however, and we now turn our attention to an examination of the geography of demand in North American markets.

Geography: Basis for Implementing Marketing Plans

Marketing plans are usually implemented in geographical units because of the ready availability of data on a geographic basis rather than its superiority as a unit of analysis in consumer behavior.

This is especially true for promotional programs. Advertising media such as television, radio, and newspapers are usually bought on a geographic basis—usually cities or the areas surrounding a city called **Area of Dominant Influence** (ADI) or **Designated Marketing Area** (DMA). Even national magazines such as *Time* or *Business Week* have regional advertising sections sold on a state or city basis. Print media are moving toward editions based on geographic divisions as specific as zip codes. As a consumer analyst, you are likely to be working with consumption and media data based on city, state, and regional units.

Regions and Economic Areas

Over 100 years ago, the Department of Commerce recognized the need to understand and classify the linkages between the natural environment of certain areas and the population statistics, economics, subcultures, and political characteristics of a primarily agricultural nation. Accordingly, U.S. geography was divided into physical regions that included lowlands, highlands, wetlands, drylands, woodlands, and grasslands.

Since 1910 these geographic areas have been combined into nine divisions frequently used for reporting census data. The divisions are fairly homogeneous in physical characteristics. The characteristics of their populations and their economic and social conditions differed originally from those of other divisions. These divisions of the United States are shown in Figure 20.10. Marketing research data are often collected or reported on the basis of these regions.

Economic Areas

Another geographic unit of analysis is **Bureau of Economic Analysis** (BEA) **Economic Areas**, which are nodal functional areas delineated to facilitate regional economic analysis. Each area consists of an **economic node**—a metropolitan or similar area—that serves as a center of economic activity including the surrounding counties and smaller cities that are economically related to the center. The areas cover the entire United States, including both metropolitan areas (cities) and the nonmetropolitan areas that are neglected when only metropolitan data are analyzed. There are 183 economic areas, defined by journey-to-work data from the census; newspaper circulation data; and country commuting data developed from Social Security and Internal Revenue Service records.

Economic area data are superior to region data because they are specific and relatively homogeneous. They are superior to city or metropolitan area data because

FIGURE 20.10 **Census Bureau Divisions**
Source: U.S. Department of Commerce, Bureau of the Census.

they cover the entire country. In addition, they give a much more accurate picture to marketing analysts of what is happening than is sometimes obtained from city data. For example, the Boston metropolitan statistical area lost population in recent years. The conclusion might be that the area should receive less emphasis in marketing plans. However, the "bedroom" metropolitan areas of Manchester, New Bedford, Portsmouth, and Worcester (treated as separate cities by the Census Bureau) grew almost as quickly as the nation as a whole did, and the nonmetropolitan areas surrounding Boston grew at an impressive rate, providing an overall growth rate for the Boston economic area for a number of years.

State and Provincial Markets

Market trends vary substantially between states and provinces. The states gaining the most population recently are California, Texas, and Florida. Florida passed Pennsylvania to become the fourth most populous state.

What will the future bring? These projections are shown in Table 20.5. Such projections are based upon the components of change: births, deaths, and net migration. California and Florida each gained more than 2 million persons through net immigration in the 1980s, and Texas gained more than 1.2 million. Those 3 states accounted for more than half of national population growth in the past decade.

Marketers can find segments of growth even in states with declining population. Every state experienced large increases in the 25- to 44-year-old age cohort.

TABLE 20.5   **Total Population in Thousands by State, 1990 to 2010; Absolute Change and Percent Change for 1990 to 2000, and 2000 to 2010**

	1990	2000	2010	1990–2000		2000–2010	
				Change	Percent	Change	Percent
U.S. Total	249,891	267,747	282,055	17,856	7.1%	14,308	5.3%
Alabama	4,181	4,410	4,609	229	5.5	199	4.5
Alaska	576	687	765	111	19.3	78	11.4
Arizona	3,752	4,618	5,319	866	23.1	701	15.2
Arkansas	2,427	2,529	2,624	102	4.2	95	3.8
California	29,126	33,500	37,347	4,374	15.0	3,847	11.5
Colorado	3,434	3,813	4,098	379	11.0	285	7.5
Connecticut	3,279	3,445	3,532	166	5.1	87	2.5
Delaware	666	734	790	68	10.2	56	7.6
District of Columbia	614	634	672	20	3.3	38	6.0
Florida	12,818	15,415	17,530	2,597	20.3	2,115	13.7
Georgia	6,663	7,957	9,045	1,294	19.4	1,088	13.7
Hawaii	1,141	1,345	1,559	204	17.9	214	15.9
Idaho	1,017	1,047	1,079	30	2.9	32	3.1
Illinois	11,612	11,580	11,495	−32	−0.3	−85	−0.7
Indiana	5,550	5,502	5,409	−48	−0.9	−93	−1.7
Iowa	2,758	2,549	2,382	−209	−7.6	−167	−6.6
Kansas	2,492	2,529	2,564	37	1.5	35	1.4
Kentucky	3,745	3,733	3,710	−12	−0.3	−23	−0.6
Louisiana	4,513	4,516	4,545	3	0.1	29	0.6
Maine	1,212	1,271	1,308	59	4.9	37	2.9
Maryland	4,729	5,274	5,688	545	11.5	414	7.8
Massachusetts	5,880	6,087	6,255	207	3.5	168	2.8
Michigan	9,293	9,250	9,097	−43	−0.5	−153	−1.7
Minnesota	4,324	4,490	4,578	166	3.8	88	2.0
Mississippi	2,699	2,877	3,028	178	6.6	151	5.2

Continued

Note: Numbers may not add to totals due to rounding.
Source: Bureau of the Census, *Current Population Reports*, Series P-25, No. 1017.

This same group, which is about a third of the nation's population, will be the rapidly growing 35 to 44 age group during the 1990s.[40]

There are pitfalls associated with concentrating only on growth. Alaska was the fastest-growing state in the 1980s and is projected to grow rapidly during the 1990s. Alaska, along with Wyoming, is also one of the least populous states, with only 576,000 people in 1990. This illustrates the trap to avoid of chasing the trend but ignoring the substance. A 10-percent market share in a no-growth market such as Ohio or Michigan may be preferable to a high market share in a rapid growth but minuscule state such as Alaska or Nevada. Additionally, the costs of doing business in areas where the infrastructure is already paid for may be lower than in areas with rapidly expanding population.

TABLE 20.5   continued

	1990	2000	2010	1990–2000		2000–2010	
				Change	Percent	Change	Percent
Missouri	5,192	5,383	5,521	191	3.7	138	2.6
Montana	805	794	794	−11	−1.4	0	0.0
Nebraska	1,588	1,556	1,529	−32	−2.0	−27	−1.7
Nevada	1,076	1,303	1,484	227	21.1	181	13.9
New Hampshire	1,142	1,333	1,455	191	16.7	122	9.2
New Jersey	7,899	8,546	8,980	647	8.2	434	5.1
New Mexico	1,632	1,968	2,248	336	20.6	280	14.2
New York	17,773	17,986	18,139	213	1.2	153	0.9
North Carolina	6,690	7,483	8,154	793	11.9	671	9.0
North Dakota	660	629	611	−31	−4.7	−18	−2.9
Ohio	10,791	10,629	10,397	−162	−1.5	−232	−2.2
Oklahoma	3,285	3,376	3,511	91	2.8	135	4.0
Oregon	2,766	2,877	2,991	111	4.0	114	4.0
Pennsylvania	11,827	11,503	11,134	−324	−2.7	−369	−3.2
Rhode Island	1,002	1,049	1,085	47	4.7	36	3.4
South Carolina	3,549	3,906	4,205	357	10.1	299	7.7
South Dakota	708	714	722	6	0.8	8	1.1
Tennessee	4,972	5,266	5,500	294	5.9	234	4.4
Texas	17,712	20,211	22,281	2,499	14.1	2,070	10.2
Utah	1,776	1,991	2,171	215	12.1	180	9.0
Vermont	562	591	608	29	5.2	17	2.9
Virginia	6,157	6,877	7,410	720	11.7	533	7.8
Washington	4,657	4,991	5,282	334	7.2	291	5.8
West Virginia	1,856	1,722	1,617	−134	−7.2	−105	−6.1
Wisconsin	4,808	4,784	4,713	−24	−0.5	−71	−1.5
Wyoming	502	489	487	−13	−2.6	−2	−0.4

The Water Belt may be a challenge to the Sun Belt for markets of the future, especially if the greenhouse effect causes widespread drought. Texas shipped valuable oil to northern states in the past, creating prosperity and expanding markets. It may be the Great Lakes states that will ship valuable water to Texas and the Sun Belt in the future.

Canada

About 80 percent of all Canadians live within 200 kilometers of the United States-Canada border, creating a market about 4,000 miles long and 125 miles wide. The fact that Canadian consumers are in a horizontal string in contrast to U.S. population clusters is a logistics problem for Canada. U.S. retailing occurs in distribution circles oriented to the clusters which tend to circle over the major Canadian markets, especially Ontario. It often is more efficient to supply Canadian markets from those efficient high-volume distribution circles than from Canada's thin linear supply line. As a consequence, Canadian firms that operate in the northern United States and use those cities as distribution points to Canada may have lower costs than firms operating solely in Canada and distributing throughout the 4,000 by 125 mile linear market. Higher distribution costs, higher labor costs, and more developed social programs add to the challenge Canadian firms face in the freer-trade environment of the 1990s.[41]

The rural areas to the north contain 80 percent of Canada's land but only about 1 percent of the population. The largest market is a 750-mile megalopolis stretching from Quebec City southwestward through Montreal, Ottawa, Toronto, and the Niagara Peninsula to Windsor. The cities in this area contain about 40 percent of the population, income, and retail sales in Canada.

The fastest-growing areas of Canada in the past were Alberta, British Columbia, and the Northwest Territories, due to the rising value of energy. It is not expected that such rapid growth will continue in the future. Ontario is regaining momentum. About 36 percent of all Canadians now live in Ontario. The moderate climate and highly developed resource and service industries of British Columbia provide a good base for future growth. The eastern provinces continue to grow the slowest.

Suburbanization and Gentrification

Population concentration is occurring in metropolitan areas throughout the world. Suburbs have been the big winners in the United States since World War II, with population growth increasing more than twice as fast as the total population and over five times as fast as that of central cities. People fled the sidewalk shops of the cities for the trees and grass of the suburbs. The shopping centers soon followed the people—in many cases becoming a magnet throughout the region.

Suburbanization   Suburbs have grown rapidly, but today **exurbs**—areas beyond the suburbs—are experiencing the fastest growth. Fast-growing counties are often non-metropolitan or rural but adjacent to suburban or metropolitan areas.

Shopping centers and many businesses often "jumped" the suburbs to build on more desirable (and cheaper) land of the exurbs. Businesses that have failed to follow the trend are often in serious difficulty, despite the major investments required to keep up with consumer movements. Affluent cosmopolitans who live in the suburbs often know their city only from its airport, an infrequent evening out, and the crime reports on the local news.

Gentrification   **Gentrification** is a process in which people move back to the city in a renaissance of neighborhoods, often displacing low-income families who had occupied the neighborhood. Gentrification usually includes growth in retail trade and industry, housing improvement, and change in the number and composition (younger, more affluent, usually white) of residents. In spite of well-publicized examples of such rejuvenated neighborhoods, however, the numbers—which must be the basis for market analysis—are overwhelmingly in the direction of the suburbs and exurbs. Zip codes of gentrified areas may be attractive targets, however, for direct marketing, remodeling services, and household furnishings and for some forms of innovative and upscale retailing and service establishments.

Cities: Winners or Losers?

Cities are the most important unit of analysis in most marketing plans. They are fundamental in the analysis of micromarketing programs. Cities are also the fundamental unit in determining the prosperity of nations, according to economist Jane Jacobs. In her book, *Cities and the Wealth of Nations*, she describes the forces that transform regional economies originating in cities that are "import-replacing" (not dependent only on producing exports but having an economy of their own). The forces that create the health of cities are their markets, jobs, technology, transplants (of prosperity to suburbs and exurbs), and capital.[42]

Downtown

The future of the "downtown" of cities or Central Business Districts (CBD) is questionable. A number of innovations have occurred recently to indicate they might experience a revival in the 1990s and beyond. Innovative growth in the past was mainly in skyscrapers or office buildings, but developments such as Eaton Centre in Toronto, City Center in Columbus, and the Harborplace in Baltimore are more consumer oriented.

The renaissance in CBDs emphasizes cities as a place to learn, to shop, to play, and perhaps even to live as well as a place to earn. The prototype for such projects is the festival marketplace known as Faneuil Hall Marketplace in Boston. Historic preservation is a "big idea" that is creating excitement as well as cultural centers, open spaces, and waterfront developments. Events such as the Boston Marathon or the Columbus Red, White, and Boom attract people to cities. The success of such projects is closely related to improved transportation, security, and living projects.[43]

Analyzing City Data

The analysis of consumer trends by cities requires use of standardized definitions. The most affluent city, for example, is Bridgeport, Connecticut, with per capita income of $24,501 in contrast to the lowest per capita income, in McAllen, Texas, at $6,800.[44] Such comparisons of market attractiveness would not be useful without standardized definitions. For many years, data were collected on the basis of **Standard Metropolitan Statistical Areas** (SMSAs). They were counties of similar social and economic character surrounding a major central city.

SMSA has been replaced by several new terms. The **Metropolitan Statistical Area** (MSA) is the most direct descendant. MSA is defined as a freestanding metropolitan area, surrounded by nonmetropolitan counties and not closely related with other metropolitan areas. A **Primary Metropolitan Statistical Area** (PMSA) is a metropolitan area that is closely related to another city. A grouping of closely related PMSAs is a **Consolidated Metropolitan Statistical Area** (CMSA). CMSAs are classified as A areas when they have more than 1 million residents, B areas with 250,000 to 1 million, C areas with 100,000 to 250,000, and D areas with a population of less than 100,000.

When you are preparing market analyses, especially those comparing cities currently with past data, you may find data reported on the basis of SMSAs, but remember that this term was deleted from usage years ago, when it was replaced by MSAs, PMSAs, and CMSAs.

Megalopolis

More than one-third of the people in the United States live in the country's 22 **megalopolises** or CMSAs. The biggest of these are huge areas made up of many counties and two or more smaller metropolitan areas. The largest of them all is New York-Northern New Jersey-Long Island, with an estimated population of 17.9 million in 1990. Even though New York City itself has declined in population, the rest of the counties in the CMSA have grown.

The Los Angeles-Anaheim-Riverside CMSA gained more than 1 million people from 1980 to 1990, placing it ahead of third-ranking Chicago-Gary-Lake County. When implementing marketing strategies, it is useful to consider that reaching the New York-Newark-Jersey City CMSA is a market larger than Canada or six of the European Common Market countries.[45]

Who wins? Who loses? The cities that are winning the battle for population growth are mostly in the West and the South. During the past 15 years only one city east of the Mississippi and north of the Sun Belt increased consistently in population—Columbus, Ohio. Columbus has the technological and computerized information economy described by John Naisbitt in *Megatrends* as more typical of the Sun Belt than the Northeast quadrant of the United States.[46] Some of the metropolitan areas of the Northeast grew, however, even though their central cities did not. In the future, most of the growing cities will be in the West and the South.

Cities are especially important for ethnic marketing. Most new immigrants settle in urban areas. New York is the most popular destination, but 37 other metropolitan areas in the United States receive at least 2,000 immigrants a year. Specific cities often attract immigrants from some countries more than others. Illinois has five times as many Polish immigrants as the rest of the United States.[47]

Collecting and Analyzing Demographic Data

You have now studied the major variables of economic demographics, the foundation of market analysis. But where do you find the data you need to make such analyses? At this point, you may be getting tired of studying so many tables and charts. Be assured that you won't have to do much more of this in this book. Demographic analysis, however, usually involves poring over numbers and questioning how they were collected and what they mean. You may have noted sources of data just by giving attention to the references for each figure in this chapter. There are so many that it is usually safe to assume data exist somewhere on the topic you need to analyze—if only you can figure out where! *American Demographics* publishes an excellent directory to where to find demographic and other information.[48]

Census Data

The first nationwide population census in the United States was conducted in 1770. In 1950, the Census Bureau introduced several sampling techniques as alternative methods to collecting census-required information. Today, many questions that are described as census data are really sampling data based on interviews of 5 to 20 percent of the population. Only a few basic questions needed for sensitive government allocation of funds are asked of 100 percent of the population queried. The 1990 Census, in spite of meticulous planning for it, has been controversial with claims that some elements of the population are underrepresented in Census statistics.

The most important source of demographic data in Canada is Statistics Canada. In the United States, it is the Bureau of the Census of the U.S. Department of Commerce. The data collected change from decade to decade, with attempts to add or delete topics or terms that are obsolete.

Accessing Census Data

The Census Bureau has become "customer oriented" in recent years to meet the needs of marketing and other organizations. In addition to the decennial census, the Census Bureau has an extensive program of sample-survey supplements on population; housing; and economic, agriculture, and government topics, issued through the Bureau's Data User Services Division.

Consumer analysts pay close attention to the Current Population Reports, known as the "P" series, based upon a monthly survey of 60,000 households. On a national basis, the "P-20" series provides reports on marital status, households and families, geographic residence and mobility, fertility, school enrollment, educational attainment, persons of Spanish origin, and other demographic topics. The "P-23" reports are special studies about such groups as blacks, youth, women, older people, and so forth. The "P-27" reports provide data about the farm population, and the "P-60" series reports on consumer income, classified by variables such as race, ethnic origin, age, sex, education, and so forth. The "P-25" series is of particular value to marketing planners because it provides projections of the future U.S. population. The U.S. Census Bureau also provides a considerable data base on international markets, although coverage is not as detailed as for U.S. markets.

Census data are available in many forms. The most useful are increasingly computerized. Waiting for hard copy requires about 4 years after a census is completed, but the most valuable product is probably Summary Tape File 3, which contains data from the long census questionnaire administered in a sample about income and income type, residence, and transportation to work for specific geographic areas.

Canada   Statistics Canada provides more comprehensive market data than is generally available about U.S. markets from government services. *Canadian Social Trends* provides data on major social indicators as well as data for studying trends in income, population, crime, education, housing, and other variables. The most current data are reported in *Statistics Canada Daily* or on a weekly basis in Informat.

Private Data Firms   Explosive growth has occurred among private firms providing analyses of demographic and economic data. Several of them have formed a consortium of firms to pay for assembly of census data by zip codes. These firms, in return, receive the right to use and sell census data in their form before it becomes available publicly.

Private firms provide specialized demographic analyses of great value to consumer analysts and marketing strategists. The goal is to match the general data with specific needs of marketers. *American Demographics*, the "Bible" of marketers interested in demographics, is a valuable source of names and addresses of the many private firms that provide specialized demographic/economic analyses and marketing assistance.

A widely used source of demographic data is *Sales Management's* "Survey of Buying Power" (SBP). Published in July of each year, the SBP contains data on population; effective buying income; and retail sales for all metropolitan areas, states, counties, and cities in the United States and for most metropolitan areas, provinces, counties, and cities in Canada.

Another widely used source is the American Research Bureau, which compiles data on the areas of dominant influence or ADI, a geographic market area of contiguous counties defined by television viewing. For each ADI, information is available concerning the estimated number of television households by county, number of adult women and adult men, and number of teenagers and children.

Environmental Scanning

Marketing organizations need systematic and timely information about the environment as it currently exists as well as projections of trends. This has given rise to the development of formal responsibility for such a function, usually called **environmental scanning**. Environmental scanning usually includes information internal to the organization, such as the cognitive maps used by executives in making decisions, as well as external variables. External variables include the following:

1. Descriptions of the *structural* properties of the environment.
2. Assumptions about the nature and sources of environmental *change*.
3. Proposed means for managers to gain *knowledge* of their environments.[49]

Environmental scanning is becoming a top priority with many firms in their search for the 3 M's of growing profits. Where should such responsibility be placed? Who should do environmental scanning? Some large corporations place such responsibility with staff departments, usually in marketing research or strategic planning. Research indicates, however, that environmental scanning is most effective when it is done by line managers who must also take responsibility for the decisions to be made with the scanning output.[50] Uncertainty about the environment is so important to line executives that it makes sense for line executives to be responsible for the scanning process, perhaps with technical assistance from centralized staff. Business planners focus on economic and customer variables, but scanning should include broader issues such as population growth, air quality, hazardous waste, land use, water quality, natural resources, and other biological and physical elements.

Sales Forecasting and Consumer Analysis

An application of environmental scanning occurs in sales forecasting. The effectiveness of sales forecasting should be evaluated by the degree to which it improves the decisions of marketing managers. Even though sales forecasting was often self-contained in the sales or finance areas of responsibility, it is increasingly a planning and strategic activity. Thus, sales forecasts should involve all the elements of the environment about which managers must make decisions. A close relationship therefore exists between sales forecasting and decision support systems (DSS).[51]

The specific techniques of sales forecasting include judgmental methods, sales-force estimation, users' expectations, traditional and advanced time-series techniques, econometric or regression modeling, input-output analysis, and various other methods. A discussion of how to use these techniques is beyond the scope of this book, but there are many sources of information about these concepts and techniques.[52] Consumer researchers generally have data and methods useful in preparing sales forecasts.

Consumer Confidence in the Future

An important determinant of what consumers will buy in the future is their confidence in the future. Surveys of consumer confidence are widely reported in connection with understanding macroeconomic conditions but firms use them for planning inventories, setting production schedules, planning human resources, capital budgeting, and many other purposes.

Two organizations are well known for their surveys of consumer confidence. The Conference Board survey of 5,000 households is conducted by mail by National Family Opinion, Inc., of Toledo, Ohio. In this survey, respondents are asked to look six months ahead and focus on the availability of jobs. The University of Michigan survey, which tends to be less volatile, questions 500 households a month by telephone. Consumers are asked, among other things, to look at family finances and overall business conditions. The types of questions asked in these two surveys are displayed in Figure 20.11.

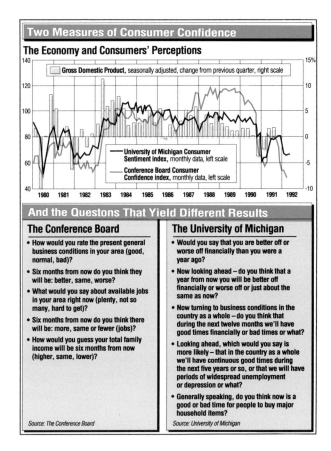

FIGURE 20.11 **Two Measures of Consumer Confidence**

Source: David Wessel, "Confidence Surveys May Help to Predict Shape of the Recovery," *Wall Street Journal* (March 5, 1992), 1ff.

Changing Values and Lifestyles

Finally, the analysis of consumer trends should consider changes in values, lifestyles, and technologies discussed in earlier chapters. Futurists use a variety of methods to project these trends and use them in new product development, planning of advertising and other purposes.[53]

Consumer analysts and marketing strategists have the responsibility to determine the possible effect on consumer behavior of broad changes in society. One such projection is shown in Figure 20.12. Some trends in Figure 20.12 are demographically based. Others are interpersonal, technological, or social in nature. These trends are just that, changes over time, and thus will also be replaced in many instances by other trends. The thoughtful marketing analyst will find implications

FIGURE 20.12   Long-Term Trends Affecting the United States

General Long-Term Societal Trends

1. Ahead is a period of U.S. economic prosperity—affluence, low interest rates, low inflation rate.
2. Rise of knowledge industries and a knowledge-dependent society.
3. Fewer very poor or very wealthy in U.S. society.
4. Rise of the middle-class society.
5. Urbanization and suburbanization of rural land.
6. Cultural homogenization—the growth of a national society.
7. Continuation of a permanent military establishment.
8. Mobility: (A) personal, (B) physical, (C) occupational, (D) job.
9. International affairs and national security as a major societal factor.

Technology Trends

10. The centrality and increasing dominance of technology in the economy and society.
11. Integration of the U.S. economy.
12. Integration of the national with the international economy.
13. Growth of the international economy.
14. The growth of research and development as a factor in the economy.
15. High technological turnover rate.
16. The development of mass media in telecommunications and printing.
17. Major medical advances.

Educational Trends

18. Expanding education and training throughout society.
19. New technologies will greatly facilitate the training process.
20. Greater role of business in training and education.
21. Education costs will continue to rise.
22. Educational institutions will be more concerned with ways to assess outcomes and effectiveness of educational programs.
23. Improved pedagogy—the science of teaching—will revolutionize learning.
24. Universities will stress development of the whole student and how the university's total environment affects that development.
25. Reduction in the size of higher educational institutions.

Trends in Labor Force and Work

26. Specialization.
27. Growth of the service sector.
28. Further decline in the manufacturing sector.
29. Growth of information industries, movement toward an information society.
30. More women will enter the labor force.
31. Women's salaries will be comparable to men's.
32. More blacks and other minority groups will enter the labor force.
33. Later retirement.
34. Decline of unionization.
35. Growth of pensions and pension funds.
36. Movement toward second and third careers and midlife changes in career.
37. Decline of the work ethic.
38. More two-income couples.
39. Shortage of low-wage workers.

Continued

FIGURE 20.12   continued

Management Trends

40. More entrepreneurs.
41. The typical large business will be information-based, composed of specialists who guide themselves based on information from colleagues, customers, and headquarters.
42. The typical large business in 2010 will have less than half the levels of management of the typical large business today and about one-third the number of managers.
43. The command-and-control model of management will be a relic of the past as the information-based organization becomes the norm.
44. The actual work will be done by task-focused teams of specialists.

Trends in Values and Concerns

45. General shift in societal values.
46. Diversity as a growing, explicit value.
47. Increasing aspirations and expectations of success.
48. Growth of tourism, vacationing, and travel (especially international).
49. General expectations of a high level of medical care.
50. Growth of physical culture and personal health movements.
51. General expectations of a high level of social service.
52. Growth of consumerism.
53. Growth of women's liberation movement.

Family Trends

54. Decline in birth rates.
55. Increase in rates of family formation and marriage.
56. Decrease in the number of divorces.
57. Growth of leisure.
58. Growth of the do-it-yourself movement.
59. Improved nutrition and the wellness movement will increase life expectancy.
60. Isolation of children from the world of adult concerns.
61. Protracted adolescence.
62. More single heads of households—the new poor.
63. Growth of the already large aged population.
64. The replacement of the extended family with other living arrangements.

Institutional Trends

65. Decrease in the size of the federal government—growth of state and local governments.
66. Growth of big business (deregulation).
67. Growth of multinational corporations.
68. Growth of futures studies and forecasting.
69. Growing demand for accountability in the expenditure of public resources.
70. Growing demand for social responsibility.
71. A phenomenon of "bimodal" distribution of institutions is emerging as the big get bigger, the small survive, and the middle-sized are squeezed out.

Source: Marvin J. Cetron, Wanda Rocha, and Rebecca Lucken, "Into the 21st Century," *The Futurist* 22 (July–August 1988), 29–40. Supporting materials for this article are also found in Marvin Cetron, *America at the Turn of the Century* (New York: St. Martin's Press, 1989).

for both consumer and goods firms, whether the trends are considered as opportunities for growing profits or threats to existing strategies and profits.

Summary

Consumer analysts have responsibilities for monitoring the environment for both macro-marketing and micromarketing reasons. Macromarketing applications focus upon determining the aggregate performance of marketing in society. Micromarketing analysis focuses on the marketing programs of specific organizations.

The primary financial goal of business firms is ESV—Enhanced Shareholder Value. The financial community attributes such value to a company's stock to the degree that the company is perceived to be able to increase profits in the future. Thus, a major role for consumer analysts is to determine trends that will allow a corporation to increase profits in the future. This can be achieved through the 3 M's—more markets, more market share, and more margin.

Consumer analysts focus upon finding markets that are growing. Markets involve people and their needs, ability to buy, willingness to buy, and authority to buy. Economic demographics involves the analysis of market trends and discovery of growing segments based upon changes in population and age distribution, buying power, geography of demand, and social and technological trends.

Population projections involve three variables: births, deaths, and net immigration. Of these, births is usually the most important determinant of population trends and the most difficult to forecast. Births are determined by four variables: age distribution, family structure, social attitudes toward family and children, and technology. All of these variables are contributing to declining fertility in industrialized countries such as the United States and Canada.

The population base of the United States and Canada is still growing but at a declining rate. It should peak at around 250 to 270 million in the United States sometime after the year 2000 and at around 28 million in Canada. During the 1990s, both countries will see fewer total but more first-order babies, more teenagers, more aging baby boomers (but less consumers in the 24 to 35 age category), a new era of expanding empty-nesters, and an enormous increase in the Young Again or older markets. Each of these categories can be attractive market opportunities for firms that recognize the specialized marketing programs required for success.

Much of the work of consumer analysts in the future will focus upon marketing to the affluent. Recognition should be given to the possibility, however, of marketing in a depression or recession and continuing concerns about consumers living near or below the poverty level.

A large part of consumer market analysis involves geodemography, the study of demand as it is related to geography. In the United States population is expanding rapidly in some states—notably California, Texas, and Florida, with slow growth in the Midwest. In Canada, the western provinces are experiencing the most growth, although not at the rate of the energy-induced boom times of the past. Ontario is recovering some of its growth, but growth of all provinces is slower as a result of decreased fertility and migration rates.

Analysis of demographic and trend data is essential for environmental scanning—the accumulation of systematic and timely information about trends. Such information focuses on the structural properties of the environment, the nature and sources of change, and the means for managers to gain knowledge of their environments. Line managers, sometimes assisted by staff, need to be involved in environmental scanning.

Review and Discussion Questions

1. Distinguish between macromarketing and micromarketing. How does the work of consumer analysts vary between these two fields?
2. Is the concept of ESV (Enhanced Shareholder Value) a socially defensible objective for business corporations? Wouldn't society be better off by focusing on the needs of society and giving the money shareholders receive to poor consumers?
3. How does the concept of ESV compare with traditional goals such as market share, profitability, and sales?
4. "Analysis of consumer trends is obviously important for firms marketing consumer products but of limited value to industrial marketers." Evaluate this statement.
5. Will there be more or fewer births in the future in the United States? What variables should be considered in answering this question?
6. How should the answer to Question 5 affect government planning? How should it affect companies such as General Electric or Johnson & Johnson?
7. Assume a marketer of major appliances is interested in the effects of the baby boomers on demand for the company's products. What are your conclusions and what, if any, research should be conducted to answer the question more fully?
8. "Maturity markets are growing in number very rapidly but they are of little interest to marketers because they have little money compared to younger markets." Analyze this statement.
9. What are the major similarities and the major differences in the population structures of the United States and Canada? Why should consumer analysts in both countries have more interest since 1988 in understanding consumer markets in the other country?
10. "Cities are the key to marketing plans." How would you evaluate this statement?
11. Find and interview a firm that specializes in the analysis of consumer trend or demographic data. How are such analyses used by marketing organizations?

Endnotes

1. Shelby D. Hunt and John J. Burnett, "The Macromarketing/Micromarketing Dichotomy: A Taxonomical Model," *Journal of Marketing* 48 (Summer 1982), 11–26.
2. George Katona, *Psychological Economics* (New York: Elsevier Scientific Publishing, 1975).
3. For more information on this topic, see Alfred Rappaport, *Creating Shareholder Value: The New Standard for Business Performance* (Glencoe, Ill.: Free Press, 1986).
4. J. Randall Woolridge, "Competitive Decline: Is a Myopic Stock Market to Blame?" *Journal of Applied Corporate Finance* 1 (Spring 1988), 26–36.
5. Martin Mayer, *Whatever Happened to Madison Avenue? Advertising the '90s* (New York: Little, Brown & Company, 1991).
6. Thomas Exter, "Birthrate Debate," *American Demographics* 13 (September 1991), 55.
7. Definitions in this section are based on Arthur Haupt and Thomas T. Kane, *Population Handbook* (Washington, D.C.: Population Reference Bureau, 1985).

8. "Family Life Styles Changing," *Better Homes & Gardens* (July and August, 1983).
9. "Fertility of American Women," Series P-20, No. 427 (Washington, D.C.: U.S. Government Printing Office, 1988).
10. "Canada Today—Results of the 1986 Census," *Consumer Markets Abroad* 6 (October 1987).
11. Joseph O. Rentz and Fred D. Reynolds, "Forecasting the Effects of an Aging Population on Product Consumption: An Age-Period-Cohort Framework," *Journal of Marketing Research* 28 (August 1991), 355–60.
12. Thomas G. Exter, "Big Spending on Little Ones," *American Demographics* 14 (February 1992), 6.
13. James U. McNeal, "The Littlest Shoppers," *American Demographics* 14 (February 1992), 48–53.
14. For additional examples, see numerous articles in a special supplement, "Marketing to Kids," *Advertising Age* (February 10, 1992).
15. "Teen Spenders," *American Demographics* 10 (June 1988), 21.
16. Roger D. Blackwell and Margaret Hanke, "The Credit Card and the Aging Baby Boomers," *Journal of Retail Banking* 9 (Spring 1987), 17–25.
17. For additional examples, see Dale Blackwell and Roger Blackwell, "Yuppies, Muppies and Puppies: They Are Changing Real Estate Markets," *Ohio Realtor* (August 1989), 11–15.
18. George Moschis, "Marketing to Older Adults," *Journal of Consumer Marketing* (Fall 1991), 33–41.
19. Paula Fitzgerald Bone, "Identifying Mature Segments," *Journal of Consumer Marketing* 8 (Fall 1991), 19–32.
20. William Lazer and Eric H. Shaw, "How Older Americans Spend Their Money," *American Demographics* 9 (September 1988), 36–41.
21. Ellen Day, Brian Davis, Rhonda Dove, and Warren French, "Reaching the Senior Citizen Market(s)," *Journal of Advertising Research* 27 (January 1988), 23–30.
22. Thomas Moehrle, "Expenditure Patterns of the Elderly: Workers and Nonworkers," *Monthly Labor Review* 113 (May 1990), 34–41.
23. Dede Ryan, *The Maturing Marketplace* (Silver Spring, Md.: Business Publishers, 1987), 33.
24. Benny Barak, "Elderly Solitary Survivors and Social Policy: The Case for Widows," in Andrew Mitchell, *Advances in Consumer Research* (1984), 27–30.
25. Ivan Ross, "Information Processing and the Older Consumer: Marketing and Public Policy Implications," in Mitchell, *Advances in Consumer Research* (1984), 31–39.
26. Nark D. Uncles and Andrew S. C. Ehrenberg, "Brand Choice among Older Consumers," *Journal of Advertising Research* 30 (August/September 1990), 19–22.
27. Charles F. Longino, Jr., "The Comfortably Retired and the Pension Elite," *American Demographics* 10 (June 1988), 22–25.
28. Elaine Sherman and Philip Cooper, "Life Satisfaction: The Missing Focus of Marketing to Seniors," *Journal of Health Care Marketing* 9 (March 1988), 69–71.
29. Ken Dychtwald, quoted in Curtis Hartman, "Redesigning America," *Inc.* 10 (June 1988), 59–69.
30. Barbara Boyle Torrey, Kevin Kinsella, and Cynthia M. Taeuber, *An Aging World* (Washington, D.C.: Bureau of the Census, 1987), 7.
31. For details, see Roger D. Blackwell, "The Rising Importance of Consumer Affairs Departments," *Mobius: Journal of Consumer Affairs Professionals* (Fall 1990).
32. Claes Fornell and Birger Wernerfelt, "Defensive Marketing Strategy by Customer Complaint Management: A Theoretical Analysis," *Journal of Marketing Research* 24 (November 1987), 337–346.

33. More examples are provided in Roger D. Blackwell and Margaret Hanke, "The Credit Card and the Aging Baby Boomers," *Journal of Retail Banking* 9 (Spring 1987), 21.

34. "Cost of the 'Good Life' Again Outpaces the CPI," *American Marketplace* 10 (March 16, 1989), 47.

35. "Family Futures," *American Demographics* 8 (May 1984), 50. Also see "Money Income of Households, Families, and Persons," Series P-60, No. 162 (Washington, D.C.: U.S. Government Printing Office, 1989).

36. Thomas J. Stanley and George P. Moschis, "America's Affluent," *American Demographics* 6 (March 1984), 28–33.

37. Ravi Batra, *The Great Depression of 1990* (New York: Random House, 1988).

38. Edward Cornish, "Start of Another Depression?" *Futurist* 10 (January–February 1988), 2ff.

39. Office of Technology Assessment, *Technology and the American Economic Transition: Choices for the Future* (Washington: U.S. Government Printing Office, 1988).

40. "State Population and Household Estimates, with Age, Sex, and Components of Change: 1981–1987," Series P-25, No. 1024 (Washington, D.C.: U.S. Government Printing Office, 1988).

41. Randall Litchfield, "Competitiveness and the Constitution," *Canadian Business* (August 1991), 18.

42. Jane Jacobs, *Cities and the Wealth of Nations* (New York: Random House, 1984).

43. John Fondersmith, "Downtown 2040: Making Cities Fun," *Futurist* 22 (March–April 1988), 9–17.

44. "The Gap Grows," *American Demographics* 10 (December 1988), 16.

45. "Megalopolis," *American Demographics* 6 (January 1984), 50–51.

46. John Naisbitt, *Megatrends* (New York: Warner Books, 1982).

47. James P. Allen and Eugene J. Turner, "Where to Find the New Immigrants," *American Demographics* 10 (September 1988), 23–27.

48. "The Best 100 Sources for Marketing Information," *American Demographics 1992 Directory*.

49. R. T. Lenz and Jack L. Engledow, "Environmental Analysis: The Applicability of Current Theory," *Strategic Management Journal* 7 (1986), 329–346.

50. Charles Stubbart, "Are Environmental Scanning Units Effective?" *Long Range Review* 12 (1987), 133–143.

51. Essam Mahmoud, Gillian Rice, and Naresh Malhotra, "Emerging Issues in Sales Forecasting and Decision Support Systems," *Journal of the Academy of Marketing Science* 16 (Fall 1988), 47–61.

52. Some sources that provide practical approaches to understanding these techniques include Lester Sartorious and N. Carroll Mohn, *Sales Forecasting Methods: A Diagnostic Approach* (Atlanta: Georgia State University, 1976); George C. Michael, *Sales Forecasting* (Chicago: American Marketing Association, 1979); Harry R. White, *Sales Forecasting: Timesaving and Profit-Making Strategies that Work* (Dallas: Scott, Foresman and Company, 1984.)

53. For an example of a report of changes in lifestyles over the past two decades, see "Who We Are, How We Live, What We Think," *Advertising Age* (January 20, 1992), 16–22.

Market Segmentation

Here's a portrait of the American man, circa 1992. He is romantic and self-centered, family-oriented and individualistic, hard-working, and leisure-loving. In other words, he is a mass of contradictions. And he is just as mysterious to businesses as men have always been to women.

Women have spent the last three decades behaving more like men in certain ways. In the 1990s, men are adapting to these changes. Women have enjoyed significant advances in educational attainment, labor force participation, career involvement, and economic independence. They have also endured significant increases in smoking, divorce, and single-parent families. The overwhelming result has been stress, as women try to play multiple roles, and increasing conflict, as women demand more from men.

"Men were thrown a curve ball," says Michael Clinton, publisher of *GQ* magazine. "The patterns they had established in terms of interacting with women were no longer relevant."

In response, men started helping out more with housework and child care. Nurturing became a manly thing in the 1980s. Advertisers became infatuated with the image of a handsome towelled man dandling a baby on his knees. Men who are full-time homemakers are still rare. But for whatever reason, men are taking on more of the everyday responsibilities of running a household. That includes shopping, child care, and cooking.

Men have mixed feelings about all of the changes going on in their lives. Some welcome the challenges and appreciate the choices, while others fight them. "Men now see that they have choices to live different kinds of lives," says Michael Clinton of *GQ*. "This is healthy not only for them but also for the women in their lives. Men are no longer following prescribed patterns and getting boxed into preordained behavioral habits."

A 1990 *GQ* study divides men into different attitudinal groups, based on their attitudes toward change. Men who like choices are called "Change Adapters." They are younger, better-educated, and more affluent than "Change Opposers."

Opposers have less money than Adapters, so they are more cautious spenders. They are more likely to shop at discount stores and to look for sales and imitation products. They are not greatly influenced by advertising, but they do a lot of background research before making a big purchase. They are not brand loyal.

Change Adapters are more likely to try new things. Within this group are two subgroups: the pragmatic "Tradition-Oriented Adapters," who roll with the changes going on around them, and the adventurous "Self-Oriented Adapters," who are the biggest spenders.

Looking good is important to many men, and romance is only part of the reason. Nearly half strongly agree that they owe it to themselves to look their best, according to *GQ*, and 39 percent say they have a strong sense of personal style. The survey found a significant increase in the amount of time men spend grooming themselves, and nearly half are pleased when others notice and comment on their appearance.

Source: Diane Crispell, "The Brave New World of Men," *American Demographics* (January 1992), 38–40. Reproduced by permission. © 1992 American Demographics, January 1992.

The male buyer is different from his female counterparts. Makers of yogurt are finding this to be disturbingly true, giving rise to the question, "Do Real Men Eat Yogurt?"[1] As Rapp and Collins have so convincingly demonstrated, the market is splintering into a bewildering variety of segments, and the marketer faces a genuine challenge in responding.[2] This is done through a **market segmentation**.

We have referred to market segmentation in many chapters and have described it as the process whereby separate products or marketing mixes are prepared for components (that is, segments) of the market that differ in distinct and meaningful ways. The goal is to develop criteria that effectively identify the segments, offering the highest potential of response to marketing efforts.

Development of these criteria (or bases) is one of the most important roles for consumer research. Once segments are identified, the task then becomes one of designing marketing strategies to capitalize upon the market potential within each segment.

Our intent in this chapter is to elaborate further on the concept of segmentation and its strategic importance. Then our primary attention focuses on the many bases that can be used for segmentation and some of the ways in which marketers have found them to be of strategic significance.

The Concept of Segmentation

In a sense, each of us is a distinct market segment, because no two people are exactly alike in their motivations, needs, decision processes, and buying behavior. Such services as tailoring, beauty care, and landscaping have long taken advantage of these differences by providing individualized attention. Also, as you have read in previous chapters, there is a groundswell in growth of direct marketing through use of computer data bases. We will say more about this phenomenon later.

Obviously, such pinpoint accuracy in reaching prospects is not possible in larger-scale marketing. The objective now shifts to identification of groups within the broader market that are sufficiently similar in characteristics and responses to warrant separate treatment.

Criteria of Usable Segments

For a segment to warrant special consideration in marketing strategy, four basic criteria must be met: reachability, identification of causal differences, economic potential, and possession of required marketing resources.

Reachability
Do you recall our discussion in Chapter 5 of the important role played by influentials (or opinion leaders) whose endorsement can make the difference between marketing success and failure? Clearly, a case can be made for treating influentials as a prime market segment, but there is one major difficulty. Usually they cannot be isolated as a distinct segment and reached efficiently and economically through advertising media. The reason is that they most often are scattered throughout other market segments.

The goal of segmented strategy ideally is to fire a rifle shot, not a shotgun blast, at the market. If there is no good way to bring the target into focus and reach it economically, the benefits may not justify the effort.

Identification of Causal Differences
When undertaking market segmentation it is important to distinguish between causal and descriptive differences. In other words, some consumer differences represent motivating influences or other factors that define and shape behavior. They would be considered causal, whereas others are merely descriptive. Unless causal differences are isolated, effective segmentation is impossible.

There is growing evidence that women are motivated and behave differently from men in automobile purchase decisions.[3] These basic designating variables represent factors that underlie and shape behavior and hence cannot be disregarded in strategy deliberations.

Let's take the driving enthusiasts as an example. These women love driving and prefer American-made performance cars. The underlying reasons for their preferences can be found in a lifestyle energized by interests in gambling, sports, and fast-paced activity. These are causal factors that lead them to favor the so-called "muscle cars." It is quite justifiable to consider marketing strategies designed to attract such women to high-performance cars.

The fact that driving enthusiasts are in their thirties, however, is probably not a causal consideration. The value seekers are in the same age bracket but are motivated differently. Hence, age is a helpful descriptor and not an underlying motivator in and of itself.

It should be noted, however, that descriptive factors find considerable use once the causal differences have been identified. The greatest value lies in expanding our understanding of the target consumer. If we know, for example, that she is under 35 and living primarily in urban areas, this information defines what can be done in advertising strategy. It obviously would be inappropriate to feature a woman in her middle fifties enjoying her grandchildren.

Descriptive characteristics help in yet another important way. Research information is available on the audience characteristics of nearly all advertising media. The objective is to match target audience characteristics against media characteristics so that media choices can be made that minimize waste coverage.

Economic Potential   A leading manufacturer of paper products designed a crayon that was demonstrably different in both its concept and characteristics. Test marketing uncovered a segment that preferred its benefits over the more familiar competitive alternatives. But this segment totalled only 2 percent of a $30 million market and offered too little revenue payout to justify the effort. Hence, it did not meet the most basic of all criteria: *the revenue projection must offer a high economic potential to justify the investment.*

Possession of Required Marketing Resources   A cable TV network designed and tested a new programming concept aimed at the nonchurch-going audience segment. The central theme was to demonstrate dramatically how lives can be changed by faith and answer to prayer. Even though all market tests, including on-air response, were positive, the program never went beyond the test stage. It soon became apparent that this program ideally should be a weekly series, but the costs of both production and air time were excessive.

The situation becomes even more critical when staff know-how and experience are lacking, even though the market opportunity is positive. As Peters and Waterman put it, an organization must "stick to its knitting" and not branch out beyond its basic mission and staff capabilities.[4]

The Market Target Decision

Once the market has been segmented properly in terms of the four criteria, the firm has three options: (1) **concentrated marketing**, (2) **differentiated marketing**, and (3) **undifferentiated marketing**.

Concentrated Marketing   In concentrated marketing, the primary focus is on one segment. For years, Plough Inc. advertised its Coppertone line of tanning products by picturing a small dog pulling at the bathing briefs of a young girl, thereby revealing her tanning line. Such a message no longer appeals to a health-oriented public. Now Plough has dropped the term *tanning* in favor of *suncare* and has targeted the "tennis set." As of 1988, it is the "Official Suncare Product" of the Association of Tennis Professionals (ATP).[5]

The obvious danger of concentrated marketing is that a niche can evaporate sometimes with amazing rapidity and the company is, in effect, eliminated as a competitor. Some diversification is always a good option, especially if there is continuing competitive turbulence.

Differentiated Marketing   An alternative approach is to concentrate on two or more segments, offering a differing marketing mix for each. There is a distinct trend toward multiple product offerings targeted at different segments. Most refrigerator manufacturers, for example, have added small units for use in offices, dormitory rooms, or other places where space is limited. These are in sharp contrast to large, split-door refrigerator/freezers designed for an entirely different segment.

There is no question that differentiated marketing offers the potential benefit of enhanced market position, but it is not without its disadvantages. One of the greatest dangers lies in loss of the core market unless precautions are taken.

The Chevrolet Division of General Motors is a case in point. At least two generations of North Americans were raised to identify the Chevrolet as one of three cars (Chevrolet, Ford, and Plymouth) made to provide safe, dependable, and affordable transportation for the "average family." The Chevy was quite different from other General Motors brands and had a clear identity.

The Chevrolet line was greatly expanded in the early 1980s, with models offered at nearly all price ranges. In so doing Chevrolet lost its traditional mass-market and low-price appeal and saw its core market dwindle because of inroads from the imports.[6] There is always the danger of blurring the established image in core markets unless precautions are taken. No product can be all things to all people.

Undifferentiated Marketing   Continuing with our earlier example of the female automobile purchaser, several manufacturers have concluded that the best approach is to include women in ads without creating a separate marketing strategy for them. This tactic worked well for Toyota, Nissan, Mazda, and Honda; and the net effect of their efforts has been to gain higher import penetration among women than among men.[7]

The problem with undifferentiated marketing, however, is that it is often exceedingly difficult to maintain market position if the needs of buyers are varied. Firms using this strategy become highly vulnerable to competitive inroads.

The General Motors Corporation, for example, tried in the late 1980s to broaden the appeal of the Cadillac Eldorado and Seville to attract young import-oriented buyers while, at the same time, retaining the loyal market core. In reality, they succeeded only in alienating core customers without attracting many import buyers, and sales were less than half of projections. Only rarely does this strategy work when there is rigorous competition.

Undertaking Segmentation Analysis

There are three ways to proceed in segmentation analysis: (1) **a priori analysis**, (2) **post-hoc analysis**, or (3) **scanner analysis**. All three strategies are very different in concept and procedure.

A Priori Analysis

Often there is good reason to define the segmentation base in advance. We might be reasonably certain, for example, that the most frequent purchasers differ from occasional users. When this is the case, we establish purchase frequency as our basis for dividing the market and do research to determine ways in which frequent users differ from others in terms of demographic and psychographic characteristics, preferred product attributes, and so on.

Here is an example of what we mean. Table 21.1 provides a summary of segmentation research undertaken by the manufacturer of a special-purpose food condiment. Extent of usage was chosen a priori to be the segmentation base and to serve as the dependent variable in the analysis which was to follow.

A nationwide survey was undertaken to differentiate between heavy users and occasional users. Each person interviewed responded to a series of questions on demographic and psychographic characteristics, usage and preferences, and media exposure. Heavy users were separated from light users by cross-classification analysis, and the resulting differences appear in Table 21.1.

It is clear from the summary data that two distinctly different segments exist. If the goal is to increase frequency of use among the first segment, it will be necessary to position the product in a traditional home setting, showing how it will please the family if used creatively.

Such a strategy, however, could alienate the heavy user who more closely fits the stereotype of the "liberated woman." Fortunately, each segment can be reached efficiently through different media without much audience overlap. This allows maximum opportunity for differentiated marketing.

Post-Hoc Analysis

In post-hoc analysis, the base for segmentation is not decided in advance but, rather, is an outcome of the analysis itself. The first step is to cluster people into homogeneous segments on the basis of similarities in responses to psychographic, demographic, motivational, and behavioral questions. There is a family of multivariate statistical techniques that can be used for this purpose.[8] Once segments are isolated, further statistical analysis is undertaken to determine whether or not there are buying preference or behavioral differences between members of the various segments.

Eight market segments were identified by Valentine-Radford Advertising from survey responses focusing on dimensions of the consumer decision-making process.[9] Referred to as CUBE (Comprehensive Understanding of Buyer Environments), segments were built post hoc from this information:

1. How people get control of their circumstances—takes control, yields control, creates own rules, accepts existing rules.
2. Method of action—acts first or thinks first.
3. Judgment of information—fact based or feeling based.

Eight primary segments have been isolated (see Table 21.2). Each then is correlated with brand use, desired benefits, and other information to provide clues on the best market target for specific products and services.

TABLE 21.1   An A Priori Segmentation Analysis for a Food Condiment

	Occasional Users (20%)	Heavy Users (41%)
Demographics	35–54; large families; middle income; suburbs and farms; southern	20–45; well educated; small families; children under 5; southeast, urban, and suburban
Usage	Mainly on holidays	At least weekly, year around
Desired attributes	Interest in creative cookery; not interested in taking risks	Exotic and exciting taste, experimental cookery preferred
Attitudes toward product	Favorable, but use only with one food category	Favorable; product is exciting and seen as asset in creative cooking
Media exposure	Women's magazines, daytime TV	Shelter group magazines, FM radio
Psychographics	Desire for self-expression constrained by maintenance of tradition; home-oriented	Contemporary; wants to express individuality; dislikes housework; not home-oriented
Social	Desire to please family	Less desire to please family

TABLE 21.2   Eight Market Segments Defined by Post-Hoc Analysis

1. *Traditionals.* Yield control, act first, and make fact-based decisions. Down-to-earth, practical, and conventional. Older, lower education and income, married, often retired.
2. *New Middle Americans.* Take control, act first, make fact-based decisions. Very sociable, achievement oriented, concerned with living standards, and are moderate risk takers. Somewhat younger, well educated, high family incomes, fewer children.
3. *Home and Community Centered.* Yield control, think first, and are fact based. Very conventional, prim, and proper. Exercise self-control, tend to go by acceptable rules of society, and are not gregarious. Somewhat older, better educated, higher incomes.
4. *Rising Stars.* Take control, think first, fact-based, intellectually curious but not socially gregarious. Has highest income and education and highest percentages of professionals, entrepreneurs, males, and singles. Oriented to cultural activities.
5. *Good Ol' Girls and Boys.* Yield control, act first, and are feeling based. Practical, down-to-earth, no nonsense, sociable, yet cynical. Lower education and income. Like soap operas, game shows, and country and western music.
6. *Young Socials.* Take control, act first, and make decisions based on feelings. Outgoing, warm, and intuitive. Low self-control—if it feels good do it. Tend to be younger and less educated and have higher family incomes, and more females.
7. *Moralists.* Yield control, think first, and are feeling based. Proper, detached, yet concerned. Older, lower education and income, factory workers, and homemakers. Attend church and are exposed to religious media.
8. *Aging Hippies.* Take control, think first, and are feeling based. Sensitive, fanciful, unrealistic, and imaginative. Younger and better educated. Unconventional living arrangements.

Source: "Ad Agency Develops Eight New Market Segments," *Marketing News* (August 26, 1987), 12. Used by special permission from the American Marketing Association.

What the Scanner Knows about You

So you thought you could slip into the supermarket and buy that diet-busting macaroni and cheese, and no one would know, eh? Wrong. Kraft knows. In fact Kraft USA knows quite a lot about macaroni-and-cheese eaters like you: how old are they and how often do they shop, for starters. The company's marketing and research folks can figure out whether they fill the grocery cart in one trip or grab a few items several times a week. Whether they spend afternoons clipping coupons. How many children they have, whether they eat out or entertain friends at home, and if they earn their living behind a desk or on the factory floor.

Has Kraft been snooping around the neighborhood again? No, the skinny on folks like you came from those supermarket scanners embedded in the grocery checkout counter. Every time a clerk whisks a purchase over the scanner, it electronically records what was bought, who makes it, the size, and the price. That information is then fortified with more telling data derived from research into what shoppers watch on television, the type of neighborhood they live in, and the kind of supermarket they shop in. The result is that manufacturers today have an even sharper picture of who their customers are than they did just five years ago.

Knowing the customer better helps companies figure out which products consumers want and what influences their decisions to buy. Are shoppers motivated by cents-off coupons, splashy displays, free sampling, or product literature? A better handle on the customer also makes manufacturers more sure-footed on the empty road of product testing. Scanner technology tells them how much of a test item is sold initially and how many—what type of—shoppers go back into the store to buy it again and again.

Source: Susan Caminiti, "What the Scanner Knows About You," *Fortune* (December 3, 1990), 51–52. © 1990 Time Inc. All rights reserved.

Scanner Analysis

As we have seen in earlier chapters, scanner analysis is finding increased application in marketing. When combined with standard surveys and other methods of data collection, scanner data, derived at point-of-sale, greatly increases a marketer's ability to define a complete profile of both company and competitor's customers. Consumer in Focus 21.1 shows you ways in which Kraft USA has gained new insights.

Some Pitfalls in Segmentation Research

In a survey undertaken among six major consumer package goods firms, only about one-half actually found segmentation studies undertaken in the past four years to be useful in strategic marketing planning.[10] Much of the problem, according to Calvin L. Hodock, lies in market researchers who "have become enamored with prestigious, sexy, multivariate techniques."[11]

We concur with this observation. Statistical "number crunching" all too often is used indiscriminately to find descriptive variables that correlate to some degree with a particular consumer characteristic or action. While the relationship may be statistically significant, of what practical value is it to discover that your best target customer is "practical," "down-to-earth," "cynical," yet "sociable?" Are these characteristics causal factors in the choices which are made? Or can be they considered as falling into the category of "interesting but irrelevant information?"

Always ask yourself this question, "What will I do differently now that I have this information?" Unless there is some reason to suspect a cause and effect relationship, such data can confuse rather than enlighten the decision maker.

Bases for Segmentation

A variety of factors (or bases) can be used to segment a market, and these fall into the following categories: (1) geographic, (2) demographic, (3) psychographic, (4) behavioristic, and (5) usage situation.

Geographic

For most of its history, Campbell Soup Company has epitomized undifferentiated marketing with its standardized red-and-white cans sold nearly everywhere. Now it is tailoring its marketing mix to fit different regions of the country and even individual neighborhoods within a city.[12] For example, its nacho cheese soup is spicier in Texas and California.

From Chapter 20 you learned the impact of changing geographic differences in terms of region, size of city or metropolitan area, density (urban, suburban, rural), and climate. All of these geographic factors have found their use in segmentation for many decades.

A more recent addition is **geodemography**. As you may recall from earlier chapters, demographic census lifestyle profiles can be generated for minute locations throughout the country. Customer penetration can be mapped within these clusters, providing a good clue both to the characteristics of present customers and the extent of penetration in such segments as "educated, affluent executives and professionals in elite metro suburbs."

This type of geodemographic information was used by Häagen-Dazs Shoppe Company, an upscale ice cream marketer, to evaluate penetration in each of 40 possible clusters. It then proved possible to develop localized programs designed to

Consumer in Focus 21.2

Geodemographic Information Breathes New Life into Equitable Strategy

James A. Sharky is assistant vice president, Market Research and Information at The Equitable Life Assurance Society of the United States. Here is what he has to say about market segmentation in the innovative 1990 marketing plan at Equitable.

We have understood market segments for years, but now we identify their size, their financial behavior, and their needs.

We define affluent households as having incomes of $50,000 and over. Families with children are the number-one subsegment, and they are growing at above-average rates when compared with all affluent households. The presence of children is still an important part of what establishes the need for life insurance, especially as it relates to insuring that the children will have a college education.

There are other affluent subsegments like Business Owners, Emerging Affluent, the Very Affluent, Pre-Retired, Already Retired, and Dual-Income No Kids (DINKS). We can analyze the affluent by median income, net worth, liquid assets, and propensity to buy security products and investment instruments. We've created an index to measure the percentage of Equitable buyers in each segment to the percentage of all U.S. households in that segment. It's an estimate of how successful we are.

Like most insurance companies, our sales force evolved over the past 130 years with no real plan for target marketing. My background in

Continued

increase both distribution and penetration.[13] Consumer in Focus 21.2 gives you further insight into the ways in which geodemography can open new doors for strategic marketing thinking.

Demographic

Market potential for any product is equivalent to the number of people who want or need it and also have the necessary resources to buy it. Hence, it is necessary to evaluate the demographic characteristics of both present and potential buyers.

Demographic information also can serve as a **proxy variable** for motivation, interests, and preferences. A proxy variable "stands in" or substitutes for something geography suggested that Equitable could benefit from planned penetration based on potential, but it wasn't until recently that we began operating in that way. For example, we didn't have defined marketing areas. We hired agents based on abilities of local managers, and the agents tended to sell in the areas around where they live.

We began providing our local offices with geodemographic information in 1986. The first thing we asked them was how they defined their market. We asked questions like "Where do you focus your efforts? Where do you recruit agents, or send direct mail?" Eventually, we developed a geographic definition for every Equitable marketing territory, defined as groups of counties. We ended up with a national map that showed about 70 territories encompassing one or more agency offices. These areas contained about 30 percent of all U.S. counties but 80 percent of the affluent population.

The latest thing we've done is to match up our customers' names and addresses with those in Donnelley Marketing's DQI² database. Donnelley has a data base of 85 million households, and there is a lot of demographic information on that list.

We've matched the Donnelley data on income and net worth of households with our individual records. We can now target direct-mail messages to individual households and develop tracking measures.

Source: "Marketing Assurance—An Interview with James A. Sharkey," *American Demographics* (November 1990), 42–43. Copyright © 1990. Reproduced by special permission.

else. If you uncover a market segment described as "upper-middle-class teenagers," you already know a great deal about what makes such people "tick" from observation and published research.

The most widely used demographic factors are age, sex, family size, family life cycle, income, occupation, education, religion, race, nationality, and social class. Often two or more factors are used in tandem. A good example is the discovery of and capitalization upon strong interest in fragrances and grooming aids by *males* between the ages of *18 and 24*.[14]

You have studied the implications of these variables for marketing strategy in many chapters in this book. Therefore, only several illustrative examples are given here.

FIGURE 21.1 **Eastpak Appeals to College-Age Consumers**

Age Age is one of the variables most often used in segmentation for two reasons. First, age is one of the most helpful proxy variables for determination of motivation and interest because of extensive secondary research on this subject.

Another reason age segmentation is so popular is that it is quite feasible to reach various age groups precisely and economically with mass media targeted specifically to them. Is there any question which age segment is the target Eastpak's ad? (See Figure 21.1.)

Here are more examples of age segmentation. At one time pickup trucks were rarely owned except by farmers, construction workers, and others who require utility vehicles for their livelihood. Today the scene is quite different. About half of sales of compact trucks are among persons under 35, 90 percent of whom are male.[15] There is particular growth among college students. According to one marketing authority:

> College students are by nature more active and more out-doorsy. Trucks fit the self-image of being a bit of a rebel. Add to that the price value of pickups, and you can see why they're a good growth category.[16]

FIGURE 21.2   Buick Is Back on Target

Next, the Buick Division of General Motors Corporation historically occupied a market position just below Cadillac as a comfortable, prestige automobile which had natural appeal for middle-income buyers in their 50s and 60s. This successful market position was lost during the 1980s as astonishingly inept top management blurred the distinctions between all GM lines.

When Edward Mertz took over as General Manager in 1986, things changed rapidly. He restored Buick's market position by concentrating anew on the generation of buyers longing for "traditional American elegance." Through such models as the LeSabre (Figure 21.2), the only American car breaking into the "Trouble-Free Top Ten" as rated by J. D. Power and Associates, Buick gained nearly a full percentage point of market share in 1991 alone.[17]

Social Class   You learned in Chapter 4 that social classes are very present in supposedly classless societies in the Western world. At one time art collecting was largely a phenomenon confined to the upper class, but now wealthy businessmen a step down the social scale are becoming avid collectors. According to one art gallery proprietor, "Ownership separates people from the masses, and is a visible sign of upward mobility and good times."[18]

Family Life Cycle   You will recall from Chapter 6 that families change over time, passing through a series of stages. This process is referred to as the family life cycle. Buying behavior often varies sharply from one stage to the next.

The Consumer Market Matrix designed by Management Horizons is a helpful analytical tool. The heavy buyers of Kentucky Fried Chicken were found to fall into this life cycle category: younger parents (head under age 45) with children at home, second-highest income quartile. It is highly likely that time is at a premium for these customers. No doubt most are willing to part with the extra money required to buy prepared food in return for gains in leisure time.

Working Women   Often there is much to be gained by investigating the potential in segments beyond the core market. Jewelers have recently discovered that working women are a responsive target for expensive jewelry traditionally marketed to mid-life families and households (head aged 45 to 65) in the "Up Market" income quartile.[19]

Psychographic   Psychographics is another term for lifestyle—those patterns by which people live and spend time and money. Personality also is a part of lifestyle, but, as we demonstrated in Chapter 12, it rarely has proved to be of much use in and of itself in segmentation analysis. Much greater use is made of AIO (Activities, Interests, and Opinion) profiles. In fact, the terms *AIO* and *psychographics* are often used synonymously.

One of the most widely cited sources of data for lifestyle segmentation, VALS (SRI International's Values and Lifestyles) is discussed in Chapter 12. While it is not used so much today in its original form,[20] VALS has provided the basis for some of the real marketing successes in the past decade. One mentioned in Chapter 12 is the change in advertising strategy for Merrill Lynch when it was discovered that the prime customer is an upwardly mobile and self-motivated achiever. Formerly the "Bullish on America" theme depicted a thundering herd of cattle. This was shifted to the lone bull designed as a "breed apart" seeking the aid of Merrill Lynch in the canyons of Wall Street.

In recent years, the subject of environmentalism has given rise to a psychographic segmentation on this dimension which previously was largely unknown. With respect to the so-called "green movement," there are five distinctly different segments[21] (see Table 21.3).

1. *True-Blue Greens* (11 percent). More than half will not buy from companies they consider to be environmentally irresponsible.
2. *Greenback Greens* (11 percent). Most willing to pay more money for environmentally safe products and will give up important elements of their lifestyle for this reason (but will not cut back on automobile use).

TABLE 21.3   Helping Out Mother—The Characteristics of Segments Defined by Interest in Protecting the Environment*

	Total Adults	True-Blue Greens	Greenback Greens	Sprouts	Grousers	Basic Browns
Total	100%	100%	100%	100%	100%	100%
SEX						
Male	47%	34%	42%	48%	46%	55%
Female	53	66	58	52	54	45
EDUCATION						
Less than high school	21%	11%	11%	15%	26%	30%
High school graduate	38	39	35	33	43	39
Some college	22	22	28	25	19	20
College graduate or more	19	28	26	28	12	11
OCCUPATION						
Executive/professional	16%	25%	17%	22%	13%	11%
White collar	18	18	28	19	18	15
Blue collar	28	19	24	22	31	36
MARITAL STATUS						
Married	62%	69%	62%	71%	55%	59%
Not married	37	30	38	29	44	41
POLITICAL/SOCIAL IDEOLOGY						
Conservative	39%	43%	37%	41%	40%	36%
Middle of the road	37	26	33	35	39	41
Liberal	20	28	29	21	18	16
REGION						
Northeast	22%	31%	24%	25%	23%	17%
Midwest	26	27	26	29	26	22
South	33	18	28	28	30	48
West	19	24	23	18	21	13
RACE						
White	85%	82%	92%	91%	80%	82%
Black	10	11	3	6	13	13
Other	4	3	4	4	6	3
WITH CHILDREN UNDER AGE 13	34%	34%	43%	33%	33%	32%
MEDIAN AGE (in years)	41	44	34	42	39	42
MEDIAN INCOME (in thousands)	$27.1	$32.1	$31.6	$32.0	$24.9	$21.2

*Demographic characterization of "True-Blue Greens," "Greenback Greens," "Sprouts," "Grousers," and "Basic Browns," 1990.
Source: The Roper Organization, New York. Reproduced in Joe Schwartz and Thomas Miller, "The Earth's Best Friends," *American Demographics* (February 1991), 28. Used by special permission.

3. *Sprouts* (26 percent). Ambivalent about regulations and forms of action, but most willing to adjust their lifestyles to accomplish environmental ends.
4. *Grousers* (24 percent). Indifferent to the environment and show lower than average interest in environmentally friendly practices. Likely to blame others for the problems that exist.

5. *Basic Browns* (28 percent). Virtually no pro-environmental interest or action largely because of a belief that there is little an individual can do that will make much difference.

About 50 percent, then, have at least a degree of environmental concern. There are obvious differences in willingness to express these values in the marketplace, but many firms pay close attention to the activists.

One of the most important lessons that has been learned is the very real danger of being perceived as crass and opportunistic when "green movement" benefits are touted for a product.[22] One of the worst examples widely cited in the trade press puts the finger once again on the beleaguered management of General Motors during the 1980s. GM surfaced on Earth Day 1990 and cited its "20 Years of Environmental Progress," a blatantly specious claim in light of GM's demonstrated record of doing all it could to sabotage government clean air efforts. As Bob Garfield put it in *Advertising Age*, "Everyone wears green on St. Patrick's Day, too—but it doesn't make them Irish."[23]

Behavioristic

Some of the most productive forms of segmentation can be classified under the generic heading of **behavioristic variables**. These include (1) extent of use and loyalty, (2) benefit, and (3) usage situation.

Extent of Use and Loyalty   Segmentation on the basis of usage usually requires extensive survey research covering a broad cross section of both present and hopefully potential users. Focus is on usage of both product and brand.

Nonusers of Product Category   The "unreached" or nonusers exert almost a seductive appeal on some marketers. Hope springs eternal that the missing strategy key will be uncovered and the "lost" will be found. Occasionally there can be positive payout when nonusers become the marketing target, but total failure is an ever-present likelihood.

If you were responsible for marketing Chivas Regal Scotch, how would you contend with the fact that young professional people between the ages of 21 and 40 have turned away from traditional distilled spirits to wine and lighter mixed drinks? Your first step should be to diagnose why this is taking place. Here are four possibilities:

1. Lagging awareness of Chivas Regal and other leading scotch whiskeys. If this is the situation, beefed-up promotion could help to reverse the trend.
2. The product has not been correctly positioned as a viable option for the young professional as opposed to those in other age groups. This too can be corrected through revamped advertising.
3. There is conflict between motivations and lifestyles in this segment and product benefits. The perceived dangers of over-consumption of alcohol, for exam-

ple, could be a major reason why many are turning to lighter beverages with less alcohol. If so, no amount of promotion will reverse the trend.

4. Scotch is no longer viewed as an "in drink" within this reference group. This also will destroy any promotional opportunity.

Chivas Regal tackled this problem by positioning the brand as a symbol of success for the upwardly mobile young professional,[24] thus capitalizing on the fact that status symbols were an important motivator to many within this segment at that time.

There are other times, however, where the marketer's hands are tied, and a prime example is the appeal of life insurance to "Asian yuppies."[25] Life insurance is commonly viewed as "death insurance" by most young Chinese. Those within this upward mobile segment shun anything that calls to mind the worst things that can happen in life.

Users of Product but Not Brand Here the objective is to make inroads into competitors' market segments. Some may be vulnerable because of inability to keep up with changes in demand and stay current with consumer preferences. Others may have alienated buyers with shoddy quality or poor customer service.

Unilever U.S. followed this strategy and vaulted over Procter & Gamble Company to grab the number one position in bar soaps during 1991, a 34 percent market share. This was done by positioning Lever 2000 as the soap "for all your 2,000 body parts" through its unique combination of moisturizing, deodorant, and anti-bacterial benefits.[26] All of P&G's chief contenders (Safeguard, Zest, and Coast) fell short of this combined set of benefits.

The best strategy, however, usually is to appeal to the **waverers** whose commitment is diminishing, rather than to attack entrenched competitors head-on. Here is a case in point.

The American Motors Corporation has experienced steady erosion in its sale of compact cars and has been bathed in red ink as a result. Therefore, it moved up to the compact segment with its new Medalion line in 1987 and backed this launch with a $10-million advertising investment.[27]

Did the Medalion have much chance of drawing sales away from such popular competitors as the Ford Escort or Honda Civic? If a competitor is to succeed with this strategy, it must offer both high credibility and significant product improvement on attributes that are important to the consumer. Disappointing sales results underscored that a head-on attack was attempted without these advantages. Shortly thereafter, the American Motors brand disappeared from the North American market.

Regardless of competitive considerations, many recommend targeting the heavy users of the product, often referred to as the **heavy half**. For example, about 20 percent of the beer market consumes around 90 percent of the total. Because of strong propensity to consume, appealing to the heavy half may be the most practical and cost-effective way of establishing a foothold. This is especially likely if there is low involvement and little brand loyalty. When involvement and brand loyalty are high, however, the probability of inroads is much less.

TABLE 21.4 **Hitting the Bull's-eye**

Brand	Heavy User Profile	Life-Style and Media Profile	Top 3 Stores
Peter Pan Peanut Butter	Households with kids headed by 18–54 year olds, in suburban and rural areas	• Heavy video renters • Go to theme parks • Below average TV viewers • Above average radio listeners	**Foodtown Super Market** 3350 Hempstead Turnpike, Levittown, NY **Pathmark Supermarket** 3635 Hempstead Turnpike, Levittown, NY **King Kullen Market** 598 Stewart Ave., Bethpage, NY
Coors Light Beer	Head of household, 21–34, middle to upper income, suburban and urban	• Belong to a health club • Buy rock music • Travel by plane • Give parties, cookouts • Rent videos • Heavy TV sports viewers	**Food Emporium** 1498 York Ave., NYC **Food Emporium** First Ave. & 72nd St., NYC **Gristedes Supermarket** 350 E. 86th St., NYC

Source: Michael J. McCarthy, "Marketers Zero In on Their Customers," *The Wall Street Journal* (March 18, 1991). Reproduced by special permission.

Users of Product and Brand Now our objective is to increase product usage and brand loyalty. It is here where research making use of scanner methods is particularly helpful. Table 21.4 shows one company's analysis of the best targets for two of its brands in the New York City area. Without scanner data, such precise segmentation would be impossible.

Benefit Segmentation Earlier chapters have discussed at length the importance of isolating those product attributes or benefits most desired by prospective customers. Often the mix of competitive products leaves gaps, thus defining an opportunity for any firm which develops a product and marketing strategy to fill the competitive gap. This is referred to as **benefit segmentation**—a customer driven response to an unmet need.[28] The ads in Figure 21.3 are just a few examples of the ways in which benefit segmentation is used.

In 1987 General Foods attempted to shore up the market share of its Sanka brand decaffeinated coffee by switching to a natural decaffeinating process as opposed to using chemicals. This was done in recognition that a substantial number of consumers have become concerned about chemical processing. Ad copy addressed the benefit of natural decaffeination by showing a woman speaking directly to a growing controversy over the decaffeinating process:

FIGURE 21.3   Benefit Segmentation Is Used Worldwide

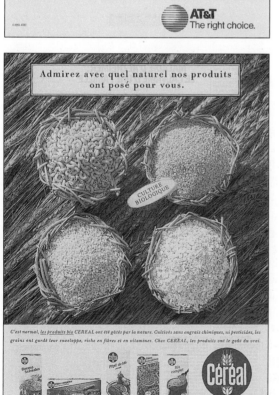

FIGURE 21.4   It's Natural to Drink Sanka

> They say decaffeinated coffee is good for you. Then they turn around and get you wondering about the way it is decaffeinated. Well, the people who make Sanka want you to know that you can enjoy cup after cup without a drop of worry.[29]

This campaign still is successful in the early 1990s (see Figure 21.4).

Skillful benefit segmentation has led to some of the most dramatic marketing successes in recent years. Among the most notable is Wal-Mart Stores, considered by many in retailing to be almost unstoppable.[30] Over the past two decades, this discount mass marketer has become the top United States retailer, even though it concentrates on small- and medium-sized communities and has yet to hit the largest population centers in the Northeastern and Northwestern states.

Wal-Mart offers a unique blend of low price, convenience, one-stop shopping, and personalized service—benefits sought by the large majority of aggressive competitors, especially Kmart Corporation and Target Stores, a division of Dayton Hudson, leading to a real head-on competitive clash. Our prognosis is that Wal-Mart will not lose the battle because of its greatest competitive edge—constant customer contact by executives and staff at all levels accompanied by instant response to their needs.

The Champ of Cheap Clones

The drive from the Sioux City, Iowa airport makes you appreciate how odd it is to find a half-billion dollar plus computer company in this neck of the woods where Iowa, Nebraska, and South Dakota come together. Yet just over the South Dakota line in North Sioux City, in an industrial park where soybean fields outnumber corporate tenants, stands Gateway 2000 Inc., which makes IBM-style PCs and will sell more of them—over 230,000—by phone this year than any other company in the country.

Gateway's owner, Ted Waitt, 28, has a simple strategy: charge the fewest bucks for the bang. For any given quantity of computing power, says industry analyst Bruce Stephen of International Data Corp., "Gateway has the lowest price out there for what's perceived as a viable product." That eases decisions for buyers. Because the technology keeps improving, nobody wants to sink pots of money into hardware that is sure to be obsolete in a couple of years. At the same time, because many computer makes use the same standard parts, PCs have increasingly become commodity products—which makes pricing crucial.

To keep on top of pricing in a low-overhead game like the PC-clone business, Waitt has to aim for the lowest costs. Gateway is strictly an assembly operation. The company's main technical person selects components from among a crowd of suppliers. Waitt has no plans to manufacture his own components or set up a research and development operation.

Also unlike chief competitor Dell Computer, Waitt sells all his product via phone order; he uses no retail outlets. That allows him to cut prices quickly and to charge as little as he wants without upsetting dealers. If a customer needs a house call for a sick machine, Gateway has a contract with TRW to do the work.

Waitt also is planning for the days when the mail-order business cools down. He wants to expand corporate sales, now about one-third of shipments. Says Waitt, "Our isolation worked for us because we snuck up on our competitors. But it worked against us because corporations didn't know about us." If he gets big companies to think as highly of Gateway as his smaller buyers do, he may be able to keep on growing. As he found out years ago, it's amazing how much money people will part with if they have faith in who they're buying from.

Source: Andrew Kupfer, "The Champ of Cheap Clones," *Fortune* (September 23, 1991), 115–120.

Another notable success example is computer assembler and distributor Gateway 2000—"The Champ of Cheap Clones."[31] You will gain further helpful insights by reading the story of this innovative "giant killer" in Consumer in Focus 21.3.

Making Segmentation Work in Marketing Strategy

Segmentation analysis plays an essential role in all phases of the marketing mix. Here is an overview of the major implications.

Uses of Segmentation

Positioning   One of the most common uses of segmentation is in **product positioning**, which refers to the ways in which consumers identify a product with a defined set of attributes such as power, sportiness, caffeine, or color. Products can be positioned or repositioned to capitalize upon untapped benefits, new uses or applications, or competitive weaknesses.

Frito-Lay, the snack-food division of PepsiCo, began its development of a new multi-grain snack chip by 10,000 consumer interviews across the country. Consumers were asked to evaluate about 50 different shapes, hundreds of names, and all kinds of flavors. The favorite proved to be a thin, rectangular chip with ridges and a salty, nutty flavor. "Sun Chip" proved to be the best name, and the prototype product was tested extensively through interviews and scanner methodology at the retail store level. From these data, it seemed highly probable that Sun Chips would exceed minimum standards of trial and four or more repurchases in at least 15–20 percent of households wherever it is marketed.[32]

Advertising and Promotion   ntation finds many uses in promotional strategy. First, and most important, the basic appeal must be designed to show how the company offering delivers expected benefits, and you have seen many examples of that in this chapter and elsewhere in the book.

The segment profile also provides a picture of the consumer in terms of demographic characteristics and lifestyle. Without such information it is difficult to speak in symbols and terms that will be processed meaningfully by those in the target segment. Refer back to Figure 21.1 for an excellent example of capturing nuances of the "new generation" in today's united Germany.

Finally, the demographic and psychographic profile is used to obtain the closest possible match between market and media audience characteristics. Frequent buyers of Stouffer's Red Box Frozen Entrees are heavy newspaper readers. A strong case can be made for concentration in food sections of both urban and suburban papers.

Distribution   Distribution strategy takes account of segmentation in many ways. Lifestyle affects how and where the consumer prefers to buy. Busy working women may prefer in-home purchase and respond to direct marketing. Retailing outlets, in turn, are designed to appeal to increasingly narrow segments, as is demonstrated by the expansion of The Limited to encompass lower price offerings (The Gap) and clothing designed for a more downscale, older segment (Lerner Stores).

Pricing   Finally, price policy is similarly affected. Income affects ability to pay. Lifestyle has an impact in that some consumers are more value and low-price conscious than others. At other times, lower price adversely affects perceptions of quality and is to be avoided.

Direct Marketing   The ultimate of sophistication in segmentation is found in direct marketing. We have given you many examples throughout the book, but here is yet another which illustrates the high degree of precision offered by this strategy.

Retailers are turning to direct marketing with stunning results. Through computer software, it is possible to reach a "segment of one."[33] Through a record of complete information on customer characteristics and preferences, highly tailored, personalized appeals can be made to buyers who otherwise are indifferent to retail advertising.

Some Sensible Precautions

Segmentation strategies offer no panacea. Indeed, there are many examples where the outcomes were decidedly unproductive. Here are some of the lessons that have been learned.

Expect Immediate Retaliation   As you are well aware, the pressures of competitive reality in mature economies can be ruinous. A short-term gain by positioning within a market niche can disappear virtually overnight as competitors retaliate. Therefore, the first thing to do is to solidify the new position with efforts to establish brand awareness and, if possible, brand preference. Next, be fully prepared to dislodge new competitors by matching them inch-by-inch if necessary through aggressive couponing and point-of-sale promotion. Finally, expect market position to be temporary and keep up continual pressure for product innovation.

Avoid Wishful Thinking   The Oldsmobile division of General Motors Company attempted to counteract its steadily deteriorating position among younger, affluent buyers by a new campaign in 1990—"This is not your father's Oldsmobile." This campaign did nothing to stop the slide in sales which led to a market share drop from 9.2 percent in 1986 to 5.5 percent by 1990.[34]

What was the problem? Oldsmobile still largely offered models appealing mostly to the post-55 segment. To think the advertising could have any impact in such a situation is naive wishful thinking. Ads run in 1992 feature attractive new models and the theme "The power of intelligent engineering." Whether the outcomes will be more favorable is still open to question.

Minimize Cannibalization   Lever 2000 surpassed all P&G brands in the hand soap category and attained number one position in the market. Lever 2000 also succeeded in reducing the share of its sister Unilever brand, Dove, from 18 percent to 16.5 percent and unseated it from its number one position.[35] This outcome is referred to as **cannibalization**.

Unilever probably has experienced a net gain from the combined effort of these two brands, but this is not always the case. It is not uncommon for a carefully positioned new product to weaken total company presence in the marketplace through ruinous in-house competition. Simply be aware that this can happen and proceed with caution.

Integrate All Phases of Marketing Strategy   All signs pointed to success when Stouffer Foods Corporation introduced its Right Course frozen entree line in September 1989. Its low-fat, low-cholesterol, low-sodium positioning seemed ideal for the fast-growing segment seeking the benefits of wellness. It was backed by a hefty $20 million marketing budget, and precautions were taken against cannibalization. Seventeen months later Right Course was pulled from national distribution because of a dismal 1.1 percent share.[36]

What went wrong? First of all, there were growing signs that frozen dinner customers do not buy entrees. This would not have been fatal, in and of itself, had care been taken to verify that all phases of the marketing mix were in synchronization. As industry observers noted according to Judann Dagnoli, "To make it stand apart from Lean Cuisine [also a Stouffer brand], the company priced Right Course too high, shelved it in the wrong section of the freezer case, made the brand's varieties too exotic, and its advertising too unfocused."[37] And others felt that the name failed to communicate.

There is a simple but highly important lesson to be learned: *make sure that everything pulls together to build a coordinated and integrated marketing strategy.* Risk is high enough in new product introduction without shooting yourself in the foot by violating such a fundamental axiom.

Summary

Market segmentation is a procedure whereby a market is divided into meaningful groups or subsets that merit separate marketing approaches. There are a number of bases or criteria used for this purpose, many of which are discussed in preceding chapters, including demographic and psychographic characteristics, geographic location, situation, and preferred benefits.

Marketers face three strategic options. One is undifferentiated marketing, in which the same mix is offered to everyone regardless of their differences. This is far less successful in today's competitive environment than it was in earlier years.

Another strategy is differentiated marketing, where two or more segments are targeted using different marketing mixes for each. The last option, concentrated marketing, focuses on one segment out of many possibilities.

In most situations some form of segmentation is a necessity rather than an option. Consumer research is essential, and the payouts can be substantial.

Review and Discussion Questions

1. Ideally, each person is a market segment. Since individualized marketing can be done only on a limited basis, what is the objective of market segmentation?
2. A regional soft drink manufacturer has marketed under one brand name since 1904 and still has the original product line consisting of root beer and orange soda. The CEO is being pressed by the board chair to consider market segmentation. You are asked to comment on this request. How would you define market segmentation? Under what conditions would you recommend it for this manufacturer?
3. You are the brand manager for a manufacturer of music systems. You have just received a research study that suggests that those who spend the most on new stereo products are more venturesome than other people. If this proves to be true, how could you capitalize on this in marketing strategy?
4. What is a proxy variable? In what ways do you think age could be a proxy variable to explain clothing preferences?
5. Many are saying that psychographic segmentation is more helpful than demographic segmentation. Why do you think this might be the case?
6. How would you describe the market segments who would be interested in upscale, expensive imported cars? Fully automatic single-lens reflex cameras? Canned soups? Motor oil?
7. Distinguish between undifferentiated, differentiated, and concentrated marketing. Under which circumstances could each be used with effectiveness?
8. In what ways does the a priori approach differ from the post-hoc approach to segmentation?
9. You have been asked by a major Protestant church denomination to discover why church attendance is declining. Some suspect that the market has become quite segmented. Would you agree? What segments do you think might exist?
10. You have now been asked to do segmentation research for this denomination. How would you tackle this request?

Endnotes

1. Judith Waldrop, "Do Real Men Eat Yogurt?" *American Demographics* (June 1991), 20.
2. Stan Rapp and Tom Collins, *The Great Marketing Turnaround—The Age of the Individual and How to Profit From It* (Englewood Cliffs, N.J.: Prentice-Hall, 1990).
3. Julie Candler, "Unlocking Mystery Surrounding Consumer Category," *Advertising Age* (September 15, 1986), S-3, S-4.
4. Tom Peters and Robert F. Waterman, Jr., *In Search of Excellence* (New York: Random House, 1982).
5. "Coppertone 'Suncare' Strategy Targets Tennis Set," *Marketing News* (April 25, 1988), 1.
6. Robert Simison, "Chevy, GM's Leader, Sustains Worst Slump in U.S. Auto Industry," *Wall Street Journal* (January 4, 1982), 1 and 4.
7. Candler, "Unlocking Mystery."

8. See, for example, Girish Punj and David W. Stewart, "Cluster Analysis in Marketing Research: Review and Suggestions for Application," *Journal of Marketing Research* 20 (May 1983), 134–148.

9. "Ad Agency Develops Eight New Market Segments," *Marketing News* (August 28, 1987), 12.

10. Calvin L. Hodock, "The Decline and Fall of Marketing Research in Corporate America," *Marketing Research* (June 1991), 11.

11. Hodock, "Decline and Fall," 11.

12. "Marketing's New Look," *Business Week* (January 26, 1987), 64ff.

13. Dwight J. Shelton, "Birds of a Geodemographic Feather Flock Together," *Marketing News* (August 28, 1987), 13.

14. "No Surprise: Modern Men Care about How They Look," *Marketing News* (September 11, 1987), 18.

15. Raymond Serafin, "Pickups Deliver a Ton of First-Time Buyers," *Advertising Age* (February 2, 1987), S-14.

16. A comment by Jim Omastiak, vice president and publisher of Campus Voice Network, as quoted in Serafin, "Pickups Deliver."

17. Alex Taylor III, "How Buick Is Bounding Back," *Fortune* (May 6, 1991), 83–88.

18. Joe Agnew, "National Art Gallery Chain Targets 'Upscale Masses,'" *Marketing News* (June 19, 1987), 8.

19. Susan Caminiti, "Jewelers Woo the Working Woman," *Fortune* (June 8, 1987), 71–72.

20. Thomas P. Novak and Bruce MacEvoy, "On Comparison Alternative Segmentation Schemes: The List of Values (LOV) and Values and Life Styles (VALS)," *Journal of Consumer Research* 17 (June 1990), 105–109.

21. Joe Schwartz and Thomas Miller, "The Earth's Best Friends," *American Demographics* (February 1991), 26–35.

22. Laurie Freeman, "The Green Revolution: Procter & Gamble," *Advertising Age* (January 29, 1991), 16ff.

23. Bob Garfield, "Beware: Green Overkill," *Advertising Age* (January 29, 1991), 26.

24. "Youthful Spirits," *Frequent Flier* (November 1987), 12.

25. Fred S. Worthy, "Asia's New Yuppies," *Fortune* (January 4, 1990), 235.

26. Pat Sloan and Bradley Johnson, "P&G Slips on Soap," *Advertising Age* (September 30, 1991), 3.

27. Raymond Serafin, "Renault Repositioning," *Advertising Age* (February 2, 1987), 60.

28. For a helpful discussion of this strategy and its rationale, see David W. Stewart, "Consumer Self-Selection and Segments of One: The Growing Role of Consumers in Segmentation," in Rebecca H. Holman and Michael R. Solomon, *Advances in Consumer Research* 18 (Provo, Utah: Association for Consumer Research, 1991), 179–186. For some helpful examples see Renee Zabor, "An Application of Segmentation Research in the Travel and Leisure Industry: The Case of Hilton Hotels," in Holman and Solomon, *Advances*, 176–177, and Ronald Hoverstad, Charles W. Lamb, Jr., and Patrick Miller, "College Benefit Segmentation Analysis: Approach and Results," in Thomas R. Srull, *Advances in Consumer Research* 16 (Provo, Utah: Association for Consumer Research, 1989), 332–338.

29. Patricia Winters, "Sanka Going Natural; Decaf War Perks Up," *Advertising Age* (January 12, 1987), 1ff.

30. Bill Saporito, "Is Wal-Mart Unstoppable?" *Fortune* (May 6, 1991), 50–59.

31. Andrew Kupfer, "The Champ of Cheap Clones," *Fortune* (September 23, 1991), 115–120.

32. Susan Caminiti, "What the Scanner Knows about You," *Fortune* (December 3, 1990), 51–52.

33. Jan Larson, "A Segment of One," *American Demographics* (December 1991), 16–17.

34. Raymond Serafin, "Olds Abandons 'New Generation,'" *Advertising Age* (July 15, 1991), 33.

35. Sloan and Johnson, "P&G Slips," 3.

36. Judann Dagnoli, "How Stouffer's Right Course Veered Off Course," *Advertising Age* (May 6, 1991), 34.

37. Dagnoli, "How Stouffer's Right Course Veered Off Course," 34.

Diffusion of Innovations

From Beer in Vending Machines to Men Giving Birth

In Tokyo, nearly every street is lined with vending machines selling everything from ice coffee and beer to underwear. In Vienna, visitors from around the world can insert their dollars, yen, francs, or pounds into a cash machine and change them into marks. Will such machines be as common in the United States and Canada in the future as they are now in Tokyo and Vienna?

A pharmaceutical firm is testing a new product that allows people to sleep only 4 hours a night and keep, at least for short time periods, the energy and alertness of a night with eight hours of sleep. If the company introduces the product to the market, will consumers buy it? Or would they rather stay in bed?

McDonald's introduced a McLean Burger made partly of kerrigean, a form of seaweed. Will the product ever replace the Big Mac in popularity? Worthington Foods produces meat analogs that look and taste like sausage, bacon, and burgers but contain no cholesterol and no animal products. Currently, about 3 percent of Americans eat only vegetarian products but the number is increasing. How much will it increase? to 10%? to 30%? to 50%?

Embryo implants are a product developed in England and now diffused throughout the world, allowing hundreds of thousands of couples to give birth to children who previously could not do so. Researchers are now experimenting with a process that would implant embryos in men. The embryos would attach to an intestine for blood supply and be delivered by Caesarian. If the medical service is perfected to allow men to give birth, will any do so? How many would adopt this new service? If men, as well as women, can have babies, what will happen to the world's birth rate?

New Products in the Marketplace

As the opening scenario to this chapter indicates, consumers are bombarded with new products to buy or reject. In Naples, New York, there is an art gallery exhibiting some of the 75,000 new products introduced in recent years.

Some new products succeed, bought by enough customers to achieve profitability. Most new products fail. This chapter discusses why some succeed and why some fail. The chapter also shows how to increase the number that succeed.

Sony is an example of a company that has experienced both success and failures. The Walkman personal stereo and other new products diffused successfully around the world. But Sony is the company that also invented the Betamax VCR. With Beta, Sony tried to keep the technology proprietary. Its competitor, Matsushita licensed its VHS format widely and as VHS spread, Betamax was doomed. Sony learned from its mistake with Beta and licensed its 8 mm camcorders and components to big names such as Fuji, Sharp, and Canon. A big new push by Sony is the Sony Data Discman electronic book shown in Figure 22.1. Notice how this innovative product is designed as a replacement for an old, old product—books in a library.[1]

The Criticality of New Product Management

Successful introduction of new products is a critical component of contemporary marketing programs. It is also one of the most misunderstood. About 5,000 new products appear each year on supermarket shelves, but as many as 80 percent are commercial duds. Both macromarketing and micromarketing reasons exist for concern about this situation.

Macromarketing   First, at the macromarketing level, much of the nation's technological and other resources are devoted to developing new products that are rejected. This causes two concerns: valuable resources are wasted that might have been channeled toward more productive uses, and products that might have helped people do things more productively or attain higher levels in their quality of life fail to be used. Perhaps the rejected products should never have been developed because they were inferior to existing products and benefits. Perhaps the rejected products failed because of ineffective communication and diffusion processes. In either instance, society is harmed by the failure to understand why and how people adopt new products. Some of the research about diffusion has produced mathematical models that can be used cross-culturally to predict the rate of adoption of products such as television.[2]

Second, at the moral or ethical level, the introduction of new products involves the attempt to change the behavior of human beings, often in rather fundamental ways. The changes usually involve more than simply switching from one brand to another, as is true in much of the material you have studied in this book. Sometimes the changes have profound effects on the people who buy the new product—as was true when some tampons produced adverse effects compared to the

FIGURE 22.1 Positioning of a New Product as Replacement for an Old Product

Source: Courtesy of Sony Corporation of America.

existing form of sanitary napkins or when silicon breast implants later created major problems. Sometimes the changes have profound effects on the people who do not adopt the product—as may be true among those who fail to adopt usage of personal computers. More than any other area of marketing, perhaps, the ability to introduce new products effectively is the ability to change how society is organized.

The desire in most diffusion research is to persuade people to accept new products or practices. The "products" have been as diverse as birth control methods, sanitation techniques, computers, and hybrid seed corn. The motivation for research on these topics stems from the notion that people should change to what is good for them or society. With personal computers, as an example, the technology has often been urged on consumers with little concern about the underlying value of the benefit or the information that consumers would derive from microcomputers.[3] People and organizations are agents for change in the behavior of other people. In a market economy, consumers are sovereign in their acceptance or rejection of products and practices, but there remain important moral and ethical questions about who should have the ability to be effective change agents.

Micromarketing   Concern about new products also exists at the microeconomic level, which is the major focus of this chapter. New products are the lifeblood of most firms in the contemporary business environment. Firms must develop and gain acceptance of new products to survive and maintain adequate profitability.

A primary reason for new product development is slow growth or declining population in industrialized countries. Firms formerly could grow profits by selling the same products to an increasing number of customers. Now firms often grow profits by developing and selling additional new products to customers.

A second reason for new product development is the role market leadership plays in a firm's profitability. Research indicates that firms that are market leaders, as measured by market share, generally have the highest Return on Investment (ROI) and Enhanced Shareholder Value (ESV). The **PIMS (Profit Impact of Market Strategy)** research indicates that market leaders achieve average rates of return three times greater than firms with low market share.[4] The PIMS data also indicate that perceived product quality is highly associated with ROI and ESV. Successful new product development is an important element in achieving long-term competitive superiority and profitability.

A successful new product can also be the beginning of a whole new company. Edison's invention of electricity was the beginning of GE. Today new entrepreneurial activity is often based upon new products rather than on attempts to compete with marketers of existing products. Thus, the path to asset accumulation for individuals often stems from a single new product. Examples include computer products of Silicon Valley entrepreneurs, new packages such as Soft Soap, and new services such as the automatic debit service of CheckFree that allows people to pay bills without writing checks each month.

Large corporations usually require a portfolio of products, some of which are new but many of which are not so new. Such a portfolio often derives the most sales not from new products but from rapid growth from products that are recent introductions. While the BCG (Boston Consulting Group) matrix of "cash cows," "dogs," and other barnyard animals has been challenged as overly simplistic,[5] most corporations do maintain a variety of products at various life cycle stages and with varying rates of growth and return on investment.

Procter & Gamble makes most of its sales and profits from detergents, coffee, peanut butter, and other products that have been in kitchen pantries for decades or longer. The focus is on brand strategies and product extensions for success. The company also devotes substantial resources to developing products that initially may be minuscule but have the potential for attracting huge markets. Procter & Gamble hoped that Pampers would become such a product. It did. It hoped Pringles would become such a product. It did not. In 1992, P&G was still struggling to reposition Pringles to flavor "niches" because the product failed to achieve widespread adoption even though many people had tried it.

Existing products sometimes can be changed so they are perceived as new. Tom Peters, in lectures to business executives, makes the point that no marketing

Perdue: Changing a Commodity into a New Product

Before Frank Perdue took over the chicken business from his father it was the quintessential commodity business. Chickens had as strong a claim to commodity status as pork bellies or crude oil. The performance of each competitor was the same on each product and service attribute. This placed Perdue and his representative competitor at the 50th percentile on relative quality, neither ahead nor behind. With no differences in performance on product and service attributes, the customer bought basically on price.

After Frank Perdue took over the chicken business, he pulled ahead on almost every nonprice attribute that counts in the purchase decision. His research showed that customers in his served market prefer their chickens plump and yellow. Careful breeding and the judicious use of feed additives enabled Frank to produce meatier, yellower chickens than competitors. His actions also produced a higher, more consistent meat-to-bone ratio.

To prevent wet pinfeathers from slipping past the torching process that's supposed to burn them off, he purchased a turbine engine to blow-dry his chickens just before they reach the torching station. This didn't get him to zero defects, but it did mean that fewer pinfeathers wound up in supermarkets

Continued

manager should accept the premise that he or she markets a "commodity." If you think such a goal is unrealistic, consider the case of Frank Perdue in Consumer in Focus 22.1. He changed consumer perceptions of "dead chickens" into a highly profitable, billion-dollar corporation. Even today, Perdue continues this progression with new packages, new methods of cooking, and new species of poultry.

Product quality in mature products is often linked to product innovation. Polaroid introduced instant photography and was, for decades, one of the nation's most innovative and successful companies. But without breakthrough products to replace the maturing instant photography, the company stagnated and quality fell behind Japanese competitors. The CEO of the company reported that this lack of innovative new products led to a Polaroid being "asleep at the switch for 20 years."[6]

Product Life Cycle

The product life cycle (PLC) is a key concept for understanding the criticality of new products. You probably studied the PLC similar to that shown in Figure 22.2 in or in family dining rooms. Notice that his particular investment in capital equipment did not expand capacity and it did not take out labor costs. It just improved the perceived quality of Perdue's chickens! Most capital appropriation requests have difficulty quantifying the justification for expenditures to improve perceived quality.

To make sure that the customer perceived and remembered his quality improvements, Perdue utilized catchy slogans in audacious media advertising: "It takes a tough man to make a tender chicken"; "Buy Perdue chickens—you get an extra bite in every breast." (Would *you* have spent millions trying to differentiate chickens?) Perdue developed a favorable difference, he made sure that it was perceived, and as a result he gets a substantial premium for what certainly *had been* a commodity. As Perdue himself says, "Customers will go out of their way to buy a superior product, and you can charge them a toll for the trip." Is your product, with all its potential associated services, really harder to differentiate than a dead chicken?

Source: Robert D. Buzzell and Bradley T. Gale, *The PIMS Principles* (New York: Free Press, 1987), 119–120.

a basic marketing course. This figure shows that just as products grow and mature, so do they decline and fail. As the process evolves, major changes are necessary in the marketing strategies and mix: price, product, place, and promotion. For the consumer as well as for marketing managers, the role of advertising may be different at varying stages of the life cycle.[7]

Profit margins vary greatly during the product life cycle, usually peaking during the latter stage of the growth phase and declining during subsequent stages. Therefore, firms systematically introduce new products not only to maintain sales volume but also to command adequate margins and profits. Firms need a portfolio of products in various stages of the PLC to achieve the growth, profitability, and capital objectives of the firm. The problem increases because of what Olshavsky and others show to be an increasing rate of adoption of innovations, causing a rapidly shortened product life cycle.[8] Shortened PLCs, caused by rapidly changed technologies and improved mass communications, create the need for shorter amounts of time in management approval of movement between phases of product introduction.[9]

The diffusion of innovations and the acceptance (and rejection) of new products are some of the most researched topics in marketing. Inadequate market research is a major obstacle to the successful introduction of new products. This

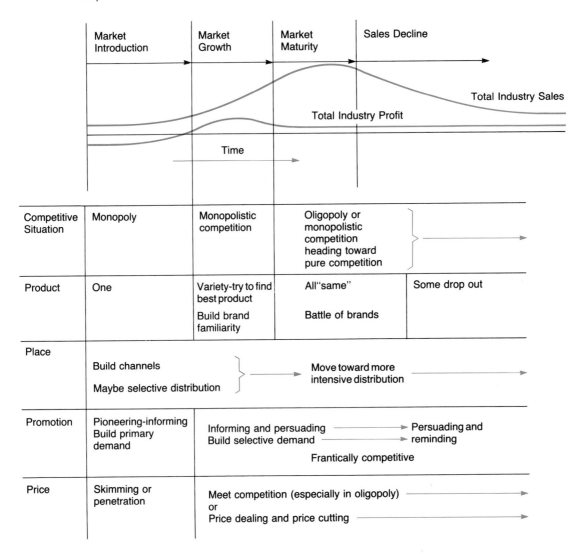

FIGURE 22.2 **Impact of the Product Life Cycle on Marketing**

Source: Adapted by permission from Jerome McCarthy and William Perrault, *Basic Marketing: A Managerial Approach* (Homewood, Ill.: Richard D. Irwin, 1985).

conclusion is shown in Figure 22.3, summarizing research by the consulting firm of Booz-Allen & Hamilton. That study also shows that major obstacles in introducing new products include lack of attention by management and delays in making decisions. Ideally, a firm and its managers would have plenty of time to perform new product research. Instead, managers must often rely on what is already known about how new products are accepted, based upon other products and theory. Fortunately,

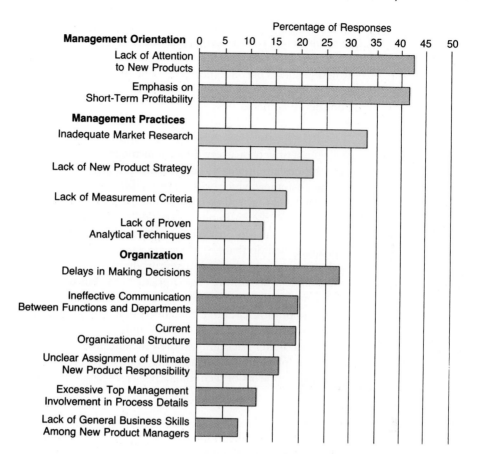

FIGURE 22.3 **Obstacles to the Successful Introduction of New Products**

Source: New Products Management for the 1980's (New York: Booz-Allen & Hamilton, Inc., 1982), 5. Reprinted by permission.

there is a great deal of both. This chapter describes both so that when you are making decisions about new products, you will have a thorough, immediate information base to help guide your decisions.

In addition to formal research, marketing managers need grass roots ways of understanding consumer reaction to new products. Campbell Soup Company has a constant need for new products in its many divisions, which include Le Menu and Swanson frozen foods, Prego spaghetti sauces, Pepperidge Farm baked products, Mrs. Paul's frozen foods, Vlasic pickles, and even Godiva chocolates. In addition to pursuing sophisticated marketing research, the president of Campbell insists that his managers do their own grocery shopping. The board of directors meets in the back room of a supermarket after roaming the store aisles and probing shoppers for comments on Campbell products. The Campbell chief executive officer spends

Saturday mornings in the neighborhood supermarket getting to know consumers. The result in one recent year was 42 successful new products for Campbell.[10] You will find many useful principles in the following pages to guide you in understanding how new products become successful. The best understanding may occur, however, because of the time you spend in the marketplace, talking to customers and reflecting on their comments.

The Growing Competitive Challenge   Contemporary firms are being attacked competitively on every dimension and from every direction. The only way to survive this onslaught, Porter has convincingly argued, is to create a "value chain" to serve the customer, which will serve to differentiate the successful firm from its competitors, and that will provide competitive superiority on the critical attributes of importance to the customer.[11] A product that will "delight the customer" is the foundational variable of marketing strategy. The challenge is to understand which new products will do that.

Innovation is not limited to new products. Innovative ideas, innovative people, and innovative processes are characteristic of the business firms and other organizations that are surviving and thriving. After careful research of over 115 innovations in major coporations, Kanter concluded that winners generate "idea power" that provides the competitive advantage, not only in new products but also in new ideas in every area: better packaging, more efficient invoicing techniques, new planning systems, and lower-cost manufacturing. The winners today are better users, adaptors, and incorporators of technology.[12]

The Diffusion Process

The criticality of new product adoption is clear, but, you might be asking, why should consumer decisions about new products be studied any differently from decisions about other products? Why not simply consider the elements of decision making and psychological and environmental variables that have been discussed in the text previously as they apply to new products rather than existing products?

The major distinction in traditional analyses of the diffusion of innovations is the emphasis on *communications within the social structure* rather than individual information processing. The **relational approach** analyzes communication networks and how social-structural variables affect diffusion flows in the system, in contrast to a **monodic approach**, which focuses upon the personal and social characteristics of individual consumers.

A Major Research Stream

A reason for a separate chapter on new product diffusion is the great quantity of research on the topic and the diversity of disciplines from which the research is drawn. Over 3,000 studies and discussions of diffusion processes have been published in at least 12 identifiable disciplines. These include anthropology, sociology, rural sociology, education, marketing, psychology, and geography. The most important contribution to the study of diffusion of innovations was a book of the same name, written by Everett Rogers in 1962 and updated in 1983.[13] According to Rogers, **diffusion** is defined as *the process by which an innovation (new idea) is communicated through certain channels over time among the members of a social system.* Under this definition, a product might be around for a long time but still be perceived as new and be an innovation in a given market.

definition

Consumer researchers and marketing analysts have been important contributors to the study of diffusion of innovations. An enumeration by Rogers of the research studies on diffusion indicates that marketing has conducted over 10 percent of all the studies in this field, surpassed only by the disciplines of rural sociology, communication, and education. The bulk of consumer behavior research, however, is on the adoption process of consumers rather than on the social structure and process variables.

The disciplines involved in diffusion studies include general sociology, anthropology, geography, and public health as well as rural sociology, communication, and education. Marketing strategists should use care when applying diffusion research. Many of the studies were conducted in primitive societies where government or some other agency had the ability to contact every member of the community. In marketing programs, effective communication with all members of the community is much more limited.

Also, many of the products involved in sociological or anthropological studies have been high-involvement and more personal products. The consistency between disciplines is one of the basic reasons, however, for the impact diffusion research has achieved. In this chapter, the important conclusions that cut across the disciplines, and have applications for marketing are summarized.[14]

Diffusion Variables

The variables that have emerged from over 3,000 studies on diffusion can be clustered to identify the critical determinants of the success of a new product. The main elements in the diffusion of innovations include:

1. *innovation* (new product, service, idea, etc.),
2. *communication* (through certain channels),
3. *time* (at which certain individuals decide to adopt the product relative to others), and
4. *social system* (interrelated people, groups, or other systems).

Each of these topics is a focus of discussion in the following pages.

The result of this process shows that some members of the social system are **adopters**—people who have made a decision to continue using a new product. Other people are **nonadopters**, and their decision not to adopt may occur for many reasons. Some will not be exposed to information about the product or will wait until other people have tried the product before doing so themselves. Some consumers will quickly decide a new product is not what they want, perhaps because of brand loyalty and satisfaction with current products. Other consumers may want a product but may not buy it for a variety of reasons.[15]

An early decision not to adopt is apparently what occurred when Gerber brought out a new product called Singles, small servings of beef burgundy and other foods that should appeal to the growing number of single households. The product was targeted to people such as college students who need a simple-to-fix, inexpensive, nutritious meal without cooking or other complications. Gerber placed the product in the same type of glass jar in which consumers had purchased baby food and identified the manufacturer as Gerber. The product was a bomb. Apparently, many consumers did not like to be identified as singles eating alone. They also associated the product with baby food even though it tasted good and was very convenient.

In the following pages, let us look closely at the four elements of diffusion that cause some people to be early adopters, late adopters, or nonadopters.

The Innovation: Which Products Are Winners?

An **innovation** can be defined in a variety of ways. The most commonly accepted definition is that an innovation is *any idea or product perceived by the potential adopter to be new.* This is a subjective definition of innovation, since it is derived from the thought structure of a particular individual.

Innovations can also be defined objectively based on criteria external to the adopter. According to this definition, *new products* are *ideas, behaviors, or things that are qualitatively different from existing forms.* This definition also has its problems because of disagreement about what constitutes a qualitative difference. Certainly TV is qualitatively different from existing communication forms, but is Liquid Tide a new product compared to the existing form of Tide? Does the addition of "blue crystals" or an improved package make a product new?

Marketing studies often define new products in relation to market acceptance. Sometimes a simple approach is used by calling any product that has recently become available in a market "new." The Federal Trade Commission sanctions such an approach but limits the use of "new" in advertising to products available in the marketplace less than 6 months.

Academic researchers have often defined a new product as any recently introduced product that has achieved less than x percent of market penetration. Innovations frequently are operationally defined as recently introduced products that have not attained 10 percent of their ultimate market share. All these definitions have problems, pointing to the need for a classification system for various types of innovations.

Types of Innovations

One system of classifying innovations is based on the impact of the innovation on behavior in the social structure. This taxonomy was described by Robertson and has been used extensively in marketing. It classifies innovations as (1) continuous, (2) dynamically continuous, and (3) discontinuous.[16]

A **continuous innovation** is the modification of an existing product rather than the establishment of a totally new one. It has the least disrupting influence on established patterns of behavior. Examples include adding fluoride to toothpaste, introducing new-model automobile changeovers, adding menthol to cigarettes or changing their length, and replacing dot matrix printers with laser printers.

A **dynamically continuous innovation** may involve the creation of either a new product or the alteration of an existing one but does not generally alter established patterns of customer buying and product use. Examples include electric toothbrushes, front-wheel-drive cars, compact discs, natural foods, and oversized tennis racquets.

A **discontinuous innovation** involves the introduction of an entirely new product that causes buyers to alter significantly their behavior patterns. Examples include television, computers, videocassette recorders, videotext products such as computerized data bases for shopping, and microwave ovens.

Most new products are of the continuous form. The best new products introduced in most years are usually just modifications or extensions of existing products, with little change in basic behavior patterns required by consumers. The information industry in the U.S. had high hopes for a wide range of products and services. But not all the predictions panned out. Figure 22.4 shows some examples of products which fell short of expectations.

Products Most Likely to Succeed

New products most likely to be adopted by consumers have some common basic characteristics. Innovations include both a hardware component and a software component. **Hardware** refers to the physical or tangible aspects of a product. **Software** is the information base that accompanies the hardware component. Just as with computers, a new product that is functionally excellent in its hardware may fail to be adopted because of inadequate software or information base. A frequent mistake is spending resources on research and development to perfect the physical attributes of the product but failing to provide adequate resources for the software necessary for success with the product. Understanding consumers' values and lifestyles in developing the software may determine success of the new product just as much as the technical R&D.

As an example, RCA devoted millions to technical perfection of the video disc, which delivered a picture quality superior to that of videocassettes. RCA later wrote off the entire new product costs (reportedly over $150 million) because the product was never accepted by consumers. For consumers, the software component of the activity—the ability to copy materials from TV or other videocassettes—apparently was more valued than the hardware component of the product.

Total Product Concept New products are often rejected because of failure to adopt a **total product concept**. Ted Levitt makes the point that products have little opportunity for profit when viewed only as *tangible attributes* or attributes (generic

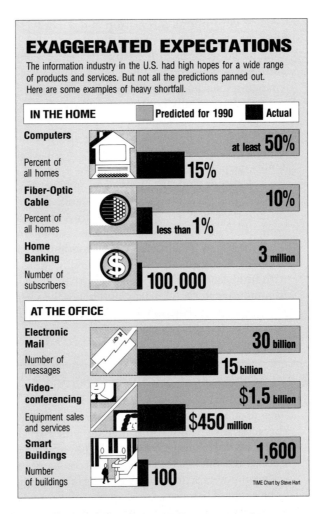

EXAGGERATED EXPECTATIONS

The information industry in the U.S. had high hopes for a wide range of products and services. But not all the predictions panned out. Here are some examples of heavy shortfall.

| IN THE HOME | Predicted for 1990 | Actual |

Computers
Percent of all homes
at least **50%**
15%

Fiber-Optic Cable
Percent of all homes
10%
less than **1%**

Home Banking
Number of subscribers
3 million
100,000

| AT THE OFFICE |

Electronic Mail
Number of messages
30 billion
15 billion

Video-conferencing
Equipment sales and services
$1.5 billion
$450 million

Smart Buildings
Number of buildings
1,600
100

TIME Chart by Steve Hart

FIGURE 22.4   Exaggerated Expectations for New Products
Source: Thomas McCarroll, "What New Age?" *Time* (August 12, 1991), 44–45.

products). The total product concept defines the *expectations* of consumers about tangible and other attributes, such as delivery conditions, postpurchase service, and so forth. The **augmented product** includes what the customer perceives the product to do to *provide more* than what is expected (and thereby provides extra "value" beyond what would be justified to pay the price of the product). All of these produce the **product potential** or everything potentially feasible that will attract and hold customers.[17] The total product concept is shown graphically in Figure 22.5. When introducing new products, marketers may be so enamored with the "new" qualities

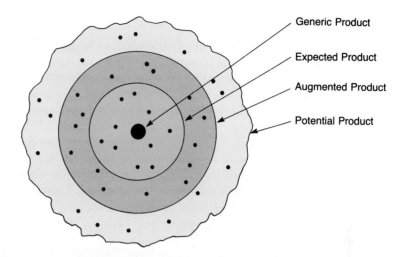

Generic Product

Expected Product

Augmented Product

Potential Product

FIGURE 22.5   The Total Product Concept

Note: The dots inside each ring represent specific activities or tangible attributes. For example, inside the "Expected Product" are delivery conditions, installation services, postpurchase services, maintenance, spare parts, training, packaging convenience, and the like.

Source: Theodore Levitt, *The Marketing Imagination* (New York: Free Press, 1986), 79.

of the product (tangible attributes) that they ignore the success requirements identified by understanding the total product concept.

Some products are winners and others are losers. Others may eventually be adopted but take much longer than expected. For example, Knight-Ridder lost about $50 million in a failed home-shopping service, and Citicorp has watched $200 million go down the drain in failed services such as one aimed at grocery shoppers. For every success story like compact discs or Nintendo, there are fizzles like picture phones and home computers.[18]

Why are some winners and some losers? What are some of the attributes or expectations and augmentations of a total product? Research by Rogers and other investigators indicates five characteristics that are associated with success with new products. These variables may not apply uniformly to all types of innovation adoption decisions. Hassan has developed an elaborate list of attributes that may be used by potential adopters to assess a particular innovation for a given situation.[19] Here we look at the five primary attributes proposed by Rogers. They include

1. relative advantage,
2. compatibility,
3. complexity,
4. trialability, and
5. observability.

Relative Advantage

The most important question to ask in evaluating the potential success of a new product is, "Will it be perceived to offer substantially greater advantage than the product it supersedes?" The issue is not whether the product is objectively better than the existing product but whether or not consumers are likely to perceive a **relative advantage**. To what degree will the new product be a substitute for existing ones or complementary with the array of products already in consumers' inventories?

New products most likely to succeed are those that *appeal to strongly felt needs*. One marketer asked consumers about their problems around home and found that many people perceive problems with collection of their garbage. Existing garbage bags were too small and too easily broken. The company brought out a new line of strong, large garbage bags, and the product was diffused quickly. Garbage disposals appeal to similar felt needs and have been one of the most widely diffused new products for homes.

Campbell, on the other hand, introduced a new instant soup consisting of single servings of highly concentrated soup. The consumer merely added boiling water. Response by consumers was tepid. They perceived it to be scarcely more instant than Campbell's regular soup, to which consumers simply add water and then boil. Although the dry product was physically quite different from liquid soup and offered many advantages to the marketers (because dry products are much more efficient to ship and store than liquid ones), the product failed because it lacked perceived relative advantage to consumers.

In banking, ATMs diffused through the social system quickly because they offer high perceived advantage to consumers who want 24-hour availability. Debit cards, in contrast, have been slow to diffuse. Although debit cards and point-of-sale (POS) may offer advantages to banks and retailers, consumers perceive little relative advantage over checks or credit cards.

Compatibility

Compatibility is an important determinant of new product acceptance. Compatibility refers to the degree to which the product is consistent with existing values and past experiences of the potential adopters. Clairol introduced a new shampoo called A Touch of Yogurt. It was unsuccessful, apparently because people found the idea of putting yogurt in their hair incompatible with their value systems, despite the fact that yogurt may be good for hair. Perhaps if the product had been called A Touch of Glamour, with yogurt as an ingredient, it might have succeeded. Glamour is part of the norm of the target market even though yogurt in the hair is not.

Radio Shack, in contrast, was successful in introducing personal computers to America because of its existing distribution system of thousands of stores. Customers whose normal behavior favored technologically innovative products were already in the stores buying products. Computers, although technically different in function, were related to consumers' product interests. The combination of distribution, personal service, and related product interests was compatible with the existing values and experiences of early adopters of computers.

FIGURE 22.6   An Innovative Product for Pet Owners
Source: Courtesy of Nestle, Inc.

Frosty Paws is an innovative product marketed by Nestle for consumers to buy as frozen treats for pets. Many pet owners feed ice cream to their dogs in spite of concern about the healthiness of eating ice cream by dogs. Frosty Paws solves this problem for consumers, as you can see in Figure 22.6, with a product that requires consumers to modify their buying behavior perhaps in a way compatible with their former usage of ice cream.

Complexity

Complexity is the degree to which an innovation is perceived as difficult to understand and use. The more complex the new product, the more difficult it will be to gain acceptance. Microwave ovens represent a discontinuous or dynamically continuous innovation, but they diffused rapidly because they are easy to use. The complexity principle makes it advantageous to build products as simple as possible during initial introduction in order to achieve simplicity in understanding and operation for consumers.

Apple Computer followed such a strategy with great success. Even the apple as a symbol communicates simplicity and a product that can be understood by all ages. IBM also used a symbol—"Charlie"—to personalize its technological image. Charlie bridged the gap to consumers who might have perceived "International Business Machines" as too complex for personal use, even though the IBM personal computer is relatively simple to use. IBM chose readily accessible software in the introduction of its personal computers, rather than less well-known software of its own. Software that is "user friendly" is initially more successful, even though complex software might be more efficient.

Products can be designed to minimize perceived complexity. When consumers read instructions for assembly or use of a new product, will such instructions be perceived as simple or complex? The more complex, the less likely the product is to succeed.

Trialability

New products are more apt to succeed when consumers can experiment with or *try the idea on a limited basis.* Sampling is an effective method of inducing trial of new products. Companies such as Procter & Gamble and General Foods give millions of new products away each year to make trial easy without economic risk.

Enhancing the trialability of new products can be accomplished through sampling in continuous innovations, especially for low-unit-value, consumer-packaged goods. How can marketers do something similar for expensive, complex, and high-involvement, discontinuous innovations? The same principles apply, but it takes more creativity.

Leasing is a strategy for such products. When computers were first introduced, IBM and other firms used leases to reduce the perceived risk for innovators. Auto manufacturers often make special offers to rental car companies on substantially changed models or cars equipped with innovative features. They know this gives consumers, especially those likely to be good prospects for new cars, an opportunity to try the new product or new feature.

New recipes and products are introduced in supermarkets through programs that demonstrate how to prepare these products. They also offer taste samples. Even communication programs can enhance the trialability of products by urging people to "Try it—you'll like it!"

The effectiveness of such programs is greatest when the trial is induced in settings likely to contain innovative consumers. An example was the introduction of Eagle Snacks, a new type of snack food consisting of nuts coated with honey. Anheuser-Busch introduced Eagle Snacks by providing small packages of the product on airlines. This setting contained large numbers of upscale consumers able to afford the relatively expensive snack food.

Observability

Observability and **communicability** reflect the degree to which results from using a new product are visible to friends and neighbors. It influences the acceptance of new products. For instance, when room air conditioners were first introduced, it was found that adoption often occurred within concentrated areas rather than throughout the city. Neighbors from next door or across the back fence saw the results of an air-conditioned room and wanted one for themselves.

Marketers can sometimes employ strategies to enhance the visibility of products by inducing celebrities to use them. Thus, the visibility of the celebrity makes the new product visible. Nike used this strategy with its tennis shoes and sporting goods. It gave them to celebrities, such as Andre Agasi, for their own use. Visible use of a new product in popular movies, TV shows, or sports events can also be an effective device for obtaining the adoption of new products. Madonna and other recording stars influence adoption of new clothing styles and other products.

Researching New Product Attributes

Developing a new product that will be a winner requires attention to the details of the total product concept. The complication with new products, compared to researching attributes of existing products, is the difficulty consumers have in thinking about products with which they have no experience. Often new product research investigates only tangible attributes and market segmentation variables rather than the lifestyle or other software details that determine the success or failure of the product.

Focus groups are a technique that can be helpful in the investigation of specific details that determine the fate of the products. Focus groups can even be used to spot the trends that indicate needs that lead to new product development. Products most likely to succeed are those that solve consumers' problems. Where do problems come from? From life; therefore consumer analysts need good methods to study lifestyles. New products, however, often must be based on emerging lifestyles, and these are difficult to measure with quantitative techniques. Emerging lifestyles and trends usually are uncovered through qualitative research. A popular method of qualitative research is focus groups to indicate consumer acceptance of items that adapt to their wants, needs, and behavior. Two approaches are inferred insights and cross-study insights.[20]

Inferred insights are observations drawn from product-specific studies, revealing whether consumers feel certain products fit their lives. **Cross-study insights** are observations based on a wide variety of product-specific studies. They help uncover demographic groups, psychographic groups, changing values, and shopping habits, as well as feelings about advertising, service, and health.

Judith Langer, president of a New York research firm, usually begins lifestyle studies by asking consumers this question, "Thinking about yourself and the people you know, how is your lifestyle different today from a few years ago?" Focusing on change by having respondents describe ways in which their lives have been altered gives clues about where they are heading and the types of products they will take with them. By asking yourself these types of questions you can readily determine why the innovations in Consumer in Focus 22.2 won or lost in the marketplace.

Winners and Losers in Product Innovation

Pop Rocks, a carbonated candy that crackled and popped when eaten, was introduced by General Foods, stirring a short-lived sensation. The candy was so effervescent that rumors swelled that children who swallowed the granules too quickly would have a carbonated stomach. The new product apparently was nothing children could sink their teeth into and eventually lost its fizz.

The first automatic teller machine (ATM) was introduced by BankOne in an upscale suburb of Columbus, Ohio, in 1970. Today, almost every city in North America has adopted the ATM. In the 1990s, Columbus bank customers stand in line to use the machine rather than deal with tellers.

Phillips, the Dutch electronics firm, developed the compact disc (CD), a technological innovation in audio and visual products that produced as much difference compared to current records and tapes as the difference between color and black-and-white television. In 1983 consumers purchased a mere 35,000 players. By 1986, sales reached nearly 2 million. By 1992, CDs had

Continued

Communications about New Products

Communication is the process by which consumers and marketing organizations share information with one another to reach a mutual understanding. Communication is critical to the widespread acceptance of new products. Communication about new products follows principles discussed throughout this book. Some of these principles are especially applicable to new product decisions of consumers, however, and are described subsequently.

Two models have been used by marketers in attempts to gain acceptance of new products. One is called the **hypodermic needle model**. It proposes that media have direct, immediate, and powerful effects on the acceptance of new products by a mass audience.

The mass media are important in brand preference or attitude formation concerning existing products and may also be important in the acceptance of continuous innovations. As new products approach higher levels of discontinuity (that is, more fundamental behavioral changes are required of adopters), however, the media appear to be limited in effectiveness. For innovations, the media are considered to be less important than interpersonal communications, especially those of opinion leaders.

replaced albums and to a large extent tapes as the preferred musical listening mode.

Procter & Gamble introduced Certain, a new brand of lotion-laced toilet paper. Consumers did not buy it in sufficient quantities to exit test markets. Undaunted, the company later introduced Puffs Special Touch, a line extension of Puffs facial tissues, hoping that consumers would like lotion in their facial tissue better than in their toilet paper.

At the same time that Procter & Gamble was introducing Puffs Special Touch, the company was also launching Liquid Tide, new "soft" cookies under the Duncan Hines brand, Ivory shampoo, and Home Fresh margarine made of a sucrose polyester that looks and tastes like fat but is not absorbed by the body (not only does it have no calories, but it actually cuts blood cholesterol levels by 20 percent or more). In late 1991, possibly as a result of a string of more losers than winners, P&G made major changes in senior management.

Off-line, electronic banking was introduced on a widespread basis in 1989 by CheckFree. The system allows consumers to pay any bill from any banking institution on a home computer and upload the information instantly, potentially saving billions of pieces of paper as well as time and money for consumers. In 1992, the service was available on leading money management programs for PCs and as a telephone service from banks. Will services of this type replace traditional checkbooks in the 1990s?

The **two-step flow model** provides another view of the role of media and personal communications. A more valid approach may be to extend the two-step concept to a multi-stage approach. In the two-step flow model, ideas flow from the media to opinion leaders and from those opinion leaders to the mass markets. The mass media accomplish the transfer of information to opinion leaders, but influence is transferred by opinion leaders to the rest of the population.

Word of Mouth: Key to Success for New Products

Word of Mouth (WOM), or interpersonal communications, plays a critical role in the adoption of new products. WOM is most important when the product is perceived to have substantial social, psychological, or economic risk involved in its purchase. WOM is also important when the choice between products is ambiguous. At later stages of the decision process to buy a new product—when people are evaluating products or confirming their decision—and when consumers have substantial experience with a product category, they may be more willing to rely upon the media. But the more innovative the product, the more likely consumers will be influenced by an existing user of the product or someone they consider an "expert" on the subject.

Speed of Diffusion   Although Word of Mouth is very important to the innovation diffusion process, marketers have little control over this variable. Marketers have more control over some factors, such as product characteristics, pricing, and resource allocations, which contribute to the speed of diffusion. Robertson and Gatignon compiled the diffusion literature into the following propositions which affect the speed of diffusion.[21]

It is believed that the greater the **competitive intensity** of the supplier, the more rapid the diffusion and the higher the diffusion level. Highly competitive firms have more aggressive pricing strategies and allocate greater resources to the product introduction. Intense competition frequently leads to price wars and an increase in demand due to the more price-sensitive customers entering the market. High competitive intensity is likely to reduce the market penetration level for any given firm within an industry, however.

The better the *reputation of the supplier* (breeding confidence among potential adopters), the faster the initial diffusion, even though the final shape of the diffusion curve may depend on the actual technology incorporated into the product. A good reputation leads to source credibility, which in turn may reduce uncertainty and risk in the purchase decision.

Products diffuse more rapidly when **standardized technology** is used. This is particularly true with products dependent upon auxiliary components, such as personal computers. Consumers may believe a purchase to be more risky if they are unsure which technology will become standard. When this risk is reduced or avoided, more consumers are likely to adopt the product. High-resolution television (HRT), for example, offers readily perceived benefits to consumers but was delayed until the 1990s in the United States because of difficulty in agreeing on either the European or Japanese standards.

Vertical coordination, which refers to a high degree of vertical dependence and an interlocking relationship among channel members, is also related to diffusion. As coordination increases, the information flow from supplier to consumer increases. As a result, diffusion increases. A corollary to this idea is that as information flows back up the channel—from consumer to supplier—innovative customers and opinion leaders can help identify new product opportunities.

Resource commitments are also important to the diffusion process. Greater research and development expenditures are positively related to innovations. As technologies become enhanced and more alternatives become available, diffusion will become broader and more rapid. As advertising, personal selling, sales promotion activities, and distribution support increase, diffusion also increases. Marketing research allocations can help guide R&D expenditures as well as develop a positioning strategy for the new technology; both of these areas are instrumental in the diffusion process.

Homophily-Heterophily: Whom Do You Trust?

Consumers tend to trust a homophilous person when they need information about new products. **Homophily** is the degree to which pairs of individuals who interact are similar in important attributes such as beliefs, education, and social status. When people share common meanings, beliefs, and a mutual language, communication between them is more likely to be effective. **Heterophilous communications** may cause cognitive dissonance because individuals are exposed to messages that are inconsistent with their own beliefs and values. Homophily and effective communication, in contrast, breed each other.

Perhaps you are beginning to understand why so many new products fail. Marketing strategies rely heavily on advertising and personal selling—messages transmitted with a definite bias in their opinion ("buy our product") from people and organizations who exist outside the interpersonal communications network. Keep in mind that the homophily principle also means that people tend to trust people of similar socioeconomic status to themselves when deciding to buy new products. Many times advertising spokespeople and sales personnel are heterophilous with the potential buyers of the new products.

Everett Rogers reviewed thousands of empirical studies concerning the diffusion of innovations, and many of these dealt with the issue of effective communications. He summarized his conclusions from this research in 17 generalizations. These, along with the number and percentage of studies that support each, are presented in Table 22.1.

Marketing Management of WOM (Word of Mouth)

Marketing organizations function as change agents—stimulating the diffusion of the new product. Change agents need to manage WOM. Public relations and sales promotion are examples of programs that accomplish the goal of stimulating WOM.

Among business or industrial firms, there is an increasing practice of bringing the key opinion leaders in an industry together for a party, seminar, laser show, or other event in which these leaders become aware of, experience, and evaluate the new product. They return home and tell opinion followers about it. This has become standard practice when firms such as IBM, Xerox, Apple, and others introduce new products. As methods of managing WOM such mega events not only are effective ways of introducing new products but they may also be used to revitalize existing products to generate positive affective response and a new vitality.

Stimulating Opinion Leadership
When LaCoste was a small, unknown marketer of premium shirts, they developed a new concept of selling quality sports apparel for everyday usage. To achieve diffusion of this concept, LaCoste gave shirts bearing their logo—a distinctive alligator—to tennis and media celebrities. Following the careful placement of these shirts with key opinion leaders who were encouraged to wear them in places other than the tennis courts, there was widespread diffusion of the concept of wearing "Alligators" in settings far removed from tennis courts. Mass media can create *awareness* and even interest in new products but personal communications are more effective in persuading people to *try* new products.

Sales Promotion
When Owens-Corning introduced a new fabric made of Fiberglas, the company developed a total promotional program that emphasized the interpersonal communications that might occur among homeowners. Among other

TABLE 22.1   A Summary of Research Evidence Supporting and Not Supporting Generalizations about Opinion Leadership and Diffusion Networks

Generalization	Support for the Generalization (Number of Research Studies)		Percentage of Research Studies Supporting the Generalization
	Supporting	Not Supporting	
8–1: Interpersonal diffusion networks are mostly homophilous.	22	13	62
8–2: When interpersonal diffusion networks are heterophilous, followers seek opinion leaders of higher socioeconomic status.	11	0	100
8–3: When interpersonal diffusion networks are heterophilous, followers seek opinion leaders with more education.	6	2	75
8–4: When interpersonal diffusion networks are heterophilous, followers seek opinion leaders with greater mass media exposure.	5	0	100
8–5: When interpersonal diffusion networks are heterophilous, followers seek opinion leaders who are more cosmopolite.	1	0	100
8–6: When interpersonal diffusion networks are heterophilous, followers seek opinion leaders with greater change agent contact.	2	0	100
8–7: When interpersonal diffusion networks are hetereophilous, followers seek opinion leaders who are more innovative.	10	1	91
8–8: Opinion leaders have greater exposure to mass media than their followers.	9	1	90
			Continued

Source: Everett M. Rogers, *Diffusion of Innovations*, 3rd ed. (New York: Free Press, 1983), 308–309.

things, the company knew that the people in the "back rooms" of fabric departments often talked with customers when they measured and installed the draperies. To ensure that even these people said good things and supported good WOM, Owens-Corning promoted a contest featuring a luxurious vacation for the "back room" that installed the most draperies made of the new Fiberglas product.

TABLE 22.1   continued

Generalization	Support for the Generalization (Number of Research Studies)		Percentage of Research Studies Supporting the Generalization
	Supporting	Not Supporting	
8–9: Opinion leaders are more cosmopolite than their followers.	10	3	77
8–10: Opinion leaders have greater change agent contact than their followers.	10	3	77
8–11: Opinion leaders have greater social participation than their followers.	11	4	73
8–12: Opinion leaders have higher socioeconomic status than their followers.	20	7	74
8–13: Opinion leaders are more innovative than their followers.	24	4	86
8–14: When a social system's norms favor change, opinion leaders are more innovative, but when the norms do not favor change, opinion leaders are not especially innovative.	7	2	78
8–15: The interconnectedness of an individual in a social system is positively related to the individual's innovativeness.	4	0	100
8–16: The information-exchange potential of communication network links is negatively related to their degree of (1) communication proximity, and (2) homophily.	2	0	100
8–17: Individuals tend to be linked to others who are close to them in physical distance and who are relatively homophilous in social characteristics.	9	0	100

Public Relations   Managing WOM well often involves public relations as an important marketing function. Too often public relations has been considered a function of finance, industrial relations, or other areas of the firm. Publicity and public relations, however, should be viewed as a major communications priority, especially among marketing managers working on new product introduction. WOM can be stimulated by well-placed publicity in the media, for example. Trade shows can be made more effective in introducing new products because of media presence and interest in the "latest and newest." Consumer electronics shows, toy shows, and clothing fashion shows are typical examples of events where firms make extensive use of publicity to stimulate WOM about their new products.

There are also cases in which unfavorable interpersonal communications can kill a new product. As an example, Anheuser-Busch introduced a soft drink called Chelsea, which contained a very small amount of alcohol, so low that labeling requirements did not even require mention of the alcohol. The word got around about the alcohol, however, and even though teenagers could drink two cases without becoming intoxicated, they would drink two or three bottles and pretend to be drunk. Parents went through the roof, forcing the withdrawal of the product from the market. The advertising was great, but that was irrelevant. WOM killed the product.

The Adoption-Decision Process over Time

Adoption of a new product is a decision process, in many ways similar to the general decision process described throughout this book. Not only does an individual consumer move through the stages of adopting the product through time, but other consumers are also moving through the process, probably at different rates and with different starting points in time. Thus, adoption of new products must be understood in a temporal context. Avoid any illusion that acceptance occurs instantly, either for an individual or a society. The rate of diffusion will vary between societies based upon cultural values. If a marketer can determine the degree to which a society is futuristic, normal, or tradition-oriented, timing and expectations of the diffusion will be modified for each market.[22]

Understanding the temporal process of adoption is very important. Otherwise, a firm might introduce a product, advertise it heavily, and commit large amounts of resources to the project, only to see it "fail." In actuality, the product may not have had enough time to move through the early stages that must inevitably be passed before arriving at the action—purchase—desired by the marketer. Frequently firms fail when introducing new products because they underestimate the time required for new products to diffuse through the market.

Business firms sometimes act as if individual consumers or markets simply decide to buy or not buy. When this fallacious assumption is made, the firm is likely not to budget properly, not to calculate return correctly, or not to plan promotional activity effectively. A further complication may arise because of confusing adoption of the physical product with the product concept or idea. People may move through the entire process of adoption but, due to situations such as their current inventory of goods or inadequate income, not buy the product until later. All elements of the firm's marketing program may have been well designed and executed, but the firm will fail if it does not understand the time and situations required for new product adoption.

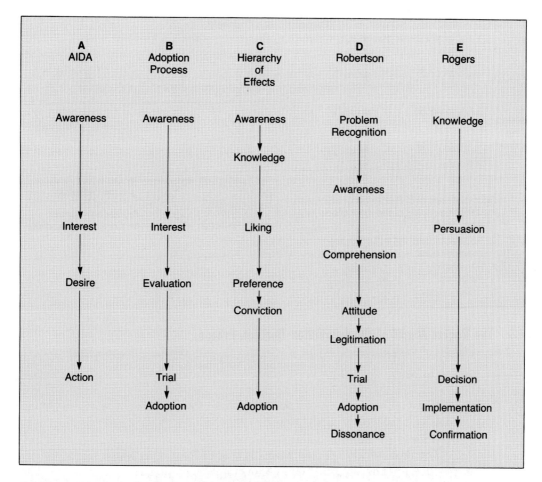

A AIDA	B Adoption Process	C Hierarchy of Effects	D Robertson	E Rogers
Awareness	Awareness	Awareness	Problem Recognition	Knowledge
		Knowledge		
			Awareness	
Interest	Interest	Liking		Persuasion
			Comprehension	
Desire	Evaluation	Preference		
		Conviction	Attitude	
			Legitimation	
Action	Trial		Trial	Decision
	Adoption	Adoption	Adoption	Implementation
			Dissonance	Confirmation

FIGURE 22.7   Models of the Adoption/Diffusion Process

Source: John H. Antil, "New Product or Service Adoption: When Does It Happen?" *Journal of Consumer Marketing* 5 (Spring 1988), 7. Used with permission.

Understanding the time and process required for adoption to occur may help explain why so many new products fail, especially when they are discontinuous innovations. Too many firms appear to believe that if they just develop a new product that fits an important need recognized by consumers and promote, price, and distribute it well, sales should result. Unfortunately, it does not work that way.

Marketing analysts have examined the process of both adoption and diffusion for many years. Models that have been used to depict the process are shown in Figure 22.7. An early conceptualization of adoption was called **AIDA** (Awareness, Interest, Desire, Action). Alternative conceptualizations of this process use different terminology but are attempts to describe the same process as Figure 22.7 shows.

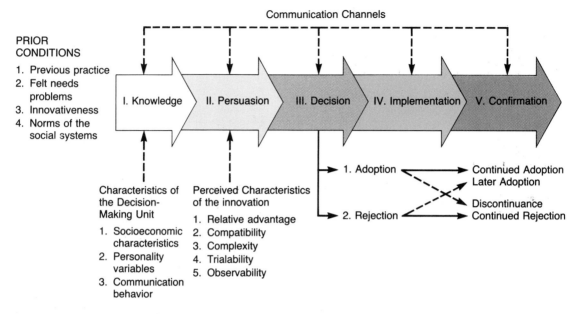

FIGURE 22.8   The Rogers Model of the Innovation-Decision Process

Source: Reprinted with permission of The Free Press, a Division of Macmillan, Inc. from *Diffusion of Innovation*, third edition by Everett M. Rogers (New York: The Free Press, 1983), 165. Copyright © 1962, 1971, 1983 by The Free Press.

The most widely adopted model is that of Rogers, in which stages are described as knowledge, persuasion, decision, implementation, and confirmation. The Rogers model of innovation decisions is compared with alternatives in Figure 22.7 and the variables associated with movement through the process are elaborated in Figure 22.8.

Knowledge

The **knowledge stage** begins when a consumer receives physical or social stimuli that give exposure and attention to the new product and how it works. In this stage, consumers are aware of the product but have made no judgment concerning the relevance of the product to a problem or recognized need. Knowledge of the new product is usually thought to be a result of selective perception. It is more likely to occur through the mass media than in later stages, which are more influenced by opinion leaders.

Persuasion

Persuasion, in the Rogers paradigm, refers to the formation of favorable or unfavorable attitudes toward the innovation. The consumer may mentally imagine how satisfactory the new product might be in some anticipated future use situation, perhaps giving the product a "vicarious trial" in the consumer's mind.

Persuasiveness is related to perceived risk in the new product or an evaluation of the consequences of using the product. When an individual considers a new product, she or he must weigh the potential gains from adopting the product against the potential losses of switching from the product now used. If the new product is adopted, it may be inferior to a present product or the cost may be greater than the increased value gained by using the new product.

Knowledge and persuasion are necessary conditions for adoption but not necessarily sufficient. Potential adopters, as we see below, may be persuaded of the advantages and the importance of accepting an innovation. Some will not do so, however, because of a variety of person and or situation-specific factors. Consumers may not have the economic resources to buy or try it. Perhaps their current technology, as in the case of many computer and communication products, may cause significant constraint on adoption.

Consumers can reduce perceived risk in adopting new products—and consequently the uncertainty that retards buying—by acquiring additional information. A person may seek out news stories, pay particular attention to advertising for the product, subscribe to product-rating services, talk with individuals who have already tried the product, talk with experts on the subject, or, in some instances, try the product on a limited basis. Each of these information-search and evaluation strategies has an economic and/or psychological cost. Moreover, they are unlikely to yield information that will completely reduce uncertainty.

Catalogs are often used to introduce new products. One reason for their effectiveness includes the ability to provide more information than the typical retail setting. Figure 22.9 provides an example. This ad for a "hair zapper" is graphic and large enough to gain attention. The copy addresses several needs and attempts to show the relative advantages over present solutions to hair problems. The endorsement in the upper right corner includes an "M.D." Attempts are made to reduce perceived risk by references to physical safety and a 30-day, money-back guarantee. This quantity of information would not be available in a retail store or affordable in most advertising media, but direct marketing firms such as Impact 2000, Sharper Image, and Land's End have been very successful in persuading consumers to buy new products. Using an "800" number and bank cards also makes the decision as easy as possible.

Decision

The decision stage involves activities that lead to a choice between adopting or rejecting the innovation. **Adoption** can be defined as a decision to make full use of an innovation as the best course of action. Adoption involves both psychological and behavioral commitment to a product over time.[23] Ordinarily, this means continued use of the product unless situational variables (lack of availability, and so on) prevent usage. **Rejection** is a decision not to adopt an innovation. **Active rejection** consists of considering adoption of an innovation, perhaps even a trial, but then deciding not to adopt it. **Passive rejection** (or **nonadoption**) consists of never really considering use of the innovation.

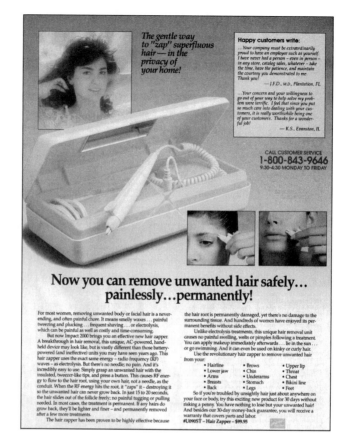

FIGURE 22.9   Persuasion to Try a New Product: Catalogs Provide Space for Information Copy

Source: Courtesy of Impact 2000 Inc., Toms River, New Jersey.

Implementation

Implementation occurs when the consumer puts an innovation into use. Until the implementation stage, the process has been a strictly mental exercise, but now behavioral change is required. The strength of the marketing plan may be the critical determinant in whether a good product that has been communicated effectively actually results in a sale.

The marketing mix should make purchase easy. To do so requires careful coordination of the channels of distribution with the new product introduction and communication process. Price is also an important ingredient. In the introduction of microcomputers, software availability, sales demonstrations in nonthreatening environments, price concessions, and educational seminars may be as important in the success of the innovation as the product itself—perhaps more so. Often consumers find ways of implementing a new product not even considered by the change agent. An example is illustrated by Post-it Notes, a new product consisting of simple notepaper with a special adhesive strip on the back. The product was introduced by 3M and has diffused throughout the world as a replacement for paper clips, note-pads, and loose pieces of paper. 3M made extensive use of sampling and because the samples were "free," office workers took the Post-it Notes home. Family members began using them for many purposes, creating rapid diffusion of the product.

Confirmation

Confirmation is the process through which consumers seek reinforcement for the innovation decision. Consumers sometimes reverse previous decisions, especially when exposed to conflicting messages about the innovation, causing dissonance.

Discontinuance is a serious concern to marketers. The rate of discontinuance may be as important as the rate of adoption, with a corresponding need for market-ing strategies to devote attention to preventing its occurrence. Pringles was intro-duced by Procter & Gamble as a new potato snack and was successful in attracting many adopters. The product eventually failed in its original form, however, because the level of discontinuers was so high, a condition the company did not observe until too late.

People who adopt the product later than early adopters may be more likely to discontinue adoption. Marketing organizations must work hard, therefore, with fol-low-up service and feedback as sales of a new product expand. Discontinuance is likely to occur when the new product is not integrated into the practices and ways of life of the purchasers or when the new product conflicts with some aspects of con-sumer lifestyles.

Consumers Most Likely to Buy New Products

Which consumers are most likely to buy new products? If you knew the answer to that question, consider how helpful it would be in concentrating the firm's resources on those people as primary targets for the marketing program of new products.

Adopter Classes

Consumers can be classified according to the time they adopt a new product relative to other consumers. In the decision to buy a specific new product, some people are innovators. Others are **early adopters**. Others can be classified as **early** or **later majority**. The ones who are last to adopt the product are called **laggards**. The distribution of people has been described as a normal distribution or, when describ-ing the cumulative total of adopters, as an S-curve. These distributions are shown in the top portion of Figure 22.10. Both curves represent the same data. The S-shaped curve represents the adoption of the innovation over time by the members of a social system, whereas the bell-shaped curves present these data in terms of individuals

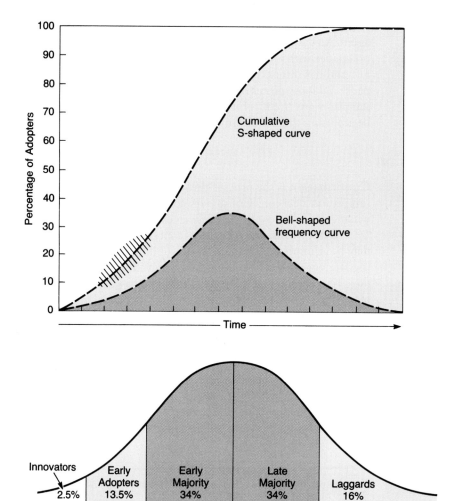

FIGURE 22.10 Classifying Adopter Categories

The bell-shaped frequency curve and the S-shaped cumulative curve for an adopter distribution

Adopter categorization on the basis of innovativeness

The innovativeness dimension, as measured by the time at which an individual adopts an innovation or innovations, is continuous. This variable, however, may be partitioned into five adopter categories by laying off standard deviations from the average time of adoption.

Source: Reprinted with permission of The Free Press, a division of Macmillan Inc. from *Diffusion of Innovations*, 3rd ed. by Everett M. Rogers (New York: The Free Press, 1983), 343 and 347. Copyright © 1962, 1971, 1983 by The Free Press.

Consumer in Focus 22.3

How to Reach Innovators

Consumers who are among the first to adopt new services or products are innovators; but, in the agricultural sector, all innovators are not the same. Empirical surveys with thousands of farmers indicate that there are three general types of farmers: proactive, reactive and open.

Proactive farmers stay current with the latest developments by talking to their neighbors, watching what works for others, attending seminars and farm shows, reading farm magazines, and searching out new-product information.

Reactive farmers are generally uninterested in new products. Their attitude is, "If it ain't broke, don't fix it." They are loyal to products and suppliers, believing that what has served them well in the past will do so in the future. This segment fits the classic stereotype of the laggard.

The open segment farmers, like the proactive, are among the first to try recently introduced products. Open farmers differ from proactive farmers and from the typical image of the innovative farmer in that they do not actively search out information about new practices and products. They don't read every available farm publication, nor do they attend numerous seminars and farm shows. They are less inclined to seek variety. They feel that trying every new product that comes on the market is just as foolish as not trying any.

What difference does it make to a marketer if the prime market is the proactive or open farmer? Lengthy copy extolling a new product's features and benefits will work fine for the proactive farmers but open farmers will not notice the ads, much less read them. Advertising messages directed toward the open farmers must be frequent, to-the-point, and attention grabbing. Because open farmers are less likely to seek variety, promotional efforts such as coupons may be necessary. The open innovator is about 20 percent of farmers operating cash grain operations and 30 percent of those who have diversified crop/livestock operations. To be effective a market strategy must capitalize on the differences between the open and the more familiar innovators.

Source: Excerpted from Brian F. Blake and Mark D. Literski, "They May Be Innovative, but They're Not the Same," *Marketing News* 25 (April 15, 1991), 12.

adopting each year. The shaded area marks the time period during which the S-curve of diffusion "takes off"—the critical interval between failure or success for most marketers. Variation among innovators can be seen in Consumer in Focus 22.3.

The pattern shown in Figure 22.10 displays what is sometimes described as an **imitation effect**. That is, the rate of adoption increases as the number of adopters increases.[24] An idea is transmitted to a few innovators who must pass through various stages to acceptance or rejection. After some innovators have adopted the product, others may follow, depending on the value of the innovation and other characteristics of the product.

Figure 22.10 vividly emphasizes the point that acceptance of a new product does not come all at once in a social system. Usually it comes much slower than marketers wish it did. The process continues throughout the social system, and its speed as well as eventual penetration of the system will be determined by many factors. Not everyone falls into these categories, of course. Some consumers may actively reject the new product from the very beginning. They are called laggards but could better be described as early rejectors. For that reason and others, adoption may be less than the 100 percent shown in Figure 22.10.

A key conclusion is possible from the phenomena expressed in Figure 22.10. Marketers must focus their attention on the innovators and early adopters, if they can be identified. If marketers do not succeed in winning adoption of the new product by these people, there is not much hope for the rest of the population.

Innovativeness

Innovativeness is the degree to which an individual adopts an innovation relatively earlier than other members in the system. A goal of marketing strategies is to understand innovativeness in order to target innovators.

The construct of innovativeness typically is measured in one of two ways in marketing studies. The first measure is based upon time of adoption, such as for those individuals who purchase in the first x weeks, months, and so on. The second is a count of how many of a prespecified list of new products a particular individual has purchased at the time of the study.

Everyone has some degree of innovativeness. Hirschman explains the importance of understanding this principle:

> Few concepts in the behavioral sciences have as much immediate relevance to consumer behavior as innovativeness. The propensities of consumers to adopt novel products, whether they are ideas, goods, or services, can play an important role in theories of brand loyalty, decision making, preference, and communication. If there were not such characteristics as innovativeness, consumer behavior would consist of a series of routine buying responses to a static set of products. The inherent willingness of a consuming population to innovate is what gives the market place its dynamic nature. On an individual basis, every consumer is, to some extent, an innovator; all of us over the course of our lives adopt some objects or ideas that are new in our perception.[25]

Innovativeness can also be measured with self-reporting instruments. The scale should be domain specific or refer to new products within a specific domain of interest. An example is provided for interest in rock music records and tapes in the research of Goldsmith and Hofacker. It asks people to indicate their agreement (or disagreement to negatives, in parenthesis) to the following statements:

- In general, I am among the first (last) in my circle of friends to buy a new rock album when it appears.
- If I heard that a new rock album was available in the store, I would (not) be interested enough to buy it.
- I will not buy a new rock album if I haven't heard it yet/I will buy a new rock album, even if I haven't heard it yet.
- I (do not) know the names of new rock acts before other people do.[26]

Three major types of variables have been studied to determine their correlation with innovativeness: socioeconomic, personality, and communication behavior. The results of studies about these variables and the conclusions about their relationships (positive, negative, or not related) are shown in Table 22.2, which summarizes years of research on the diffusion process.

Socioeconomic Variables

Analysis of socioeconomic variables indicates that people of high social status, who are upwardly mobile, educated, and/or literate, and who are privileged relative to others in the social system are likely to be high in innovativeness. Income is almost always useful in profiling innovativeness. Higher income people not only have the ability to buy more new products, but they also have the ability to take the risk of trying new products. For low-priced products, this relationship may not be as important.

Personality and Attitude

Personality and attitudinal variables associated with innovativeness in consumers include venturesomeness or openmindedness, intelligence, higher aspirations for themselves and their children, rationality, and ability to deal with abstractions or to be creative. Dogmatism and rigidity, however, are likely to be negatively associated.

Consumers may react to new products based on their cognitive style of problem solving. Kirton indicates people can be placed on a continuum between two extremes: adaptors or innovators. Extreme adaptors will adopt solutions that improve technical efficiency but involve practices and objects similar to those previously employed for the same purpose. Innovators are less likely to seek solutions within the context of previous solutions to the problem. They tend to produce different ways of organizing, deciding, and behaving that entail radical change and the incorporation of novel activities, techniques, and objects.[27]

Using the Kirton Adaption-Innovation Inventory (KAI), Foxall and Hawkins found relationships between this measure of personality and innovative brand choice.[28]

Communication Variables

Communication behavior variables include cosmopolitanism, social participation, contact with change agents, mass media exposure, higher amounts of interpersonal communication, active information seeking, knowledge of innovations, opinion leadership, and other variables. As you can see in Table 22.2, there are many studies (as is also true of socioeconomic variables) that

TABLE 22.2   A Summary of the Research Evidence Supporting and Not Supporting Generalizations about the Characteristics of Adopter Categories

Generalization	Direction in Which the Independent Variable Is Related to Innovativeness	Support for the Generalization (Number of Research Studies)		Percentage of Research Studies Supporting the Generalization
		Supporting	Not Supporting	
I. Socioeconomic Characteristics				
7–2	Age (not related)	108	120*	48
7–3	Education (positive)	203	72	74
7–4	Literacy (positive)	24	14	63
7–5	Higher social status (positive)	275	127	68
7–6	Upward social mobility (positive)	5	0	100
7–7	Larger-sized units (positive)	152	75	67
7–8	A commercial, rather than a subsistence, economic orientation (positive)	20	8	71
7–9	A more favorable attitude toward credit (positive)	19	6	76
7–10	More specialized operations (positive)	9	6	60
II. Personality Variables continued				
7–11	Empathy (positive)	9	5	64
7–12	Dogmatism (negative)	17	19	47
7–13	Ability to deal with abstractions (positive)	5	3	63
7–14	Rationality (positive)	11	3	79
7–15	Intelligence (positive)	5	0	100
7–16	A more favorable attitude toward change (positive)	43	14	75
7–17	Ability to cope with uncertainty (positive)	27	10	73
7–18	A more favorable attitude toward education (positive)	25	6	81

Continued

*Of these 120 studies, 44 show that earlier adopters are younger and 76 show that earlier adopters are older.

Source: Reprinted with permission of The Free Press, a Division of Macmillan, Inc. from *Diffusion of Innovation*, 3rd ed. by Everett M. Rogers (New York: The Free Press, 1983), 260–261. Copyright © 1962, 1971, 1983 by The Free Press.

TABLE 22.2   **continued**

Generalization	Direction in Which the Independent Variable Is Related to Innovativeness	Support for the Generalization (Number of Research Studies)		Percentage of Research Studies Supporting the Generalization
		Supporting	Not Supporting	
	II. Personality Variables			
7–19	A more favorable attitude toward science (positive)	20	7	74
7–20	Fatalism (negative)	14	3	82
7–21	Achievement motivation (positive)	14	9	61
7–22	Higher aspirations for education, occupations, etc. (positive)	29	10	74
	III. Communication Behavior			
7–23	Social participation (positive)	109	40	73
7–24	Interconnectedness with the social system (positive)	6	0	100
7–25	Cosmopoliteness (positive)	132	42	76
7–26	Change agent contact (positive)	135	21	87
7–27	Mass media exposure (positive)	80	36	69
7–28	Exposure to interpersonal communication channels (positive)	46	14	77
7–29	More active information seeking (positive)	12	2	86
7–30	Knowledge of innovations (positive)	61	19	76
7–31	Opinion leadership (positive)	42	13	76
7–32	Belonging to highly interconnected systems (positive)	8	7	53

indicate the association of communication variables, some of which can be influenced directly by marketing, and the adoption of new products. In the past, it was felt that innovators and early adopters use the mass media more but that later adopters used interpersonal sources more. Some research indicates that earlier adopters use both mass media and interpersonal sources more than later adopters.[29]

Polymorphism   **Polymorphism** is the degree to which the innovators and early adopters for one product are likely to be innovators for other products. Consumers who are innovators for many products are said to be polymorphic, whereas those who are innovators for only one product are **monomorphic**. If innovativeness is monomorphic, the process of finding innovators for a specific new product may not be worth the cost, but if it is polymorphic, the search would be justified more.

Findings are conflicting in this area, but a position may be emerging that identifies categories of products that have the same innovators. For example, perhaps the people who are the first buyers of component stereo systems are likely to be innovators for microcomputers or a wide range of consumer electronics but are unlikely to be innovators for fashion clothing, food, or other products.

Interaction occurs between type of innovator and innovation. Consumer in Focus 22.4 shows how cognitive and sensory innovators place different values on attributes of the innovation. Innovators, or people who translate their desire for new experiences into new product purchase or adoption, can be separated into those who are motivated toward new experiences that stimulate the mind (cognitive) and those that stimulate the senses (sensory). Cognitive innovators enjoy thinking, problem solving, puzzling over issues and other mental exertions while sensory innovativeness involves new experiences such as fantasy and daydreaming and externally available new thrilling and adventurous activities.[30]

Predicting Diffusion and Adoption Success

Marketing strategies often have a need for predicting the ultimate sales that will be achieved for new products in future time periods. There are a number of mathematical approaches that are used for this purpose.[31]

Fundamental diffusion models are called **penetration models**. These predict the level of penetration by a new product in a given time period based upon early sales results. **Epidemiological models** predict acceptance based upon the view that new product diffusion is a process of social interaction in which the innovators and early adopters "infect" the rest of the people, similar to disease epidemics that move through a population. These models are stochastic in nature. Analysis in the marketing literature has generally focused on the structural or mathematical properties of the models rather than on a comparison of their ability to generate forecasts of new product sales in empirical studies. An excellent review of these models is available in Mahajan and Peterson.[32]

Which Attributes Will Appeal to Sensory or Cognitive Innovators?

Innovators can be segmented into cognitive innovators and sensory innovators. Cognitive innovators have a strong preference for new mental experiences. Sensory innovators have a strong preference for new sensory experiences. Some innovators prefer both.

Research about personal computers (PC), video cassette recorders (VCR) and food processors (FP) was conducted when they were perceived to be new products. The VCR was found to be more hedonic in its benefits, the FP more functional, and the PC as both functional and hedonic.

There are dramatic differences in the demographic profile of each segment. Advertising and other communication messages can be targeted to cognitive and sensory innovators. For cognitive innovators, communications should emphasize the relative advantages of the innovation in comparison to other existing products and services and deemphasize the enjoyment risk. For sensory innovators, communications should emphasize the uniqueness of the product and reduce its complexity, performance, and economic risks. For sensory innovators, marketers should reduce complexity and risk with long warranties, manufacturer-supported service centers, toll-free lines, and easy-to-read and understand instructions. For cognitive innovators, product manuals and other product information can be comprehensive and detailed, including sections on the technology and advanced applications. For sensory innovators, it is important to make the set-up and operating instructions very simple. Sensory innovators typically are younger males; cognitive innovators have higher educations. This makes it possible to select the media to reach these segments with the communication messages that can be tailored to the attributes they are seeking.

Source: Meera P. Venkatraman, "The Impact of Innovativeness and Innovation Type on Adoption," *Journal of Retailing* 67 (Spring 1991), 51–67.

Adoption models are deterministic. They include internal variables that describe consumer decision making concerning the new product and the effects of external variables that may affect the penetration rates and timing of acceptance. These models, and hybrids that relate external variables to diffusion models, can be useful to show effects of marketing mix variables. Horsky and Simon, for example, show that advertising can accelerate the diffusion process. Optimal effects on

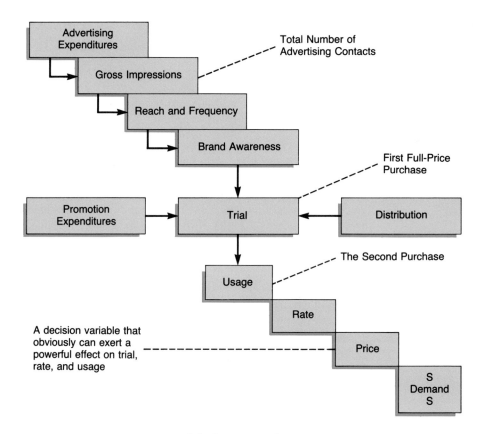

FIGURE 22.11   DEMON Model of New Product Acceptance

Source: James K. DeVoe, "Plans, Profits, and the Marketing Program," in Frederick E. Webster, Jr., ed., *New Directions in Marketing* (Chicago: American Marketing Association, 1965).

profitability occur when a firm advertises heavily when the product is introduced and reduces advertising as the product moves through its life cycle and interpersonal communications take effect.[33]

Many adoption models, incorporating market structure variables, are used by advertising agencies and other organizations involved in new product introductions. One of the foundational models for these approaches was the DEMON model, later revised to the NEWS (new product, early warning system) model, developed by the advertising agency of Batten, Barton, Durstine, and Osborne. The variables involved in DEMON are shown in Figure 22.11.

Both DEMON and NEWS are recursive, which means that each variable is first the dependent and then the independent variable. Thus, trial depends on awareness but, once activated, trial becomes the independent variable for prediction of usage. Each of these variables is influenced in turn by variables (such as advertising) that are marketing dominated. Awareness is important and is predicted by measuring the ratio of advertising dollars spent to the number of delivered gross impressions and the ratio of impressions to the level of attained reach and frequency.

N. W. Ayer Advertising's model includes recall of advertising claims as an important determinant of initial purchases of new products. SPRINTER, developed by Urban, simulates new product adoption. It is based upon an assumption of buying activity leading to trial in the following stages: (1) awareness, (2) interest, (3) search, (4) selection, (5) postpurchase behavior. There are many other models, usually drawing upon test-market data that can be used with the simulation model, which when combined with early returns in the marketplace are used to forecast future sales and profitability of the new product. Most of these models are the proprietary work of marketing organizations. Although they may be very useful in managing marketing programs, they are not generally published for scholarly examination. A fair conclusion, however, is that models to forecast new product performance have evolved from the academic interest of a few management scientists to standard practice in many good marketing organizations.[34]

The increasing availability of scanner data in some markets should allow more development of models that predict ultimate market acceptance based upon early information about the new product.

The Diffusion of Diffusion

Information about the diffusion process has been circulated widely through academic and business organizations. Perhaps no topic of discussion has been affected by, and affected, so many diverse disciplines. Marketing managers could greatly improve the introduction of new products by simply reviewing plans on the basis of principles that are well established in the diffusion literature as it has been described in this chapter.

There is still room for improvement. Much of the diffusion research was conducted in social systems that are much more controlled than those faced by marketing managers. Many of the studies were conducted with discontinuous, high-involvement products that are different from the more mundane products marketing managers often must introduce. There is much more to be learned, therefore, about diffusion research by those involved in the study of marketing. Robertson reviewed the literature of marketing and the literature of diffusion and prepared a summary of the most critical needs. Although we do not have the luxury of space to discuss all of these, they are neatly summarized in Table 22.3. If you want to go further in your study of the diffusion of innovations, this table will provide a number of good suggestions.[35]

TABLE 22.3 New Directions for Consumer Diffusion Theory

Extant Theory and Assumptions	Needed Conceptual Developments
The Innovation	*The Innovation*
Generally assumed to be important and can be classified as to its: relative advantage, compatibility, complexity, trialability, observability	A broader framework for classifying and assessing innovations from high technology to line extensions
Value of the innovation can be measured with a rational yardstick and scientific authority is often available	A framework for consumer evaluation of innovations when value cannot be measured by a rational yardstick and when there is no scientific authority
Expectations on innovation performance are well developed and assumed to be an extension of the consumer's existing experience base	A framework for assessing innovations when consumers are required to develop new patterns of experience
The Diffusion Process	*The Diffusion Process*

Generally assumed to be an S-shaped (logistic) pattern
A single curve assumed for the entire market
	Specification of diffusion process to be expected as a function of:
	    innovation characteristics
	    marketing variables
	    competitive variables
	    social contagion effect
	    environmental factors
	Recognition of varying diffusion processes by market segment

The Adoption Process	*The Adoption Process*
Assumed to follow a single hierarchical process from awareness to knowledge, evaluation, trial, and adoption	Recognition of multiple models: hierarchical, low involvement, dissonance/attribution and specification of variables (including marketing

Continued

Source: Thomas S. Robertson, "Marketing's Potential Contribution to Consumer Behavior Research: The Case of Diffusion Theory," in Thomas C. Kinnear, *Advances in Consumer Research* 11 (Provo, Utah: Association for Consumer Research, 1984), 485.

New Product Diffusion and ESV

As a concluding perspective to this chapter on Diffusion of Innovations, study Consumer in Focus 22.5. It provides a realistic application of many of the materials in this chapter. Perhaps it will suggest some things that must be done to manage the development of new products, a topic that space does not permit discussion of here.[36]

Ford Taurus was the most successful introduction of a new car by an American manufacturer in recent years. When it was first introduced, it received little mass acceptance. The innovators and early adopters who first bought it were probably thought a bit weird. The car was thought to be a bit weird—a jelly bean, some called it. Yet advertising communicated the idea to a relatively upscale, educated market

TABLE 22.3   continued

Extant Theory and Assumptions	Needed Conceptual Developments
The Adoption Process (continued)	*The Adoption Process (continued)*
Generally assumed to be an individual consumer adoption decision Measures only initial adoption Ignores effect of adoption on the consumption system or innovator	program design) which determine the form of the adoption process Further development of organizational adoption and family adoption models Development of concepts and methods as to the width and depth of usage and adoption Assessment of adoption potential conditional on current consumer inventory of goods and services and consumption system
The Communication Process	*The Communication Process*
Change agent is assumed to be non-self-serving Information is generally available—often from impartial sources Mass media and personal selling information sources are accorded limited attention	Research needed on marketing-controlled sources which are biased and self-serving Research needed when information is lacking or when impartial standards are non-existent An enriched conceptualization needed on the role of mass media in diffusion
Opinion Leadership and Personal Influence	*Opinion Leadership and Personal Influence*
Assumed important for all innovations Assumed to occur in a two-step manner Assumed to occur within the boundaries of social systems	A better delineated model for when personal influence will occur Recognition of the multiflow nature of consumer influence and the lesser importance of opinion leaders More explicit research on the interaction of mass media influence and personal influence beyond social systems

target augmented by favorable publicity in consumer and auto magazines. The innovators "tried" it, and their decisions were confirmed sufficiently that they became opinion leaders, evangelizing others about the relative advantage, simplicity, and other attributes of the car.

Market research in the auto industry often asks consumers what they want (attitudes), but Taurus research asked consumers about their behavior—what they liked and disliked about their present behavior in buying and using cars. The success took time to build, but Taurus (and its Mercury sister, Sable) increased in sales until it beat out traditional rival Chevrolet and became the profit leader for Ford. The result was ESV; the cause was successful management of a new product that diffused through society just the way the textbooks say it should!

Ford Taurus Copycat Stuff? Hardly!

When Ford Motor Co. set out to design the Taurus, it looked hard at the competition: Let's see what we can learn from those guys. But the way they went about it was different, intriguing, and a focus forcer.

Under Vice President Lew Veraldi's direction, Team Taurus identified some 40 cars in the rough class category they were examining (midsize, four door). The idea was to pick the best cars they thought they could learn from—the "best of class"—and see what rival companies and vehicles from all over the world had to teach Ford.

Of the 40, they selected about a dozen cars (most of them foreign), which were then subjected to the indignity of what they call the "layered stripdown." They took them apart piece by piece to see how the cars were made.

They learned a lot. The stripdown helped them identify 400 features that went on their Taurus wish list—items they thought they might be able to beat, or at least emulate. The feature might be something as visible to the customer as a better lumbar support system in the seats, or as innocent and invisible as an engine part designed to be more accessible to the mechanic.

Of the 400, Ford reckons it either met or bettered the competition in 360 of them. It sounds like copycat stuff. Maybe that's why companies don't look at competition in this way more often. But Ford people will tell you that this is the first time in a long while that they *haven't* felt like imitators following a me-too strategy. It's a paradox—by taking little pieces of others, you become a better version of yourself.

Source: Robert H. Waterman, Jr., *The Renewal Factor: How the Best Get and Keep the Competitive Edge* (New York: Bantam Books, 1987).

Summary

The diffusion of innovations, a topic of study and research that has grown rapidly in the past few decades, deals with how a new product is adopted in a society. It is of high importance to marketing organizations because new products must be brought out continuously in order for firms to survive.

The elements of the diffusion process include the innovation, the communication of the innovation, time, and the social system. The most commonly accepted definition of an innovation is any idea or product perceived by the potential innovator to be new.

Everett Rogers is the most influential change agent in the diffusion of the diffusion research. He has identified the types of consumers adopting a new product classified by the time of adoption as innovators, adopters, early majority, late majority, and laggards. Consumers who have a high amount of innovativeness can be identified in terms of socioeconomic (privileged), personality (venturesome), and communication behavior (contact with the mass media and other people) variables.

Review and Discussion Questions

1. What are the major differences in perspective on diffusion of innovations of those who are studying macromarketing issues compared to micromarketing issues?
2. Sun Tzu, the famous Chinese strategist, once said, "He who occupies the field of battle first and awaits his enemy is at ease; he who comes later to the scene and rushes into the fight is weary." Does this quotation apply to the study of diffusion of innovations? Explain.
3. How would you define innovation? How does the choice of your definition affect research that might be conducted on the topic?
4. Explain as precisely as possible the differences between continuous, dynamically continuous, and discontinuous innovations. Give some examples of each, other than those mentioned in the text.
5. What are the major competitive challenges facing firms in which understanding of diffusion of innovations might be helpful?
6. Prepare a short essay that explains how to pick winners from the many candidates for new product introduction.
7. Assume that a firm is introducing a new car. How would you suggest they manage Word of Mouth for this introduction?
8. The manufacturer of a new product is attempting to determine who the innovators for the product might be. The product is a game that requires players to answer each other with phrases from various foreign languages. Whom would you identify as the most likely innovators? What appeals would you suggest to be used in promoting the product?
9. A large manufacturer of drug and personal grooming products wants to introduce a new toothpaste brand in addition to the three already marketed. Evaluate for the firm what information might be used for innovation studies to guide introduction of the product.
10. How would you justify ESV (Enhanced Shareholder Value) as a firm's primary financial goal? What should be the role of new product development in this goal?

Endnotes

1. Andrew Tanzer, "Sharing," *Forbes* 149 (January 20, 1992), 82.
2. Grahame R. Dowling and Paul K. Walsh, "Describing the New Product Adoption Behavior of Countries Using a New Product Growth Model," *Behavioral Science* 35 (October 1990), 259–280.
3. Douglass K. Hawes, "The Role of Marketing in Facilitating the Diffusion of Microcomputers and the Information Society," *Journal of the Academy of Marketing Science* 15 (Summer 1987), 83–89.

4. Robert D. Buzzell and Bradley T. Gale, *The PIMS Principles* (New York: Free Press, 1987).

5. Buzzell and Gale, *The PIMS Principles*.

6. "Where Did They Go Wrong?" *Business Week Quality Imperative* (January 1992), 34–38.

7. Gerald J. Tellis and Claes Fornell, "The Relationship between Advertising and Product Quality Over the Product Life Cycle: A Contingency Theory," *Journal of Marketing Research* 25 (February 1988), 64–71.

8. Richard Olshavsky, "Time and the Rate of Adoption of Innovations," *Journal of Consumer Research* (March 1980), 425–428.

9. Milton D. Rosenau, Jr., "Speeding Your New Product to Market," *Journal of Consumer Marketing* 5 (Spring 1988), 23–35.

10. Christopher S. Eklund, "Campbell Soup's Recipe for Growth: Offering Something for Every Palate," *Business Week* (December 14, 1984), 66–67.

11. Michael E. Porter, *Competitive Advantage* (New York: Free Press, 1985).

12. Rosabeth Moss Kanter, "Highlights" from *The Change Masters: Innovation and Entrepreneurship in the American Corporation* (New York: Free Press), 1987.

13. Everett M. Rogers, *Diffusion of Innovations*, 3rd ed. (New York: Free Press, 1983), 5.

14. An excellent source for application materials is Thomas Robertson, *Innovative Behavior and Communication* (New York: Holt, Rinehart, and Winston, 1971).

15. John O'Shaugnessy, *Why People Buy* (New York: Oxford University Press, 1987), 25–38.

16. Thomas S. Robertson, "The Process of Innovation and the Diffusion of Innovation," *Journal of Marketing* (January 1967), 14–19.

17. Theodore Levitt, *The Marketing Imagination* (New York: Free Press, 1986), 74–93.

18. Thomas McCarroll, "What New Age?" *Time* (August 12, 1991), 44–45.

19. Salah Hassan, "Attributes of Diffusion Adoption Decisions," Proceedings of the Academy of Marketing Science, 1990.

20. The information in this and the next two paragraphs is adapted from "Researcher: Focus Groups Are the Best Way to Spot Trends," *Marketing News* 22 (March 28, 1988).

21. Thomas S. Robertson and Hubert Gatignon, "Competitive Effects on Technology Diffusion," *Journal of Marketing* 50 (July 1986), 1–12.

22. James Wills, A. C. Samli, and Laurence Jacobs, "Developing Global Products and Marketing Strategies: A Construct and a Research Agenda," *Journal of the Academy of Marketing Science* 19 (Winter 1991), 1–10.

23. John M. Antil, "New Product or Service Adoption: When Does It Happen?" *Journal of Consumer Marketing* 5 (Spring 1988), 5–15.

24. Ram C. Rao and Frank M. Bass, "Competition, Strategy, and Price Dynamics: A Theoretical and Empirical Investigation," *Journal of Marketing Research* 22 (August 1985), 283–296, at 284.

25. Elizabeth C. Hirschman, "Innovativeness, Novelty Seeking, and Consumer Creativity," *Journal of Consumer Research* (December 1980), 283–295, at 283.

26. Ronald E. Goldsmith and Charles F. Hofacker,"Measuring Consumer Innovativeness," *Journal of the Academy of Marketing Science* 19 (Summer 1991), 209–222.

27. M. J. Kirton, "Adaptors and Innovators: A Theory of Cognitive Style," in K. Gronhaug and M. Kaufman, eds., *Innovation: A Crossdisciplinary Perspective* (New York: John Wiley & Sons, 1986).

28. Gordon Foxall and Christopher G. Hawkins, "Cognitive Style and Consumer Innovativeness: An Empirical Test of Kirton's Adaption-Innovation Theory in the Context of Food Purchasing," *European Journal of Marketing* 20 (1986), 63–80.

29. Linda Price, Lawrence Feick, and Daniel Smith, "A Re-Examination of Communication Channel Usage by Adopter Categories," in Richard Lutz, ed., *Advances in Consumer Research* 13 (Provo, Utah: Association for Consumer Research, 1986), 409–412.

30. E. C. Hirschman, (1980), and M. P. Vekatraman and L. P. Price, "Differentiating between Cognitive and Sensory Innovativeness: Concepts, Measurement and their Implications," *Journal of Business Research* 20 (1990), 293–315.

31. Space does not permit more detailed discussion of these models. If you are interested, you will find them described, along with appropriate citations to source materials, in earlier editions of this text. See James Engel and Roger Blackwell, *Consumer Behavior*, 4th ed. (Homewood, Ill.: Dryden Press, 1982), 401–409. For a review of these models, see C. Naqrasimhan and S. K. Sen, "Test Market Models for New Product Introduction," in Yoram Wind, Vijay Mahjan, and Richard Cardozo, eds., *New Product Forecasting: Models and Applications* (Lexington, Mass.: Lexington Books, 1981).

32. Vijay Mahajan and Robert A. Peterson, *Innovation Diffusion: Models and Applications* (Beverly Hills: Sage Publications, 1985).

33. Dan Horsky and Leonard S. Simon, "Advertising and the Diffusion of New Products," *Marketing Science* 2 (Winter 1983), 1–17.

34. Robert S. Shulman and Kevin J. Clancy, "Refinements Improve New Product Models' Predictions," *Marketing News* (August 31, 1984), 15.

35. Also see Hubert Gatignon and Thomas S. Robertson, "A Propositional Inventory for New Diffusion Research," *Journal of Consumer Research* 11 (March 1985), 849–867.

36. This topic is addressed well in William E. Souder, *Managing New Product Innovations* (New York: Lexington Books, 1987).

23

Global Consumer Markets

Like many European entrepreneurs these days, Julian Riedlbauer does business in a number of countries. He calls Vienna one minute and flings a fax across the Atlantic the next. But unlike most of Europe's international business owners, Mr. Riedlbauer is only 17 years old.

At 15, he started selling discount modems. Now he also sells facsimile machines, personal computers, and other gear with sales of more than $300,000. Traditionally, few teenagers in Europe have worked in business because they focused their efforts on schoolwork.

His company, DTP Service Riedlbauer, occupies three rooms of the family's home in Meerbusch, near Duesseldorf. Recently he was an exchange student in Connecticut, keeping in touch with his company by telephone and fax between classes. Julian says he came to the U.S. mostly to improve his English for use in negotiations with U.S. suppliers.

Mr. Riedlbauer started with $1,200 with which he bought 10 Taiwanese-made modems. He resold the modems, mostly by mail, at a 30 percent markup to customers located through computer bulletin boards. Soon he was buying 30 modems at a time and advertising in computer publications. He always asked customers where they had seen his ads; then he increased advertising in the magazines whose readers were responding. As sales grew, Mr. Riedlbauer added products and hired three employees, all of whom are older than he is.

Mr. Riedlbauer doesn't feel constrained by borders, with customers in Austria and Switzerland as well as his native Germany. About 10 percent of his volume comes from the former East Germany. While living in Connecticut, he obtained a driver's license, even though not old enough to qualify for one in Germany where the minimum age is 18. Because of reciprocity between Germany and the U.S., he can drive his car, which he uses to pay visits to customers. Mr. Riedlbauer clearly has learned to live in the global economy.

Source: Excerpted from Jeffrey A. Tannenbaum, "Teenager Shows Allure of Business for Europe's Youth," *Wall Street Journal* (November 19, 1991), B2.

Global Marketing Strategy

Ethnocentricity is a disease that has infected many an American corporation for decades. Focusing only on one's own way of doing things with little sensitivity or interest in the ways of the rest of the world is the most common symptom of this disease. Ethnocentric managers are increasingly an endangered species, however.

Perhaps no manager should be promoted to a position of major responsibility in contemporary business organizations if that individual cannot "think globally." Thinking globally involves the ability to understand markets beyond one's own country of origin with respect to

1. sources of demand,
2. sources of supply, and
3. methods of effective management and marketing.

Consumer in Focus 23.1 examines three different companies and how they think globally in their business practices according to this definition.

Consumer in Focus 23.1

Going Global: Different Strokes for Different Folks

Global Sources of Demand: Toys R Us Sells to the World

Toys R Us opened its second store in Kashihara, Japan, in January 1992 after three years of planning and negotiating with the Japanese government. Building on its success in Europe, Toys R Us has come to symbolize the heroic efforts often needed to open retail stores in the protected market of Japan. President Bush was present for the opening and commented on how Toys R Us has helped pave the way for other U.S. retailers to do the same.

Toys R Us chairman and chief executive officer, Charles Lazarus, saw firsthand how the opportunities in the $6 billion Japanese toy market far outweighed the obstacles Toys R Us faced. One hundred sixty thousand shoppers

Continued

Consumer in Focus 23.1 continued

filed through the doors of the Japanese outlet that day. Consumers who place a high value on their children were pleased with the great selection and the relatively low prices. The independent Japanese toy store owners which the government was trying to protect, however, probably did not react as enthusiastically to the presence of the U.S. toy powerhouse.

Global Sources of Supply: The Limited Sources the World

One of the world's most successful retailers of apparel, The Limited, achieved its status because of its ability to think globally. With all of its retail outlets located inside the U.S., it can be described as a global company because of its global sourcing practices.

The process of getting the products on the store shelves begins with the inception of the product design and ends with the shipment of the garments to the individual stores, which at The Limited only takes approximately 1,000 hours. Other retailers wait 6 to 9 months for their products. Besides superior logistics, one reason for the efficiency and economy of this cycle is global sourcing. The designs are conceived in Italy and other European countries, the garments are produced in Asian and other countries by local manufacturers, and shipped over global logistics networks to Columbus, Ohio, from where they are distributed to the 3,600 retail outlets which include The Limited, Express, Victoria's Secret, Abercrombie and Fitch, Lerner, Lane Bryant, and Henri Bendel.

Global Management and Marketing: Honeywell, Inc., Employs the World

As companies become global in scope, managers face increased responsibility for marketing to foreign countries and managing adaptation to cultural differences. European expansion often requires a "Euromanager" who can manage cultural diversity, understand foreign markets, and is willing to travel or take temporary assignments in other countries to increase his/her understanding of a foreign market. Firms such as Honeywell are recognizing the increased need for hiring and promoting managers for such services.

Companies such as 3M are experimenting with international project teams as an alternative to relocation for their young managers to gain international experience. But Honeywell believes strongly in the value gained by the company and the individual when managers work abroad. Honeywell Europe offers as an incentive for temporary relocation an increased likelihood of promotion. This incentive is supported by the fact that 12 of the 13 top positions at Honeywell Europe are held by non-Americans and Mr. Rosso, a Frenchman, heads the operation. His hope is that a European executive will soon sit on the board of Honeywell in the U.S.

Sources: "Bush Finds Selling Toys, Burger Isn't Just Child's Play in Japan," Columbus *Dispatch* (January 8, 1992), F1; The Limited, Inc., Annual Reports, 1989 and 1990; "Firms in Europe Try to Find Executives Who Can Cross Borders in a Single Bound," *Wall Street Journal* (January 25, 1991), B1.

The globalization of marketing requires managers of all types, but especially those dealing with consumer behavior, to understand the broad forces that characterize contemporary markets. The forces affecting globalization of markets and international competition have been identified by Michael Porter to include the following:

1. Growing similarity of countries in terms of available infrastructure, distribution channels, and marketing approaches;
2. Fluid global capital markets—national capital markets are growing into global capital markets because of the large flow of funds between countries;
3. Technological restructuring—the reshaping of competition globally as a result of technological revolutions such as in microelectronics;
4. The integrating role of technology—reduced cost and increased impact of products have made them accessible to more global consumers;
5. New global competitors—a shift in competitors from traditional country competitors to emerging global competitors.[1]

Some countries have more experience than others. The Netherlands is such a country. It has a history of global trading and operations stretching over 400 years, as Figure 23.1 shows. The Dutch East Indies Company dominated the world economically for many years and Holland was the second largest owner of U.S. investments until recently. It is no wonder that companies such as Unilever, Shell, KLM, and many others have achieved such global success. They understand local markets and work well with them.

Importance of Global Thinking in Marketing

Emergence of the Multi-National Enterprise (MNE) or corporations with operations in multiple countries makes it essential that managers have the ability to "think globally." Corporations such as Coca-Cola, IBM, Gillette, Nestle, Sony, Phillips, and Unilever derive over 50 percent of their sales outside their country of domicile.

Globalization is not limited to large corporations. Small, relatively obscure companies with specialized "niches" that transcend national boundaries are likely to export and be successful. In fact 80 percent of the 100,000 U.S. companies that export are small businesses.[2] Because of their size, small firms tend to be flexible and adapt to local markets well. The Brooklyn Brewery, a small New York brewery, found much success in Japan because of a gimmick its Japanese distributor developed. By flying the beer to Tokyo versus shipping it by boat and dating each bottle, Brooklyn Brewery positioned its beer as "fresh from the brewery." This attribute impressed the Japanese consumer so much that the beer now sells for $15 per bottle.[3]

Exporting is the form of global business and global thinking most commonly discussed because it has been practiced for hundreds of years; however, global sourcing has proven profitable for companies in recent decades. Resource capabilities may emphasize labor costs in one country, raw materials in another, and information technologies in still others. Lincoln Mercury introduced the Capri in 1990. The design came from Italy, the parts came from Japan, and the assembly was performed in Australia, yet it is considered an American car. A company that sources globally

FIGURE 23.1 **Global Companies Do Well in an Environment That Understands Global Business**

Source: Courtesy of Netherlands Foreign Investment Agency.

can be considered a global company even if it never sells a product outside its country of domicile.

The corporate cultures of today's successful organizations also are increasingly global. Volkswagen in Germany recently appointed a new president from the United States. The president of Coca-Cola came from Cuba. IBM for the first time recently appointed an American to head its far-flung European Division, which includes Africa and the Middle East. Global managers must be able to learn a new language quickly, understand the structure and culture of any country in the world, and work effectively with people from any country. Consumer analysts can play a key role in this process by identifying structural, cultural, and ethnic differences and similarities among markets in different countries.

Global market analysis starts with understanding the structure of markets on a global basis—people, their needs, and the ability to buy. Today's consumers choose not only from products made in many countries, but from ideas, advertisements, and friends representing a diversity of nations and cultures. Consumer analysts must, therefore, be global thinkers to design strategies to reach today's consumers.

Global market analysis also involves willingness to buy—often affected by cultural, ethnic, and motivation variables. The following pages discuss how to analyze these variables using a cross-cultural perspective. In the last part of the chapter, these variables are considered as well as marketing institutions to examine marketing opportunities in some specific countries of the world other than North America.

Structure of Global Markets

The world population is approximately 5.4 billion and growing at the rate of about 1.7 percent annually.[4] That represents a decline from a 2.04 percent growth rate in the 1960s and a reversal of 2 centuries of increasing growth rates. Demographers expect the growth rate to continue to decline to between 1.4 and 1.5 percent in 2000 and zero toward the end of the twenty-first century. Even though the *rate* is declining, the *numbers added* are still growing about 83 million people each year and will increase to about 86 million people added each year in the 1990s, peaking at 89 million added in the year 2000 when the world's population is estimated by the United Nations to be about 6.1 billion. After that, the numbers added each year are projected to decline but will still produce a world population of 10.2 billion by the last decade of the twenty-first century, when population in absolute numbers should begin to decline.[5]

The population of a country is affected by natural growth variables of fertility and death rates as well as migration rates. Fertility is declining in industrialized nations. The primary reasons are higher educational attainment, urbanization, rising standards of living, legal abortion, more effective methods of contraception, widespread sterilization, increased labor force participation of women, high divorce rates, and delayed marriage and childbearing. Emigration from developing countries to developed countries is increasing rapidly. The best-educated and relatively affluent segments of the population are often the ones who emigrate.

Strategic planning involves committing corporate resources to the most promising areas of the world. This process requires accurate projection of world population trends over the next few decades. Table 23.1 displays current and projected population for major countries of the world by age distribution. This table serves as a reference point for many of the global trends discussed in this chapter. When studying this chart, look for changes occurring in specific countries.

Important global population trends can be summarized as

1. prolonged below-replacement fertility in developed nations;
2. rapid growth despite falling fertility in developing nations; and
3. rapid urbanization in less developed countries, with unprecedented migration from poor LDCs to more affluent industrialized nations.

Fast and Slow Growth Markets

Growth-oriented firms, striving for ESV (Enhanced Shareholder Value), need to find growth markets to increase profits. This is often the responsibility of the consumer

TABLE 23.1   World Population Trends, by Age: 1985 and 2025 (numbers in thousands)

1985

Country	Total all ages*	0 to 24 years	25 to 54 years	55 to 59 years	60 to 64 years	65 to 69 years	70 to 74 years	75 to 79 years	80 years and over
United States	238,631	91,578	96,256	11,245	10,943	9,214	7,641	5,556	6,198
WESTERN EUROPE									
Austria	7,502	2,643	2,953	420	425	256	319	256	228
Belgium	9,903	3,402	4,007	593	571	352	392	299	287
Denmark	5,122	1,747	2,081	262	268	235	205	161	162
France	54,621	20,093	21,789	3,086	2,905	1,594	1,769	1,644	1,741
Germany, Federal Republic	60,877	19,410	25,662	3,618	3,374	2,133	2,539	2,189	1,951
Greece	9,878	3,626	3,865	625	463	382	372	284	261
Italy	57,300	20,249	22,908	3,459	3,243	1,982	2,324	1,701	1,436
Luxembourg	363	119	157	23	18	13	14	11	8
Norway	4,142	1,483	1,578	208	230	207	173	131	133
Sweden	8,351	2,714	3,291	446	485	434	381	305	295
United Kingdom	56,125	19,901	21,520	3,069	3,171	2,543	2,367	1,824	1,732
EASTERN EUROPE									
Bulgaria	9,071	3,266	3,651	586	544	301	328	228	167
Hungary	10,697	3,663	4,436	650	614	363	420	310	240
Poland	37,187	14,669	15,379	2,000	1,655	980	1,017	837	650
OTHER DEVELOPED COUNTRIES									
Australia	15,698	6,385	6,279	757	686	559	454	310	268
Canada	25,426	9,732	10,734	1,196	1,113	896	731	511	513
Japan	120,742	43,445	52,896	6,920	5,356	4,164	3,522	2,439	2,000
New Zealand	3,318	1,415	1,268	150	140	118	98	70	59
DEVELOPING COUNTRIES									
Bangladesh	101,147	66,246	27,807	2,262	1,712	1,262	959	623	275
Brazil	135,564	76,932	45,799	3,909	3,098	2,283	1,718	1,037	790
China	1,043,204	545,766	378,000	36,697	29,851	22,340	15,471	9,381	5,697
Guatemala	7,963	5,197	2,198	191	143	97	66	38	34
Hong Kong	5,548	2,383	2,289	252	204	167	120	76	56
India	758,927	428,856	254,102	24,135	19,137	14,380	9,824	5,581	2,913
Indonesia	166,440	97,940	54,277	4,827	3,495	2,529	1,808	1,047	517
Israel	4,252	2,088	1,484	154	147	129	97	89	64
Mexico	78,996	49,882	23,166	1,715	1,436	1,008	798	532	459
Philippines	54,498	33,158	17,129	1,297	990	780	571	304	219
Singapore	2,559	1,148	1,125	88	65	52	40	25	15
Uruguay	3,012	1,296	1,091	163	139	109	94	62	57

TABLE 23.1 continued

Country	2025								
	Total all ages*	0 to 24 years	25 to 54 years	55 to 59 years	60 to 64 years	65 to 69 years	70 to 74 years	75 to 79 years	80 years and over
United States	301,394	91,851	113,153	18,071	19,547	18,352	14,836	11,235	14,348
WESTERN EUROPE									
Austria	7,279	2,041	2,671	562	570	473	364	287	311
Belgium	10,054	3,000	3,659	691	717	654	539	408	387
Denmark	4,690	1,144	1,785	367	352	303	268	237	235
France	58,431	17,242	22,141	3,917	3,858	3,531	3,123	2,508	2,111
Germany, Federal Republic	53,490	13,862	18,460	4,522	4,628	3,827	3,088	2,247	2,855
Greece	10,789	3,357	4,136	726	648	583	482	400	457
Italy	57,178	16,268	21,271	4,292	4,126	3,441	2,868	2,427	2,485
Luxembourg	339	93	124	25	25	24	20	14	14
Norway	4,261	1,186	1,598	323	291	266	229	192	175
Sweden	7,707	2,048	2,842	576	532	466	433	405	404
United Kingdom	55,919	16,894	20,608	4,030	3,949	3,263	2,654	2,309	2,211
EASTERN EUROPE									
Bulgaria	10,070	3,342	3,914	579	549	513	459	367	347
Hungary	10,598	3,196	4,189	647	550	615	610	401	391
Poland	45,286	14,997	17,836	2,311	2,406	2,663	2,320	1,510	1,243
OTHER DEVELOPED COUNTRIES									
Australia	22,575	7,167	9,011	1,460	1,351	1,206	985	745	649
Canada	33,261	10,376	12,410	1,997	2,238	2,069	1,672	1,264	1,235
Japan	132,082	40,389	49,052	8,348	7,451	6,700	6,940	6,671	6,531
New Zealand	4,202	1,266	1,665	299	287	237	182	144	123
DEVELOPING COUNTRIES									
Bangladesh	219,383	103,492	92,273	8,114	6,119	4,463	2,559	1,472	892
Brazil	245,809	99,425	100,520	11,982	11,038	8,635	6,383	4,154	3,672
China	1,388,431	449,084	558,616	113,599	88,981	64,697	56,554	31,691	25,208
Guatemala	21,668	11,293	8,108	667	530	403	298	189	181
Hong Kong	7,617	2,361	2,866	493	560	517	375	245	199
India	1,228,829	441,190	540,386	69,710	58,574	46,980	33,989	21,564	16,435
Indonesia	272,744	103,677	118,444	14,971	11,989	9,700	6,612	4,027	3,324
Israel	6,865	2,578	2,770	380	318	269	227	179	144
Mexico	154,085	62,898	65,604	7,671	6,063	4,609	3,280	2,066	1,894
Philippines	102,787	41,350	44,598	5,025	4,127	3,230	2,263	1,298	896
Singapore	3,323	1,028	1,232	218	252	236	173	112	73
Uruguay	3,875	1,422	1,569	209	200	163	120	89	104

*The sum of the age groups may not add to the total because of rounding.
Source: Bureau of the Census, *An Aging World*, International Population Reports Series P-95, No. 78 (Washington, D.C.: U.S. Department of Commerce, 1987), 48–49.

analyst. Let's examine where the growth markets are—and are not—focusing on the variables of population and ability to buy.

Birth Dearth The ability to buy has been concentrated historically in North America, Europe, and Japan. However, these affluent countries are expecting either a decline or slight increase in population in the next decade. Industrialized countries (North America, Europe, Israel, Japan, Australia) are projected to decline from 15 percent of the world's population in 1985 to barely 5 percent in the year 2100.[6] Table 23.2 shows that population in the European Common Market is expected to increase 2.55 percent between 1991 and 2010. Actual decline in population is projected in some European countries. In that same time period, Japan is projected to increase about half the rate of the United States and Canada. It is not difficult to see why MNEs have been pouring their capital into North America, why Europeans are developing a single market in 1992, and why the Russian market has been opened for economic development.

Fast-Growth Populations Some countries are projected to grow rapidly. These countries can be identified in Table 23.1. Relative changes are easier to observe by

TABLE 23.2 Population Growth in European Common Market and Some Other Countries (population in millions)

	1991	2010	Percentage Change
France	56.7	58.8	3.7%
Germany	79.5	82.2	3.3
Italy	57.7	55.9	-3.2
Netherlands	15.0	16.1	7.3
Belgium	9.9	9.7	-2.0
Luxembourg	.4	.4	0.0
United Kingdom	57.5	59.8	4.0
Ireland	3.5	3.4	-2.9
Denmark	5.1	5.1	0.0
Greece	10.1	10.2	.9
Spain	39.0	41.2	5.6
Portugal	10.4	10.8	3.8
Total Europe	344.8	353.6	2.55
Poland	38.2	40.6	6.2
Czechoslovakia	15.7	16.8	7.0
Hungary	10.4	10.5	1.0
Total Eastern Europe	64.3	67.9	5.5
Former U.S.S.R.	292.0	333.0	14.0
U.S.A.	252.8	299.0	18.2
Canada	26.8	31.5	17.5
Japan	123.8	135.8	9.7
World Total	5384.0	7189.0	33.5

Source: 1991 World Population Data Sheet, The Population Reference Bureau, Inc. (1991).

identifying population percentage changes in Table 23.2 and the changing rank of countries, as is done in Table 23.3.

The fastest-growing country in the world is India. If current trends continue, India will surpass China as the most populous country in the world in the next century. Kenya is the fastest growing country by percentage increase, rising at the rate of 4.2 percent annually. Kenya is not shown in Table 23.1 because of its relatively small size, but its 1988 population of 23 million is expected to quadruple by 2025. Kenya is a land of economic potential because of export commodities such as coffee and tea. It also has relative political stability, freedom, and increasing prosperity. The problems of Kenya as a consumer market are described, however, in this demographic analysis, which appears on the following page.

TABLE 23.3 Countries Ranked by Population Size: 1950, 1987, 2025, and 2050

1950	1987	2025	2050
1. China	1. China	1. China	1. India
2. India	2. India	2. India	2. China
3. Soviet Union	3. Soviet Union	3. Soviet Union	3. Nigeria
4. United States	4. United States	4. Indonesia	4. Pakistan
5. Japan	5. Indonesia	5. Nigeria	5. Soviet Union
6. Indonesia	6. Brazil	6. United States	6. Brazil
7. Brazil	7. Japan	7. Brazil	7. Indonesia
8. United Kingdom	8. Nigeria	8. Pakistan	8. United States
9. West Germany	9. Bangladesh	9. Bangladesh	9. Bangladesh
10. Italy	10. Pakistan	10. Iran	10. Iran
11. Bangladesh	11. Mexico	11. Ethiopia	11. Ethiopia
12. France	12. Vietnam	12. Mexico	12. Philippines
13. Nigeria	13. Philippines	13. Philippines	13. Mexico
14. Pakistan	14. West Germany	14. Vietnam	14. Vietnam
15. Mexico	15. Italy	15. Japan	15. Kenya
16. Spain	16. United Kingdom	16. Egypt	16. Zaire
17. Vietnam	17. France	17. Turkey	17. Egypt
18. Poland	18. Thailand	18. Zaire	18. Tanzania
19. Egypt	19. Turkey	19. Kenya	19. Turkey
20. Philippines	20. Egypt	20. Thailand	20. Japan
21. Turkey	21. Iran	21. Tanzania	21. Saudi Arabia
22. South Korea	22. Ethiopia	22. Burma	22. Thailand
23. Ethiopia	23. South Korea	23. South Africa	23. Uganda
24. Thailand	24. Spain	24. Sudan	24. Sudan
25. Burma	25. Burma	25. South Korea	25. Burma
26. East Germany	26. Poland	26. France	26. South Africa
27. Argentina	27. South Africa	27. United Kingdom	27. Syria
28. Iran	28. Zaire	28. Italy	28. Morocco
29. Yugoslavia	29. Argentina	29. West Germany	29. Algeria
30. Romania	30. Colombia	30. Uganda	30. Iraq

Note: Developing countries are shown in boldface.
Source: Bureau of the Census, *World Population Profile, 1987* (Washington, D.C.: U.S. Department of Commerce, 1987), 5.

The total fertility rate—or the average number of children a woman will bear in her lifetime—is well above 2.6 to 5 children per woman, the figure considered necessary to indicate that a country may be a good potential market. With the average woman bearing about 8 children in her lifetime and with little prospect for change in the near future, the country shows small promise as a consumer market in this century. Just keeping up with the basic needs of a surging population will strain already limited resources. And Kenya's record-high population growth of about 4.2 percent per year is far above the 1.5 to 2.5 percent considered indicative of a good potential market.[7]

Another fast-growing country is Bangladesh, the eighth most populous nation in the world and growing rapidly. Between 1983 and 2000, 52 million people are projected to be added to Bangladesh's population. That is roughly equivalent to a country with the population of France being added to a state the size of Georgia.[8]

The difference between growth rates of developed and developing countries is dramatically indicated in Table 23.3. In 1950, only 8 of the top 15 countries were developing countries. Currently the number is 10, and by 2050, it is projected to rise to 13.

The changing rank of developing countries produces some dramatic changes over the next few decades. By 2025, Iran and Ethiopia will join the list of 15 largest countries, while Japan is expected to drop from 7th to 20th. Perhaps the greatest changes for consumer analysts to monitor are countries such as Nigeria and Pakistan, which were 13th and 14th in 1950 but which are expected to move to 3rd and 4th place by the year 2050. Among Latin American countries, Brazil is expected to retain its rank as one of the 10 largest countries in the future.

From a market perspective, the greatest challenge for the "rich" countries that hope to have growing markets for their products in the future is to assist the "poor" countries in developing themselves to where they also are rich enough to be economically strong markets.

Economic Resources and Market Attractiveness

The most attractive markets are countries that are growing both in population and in economic resources. An important task of consumer analysis is to identify such countries.

Economic resources, or ability to buy, can be measured in various ways. Per capita income is an important indicator, although there are problems, such as the currency with which it will be measured and the purchasing power of income within a country. One of the most valid indicators is "hours required to purchase" standard consumer goods. For example, consumers might require 11 hours at an average wage to purchase a standard television receiver in the United States but as much as 11 months in some developing countries. Unfortunately, such data are not readily available for market analysis purposes.

A useful indicator of "ability to buy" is Gross National Product (GNP) or Gross Domestic Product (GDP) per capita in a country. Even though the statistic does not reflect variations in distribution between countries, per capita GNP or GDP is a commonly accepted indicator of market attractiveness. These data for some major countries are presented in Table 23.4.

TABLE 23.4   **Market Data for Selected Major Countries, 1991**

Country	Natural Increase %/Yr	Life Expectancy (Years)	Per Capita GNP (US$)
NORTH AMERICA	.9	75	20,900
United States	.8	75	21,100
Canada	.7	77	19,020
EUROPE	.2	75	12,920
Austria	.1	75	17,360
Belgium	.1	74	16,390
Denmark	0.0	75	20,510
France	.4	77	17,830
Germany	0.0	75	16,200
Greece	.1	77	5,340
Italy	.1	76	15,150
Luxembourg	.2	74	24,860
Norway	.3	76	21,850
Sweden	.3	78	21,710
United Kingdom	.2	75	14,750
EASTERN EUROPE	.3	71	n.a.
Czechoslovakia	.2	72	n.a.
Hungary	−.2	70	2,560
Poland	.5	72	1,760
OTHER DEVELOPED COUNTRIES			
Australia	.8	76	14,440
Japan	.3	79	23,730
New Zealand	.9	74	11,800
DEVELOPING COUNTRIES			
Bangladesh	2.4	53	180
Brazil	1.9	65	2,550
China	1.4	69	2,720
Guatemala	3.0	63	920
Hong Kong	.7	77	10,320
India	2.0	57	350
Indonesia	1.7	61	490
Israel	1.6	76	9,750
Mexico	2.3	70	1,190
Philippines	1.7	61	490
Singapore	1.3	75	10,450
South Africa	2.7	64	2,460
Uruguay	.8	72	2,620
LATIN AMERICA	2.1	67	1,190
AFRICA	3.0	53	610
WORLD	1.7	65	3,760

Source: *World Population Data Sheet* (Washington, D.C.: Population Reference Bureau, Inc., 1991).

Three other indicators of market attractiveness are *natural increase* (percentage increase in population each year considering births and deaths), *life expectancy*, and *urban population* (as a percentage of total population). Market indicators are shown in Table 23.4 where data are presented for some of the countries as in Table 23.1. Data for additional countries are available from the Population Reference Bureau.[9]

The search for both population growth and ability to buy increasingly takes consumer analysts to the Pacific Rim. Hong Kong, Singapore, Malaysia, and South Korea have much faster population growth than Europe and relatively high income. China and India currently have low per capita GNP but attract the interest of world marketers because of the size of the population bases and the rapidity of their growth.

Cultural Analysis of Global Markets

After the structure of markets is examined, the next major area of understanding that must be developed by consumer analysts involves **cultural analysis**. This involves the ability to understand and be effective in communicating with the core values of a society. Ethnographic analysis of marketing focuses on the interactive processes of exchange with particular attention on the subtle nuances and orderliness of the selling process.[10]

Marketing practitioners need **cultural empathy**, defined as the ability to understand the inner logic and coherence of other ways of life. Cultural empathy includes restraint not to judge the value of other ways of life. Consumer analysis focuses on "meaning systems" of consumers in a nation that are intelligible within the cultural context of that country.

Global strategies need to be adapted to meaning systems of the market rather than attempting to change the market to the customary marketing programs of the firm. For example, firms in the United States typically spend about 3 percent of sales on advertising. In nations such as Australia, the advertising/sales ratio is typically between 7 and 8 percent, in Sweden about 5 percent, in Mexico a little over 5 percent, and in Canada between 4 and 5 percent.[11] An American company entering Australia may under budget for advertising according to local practices.

The marketplace is changing rapidly. Global marketers find it useful to track global trends to predict and better understand how consumers in various parts of the world will be changing. Table 23.5 lists some of the trends shaping the world. See how many ideas you can formulate as to how the global marketplace might change in the next decade and how as a marketer these changes would affect your marketing strategies.

Cross-Cultural Analysis

Cross-cultural analysis is the systematic comparison of similarities and differences in the material and behavioral aspects of cultures. Anthropologists have developed

TABLE 23.5   Trends Shaping the Global Marketplace

1. The West will continue its concern for personal health and physical culture, but the developing countries will adopt the bad habits of the richer nations including smoking and high-fat diets.
2. The gap between rich and poor countries will widen in the next decades because populations in poor countries will continue to increase faster than their incomes.
3. The technology gap between developed and developing countries will widen. This will aggravate trade between countries of the Northern and Southern hemispheres.
4. People in industrialized countries will increase mobility in terms of residences, jobs, and occupations in the next decade.
5. The proportion of illiterate adults in developing countries will drop from 39 percent in 1985 to 28 percent by 2000, although the absolute number will increase by 10 million people.
6. By 2000, many or most of the Eastern European countries will be associate members of the EC.

Source: Excerpted from "50 Trends Shaping the World," *The Futurist* 25 (September–October 1991).

techniques to catalog similarities and differences among peoples of various cultures. Remarkable similarities are found in the methods people use to handle common problems among societies located so far apart that they could not possibly have come into contact with each other.

Cross-cultural research methodology involves standard research techniques adapted to the special requirements of different languages, structural characteristics of the societies, and values of the investigator. Cross-cultural studies in anthropology often focus upon social organization, child rearing, belief systems, and similar topics. In marketing, the elements studied are more likely to be distribution systems, beliefs about sales and pricing activities, and communications channels.

Cultural analysis provides an approach to understanding the consumer behavior of diverse nations and diverse groups within a nation. In Africa, for example, tribal cultures within countries such as Zambia, Nigeria, Zimbabwe, and South Africa may be more influential than differences that exist between these countries. Many of the ethnic influences cut across national boundaries established by white colonists with little regard for cultural or tribal boundaries. In Europe people in the south of Switzerland may have more cultural similarity to France than to the north of Switzerland. Cross-cultural analysis provides an approach for understanding such situations and is likely to be even more important as Europe moves toward a "single market."

Consumer research and global consumer behavior play special roles in global marketing. Consumer research can also help firms by influencing the strategic decisions made about a specific country or market based on the communalities and differences between the various markets. Kentucky Fried Chicken chose to test market its breakfast menu in Singapore because research showed that breakfast was becoming an eating occasion of growing importance in Singapore.[12] When research

TABLE 23.6 Outline of Cross-Cultural Analysis of Consumer Behavior

Determine Relevant Motivations in the Culture

What needs are fulfilled with this product in the minds of members of the culture? How are these needs presently fulfilled? Do members of this culture readily recognize these needs?

Determine Characteristic Behavior Patterns

What patterns are characteristic of purchasing behavior? What forms of division of labor exist within the family structure? How frequently are products of this type purchased? What size packages are normally purchased? Do any of these characteristic behaviors conflict with behavior expected for this product? How strongly ingrained are the behavior patterns that conflict with those needed for distribution of this product?

Determine What Broad Cultural Values Are Relevant to This Product

Are there strong values about work, morality, religion, family relations, and so on, that relate to this product? Does this product connote attributes that are in conflict with these cultural values? Can conflicts with values be avoided by changing the product? Are there positive values in this culture with which the product might be identified?

Determine Characteristic Forms of Decision Making

Do members of the culture display a studied approach to decisions concerning innovations or an impulsive approach? What is the form of the decision process? Upon what information sources do members of the culture rely? Do members of the culture tend to be rigid or flexible in the acceptance of new ideas? What criteria do they use in evaluating alternatives?

Evaluate Promotion Methods Appropriate to the Culture

What roles does advertising occupy in the culture? What themes, words, or illustrations are taboo? What language problems exist in present markets that cannot be translated into this culture? What types of salesmen are accepted by members of the culture? Are such salesmen available?

Determine Appropriate Institutions for This Product in the Minds of Consumers

What types of retailers and intermediary institutions are available? What services do these institutions offer that are expected by the consumer? What alternatives are available for obtaining services needed for the product but not offered by existing institutions? How are various types of retailers regarded by consumers? Will changes in the distribution structure be readily accepted?

results are positive, they can stimulate interest and enthusiasm for specific marketing programs from the local organizations.[13] The global expansion of markets furthers the need for study in the field of global consumer behavior. Consumer behavior is not only an American topic. It must be researched and discussed in international terms.[14]

An outline for conducting cross-cultural studies from a marketing perspective is shown in Table 23.6. This outline can be used by a marketing organization to discover if unmet needs exist for which a company might adapt or develop new products. The information gathered by use of this outline also helps develop a successful marketing program to meet those needs.

Cross-cultural studies may be **descriptive** or **analytical**. Descriptive studies describe structural components and are used to contrast or compare societies. Analytical or functional studies attempt to deduce general principles of behavior that apply in one or more cultures.[15]

Can Marketing Be Standardized?

Can one marketing program be used in all or at least many countries? Or must marketing programs be modified for each country? If marketing programs must be modified to each culture, firms will fail if they do not develop specific products, promotions, and organizations for each country. Enormous economies are achieved, however, if the marketing program is standardized.

Is consumer behavior subject to cultural universals? Erik Elinder answered this question affirmatively and advanced the position that advertising can be standardized.[16] Elinder's question and the validity of his answer have intrigued marketers since Elinder first raised the issue. It was a major topic addressed in the first edition of this text over 20 years ago.

The issue of standardization has become more important because of increased global competition facing marketers. The debate was intensified by a controversial article by Ted Levitt describing the globalization of the marketplace.[17]

The need for globalized marketing strategies arises not only from market characteristics but also from technological and organizational characteristics. To compete, a firm must use technology that is not limited to national borders and people operating in worldwide organizations. Measures of marketing efficiency must now include global market share, requiring firms to understand their market niche in terms of customer types, not geodemographic segments.[18]

As Europe moves beyond the 1992 goal of a single market, firms are increasingly defining market segments to consist of similar types of customers and cultures throughout Europe rather than groups within a specific country. But if Europe is treated as one common market, will the cultural identities of each country disappear? Will the French become more or less French if treated as a generic European? The answer depends on whether a firm's marketing strategies are based on the similarities of consumers or the differences among consumers.

Standardization Based on Similarities

Standardization should be based on a solid understanding of the similarities as well as the differences between countries. Marketing organizations want such standardization in international marketing programs.[19]

A study of 27 MNEs, including companies such as General Foods, Nestle, Coca-Cola, Procter & Gamble, Unilever, and Revlon, found that 63 percent of the total marketing programs could be rated as "highly standardized." The authors of that study describe the need for cross-cultural (or "cross-border") analysis:

> Management of multi-nationals should give high priority to developing the ability to conduct systematic cross-border analysis, if they are not already doing so. Such analysis can help management avoid the mistake of standardizing when markets are significantly different. At the same time, systematic cross-border analysis can help avoid the mistake of excessive custom-tailoring when markets are sufficiently similar to make standardized programs feasible.[20]

People are basically the same around the globe. They vary in specific traits, often influenced by structural elements such as economic resources, urbanization, population age, and other variables. The challenge is to build the core of the marketing strategy on the *universals* rather than on the differences.

An example of standardization based on universals would be the desire to be beautiful. In a sense, young women in Tokyo and those in Berlin are sisters not only "under" the skin but "on" their skin, lips, fingernails, and even in their hairstyles. Consequently, Fatt states, they are likely to buy similar cosmetics with similar appeals. If they could, Fatt believes, the women of Moscow would follow suit, and some of them do.[21] Appeals to such images as mother and child, freedom from pain, glow of health, and so forth may cut across many boundaries.

Nestle has recognized the similarities among coffee consumers around the world. Consumer in Focus 23.2 describes how this traditionally decentralized firm is marketing its Nescafe brand based on a standardized approach.

Localization Based on Differences

True localization of marketing strategies would argue for different products and ads in every country of the world. While this is economically inefficient and impractical, it is necessary to examine the needs and wants of specific markets and to adapt products, packaging, and advertising based on the differences between markets and the consumer behavior patterns of the target markets. Therefore, *going global and acting local* has become the choice of many marketers.

While Pepsi is basically the same around the world, it had to adapt slightly to the market when it entered India. At the request of the Indian government, Pepsi will "Indianize" its soft drinks by adopting the prefix Lehar, meaning "wave" in Hindi, which will coordinate with the "wave" advertising. Similarily, McDonald's recognized the strong demand for spaghetti among Filipinos, so it added McSpaghetti to the menu in its stores located in the Philippines. Before Japanese cars were introduced into the U.S. market, the cars had to be redesigned so that the steering wheels were on the left side of the car. How many Americans would have bought Hondas had the steering wheels been on the "wrong" side? You might think that medicines would be the same around the world because they are used for the same human species. Yet it is not uncommon to see the same medicine dispensed according to local preferences: capsules in the U.S. and Canada, tablets in England, injections in Germany, and suppositories in France.

Nestle's Global Strategy

Nestle is a huge worldwide company whose historic roots put it toward decentralization on the global continuum. Because of its early international start over a hundred years ago, long before intercontinental communications and travel were improved—and when wars often disturbed Swiss control—strong local managerial authority was a way of life at Nestle. Only recently has Vevey headquarters moved toward tighter global coordination. But Nestle does it globally with its Nescafe brand, despite the fact that the definition of coffee varies according to the local culture.

Do you have a tea culture like Japan? Or, like the United Kingdom, a tea culture that has also become an instant coffee culture? Or, ground coffee cultures like France, Germany, and Brazil? It's a confusing and steadily changing advertising environment, but Nescafe has given it one common emotional link: "Whatever good coffee means to you and however you like to serve it, Nescafe has a coffee for you."

So wherever you sell Nescafe, you sell coffee-ness. The ingredients, the appetite appeal, the warmth of the shared moment—stir the mixture to suit the context. In fact, whatever consumers want their coffee to be, that coffee is Nescafe. This broad approach overcomes cultural differences and links Nescafe advertising today in 50 countries.

Source: Gordon L. Link, "Global Advertising: An Update," *Journal of Consumer Marketing* 5 (Spring 1988), 69–74, at 72.

Global Advertising Effectiveness

In this rapidly changing environment, advertising agencies often serve as the primary link between the MNE and its consumers. And with the diversity of consumers within these markets and the global vision of these MNEs, the agency's role may become more important than ever.[22] This has led to the creation of mega advertising agencies with offices around the globe. One of their strengths is that they are very efficient in implementing globalized advertising campaigns that relay the same message to each market regardless of geographical location. This strategy has worked well for John Deere. The tractor is used and perceived similarly in most markets and lends itself well to a global strategy. The result has been a uniform image worldwide.

Some advertising messages and specific product characteristics tend to be suited better than others for a globalized advertising approach. These characteristics are summarized as follows:

1. The communications message is based on similar lifestyles.
2. The appeal of the ad is to basic human needs and emotions.
3. The product satisfies universal needs and desires.[23]

While global advertising campaigns might be effective for some products and firms, others need to recognize cultural differences and adapt their campaigns accordingly.[24] Nivea failed to consider that what is appropriate, acceptable, and allowed in one country may not be in another. A Nivea print ad was published in the U.S. and was ultimately banned from further publication due to what in the U.S. was considered to be indecent exposure. The same message and image had been used in Germany, however, without any controversy. McCain Foods, the distributor of a highly successful brand of frozen French fried potato, decided to adapt its advertising to the local tastes and norms of the specific markets. Television commercials seen in Germany show the potatoes served at the dinner table with a glass of beer nearby. If the same ad were shown in France, consumers would probably find it offensive and ineffective because wine is the usual drink with meals. Consumer in Focus 23.3 shows how American Express is solving this problem in Europe with its new advertising campaign.

MNEs are faced with the tradeoff between the efficiencies of standardized advertising and the effectiveness and cultural sensitivity of localized campaigns. This has traditionally been directly related to the tradeoffs between mega advertising agencies and smaller, local agencies. For many MNEs the solution to choosing an agency is to have a portfolio of advertising agencies. Marketers with a global vision may select a domestic or localized advertising agency, but increasingly it will probably be one that maintains a global network of agencies available to the agency and its client. This network decreases the probability of marketing mistakes occurring due to a lack of knowledge or misinterpretation of a culture.

Overcoming Language Problems

Language problems must be overcome to standardize marketing programs. General Motors used the phrase "Body by Fisher" in its marketing. Some problems occurred, however, when it was translated into Flemish and took on the meaning of "Corpse by Fisher." The phrase "Come alive with Pepsi" experienced problems when it was translated in German ads as "Come alive out of the grave" and in Chinese as "Pepsi brings your ancestors back from the grave." Coors used a slogan in English as "Turn It Loose," but the phrase in Spanish became "Suffer from Diarrhea." When Frank Perdue's "It Takes a Tough Man to Make a Tender Chicken" was translated into Spanish, it became "It Takes a Sexually Stimulated Man to Make a Chicken Affectionate." And Budweiser's "King of Beers" became "Queen of Beers" in Spanish because the Spanish word for beer, "cerveza," has a feminine

Amex Euro Ads: A Global Message with Local Flair

American Express believes in localizing of its global advertising campaigns. It will begin running television ads that combine common footage with local (country specific) variations.

The commercial features a young photographer who is on her way to a photo shoot when her equipment is sent out on the wrong flight to an unknown destination. She is faced with paying a high rental fee to rent photo equipment, which she charges on her AmEx card.

The second portion (local portion) of the ad takes place in a restaurant when she tells a friend of her mishap, but the restaurant scene is different in each country the commercial airs. Different women play the role of the photographer in different countries and local props are used to localize the restaurant scene. For example a blue-eyed blonde in a German *Gasthof* may be featured in Germany, while a woman with olive skin in an Italian *trattoria* might be featured in the Italian version.

Initial research indicates the "localization" of the ads does not adversely affect the delivery of a universal message or the global image of American Express. The solution to the question of globalization or localization in advertising for American Express is a "multi local approach."

Source: Laurel Wentz, "New Euro ads get localized element," *Advertising Age* (November 25, 1991), 28.

ending.[25] Linguistics techniques borrowed from cross-cultural methodologies are helpful to marketers in overcoming such problems.

Back-Translation   A useful technique for overcoming language problems is **back-translation**. In this procedure, a message (word or a series of words) is translated from its original language to the translated language and back to the original by a number of translators. This process may be repeated several times, with the translated versions being interchanged with the original among the translators. The purpose of the iterations is an attempt to achieve conceptual equivalency in meaning by controlling the various translation biases of translators.[26]

Marketing research questionnaires often need to be translated into additional languages. This process can be more reliable with back-translation. Sometimes, however, it is necessary to use scales other than verbal or quantitative. Figure 23.2 shows an example from Holiday Inn in which questions are given in English and Afrikaans. Responses are given with smiling or unhappy faces.

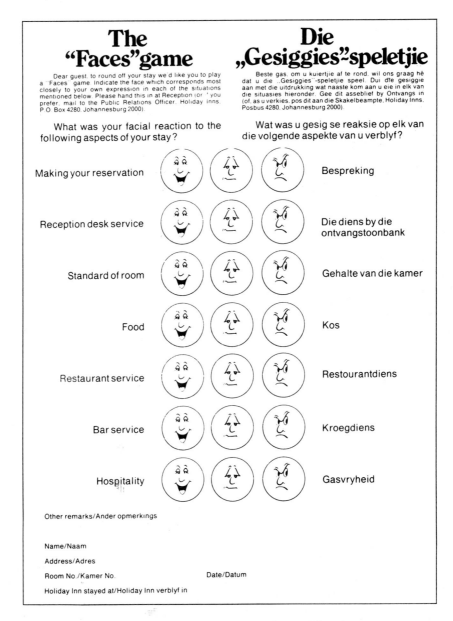

FIGURE 23.2 Cross-Cultural Questionnaire for Holiday Inn

Source: Courtesy of the South African division of Holiday Inns. Reprinted by permission.

Brand Names

Brand names should be evaluated from a cross-cultural perspective even when they are currently used only in domestic markets. "Thinking globally" includes considering the possibility that the brand will someday be extended to other countries, as well as making it more appealing to diverse cultures within the current country. Coined names are increasing in popularity among Fortune 500 companies because they do not need to be translated and avoid awkward translation. This makes names like Exxon and Xerox very effective in a global market.[27]

The steps that should be used for a cross-cultural approach, in addition to legal search, in finding an English name acceptable on a global basis include the following:

1. Does the English name of the product have another meaning, perhaps unfavorable, in one or more of the countries where it might be marketed?
2. Can the English name be pronounced everywhere? For example, Spanish and some other languages lack a "k" in their alphabets, an initial letter in many popular U.S. brand names.
3. Is the name close to that of a foreign brand, or does it duplicate another product sold in English-speaking countries?
4. If the product is distinctly American, will national pride and prejudice work against the acceptance of the product?[28]

There are many other ways companies can prepare for increasing globalization of marketing. Look at the top of Figure 23.3 which shows a Pizza Hut restaurant in Brussels. In this location, consumers may speak any one of several languages. The menu rack simplifies the process for both the customer and restaurant personnel who may not be able to speak all the languages. *Visual language* is another solution to the problem of cross-cultural communications. A Brussels hypermarket and many European grocery stores solve the language problem by using scales that have pictures of all the produce rather than words. Consumers from any country need only push the button with the correct picture to determine the weight and price of their produce.

Research Methodology for Cross-Cultural Analysis

Consumer behavior and marketing have borrowed from disciplines such as anthropology, linguistics, and sociology to obtain needed methodology for cross-cultural studies. This is reflected in the increased application of standard marketing research techniques on a cross-cultural basis.

Multiattribute methodology has dominated recent consumer behavior literature, as we see in earlier chapters. Berger, Stern, and Johansson have demonstrated that it can be used across cultures in comparing American and Japanese car buyers.[29] Japanese respondents tend to answer more in intermediate ranges of the scales, whereas Americans respond more at the extreme ends of scales.

Focus groups, a traditional form of consumer research, are also applicable on a global basis. Global focus groups take place in multiple locations and are linked through the use of video conference centers. BMW sends executives from Munich to its ad agency in New York via this video technology to watch focus groups.[30] It also enables them to interact with consumers around the world during focus groups without extensive travel.

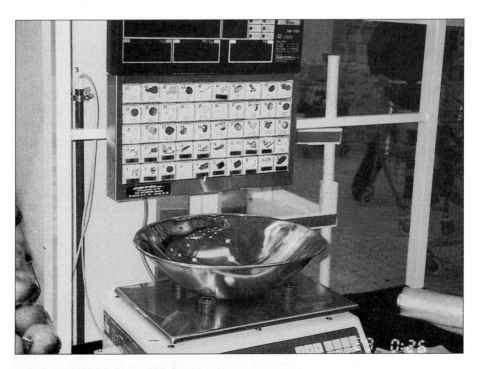

FIGURE 23.3   **Solving Global Language Problems**

Psychographic studies of the type you studied in Chapter 12 are also useful in cross-cultural applications. Boote demonstrated their usefulness in a cross-cultural study in the United Kingdom, Germany, and France.[31] Using an approach based upon Rokeach's instrumental value scales, Boote found the methodology (coupled with Z-Methodology factor analysis) useful in discovering substantial differences between those three countries, belying what some believe to be a homogeneous common market. Germans scored high on an "appearance conscious" segment, whereas the French scored high on an "outside interest" in the environment segment. The British were more directed toward home interests.

Family purchasing roles have also been studied on a cross-cultural basis by numerous researchers. Green and his colleagues reviewed many of these studies and administered questionnaires in English and other languages in major cities of the United States, France, Holland, Venezuela, and Gabon. The researchers found a substantial range in purchase roles along the lines that family decision-making theory had suggested.[32]

Participant-Observer Studies

Participant-observer studies involve an investigator or team of investigators living in intimate contact with a culture. The investigator makes careful and comprehensive notes of observations about the culture. Data collection includes records of what is observed, interviews with "key" informants, and perhaps structured questionnaires, attitude scales, and projective tests.

Content Analysis

Content analysis is a technique for determining the values, themes, role prescriptions, norms of behavior, and other elements of culture. Analysis is based on objective materials produced by the people of a culture in the ordinary course of events.[33] Usually the content studied is verbal in nature, such as newspaper or magazine stories. It could be derived from advertisements or any other objective material, such as art, products, or even the garbage discarded by consumers. Some of the more interesting of these approaches are described in Webb's *Unobtrusive Measures*.[34]

Content analysis is used in domestic marketing studies as well as cross-nationally, often concerning advertising themes. Kassarjian analyzed occupational roles of blacks in America, discovering some changes in occupational roles but the continuation of many stereotypes.[35] Pollay conducted a content-analytic study of American advertising during the past 80 years. He found that American advertising has become more focused, is more forceful, and attempts fewer total value appeals.[36] One study based on content analysis, Naisbitt's book *Megatrends*, became a bestseller.[37]

While many of the methodologies described here are not fundamentally different from routine marketing research, the consumer analyst or marketing researcher equipped for the future can be expected to understand how to conduct research on a global basis, including the specific techniques involved in cross-cultural analysis.

Global Marketing Strategies

Business without borders will probably not be the reality, but global relationships between MNEs will be in the future environment facing consumer analysts and marketing strategists. It is the responsibility of consumer analysts, perhaps more than other individuals in an organization, to be on the "cutting edge" of knowledge about how global markets are changing, including the inter-environmental elements as well as the intra-environmental elements.

What are some of the specifics of how consumer analysts and their knowledge of cultural aspects can benefit an organization? Look at Figure 23.4, which displays the meaning of some common gestures. After you have read each one, ask yourself if this is the meaning you intend to communicate when you are in that country.

Network marketing is increasingly global. News reports indicate that corporate alliances between firms in different countries increased 47 percent *annually* during the past decade, and a survey of U.S.-based companies reported some 12,000 in which American firms owned 10 to 50 percent equity position in a foreign firm.[38] These networks are required for access to markets as well as resources. Such alliances may be essential for global dominance. This was apparently the motivation in an alliance between Du Pont, the largest American chemical firm, and Phillips, the largest Dutch electronics firm, but they needed each other in a joint venture to develop optical-disc products expected to be a $4 billion market. In centrally planned economies such as China, a local partner may be legally required to do business in the alien system.

In this final section of the chapter, we briefly spotlight some of the opportunities for consumer analysts seeking growth opportunities for organizations that are increasingly global in their operations.

Consumer Behavior in Developing Countries

Population is growing rapidly in Africa, some Asian countries, and in Latin America. But most also have low incomes. Great care must therefore be used to design effective marketing strategies for developing countries.

What are the most important attributes of the developing countries? Youthfulness is one, specifically a large number of babies. In some developing countries, women bear 7 or 8 children, but infant mortality is high. The 10 countries with the highest birth rates in the world (in order) are Kenya, Pakistan, Saudi Arabia, Egypt, the Philippines, Peru, South Africa, India, Venezuela, and Brazil.

Most developing countries are predominantly rural. In spite of the rural nature, consumers are usually dependent upon other countries for food supplies. Often other countries are also responsible for educating the nation's youth.

Observe how Johnson & Johnson has positioned its marketing strategy in Figure 23.5 for the African market. The photograph communicates the love and concern of a mother for her baby without the need for words. The copy, however,

---

International Gesture Dictionary

Gestures Using the Face

Eyebrow Raise: In Tonga, a gesture meaning "yes" or "I agree." In Peru, means "money" or "Pay me."

Blink: In Taiwan, blinking the eyes at someone is considered impolite.

Wink: Winking at women, even to express friendship, is considered improper in Australia.

Eyelid Pull: In Europe and some Latin American countries, means "Be alert" or "I am alert."

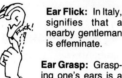

Ear Flick: In Italy, signifies that a nearby gentleman is effeminate.

Ear Grasp: Grasping one's ears is a sign of repentance or sincerity in India. A similar gesture in Brazil—holding the lobe of one's ear between thumb and forefinger—signifies appreciation.

Nose Circle: The classic American "okay" sign—the fingers circle—is placed over the nose in Colombia to signify that the person in question is homosexual.

Nose Tap: In Britain, secrecy or confidentiality. In Italy, a friendly warning.

Nose Thumb: One of Europe's most widely known gestures, signifying mockery. May be done double-handed for greater effect.

Nose Wiggle: In Puerto Rico, "What's going on?"

Cheek Screw: Primarily an Italian gesture of praise.

Cheek Stroke: In Greece, Italy, and Spain, means "attractive." In Yugoslavia, "success." Elsewhere, it can mean "ill" or "thin."

FIGURE 23.4   International Gesture Dictionary

Source: Reprinted from the book "Do's and Taboos Around the World—A Guide to International Gift-Giving" published by Parker Pen U.S.A. Limited. To obtain a copy of the complete book contact John Wiley and Sons, Inc., 608 Third Ave., New York, New York 10158.

features an economy appeal by saving 20 cents. Additionally, however, Johnson & Johnson has positioned itself as concerned about all children in the culture by donating 20 cents to the Child Welfare Fund with each purchase. Figure 23.5 provides a useful example of effective strategy based upon an understanding of the economic and cultural realities of the African market.

Cultural sensitivity is especially needed in developing countries because pictures may be much more important than words. As an example, one marketer attempted to export the firm's detergent to a Middle Eastern country. Advertising for

FIGURE 23.5   Advertising Appeals Based on African Culture
Source: Johnson & Johnson Company, Africa.

the detergent featured dirty clothes piled on the left and clean clothes stacked on the right. Reading right to left, as consumers in the Middle East frequently do, the message was clear: Soap soiled the clothes.

Consumer Behavior in the Pacific Rim

The Pacific Rim provides some of the most attractive markets for growth-oriented marketing strategies. The area includes many low-income but fast-growing population bases in Southeast Asia, as well as some of the most affluent markets in the world, such as Japan, Singapore, and Australia (refer to Tables 23.1 and 23.4).

India   As a country projected to become the largest in the world, India is attracting worldwide interest among marketers. Although poor by western standards, the attractiveness of India is based upon its infrastructure; well-developed legal system; and large numbers of well-educated doctors, engineers, and others needed for growth of a thriving middle class. India is a country with growth in national income and productivity but major problems due to its large debt, shortage of foreign exchange, and unsettling coalitions of government.[39] Even though facing a period of uncertainty, the long-run future of the market is promising for global marketers.

The middle class is the key to understanding India's consumer markets. Although the government does not publish statistics on this politically sensitive subject, some economists estimate the number at 7 to 12 percent of the population or a market range from 60 million to 100 million, larger, for example, than that of West Germany and France.[40]

Consequently, the demand for consumer goods is rising rapidly. Yearly car sales have tripled since 1980, sales of motorbikes and scooters have more than tripled in recent years, and production of consumer durables in general is rising at the rate of 20 percent annually. Movie theaters have doubled in the past decade. The middle-class family with a yearly income of about $1,400 does not live in luxury but may be buying a television; a radio; appliances such as an electric iron, clocks, and so forth; and a respectable wardrobe of shoes, jewelry, and silk saris.[41] There are more than 14 million television sets in middle-class homes. Consumer purchases are often deliberate, with the wife acting as information gatherer but with long discussions and interaction about the best choice.[42]

The middle class is a small minority, however, and marketers accustomed to mass class affluence of industrialized economies make serious mistakes by assuming such market conditions in countries such as India. Television has far less impact in India, for example, because access is restricted to those with the means to buy TV sets. When the least expensive black and white TV set costs the equivalent of three months of an assembly worker's wages, access is restricted! Add to that the fact that most programs are in Hindi, understood only by Northerners and the highly educated minority of the country and marketers are faced with a significant cross-cultural difference.[43]

South Korea

Ability to buy has increased at an astounding rate in South Korea. Annual per capita GNP soared from $120 in 1965 to $4,400 in 1991. Private consumption in recent years has been growing at an annual rate of 5.5 percent. Soaring income and plummeting birth rates (from 5.4 lifetime births in the 1960s to 1.6 in 1991); good health care; a high regard for religious values; and a young, increasingly well-educated population give South Korea many strengths upon which to build.

A key element in the success of Korea has been export capabilities, strongly assisted by governmental policies. The most successful auto ever to be imported into the North American market is Hyundai, first in Canada and later in the United States. Consumers in North America might not have heard of Korean firms such as Daewoo, a massive industrial firm (see Figure 23.6), but its recent ads in the United States designed to correct that situation appear to have done so.[44]

Australia

Australia is a market similar in characteristics to European and North American markets. High income and an older population are characteristics shared with other industrialized economies.[45]

Australia has a well-developed infrastructure and plenty of room to grow. At one time, immigration was mostly European, but in recent years nearly 50 percent of immigration has been Asian. Marketers find the nation attractive because it also has a well-developed advertising and marketing research support system and, as

FIGURE 23.6   Developing U.S. Acceptance of a Korean Firm
Source: Courtesy of Daewoo.

sailing enthusiasts and *Crocodile Dundee* fans both can attest, the influence of Australia on the rest of the world is considerable.

China   China is the largest nation in the world. The pent-up demand of a billion consumers excites marketers all over the world. In the past, most of China's imports have been industrial goods, but new government priorities caused marketers to begin to consider the potential for consumer markets, at least prior to the political instabilities and tragic demonstrations that occurred in Tiananmen Square.

Private consumption makes up 70 percent of all final demand in China, so that when consumers increase their demand for food, this initially puts money in the pockets of agriculture. Suppliers to agriculture and food manufacturers then place orders with their suppliers, and the demand for any consumer good multiplies throughout the economy. While most of the demand in China for imports from other nations will be producer goods for many years, the internal demand for consumer goods is so high that joint ventures to produce them may present substantial opportunities for foreign marketers to provide as well a broad range of industrial goods related to the production of consumer goods.[46] This process is expected to double per capita consumption by the year 2000. If government policies favoring market incentives continue, a growth in the 4.7 to 5.0 percent range is projected by the World Bank.

What do Chinese consumers want to buy most? Refrigerators top the list in a study made in two of China's largest cities, Beijing (with a population of 9.5 million) and Guyangzhou (with a population of 7 million).[47] Washing machines are equally wanted, although television sets are the electrical appliance most often owned. Chinese consumers are also interested in cameras and radio/cassette recorders, according to the study. With the results of the sixth Five-Year Plan producing an increase of salaries of urban workers by 68 percent and farmers by 109 percent, many more are now able to consider a broader array of consumer goods.[48]

Procter & Gamble entered into a joint venture with three China-based organizations in 1988 to produce and sell dishwashing detergents, shampoo, bath foam, and other personal care products in China. Until then, P&G sold small quantities of its products through "friendship stores," which exist mostly to serve foreign visitors. The joint venture included provisions for manufacturing the products in China.

The shift toward deregulation and more of a market-driven system is producing enormous change and conflict in China. There are major issues about the proper role of marketing activities, however.[49]

Japan Japan is smaller in land area than California and smaller in population than other nations. Yet its 123 million people consume more goods and services than every other country in the world, except one. The population of Japan is also aging more rapidly than in any other country.

Land is perhaps the most scarce and valuable resource in Japan. Japan also lacks petroleum and other natural resources. Japan's major assets are its culture and its people, which have both contributed to the development of its powerhouse economy.

Opportunities for non-Japanese firms will increase in the future perhaps as never before because of the emphatic shift in the Japanese economy to consumer goods. Wealth and economic power have been accumulated by efforts to stimulate export of goods, but a combination of accumulated affluence, world pressure to encourage more imports by Japan, and the relative inefficiency of consumer goods distributed in Japan is creating the opportunity for European and North American consumer goods firms to export more to Japan in the future.

Limited space does not permit close examination of the Japanese market; however, Table 23.7 examines how Americans and Japanese view each other. Americans were asked about their feelings toward the Japanese on the specific attributes shown in the table, while the Japanese were asked about their view of Americans on each attribute. Japanese culture has received much attention in other places.[50] We will look, however, at how advertising is affected by consumer behavior in Japan.

TABLE 23.7 Americans and Japanese: How They See Each Other

Attribute	American View	Japanese View
Which of the following do you admire the most about Japan (asked of American respondents)/America (for Japanese respondents)?		
1. Form of Government	23%	63%
2. Freedom of Expression	27	89
3. Variety of Lifestyles	25	86
4. Industriousness	88	27
5. Educational Institutes	71	48
6. Leisure Time Available to Workers	15	88
7. Respect for Family Life	75	87
8. Treatment of Women	20	68
Which of the following words describe what people in Japan (asked of Americans)/in America (asked of Japanese) are like?		
1. Friendly	59%	64%
2. Competitive	94	50
3. Devoted to Fair Play	35	43
4. Lazy	4	21
5. Crafty	68	13
6. Poorly Educated	12	21
Which country will be the strongest economic power 10 years from now?		
1. United States	51%	14%
2. Japan	27	35
3. Other	11	30

Source: "Japan in the Mind of America, America in the Mind of Japan," *Time* 139 (February 10, 1992), 16–23.

Japanese Advertising   The purpose of advertising is the same in Japan as it is in the West—to stimulate consumption. In Japan, however, one tries not to upset people. Outspoken opinions are not welcome. Advertising reflects a concern for harmony to the extent that Westerners often fail to understand the message of a particular advertisement. Rather than pushing for a sale, the underlying idea is that the more the advertisement pleases customers, the more likely it is to move the product.

Japanese consumers react more to beautiful background scenery, a star of the entertainment world, or the development of a story than to product recommendations. Among younger consumers especially, the presence of American pop culture in advertising is influential in the buying decision. Japanese viewers dislike garrulous and argumentative sales talk. Product information should be short and conveyed with a song that sets a mood. The great majority of Japanese TV commercials are directed toward affective rather than cognitive components of attitude. This is an important point for foreign manufacturers more accustomed to the American hard-sell advertisements. Japanese advertising is more likely to develop a story, describe the expression of people, and enhance poetically the mood of the product. The product message comes at the end of the commercial, almost as an afterthought to the rest of the commercial.

Commercials in Japan constructed around a comparison of products are virtually nonexistent. Commercial practices are based, at least at the visible level, on the principle of respect for one another. Attacking and putting down a rival openly is avoided. Comparative advertising is not permitted by the Advertising Code, which explains, "Let us avoid slandering, defaming and attacking others."[51] Marketing programs in Japan are strongly influenced by Confucianism, which places high value on self-esteem, reciprocity, and harmony. Rudeness is intolerable even to the point that polite lies are acceptable rather than the expression of contradictory opinions. From Buddhism, values are also derived leading to a need for simplicity and a dominant aesthetic sense as well as loyalty and satisfaction in interpersonal relationships.[52]

The Communist-Capitalist Continuum

Communism challenged capitalism for half a century as a viable method of organizing society and markets. It crumbled rapidly in recent years. When a new flag was raised in Moscow in 1992, it symbolized much more than a change from one nation to another. It symbolized change from centralized control of the soviet republics and, in reality, many other countries throughout the world to decentralized nations representing a continuum of approaches to government and market control. Although bastions of communism remain in places such as Cuba and North Korea, other nations such as China had begun the trek toward more market control, while Russia and other republics as well as most of Eastern Europe were steaming ahead to something other than central planning.

Russia and the Republics   Russia and other former members of the Union of Soviet Socialist Republics offer some of the most challenging markets in the world. Together they are a huge market, industrially developed in some ways, with enough spending power to represent one of the great growth markets of the future. The "iffy" part of the scenario is whether or not that spending power can change from one market centrally planned for the production of industrial and defense goods to one capable of producing and distributing large amounts of consumer goods and services in a market-driven economy.

The change in direction was stimulated by policies advocated by Mikhail Gorbachev and his advocacy of *glasnost* and *perestroika*—the opening up of society.[53] In these restructured economies, the goal is to achieve market-directed production with an emphasis on more consumer goods. In the long run, market efficiencies and higher motivation should lead to a higher standard of living if the society can survive the suffering and starvation associated with the transition. There was no entrepreneurial culture under either the Communists or the czars. Developing such a culture is essential in a market-driven society but achieving that quickly enough to prevent collapse of the production and distribution of such essential products as food and energy is an issue of monumental proportions.

Advertising is both a blessing and a bane in Russia and the former Soviet Republics. On the one hand, there are few consumer goods to buy. Even the Russian products, whose poor quality was a staple of Russian humor, are not very available. Yet, on the other hand, the sudden opening of market possibilities and the lure of hard currency have led to the appearance of advertisements in most of the media for these virtually nonexistent products. A general euphoria about advertising has given way to a recognition of many problems: the absence of a precise advertising policy, the shortage of specialists, and the lack of a code of ethical norms for advertising. They have resulted in Soviet television viewers being bombarded with low-quality advertising and rejection by consumers on the basis that the gap between advertising and real life is too great.[54]

The market structure of the former U.S.S.R. is complicated. There are two, or more, major groups separated more or less as Slavic and non-Slavic. European-oriented Russia has provided leadership and much of the population. At the same time, there is a tremendous increase in the Muslim republics of Central Asia and their high birth rates. In Russia and most Eastern European countries, a high proportion of women is employed in the labor force, often in the professions. That fact, and the traditional system of labor-intensive distribution (reflecting a political philosophy that emphasizes labor rather than capital), has created a massive demand for labor-saving appliances and services.

Shopping is usually an arduous and time-consuming activity. Shortages and high prices are characteristics of the buying environment. Coffee has skyrocketed in price. Toilet paper is chronically in short supply, requiring consumers to use substitutes such as newspaper ripped in square pieces. Laundry soap has virtually disappeared except for a few luxury brands.[55]

About 65 percent of Soviet households have a refrigerator, 55 percent have a washing machine, 38 percent have a television, and 40 percent have a radio.[56] With one of the lowest ownership levels of refrigerators of any country in the world, and one of the most advanced technological capacities in such areas as nuclear engineering and theoretical physics, significant opportunities surely must exist for growth. These probably will occur from joint ventures and other market development strategies with firms from other countries. Success is possible. Consumer in Focus 23.4 describes one of the most famous of those successes, McDonald's.

Youth lead the way to change in most societies. In Russia and other republics of the Confederation, this principle appears to be true. Western consumer goods such as jeans and boomboxes dramatized alternative lifestyles before perestroika. Rock lyrics and ads for Western beauty products also offer teenagers formulas to express their search for love. To some extent, the intensity of Soviet youth culture is owed, as in many other developing countries, to relatively recent massive migration to the cities.

Consumer in Focus **23.4**

Expansion into the Wild, Wild East

McDonald's Corporation opened its 12,418th location in 1991, marking yet another "McMilestone" in the firm's 33-year history, during which it grew from a single hamburger joint to a household word across the country and around the world. In recent years McDonald's has focused its marketing efforts on foreign market expansion, with foreign sales more than tripling since 1980 to 7.41 billion in 1991 representing 37 percent of total sales.

Perhaps the most significant event in McDonald's history, however, occurred in 1990 when Moscow became the new home for the world famous golden arches. Fast food took on new meaning as enthusiastic patrons waited 2½ hours for their "Beeg Maks" even as staffers served an average of 5,000 sandwiches an hour. But even after 4 hours at this hectic pace, the Soviet staffers served up salty, golden fries and polite smiles. For Soviet consumers used to frowning, unfriendly retail clerks, this was a welcome change and a reason to revisit McDonald's.

McDonald's expected an overwhelming demand for its "taste of the U.S." in the Soviet market, but was surprised at the 30,000 meals per day sales figure when it opened. Stunned might best describe the reaction of managers at the more recent figure of 50,000 meals per day making this store, operated by a Canadian McDonald's franchisee, the busiest store in the chain, at least until an even larger store opened in China.

Among the reasons for its success, McDonald's executives point to the firm's commitment to local communities. Since many of the food supplies needed for the traditional McDonald's hamburger and fries were not available in Moscow, it built a $50 million food factory in Moscow and taught Soviets how to produce the potatoes needed for good fries. These steps ensured consistency among McDonald's meals from store to store and country to country, a key to its long-term success. It also aided in the development of this foreign market as a long-term investment, a key to McDonald's continued worldwide growth.

Sources: American Marketplace (March 31, 1988), 9, 49; "No fast food in Moscow," Columbus *Dispatch* (July 21, 1990), 2H; and McDonald's Corporation 1991 Annual Report.

Eastern Europe   Eastern European economies are opening up for trade with the rest of the world, some with much more success than others. Hungary has been among the most receptive to a market economy, especially for tourism and other industries that bring hard currency quickly. Poland generates high interest in the

United States for trading relationships but the country suffers from massive debt along with severe shortages and sweeping price hikes. Czechoslovakia and Romania have stimulated interest among many global firms as offering significant opportunities for companies that serve consumers well and can develop market-oriented strategies.

The attractiveness of Eastern European markets for global marketers is the similarity with preferences of Western consumers. The most desired durable products in Eastern Europe are Western cars (58 percent), video recorders (42 percent), and microwaves (35 percent) while the most wanted nondurables are perfume and athletic shoes. Television viewing is the most frequent leisure-time activities but 85 percent of East Europeans shop every day, spending an average of 2 hours a day.[57]

Companies such as Procter & Gamble are now significant marketers in countries such as Hungary, Poland, and Czechoslovakia. Products include Pampers disposable diapers and Blend-a-Med toothpaste in Hungary, Vidal Sassoon Wash & Go shampoo and Pampers in Poland, and Vizir and Ariel laundry detergents in Czechoslovakia through the acquisition of a leading producer of detergents and cleaning products. All brands are backed by TV advertising from international advertising agencies with creative strategies that avoid authoritarian approaches that might offend sensitivities of consumer developed in the past 40 years. Unlike marketing in North America, all advertising for P&G carries the P&G logo and emphasizes corporate identity in order to develop a degree of credibility for future product introductions.[58]

European Single Market

The European Community or EC set the beginning of 1993 as the time when its 12 members become a free internal market. People, money, and goods are supposed to move across borders without passports, exchange controls, or customs. As this is accomplished, Europe becomes a larger single market than the United States.

As you saw earlier in this chapter, population growth slowed or has become nonexistent in Europe. But from Euro-stagnation of the early 1980s, countries have unified economically in an attempt to develop efficiencies and growth in the 1990s in a way that well may be the pattern for a North American Common Market in the future. Factories become more efficient as they serve a market of 344 million people expected to purchase $4 trillion in goods and services. Greater efficiencies in the physical movement of goods and the financial movement of funds are some of the results of the single market. The result is also tougher competition for many firms as companies take a Europe-wide approach to marketing. You can see how one of the most successful marketers in the world, Mars, markets in Europe in Consumer in Focus 23.5.

The EC consists of 12 members: Britain, Ireland, Denmark, Germany, France, Spain, Portugal, Italy, Greece, Belgium, the Netherlands, and Luxembourg. A "White Paper" was adopted in 1985 containing the 300 legislative changes needed to create the single European market on December 31, 1992. Some of the benefits of the EC have been extended to the seven members of the European Free Trade

Consumer in Focus 23.5

Mars Lands in Europe

Smart marketers began to take advantage of the burgeoning opportunities in Europe some time ago. Many have switched to European factories, moved marketing to a more pan-European basis, and aligned brands' ad agencies across the region.

Mars, for instance, has been furiously renaming established local brand names for confectionery and pet foods. Previously, the marketer used a variety of local names. Mars has made pan-European advertising and packaging a priority.

After renaming Marathon candy bars in the U.K. to Snickers, the name already used on the Continent, Mars is now changing the name of its Raider candy bars on the Continent to Twix, which is the U.K. and U.S. name. TV spots by Backer Spielvogel Bates Europe announced the rebranding of Raider in nine Continent countries.

On the pet food side, Mars followed up massive rebranding with the creation of Mars Europet, overseeing everything from marketing to accounting for key pet food brands across Europe. Pedigree is run from Germany, Kit-e-Kat and Whiskas cat foods from the U.K., and Sheba premium cat and Cesar premium dog food from France.

In recent years, all Mars European pet food and confectionery advertising has been realigned with Backer, Grey Advertising, D'Arcy Masius Benton & Bowles, and Saatchi & Saatchi Advertising.

Source: Excerpted from Laurel Wentz, "Europe: How Smart Marketers Cash In," *Advertising Age* (December 2, 1991), S-1.

Association (EFTA) consisting of Austria, Finland, Iceland, Liechtenstein, Norway, Sweden, and Switzerland, possibly setting the stage for those countries' full integration into the common market. If all of the countries that have expressed interest in joining the EC were to do so, the number of members would be about 25.

Increasingly, business managers and some consumers are referring to themselves as "we Europeans" rather than the national identity. Borders between countries may have only a sign noting the country but featuring the EC symbol prominently. Firms are beginning to do the same. Notice the point-of-purchase sign for Miele (a European appliance manufacturer) in Figure 23.7, which carries the EC emblem. Also notice that the company has chosen words to describe its product that can be readily understood by consumers regardless of whether their first language is German, Dutch, English, or a romance language.

FIGURE 23.7   **Euromarketing by Miele**

The largest market in the world is now the EC. The dominant force in that market is Germany, which receives its importance not only for its role in the EC but for its favorable position to trade with Eastern Europe and the former Soviet republics. Although Brussels is the capital city of the EC, from a marketing perspective Berlin may well be the capital of all of Europe. For this reason, we conclude this chapter with a closer look at the economic power that is emerging as a new world super power, alongside the United States and Japan.

Unified Germany

Germany has undergone drastic changes in almost every measurable area including population, average income, average age, even geographical size of the country. Consumer analysts forecast growth in other countries; reunification achieved it almost instantly. The German economy and corporations have had to adjust to the addition of 17 million people to increase its population base to roughly 78 million, 20 million stronger than the next largest European country, Italy with 58 million.

German corporations are increasing profits at rates comparable or faster than their U.S. and Japanese counterparts but with substantially different methods and radically different effects on employee lifestyles. These differences are of particular interest to consumer analysts who increasingly study consumption as well as buying behavior.

The German form of capitalism is somewhere between the Japanese form of government, which promotes business, and the American form, which regulates business. The blend of business, government, and unions based on a structured value system has created a standard of living that is among the highest in the world and a quality of life for the masses of workers that would be the envy of most of the elite in the world. Germans do not have as high per capita income as Japanese but have large homes, excellent food, world-class cars, fast highways, environmentally concerned cities ringed by green forests, and very good beer!

The German market has created its high standard of living without giving up the one resource that Japanese and Americans have the least: leisure. As you may recall from Chapter 8, 80 percent of American workers would trade lower pay for more leisure. The Germans already have the leisure with a standard work week of 37½ hours and vacations mandated by law at 4 weeks but that are commonly 6 to 8 weeks. Leisure products from spas to boats are booming. While Americans are still more productive than anyone in the world, Germans are closing the gap fast with productivity gains faster than in the United States or Japan.

Does reunification translate into a liability or an opportunity for marketing in Germany? East Germany could be characterized as 17 million people with the need and desire to buy everything. Under communist rule they sometimes had the money, but lacked available goods to buy. Since reunification they lack many of the resources needed to satiate their appetite for goods, but they are willing to work to gain resources to spend. As Eastern Germans are brought into the reunified economy, they become a large, viable market for almost every type of product from cars to fresh fruit. Trade barriers of the EC somewhat guarantee they won't buy too many Toyotas. The question is will they buy Volkswagens or Fords?

Germany has made economic sacrifices in the short term to invest in its long-run future which include a new labor supply made up of people with similar values and good positioning for market dominance in other Eastern European countries. Figure 23.8 shows an ad sponsored by the Economics Ministry of the Federal Republic of Germany to further the understanding of the New Federal States of Germany and its goals and stimulate investment in its future. In the long run it will be recognized that culture and language form a bond among people that not even walls can destroy. It is values that make a country wealthy, not its natural resources.

Global Thinking—A Final Perspective

Perhaps the most important aspect of global thinking is not knowledge of how to sell in other countries or how to source in other countries. Those are very important but even more important is the ability to understand marketing and management globally, to adopt the best methods from around the globe, and to avoid the worst. A study of firms that are successful around the world—Coca-Cola, Unilever, Toyota,

MADE IN GERMANY

For decades, the words "Made in W. Germany" have set the global standard for product excellence. And for decades, West Germany has been equal to the challenge this standard implies.

Now we face a new challenge. By dropping the 'W,' we extend this mark of excellence to include the New Federal States of Germany. And in realizing this aim, we create investment opportunities of unparalleled proportion for companies large and small around the globe.

Find out how you can put "Made in Germany" to work for you. For information on investment incentives and opportunities in the New Federal States of Germany, please give us a call at 1-800-551-8545 (U.S. and Canada).

THE NEW FEDERAL STATES OF GERMANY

For on-the-spot information about investment opportunities in the New Federal States, you can also call our new Foreign Investor Information Center in Berlin directly at 011-49-30-39985-100

© Economics Ministry of the Federal Republic of Germany.

FIGURE 23.8   Ad for German New Federal States

and Aldi—helps to achieve this goal. Aldi is a family owned grocery chain based in Germany, but which operates in many countries including the United States. It is a niche player, however, and its niche is the cost sensitive segment whether that be in the cities of the U.S. or the rural villages of the Benelux. How does a firm keep its prices dramatically lower than the competition throughout the world? By unrelenting pressure to lower costs. Look at Figure 23.9 and you will see a shopper selecting a shopping cart in an Aldi supermarket. There is an interesting detail. She must first place a coin into the cart before taking it. The coin is refunded when the cart is returned from the parking lot. A small idea but think of the reduction in labor costs (from pushing the carts back from the parking lot), reduction in theft, and reduction in maintenance costs because the carts are not left out in bad weather. Perhaps the idea would not work in affluent suburbs of the U.S.—but that's not Aldi's market segment, although it does attract some members of this group.

Too often American business managers have been ethnocentric or simply unaware of management and marketing solutions around the world. Consumer analysts need the skills to lead the way in understanding behavior on a cross-cultural basis.

FIGURE 23.9 **Cost Reduction with Coin-Operated Shopping Carts**

Summary

Consumer behavior analysts are increasingly required to understand buying and consumption decisions on a global basis. Population growth is slowing so rapidly in industrialized countries that consumer analysts must find and understand the cultures of new markets that have both population vitality and ability to buy.

The fastest-growing country in the world population is India. African countries such as Kenya and Nigeria have rapid population growth but low income. The search for markets that have both population growth as well as good or improving economic conditions often leads to the Pacific Rim.

Cross-cultural analysis is the systematic comparison of similarities and differences in the behavioral and physical aspects of cultures. Cross-cultural analysis provides an approach to understanding market segments both across national boundaries and between groups within a society. The process of analyzing markets on a cross-cultural basis is particularly helpful in deciding which elements of a marketing program can be standardized in multiple nations and which elements must be localized.

Major changes in markets are caused by the continuum of change found in countries that formerly were communist and are now moving toward capitalism. Russia and its fellow republics provide a hope for huge markets in the future because of the size of the nations and the historical base of technology although currently there is enormous suffering and struggle due to the inefficiencies of the distribution system. Eastern European countries provide some of the best opportunities for purchase of Western products and services produced and marketed by global marketing organizations.

Europe (EC) is now the largest market in the world with 344 million people in 12 countries. The addition of EFTRA creates more market opportunities and potentially this market could encompass as many as 25 countries. The economic powerhouse of this area and increasingly the world is reunified Germany. Germany has solved one of the classic consumption problems. Not only has it achieved a high level of economic resources for its citizens approaching the level of the U.S. and Japan, Germany has also achieved the goal of providing leisure by developing an economy that achieves productivity levels that permit large amounts of leisure time.

Review and Discussion Questions

1. Is it really necessary to "think globally" in the study of consumer behavior? Why?
2. Which countries of the world will provide the best consumer markets in the next 5 to 10 years? In the next 10 to 30 years? Why?
3. How do you reconcile the belief that India represents an attractive market when Table 23.4 reports such a low per capita GNP?
4. Assume that a soft drink marketer wanted to enter the Russian market. Prepare a set of recommendations for doing so.
5. Assume that a manufacturer of shoes wishes a market analysis on how to enter the most profitable markets in Africa. What should be included in the report?
6. Assume that a French manufacturer of women's apparel is seeking to expand markets by exporting to Canada or the United States. What would you recommend for maximum effectiveness?
7. What is meant by the term cross-cultural analysis? Why is it important for marketers?
8. What are the opportunities for trade or joint ventures in Russia or other former Soviet republics? What are the major elements that you would include in a market analysis of such ventures?
9. "If a firm were entering Europe now, it should probably place its headquarters in Berlin." Evaluate this statement.

Endnotes

1. Michael E. Porter, ed., *Competition in Global Industries* (Cambridge, Mass.: Harvard Business School Press, 1986).
2. "Three Small Businesses Profit by Taking on the World," *Wall Street Journal* (November 8, 1990), B2.
3. Ibid.
4. 1991 World Population Data Sheet, Population Reference Bureau, Inc. (1991).

5. Thomas W. Merrick, "World Population in Transition," *Population Bulletin* 41 (April 1986), 3.

6. Ben J. Wattenberg, *Birth Dearth* (New York: Pharos Books, 1987).

7. *Trends & Opportunities Abroad, 1988* (Ithaca, N.Y.: American Demographics, Inc., 1988), 1.

8. Bryant Robey, "Some Numbing Numbers," *American Demographics* 6 (April 1984), 11. For additional discussion on world population trends, see Rafael M. Salas, "Beyond 2000: State of the World Population," *Populi: Journal of the U.S. Fund for Population Activities* 8 (1981), 3–11.

9. World Population Data Sheet (published annually) (Washington, D.C.: Population Reference Bureau, Inc.). Data presented in Table 23.4 are from 1987.

10. Robert Prus, *Pursuing Customers: An Ethnography of Marketing Activities* (Newbury Park, Calif.: Sage Publications, 1989).

11. Charles F. Keown, Nicolas Synodinos, Laurence Jacobs, and Reginald Worthley, "Can International Advertising Be Standardized?" World Congress of the Academy of Marketing Sciences, Barcelona, 1987. For a macroeconomic perspective on this issue, see Seymour Banks, "Cross-National Analysis of Advertising Expenditures," *Journal of Advertising Research* 26 (April/May 1986), 11–23.

12. "Colonel serves test breakfast in Singapore," *Marketing News* 25 (June 10, 1991), 6.

13. Kamran Kashani, "Beware the Pitfalls of Global Marketing,"*Harvard Business Review* (September–October 1989), 97.

14. James Wills, Coskun A. Samli, and Laurence Jacobs, "Developing Global Products and Marketing Strategies: A Construct and a Research Agenda," *Journal of the Academy of Marketing Science* 19 (Winter 1991), 7.

15. An introduction to cross-cultural methods is found in R. W. Bristin, W. J. Lonner, and R. M. Thorndike, *Cross-Cultural Research Methods* (New York: John Wiley & Sons, 1973), and Walter J. Lonner and John W. Berry, *Field Methods in Cross-Cultural Research* (Beverly Hills: Sage Publications, 1986).

16. Erik Elinder, "How International Can European Advertising Be?" *Journal of Marketing* 29 (April 1965), 7–11.

17. Theodore Levitt, "The Globalization of Markets," *Harvard Business Review* 61 (May–June 1983), 92–102. For the contrasting perspective see Yoram Wind, "The Myth of Globalization," *Journal of Consumer Marketing* 3 (Spring 1986), 23–26.

18. James Leontiades, "Going Global—Global Strategies vs. National Strategies," *Long Range Planning* 19 (1986), 96–104.

19. Robert D. Buzzell, "Can You Standardize Multinational Marketing?" *Harvard Business Review* 46 (November–December 1986), 102–113; Theodore Levitt, "The Globalization of Markets," *Harvard Business Review* 61 (May–June 1983), 92–102; "Multinationals Tackle Global Marketing," *Advertising Age* (June 25, 1984), 50ff. Also see "Marketers Turn Sour on Global Sales Pitch Harvard Guru Makes," *Wall Street Journal* (May 11, 1988), 1.

20. Ralph Z. Sorenson and Ulrich E. Wiechmann, "How Multinationals View Marketing Standardization," *Harvard Business Review* 53 (May–June 1975), 38–56. Also see William H. Davidson and Philippe Haspeslagh, "Shaping a Global Product Organization," *Harvard Business Review* 60 (July–August 1982), 125–132.

21. Arthur Fatt, "The Danger of 'Local' International Advertising," *Journal of Marketing* 31 (January 1967), 60–62.

22. Roger Blackwell, Riad Ajami, and Kristina Stephan, "Winning the Global Advertising Race: Planning Globally, Acting Locally," *Journal of International Consumer Marketing* 3 (1991), 108.

23. Ibid.

24. For an in-depth description of what can go wrong in global market situations see David Ricks, *Big Business Blunders: Mistakes in Multinational Marketing* (Homewood, Ill.: Dow Jones-Irwin, 1983). A valuable guide to avoiding global blunders is found in Vern Terpstra and Kenneth David, *The Cultural Environment of International Business* (Cincinnati: South-Western Publishing, 1985).

25. Kevin Lynch, "Adplomancy Faux Pas Can Ruin Sales," *Advertising Age* (January 15, 1979), S-2ff, and "When Slogans Go Wrong," *American Demographics* 14 (February 1992), 14.

26. Richard W. Brislin, "Back-Translation for Cross-Cultural Research," *Journal of Cross-Cultural Psychology* 1 (September 1970); Oswald Werner and Donald T. Campbell, "Translating, Working through Interpreters and the Problems of Decentering," in Raoul Naroll and Ronald Cohen, eds., *A Handbook of Method in Cultural Anthropology* (Garden City, N.Y.: National History Press, 1970), 298–420.

27. "Firms Pick Their Names to Fit New Global Economy," *Marketing News* 24 (October 1, 1990), 2.

28. Walter P. Margulies, "Why Global Marketing Requires a Global Focus on Product Design," *Business Abroad* 94 (January 1969), 22.

29. Karen A. Berger, Barbara B. Stern, and J. K. Johansson, "Strategic Implications of a Cross-Cultural Comparison of Attribute Importance: Automobiles in Japan and the United States," in *Proceedings of the American Marketing Association Educators' Conference* (Chicago: American Marketing Association, 1983), 327–332.

30. Cyndee Miller, "Anybody Ever Hear of Global Focus Groups?" *Marketing News* 25 (May 27, 1991), 14.

31. Alfred S. Boote, "Psychographic Segmentation in Europe," *Journal of Advertising Research* 22 (December 1982), 19–25.

32. Robert T. Green, Jean-Paul Leonardi, Jean-Louis Chandon, Isabella C. M. Cunningham, Bronis Verhage, and Alain Strazzieri, "Societal Development and Family Purchasing Roles: A Cross-National Study," *Journal of Consumer Research* 9 (March 1983), 436–442.

33. For details of this methodology see Bernald Berelson, *Content Analysis in Communications Research* (New York: Free Press, 1952); and Klaus Krippendorff, *Content Analysis* (Beverly Hills: Sage Publications, 1980).

34. Eugene J. Webb et al., *Unobtrusive Measures* (Chicago: Rand McNally, 1966).

35. Harold H. Kassarjian, "The Negro and American Advertising, 1946–1965," *Journal of Marketing* 6 (February 1969), 29–39.

36. Richard W. Pollay, "The Identification and Distribution of Values Manifest in Print Advertising 1900–1980," in Robert E. Pitts, Jr., and Arch G. Woodside, eds., *Personal Values and Consumer Psychology* (Lexington, Mass.: Lexington Books, 1984), 111–135.

37. John Naisbitt, *Megatrends* (New York: Warner Books, 1982).

38. "Business Without Borders," *U.S. News & World Report* 104 (June 20, 1988), 48–53.

39. "Caged, A survey of India," *The Economist* 319 (May 4, 1991).

40. Anthony Spaeth, "A Thriving Middle Class Is Changing the Face of India," *Wall Street Journal* (May 19, 1988), 22.

41. Spaeth, "A Thriving Middle Class Is Changing the Face of India."

42. K. Ambarish Kumar and C. P. Rao, "Problems of Researching Household Consumer Behavior in India," World Congress of the Academy of Marketing Sciences, Barcelona, 1987.

43. Arvind Singhal and Everett M. Rogers, *India's Information Revolution* (Newbury Park, Calif.: Sage, 1989).

Consumer Analysis and Marketing Strategy

Part 6 provides further testimony to the importance of understanding behavior in developing sound marketing strategy. The following full-color ads, as explained by the short description accompanying each, illustrate the role of consumer analysis in developing marketing strategy and action.

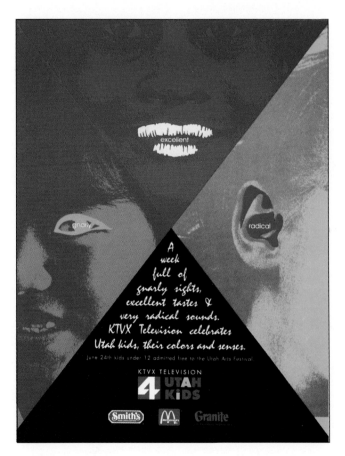

Consumer Trends

Beginning in the late 1960s, artists and musicians began to gather in festivals to show their works and perform. These festivals now draw millions to their vending booths and performances across the United States and Canada. The Utah Arts Festival includes creative activities for children as an added incentive to attend.

Can we arrest the disease that robs people of their minds?

Over 4 million people suffer from it, and nearly half of all nursing home patients are its victims.

It's Alzheimer's, the disease that steals a person's mind, dignity and independence, and exacts costs of over $88 billion a year for institutional and home care.

Leading the way in the search for relief from this mysterious disease is the pharmaceutical industry, which is making the nation's largest investment in drug research.

Since 1988 alone, the industry has been conducting research on over 40 medicines for Alzheimer's, and currently has 13 in test. While these efforts hold hope for breakthroughs, the process is long and difficult, with only a few of the thousands of compounds developed ever achieving success.

This exhaustive, high risk research increases the industry's cost of doing business, and in turn the price of drugs. But it also leads to the kind of discoveries that can break the grip of an enormously costly disease like Alzheimer's.

To learn more about pharmaceutical research, and the critical role it plays in health care, call or write for our free booklet, "Good Medicine."

The Pharmaceutical Manufacturers Association, 1100 15th St, NW, Box N, Wash., DC 20005. 1-800-538-2692.

PHARMACEUTICALS
Good Medicine For Containing Health Costs.

Segmentation

Pharmaceuticals Manufacturers Association explains the value of pharmaceuticals to the mature market. The ad includes photography, subject matter, and facts of keen interest to the target audience, portrayed in very human terms.

Diffusion of Innovation

Apple's PowerBook™ addresses several different expressed computer customer needs: portability, versatility, adaptability, implied power, and implied cost consciousness. Apple has created an innovative product by packaging all these potential competitive advantages in one product. Because several laptop computers were on the market before Apple's entry, PowerBook™ is an example of *dynamically continuous innovation*.

WAS TRAGEN SIE DIESEN SOMMER?

Das BMW M3 Cabrio aus der 3er-Reihe. Kauf, Finanzierung oder Leasing – Ihr BMW Händler ist der richtige Partner. BMW in Btx ✱ 20900 #

Freude am Fahren

Global Consumer Markets

Similar appeals work for similar market segments worldwide. The German ad copy translates, "What are you wearing this summer?" This appeal to fashion consciousness is an appropriate offer to the affluent in any nation.

44. Inder Khera, "The Broadening Base of U.S. Consumer Acceptance of Korean Products," World Congress of the Academy of Marketing Science, Barcelona, 1987.

45. Grame Hugo, *Australia's Changing Population: Trends and Implications* (Oxford: Oxford University Press, 1987).

46. Jeffrey R. Taylor and Karen A. Hardee, *Consumer Demand in China* (Boulder: Westview Press, 1986).

47. Doris L. Walsh, "Refrigerators Top List in China," *American Demographics* 9 (October 1986), 49.

48. Jerry Stafford, "Vast China Market Just Waiting to Be Researched," *Marketing News* 20 (September 12, 1986), 1.

49. Richard Semenik, Nan Zhou, and William Moore, "Chinese Managers' Attitude Toward Advertising in China," *Journal of Advertising* 15 (1986).

50. The classic book to understand Japanese culture for business persons is probably William Ouchi, *Theory Z* (New York: Addison-Wesley, 1981).

51. This section abstracted from Dentsu Incorporated, *Marketing Opportunity in Japan* (London: McGraw-Hill, 1978), 84–114. Dentsu is one of the largest advertising agencies in the world.

52. Walter A. Henry, "Impact of Cultural Value Systems on Japanese Distribution Systems," in Robert E. Pitts, Jr., and Arch G. Woodside, *Personal Values and Consumer Psychology* (Lexington, Mass.: Lexington Books, 1984), 255–270.

53. Mikhail Gorbachev, *Perestroika: New Thinking for Our Country and the World* (New York: Harper & Row, 1988).

54. Svetlana Kolesnik, "Advertising and Cultural Politics," *Journal of Communication* 41 (Spring 1991), 46–54.

55. "Why the Bear's Cupboards Are Bare," *Time* (January 16, 1989), 33–36.

56. *Trends and Opportunities Abroad, 1988*, 190.

57. Perestroika: The Consumer Signals," *Euromarketing Insights* 2 (February 1991), 4.

58. Jennifer Lawrence, "P&G Marches into E. Europe," *Advertising Age* (September 30, 1991), 10.

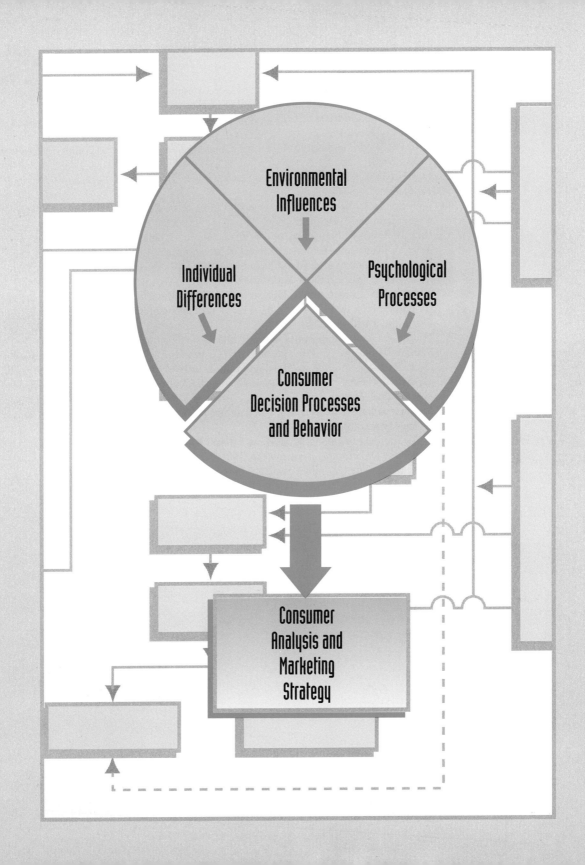

Environmental
Influences

Individual
Differences

Psychological
Processes

Consumer
Decision Processes
and Behavior

Consumer
Analysis and
Marketing
Strategy

PART 7

Epilogue

No study of consumer behavior would be complete without careful reflection from the broader perspective of ethics and consumer rights. Chapter 24 looks at basic consumer rights that must be guaranteed and affirmed by an economic system and its agencies that take consumer interests seriously.

There are many implications. We challenge you to think seriously about your own sense of ethics and moral values. The choices you make can have far-reaching implications.

24

Consumerism and Ethical Responsibility

A federal judge soon will be hearing from Kellogg Co. and General Foods about raisins, specifically about the fact there's sugar-coating on the raisins in Kellogg's Raisin Bran and no sugar on the raisins in Post Natural Raisin Bran. But he'll also be hearing that there *is* sugar in the Post cereal, even though it doesn't happen to be on the raisins.

According to GF's own Consumer Nutrition Center, there are nine grams of sugar per 1-oz. serving of Post Natural Raisin Bran. That happens to be the same amount of sugar in the Kellogg's cereal. Does John Denver know that? There he is, wholesomely pitching Post's "naturally sweet" raisins in TV commercials, but failing to mention that the cereal itself is unnaturally sweet because it has added sugar.

A lot of people who aren't sitting around on a Rocky Mountain peak now do know of this advertising weasel. It has become part of a public squabble between two major manufacturers. The advertising business has already been found guilty. Consumer respect and trust is lost because Post and its ad agency sought to create the impression that Post Natural Raisin Bran doesn't contain sugar.

This is another example of an ad claim blowing up in our faces. It was supposed to set one product apart from a competitor's, but because the claim was strained and artificial, it boomeranged. Consumers who insist "you can't believe advertising" sure are going to make a hot three-course meal out of this cold break-fast cereal controversy.

Source: "Sour Grapes from Sweet Raisins." Editorial reprinted with permission from *Advertising Age* (September 7, 1987), 16. Copyright Crain Communications, Inc. All rights reserved.

This *Advertising Age* editorial titled "Sour Grapes" quickly found its way around the ranks of the account executives at a Philadelphia advertising agency. Not surprisingly, it became the subject of many coffee break discussions.

Let's listen in on one:

SARAH: This is disgusting and makes me ashamed to be in this business. I'm glad *Ad Age* socked it to them. It's about time some of us speak out.

TED: Wait a minute—get off your high horse. This kind of thing is done every day.

SARAH: That's my point exactly. It is done every day, and it's tarring us all with a bad brush.

TED: Yeah, what makes you so high and mighty? Those Post guys were dead right when they nailed Kellogg for those sugar-coated raisins.

SARAH: I can't believe what I'm hearing. They're making it look like Post is sugar free, and that's an outright lie.

TED: That's not a lie. All they said is that there's no sugar on *the raisins* in Post Raisin Bran. And that's the absolute truth.

SARAH: Look hot shot, their claim can only be interpreted one way—Post is sugar free when it isn't. A lie is a lie no matter how you try to cover it up. And that's wrong!

TED: So, Ms. Lily White, you're one of those purists, huh? Show me what law was violated. Was the consumer in any way hurt? After all, anyone with common sense would look at the box, and Post says right there that they added sugar.

SARAH: For crying out loud, who looks at the box? Don't all consumers, including you and me, have a right to expect truthful advertising? I'm glad at least one of us around here pays attention to ethics. It ticks me off plenty that they cheated me in this way. I'm not about to pull such a trick on someone else.

TED: I'm sick of moralists like you. Don't swing your personal code of ethics at me. You won't last long here if you keep that up. We've got just one duty to the client—to make as much money as possible as long as we don't break the law.

A real hot potato, isn't it? And who's right? On what basis can we decide?

Our concern in this chapter lies with ethical responsibility to the consumer—managerial behavior that is consistent with accepted standards of what is right and what is wrong. Lantos puts it this way:

Ethics can be defined as the study of morality, i.e., standards that determine what is right and wrong, good and evil, helpful or harmful, acceptable or unacceptable. It is the name given to the attempt to think through the moral implications of human actions. Ethics is concerned with any situation where there is actual or potential harm to any individual or group from a particular course of action.[1]

Although such eminent management authorities as Peter Drucker have long stressed the central role of social responsibility and ethics,[2] most evidence indicates that this has not been taken especially seriously until recently.

Fortunately business enterprises are facing a consumer uprising they cannot ignore. A movement that has become known as **consumerism** has grown from a small voice to a formidable outcry for consumer interests.

It is necessary to tackle the issues of consumerism head on because public pressure does not allow any enterprise to rest for long on its ethical haunches. If we are to do this, however, we must put in place a framework to guide ethical thinking and reasoning.

This is followed by an overview of the historical and sociological context in which consumerism has arisen. Then we discuss the basic dimensions of a proper ethical response to consumer interests. The subject of corporate and individual ethics is basic in this context.

Ethical Thinking and Reasoning*

As Sarah and Ted talked, you saw that there was little real common ground between them regarding the alleged violation by Post of the second consumer right focusing on the question of truthfulness in advertising. While many, perhaps most, readers will side with Sarah and her ethical perspective, we will also see that Ted has an ethical perspective—a different and contradictory one based on a set of different standards and reasoning.

Which ethical perspective is best? To answer this question with any degree of clarity and objectivity, we must delve a bit into the nature and premises of ethical reasoning. We recognize that some readers who have extensive background in philosophy will find our discussion unduly brief. For others, however, it hopefully will provide sufficient foundation for you to grapple with where you stand on such issues.

Three Ethical Perspectives

There are many bases or principles for ethical reasoning that have relevance for our discussion, but space limits us to only three: (1) utilitarianism, (2) justice and fairness, and (3) personal rights.

*The authors gratefully acknowledge the significant contribution of Van B. Weigel, Professor of Ethics and Economic Development at Eastern College. We also have been influenced by Geoffrey Lantos of Stonehill College. Many of his perspectives are reflected here (see Endnote 1 at the end of this chapter).

Utilitarianism   Utilitarianism has its roots in the 18th century thinking of Adam Smith, Jeremy Bentham, and John Stuart Mill. The objective is to produce the greatest good for the greatest number as opposed to the concerns of a single individual or enterprise. Moral worth is determined by the *consequences* of an act, making use of these two criteria:

1. Is there a net increase in the well being or welfare within a society?
2. Have the means used to achieve this end been *efficient*—that is, has optimal use been made of productive resources from the perspective of both the enterprise and society as a whole?

In other words, has there been a positive impact in terms of pleasure, satisfaction, and well-being in terms of a societal cost/benefit ratio?

This ethical perspective requires the following steps in reasoning:[3]

1. Identify all relevant *stakeholders* (those who are impacted in any way—consumers, workers, stockholders, and so on).
2. Identify alternative strategies.
3. Estimate the cost and benefit impact on each stakeholder group.
4. Select the option which gives the best cost/benefit outcome.

In our scenario Ted was, at least in part, thinking as a utilitarian. He was contending that the consequences of this advertising claim were mostly positive. Who was hurt? Why get uptight just because the truth was stretched a bit? Furthermore, it worked and increased the profit bottom line. Isn't that worthwhile?

Sarah, on the other hand, was using the standard that the consumer has a right to the absolute truth. To her, the act is immoral in its own right regardless of utilitarian consequences.

So who is right and who is wrong in this argument? Utilitarian theory probably will not provide a clear answer. Costs and benefits are extraordinarily hard to compute. Furthermore, it focuses only on the interests of the majority and does not explicitly take individual rights into account. Nevertheless, it provides a way of thinking that often proves helpful.

Justice and Fairness   Aristotle and Plato are traditionally considered to be the fathers of this influential perspective which holds that impartiality and fairness are the criteria for ethical decision making. Justice is attained when the benefits and burdens of society are distributed fairly to stakeholders unless there are clear and defensible reasons for differential treatment. Everyone has a right for equal opportunity and treatment. Many legal codes are rooted in this philosophy. Rules for fair treatment are established and enforced as the norms and methods for restitution.

Sarah also is using justice as a criterion in her reasoning when she contended that she and others were cheated by not having full information upfront. From her perspective this action is a moral violation. Ted, of course, was not in the least bit motivated by such an argument.

The Theory of Personal Rights   From the earliest recorded times, there has been a recognition that individuals have rights ensuring their dignity, respect, and autonomy. These are inherent within the great religions of the world and also appear in the writings of such 17th century philosophers as Hobbes, Locke, and Kant.

A *right* implies that an individual, ourself or others, is entitled to something. Often rights are captured in legal documents such as a national constitution. But they also exist in moral codes that exist apart from any legal system. Velasquez puts it this way:

> Rights are powerful devices whose main purpose is that of enabling the individual to choose freely whether to pursue certain interests or activities and of protecting those choices.[4]

Personal rights and the accompanying ethical responsibilities are expressed eloquently in the Judeo/Christian tradition in form of the familiar Golden Rule of Jesus—"Love your neighbors as you love yourself" (often rephrased as "Do unto others as you would have them do unto you"). It also is widely attested to in other religious traditions. At its heart, the Golden Rule calls for moral and ethical reasoning to be based on the highest principle that the rights of others should be paramount to our own.

One also finds a very similar expression in the writings of philosopher Immanuel Kant (1724–1804). His reasoning was based on a moral principle he referred to as the "categorical imperative" worded in this way in its original formulation: "I ought never act except in such a way that I can also will that my maxim become a universal law."[5] For Kant, the word maxim designated the basis of reasoning that shapes behavior in a particular situation. A maxim, in turn, would become a universal law if everyone based their choices upon it in a similar situation.

Here is a rephrasing that may make this principle easier to understand:

> An action is morally justifiable if and only if a person's rationale for carrying out that action in a given situation is a rationale which the person would be willing to have everyone else use in a similar situation.

Kant amplified his imperative by a second formulation worded in this way: "Act in such a way that you always treat humanity, whether in your own person or in the person of any other, never simply as a means, but always at the same time as an end."[6] In other words, *don't use others only to advance your own interests but also develop their capacity to choose for themselves.*

Can the teachings of Kant and Christ be synthesized? Many contend that they touch a common theme—*the principle of equal regard.* In other words, *the rights of others are to be viewed, at the very least, as equal to your own.* Traditional Christian teaching would take this even a step further and affirm that the highest principle is to put others' rights *above* your own. No matter how this is interpreted, the rights of others will be affirmed and protected.

Sarah is straightforward in her assertion that consumers have individual rights. Her ethical code embraces these rights and the necessity to protect them in all she does. Ted may not disagree explicitly, but it's obvious that he takes the issue of consumer rights much less seriously. What will he do when profit considerations contradict with the consumer's best interests? No doubt profit will be the determining criterion. Now he finds himself on ethical thin ice from this perspective.

The Issue of Relativism

In approaching ethical dilemmas such as the one discussed here, there always will be three standards to use in the process of reasoning regardless of the ethical perspective you embrace: (1) legal codes, (2) cultural norms and behavioral codes, and (3) moral absolutes.

Legal statutes, cultural norms, and behavioral codes are closely related. They arise through a process of regulation or consensus and are often situation- and context-specific—what applies in one situation will not necessarily apply elsewhere.

Moral absolutes, on the other hand, are universal and transcend context. They may be reflected in the law and cultural norms, but this is by no means a certainty.

Many are uneasy when moral absolutes are introduced into ethical reasoning, contending that they fall into the category of philosophical and religious moralizing, which has no place in a pluralistic world. Those who reason this way are referred to as **relativists**. They will fall back to **relativism**, which holds that morality is relative to or dependent upon some cultural, social, or personal standard—there cannot be an absolute.[7]

Certainly Ted is a moral relativist. First of all, he justified an action that skirts the borderline of many people's ethical standards by referring to "our clients' profit interests." Also, he made it quite clear that "what's right for you may not be right for me."

In one sense, relativism legitimately recognizes complexity and affirms individual diversity in ethical matters. But it also can have consequences that stifle moral reasoning because, first of all, it cuts off rational moral discourse. If "it all depends," what basis is there for any kind of serious discussion on ethics? This becomes an especially acute problem in transcultural situations.

The Nestle Corporation, for example, unexpectedly found itself enmeshed in a problem when its marketing of baby formula to third world nations began to prove successful. It could argue, on the one hand, that there are some undeniable benefits brought about through better nutrition. On the other hand, minimization of breast feeding goes against cultural mores in many societies, and there has been a strong outcry that acceptance of this product only contributes to impoverished conditions among the poor. If everything is relative, there is no ultimate basis to determine ethical validity.

Some relativists argue that we should be tolerant of everyone as long as they are acting *sincerely* and *in accord with their own belief or role expectations*. In making such a statement, however, the relativist says *always be tolerant—it all depends*. Strangely enough, tolerance now becomes expressed as an *absolute moral view* in and of itself.

Individual, social, and cultural diversity does not require that we conclude that there are no universal norms and values to guide morality. If there are no universals, ethical questions all-too-often can only be resolved as the shifting basis of arbitrary whims, biases, or traditions.

It was, in our opinion, perfectly fair game for Sarah to push Ted on his dictum that the agency's role is to make a profit for clients as long as one lives somewhere within the broad confines of the law. He ventures into troublesome territory when he puts her down and rules out further deliberation of right and wrong. In effect, he puts himself into the role of having the "highest standard."

Where Do You Stand?

You will be faced with many issues in the coming pages. How will you determine where you stand? We urge you to go beyond the law and societal norms and bring your own code of personal values to the forefront. Personal values must, of necessity, be an essential part of moral dialogue. Van Weigel offers good counsel:

> Bare ethical principles are rarely able to inspire the energy and devotion necessary for carrying them out. Just actions thrive upon the religious and moral ideals that belong to the human heritage.[8]

Back now to the dialogue about Post and Kellogg. Ted never evidenced any sensitivity to the rights and concerns of others. Sarah, on the other hand, was explicit in her embrace of justice and the Principle of Equal Regard. In so doing, she has, in our opinion, based her thinking on a standard that goes far beyond utilitarianism and narrow self-centered interests.

It is not our intent in this all-too-short ethical overview to endorse any point of view, let alone any religion or school of philosophical thought. Nevertheless, it is our hope that each reader will be challenged to reason more deeply as we explore the Consumer Bill of Rights.

Ultimately it all comes down to the individual. We have given you much to think about here and affirm your integrity in arriving at your personal code of ethics. We like the way in which Dickson has fleshed out a personal ethics checklist for managers. We present this checklist for your consideration in Figure 24.1.

You will soon discover that application of any ethical code is difficult. Terms, concepts, and outcomes must be defined precisely. Often there will be no clear answer at all. The best that any of us can do, within our own limitations, is to approach these issues with an attitude of selfless integrity.

FIGURE 24.1 **A Personal Ethics Checklist**

1. Am I violating the law? If yes, why?
2. Are the values and ethics that I am applying in business lower than those I use to guide my personal life? If yes, why?
3. Am I doing to others as I would have them do to me? If not, why not?
4. Am I willfully risking the life and limb of consumers and others by my action? If yes, why?
5. Am I willfully exploiting children, the very elderly, the illiterate, the feeble minded, naive or the poor? If yes, why?
6. Am I keeping my promises? If not, why not?
7. Am I telling the truth—all the truth? If not, why not?
8. Am I exploiting a confidence or a trust? If yes, why?
9. Am I misrepresenting my true intentions to others? If yes, why?
10. Am I loyal to those who have been loyal to me? If not, why not?
11. Have I set up others to take responsibility for any negative consequences of my action? If yes, why?
12. When it comes to a marginal call am I fair and considerate or ruthless and greedy?
13. Am I prepared to redress wrongs and fairly compensate for damages? If not, why not?
14. Are my values and ethics as expressed in my strategy offensive to certain groups? If yes, why?
15. Am I being as efficient as I can? If not, why not?

Source: Peter Dickson (unpublished manuscript. The Ohio State University, 1988).

Understanding and Responding to Consumer Rights

The consumerist voice was given its marching orders in 1962, as you may recall from Chapter 1, by President John F. Kennedy who proclaimed four basic consumer rights, which since have been expanded to six:[9]

1. *The right to safety*—protection against products or services that are hazardous to health and life.
2. *The right to be informed*—provision of facts necessary for an informed choice; protection against fraudulent, deceitful, or misleading claims.
3. *The right to choose*—assured access to a variety of products and services at competitive prices.
4. *The right to be heard (redress)*—assurance that consumer interests receive full and sympathetic consideration in formulation and implementation of regulatory policy; prompt and fair restitution.
5. *The right to enjoy a clean and healthful environment.*
6. *The right of the poor and other minorities to have their interests protected.*

A Historical Perspective

Consumerism has roots reaching far beyond the last two decades, when this name was assigned to the activities of such well-known leaders as Ralph Nader. The Bible, especially the Book of Proverbs, has many references to deceptive and irresponsible business practices. In their time, Thomas Aquinas, Martin Luther, John Calvin, and other reformers also represented a kind of consumerism. Specific attacks were made on deceptive selling practices.

A historical analysis reveals that consumerism increases most sharply when an era of rapidly rising income is followed by a decrease in real purchasing power coming from rising prices.[10] In addition, the environment must be conducive to the rise of leadership for the movement, which normally centers among those with greater-than-average wealth and income.

Alienation is another major triggering factor. It arises when the basic causes fueling consumer discontent are not dealt with satisfactorily or relief is only transitory. Feelings of powerlessness, alienation, and isolation lead essentially to defensive responses in the forms of boycotts, pressures for legislation, and so on.

Consumerism as it is known today generally is attributed to President John F. Kennedy's message to Congress on March 15, 1962, in which he put forth the original version of the Consumer Bill of Rights quoted at the beginning of this chapter. Kennedy was explicit that government is the ultimate guarantor of these rights and hence built the foundation for much of the role federal consumerism plays today.

Other well-known issue advocates galvanized a movement that was to have many facets: women's liberation, Gray Panthers, and so on. Ralph Nader was one major catalyst with his book on the automobile industry, *Unsafe at Any Speed*. Rachael Carson polarized the pollution issue with *Silent Spring*. And these are only two examples from a large group.

Government took Kennedy seriously and began an activist role. False and misleading advertising was a major target of the FTC. Product safety also became a major issue, especially in the automobile industry, which became characterized by government-ordered recalls. Products were withdrawn from the market because of pollution and public health danger—DDT being a leading example.

History often records a moderating trend or pendulum swing after a period of extensive activism. Many came to feel that governmental regulation was more of a hindrance than a help. This conservatism was expressed in the election of both Jimmy Carter and Ronald Reagan, although it was to achieve its full expression under the latter president.

The outcome was substantial deregulation in many industries or, more precisely, a return to reliance on regulation by the marketplace through its own corrective influences.

The jury is still out on the impact of President George Bush's policies on consumer interests. One should not assume that consumerism concerns have abated, for that is not the case. Among the greatest worries are low product quality and deficient after-sale service,[11] indiscriminate use and resale of private information in data bases,[12] and business indifference to environmental issues.[13]

Taken together, studies show that public attitudes toward consumerism in general are favorable and should remain strong.[14] Moreover, there is a trend toward more rigorous enforcement by regulatory agencies.

What does the future hold? There is one helpful clue to use in making such a prognosis. Do not fail to grasp the essential lesson: consumerism arises because of the failure of business or other organizations in the exchange relationship to meet and respond to legitimate consumer demands. Business still is guilty in these terms.

Socially responsive business practices could have anticipated these movements and responded before alienation became widespread. Unfortunately, however, one basic law of history seems to be that its lessons are not heeded until it is too late.[15]

The Importance of a Research Perspective

Consumer research is essential if disparate views of diverse groups are to be resolved. All parties, especially business and government, need the objectivity that well-designed research can provide in problem identification, problem clarification, and evaluation of proposed solutions.

Few disagree with the need for objectivity, but there are inevitable difficulties in the use and interpretation of research. Differing values and resulting self-interest can lead to varying agendas from one party to the next.

How, for example, do we interpret and use a finding that 11 percent of consumers misunderstood an ad and formed beliefs about the advertised product that contradict actual fact? An ardent consumer advocate could label this as a blatant indication of deception. The advertiser, on the other hand, could contend, with some merit, that a certain amount of misperception will occur regardless of the wording that is used. It is precisely at this point that the propositions developed over the years in consumer research as a discipline and field of study find fruitful application.[16]

As you have seen throughout this book, it is now possible to state with a fairly high degree of confidence how consumers process and use information. Therefore, there is an increasingly firm basis of theory and evidence on which to resolve disagreements more objectively. The resolution now relies less on theories of what consumers *ought to do* and shifts instead to *actual responses* to current or contemplated strategies.

Consumer research also offers the benefit of test marketing proposed consumerism programs, just as it is used in all phases of marketing practices. Often there is need for sophisticated experimental designs.[17] Agencies such as the Federal Trade Commission (FTC) are increasingly research sensitive, and this is an encouraging trend.

The Right to Safety

ISSUE: One of the models of a popular automobile make can be purchased with a hatchback design. This allows much more interior space. The lid on the hatchback is automatically self-supporting. It was recognized in design that the pneumatic self-support mechanisms will fail in 11 out of 5,000 cars, potentially resulting in serious or even fatal injury. The actual incidence of failure is 39 out of 5,000. Should there be a product recall? Thus far sales are below the breakeven point. It will cost $500 for each repair, and the total costs required will drive losses up significantly.

How would you approach this issue? The first plank in the Consumer Bill of Rights reads, "Consumers have the right to be protected against products or services that are hazardous to health and life."[18] The right to safety has been made specific under the Consumer Product Safety Act, which established the Consumer Product Safety Commission (CPSC).[19]

The CPSC has the mandate to protect consumers against unreasonable risk of injuries caused by hazardous household products. Manufacturers have always had some safety liability under common law, but now the manufacturer must assume explicit responsibility for designing the product in accordance with safety considerations.

Since 1980, however, the activity of the CPSC has been cut back, reflecting the move toward voluntary industry self-regulation. When enforcement and redress are necessary, increasing use has been made of cost/benefit criteria, assessing whether or not the benefits of a proposed remedial action are justified by its costs. This is not an easy issue to resolve.[20]

Using Consumer Research Consumer research has two specific functions here. The first is to document product-usage patterns, especially unexpected safety hazards. The second is to establish the expected probability of injuries or levels of safety.

A particular doctrine, **foreseeability**, is often a matter of contention between manufacturer and government. This doctrine holds that the manufacturer should be able to *foresee* (anticipate and evaluate) risks inherent in product use and find out ways to avoid them.

Complaints about safety and poor performance often arise, of course, because of incorrect consumer usage. The real difficulty, however, lies in anticipating and minimizing the problems arising when so-called "normal" people use the product in a distinctly abnormal way. The manufacturer often is held liable in such situations. Therefore, extensive usage testing may be required.

The Issue of Costs versus Benefits What would your solution be in the automotive safety issue discussed at the beginning of this section? Everyone feels uneasy when a monetary value is placed on human life. Many would not hesitate to recommend the change, regardless of its cost, because of the consumer's right to safety. If this is your position, you have reasoned **deontologically**. This term comes from the Greek word, *deon*, which refers to right or duty. You have reasoned that rightness or wrongness is inherent within the act itself.

Others would be more hesitant, because matters of this type are never as simple as they seem. What effect will this have on lower-income buyers? Is a potential increased price because of the recall justified if it is demonstrated that potential buyers with lower incomes are, in effect, priced out of the market? Those raising this type of issue are reasoning **teleologically**—you are placing emphasis on rightness or wrongness of ends (*teleos*) or consequences.

Frankly, this creates an almost unavoidable dilemma for anyone attempting to make use of the Principle of Equal Regard (Categorical Imperative or Golden Rule).

One could build a reasonable case from either side, thus making absolute certainty elusive.

The authors' position here is strictly deontological—everything possible should be done to build a zero defect policy that attempts to eliminate accidents resulting from foreseeable product failure even if it causes low income people to not be able to afford cars. Diminished profitability, while never to be dismissed, should not be the determining criterion.

A Multicultural Ethical Dilemma   It has been illegal for more than two decades to advertise cigarettes on TV in the United States. Print ads are allowed only if there is a prominent warning, also appearing on each package, that cigarette smoking may be dangerous for your health. Growing antipathy toward smoking has led to a decrease in the number of smokers except on college campuses where it has been increasing since 1986. As Consumer in Focus 24.1 indicates, however, manufacturers are more than making up for these lost sales by turning to Africa, Asia, and elsewhere.

The cigarette manufacturers are not alone in pursuing such marketing policies in the so-called Third World. Cosmetics and self-medication products now abound. "So what's the problem?" is the frequent response. "After all, there is no law against it, and people are just exercising their freedom when they make the purchase."

We have stepped into a sensitive arena here. Regulators often contend that the evidence linking smoking and cancer is incontrovertible and have enacted rules to curb cigarette advertising.

Rather than spend money to advertise cigarettes, would it not be better to invest these funds introducing products that are both beneficial and healthy, especially in under-developed countries? Practices such as the one described above often draw money from survival necessities. Such practices should be labeled for what they really are—blatant attempts at profit maximization with little regard shown for consumer interest.

The Right to Be Informed

We started the chapter with an example of questionable advertising veracity. Here's another example for you.

> ISSUE: For months, the Food & Drug Administration had been writing letters to Procter & Gamble Co., complaining that it was misleading to use the word "fresh" on Citrus Hill packages because the orange juice is made up of concentrate. And despite a long day of meetings between agency and company representatives, P&G would not back down and remove the offending word.[21]

Procter & Gamble management played "hardball" here with the Food and Drug Administration (FDA). Were they right in what they did? What would your decision have been?

Ultimately P&G lost in a big way. The FDA immediately confiscated a shipment of Citrus Hill and won the battle in having the questionable wording removed

Consumer in Focus 24.1

U.S. Tobacco Firms Set Their Sights on Asian Market

With Asia's $90 billion-a-year cigarette market in their sights, U.S. tobacco firms are moving hungrily into markets from Tokyo to Thailand. All international companies are anxious to carve their own slices of an industry that is adding millions of smokers every year. The job, however, is complicated by economic, political, and cultural factors that are often difficult to correlate.

Executives attacked the Asian markets with the same enthusiasm as their predecessors attacked markets back home during the '50s and '60s. Western models and lifestyles create glamorous standards to emulate, and Asian smokers can't get enough.

Smoking-related deaths have overtaken communicable diseases as Asia's top killer, according to Judith Mackay, head of Hong Kong's Council on Smoking and Health (one of at least three such agencies in Asia), who said the problem is well past the finger-pointing stage.

With brand names such as "Long Life" (Taiwan) and tepid health warnings such as "Please don't smoke too much" (Japan), Asian governments should clean their own nests first, said one U.S. executive.

International marketers said their strategies break no rules, their products' quality is higher than local varieties, and brand equity is responsible for recent growth. Yet they face increasingly tough ad restrictions, which, in effect, protect local producers and their employees.

Source: Mike Levin, "U.S. Tobacco Firms Push Eagerly Into Asian Market," *Advertising Age* (January 21, 1991), 2 and 14. Reproduced by special permission.

from all packaging and promotional material. Furthermore, management was tarred with the brush of playing free and easy with consumer rights.

The Consumer Bill of Rights advocates that the consumer has the right "to be protected against fraudulent, deceitful, or grossly misleading information, advertising, labeling, or other practices, and to be given the facts he [or she] needs to make an informed choice."[22]

How do we tackle this issue? First of all, we need to clarify what the phrase *informed choice* means. Even more important is to determine when a message is misleading. Both of these issues are more difficult than they might seem.

What Is an "Informed Choice"?

Hans Thorelli has this to say on information adequacy: "Informed consumers are protected consumers— more than that, they are liberated consumers."[23] But how much information does the consumer want and need? How should it be provided? Can we provide too much information?

When Is an Appeal Informative? As you might expect, there is disagreement on what the word *informative* means. Contrast the two ads appearing in Figure 24.2. The Colgate ad was aimed at middle-class Kenyan families, whereas the China Airlines ad was designed for English speakers in Asian countries. Which do you think is most informative?

Most readers probably will vote for the Colgate ad because of the product-feature demonstration and endorsement by the Kenya Dental Association. Empirical studies show, however, that less than half of all ads are informative in the sense that focus is on such objective features as price, quality, performance, and availability.[24]

But what about the China Airlines appeal? Would you say that it is noninformative because of its decidedly subjective (that is, more emotional) message? We would seriously caution against such an interpretation because the focus on Chinese tradition and ambiance is a benefit in and of itself, even though it cannot be quantified or objectified. It is entirely possible that the decision process of an Asian consumer is enhanced far more by the psychological and emotional associations than in any other way.

The issue comes down to this important point: *only the consumer can decide whether useful information has been provided.* It can be a serious mistake to allege, following some consumerists, that valid information is confined only to the factual and objective.

How Much Is Enough? It has been made clear in many chapters that both the amount and type of information needed will depend upon the degree of involvement and resulting extended problem solving. Furthermore, there are individual differences in desire to search and willingness to act on limited information.

The problem is further complicated by **information overload**. You will remember from our discussion of information processing that provision of too much information can impair decision making. There are distinct limits on information-processing capacity. Many well-meaning consumer advocates mistakenly assume that "more is better" and wind up hindering rather than helping the consumer.

Therefore, it is impossible to give a simple answer to the question of how much is enough. It can only be resolved on the basis of research that verifies actual information acquisition and use. If there are deficiencies resulting in unwise buying decisions, then action can be taken in the form of revamped promotion or consumer education efforts.

Day's conclusion regarding well-intended consumerism efforts on this dimension has stood the test of time:

> What is clear . . . is that it is not enough to simply provide consumers with more information. That is simply the first step in a major educational task of getting consumers to understand the information, and persuading them to use it. Consumer researchers can make a significant contribution to both these tasks.[25]

Information Veracity No issue has given rise to greater concern over the years than deception and misrepresentation because such practices materially interfere with the consumer's legitimate rights.

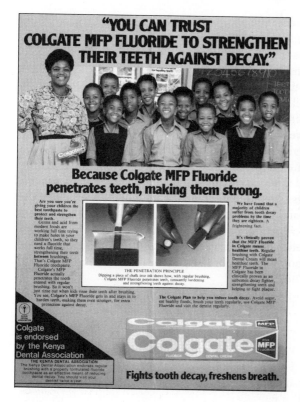

FIGURE 24.2   Which Ad Is More Informative?

Source: Courtesy Colgate-Palmolive East Africa and China Airlines.

What Represents Deception?   As you can well imagine, P&G's contention with the FDA was that their claim of freshness was not deceptive or misleading, even though the product comes from reconstituted juice. How can the question of deception be decided?

First of all, what is deception? Definitional issues are of central importance here, because nuances of wording can have great significance. According to Gardner and Leonard, the following points comprise the common elements in all definitions used since 1970:

1. The consumer has a set of experiences, beliefs, and attitudes.
2. The advertisement as stimulus interacts with the experiences, beliefs, and attitudes of the consumer.
3. The impressions, beliefs, or attitudes that follow from the advertisement/consumer interaction are the basis for the determination of deception.[26]

In its 1983 policy statement, the Federal Trade Commission defined deception as "a representation, omission, or practice that is likely to mislead the consumer acting reasonably in the circumstances, to the consumer's detriment."[27] Its current standard of deception requires that the representation, omission, or practice be "material." The representation becomes "material," in turn, when it is likely to affect consumer decision processes.[28]

The issue thus becomes resolved on the basis of the effect on consumers. In recent actions courts have ruled that this impact comes from what can be reasonably inferred by the consumer, as well as what is literally said.[29] Also, for a claim to be judged misleading, there generally must be evidence that more than 22 percent of actual or prospective buyers have been misled.[30]

Further, an evaluation of whether deception has occurred also must take into account that all forms of mass media content will be misperceived at times. Jacoby and Hoyer undertook a national study of consumer perception of 54 magazine ads and 54 editorials. Their findings showed that 21.4 percent of the material, on the average, was miscomprehended and an additional 15.5 percent said they didn't know what it meant.[31]

A standard that can be used is provided by Shimp and Preston who conclude that the following conditions should be demonstrated before arriving at a conclusion that deception has taken place:

1. The claim is *attended to* by the consumer.
2. The claim (or its implication) *affects beliefs*.
3. The claim (or its implication) is *important* to the consumer.
4. The claim (or its implication) becomes *represented in long-term memory*.
5. The claim (or its implication) is *objectively false*.
6. *Behavior* is influenced as a result of either the claim itself or implications which can reasonably be derived from it.[32]

The Impact of Anti-Deception Efforts   During the 1960s and 1970s the FTC was vigorous in its pursuit of advertising truthfulness. This abated substantially under the Reagan administration in the belief that a free market will provide correctives if left alone. The FTC also relaxed its standards for ad substantiation in that less evidence now is required to prove the veracity of claims.

Traditionally the FTC and other agencies have performed the function of providing a "well-lighted street." The theory is that the threat of enforcement will deter violations. Fortunately, this light is becoming much brighter recently due to stepped-up enforcement efforts.[33] Also, much greater lip service is paid to voluntary enforcement efforts which, frankly, have had a mixed record of success.[34]

But, can we make a case that the consumer's right for honest and verifiable information is being better met at this point in history? The safest conclusion is that the brighter legal streetlight is making potential offenders more cautious.

It may be premature, however, to give an affirmative answer to this question. Consider these specific instances:

1. Volvo Cars of North America reinforced the cars which were used in an ad to demonstrate how the Volvo withstands unusual crushing because of its strength.
2. Adolph Coors Company was sued for improperly claiming that it uses Rocky Mountain spring water as its source for its popular beers.

3. Quaker Oats Co. faced the charge over untrue claims that its oat bran cereals cut the risk of heart attack.
4. The makers of Mazola corn oil were charged for making the untruthful claim that cholesterol levels are lowered by corn oil use.

We could go on and on about the charges brought against supposedly reputable marketers. This doesn't say much about ethics and self-regulation, does it? It all comes down to this question: *Do consumers have a right to receive truthful information or not?*

The definitional and interpretation problems mentioned above need to be considered fully. Yet, far too many decision makers use the shoddy ethical standards of Ted mentioned at the opening of this chapter. Is it asking too much to expect everyone to show the ethical integrity of Sarah? A *deontological* (literal) view would require consumer analysts to stand up and be counted!

The Right to Choose

ISSUE: Japan bashing has become a widespread practice in the United States because of allegedly unfair trade practices. The chief finger pointers are the three leading (or should we say lagging) automobile manufacturers who are trying to make the case that Japan is responsible for their across-the-board slump in market share and profitability. But the automobile manufacturers are not alone in this lament. There are widespread voices calling for trade restrictions against Japan.

Beneath these advocates of trade restrictions stands the third plank in the Consumer Bill of Rights:

Consumers have the right to assured access, whenever possible, to a variety of products and services at competitive prices. In those industries in which competition is not workable, government regulation is substituted to assure satisfactory quality and service at fair prices.[35]

Would you call for restrictions on trade? Would you advise saving jobs of some workers or protecting certain corporations if the result is raising the price of cars to everyone else? To tackle this issue, first of all, we must explore the problem of monopoly and the ways in which this has been dealt with legally. Then we can begin to assess whether or not restrictions are in the consumer's best interests. We also will tackle the question of responsibility, if any, to those who choose "unwisely."

Monopoly Power and Barriers to Entry
Traditionally, the laws of market-based economies embody the principle of laissez-faire, which contends that the consumer is best served when firms freely compete, offering an unrestrained choice. Anti-trust legislation has long been a potent weapon against monopolies that allegedly curb this freedom—hence the well-publicized breakup of AT&T into smaller, independent competitive units.

Consumerists usually have not made monopoly power into an issue because of the adequacy of both legislation and enforcement machinery. On the other hand, there has been pressure from many quarters other than consumerists for *deregulation* in certain industries and greater freedom for firms to compete.

Deregulation, of course, became a major theme of both the Reagan and Bush administrations. But, has this had a discernible influence on consumer interest? Those who have looked at this question most thoroughly cannot come to a conclusion one way or the other, but there is some hope that consumers ultimately will be the beneficiaries.[36]

There is growing concern as of this writing, however, about the impact of corporate takeovers in some industries. Admittedly the numbers of competing firms have been reduced, but this does not necessarily imply consumer disadvantage. Even if there is no evidence of intent to create a monopoly, there is no denying the fact that entrenched firms with marketing muscle are often difficult and even impossible to dislodge.

As a case in point, how many upstart airlines have been absorbed by the "big four" in the past few years? We no longer see Pan American, Midway, People Express, or Braniff, and others are either in Chapter 11 or are close to bankruptcy. The price of being competitive simply proved to be too high.

Fortunately, such barriers to entry rarely are permanent because of competitive counterattack. Just compare the lists of the top firms in any product field from one decade to the next and you will see substantial variation. The crumbling of the General Motors empire and the diminished market share of each of its divisions is ample evidence of competitive vulnerability.

In fact, there is growing evidence that smaller and more aggressive marketers often gain a competitive edge over their larger and more inflexible counterparts. Who would have believed that upstarts such as Apple Computers or Compaq could reach a position from which they could challenge mighty IBM for world leadership? Many other examples can be given.

Trade Restrictions

Consumerists usually are not found among those advocating trade restrictions. Dardis explains why:

> . . . trade restraints impose high costs on consumers and the economy. The direct costs are higher prices paid by consumers and the reduction in consumer choice due to product upgrading. The indirect costs include the lack of incentive for the domestic industry to respond to changes in product and consumption and the pervasive effects of protectionist measures on economic efficiency and economic growth.[37]

Let's face it—any attempt to restrict competition seldom benefits the consumer. You can be sure that the right of freedom of choice played no role in the calls from Chrysler President Lee Iacocca and others for a clamp on Japanese car imports.

We completely agree with those in Japan who reacted with understandable contempt that the Americans were beaten by the Japanese at their own game—consumer-oriented marketing. Consumers in the United States pay much less for cars than those in most other countries, partly as a result of allowing global competitors the right to compete freely in this country.

The Problem of Unwise Choice

Here is a challenging question: Does the buyer have a right to choose even if there is evidence that actions are unwise? Should choice be regulated and restricted in such situations? This has been an unresolved issue since the very onset of consumerism nearly a century ago.

Some have doubts that people can make a sound, reasoned choice given the plethora of product alternatives and promotional claims. Others contend that consumers should be forced to do what is best for them, regardless of personal preferences.

Both points of view, if enacted, inevitably lead to some restriction of choice. The auto seat belt laws in many states are a case in point. Even though usage is mandated by statute, compliance is less than 50 percent in most states.

Unfortunately this is a "no-win" issue. On the one hand, certain clearly unwise and destructive behaviors, such as heroin or cocaine use, must be regulated. Few would have any quarrel with this position, given extensive documentation of disastrous personal and social outcomes of addiction.

But what if similar legal limits were placed on the consumption of whole milk, which is known to produce allergies in some adults? Or chocolate? Now we have entered into the domain where any position taken inevitably will be arbitrary.

How can a line be drawn between wise and unwise buying and consumption behavior? In its most general sense, the principle of unrestrained free choice must remain at the bedrock of a market economy except in extreme cases of public health or safety dangers.

A more defensible and increasingly popular approach is to move away from regulation and restriction toward education designed to bring about a more intelligent choice.[38] The goal is to enhance the ability to cope with complex choice processes in a mass consumption society. Such educational programs should cover these elements:

1. Formal knowledge about criteria used to evaluate complex technical products, and ways to choose logically.
2. Consumer managerial and decision-making skills comparable to those developed in professional education.
3. Increased consumer knowledge of the workings of business, government, and the marketplace.
4. Values and consciousness that will encourage respect and concern for others in their pursuit of collective consumption.

The Right to Be Heard (Redress)

> ISSUE: A person has bought an electric range with a one-year warranty against defective parts. Several repairs were required during the first year and were done at no charge. Problems continued unabated, however, after the warranty expired, and the buyer appealed, asking for replacement of a product that has become a "lemon." The manufacturer declined, pointing to the fact that all liability ceased once the warranty expired.

Does the consumer have a right of redress in such situations? The fourth plank of the Consumer Bill of Rights, as originally stated, is somewhat ambiguous:

Consumers have the right to be assured that consumer interests will receive full and sympathetic consideration in the formulation of government policy and fair and expeditious treatment in its administrative tribunals.[39]

Its focus as written was entirely on regulatory behavior, although its application has been broadened to encompass the responsibility of the enterprise for redress.

Legislative Protection   There is a substantial body of federal legislation controlling restitution and punishment, and this is detailed in Figure 24.3. The major avenues of redress are summarized in Figure 24.4.

Despite these legal remedies, authorities are unconvinced that consumer interests are fully protected.[40] Fortunately, there is constant consumerist activity in this arena. Our greater concern lies with prevention, for it is here that ethics plays its greatest role.

Prevention   Ideally, the consumer voice needs to be heard before problems develop and redress becomes necessary.

Codes of Ethics   One means of prevention can be found in industry codes of ethics, an example of which is presented in Figure 24.5. Such creeds are often little more than window dressing because of the lack of enforcement mechanisms. Nonetheless, consumerism problems would diminish sharply if such standards were internalized and enforced by top management.

Quality and Guarantees   As we have mentioned throughout the book, consumer dissatisfaction levels are increasing. In fact, one consumer researcher sees "almost the Naderistic feel of the '60s" in a "fight-back trend" that is making consumers "more conscious about getting ripped off."[41]

Consumer rebellion inevitably will be felt in lost sales and bad word of mouth. The business solution lies in recognition that *quality is a marketing problem, not just a production problem*. When quality levels are improved and backed by stringent guarantees, it is possible to regain or solidify market position while, at the same time, contributing to legitimate consumer interests.

Restitution   Legal restitution for wrongs can be made many ways as Figure 24.4 indicates. Among the most visible is the almost daily incidence of mandatory automobile recalls ordered to remedy safety defects.

You may recall our previous discussion in Chapter 18 of the initial resistance of management when such an order was issued to rectify engine surge problems with the Audi 5000 model. Many would regard this as a clear case of ethical disregard.

Issues of restitution should not have to reach the point where legal authorities must step in. The consumer has every right to expect response from the manufacturer or retailer when complaints are made. History has proven time and time again that the gains in consumer loyalty far offset costs. But this type of lesson does not seem to sink in as it should, if complaint levels are any indication.[42]

FIGURE 24.3   Selected Federal Consumer Protection Laws

Act	Purposes
Pure Food and Drug Act (1906)	Prohibits adulteration and misbranding of foods and drugs sold in interstate commerce
Food, Drug, and Cosmetic Act (1938)	Prohibits the adulteration and sale of foods, drugs, cosmetics, or therapeutic devices that may endanger public health; allows the Food and Drug Administration to set minimum standards and to establish guides for food products
Wool Products Labeling Act (1940)	Protects producers, manufacturers, distributors, and consumers from undisclosed substitutes and mixtures in all types of manufactured wool products
Fur Products Labeling Act (1951)	Protects consumers and others against misbranding, false advertising, and false invoicing of furs and fur products
Flammable Fabrics Act (1953)	Prohibits interstate transportation of dangerously flammable wearing apparel and fabrics
Automobile Information Disclosure Act (1958)	Requires automobile manufacturers to post suggested retail prices on all new passenger vehicles
Textile Fiber Products Identification Act (1958)	Guards producers and consumers against misbranding and false advertising of fiber content of textile fiber products
Cigarette Labeling Act (1965)	Requires cigarette manufacturers to label cigarettes as hazardous to health
Fair Packaging and Labeling Act (1966)	Declares unfair or deceptive packaging or labeling of certain consumer commodities illegal
Child Protection Act (1966)	Excludes from sale potentially harmful toys; allows the FDA to remove dangerous products from the market
Truth-in-Lending Act (1968)	Requires full disclosure of all finance charges on consumer credit agreements and in advertisements of credit to allow consumers to be better informed regarding their credit purchases
Child Protection and Toy Safety Act (1969)	Protects children from toys and other products that contain thermal, electrical or mechanical hazards
Fair Credit Reporting Act (1970)	Ensures that a consumer's credit report will contain only accurate, relevant, and recent information and will be confidential unless requested for an appropriate reason by a proper party
Consumer Product Safety Act (1972)	Created an independent agency to protect consumers from unreasonable risk of injury arising from consumer products; agency is empowered to set safety standards
Magnuson-Moss Warranty-Improvement Act (1975)	Provides for minimum disclosure standards for written consumer product warranties; defines minimum content standards for written warranties; allows the FTC to prescribe interpretive rules and policy statements regarding unfair or deceptive practices

Source: William M. Pride and O. C. Ferrell, *Marketing: Basic Concepts and Decisions*, 4th ed., 481. Copyright © 1985 by Houghton Mifflin Company. Used by permission.

Ethical Response   Now, back to the issue that opened this section of the chapter—would you refund the buyer's money in this situation? Or would you enforce the guarantee? If you are using the Categorical Imperative or the Golden Rule, you

FIGURE 24.4   Remedies for Consumer Protection

Prevention	Restitution	Punishment
Codes of conduct	Affirmative disclosure	Fines and incarceration
Disclosure of information requirements	Corrective advertising	Loss of profits
Substantiation of claims	Refunds	Class action suits
	Limitations on contracts	
	Arbitration	

Source: Dorothy Cohen, "Remedies for Consumer Protection: Prevention, Restitution, or Punishment," *Journal of Marketing* (October 1975), 25. Reprinted from the *Journal of Marketing* published by the American Marketing Association.

FIGURE 24.5   The Advertising Code of American Business

1. **Truth.** Advertising shall tell the truth, and shall reveal significant facts, the concealment of which would mislead the public.
2. **Responsibility.** Advertising agencies and advertisers shall be willing to provide substantiation of claims made.
3. **Taste and Decency.** Advertising shall be free of statements, illustrations, or implications which are offensive to good taste or public decency.
4. **Disparagement.** Advertising shall offer merchandise or service on its merits, and refrain from attacking competitors unfairly or disparaging their products, services, or methods of doing business.
5. **Bait Advertising.** Advertising shall offer only merchandise or services which are available for purchase at the advertised price.
6. **Guarantees and Warranties.** Advertising of guarantees and warranties shall be explicit. Advertising of any guarantee or warranty shall clearly and conspicuously disclose its nature and extent, the manner in which the guarantor or warrantor will perform and the identify of the guarantor or warrantor.
7. **Price Claims.** Advertising shall avoid price or savings claims which are false or misleading, or which do not offer provable bargains or savings.
8. **Unprovable Claims.** Advertising shall avoid the use of exaggerated or unprovable claims.
9. **Testimonials.** Advertising containing testimonials shall be limited to those of competent witnesses who are reflecting a real and honest choice.

Note: This code was part of a program of industry self-regulation pertaining to national consumer advertising announced jointly on September 18, 1971, by the American Advertising Federation, the American Association of Advertising Agencies, the Association of National Advertisers, and the Council of Better Business Bureaus, Inc.

probably would swallow your profit and make restitution. Where this becomes tough, of course, is when it impinges upon the bottom line, threatening the survival of the firm. But what is the higher concern here? It all depends upon your values (and your courage).

Punishment   If nothing else works, it is possible to take more extreme action in the form of fines and incarceration, loss of profits, and class action suits.

Various members of the security and exchange industry have discovered to their dismay that fraudulent stock manipulation can lead to a stint behind bars. Such legal proceedings unfortunately can be extremely costly and time consuming.

The Right to Enjoy a Clean and Healthful Environment

ISSUE: The so-called "green movement" is pressuring business firms to lessen the extent to which their products pollute the environment. McDonald's agreed to let an advocacy group, The Environmental Defense Fund, put together a plan for recycling and cutting waste. The company has agreed to test 42 initiatives that will reduce waste by 80 percent. Among these are reusable lids for salad containers and pump-style dispensers for condiments.[43]

Environmental pollution is an unfortunate byproduct of a high and rising standard of living in a technological age, thus necessitating an addition to the Consumer Bill of Rights—the right to enjoy a clean and healthful environment. North America has fallen far behind some other countries such as Japan and Germany in this regard.

Would you have agreed with the above steps if you had been a member of the McDonald's executive team? Keep several factors in mind as you make this judgment:

1. Remember that they, along with other companies, have been the targets of tremendous consumer pressure for change.
2. Also, remember that there are some firms who have given in to pressure, only to discover that their actions boomeranged seriously. The most notable case in point is Mobil's Hefty brand plastic trash bag.[44] It was reissued in a biodegradable form at great cost, but it later turned out that it would biodegrade only if it remains exposed to air, a condition that does not happen in most disposal situations. They and others have discovered that the "definition of what's good keeps changing,"[45] thus making this a "Catch-22" situation.
3. Consumers, 80 percent or more, are quick to say that they place primary importance on buying environmentally safe products.[46] But other desires such as convenience may overwhelm their idealism.[47] Therefore, their response may be quite different than their voiced convictions.

If we were acting on ethical considerations alone, most of us probably are willing to apply the Principle of Equal Regard here and respond affirmatively. After all, pollution affects us all in increasingly direct ways.

Even our friend Ted, whom we met early in the chapter, most likely would agree. But he would be more likely to acquiesce simply because "doing so is good business—ethics has nothing to do with it."

It becomes more difficult, doesn't it, when the pragmatic issues mentioned above are taken into account. Environmentalism is a recent phenomenon and scientific knowledge is changing rapidly. In our opinion, we must, of necessity, become more *teleological* and consider seriously the consequences of any proposed step, no matter how good it seems on the surface. All that can be asked is that this consumer right be taken seriously and not subjugated to self-centered profit considerations.

It becomes more difficult when environmental necessity compels such dramatic steps as eliminating internal combustion engines in order to reduce pollutants to levels that are not life threatening. At this point made firms will face the unmistakable necessity of engaging in **demarketing**—a deliberate attempt to induce consumers to buy *less* or cease consumption altogether.

It is likely that this situation will be faced in a very few years in many parts of the world. Mexico City is at the point of no return right now. It requires quite a measure of faith to believe that business ever will demarket voluntarily if it means sacrifice of potential profit.

Here is where governments may have no other choice but to force compliance. Yet, such agencies often are greater polluters than anyone else, prompting suits by the U.S. Environment Agency against the Corps of Engineers, state governments, and other agencies who flout existing laws.

Protection of the Interests of Special Interest Groups and the Poor

Most readers will know immediately what the following issue is all about, but a word of explanation is perhaps necessary. American beer manufacturers are prone to advertise their products using attractive and sexy female models who are displayed in highly provocative ways, hence the term, "bikini-clad-bimbo-on-the-beach." This has given rise to quite justified cries of outrage from many feminists.

> ISSUE: "The bikini-clad-bimbo-on-the-beach approach to beer advertising lives on. It has even seemingly survived a lawsuit against Stroh Brewing Co., charging that its ads featuring scantily dressed women led to sexual harassment in the workplace. Millers and Coors say they have no reason to change their ads. 'We have been and continue to feel very positive about how beer drinkers, both men and women, are portrayed. They're sociable, fun, and are presented in a realistic manner,' said David Fogelson, a spokesman for Miller Brewing Co., Milwaukee."[48]

There has been a marked increase in efforts to determine whether a unique set of problems exists among special interest groups and the poor toward which special regulative and informational efforts should be directed. This has given rise to the last component of the Consumer Bill of Rights—protection of the interests of the poor and other interest groups which have experienced some oppression.

Insensitivity to Special Interest Groups
The so-called bimbo-on-the-beach advertising is an aggravation to many women who, frankly, are tired of being stereotyped as sex symbols in a male-dominated world. Women's interests must be taken more seriously because there will be an inevitable backlash through lost sales unless changes are made.

But the issue goes far beyond women. What about improper advertising to children? Consider the case of "Old Joe," the Camel cigarette character discussed in Consumer in Focus 24.2. These situations will occupy ethicists for decades to come.

I'd Toddle a Mile for a Camel

From 1987 to 1990, R. J. Reynolds Tobacco Co. saw its share of Camel filter cigarettes jump from 2.7 percent to 3.1 percent—some jump for an aging brand when U.S. cigarette sales are sinking.

The No. 2 tobacco manufacturer resuscitated the brand largely through a four-year-old ad campaign featuring a cartoon character of its Camel mascot. Now, it's looking as if the extra market share may have come at a steep price.

Antismoking crusaders and health officials have repeatedly criticized the cartoon dromedary as an effort to target underage smokers. After long denying these charges, Reynolds now must fend off dramatic new evidence that reports that Old Joe Camel, as the character is called, entices kids to light up.

According to the studies, teenagers are far better able than adults to identify the Camel logo. One study even found that kids as young as three identify the cartoon with cigarettes. More chilling: One study concluded that Camel's share of the market of underage children who smoke is nearly 33 percent—up from less than a point before the Old Joe campaign got rolling.

Reynolds contests the studies' results. The average Camel smoker, Reynolds says, is 35. "Just because children can identify our logo doesn't mean they will use the product," a Reynolds spokeswoman says.

Source: Walecia Konrad, "I'd Toddle a Mile for a Camel," *Business Week* (December 23, 1991), 34. Reproduced by special permission.

Since you've just read about "Old Joe, the Camel," would you like to hear the defense from the manufacturer? The first recourse is to the ancient excuse that the quoted scientific studies are false. James W. Johnston, chairman-CEO of R. J. Reynolds Tobacco Company, offers this rebuttal:

> The fact that children see and recognize tobacco advertising is not a justification for eliminating those ads or for depriving a company of its right to advertise a legal product. If advertising were the true culprit, then perhaps all ads should be banned.[49]

The issue is often considered to be one of free speech. The creators of "bimbos-on-the-beach" ads could say exactly the same thing. A teleological view would look at the consequences, however. Does free speech give license to offend or directly hurt another party? Historical precedent and case law supports this fundamental right but places limits when the consequences are unacceptable.

There also is the strong rebuttal that this kind of advertising sells the product—what's good for the profit bottom line is what counts. And we are only poking fun. Why would anybody be offended?

This opinion, however, takes on quite a different perspective when it is subjected to this standard: *"Is this the way you would talk to your husband [wife] or kids?"* Or, put differently, *"How would you feel if the shoe were on the other foot and you were parodied or appealed to with such tactics?"*

Free speech? Yes, technically such comments are protected constitutionally. But many reason from a higher law such as the Principle of Equal Regard that would affirm and protect the legitimate interests. They would not believe in exceptions such as those cited here.

You will find on the pages of *Advertising Age* and other industry forums that many observers and participants in marketing are expressing such objections to industry practices. Pressures are getting so great that failure to heed these concerns could lead to increased regulation in the United States.

The Dilemma of the Poor   Potentially even more serious are the problems of poverty. These become especially acute in urban areas that are burgeoning around the world. Nairobi, Kenya, for example, must generate *1,000 new jobs each day* to cope with urban population growth.[50] Certainly the former Communist countries are now facing poverty in massive and perhaps unexpected ways, and it is entirely likely that this problem will be all the more aggravated by unethical free enterprise practices.

Businesses in general and consumer researchers specifically cannot avoid playing a role in determining the kind of urban environment to be built for the future and the ways in which greater equality can be achieved.

Consumer researchers have investigated the problems of how those who have been most subject to discrimination can more efficiently allocate their limited resources. A second contribution is improvement of marketing efficiency among firms and organizations that serve disadvantaged segments. Minority-owned businesses, for example, are being helped to achieve greater market penetration.

A third contribution is made when research evidence documents the ways in which those who are not disadvantaged enhance the problems of those who are. A case in point is the potent curb on upward mobility when those who are white rapidly sell their homes as blacks move in. Legitimate corrective action can be taken on such a foundation.

Organizational Ethics and Consumerism

There is no question that contemporary enterprises—business and nonbusiness—are faced with changing realities. The need is for *preventive approaches* to these issues of consumerism rather than *reactive ones*. Consumerism, after all, is not anti-business per se. It is, as we have stressed, a natural countervailing force in response to alienation. If abuses were not present, it would not exist.

Any market-controlled free enterprise system is built on the assumption that profit and material gain will be the guiding motive with the constraint that the market must be truly served with a focus on long-run consumer interest.

This doctrine presupposes a set of managerial ethics, a code of right and wrong, that is both workable and actively followed. We have seen at many points

FIGURE 24.6   IBM's Guidelines for Business Conduct

- Do not make misrepresentations to anyone you deal with.
- Do not use IBM's size unfairly to intimidate or threaten.
- Treat all buyers and sellers equitably.
- Do not engage in reciprocal dealing.
- Do not disparage competitors.
- Do not make premature disclosure of unannounced offerings.
- Do not engage in further selling after competitor has the firm order.
- Contact with the competition must be minimal.
- Do not make any illegal use of confidential information.
- Do not steal or obtain information by willfull deceit.
- Do not engage in violation of patents or copyrights.
- No bribes, gifts or entertainment that might be seen as creating an obligation should be accepted or given.

Source: Gene R. Laczniak and Patrick E. Murphy, *Marketing Ethics: Guidelines for Managers* (Lexington, Mass.: Lexington Books, 1985), 117–123.

what can happen when short-term financial gain becomes the guiding consideration. Ethical mandates quickly fall by the wayside, as economic history (and indeed the entire history of mankind) so amply reveals. Unfortunately, the public only becomes aware of the most flagrant instances of resulting compromise behavior. Small wonder that "Businesses Are Signing Up for Ethics 101."[51]

The ultimate dilemma faced in constructing any ethical philosophy is determining *what is right and what is wrong.* Company-wide codes of ethics such as IBM's Guidelines for Business Conduct can be helpful (see Figure 24.6). If these are to work, however, they must be endorsed consistently by top management and find their way into job descriptions, standards of performance, and managerial evaluation.[52]

Phasing Ethics and Social Responsibility into Marketing Planning

Corporate values of profit and efficiency will dominate unless there is the addition of counterbalancing ethical values. Robin and Reidenbach have diagrammed how this might look (see Figure 24.7).

A Consumerism Management System   Consumerism obviously is not going away, and it must be managed in the same way as every other environmental challenge. Here are the steps in a management system that are both workable and promote responsibility:

1. Orienting top management to the consumer's world.
2. Organizing for responsive action.

FIGURE 24.7 **Parallel Planning Systems for Integrating Ethical and Socially Responsible Plans into Strategic Marketing Planning**

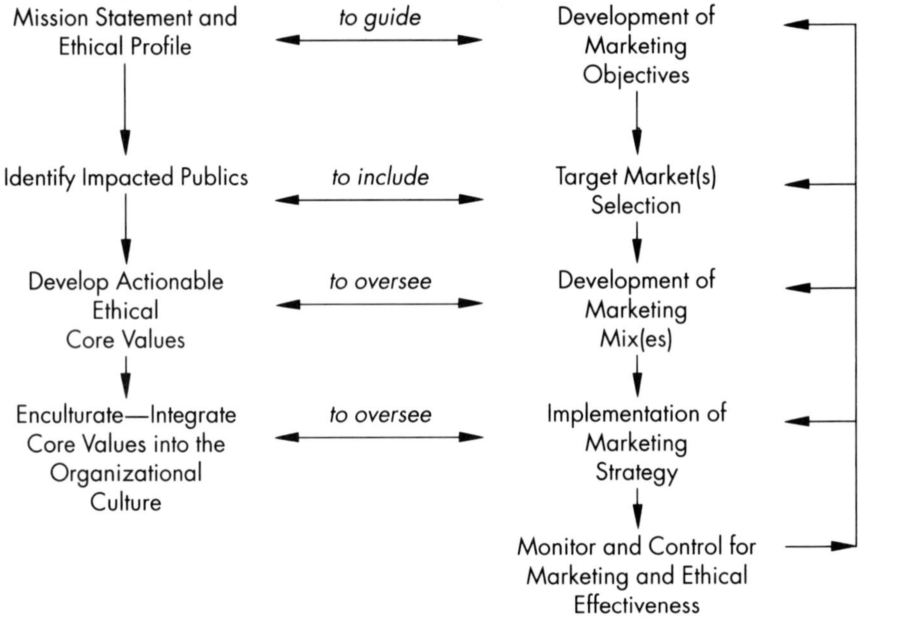

Mission Statement and Ethical Profile	← *to guide* →	Development of Marketing Objectives

Identify Impacted Publics	← *to include* →	Target Market(s) Selection

Develop Actionable Ethical Core Values	← *to oversee* →	Development of Marketing Mix(es)

Enculturate—Integrate Core Values into the Organizational Culture	← *to oversee* →	Implementation of Marketing Strategy

Monitor and Control for Marketing and Ethical Effectiveness

Source: Donald P. Robin and R. Eric Reidenbach, "Social Responsibility, Ethics, and Marketing Strategy: Closing the Gap between Concept and Application," *Journal of Marketing* 51 (January 1987), 52.

3. Improving customer contact.
4. Redressing grievances.
5. Providing consumer information and education.

Top Management Orientation   There now is a consensus that the first step is to ensure that both the board of directors and top management are acquainted with the realities of the consumer world, including economic and financial fears, negative attitudes toward business practice, and perceived grievances. This level of knowledge also must be backed consistently by a commitment to take responsible action when needed.

The number one managerial productivity problem in America is, quite simply, managers who are out of touch with their people and out of touch with their customers. And the alternative, "being in touch," does not come via computer printouts or the endless stream of overhead transparencies viewed in the endless darkened meeting rooms stretching across the continent. Being in touch means being informed via tangible, visceral ways.[53]

Organizing for Responsible Action   A logical starting point is a written consumer rights policy specifying in detail what the company is prepared to do in the way of implementation when shortcomings arise. We also recommend the establishment of a consumer affairs department that is empowered to have a real voice in marketing decision making and responsibility to provide redress.

The head person of the consumer affairs department, in turn, should be a member of top management assigned the responsibility and authority to assure that product quality and safety are maintained, that promotional strategies are truthful and not misleading, and that there is no deception in other phases of the marketing program. If this position is seen as merely advisory without management power and sanctions, it will be little more than window dressing.

Improving the Quality of Customer Contact   One of the greatest challenges for any management team is to create customer credibility. Some logical steps include community involvement, soft-sell institutional ads, and just plain human friendliness and decency in all dealings. The intent is to break down and hopefully eliminate barriers.

One of the best strategies is a continual customer satisfaction monitoring program following our discussion in Chapter 18. This provides an ongoing evaluation of service as opposed to an occasional "snapshot," thus allowing immediate remedial action when needed.

Providing for Redress   It is essential to respond to grievances and injuries. This requires prompt and direct means of reacting to complaints and inquiries through a consumer affairs department. There must be a clear recognition that commitment to information feedback and post-sale communication is an ethical mandate, to say nothing of the extent to which this response is significant in building long-term consumer loyalty, a phenomenon that is becoming increasingly rare.

Providing for Customer Education   There is a true consumer education movement in some firms, and we find such responses to be encouraging indeed. The focus lies on moving beyond the usual forms of promotion, as important as these are, to efforts that clearly are designed to help the consumer buy wisely.

Conclusion

We have noticed a disturbing trend since the first edition of this book in 1968 that, hopefully, may be abating somewhat at the present time.

The majority of students in the 1960s and 1970s developed a high sense of moral outrage over political and economic shortcomings. For a period, of course, this was expressed through campus protest, but a large percentage carried a commitment to ethically responsible action into their professional lives. Consumerism is a central part of the social agenda of that generation of business managers, and many of the most laudable corporate actions have come from their initiative.

It seems, however, that this moral outrage gave way to a sense of individualistic opportunism. Social and moral issues are not seen negatively; rather, such concerns are at the distinct periphery of life.

We have tried to make a case that each of us can live responsibly only by focusing on the best interests of consumers as well as the financial bottom line. It's time for a pendulum swing back once again to moral and ethic responsibility.

Summary

The consumer has the right to safety, the right to be informed, the right to choose, and the right to be heard. These tenets have been reaffirmed by decree and administrative action ever since they were declared in 1962 by President John F. Kennedy. Yet, there is ample evidence that these rights are consistently violated, creating a rising interest in consumerism.

Consumerism is not a recent phenomenon. A historical review showed some ancient antecedents as well as specific activity that began in the United States around the turn of the century. Consumerism as we now know it, however, received its greatest impetus from the Kennedy declarations. The 1960s and 1970s were characterized by a frenzy of activity on many fronts, but there has been a pendulum swing toward a return to market forces as opposed to regulation as a corrective during the 1980s.

Our focus throughout has been two-fold: (1) use consumer research to help assure consumer rights and (2) undertake responsible ethical action which puts consumer interests above such bottom line concerns as profitability.

We saw that consumer research can play the unique role of providing facts for responsible policy and activity. Otherwise, there often is recourse to normative authoritarianism based on opinion and arbitrary fiat. In a sense, then, a research approach has the potential of becoming a boundary-spanning agent between the conflicting interests of business, government, and consumer advocacy groups.

Research is of no value, however, unless our corporate and individual response is governed by ethics. We reviewed the nature of ethical thinking and put forth the principle that all decision makers need to be guided by the Golden Rule or other philosophical axioms that place primary focus on the best interests of another.

Each of the six consumer rights was evaluated comprehensively from both a research and an ethical perspective. Unfortunately, it becomes apparent that these rights are often treated in a cavalier manner, and this underscores the need for serious attention once again to the integration of ethics into strategy.

Consumerism is just an interesting textbook topic, however, unless recognized as a legitimate force and responded to by business accordingly. A number of suggestions were given in the spirit that responsible action is needed if a free market economy is to function in the best interests of all parties.

Review and Discussion Questions

1. As this book is being written, Dow-Corning has just abandoned a product line for which it had been the world leader—silicone breast implants. Such products are unusual outside of the West. In brief, their primary use is after breast surgery to restore normal feminine appearance. Others use them to enhance breast size.

Dow Corning took this step because of scathing public attack for allegedly having concealed damaging safety information regarding the use of its silicone breast implants. If indeed these charges are justified, what would your verdict be? Is there any justification for such actions other than to prevent damage to sales? Can this defense ever be used ethically?

2. What if further legal inquiry sustains that Dow-Corning executives indeed withheld safety information but that there was no evidence of intentional legal violation. Assume further that all evidence collected largely affirms the danger if these implants rupture, even though some serious scientists disagree that consumer injury actually has resulted. What responsibility do you feel Dow-Corning has, if any, to women who feel their health was demonstrably damaged by defective implants? Clarify the reasons for your conclusion.

3. You have been charged with writing ad copy that has been charged in court as being false and misleading. The question now is the nature of the defense that you will undertake.

   a. What definitional standard(s) should be used to determine whether or not the appeal truly is false and misleading?

   b. You can make a clear case, based on written memoranda, documenting that senior management directed you to write the copy you did. It is clear that you could have lost your job had you not acquiesced. Would you use this in your defense? Is it ethical to do so?

4. Examine your own experiences as a consumer in the past year. Have you experienced feelings of alienation? From what sources? What might have been done by the offending organizations to have prevented this?

5. *Unsafe at Any Speed* was the title of Ralph Nader's book castigating the automobile industry, and he alleges that things have not improved to any degree. Following a research approach, how would you go about substantiating his claim? What types of safety standards could legitimately be proposed, taking cost-benefit analysis into account?

6. William Lazer, a former president of the American Marketing Association, advocated during the 1960s that marketing should work toward the end of helping the consumer to accept self-indulgence, luxurious surroundings, and nonutilitarian products. Do you agree?

7. A former president of Hunt-Wesson Foods proposed a number of years ago that business must divert some of its profits to help solve social problems and issues such as consumerism. Many today are making similar statements. However, such a practice might adversely affect financial returns, thus giving rise to potential conflict of interest. Can this be resolved?

8. "Get government out of the business of regulating automotive safety. The industry will police itself." What is your response?

9. This is not the typical end-of-chapter question, but we leave it with you anyway. You are selling a name brand headache remedy containing only pure aspirin. You are fully aware that generic brands containing exactly the same ingredients sell for half the price or less. Yet, your brand is marketed with such claims as "purity," "a name you can trust," "speed of relief."

   Examine your own code of ethics carefully, and answer this question: Can you justify this marketing strategy? What would your answer be to the charge that the advertising is deceptive from a belief-claim interaction perspective? Is it justifiable to continue selling as long as people keep buying? Try to make explicit the ethical principles underlying your initial responses.

Endnotes

1. Geoffrey P. Lantos, "Arthur Anderson & Co. Business Ethics Overview: A Summary and Critique," Stonehill College Working Paper, Copyright 1991 by Geoffrey P. Lantos.
2. See, for example, Peter F. Drucker, *An Introductory View of Management* (New York: Harper & Row, 1977), pt. 4.
3. Lantos, "Business Ethics Overview," 4.
4. Manuel G. Velasquez as quoted in Van B. Weigel, *Business Ethics and Transitional Economies*, Unpublished Manuscript, Eastern College, Copyright 1991 by Van B. Weigel, 187.
5. Kant's categorical imperative as cited in Manuel G. Velasquez, *Business Ethics: Concepts and Cases*, 2nd ed. (Englewood Cliffs, N.J.: Prentice-Hall, 1988), 196.
6. Velasquez, *Business Ethics*.
7. See Nancy Gifford, *When in Rome: An Introduction to Relativism and Knowledge* (Albany, N.Y.: SUNY Albany Press, 1983).
8. Weigle, *Business Ethics and Transitional Economies*, 7th ed. (New York: McGraw-Hill, 1980), 87.
9. Robert J. Lampman, "JFK's Four Consumer Rights: A Retrospective View," in E. Scott Maynes, ed., *The Frontier of Research in the Consumer Interest* (Columbia, Mo.: American Council on Consumer Interests, 1988), 19–36.
10. Robert O. Herrman, "Consumerism: Its Goals, Organizations and Future," *Journal of Marketing* 35 (October 1970), 55–60.
11. "Detroit May Be Missing the Market that Matters Most—Business Week/Harris Poll" *Business Week* (October 22, 1990), 91.
12. Scott Hume, "Consumers Target Ire at Data Bases," *Advertising Age* (May 6, 1991), 3.
13. "Americans Favor a Tight Leash on Business," *American Demographics* (August 1991), 20.
14. Darlene Brannigan Smith and Paul N. Bloom, "Is Consumerism Dead or Alive? Some New Evidence," in Thomas C. Kinnear, ed., *Advances in Consumer Research* 11 (Provo, Utah: Association for Consumer Research, 1984), 469–473.
15. For a sobering analysis on this point see Will and Ariel Durant, *The Lessons of History* (New York: Simon and Schuster, 1968).
16. For helpful examples on the role of consumer research, see William L. Wilkie, *Consumer Behavior* (New York: John Wiley & Sons, 1986), chap. 21.
17. See, for example, Lynn Phillips and Bobby Calder, "Evaluating Consumer Protection Laws, Promising Methods," *Journal of Consumer Affairs* 14 (Summer 1980), 9–36.
18. "The Consumer Bill of Rights," in *Consumer Advisory Council, First Report* (Washington, D.C.: U.S. Government Printing Office, 1963).
19. For a thorough review of product safety issues, see Jennifer L. Gerner, "Product Safety: A Review," in Maynes, *The Frontier of Research*, 37–60.
20. See Robert W. Crandall, "The Use of Cost-Benefit Analysis in Product Safety Regulation," in Maynes, *The Frontier of Research*, 61–76. Also Eric B. Ault, "CPCS'S Voluntary Standards: An Assessment and a Paradox," in Maynes, *The Frontier of Research*, 77–82.
21. "Procter & Gamble: On a Short Lease," *Business Week* (July 22, 1991), 76.
22. "The Consumer Bill of Rights."
23. Hans Thorelli, "The Future for Consumer Information Systems," in Jerry C. Olson, ed., *Advances in Consumer Research* 8 (Ann Arbor: Association for Consumer Research, 1980), 222.

24. Alan J. Resnik and Bruce L. Stern, "An Analysis of Information Content in Television Advertising," *Journal of Marketing* (January 1977), 50–53.

25. See George S. Day, "Assessing the Effects of Information Disclosure Requirements," *Journal of Marketing* (April 1976), 42–52.

26. David M. Gardner and Nancy H. Leonard, "Research in Deceptive and Corrective Advertising: Progress to Date and Impact on Public Policy," in James H. Leigh and Claude R. Martin, Jr., *Current Issues & Research in Advertising* 12 (Ann Arbor, Michigan: Division of Research, School of Business Administration, University of Michigan, 1991), 278.

27. Resnik and Stern, "An Analysis of Information Content."

28. Dorothy Cohen, "Legal Interpretations of Deception Are Deceiving," *Marketing News* (September 26, 1986), 12.

29. Cohen, "Legal Interpretations."

30. Cyndee Miller, "Ads Must Back up Their Claims—or Pay the Legal Price," *Marketing News* (February 1, 1988), 22.

31. Jacob Jacoby and Wayne D. Hoyer, "The Comprehension/Miscomprehension of Print Communication: Selected Findings," *Journal of Consumer Research* 15 (March 1989), 434–443.

32. Terence A. Shimp and Ivan L. Preston, "Deceptive and Nondeceptive Consequences of Evaluative Advertising," *Journal of Marketing* (Winter 1981), 22–32.

33. Howard Schlossberg, "The Simple Truth: Ads Will Have to Be Truthful," *Advertising Age* (December 24, 1990), 6.

34. For a helpful review of voluntary regulation practices, see Gordon E. Miracle and Terence Nevett, *Voluntary Regulation of Advertising* (New York: Lexington Books, 1987).

35. "The Consumer Bill of Rights."

36. John E. Kushman, "Increasing Competition Through Deregulation: Do Consumers Win or Lose?" in Maynes, *The Frontier of Research*, 413–439.

37. Rachel Dardis, "International Trade: The Consumer's Stake," in Maynes, *The Frontier of Research*, 355.

38. See, for example, Marilyn Kourilsky and Trudy Murray, "The Use of Economic Reasoning to Increase Satisfaction with Family Decision-Making," *Journal of Consumer Research* 15 (September 1981), 183–188.

39. "The Consumer Bill of Rights."

40. See George L. Priest, "The Disappearance of the Consumer from Modern Products Liability Law," in Maynes, *Frontiers of Consumer Research*, 771–791.

41. Faith Popcorn as quoted in Janet Neiman, "Values-Added Marketing," *ADWEEK* (April 6, 1987), 19.

42. Claes Fornell and Robert A. Westbrook, "The Vicious Cycle of Consumer Complaints," *Journal of Marketing* 48 (Summer 1984), 68–78.

43. Jaclyn Fierman, "The Big Muddle in Green Marketing," *Fortune* (June 3, 1991), 92.

44. Fierman, "The Big Muddle in Green Marketing," 91.

45. Fierman, "The Big Muddle in Green Marketing," 92–102.

46. Howard Schlossberg, "Americans Passionate about the Environment? Critic Says that's 'nonsense,'" *Advertising Age* (September 16, 1991), 8.

47. Rose Gutfield, "Eight of 10 Americans Are Environmentalists, At Least So They Say," *The Wall Street Journal* (August 2, 1991), 1.

48. Walecia Konrad, "I'd Toddle a Mile for a Camel," *Business Week* (December 23, 1991), 34.

49. James W. Johnston, "For Old Joe: Free Speech Is the Issue," *Advertising Age* (January 27, 1992), 22.

50. Comments made by the Hon. B. L. Kiplagat, Permanent Secretary of State, The Republic of Kenya, March 6, 1988.

51. John A. Byrne, "Businesses Are Signing Up for Ethics 101," *Business Week* (February 15, 1988), 56–57.

52. Shelby D. Hunt, Van R. Wood, and Lawrence B. Chonko, "Corporate Ethical Values and Organizational Commitment in Marketing," *Journal of Marketing* 53 (July 1989), 79–90.

53. Tom Peters and Nancy Austin, *A Passion for Excellence* (New York: Random House, 1985), 8.

GLOSSARY

absolute standards categorical moral revelations and religious laws used as the basis for ethical decision making.

absolute threshold the amount of stimulus energy or intensity necessary for sensation to occur.

abstract elements intangible elements of culture, such as values, attitudes, ideas, personality types, and summary constructs, such as religion.

abstract words those that express a quality apart from an object (e.g., justice, equality).

acceptance a stage of information processing representing the degree to which a stimulus influences the person's knowledge and/or attitudes.

active rejection the decision not to adopt an innovation.

Actual State Types consumers in whom need recognition results from changes in the actual state.

adaptation level the level at which an individual becomes so habituated to a stimulus that it is no longer noticed.

adopter one who makes the decision to continue using a new product.

adoption the decision to make full use of an innovation.

advertising wearout the reduction of advertising effectiveness as a result of excessive ad repetition.

affect feeling states that influence consumer behavior.

affective responses the feelings and emotions that are elicited by a stimulus.

affect referral a decision rule that assumes that a consumer has previously formed overall evaluations of each choice alternative, rather than judging them on various evaluative criteria.

AIDA an early conceptualization of the adoption process, including Awareness, Interest, Desire, Action.

aided recall measures measures that provide cues for retrieving learned information.

AIO measures measures of activities, interests, and opinions.

alienation feelings of powerlessness and isolation which, when experienced in regard to the business world, often results in consumerism.

alternative evaluation the third stage of the nonhabitual decision-making process in which a choice alternative is evaluated and selected to meet consumer needs.

analytical cross-cultural studies studies that attempt to deduce general principles of behavior that apply in one or more cultures.

anomie social instability resulting from a weakened respect for social norms and values.

approach in motivation, the theory that some forces promote or produce movement toward a goal object.

a priori segmentation analysis defining the segmentation base in advance.

Area of Dominant Influence an area for which advertising media is purchased, usually cities or areas surrounding them.

argument a message element relevant to forming a rational, reasoned opinion.

arousal a person's degree of alertness along a continuum ranging from extreme drowsiness to extreme wakefulness.

aspirational group a reference group whose members wish to adopt the norms, values, and behaviors of others.

association a variable of social class concerned with everyday relationships between people.

association measures *see* evaluated participation studies

associative network a conceptualization according to which memory consists of a series of nodes (representing concepts) and links (which represent associations between nodes).

attention a stage of information processing representing the allocation of cognitive capacity. *see also* direction of attention and intensity of attention

attitude an overall evaluation that can range from extremely positive to extremely negative.

attitude change a term used to characterize conditions under which a person holds a preexisting attitude that is changed subsequently.

attitude formation a term used to characterize conditions under which a person has yet to develop an attitude.

attraction effect a phenomenon in which a given alternative's attractiveness is enhanced when an inferior alternative is added to the set of choice alternatives.

attribute a characteristic or property of a product; generally refers to a characteristic that serves as an evaluative criterion during decision making.

attribute evaluation measures measures used to assess the goodness or badness of an attribute.

attribute importance measures measures used to assess the concept of salience or potential influence of product attributes.

attribute search sequence brand information is collected on an attribute-by-attribute basis.

attribution theory a theory stating that an individual encountering a situation is motivated to ascertain whether the causal influence on the person is internal or external (e.g., if a product fails, is the failure in the product or in an adjunct system, such as wiring?).

augmented product   the tangible attributes of a product plus its additional value to the consumer.

avoidance   in motivation, the theory that some forces promote or produce movements away from a goal object.

awareness analysis   a technique for assessing brand awareness by asking consumers to recall or recognize brand names.

awareness set   the set of brands familiar to a consumer.

baby boomer   one of the cohort of 77 million Americans born between 1946 and 1964.

background noise   a description of the way in which advertising may strike the consumer.

back-translation   a procedure in which a message is translated from its original language to the translated language and back to the original by a number of translators.

backward conditioning   classical conditioning in which the conditioned stimulus follows the unconditioned stimulus.

behavioral consistency   a phenomenon that exists when the purchase behavior of individuals in a submarket remains constant over time.

behavioral intention measures measures of the perceived likelihood that a particular behavior will be undertaken by the person.

behaviorist approach   an approach to learning in which learning is demonstrated by changes in behavior and the role of mental processes is ignored.

behavioristic variables   variables used for segmentation, including extent of use, loyalty, benefit, and usage situations.

belief   a link between two nodes in an associate network, such as "IBM is an expensive brand."

benefit segmentation   a marketing strategy oriented toward meeting a benefit or felt need in a target market segment.

birthrate   the number of live births per 1,000 population in a given year.

brand loyalty   a motivated, difficult-to-change habit of purchasing the same item or service, often rooted in high involvement.

brand personality   the attributes of a product and the profile of perceptions received by consumers about a specific brand.

brand search sequence   brand information is collected on a brand-by-brand basis.

breaking point   in location analysis, the point at which 50 percent of the market trade is attracted to each of two locations.

Bureau of Economic Analysis Economic Area   an area of geographic analysis designated by the Bureau of Economic Analysis and consisting of an "economic node" and the surrounding counties.

buyer's regret   a feeling of remorse following a purchase decision with high involvement.

cancellation rate   the proportion of customers who do not repurchase.

cannibalization   a new product reduces the market share of another product produced by the same company.

capacity   the cognitive resources that an individual has available at any given time for processing information.

category killer   a retailer that carries a broad assortment in one category of merchandise.

causal differences   consumer differences that represent motivating influences or other factors that define and shape behavior.

Censal-Ratio method   a population estimate method comparing an area's population from the most recent census with a variable that changes as the size of population changes.

Central Business District   the traditional "downtown" shopping district.

central route   a form of persuasion in which issue relevant thinking is high and message elements or arguments relevant to forming a reasoned opinion are influential.

chunk   a grouping or combination of information that can be processed as a unit.

classical conditioning   a form of learning in which a conditioned stimulus (e.g., the sound of a bell) is paired with an existing unconditioned stimulus (e.g., the sight of food) until the conditioned stimulus alone is sufficient to elicit a previously unconditioned response (e.g., salivation), which is now a conditioned response.

classification dominance   the state a retailer achieves when giving the customer the impression that the merchandise assortment contains virtually any item that could be desired.

closure   the tendency to develop a complete picture or perception even when elements in the perceptual field are missing.

cognitive approach   an approach to learning in which learning is seen as reflected in changes in knowledge, and emphasis is on understanding the mental processes that determine how people learn information.

cognitive consistency theories theories, such as balance theory and congruity theory, that propose that people strive to maintain a consistent set of beliefs and attitudes.

cognitive map   consumer perceptions of store locations and shopping areas, as opposed to actual locations.

cognitive responses   the thoughts that occur to an individual during the comprehension stage of information processing.

cohesion   the emotional bonding that family members have toward one another.

cohort   any group of individuals linked in some way, usually by age.

cohort analysis   a method of investigating the changes in patterns of behavior or attitudes or groups called cohorts.

communicability   the degree to which results from using a new product are visible to friends and neighbors.

communication   a facilitating dimension, critical to movement on the other family dimensions of cohesion and family adaptability.

communication situation   the setting in which the consumer is exposed to either personal or nonpersonal communications.

comparative advertising advertising that makes comparisons between products.

compatibility the degree to which a product is consistent with the existing values and past experiences of a potential adopter.

compensatory strategy a strategy in alternative evaluation in which a perceived weakness on one attribute may be compensated for or offset by strength on others.

competitive intensity the degree of a firm's competition.

completed fertility rate the total number of children ever born to women of a specific age group.

complexity the degree to which an innovation is perceived as difficult to understand and use.

component method a population estimate method that divides population into its components of change: births, deaths, and migration.

comprehension a stage of information processing in which interpretation of a stimulus occurs.

concentrated marketing marketing in which the primary focus is on one segment.

concrete words those that name a real thing or class of things.

conditioned response (CR) *see* classical conditioning

conditioned stimulus (CS) *see* classical conditioning

confidence the degree of conviction with which an attitude is held.

confirmation the process through which consumers seek reinforcement for the innovation decision.

conjunctive decision rule a non-compensatory decision rule involving processing by brand in which cutoffs are established for each salient attribute and each brand is compared to this set of cutoffs.

consideration set the set of alternatives from which choice is made.

Consolidated Metropolitan Statistical Area a grouping of closely related PMSAs.

constructive decision rule a decision rule that a consumer builds using elementary processing operations

(fragments of rules) available in memory that can accommodate the choice situation.

consumer behavior those actions directly involved in obtaining, consuming, and disposing of products and services, including the decision processes that precede and follow these actions.

consumerism policies and activities designed to protect consumer interests and rights as they are involved in an exchange relationship with any type of organization.

consumer knowledge information relevant to the functioning of consumers in the marketplace.

consumer satisfaction/dissatisfaction (CS/D) a judgment as to whether purchase outcomes meet expectations.

consumer socialization the acquisition of consumption-related cognitions, attitudes, and behavior.

content analysis a technique for determining the values, themes, role prescriptions, norms of behavior, and other elements of culture.

contextualized marketing a marketing strategy designed to take into account cultural differences in consumer motivation and behavior by adapting marketing efforts in such a way that they are perceived as culturally relevant.

continuous innovation the modification of an existing product.

core merchandise the basic group of products essential to a store's traffic, customer loyalty, and profits.

core values values that are basic to understanding human behavior.

corrective advertising advertising used to rectify deception that occurred in previous advertising.

counterargument a cognitive response that opposes the claims made in a communication.

credence claims claims that a consumer cannot evaluate or verify (e.g., "Millions of research dollars are behind this product").

credit an amount or sum placed at a person's disposal by a bank or other financial institution, which extends the income resource, at least temporarily.

cross-cultural analysis the systematic comparison of similarities and dif-

ferences in the material and behavioral aspects of cultures.

crude birthrate *see* birthrate

CUBE (Comprehensive Understanding of Buyer Environment) post-hoc segmentation analysis identifying eight primary segments.

cultural analysis studies whose goal is to create the ability to understand and be effective in addressing the core values of a society.

cultural artifacts *see* material components

cultural empathy the ability to understand without judging the inner logic and coherence of other ways of life.

cultural functionalist an anthropologist holding the view that culture is an entity that serves humans in their efforts to meet the basic biological and social needs of the society.

culture the values, ideas, artifacts, and other meaningful symbols that help individuals communicate, interpret, and evaluate as members of society.

customer satisfaction monitoring program a policy of using ongoing customer surveys to continually monitor and evaluate service.

cutoff a restriction or requirement for acceptable attribute values, used in alternative evaluation.

decay theory a theory positing that the strength of a memory trace will fade over time.

decision rule a strategy that a consumer uses to make a selection from the choice alternatives.

declarative knowledge knowledge of information facts, which are subjective in that they need not correspond to objective reality.

defensive marketing marketing that encourages and resolves consumer complaints.

deference the granting of social honor.

degree of search a dimension of search indicating the total amount of search.

demarketing a deliberate attempt to induce consumers to buy less in a product class.

demographics   the characteristics of human populations, such as size, growth, density, distribution, and vital statistics; used in consumer research to describe segments of consumers in such terms as age, income, and education.

demographic segmentation   directing marketing efforts toward differing segments as defined by demographic characteristics.

demography   the study of demographics.

demonstrated recall measure   a measure utilizing a survey to determine what percentage of viewers can recall the name of the advertised product and one point from the advertising copy.

deontologically   reasoning based on one's right or duty or the inherent morality within the act itself.

depth interview   the interviewing of a small sample (50 or fewer), one at a time, in a lengthy, unstructured session.

descriptive cross-cultural studies   studies that describe structural components and are used to contrast or compare societies.

descriptive differences   consumer differences that are merely descriptive, as opposed to causal.

Designated Marketing Area   *see* Area of Dominant Influence

Desired State Types   consumers in whom need recognition results from changes in the desired state.

determinant attribute   a salient attribute on which choice alternatives differ in their performance.

dialectical materialism   the view that culture moves in a determined direction through a process of exchange and social interaction in competition for scarce resources.

difference threshold   the smallest change in stimulus intensity that will be noticed by an individual.

differentiated marketing   marketing that concentrates on two or more segments, offering a differing marketing mix for each.

diffusion   the process by which an innovation is communicated through certain channels over time among the members of a social system.

directed learning   learning that occurs when learning is the primary objective during information processing (i.e., motivation is high).

direction of attention   a dimension of attention representing the focus of cognitive capacity.

direction of search   a dimension of search representing the specific content of search.

direct marketing   activities by which products and services are offered for information purposes or to solicit a direct response from a present or prospective customer or distributor by mail, telephone, or other access.

discontinuance   ceasing to use a previously adopted innovation.

discontinuous innovation   an entirely new product that causes buyers to significantly alter their behavior patterns.

discrimination   in classical conditioning, the process whereby an organism learns to emit a response to one stimulus but avoids making the same response to a similar stimulus.

discriminative stimuli   stimuli that serve as cues about the likelihood that performing a particular behavior will lead to reinforcement.

dissatisfaction   the outcome of purchase when the consumer perceives the choice as falling short of expectations.

dissociative group   a reference group whose members are motivated to avoid association.

door-in-the-face   a multiple-request procedure under which compliance with a critical request is increased if this request is preceded by an even more demanding request which is refused.

doubling rate   the length of time required for the population to double in size based on current growth rates.

drive   a condition of arousal that occurs when there is sufficient discrepancy between a present state and a desired or preferred state of being.

dynamically continuous innovation   either the creation of a new product or the alteration of an existing one; either way, there is no alteration in established patterns of customer buying and product use.

early adopter   a consumer who adopts an innovation later than innovators.

early majority   consumers who adopt an innovation after early adopters.

echoic   the term used to describe auditory processing at the sensory-memory stage.

economic demographics   the study of the economic characteristics of a nation's population.

economic node   a metropolitan or similar area that serves as center of economic activity.

economic role   *see* instrumental role

elaboration   the amount of integration between new information and existing knowledge stored in memory (or, the number of personal connections made between the stimulus and one's life experiences and goals).

Elaboration Likelihood Model   the theory of persuasion which proposes that the influence exerted by various communication elements will depend on the elaboration that occurs during processing.

elimination by aspects decision rule   a noncompensatory decision rule involving processing by attribute in which cutoffs are established for each salient attribute and brands are compared on the most important attribute; if several brands meet the cutoff, the next most important attribute is selected until the tie is broken.

empty-nester   an older adult whose children have left home and the university.

enhanced shareholder value   long-term, consistent appreciation of shareholder value.

enthography   a research method, borrowed from cultural anthropology, which includes a guided interview supplemented by participant observation of buying and consumption behavior.

entrepreneurship   organizing, managing, and assuming the risks of a business or enterprise. Refers not only to the traditional small business, but also to the value of individual effort and accomplishment in large corporations.

environmental scanning   analysis of the current environment and projected trends, including internal and external variables.

epidemiological model   a diffusion-prediction model assuming that diffusion is a process of social interaction in which innovators and early adopters "infect" other consumers.

episodic knowledge   knowledge involving information that is bound by the passage of time (e.g., knowing when one last purchased clothing).

equitable performance   in purchase expectations, a normative judgment reflecting the performance one ought to receive.

ergonomics   the study of the human factors involved with product design.

ethnic patterns   the norms and values of specific groups within the larger society.

ethnocentricity   an attitude that one's own group, race, or nationality is superior.

ethnographic research   research in which researchers place themselves in the culture or its artifacts in order to "soak up" meaning.

evaluation   the measure used to assess the "goodness-badness" of an attribute or product.

evaluative criteria   the standards and specifications used by consumers to compare different products and brands.

evaluative participation studies   studies in which researchers count the number and nature of personal contacts in people's informal relationships, using data collected from respondents as well as their own observations of the community and its formal and informal networks.

event marketing   creating events at which opinion leaders are brought together to experience and evaluate a new or existing product.

evoked set   *see* consideration set

executional elements   elements in a communication other than the message content, such as visuals, sounds, colors, and pace.

expectancy disconfirmation model   a theory of the process by which performance of a product or service is evaluated and a satisfaction/dissatisfaction outcome is reached.

expected performance   in purchase expectations, a normative judgment reflecting what the performance probably will be.

experience claims   claims that a consumer can fully evaluate only after product consumption.

experiential benefits   the symbolic value of a consumption object in terms of emotional response, sensory pleasure, daydreams, or aesthetic considerations.

exposure   physical proximity to a stimulus that allows the opportunity for one or more senses to be activated.

expressive role   role behavior involving support to other family members in the decision-making process and expression of the family's aesthetic or emotional needs.

extended family   nuclear family plus such other relatives as grandparents, uncles and aunts, cousins, and in-laws.

extended problem solving   detailed and rigorous decision-making behavior, including need recognition, search for information, alternative evaluation, purchase, and outcomes. Often used in making major or critical purchases.

external search   a stage of the consumer decision process in which relevant information is acquired.

extinction   in classical conditioning, when the conditioned stimulus no longer evokes the conditioned response.

exurbs   areas beyond the suburbs.

family   a group of two or more persons related by blood, marriage, or adoption who reside together.

family adaptability   the ability of a family or marital system to change its power structure, role relationships, and relationship rules in response to situational and developmental stress.

family branding   the strategy of placing the same brand name on various company products to encourage generalization.

family life cycle (FLC)   the stages a family passes through during its lifetime.

family of orientation   the family into which an individual is born.

family of procreation   the family which is established by marriage.

favorability   the degree of negativeness or positiveness of an attitude.

fertility rate   the number of live births per 1,000 women of childbearing age (15 to 44).

festival marketplace   a large complex of shops and restaurants, such as Boston's Faneuil Hall Marketplace or New York City's South Street Seaport.

figure   those elements within a perceptual field that receive the most attention (*see also* ground).

first-order child   first-born child

focus   direction of attention.

focus group   a group of about 10 individuals, brought together with a trained leader for about 1 hour to discuss motivations and behavior.

foot-in-the-door   a multiple-request procedure under which compliance with a critical request is increased if the person first agrees to an initial smaller request.

forced-choice recognition measures   measures that require respondents to choose among a set of fixed answers (as in a multiple-choice instrument) to demonstrate their memory of specific ad and brand elements.

foreseeability   the doctrine that a manufacturer should be able to anticipate and evaluate risks inherent in product use and find out ways to avoid them.

formal group   a reference group characterized by a defined, known list of members and an organization and structure codified in writings.

forward conditioning   conditioning in which the conditioned stimulus precedes the unconditioned stimulus.

framed ad   one in which the message relates the picture to the product.

fully planned purchase   a purchase in which both the product and the brand are selected as intended.

functionality   the degree to which a product's features meet a consumer's needs.

functional role   *see* instrumental role

general fertility rate   *see* fertility rate

generalization   in classical conditioning, when a new stimulus similar to the existing one elicits the same response.

generic branding   descriptive labeling of products that sell at lower prices than nationally advertised brands.

generic need recognition   the activation of a need for a particular product category; the need is not brand specific as in selective need recognition.

gentrification   a process in which people move back to revitalized city neighborhoods, often displacing low-income families.

geodemography   the analysis of demographic lifestyle profiles for areas as small as a neighborhood.

geographic segmentation   analysis of geographic differences in terms of region, size of metropolitan area, and density.

Gestalt psychology   a theory that focuses on how people organize or combine stimuli into a meaningful whole.

global marketing   the technique of using the same marketing strategy in all cultural contexts.

global thinking   the ability to understand markets beyond one's own country of origin with respect to sources of demand, sources of supply, and methods of effective management and marketing.

Gross Domestic Product (GDP)   a measure of goods and services produced in the United States, including those produced or provided by foreign companies operating in the United States.

ground   the elements, other than figure, that comprise the background in a perceptual field.

group norms   stable expectations arrived at by consensus concerning behavioral rules for individual members.

growth rate   the increase in population due to natural increase and net migration, expressed as a percentage of base population.

habitual decision making   decision making based on habits of repeat purchasing, often formed to simplify decision-process activity.

hardware   the physical or tangible aspects of a product.

heavy half   the heavy users of a product.

hedonic benefits   *see* experiential benefits

heterophilous communications   a situation in which individuals are exposed to messages that are inconsistent with their own beliefs and values, which may cause cognitive dissonance and be a less effective method of communicating.

higher-order child   any child born after a first-born child.

historicalist   *see* structuralist

homophilous influence   influence brought about by information transmission between people similar in social class, age, education, and other demographic characteristics.

homophily   the degree to which pairs of individuals who interact are similar in important attributes, such as beliefs, education, and social status.

household   all the persons, related and unrelated, who occupy a housing unit.

Housing-Unit method   a population estimate method that multiplies occupied housing units by the average household size.

hypermarket   a retail store in the 60,000- to 200,000-square-foot range that carries both convenience and shopping goods, with a heavy emphasis on general merchandise as well as on food.

hypodermic needle model   a theory of marketing communications proposing that media have direct, immediate, and powerful effects on new product acceptance.

iconic   the terms used to describe visual processing at the sensory-memory stage.

ideal performance   in purchase expectations, a normative judgment reflecting the optimum or ideal performance level.

ideology of consumption   the social meaning attached to and communicated by products.

image analysis   the examination of consumers' knowledge or beliefs about a product's properties.

imagery   a process by which sensory information and experiences are represented in working memory.

imitation effect   a phenomenon in which the rate of adoption increases as the number of adopters increases.

implementation   the process by which a consumer puts a product into use.

importance   the measure used to operationalize the concept of salience.

impulse purchase   a spur-of-the-moment purchase triggered by product display or point-of-sale promotion.

inbound telemarketing   use of the telephone to place orders for goods or services.

incentive   an anticipated reward from a course of action that offers need-satisfying potential.

incidental learning   learning that occurs even when learning is not the primary objective during information processing.

indepth (or guided) interview   a research method, borrowed from clinical psychology, using a small sample (50 or less), one at a time in a lengthy, unstructured interview session.

individualized standards   situational or individual ethic strategies used as the basis for ethical decision making.

inertia   a motivation that leads to habitual decision making due to a lack of sufficient incentive to consider alternative brands.

influential   a transmitter of opinions about products and services.

informal group   a loosely structured reference group based on friendship or collegial associations. Norms, even when stringent, seldom appear in writing.

information adequacy   the degree to which a consumer has the facts needed to make an informed choice.

informational advertising   advertising that attempts to influence consumers' product knowledge and attitudes by providing information that elicits favorable cognitive responses.

informational influence   the influence of friends or spokespeople, which consumers often accept as providing credible and needed evidence about reality.

information environment   the entire array of product-related data available to the consumer.

information overload   a situation that occurs when the amount of information in a choice environment exceeds cognitive capacity.

information processing   the process by which a stimulus is received, interpreted, stored in memory, and later retrieved.

information veracity   the degree to which advertising is free of deception and misrepresentation.

inner-directed consumers   consumers whose lives are directed more toward their individual needs than toward values oriented to externals.

innovation   any idea or product perceived by the potential adopters to be new.

innovativeness   the degree to which an individual adopts an innovation relatively earlier than other members in the system do.

innovator   a consumer who adopts a new product early.

instrumental learning   a form of learning in which the consequences of a behavior affect the frequency or probability of the behavior being performed again.

instrumental role   role behavior based on knowledge of functional attributes, such as financial aspects, performance characteristics, or conditions of purchase.

Integrated Marketing Communications (IMC)   a comprehensive, unified marketing program emphasizing the same theme or themes in advertising, public relations, investor relations, and other communications, with a targeted market.

intensity   the strength of an attitude.

intensity of attention   the amount of attention focused in a particular direction.

interactive picture   one in which both the product class and brand name are represented visually.

inter-environmental considerations the concept, important in global marketing strategy, of considering the characteristic ways a culture responds to marketing.

interference theory   according to this theory, forgetting is due to the learning of new information.

internal search   retrieval of knowledge from memory.

intra-environmental considerations the methods of marketing that are characteristic of a firm in its own culture.

involvement   strong motivation, as reflected in high perceived personal relevance of a stimulus in a particular context.

key-informant method   a research method in which knowledgeable people are used to identify the influentials within a social system.

knowledge   the information stored within memory.

knowledge stage   the first Rogers innovation-decision stage, in which a consumer receives physical or social stimuli that give exposure and attention to the new product.

labeling   a behavior modification technique in which attaching a label or description to a person increases the likelihood of her or him behaving in a manner that is consistent with the label.

laddering   in-depth probing directed toward uncovering higher-level meanings both at the benefit (attribute) level and at the value level.

laggard   consumers who are the last to adopt a new product.

later majority   consumers who adopt an innovation after the early majority.

learning   the process by which experience leads to changes in knowledge, attitudes, and/or behavior resulting from experience.

leisure   discretionary or uncommitted time.

lexicographic decision rule   a noncompensatory rule involving processing by attribute in which brands are compared on the most important attribute; if more than one brand qualifies, the next most important attribute is selected until the tie is broken.

life chances   the fundamental aspects of a person's future possibilities.

lifestyle   patterns by which people live and spend time and money.

lifestyle retailing   the policy of tailoring a retail offer closely to the lifestyles of specific target market groups of consumers.

limited problem solving   limited decision-making behavior using a reduced number and variety of information sources, alternatives, and evaluation criteria.

lowballing   the behavior modification technique of citing a low price to gain customer commitment, then raising the price.

lower threshold   *see* absolute threshold

macroculture   the set of values and symbols that apply to an entire society.

macromarketing   macroanalysis of consumer behavior focused on determining the aggregate performance of marketing in society.

Management by Wandering Around   the practice of keeping open channels of communication with subordinates and customers by direct personal contact.

market-driven   a firm using a strategy that involves identifying high-growth opportunities in consumer, merchandise, and geographic markets, and having well-defined marketing strategies geared to some form of dominance.

marketing   the process of planning and executing the conception, pricing, promotion, and distribution of ideas, goods, and services to create exchanges that satisfy individual and organizational objectives.

marketing communications   shared meanings between retailing organizations and persons, with exchange as their objective.

marketing mix   a marketing strategy integrating product, price, promotion, and distribution.

market segment   one of various groupings of buyers who expect benefits from a given transaction.

market segmentation   a marketing strategy involving viewing each segment as a distinct target with its own requirements for product, price, distribution, and promotion.

market types   classifications of products, including consumer package goods, consumer durable goods, industrial support consumables, industrial process consumables (commodities), make-or-buy consumables, and industrial capital goods.

massification theory   the theory that social class distinctions among the working and middle classes are disappearing.

material components   the physical components of culture, such as books, computers, tools, buildings, and specific products.

measurement correspondence   the degree to which a measure captures the action, target, time, and/or contextual elements that make up the to-be-predicted behavior.

megalopolis   *see* Consolidated Metropolitan Statistical Area

me-too product   one whose packaging mimics that of a highly successful brand.

Metropolitan Statistical Area   a freestanding metropolitan area, surrounded by nonmetropolitan counties and not closely related with other metropolitan areas.

microculture   the set of values and symbols of a restrictive group, such as a religious, ethnic, or other subdivision of the social whole.

micromarketing   microanalysis of consumer trends and demographics that focuses on the marketing programs of specific organizations.

microspecialization   the identification of specific market targets and the development of specialized retailing formats that provide a high level of satisfaction to those market targets.

mid-range problem solving   decision-making behavior falling between extended problem solving and limited problem solving on the problem-solving continuum.

mini-mall   small and medium-size shopping centers of various formats, usually with less than 100,000 square feet. Some are fully enclosed or have an all-weather format.

misperception   inaccurate knowledge.

mobility and succession   a dual concept related to the stability or instability of stratification systems.

modeling   a form of learning in which an individual observes the behaviors of others and the consequences of those behaviors.

monodic approach   in innovation-diffusion research, a focus upon the personal and social characteristics of industrial consumers.

monomorphic   describes consumers who are innovative for only one product.

monomorphic influence   influence that relates to one product only.

motivation research   research into the classification of consumer motives and whether they are conscious or unconscious.

motive   an enduring predisposition that arouses and directs behavior toward certain goals. Motives can be rational (utilitarian) or emotional (hedonic).

multiattribute attitude models   models that propose that overall attitude depends on beliefs about the attitude object's attributes weighted by the salience of these attributes.

multi-stage interaction   a theory of personal influence that holds that both influentials and information seekers are affected by the media.

natural increase   the surplus of births over deaths in a given time period.

need   a perceived difference between an ideal state and the present state, sufficient to activate behavior.

need-driven consumers   consumers who exhibit spending driven by need rather than preference.

need for cognition   a personality trait representing an individuals' tendency to undertake and enjoy thinking.

need recognition   perception of a difference between the desired state of affairs and the actual situation sufficient to arouse and activate the decision process; the first stage of the decision-making process.

negative disconfirmation   a CS/D judgment that performance is worse than expected.

negative reinforcement   in operant conditioning, a behavior leading to the removal of some adverse stimulus which increases the odds of the behavior being repeated.

network marketing   the development of a firm's marketing mix in close relationship to the marketing program of other firms.

new consumerism   contemporary consumerism, generally thought to begin with President Kennedy's 1962 address on the consumer bill of rights.

niche retailer   a retailer offering a narrow but deep assortment, such as Banana Republic.

nonadopter   one who makes the decision not to adopt a new product.

nonadoption   *see* passive rejection

no-name brand   *see* generic branding

noncompensatory strategy   a strategy in alternative evaluation in which a brand's weakness on one attribute cannot be offset by a strength on another attribute.

noninteractive pictures   pictures in which either product class or brand name, but not both, are shown visually.

normative influence   *see* utilitarian influence

norms   beliefs held by consensus of a group concerning the behavior rules for individual members.

nuclear family   immediate group of father, mother, and children living together.

objective knowledge measures   measures that assess the knowledge actually stored in memory.

objective research methods   assigning status to respondents on the basis of a stratified variable such as occupation, income, or education.

observability   *see* communicability

observation   a measure for observing consumer search based on how much people seek information before making a decision.

one-sided message   a communication presenting only the pros of the advocated position.

ongoing search   a type of external search in which information acquisition occurs on a relatively regular basis regardless of sporadic purchase needs.

operant conditioning   *see* instrumental learning

opinion leader   person from whom a consumer seeks consumer-related advice.

order effects   the differences in consumption between families caused by birth order (first-order babies generate more economic impact than higher-order babies).

outbound telemarketing marketing telephone contact by the seller to the consumer.

outcomes the fifth stage in decision making, in which the consumer evaluates whether or not the chosen alternative meets needs and expectations once it is used.

outer-directed consumers consumers who generally buy with awareness of what other people will attribute to their consumption of the purchased product.

outshopper a consumer who shops outside a local trading area.

PAD paradigm A categorization of emotional responses including the dimensions of pleasure, arousal, and dominance.

parody display the mockery of status symbols and behavior, as in the wearing of "work clothes" by upper-class youth.

partially planned an intention to buy the product but brand choice is deferred until shopping.

partial reinforcement a schedule of reinforcement in which the desired response is reinforced only part of the time; it may be systematic (e.g., every third response) or random.

passive rejection never really considering use of an innovation.

penetration model model that predicts the level of penetration by a new product in a given time period based on early sales results.

pension elite 3 million older adults, mostly between 65 and 74, with enough income from multiple sources to support an active, independent, and healthy lifestye.

peripheral cues elements in a communication that are irrelevant to developing a reasoned opinion.

peripheral route a form of persuasion in which issue relevant thinking is low and peripheral cues become influential.

personal determinants of attention the characteristics of an individual that influence attention.

personality the consistent responses of an individual to environmental stimuli.

person-situation segmentation a segmentation strategy that takes into account the fact that different consumers seek different product benefits, which can change across different usage situations.

persuasion the formation of favorable or unfavorable attitudes toward an innovation.

phased decision strategy a process using one decision rule as a screening device to help narrow the choice set to a more manageable number, and a different rule or rules to make the final choice.

piece part and tooling costs a reflection of whether a product is designed to be produced with processes and materials suited to the manufacturer's product levels and target costs as well as the product's actual purpose.

polymorphic influence influence that relates to several product areas.

polymorphism describes consumers who are innovators for many products.

positive disconfirmation a CS/D judgment that performance is better than expected.

positive reinforcement in operant conditioning, a behavior leading to receiving some positive stimulus which increases the odds of the behavior being repeated.

post-hoc segmentation analysis defining the segmentation base as an outcome of analysis.

power potential of individuals or groups to carry out their will over others.

power mall *see* mini-mall

prepotency the theory that needs are organized in such a way as to establish priorities and hierarchies of importance.

prepurchase search a type of external search that is motivated by an upcoming purchase decision.

prestige a variable of social class reflecting other people's attitude of respect or deference to a person.

primacy an order effect wherein stimuli appearing at the beginning of a sequence are given more weight in the resulting interpretation.

primary group a social aggregation (reference group) sufficiently small to permit and facilitate unrestricted face-to-face interaction.

Primary Metropolitan Statistical Area a metropolitan area closely related to another city.

proactive inhibition a form of interference in which prior learning hinders the learning and retrieval of new information.

problem solving thoughtful, reasoned action undertaken to bring about need satisfaction.

procedural knowledge the understanding of how the facts of declarative knowledge can be used.

processing by attribute *see* attribute search sequence

processing by brand *see* brand search sequence

producibility the degree to which a product can be made with a firm's normal capabilities.

product category the category of goods (e.g., clothing, appliances).

product knowledge information stored in memory about a product category, such as the brands within it, product terminology, product attributes, and beliefs about the product category and specific brands.

product life cycle the cycle of introduction, growth, and decline of a product. Marketing strategy and mix must be adapted to the changing stages of the life cycle.

product positioning the ways in which consumers identify a product with a defined set of attributes such as power, sportiness, caffeine, or color.

product potential the tangible attributes, augmented product, and consumer expectations for the product, all combined to incorporate every factor that might attract and hold customers.

product semantics *see* semiotics

Profit Impact of Market Strategy Research research into how market strategy affects practitioners economically; it indicates that market leaders achieve average rates of return three times greater than firms with low market share.

programmed resource relationship a retailer-supplier relationship in which the retailer is a powerful controlling factor.

projective test a questioning technique that allows the respondent to reply in the third person.

prompting a behavior modification technique in which consideration of product purchase is gained by a simple request (e.g., offering or suggesting a side dish in a restaurant).

proposition *see* belief

proxy variable a variable that stands in for another (e.g., demographic data can serve as a proxy variable for motivation and interests).

psychoanalytic theory a personality theory that posits that the human personality system consists of the id (the source of psychic energy), the superego (representing societal or personal norms), and the ego (which mediates the hedonistic demands of the id and the moralistic prohibitions of the superego).

psychographics research into psychological profiles of groups or individuals, especially regarding personality traits, values, beliefs, preferences, and behavior patterns.

psychographic segmentation analysis of lifestyle factors for segmentation purposes.

psycholinguistics the study of psychological factors involved in the perception of and response to linguistic phenomena.

pull strategy a marketing strategy for creating product demand by appealing to the ultimate consumers, who, in turn, encourage the channel to carry the product.

punishment in operant conditioning, a behavior leading to the appearance of an adverse stimulus which decreases the odds of the behavior being repeated.

purchase the fourth stage in the decision-making process, in which the consumer acquires the preferred alternative or an acceptable substitute.

purchase knowledge information stored in memory that is germane to acquiring products.

purchase situation those settings in which consumers acquire products and services.

push strategy a marketing strategy that involves focusing selling efforts on the channel, which is then responsible for attracting consumers.

Quality Function Deployment the use of customer input throughout the design, engineering, manufacturing, and distribution of a product.

ratio-correlation method a population estimation method that uses multiple regression to mathematically compute a population estimate.

rational decision making problem solving based on the careful weighing and evaluation of utilitarian or functional product attributes.

recall measures measures of cognitive learning that do not provide cues to prompt memory.

recency an order effect wherein stimuli appearing at the end of a sequence are given more weight in the resulting interpretation.

reciprocity a principle that states that we should try to repay what others have done for us.

recognition measures measures of cognitive learning that provide cues to prompt memory.

reference group a person or group of people that significantly influences an individual's behavior and attitudes.

rehearsal the mental repetition of information (i.e., the recycling of information through short-term memory).

rejection the decision not to adopt an innovation.

relational approach in innovation-diffusion research, a focus on communication networks and how social-structural variables affect diffusion flows in the system.

relative advantage the degree to which consumers perceive a relative advantage of a new product over the existing product.

relativism a belief that morality is relative to or dependent on some cultural, social, or personal standard. There cannot be an absolute moral standard.

relativists people who do not believe in moral absolutes, but instead believe that morality depends on cultural, social, and personal standards.

repeated problem solving decision-making dynamics that lead the consumer to buy a different brand than previously purchased.

replacement rate the fertility rate required to replace the current population, with allowance for some infant mortality.

reputational research methods methods utilizing people's rankings of the social position or prestige of other people.

resource commitments the degree to which research and development, advertising, personal selling, sales promotion, and distribution support are devoted to the diffusion process.

retail image the way a store is defined in a shopper's mind, partly by its functional qualities and partly by an aura of psychological attributes.

retail image measurement measures of image include many attitude-measurement techniques, including semantic differential and psycholinguistics.

retailing portfolio a group of specialty stores, each programmed for a specific lifestyle, owned by one retailer.

retention the transfer of information to long-term memory.

retrieval the process by which knowledge stored in long-term memory is activiated.

retrieval set a consideration set obtained by recall of alternatives from memory.

retroactive inhibition a form of interference in which recently learned information inhibits the retrieval of previously learned information.

retrospective questioning a measure for consumer search based on recall of search activities during decision making.

role what the typical occupant of a given position is expected to do in that position in a particular social context.

role overload a situation in which the total demands on time and energy associated with the prescribed activities of multiple roles are too great to allow an individual to perform the roles adequately or comfortably.

salience the potential influence that a criterion exerts during the alternative evaluation process, often measured in terms of importance.

satisfaction a postconsumption evaluation that a chosen alternative meets or exceeds expectations.

schema a high-order knowledge structure made up of a combination of propositions or beliefs.

script one type of schema, which contains knowledge about the temporal action sequences that occur during an event.

search the motivated activation of knowledge stored in memory or acquisition of information from the environment; the second stage of the decision-making process.

search claims claims that a consumer can accurately evaluate before purchase through external search.

secondary group a reference group exhibiting face-to-face behavior that is more sporadic, less comprehensive, and less influential in shaping thought and behavior than that of a primary group.

selective need recognition the activation of a need for a specific brand within a product category.

self-actualization the desire to know, understand, systematize, prioritize, and construct a system of values.

self-concept an organized configuration of perceptions of the self which are admissible to awareness, including perceptions of one's characteristics, values, and relationships.

self-designation method a research method by which people are asked to evaluate the extent to which they are sought out for advice.

self-monitoring a personality trait representing the degree of sensitivity to situational and interpersonal considerations.

self-perception theory a theory stating that individuals come to know their own attitudes, emotions, and other internal states by inferring them from observations of their own behavior.

self-referencing relating information to one's own self and experiences.

self-serving strategy a technology-development strategy in which a firm develops innovations but waits to introduce them until sales of its current products decline.

semantic knowledge generalized knowledge that gives meaning to an individual's world.

semiotics the study of the symbolic qualities of products in the context of their use.

sensation the activation of sensory receptors, following which the encoded information about the stimulus is transmitted along nerve fibers to the brain.

sensation seeker an individual motivated by the need for continued high-level stimulation.

sequence of search a dimension of search representing the order in which search activities occur.

shaping the reinforcement of successive approximations of a desired behavior pattern or of behaviors that must be performed before the desired response can be emitted.

simple additive decision rule a compensatory decision rule under which the consumer counts the number of times each alternative is judged favorably in terms of the set of salient evaluative criteria.

simple confirmation a CS/D judgment that performance equals expectations.

simple recognition measures measures that involve presenting ads to people and asking whether they remember seeing them previously.

simultaneous conditioning classical conditioning in which the conditioned stimulus and unconditioned stimulus are presented at the same time.

situational influence the influence arising from factors that are particular to a specific time and place and are independent of consumer and object characteristics.

social class divisions within society composed of individuals sharing similar values, interests, and behavior.

socialization the process of absorbing a culture and all of its values and symbols.

sociometric measures *see* evaluative participation studies

sociometric method a research method in which individuals are asked to identify others they seek out for advice or information for decision making.

socio-psychological theory a personality theory that posits that social variables (not biological instincts) shape personality and that behavioral motivation is directed to shape those needs created by the social variables.

software the information base that accompanies a product's hardware component.

stability a dimension of one's attitude determining its endurance and longevity.

standardized technology technology that has become standardized among firms; its presence encourages diffusion.

Standard Metropolitan Statistical Area the old term for Metropolitan Statistical Area.

status group a group that reflects a community's expectations for style of life among each class as well as the positive or negative social estimation of honor given each class.

stimulus categorization the classifying of a stimulus during the comprehension stage of information processing using concepts stored in memory.

stimulus determinants of attention the characteristics of a stimulus that influence attention.

store atmospherics the physical properties of the retail environment.

store image *see* retail image

structuralist an anthropologist who believes that culture follows a logic based on the patterns of the human mind.

subjective knowledge measures measures that assess a person's perception of the amount of knowledge he or she possesses, which may or may not correspond to her or his actual knowledge.

subjective research methods methods assigning status to individuals based on the perceptions of other people and the subjective insights or theories of the researchers.

subliminal persuasion the theory that stimuli below the lower or absolute threshold can influence attitudes and behavior.

supplier-style retailing in contrast to lifestyle retailing, supplier-side retailing emphasizes homogeneity and gives little or no recognition to customer differences.

support argument a cognitive response that is favorable to the claims of a communication.

surrogate shopping list a list of products obtained in response to product display rather than through cognitive planning.

telologically reasoning based on the morality of the consequences of one's actions.

terminal threshold the point at which additional increases in stimulus intensity have no effect on sensation.

time goods products and services classified by their time properties.

time guarantee a promise by the seller that the customer will not have to devote an unreasonable amount of time to getting product and service problems resolved.

total fertility rate the average number of children that would be born alive to a woman if she were to pass through all her childbearing years conforming to the age specific fertility rates of a given year.

total product concept the combination of the generic product, expected product, augmented product, and potential product; successful introduction of new products requires understanding of this concept.

total reinforcement a schedule of reinforcement in which the desired response is always reinforced.

trait any distinguishable, relatively enduring way in which one individual differs from another.

trait-factor theory a personality theory that postulates that an individual's personality is composed of definite predispositional attributes called traits.

transformational advertising advertising that attempts to influence consumers' perceptions of a product's emotional and symbolic features by eliciting favorable affective responses.

trend analysis the analysis of marketing opportunities that arise as a result of changes in the environment.

trend following a technology-development strategy in which a firm capitalizes on the developments of other firms in the industry while minimizing its own research and development expenses.

trend setting a technology-development strategy in which a firm continuously develops innovations for current and future product developments, and introduces these innovations as soon as feasible.

trickle-down theory a theory of personal influence that holds that lower classes emulate the behavior of their high-class counterparts.

two-sided message a communication presenting the pros and cons of the advocated position.

two-step flow model a theory of personal influence that holds that new ideas first flow to influentials, who then pass them on to the rest of the population.

unaided recall measures measures that do not provide cues for retrieving information from memory.

unconditioned response see classical conditioning

unconditioned stimulus see classical conditioning

undifferentiated marketing marketing that targets all available segments.

unframed ad one in which the message does not relate the picture to the product.

unplanned purchase a purchase for which a conscious intention was not articulated in advance.

usage knowledge information in memory about how a product can be used and what is required to actually use it.

usage situation the setting where consumption occurs.

usage situation segmentation segmentation derived from information on product usage.

utilitarian benefits benefits resulting from purchase or other consumer decisions that are objective, functional product attributes.

utilitarian influence pressure that the reference group applies to the individual to comply with group norms.

value an enduring belief that a specific mode of conduct or end-state of existence is personally or socially preferable to an opposite or converse mode of conduct or end-state of existence.

value-expressive influence the pressure to experience psychological association with a group by conforming to its norms, values, or behaviors, even if membership is not sought.

value-oriented retailer a retailer who offers low prices and basic levels of product selection, and appeals to the economic shopper.

value platform the manner in which a firm differentiates itself from its competitors in the minds of the consumers it intends to serve.

values shared beliefs or group norms that have been internalized by individuals.

variety seeking switching of brands simply in the interest of variety; often used when many similar alternatives are available.

vertical coordination the flow of information from supplier to consumer that affects the diffusion of information.

vicarious learning see modeling

videotex interactive electronic media used for in-home shopping and information.

waverer a consumer whose commitment to the product is diminishing.

wealth net worth or assets, in consumer terms correlated with income.

Weber's Law a rule stating that the amount of change necessary to reach the difference threshold will depend on the initial starting point; e.g., as stimulus intensity increases, a greater amount of change is required to produce a just noticeable difference.

weighted additive decision rule a compensatory decision rule in which judgments about an alternative's performance on evaluative criteria are weighted by the relative salience of the evaluative criteria.

PHOTO CREDITS **Figure 1.1** Nike ad: Reprinted with Permission of NIKE, Inc. **Figure 1.1** Pizza Hut ad: Reproduced with permission of Pizza Hut, Inc. Copyright © 1990 Pizza Hut, Inc. **Figure 1.2** Courtesy of 3M Commercial Supply Division. **Figure 3.2** O. Toscani for United Colors of Benetton. **Figure 3.3** Courtesy of Robert Schuller Ministries. **Figure 3.5** Reproduced with permission of Pepsico, Inc. 1992, Purchase, NY. **Figure 3.6** Courtesy of Ford Motor Company, Agency: Hispania. **Figure 4.1** Source: Leonard Beeghley, *Social Stratification in America* (Santa Monica, Calif.: Goodyear Publishing Company, Inc., 1978), 102. Reprinted by permission. **Figure 4.2** Movado Ad: Courtesy of The Movado Watch Corporation. **Figure 4.3** Source: Richard P. Coleman, "The Continuing Significance of Social Class to Marketing," *Journal of Consumer Research* 10 (December 1983), 265–280. **Figure 4.5** © 1991 Russell Athletics. **Chapter 5/Opening Vignette Photo** © 1991 *The Philadelphia Inquirer/*J. Kyle Keener. **Figure 5.3** Courtesy of the Coca-Cola Company. **Figure 5.7** Courtesy Columbia Crest Winery, Patterson, WA. **Figure 5.8** William O. Bearden and Michael J. Etzel, "Reference Group Influence on Product and Brand Purchase Decisions," *Journal of Consumer Research* 9 (September 1982), 185. Used with permission. **Figure 6.7** Calgon ad: Benckiser Consumer Products, Inc. Calgon Ad Campaign 1991. **Figure 6.7** Nedbank ad: Courtesy of Nedbank. **Figure 6.7** Toyota ad: © Toyota Motor Sales, USA, Inc. **Figure 6.7** ASICS ad: Courtesy of ASICS TIGER Corporation. **Figure 7.1** Reprinted by permission of *The Wall Street Journal*, © 1992, Dow Jones & Company, Inc. All Rights Reserved Worldwide. **Figure 7.2** SANKA Ad: SANKA is a registered trademark of General Foods Corporation and is used with permission, © 1985, General Foods Corporation. **Figure 7.3** Wet Ones Ad: Courtesy of Lehn & Fink Products Group. Agency: Jordan McGrath Case Taylor. **Figure 7.4** © Wm. Wrigley, Jr. Company, 1991. **Figure 7.5** Peter R. Dickson, "Person-Situation: Segmentation's Missing Link," *Journal of Marketing* 6 (Fall 1982), 56–64. Used with permission. **Figure 8.1** Bureau of Labor Statistics and Bureau of the Census. **Figure 8.2** Godiva Ad: Reprinted with permission of Godiva Chocolatier, Inc. All rights reserved © 1988 Godiva Chocolatier, Inc. **Figure 8.6** Advertisement courtesy of CompuServe Incorporated. **Figure 9.4** © Parker Pen USA Limited. **Figure 9.6** Reprinted courtesy of General Foods Cor-

poration. **Figure 9.7** Adapted from Judith L. Zaichkowsky, "Conceptualizing Involvement," *Journal of Advertising* 15 (1986), p. 6. **Figure 9.8** Source: Judith L. Zaichkowsky, "Measuring the Involvement Construct," *Journal of Consumer Research* 12 (December 1985), 350. Used by special permission. **Figure 9.12** Source: Sara Lee Personal Products-HHW Socks. **Figure 10.1** Interceptor Ad: CIBA-GEIGY Annual Health, Greensboro, NC. **Figure 10.1** Source: The Kroger Company, Atlanta Division, Atlanta, Georgia. Design Photography and Printing by WEBCO, Atlanta, Georgia. **Figure 11.5** Source: Alvin C. Burns, "Generating Marketing Strategy Priorities Based on Relative Competitive Position," *Journal of Consumer Marketing* 3 (Fall 1986). **Figure 11.6** Reprinted with permission of IBM Corporation. **Figure 12.1** Reprinted with permission of NIKE, Inc. **Figure 12.3** Courtesy of Coty Wild Musk. **Figure 12.4** Reprinted with permission of NIKE, Inc. **Figure 12.5** Source: Thomas J. Reynolds and Jonathan Gutman "Laddering Theory, Method, Analysis, and Interpretation," reprinted from *Journal of Advertising Research* 28 (February/March 1988), 19. © 1988 by the Advertising Research Foundation. **Figure 12.7** Reproduced with permission of PepsiCo, Inc. 1992, Purchase, NY. **Figure 13.2** Reprinted with the permission of The Little Tikes Company © 1987. **Figure 13.4** Courtesy of Hershey Foods Corporation. HELPS is a registered trademark and is used with permission. **Figure 13.8** Courtesy of Champion Motor Coach Inc., a subsidiary of Champion Enterprises, Dryden, Michigan. **Figure 14.1** Reprinted with permission from Bull HN Information Systems, Inc., Billorica, MA. **Figure 14.7** © 1988 Canon USA, Inc., FAXPHONE is a registered trademark of Canon, Inc. **Figure 14.10** Macintosh ad: Reprinted by permission of Apple Computer, Inc. Apple and the Apple logo are registered trademarks of Apple Computer Inc. Macintosh is a trademark licensed to Apple Computer Inc. **Figure 14.11** Plymouth ad: Reprinted with permission of the Chrysler Corporation—Bozell, Inc., Advertising. **Figure 14.12** Source: *Insights*, NPD Research, Inc., 1979–1982. **Figure 15.2** Source: Richard E. Petty, John T. Cacioppo, and David Schumann, "Central and Peripheral Routes to Advertising Effectiveness: The Moderating Role of Involvement," *Journal of Consumer Research* 10 (September 1983), 135–146. Used with permission. **Figure 15.3** © Oldsmobile Division, General Motors Corporation.

Figure 15.4 Source: Marvin E. Goldberg and Jon Hartwick, "The Effects of Advertiser Reputation and Extremity of Advertising Claim on Advertising Effectiveness," *Journal of Consumer Research* 17 (September 1990), 172–179. **Figure 15.5** Reprinted with permission of NIKE, Inc. **Figure 15.6** © Eastman Kodak Company. Reprinted courtesy of Eastman Kodak Company. **Figure 15.7** Source: David M. Zeitlin and Richard A. Westwood, "Measuring Emotional Response," *Journal of Advertising Research* 26 (October/November 1986), 34–44, Table 3. **Figure 15.11** Source: *Insights*, NPD Research, Inc., 1979–1982. **Figure 15.12** Reprinted by permission of the Coca-Cola Company. **Figure 16.5** Nicoderm ad: Marion Merrell Dow, Inc., which markets Nicoderm® in the United States. **Figure 16.5** Dannon ad: Courtesy of The Dannon Company, Inc. **Figure 16.6** Source: William L. Wilkie and Peter R. Dickson, "Shopping for Appliances: Consumers' Strategies and Patterns of Information Search," Marketing Science Institute Working Paper No. 85–108, 1985, Figure 2. Used with permission. **Figure 17.2** Courtesy of Plymouth, Chrysler Corporation. **Figure 17.5** © Xerox Corporation. **Figure 17.6** Copyright Bankers Life Company. Reprinted by permission. **Figure 18.2** Courtesy Delta Airlines, Inc. **Figure 18.3** Courtesy of Lufthansa German Airlines. **Figure 19.2** Reprinted by permission of the publisher from *Location Strategies for Retail and Service Firms* by Avijit Ghosh and Sara L. McLafferty (Lexington, Mass.: Lexington Books, D. C. Heath and Company, 1987, 34, Copyright 1987; D. C. Heath and Company). **Figure 19.3** Source: Urban Decision Systems, Inc., Los Angeles, California. **Figure 19.4** Source: "Tiny Targets: Pinpointing the Possibilities of Online Demographic Research," *Online Access* 2 (November/December 1987), 29 and 44. **Figure 19.5** Source: *The Evolution of Regional Shopping Centers* (Atlanta: Equitable Real Estate Investment Management Inc., 1987). Left photo courtesy of J. C. Nichols Company. Right photo courtesy of West Edmonton Mall. **Figure 19.7** Courtesy of Jacobs, Visconsi, & Jacobs Co., Cleveland, Ohio. **Figure 19.9** Courtesy of Cheryl & Co. **Figure 19.10** Courtesy Woolworth, Inc. **Figure 20.2** Source: Lowest, medium, and highest fertility series. U.S. Bureau of the Census. **Figure 20.3** Source: *Statistics Canada*, The Daily, July 9, 1987. **Figure 20.5** Courtesy of Levi Strauss & Co. **Figure 20.10** Source: U.S. Department of Commerce, Bureau of the Census. **Figure 20.12**

NAME INDEX

SUBJECT INDEX